York City
The Complete Record

York City

The Complete Record

1922-2008

Every game, every scorer, every player and every attendance. memorable matches, complete history, pen pictures, manager profiles, appearance records

David Batters

Acknowledgments

Many thanks to the York City FC board of directors for their help and support.
Grateful thanks to my son Ian for his invaluable and tremendous help in typing up much of the material plus helping proof read.
Many thanks to Jason McGill, Jon Champion and Malcolm Huntington for writing forewords.
Last but not least, many thanks to my family and friends, especially Norma, for their support, understanding and patience.

Bibliography

Acknowledgement to the following publications.

Citizens and Minstermen by Dave Windross and Martin Jarred.
Premier League and Football League Players' Records compiled by Barry J. Hugman.

Thanks to Paul Bowser for his help with the FA Youth Cup results.

Photographic Credits

Many thanks to *The Press* for allowing the extensive use of photographs from their archives.
Also thanks to the following for allowing photographs from their private collections to be used:
Graham Bradbury, Judith Brisby, daughter of Tom Lockie,
Terry Fowler, daughter of G.W. Sherrington,
Andy McMillan, Alf Patrick, Chris Topping and Dave Windross.

First published in Great Britain in 2008 by The Breedon Books Publishing Company Limited, Breedon House, 3 The Parker Centre, Derby, DE21 4SZ.

Paperback edition published in Great Britain in 2012 by The Derby Books Publishing Company Limited, 3 The Parker Centre, Derby, DE21 4SZ.

This edition published in Great Britain in 2013 by DB Publishing, an imprint of JMD Media Ltd

ISBN 978-1-78091-133-5

Printed and bound by Copytech (UK) Ltd, Peterborough

Contents

Foreword

It is a great pleasure to be asked to write a foreword to the second edition of *York City – The Complete Record.*

I must confess that when the Board were approached for agreement to publish I reacted with some hesitation. It would have been attractive to publish on a high note, hopefully having recovered our Football League membership, rather than against the background of the tribulations of recent years. However, since the manipulative attempts to put the club into administration in 2002, enormous credit is due to supporters, supporters' groups, fundraisers, loyal sponsors, staff and individuals who have dedicated an immense amount of time and effort to keeping York City in existence. This book is a tribute to this army of well-wishers and passionate defenders of our community football club.

Football is an emotive, success-based industry. When you're winning, you're winning; when you're not winning, there is trouble ahead. I have been in stewardship of York City for five years and the pressures on personal and business life in managing a smaller club with limited resources are considerable. I am often asked if I would do it all again and I suspect, like my fellow directors, there is sometimes a hesitation when considering the level of commitment and responsibility necessary in running a professional football club. There is always a hard road to follow, but we are hopeful and enthusiastic about the future and diligently seek the solution to the issue of the new stadium, new beginnings and the success I believe we all deserve.

I recommend David Batters's book to all football-lovers. It is carefully researched and presented, and a credit to David and his family, who are longstanding supporters and contributors to the welfare of York City FC. I wish David every success with the publication.

Jason McGill
Managing Director
York City Football Club
June 2008

Foreword

It is a great pleasure to be asked to contribute a few words to the definitive history of York City Football Club. The original edition is one of the most thumbed through books in my collection, so a new version embracing another two turbulent decades is most welcome!

I have had a close connection with the club since the age of five, when I turned up for my first day as a pupil at Shipton Street Infants School. The school playground backed onto the Shipton Street End terracing, and so wayward were my finishing skills that lunchtime football matches often ended in a surreptitious trip down the alleyway and into the ground to retrieve our ball.

Happily, that was an era when Paul Aimson was exhibiting rather more accuracy on behalf of York City, and by the time Jimmy Seal and Chris Jones were firing the club into the old Second Division, I was haranguing my father to let me go to watch.

It was a battle that took a while to win, and so it wasn't until the age of 12 that I was allowed to set foot – officially – inside Bootham Crescent. By then, Wilf McGuinness had fulfilled his promise to take York City out of Division Two. So effective was his work that my first game on 7 January 1978 was a Fourth Division fixture against Newport County. Less than 2,000 were present to watch Charlie Wright's team win 2–0. Peter Scott scored the first and by the time Gordon Staniforth netted a penalty, I was hooked.

For several years I travelled the length of the country watching a struggling team suffer indignities like Bruce Grobbelaar's penalty at Crewe. By the time Denis Smith and Viv Busby brought a brave new world to the club, I was cutting my broadcasting teeth and players like Keith Walwyn and John Byrne were cutting a swathe through most opposition. Will York City ever have a more dynamic and exciting team than the Division Four champions of 1983–84?

More recently, I have had to put partiality to one side to commentate on a Play-off win at Wembley and that League Cup victory over Manchester United. Beacons of achievement for a club where life is rarely dull. And that, I suppose, is a euphemistic way of describing the horrible combination of circumstances – both footballing and financial – that swept York City out of the Football League.

I am convinced there will be more great days in the future. But for now we should take solace in the fact that in this age of foreign ownership, and a preference for style over substance, ours remains a 'proper' football club, still looked at with affection by prominent football folk, still run and followed by people that genuinely care, still there to act as a dream factory for future generations, just as it was for me – and you.

Jon Champion
ITV/Setanta Sports Commentator
June 2008

Foreword

It seems only yesterday that my old friend David Batters asked me to write a foreword to his first York City book, which covered the period from 1922 to 1990. But I see that it was, in fact, 18 years ago.

It has been my great fortune – perhaps cynical City supporters might regard it otherwise – to write about City affairs for exactly 40 years. During this time I have watched some 2,000 games and have visited every League ground in the country and a few more, such as Barrow, Workington, Aldershot, Exeter, Southport and Maidstone, who have dropped out of the Football League for one reason or another.

It has been a memorable journey. Whoever thought, for example, that City would perform giant-killing acts on Manchester United, Arsenal and Everton? And what about the superb promotion season of 1973–74, when City reached the Second Division (now the Championship), playing the likes of Manchester United and Aston Villa.

Then, in 1983–84, City became the first Football League club in history to reach 100 points in a season, running away with the Fourth Division Championship by 16 points, with Doncaster, Reading and Bristol City the other teams to go up. The year 1993 produced another wonderful moment in City's history, with promotion at Wembley. What a day that was.

There have, of course, been low spots as well, with relegations from the Second, Third and Fourth Divisions, the death of David Longhurst on the pitch during a home game and the awful more recent period when the club had to borrow £2 million to buy the ground back from the owners, resulting in huge interest repayments. Recovering from that monumental blow will take a long time.

But throughout all these triumphs and disasters, one thing has been very constant, and that has been the help and advice David Batters has been able to offer to writers such as myself, in addition to keeping a historical record.

It is all very well to be able to report a match with details of who passed the ball that resulted in a centre from which someone headed the winner in the 89th minute. But when, if ever, did he last head the winner? Where was he born? And have City ever played a team containing four left-footed players? Obtaining such obscure facts and figures is an art in itself, and people like David always seem to have them at their fingertips because of their deep love of the game. A supporter since 1948, he has charted the progress of the club over the years with meticulous care, and all those who delight in watching football, and York City in particular, owe him a great debt of gratitude.

The first City book sold out. This updated version will as well, so do be sure to have plenty printed, David. It will be a treasured addition to all our soccer bookshelves.

Malcolm Huntington MBE
Sports Writer
June 2008

Editor's note

Malcolm Huntington is one of only five football writers to have covered York City for *The Press* (formerly *The Yorkshire Evening Press*) since the club was formed in 1922. Wilf Meek reported on City matches from 1922 to 1968, and when he retired Malcolm took over from 1968 to 1995, during which time he covered 1,302 games. Tony Kelly was next, followed by Dave Stanford. Dave Flett, the current writer, took over in December 2003.

Malcolm, who has worked as a freelance covering City matches for *The Yorkshire Post* since his retirement from full-time writing in May 1995, was made an MBE for 'services to Yorkshire sports journalism' in January 1997.

Introduction

It is 60 years – Saturday 23 October 1948 – since I was taken by my Uncle Les to watch my first-ever game at Bootham Crescent, aged nine. It was a Division Three North fixture between City and Mansfield Town, and among a crowd of nearly 11,000 I was pushed to the front of the Popular Stand. Peering over the wooden railing fence that then surrounded the pitch, I was swept away by the excitement and atmosphere as City won 2–1. I well remember that day and the team of Jack Frost, Harry Brigham, John Simpson, Bert Brenen, Tommy Gale, Bill Allen, George Ivey, Matt Patrick, Alf Patrick, Sid Storey and Jimmy Rudd, all of whom became my immediate heroes, and from that moment I was a City fan. Those were the days of the post-war soccer boom, with record attendances up and down the country. The third game I saw was a 6–1 victory over Northern Section leaders Rotherham United, when a crowd of 19,216 saw Alf Patrick score five goals.

Happily, there was no segregation in those days and fans used to regularly change ends at half-time using the tunnel at the back of the Popular Stand. Floodlit football was some years in the future, and in the late 1940s kick-off times in mid-winter were brought forward to 2.30pm and 2.15pm. Midweek fixtures were restricted to the beginning and end of the season and FA Cup replays were staged on midweek afternoons. It was long before television and local radio, and on Saturday evenings one eagerly awaited the *Sports Press* to read Wilf Meek's (Citizen) report on the game. There was no sponsorship or club shop, but on big occasions, especially Cup ties, rattles, bells, rosettes and scarves were the order of the day.

So many memories of good and bad days over the years: the great FA Cup triumphs in the 1950s; the promotion successes and the spell in the 1970s when City spent two seasons in the second tier of English football; the memorable trip to Wembley plus the Cup victories over Arsenal, Manchester United and Everton in recent times. On the down side there were the relegations, applications for re-election, Cup reverses and the biggest blow of all – dropping out of the Football League in 2004. Older supporters will recall the early days of the club, the FA Cup exploits in the 1930s and wartime football, and I hope that this book will revive many memories of York City FC for supporters and fans of all ages.

The club can boast a number of fine achievements and can proudly look back at the contribution they have made to the sporting annals of the historic city they represent. Thanks to sterling efforts by so many people, City have survived recent dark times and will, hopefully, continue to play an important part in the sporting life of the community of York and district in the years ahead.

David Batters
June 2008

The History of York City

The Early Days (Pre-1922)

Association football was played by several clubs in the York area in the latter part of the 19th century, but with rugby union holding sway, the handling code claimed the only representative City side.

In the 1890s local soccer was not run on an organised basis, and as teams were not affiliated to any association or competition, only friendly games were played. Some of the early clubs in the York area were York Wednesday, who claimed to be the oldest club in the city, St Clements, Heworth, Ebor Wanderers and school teams Bootham, St John's College and Elmfield College. This latter school produced a great soccer enthusiast, Mr S.R. Slack, who was its headmaster for many years. A fine player in his younger days, he was later president of the York Football Association for more than 30 years, until his death in 1946.

In the 1890s, with leagues developing throughout the country, moves were made to organise such a competition in York, and in 1897 the York & District League was established. Ten clubs were divided into two divisions, and these pioneers were St Clements, Rowntrees, Acomb, Sycamore, Heworth, Groves Wesley, Selby, Easingwold, Ulleskelf and Ebor Wanderers. Two men who were largely involved in the setting up of the organisation were C.M. Rawes and A. Lumley.

In 1900 the York & District Football Association was formed and local Cup competitions launched – the Riley Smith Cup, which was to become the Junior Cup, and the Faber Cup, which became the Senior Cup. A prominent figure in local football at this time was Mr J.A. MacGregor. Under the umbrella of the local FA, the York League was supplemented by the Half-Holiday League, which catered for games played on Wednesdays. The Minor and Junior Leagues were formed, and the Schools League and the York FA ran four Cup competitions together with two Charity Cup tournaments. Military clubs entered these competitions – Northumberland Fusiliers, York & Lancaster Regiment, 18th Hussars, 5th Irish Lancers and the Border Regiment.

In those early days, the Rowntree club was the most successful, and their chief rivals were St Clements, Heworth, St Paul's, Sycamore and Hungate Mission. The league continued to expand, and Knaresborough and Malton United joined the fold. By the 10th year of its existence, in 1907, the league operated with three divisions and over two dozen clubs. Amateur soccer was thus prospering in the city.

At this time, the York FA council members were Messrs J. Ernest Trees (honorary secretary), J.W. Biscomb (president), C.M. Rawes (vice-president), T.K. Wilson (vice-president), J. Bond, J.W. Cundall, A. Bell, F. Butler, C.H. Page, G. Dinsdale, W.W. Milburn, A.R. Crowe, F. Taylor, G.F. Andrew (honorary treasurer) and J.G. Bruce (assistant honorary secretary).

The demand grew for a club representative of the city, and in 1908 the first York City Football Club was formed as an amateur concern and entered the Northern League. The honorary secretary was Mr Trees, and the newly formed club obtained a ground in Holgate Road at the end of Lindley Street and Murray Street. The only stand accommodation was a couple of open stands from York Racecourse. One was canvas-topped, and 300 people could be accommodated.

The first captain of York City Football Club was Tom Hillary, who was born in Guisborough, Cleveland, in 1883 and arrived in York in November 1899, when he joined the St Paul's club. Hillary later appeared for St Clements and NER United, as well as playing for York in inter-city games against Sheffield and Middlesbrough.

City's first game, at home to South Bank, was won 2–1, and opponents that season included West Hartlepool, Saltburn, Bishop Auckland, West Auckland and Leadgate. The club entered the FA Amateur Cup and, after knocking out Withernsea and St Paul's, lost to Scarborough in a replay.

In two seasons in the Northern League, York City met with little success, finishing second from bottom and then bottom, winning just 10 out of a total of 44 league games during this period. In order to reduce travelling, they competed in the Yorkshire Combination from 1910 to 1912. Mr J.E. Wright took over as secretary from Mr Trees in 1911 and quickly came to the conclusion that amateur football would not thrive in a rugby stronghold, and he paved the way by signing a professional by the name of Corrighan (amateur clubs in the Yorkshire Combination were allowed to field one paid player at the time). Corrighan, therefore, became the first professional to play soccer for a club in the city of York, but Wright had bigger ideas and advocated the formation of a limited liability company to run a professional club.

Several well-known citizens expressed interest, including the Lord Mayor, Alderman Norman Green, who became chairman of the board, Frank Marks, who kept the Greyhound Hotel, and Bert Rutter, who ran the old Victoria Hall Cinema in Goodramgate. Mr J.T. Clarke, Mr S.R. Slack and Fred Airey were the other directors.

The new professional club was formed in 1912, and 592 five-shilling shares were issued. A plot of rough land in Burton Stone Lane, known as Field View and not far from the present club's headquarters at Bootham Crescent, was obtained. One of the early directors was Alderman Sir William Forster Todd, who later moved over to Clarence Street, where he was a very influential figure at York RLFC between the wars.

York City line up pre-1912.

In May 1912 a deputation went to the Midland League's annual meeting in Nottingham, and the club was admitted to that competition. The directors appointed Peter Boyle, a former Sheffield United, Sunderland and Irish international full-back, as player-manager. Another personality to join the club was Roddie Walker, a full-back from Hearts who had represented the Scottish League against the Football League in 1910–11.

The opening of the ground at Field View, with a game against Midland League champions Rotherham Town, was an auspicious occasion. One of York's two Members of Parliament, Sir John Butcher, was in attendance together with the Lord Mayor, General Plumer and General Reade. The ceremony was filmed and the picture shown at the Empire and the Victoria Hall in Goodramgate. For the match, there were 5,000 paying spectators – sixpence for men, threepence for boys and ladies admitted free. Season tickets were 7s 6d (37½p).

Players who appeared for the club in those early professional days included goalkeeper Jimmy Atherton and David Melville, a right-back from Bradford City. His left-back partner was Dick Waterworth of Rowntrees. The half-back line was A. Lawson of the Scots Greys, Bob Black, a Scottish Junior international, and George Sykes, who attracted the attention of Herbert Chapman – then manager of Leeds City. In attack was David Galbraith of Raith Rovers, J. McMahon, Scotsman W. Lomas from Bury, who was valued at £500 – a big sum in those days – T. Shanks, an Irish international inside-left, and W. Robertson, a former Portsmouth winger. Added to these experienced players were a number of noted local lads: Dick Tindale from Rowntrees, who would later play for the newly formed club in 1923, was recruited along with Teddy Ledgard, a talented inside-forward from the top York amateur side Lowther United. As part of Ledgard's transfer deal, City sent their team of professionals to play United at Mille Crux, Rowntrees, and lost 4–0.

After the enthusiasm of the introduction of professional football, the club struggled to establish itself and fixture clashing with York RLFC frequently occurred. The rugby hold was formidable. The Football Association granted York a representative North versus South fixture but the receipts totalled only £36. When told of the 'gate', FA secretary Sir Frederick Wall remarked to the City secretary 'Never again, sir!'

Tommy Collier succeeded Peter Boyle as manager, and after him came Archie Taylor, who had captained Barnsley when they won the FA Cup in 1912. Features in those far-off days were a visit from Newcastle United, for a friendly game, and hard-fought FA Cup tussles against Goole Town. In August 1914 City were invited to a meeting by the Nelson club to discuss the formation of a Third Division of the Football League, but war was declared and this never took place. Otherwise York City might have been original members of the Third Division.

The club completed its third season in the Midland League in 1914–15, but then the competition was suspended because of hostilities. In 1915–16 a few friendly games were played but the club folded in 1917. Pressed by a creditor, York City went into liquidation through the bankruptcy court almost overnight. The stand and equipment were disposed of, and Field View was turned into allotments and then a building estate. The current overdraft at the bank had only been £518, but with the stand unpaid for and one creditor pressing for payment, the end came after only five years as a professional club. It was to be another five years before the new and present York City FC emerged.

Their record in the Midland League was as follows:

Season	P	W	D	L	F	A	P	POS
1912–13	38	16	6	16	69	80	38	10
1913–14	34	13	5	16	48	60	31	12
1914–15	38	12	7	19	45	72	31	16

The Formation of the Present Club and the Midland League Days (1922–29)

Local football continued to prosper and expand after World War One, but with no professional club in the city, York's rugby league side had the stage to themselves. Junior soccer was proving popular, however, and so many clubs were springing up that the York League was constantly having to be revised. Local Cup competitions, promoted by the York FA, attracted good crowds and receipts exceeding £100 were taken at a Senior Cup Final with an admission fee of 6d (2½p).

Shortly after the war, the Yorkshire League was formed. This catered for clubs with part-time professionals, and three York clubs entered the new competition – Acomb WMC, Rowntrees and York YMCA. This brought the reserve teams of a number of senior professional clubs and a good standard of football to the York area. Acomb, particularly, had a fair degree of success, and among their players of note were Tom Maskill, later to play for York City, Jack Robson, who was a fine centre-half, Tommy Holmes, 'Sandy' Acklam, the Halder brothers and 'Mike' Dennis. YMCA recruited an Aberdeen full-back, McRobbie, as trainer, and it was with this club that Joe Hulme, who went on to have an illustrious professional career with Arsenal and England, played his early football.

Without doubt these Yorkshire League games helped to create a demand for another senior team in the city of York. With public opinion growing, a number of private meetings and discussions took place, and then, on 31 March 1922, Harry Hayhurst called together enthusiasts for a public meeting at the Guildhall. Great interest was aroused and 400 people attended. The chairman of the meeting was C. Horner, and among those present were Hammond Richmond, who contributed articles in the Football Press under the pseudonym of 'Nomad', Arthur Brown, Councillor W.H. Shaw, H. Hayhurst, H. Rusholme, J. Hutchinson and J. Scott. A committee of 20 was formed, with Richmond as secretary. Amid a good deal of enthusiasm, a resolution proposed by Councillor W.H. Shaw and seconded by J. Hutchinson was passed that 'in the opinion of this meeting, the present is an opportune time for the formation of a York City Association Football Club'.

At a further meeting on 4 April 1922, C. Horner was elected chairman and George Robinson of the Blue Bell, Fossgate, became honorary treasurer. A number of early meetings regarding the formation of the club had been held in this public house, which is still a popular hostelry today. Five trustees were elected, among them John Fisher, who was to prove a good benefactor.

Councillor W.H. Shaw, the club's first chairman.

On 6 May 1922 the decision was made at a meeting in the Co-operative Hall to form the York City Association Football and Athletic Club Limited. The meeting fixed the sum of £5 as a minimum share investment for a director's financial responsibility. The first five directors elected were Messrs J. Fisher, G.W. Sherrington, G.E. Robinson, A. Brown and H. Watson. Later additions resulted in W.H. Shaw being elected chairman, and secretary Harry Rusholme was put on the board. One of the first things on the

directors' agenda was to make what could only amount to a cheeky application to join the Football League. The following letter was circulated to Football League clubs in support of the application:

YORK CITY ASSOCIATION FOOTBALL & ATHLETIC CLUB

Headquarters
Y.M.C.A.
Clifford Street
York
24 May, 1922
Sir,

Following a series of public meetings held in the City of York, a Limited Company is being formed for the purpose of raising an Association Football Club.

As you are aware, application has been made for inclusion in the Third Division of the Northern Section.

In seeking your support in furtherance of our election, we beg to place before you the following facts:-

(a) The population of the City of York is approximately 85,000: there is a growing demand for a better class of football & there are at present, some 70 clubs playing the Association Code in the City and neighbourhood of York.

(b) The purchase of a ground covering seven acres, is on the point of completion, and it is intended to equip this in the most up to date style. The ground is conveniently situated on a main tram route.

As the geographical position of York is second to none, and its railway facilities of the best, the travelling expenses of visitors will be reduced to a minimum.

(c) It is the intentions of the club to get together a strong workmanlike team by the commencement of next season, and in this connection it may be stated that applications have already been received from several prominent players.

(d) Financially, the capital of £5,000 is practically assured; already there are upwards of 1,000 shareholders of £1 0s 0d in addition to those of larger amounts.

(e) A strong Supporters' Club has already been formed and is working hard for success in all directions.

We are making application in confidence that we should be able to carry out all that is required of us.

Thanking you in anticipation of your kind support.

Yours faithfully

(signed) ARTHUR BROWN, Chairman.
(signed) HAMMOND N.RICHMOND, Hon.Secretary.

They had neither ground (Fulfordgate was not yet equipped – see Homes of York City) nor players, yet Fisher and Rusholme were sent to the Football League's annual meeting in London to apply for membership to the Third Division North. Halifax Town and Rochdale were both re-elected, and although the infant York City received one vote, the president of the Football League, John McKenna, and committeeman Charles Sutcliffe told the York delegation to go back home, establish a club, work a bit and then come back another day.

Shortly afterwards, directors attended the Midland League annual meeting in Sheffield, and on 10 June 1922 York City were elected to that competition. It was a close call, however, as seven clubs competed for six vacancies. City finished sixth, only three votes ahead of Sutton. With the problem of which league to play in now solved, the task of recruiting players was embarked upon.

Hughie 'Spud' Murphy became trainer after long service in the army, and one of the first players to be signed was Nicol Hendry, Hull City's goalkeeper for many years. Other former Hull players acquired were centre-half Billy Smith, who was appointed the club's first captain, and outside-left Joe Harron. There were links with the old Field View club with the signing of 'Ginger' Lynch, Tommy Holmes and Dick Tindale. From the Acomb club came Tom Maskill, who had been a Schoolboy international, and 'Sandy' Acklam. There was also a strong contingent of Sheffield players – Ted Thorpe, Charlie Elliott and Charlie Lemmons.

In the summer of 1922, there were financial problems. The formation of a limited liability company had been decided with an authorised share capital of £4,000 in £1 shares. Before the directors could go to allotment, it was necessary to raise £1,250, but this capital was very slow in coming. One of the schemes introduced was one whereby shares could be purchased in weekly instalments and, as a result, many supporters became shareholders. The establishment of York City FC arose from a desire to provide sport for the working men of the city; consequently, it was largely the working men who brought it into being. A ground at Heslington Lane, Fulfordgate, was obtained and the necessary minimum capital raised.

Nicol Hendry was appointed as player-coach at a salary of £4 per week and his duties, as spelled out in the club's Minute Book, were as follows:

PROSPECTUS.

THE Company has been formed for the purposes mentioned in its Memorandum of Association, and primarily to adopt and carry into effect an Agreement for the purchase of a piece of freehold land situate in Heslington Lane, Gate Fulford, in the County of York, for the purpose of a Football and Athletic Ground, and to form an Association Football Club for the City of York and District.

The supporters of first-class Association Football are completely neglected in York, and the Directors are confident of strong support in their effort to form an Association Football Club.

The City of York, being one of the principal Railway Centres and Junctions in the United Kingdom, is easily accessible, and, therefore, the Company will be able to obtain supporters from a wide area, and also arrange fixtures with leading clubs.

The Directors have secured a most suitable ground situate in Heslington Lane, Gate Fulford—the ground is pleasantly situated, level, and well drained. Trams run from all parts of the City to within a very short distance from the ground. As the ground is situate just beyond the City Boundary the Company will have the advantage of rural instead of urban rates, a matter of great importance.

The cost of the ground to the Company is £2000 (exclusive of legal expenses and stamps on transfer). The Vendor has agreed to leave £1250 of the purchase-money on mortgage at £5 10s. per centum per annum, thus facilitating the provision of funds for the equipment of the ground, and working capital. The Contract (hereinafter referred to) for the purchase of the ground has been made in the names of six of the Directors and The Reverend DAVID GRAHAM EVANS, St. Luke's Parsonage, Burton Lane, York (who are the promoters of the Company), on behalf of the Company. The Company is liable to reimburse the Vendor all moneys, not exceeding £50, payable by him to the present tenant of the land to secure vacant possession. The Company are entitled to vacant possession on completion of the purchase.

The said Directors and promoters have paid the deposit payable on the purchase of the said ground, and, except that they will be reimbursed such deposit by the Company, are not further interested in the said purchase or promotion.

No Promotion Profits have or will be paid to the promoters.

The Directors have applied for and obtained admission into the Midland League, and in preparation for the coming Season have entered into negotiations with several Professional Players of good standing.

The Directors hope to have the ground ready for play in September.

The Football Association regulates the maximum Dividend allowed to be paid, and at present no larger Dividend than Seven and a Half per centum per annum, as now allowed by the Association, can be declared.

No Shares are to be issued as fully or partly paid up otherwise than in cash.

The prospectus and share advice.

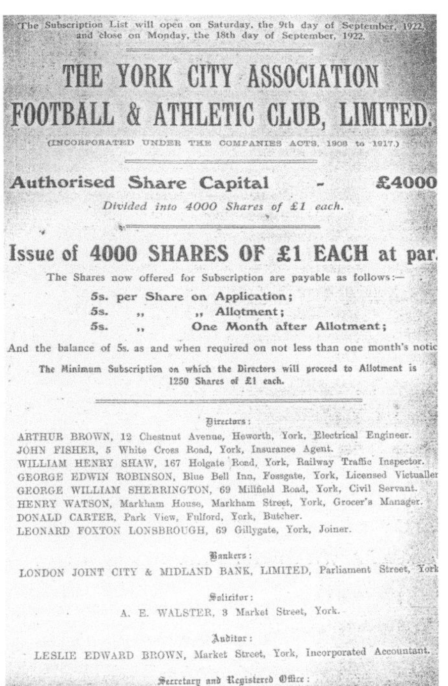

The Subscription List will open on Saturday, the 9th day of September, 1922, and close on Monday, the 18th day of September, 1922.

THE YORK CITY ASSOCIATION FOOTBALL & ATHLETIC CLUB, LIMITED.

(INCORPORATED UNDER THE COMPANIES ACTS, 1908 to 1917.)

Authorised Share Capital - £4000

Divided into 4000 Shares of £1 each.

Issue of 4000 SHARES OF £1 EACH at par.

The Shares now offered for Subscription are payable as follows:—

5s. per Share on Application;
5s. ,, ,, Allotment;
5s. ,, One Month after Allotment;

And the balance of 5s. as and when required on not less than one month's notic

The Minimum Subscription on which the Directors will proceed to Allotment is 1250 Shares of £1 each.

Directors:

ARTHUR BROWN, 12 Chestnut Avenue, Heworth, York, Electrical Engineer.
JOHN FISHER, 5 White Cross Road, York, Insurance Agent.
WILLIAM HENRY SHAW, 167 Holgate Road, York, Railway Traffic Inspector.
GEORGE EDWIN ROBINSON, Blue Bell Inn, Fossgate, York, Licensed Victualler
GEORGE WILLIAM SHERRINGTON, 69 Millfield Road, York, Civil Servant.
HENRY WATSON, Markham House, Markham Street, York, Grocer's Manager.
DONALD CARTER, Park View, Fulford, York, Butcher.
LEONARD FOXTON LONSBROUGH, 69 Gillygate, York, Joiner.

Bankers:

LONDON JOINT CITY & MIDLAND BANK, LIMITED, Parliament Street, York

Solicitor:

A. E. WALSTER, 3 Market Street, York.

Auditor:

LESLIE EDWARD BROWN, Market Street, York, Incorporated Accountant.

Secretary and Registered Office:

1. To have supervision of all players and trainer.
2. To coach the players in football playing.
3. To attend the directors' weekly meeting, and give report of players attending practice.
4. To receive report from trainer as to the fitness or otherwise of players, and report to the directors at their weekly meeting.
5. To act as medium between players and directors.
6. To sign on amateur players on the instruction of the secretary.
7. To introduce local lads to sign on for the reserve team, with the object of their becoming fit for the first eleven.
8. To obtain the authority of the secretary for the expending of any money, and obtain his counter signature before issuing orders for work or materials required.
9. To report to directors as to the suitability or otherwise of new players.
10. To perform any special duty that may be requested by the directors at any time in the interests of the club.
11. That he be invested with power to settle disputes but in case of any disputes which he settles, the same to be immediately reported to the secretary, so that the same may be put before the directors at their next meeting.

The duties of Hughie Murphy – trainer and groundsman – were as follows:

1. To see that all players are properly prepared before turning out in a match and to see that they are all supplied with equipment.
2. To see that all players' equipment is kept in good condition and ready for use by the players.
3. To give attention to minor injuries.
4. To keep in good condition the rooms and equipment and have the ground marked out for matches, and to do any other work on the ground in the interest of the club, either with or without assistance when authorised or requested to do so by the directors.
5. To report to the player-coach any serious injury.
6. To make requisition to the player-coach of any materials required.
7. To obtain authority from the player-coach before expending any money.

The first match for the club was away to Notts County reserves on Wednesday 6 September 1922. Against strong opposition, City put up a good display before losing 4–2. The first ever City goal was scored by Billy Smith, direct from a free-kick, and Jack Woods, who had previously been with Halifax Town, was the other marksman. The City team lined up as follows: Hendry, Holmes, Thorpe, Lynch, Smith, Acklam, Elliott, Moult, Woods, Lemmons and Harron. The club colours were maroon and white-striped shirts and white shorts – or knickers as then described.

With Fulfordgate not yet ready, City had to play their first home match three days later at Mille Crux, Haxby Road – the ground of Messrs Rowntree & Company Limited. Lincoln City reserves were the visitors, and York won 3–2 with goals from Acklam, Elliott and Woods. The gate receipts at a 9d fee (just under 4p) were £122, and this figure remained a record for a long time. Rowntrees again kindly loaned their ground a week later, when City lost to Boston Town 4–2, and the first game was played at Fulfordgate on Wednesday 20 September 1922. City celebrated with a 4–1 victory over Mansfield Town and generally performed creditably that season, but after occupying a mid-table position in early March, the side failed to win any of its last 14 fixtures and finished in 19th position.

York City line up prior to their home game against Lincoln City reserves on 9 September 1922. Back row, left to right: Harry Rusholme (honorary secretary), Tommy Holmes, Nick Hendry, Ted Thorpe, Hughie Murphy (trainer). Middle row: 'Ginger' Lynch, Charlie Elliott, Billy Smith, Charlie Lemons, Joe Harron. Front row: 'Sandy' Acklam, Jack Woods, Tom Maskill.

The team did very well, however, in the North Riding Senior Cup, and they reached the Final. A 7–1 victory at Scarborough in a qualifying-round match was followed by home wins over Stockton Catholics and Darlington RA. The Final against Middlesbrough reserves was played at Ayresome Park on 10 March 1923. City took the lead through Jack Woods but eventually lost 4–2 to the experienced and powerful Boro side. Joe Harron was the other scorer that day, and it was to be his last game for the club, as on 12 March he became the first City player to figure in a transfer when he went to Sheffield Wednesday for £200.

At the end of the season local lad Tom Maskill moved to Coventry City. Tom was one of two talented local brothers, both of whom gained Schoolboy international honours. The younger lad, George, made his senior City debut in January 1924 and moved to Scarborough in 1927. Both players returned to the club in 1932–33 and played in the Third Division North side. Meanwhile, the board of directors had been increased to 12, and Leslie Brown had succeeded Rusholme as secretary in December 1922.

Financially, the first season proved disappointing and a little worrying. A loss of £718 was reported, and only £1,260 of the share capital had been subscribed. Councillor Shaw relinquished the chairmanship to Arthur Brown, and the small band of enthusiasts renewed their efforts to build a successful and soundly based club. On 20 April 1922 just prior to the formation of the City club, the supporters' club had been formed, and in the summer of 1923, under their sponsorship, many improvements were made to the ground.

In 1923–24 the club entered a reserve team in the Yorkshire League and competed for the first time in the FA Cup. The previous season, the club had not been formed in time to enter the competition. In the extra preliminary round, Castleford and Allerton United were beaten 2–1 at Fulfordgate. The honour of scoring the first FA Cup goal for York City went to Tommy Rippon. One other player who established himself in the team that season was 'Mickey' Albrecht, who had joined the club from Inniskilling Dragoons. Described as being as 'hard as nails', he was quite a character.

In the next round, City won at Cudworth, but in the first qualifying round they lost to Mexborough in a second replay. Humble beginnings, therefore, in the competition that was to provide such thrills and excitement for York City in the years to come.

Further transfers took place, with the departure of goalkeeper Len Boot to Huddersfield for £300 in October 1923, and then in February the following year, teenager Joe Hulme moved to Blackburn Rovers for £250. City received a further £50 after the right-winger played in six first-team games, and Rovers played a friendly match at Fulfordgate as part of the deal. The 19-year-old Hulme had made a total of only 28 Midland League appearances and scored three penalties but had immense natural football ability, and quite a few clubs, including Hull City and Barnsley, were very keen on his signature. The Ewood Park club won the race for his services, and within 18 months he had been transferred to Arsenal, then managed by Herbert Chapman, for almost £3,000. Hulme went on to be one of the best outside-rights of his generation, winning League and FA Cup honours with Arsenal, as well as being capped for England nine times.

Travelling to games in those far-off days could be quite difficult as the following experience proved. In December 1923 City were away to Grimsby Town reserves, and they made the journey to Hull to cross the Humber by ferry to New Holland. The boat went off-course, hit a sandbank and the City party were stuck in mid-river for a long time. A belated arrival at New Holland caused the rest of the trip to be made by dock tramcar and taxi, and the match began nearly an hour late. To complete City's woe, Town won 9–0, and the game finished in almost total darkness.

City ended 1923–24 again in 19th position with an almost identical record to the previous year. The best performance of the season was a 5–0 win at Rotherham County reserves, with Tommy Rippon netting a hat-trick. Hulme, in what was to be his last game for the club, scored from the penalty spot, and the other marksman was Arthur Charlesworth.

At the annual meeting in September 1924, shareholders were told of an 'encouraging outlook' by the directors. Wages, salaries and bonuses paid to players in that second season had amounted to £1,494. Travelling expenses and refreshments cost £497 6s 9½d. Items on the revenue side included gate receipts of £2,119 19s 4d, and sale of programmes totalled £62. Overall, the loss on the season was £350 – a big improvement on the first year's figures – and the directors felt that they were on the right path. To be able to reduce the loss by nearly £400, in what had only been a moderate playing season, was no mean achievement and the directors' report concluded:

> The presence of so many York-born players with the club should appeal to sportsmen in the city and the directors are looking forward to a very successful season and hope that the public will give them every support in their endeavour to establish and popularise the Association game in the city. There is still one goal ahead, namely the Third Division, and we appeal to all to give us the necessary financial support to achieve this object at the earliest possible moment.

During the summer of 1924, the old established Midland League was faced with a crisis. Eight reserve teams of Football League clubs withdrew from the competition to help form the Midland Combination. The split came at such short notice that, to ensure a full complement of fixtures, the Midland League formed a principal competition to end in February and then followed this with subsidiary north and south sections.

The 1924–25 campaign proved a successful one for the club. They finished sixth in the Principal Competition and runners-up to Denaby United in the North Subsidiary Competition. Club captain, top scorer with 17 goals, and star player was Jimmy Miller, who had previously been on the books of Grimsby Town and Manchester United. Other players who made their mark were Joe Laws, a tricky little left-winger, and Fred Walker, a local centre-half from Heslington. The latter made such good progress that he was transferred to Tottenham Hotspur in the summer of 1925. As City did not pay summer wages to retain players in those days, Spurs got Walker without a fee (as did Coventry with Tommy Maskill in 1923). In November 1925, however, it was announced that Tottenham had made a generous donation that had been gratefully received by the City directors.

A local full-back, Lester Marshall, hit the headlines when he was tried at centre-forward. He hit five goals in the FA Cup tie against Horsforth, five goals in a League match against Castleford and, in a North Riding Senior Cup tie, he netted six in an 11–1 win over Grangetown St Mary's. In January 1925 he moved to Lincoln for £100. Brothers Joe and Reg Baines also made appearances in the first team. Reg was to play a big part in the club's history in the years ahead. The reserve side also did well that season, winning the York Senior Cup and York Charity Cup.

It was in 1924 that George William Sherrington, one of the directors, took over the role of honorary secretary. Billy, as he was known, was to serve the club as secretary for 37 years. One of the founder members of the club in 1922, he was indeed 'Mr York City'. Upon taking over the secretaryship, he inherited a legacy of administrative problems, but he applied all his enthusiasm to the job together with diligence and hard work. When the club gained election to the Football League in 1929, the secretarial work plus the financial administration became much more intensive, and on 1 February 1930 he was appointed full-time secretary and relinquished his place on the board. He was to give the club many years' outstanding and loyal service, which included spells as secretary-manager (see York City Managers). In 1951 he received the Football League long service medal and, upon his retirement in 1961, Sherrington became the club's first-ever vice-president. He was appointed president six years later following the death of Mr W.H. Sessions.

The mid-1920s were difficult days economically, especially for football clubs like City, still striving to establish themselves. In the dark days of 1925, York City had to fight to keep their head above water, and the club was only kept going by the enthusiasm and generosity of the directors, especially chairman John Fisher, who loaned several sums of money.

The Midland League was restored in size in readiness for 1925–26, and new clubs elected included Alfreton, Loughborough, Long Eaton, Sutton, Shirebrook and Ilkeston. With only one point from the first six games, City made a bad start from which they never really recovered, and finished a disappointing 16th. The captain was a strong centre-half by the name of Jimmy Loughran, and under his leadership the side did, however, have their best run so far in the FA Cup, reaching the third qualifying round before losing to Wath. In the preliminary round at Maltby Main, they were winning 7–0 when a violent rainstorm caused the match to be abandoned after 71 minutes. The game was replayed at Fulfordgate, and City had to battle hard to win 5–3.

With the arrival of the new clubs in the League, City had a number of long trips to make. Invariably for these matches in Nottinghamshire and Derbyshire, a small party assembled in York as few of the players then lived in the city and the team was collected en route. On a trip to Alfreton on 21 November 1925, City were one man short, and Sherrington recruited a man from a local pub by the name of Jones, who was reported to be useful. Less than an hour before the game, he was drinking pints – in the game, he scored City's only goal in a 5–1 defeat.

During this time, there was a prolonged strike in the coal mines, and there was considerable depression. Visiting one mining town, City officials called on a local hostelry that was full of out-of-work

York City 1926–27. Back row, left to right players only: A. Flynn, C. Flood, G. Thompson, E. Harvey, R. Shanks. Middle row: L. Redfern, J. Loughran, J. Middlemiss, R. Merritt. Front row: L. Duckham, S. Ranby.

miners before the game. It was customary for the City players to be paid their wages on the day of the match and, to the consternation of the landlord, the director in charge of the party took out his wallet and started to check the wages cash. He was the object of much attention in the crowded pub; after a hint from the landlord, the group of City officials grabbed their hats and coats and bid a hasty retreat.

The 1926–27 season was the most successful one that City experienced as a non-League club. They finished sixth in the table, scoring 96 goals in their 38 League matches, and reached the second-round proper of the FA Cup.

City strengthened their side with more experienced players, and this reaped dividends. Goalkeeper George Thompson proved an outstanding discovery. In July 1927 he was transferred to Southampton, and in the 1950s his son was to play for City. Former Exeter player Andy Flynn was an excellent right-back. Jimmy Loughran was again an inspiration at centre-half, and the ever-reliable Jack Middlemiss was at left-half. At centre-forward was Charlie Flood, who had previously been with Plymouth, Hull, Bolton and Nottingham Forest. He rattled in 17 goals in 15 League appearances and was transferred to Swindon in February 1927. Dicky Merritt, an ex-Lincoln player, was at outside-left and was a match-winner on his day. Skilful inside-forward Sam Ranby was in his second season with the club, and Tom Fenoughty, destined to have a long career with City, made his debut. Levi Redfern, a talented half-back recruited from Denaby, was transferred to Huddersfield late in the campaign.

Subsequently, there were some high-scoring performances in the League. Alfreton Town were beaten 7–0 at Fulfordgate, with Len Duckham netting five goals. Flood hit four in a six-goal win over Ilkeston, and he also grabbed a hat-trick in a 7–1 thrashing of Wath Athletic. The same player also netted three in a 4–4 draw at home to Heanor Town. Another hat-trick scorer was Arthur Clayton against Wombwell (7–1). The team suffered only one League defeat at Fulfordgate, and that was to runaway champions Scunthorpe United. A young, local outside-left, Ron Clancey, made his debut on New Year's Day in 1927 in a home game against Sutton Town. He scored the only goal of the match but then broke his ankle and, sadly, never played again.

It was, however, the FA Cup run of 1926–27 that put the club on a sound basis. For the first time, City were switched from south to north Yorkshire in the qualifying stages. In the early rounds Guisborough Belmont, South Bank and Whitby United were disposed of, and then in the fourth qualifying round, City entered a bigger geographical area and were drawn away to Ilkeston, where they swept to a 5–1 victory. Reaching the competition proper for the first time in their history, they were drawn at home to Worksop. A 4–1 success in front of 3,500 at Fulfordgate sent City into the second round and a trip to Second Division Grimsby Town. After a tremendous tussle, City lost narrowly by 2–1 in front of 11,000 fans, paying receipts of £750. The demand grew for Third Division football, and the club made its first serious attempt for election to the Football League in 1927.

Wilf Meek, a sports journalist on the staff of the *Yorkshire Evening Press*, reported on City's activities from the club's inauguration in 1922 until his retirement in 1968. For many years, Meek used the pseudonym 'Citizen', and York City received much publicity and support through his columns. In turn, Meek received many letters of encouragement from notable football personalities including Ivan Sharpe, the editor of *Athletic News*, and Charles Buchan, the famous Arsenal and England inside-forward. Meek later became a club director.

Meanwhile, the application for election was not successful, and both retiring clubs, Barrow and Accrington Stanley, were re-elected. City received only six votes, but the club were able to give an optimistic report at the club's AGM in July. For the first time, the balance sheet showed a surplus of income (£850) over expenditure. Gate receipts for 1926–27 were £2,783 compared with £1,776 for the previous year, and one interesting item of expenditure was police charges at £3 12s. Considerable improvements, with the co-operation of the supporters' club, were in hand at the Fulfordgate ground. Summing up, the directors expressed great optimism regarding the club's future. As the report said, 'The club has weathered stormy seas and pulled through to calmer waters. Well-established York City need not fear the coming years.'

After the excitement and progress made in 1926–27, the following season was a little disappointing, although the side finished a very creditable seventh in the league. The most outstanding performance was a remarkable 7–1 win away to Nottingham Forest reserves in March. City also beat Heanor 7–1 at home, with John Hammerton scoring four. There was also a controversial game away to Mansfield in January 1928, when City played with only nine men for 75 minutes. Goalkeeper George Crowther was carried off injured, and then Fenoughty was sent off. Mansfield won 5–1, and later in the season Town completed the double with a 5–2 win at York.

In the FA Cup, York were knocked out in a fourth-round replay at home to Shildon. In an earlier round they had been drawn against Scarborough, who were in their first season of Midland League football. The tie at Fulfordgate attracted tremendous interest, and a record crowd of 6,422 (with receipts of £311) saw a 1–1 draw on 15 October 1927. In the replay at Scarborough, watched by 4,073, City won surprisingly easily by 4–0. City relied chiefly on the players who had appeared the previous year, but two promising youngsters who sprang to the fore were 'keeper Crowther and Dunnington-born Jack Everest. In May 1928 these two players were snapped up by Stockport County. That summer, City made another bid for League status. With only seven votes, they failed again, and Carlisle United were successful at the expense of Durham City.

Arthur Brown again became chairman, and he held this position until 1939. Brown had a lifelong interest in soccer and had taken up refereeing in the Middlesbrough area in 1894. He was appointed secretary of the Middlesbrough League and then, when he moved to Otley at the beginning of the

England Schoolboy international Jack Pinder.

century, he refereed in the Leeds and Bradford area. He came to York in 1905 and continued his 'whistling', taking charge of local Cup Finals over the years and completing over 30 seasons as a referee. In 1908 he assisted in the formation of the original York City amateur club and was the first chairman of that organisation. He helped form the present City club and served as a director for 20 years, most of these as chairman. He was also involved for many years on the executive of the York and District Referees' Association.

In June 1928 the York City Supporters' Club were able to announce at their annual meeting that they had a record membership of 632, with receipts of £837. During the 1927–28 season they had been able to donate £325 to the City club and, in the six years of their existence, the supporters' club had handed over £1,250 to the parent body. At the time the officials of the supporters' club were Arthur Russell (chairman) and H. Ward (secretary), and the committee members were Messrs Taylor, Barnes, Dunn, Dungate, Deighton, Houghton, Hardcastle, Innes, Morton, Marshall, Pinder, Pearson, Shepherd, Shaw, Thompson, Topping, Temple, McAdams, Pratt, Ledward, Trebich and Waite.

Although disappointed at their failure to get into the Football League, City planned ahead and in the summer of 1928 appointed John 'Jock' Collier, the former Hull City and Queen's Park Rangers half-back, as player-manager. Scotsman Collier recruited no fewer than seven players from over the border, most notably centre-forward Jimmy Cowie from Raith Rovers. Cowie's scoring feats in the last season of Midland League football were legendary. In 49 League games he totalled 49 goals and was top marksman in the Midland League. The cry of 'give it to Cowie' became a slogan at Fulfordgate. Twice, he scored six goals, once five and twice four, and in one sequence of seven games in January–February 1929, he scored in every match, netting a total of 17 goals. At the end of the season, he was selected for the Rest of the Midland League against the champions, Mansfield Town, as was outside-left Dicky Merritt. Also outstanding was Sam Charnley, a centre-half signed from Wolves. A skilful left-half was Johnny Duthie, who had been with Collier at QPR.

The club finished ninth, playing a total of 50 League games in the newly extended Midland League, and there was no shortage of goals, thanks chiefly to Cowie. The biggest win was 8–2 against bottom-of-the-table Worksop Town. In what was to be the last non-League game for the club until 2004 City played Gainsborough Trinity at Fulfordgate on 1 May 1929. Duthie scored the only goal but, to the disappointment of all concerned, Jimmy Cowie failed to get his 50th goal of the season, although certainly not for the want of trying, according to all reports.

It was the FA Cup that again provided the real excitement. City won their way through to the fourth qualifying round, and at this stage they had three tremendous tilts with Jarrow. The tie went to a third meeting, which was staged at St James' Park, Newcastle, and a crowd of 6,843 saw City win 3–2. In the first round, the club were drawn at home to Third Division Barrow – the first time they had entertained a League club in a competitive match. The attendance of 6,957 (receipts £352) set new club records, and the visitors rather luckily scraped home 1–0.

ork City Association Football & Athletic Club, Ltd.
(Members of the Midland Counties Football League and Yorkshire League)

Telephone:
Ground, FULFORD, 43.
(During Match).

Secretary:
G. W. SHERRINGTON.

Ground: FULFORDGATE.
Registered Office:
37, MARKET STREET,
YORK.

13th May, 1927.

Dear Sir,

Our application for admission to the Third Division of The Football League - Northern Section has been forwarded to Mr. Charnley, and we give below a few particulars to enable you to judge our merit.

This City itself has a population of 85,000 exclusive of the military, and the area served by the 2d. tram route covers more than 100,000 population. There are not six towns larger that are represented in the Northern Section.

There is no Football League Club nearer than Leeds 26 miles, Darlington 45 miles, Sheffield 50 miles, Hull 45 miles, so that there is no counter attraction to our matches if we are elected. There are a number of smaller towns and villages near at hand from whom we can expect a measure of support if we can provide League Football.

The excellent railway facilities, are a feature in our favour. There is no other place in the section so well situated. There are a number of first class hotels in the City.

Our ground is the property of the Club, splendidly drained, well equipped, spacious and capable of being extended to hold any number up to 40,000 spectators. It is our intention to carry out necessary improvements during the Summer.

The Club is controlled by a popularly elected Board of Directors comprising business men of experience.

For five seasons we have been members of the Midland League and have earned a name for always playing attractive football.

This season we have had an excellent team, having lost only nine League matches, whilst in the second round of the F. A. Cup we played at Grimsby Town to lose 2. - 1.

We honestly believe our Club would be a credit to the League.

We hope you will give us your support, and if we are elected you will have nothing to regret.

Yours truly,

Chairman.

Secretary.

Letter of application to the Football League, 1927.

The end of the season saw the departure of Jack Middlemiss, who had been first choice at right-half for six seasons. He had given splendid service, travelling from Durham for every game, and he became the first City player to be rewarded with a benefit. Middlesbrough sent a team for the occasion, and Jack received a cheque for £111.

City's bid for Third Division football grew stronger, and on 24 April 1929 they derived great encouragement when Northern Section clubs, meeting in Manchester, voted that City be elected and Hartlepool be re-elected. Although this only recommended the change to First and Second Division clubs, City's hopes were considerably boosted.

In making what was their fourth bid for League status, York City stressed the following points: they owned their own ground, which could accommodate 17,000 spectators; revenue for 1928–29 was almost £5,000; and York was one of the largest places not represented in the Football League. On 3 June 1929 the York City delegation of Messrs D.A. Pratt, H. Rusholme, J. Fisher, G.H. Douglas and G.W. Sherrington made the journey to London for the League meeting in an optimistic mood. The voting for the Northern Section resulted as follows:

Hartlepools United	33 votes
York City	24 votes
Mansfield Town	16 votes
Ashington	14 votes
Manchester Central	2 votes
Prescot Cables	1 vote

Chester, Rhyl and Workington received no support.

So City took the place of Ashington in the Third Division North and had achieved their great ambition, seven years after being told to go back and work by John McKenna. The news was received with great enthusiasm and the Lord Mayor of York (Councillor Rymer) telegraphed his congratulations to the York directors at the Hotel Imperial, London, and York MP F. Burgess sent a tribute too. After the declaration of the result, the York deputation received further messages of congratulation, especially from representatives of Yorkshire clubs. The list of directors and officials at York City at the time of their joining the Football League was as follows:

President:	Capt H. Whitworth, MFH
Chairman:	A. Brown
Directors:	Messrs G.H. Douglas, J. Fisher, H. Hayhurst, W. Mason, D.A. Pratt, N. Pratt, G.E. Robinson, J.W. Rosindale, H. Rusholme, G.W. Sherrington, Councillor J. Wilkinson
Hon Secretary:	G.W. Sherrington
Manager:	J. Collier

The seventh annual meeting of the club was held on 17 July 1929. Seconding the adoption of the report, director D.A. Pratt said that the optimism expressed at the last annual meeting had been well justified. York City had been regarded as the most attractive team in the Midland League. By gaining admission to the Football League, they were creating history in the ancient city of York. Pratt stated there was a good deal more optimism ahead and every incentive for them to work hard.

Football League Plus FA Cup Triumphs (1929–39)

In the 10 seasons prior to the outbreak of World War Two, City steadily established themselves in the Football League, chiefly occupying a mid-table position in Division Three (North). Their highest placing was in their initial season, when they finished sixth, while twice they finished 20th, just avoiding application for re-election. The club figured in the third round of the FA Cup no less than six times in this decade, progressing to round four in 1936–37 and the quarter-finals the following campaign.

The summer of 1929 was a busy time for City manager Jock Collier, as he recruited a virtually new team in preparation for life in the Football League. Of the side that represented the club on their League baptism at Wigan Borough on 31 August 1929, only ace marksman Jimmy Cowie had played for City in the Midland League the previous season, but the Scot was not able to repeat his scoring feats of 1928–29. Goalkeeper Jack Farmery had been signed from Doncaster Rovers, full-back David Archibald was recruited from Morton, and Sam Johnson, another full-back, had been with Stoke City and Swindon Town. An experienced half-back line consisted of ex-Walsall and Barrow player Harry Beck, Charlie Davis from Torquay United and captain Oliver Thompson, who had previously been on the books of Chesterfield and Queen's Park Rangers. Other signings included Scottish right-winger Sam Evans from Reading and experienced inside-forward Wally Gardner, who had played for Derby County and Grimsby Town. In his early days, Gardner had been a notable amateur player, appearing in the 1915 FA Amateur Cup Final for Bishop Auckland and winning two England amateur caps.

Also in the line up in that opening game were two lads who had joined the club from local football – Tom Smiles and Reg Stockill. The latter, who was drafted into the side at the last minute, was born in York on 23 November 1913, and at 15 years and 281 days he remains the youngest player to represent the club in a senior competitive match. He also had the honour of scoring City's first-ever goal in the Football League as the side recorded a 2–0 win. Stockill, an England Schoolboy international, played only one other League game for City, on the opening day of the following season, before moving to Scarborough. He later went on to have success with Arsenal, Derby County and Luton Town before injury prematurely ended his League career in the late 1930s.

The Sunday Dispatch reported that York gave a capital display and well-deserved their first points. A report in the *Athletic News* said:

> York City fully justified their election to the Football League not only by their win but by their play. They should do well in the Northern Section – well endowed with physique they can play the robust game and have skill too. They have a goalkeeper of more than average ability plus a pair of fine full-backs. The half-back line is a spoiling force rather than constructive while the attack is speedy and thrustful.

The first home match on 4 September 1929, which ended goalless against Wrexham, attracted a crowd of 8,726 to Fulfordgate. The club went on to experience a successful first season partly thanks to the strength of the defence. No less than 16 games were drawn and they finished sixth, which was to be the highest placing until 1952–53.

Other players who figured prominently in that historic first League campaign were Billy Bottrill, top scorer with 18 goals, Glaswegian wingman Willie Millar, who joined the club from Middlesbrough, and Tom Fenoughty, who bridged the gap between the Midland League and Division Three North with ease. Formerly with Middlesbrough, Nelson and Rotherham United, Bottrill recorded the first League hat-trick for the club in a 4–0 win over Wigan Borough in December 1929. At the end the season, he moved to Wolverhampton Wanderers.

The biggest win of the campaign was a 6–0 success over Rochdale, and the biggest crowd was 10,120 on Easter Monday 1930, when champions-elect Port Vale won 2–0. The FA Cup provided the highlight of the campaign, however, as the club reached the third round of the competition for the first time. To reach that stage, City beat Tranmere Rovers and Southend United, as well as Scarborough in a fourth qualifying-round tie – the next time the club played in the qualifying round was 2004–05. All these victories were away, and Fenoughty netted five goals in the process.

On 11 January 1930 City travelled to First Division giants Newcastle United and forced a 1–1 draw (see Matches To Remember).The replay four days later attracted tremendous interest; the gates were closed an hour before the start and many supporters were locked out, including 700 late Newcastle fans. A new record crowd of 12,583 saw a titanic battle, with United winning 2–1 after City had taken the lead through Evans.

A successful season generated total revenue of £10,574, and the end-of-season 1929–30 programme stated:

> We have reason to remember 1929–30 for in this season City attained Football League status and we realise how well the club have done to justify this. The memorable FA Cup ties will never be forgotten nor will the way the team rose to the occasion in League matches. We have all had a great time, a feast of good football and can await the future with every confidence.

Jock Collier relinquished his position as manager at the end of the campaign and became a publican in the city. Billy Sherrington, who had been appointed full-time secretary in February 1930, was to combine his secretarial work with the manager's job for the next three years.

The club relied chiefly on the same squad of players for 1930–31 and finished mid-table, averaging a point per game. They reached the third round of the FA Cup once more and again drew away at First Division opposition, when they held Sheffield United 1–1 at Bramall Lane. The replay set an all-time record crowd for Fulfordgate, when 12,721 saw the Blades win 2–0.

At the shareholders' meeting in the summer of 1931, chairman Arthur Brown stated that they had reached the stage when they might consider themselves well-established as a company and a Football League club. One important move was switching the reserve side from the Yorkshire League to the Midland League.

During the close season, a number of signings were made. Reg Baines returned to the club from Scarborough, and other arrivals were Peter Spooner from Bradford Park Avenue, Tommy Mitchell from Leeds and experienced players Tommy McDonald and Joe Harris from Newcastle United. Stan Fox and Ted Wass made their debuts during the campaign, and City entered the Christmas period second in the table, behind Gateshead, with the following record: P 19, W 11, D 4, L 4, Pts 26.

Support was disappointing, however, with average crowds of only 5,000, and in December 1931 the directors appealed for bigger attendances. In return for an increase of at least 1,000 per game, they said they would do everything possible to strengthen the side in a bid to reach Second Division status, just three seasons after joining the League. Consequently, a crowd of 8,000-plus saw the Boxing Day fixture against Doncaster Rovers, but three successive defeats dented the promotion challenge, and the club again finished in a mid-table position.

During the campaign Reg Baines hit 29 League goals, including three hat-tricks, and set a club scoring record in the Football League, which remained unbeaten until 1951–52. Generally, City were involved in some high-scoring games. They beat Halifax Town 7–2 on 23 April 1932, in what was to be the last League game staged at Fulfordgate. On the other side of the coin, they suffered heavy defeats at Crewe (8–1), Hartlepool (7–2) and Gateshead (6–0).

Action from the last Football League game to be played at Fulfordgate on 23 April 1932, when City beat Halifax Town 7–2. City's 'keeper Richard Thornton makes a save with defender Joe Harris on the right.

In October 1931 Wigan Borough dropped out of the League with mounting financial problems, and Rochdale finished bottom of the table with just 11 points. Over Easter 1932, City completed a 5–2 and 5–3 double over the hapless Spotland club, with Baines netting a total of five goals in these games. The end of the season saw the departure of stalwarts Oliver Thompson, Harry Beck and Jack Brooks, who had served the club so well in those early days of League football.

In the FA Cup, City suffered a first-round defeat at New Brighton. The resultant loss of revenue from this early dismissal, plus disappointing average home crowds of 4,330, resulted in a deficit of £1,539 over the season. The continued lack of support was one of the chief factors in the move to Bootham Crescent (see York City Grounds).

At the AGM in the summer of 1932, the directors were commended by shareholders for the bold policy they had pursued in moving to the new ground in such a short time. With a new permanent home that was well-equipped and capable of development, a new era dawned for York City Football Club. They also sported new colours – chocolate and cream striped shirts and white shorts, considered to be in recognition of the confectionery industry in York.

The 1932–33 campaign started with a defeat at Crewe, and then in the official opening match at Bootham Crescent on 31 August 1932, a crowd of 8,106 saw a 2–2 draw against Stockport County. The scorer of City's first-ever goal at the new ground was Tommy Mitchell, with Reg Baines netting the other goal from the penalty spot. City lost the next home game against Rochdale (6–2) and went on to experience their worst season in the Football League to date, only avoiding having to seek re-election by winning their last game of the campaign 6–1, at home to bottom club Darlington.

A number of players were released at the end of the season, including Sam Johnson and David Archibald, who had served the club so well since 1929. The former was later to return as second-team trainer. Reg Baines moved to Sheffield United for a fee of £500 in May 1933, and Peter Spooner also made the move to Bramall Lane for a similar fee, but both these players were to return to figure in the FA Cup triumphs that lay ahead in the late 1930s. Impressive players during the season included 'keeper Desmond Fawcett, who had previously been with Preston North End, and the promising Jack Pinder, who made his senior debut that term and had captained England Schoolboys in the mid-1920s (see picture page 22).

City again fell at the first hurdle in the FA Cup when Midland League side Scarborough won 3–1 at Bootham Crescent in front of 8,958. To rub salt in the wounds, two of the visitors' goals were netted by former City player Matt Jenkinson and York-born Dave Halford, who went on to play for Derby County. Jenkinson was to rejoin City later that season.

As well as being disappointing from a playing point of view, 1932–33 was a bad season financially. With a deficit of £624 plus the expense of moving to the new ground, the total adverse balance carried forward amounted to £3,388. The average home crowd of 4,370 was almost identical to the last season at Fulfordgate.

Meanwhile, the supporters' club announced a record membership of 1,100. The death of the club's president, Sir John Hunt, was announced in June 1933, and the directors expressed their sense of deep

York City, 1933–34. Back row, left to right: G. Ivory, M. Jenkinson, H. Murphy (trainer), D. Fawcett, T. Fenoughty, J. Scott. Middle row: W. Dawson, T. Lockie, S. Wilcockson. Front row: W. Clayson, J. Pinder, H. King.

loss for a generous man who had taken an active interest in the club. Subsequent presidents in the pre-war period were Lord Milton and Viscount Halifax.

During this summer, Jock Collier was reappointed as manager. Among his signings was Maurice Dando, a centre-forward from Bristol Rovers, who made a big impact by finishing top marksman with 25 goals in 1933–34. Half-back Ted Hathway joined the club from Bolton Wanderers, and he was to give City six seasons' excellent service. Another newcomer was centre-half Tom Lockie from Barnsley.

The club experienced a better campaign, finishing 12th and scoring six goals on three occasions, in games against Barrow and home and away encounters against Rochdale. The biggest disappointment was in the FA Cup when, for the third successive campaign, they fell at the first hurdle, losing at home to Hartlepools United. Consequently, this had an adverse effect on finances, and the total debt rose to £5,446. The club's financial situation was one of the factors involved when they reluctantly released Tom Fenoughty in January 1934. He had spent eight seasons with City, serving the club well in the Midland League and Football League at Fulfordgate and Bootham Crescent, scoring 104 goals in 252 senior appearances. Another economy measure involved switching the reserve side back to the Yorkshire League to save on travelling costs.

At the AGM in the summer of 1934, anxiety was expressed regarding finances, but the directors remained confident that the move to Bootham Crescent would prove beneficial to the club in the years ahead. The chairman claimed the widening of the road approaching the ground would greatly facilitate the arrival and departures of fans to and from matches and that this improvement was being made at no expense to the club. Once again, tribute was paid to the supporters' club, which had undertaken the task of raising £1,500 to pay for the Popular Stand at the new ground, and it was announced that over £950 had already been collected.

Jock Collier's recruits for 1934–35 included newly appointed captain Jack Eyres, an inside-forward from Bristol Rovers, and goalkeeper Joe Cunningham, who had been in Walsall's giant-killing side when they had beaten Arsenal in the FA Cup in 1932–33. Powerfully built centre-half Bill Routledge, another ex-Bristol Rovers player, also joined the club, as did Fred Speed from Hull City.

Maurice Dando was top marksman again, notching 21 goals with two hat-tricks, including one in a 7–0 win over Carlisle United in April 1935 – the club's biggest win in the Football League until 1956–57. Another big win came in February 1935 when Crewe Alexandra were vanquished 7–3. In the close season Dando moved to Chesterfield, and the club finished 15th in the Northern Section.

After three barren years in the FA Cup, City experienced some excitement and success in the competition, starting with a 3–2 win at non-League Burton Town in a stormy first-round affair. Left-winger George Bowater scored a disputed late winner, and at the end of the game hundreds of spectators ran onto the pitch and the referee was attacked. The Burton secretary was injured as he tried to protect the official, Mr G. Dutton from Warwick, and press reports said 'it was a disgusting final scene as players and officials tried with utmost difficulty to reach the dressing rooms'. The Burton ground was later closed for a period by the Football Association.

In the second round, Speed scored a fine goal in a home win over New Brighton, and City's reward was a pairing with First Division Derby County. Thus on 12 January 1935 Bootham Crescent staged its first big game, and a then record crowd of 13,612 were in attendance. The Rams had a strong side with three internationals in their attack – namely Sammy Crooks, Dally Duncan and old adversary Hughie Gallacher. City put on a fine display, with Routledge and Stan Fox in outstanding form along with 'keeper Cunningham, but Derby ran out winners thanks to a late goal from Crooks. The gate receipts amounted to £1,040, and it is interesting to note how these were allocated: entertainment tax

– £175; printing, advertising and so on – £6; referee and linesmen – £8; visitors' expenses – £12; sundry items – £4; and £415 to each club.

A deficit of £229 was announced at the end of the season, which was an improvement on the previous year, thanks chiefly to savings made on wages and travelling. New member of the board Mr W.H. Sessions felt that the 'football habit' had still to be cultivated in the city, and discussions took place regarding the establishment of a trust fund, with the idea of purchasing the ground before the lease ran out in 1953. Mr D.A. Pratt, who had been associated with the club since its inception, relinquished his seat on the board for business reasons.

In the summer of 1935, Peter Spooner returned to the club. Other new faces included right-winger Harry Green from Bristol City and experienced Scottish centre-forward Duncan Lindsay, who had made his mark at Newcastle United, Bury and Hartlepools United. The 1935–36 season, however, was a very poor one. Not only did the club struggle throughout in the Northern Section, finishing 19th, but they were swept out of the FA Cup in the first round when Burton Town gained full revenge for the previous season, winning 5–1 at Bootham Crescent. Bowater, now in Burton colours, scored one of the visitors' goals. It was a black day for the club, and there were a few more that season, including a record 12–0 reverse at Chester on 1 February 1936. They also went down 7–2 at Accrington, 6–0 at Walsall, 6–2 at Oldham and 5–0 at Rotherham and Mansfield. In the return game against the Stags, City won a remarkable 7–5. The total of 95 goals conceded that season has only been exceeded once in their history (106 in 1965–66).

The loss on the season's workings was £1,352, and the total debt now stood at £7,048. The annual report said that increased support must be forthcoming if the club was to retain its Football League status. Individual directors continued to dig into their pockets to help ease matters, and in June 1936 the club launched a 'Shilling Fund'. Weekly publicity of subscription lists appeared in the *Evening Press,* and together with tremendous work done by the supporters' club in organising collections and so on, a useful sum of money was raised over a period of months.

No fewer than 10 players were released in May 1936, and several players were signed during the close season. These included goalkeeper Norman Wharton from Doncaster Rovers, ex-Rotherham United half-back Dick Duckworth and inside-forward Malcolm Comrie, who had previously been with Manchester City, Burnley and Crystal Palace. Promising local left-winger George Lee was signed on his 17th birthday, and right-winger Alf Agar was signed from Oldham Athletic. In addition, the club appointed Tom Lockie as trainer and coach that summer. He had spent 1933–34 as a player for the club and then, after spells at Accrington Stanley and Mansfield Town, returned to give 31 years' outstanding and loyal service as trainer, coach, physiotherapist and manager.

For the third time in their history, the club colours were changed – this time to red shirts with white collars, white shorts and red stockings. The campaign got off to a bright start, and City were unbeaten in the opening five games. The visit of Chester on 19 September 1936 drew a then record League crowd of 10,629. In October, Welshman and regular soldier Albert Thompson joined the club from Bradford Park Avenue, and he went on to score 28 goals in 29 League and Cup games. The team's overall form was inconsistent, however, and the final placing of 12th was a little disappointing.

The highlight of the 1936–37 campaign came when the club reached the fourth round of the FA Cup for the first time. At the first hurdle they swept aside Hull City 5–2 at Bootham Crescent, with Agar scoring a hat-trick, and then beat Southend United 2–1 after extra-time in a replay at York, following a 3–3 draw in Essex. At the next stage, they were drawn away to Second Division Bradford City and fought back in fine style to force a replay, after trailing by two goals. The replay attracted

York City, 1937–38. Back row, left to right: Tom Lockie (trainer), Dick Duckworth, Jack Pinder, Ted Wass, Claude Barrett, Ted Hathway, Norman Wharton, Tom Mitchell (manager). Front row: 'Mascot', Sam Earl, Jimmy Hughes, Reg Baines, Malcolm Comrie, Peter Spooner.

12,226 fans, and amid great excitement James Nicol scored an 87th-minute winner to send City into round four. The forward, who had joined City at the start of the season from Hull City, had scored twice for Burton in their 5–1 FA Cup win at York in November 1935. It marked the first time City had beaten opposition from a higher division, and their reward was a trip to another Second Division club – Swansea Town.

The game at Vetch Field was played in terrible conditions. Heavy rain fell throughout and turned the snow-covered pitch into a muddy morass. The markings were washed out and pools of water covered the ground. At half-time the referee inspected the pitch but decided to continue in near-farcical conditions. Full credit to both sides, who battled on, but near the end of the game the players could hardly kick the ball more than three yards. Swansea had the better of the first half but Wharton gave a magnificent display in goal. With the defence in heroic form, City held on and thoroughly deserved the goalless draw. Players from both sides were exhausted at the end, and Fox actually collapsed in the dressing room. In view of the ordeal, the club cancelled the all-night journey home and stayed in a Swansea hotel.

The teams faced another heavy pitch in the replay at Bootham Crescent. The Welsh club took an early lead but City fought back to equalise before half-time thanks to a Hathway header. After the interval, City were on top but Town's goalkeeper made a number of fine saves. It was against the run of play when the visitors regained the lead in the 80th minute and grabbed a third goal on the final whistle. Sunderland went on to beat Swansea in the fifth round, en route to winning the Cup. The Cup run had grossed receipts of £4,666, and the season's profit of £1,088 helped to reduce the overall debt.

In March 1937 Jock Collier requested to be released from his post as coach-manager to go into business with one of his brothers in his native Scotland, and former player Tom Mitchell took over the managerial reins. Before the end of the campaign, two young wingers made their first-team debuts –

right-winger Fred Scott, who had joined the club from Bradford Park Avenue, and 17-year-old outside-left George Lee. Prolific marksman Thompson left for Swansea during the summer, signing off with a hat-trick on the last day of the season in a 5–2 home win against Carlisle United. After a couple of seasons at Bramall Lane, Reg Baines had helped Doncaster Rovers win promotion to the Second Division, so, as Thompson's replacement, City brought Baines back for his third spell with the club. Claude Barrett was signed from Port Vale and right-winger Sam Earl joined from Bury, but City retained basically the same squad as they prepared for their ninth campaign in the Football League.

During the first part of 1937, two directors died – Mr G.W. Halliday, who was instrumental in the move to Bootham Crescent, and Mr S.M. Gawthorne, who sadly did not see the establishment of the social club, which was his brainchild, at the ground. Nevertheless, the 1937–38 season was a memorable campaign, which put York City firmly on the football map. This was the first of the two great FA Cup runs that captured the imagination and attention of football fans throughout the country. In the first two rounds they needed replays to progress but then, favoured with home draws, it was a case of records being broken all along the way as City progressed to the quarter-finals. Record attendance figures and gate receipts were established at each stage, culminating in the all-time record Bootham Crescent attendance in the sixth round.

City played a total of nine ties and used only 13 players, whose names go down in the club's 'Hall of Fame'. They were Norman Wharton (goalkeeper), Jack Pinder, Eddie Legge and Claude Barrett (full-backs), Dick Duckworth (captain), Ted Wass and Ted Hathway (half-backs), Fred Scott, Sam Earl, Reg Baines, Malcolm Comrie, Jimmy Hughes and Peter Spooner (forwards). Legge and Scott played in the first two rounds, and after that the side was unchanged.

In the first round, City had to come from behind to draw against Halifax Town, with Hughes netting the equaliser. In the replay at the Shay Baines scored the only goal of the game. In round two, they were drawn away to Division Three South club Clapton Orient, their first-ever game in the capital. With just 15 minutes remaining, City were losing 2–0 and heading out of the competition, but then, in a tremendous finale, Scott and Comrie scored to force a replay, which was played in front of 7,599 fans. Hughes netted a 78th-minute goal to earn a well-deserved win, and for the fifth time in their history, the club had reached the third round.

Their opponents at this stage were Coventry City, who at the time were joint-leaders of Division Two. The week before, York had crashed 5–0 at home to Rochdale in a League match but rose to the occasion in the Cup tie, watched by 13,917. In a thrilling contest, Spooner opened the scoring in the fifth minute, only for the visitors to quickly equalise. Playing some exciting football, City took control and goals from Hughes and Earl gave them a 3–1 interval lead. Coventry put City under tremendous pressure after the break and reduced their arrears in the 66th minute. However, they defended resolutely and in a dramatic finish, with Earl going off injured in the closing stages and Wass suffering from a cut head, the depleted side held on to record a famous victory.

First Division West Bromwich Albion, who had won the Cup in 1931 and were runners-up in 1935, were the visitors in the next round. City won a thrilling game 3–2, courtesy of a Reg Baines hat-trick (see Matches to Remember).

Middlesbrough, who finished fifth in the First Division that term, travelled to York on 12 February 1938 and 23,860 fans packed into Bootham Crescent. In windy conditions, City had a lot of defending to do against the strong visitors' attack in the opening stages, but they held firm and gradually started to match their First Division opponents. After the break, with the wind in their favour, they resumed well and scored a fine goal in the 53rd minute. Inside-forward Comrie slipped

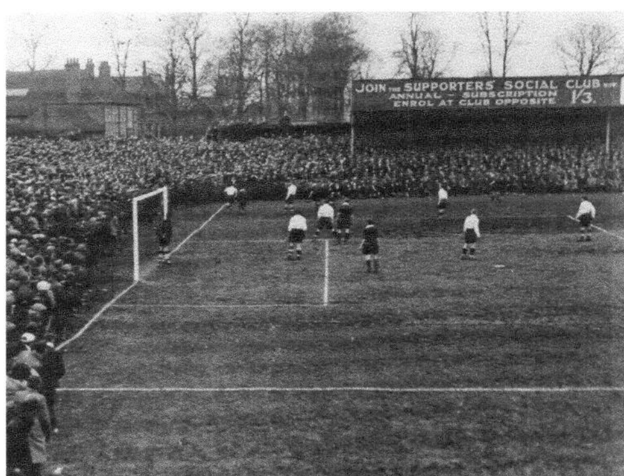

City v Middlesbrough in the fifth round of the FA Cup, 12 February 1938.

the ball to Spooner out on the left, and with a fine left-footed drive the winger beat Dave Cumming sending the City fans wild with excitement. In the next minute, Baines sent in a fierce shot that was parried by the 'keeper and Spooner headed just over. Middlesbrough desperately tried to save the game in the closing stages but City's defence was outstanding and held the much-vaunted Middlesbrough attack in masterly fashion. There were incredible scenes at the end as City fans dashed onto the field to mob their heroes. York City, less than 16 years since their formation, had reached the last eight of the FA Cup.

Newspaper headlines included 'City March On – Amazing Odd Goal Victory. Every Player a Hero in a Merited Win' (*Sports Press*), 'York City's £50 Team Still Making History' (*Northern Echo)* and 'York Goes Wild as City Triumph Again' (*Sunday Express*). The £50 team referred to the fee paid to Sheffield United for match-winner Peter Spooner, while none of the other players had cost any money.

City's winning goal against Middlesbrough scored by Peter Spooner (out of picture), watched by Sammy Earl, Reg Baines and Malcolm Comrie.

The draw for the sixth round produced another all-Yorkshire clash at Bootham Crescent as City entertained First Division Huddersfield Town, who, between the wars, were one of the top clubs in the land. As preparation for the game, the City players spent a few days in Scarborough. The club were now the football talk of the country, and the quarter-final tie was described as one that was going to be an epic game in their history. Hopes were high that City could emulate the feat of Millwall, who had reached the semi-final when in Division Three South the previous season.

The great day dawned – 5 March 1938 – and in spring-like weather, the crowd began to assemble several hours before kick-off. Appropriately, the *Press* stated 'The Eyes of the Country are on York City.' The turnstiles were closed shortly before the start and every vantage point was taken. The all-time record crowd of 28,123 (receipts of £2,736) gave both teams an ovation as they took to the field. The fast and furious Cup tie ended 0–0 (see Matches To Remember).

The replay at Leeds Road on Wednesday 9 March attracted a crowd of 58,066. There were remarkable scenes of traffic congestion on the Leeds to Huddersfield road, and a number of fans abandoned their vehicles and walked several miles to the ground. City bowed out 2–1 after another full-blooded encounter. Town took the lead in the second half, but City quickly equalised when Baines collected a Hathway pass to beat Bob Hesford. In the 68th minute, the First Division side scored the decisive goal, following a goalmouth scramble. In the end, Huddersfield deserved their victory but for City there was no disgrace – only honour and added prestige in defeat. Town went on to reach Wembley, where they lost to Preston North End.

In the nine Cup ties played, a total crowd of 171,336 had watched City, and the receipts amounted to £12,865. Along with the players, great praise was due to manager Tom Mitchell and trainer Tom

City players about to board the team bus during the 1937–38 season, including trainer Tom Lockie (second left), captain Dick Duckworth (centre) and manager Tom Mitchell (right).

Trainer Tom Lockie with three 1937–38 FA Cup heroes – Jack Pinder, Reg Baines and Norman Wharton.

Tom Mitchell and Tom Lockie supervise a training session in 1937–38.

City players relax in a Scarborough hotel prior to the sixth-round FA Cup tie against Huddersfield Town. Norman Wharton is at the piano.

Cartoon of the 1937–38 City team.

OUT OF THE MOUTHS OF EVERY FOOTBALL FAN IN THIS COUNTRY, MUST COME A WONDERFUL DESCRIPTION OF A GREAT LITTLE TEAM
YORK CITY !!

Lockie. It had been, as the *Football Press* described, 'A glorious chapter in York City's history – the victories against teams from every section in the Football League – the crowds – the almost worldwide publicity. City supporters will never forget 1937–38. It may be years and years before a York City team equals the Cup performances of the present side'. It was in fact 17 years before City next hit the national headlines.

In Division Three North that season, City started quite well, but four successive defeats in October were a setback. The next 17 League games yielded nine wins and six draws, and when the Cup run ended in March they were on the fringe of the promotion race, with games in hand against all their rivals. However, they faltered in the closing weeks and ended in 11th place, finishing with five successive defeats. Baines topped the scoring chart with 28 League and Cup goals, but the strength of the side was in the defence, especially at half-back, where Duckworth, Wass and Hathway had outstanding seasons. Profit from the Cup run amounted to £3,518, and the overall deficit was reduced to £3,674. Meanwhile, the reserves had a successful campaign and won the Yorkshire League Championship.

During the year, Mr J.A.(Arthur)Wright joined the board of directors and was to prove an influential figure for the club in the early years of the war. At the end of the season, Stan Fox retired after seven outstanding years' service, and he was rewarded with a benefit game. Reg Baines could not agree terms and moved to Halifax Town, and Malcolm Comrie departed for Bradford City; apart from these two, all the FA Cup heroes were retained. As replacement for Baines, City signed experienced centre-forward Bob Mortimer from Blackburn Rovers for a then club record fee paid of £300.

After the excitement of the previous campaign, City entered their 10th season in the League with a degree of confidence, but 1938–39 was to prove very disappointing. Mortimer was a prolific scorer, totalling 22 goals. He netted in five successive games early in the campaign as the club made a reasonable start, but a disastrous sequence of seven successive defeats in October and November plunged them down the table and into a long battle against having to apply for re-election. A win in

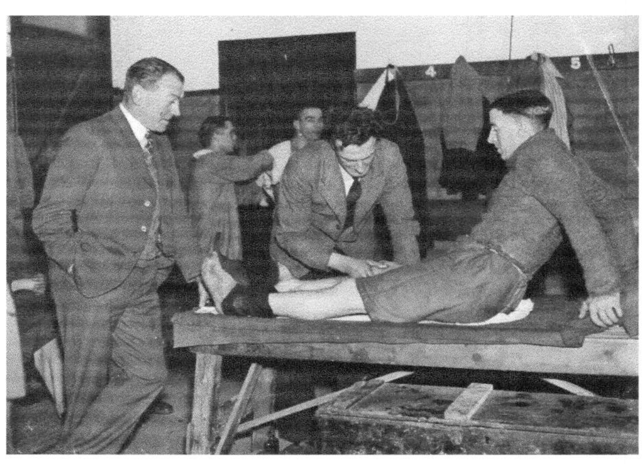

Malcolm Comrie receives treatment from Tom Lockie.

the penultimate game at Darlington avoided that indignity, but there was no doubting it had been a poor season. City suffered some heavy reverses against Crewe Alexandra (8–2), Bradford City (6–0) and Oldham Athletic (6–0), and in January 1939 Rochdale won 7–0 at York to inflict City's biggest-ever home defeat.

As a reward for their feats in the FA Cup the previous campaign, City were exempt until the third round, but there was no glory this term as they crashed out 5–0 to Second Division Millwall at Bootham Crescent. Another reward for their 1937–38 Cup performances was an invitation from the Dutch Football Association to visit Holland and play a Dutch National XI in Rotterdam. The City party of players and officials sailed from Harwich on 11 October 1938 and, although they lost the game 8–2, had a very enjoyable trip. It must be stated that no English club had won in Rotterdam in five years, and Arsenal were among the teams beaten there. City formed good impressions from their continental trip and could report that Holland had little to learn from English clubs, both in regard to playing ability and ground facilities. The group left Rotterdam on the Berlin Boat Express and experienced an air-raid test. All stations were blacked out and the train coaches heavily screened – a sign that war clouds were gathering over Europe.

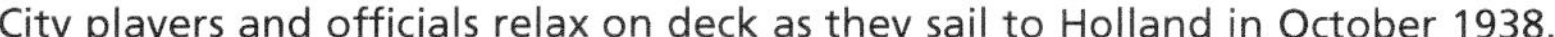

City players and officials relax on deck as they sail to Holland in October 1938.

The reliable Hathway was an ever present that season, while wingmen Scott and Lee made good progress. Bert Brenen, who was to serve the club well in the years ahead, made his debut in the closing weeks of a campaign that saw them finish third from bottom. A big clear out at the end of the season saw the departure of Wharton, Duckworth, Earl, Hughes, Spooner and Wass, among others.

Although the threat of war clouded events, preparations went ahead for the 1939–40 season. Among the new signings were goalkeeper Bob Ferguson from Middlesbrough, inside-forward Bill Allen from Chesterfield, ex-Blackburn Rovers and Manchester United centre-forward John Thompson and, most notably, inside-forward Fred Tilson from Northampton Town. A former England international, Tilson had won League and Cup honours while with Manchester City and scored twice in the 1934 Cup Final, when City beat Portsmouth 2–1.

City opened the season with a 2–2 home draw against Chester and then lost successive away games at Rotherham (2–1) and Rochdale (1–0). The side that represented the club in these three games was as follows: Ferguson, Kelly, Boyle, Hathway, Hawkins, Gledhill, Scott, Allen, Thompson, Tilson and Lee.

War was declared on Sunday 3 September 1939, the day after the match at Spotland, and on the Monday the players were called together at Bootham Crescent. Secretary Billy Sherrington explained that all football had been suspended indefinitely and consequently the club would have no revenue or income. In consultation with the newly appointed chairman, Mr W.H. Sessions, the players were given their insurance cards and told they were free to return to their homes. They were thanked for their services and wished the best of luck in whatever sphere they found themselves. It was to be seven long years before football was back on a normal peacetime footing.

Wartime Football (1939–46)

Upon the declaration of war, football was put on hold, but within a few weeks the stringent conditions were gradually eased, and the government gave permission to the Football Association for the game to proceed on a wartime footing.

In October 1939 the Football League organised regional competitions. The City club had effectively closed down on 4 September when the players were given their insurance cards, but after long discussions the board decided unanimously to carry on. So began an interesting and glorious chapter in the club's history. One ruling instituted by the League allowed clubs to use the services of players (known as guest players) who lived or were stationed nearby, and with York being a military centre, the club were to benefit greatly from this. Players were to be paid 30 shillings a match (£1.50), which was increased to £2 in 1943.

The first wartime season was very experimental. City were placed in the North East League, where their opponents included Newcastle United, Middlesbrough and Leeds United. Quite a few of City's old squad were still available, namely Bob Ferguson, Sam Gledhill, Bert Brenen, Bill Allen, Jack Pinder, Walter Porritt and George Lee. Guest players included former City players Jack Everest and Reg Stockill, who had started their careers with the club back in the 1920s. After a friendly home match against Sheffield United on 14 October, City started their programme the following week when they lost at Bootham Crescent, 3–1 to Middlesbrough. To add to their problems, the winter of 1940 was one of the most severe of the century. Snow and ice caused a virtual shutdown, and City did not play a competitive game from Christmas Day until 16 March 1940. City finished eighth in their section of 11 clubs, winning eight and drawing one of their 20 games. A number of friendly games supplemented the programme, and in the closing weeks the Football League War Cup was instituted, with City losing to Hull City. Although the season had been difficult and the club had lost money, the directors were determined to carry on and the supporters' club carried on their activities with their chairman, Mr J.H. Edwards, pledging full support.

City were placed in the North Regional League in 1940–41, which comprised 36 clubs. Placings were decided by percentages, because teams did not all meet each other. City finished fifth from bottom, winning seven and drawing four of their 25 fixtures, but were involved in some entertaining football that put the emphasis on goals. Left-winger Lee continued to make good progress and Brenen, Pinder and Gledhill were prominent. Among the guests that season were Scottish player Matt Patrick, who was to have a long career with City after the war, and his namesake Alf, a local lad who also made an appearance. Others included George Eastham of England and Blackpool fame, and Tommy Dawson from Charlton Athletic. Another local lad who joined the team was Gordon Jones, a talented left-back from Dringhouses, who quickly made a big impression.

In the League North War Cup, City beat Sheffield Wednesday 7–0 in a preliminary-round tie, with Brenen scoring four goals. Unfortunately, they bowed out to Newcastle United in the second round. In December 1940, the death of City's first manager, Jock Collier, was announced.

The format for 1941–42 was altered. The first half of the season comprised 18 League games, with the points system now operating instead of percentages. With four wins and four draws, the club finished 32nd out of 38 in the Northern League. The League Cup was organised in the second half of the campaign, and the qualifying stages were on a League basis. Fifty-four clubs competed and the top 32 entered the knock-out stages, but City narrowly missed out, finishing 33rd.

York City, winners of the Combined Counties Cup in 1941–42.

In the closing weeks of the season, City played in the Combined Counties Cup along with Chesterfield, Halifax Town, Bradford City, Middlesbrough and Huddersfield Town. They made it to the Final and won the trophy, beating Halifax Town 5–2 over two legs. The players featured in both these games were as follows: Ferguson, Gledhill, Jones, Hodgson (Grimsby Town),Wilson (Reading), Atkinson (Bolton Wanderers), Porritt, Brenen, O'Donnell (Aston Villa), Brown (Charlton), Lee.

Centre-forward Frank O'Donnell was a Scottish international, while inside-forward Bert Brown made a number of wartime international appearances for England. Brown, nicknamed 'Sailor' for his rolling gait, played over 50 times for City and formed an outstanding left-wing partnership with Lee. Two other famous players wore City colours that term – Raich Carter of Sunderland and England fame and the legendary Dixie Dean, winner of 16 England caps and a record-breaking marksman for Everton. Dean played in the home game against Gateshead on 22 November 1941 and fittingly scored with a header, while Carter's appearance was at Bootham Crescent against Grimsby Town on 3 January 1942. Jimmy Rudd (Manchester City) and Len Butt (Blackburn Rovers), both of whom played for the club in post-war football, also made guest appearances. Lee top scored again and hit 26 goals, including four in a 9–5 win over Middlesbrough.

Cecil McCormack (second left) challenges for the ball with Sheffield Wednesday defender Walter Millership, as George Lee (No. 11) looks on in the Football League North War Cup semi-final in April 1943. Note the spectators on the top of the Popular Stand in City's biggest wartime attendance.

Former chairman Arthur Brown resigned his place on the board after almost 20 years' service and retired to live in the South. A profit of £1,041 was made during 1941–42, and the level of support was encouraging. At the club's 20th annual meeting, tribute was paid to Arthur Wright for his tireless work as acting team manager and to trainer Tom Lockie. Praise was also given to Wilf Meek, who wrote under the pseudonym 'Citizen' in the *Yorkshire Evening Press* for his balanced reporting and judgement.

City's most successful wartime season was 1942–43, when outstanding goalkeeping personality Sam Bartram from Charlton Athletic teamed up with the club. Also continuing to guest were Brown, O'Donnell and Reading centre-half Joe Wilson, who gave great service to the club, making 114 appearances during the war. The Arsenal centre-half and Middlesex cricketer Leslie Compton played three games, and an appearance was made by local lad Neville Tutill. Many years later, his son Stephen played for the club. Fred Scott, who had played for the club before the war, was also available for selection that season.

George Lee scoring from the spot against Sheffield Wednesday.

British prisoners of war line up for a game in German camp Stalag No. 5947. Third from right in the front row is Jimmy Hughes, one of City's FA Cup heroes of 1937–38.

On 17 October 1942 the Football League staged a representative game at Bootham Crescent between the League and the Northern Command. At left-back for the League was City's highly rated Gordon Jones. A great future was predicted for the local lad, but sadly he was struck down by a serious illness in 1943 from which he was unable to recover, and he died in January 1947.

The same fixture format applied as in the previous campaign in League North, and with nine victories and three draws, the club finished 17th out of 47. One individual scoring feat is worth recalling: in a 4–3 win over Newcastle United in October, all four City goals were scored by O'Donnell.

After the disappointment of the previous season, City waltzed through the League qualifying stages this time, winning six and drawing one of their nine games. City then embarked on an outstanding run to the Football League North Cup semi-finals. The knock-out stages were on a two-leg basis, and Newcastle United were beaten 4–3 on aggregate in the first round. Bradford Park Avenue were vanquished 5–1 and Chesterfield were beaten 4–0. For the first time in their history, City had reached the semi-final of a major Cup competition, and enthusiasm in the area was almost on a par with the great days of 1937–38. Sheffield Wednesday provided the last hurdle before the Final, and in the first leg at Hillsborough in front of 35,253, Wednesday established a 3–0 lead. Unfortunately, 'Sailor' Brown was not available that day, as Charlton had recalled him for their Southern semi-final. He did play in the second leg, but in front of a record wartime crowd at Bootham Crescent (16,350), the task was too hard for City, who drew 1–1 and bowed out 4–1 on aggregate. City's line ups for this famous Cup run were:

Newcastle United (A) Bartram (Charlton Athletic), Pinder, Gledhill, Hodgson (Grimsby Town),Wilson (Reading), Campbell (Luton Town), Scott, Dawson (Charlton Athletic), Brenen, Brown (Charlton Athletic), Lee.

Newcastle United (H) Ferguson, Pinder, Jones, Hodgson (Grimsby Town), Wilson (Reading), Campbell (Luton Town), Scott, Black (Hearts), Brenen, Brown (Charlton Athletic), Lee.

Bradford PA (H) Bartram (Charlton Athletic), Pinder, Jones, Hodgson (Grimsby Town),Wilson (Reading), Gledhill, Scott, Dawson (Charlton Athletic), Brenen, Brown (Charlton Athletic), Lee.

Bradford PA (A) Bartram (Charlton Athletic), Pinder, Jones, Hodgson (Grimsby Town), Wilson (Reading), Gledhill, Scott, Dawson (Charlton Athletic), McCormack (Gateshead), Brown (Charlton Athletic), Lee.

Chesterfield (H & A) Bartram (Charlton Athletic), Pinder, Jones, Hodgson (Grimsby Town), Wilson (Reading), Gledhill, Scott, Dawson (Charlton Athletic), McCormack (Gateshead), Brown (Charlton Athletic), Lee.

Sheffield Wednesday (A) Bartram (Charlton Athletic), Pinder, Jones, Hodgson (Grimsby Town), Wilson (Reading), Gledhill, Scott, Dawson (Charlton Athletic), McCormack (Gateshead), Brenen, Lee.

Sheffield Wednesday (H) Bartram (Charlton Athletic), Pinder, Jones, Hodgson (Grimsby Town), Wilson (Reading), Gledhill, Scott, Powell (Leeds United), McCormack (Gateshead), Brown (Charlton Athletic), Lee.

The eight ties attracted a total of 136,935 spectators and grossed £9,156. City made a profit of £2,188 over the season. The Cup run had attracted not only attention at home but also many messages of congratulations from York servicemen abroad, especially from the victorious Eighth Army in North Africa.

The sad news of the death of Arthur Wright was announced in June 1943. A leading York chemist, he had shown much enthusiasm in his time as a director and had been instrumental in bringing so many notable guest players to the club. On a brighter note, it had been another fine year for George Lee, who netted 26 goals and topped the scoring charts for the fourth successive season. Benefits were granted to Sam Gledhill and Ted Hathway.

The summer of 1943 marked the coming of age of York City. At a special meeting to mark the club's 21st anniversary, a tribute was made to Billy Sherrington. Chairman Mr W.H. Sessions summed him up by saying 'Billy is York City and what more can I say than that.' His life's work had seen the club grow from an idea to a soccer stronghold. At the outbreak of war, he had resumed civil service duties but continued to work tirelessly for the club during this difficult period.

The fifth season of wartime football again produced some excellent football at Bootham Crescent, watched by sizeable crowds. In the pre-Christmas League programme, City finished 31st out of 50 clubs, with seven wins and two draws. In the League Cup qualifying group, they went into their last match needing to beat Leeds United by a big score and did just that, winning 8–1 at home! In the knock-out stages, Barnsley were beaten 5–4 on aggregate, with a crowd of over 14,000 at Oakwell. Bradford Park Avenue were too strong in the second round, and City lost 7–2 overall. Shackleton, who went on to have a very successful career with Newcastle United and Sunderland, netted four of Bradford's goals in the two games.

One notable guest player that season was Benny Fenton, who had a long and illustrious career with London clubs West Ham United, Millwall and Charlton Athletic. Also, promising local 'keeper Peter Pickering made his debut away at Chesterfield in April. Meanwhile, George Lee scored his 90th wartime goal during the 1943–44 campaign, which took his tally to 100 for the club. He joined the army in March 1944, and his future appearances were limited.

At the AGM in the summer of 1944, another profit for the season was announced and tribute was paid to two players who had lost their lives on active service, namely Len 'Taffy' Milner and G.Reynolds, a Charlton Athletic centre-half who guested for City that season. Others killed were Nottingham Forest player Grenville Roberts, who had played for the club in 1940, and Albert Bonass, who died in a training flight crash at Tockwith in October 1945. A local lad, he played for City in 1933–34 and then Hartlepools United and Chesterfield.

The 1944–45 season caused great selection problems. Many players had left for the war fronts, and with constant troop movements there were considerable alterations to team personnel. No fewer than 57 players appeared for the club; remarkably, centre-half Joe Wilson was an ever present. Although 'Sailor' Brown was no longer available, his Charlton colleague Sam Bartram still made regular appearances and took over the role of penalty-taker towards the end of the campaign.

There was no shortage of goals this season, and Gateshead were beaten 10–2 in October, with guest player Harry Hawkins (ex-Southport and Middlesbrough) scoring four times. Hawkins finished top scorer with 21 League and Cup goals. With six wins and one draw from their 18 League games, City finished 42nd out of 54 and also failed to qualify for the League North Cup knock-out stages. To supplement their programme, they competed in the Tyne, Wear and Tees Cup, along with Darlington, Middlesbrough, Sunderland and Newcastle United. It was in this competition that Bartram, in a game against the Quakers, netted twice from the same spot.

In March 1945 Harry Hayhurst, who had been involved with the club since its formation, resigned from the board of directors due to ill health, and Hugh Kitchin was co-opted to succeed him. At the summer AGM, Messrs B. Littlefair and D. Blundy took the places of Messrs E.J. Pulleyn and W. Newton on the board.

Although hostilities had finished by the start of 1945–46, there was not sufficient time to restore soccer to its usual pattern, but changes were made to the format in preparation for the resumption of peacetime football. In the first half of the campaign, City figured in Division Three East and finished mid-table, winning six and drawing six of their 18 fixtures. In the second half, they played in the Third Division (East) Cup and reached the second round after qualifying through the group stages.

The reserves resumed their programme in the Yorkshire League and the FA Cup was restored. And for the first and only time, ties were on a two-leg home and away basis – the highlight of the campaign for the club. Halifax Town and Bishop Auckland were beaten in the first two rounds, and City were drawn against strong Second Division side Chesterfield, who at the time were top of League North. Signed just in time for the clash was Harry Thompson from Sunderland for an undisclosed club record fee paid. The skilful inside-forward, who had played previously as

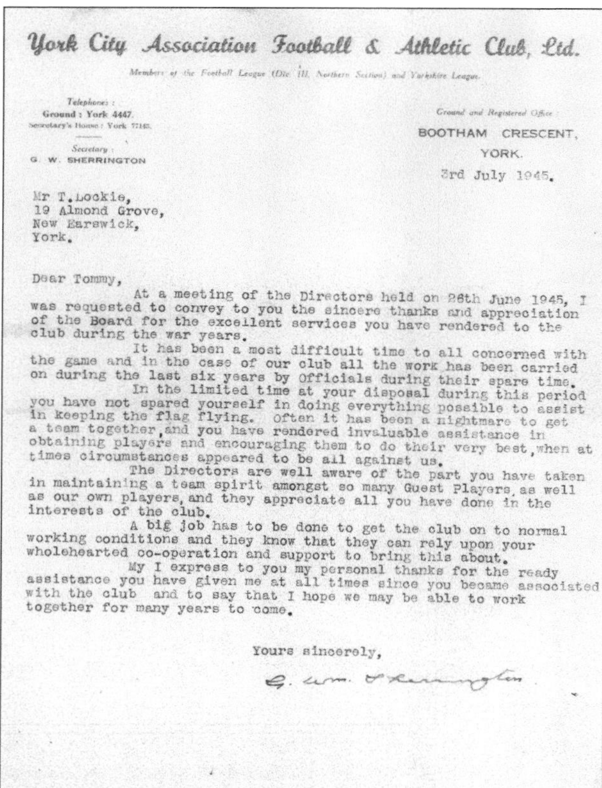

York City Association Football & Athletic Club, Ltd.

Members of the Football League (Div. III, Northern Section) and Yorkshire League.

Telephones:
Ground: York 4447.
Secretary's House: York 77145.

Secretary:
G. W. SHERRINGTON

Ground and Registered Office:
BOOTHAM CRESCENT,
YORK.

3rd July 1945.

Mr T. Lockie,
19 Almond Grove,
New Earswick,
York.

Dear Tommy,

At a meeting of the Directors held on 26th June 1945, I was requested to convey to you the sincere thanks and appreciation of the Board for the excellent services you have rendered to the club during the war years.

It has been a most difficult time to all concerned with the game and in the case of our club all the work has been carried on during the last six years by Officials during their spare time.

In the limited time at your disposal during this period you have not spared yourself in doing everything possible to assist in keeping the flag flying. Often it has been a nightmare to get a team together, and you have rendered invaluable assistance in obtaining players and encouraging them to do their very best, when at times circumstances appeared to be all against us.

The Directors are well aware of the part you have taken in maintaining a team spirit amongst so many Guest Players, as well as our own players, and they appreciate all you have done in the interests of the club.

A big job has to be done to get the club on to normal working conditions and they know that they can rely upon your wholehearted co-operation and support to bring this about.

My I express to you my personal thanks for the ready assistance you have given me at all times since you became associated with the club and to say that I hope we may be able to work together for many years to come.

Yours sincerely,

G. Wm. Sherrington

A letter of thanks to Tom Lockie for his excellent service to the club during the war years.

a guest for the club, went to Roker Park from Wolverhampton Wanderers in 1938 for the then sizeable fee of £7,500. Another newcomer was Alf Young, the former Huddersfield Town centre-half.

City drew the first leg 1–1 at Saltergate, and the game at Bootham Crescent attracted a 14,207 crowd on a Wednesday afternoon. In a thrilling affair, City led through an own-goal and an Ian Winters header, but the Spireites hit back and levelled the score with five minutes left. Consequently, 20 minutes of extra-time was played in semi-darkness. Amid great excitement, City regained the lead when Winters volleyed the ball into the net after good work by Thompson. In a terrific finish, they withstood tremendous pressure and held on to record another famous FA Cup success. They had reached the fourth round for the third time, but at this stage they were swept aside 11–1 on aggregate by Sheffield Wednesday.

The 1945–46 season ended on a sad note when former chairman and director Arthur Brown collapsed and died after attending the FA Cup Final. Five of the seven seasons of wartime football had produced a profit and the York public had been well-entertained, so the decision to carry on back in 1939 had been fully vindicated. City were indebted to many guest players during those seven years but tribute had to be paid to five of their own players who gave such outstanding service during this time – Sammy Gledhill, who made a total of 219 appearances, Jack Pinder (173), George Lee (153 with 90 goals), Bob Ferguson (106) and Bert Brenen (127), who played in every position, including 'keeper in an emergency. Pinder received his second benefit when Huddersfield Town provided the opposition on 1 May 1946, and an attendance of almost 6,000 was just reward for the stalwart full-back, who had completed 17 years with the club. Praise was also due to the backroom staff especially secretary Billy Sherrington and trainer Tom Lockie.

The soccer flag had been kept flying by York City, and the club looked ahead with confidence and eagerness to the resumption of peacetime football in August 1946.

The Post-war Soccer Boom (1946–54)

In the late 1940s and early 1950s, big crowds flocked to grounds throughout the country as people shook off the effects of war in pursuit of sport and entertainment. They were the days before widespread ownership of televisions and cars, so clubs boasted record attendances – in 1948–49 City's average League attendance was 10,412, which remains a club record. Reserve fixtures drew crowds of 3,000-plus.

In the eight immediate post-war seasons, City had a moderate playing record and only finished in the top half of the Northern Section twice. There wasn't much success in the FA Cup either, as the club made only one appearance in the third round. Nonetheless, there was some exciting football played during this time at Bootham Crescent, and the big crowds were well-entertained in those austere days.

Not surprisingly, the 1946–47 campaign was one of reconstruction, not only at York but throughout the Football League. The fixture list was the one that had been scheduled for 1939–40, so City entertained Chester on 31 August 1946. Seven years earlier, the game was drawn 2–2 and this time it finished 4–4. Bill Allen, who had netted twice in the pre-war fixture, scored once on his official debut in 1946, and the other men on the mark were Frank Carr and Ernie Nettleton. Of the side that had played at Rochdale in September 1939, there were four survivors – Bob Ferguson, Sammy Gledhill, Fred Scott and Allen. Also in the team for the opening game were pre-war players Jack Pinder, Bert Brenen and Austin Collier. Tom Mitchell resumed his duties as manager following his service in the RAF so, unlike at a number of clubs, there was a good deal of continuity.

Within a week of the start of the season, right-winger Scott was transferred to Nottingham Forest for a new club record fee received of £3,000. Harry Thompson, who had joined City the previous season, was released from his contract and moved to Northampton Town a few weeks later. No fewer than 34 players appeared for City in this first post-war campaign, and notable debutants included Alf Patrick – top scorer with 17 goals – and Matt Patrick, along with Sid Storey and Jimmy Rudd. Two Polish army players also made appearances – goalkeeper Eddie Wojtczak and left-winger Eryk Kubicki.

The winter of 1947 was severe, and in February and March the country was in the grip of ice and snow, followed by floods. These were days long before floodlights, and there was also a government ban on midweek football because of the early post-war economic crisis. Consequently, City did not play between 1 February and 22 March, and the season was extended until 7 June. It was a mixed year for City, who finished 15th, chiefly because of poor home form – just six wins at Bootham Crescent. They also lost at home to non-League Scunthorpe United in the first round of the FA Cup.

Meanwhile, at the supporters' club annual dinner that winter, a tribute was paid to their secretary Mr H.Ward, who had held the post for over 20 years. In the summer of 1947, at the club's silver jubilee AGM, a profit of £3,651 was announced, and Mr Eric Magson was elected to the board of directors.

For the new season, the second team transferred back to the Midland League. Just before the start of the campaign, George Lee was transferred to Nottingham Forest for £7,500, which more than doubled the club record fee received. At Forest, he teamed up with former teammate Scott and his wartime mentor, 'Sailor' Brown.

City made a good start to 1947–48 and, unbeaten after six games, topped the table. Form dipped, however, and they finished in 13th place and also again fell at the first hurdle in the FA Cup, when

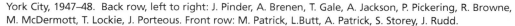

York City, 1947–48. Back row, left to right: J. Pinder, A. Brenen, T. Gale, A. Jackson, P. Pickering, R. Browne, M. McDermott, T. Lockie, J. Porteous. Front row: M. Patrick, L.Butt, A. Patrick, S. Storey, J. Rudd.

Rochdale won at Bootham Crescent. Newcomers this term included centre-half and captain Tommy Gale from Sheffield Wednesday and full-back John Simpson, who became the first £1,000 signing when he was recruited from Huddersfield Town in March 1948. Percy Andrews and Ron Spence made their debuts this season, while stalwart full-back Pinder hung up his boots at the end of the campaign. Alf Patrick made an impact, hitting 19 goals, including four in a 6–0 win over Halifax Town – the first City player to achieve this feat in League football. Outstanding during the season was 'keeper Peter Pickering, who in May 1948 was transferred to Chelsea for £6,750. Average crowds were over 9,000, and takings that season of £16,213 were a record for Bootham Crescent. With a net profit of £4,914, the club were able to carry forward a plus balance of £1,843.

In September 1948 the club announced the purchase of the Bootham Crescent ground (see Homes of York City). Mr N.J. Hopwood was elected to the board, and £75 was donated to former centre-forward Maurice Dando, who was suffering from paralysis. Later, vice chairman Mr H. Rusholme died. He had been the club's longest-serving director and its first secretary back in 1922.

The 1948–49 season was the peak of the soccer boom period, with record-breaking attendances throughout the country. Takings at Bootham Crescent rose to a new high of £19,035, as no fewer than 17 of City's League games, home and away, drew five-figure crowds. These included the two matches against Northern Section champions-elect Hull City in April 1949, which drew an aggregate attendance of over 61,000 – 40,002 were at Boothferry Park; and for a midweek encounter, which City won 3–2, Bootham Crescent's all-time record League attendance of 21,010 saw the Tigers gain revenge 3–1 on 23 April. In November 1948 over 19,000 watched City thrash then League leaders Rotherham United 6–1 (see Matches to Remember), when Alf Patrick netted five times. The centre-forward was top scorer again with a total of 26 goals.

City showed outstanding home form in the first half of the campaign and won eight successive League games at Bootham Crescent, scoring 31 goals in the process. With the exception of the win at

Alf Patrick (on the ground) scoring against Accrington Stanley on 1 October 1949.

Hull, they fell away in disappointing fashion in the closing weeks and finished 14th. Early in the new year, the mercurial Jimmy Rudd was transferred to Leeds United, and at the end of the season Sammy Gledhill retired. In the FA Cup, City lost at home to Southport in a second-round replay.

One newcomer to the ranks was centre-half Alan Stewart from Huddersfield Town, but a bad start was made to the 1949–50 season. With just one win in the opening 10 games, City never fully recovered and finished bottom of Division Three North and had to apply for re-election for the first time in their history. Along with Halifax Town, Newport County and Millwall from the Southern Section, they did not have to enter a ballot, as the Football League was increased in 1950 to 92 clubs. Twenty non-League clubs competed for the four additional places, and the successful ones were Scunthorpe United, Shrewsbury Town, Colchester United and Gillingham.

In February 1950 Tom Mitchell announced his resignation as manager, and the new boss was Dick Duckworth, who had captained the side in the memorable FA Cup run 12 years earlier. In March the death of City's first trainer, Hughie 'Spud' Murphy, was announced. However, it was not all doom and gloom that season, as the reserves finished in the top six of the Midland League, scoring over 100 goals, and won the North Riding Cup for the first time in the club's history, beating Middlesbrough reserves 3–0 at Ayresome Park on 7 April 1950. The line up was: Frost, Brown, Duthoit, Spence, Burgin, Jackson, Ivey, Coop, Walker, Collins and Birch.

The club entered a third team in the Yorkshire League in 1950–51, and new signings included right-winger John Linaker and inside-forward Gordon Brown from Nottingham Forest. The season got off to a disastrous start with a 7–2 defeat at Tranmere Rovers. Making his one and only appearance in goal that day was Jimmy Pegg, who had played a couple of First Division games for Manchester United in

York City squad, 1950–51.

A heading duel between George Hardwick, ex-England and Middlesbrough, and Alf Patrick in a Division Three North game between City and Oldham Athletic on 30 December 1950.

1947. It turned out to be a better season, however, with a final placing of 17th, and the third round of the FA Cup was reached for the first time since 1946. At that stage, they bowed out 2–0 to First Division Bolton Wanderers. City put up a resolute display but were handicapped early in the second half when Alan Stewart had to go off with a badly cut eye after a collision with England centre-forward Nat Lofthouse. In his absence, Wanderers took the lead. Stewart returned to play on the right wing, and it was not until the last minute that the First Division side clinched the win with a second goal after a gallant City effort.

Promising 'keeper Des Thompson made his debut in the second half of the campaign, and Bert Brenen received a record benefit at the end of that season – a just reward for 13 years' outstanding service. The utility player moved to Scarborough, however, in August 1951 after failing to agree terms with City.

In his first season with the club, Linaker was an ever present and joint-top League scorer with Matt Patrick. A top-class golfer, he became a professional and managed a number of top golf clubs when his footballing days were over, including Fulford, Royal North Devon (Westward Ho), Moor Park and Gullane in Scotland. Linaker also won a number of tournaments and represented Yorkshire, Devon and Lothian.

As part of the Festival of Britain celebrations, a series of special matches were played throughout the country. For their part, City entertained League of Ireland clubs Sligo Rovers and Transport. They won the games 4–0 and 5–0 respectively, and making his debut in these matches was a young right-winger by the name of Billy Hughes.

In readiness for 1951–52, several signings were made, notably left-winger Billy Fenton from Blackburn Rovers and experienced inside-forward Steve Griffiths, formerly with Portsmouth and Barnsley, who was made captain. These players made a big impact as City enjoyed their best post-war season to date, and they rose to 10th place. Under the skilful leadership of the veteran Griffiths, City played some fine football and were well-nigh invincible at home, with 16 wins and four draws. Some big victories were recorded, including 6–1 versus Accrington Stanley, 6–2 versus Halifax Town, 5–0 versus Oldham Athletic and 5–1 versus Workington.

During the season, Alf Patrick completed 100 Football League goals for the club – the first City player to achieve this feat – while Fenton hit 31 goals to beat Reg Baines's record of 29, set in the early 1930s. Upon the departure of Linaker to Hull City early in the campaign, Hughes established himself on the right wing, and local centre-forward David Dunmore scored on his senior debut in the last game of the season. In the FA Cup City lost to Bradford Park Avenue in a first-round second replay at Elland Road.

Tom Lockie is congratulated by Sam Bartram after his testimonial game against a Football League XI in April 1952. On the right is Sunderland's Len Shackleton.

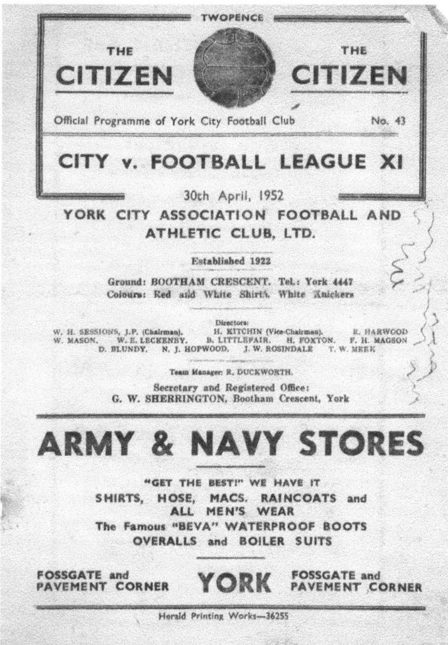

TWOPENCE

THE CITIZEN THE CITIZEN

Official Programme of York City Football Club No. 43

CITY v. FOOTBALL LEAGUE XI

30th April, 1952

YORK CITY ASSOCIATION FOOTBALL AND ATHLETIC CLUB, LTD.

Established 1922

Ground: BOOTHAM CRESCENT. Tel.: York 4447
Colours: Red and White Shirts. White Knickers

Directors:
W. H. SESSIONS, J.P. (Chairman). H. KITCHIN (Vice-Chairman). R. HARWOOD
W. MASON. W. E. LECKENBY. B. LITTLEFAIR. H. FOXTON. F. H. MAGSON
D. BLUNDY. N. J. HOPWOOD. J. W. ROSINDALE T. W. MEEK

Team Manager: R. DUCKWORTH.

Secretary and Registered Office:
G. W. SHERRINGTON, Bootham Crescent, York

ARMY & NAVY STORES

"GET THE BEST!" WE HAVE IT
SHIRTS, HOSE, MACS. RAINCOATS and ALL MEN'S WEAR
The Famous "BEVA" WATERPROOF BOOTS
OVERALLS and BOILER SUITS

FOSSGATE and PAVEMENT CORNER YORK FOSSGATE and PAVEMENT CORNER

Herald Printing Works—36255

Tom Lockie's testimonial game programme cover.

In March 1952 Wilf Meek was appointed to the board, and at the end of the season Tom Lockie was rewarded with a benefit match when City met a Football League XI. In the representative side were Sam Bartram, Len Shackleton and young Sheffield United forward Arthur Bottom, who was to make an enormous impact when he joined City two years later.

City relied on virtually the same squad for the 1952–53 season and experienced their best campaign to date in the League. Fenton was again top marksman with 25 goals, but the main strength of the side was the defence, with Andrews and both Spences outstanding. At the halfway stage, City were well-placed in third position. However, on 3 January 1953, in front of 15,222, they narrowly lost at home to leaders Oldham Athletic and then followed a sequence of just one win in 10 outings. They failed to record a win at Bootham Crescent from

City line up on 14 April 1953 prior to a Northern Section game at Southport. Back row, left to right: M. Patrick, G. Brown, H. Searson, P. Andrews, R. Spence, J. Simpson. Front row: W. Hughes, R. Warrender, A. Patrick, S. Storey, W. Fenton.

Boxing Day until 28 March and the promotion dream faded, although fourth position and 53 points were new club records.

There were two significant departures in the autumn of 1952. Firstly, in October, Dick Duckworth was reluctantly released from his contract and took over at Stockport County. His successor was Charles Spencer, the former England and Newcastle United centre-half and previous boss at Grimsby Town, but sadly he died after less than three months in office. Secondly, in November, 'keeper Des Thompson was transferred to First Division Burnley for £7,350, just prior to an FA Cup first-round match at home to Barrow. Local lad Mick Granger, who was doing his National Service, was pressed into action. Although Granger had a good game, City went down 2–1.

In May 1953 Jimmy McCormick, the former Tottenham Hotspur and Fulham winger and Sheffield United coach, was appointed the new manager. Three seasons of steady progress had seen the club rise from the foot of the Northern Section to fourth place, and hopes were high at the start of the 1953–54 campaign. However, injuries to key players proved a setback, and the season was bitterly disappointing. The average League attendance of 5,636 was the smallest since the war. At the halfway mark, City were bottom of the table. Although they staged a recovery, only a victory in the last game of the season at Halifax Town spared them the indignity of having to apply for re-election.

Mr W.H. Sessions stood down as chairman after 14 years. His successor was Mr H.F.(Hugh) Kitchin, and Mr D. Blundy was vice-chairman. In the FA Cup City fell at the first hurdle – for the sixth time in eight seasons – when they crashed 5–2 at Barnsley. The one bright spot this term was the form showed by Dunmore. The powerful young centre-forward had 20 goals to his credit when signed by Tottenham Hotspur just after his 20th birthday in February 1954, for a new club record fee received of £10,500.

The Happy Wanderers (1954–58)

The 1954–58 period was arguably the best and most successful spell in the club's history as, along with the glorious FA Cup triumphs, City were one of the leading Division Three North clubs. With the team playing some outstanding football, the crowds flocked back to Bootham Crescent.

With monies available from the Dunmore transfer plus financial help from the supporters' club and its fund-raising branch formed earlier that year, the auxiliary supporters' club, several players were signed in the summer of 1954. The auxiliary supporters' club committee included Jack Burke, Frank Cawood, Jim Edwards, Eric Thompson, Norman Clay, Tommy Roebuck and Billy Hill. At one time, the scheme boasted 16,000 members and raised over £100,000 over a period of 10 years. Jack Burke was a tireless worker for City for many years, and he helped start the scheme and acted as secretary. Ill health caused him to stand down in 1960, and in recognition of his loyal and valuable service, the club made him a life member of York City.

All the profits and monies raised were ploughed back into the club, and the new captures included Tommy Forgan, Ernie Phillips and Norman Wilkinson (all from Hull City); ex-Huddersfield Town player George Howe; Arthur Bottom and Sam McNab from Sheffield United; and Les Slatter from Aston Villa. The new-look team, under the captaincy of Phillips, made a sensational start with a 6–2 win at Wrexham (see Matches to Remember). A home win over Hartlepool was then followed by defeat against Scunthorpe United at Bootham Crescent. After this game a dispute over team selection arose between McCormick and the directors. It was not resolved, and a few days later the manager's resignation was accepted. Team affairs were subsequently handled by trainer Tom Lockie and secretary Billy Sherrington – it was to be 18 months before a new manager was appointed.

A run of eight games without a win saw the club drop to near the foot of the table, and attendances plummeted from 12,000 to under 6,000. With the recall of Billy Hughes and Sid Storey to the attack, the team began to blend and the obvious potential in the side was realised. On 16 October 1954, in a home win over Darlington, City fielded a side that was to become, perhaps, the most famous in their history: Forgan, Phillips, Howe, Brown, Stewart, Spence, Hughes, Bottom, Wilkinson, Storey, Fenton.

With the emphasis on close-passing, attacking football, the side embarked on a ten-match unbeaten run prior to the start of the FA Cup. In the first round, they had a scare before beating neighbours Scarborough. This was followed by a 5–2 win at Dorchester Town, with Bottom hitting a hat-trick. After the match, the Dorchester secretary made a prophetic statement when he said 'I pity any First Division team who meet these continental Yorkshiremen.'

The draw for the third round pitched City against glamour side Blackpool at Bloomfield Road and City recorded a 2–0 victory in a magnificent display (see Matches to Remember).Top amateur side Bishop Auckland were then vanquished 3–1 at their Kingsway Ground, with Bottom scoring twice along with Storey. It should be noted that the Bishops had several amateur internationals in their side, including captain Bob Hardisty, who had led Great Britain's side in the 1948 Olympics.

The famous victory over Spurs (see Matches to Remember) put City into the last eight, equalling the record of the 1937–38 side, and City were drawn away to Second Division Notts County in the quarter-finals. An all-ticket crowd of 47,301 saw the game, including 11,225 City fans. A tense and keenly contested Cup tie was decided by a 78th-minute Bottom goal following a Hughes free-kick.

In that night's *Sports Press*, Wilf Meek wrote 'Amidst scenes which I have never seen equalled before on a football ground this amazing York City team could hardly fight its way to the dressing room after

Stanley Matthews and George Howe tussle for the ball at Bloomfield Road on 8 January 1955.

their 1–0 victory.' Other headlines read 'York City's famous Cup victory was well deserved' (*Yorkshire Post)* and 'This Was York City's Finest Hour' (*Yorkshire Evening Press*).

There was great excitement in York as news came through of the result. Progress of the match had been relayed to Clarence Street, where York RL were in action, and there was cheering in local cinemas as the result was flashed on the screens. The scenes in York that Saturday night were quite incredible. The first of the 14 special trains arrived back at 8 o'clock, and many people assembled at the station to greet those who 'had been there'. The station was a cauldron of noise and excitement with the roar

Arthur Bottom scores against Notts County to put City into the semi-final.

of rattles, bells and cheering. The players were given a heroes' welcome as several hundred people congregated in Blossom Street to cheer the arrival of the City team coach, escorted by a police car down Tadcaster Road. It was, as Wilf Meek appropriately put it, 'The day you dream about but seldom experience'.

City had become the third club from Division Three to reach the last four (after Millwall in 1937 and Port Vale in 1954) and were consequently billed as 'The Happy Wanderers' – the name of a popular song at the time. It was also the title of a souvenir brochure compiled by Meek, which provided a pictorial record of the Cup feats. It is now a collectors' item and a prized possession from those far-off days.

The draw for the semi-finals paired City with either Newcastle United or Huddersfield Town at Hillsborough. The Magpies won their replay, and an-all ticket crowd of 65,000 was fixed for Hillsborough. The build-up was one of great excitement and anticipation, and there was only one topic of conversation in pubs, clubs and workplaces. Letters of congratulation were received from all over the world, including one from Yorkshire cricketer Vic Wilson, who was with the MCC party in Australia. The England side, who retained the Ashes that winter, had kept a close interest in City's fortunes.

A quarter-final ticket stub.

A semi-final ticket stub.

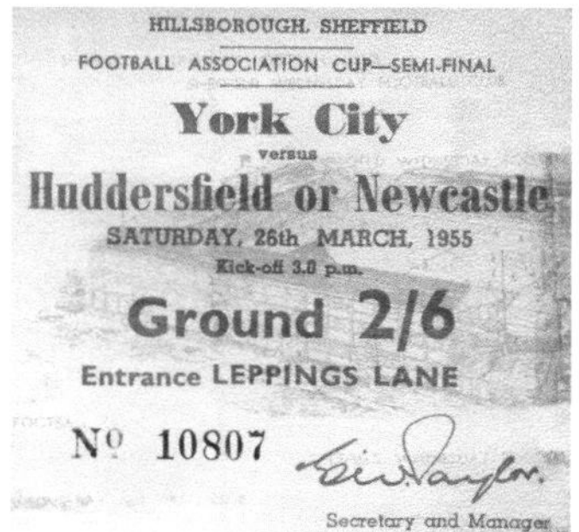

City players embark for their Matlock headquarters prior to the semi-final at Hillsborough. From left to right: G. Brown, T. Lockie, W. Hughes, N. Wilkinson, R. Spence, E. Phillips, S. Storey, G. Howe, S. McNab, E. Wardle, A. Bottom, T. Forgan, W. Fenton, A. Stewart.

The City party, as in the previous round, made their headquarters at the Lilybank Hydro Hotel in Matlock. On Saturday 26 March 1955, 21,000 – one-fifth of the city's population – made the exodus to Sheffield. The match finished goalless (see Matches To Remember), and City became the first Third Division club to force a semi-final replay, which was arranged for the following Wednesday afternoon at Roker Park. The club were allocated 12,000 tickets, which were immediately snapped up. Although City welcomed back Storey, after he had missed the Hillsborough game through injury, City's record-breaking run ended when they went down 2–0. The team had gained great prestige in defeat, and many tributes were made afterwards, including one from Sir Stanley Rous, the secretary of the FA. The Sunderland chairman said 'York City's football would not only be a credit to the Second Division but also the First.'

A total of 247,916 had watched City's eight games in the competition. Receipts amounted to £45,776, of which City's share after tax and other deductions amounted to approximately £8,000. As in 1937–38, 13 players figured in the Cup exploits – the regular 11 plus Mick Granger, who kept goal in the opening two ties, and Sam McNab, who deputised for Storey at Hillsborough. Of the backroom staff, Lockie and Sherrington, who were involved 17 years earlier, again received fulsome praise for their tremendous part in the success.

A civic reception was held later in the Mansion House, and in May 1955 the club undertook a week's tour of Ireland in recognition of their fine achievement. They drew 3–3 with Bohemians at

City take the field at Hillsborough, led by skipper Ernie Phillips.

Dalymount Park, Dublin, and beat Linfield 3–1 at Windsor Park, Belfast. The City party received warm Irish hospitality throughout the trip and attended a number of civic receptions.

From mid-September to late April, City won 21 and drew nine of 33 League games. Following their Cup exit, they were on the fringe of the promotion race. On Good Friday 1955, the gates had to be closed with up to 3,000 locked out, as just under 20,000 saw a top-of-the-table clash with Accrington Stanley. In the final analysis, City were not quite able to make up for the poor start. A crop of injuries in the closing weeks, plus a crowded fixture list of 12 games in April, saw them finish in fourth position. Barnsley were the Northern Section champions, and their double over City proved crucial. Bottom, who missed the closing matches through injury, set a new club scoring record with 39 League and Cup goals. It had been a truly outstanding campaign, although it was disappointing that the club had so narrowly missed out on promotion and a trip to Wembley.

The quality of football played that season was way above the Third Division. Reporting on City's win at Stockport County two days after the triumph over Spurs, noted sports journalist Henry Rose of the *Daily Express* said 'York City are First (Premiership) Division class. On a snow-covered pitch they played top-notch football. They found their men, used the open spaces and switched defence to attack with precision passes. There were no weak spots in this First Division side masquerading in Third Division shirts.' The average League attendance rose to 9,630 and gross receipts amounted to £38,227 compared to £17,930 the previous season. Benefit cheques of £500 each were given to Alan Stewart, Sid Storey, Matt Patrick and Ron Spence as reward for their fine service over a number of seasons.

Arthur Bottom equalising against Accrington Stanley in a top-of-the-table Division Three North clash on Good Friday 1955.

The Happy Wanderers of 1954–55. Back row, left to right: N. Wilkinson, G. Brown, T. Forgan, A. Stewart, R. Spence, G. Howe, T. Lockie (trainer). Front row: W. Hughes, A. Bottom, E. Phillips, S. Storey, W. Fenton.

New signings from Leeds United were winger Clive Colbridge, who made his debut on the Irish tour, and midfielder Ron Mollatt. Optimism was naturally high for 1955–56, and despite losing their opening fixture to Wrexham at Bootham Crescent, City topped the Northern Section after 10 games. Then followed a bad run of seven games without a win, and the club never got back into the promotion race, finishing 11th. Support and enthusiasm remained high. The average home League crowd of 10,291 was the second-highest in the club's history, and 10 home games attracted five-figure attendances. Although lacking consistency, the team played some fine football and provided tremendous entertainment as they embarked on the FA Cup trail once again.

After knocking out Rochdale and Mansfield Town, City were paired with Swansea Town, who were riding high in Division Two at the time. On 7 January 1956 City gained one of their finest-ever Cup victories when they beat the Swans, who had eight Welsh internationals in their side, 2–1 at Vetch Field. City's reward was a home tie against First Division Sunderland, then billed as the 'Bank of England' side because of their big-money signings. The previous season, City and Sunderland had been the beaten semi-finalists. An all-ticket 21,000 Bootham Crescent crowd saw an epic battle with City having much the better of a goalless draw. 'Keeper Willie Fraser made a number of fine saves for Sunderland, who were lucky to survive.

The replay was played on an icy pitch, and defences were generally on top. City fell behind on the stroke of half-time when Forgan punched the ball into his own net, but they fought back to equalise with a Fenton header before Charlie Fleming netted a late winner for the First Division side. So for the second successive season, City went out of the competition at Roker Park.

For the second year running, Bottom hit 31 League goals, and Fenton completed 100 goals for the club during the campaign. The reserve side finished in the top six of a very competitive Midland League, and the third team, who had been reformed this season, won promotion to the First Division of the Yorkshire League. Making his mark in this side was promising young player Colin Addison.

During the season, serious consideration was given to filling the vacant managerial position. In December 1955 Don Roper, the current Arsenal captain and inside-forward, was offered the post of player-manager, but after prolonged negotiations he turned down the deal. Charlie Wayman, the Middlesbrough centre-forward, and George Hardwick, the former England and Middlesbrough full-back, were also on the shortlist before Sam Bartram was appointed in March 1956. The Charlton goalkeeper was a popular choice, having been a great favourite with City fans when guesting for the club during the war.

At the end of the season, Gordon Brown received a benefit cheque for £500, and long-serving Storey was released and moved to Second Division Barnsley. City beat Hull City 7–4 on aggregate to win the East Riding Invitation Cup, with the second leg at Bootham Crescent, which City won 5–0, attracting a crowd of 8,881. At the AGM, record receipts and a profit of £8,453 were reported, and the accumulated credit balance was over £22,000. The Bootham Crescent ground and equipment was valued at £19,832.

Prior to the start of the 1956–57 season, the club spent a good deal of money on transfers. Centre-forward Alan Monkhouse (from Newcastle United), Jim Cairney (a centre-half from Portsmouth) and Peter Wragg (an inside-forward, formerly with Sheffield United) were signed for an outlay of £12,000, which was sizeable by 1956 standards. Everything was geared for a determined bid for promotion to the Second Division. A crowd of 7,099 watched the public

Alan Stewart, Sid Storey and Gordon Brown with new manager Sam Bartram in March 1956.

practice match between Reds and Blues, and it was in this game that a youthful Barry Jackson made his debut.

Enthusiasm was at a new high, and 15,318 fans saw the opening home fixture against Workington. The team never quite made the impact they hoped for and had to be content with seventh place. A good run of results early in the New Year – six wins including a club record 9–1 victory over Southport (see Matches to Remember) and a draw in eight games – rekindled hopes, but the momentum was not maintained. In the FA Cup they were knocked out in the second round at Hull City. Bottom was top scorer again, and the average home League attendance was 9,414. Percy Andrews received a benefit game after 10 years' excellent service, and Matt Patrick and Alan Stewart both retired. The reserves had another good season but the third team were relegated. At the AGM, the directors announced in their annual report that the financial position was one that many clubs would be proud to possess.

The 1957–58 season was a crucial campaign for Third Division clubs. It was the last season of regionalised football. At the end of the term, the top 12 clubs in the Northern and Southern Sections would form the new Third Division, with the bottom clubs becoming founder members of Division Four. After three good seasons, City's form deserted them at just the wrong time. They went into the Easter programme in an apparently hopeless position – third from bottom with only 29 points from 36 games, then staged a tremendous last-ditch effort in a bid to retain their Third Division status, recording seven wins and three draws in their last 10 games. In the end, only an inferior goal average caused them to miss out on a top-12 position. Heavy defeats had cost them dear, including 6–1 at

Tranmere Rovers and 9–2 at Chester, their biggest defeat since the war. One notable debutant this season was Colin Addison.

Amid the traumas in the League, the club again embarked on an FA Cup run. They beat Chesterfield and South Shields, then entertained First Division Birmingham City, winning 3–0 (see Matches to Remember). The fourth-round tie against Bolton Wanderers drew the biggest crowd to Bootham Crescent since the war, with 23,600 watching a hard-fought tussle that ended 0–0. Eight of the famous Cup team of three years earlier figured in this match; however, following a 3–0 defeat at Burnden Park in the replay, Arthur Bottom was transferred to Newcastle United, and the end of the season saw the departure of three other Happy Wanderers – Ernie Phillips, Gordon Brown and Billy Fenton.

A glorious chapter had come to an end, and City now faced life in Division Four. The reserves were also to compete in a new section – the North Regional League – and so the club's long connection with the Midland League came to an end.

The Yo-Yo Years (1958–70)

The 1958–70 period was a time of mixed fortunes for the club. Twice City gained promotion only to suffer immediate relegation, and they also had to make four applications for re-election to the Football League. In the FA Cup, they enjoyed only moderate success but reached the quarter-finals of the newly constituted Football League Cup in 1961–62.

City's first game in Division Four was on 23 August 1958. They opened with a 1–0 win, thanks to a Ron Greensmith goal. Making his debut was 20-year-old Barry Jackson, replacing the injured Howard Johnson, and the towering centre-half made an immediate impact. Under the captaincy of Peter Wragg, the club achieved their objective and won promotion to quickly restore their Third Division status, which they had lost rather unluckily a year earlier. They made an excellent start and led the table until the end of October, with just one defeat in the opening 16 games. They faltered a little midterm but continued well. With only one reverse in the last 20 outings, they finished third behind Port Vale and Coventry City to gain promotion for the first time in their history. They lost only once at home in a season of unspectacular success that owed much to a very strong rearguard, with Tommy Forgan and George Howe as reliable as ever and Jackson outstanding at the heart of the defence. In midfield, Ron Mollatt and George Patterson were key figures, and Wragg proved a fine leader up front, leading the scoring with 14 goals. Colin Addison made good progress, and a newcomer was left-winger Charlie Twissell from Plymouth Argyle, a former amateur international.

In their first campaign in the North Regional League, the reserves finished fifth, and the top marksman was Barrie Tait with 24 goals. For the first time since 1953–54, City fell at the first hurdle in the FA Cup when they lost at Bury.

In the summer of 1959, floodlights were installed at Bootham Crescent. Back in the Third Division, City crossed swords for the first time with the likes of Norwich City, Southampton, Bournemouth, Reading and Queen's Park Rangers. Apart from new signings, a half-back John Battye from Huddersfield Town, and ex-Gillingham forward John Edgar, they relied chiefly on the players who had won promotion. Goals were hard to come by, but City held their own in the opening weeks and support was good, especially in the floodlit games. The lights were first used in a game against QPR on 7 September 1959 in front of 10,593, and almost 12,000 saw the visit of Grimsby Town later that month. At the end of February 1960, City were mid-table with the following record: P 33, W 11, D 11, L 11, F 43, A 48, Pts 33.

A disastrous finish, with just two wins and one draw in the last 13 games, saw them slip into the bottom four and drop back to the Fourth Division. In the FA Cup City were knocked out at Bournemouth in the third round. Average attendances were 7,507, and the end of the season saw the departure of long-serving Ron Spence. Other departures included Terry Farmer, Ron Greensmith, Billy Hill and Johnny Powell. The 38th annual report, while expressing 'keen disappointment' in the playing record of 1959–60, was still able to confirm a satisfactory position as to the financial stability of the club.

The summer of 1960 saw many changes at the club. Sam Bartram was released from his contract and took over as manager of Luton Town, and the directors unanimously appointed Tom Lockie as his successor. Since 1936 the loyal clubman had been trainer, physio and coach, and Sid Storey returned to the fold as chief trainer. Ernie Phillips was appointed to look after the third team, and a number of new signings were made. These included winger Jimmy Weir from Fulham, midfielder Alan Woods from Swansea, and ex-Swindon Town players Walter Bingley and Jack Fountain.

Under the new managerial team, the side started well and were in the top four by mid-November, but a run of five successive defeats checked their progress. A good run in the New Year revived promotion hopes but they finished fifth with only one win in the last seven games, nine points behind fourth-placed Bradford Park Avenue.

During the season, wing-man Wally Gould was signed from Sheffield United, and Norman Wilkinson completed his 100 goals for the club. Following the FA Cup defeat at Norwich City in a third-round replay, Colin Addison was transferred to Nottingham Forest for a club record fee received of £12,000. The Football League Cup was instituted this season, and Addison scored City's first-ever goal in the competition, in a 3–1 defeat at the hands of Blackburn Rovers.

At the end of the season, Billy Sherrington retired as secretary after filling the role with distinction for 37 years, and he was one of the best-known and respected officials in the Football League. His successor was George Teasdale, who had served in the RAF for many years and been manager of Selby Town and Goole Town. Messrs W.H. Sessions and J.W. Rosindale both stepped down as directors after many years, and former player and manager Tom Mitchell joined the board.

New signings for the 1961–62 campaign included full-back Tommy Heron from Manchester United and centre-forward John Stainsby from Barnsley. Billy Rudd was also signed from Birmingham City in November 1961 for a sizeable fee. Throughout the season, City were on the fringe of a top-four place, but poor form on their travels let them down. At home they recorded several impressive victories, including

G.W. 'Billy' Sherrington.

5–0 wins over League leaders Colchester United and Barrow. They went into the last game of the season at Bootham Crescent, against Aldershot, needing a victory to ensure promotion. In a bitterly disappointing finale, they suffered a rare home defeat and were condemned to another season of Fourth Division football.

Jimmy Weir had a fine season and top scored with 29 League and Cup goals, which included a couple of hat-tricks. Although bowing out of the FA Cup in the first round at Bradford City, the club embarked on a successful run in the Football League Cup. En route to the last eight, they knocked out Third Division clubs Bristol City, Watford, Bournemouth and most notably First Division Leicester City. A crowd of 13,273 saw City give a fine display, and goals from Peter Wragg and John Stainsby ensured a 2–1 win. Scenes at the end of the game were reminiscent of the FA Cup triumphs of the mid-1950s. Having done so well in the competition, it was a big disappointment when they lost to fellow Fourth Division club Rochdale at Spotland in the quarter-finals. At the end of the campaign, George Howe and Billy Hughes – two more of the 1954–55 heroes – left the club, as did reliable understudy goalkeeper Mick Granger.

After narrowly missing promotion in each of the two previous seasons, there was little change in personnel for 1962–63, but Weir was transferred to Mansfield Town early in the campaign. The club had a poor first half of the season and were second from bottom at Christmas. This was the winter of the big freeze, and City did not play a League game from 22 December 1962 until 8 March 1963. During this period, City's third-round FA Cup tie at Southampton was postponed no less than nine times, and when it was eventually played they crashed out 5–0.

Upon the resumption of the League programme, City showed improved form and pulled well clear of the bottom four, finishing a respectable 14th. Nonetheless, it had been a disappointing campaign, and the average League attendance of 4,515 was a new post-war low. Players who departed at the end of the campaign, which had been extended until the end of May, included Wragg, Bingley and Stainsby. The annual report stated that the club's financial stability was largely due to the continued and welcome support and assistance of the auxiliary club, supporters' club and the social club. As an economy measure, the third team was disbanded.

Several newcomers joined the club in the summer of 1963, including Republic of Ireland and Leeds United inside-forward Noel Peyton and ex-Nottingham Forest full-back Gerry Baker. Ron Spence took over from Sid Storey as trainer and physio, but the 1963–64 campaign was one of the worst in the club's history, and they never recovered from a dreadful start that saw them lose their first four home games. They were in the bottom four for virtually the whole of the season and finished 22nd so having to apply for re-election for the second time in their history. The average home crowd fell to 3,937, and the match at Bootham Crescent on 22 December 1963 drew only 1,653 – the smallest in their history at the time.

City were also knocked out of both Cup competitions in the early stages, but overshadowing everything was the football bribery scandal exposed by the *Sunday People*. One of the players involved in fixing match results was City half-back and former captain Jack Fountain. Reporting the matter in the *Sports Press,* Wilf Meek said 'Without doubt this has been the most unfortunate and sickening week in the 42-year history of York City Football Club'. The City matches that were allegedly fixed were a home game against Tranmere on 21 October 1961, which was lost 2–1, and a game at Oldham on 1 December 1962, which City lost 3–2 after leading 2–0. Fountain's contract with City was terminated, and he was subsequently banned from football for life and served a prison sentence. Other players involved included England internationals Tony Kay and Peter Swan.

At the Football League's AGM, City polled the maximum 48 votes and were re-elected. The year had seen the foundation of the Development Association, and donations from the organisation raised £12,865. So, after the trials and tribulations of 1963–64, the next season saw City rise from the ashes. New recruits included centre-forward Paul Aimson from Manchester City, wingers Andy Provan from Barnsley and Derek Weddle from Darlington, and midfielder Dennis Walker from Manchester United. Under the inspired leadership of Billy Rudd, the side found the right blend, and producing some of the best football since the glory days of 10 years earlier won promotion in fine style.

In midterm, City had a sequence of 10 wins and two draws in 12 matches, including a 7–1 Boxing Day victory over Chesterfield. The average League crowd of 7,185, including four five-figure attendances, was almost double that of the previous season, and they won a club record 20 League games at home. City finished third, just one point behind champions Brighton. Aimson was top scorer, with 30 League and Cup goals, and he had good support from Provan, Walker and Weddle. Forgan and Wilkinson – the two survivors of the 'Happy Wanderers' – also played their part, and the sun once more shone on the club after its darkest hour. Sadly, in March 1965 the club's longest-serving director, William Mason, died. He had been on the board since 1927 and had worked exceptionally hard to help secure admission to the Football League in the late 1920s.

In preparation for their first season back in Division Three since 1960, City signed talented Irish inside-forward Eamon Dunphy from Manchester United and welcomed back centre-forward David Dunmore. Following an injury to Forgan early in the season, Harry Fallon was signed from St Johnstone. Hopes were high and early results were encouraging, with away wins at Brentford, Southend

York City, 1964–65. Back row, left to right: T. Lockie (manager), G. Baker, B. Jackson, T. Forgan, A. Woods, D. Walker, T. Heron. Front row: D. Weddle, N. Wilkinson, W. Rudd, P. Aimson, A. Provan.

Paul Aimson scoring against Halifax Town on 24 April 1965 in the 4–0 win that clinched promotion from Division Four.

Skipper Billy Rudd scoring in the same game.

United and a magnificent 4–1 success at Hull City (see Matches to Remember). Sadly their home form deserted them, and only five wins were recorded at Bootham Crescent – in direct contrast to the previous campaign.

By Christmas, City had dropped into the bottom four, and in March they sunk to the foot of the table and stayed there, and so made another immediate return to the Fourth Division. They conceded a club record number of 106 goals and suffered a number of heavy defeats, including 7–2 at QPR and Swansea and 6–0 at Swindon. Dunphy, who became the first player to be capped while with the club, for the Republic of Ireland against Spain in November 1965, moved to Millwall in January 1966. Two months later, leading scorer Aimson was transferred to Bury for £10,000. Attendances of over 9,000 early in the season slipped to under 3,000, and the average was 5,921. The biggest crowd was 19,420 in March 1966, when Hull City were the visitors.

To complete a poor season, City lost to non-League opposition in the FA Cup for the first time since 1946–47 when they went down at South Shields. The end of the season saw the departure of the last two members of the great 1954–55 side, Wilkinson and Forgan. Between them they had made 829 senior appearances, and Wilkinson's tally of 143 goals remains a club record. Others to leave were Rudd, Woods, Heron and Ken Boyes, who had served the club loyally for 11 years, chiefly as understudy to Barry Jackson. In recognition of their service, Boyes, Forgan and Wilkinson were presented with inscribed gold watches by the chairman.

Manager Tom Lockie chats to players in August 1965 prior to City's return to Division Three. Back row, left to right: Gerry Baker, Paul Aimson, Barry Wealthall, Barry Jackson, David Dunmore, Bobby Cunliffe, Ken Lowe, John Pearson, Ken Morton. Front row: Billy Rudd, Tommy Heron, Alan Woods, Andy Provan.

The next three seasons saw the club in the doldrums, and three successive applications for re-election back to the Football League were made, under three different managers.

In 1966–67, ex-Southampton player Tommy Spencer top scored with 23 League and Cup goals. Among the newcomers was 'keeper Mike Walker, who was capped for Wales at Under-23 level while with the club. City struggled throughout and won just one of 19 League games during one spell, which included a club record eight defeats in succession. The away form was dismal, with just one victory on their travels. In the FA Cup City had three exciting tussles with Middlesbrough before losing in a second-round second replay at St James' Park, Newcastle. The reserve team had switched to the Second Division of the Yorkshire League and won promotion at the first attempt. The club were duly re-elected, receiving 45 votes.

In November 1966 W.H. Sessions died. He had served the club for over 30 years, as director, chairman and latterly as president – a position that was taken over by G.W. 'Billy' Sherrington. In June 1967 Hugh Kitchin resigned from the board for business reasons. He had been a director since 1945 and chairman for 13 years. The new chairman was Derrick Blundy, but after 16 months Eric Magson took over with Wilf Meek as vice-chairman.

For the first time in 31 years there was a change of club colours, and City sported an all-white kit for the 1967–68 season. Among the newcomers in attack were Tommy Ross from Peterborough United and Ted MacDougall, a £5,000 signing from Liverpool. A dreadful start was made as City failed

City line up prior to FA Cup first-round match against Doncaster Rovers on 9 December 1967. Back row, left to right: Ron Spence (trainer), Dennis Walker, Ted MacDougall, Mike Walker, Barry Jackson, Joe Shaw (manager). Middle row: David Joy (sub), Ken Turner, Tommy Ross, John Hawksby, Phil Burrows, Gerry Baker. Front row: Andy Provan, Rowland Horrey.

to win any of their first 13 games, and it was mid-October before they recorded their first victory. By then, manager Lockie had been dismissed, becoming the first City boss to suffer that fate. His successor was Joe Shaw, the former Sheffield United centre-half, who recruited Billy Hodgson, his former Bramall Lane colleague and inside-forward, as assistant and player-coach. Results improved, and the club rose from the bottom of the table to 14th position by the beginning of April. They failed to win any of their last eight games, however, and again had to go cap in hand to the League AGM, where they were duly re-elected with 46 votes. MacDougall was top scorer, and at the end of another poor season, players to leave included Walker and Fallon.

May 1968 marked the end of an era, with the retirement of Wilf Meek, sports editor of the *Yorkshire Evening Press.* He had reported on City matches for 46 years since their formation, and his son David covered Manchester United's games for the *Manchester Evening News.* From 1968 to 1995, Malcolm Huntington, the chief sports writer at the *Yorkshire Evening Press*, chronicled the club's affairs.

In the summer of 1968 it was decided to scrap the second team. There was to be a first-team pool of 16 professionals, and an intermediate side of players, aged up to 19, would operate in the Northern Intermediate League. The most notable new signing was Phil Boyer, a highly rated young forward from Derby County, whose partnership with MacDougall was to blossom later at Bournemouth and Norwich City.

The season was only a week old when manager Shaw resigned for personal reasons and Tom Johnston, the former boss at Rotherham United, Grimsby Town and Huddersfield Town, took over the reins at the end of October. At the time of his arrival, City were again struggling in the lower reaches of the Fourth Division, chiefly because of continued poor away form. They were to lose their last 11 away games and had won only five of 69 outings in three seasons back in Division Four.

New signings during the season were Dick Hewitt, an inside-forward from Barnsley, speedy winger Archie Taylor from Bradford City and ex-Leeds United defender Bob Sibbald. In December 1968 17-year-old Chris Topping – the club's first-ever apprentice professional – made his debut in the defence, and young amateur 'keeper John Andrews deputised for the injured Bob Widdowson in the last few matches. Provan and goalkeeper Walker departed, while Gerry Baker had to retire through injury.

For the first time since 1962–63, the club reached the third round of the FA Cup. In the first round they gained their biggest-ever away victory in the competition when they won 6–0 at South Shields. Then, after a home win over Morecambe, they were drawn at home to First Division Stoke City. In front of 11,129 – the biggest crowd for nearly three years – City put up a good fight before losing 2–0.

At the end of the campaign, top scorer MacDougall moved to Bournemouth and so ended a fourth successive season of disappointment and failure – relegation followed by three applications for re-election. In June 1969 City received 45 votes and once more were re-elected without any undue anxiety. Changes in the boardroom included the resignation of Tom Mitchell. Club colours were changed to maroon shirts and white shorts, the reserve side was reinstated and joined the North Midlands League, while the intermediate side was retained.

After four years in the doldrums, the club experienced much better fortunes in 1969–70. In the early weeks of the season, a promotion challenge looked likely as they won four and drew one of their first five games, and they were in the top four after 12 matches. New signings settled in well. These included Ian Davidson, a midfielder from Hull City, full-back John Mackin from Lincoln City and forward Kevin McMahon from Newcastle United. Early in the season, the club welcomed popular centre-forward Paul Aimson back to Bootham Crescent, and in October 1969 another notable signing was made – centre-half Barry Swallow from Bradford City.

Although the promotion challenge faded, the side finished in a comfortable mid-table position, well clear of the bottom four. After a number of lean seasons in the FA Cup, at last City gave their supporters something to cheer as they reached the fourth round for the first time since 1957–58. After knocking out non-League Whitby Town and Bangor City in the first two rounds, high-flying Second Division Cardiff City were the visitors in round three. An exciting match followed, which was drawn 1–1, and the sides were involved in another 1–1 thriller at Ninian Park. At the third attempt at St Andrews, City overcame their Welsh opponents 3–1 after extra-time. Swallow scored twice and Aimson supplied another as City put on one of their special giant-killing displays. Outstanding in defence was Jackson who, for the third successive game, snuffed out the threat of the young Welsh star John Toshack. City's run ended at Ayresome Park at the next stage, when a crowd of 38,283 saw Middlesbrough win 4–1.

During the season, teenage defender Topping continued to make good progress, and 17-year-old Ron Hillyard made his debut in goal. Hodgson was released at the end of the season, as was Barry Jackson. He had been a virtual ever present at the heart of defence for 12 years and his club record total of 539 senior appearances is unlikely to be beaten, but sadly his last season was clouded with controversy. Sent off in a game at Scunthorpe in January 1970, he was suspended for eight weeks and missed his testimonial match against Hull City. He had a magnificent career, however, and his enthusiasm and commitment has rarely been equalled.

The 1960s had largely been a disappointing decade, apart from the promotion success of 1964–65, but the 1970s were to provide the highpoint of City's Football League career.

The Rise and Fall of the Minstermen (1970–80)

The 1970–80 period was an eventful decade of League football for the club. City started and finished the 1970s in Division Four but in between, after a couple of promotions, experienced two memorable seasons in the second tier of English football. Known by now as the Minstermen, with obvious reference to the city of York's world-famous landmark, they had been previously nicknamed the Citizens, Robins, Happy Wanderers and City.

In August 1970 the death of Wilf Meek, vice-chairman and a director for 18 years, was announced. An outstanding figure in the club's history, he had reported on City matches from 1922 to 1968 and helped compile the programme for 40 years. Ken Lancaster became vice-chairman, and a newcomer on the board was R.B. (Bob) Strachan. The death also occurred of Jack Wright, one of the stalwarts of the supporters' club.

New signings included Albert Johanneson from Leeds United. A good start was made to the 1970–71 campaign, but City faltered midterm and were in 10th position at the end of January. City then embarked on an unbeaten run of 16 games (10 wins and six draws) that thrust them into the top four. Two notable successes were a 4–1 win at home to Northampton Town and a 5–4 victory at Lincoln. The run ended on 19 April 1971, when Oldham Athletic won a vital promotion clash 1–0. It was City's first home defeat since 31 January 1970 – a club record sequence of 36 consecutive unbeaten League and Cup games at Bootham Crescent. Despite losing three of their last four games, City held onto fourth place to gain promotion for the third time. The tally of seven away wins equalled the number of the previous four seasons totalled together. The back four of Mackin, Burrows, Swallow and Topping were outstanding, and they missed only six games between them. Hewitt and Davidson did well in midfield and Aimson, as in the promotion campaign of six years earlier, top scored with 26 League goals. In December 1970 Boyer was transferred to Bournemouth for a new club record fee received of £20,000, and McMahon re-established himself in the side as a result.

For the second successive campaign, the fourth round of the FA Cup was reached. Non-League Tamworth and Boston United were knocked out – the former in a 5–0 replay, with Aimson notching a hat-trick – and then City beat Second Division Bolton Wanderers 2–0 at home, with Davidson scoring both goals. Then followed a classic Cup tie (3–3) at Bootham Crescent against First Division Southampton (see Matches to Remember). City bowed out 3–2 in the replay after another exciting affair.

Back in Division Three after a five-year absence, City recruited utility player John Woodward from Arsenal, Pat Lally from Millwall and forward Eddie Rowles in an exchange deal which took Davidson to Bournemouth. The first two seasons back in the Third Division were nail-biting affairs, as City just avoided the drop back to the Fourth on goal average, twice. They started 1971–72 quite well with good away wins at Brighton and Bolton, but an 11-match run without a win saw them drop into the bottom four, and they had to wage a long battle to avoid another immediate return to the basement division.

The Football League Cup provided the highlight of the campaign and for the first time since 1966–67 the club reached the third round. At the second hurdle, they had two tremendous tilts with Second Division Middlesbrough, winning the replay 2–1 at Ayresome Park. They then travelled to Sheffield United, who were top of the First Division, and a crowd of just under 30,000 saw City give the Blades a real fright as Swallow and Topping netted for City. With the score 2–2, substitute Rowles

Paul Aimson challenges Bolton's 'keeper in the third-round FA Cup tie on 2 January 1971.

missed a great chance to provide another giant-killing feat in the closing stages. United responded by scoring a spectacular goal in the 88th minute when Alan Woodward drove a 25-yard shot into the net.

During the season, goalkeeper Graeme Crawford was signed from Sheffield United and 17-year-old local lad Brian Pollard made his debut on the wing. The average home League crowd of 5,597 was the highest for six years. To celebrate the 50th anniversary of the club, the supporters' club produced a souvenir handbook, which was compiled by committee members Jeff Mortimer and Norman Clay.

Centre-forward Jimmy Seal joined from Barnsley and full-back John Stone came from Middlesbrough, but 1972–73 was a difficult season, and the side never really recovered from a nightmare start that saw them fail to win any of their first 11 fixtures, including a sequence of seven games without a goal. Results improved mid-season and City reached the top half of the table in early March, but another slump followed and only a dramatic win in the last game of the season at Rotherham United saved them from the drop. Left-winger Dennis Wann, signed from Blackpool the previous season, broke his leg in a Boxing Day

Chris Topping stops a Brighton attack at the Goldstone Ground in a Division Three encounter on 4 September 1971.

fixture at Oldham, and Aimson moved to Bournemouth in March. Left-winger Billy Fenton, one of the stars of the 1954–55 team, died suddenly at the age of 46 in April 1973, 17 months after George Howe, the left-back in that famous side, had passed away, also in his forties.

In readiness for 1973–74, a number of important signings were made. Barry Lyons came from Nottingham Forest for a then club record fee paid of £12,000. Other signings were midfielder Ian Holmes from Sheffield Wednesday, forward Chris Jones from Walsall and left-winger Ian Butler from Hull City. This was an historic campaign that saw York City win promotion and so achieve Second Division status for the first time. Having escaped relegation by winning the last game of the previous season, this was a remarkable achievement.

City started with an impressive 4–2 win at Charlton Athletic on the opening day but lost 4–0 at Blackburn Rovers in their third match on 8 September. Then followed a club record run of 21 League games without defeat, which was ended on 19 January 1974 when Charlton gained revenge with a 1–0 win at York. During this period, City equalled a Football League record by going 11 matches without conceding a goal. This was the first season of 'three up, three down' in the top three divisions, and after beating Southend United on 10 November City were never out of the top three. Promotion was clinched on 27 April 1974 when the biggest home crowd for eight years (15,583) saw a 1–1 draw against Oldham Athletic, whose progress and fortunes were so interwoven with City's in the early 1970s. After 38 seasons in the Football League, City had reached the second tier of English football.

The season was also notable for a good run in the Football League Cup, progressing beyond the third round for the second time. After beating Huddersfield Town, they knocked out Second Division clubs Aston Villa and Orient and then met First Division Manchester City in the fourth round at Bootham Crescent. Owing to a floodlight ban, the game was staged on a Wednesday afternoon and 15,360 saw a 0–0 draw. In the replay at Maine Road, City went down 4–1, with Rodney Marsh scoring a hat-trick for the home side.

In January 1974 Bob Strachan took over as chairman and served on the FA Council during his tenure – the first City official to do so. It had been a memorable season and a great team effort under the fine leadership of Barry Swallow. The defenders – 'keeper Crawford and back four of Stone, Swallow, Topping and Burrows (the first winner of the Billy Memorial Trophy Clubman of the Year) – missed just six games between them. Lyons and Holmes were very influential on the right side of midfield, with Butler providing the skill and experience down the left. Up front, Seal and Jones proved a fine striking duo, finishing with 35 goals between them. Utility players Woodward and Cliff Calvert also figured prominently, as did young winger Pollard.

Shortly before the start of the 1974–75 season, Phil Burrows was transferred to Plymouth Argyle for £20,000. An outstanding left-back, he had been a virtual ever present for eight years and a key figure in City's rise from the Fourth to the Second Division. Midfielder Micky Cave was signed from Bournemouth for a club record fee of £18,000, and another newcomer was centre-forward Jim Hinch from Hereford United. The club appointed its first commercial manager but Keith Hunt's stay was short – in a stormy five months, he clashed with the directors and the supporters' club on a number of occasions. His legacy was a new strip, designed with the help of former reserve player Peter Turpin, of maroon shirts with a white 'Y' on the front – these colours were reversed two years later. Hunt also devised a new match day magazine style programme. One of the club's best-known supporters, Raymond 'Nobby' Clarke, died in September 1974. On big occasions, he would dress as a 'pearly king' and parade around the pitch.

Saturday 17 August 1974 was a red-letter day in the history of York City Football Club, as they played their first game in Division Two, at home to Aston Villa (see Matches to Remember). So began two seasons in which City competed at the same level as Sunderland, Nottingham Forest, Sheffield Wednesday, West Bromwich Albion, Chelsea and Manchester United. Just six years earlier, while United were winning the European Cup, City were applying for re-election!

Lyons scored City's first goal at the higher level, and Chris Jones was the marksman when the club recorded their first win, against Cardiff City. They made a good start and on 19 October 1974, following a win at Oldham, were fifth in the table – their highest-ever placing in the Football League. A final position of 15th was very creditable, and high spots were doubles over Norwich City, who won promotion, and Fulham, who were FA Cup runners-up that season.

For the first time since 1938–39, City were exempt until the third round of the FA Cup, at which stage they were paired with Arsenal. City gave a great display at Highbury and took the lead with a magnificent goal by Seal. Eddie Kelly equalised for the Gunners, who won the replay at Bootham Crescent 3–1 after extra-time, with Brian Kidd scoring a hat-trick.

Following the Cup defeat came the shock announcement that Tom Johnston had been released from his contract to take over at Huddersfield. Arguably the best manager in the club's history, he had been at the helm since October 1968. Trainer-coach Clive Baker acted as caretaker manager until Wilf McGuinness was appointed manager in February 1975. The former England international had been manager of Manchester United for a spell when he took over from Matt Busby in 1970.

Chris Jones tussles with Portsmouth 'keeper Grahame Lloyd on the opening day of the 1975–76 Second Division season.

Chris Jones scores against Bolton Wanderers in the Second Division on 30 August 1975.

The second season of Second Division football was to prove very disappointing. City made a reasonable start, with new signing Eric McMordie from Middlesbrough scoring in an opening day win over Portsmouth, followed by draws at West Bromwich Albion and Chelsea in the early weeks. Then followed a run of nine defeats in 10 games, which sent them to the foot of the table, and a sequence of seven successive defeats in the New Year sealed their fate.

In the closing weeks, results improved and notable wins were recorded against Southampton, Nottingham Forest and Bolton Wanderers. Chelsea, who had knocked City out of the FA Cup in the fourth round, drew the curtain on Second Division football at York, in a 2–2 draw on 24 April 1976. Graeme Crawford and Chris Topping played in every game at this level and the latter, who was Clubman of the Year in 1974–75, had been an ever present for five successive seasons. So ended City's days in Division Two – two heady seasons of triumph, drama and disappointment. It had been an unforgettable chapter in the club's history.

Cup drama this season occurred in the Football League Cup, when swords were crossed with Liverpool for the first time. The Reds won a second-round tie with a controversial late penalty, when Topping was adjudged to have fouled Kevin Keegan. Shortly after this game, Chris Calvert was transferred to Sheffield United for a record £30,000, and physio Ron Spence left the club in September 1975. As a player and in the backroom, Spence had served the club since 1948, apart from a short spell in the early 1960s.

A number of players left the club at the end of 1975–76, including Lyons, Stone, Wann and Swallow, who had been such an inspirational skipper and led the side to two promotions. Early in the new season, the successful scoring duo of Jones and Seal departed to Huddersfield Town and Darlington respectively. Also, long-serving director and former chairman Derrick Blundy retired after 31 years on the board.

Micky Cave (right) beats Chelsea's Ian Hutchinson in the air at Stamford Bridge on 4 October 1975.

Brian Pollard takes on Southampton's defence at The Dell on 25 October 1975.

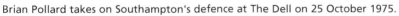

Ian Holmes scores from the spot against Fulham on 15 November 1975 to end a run of seven successive Second Division defeats.

Jimmy Seal cracks home City's consolation goal in a 4–1 defeat at Bristol City – a game featured on BBC's *Match of the Day* on 22 November 1975.

A bad start was made to 1976–77, and City were bottom of the table for most of the first half of the season. One of the worst defeats was in front of BBC TV's *Match of the Day* cameras, when they crashed 7–2 at Brighton in September. In midterm Gordon Staniforth and Chris Galvin joined from Hull City, the latter on loan, and the signings of these two talented forwards marked an upturn in fortunes. However, with only one win in the last 15 outings, they dropped back to the foot of the table and were again relegated. The average League attendance was 2,986 – the first time it had slipped below 3,000. For the sixth successive season, Topping was an ever present, and to mark his 300th consecutive League appearance during the season, the club presented him with a silver tray and seven crystal goblets.

Meanwhile, Michael Sinclair joined the board of directors in May 1977, and two great stalwarts sadly passed away in the summer – president 'Billy' Sherrington and Tom Lockie. Coach Clive Baker left and former player John Simpson took over as trainer and physiotherapist. 'Keeper Crawford was transferred to Scunthorpe United, and promising 16-year-olds Gary Ford and John Byrne joined the club.

Back in the Fourth Division for the first time since 1971, City completed an unenviable hat-trick – two successive relegations followed by a re-election application for the sixth time in their history. The 1977–78 season started badly, and it was no surprise when McGuinness was dismissed in October. A flurry of activity followed, with the signing of forwards Kevin Randall and Ian McDonald from Mansfield Town, along with the transfer of Ian Holmes to Huddersfield Town and Brian Pollard to Watford for a new club record fee received of £33,000.

In November Charlie Wright was appointed as the new manager. The dismal campaign completed its unhappy course, and the club finished in the bottom four. For only the second time, City were knocked out of both Cup competitions at the first hurdle. To complete their grief, non-League Wigan Athletic beat them in the FA Cup, and the average League attendance of 2,139 was a record low for the club.

At the end of the campaign, John Woodward left after seven seasons' service, and the last link with the Second Division days was broken when Chris Topping was transferred to Huddersfield Town for £20,000. Since making his debut in December 1968, Topping had been a model of consistency in the centre of defence. He was an ever present in his last seven seasons at Bootham Crescent – a magnificent sequence of 355 successive League appearances – and his total of 463 senior games for the club is bettered only by Barry Jackson and Andy McMillan.

With financial problems mounting, there took place in April 1978 the biggest boardroom shuffle in the club's history. Sinclair took over as chairman and Messrs Ken Lancaster, Gordon Winters and Dr Angus MacLeod retired, the latter continuing as the club's medical officer. Former chairman Strachan and long-serving director Eric Magson remained on the board and were joined by Douglas Craig in September 1978. The detail of these financial problems came to light at the shareholders' meeting in January 1979. But for a loan of £54,000 from the directors, the club would have ended the financial year with a £100,000 deficit.

Sinclair promised new ideas and a fresh approach, and he and his fellow directors received a boost when the club were re-elected at the League AGM, with a maximum number of votes. A new club logo was introduced, and the strip was changed to red shirts, navy blue shorts and red stockings; the 'Y' design was dispensed with. A new weekly lottery under the guidance of Maureen Leslie was launched, as was a travel club for away games. The main stand was repainted and the car park resurfaced, and spectators were to be provided with a free match-day programme. To complete a summer of high activity, seven signings were made: defenders Roy Kay from Hearts, Steve Faulkner from Sheffield Wednesday and Jimmy Walsh from Watford; midfielder Peter Stronach from Sunderland; and forwards Neil Warnock from Barnsley, Barry Wellings from Everton and David Loggie from Burnley, a £20,000 capture.

In September secretary George Teasdale resigned for health reasons. Shane Winship, who had worked in the club offices since leaving school, took over the role and at the age of 21 became the youngest secretary in the Football League.

After three years in the doldrums, 1978–79 was a much better campaign. The club finished in the top half of the table and reached the fourth round of the FA Cup. Second Division Luton Town were beaten in the third round, and City were drawn away to reigning First Division champions and European Cup winners-elect Nottingham Forest (the clubs were competing together in Division Two only three years earlier). City put up a gallant fight on a snow-covered pitch, with 'keeper Graham Brown outstanding, but lost 3–1. During the season, 17-year-old Gary Ford made his debut, and City were awarded a grant of over £18,000 by the Sports Council to enable them to institute a Youth Development Scheme and reinforce the club's commitment to a new youth policy. In June 1979 former City favourite Barry Lyons was appointed youth coach.

At the AGM, the accounts reflected an improvement in the financial position, and in 1979 the share capital was increased to £100,000 from £4,000. The majority of the new shares were bought by existing holders, with 20,000 offered to the general public. The loan of £54,000, which had ensured the survival of the club, was converted into shares. At this point, Brian Houghton and Colin Webb joined the board, which now had a complement of six.

The 1979–80 season marked the 50th anniversary of the club's election to the Football League, and the *Yorkshire Evening Press* marked the occasion by issuing a souvenir edition. After the improved performances of the previous campaign, 1979–80 was disappointing, and City had to wage a long battle against having to make another application for re-election. The most notable newcomer was former Scotland and Leeds United star Peter Lorimer, while Gordon Staniforth moved to Carlisle United for a reported fee of £120,000 – a new record amount received. In each of his two full seasons at Bootham Crescent, he had been top marksman and Clubman of the Year. Youngster John Byrne made his debut, and Derek Hood was signed from Hull City. Graeme Crawford returned to the club for the second half of the season in an exchange deal that took Joe Neenan to Scunthorpe United. In March 1980, with the club in the lower reaches of the Fourth Division, Wright was dismissed and Lyons took over the managerial reins, initially on a caretaker basis, and Kevin Randall became youth coach. Sadly, the death of former chairman Derrick Blundy was announced, and the club's longest-serving director, Eric Magson, retired in the summer of 1980. In recognition of his 33 years' service, he was presented with a silver salver and was made club president.

The Team of the Century and Silverware (1980–90)

The 1980s followed a rather similar course to the previous decade, with City starting and finishing in the Fourth Division of the Football League. In between came the record-breaking campaign of 1983–84, when City finished runaway champions, lifting the first major trophy in their history and becoming the first Football League club to reach 100 points in a season. Under the successful managerial team of Denis Smith and Viv Busby, the club twice reached the fifth round of the FA Cup in the mid-1980s.

The decade started badly. The 1980–81 season was one of the worst in City's history, as they finished bottom of the Football League and so had to make their seventh application for re-election. Peter Lorimer's contract was not renewed, while newcomers included 'keeper Eddie Blackburn from Hull City, who was Clubman of the Year. Also, 16-year-old 'keeper Mick Astbury and 17-year-old full-back Steve Senior made their debuts during the season.

The season began quite brightly, and City were unbeaten in the opening seven League and Cup games. Early in the New Year they occupied a mid-table position, but the campaign ended with just three wins in the last 18 games, including 10 defeats in 11 matches, and the side slumped to the foot of the table. The average attendance was 2,162, and the crowd of 1,167 for the last game of the season against Northampton Town remains the smallest-ever League crowd at Bootham Crescent.

With 46 votes City were duly re-elected, and in the summer Barry Swallow joined the board. He thus became only the second former player to become a director, the first one being Tom Mitchell. City's disastrous season was reflected in a loss of over £33,000. Shane Winship stepped down from his secretarial duties to take over the social club and also act as sales executive. Tom Hughes became the new secretary, having been involved in football administration in the Selby and West Riding leagues for many years.

Manager Barry Lyons's most notable capture for the 1981–82 season was Keith Walwyn, signed from Chesterfield for £4,000, and the big and powerful centre-forward became the first City player to top 20 League goals since Paul Aimson in 1970–71. Brian Pollard returned to the club, midfielder Malcolm Crosby joined City from Aldershot in a player-exchange deal involving Ian McDonald, and local lad Richard Dawson established himself in the defence.

This 1981–82 season – the first with three points for a win – was another poor one, and City flirted with the bottom four for most of the time, also losing in the FA Cup to non-League Altrincham. The chief problem was their dreadful home form, which saw them go a club record sequence of 12 League

Gary Ford (right) scores against Sheffield United in a Fourth Division encounter on 3 October 1981, which the Blades won 4–3.

games without a win at Bootham Crescent. They did, however, finish their home programme with a number of convincing victories, including 6–0 against Crewe Alexandra, which was their biggest win since 1964–65, and their final placing was 17th.

On the managerial front, this was a season of great upheaval. In December 1981 Barry Lyons was dismissed as manager and resumed as youth coach, with Kevin Randall taking over as caretaker boss. Results did not improve. With the club in the bottom four, Randall was relieved of his duties, and a caretaker managerial team of Swallow, new signing Gerry Sweeney from Bristol City and former coach Colin Meldrum was formed. One of their first acts was to get Stoke City centre-half Denis Smith on loan. This was to prove a most significant move, as he was appointed player-manager in May 1982, with Viv Busby as his assistant player-coach. Smith thus became City's first player-manager since Jock Collier back in the late 1920s.

Careful housekeeping kept the loss, on what had been another poor season, to under £20,000, but once again the club were indebted to the development association and other commercial activities, which had raised nearly £100,000.

The major problems in 1981–82 had been in defence, and the record of 91 goals conceded was the worst in the Football League. Smith's priority was obvious, and in the summer of 1982 he recruited a new rearguard – experienced ex-Bournemouth and Blackburn Rovers goalkeeper Roger Jones, full-backs Chris Evans and Alan Hay from Stoke City and Bristol City respectively, and Ricky Sbragia, formerly with Birmingham City and Walsall, who would team up with the manager in the centre of defence. Later in the campaign, John MacPhail from Sheffield was another notable signing.

The 1982–83 season marked the diamond jubilee of the club and the 50th anniversary of the move to Bootham Crescent, and, after a number of lean years, the season also marked a noticeable upturn in the club's fortunes. They finished seventh and just missed out on promotion, chiefly because of indifferent away form in the first half of the season. They were well-nigh invincible at Bootham Crescent, with one sequence of 13 League and Cup wins, in which they scored 47 goals. In total City scored 100 goals – 88 League and 12 Cup – and Walwyn topped the scoring chart again. The average League crowd of 3,243 was the highest since the Second Division days, and a small profit was announced.

Earlier in the year, Jack Miller, a former Rowntree Mackintosh executive, had been appointed sales executive. Meanwhile, physiotherapist Gerry Delahunt replaced John Simpson, who retired and was rewarded with a testimonial game against Leeds United. Also this term, long-serving chairman of the supporters' club Arthur Butler died and was suceeded by Jeff Mortimer, while Ray Wynn became secretary.

Hopes were high at the start of the 1983–84 season, and these were fully realised in a magnificent record-breaking campaign in which the club was never out of the top two. The North Midlands League had folded, so City's reserve side played a number of friendlies this season.

Midfielder Sean Haslegrave was a notable addition to the squad, and the season began with three successive wins. A win at Northampton Town on 29 October sent them to the top of the table, and they stayed there. They suffered only one home defeat and twice won five successive away games.

The top-of-the-table clash on 8 April 1984 attracted 11,297 – the biggest Bootham Crescent crowd for eight years, and the average attendance rose to 5,008. Promotion was clinched in a draw at Chester on 18 April, and the Championship was assured 10 days later when Hartlepool United were beaten.

A 3–0 success against Bury in the last home game lifted the points total to 101 and earned City the *Yorkshire Evening Press* billing of 'The Team Of The Century'. There were tremendous scenes of enthusiasm at the end of this game, and Ian Jones – a member of the Football League Management

Keith Walwyn opens the scoring in a 2–0 win over Hartlepool United on 28 April 1984, which clinched the Fourth Division title. In goal for United was former City 'keeper Eddie Blackburn.

The players carry successful managerial duo Viv Busby and Denis Smith, after City become the first club in Football League history to reach 100 points.

The open-top bus outside the Mansion House following City's win over Bury on 7 May 1984.

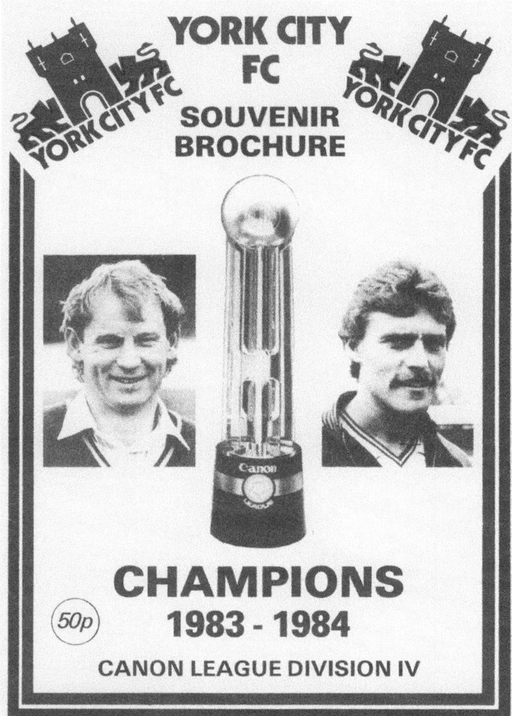

Front cover of the souvenir brochure.

Committee – presented the Fourth Division Canon Trophy to skipper Roger Jones. Later, the team travelled on an open-top bus, driven by former City star Sid Storey, to the Mansion House for a reception.

It was a season of many achievements, including finishing 16 points clear of second club Doncaster Rovers plus achieving 100 points, which were both new Football League records. New club records were 31 wins, most away wins (13) and most goals (96). Also, for the first time they scored in every home game, and for the second successive campaign they only lost once at Bootham Crescent.

Only 16 players were utilised and three were ever present – MacPhail, Ford and Byrne – with Walwyn and Sbragia missing just one game each. Hay and Jones each made over 40 appearances, and others who played a big part were midfielders Hood, Haslegrave and

Michael Sinclair, chairman from 1978–91.

Crosby, together with wingmen Pollard and Alan Pearce. The other players who figured were Evans, Astbury and newcomer Keith Houchen (from Leyton Orient), while Busby and Brian Chippendale made substitute appearances.

As Fourth Division champions, City received £8,000 plus £2,000 for finishing as top scorers. And to mark the achievement of reaching 100 points, Canon – the sponsors of the Football League – awarded an additional £1,000. This truly unforgettable season was reflected in the balance sheet, with a profit of almost £15,000 announced at the AGM. Optimism was expressed for the future, with the club setting its sights on further progress and promotion. One sad note was the death of club president Eric Magson in March 1984.

For 1984–85 the reserve side was resurrected and operated in the second division of the Central League. City relied on the same squad of players, with the addition of left-winger Gary Nicholson from Mansfield Town, and made an outstanding start to the season. A 1–0 home win over Bristol Rovers on 2 October 1984 sent them top of Division Three (League One) with six wins and two draws in eight games. It also marked the 100th League game of the Smith-Busby regime, which could boast the following magnificent record: P 100, W 59, D 23, L 18, F 200, A 104, Pts 200.

City lost the next game at home to Bristol City and a mini slump of only two wins in 11 matches saw them lose touch with the leading pack, but a final position of eighth was regarded as satisfactory. The 7–1 win against Gillingham in November 1984 was City's biggest score for 20 years, and the average crowd of 5,550 was the biggest at Bootham Crescent since 1974–75.

Meeting of champions: jockey Willie Carson with City players at York Racecourse on 15 May 1984.

City played no less than 14 Cup ties in 1984–85, and the overall total of 60 games in the season is a club record. In the Football League Cup they knocked out Doncaster Rovers 8–2 on aggregate and then had two tremendous tilts with Queen's Park Rangers before bowing out. Shortly after the second leg at Loftus Road, John Byrne was signed by Rangers for £100,000, and Dale Banton joined City from Aldershot for a new club record fee paid of £50,000.

By now the FA Cup was under way, and City progressed to the fifth round for the third time in their history. Blue Star, Hartlepool United and Walsall were beaten without conceding a goal, and Arsenal were the visitors to Bootham Crescent in round four. City recorded one of their most memorable giant-killing acts, and this encounter is featured in Matches To Remember.

In the next round, they received a plum home draw against Liverpool and, for the first time since the mid-1950s, Cup fever hit the city. An all-ticket crowd of 13,485 was fixed, and the office staff of Tom Hughes, Sheila Smith and newcomer Tricia Westland were inundated with requests for tickets. As City launched a voucher scheme, a crowd of 10,940 saw a League game against Wigan Athletic.

Houchen, the penalty hero of the Arsenal game, missed the Liverpool tie, which kicked off in an electric atmosphere in front of the sell-out crowd that produced new club record receipts of £29,138. Martin Butler had an early goal ruled out for offside, and honours were even in the first half. The deadlock was broken in the 52nd minute when, following a free-kick, Ian Rush scored for the First Division side. It was the first goal City had conceded in nine games and the first in their FA Cup run. The reigning European champions threatened to take control, and only a goalline clearance by MacPhail prevented them from going further ahead. City kept battling and sent their supporters wild with delight when they equalised with five minutes remaining. Pearce's free-kick on the left was knocked back into the middle by Ford. In quick succession, Sbragia hit the post, Walwyn's header struck the crossbar, MacPhail's shot rebounded off Bruce Grobbelaar's legs and finally Sbragia lashed the ball into the net. In a pulsating finish, Ronnie Whelan had a goal disallowed, but City fully deserved the draw and a lucrative trip to Anfield. There was some crowd trouble at the end, but it did not spoil another great day in the club's history.

York City, 1984–85. Back row, left to right: Malcolm Crosby, Chris Evans, Steve Richards, Alan Hay, Keith Houchen, Mick Astbury, John MacPhail, Keith Walwyn, Derek Hood, Gary Nicholson, Garry Delahunt. Front row: Brian Chippendale, Ricky Sbragia, Steve Senior, Viv Busby, Sean Haslegrave, Denis Smith, Alan Pearce, Martin Butler, Gary Ford.

Nearly 10,000 fans made the trip for the replay in the biggest exodus for 30 years, and Houchen returned to the side in place of Hood. On the night, City were swept aside 7–0 by a Liverpool team in top gear, with John Wark netting a hat-trick. The crowd of 43,010 was the Merseysiders' biggest for two seasons. Manager Denis Smith summed it up by saying 'We cannot compete at world level. We have a good Third Division side, possibly capable of doing well in the Second, but when you play against the best team in Europe and probably one of the best three or four club sides in the world you realise what a gap there is.' City were still on the Wembley trail in the Freight Rover Trophy but lost at home to Lincoln City in the Northern quarter-finals.

Two debutants in the closing weeks of the season were amateur Tony Canham, who scored in his first League game, and 17-year-old Marco Gabbiadini. At the end of the season, Roger Jones left after three fine seasons and Ricky Sbragia took over the captaincy. Other newcomers as City prepared for their 50th season in the Football League were midfielder Simon Mills from Sheffield Wednesday and central-defender David McAughtrie from Carlisle United. Bob Baldwin, a freelance journalist who had been the editor of the *League Review* published in the 1960s–1970s, was appointed the new commercial manager.

The 1985–86 season followed a remarkably similar pattern to the previous one, with solid League success and another FA Cup run. For the fifth successive season City improved their position in the Football League, but the final placing of seventh was a little disappointing as promotion hopes had been high at the beginning of the campaign. A good start was made, and by the end of November they were second behind runaway leaders Reading in Division Three, with 36 points from 20 games.

In October they had beaten Darlington 7–0 to equal their second-highest Football League win and Canham, now signed on as a professional, had scored a hat-trick. A bad midterm spell, from which they only collected 10 out of a possible 39 points, dented promotion hopes but the season ended on a better note with an unbeaten run of nine games. Home form was good, with 16 wins and 49 goals, but City only recorded four victories on their travels.

For the second successive season, they reached the last 16 of the FA Cup and had the unique experience of being drawn at home to non-League opposition in the first four rounds. By a remarkable coincidence, they once again entertained Liverpool in round five, and again the outcome was a 1–1 draw (see Matches To Remember). There was no repeat of the seven-goal drubbing in the replay, as City forced extra-time with Canham equalising after Wark had given the Reds the lead. Walwyn forced the ball into the net in the second half, but his goal was controversially ruled out, and Liverpool survived this scare to score through Jan Molby and Kenny Dalglish in extra-time. It had been a wonderful effort by City, who received a standing ovation at the end.

In the four games with Liverpool over the two seasons, City had drawn three times over 90 minutes. The Merseyside giants went on to reach the Cup Final, and in the Wembley programme their midfielder Craig Johnston praised City for their performance at Anfield, admitting that he could not see a lot wrong with Walwyn's disallowed goal. 'We were very fortunate and York gave us two hard battles,' he said.

During the season, Walwyn netted his 100th goal, while Gary Ford became the 10th player to complete 300 League games for the club – only Chris Topping had reached this milestone at a younger age. Shortly after the Cup exit, Houchen moved to Scunthorpe United.

In July 1986 the *Sports Press* was printed for the last time. It had been first published in 1905, and City news and match reports had featured prominently over the years. In March 1955, when the club played in the semi-final of the FA Cup, a record 25,000 copies were sold. The match reports of Wilf

Meek (known as 'Citizen') and Malcolm Huntington were always eagerly awaited, and it was a sad day when the decision to stop publication was announced.

City made a profit of nearly £40,000, and new director John Quickfall was made responsible for financial matters. Tribute was paid at the AGM to Bob Godfrey, who for many years had dealt ably with the day-to-day accounting.

After the successes and triumphs in the League and Cup over the previous four seasons, the 1986–87 campaign was disappointing, with the club just avoiding relegation and suffering an FA Cup defeat at the hands of Caernarfon Town in a second-round replay at Bootham Crescent. It was the first time that the club had lost to non-League opposition in a replay at home. A little improvement was made in the Football League Cup when they beat Sunderland 4–2 at Roker Park, with Walwyn hitting a hat-trick, and despite losing at home they went through on the away goals rule. In the next round, they beat Chelsea 1–0 at Bootham Crescent but lost on aggregate when they went down 3–0 at Stamford Bridge.

Just prior to the start of the season, MacPhail moved to Bristol City and Hay went to Tranmere Rovers, but these key defenders were not effectively replaced. Another departure was reserve-team coach Malcolm Crosby, who took up a coaching appointment in Kuwait.

A good start to the season was made, and at the end of September the club were second with 16 points from the opening eight games. But from then it was all downhill, and only seven victories were recorded in the remaining 38 fixtures, and City went into the last match needing one point to guarantee their Third Division status. Their away form was very poor, with just one win and 17 defeats. The best League performance was against Middlesbrough on New Year's Day, when they won 3–1 in front of the biggest home crowd of the season (8,611), although the average attendance dropped to 3,432.

At the end of a traumatic season, there was a mass exodus in the summer of 1987. Players to leave included Sean Haslegrave to Torquay United, 'keeper Andy Leaning to Sheffield United and Steve Senior to Northampton Town, while Gary Ford was transferred to Leicester City for £25,000. Ford had been a virtual ever present for seven seasons, and at the time only Barry Jackson, Chris Topping and Tommy Forgan had bettered his 366 League appearances. It was the departure of Denis Smith and Viv Busby to Sunderland that provided the biggest bombshell. In charge for five years, they had guided the club from the lower reaches of the Fourth Division to the title in 1983–84 and to successive seasons in the top eight in the Third, plus two successful FA Cup runs.

The man appointed to the hot seat in June 1987 was Bobby Saxton, who had previously been manager at Exeter City, Plymouth Argyle and Blackburn Rovers. He was faced with a massive team-building effort, as Keith Walwyn became another player to leave when he moved to Blackpool for a tribunal fee of £35,000. In six splendid seasons, Walwyn had scored 140 League and Cup goals, which made him the second-highest scorer in the club's history. Ricky Sbragia hung up his boots to become youth-team manager, and of the side that had won the Fourth Division Championship just three years earlier, only Derek Hood remained.

There were also changes on the administrative and commercial side. Tom Hughes, who had been secretary for six years, took up a similar appointment at Middlesbrough, and commercial manager Bob Baldwin left for Leeds United. The new secretary was Keith Usher, who had been secretary of both the York FA and York & District League. He had also been a member of the North Riding County FA. Sheila Smith was later to take over as commercial manager, and replacing physiotherapist Gerry Delahunt was Jeff Miller, who had experience both as player and physio in the Northern League.

At the 65th annual meeting of the shareholders in December 1987, it was disclosed that the club had lost £65,000 on the day-to-day football running costs for the year ending June 1987. At a lively meeting, Sinclair said that the club's slide had started in April 1986, when Smith had turned down a substantial sum of money to strengthen the side. The chairman continued, 'The manager declined the offer, feeling that he had a strong enough squad. During the close season he failed to agree terms with MacPhail, and replacement Mike Pickering was not good enough.' Sinclair, however, paid tribute to Denis Smith and his success in putting York City back on the football map.

It was obvious that 1987–88 was going to be a difficult season, and Saxton was faced with an almost impossible task as only two players had signed contracts when he arrived. His hastily arranged squad struggled from day one, and they did not record their first win until the 16th attempt at the end of October. By then, Marco Gabbiadini had joined his former boss at Sunderland for an initial fee of £80,000, and before Christmas Simon Mills moved to Port Vale. As City tried to halt the slide, they utilised 31 players that season, including Gordon Staniforth, who returned on a non-contract basis, plus new signings Gary Howlett from Bournemouth and Ian Helliwell from Matlock Town. A big plus was the promise showed by youngsters Steve Tutill, Gary Himsworth and Andy McMillan, who all made their Football League debuts.

One of the few highlights of the season was a remarkable 2–1 home win over Sunderland in March 1988 (see Matches to Remember), while a victory at Brentford on the last day saw them move off the bottom of the table. Statistically, it had been the club's worst season in the Football League, with the fewest wins (8), most defeats (29), fewest points (33 or 25 under the old system of two points for a win) and an away record that had been extended to 38 League games without victory. City had gone from September 1986 until March 1988 without a win on their travels, drawing six and losing 32! At the end of the campaign, several players were released, including long-serving Derek Hood, who was rewarded with a testimonial game in November 1988.

The club received a boost in the summer when their sponsorship deal with Cameron Breweries was extended for a further two years. They had first sponsored City in 1983, and the word HANSA still appeared on the shirts. The club also announced a £100,000 share issue, with Sinclair's family company, Mulberry Hall, agreeing to underwrite virtually the whole sum. That took the chairman and his company's stake in the club from 53 per cent to 75 per cent. John Greenway MP became the new club president.

The club earmarked £100,000 for the manager to spend on new players in a determined bid to make a speedy return to Division Three, and close season captures included 'keeper Chris Marples from Chesterfield (£28,000), ex-Coventry City central-defender Kevan Smith (£35,000) and midfielder and new skipper Steve Spooner from Hereford United (£29,000). Former long-serving Blackburn Rovers defender Derek Fazackerley became the new player-coach.

A bad start was made to 1988–89, and following a home defeat to Scunthorpe United on 17 September, which dumped the club to the bottom of the Football League, Saxton resigned. He stated that he took this decision for the sake of York City and that he had put the players under too much pressure. As in 1982, director Barry Swallow took over as caretaker boss prior to the appointment on 10 October 1988 of John Bird, who became the club's 15th official full-time manager. Previously in charge at Hartlepool United, he brought Alan Little with him from Victoria Park as his assistant and coach. Dale Banton was transferred to Walsall for £80,000 and midfielder Shaun Reid was signed from Rochdale for £35,000, and the club gradually climbed the table.

In the second half of the campaign, City showed good form on their travels, winning five and drawing three of their last 10 away games. They went into the last week of the season with an outside chance of reaching the Play-offs. They missed out, but a mid-table position was reasonably satisfactory after the bad start.

At the shareholders AGM in December 1989 tribute was paid to Bob Strachan, who had retired after 19 years on the board. In the financial year ending June 1989, City had lost £190,000 – the highest in their history – but thanks to interest-free loans from directors plus the £100,000 share issue, the club were not carrying an overdraft. The balance sheet reflected more than two years' poor playing results, but the chairman was not too discouraged or pessimistic. He said in the annual report 'As a board we will continue in our efforts to meet all the responsibilities during the forthcoming year, as well as supporting to the best of our ability the manager and coach in their quest for success on the field.'

In the summer of 1989 Michael Sinclair was elected unopposed as the Third and Fourth Division representative on the Football League Management Committee. Newcomers to the squad in preparation for the 1989–90 campaign included Ray Warburton, a central-defender from Rotherham United.

Results were good in the first half of the season and City went into the Christmas programme in fourth place, poised to make a promotion bid. Successive home defeats over the holiday period heralded a decline that saw the club finish mid-table with 64 points – identical to the previous season. Injuries did not help, especially when new forward David Longhurst, who had been signed from Peterborough United in January 1990 for £30,000, was sidelined after just four games.

An attractive clock in club colours was erected on the top of the Popular Stand in April 1990. This was presented to the club by the family of Phil Dearlove, a keen young City fan who had died a year earlier.

After nearly 25 years, Dr Angus MacLeod retired from the post of honorary medical officer and was succeeded by Robert Porter. The new club sponsors were Flamingo Land Funpark and Zoo at nearby Kirby Misperton, Malton.

Six Seasons in the Third Tier and Triumphs at Wembley and Old Trafford (1990–2000)

The 1990s were another decade that started and finished on a low key but provided plenty of high drama, excitement and triumph in between. A sixth promotion was achieved on a memorable afternoon at Wembley – City's first-ever visit to the famous stadium – and this was followed by a club record six seasons in the third tier of the Football League. In the mid-1990s City achieved two of their finest Cup feats when, in successive seasons, they knocked out Premiership giants Manchester United and Everton in the Football League Cup.

The first two campaigns in this period were very disappointing, as the club struggled in the lower reaches of the Fourth Division almost throughout.

Overshadowing everything in 1990–91 was the tragedy on 8 September 1990 when 25-year-old striker David Longhurst collapsed and died in a home game against Lincoln City. With the side having already lost their opening four games in the League and Football League Cup, the campaign never got off the ground.

One notable new signing was midfielder Nigel Pepper from Rotherham United, and forward Ian Blackstone joined from Harrogate Town. Defensively the side were sound, with full-backs Andy McMillan and Wayne Hall making good progress along with Steve Tutill, who was Clubman of the Year. Once again, goals were in short supply, and although Ian Helliwell was top scorer for a third successive season, his tally of seven League goals equalled the club's lowest individual scoring record.

Departures during the term included Gary Howlett, who returned to his native Ireland, and Gary Himsworth, who moved to Scarborough. Looking ahead to more promising days, 'keeper Dean Kiely, midfielder Steve Bushell and winger Jon McCarthy all made their debuts. And at the end of the campaign, work started on the new covered stand at the Shipton Street end of the ground.

In March 1991 Michael Sinclair announced that he would stand down as chairman after 13 years and leave the board in the summer. In 1978 he had ensured the survival of the club and had worked tirelessly to maintain financial stability during his term of office. In recent years, he had also been chairman of the Associate Member Clubs (Third and Fourth Divisions). Vice-chairman Douglas Craig, a retired civil engineer who had been on the board since 1978, was appointed chairman-elect and would take over in July 1991.

Towards the end of the 1990–91 season, there was a war of words with Robert Gibb, the chairman of the club's sponsor Flamingo Land, who made claim that there was a crisis at York City and proposed a takeover bid. In a statement, Craig said:

> Mr Gibb talks about a crisis at Bootham Crescent, but this is not the case. The truth is that York City is one of the best-run clubs in the Third and Fourth Division. We own our ground, which is one of the best in the lower divisions, and our overdraft of less than £100,000 is also one of the lowest in Division Three and Four, and we have no hidden or outstanding bills. Talk of a £1.5 million bid bears no resemblance to reality, and we will be having no further negotiations of any kind with him about York City.

Just prior to the start of the 1991–92 season, Ian Helliwell was transferred to Scunthorpe United for £80,000, and central-defender Paul Stancliffe, who had previously been with Rotherham United, Sheffield United and latterly at Wolverhampton Wanderers, was a major signing. Another significant newcomer was defender/midfielder Paul Atkin from Bury. New sponsors were local company Portakabin, and the covered stand at the 'Shippo end' was officially opened and named the David Longhurst Stand.

In September 1991 the club's coffers received a big boost when they netted over £300,000 from Marco Gabbiadini's move from Sunderland to Crystal Palace. This was the result of a clause in the deal when the player had moved to Roker Park in 1987, in which it was agreed that City would receive 25 per cent of any sell-on fee over £80,000.

It was to be another frustrating campaign, with injuries to key players including Stancliffe proving a big handicap. With just two wins in the opening 14 League and Cup outings, John Bird was dismissed in mid-October after exactly three years at the helm. His successor was John Ward, who had been Graham Taylor's assistant manager and coach at Watford and Aston Villa. Results initially improved, but the side struggled in the second half of the campaign and finished fourth from bottom for the second successive season. The total of just eight wins equalled the club record low, and lack of scoring power was again the major problem. The average League attendance of 2,506 was almost identical to the previous season, but new club record receipts of £33,000 were announced following the game against Burnley on 28 April 1992, which attracted a crowd of 7,620, including 4,849 away supporters.

After several seasons in the doldrums, 1992–93 was a memorable campaign, culminating in a first-ever trip to Wembley, where, in a dramatic and nail-biting penalty shoot-out, they beat Crewe Alexandra to win promotion. The big summer signing of 1992 was centre-forward Paul Barnes from

Dean Kiely makes the vital save in the penalty shoot-out.

Stoke City for £50,000, and he was an immediate success, scoring on his debut and finishing top marksman with 21 goals. In February 1993 he netted four goals in a win over Scunthorpe United – the first City player to achieve this feat for 32 years – and the following month hit a hat-trick in a 5–1 win at Barnet. Another important signing was Gary Swann from Preston North End, who proved an influential figure in midfield.

The season opened with a club record start of four wins, and they led the table up to the end of 1992. At that stage, not only automatic promotion but also the Championship looked a distinct possibility, but then came a mid-season slump that produced only two victories in 15 games, including six successive draws. Just prior to the win at Barnet in mid-March 1993, John Ward moved to Bristol Rovers, and Alan Little, who had

Barclays League Division Three Play-off winners.

been assistant boss since 1988 under Bird and then Ward, took over. City finished strongly but finished fourth and met Bury in the Play-offs.

After a 0–0 draw at Gigg Lane, they won the second leg at Bootham Crescent thanks to Swann's first goal of the season. The crowd of 9,206 was the biggest since the visit of Liverpool in February 1986. The Play-off Final on 29 May 1993 is featured in Matches To Remember, as City finished on a triumphant note. Overall, it had been a fine team effort. Kiely maintained his fine progress in goal, and McMillan and Hall along with skipper Stancliffe and Atkin were a solid and reliable back four. In midfield were Swann and driving force Pepper, who was the penalty expert, with McCarthy and Canham providing the skill and pace down the flanks. Up front, Barnes and Blackstone provided the fire-power, with John Borthwick, formerly with Darlington, playing his part in the first half of the campaign.

To complete a fine season, the reserves won promotion to the First Division of the renamed Pontins League, while the intermediates, under the guidance of Ricky Sbragia, reached the quarter-finals of the FA Youth Cup, losing to Manchester United. The only disappointment was City's lack of success in the Cup competitions, where in each instance they fell at the first hurdle.

Back in the third tier (now called Division Two following the formation of the Premiership in 1992) after an absence of five years, City had another successful campaign and reached the promotion Play-offs. The squad was strengthened with the signing of forward Steve Cooper from Tranmere Rovers, and the season started well with victories at Exeter and Fulham and a 5–0 win over Cardiff City. A lean spell followed, and by the end of November they had slipped to 17th. They found their feet again and finished fifth with only five defeats in the last 30 games – their highest placing since the days in the old Second Division in the mid-1970s. One of the highlights was a 5–0 win at Blackpool – their biggest-ever away victory in the Football League. In the Play-offs they narrowly lost to Stockport County, 1–0 on aggregate, just failing to make another trip to Wembley.

With just 40 goals conceded, City had the best defensive record in the Second Division, and at home they let in only 13, which was a new club best. A total of 20 clean sheets equalled a club record, and one of the biggest factors in this success was their ability to field a settled side, with Kiely, McMillan and Tutill ever present in defence and Hall missing only one game. Tony Canham in his testimonial year was as consistent as ever, and Paul Barnes again topped 20 goals. One notable debutant this term was promising youngster Graeme Murty. The average attendance of 4,677 was the best since 1984–85, and the club record receipts were broken on no less than three occasions.

Departures during the summer of 1994 included Gary Swann, who was unable to agree new terms; Ray Warburton, who moved to Northampton Town; and Ian Blackstone, who switched to Scarborough. Early in the new season, the successful youth manager Ricky Sbragia, who had served the club well over 12 years as player and coach, left to take up a similar appointment at Sunderland. His replacement was Derek Bell, a former striker with Halifax Town and Lincoln City, who had been the club's chief scout in recent months. A new recruit was central-defender Tony Barras from Stockport County. Cooper left for Airdrie early in the campaign, and Paul Baker was signed from Gillingham as his replacement.

City recovered from a poor start to 1994–95, and early in the New Year a run of four straight wins raised hopes of another promotion challenge, but they were to remain just on the fringe of the leading pack and finished ninth. Notable victories were recorded over Birmingham City and Huddersfield Town, who both won promotion, and, remarkably, City repeated their 5–0 win at Blackpool. Barnes was top scorer again and notched a couple of hat-tricks.

Tony Canham in typical action.

The intermediates, with Richard Cresswell and Darren Williams to the fore, had a fine campaign and were just pipped on goal difference by Newcastle United for the Northern Intermediate League title. Once again, there was disappointment in the FA Cup as City did not progress beyond the second round – and had not done since 1985–86.

At the end of the season, Tony Canham left the club after 11 splendid years and a total of 413 senior appearances. Commercial manager Sheila Smith retired in May 1995. She had held the post since 1987 and had been at the club for over 17 years when she joined the office staff. Maureen Leslie, who had been in charge of the lottery department, was her replacement.

In the close season, Paul Stancliffe, who had finished his playing days the previous season, was appointed assistant manager and Paul Baker, as player-coach. The latter was to leave midterm for Torquay United. Just before the start of the 1995–96 campaign, Jon McCarthy was transferred to Port Vale for a new record fee received of £450,000, and Paul Stephenson was signed from Brentford. Another newcomer was forward Rob Matthews, who moved to Bootham Crescent from Luton Town for a new record fee paid of £90,000. In December this record was raised to £140,000 when midfielder Adrian Randall was signed from Burnley. Among the new intake in the youth training scheme was a youngster by the name of Jonathan Greening.

This campaign was a roller-coaster affair, and in the final analysis City only just managed to retain their Second Division status by winning at Brighton in a rearranged last match of the season, played on a Thursday morning. The original fixture on 27 April 1996 was abandoned following crowd disturbances caused by Brighton fans protesting against their directors.

City never really recovered from a bad start, which saw them collect just two points from the first six games. Four successive victories followed, but then came another slump, including a 6–1 defeat at Peterborough. They remained in the danger zone for the rest of the campaign, although notable wins were recorded against promoted clubs Swindon Town and Oxford United, plus their customary success at Blackpool.

The highlight of the season was undoubtedly the remarkable success over Manchester United in the Football League (Coca-Cola) Cup. The 3–0 victory at Old Trafford (see Matches to Remember) hit the national headlines, and City held on in the second leg to knock United out 4–3 on aggregate. Making his debut in the game at Bootham Crescent was 19-year-old 'keeper Andy Warrington, in place of the injured Dean Kiely.

In the third round, City lost away to Premiership side Queen's Park Rangers after a very creditable display. Richard Cresswell made his senior debut, and in March 1996 top marksman Paul Barnes moved to Birmingham City for a reported fee of £350,000, with Gary Bull moving from St Andrews to York. In just under four seasons, Barnes scored 85 goals in 179 League and Cup games, which puts him among the top ten marksmen for the club. Also this term, the death was announced in April 1996 of Ron Spence, one of the FA Cup heroes of the mid-1950s.

In the annual report made at the AGM in October 1996, it was disclosed that although net income from transfers for the year amounted to over £600,000, the club had made an operating loss of £173,000. These transfers included the major summer signing of centre-forward Neil Tolson for

Eric Cantona and Andy McMillan in close contention in the Football League Cup second-leg tie between City and Manchester United in October 1995.

David Beckham and Tony Barras tussle for the ball in the League Cup tie at Bootham Crescent.

City's midfielder Scott Jordan, who scored the vital goal that knocked the Red Devils out of the League Cup.

£80,000 from Bradford City and, on the eve of the campaign, Dean Kiely's departure for Second Division rivals Bury. After a prolonged and acrimonious Football League tribunal wrangle, City received a fee of £125,000, which was way below their valuation of £400,000 for the 'keeper.

The 1996–97 season was almost a carbon copy of the previous one, with City again finishing 20th with an identical record of 13 victories, 13 draws and 20 losses, and they did not secure safety until they won at Rotherham United in their penultimate game. Their record up to December was reasonable, and a home win in mid-December lifted them into the top half. However, with only five wins in the last 24 outings, they again walked the relegation tightrope.

The 1995–96 squad.

It was a season of comings and goings, with Rodney Rowe, ex-Huddersfield Town, and Mark Tinkler from Leeds United among the newcomers – both for sizeable fees. Departures included young midfielder Darren Williams, who moved to Sunderland in October 1996 for an initial fee of £50,000 and possibly more, depending on his first-team appearances. Record signing Adrian Randall moved to Bury after less than a year at Bootham Crescent, and in February 1997 Nigel Pepper was transferred to Bradford City for £100,000. He had been the driving force in midfield for almost seven seasons and had 281 senior appearances to his credit.

In the FA Cup City reached the third round of the competition for the first time in 11 years, but after knocking out Hartlepool United and Preston North End, they lost in disappointing fashion, away to Conference side Hednesford Town. The high point in the campaign again came in the Football League Cup, when Everton were beaten 4–3 on aggregate in the second round. It was the first time City had met the Toffeemen, and Tolson scored in a 1–1 draw in the first leg. The second leg (featured in Matches To Remember) was another memorable night in the club's long and distinguished list of Cup triumphs. In a backroom shuffle, Derek Bell became first-team coach and assistant manager, and Paul Stancliffe took over as youth-team manager.

In July 1997 Steve Tutill's testimonial game against Middlesbrough drew an attendance of 7,123. As part of the central-defender's testimonial year, a sportsmen's dinner had been held, and members of the 1954–55 side joined 450 guests at the Ebor Suite, York Racecourse.

Early in the 1997–98 campaign, Tutill moved to Darlington after 10 years' stalwart service. The season was a classic case of two halves. At Christmas they were well poised to make a promotion challenge but form dipped in the New Year, especially at Bootham Crescent. Eight of the first 11 home games were won, but only one of the last 12 matches resulted in a victory. The chief problem was the lack of scoring power. Leading marksman Rowe notched 16 goals, but he only found the net in one League game after mid-November, and that was when he scored twice in a defeat at Preston.

Newcomers during the campaign were defender Barry Jones from Wrexham and full-back Neil Thompson, ex-Barnsley, while Marco Gabbiadini rejoined the club for a short spell in the closing weeks. In March 1998 highly rated 19-year-old forward Jonathan Greening was signed by Manchester United for a reported initial fee of £350,000. He had started just five League games for City and made 20 substitute appearances. At the end of the season, Graeme Murty also left the club when he was transferred to Reading for £700,000, and Clubman of the Year Steve Bushell moved to Blackpool. Adie Shaw, who had a short spell as a player with City in the late 1980s, was appointed youth development coach to work alongside Stancliffe.

At the AGM in December 1998, a profit for the year ending June 1998 amounted to £170,000, but the day-to-day trading loss was £468,000. At the meeting, tribute was paid to Brian Houghton, who had resigned after 20 years on the board.

Manager Alan Little, now in his sixth season in charge, was granted a testimonial match, and the game against Middlesbrough, including Paul Gascoigne, drew a crowd of 6,215. Newcomers for the 1998–99 campaign included Steve Agnew from Sunderland and Gordon Connelly, a right winger from

York City, 1996–97. Back row, left to right: Pepper, Campbell, Atkin, Barras, Tolson, Tutill, Sharples, Cresswell, Randall. Middle row: Miller (physio), Naylor, McMillan, Reed, Warrington, Osborne, Pouton, Stephenson, Stancliffe (assistant manager). Front row: Williams, Himsworth, Atkinson, Bull, Little (manager), Bushell, Jordan, Hall, Murty.

Eleven players from City's Hall of Fame at Steve Tutill's testimonial dinner in July 1997. Back row, left to right: Norman Wilkinson, Billy Hughes, Phil Burrows, Chris Topping, Gordon Brown, Derek Hood. Front row: Sid Storey, Andy McMillian, Steve Tutill, Tony Canham, Gary Ford. In total these players between them made 4,399 appearances for the club.

Airdrie, for a reported fee of £70,000. Experienced goalkeeper Bobby Mimms, whose previous clubs included Everton and Tottenham Hotspur, joined the club early in the campaign.

On 13 October 1998 Manchester United manager Alex Ferguson officially opened the club's new training ground near Wigginton. Three years earlier, United had signed 17-year-old City intermediate 'keeper Nick Culkin for £100,000, and this money had provided the initial outlay for the training complex, which cost upwards of £250,000. Impressed with the set-up, Ferguson stated 'the facilities are first class and are better than most Premiership teams.'

City made an encouraging start to the season and were placed eighth in the table in mid-October. A bad sequence then followed, with just one point taken from a possible 21, and they slithered into the lower reaches. They were knocked out of the FA Cup at Wrexham in a game in which they had two players sent off. This match also marked the debut of 17-year-old midfielder Lee Bullock, while another promising youngster who made his mark this season was left-winger Martin Garratt.

Results improved over the Christmas period, with a notable 2–1 success over Manchester City and successive away wins at Oldham and Wycombe, leaving City ninth in the table on 2 January 1999. The sequence that followed in this topsy-turvy season proved disastrous – just two draws and nine defeats in 11 outings, including five successive home defeats. With the club hovering just above the bottom four, Little was sacked on 15 March after over 10 years at Bootham Crescent, virtually six years to the day since he took over as manager. Player-coach Neil Thompson was appointed caretaker boss, and there was a flurry of transfer activity, most notably the departure of leading marksman Richard Cresswell to Premiership club Sheffield Wednesday for an all-time record fee received of £950,000. A month earlier he had become the first City player to gain representative honours for England when he was capped for the Under-21 side. Tony Barras moved to Reading, while incoming players included former Leeds United central-defender Chris Fairclough, Halifax Town striker Marc Williams and Hull City defender Matt Hocking.

With four wins and two draws in their next 10 outings, City went into their last game at Manchester City needing a point to ensure safety. In front of 32,471, they lost 4–0 and, with Oldham Athletic and Wycombe Wanderers both winning, City dropped into the bottom four for the first time that season, and six seasons of Second Division football – the club's longest spell in the third tier – was brought to an end.

One bright note was the success of the youth team who, under the guidance of Stancliffe and Shaw, reached the last 16 of the FA Youth Cup, bowing out to a West Ham United side featuring Joe Cole.

Players who were released at the end of the season surprisingly included ever-reliable right-back Andy McMillan, who, with 492 senior appearances, is second to Barry Jackson in the all-time appearance list. His testimonial year included a game against Leeds United in July 1999. Mark Tinkler, Gordon Connelly and Neil Tolson all moved to Southend United to join Alan Little, who was now manager at Roots Hall. Andy Warrington signed for Doncaster Rovers and Alan Pouton was transferred to Grimsby Town for £150,000. Neil Thompson was officially appointed player-manager, and his assistant was Adie Shaw. Derek Bell, who had been Little's number two, had left for Lincoln City in January 1999.

As City faced the last season of the millennium back in the basement division of the Football League, one important signing was Irish centre-forward Barry Conlon from Southend United for £100,000 – the second-biggest fee in the club's history. Other newcomers were Mark Sertori and Kevin Hulme from Halifax Town. The club appointed Sophie McGill as their first public relations executive, and her role was to boost City's profile and transform Bootham Crescent into a fan-friendly venue for 21st-century football.

City announced a record profit of £1,274,202 for the year ending 30 June 1999, due to the big-money transfers, but the overall trading loss on the season amounted to £483,000. The stark reality was that the club had to sell to survive. Although gate receipts broke the £500,000 barrier for the first time, the annual report stated that they were not sufficient to sustain the club, especially in a year when the Bootham Crescent payroll was £1,427,028 and repairs and safety work at the ground amounted to £45,000.

During the summer of 1999 the board received the backing of shareholders for a move to safeguard the club's assets in the event of liquidation. Directors at the club were concerned about a clause in Football Association rules that would force them to give up any surplus assets if that situation ever arose, such as the Bootham Crescent ground and the Wigginton training ground complex. This was confirmed at the December 1999 AGM by the following statement:

> The directors had decided that it would be in the best interests of the shareholders to re-structure the Company by creating a holding Company, known as Bootham Crescent Holdings Plc, with the York City Association Football and Athletic Club Plc (YCFC) as its wholly owned subsidiary and with the real property assets of YCFC being transferred to the holding company. In the view of the directors the new structure will enable the football club to be secure in its activities and provide a base from which a determined effort can be made to seek promotion.

The 1999–2000 campaign started reasonably well but a bad slump in midterm produced just one win in 18 League outings. Alarm bells were ringing as the drop into the Conference beckoned. During this period, centre-forward Colin Alcide was signed from Hull City for £80,000, and Rodney Rowe moved to Gillingham.

In February 2000 Thompson was dismissed after just 11 months in charge, and former Bradford City and Hull City manager Terry Dolan took over the hot seat. He bolstered the defence with newcomers including Northern Ireland goalkeeper Alan Fettis from Blackburn Rovers, two full-backs – Peter Hawkins on loan from Wimbledon and ex-Huddersfield Town player Darren Edmondson – plus two central-defenders – Peter Swan, previously with Leeds United and Hull City, and Mark Bower, on loan from Bradford City. Consequently, only five goals were conceded in the last 12 League games, of which one was lost, and eight clean sheets were kept as the club scrambled its way to safety.

During the season, Wayne Hall became the eighth player to make 400 senior appearances for the club. The average home League crowd of 3,048 was the lowest since 1991–92, and the 35 players used during the campaign was a club record. Promising youngsters who made their debut this term included 'keeper Russell Howarth, Christian Fox and Marc Thompson. James Richardson took over from Maureen Leslie as commercial manager early in 2000. He had previously been her assistant and was the match-day programme editor. The death was announced of Bob Strachan who had been chairman when the club were in the old Second Division in the mid-1970s.

Relegation from the Football League and Off-field Traumas and Upheavals (2000–08)

The early years of the new millennium proved to be a rocky and tempestuous period in the history of York City Football Club. In May 2004 75 years' membership of the Football League ended following relegation to the Conference, but overshadowing everything were the off-field problems that threatened the very future of the club.

In the summer of 2000 chairman Douglas Craig admitted that the board had relaxed their grip on the club's purse strings as a calculated risk in the hope of brighter times. 'I think it would be fair to say that we have gambled a bit. If that has been a wise thing to do, we will have to wait and see,' he said. In his report to the shareholders of Bootham Crescent Holdings later that year, it was announced that losses for the year ending 30 June 2000 amounted to nearly £700,000 after the previous year's profit of £1.25 million. It was also revealed that the wage bill of £1,635,736 for the year was more than double that in 1995. (It later transpired that in the 1999–2000 and 2000–01 seasons, City had one of the worst wages/turnover ratios in the history of British football.) The chairman stated how important the investment in a strong youth policy had been over the years. This had shown returns when young players developed by the club were transferred, bringing fees into the club that ensured its survival, although a threatened change to the transfer system could spell real problems and spark a 'radical review' of the club's affairs.

Early in 2001 it was revealed that the club had tabled an undisclosed bid for the barracks site adjacent to the ground, but this proved unsuccessful. On the playing side, 2000–01 was another disappointing campaign, and the club did not clinch safety from relegation until the penultimate game, drawing 2–2 at Torquay United thanks to a dramatic last-gasp equaliser direct from a Graham Potter corner. The left-back was one of a number of newcomers, with others including Gary Hobson from Hull City, ex-Oldham Athletic player David McNiven, who finished top scorer, and Peter Duffield from Darlington, who had the misfortune to break his leg early in the season. Notable signings later in the campaign were experienced striker Lee Nogan, a former Welsh international whose previous clubs included Oxford United,Watford and Grimsby Town, and Chris Brass from Burnley. These two players played an important part as City clawed their way to safety in the closing weeks. In mid-February, following a 3–0 home defeat against Exeter City, the club had dropped to the foot of the table but lost just two of their last 16 outings to finish 17th. Goalkeeper Alan Fettis was Clubman of the Year, and a record number of 38 players were used during the campaign.

For only the second time since 1986, the third round of the FA Cup was reached; at that stage, they bowed out 3–0 away to Premiership club Leicester City. The highlight of the season was the visit of Manchester United for a friendly match in July 2000 as part of the deal that had seen youth player Nick Culkin move to Old Trafford back in 1995. A crowd of 9,003 saw a strong United side win 2–0, with Roy Keane scoring both goals. Departures at the end of the season included Barry Conlon, who moved to Darlington, Barry Jones and Scott Jordan.

At the annual meeting of Bootham Crescent Holdings on 20 December 2001, a record loss of more than £1.2 million was reported, and chairman Douglas Craig made the shock announcement to shareholders that 'at the end of the season the board of York City Football Club intend to resign and, in the interim, invite anyone interested in acquiring the football club to write to the chairman to obtain further details'. The full statement read:

> By the end of February 2002 York City FC will be at the limit of its current overdraft facility at the bank. The current facility has been possible because of a joint security provided by Bootham Crescent Holdings Plc and York City Association Football and Athletic Club (The Football Club). Unless further security is provided to allow an increase in the overdraft facility, or the provision of a bridging loan, it follows that The Football Club will not be in a position to continue beyond the end of February 2002. In order to prevent this happening, the Board of Bootham Crescent Holdings Plc are prepared to provide additional security for sufficient funds to enable the Football Club to complete the current season but not for any period beyond that date. Anyone who believes they can make a success of running the club will not be required to make any payment, or assume responsibility for the overdraft and/or bridging loan, but they will have to provide certain guarantees and undertake certain obligations. The club's many supporters may wish to form a trust and proceed on that basis. The provision of additional security by Bootham Crescent Holdings Plc will not, however, continue to apply if actions by others precipitate a worsening of the anticipated financial position.

The *Evening Press*, who had taken over as the club's sponsors during the summer, immediately launched a 'Save City' campaign. A meeting in their Walmgate offices in late December with supporters' representatives including Josh Easby, who had recently been appointed to the City board, led to a public meeting in the Temple Anderson Hall on 7 January 2002. Over 300 people, including club captain Chris Brass and a number of Bootham Crescent staff, packed into the venue with many locked out, and a unanimous decision was taken to form a supporters' trust. The chairman of the meeting was Paul Rawnsley, a City fan with specialist knowledge of football finances through his work with Deloitte and Touche. He echoed the feelings of all present when he said 'we must not let York City die and must do everything we can to ensure the club survives for future generations.'

Two days later, another bombshell was delivered with the announcement that it was proposed that Bootham Crescent, the club's home since 1932, would close by 30 June 2002. Any buyer would have to vacate the ground by this date and relocate to another stadium. It was also disclosed that talks over a move to Huntington Stadium had been held and that York City FC would quit the Football League at the end of the 2001–02 season if no buyer was found. The capital needed to buy the club and ground was £4.5 million.

Amid claims of 'moral guardianship' and that directors merely looked after the club's assets for future generations, chairman Craig was defiant. 'Since when did the moral guardians of the club have to sit and take abuse, vilification and vandalism and continue to hold the role. The supporters are getting what they have wanted and shouted for over the years – getting shot of me and the board.'

Two stalwarts and former directors – Hugh Kitchin and Arthur Brown – expressed sadness and surprise at the situation. The former, who had been chairman during the glory days in the mid-1950s, said 'I do not want to be critical of the present board because I know how difficult it is to run a club. I would say, however, that things have changed. Directors in my day did not regard it as their club to make money from. We were merely looking after it on behalf of the public of York and district.' Brown, who was a director from 1954 until 1970, said 'There is no point in me being critical of the present set-up because things change in football, but I would add that when you have had enough as a director you should pack it in instead of cashing in.'

Former City players including Chris Topping, Graeme Crawford, Jimmy Seal, Chris Jones, Phil Burrows, John Stone, Brian Pollard and Ian Holmes signed a letter pledging their full support for the Save City campaign, and almost 1,000 fans attended the formal launch of the Supporters' Trust on 1 February 2002 at the Barbican. ITV sports commentator Jon Champion, a keen City fan, hosted the meeting, and many former City players including 89-year-old Jack Pinder were in the audience along with York-born Steve McLaren, the Middlesbrough manager and future England boss.

Two major bidders for the club emerged – the York Rugby League duo of John Stabler and Russell Greenfield, and John Batchelor, a self-styled motor racing tycoon and owner-driver of the B&Q-sponsored Honda Integrity Racing team, who competed in the British Touring Car Championship. It was Batchelor who won the race to take over the club, and the announcement on 15 March 2002 was greeted with enthusiasm from most quarters, including the Supporters' Trust. He promised to make City the 'most unusual team' in the Football League and also pledged that the Supporters' Trust would be given two seats in the boardroom. One of his first announcements was of a three-year sponsorship package deal with York builders Persimmon Homes, in which a then undisclosed sum of money would be split between the football club and his racing team. Sadly, the Batchelor regime was to prove disastrously ill-fated.

On the playing front, the 2001–02 season was to prove disappointing as the club once again flirted with relegation. In January they were second from bottom in the table but then staged their customary second-half-of-season rally and finished 14th – their highest placing since their return to the bottom division in 1999. Top marksman was striker Michael Proctor on loan from Sunderland. There was long-awaited success in the FA Cup when the fourth round was reached for the first time since 1985–86. For the second successive season, they knocked out Reading at the second stage and then, after beating First Division (Championship) Grimsby Town, entertained Premiership club Fulham. The tie was played in the middle of the off-field problems, and the Cottagers, who won 2–0, generously

The programme cover for 23 March 2002 welcomes new owner John Batchelor – a false dawn and a costly one for the club.

donated their share of the gate receipts through owner Mohammed Al Fayed, which amounted to £25,000 going to the Supporters' Trust.

One new signing during the season was Jon Parkin from Barnsley, who could play either up front or in the centre of defence. On the administrative side, Peter Salter took over as commercial manager, with James Richardson becoming communications manager.

The John Batchelor bandwagon rolled on during the summer of 2002. The name was changed to York City Soccer Club as part of his plan to market the club in the USA, and a new strip incorporated a black-and-white-chequered design on the right sleeve. Former England striker Luther Blissett was appointed coach, but he was to remain with the club only a few months. Batchelor proposed to establish a new rugby league team following the demise of York Wasps earlier in the year and revealed he wanted to build City's new stadium at Clifton Moor. Ian McAndrew was appointed a new director, and his role was to oversee the move from Bootham Crescent. Another newcomer to the board was Nick Townend.

The names of the first elected board of the Supporters' Trust were unveiled at the first annual meeting. They were Sophie McGill, Paul Rawnsley, Terry Herbert, Kirsten Gillies, Steve Beck, Graham Kilby, Richard Willis, Michael Shannon, Michael Brown, Richard Snowball and John Catton.

Persimmon Homes, who had acquired 10 per cent of the shares in Bootham Crescent Holdings, announced that they were submitting planning applications for 93 homes on the Bootham Crescent site, while Batchelor branded council planners as inept and shambolic as he ran into problems regarding the proposed new City ground. Craig resigned from the board of the football club but remained as chairman of BCH, and Townend also ceased to be a director.

Season-ticket sales reached 1,500. Amid all the mayhem, 2002–03 was a successful campaign, as a strong bid was made for the Play-offs, but off-field problems deepened and the club was brought to the brink of extinction.

Half-price season tickets for 2003–04 were offered for sale in October 2002, and with warning bells sounding, Batchelor called a press conference the following month to deny there were financial problems and to refute claims that the club was poised to go into administration. That month, the Supporters' Trust announced their first intention to launch a bid to secure full ownership. Batchelor subsequently broadcast, at half-time in an FA Cup tie against Swansea City, that he would hand over control. Twenty-four hours later, he did an about-turn on this statement.

On 28 November 2002 the club entered a creditors' voluntary agreement as they attempted to survive, and the *Evening Press* said the club had been plunged into the darkest and coldest days of its history. It was revealed that the players' pay packets had been delayed for a second month running and that a considerable sum of money was owed to the Inland Revenue. The players and staff were dismayed that Batchelor had not made them fully aware of the crisis, and as Alan Fettis said 'The chairman was hailed as the knight in shining armour, but it now turns he has not got any armour.' Pressure group Friends of Bootham Crescent, whose spokesman was Ian Savage, did a tremendous amount of work with the Supporters' Trust in organising emergency fundraising projects.

At a court meeting held at Leeds Combined Courts, attended by insolvency experts Jacksons Jolliffe Cork, it was announced that the club had just five weeks to find a buyer or face going bankrupt, which meant that City's game against Swansea on 18 January 2003 could be the last for the club. An unnamed bidder came forward at the 11th hour, and £92,000 of Supporters' Trust money was injected into the club, giving a temporary last-gasp reprieve and meeting the initial mid-January deadline. The mystery bidder was revealed as Jon Heynes, a millionaire businessman based in Oxfordshire with motor racing connections, who would work in tandem with Batchelor. Another interested party was thought to be Brooks Mileson, an insurance tycoon. He later became the owner of Gretna FC.

Boosted by a cash donation reported to be £50,000 by lifelong fan Jason McGill, owner of JM Packaging Ltd based in Malton, Yorkshire, the Trust made their official bid to take over the club. As another deadline was reached, fans raised more than £50,000 in 72 hours, including a staggering £20,000 in bucket collections at a game against Bury on 23 February. After much discussion, the Supporters' Trust offer was accepted by administrator David Willis, who revealed that City owed £1.85 million. Of this, £890,000 would be due to the players to honour their contracts, with £98,000 owed to the taxman. After several days' negotiation and hard work, the final obstacle was cleared when the Inland Revenue accepted 63 pence in the pound, and the Supporters' Trust took over control of the club on 26 March 2003. As the new chairman Steve Beck said, 'We are so pleased to have got to this stage but, to be honest, now the hard work starts.'

The newly incorporated company was York City Football Club Ltd, and the other directors were Sophie McGill, previously a public relations executive at Bootham Crescent, Michael Brown, Jason McGill and Ian McAndrew. Terry Doyle joined the board as finance director a few weeks later. The York City Soccer Club sign at the ground was dismantled, and to complete the celebrations, a 2–0 win over Southend United in the first match under the new regime on 29 March lifted the club up to third place. It had been a tremendous effort by supporters, and particular praise was due to Paul Rawnsley for all his tireless work from day one back in December 2001. The slogan had been 'They'll Never Kill York City' and, thanks to the magnificent efforts of so many people, the club did not die.

At the end of the season, the Football Supporters' Federation gave its coveted Services to Supporters award to City. John Quickfall, one of Bootham Crescent Holdings' directors, resigned, saying 'I should like to make it clear that I will not make any personal profit out of my shares in BCH. It is my intention that any such profit which may become due to me will be put toward securing a new home for the club.' It was later disclosed that he made a donation of over £20,000.

It transpired that Batchelor had made a bad situation worse. He acquired the club from BCH for just £1 and, unbeknown to the Trust, diverted nearly all the £400,000 Persimmon Homes sponsorship money away from the football club to his racing team, and his promise of having Supporters' Trust members on the board of directors never materialised. Batchelor later admitted he walked away with a profit of £120,000 from a club he took into administration and that he was guilty of 'asset-stripping' during his time as owner. It was also disclosed that at the time of his takeover he agreed that the Minstermen would vacate Bootham Crescent by the end of the 2002–03 season, so ending the club's 25-year lease with BCH. It was revealed in the summer of 2004 that £42,500 – season-ticket money that Batchelor had used in advance of the 2003–04 season – had not been returned, but owing to a breach of the confidentiality clause, City were unable to pursue this matter through the courts.

In view of all the massive problems off the field, events on it in 2002–03 proved much better, and great credit went to manager Terry Dolan and his players for their determined bid to reach the Play-offs. At the end of March, they were in an automatic promotion position, but without a win in the last six games they just failed to reach a top-seven place. Special praise went to skipper Chris Brass, who led from the front both on and off the pitch. During the height of the problems in midterm, Peter Duffield and Alan Fettis left Bootham Crescent. The team battled on and, at the end of the campaign, Dolan received a Special Achievement Award in the north-east football awards ceremony, hosted by Tyne-Tees television, for steering the Minstermen to the verge of the Third Division Play-offs despite the club teetering on the brink of extinction.

At the end of May 2003, however, Dolan's three-and-a-half-year reign at the club ended when it was announced that he had been relieved of his duties, along with his assistant Adie Shaw. The board insisted that the decision was made for financial reasons. The new managerial team was player-boss Chris Brass with Lee Nogan as his assistant. At the age of 27, Brass became the youngest Football League manager since 1946. New club sponsors were Phoenix Software, and the present club badge and logo were introduced.

Jon Champion interviews 90-year-old Jack Pinder at a York City Legends dinner in March 2003.

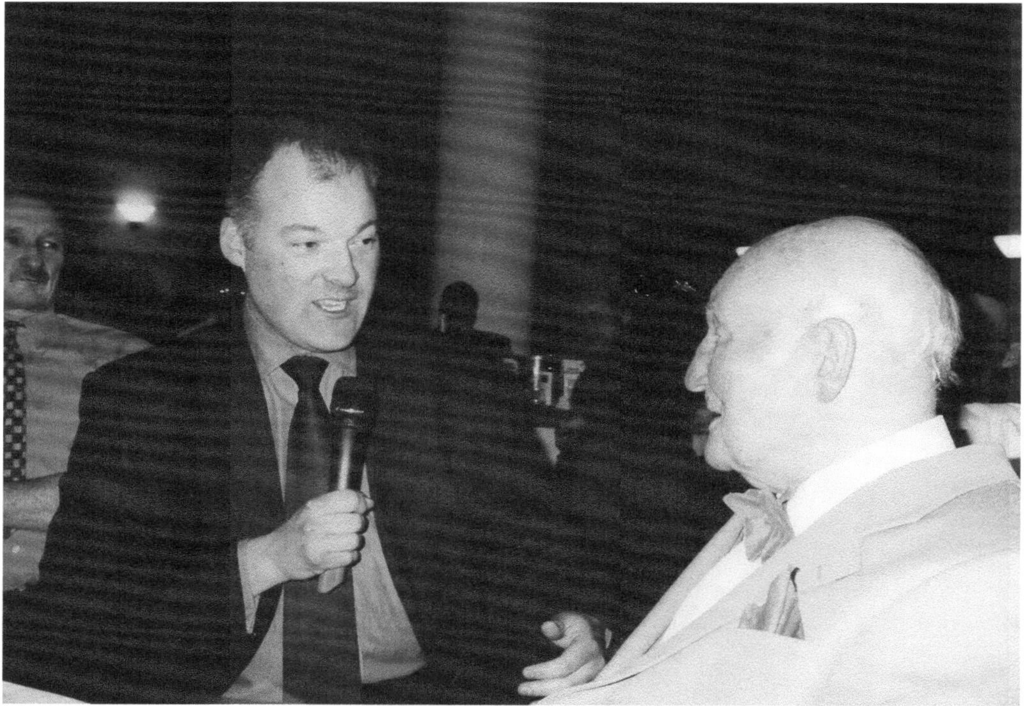

The club's lease to stay at Bootham Crescent was extended to May 2004, and plans proceeded with the development of Huntington Stadium as their new home, but mounting planning problems arose regarding bringing the ground up to Football League standards. It was disclosed that the City board were working behind the scenes to stay at Bootham Crescent and that this was the preferred option. At the annual meeting of BCH in January 2004, Douglas Craig stated that it would cost £2.6 million for the football club to assume ownership of Bootham Crescent and confirmed that he would be unwilling to extend the club's lease beyond the end of the season. He also defended his role in the transfer of the club's assets to Bootham Crescent Holdings in 1999, saying 'The football club would not be in existence at all if I had not done what I did.'

At the beginning of February 2004 came the announcement that after months of behind-the-scenes negotiations, the club had won their two-year battle to stay at Bootham Crescent. A joint statement from the club ground owners, Bootham Crescent Holdings and Persimmon Homes, revealed 'an agreement has been reached in principle to enable the football club to continue to play professional football at Bootham Crescent.' Six months of hard work under the code name Project Gold had paid dividends, as the club regained control of its destiny. Club director Jason McGill said 'We are delighted to have reached this agreement. It has taken much hard work and many sleepless nights, but we have achieved our aim of ensuring York City has a home for next season and for the future.' He also paid tribute to his fellow director Ian McAndrew, who had worked so hard on putting a feasible plan together for moving to Huntington, which had remained the only option for the club's survival for some time. Many tributes were paid to the tremendous work done by the board, and trust board member Paul Rawnsley said 'Great tribute is due to Jason McGill and those around him (Steve Beck, Sophie McGill and Terry Doyle) who have supported the aim of staying at Bootham Crescent.' The Supporters' Trust, which had been awarded the national Trust of the Season award for their achievements, expressed their great delight through their chairman Richard Snowball, and City manager Chris Brass described it as wonderful news.

Newcomers for the 2003–04 campaign included experienced midfielder Mitch Ward from Barnsley, ex-Luton Town forward Liam George, goalkeeper Mark Ovendale from Bournemouth and midfielder Darren Dunning, who had been with Premiership club Blackburn Rovers. Under the new managership team and captaincy of Darren Edmondson, the side made a wonderful start and equalled a club record by winning the first four games. Form dipped but Play-off aspirations were maintained, and victory over bottom club Carlisle United on 10 January 2004 put them 10th, just three points off a top-seven position. Their record at this stage of the campaign read: P 26, W 10, D 9, L 7, F 25, A 28, Pts 39.

Brass and Nogan were given extended contracts, and City were 18 points clear of the bottom two clubs, but then came a dreadful slump that saw them fail to win any of their remaining 20 games and gain just five more points. Unbelievably, City finished bottom of the table and were relegated to the Conference along with Carlisle. Their fate was sealed in a 3–1 defeat at Doncaster Rovers on 24 April, and there were tearful scenes at the end of their last home match the following week, against Leyton Orient.

City's 75 years in the Football League ended on 8 May 2004 at Swansea. Two crucial departures during the club's alarming slump were Jon Parkin, who moved to fellow strugglers Macclesfield Town in February, and Lee Bullock, who joined Cardiff City, initially on loan. At the end of the campaign, a number of players were released, including Darren Edmondson and Christian Fox.

Brass hails fans as tears fall at final whistle

AN emotional Chris Brass paid tribute to York City's "fabulous" fans after Saturday's 2-1 home defeat against Leyton Orient marked the end of 75 years of league football in the city.

Hundreds of Minstermen supporters spilled on to the pitch at the final whistle and shouted their continued support for Brass and the club when the manager and his players left the dressing room to receive a rousing reception from the Main Stand.

They were scenes more reminiscent of a promotion party rather than the relegation wake the national media's cameras had hoped to capture and even Brass admitted that at other clubs he would have expected to be showered by abuse rather than platitudes.

A newspaper report on the club's last home game in the Football League, on 1 May 2004.

In December 2003 the death was announced of Frank Cawood, aged 85. A supporter for over 70 years, he had assisted in the move from Fulfordgate to Bootham Crescent by helping to carry railway sleepers for the building of the Popular Stand. A former secretary of the supporters' club, he had been involved in tremendous fundraising work for many years and had also been chief steward at Bootham Crescent. The club paid tribute, saying 'Frank was "Mr York City" and made a huge contribution to City over a long period of time.' In January Ernie Phillips, the captain of the Happy Wanderers, died, aged 80.

Details of the deal that had allowed the club to buy back Bootham Crescent were released in the summer of 2004. Negotiations had started with the Football Foundation in July 2003. This organisation is the UK's largest sports charity and was launched in 2000 by the football authorities and the government to provide investment into the grass roots of football. It represents a partnership of the FA Premier League, the Football Association, the Department of Culture, Media and Sport, and Sport England who jointly contribute money. The foundation distributes this in grants through, in this instance, the Football Stadia Improvement Fund (FSIF). In a series of meetings over the next six months, City's requests for help were turned down no less than four times. However, through sheer persistence and hard work, and with Jason McGill determined not to take no for an answer, the club were finally granted a £2 million loan. Under the deal, City owned 75.89 per cent of BCH shares and bought all the 20,000 shares owned by Persimmon Homes. Former chairman Douglas Craig received a £1,084,000 pay-off as a result of the deal, his fellow directors Barry Swallow and Colin Webb received £172,661 each, and they retained a combined total of 8.5 per cent of shares. The conditions of the loan required that the club had to identify a site for a new stadium by 2007 and detailed planning permission by 2009 to avoid financial penalties. The loan gave the club overall control of Bootham Crescent, the training ground near Wigginton and land near the Bumper Castle public house. Once plans for a new stadium were in place, the loan would turn into a grant to assist in funding the relocation. The combined cost of paying BCH directors, Persimmon Homes and stamp duty left a shortfall of £100,000, and in January 2005 Nestle Rowntree donated this sum. In recognition of their contribution, the ground was renamed KitKat Crescent. Prior to a pre-season friendly match against Sheffield Wednesday on 24 July 2004, the club were presented with the cheque for £2 million from the foundation.

The most traumatic period in the club's history had begun in December 2001, but City could now look ahead. Michael Brown resigned as a director owing to business and family commitments, and in September 2004 Steve Beck renounced his title of chairman, favouring a more democratic approach for a supporter-owned club. The board was restructured with Jason McGill becoming managing director, and Steve Beck took over as youth development and fans liaison director. Terry Doyle remained financial director, Sophie McGill was in charge of communications and community and Ian McAndrew continued as the stadium development director.

As the club prepared for their first season of non-League football since 1928–29, a number of experienced players were signed in a bid to make an immediate return to the Football League. Steve Davis, the former Burnley, Blackpool and Luton Town centre-half, was made captain. Other newcomers were defender Shaun Smith from Crewe Alexandra and midfielder Paul Groves from Grimsby Town, who both had vast League experience. Strikers Paul Robinson, ex-Newcastle United and Wimbledon, and Andy Bishop from Walsall were also recruited. The season was a big disappointment as the club struggled to come to terms with the lower echelons, and a further relegation threatened by midterm.

Chris Brass was relieved of his managerial duties early in November following a home defeat at the hands of Forest Green Rovers, which left the club fourth from bottom. After a brief spell with former hero Viv Busby at the coaching helm, Billy McEwan was announced as the new boss on 10 February 2005. His immediate brief was to avoid the drop into Conference North, and this was just achieved, with the club finishing 17th.

To celebrate the 50th anniversary of the club's FA Cup feats in 1954–55, a tribute dinner was held at the Voltigeur Suite at York Racecourse on 30 March 2005. Members of the semi-final team were among over 300 people who attended, and newsreel film of the matches of 50 years earlier were shown in an evening of celebration and nostalgia. This was one of a number of events organised in recent years by keen City fan and former referee Graham Bradbury. Keith Usher, the club's chief executive and secretary, left the club that month for personal reasons with, he said, 'much sadness' after 18 years' service. Nigel Pleasants, who had previously worked for Norwich City and Leeds United, became the new secretary but stepped down later in the year, and his successor was Nick Bassett. Another departure was youth coach Brian Neaves, who had been with the club several years, and the 12 players released included Nogan.

A trading loss of £83,568 was announced for the first season of non-League football, following a similarly sized profit the previous year. As City's search for a site for the new ground continued, it was reported that two venues were being considered – Leeman Road near York Railway Station and the Terry's factory near the racecourse. The new club sponsors were CLP Industries Ltd, and Elliot Stroud became the new commercial manager.

New faces for 2005–06 included striker Clayton Donaldson from Hull City; midfielders Manny Panther, who had played in Scotland for Partick Thistle and St Johnstone, and ex-Darlington player Mark Convery; and new defenders were Mark Hotte from Scarborough, Nathan Peat, who had League experience with Hull City and Lincoln City, and James Dudgeon, who had been on the books of Barnsley and Halifax Town. Centre-half David McGurk

Goalscoring hero of the 1950s Arthur Bottom with his silver salver, presented to the 1954–55 FA Cup semi-final players in 2005.

returned to the club on a long-term loan deal from Darlington, and Colin Walker joined the coaching staff as right-hand man to Billy McEwan.

The new players settled in well and a much better season was experienced, with Donaldson and Bishop proving an effective strike force. They netted 43 goals between them, and the former scored in six successive games in the first half of the season – just one match short of the club record held jointly by Jimmy Cowie in 1928–29, Billy Fenton in 1952–53, Arthur Bottom in 1954–55 and Paul Aimson in 1970–71.

After a third of the campaign, City were in second place, averaging two points per game, but then came a midterm slump that saw them slip down the table. Chris Brass left the club after loan spells with Harrogate Town and Southport and, in the New Year, midfielder Neal Bishop was signed from Scarborough for an undisclosed fee – the first money transfer made by the club since June 2000, when Terry Dolan bought Peter Duffield from Darlington for £10,000.

A run of six straight wins thrust City back into the promotion race and a renewed bid for the Play-offs, only for them to falter in the final run-in and finish eighth. The average home League attendance of 2,871 was the second best in the Conference, and the club won the North Riding Senior Cup for the 10th time when they beat Northallerton Town. Andy Bishop, top Conference marksman with 25 goals, moved to Bury; owing to a clause in his contract, he was allowed to leave for free.

Financial problems arose again, and a loss of £150,000 was reported for the season, plus there had been problems meeting the first annual payment of £100,000 to FSIF in respect of the £2 million loan. JM Packaging, owned by City's managing director, Jason McGill, put forward a proposal to the Supporters' Trust offering to become 75 per cent majority shareholders in the club. They offered to convert a £300,000 loan they had made to the club in January 2005 into shares and would further invest £650,000 to cover the current losses and meet the loan repayments for the next five years. This new injection of funds would be treated as a loan with an interest of 11 per cent secured against KitKat Crescent. This loan would only be repayable in the case of insolvency. Otherwise, only the interest would be payable on the assumed sale of the ground when the club were in a position to move to a new stadium. Supporters' Trust chairman Steve Beck, in a letter to the 1,250 members, strongly recommended that the proposal be accepted. He stressed that if additional funding was not put in place very quickly then the club's directors would be obliged to consider the solvency of the club.

In a meeting on 6 June 2006 at the Barbican, the proposal to make JM Packaging the new owners of York City Football Club was passed by an overwhelming majority of 78 per cent. The new owners would have 75 per cent of the company. The trust's previous share of 85 per cent ownership was reduced to 25 per cent. In a statement, Jason McGill said:

> If there is one thing nobody should doubt it is that my sister Sophie and myself love York City Football Club. [As Supporters' Trust members they had played their part in helping save the club from extinction in 2003.] Myself and my family are all from York and have been supporters through my father since he came to live in the area in 1955. JM Packaging will ensure that York City remains a professional club with a professional set-up, a youth system, reserve team, a full first-team squad, professional manager and coaches. We want to keep the infrastructure we have got, which is a Football League structure, because that is the way forward.

In some quarters, regret was expressed that the Supporters' Trust, which had worked so hard to keep the club afloat in the darkest days, were relinquishing control, but the vast majority welcomed the move and the fact that the club had been given security and stability for the foreseeable future.

Rob McGill, father of Jason and Sophie, joined the board as business development director after the resignation of Pete Davis, who had a short spell as commercial director. And in the summer of 2006, the death occurred of Hugh Kitchin at the age of 92. He had been chairman at the time City had reached the semi-finals of the FA Cup in 1954–55.

The 2006–07 season was the most successful campaign since the mid-1990s, and the club came so close to regaining their Football League status. McEwan's new signings included goalkeeper Tom Evans from Scunthorpe United; full-backs Darren Craddock from Hartlepool United and Anthony Lloyd from Torquay United; midfielder Steve Bowey, captain of Scottish First Division side Queen of the South; and forward Craig Farrell, previously with Leeds United, Carlisle United and Exeter City. Central-defender Danny Parslow was signed from Cardiff City, David McGurk joined the club on a permanent basis, and talented young winger Martyn Woolford was signed for a fee from Frickley Athletic early in the campaign.

A good start was made, and City were never out of the top five from the beginning of November. Their away form was excellent, and the record of 13 wins and five draws on their travels was the best in the club's history. A Play-off position was clinched with a 1–0 victory over Oxford United in front of 5,378 – the biggest home crowd since they dropped out of the Football League – and City finished fourth with 80 points, their second-highest tally ever.

The first leg of the Play-off against Morecambe, which attracted a crowd of 6,660, was dominated by City but ended goalless. In the return game at Christie Park, a Bowey penalty gave them the lead, only for the home side to draw level just before the interval, when Evans misjudged a free-kick and was beaten by a header. Morecambe notched the winner early in the second half to go through 2–1 on aggregate, and the Lancashire club went on to beat Exeter City at the new Wembley Stadium to take their place in the Football League. For City, it was a case of so near yet so far.

Two key players left the club at the end of the campaign. Clubman of the Year Neal Bishop moved to League One Barnet, and top marksman Clayton Donaldson, who notched 26 goals, joined Hibernian in a controversial transfer deal. City had turned down a bid of £200,000 from Scunthorpe United in midterm, but the player's agent brokered a deal with the Scottish Premiership club in January 2007, when a pre-contract agreement was signed. The striker was rated at £500,000, but his move north of the border in May robbed City of a transfer fee because Scotland was not covered by FA rules, which insist that clubs are entitled to compensation when players aged under 24 move elsewhere. During the season, youth coach Ian Kerr resigned for health reasons, and former Barnsley player and coach Eric Winstanley was appointed head of youth development.

Newcomers for City's fourth season out of the Football League included striker Onome Sodje from Gravesend and Northfleet, defender Mark Robinson from Torquay United and experienced midfielder Stuart Elliott from Northwich Victoria. Early in the season, central-defender Darren Kelly was signed from Derry City for a reported sizeable fee, and the former Northern Ireland Under-21 international made his debut in a home game against Rushden and Diamonds on 30 August. This match marked the 75th anniversary of City's move to Bootham Crescent, and a special birthday cake was cut on the pitch by the club's patron, Archbishop of York Dr John Sentamu. During the previous season, striker Richard Brodie had joined the club from Newcastle Benfield, and in September 2007 physiotherapist Jeff Miller celebrated 20 years' outstanding service for the club.

A bad start was made to the 2007–08 campaign, and City only won one and drew two of the opening 10 games. Form improved, but the home record remained poor, and successive defeats at KitKat Crescent at the hands of Havant and Waterlooville in the FA Cup and Salisbury brought an end to Billy McEwan's reign as manager in November. Upon leaving, McEwan spoke of his regret at being unable to 'see the job

York City 2007–08. Back row, left to right: Darren Craddock, Chris Beardsley, Danny Parslow, Ben Purkiss, Richard Brodie, David McGurk, Martyn Woolford, Craig Farrell. Middle row: Jeff Miller (physio), Stuart Elliott, Phillip Turnbull, Tom Evans, Ross Greenwood, Paul Brayson, Colin Walker (coach). Front row: Chas Wrigley, Alex Meechan, Manny Panther, Billy McEwan (manager), Onome Sodje, Mark Robinson, Alex Rhodes.

Richard Brodie nets with a close-range header in a 2–0 win over leaders Aldershot Town on 26 January 2008.

through' at York City. Colin Walker took over as caretaker manager and was appointed manager on Boxing Day following a successful run of results. Apart from a penalty shoot-out defeat against Northwich Victoria in the Setanta Shield, City went unbeaten under Walker from mid-November until mid-February – a run of 17 games – and rose from 19th to 10th in the Blue Square Premier. A sequence of seven successive away wins from mid-October to New Year's Day created a new club record.

Eric Winstanley became head coach and right-hand man to Walker, and to complete the Barnsley connection, Neil Redfearn was appointed youth coach. Any hopes of another Play-off challenge, however, ended in the later stages of the season when just two points were collected from five games, including a heavy defeat at Crawley Town.

After several lean seasons in Cup competitions, City embarked on a run in the FA Trophy that took them to the semi-finals. At that stage, they lost 2–1 on aggregate to Torquay United and narrowly missed out on a trip to Wembley for the second successive season. The financial reward for reaching the Final would have provided much vital income. In his programme notes on 25 March 2008 against Northwich Victoria, managing director Jason McGill spelled it out:

> I must reiterate that the financial burden on York City Football Club at present is a constant struggle. As most of you are aware the £140,000 per annum interest repayment to the Football Stadia Improvement Fund, as a result of securing a £2 million loan to purchase Bootham Crescent from previous directors Douglas Craig, Barry Swallow and Colin Webb, is a considerable liability. Added to this is the annual cost of some £60,000 for the maintenance and upkeep of a 1932 stadium with few commercial and income-generating opportunities. A new stadium with all the potential new revenue opportunities would of course change the economic pressures on the club overnight. The current FSIF loan would be converted into a £2 million grant and with further equity released from the sale of Bootham Crescent would go a long way towards financing the construction of a new community sporting arena. The major stakeholders and decision-makers in the city must now decide once and for all if a professional football club, which can have a positive influence on the people of York and enhance the national reputation of the city in general, is viewed as an important asset for the local community. Despite several years of negotiation, at all levels, the board of directors is acutely disappointed by the lack of progress in determining the club's new stadium ambitions. In the short term there must be a consensus and general agreement from all interested parties on the need and desire for a new community facility for the city. This is a vital component and will be hugely influential in deciding the future of the club, not only in the long term but also over the coming weeks, when the board will have the difficult task of financial budget preparation for season 2008–09.

During the summer of 2008 the club received a big boost when the City of York Council proposed to take over the repayment of the £2 million FSIF loan (subject to a review of the football club's books). The council also confirmed its commitment to building a community stadium in York by using cash generated from the sale of Huntington Stadium, the home of York City Knights RLFC and Bootham Crescent.

City finished a rather disappointing 14th, but a number of promising youngsters from the youth squad were successfully blooded towards the end of the campaign proving how vital the youth system is to the club's future. The continuation of this system along with the retention of the reserve side is, therefore, of immense importance.

As City approached their fifth season of non-League football, manager Colin Walker looked ahead with confidence as he planned a squad of 18 quality senior players supplemented by the young brigade.

In May 2008 his first signings for 2008–09 were revealed. 'Keeper Michael Ingham, who had a successful loan spell with the club in 2003, joined from Hereford United and experienced central-defender/midfielder Mark Greaves arrived from Burton Albion. He had previously been at Hull City and Boston United.

In the words of the often-used expression at the club – KEEP THE FAITH.

Homes of York City

Fulfordgate (1922–32)

When York City Football Club was formed in 1922, eight acres of land were purchased for £2,000 in Heslington Lane, Fulfordgate. This was in the south-east of the city, away from the centre and not far from where the university is now situated. It was very much a rural setting and the land was known as Gate Fulford, although the name was soon changed to Fulfordgate. Hawthorn hedges formed its boundaries and it was very well drained. Initially there were no covered stands and the dressing rooms consisted of an old army hut. Open stands were bought from York Race Committee as an addition to the ground.

The first match at Fulfordgate was played on Wednesday 20 September 1922, against Mansfield Town. The game went ahead only after the requisite deposit, which amounted to £180, was paid. This cash, courtesy of one of the directors, Mr John Fisher, was produced literally at the last minute.

Gradually, the ground was built up and improved and, within a couple of years, covered accommodation was available. In the letter of application for admission to the Football League in 1927, York City were able to say that the ground was 'splendidly drained, well equipped, spacious and capable of being extended to hold up to 40,000 spectators'. Furthermore, considerable improvements were made that year. New turnstiles were fitted and stronger fencing was built around the pitch. It was reported that when the fencing was completed, it would be much more difficult for a spectator to surmount it and go on to the pitch. Behind one of the goals, nine-tier terracing replaced the old banking. The covered 'popular' stand was extended to house 1,000 and a small, seated stand was incorporated.

Before City were elected to the Football League, the biggest crowd housed at the ground was 8,318 (receipts were £366) to see the English Schools Trophy semi-final between York Boys and Brighton Boys on 12 May 1928. In the York team were Reg Stockill and Dave Halford, both of whom went on to have distinguished football careers. By the time of election to the League the following year, it was estimated that Fulfordgate could accommodate 17,000.

Mr J. Fisher was a tremendous benefactor of the club in its early days and loaned several sums of money, including the £180 deposit that City needed to play their first match at Fulfordgate in September 1922. He was chairman from 1925–27.

The ground was to stage two big FA Cup third-round replay matches. For the visit of Newcastle United in January 1930, 12,583 congregated, paying receipts of £900 5s 3d. The following year, Fulfordgate records were set when 12,721, paying £1,058 16s, saw Sheffield United provide the opposition. In November 1931 an amateur international between England and Ireland was played at the ground.

Towards the end of the third season in the Football League, concern was expressed at City's poor support. One of the directors, Mr G.W. Halliday, was convinced that the only solution was a change of ground. A major problem about Fulfordgate was the relative inaccessibility of the place. It was a good distance from the railway station and the tram service to Fulford had only a single track. The loop system for tramcars passing one another also restricted the service. In addition, the bus routes had not been fully developed and, with general car ownership still a long way in the future, Fulfordgate, without a doubt, was not an easy ground for the majority of supporters to reach.

Early in 1932, a ground ideally situated near the centre of the city became vacant. For a number of years York Cricket Club had played at Bootham Crescent, but they decided to move to new headquarters at Wigginton Road, which is now the site of York District Hospital. Yorkshire Gentlemen's Cricket Club had previously played at Wigginton Road but they, in turn, had transferred to Escrick Park.

After preliminary discussions and visits to the Bootham Crescent ground, the directors were unanimous that a change should be made, and a special meeting of the shareholders was held in St George's Hall, Castlegate, on 26 April 1932 to consider and approve the intended move. At the meeting the chairman, Mr Arthur Brown, drew attention to the average 'gate' receipt figures in the three seasons of League football at Fulfordgate (1929–30: £261; 1930–31: £183; and in 1931–32, when the club were near the top of the table for the first half of the campaign, £198). This represented average League crowds of approximately 4,000 and, at the end of the day, a deficit on the balance sheet. The board felt that the class of football had been good enough but the distance to Fulfordgate from the main parts of the city, coupled with the inadequate transport services, had a serious effect on attendances especially in bad weather and for early kick-offs. Mr Halliday pointed out that in a one-mile radius of Bootham Crescent the population was 30,000, whereas for a similar radius at Fulfordgate it was only 3,000. On the question of ownership over tenancy, Mr Brown stated that Fulfordgate was mortgaged as far as possible and that the present mortgage, bank interest and overdraft would exceed the rent and rates at Bootham Crescent by £40 per annum.

The directors were satisfied that the new ground would fulfil all requirements. There were no restrictions as to banking, terracing and the erection of stands, and the property of the shareholders would be fully protected if the lease, which was for 21 years, expired.

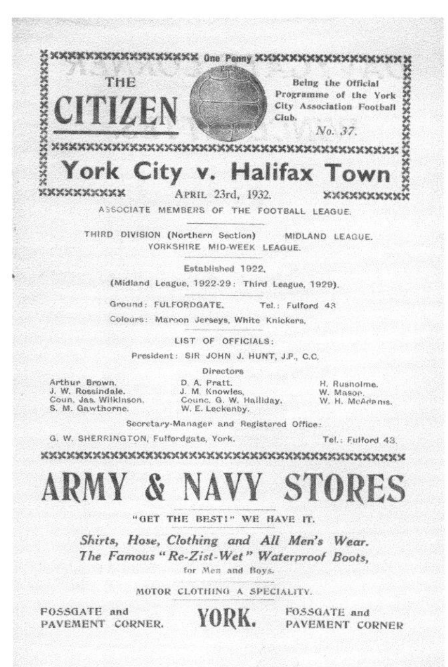

One Penny

THE CITIZEN

Being the Official Programme of the York City Association Football Club.

No. 37.

York City v. Halifax Town

APRIL 23rd, 1932.

ASSOCIATE MEMBERS OF THE FOOTBALL LEAGUE.

THIRD DIVISION (Northern Section) MIDLAND LEAGUE.
YORKSHIRE MID-WEEK LEAGUE.

Established 1922.
(Midland League, 1922-29: Third League, 1929).

Ground: FULFORDGATE. Tel.: Fulford 43
Colours: Maroon Jerseys, White Knickers.

LIST OF OFFICIALS:
President: SIR JOHN J. HUNT, J.P., C.C.

Directors

Arthur Brown.	D. A. Pratt.	H. Rusholme.
J. W. Rossindale.	J. M. Knowles,	W. Mason.
Coun. Jas. Wilkinson.	Counc. G. W. Halliday.	W. H. McAdams.
S. M. Gawthorne.	W. E. Leckenby.	

Secretary-Manager and Registered Office:
G. W. SHERRINGTON, Fulfordgate, York. Tel.: Fulford 43.

ARMY & NAVY STORES

"GET THE BEST!" WE HAVE IT.

Shirts, Hose, Clothing and All Men's Wear.
The Famous "Re-Zist-Wet" Waterproof Boots,
for Men and Boys.

MOTOR CLOTHING A SPECIALITY.

FOSSGATE and PAVEMENT CORNER. YORK. FOSSGATE and PAVEMENT CORNER

The programme cover for York City's last match at Fulfordgate.

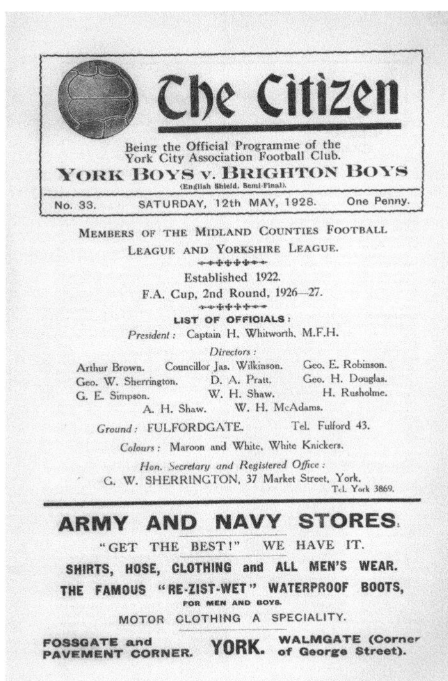

The Citizen

Being the Official Programme of the York City Association Football Club.

YORK BOYS v. BRIGHTON BOYS

(English Shield. Semi-Final).

No. 33. SATURDAY, 12th MAY, 1928. One Penny.

MEMBERS OF THE MIDLAND COUNTIES FOOTBALL LEAGUE AND YORKSHIRE LEAGUE.

Established 1922.

F.A. Cup, 2nd Round, 1926—27.

LIST OF OFFICIALS:

President: Captain H. Whitworth, M.F.H.

Directors:

Arthur Brown. Councillor Jas. Wilkinson. Geo. E. Robinson.
Geo. W. Sherrington. D. A. Pratt. Geo. H. Douglas.
G. E. Simpson. W. H. Shaw. H. Rusholme.
A. H. Shaw. W. H. McAdams.

Ground: FULFORDGATE. Tel. Fulford 43.

Colours: Maroon and White, White Knickers.

Hon. Secretary and Registered Office:
G. W. SHERRINGTON, 37 Market Street, York.
Tel. York 3869.

ARMY AND NAVY STORES.

"GET THE BEST!" WE HAVE IT.

SHIRTS, HOSE, CLOTHING and ALL MEN'S WEAR.

THE FAMOUS "RE-ZIST-WET" WATERPROOF BOOTS, FOR MEN AND BOYS.

MOTOR CLOTHING A SPECIALITY.

FOSSGATE and PAVEMENT CORNER. YORK. WALMGATE (Corner of George Street).

The progamme cover for York Boys v Brighton Boys, which attracted the biggest pre-Football League crowd to York.

The oldest stand at Fulfordgate needed replacing and it was pointed out that the club could put up a structure three times the size on the new ground. New dressing rooms were also required at Fulfordgate.

There was some opposition to the move. A former director, Mr J. Fisher, who had been a benefactor back in 1922, said that during the club's 10-year existence it had built a playing history and a ground second to none in such a short time. He pointed out that it had been a bad time for football clubs generally with regard to crowds and said that good times would come again to Fulfordgate. He condemned the proposal as a bad policy when it involved renting a ground instead of owning it. The Fulfordgate pitch had an excellent playing surface, while the new ground was on land subject to severe flooding. There was also a danger of Bootham Crescent being more heavily rated once more valuable equipment was on it. Another former director, Councillor W.H. Shaw, also opposed the scheme and expressed doubts regarding the approaches and, looking to the future, car-parking limitations at the new ground.

After much discussion, the matter was put to the vote, and by a majority of over three to one (115 for, 37 against) the shareholders approved the move to take on a lease at the Bootham Crescent ground. The Fulfordgate site was subsequently sold and developed as a building estate. Sadly, there is nothing now to identify it as the birthplace of the club back in 1922.

Top 10 crowds at Fulfordgate

12,721	FA Cup third round	Sheffield United	14 January 1931
12,583	FA Cup third round	Newcastle United	15 January 1930
10,120	Division Three North	Port Vale	21 April 1930
8,726	Division Three North	Wrexham	4 September 1929
8,318	English Schools Trophy	York Boys v Brighton Boys	12 May 1928
8,183	Division Three North	Doncaster Rovers	26 December 1931
7,834	Division Three North	Barrow	26 December 1929
7,462	Division Three North	Carlisle United	7 September 1929
6,957	FA Cup first round	Barrow	24 November 1928
6,422	FA Cup second qualifying round	Scarborough	15 October 1927

Bootham Crescent/KitKat Crescent (1932 to date)

The summer of 1932 saw a period of feverish activity as the new ground was equipped. The area was first drained and then built to the design of York architects, Messrs Ward & Leckenby. Two stands were erected – the Main (members') Stand and the Popular Stand. The supporters' club undertook the responsibility for defraying the cost of the latter stand and found many willing hands. Within four months, the club had set up the new ground in readiness for the 1932–33 season.

The official opening of the ground was on 31 August 1932, for a Third Division North game against Stockport County. The club president, Sir John Hunt, formally opened the ground by cutting a chocolate and cream-coloured ribbon – the colours of the club. Also in attendance were the Sheriff of York, Mr Arnold Rowntree; Mr Roger Lumley MP; Mr Arnold Kingscott, treasurer of the Football Association; and other personalities in the football world. The attendance was 8,106, receipts were nearly £400 and the result was a 2–2 draw.

The first big match staged at the ground was on 12 January 1935, when Derby County were the visitors in a third-round FA Cup tie. The attendance of 13,612 set a new club record. Three seasons later, when York City reached the quarter-finals of the FA Cup, attendance records were established at four successive stages, culminating in the 28,123 who attended the sixth-round match against Huddersfield Town on 5 March 1938. In 1937 a social club was established at the ground. This was the brainchild of one of the directors, Mr S.M. Gawthorne.

During the war the tunnel at the back of the Popular Stand was used as an air-raid shelter for pupils and staff of the nearby Shipton Street School. The ground suffered slight damage after the air-raid on York in April 1942. Houses at the Shipton Street end were bombed. A representative match was staged at the ground on 17 October 1942 when a Football League XI defeated the Northern Command 9–2, watched by 5,500. After the match Mr Fred Howarth, the secretary of the Football League, wrote the following letter to the club:

> May I take this opportunity, on behalf of the League, of congratulating your club, directors and officials alike, for the excellence of the arrangements. You will appreciate that always in representative matches our chief concern is the smoothness of the arrangements. You did your part splendidly.
>
> The League thanks you for staging the match, which was a complete success, both from the entertainment side and from the financial side. They are grateful for the kindly attention of your directors and will remember with pleasure their first official visit to your lovely city.

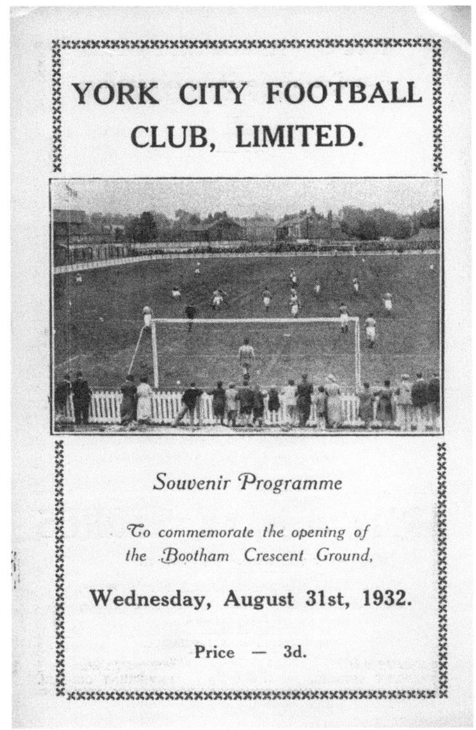

A souvenir programme cover for the first match at Bootham Crescent on 31 August 1932.

A dinner at the Royal Station Hotel, celebrating the purchase of the Bootham Crescent ground in 1948.

In the early post-war period, considerable improvements were made to the ground. Deeper drainage was completed, as was the concreting of the banking at the Bootham Crescent end of the ground. Loudspeaking equipment was also installed.

At the shareholders' annual meeting in September 1948, it was announced that the club had purchased the Bootham Crescent ground, which had been on lease since 1932. The chairman, Mr W.H. Sessions, stated that an agreement had been signed and the club now owned one of the best grounds in the Third Division. The club's finances were very sound at the time. The company had £6,000 invested in Government stock, and there was a balance on transfer deals of £5,570, with donations, chiefly from the social club, of £2,105. The balance sheet revealed that the ground was bought for £4,075 and the buildings, which cost £7,444, had been depreciated so that the whole ground and equipment's value was listed at £7,204 in 1949.

To celebrate the purchase of the ground, a dinner was held at the Royal Station Hotel, at which the deeds were handed to the chairman. Among those present were past and present directors and many enthusiasts who had worked for the club over the years. Also in attendance was Billy Smith, the club's first captain back in 1922.

In May 1952 England met Ireland in the first Schoolboy international to be played at Bootham Crescent. The attendance was 16,000 and England, who won 5–0, were captained by Wilf McGuinness, who was to become manager of York City some 23 years later.

In the late 1940s and early 1950s concreting was completed on the terracing in the Popular Stand – thanks to the efforts of the supporters' club – and the Shipton Street end. The next major work was carried out in the summer of 1955, when the

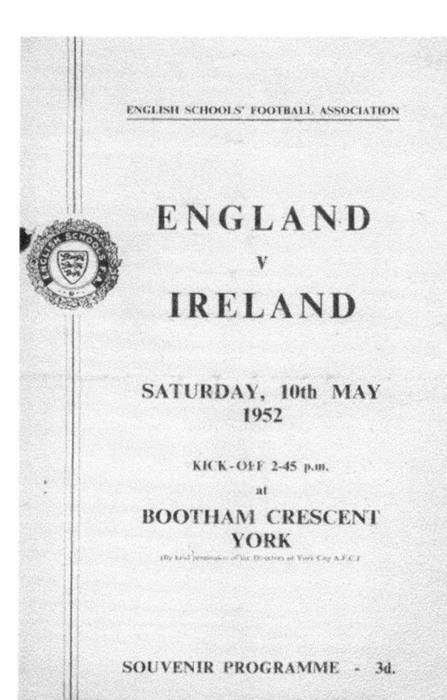

England v Ireland Schoolboy international, 10 May 1952.

York City v Newcastle United, 28 October 1959, in a friendly to officially 'switch on' the floodlights.

Main Stand was extended towards Shipton Street. Profits from the FA Cup run, together with a stand extension fund, helped in this project.

The following year a concrete wall was built at the St Olave's Road (Bootham Crescent) end. The project, which cost more than £3,000, had a two-fold purpose – a safety precaution and a support for additional banking and terracing. The FA Cup tie in 1955 against Tottenham Hotspur had been restricted to a 21,000 capacity by the police but, with the improvements made, the limit had risen to 23,600 when Bolton Wanderers provided the opposition in January 1958.

In the summer of 1959 floodlights were installed at the ground at a cost of £14,500, a substantial part of which was raised by the auxiliary supporters' club. The installation was based on a system of lighting developed by the General Electric Company, which designed and supervised the project. Messrs Shepherds of York were responsible for the concrete bases and erection of the four 100-foot towers. The electrical sub-contractors were Messrs F.H. Wheeler of Scunthorpe. The lights were

Souvenir programme for the York City v Newcastle United friendly, 1959.

YORK CITY A.F. & A.C. LTD.

Established 1922

President:
Mr. W. H. Sessions, J.P.

Directors:
Mr. H. F. W. Kitchin (*Chairman*); Messrs. A. G. D. Blundy, W. H. Sessions F. Harwood, W. Mason, H. Foxton, F. H. Magson, N. J. Hopwood, J. W. Rosindale, T. W. Meek and A. Brown.

Team Manager: Mr. S. Bartram.

Honorary Medical Officer: J. B. McKenna, M.B., B.Ch.

Secretary and Registered Office:
G. W. Sherrington, Bootham Crescent, York
Telephone 24447

Colours:
Red Shirts, White Knickers.

No. 10 CITY v NEWCASTLE UNITED 28th Oct.

OFFICIAL OPENING OF THE BOOTHAM CRESCENT LIGHTS

Tonight's match marks the official opening of the floodlit installation at Bootham Crescent and we welcome Newcastle United, whose visit brings back memories of our great F.A. Cup semi-final tussles in 1955, when United beat us in a replay and went on to win the Cup against Manchester City.

In opening these floodlights, it is only fitting to put on record that such a standard of installation would not have been possible without the help of the Auxiliary Club, which every season raises such a substantial sum. As some slight recognition of the hard and enthusiastic work put in, about 200 agents are the guests of the club at tonight's game.

The installation is based on a system of floodlighting developed in the research laboratories of the General Electric Co. Ltd. some years ago, and used as a basis for recommendation by the Football Association.

This system has been used in the majority of major floodlighting installations throughout the country, including such well-known grounds as Wembley, Sheffield Wednesday, Chelsea, Manchester United and many others, both large and small.

Four Tubewrights Towers are used, situated at each corner of the field, and each carrying 24 specially designed G.E.C. 1,500 watt floodlight units, and provision is made for the addition of further floodlights should future recommendations be for a higher level of illumination.

Each floodlight is focused and trained to a particular section of the field, ensuring an overall covering of even illumination and a complete absence of disability glare. The height of the towers is determined by a minimum angle from the centre point of the playing area to the lowest row of floodlights on each tower, thus ensuring a clear sight of the ball by players on any portion of the playing area.

Tubewrights Towers were chosen because of their particular suitability to the surrounding area, being unobtrusive, attractive in design with the necessary strength and durability.

Herald Printing Works—52406

Bryan Foster, City's head groundsman, with the gold watch presented to him in recognition of his 25 years' service to the club in March 1988.

officially switched on in a match against Newcastle United on 28 October 1959. In an entertaining exhibition game, United won 8–2 in front of a 9,414 crowd.

The year before, in August 1958, a young man by the name of Bryan Foster joined the ground staff. He duly became head groundsman and apart from 1971 to 1975, when he held similar appointments at Bury and then Preston, he served the club until 1994. For many years the Bootham Crescent pitch had an excellent playing surface and, in recognition of his long and outstanding service, Bryan was presented with a gold watch by the directors in March 1988. He remained head groundsman until his untimely death in February 1994. His successor was Bryan Horner, who spent eight years at the club and was voted Division Two groundsman of the year in 1999. Since then the post has been held by Jez Milner and Mark Hirst.

The 1960s were a relatively quiet period in the history of the ground. In 1965 the half-time score-board at the Shipton Street end ceased to be used for that purpose but remained as an advertising hoarding. In March 1966 an attendance of 19,420 saw the Third Division fixture against Hull City and, in February 1968, Bootham Crescent staged its first major neutral match when Hull played Middlesbrough in an FA Cup third-round second replay. Boro won 1–0 in front of 16,524.

Part of the record crowd of 28,123 that saw York play Huddersfield on 5 March 1938, with ambulance men busy on the touchline.

FOOTBALL ASSOCIATION CUP
Third Round — Second Replay

BOOTHAM CRESCENT

WEDNESDAY, 7th FEBRUARY, 1968

at 7.30 p.m.

HULL CITY

VERSUS

MIDDLESBROUGH

OFFICIAL PROGRAMME — Price Sixpence

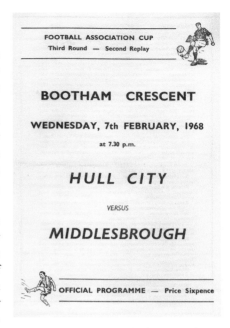

A programme for Bootham Crescent's first major neutral match, Hull City v Middlesbrough.

The next major alteration to the ground was in the summer of 1974, when seats were installed in the Popular Stand prior to the start of Second Division football. This increased the seating capacity to 2,762.

In 1980 the floodlights were updated and improved at a cost of £20,000. They were officially switched on by former Wolves and Northern Ireland international Derek Dougan, prior to a friendly game against Grimsby Town on 1 August. The referee for this game was Keith Usher, who was later to become club secretary.

Early in 1981 a gymnasium was built at the Bootham Crescent end at a cost of £50,000. To help towards this, City received £15,000 from the Sports Council and £20,000 from the Football League Improvement Trust. In the summer of 1983 improvements were made to the administration facilities. New offices for the manager, secretary, matchday and lottery manager were built, together with a vice-presidents' lounge. Jack Dunnett, chairman of the Football League, officially opened the lounge prior to a game against Wrexham in November 1983.

By the early 1980s cracks had appeared in the concrete wall built in 1956 at the back of the Bootham Crescent end. The rear of the terracing was cordoned off and the capacity of the ground reduced to under 13,500, less than half the attendance record set in 1938. For segregation purposes, the Bootham Crescent end was allocated to visiting supporters and, before the FA Cup tie against Liverpool in February 1985, fencing was erected for the first time at the ground. By the early 2000s all the fencing had been dismantled.

During the successful seasons of 1983–84 and 1984–85 many problems had arisen in handling big crowds. This was due to the problem of the ground having only two of its four sides available for entry and exit, plus the fact that home supporters funnelled through the car park to the Shipton Street end. In the summer of 1985, therefore, extensive improvements were made at a cost of approximately £100,000, and eight new turnstiles were installed at that end. At the same time the dressing rooms were refurbished, incorporating new baths and showers, a new referees' changing room and physiotherapist's treatment room. New toilets were also built at the Shipton Street end and a modern club shop was built in 1985.

In 1986–87, hospitality boxes were built into the Main Stand. Video equipment was installed inside the ground and crash barriers were strengthened. Ground safety requirements were met and in September 1989 it was announced that capacity had been increased to 14,628, divided as follows:

Main Stand (seats)	1,102
Popular Stand (seats)	1,957
Shipton Street End	5,105
Shipton Street Enclosure	867
Grosvenor Road End	4,747
Grosvenor Road Enclosure	850

A souvenir programme for the game against Leeds on 14 October 1991, celebrating the opening of the new David Longhurst Stand.

The lack of covered standing accommodation was the ground's one major drawback. For many years a stand at the Shipton Street end had been talked about but the cost had been prohibitive. In the spring of 1988 two supporters, Chris Forth and Frank Ormston, launched the Shipton Street Roof Appeal Fund in an endeavour to raise money for the building of a stand. With the blessing of the directors, a committee was formed and various fund-raising schemes were put into operation. In August 1989, Middlesbrough were the visitors for a special match, with all the proceeds going into the fund.

On 8 September 1990, a tragic day in the history of the club, David Longhurst collapsed and died at Bootham Crescent during a Fourth Division game against Lincoln City. The 25-year-old striker had joined City from Peterborough United earlier that year and it was disclosed at the inquest that he had suffered from a rare heart disorder. With the approval and consent of David's family, a David Longhurst Memorial Fund was set up and all donations were added to the monies already raised for the roof appeal.

The Football Trust contributed 50 per cent of the £150,000 cost of the stand and it was constructed in the summer of 1991. The architects were Ronald Sims, Ann Teasdale and Keith Parbutt; the consulting engineers were John Dosser and Partners; and the stand was constructed by John Laing Construction. The stand was officially opened on 14 October 1991 when a crowd of 4,374 saw a very entertaining exhibition match against Leeds United end 2–2. Before the game Vic Longhurst, father of the late David, officially unveiled the David Longhurst Stand.

In 1992 the Family Stand was opened in the Main Stand. The then manager John Ward was instrumental in the project and helped raise funds by running the London Marathon. In the summer of 1995 new floodlights were installed at a cost of £122,000. The new lights were shorter in height but twice as powerful. The old pylons were re-erected at New Lane, the home of York Railway Institute FC.

In recent years the ground has hosted a number of Youth internationals. The most notable was on 13 October 1996, when 16-year-old Michael Owen scored all four goals in a 4–0 win for England Under-18s against Northern Ireland. Also playing for England that day was Rio Ferdinand.

A number of non-footballing events have taken place at the ground over the years. A pop concert was held in September 1979 and a grand firework display in October

Programme for the England Under-18 match against Northern Ireland, 13 October 1996. In the England side that day were a young Michael Owen and Rio Ferdinand.

Aerial shot of Bootham Crescent.

1982 celebrated the centenary of the *Yorkshire Evening Press*. An American football game was staged in the summer of 1988 and, in January 1989, rugby league was played at Bootham Crescent for the first time. In the first round of the RL Challenge Cup, York entertained Leeds in front of 11,347.

In January 2005 the ground was renamed KitKat Crescent as part of a deal that saw Nestlé Rowntree make a donation of £100,000 to the club.

The capacity for the 2007–08 season was 9,196, divided as follows:

Main Stand (seats) including Family Stand	1,757
Popular Stand (seats)	1,652
David Longhurst Stand (standing)	3,062
Grosvenor Road End (standing)	2,725

Top 10 crowds at Bootham Crescent

28,123	FA Cup sixth round	Huddersfield Town	5 March 1938
23,860	FA Cup fifth round	Middlesbrough	12 February 1938
23,600	FA Cup fourth round	Bolton Wanderers	25 January 1958
22,000	FA Cup fourth round	Sunderland	28 January 1956
21,010	Third Division North	Hull City	23 April 1949
21,000	FA Cup fifth round	Tottenham Hotspur	19 February 1955
19,843	Third Division North	Accrington Stanley	8 April 1955
19,750	FA Cup third round	Birmingham City	8 January 1958
19,420	Division Three	Hull City	12 March 1966
19,216	Third Division North	Rotherham United	20 November 1948

Matches to Remember

11 January 1930
Newcastle United 1 York City 1
FA Cup third round

One of the first-red letter days in the club's history was this visit to St James's Park as City, just eight years after their formation and in their first season in the Football League, were paired against First Division giants Newcastle United.

The match was played in dreadful conditions as a severe snowstorm had almost obliterated the line markings and the surface was treacherous. The ball was very heavy, but the game was played at a fast and thrilling pace. City, playing a direct, open game, had the edge in the first half and were unlucky not to take the lead when Wally Gardner hit the post with a fine shot in the 20th minute. Jack Farmery made some excellent saves to foil Hughie Gallacher and Andy Cunningham but was beaten just before the interval when the former headed home a Sam Weaver cross.

City defended stoutly early in the second half and then drew level in the 61st minute with a magnificent goal by Gardner. He collected a pass from Sam Johnson, burst through United's defence and netted with a fine right-foot shot. In the closing stages the First Division side threw everything into attack but City's defence, with Farmery and centre-half Charlie Davis outstanding, held firm and the team received a great ovation at the final whistle.

Supporters clamoured around the entrance to the dressing rooms and pursued the players to the railway station to watch them depart on the train to York. As described at the time, 'these happy City enthusiasts then went back into the centre of Newcastle and revelled in the gayest spirits.' When the team arrived back in York 1,000 people greeted them amid scenes of great enthusiasm.

The Football League babes had held a team containing seven internationals and shown great team spirit and determination. As described in the *Sports Press* 'The great exodus to Tyneside of 5,000 exuberant and boisterous Yorkshire spirits witnessed a remarkable City display.'

YORK CITY REVEAL CUP FIGHTING ABILITY.

Newcastle United, 1 ; York City, 1.

York City, the youngest club in the Football League, accomplished the most sensational feat in the third round games of the Football Association Cup competition on Saturday, when they drew with Newcastle United at St. James's Park. The teams will meet again on Wednesday at 2.15, this time at Fulfordgate.

Few expected the Third Division team to prove equal to holding their exalted rivals, and their display astonished the Tyneside crowd. York City revealed that they were formidable cup fighters, and there is little doubt that ground records with be established on Wednesday, and that the York team will make a great effort to dismiss a club which has six times appeared in the final.

Farmery emerged with great triumph, fielding some great shots from Gallacher and Cunningham. Johnson was the best back in the game, and thoroughly subdued Urwin long before the end. Brooks, in a different way, was just as valuable, introducing rare dash and energy into his tackling. Perhaps chief honours in defence are due to Davis. His mission was to stop Gallacher, and he did it so effectively that the International could not find a loophole. It was a tribute to the York player that not once was he pulled up for an illegitimate tackle against his famous opponent. Neither did he neglect his other duties simply to "play the policeman" to Gallacher.

Newspaper report on the game against Newcastle.

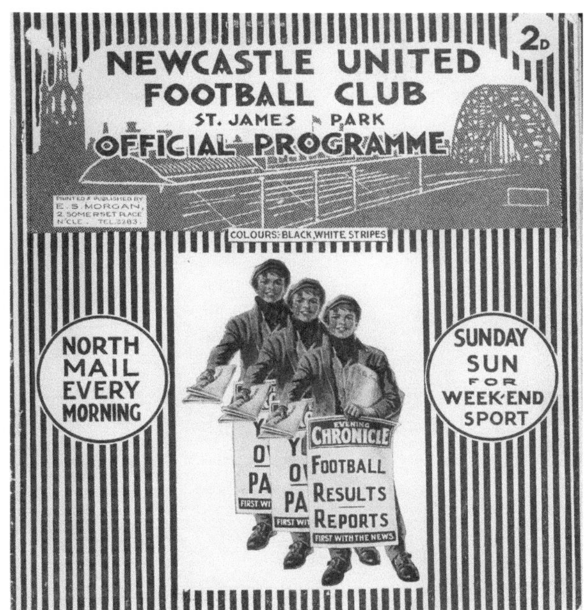

A programme cover for the game against Newcastle.

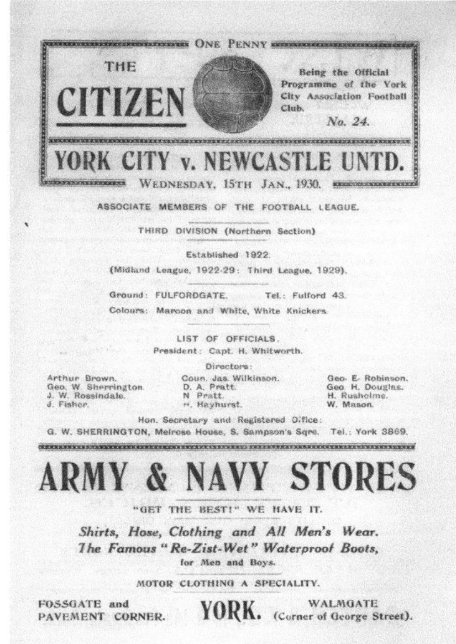

The replay programme cover.

Newcastle United: McInroy, Fairhurst, Thomson, McKenzie, Hill, Weaver, Hutchinson, McDonald, Gallacher, Chalmers, Scott.
York City: Farmery, Brooks, Johnson, Beck, Davis, Thompson, Evans, Bottrill, Gardner, Fenoughty, Millar.
Attendance: 38,674

Footnote: The Magpies won the replay 2–1 at Fulfordgate in front of 12,583. Sam Evans gave City the lead in the 23rd minute, legendary Scottish international centre-forward Hughie Gallacher equalised before the interval and United got the winner through Hutchinson midway through the second half.

22 January 1938
York City 3 West Bromwich Albion 2
FA Cup fourth round

On one of the great days in the club's history, City knocked out First Division Albion in a sensational finish and so reached the last 16 of the FA Cup.

In front of a record Bootham Crescent crowd, City, then in the Third Division North, made a lively start and the visitors were forced on the defensive in the early stages. Albion 'keeper Adams made a fine save to keep out a Reg Baines header and then Peter Spooner shot just wide. It was somewhat against the run of play when the Baggies took the lead in the 23rd minute with a fortunate goal. Billy

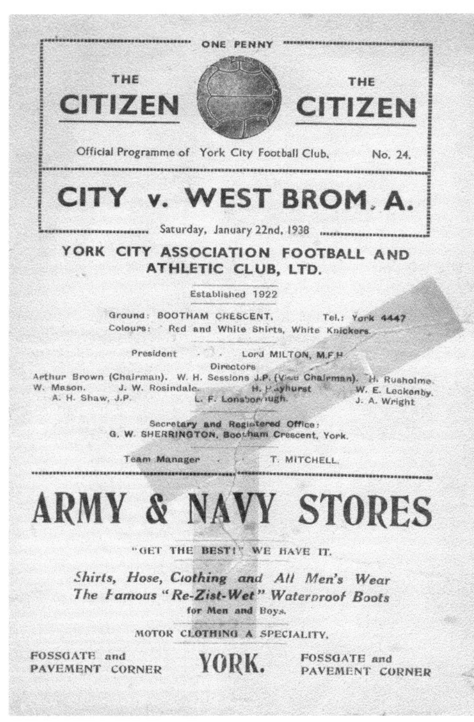

ONE PENNY

THE CITIZEN — THE CITIZEN

Official Programme of York City Football Club. No. 24.

CITY v. WEST BROM. A.

Saturday, January 22nd, 1938

YORK CITY ASSOCIATION FOOTBALL AND ATHLETIC CLUB, LTD.

Established 1922

Ground: BOOTHAM CRESCENT. Tel.: York 4447
Colours: Red and White Shirts, White Knickers.

President - - Lord MILTON, M.F.H.

Directors

Arthur Brown (Chairman). W. H. Sessions J.P. (Vice Chairman). H. Rusholme.
W. Mason. J. W. Rosindale. H. Hayhurst W. E. Leckenby.
A. H. Shaw, J.P. L. F. Lonsborough. J. A. Wright

Secretary and Registered Office:
G. W. SHERRINGTON, Bootham Crescent, York.

Team Manager - - T. MITCHELL.

ARMY & NAVY STORES

"GET THE BEST!" WE HAVE IT.

Shirts, Hose, Clothing and All Men's Wear
The Famous "Re-Zist-Wet" Waterproof Boots
for Men and Boys.

MOTOR CLOTHING A SPECIALITY.

FOSSGATE and PAVEMENT CORNER — YORK. — FOSSGATE and PAVEMENT CORNER

The programme cover for the West Brom game.

Richardson's shot was going wide but struck full-back Jack Pinder and was deflected into the net. City fought back and Malcolm Comrie went close, and penalty appeals were turned down when Baines was brought down in the area. Norman Wharton made one good save to thwart Albion right-winger Jones but City scarcely deserved to be in arrears at the interval.

The visitors almost increased their lead when Jones hit the post and Wharton made a fine save from the rebound. City battled away and were rewarded in the 55th minute with an equaliser. Baines was brought down in the penalty area and, from the resultant spot-kick, the local centre-forward drove the ball into the net. With the crowd urging them on, City started to get on top but Pinder was injured midway through the half and, while he was off the field, Albion regained the lead when Richardson netted from close range. Pinder returned to the fray but the First Division side were in the driving seat and City's Cup run looked to be over with just six minutes remaining. However, then came the high drama – in the 84th minute Pinder's free-kick was headed home by Baines and with only three minutes remaining he completed his hat-trick. Sam Earl crossed the ball from the right and the centre-forward forced the ball past Adams. The closing seconds were played amid scenes

This header by Baines was well saved by Albion's 'keeper.

of incredible excitement and, at the final whistle, thousands spilled on to the pitch to mob the City team. The *Yorkshire Evening Press* described it as 'York's biggest football thrill' and went on to claim 'it was a stirring sight to see those red shirted players simply refuse to be beaten'.

York City: Wharton, Pinder, Barrett, Duckworth, Wass, Hathway, Earl, Hughes, Baines, Comrie, Spooner.

West Bromwich Albion: Adams, Finch, Shaw, Murphy, Robbins, Sankey, Jones, Clarke, Richardson, Boyes, Johnson.

Attendance: 18,795

5 March 1938
York City 0 Huddersfield Town 0
FA Cup sixth round

The then biggest day in the club's history saw them entertain Yorkshire rivals and First Division giants Huddersfield Town, in front of Bootham Crescent's all-time record crowd of 28,123.

The match was played in spring-like conditions and both teams received a tremendous reception when they took the field. The game proved to be a typical Cup tie – fast and furious. City made the early running and in the opening 15 minutes Town had to defend resolutely. The ground was absolutely full and spectators in some parts spilled over the barriers and lined the touchlines. The visitors gradually settled down but the first half belonged to City, with Huddersfield unsettled by the pace and strong tackling of the Third Division side.

After the break, Town resumed strongly and it was City's turn to defend. Norman Wharton made one fine save to stop an effort by Watson and then a Beasley shot struck the crossbar. Thrills were coming thick and fast, and City came close to breaking the deadlock in the 71st minute. Sam Earl crossed from the right and Peter Spooner headed the ball over the advancing 'keeper Bob Hesford but, with the crowd ready to greet a goal, full-back Mountford made a spectacular goalline clearance. A Watson shot hit the York crossbar with Wharton beaten, City forced a series of four corners and Ted Wass cleared one Town shot off the line.

In a tense and nail-biting finish the crowd were in a ferment of excitement but in the end

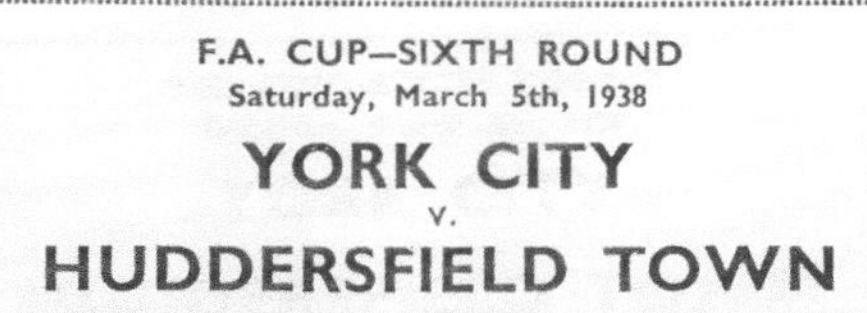

The souvenir programme for the match, which saw a record attendance of 28,123.

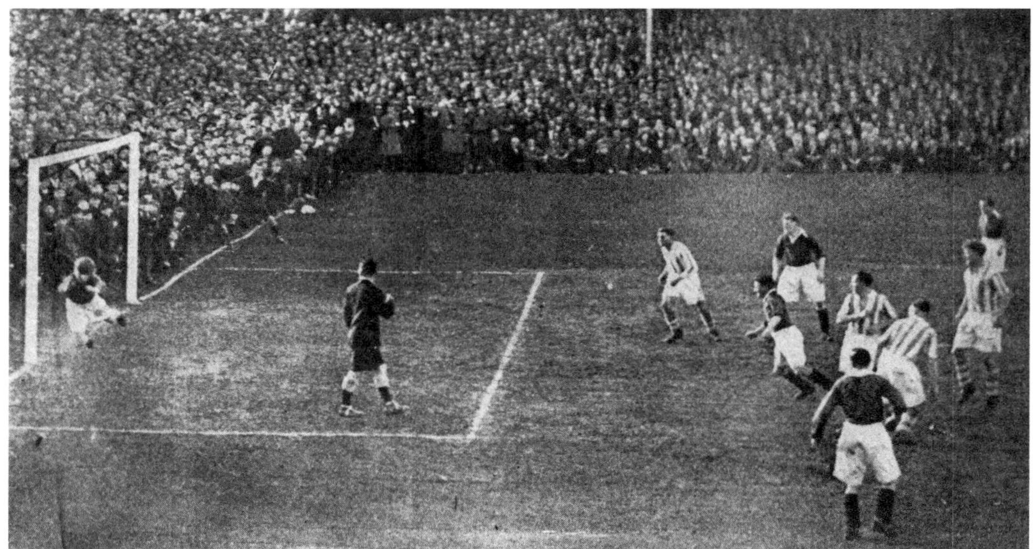

Huddersfield 'keeper Bob Hesford dives to save Comrie's shot.

honours were even, with both defences coming out on top. City's rearguard all had fine games, with Jack Pinder outstanding, while Town centre-half Alf Young (later to play for City in 1945–46) kept a tight grip on Reg Baines.

York City: Wharton, Pinder, Barrett, Duckworth, Wass, Hathway, Earl, Hughes, Baines, Comrie, Spooner.

Huddersfield Town: Hesford, Craig, Mountford, Willingham, Young, Chivers, Wienand, Barclay, McFadyen, Watson, Beasley.

Attendance: 28,123

Footnote: Huddersfield won the replay 2–1 at Leeds Road in front of 58,066. Watson and Chivers scored for Huddersfield, with Baines the City marksman. Town went on to reach the Final, losing at Wembley to Preston North End.

20 November 1948

York City 6 Rotherham United 1

Division Three North

This was arguably City's most sensational League victory and an afternoon of triumph for local centre-forward Alf Patrick. Rotherham travelled to Bootham Crescent as Division Three North leaders, having won 15 and drawn one of their 17 matches. City were fifth in the table and in the middle of an excellent run of six successive home wins, scoring 23 goals with only two against. The stage was set for a tremendous tussle, and a huge crowd – including a big following from Rotherham – created a magnificent atmosphere.

Honours were even in the early stages, but with Jimmy Rudd showing fine footwork down the left wing, City began to take command and took the lead in the 28th minute. Rudd and Storey combined down the left and, from a cross, Alf Patrick turned the ball into the net at the far post. United hit back but City's defence held firm, with 'keeper John 'Jack' Frost making one fine save from Wally Ardron.

Three minutes after the break, City scored a picture-book second goal. Matt Patrick sent George Ivey racing down the right wing. The diminutive winger crossed the ball perfectly for Alf Patrick to crack a tremendous right-foot shot into the roof of the net. Again the visitors hit back with some fine attacking football but were shaken in the 57th minute when City were awarded a debatable penalty for hand-ball by Arthur Radford. Full-back Harry Brigham converted this and Alf Patrick completed his hat-trick five minutes later, beating United's 'keeper Danny Bolton with a right-foot shot after clever work by Storey. United finally got on the score sheet in the 70th minute when Ardron netted a spectacular goal, but City were to set the seal on a famous victory as Alf Patrick completed his nap hand with two more goals. In the 83rd minute he outpaced the defence to score a fine individual effort and netted from close range four minutes later following a goalmouth scramble. The local lad received a tremendous ovation and in the closing moments the crowd chanted the goals in sequence, 'one, two, three, four, five, six'.

City had outplayed the League leaders, who had no answer to York's quick-moving, short-passing attack. The defence also played their part in keeping United at bay in what was a superb

Alf Patrick nets against Halifax Town on 16 February 1952, four years after scoring five against Rotherham.

all-round City effort. Furthermore, Alf Patrick's five-goal feat established an individual club record in the Football League, and the then record League attendance of 19,216 saw what was truly a match to remember.

York City: Frost, Brigham, Simpson, Brenen, Gale, Allen, Ivey, M. Patrick, A. Patrick, Storey, Rudd.

Rotherham United: Bolton, Selkirk, Radford, Edwards, H. Williams, D. Williams, Grainger, Guest, Ardron, Shaw, McMahon.

Attendance: 19,216.

21 August 1954
Wrexham 2 York City 6
Division Three North

The opening day of what was to be a memorable campaign for the club saw a remarkable performance by a City team fielding no less than seven newcomers. Making their debuts that afternoon were Tommy Forgan, Ernie Phillips, George Howe, Arthur Bottom and Norman Wilkinson, along with Les Slatter and Sam McNab.

It was a great team effort but the hero was Bottom, who hit a hat-trick. The former Sheffield United player opened the scoring after just 90 seconds with a 20-yard shot following a Gordon Brown free-kick. New 'keeper Forgan made one fine save but City, playing some classy football, increased their lead when Bottom crashed home a pass from Billy Fenton. The home side hit back immediately and reduced their arrears through Tommy Bannan, but before the interval City had swept into a 4–1 lead. Wilkinson ran on to a Bottom through-ball to net his first goal for the club in the 40th minute and Bottom completed his hat-trick on the stroke of half-time, following a fine four-man move. Within a minute of the restart City increased their lead, when Bottom hit the post with a fine drive and McNab shot the rebound into the net. Shortly afterwards, the Welsh side scored through a Johnnie Tapscott header, and for a time they fought desperately to get back into the game. City swung back to take full command and completed the scoring in the 73rd minute, when McNab pinpointed a pass to Wilkinson, who netted from 12 yards.

The *Sports Press* wrote 'City gave an exhibition of classy, attacking football, the like of which has seldom been seen in the Northern Section.' Additionally, a Wrexham reporter summed it up

The programme cover for Wrexham v York City.

Arthur Bottom in action against Notts County in the sixth round of the FA Cup on 12 March 1955, in the same season he hit a hat-trick against Wrexham.

when he said 'York's football was such a delight to watch and they played with understanding and precision. The sheer speed and brilliance of some of the York moves left Wrexham floundering.'

Wrexham: Eggleston, Speed, McGowan, Griffiths, Wynn, Tapscott, Hughes, Hewitt, Bannan, Samuels, Richards.

York City: Forgan, Phillips, Howe, Brown, Stewart, Spence, Slatter, Bottom, Wilkinson, McNab, Fenton.

Attendance: 11,695

8 January 1955
Blackpool 0 York City 2
FA Cup third round

This was a memorable afternoon for City, who recorded a magnificent victory over a star-studded Blackpool side. Only 18 months earlier the Lancashire club had won the FA Cup against Bolton Wanderers in the famous Final of 1953, and no less than eight of that triumphant team were on duty against City. The *Sports Press* headline that evening spelled it out – '5,000 did like to be beside the seaside.'

This was a glamour tie for City as, apart from the legendary Stanley Matthews on the right wing, the Tangerines also fielded international stars Stan Mortensen, George Farm, Harry Johnston and Ernie Taylor. City gave a superb performance, though, and fully deserved their success. It remains the

The programme cover for Blackpool v York.

only occasion that they have beaten top-flight opposition away in the FA Cup.

After weathering early pressure, City settled into their familiar skilful close passing, push-and-run style. With the half-back line in outstanding form and George Howe's intelligent positional play keeping Matthews quiet, City began to take control and took the lead in the 37th minute. Sid Storey out on the left sent in a swerving centre-cum-shot, Farm misjudged it and the ball finished in the net. Encouraged by this, City finished the half strongly and made a number of menacing attacks.

Blackpool started the second half in determined fashion but City held firm, even when handicapped by an injury to right-winger Billy Hughes, who limped badly for most of the second half. There was no question, however, of City sitting back and hanging on to their lead, and Farm was kept busy in the home goal. In the 70th minute they scored a classic second goal. Norman Wilkinson placed a perfect pass to Billy Fenton, who ran on to score from 12 yards with a fine shot. With 12 minutes remaining Blackpool were awarded a controversial penalty, but Tommy Forgan rose to the occasion and turned Jim Kelly's spot-kick over the bar.

Sid Storey (out of picture) beats Blackpool 'keeper George Farm to open the scoring.

It had been a tremendous team effort, with particular praise going to Alan Stewart, Gordon Brown and Howe. The City fans mobbed the players at the final whistle – it was a day they would never forget.

Blackpool: Farm, Gratix, Garrett, J. Kelly, Johnston, H. Kelly, Matthews, Mudie, Mortensen, Taylor, Perry.

York City: Forgan, Phillips, Howe, Brown, Stewart, Spence, Hughes, Bottom, Wilkinson, Storey, Fenton.

Attendance: 26,030

19 February 1955
York City 3 Tottenham Hotspur 1
FA Cup fifth round

In arguably the finest display in their history, City swept to a magnificent victory over their illustrious opponents on an unforgettable afternoon in front of an all-ticket crowd of 21,000.

The groundstaff had done a good job to get the pitch playable but conditions were tricky for the players. Although Spurs opened the scoring in the 11th minute when George Robb netted from close range, City played some superb football and went on to outplay their First Division opponents for long periods. The visitors were forced to defend and conceded a number of corners before City scored twice in the space of two breathtaking minutes. In the 29th minute Billy Fenton went on a crossfield run pursued by Alf Ramsey. He back-heeled the ball to Billy Hughes, who crossed perfectly from the right, for Norman Wilkinson to head a glorious goal. In the next attack Arthur Bottom beat two defenders and passed to Wilkinson, whose fierce shot was parried by Ron Reynolds to Fenton, who slammed the loose ball into the net. Pandemonium broke out as the crowd roared with excitement, and there was no doubt that City deserved their lead. They kept up the pressure and Spurs had to defend desperately at times as Fenton's pace caused them problems. Tottenham's forwards played some clever football at times but the home defence coped well and the City side left the field at half-time to a great ovation.

In the second half the Londoners fought hard to get back into the game and came near to equalising when Eddie Baily's header was cleared off the line by George Howe. City

F.A. CUP, FIFTH ROUND
York City v. Tottenham Hotspur
SATURDAY, 19th FEBRUARY, 1955
Official Programme
Price THREEPENCE
ARMY & NAVY STORES
"GET THE BEST!"—WE HAVE IT
SHIRTS, HOSE, MACS., RAINCOATS and ALL MEN'S WEAR
The Famous "BEVA" WATERPROOF BOOTS
OVERALLS and BOILER SUITS
FOSSGATE and PAVEMENT CORNER
YORK
FOSSGATE and PAVEMENT CORNER
Herald Printing Works—42257

The programme cover for York v Spurs.

Norman Wilkinson scores the third goal against Tottenham.

roared back and twice went close to increasing their lead. First Fenton shot inches too high, then Reynolds rather luckily saved a Bottom shot with his feet. Tommy Forgan made a fine save to keep out a Len Duquemin header but City, playing Spurs at their own traditional short-passing game, remained in control and clinched victory with 10 minutes to go. Fenton beat Ramsey down the left and his cross was steered into the net by Wilkinson. Only a magnificent diving save by Reynolds prevented the centre-forward from scoring a hat-trick when he shot powerfully from 20 yards. At the final whistle the crowd swarmed on to the pitch to acclaim the team that had equalled the club's 1938 record by reaching the last eight of the FA Cup. They had also become the first Northern Section team to reach the quarter-finals twice.

York City had given a display of outstanding football and earned nationwide tributes and praise. Some of the headlines read:

News Chronicle: 'York City looked like 1950 Spurs side.'
Daily Express: 'No fluke – it might have been six.'
Yorkshire Post: 'A footballing triumph.'
Sports Press: 'Spurs outplayed from start to finish.'

Tottenham player Danny Blanchflower praised City when he said 'York's standard of play left us speechless. They were better in all departments. They played so well we could not blame the state of the pitch. I think they would have won whatever the conditions.' Spurs captain Alf Ramsey commented 'York were the better team and deserved to win. They showed they could play good football on a difficult pitch.'

The game had been billed as a classic and it had certainly been a classic display by the Third Division side. Although Norman Wilkinson was the two-goal hero, it had been a marvellous team effort.

York City: Forgan, Phillips, Howe, Brown, Stewart, Spence, Hughes, Bottom, Wilkinson, Storey, Fenton.

Tottenham Hotspur: Reynolds, Ramsey, Hopkins, Blanchflower, Clarke, Marchi, Walters, Baily, Duquemin, Brooks, Robb.

Attendance: 21,000.

26 March 1955
York City 1 Newcastle United 1
FA Cup semi-final

This was the biggest day in York City's history and, in a mass exodus, 21,000 fans travelled to Hillsborough by road and rail to cheer on their heroes, and heavy, persistent rain that fell throughout the day did not dampen spirits. For the first time since the third round, City had to make a change, as Sam McNab deputised for Sid Storey, who had to drop out owing to a back injury. The pitch, although very heavy, had stood up well to the incessant rain, and the Dagenham Girl Pipers' Band formed a tunnel as the teams entered the field to a thunderous reception. The *Yorkshire Post* sportswriter Richard Ulyatt described the roar as the most deafening he had heard at a sporting occasion, and it should be noted that he had reported on many a game at Wembley and Hampden Park.

Both sides made early attacks but after settling quite well City fell behind after 14 minutes. Bob Cowell and Reg Davies set up Vic Keeble, who slipped the ball past Tommy Forgan into the net. Undismayed, they hit back and Jimmy Scoular had to make a last-ditch tackle to stop Billy Fenton. The First Division side went close through Keeble and then, after half an hour, City equalised. Arthur Bottom took the ball off Scoular in midfield and ran 30 yards before drawing Ron Simpson out of goal and placing the ball into the empty net, then he jigged back to the halfway line pursued by his delighted teammates. United were clearly knocked out of their stride and had to defend resolutely for a time. Half-time came with honours even.

With conditions deteriorating, both sides found the game tough. For the first 25 minutes of the second half, United did most of the attacking and Jackie Milburn shot over the bar from point-blank range. But City defended soundly and came back well in the latter stages, finishing the stronger side. Fenton shot straight at Simpson when well placed, and then, in the 80th minute, came an incident still talked about over 50 years later. A tremendous scramble in United's penalty area saw Bottom's header scooped off the line by Simpson's despairing one-handed save. Many thought the ball had crossed the line but amid controversial scenes the referee awarded a free-kick against Bottom. In a thrilling finish, Forgan made a brave save at Keeble's feet and Gordon Brown headed just wide from a last-minute corner.

In the end, a draw was a just result after a gruelling match in terrible conditions. City had become the first-ever Division Three side to force a semi-final replay. At the time there was a national

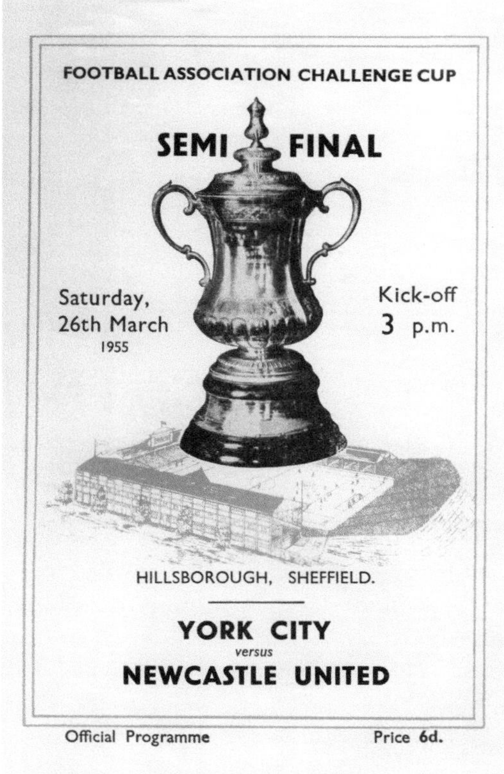

The programme cover for York versus Newcastle.

newspaper strike so City's feat did not receive the attention it deserved. The *Northern Echo* headline read 'York City merited second chance after great struggle', while the local *Sports Press*, which sold a record 25,000 copies that night, spelled out 'City Live To Fight Again'.

York City: Forgan, Phillips, Howe, Brown, Stewart, Spence, Hughes, Bottom, Wilkinson, McNab, Fenton.

Newcastle United: Simpson, Cowell, Batty, Scoular, Stokoe, Casey, White, Davies, Keeble, Milburn, Mitchell.

Attendance: 65,000 (the largest ever to watch a City match)

Footnote: United won the replay 2–1 at Roker Park on 30 March in front of 58,239, with goals from Len White after three minutes and Vic Keeble in the 90th minute. City, who had Sid Storey back in the line up, were handicapped when centre-half Alan Stewart suffered a badly cut head just after half-time and, after a 12-minute absence, had to finish the game on the right wing.

Norman Wilkinson watches an effort go wide at Hillsborough against Newcastle United.

2 February 1957
York City 9 Southport 1
Division Three North

This was the day when City went one over the eight to record their biggest win in the Football League. City were on the fringe of the promotion race in Division Three North while the visitors were second from bottom, but no one could have anticipated the goal rush and the rout which was to ensue.

On a greasy pitch, Southport made the better start but City opened the scoring in the 14th minute with an Arthur Bottom special. Norman Wilkinson crossed from the left and Bottom hit a tremendous shot that flew into the net from outside the penalty area. Shortly afterwards, Southport full-back Peter Lomas was badly injured and was unable to take any further part in the game. City took command and Bottom increased the lead after 27 minutes, converting a penalty after being brought down in the area. Just before the interval he secured his hat-trick when he collected a Peter Wragg pass and netted with a low shot via the inside of a post, and the next minute he rattled the crossbar with a tremendous shot.

After the break, City continued to dominate and Billy Hill went close twice. On the hour, City made it 4–0 when Wilkinson headed home a Billy Fenton centre. Southport 'keeper Jack Richardson made a number of fine saves but Southport's hard-pressed defence collapsed and City scored five times in the space of eight minutes, from the 75th to the 83rd. First, Bottom stabbed in a Hill pass then straight from the kick-off, Fenton raced through to beat Richardson. Gordon Brown got on the score sheet when he cracked the ball home after a Bottom shot rebounded to him. The City inside-forward seemed to mesmerise the Southport defenders whenever he had the ball and, after one of his dribbles, he supplied the perfect pass to Wilkinson for goal number eight. Finally, Wragg headed a cross from the right past the bemused Southport 'keeper. The last goal of the game, however, was scored by the visitors when George Howe handled the ball and Wilf Charlton netted from the penalty spot in the 89th minute.

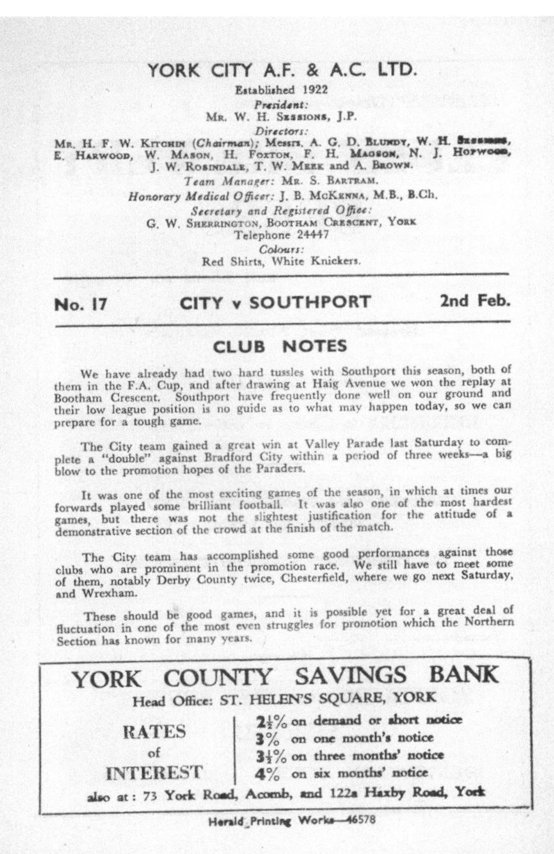

YORK CITY A.F. & A.C. LTD.

Established 1922

President:
Mr. W. H. Sessions, J.P.

Directors:
Mr. H. F. W. Kitchin (*Chairman*); Messrs. A. G. D. Blundy, W. H. Sessions, E. Harwood, W. Mason, H. Foxton, F. H. Magson, N. J. Hopwood, J. W. Rosindale, T. W. Meek and A. Brown.

Team Manager: Mr. S. Bartram.

Honorary Medical Officer: J. B. McKenna, M.B., B.Ch.

Secretary and Registered Office:
G. W. Sherrington, Bootham Crescent, York
Telephone 24447

Colours:
Red Shirts, White Knickers.

No. 17 CITY v SOUTHPORT 2nd Feb.

CLUB NOTES

We have already had two hard tussles with Southport this season, both of them in the F.A. Cup, and after drawing at Haig Avenue we won the replay at Bootham Crescent. Southport have frequently done well on our ground and their low league position is no guide as to what may happen today, so we can prepare for a tough game.

The City team gained a great win at Valley Parade last Saturday to complete a "double" against Bradford City within a period of three weeks—a big blow to the promotion hopes of the Paraders.

It was one of the most exciting games of the season, in which at times our forwards played some brilliant football. It was also one of the most hardest games, but there was not the slightest justification for the attitude of a demonstrative section of the crowd at the finish of the match.

The City team has accomplished some good performances against those clubs who are prominent in the promotion race. We still have to meet some of them, notably Derby County twice, Chesterfield, where we go next Saturday, and Wrexham.

These should be good games, and it is possible yet for a great deal of fluctuation in one of the most even struggles for promotion which the Northern Section has known for many years.

Herald Printing Works—46578

The programme cover for York versus Southport.

Lomas, Southport's right back, heads clear a centre with Bottom and Wilkinson, the City forwards, in close attendance, while Taylor (centre half) looks on.

Bottom star in dazzling forward line

York City ... ... 9 Southport 1

A newspaper cutting after the win over Southport.

Even allowing for the fact that Southport played with only 10 men for much of the game, they seldom looked like holding a City team firing on all cylinders. The forwards played some devastating football and their positional play was of the highest standard. Bottom had an outstanding game and his tally of four goals was to be his best return for the club.

York City: Forgan, Phillips, Howe, Brown, Cairney, Mollatt, Hill, Bottom, Wilkinson, Wragg, Fenton.
Southport: Richardson, Lomas, Forsyth, Gryba, Taylor, Charlton, Miles, Evans, Bromilow, McIlvenny, McDermott.
Attendance: 8,801

8 January 1958
York City 3 Birmingham City 0
FA Cup third round

In the middle of a poor League run of just two wins in 14 outings, City produced one of their best FA Cup performances by comprehensively beating First Division Birmingham City 3–0 at Bootham Crescent. The match was played on a Wednesday afternoon, following a postponement the previous Saturday because of a waterlogged pitch. City were 19th in Division Three North at the time, while the Blues were just below mid-table in the First Division and, in the two previous campaigns, had been FA Cup runners-up and beaten semi-finalists.

Conditions were good for the rearranged game and City, fielding eight of the side who figured in the 1954–55 FA Cup run, took immediate control and completely outfought and outplayed the visitors in the first half. They took the lead in the 13th minute when former England 'keeper Gil Merrick got one hand to a Billy Fenton shot and Arthur Bottom cracked home the rebound. Two minutes later, following a Ron Spence free-kick, Peter Wragg smashed a half-volley into the net with the Birmingham defence all at sea. City went three up in the 28th minute when a Billy Hughes free-kick from the right was smartly headed into the roof of the net by Norman Wilkinson, and the side got a standing ovation at the break.

In the second half the First Division side desperately strove to get back into the game but City's defence held firm, with skipper Ernie Phillips and centre-half Howard Johnson in outstanding form. Centre-forward Eddie Brown went close for the visitors when his shot hit the bar, and George Howe had to clear one effort by Harry Hooper off the line. 'Keeper Mick Granger made a number of fine stops, including

The programme cover for York against Birmingham.

one magnificent diving save to keep out a Peter Murphy header. City survived the pressure and ran out deserved winners with the crowd singing *The Happy Wanderer*, the theme song from the FA Cup semi-final days of three years earlier.

After the game the Birmingham chairman said 'York won deservedly. We rarely looked like scoring.' Manager Arthur Turner added 'We have no complaints – York dictated the game.' It was another famous FA Cup success, and the three-goal winning margin is the club's biggest against opposition from the top division in the competition.

York City: Granger, Phillips, Howe, Brown, Johnson, Spence, Hughes, Bottom, Wilkinson, Wragg, Fenton.

Birmingham City: Merrick, Hall, Farmer, Watts, Smith, Neal, Hooper, Kinsey, Brown, Murphy, Astall.

Attendance: 19,750

City's forward line against Birmingham relax after the victory. From left: Billy Fenton, Peter Wragg, Norman Wilkinson, Arthur Bottom, Billy Hughes.

18 September 1965
Hull City 1 York City 4
Division Three

The 1965–66 campaign was disastrous for City, finishing rock-bottom of Division Three (League One). By contrast, their neighbours on Humberside had a season of triumph, running away with the Championship. This result, therefore, on a sunny September afternoon at Boothferry Park, was one of the surprises of the season and a richly deserved success.

After early skirmishes City missed a great chance when Andy Provan shot wide from close range, but City shook the Tigers in the 22nd minute when Paul Aimson headed in a Provan centre. The game swung from end to end as each team attacked in turn and Harry Fallon, playing in only his second game in goal for City, made a brilliant save to keep out a Ken Wagstaff header. Ian Butler, later to play for York, went close but City were playing clever and skilful football and held on to their lead until the interval.

Hull had their best period in the 20 minutes after the resumption. After Butler had skimmed the crossbar, the left-winger equalised from close range in the 57th minute following good work by Chris Chilton. Spurred on by their fans, the Tigers put pressure on the visitors' defence but, with centre-half Barry Jackson in commanding form, City held firm and regained the lead midway through the second half. Provan split the Hull defence with a through-ball and Aimson ran clear to finish in fine style. Three minutes later, a long-range John Pearson shot was deflected to David Dunmore, who made no mistake with a low drive into the net. City were now in total command and sent their large band of supporters wild with delight when Aimson set the seal on a famous win with a great volley from the edge of the penalty area, which flew past Hull 'keeper Mike Williams in the 77th minute. It completed the perfect hat-trick for Aimson – a header, and shots with his right and left feet – but this was a fine team effort with outstanding displays from Dunphy, Walker, Jackson and Pearson. Newspaper reports bore witness to City's achievement:

> *Yorkshire Evening Press:* 'Hull were beaten by an immaculate and brilliant display of football.'
> *Hull Daily Mail:* 'A generally livelier and nippier York City had the edge all round over Hull City.'
> *Daily Express:* 'The team that Tom Lockie has built is a credit to the Third Division.'
> *Sunday Telegraph:* 'Nimble York City coasted to a remarkable victory.'

The programme cover for Hull versus York.

It was indeed a remarkable win but City were not able to maintain the high standards achieved on that glorious afternoon, and Hull gained revenge with a 2–1 win at Bootham Crescent later in the season, in front of 19,372.

Hull City: Williams, Davidson, D. Butler, Collinson, Milner, Simpkin, Heath, Wagstaff, Chilton, Houghton, I. Butler.

York City: Fallon, Baker, Walker, Woods, Jackson, Dunphy, Pearson, Dunmore, Aimson, Rudd, Provan.

Attendance: 20,554

23 January 1971
York City 3 Southampton 3
FA Cup fourth round

This epic Cup tie was regarded by many as one of the finest and most exciting ever seen at Bootham Crescent. City went into the game mid-table in Division Four, while Southampton were seventh in the First (Premiership).

The first half was goalless but City outclassed the Saints with a magnificent display of football in which Paul Aimson, Albert Johanneson, Kevin McMahon and Phil Burrows all went close to scoring.

The First Division side came into the game more after the interval but it was against the run of play that they took the lead in the 66th minute. Mike Channon crossed from the left and Jimmy Gabriel headed past Ron Hillyard. The young 'keeper made a fine save to thwart Ron Davies but was beaten again in the 78th minute, when Channon ran clear to score with City appealing for offside. Tommy Henderson came on for Archie Taylor and combined with Aimson to set up McMahon, whose header beat Eric Martin with ten minutes remaining.The visitors looked to have clinched the tie when Davies headed home from close range following a Terry Paine centre in the 84th minute. Then came City's dramatic fightback, with two late goals earning a richly deserved draw. First, Dick Hewitt blasted a shot into the roof of the net with three minutes remaining after an Aimson header had set up the opening, then, amid scenes of great excitement, City equalised in the last minute of normal time. John Mackin centred from the right and Aimson placed a magnificent header just inside Martin's left-hand post to make it 3–3.

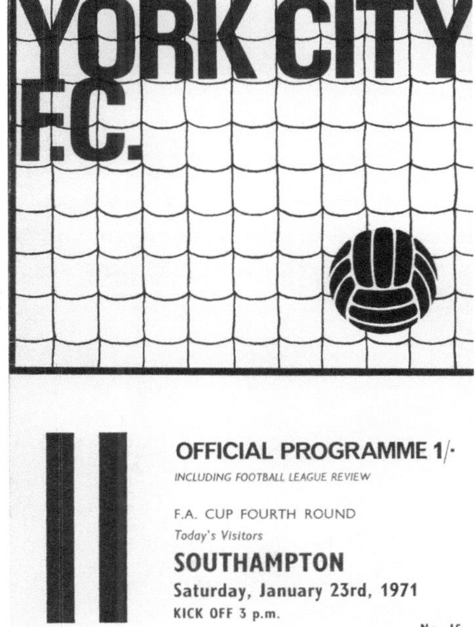

YORK CITY
F.C.
OFFICIAL PROGRAMME 1/-
INCLUDING FOOTBALL LEAGUE REVIEW
F.A. CUP FOURTH ROUND
Today's Visitors
SOUTHAMPTON
Saturday, January 23rd, 1971
KICK OFF 3 p.m.
No. 15

The programme cover for York versus Southampton.

After the match, Southampton manager Ted Bates said 'What a wonderful game. I was very happy

Paul Aimson heads the dramatic late equaliser against the Saints.

to get to the interval still level. We sorted out our problems at half-time by moving Gabriel up front and should not have let our lead slip. Full marks to York, though – they played excellent football and fully deserved their draw.'

City certainly deserved the replay after a magnificent display and it was truly a game to remember.

York City: Hillyard, Mackin, Burrows, Davidson, Swallow, Topping, Taylor (Henderson 78), McMahon, Aimson, Hewitt, Johanneson.

Southampton: Martin, Kirkup, Hollywood, Fisher, McGrath, Gabriel, Paine, Channon, Davies, O'Neill, Walker.

Attendance: 13,775

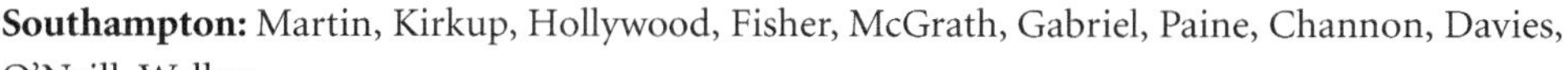

Footnote: City lost the replay 3–2 in front of 25,034 at The Dell after another exciting game. Aimson and Johanneson were the scorers for City while Brian O'Neill, Joe Kirkup and Davies netted for Southampton.

17 August 1974

York City 1 Aston Villa 1

Division Two

This was a famous day in the history of York City – the occasion of their first-ever match in the second tier of English football. Ever since promotion had been gained from Division Three, the start of the 1974–75 campaign had been eagerly awaited and the home crowd gave the players a huge ovation when skipper Barry Swallow led the side out at Bootham Crescent for this historic first fixture.

Urged on by the excited fans, City almost took the lead in the first minute when Swallow headed an Ian Butler free-kick just over the bar. Playing very entertaining football in the early stages, City put the Villa defence under considerable pressure and the crowd roared with delight when they took the lead in the eighth minute.

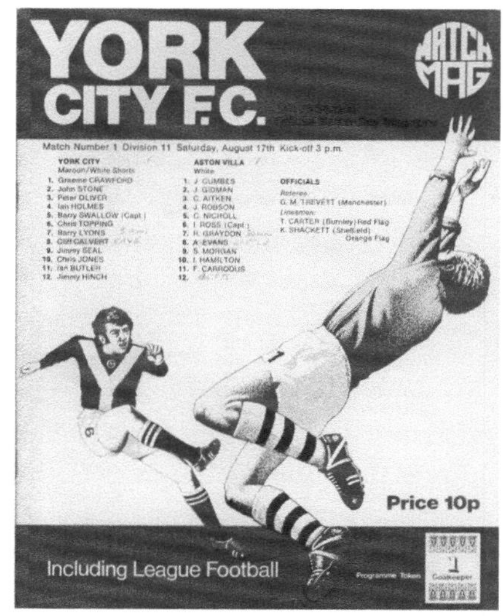

The programme cover for York versus Villa.

City's first-ever goal in Division Two. Barry Lyons (out of picture) beats Villa 'keeper Jim Cumbes.

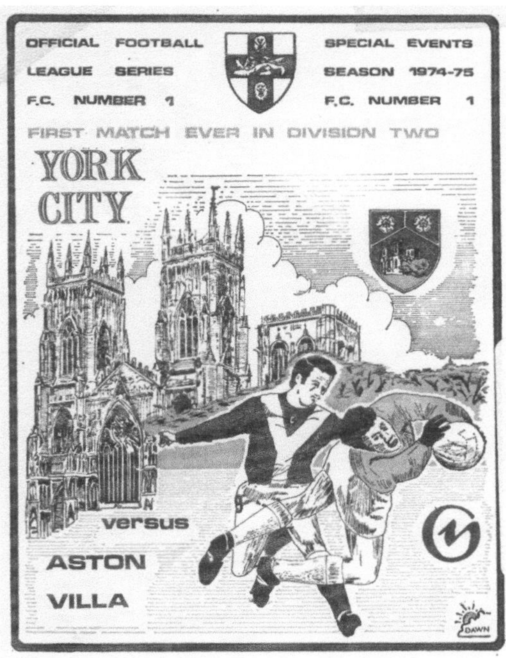

Commemorative postcard to mark City's first game in Division Two.

Cumbes was penalised for carrying the ball too many paces and, from the resultant indirect free-kick, Ian Holmes placed a short pass to Barry Lyons, who cracked a low shot through the defensive wall and just inside the 'keeper's right-hand post. The visitors hit back and Graeme Crawford made two magnificent saves to thwart John Gidman. In the 27th minute City came within an ace of increasing their lead when Jimmy Seal rounded Cumbes, only for his shot to be kicked off the line by full-back Charlie Aitken. Villa equalised against the run of play after half an hour, when Ray Graydon headed home from close range. Encouraged by the goal, Aston Villa began to get on top and City were kept at full stretch in the closing stages of the first half.

On the resumption, the visitors again began to dominate proceedings and were indebted to strong work by Swallow and Crawford. Gradually, City got back into the game and both Jones and Seal went close to scoring. Villa had a goal disallowed for an infringement, City had appeals for a penalty turned down, and Chris Topping did well to clear two dangerous crosses.

In the end, City were pleased to collect a point from what had been a stern baptism. In retrospect, it was a useful performance as Villa finished runners-up to Manchester United that season, and won promotion back to the top flight.

York City: Crawford, Stone, Oliver, Holmes, Swallow, Topping, Lyons, Cave, Seal (Hinch 85), Jones, Butler.

Aston Villa: Cumbes, Gidman, Aitken, Ross, Nicholl, Robson, Graydon, Little, Morgan, Hamilton (Betts 75), Carrodus.

Jimmy Seal and Ian Butler greet Chris Jones's (out of picture) opening goal against Fulham.

22 March 1975
York City 3 Fulham 2
Division Two

This match was a thrilling Second Division encounter. It marked Fulham's first-ever trip to York and the Cottagers were in the middle of a very good run of 13 League and Cup games without defeat. The London club went on to reach Wembley that season, finishing FA Cup runners-up to West Ham United. At the time of their visit to Bootham Crescent they were in mid-table, while City were just above the relegation zone.

In the visitors' line up were World Cup-winning captain Bobby Moore and former England teammate Alan Mullery. In attack was Viv Busby, who would play a big part in City's fortunes a few years later.

The game had an electrifying start and the scoreline read 2–2 after only 20 minutes. City struck first in the seventh minute when Chris Jones, who had scored twice in a 2–0 win at Craven Cottage earlier that season, ran onto a pass from Brian Pollard and chipped a curling shot over 'keeper Peter Mellor. The Londoners hit back four

The programme cover for York versus Fulham.

minutes later when Alan Slough hit a low shot past Graeme Crawford. In the 19th minute Busby hit a spectacular goal from outside the penalty area, but straight from the kick-off Jones glanced in a header from a Pollard cross. The game swung from end to end in thrilling fashion and there were plenty of goalmouth incidents to keep the crowd on their toes.

The pace and excitement continued in the second half and Jones raced clear in the 51st minute. As he was about to shoot, he was challenged by Moore and the referee awarded a penalty. Ian Holmes converted the spot-kick in his usual calm manner and City regained the lead. The thrills and spills continued and Crawford made two magnificent saves as Fulham went flat out for the equaliser, but City held firm and deserved the points after a fine contest that could have produced a dozen goals. City, therefore, ended Fulham's unbeaten run and completed a League double over their London opponents. It was indeed a match to remember and the crowd gave the teams a standing ovation at both half-time and the final whistle.

York City: Crawford, Calvert, Oliver, Holmes, Swallow, Topping, Pollard, Cave, Seal, Jones, Butler.
Fulham: Mellor, Fraser, Strong, Mullery, Lacy, Moore, Dowie, Mitchell, Busby, Slough, Barrett.
Attendance: 7,495

26 January 1985
York City 1 Arsenal 0
FA Cup fourth round

This was an afternoon of high drama as City beat their famous opponents thanks to a late Keith Houchen penalty. At the time City were mid-table in Division Three (League One) while the Gunners were fifth in the First Division. Arsenal fielded eight internationals that day and their side was worth £4.5 million, while City's team cost £19,000 in transfer fees. The groundstaff had to work hard when three inches of snow was cleared from the playing area on the morning of the tie.

On a tricky and, in places, icy pitch, City adapted themselves better to the difficult conditions. The visitors made an early attack but Paul Mariner's header was saved by Mick Astbury, and Tommy Caton sent a free-kick just wide. City settled and Houchen went close after good work by Alan Hay and John MacPhail. Eighteen-year-old Martin Butler was prominent and his shot was charged down, only for Gary Ford to hit the rebound wide. Both defences were on top and chances were few and far between in the first period.

After the interval Arsenal threatened for a while, and Mariner and Tony Woodcock forced Astbury into making two fine saves. At the other end, Caton had

Keith Houchen scores the dramatic penalty against the Gunners.

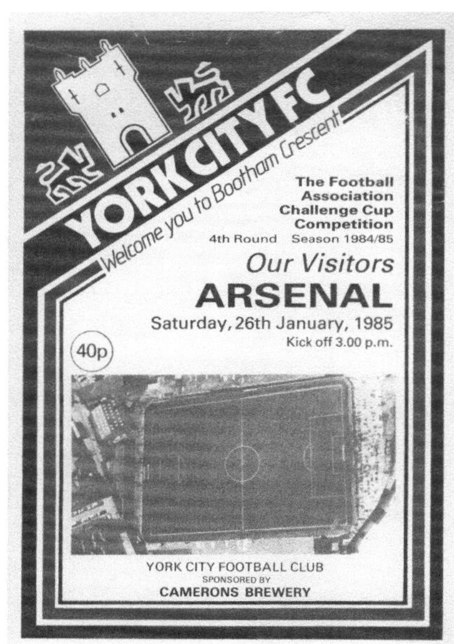

The programme cover for York versus Arsenal.

to clear Walwyn's lob off the line after the striker had beaten 'keeper John Lukic. City continued to show more determination and Houchen just failed to get on the end of a Walwyn cross after a strong run by the centre-forward. In the last minute of normal time, their sterling efforts were rewarded. With the tie looking set for a replay at Highbury, City launched an attack down the right involving Walwyn and Butler and, as the ball was crossed, Houchen went down in the penalty area under a challenge by Steve Williams. Amid great excitement, City's inside-forward calmly side-footed the resultant spot-kick just inside Lukic's right-hand post.

City's courage, spirit and commitment earned them this deserved victory, and another famous chapter in their FA Cup history was recorded. Although Houchen earned the plaudits, it had been an excellent all-round performance. Manager Denis Smith summed it up when he said 'I demanded passion and commitment and I got it.'

York City: Astbury, Senior, Hay, Sbragia, MacPhail, Haslegrave, Ford, Butler, Walwyn, Houchen, Pearce.

Arsenal: Lukic, Anderson, Sansom, Talbot, O'Leary, Caton, Robson, Williams, Mariner, Woodcock, Nicholas (Allinson 77).

Attendance: 10,840

15 February 1986
York City 1 Liverpool 1
FA Cup fifth round

For the second successive season, City were paired at home against the Merseyside giants at the same stage of the FA Cup and once again the match was drawn 1–1. To get to the fifth round this time, City had the unique experience of beating non-League opposition at each of the four previous hurdles and went into the tie mid-table in Division Three (League One). Liverpool, who were destined to do the League and Cup double, were third in Division One.

On a hard pitch, heavily sanded in areas, City made a lively start, and in the fourth minute Dale Banton raced on to a Gary Ford through-ball and shot inches wide of Bruce Grobbelaar's right-hand post. Liverpool settled down with player-manager Kenny Dalglish prominent and Ian Rush had a hard shot well saved by Andy Leaning. City continued to have the edge, however, and only a brilliant save by Grobbelaar in the 37th minute prevented them taking the lead. Keith Walwyn and David McAughtrie combined to set up a chance for John MacPhail, who cracked in a fierce shot from 12 yards, only for the Liverpool 'keeper to turn the ball over the bar in breathtaking fashion. City could have been two goals

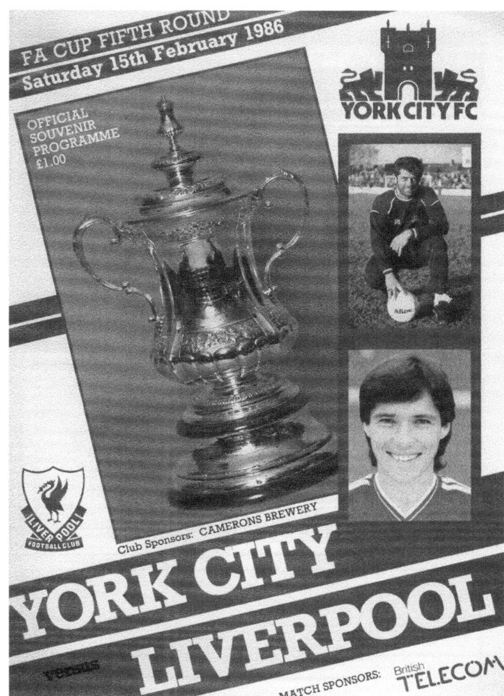

The programme cover for York versus Liverpool.

ahead and the visitors were happy to reach half-time on level terms.

Liverpool resumed in more purposeful fashion and City had to defend strongly for a while but then, in the 61st minute, took the lead. Tony Canham chipped the ball into the area from the left, Banton headed it on and Walwyn slipped it to Ford, who scored with a low shot from 10 yards, just inside Grobbelaar's left-hand post. City held the lead for just four minutes before the visitors equalised from a Jan Molby penalty, after Steve Senior was adjudged to have handled the ball under pressure from Craig Johnston. With Simon Mills having a fine game in midfield, City battled on but with five minutes remaining Liverpool almost won the tie when Rush lobbed the ball over the bar after being put through by John Wark.

It had been another memorable day in the club's illustrious FA Cup history and they had deserved the replay at Anfield. Dalglish complained about the state of the pitch but admitted it was the same for both sides and was relieved to have gone away unbeaten.

York City: Leaning, Senior, Hood, McAughtrie, MacPhail, Mills, Ford, Banton, Walwyn, Haslegrave, Canham.

Liverpool: Grobbelaar, Lee, Beglin, Lawrenson, Wark, Hansen, Dalglish, Johnston, Rush, Molby, Seagraves.

Attendance: 12,752

Footnote: There was to be no repeat of the 7–0 scoreline in the replay, as in the previous campaign. City forced the game into extra-time before losing 3–1. Tony Canham scored the equaliser and Keith Walwyn had a goal disallowed in normal time.

Gary Ford gives City the lead against Liverpool.

26 March 1988
York City 2 Sunderland 1
Division Three

This was one of the surprise League results of 1987–88. City were at the foot of Division Three with only four wins and 20 points in 37 games, while Sunderland were second with 72 points and destined to finish top. On paper, it was a banker away win. The game had been eagerly awaited, with the visitors' management team of Denis Smith and Viv Busby making their first visit back to Bootham Crescent since their dramatic departure in May 1987.

In Sunderland's line up were former City favourites John MacPhail and Marco Gabbiadini, and the game kicked-off in a Cup tie atmosphere. The Roker Park outfit dominated the early proceedings but City held firm thanks to fine performances from centre-half Steve Tutill, returning after three months out with a broken ankle, and 'keeper Scott Endersby. Gradually City settled, shaking the visitors and their big following of fans by taking the lead in the 34th minute. Gary Howlett found Ian Helliwell with a fine pass and the big centre-forward cut in from the left and scored with his low-angled shot, ending up in the net after hitting both posts.

Sunderland continued to press after the break and City had to defend for long periods, with Endersby making a series of outstanding saves. The home side held on and in the 75th minute scored a magnificent second goal. Helliwell's pass set Gary Himsworth free down the left and the young winger's perfect centre was met by Dale Banton, who rocketed a tremendous header into the roof of the net. With eight minutes

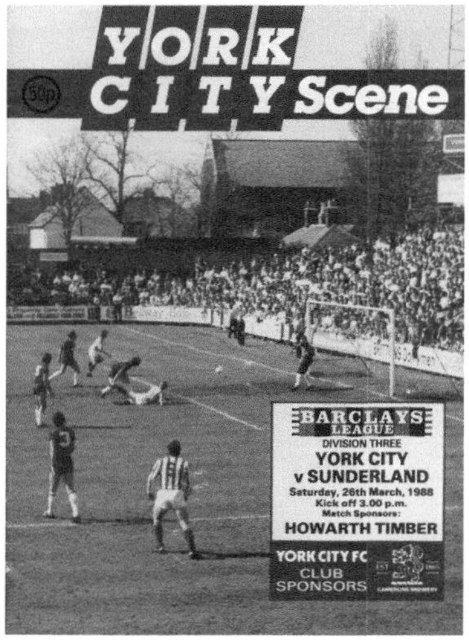

The programme cover for York versus Sunderland.

Dale Banton's spectacular header puts City 2–0 ahead against Sunderland.

left, Sunderland finally scored when Colin Pascoe netted from close range, setting up a dramatic and frantic finale. City's defence held on, amid great tension, to record a remarkable victory. One of City's many heroes that day was Tutill, who kept such a tight hold on his close friend and former teammate Gabbiadini.

Unfortunately, the afternoon was marred at the end when some of the visiting fans invaded the pitch and smashed the goalposts.

York City: Endersby, McMillan, Johnson, Clegg, Tutill, Branagan, Howlett, Bradshaw, Helliwell, Banton, Himsworth.

Sunderland: Hesford, Kay, Bennett, MacPhail, Agboola, McGuire (Pascoe 46), Owers (Gray 82), Doyle, Armstrong, Gabbiadini, Gates.

Attendance: 9,183

29 May 1993
York City 1 Crewe Alexandra 1
(City won 5–3 on penalties)
Third Division Play-off Final

York City's first-ever visit to Wembley Stadium provided an afternoon of incredible excitement and drama, and ended with the club winning promotion to Division Two (League One).

City's estimated 10,000 followers that day experienced just about every emotion possible in a thrilling contest. The first half was dominated by City, who played some tremendous flowing football. Tony Canham rattled the crossbar with a fine shot from 20 yards in the 25th minute and, with Jon McCarthy in sparkling form, Crewe had to defend desperately at times. At the back, Paul Stancliffe marshalled the defence in his usual composed fashion and City should have had at least a two-goal lead by the interval.

Alexandra improved after the break but City still looked the better side and McCarthy went close when he hit the woodwork after an hour. City kept their

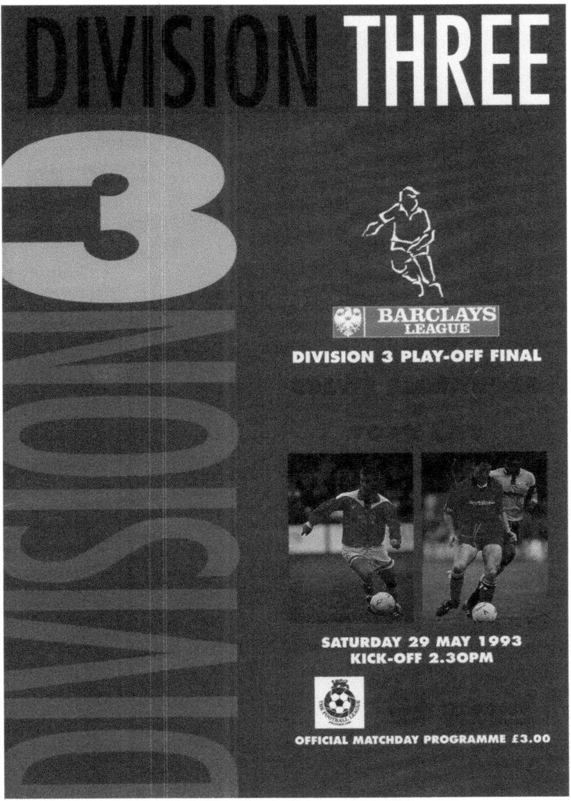

The programme cover for the Play-off Final.

Wayne Hall and Dean Kiely celebrate the promotion success.

shape and, playing with pace and determination, rarely allowed Crewe to settle. In the last minute of normal time McCarthy broke free on the right and ran 50 yards, only to scoop the ball over the bar from close range.

In extra-time City broke the deadlock in the 104th minute. Andy McMillan started the move and Paul Barnes slipped the ball through for local born Gary Swann to finish in fine style with a low shot. Steve Tutill came on as substitute for skipper Stancliffe but, with just one minute remaining, inexplicably handled the ball following a Crewe corner. Dave McKearney converted the spot-kick to take the encounter to a penalty shoot-out.

Jon McCarthy, Paul Barnes and Tony Canham all scored for City, and McKearney and Shaun Smith (later to play for City in the Conference) did so for Crewe but Gareth Whalley saw his effort saved by Dean Kiely. Nigel Pepper made it 4–2 and Ashley Ward narrowed the gap. Wayne Hall then coolly converted his left-footed penalty just inside Mark Smith's left-hand post to win promotion, and was immediately mobbed by his excited teammates.

A truly memorable afternoon and a triumph for the players and manager Alan Little, who had only been in charge for two months.

York City: Kiely, McMillan, Hall, Pepper, Stancliffe (Tutill 108), Atkin, McCarthy, Blackstone, Barnes, Swann, Canham.

Crewe Alexandra: M. Smith, McKearney, S. Smith, Evans, Carr, Whalley, Ward, Naylor, Lennon, Walters (Clarkson 104), Edwards (Woodward 79).

Attendance: 22,416

20 September 1995
Manchester United 0 York City 3
Football League (Coca-Cola) Cup second round, first leg

City hit the national headlines with an astonishing victory at Old Trafford that brought back memories of the glory days of the mid-1950s.

The club went into the game second from bottom of Division Two (League One) while the Red Devils were joint leaders of the Premiership, and although Alex Ferguson included some of his

Tony Barras celebrates his goal against United.

promising less experienced younger players, United still fielded a strong side. Old Trafford was virtually full, with one side of the ground closed because of redevelopment.

City started the game at a good tempo and were not in awe of their opponents or their surroundings. Scott Jordan and Nigel Pepper were excellent in midfield and both went close with shots before Dean Kiely made a fingertip save to keep out a Brian McClair header. Paul Barnes opened the scoring in the 24th minute. Graeme Murty won the ball off Phil Neville with a great tackle and fed Barnes, whose 25-yard shot took a slight deflection and flew past Kevin Pilkington. McClair went close following good work by Ryan Giggs but City fully deserved their lead at the interval.

Within eight incredible minutes at the start of the second period, City had raced into a 3–0 lead.

The programme cover for Manchester United versus York.

City celebrate their aggregate win over Manchester United after the second leg at Bootham Crescent.

In the 51st minute Barnes raced through United's defence and was fouled by Pat McGibbon. The referee awarded a penalty and sent off the defender, and Barnes dusted himself down to fire home the spot-kick. Two minutes later, the home side were stunned when Tony Barras rose high to head Pepper's free-kick into the net. Soon afterwards, Barnes found the net again but his effort was narrowly ruled offside. United played substitute Steve Bruce up front as they desperately tried to retrieve the situation, and Barnes cleared one of his shots off the line. City were reduced to 10 men when substitute Paul Baker was dismissed for two bookable offences, and although they were put under pressure in the closing stages, the defence held firm.

At the end, City fully merited the tremendous standing ovation, not only from their own ecstatic fans but also United's. It had been a superb team effort and an unforgettable night for York City.

Manchester United: Pilkington, Parker, McGibbon, Pallister, Irwin, Beckham, P. Neville (Cooke 46), Davies (Bruce 58), Sharpe, McClair, Giggs.

York City: Kiely, McMillan, Tutill, Barras, Hall, Williams, Pepper, Jordan, Murty, Peverell (Baker 67), Barnes (Atkin 89).

Attendance: 29,049

Footnote: For the return leg at Bootham Crescent two weeks later, United brought back some of their big guns, including Eric Cantona and Peter Schmeichel. United won 3–1 but bowed out, with City going through 4–3 on aggregate. United went on to win the Premiership and the FA Cup that season.

24 September 1996
York City 3 Everton 2
Football League (Coca-Cola) Cup second round second leg

For the second successive season, Second Division (League One) City knocked out Premiership opposition in the Coca-Cola Cup. Everton were the victims this time as the club added another illustrious name to their long list of scalps accumulated over the years. The clubs' first-ever meeting had been at Goodison Park in the first leg the previous week, and City had earned an excellent 1–1 draw with Neil Tolson's goal cancelled out by Andrei Kanchelskis's equaliser.

City were having a moderate season in the League but raised their game again in the second leg and were undaunted after falling behind in the 24th minute. Joe Parkinson's shot was deflected to Paul Rideout, who netted easily from close range. City were level 11 minutes later when, in a move involving Paul Stephenson and Adrian Randall, the ball was flicked home by Neil Tolson. Andy Warrington made a great save just before half-time to deny Anders Limpar, and City withstood early pressure after the break, with Mike Branch shooting inches over the bar. Neil Tolson then went close before City took the lead in the 57th minute. Andy McMillan, who had an outstanding match, played a magnificent cross-field pass to Stephenson, who beat Neville Southall, only to see his shot hit the post, but Gary Bull followed up and prodded the rebound into the net. Shortly afterwards, Tolson again almost scored and the tie reached a terrific climax as the visitors desperately fought back. Twice Kanchelskis went close and Limpar had a shot deflected wide. City survived, and with three minutes remaining Graeme Murty raced on to a long pass from Stephenson, shook off a challenge by Andy Hinchcliffe and knocked the ball past Southall to make it 3–1. Deep in stoppage time, Gary Speed back-heeled a consolation goal for the Toffeemen but City were safely through 4–3 on aggregate.

It had been another glory night for the club, and a fine display of skill and tenacity. Everton manager Joe Royle, although disappointed with his team's display, paid full credit to City. 'They played well, scored three goals and could have had more. They deserved it.'

York City: Warrington, McMillan, Sharples, Barras, Hall, Murty, Pepper, Randall, Stephenson, Tolson, Bull.

Everton: Southall, Hottiger, Barrett, Unsworth, Hinchcliffe, Kanchelskis, Parkinson, Speed, Limpar, Rideout (Branch 46), Stuart.

Attendance: 7,854

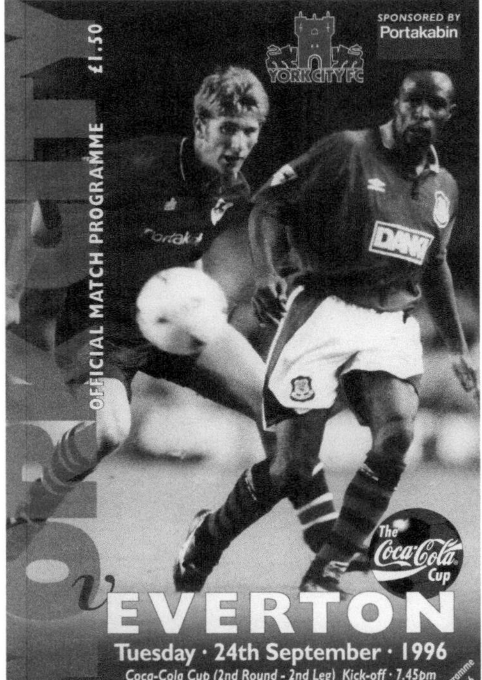

The programme cover for York versus Everton.

Top York City Players

Colin Addison

Although born in the West Country on 18 May 1940, Colin Addison moved to York as a youngster with his family and joined City from local minor League club Cliftonville in 1956. He turned professional the following year and made his debut as a 17-year-old in a Division Three North fixture against Bury on 14 September 1957. The following season the skilful inside-forward established himself in the City side that won promotion from the Fourth Division, and netted 10 goals in 25 League outings. He maintained his progress and in 1960–61 hit a hat-trick in a 4–0 win over Workington and scored a spectacular goal against First Division Blackburn Rovers in the Football League Cup – City's first-ever goal in the competition. He was leading scorer with 16 goals when he was transferred to First Division Nottingham Forest in January 1961 for a then club record fee received of £12,000. He spent five years at Forest and then moved to Arsenal and Sheffield United before joining non-League Hereford United in 1971. As player-manager, Addison guided Hereford to FA Cup glory when they beat Newcastle United and then to election to the Football League. His playing days ended in 1972 and he went on to have a long and varied coaching and managerial career both at home and abroad. The British clubs he managed included Newport County, West Bromwich Albion, Derby County, Scarborough and Swansea City, while overseas he managed Durban City in South Africa, Real Celta and Atletico Madrid in Spain, and coached in Kuwait and Qatar. Colin scored 31 goals in 97 senior appearances for City.

Appearances

	League		FA Cup		League Cup		TOTAL	
SEASON	Apps	Gls	Apps	Gls	Apps	Gls	Apps	Gls
1957–58	8	0	0	0	0	0	8	0
1958–59	25	10	1	0	0	0	26	10
1959–60	31	4	2	1	0	0	33	5
1969–61	23	14	6	1	1	1	30	16
TOTAL	87	28	9	2	1	1	97	31

Paul Aimson

Centre-forward Paul Aimson had two successful spells with the club, figuring prominently in the promotion campaigns of 1964–65 and 1970–71.

The fifth-highest marksman in City's history with 113 League and Cup goals in 248 appearances, he finished top scorer in four of his six seasons at York. He hit a total of five hat-tricks for the club, including a memorable treble at Hull in September 1965. Born in Macclesfield on 3 August 1943, Aimson joined Manchester City as a junior and turned professional in 1960. He made a number of League appearances while at Maine Road before joining City for £1,000 in the summer of 1964. He made his debut on the opening day of the 1964–65 campaign and scored in a win over Rochdale going on to net 30 League and Cup goals in that promotion season. In March 1966 he moved to Bury for £10,000 and after spells at Bradford City and Huddersfield Town returned to Bootham Crescent in August 1969 for a fee of £8,000. In 1970–71 he scored 31 League and Cup goals as City again won promotion from the Fourth Division and also reach the fourth round of the FA Cup. It was at that stage of the competition that Paul scored one of his most famous goals – a last-minute headed equaliser in a 3–3 thriller against First Division Southampton. He finally left the club in March 1973 and moved to Bournemouth, finishing his playing days at Colchester in 1974. In his career he scored 141 League goals, 98 of them for City. Paul Aimson was the complete centre-forward: he could shoot with either foot, was excellent in the air and was a very skilful and intelligent leader of the attack. He died in January 2008, aged 64.

Appearances

	League		FA Cup		League Cup		TOTAL	
SEASON	Apps	Gls	Apps	Gls	Apps	Gls	Apps	Gls
1964–65	45	26	2	4	1	0	48	30
1965–66	32	17	1	1	3	3	36	21
1969–70	29+4	8	5	2	0	0	34+4	10
1970–71	42+1	26	6	5	2	0	50+1	31
1971–72	42+1	16	3	0	4	0	49+1	16
1972–73	20+3	5	0+2	0	0	0	20+5	5
TOTAL	210+9	98	17+2	12	10	3	237+11	113

William (Billy) Allen

Half-back/inside-forward Billy Allen was born near Newcastle upon Tyne on 22 October 1917 and played for Chesterfield prior to joining City in August 1939. He netted both goals in a 2–2 draw at home to Chester on the opening day of the 1939–40 campaign, but a week later the Football League closed down owing to the outbreak of war.

Allen made a number of wartime appearances for City but his official League debut was not until 31 August 1946, when peacetime football resumed. Chester again provided the opposition and Billy was again on target in a 4–4 draw. For the first four post-war seasons Allen was a regular and consistent performer, mostly in midfield, and scored 24 goals in 136 League and Cup games for the club. He moved to Scunthorpe United in the summer of 1950 and figured in their first two seasons in the Football League. Billy died in 1981.

Appearances

	League		FA Cup		TOTAL	
SEASON	Apps	Gls	Apps	Gls	Apps	Gls
1945–46	0	0	1	1	1	1
1946–47	33	13	1	0	34	13
1947–48	29	4	1	0	30	4
1948–49	33	3	3	0	36	3
1949–50	35	3	0	0	35	3
TOTAL	130	23	6	1	136	24

Percy Andrews

Equally at home at either right-back or centre-half, Percy Andrews gave City 11 years' outstanding service in the 1940s and 1950s. Born in Alton, Hampshire, on 12 June 1922, Andrews was on Portsmouth's books as an amateur. He joined the Royal Signals at the age of 16 and had a distinguished army career. During the war he captained the British Army team and won several wartime football medals. He joined City at the

start of the 1947–48 season and made his debut in a 1–1 draw at Carlisle United on 4 September 1947. For a number of seasons he was a key member of City's defence with his determined and fearless play and was an ever present in 1952–53 and 1953–54. His first-team days ended following an injury in a game at Gateshead in October 1954 but he continued to play for the second and third teams for the next four years, helping and encouraging the younger players until his retirement in 1958. Percy made a total of 181 League and Cup appearances for the club and in May 1957 was rewarded with a testimonial match against an All Stars XI in front of a crowd of 7,000 at Bootham Crescent. He died at Pocklington in February 1985, aged 62.

Appearances

	League		FA Cup		TOTAL	
SEASON	Apps	Gls	Apps	Gls	Apps	Gls
1947–48	1	0	0	0	1	0
1948–49	5	0	0	0	5	0
1949–50	27	0	0	0	27	0
1950–51	21	0	3	0	24	0
1951–52	26	0	0	0	26	0
1952–53	46	0	1	0	47	0
1953–54	46	0	1	0	47	0
1954–55	4	0	0	0	4	0
TOTAL	176	0	5	0	181	0

Paul Atkin

Utility player Paul Atkin served City well in both defence and midfield in his six seasons with the club.

Born in Nottingham on 3 September 1969, he played for England Schoolboys Under-16s and Under-17s and spent two years at the FA's School of Excellence. He turned professional for Notts County in 1987 and made his League debut for Bury before joining City in the summer of 1991. He made 31 League appearances in the promotion season of 1992–93 and played against Crewe Alexandra in the Play-off Final at Wembley. A quietly efficient and thoughtful player, Atkin was a key member of the first-team squad throughout his time at York and captained the side on a number of occasions. Paul made 179 senior appearances for the club and scored three goals, two of them in a win over Crewe Alexandra in November 1992. After a spell on loan at Leyton Orient in 1996–97, he left City in June 1997 and finished his League days with Scarborough.

Appearances

	League		Play-offs		FA Cup		League Cup		Others		TOTAL	
SEASON	Apps	Gls	Apps	Gls	Apps	Gls	Apps	Gls	Apps	Gls	Apps	Gls
1991–92	29+4	1	0	0	3	0	1+1	0	1	0	34+5	1
1992–93	28+3	2	3	0	1	0	0	0	2	0	34+3	2
1993–94	13+1	0	0	0	0	0	2	0	1	0	16+1	0
1994–95	30+4	0	0	0	2	0	0	0	1+1	0	33+5	0
1995–96	25+4	0	0	0	0	0	1+3	0	2	0	28+7	0
1996–97	6+6	0	0	0	0	0	1	0	0	0	7+6	0
TOTAL	131+22	3	3	0	6	0	5+4	0	7+1	0	152+27	3

Reg Baines

Local lad Reg Baines was City's scoring hero in the 1930s and figured prominently in the 1937–38 FA Cup run. Born in York on 3 June 1907, he had a brief period with the club in the mid-1920s in the Midland League before having spells with Scarborough and Selby Town. He returned to City in September 1931 and scored on his Football League debut on 3 October 1931, in a home game against Carlisle United. He went on to net 29 League goals that campaign, a feat he emulated in 1932–33. This seasonal tally remained a City record in the Football League until 1951–52, when Billy Fenton notched 31 goals. In May 1933 Baines moved to Sheffield United for a fee of £500 and the following season moved to Doncaster, helping Rovers win promotion to Division Two in 1934–35. He returned to Bootham Crescent for his third spell with the club in the summer of 1937. Once again he proved a prolific marksman, and the highlight was a hat-trick in a sensational 3–2 win over First Division West Bromwich Albion in the fourth round of the FA Cup. An old-fashioned, bustling centre-forward, Reg hit a total of eight League and Cup hat-tricks for City – a club record. In 140 senior appearances he scored 93 goals and is the eighth-highest-scoring marksman in City's history. In May 1938 he was transferred to Barnsley and joined Halifax Town just prior to the outbreak of war. A part-time player, he worked for the confectionery company Rowntrees for over 50 years and was a very good local cricketer. Reg died suddenly while on holiday in Israel in 1974, aged 67.

Appearances

	League		FA Cup		TOTAL	
SEASON	Apps	Gls	Apps	Gls	Apps	Gls
1924–25*	9	1	0	0	9	1
1925–26*	10	6	0	0	10	6
1931–32	32	29	1	0	33	29
1932–33	39	29	1	0	40	29
1937–38	39	23	9	5	48	28
TOTAL	129	88	11	5	140	93

* Midland League

Gerry Baker

Born on 16 September 1938, Gerry Baker had been on the books of Bolton Wanderers, Nottingham Forest and his home-town club Wigan Athletic but did not make his Football League debut until joining City. Signed in the summer of 1963, he played his first game for the club at Tranmere Rovers in Division Four on 26 August 1963 and until injury cut short his career in 1969 was a virtual ever present. Baker was a strong-tackling and consistent right-back, and he also made a number of appearances at centre-forward with

some degree of success. He played a big part in the promotion-winning campaign of 1964–65 and in October 1969 was awarded a testimonial game against the 1954–55 FA Cup semi-final side. An excellent servant to the club, he made 234 senior appearances and scored nine goals.

Appearances

	League		FA Cup		League Cup		TOTAL	
SEASON	Apps	Gls	Apps	Gls	Apps	Gls	Apps	Gls
1963–64	33	5	1	0	4	1	38	6
1964–65	41	1	2	0	0	0	43	1
1965–66	43	0	1	0	3	0	47	0
1966–67	40	0	4	0	2	0	46	0
1967–68	41	1	1	0	0	0	42	1
1968–69	16	0	2	1	0	0	18	1
TOTAL	214	7	11	1	9	1	234	9

Dale Banton

Striker Dale Banton was signed for a then club record fee paid of £50,000 in November 1984 following the departure of John Byrne. Born in Kensington, London, on 15 May 1961, Banton served his apprenticeship with West Ham United and made a number of senior appearances for the Hammers before moving to Aldershot in 1982. In his first season with the Hampshire club he was the leading marksman in Division Four with 28 goals. He scored on his City debut in a Third Division (League One) game at Lincoln on 24 November 1984 and for the next four years was a regular in City's attack, impressing with his skilful play and finishing ability. In his first full season at York he struck up a good partnership with Keith Walwyn and was a key figure as the club reached the fifth round of the FA Cup. In 1987–88 he was top marksman with 18 League and Cup goals and was voted Clubman of the Year. Banton moved to Walsall in October 1988 for £80,000 after scoring 55 goals in 173 appearances for City. Dale finished his Football League days back at Aldershot before joining non-League Goole Town as player-manager in 1991. He scored exactly 100 League goals in his career.

Appearances

	League		FA Cup		League Cup		Others		TOTAL	
SEASON	Apps	Gls	Apps	Gls	Apps	Gls	Apps	Gls	Apps	Gls
1984–85	29+1	12	0	0	0	0	4	1	33+1	13
1985–86	33+2	11	7	1	3	1	2	0	45+2	13
1986–87	24+5	6	3	1	4	0	0	0	31+5	7
1987–88	32+1	16	4	1	4	0	2	1	42+1	18
1988–89	11	4	0	0	2	0	0	0	13	4
TOTAL	129+9	49	14	3	13	1	8	2	164+9	55

Paul Barnes

In July 1992 Paul Barnes became the then joint record City signing when manager John Ward paid £50,000 to bring him from Stoke City. Born in Leicester on 16 November 1967, he began his career as an apprentice at Notts County and turned professional in 1985. He made over 50 League appearances for County before his move to Stoke in 1990. Barnes scored on his City debut on the opening day of the 1992–93 season in Division Three (League Two) against Shrewsbury Town (15 August) and quickly made an impact with his neat control and finishing. He scored 21 goals as the club went on to win promotion, and he became the first City player in over 30 years to net four times in a game when Scunthorpe United were beaten 5–1 in March 1993. He also netted a hat-trick in a 5–1 victory at Barnet later that month, and in City's penalty shoot-out win over Crewe Alexandra at Wembley he converted one of the spot-kicks. As City reached the Second Division (League One) Play-offs the following year, Barnes was again top marksman with a tally of 24 goals and was Clubman of the Year. In September 1995 Paul hit the national headlines when he scored twice in City's sensational 3–0 win at Old Trafford against Manchester United. Later that term he moved to Birmingham City in March 1996 for a reported fee of £350,000. Barnes made 179 senior appearances for York City and netted 85 goals. He was the leading marksman in each of his four seasons, netted a total of four hat-tricks and is the 10th-

highest-scoring player in the club's history. Barnes later played for Burnley, Huddersfield Town and Bury and top scored for Doncaster Rovers when they won promotion from the Conference in 2002–03. In his Football League career he scored 140 goals in 397 games.

Appearances

	League		Play-offs		FA Cup		League Cup		Others		TOTAL	
SEASON	Apps	Gls	Apps	Gls	Apps	Gls	Apps	Gls	Apps	Gls	Apps	Gls
1992–93	40	21	3	0	1	0	2	0	1	0	47	21
1993–94	42	24	2	0	1	0	1	0	3	1	49	25
1994–95	35+1	16	0	0	2	0	2	0	2	1	41+1	17
1995–96	30	15	0	0	1	0	5	5	5	2	41	22
TOTAL	147+1	76	5	0	5	0	10	5	11	4	178+1	85

Tony Barras

A central-defender, Tony Barras joined City from Stockport County in the summer of 1994 and in almost five seasons at Bootham Crescent was a virtual ever present at the heart of the defence. Born in Stockton-on-Tees on 29 March 1971, he started his League career at Hartlepool United

before moving to Edgeley Park in 1990. A sound defender and very strong in the air, he made his City debut in a Football League Cup tie at Burnley on 16 August 1994 and quickly established himself in the side. Tony was a very consistent and reliable player, and he was Clubman of the Year for 1996–97. Barras also scored a number of goals for the club, the most notable being his header in the famous win at Old Trafford in September 1995. After over 200 senior appearances and 15 goals for City, he was transferred to Reading in March 1999 and later played for Walsall and Notts County before ending his League days at Macclesfield in 2005.

Appearances

	League		FA Cup		League Cup		Others		TOTAL	
SEASON	Apps	Gls	Apps	Gls	Apps	Gls	Apps	Gls	Apps	Gls
1994–95	27+4	1	2	0	2	0	2	0	33+4	1
1995–96	32	3	1	0	5	1	3+1	1	41+1	5
1996–97	46	1	4	1	5	0	2	0	57	2
1997–98	38	6	2	0	4	1	0	0	44	7
1998–99	24	0	1	0	0	0	1	0	26	0
TOTAL	167+4	11	10	1	16	2	8+1	1	201+5	15

Walter Bingley

In his three seasons with City, right-back Walter Bingley was a model of consistency and missed just six games. Born in Sheffield on 17 April 1930, he started his League career at Bolton Wanderers in 1949–50 and made a handful of First Division

appearances for the Trotters before moving to Sheffield Wednesday in 1955. He was transferred to Swindon Town in 1958 and for two seasons was a regular in their defence before his move to Bootham Crescent in the summer of 1960. His debut for City was on the opening day of the 1960–61 campaign (22 August) at home to Millwall in Division Four, and he became a fixture in the defence with his solid and reliable play. In 1961–62 he helped the club reach the quarter-finals of the Football League Cup. The following season Walter took over the role of penalty taker and in a 15-match spell converted five spot-kicks out of six in typical no-nonsense style. In 1963 Bingley moved to Halifax Town, where he spent his last two seasons in the Football League. In total he made 339 League appearances, 130 of which were at York.

Appearances

	League		FA Cup		League Cup		TOTAL	
SEASON	Apps	Gls	Apps	Gls	Apps	Gls	Apps	Gls
1960–61	44	0	6	0	1	0	51	0
1961–62	44	0	1	0	7	0	52	0
1962–63	42	5	4	0	2	0	48	5
TOTAL	130	5	11	0	10	0	151	5

Ian Blackstone

Born in Harrogate on 7 August 1964, Ian Blackstone was signed by City from non-League Harrogate Town in September 1991 as a part-time professional, and made his debut on 2 October

1990 at Chesterfield in a Division Four fixture. He notched a hat-trick in a 4–0 win at Wrexham in December that term and in March 1991 became a full professional. Playing either up front or wide left, Blackie soon proved popular with the fans. He scored twice in an FA Cup win at Bridlington in November 1991 and played a big part in City's promotion-winning campaign of 1992–93, when he finished second-top scorer with 16 goals and figured in the club's Wembley success. The following season he helped the club reach the Second Division (League One) promotion Play-offs but was released in the summer of 1994. Blackstone moved to Scarborough after scoring 42 goals in 148 senior appearances for York City, including five Play-off games. He later had a spell playing in Hong Kong before returning to play in non-League football.

Appearances

	League		Play-offs		FA Cup		League Cup		Others		TOTAL	
SEASON	Apps	Gls	Apps	Gls	Apps	Gls	Apps	Gls	Apps	Gls	Apps	Gls
1990–91	20+8	6	0	0	0	0	0	0	2	2	22+8	8
1991–92	26+4	8	0	0	3	2	2	1	1	0	32+4	11
1992–93	37+2	16	3	0	0	0	1+1	0	2	0	43+3	16
1993–94	24+8	7	2	0	0+1	0	0	0	1	0	27+9	7
TOTAL	107+22	37	5	0	3+1	2	3+1	1	6	2	124+24	42

Arthur Bottom

One of City's all-time scoring heroes, Arthur Bottom was without doubt one of the best marksmen in the club's history. He netted a hat-

trick on his debut in a 6–2 win at Wrexham on the opening day of the 1954–55 campaign and equalled the club scoring record of 31 goals in the Football League in his first season. In total that season he scored 39 times, which included eight goals in the club's run to the FA Cup semi-finals. In that memorable campaign he notched a hat-trick at Dorchester, two goals at Bishop Auckland, the winner at Notts County in round six and the equaliser against Newcastle United at Hillsborough. In 1955–56 he again totalled 31 League goals, and the following season claimed his best tally in one game when he scored four goals in a 9–1 win over Southport in February 1957. Born in Sheffield on 28 February 1930, Bottom joined Sheffield United as a junior and turned professional in 1947. He made a number of senior appearances for the Blades before joining City in the summer of 1954. In total he scored 105 goals in 158 League and FA Cup games and is sixth in City's all-time scoring list. Arthur thrilled the Bootham Crescent crowds in the mid-1950s with his explosive finishing and aggressive style. A sometimes controversial figure on the field, he was quiet and retiring off it. Truly a City legend, his name lives on in the club's worldwide electronic newsletter, which is entitled 'There's Only One Arthur Bottom'. Bottom was transferred to Newcastle United in February 1958 and scored 10 goals in 11 matches to save the Magpies from relegation to Division Two. He later played for Chesterfield and finished his playing days with non-League Alfreton Town.

Appearances

	League		FA Cup		TOTAL	
SEASON	Apps	Gls	Apps	Gls	Apps	Gls
1954–55	38	31	8	8	46	39
1955–56	43	31	5	2	48	33
1956–57	37	21	3	1	40	22
1957–58	19	9	5	2	24	11
TOTAL	137	92	21	13	158	105

Philip Boyer

One of the most talented and skilful players in the club's history, Phil Boyer was signed from Derby County by manager Joe Shaw for a fee of £3,000 in July 1968 and made his debut on the opening day of the 1968–69 campaign at Chester (10 August) in Division Four. A most exciting and lively player

with good ball skills, the forward quickly proved a favourite with fans and struck up an effective partnership with Ted MacDougall (this combination was to continue when the players met up again at Bournemouth, Norwich City and Southampton in the 1970s). Phil was a virtual ever present in his time with City and had scored 34 goals in 126 senior appearances by the time he moved to Bournemouth in December 1970 for a then club record fee received of £20,000. Boyer was born on 25 January 1949 in Nottingham and later played for Norwich, Southampton and Manchester City. In his career he made a total of 520 Football League appearances, scored 159 goals and was capped for England in 1976.

Appearances

	League		FA Cup		League Cup		TOTAL	
SEASON	Apps	Gls	Apps	Gls	Apps	Gls	Apps	Gls
1968–69	46	9	3	0	1	0	50	9
1969–70	40+1	9	6	3	0	0	46+1	12
1970–71	22	9	3	1	4	3	29	13
TOTAL	108+1	27	12	4	5	3	125+1	34

Christopher Brass

Chris Brass joined City from Burnley in March 2001 after spending seven seasons with the Turf Moor club. A very keen and enthusiastic player, equally at home in defence or midfield, he quickly settled at the club and over the next three years was a virtual ever present. Appointed captain, he proved very popular with the fans for his leadership and energetic style of play and in 2002–03 was voted Clubman of the Year. By the following season he had become player-manager (see York City Managers) but in May 2004 the club dropped out of the Football League. In November that year he was relieved of his managerial duties as the club struggled in the Conference, but he continued as a player. A serious injury, however, in December 2004 ended his first team playing days and he later left the club. After spells with Harrogate Town and Southport he resumed his League career with Bury.

Appearances

	League		FA Cup		League Cup		Others		TOTAL	
SEASON	Apps	Gls	Apps	Gls	Apps	Gls	Apps	Gls	Apps	Gls
2000–01	8+2	1	0	0	0	0	0	0	8+2	1
2001–02	41	2	5	1	1	1	1	0	48	4
2002–03	40	1	2	0	1	0	0+1	0	43+1	1
2003–04	39	1	1	0	1	0	0	0	41	1
2004–05*	20+2	1	1	0	0	0	0	0	21+2	1
TOTAL	148+4	6	9	1	3	1	1+1	0	161+5	8

* Conference

Albert (Bert) Brenen

One of the most versatile players to appear for the club, Bert Brenen's career with City spanned 13 years (1938–1951). Born in South Shields on 5 October 1915, he was a student at St John's College in York when he was signed by City boss Tom Mitchell in August 1938. He scored on his League debut at home to Chester on 4 March 1939 and kept his place in the closing weeks of that last season before the war. During the war years he made 127 appearances for the club and

scored 51 goals. In the five seasons after hostilities ended Bert was a virtual ever present and captained the side on a number of occasions. Although his best place was at right-half, he could boast that he played in every position for the club, including keeping goal in a wartime fixture. He was rewarded for his outstanding service to the club with a testimonial match against Leeds United in May 1951. In total he made 218 League and Cup appearances and scored 15 goals, and throughout his time at Bootham Crescent he was a part-time player, being a schoolmaster by profession. In 1951 Brenen joined Scarborough, where he spent four seasons before hanging his boots up. He went on to manage Goole Town and then had a spell coaching City's intermediate and junior sides. In later years he commentated on City games for York Hospital Radio and died in February 1995, aged 79.

Appearances

	League		FA Cup		TOTAL	
SEASON	Apps	Gls	Apps	Gls	Apps	Gls
1938–39	12	5	0	0	12	5
1945–46	0	0	5	1	5	1
1946–47	36	1	1	0	37	1
1947–48	41	2	1	0	42	2
1948–49	38	1	3	0	41	1
1949–50	41	1	1	0	42	1
1950–51	36	3	3	1	39	4
TOTAL	204	13	14	2	218	15

Gordon Brown

One of City's stalwarts and heroes of the 1950s, Gordon Brown was signed from Nottingham Forest in June 1950. Born on 21 March 1929 at Warsop, Nottinghamshire, he had spent four years with Forest but had been unable to claim a place in the first team. Initially an inside-forward, he scored in his first game for City at Tranmere Rovers in Division Three North on 19 August 1950, a match which was lost 7–2. He quickly established himself in the side, and for eight seasons he was a first-team regular, later switching to right-half. His fine attacking style and consistency was a vital cog in City's midfield, and Gordon starred in the FA Cup run of 1954–55 and figured in all the club's FA Cup triumphs of the 1950s. A part-time player while with the club, he worked as a storeman near his home in Mansfield. In total he played in 351 League and Cup games and scored 25 goals. After

leaving Bootham Crescent in May 1958, Brown played for non-League Sutton United and then Shirebrook Miners' Welfare.

Appearances

	League		FA Cup		TOTAL	
SEASON	Apps	Gls	Apps	Gls	Apps	Gls
1950–51	31	8	3	0	34	8
1951–52	42	4	3	0	45	4
1952–53	45	1	1	0	46	1
1953–54	43	1	1	0	44	1
1954–55	44	5	8	0	52	5
1955–56	42	2	5	0	47	2
1956–57	43	3	3	0	46	3
1957–58	32	1	5	0	37	1
TOTAL	322	25	29	0	351	25

Lee Bullock

Born in Stockton-on-Tees on 22 May 1981, Lee Bullock joined City as a youngster and developed through the club's junior ranks. He made his senior debut in an FA Cup tie at Wrexham in December 1998, aged 17. He turned professional in the summer of 1999 and in 1999–2000 made gradual progress. Lee established himself in the first team the following campaign and for four seasons was a regular in City's midfield, impressing with his attacking skills, vision and creativity. He also netted 27 goals and made 189 League and Cup appearances for City. In March 2004 Bullock moved to Cardiff City on loan and in the summer was signed by the Welsh club for a fee of £100,000.

He later played for Hartlepool United and Bradford City.

Appearances

	League		FA Cup		League Cup		Others		TOTAL	
SEASON	Apps	Gls	Apps	Gls	Apps	Gls	Apps	Gls	Apps	Gls
1998–99	0	0	1	0	0	0	0	0	1	0
1999–2000	16+8	0	0	0	1	0	0	0	17+8	0
2000–01	29+4	3	1+1	1	1+1	0	0	0	31+6	4
2001–02	39+1	8	5+1	0	1	1	0	0	45+2	9
2002–03	38+1	6	2	1	1	0	0	0	41+1	7
2003–04	34+1	7	1	0	1	0	0	0	36+1	7
TOTAL	156+15	24	10+2	2	5+1	1	0	0	171+18	27

Phil Burrows

Left-back Phil Burrows gave the club outstanding service in his eight seasons at Bootham Crescent. Fast and skilful and a good passer of the ball, he was also a strong tackler. He made his City debut on the opening day of the 1966–67 campaign at home to Chesterfield (20 August 1966) in the Fourth Division and immediately established himself in the side, initially at left-half. Born in Stockport on 8 April 1946, he joined Manchester City as a youngster and turned professional in 1962 but was unable to break into the first team at Maine Road. He was signed by City manager Tom Lockie in June 1966 and played a big part in the promotion seasons of 1970–71 and 1973–74, which saw the club rise from the Fourth to the Second Division. He was an ever present in his last five seasons with the club and, ever popular with the fans, was voted City's first-ever Clubman of the Year. He received the newly instituted trophy on the day promotion to Division Two was clinched in April 1974. He was not to play for City in the second tier, however, as in July 1974 he was transferred to Plymouth Argyle for £20,000, helping the Pilgrims win promotion from Division Three in his first season at Home Park. He later played for Hereford United before finishing his playing days with non-League Witton Albion. Burrows made a total of 390 League and Cup appearances for the club and was one of the most consistent and reliable players in City's history.

Appearances

	League		FA Cup		League Cup		TOTAL	
SEASON	Apps	Gls	Apps	Gls	Apps	Gls	Apps	Gls
1966–67	32+1	2	6	0	4	0	42+1	2
1967–68	32+2	2	1	0	1	0	34+2	2
1968–69	40	1	3	0	1	0	44	1
1969–70	45+1	1	7	0	1	0	53+1	1
1970–71	46	1	6	0	4	0	56	1
1971–72	46	3	3	0	4	0	53	3
1972–73	46	1	3	1	1	0	50	2
1973–74	46	3	2	0	6	0	54	3
TOTAL	333+4	14	31	1	22	0	386+4	15

Stephen Bushell

Steve Bushell was born in Manchester on 28 December 1972 and came through the club's youth system before turning professional in February 1991 and making his Football League debut that month as a substitute in a Fourth Division game at Northampton. The hard-working midfielder played a handful of games in the 1992–93 promotion season but established himself in the senior side the following campaign as the club reached the Second Division promotion Play-offs. Injuries curtailed his appearances over the following two seasons, but he fought back to claim his first-team place and again took the eye with his combative play and passing skills. In 1997–98 he was Clubman of the Year but in the summer of 1998 moved to Blackpool after playing in over 200 League and Cup games for the club. He later played for Halifax Town.

Appearances

	League		Play-offs		FA Cup		League Cup		Others		TOTAL	
SEASON	Apps	Gls	Apps	Gls	Apps	Gls	Apps	Gls	Apps	Gls	Apps	Gls
1990–91	10+5	0	0	0	0	0	0	0	0	0	10+5	0
1991–92	15+1	0	0	0	0	0	0	0	0	0	15+1	0
1992–93	8	0	0	0	0	0	0	0	2	0	10	0
1993–94	30+1	4	2	0	2	0	0	0	2	1	36+1	5
1994–95	10	1	0	0	0	0	2	0	0	0	12	1
1995–96	17+6	0	0	0	0	0	1	0	3+2	0	21+8	0
1996–97	26+5	3	0	0	1	0	1+1	1	1	0	29+6	4
1997–98	40	3	0	0	2	0	4	1	1	0	47	4
TOTAL	156+18	11	2	0	5	0	8+1	2	9+2	1	180+21	14

John Byrne

One of the most talented and skilful players to appear for the club, John Byrne joined City as an apprentice in July 1977 after being recommended to City boss Wilf McGuinness by a taxi driver, who had spotted John playing in a Manchester park. Born in Manchester on 1 February 1961, he turned professional aged 18 and made his senior debut on 25 August 1979 in a Division Four fixture against Lincoln City. A naturally gifted forward, John developed gradually and the following campaign established himself in City's attack. Under the guidance of coach Viv Busby in 1982 his shooting skills improved, and in the Fourth Division Championship campaign of 1983–84 he was top scorer with 27 goals and was voted Top Fourth Division Player of the Season in the *Sunday People*/Bukta Merit Awards. He netted two hat-tricks that season in home games against Chester and Halifax Town and struck up a fine partnership up front with Keith Walwyn. He made a total of 199 League and Cup appearances for the club and scored 64 goals prior to his transfer to First Division Queen's Park Rangers in October 1984 for £100,000. He appeared in the 1986 Football League Cup Final for the London club and later played in France for Le Havre and then Brighton,

Sunderland (for whom he played in the 1992 FA Cup Final) Millwall and Oxford United. Byrne was capped 23 times for the Republic of Ireland, the country of his father's birth, and was a member of their World Cup squad in 1990. In his Football League career he played in 503 games and scored 134 goals.

Appearances

	League		FA Cup		League Cup		Others		TOTAL	
SEASON	Apps	Gls	Apps	Gls	Apps	Gls	Apps	Gls	Apps	Gls
1979–80	5+4	2	1+1	1	0	0	0	0	6+5	3
1980–81	36+2	6	2	1	0+2	0	0	0	38+4	7
1981–82	28+1	6	0	0	2	1	0	0	30+1	7
1982–83	42+1	12	4	1	2	1	0	0	48+1	14
1983–84	46	27	3	1	2	0	1	0	52	28
1984–85	10	2	0	0	4	3	0	0	14	5
TOTAL	167+8	55	10+1	4	10+2	5	1	0	188+11	64

Anthony (Tony) Canham

One of the most popular players to wear City's colours, Tony Canham did not turn professional until he was 25. Born in Leeds on 8 June 1960, he played for Harrogate Railway and joined the club as a non-contract amateur early in 1985. He made his debut in a Freight Rover Trophy game in January that year and his Football League debut on 2 March 1985 against Brentford, when he netted the winner in a Third Division (League One) encounter. He turned professional that summer and for the next 10 seasons was a regular in the City side, chiefly operating down the left wing. He quickly proved a favourite with the fans thanks to his exciting dribbling skills and finishing. In his first full season he was second-top scorer with 14 goals, including a hat-trick in a 7–0 win over Darlington. That term he also figured in the club's FA Cup run and netted City's equaliser at Anfield in a fifth-round replay, which took the game into extra-time against Liverpool. The following season he scored the winner against Chelsea in the first leg of a Football League Cup second-round game. Canham played an important part in the promotion-winning season of 1992–93, scoring one of the penalties in the shoot-out against Crewe Alexandra at Wembley, and also helped the team reach the Second Division (League One) Play-offs the following campaign. In 1994–95 Tony was awarded a testimonial season, culminating in a game against Sunderland. He played in a total of 413 League and Cup games for the club and scored 70 goals, putting him seventh in City's all-time list for appearances and making him 11th-top marksman. In the summer of 1995 he moved to Hartlepool United and finished his playing days with former club Harrogate Railway.

Appearances:

	League		Play-offs		FA Cup		League Cup		Other		TOTAL	
SEASON	Apps	Gls	Apps	Gls	Apps	Gls	Apps	Gls	Apps	Gls	Apps	Gls
1984–85	3	1	0	0	0	0	0	0	1+1	0	4+1	1
1985–86	40+1	13	0	0	5	1	4	0	2	0	51+1	14
1986–87	36+2	9	0	0	3	1	4	1	2+1	1	45+3	12
1987–88	13+5	2	0	0	0	0	2	0	0	0	15+5	2
1988–89	40+1	9	0	0	1	0	0	0	3	1	44+1	10
1989–90	28+6	3	0	0	1	0	0	0	3	2	32+6	5
1990–91	39+2	6	0	0	3	2	1	0	3	0	46+2	8
1991–92	28+3	5	0	0	2	0	2	1	2	0	34+3	6
1992–93	16+13	4	3	0	1	1	1	0	0+1	1	21+14	6
1993–94	36	3	2	0	2	1	2	0	1+1	0	43+1	4
1994–95	30+5	2	0	0	2	0	2	0	2	0	36+5	2
TOTAL	309+38	57	5	0	20	6	18	2	19+4	5	371+42	70

Michael Cave

Micky Cave became City's then record signing when he moved to Bootham Crescent from Bournemouth in August 1974 for a fee of £18,000. He made his debut for the club on the opening day of City's first ever season in Division Two (Championship) against Aston Villa on 17 August 1974. Born in Weymouth on 28 January 1947, Micky played for his home-town club in non-

League football before joining Torquay United in 1968 and then Bournemouth three years later. A talented midfielder with good passing skills, Micky was very popular in his time at York and was voted Clubman of the Year in 1975–76, when he finished top scorer with eight goals. He totalled 109 senior appearances for City, most of them in the Second Division, before rejoining Bournemouth in February 1977. Cave moved to America in the late 1970s and played in Seattle and Los Angeles before taking a coaching appointment in Pittsburgh, where he died from accidental carbon monoxide poisoning in November 1985, aged 38.

Appearances

	League		FA Cup		League Cup		TOTAL	
SEASON	Apps	Gls	Apps	Gls	Apps	Gls	Apps	Gls
1974–75	39	1	0	0	1	0	40	1
1975–76	32+2	8	1	0	3	0	36+2	8
1976–77	23	4	5	2	3	0	31	6
TOTAL	94+2	13	6	2	7	0	107+2	15

Malcolm Comrie

One of City's stars of the 1930s, Malcolm Comrie was a typical Scottish ball-playing inside-forward, whose skilful performances were a big factor in the club's FA Cup exploits of 1936–37 and 1937–38. He was born in Denny, near Falkirk, and after

playing in junior football and winning Scottish junior international caps, he signed for Brentford. He later moved to Manchester City (where he made First Division appearances), Burnley and Crystal Palace before joining City in the summer of 1936. Malcolm made his debut against Halifax Town on 29 August 1936 and in his two seasons at York was a key player in City's attack. During this time he played in 16 FA Cup ties, helping the club reach the fourth round and quarter-finals. He moved to Bradford City in 1938 and later returned to Bootham Crescent when he became steward of the social club at the ground.

Appearances

	League		FA Cup		Others		TOTAL	
SEASON	Apps	Gls	Apps	Gls	Apps	Gls	Apps	Gls
1936–37	42	8	7	2	3	1	52	11
1937–38	37	12	9	1	0	0	46	13
TOTAL	79	20	16	3	3	1	98	24

James Cowie

The Scottish centre-forward was a prolific scorer for the club in the late 1920s and early 1930s, and in City's last season in the Midland League (1928–29) he netted a remarkable 56 goals in 56 games. Born in Keith on 8 June 1904 Jimmy played for his home-town club before joining Raith Rovers in 1926. He was signed by City boss Jock Collier in August 1928, making his debut that

month in a home game against Shirebrook. The stocky forward's scoring feats in his first season at York were phenomenal. He hit six goals in a game twice – against Worksop in the League and Stockton in the FA Cup – plus five against Hull City reserves and two tallies of four goals. The regular cry from the terraces was 'Give it to Cowie' and in one spell he hit 17 goals in seven games. At the end of that season he played for the Rest of the Midland League against champions Mansfield Town. Jimmy scored in City's opening game in the Football League in August 1929, a 2–0 win at Wigan Borough, but over the next two seasons was unable to repeat the sensations of 1928–29. He did record a League hat-trick in a win over Hartlepools United in February 1931 but at the end of that season left the club and returned to play for Keith, where he played in the same side as two of his sons. Cowie died in October 1964.

Appearances

	League		FA Cup		TOTAL	
SEASON	Apps	Gls	Apps	Gls	Apps	Gls
1928–29*	49	49	7	7	56	56
1929–30	14	4	3	1	17	5
1930–31	4	5	0	0	4	5
TOTAL	67	58	10	8	77	66

*Midland League

Graeme Crawford

One of the outstanding goalkeepers in the club's history, Graeme Crawford was born in Falkirk on 7 August 1947. He started his career with East Stirling and moved to Sheffield United in 1969. His first-team opportunities were limited at Bramall Lane and he joined City in October 1971, initially on loan. He made his debut for the club on 5 November 1971 in a Division Three (League One) fixture at Tranmere Rovers and for the next five and a half seasons was first choice 'keeper. During the promotion-winning campaign of 1973–74 Graeme kept a clean sheet in 11 successive games, equalling a Football League record that had been set by Millwall in the 1920s, and he played in every game in City's two seasons in Division Two (now the Championship). In July 1977 Crawford moved to Scunthorpe United, but in January 1980 he returned to Bootham Crescent in a player-exchange deal involving Joe Neenan. His second spell was only brief and in September 1980 he moved to Rochdale, where he spent three seasons. He finished his playing days at Scarborough but in an emergency came out of retirement to play for Goole Town in the FA Cup at the age of 42.

Appearances

	League		FA Cup		League Cup		TOTAL	
SEASON	Apps	Gls	Apps	Gls	Apps	Gls	Apps	Gls
1971–72	28	0	0	0	0	0	28	0
1972–73	42	0	3	0	1	0	46	0
1973–74	43	0	2	0	6	0	51	0
1974–75	42	0	2	0	1	0	45	0
1975–76	42	0	2	0	3	0	47	0
1976–77	38	0	5	0	3	0	46	0
1979–80	17	0	0	0	0	0	17	0
TOTAL	252	0	14	0	14	0	280	0

Richard Cresswell

Born in Bridlington on 20 September 1977, Richard Cresswell developed through the club's productive youth system in the 1990s and made his senior debut as a substitute on 20 January 1996 in a Second Division (League One) game at Brentford. The talented centre-forward with good all-round skills was gradually nursed into the first team and by 1998–99 had fully established himself at League level. Richard hit 19 goals that season and attracted a lot of attention with a number of outstanding displays. In February 1999 he became the first City player to win representative honours for England when he was capped for the Under-21s against France. The following month he was transferred to Premiership club Sheffield Wednesday for a record club fee received of £950,000. Cresswell later played for Leicester City, Preston North End, Leeds United and Stoke City.

Appearances

	League		FA Cup		League Cup		Others		TOTAL	
SEASON	Apps	Gls	Apps	Gls	Apps	Gls	Apps	Gls	Apps	Gls
1995–96	9+7	1	0	0	0	0	1	0	10+7	1
1996–97	9+8	0	0+1	0	1+2	0	1	0	11+11	0
1997–98	18+8	4	1+1	0	0+1	0	1	0	20+10	4
1998–99	36	16	3	3	2	0	1	0	42	19
TOTAL	72+23	21	4+2	3	3+3	0	4	0	83+28	24

Malcolm Crosby

Malcolm joined City in an exchange deal with Aldershot that took Ian McDonald to the Recreation Ground in November 1981, and he made his debut that month in a Fourth Division game at Scunthorpe United. Born in South Shields on 4 July 1954, Malcolm Crosby joined Aldershot as an apprentice, turned professional in 1972 and made nearly 300 League appearances for the Shots. An industrious midfielder and likeable character, Malcolm quickly settled in at York and played his part in the Fourth Division Championship-winning side of 1983–84. In the latter part of his time with the club he helped with the coaching of the juniors, and in August 1986 he left to take up a coaching appointment in Kuwait. He returned to join the backroom staff at Sunderland, where he teamed up again with his former York colleagues Denis Smith and Viv Busby. Crosby later took over the managerial reins at Roker Park and led the club to the 1992 FA Cup Final against Liverpool, and he was later assistant boss to Smith at Oxford United. He went on to take coaching roles at West Bromwich Albion, Derby County, Swindon Town and Middlesbrough.

Appearances

	League		FA Cup		League Cup		Others		TOTAL	
SEASON	Apps	Gls	Apps	Gls	Apps	Gls	Apps	Gls	Apps	Gls
1981–82	19+4	2	3	0	0	0	0	0	22+4	2
1982–83	38	2	4	0	0	0	0	0	42	2
1983–84	31	0	3	0	2	0	1	0	37	0
1984–85	11	0	1	0	0	0	0	0	12	0
TOTAL	99+4	4	11	0	2	0	1	0	113+4	4

Maurice Dando

Born in Bristol in July 1905, Maurice Dando had two successful seasons with City in the mid-1930s. A lively and energetic centre-forward, he joined City from Bristol Rovers in the summer of 1933, having started his career with Bath City. Maurice made his debut for City in a Division Three North game at Crewe Alexandra on 30 August 1933 and scored twice in a 5–3 defeat. He proved a consistent and reliable marksman during his period at Bootham Crescent and notched three hat-tricks, top scoring in each of his two seasons and taking over the mantle from Reg Baines. He scored 52 goals in 92 League and Cup games before moving to Chesterfield in 1935. In his first season at Saltergate he helped the Spireites win the Northern Section Championship by scoring 27 goals. Dando finished his League days with Crewe. Troubled by ill health, he suffered from paralysis for a number of years before dying in 1949, aged 44.

Appearances

	League		FA Cup		Others		TOTAL	
SEASON	Apps	Gls	Apps	Gls	Apps	Gls	Apps	Gls
1933–34	41	25	1	0	3	4	45	29
1934–35	41	21	3	0	3	2	47	23
TOTAL	82	46	4	0	6	6	92	52

Ian Davidson

A talented and stylish midfielder, Ian Davidson joined the club from Hull City in June 1969. Born in Goole on 31 January 1947, he had turned professional for the Tigers in 1963 and made a handful of Second Division appearances for the club. Ian made his City debut in a Fourth Division encounter at Newport County on 9 August 1969. His attacking midfield play was a key factor as City won promotion to Division Three in 1970–71. Davidson also played an important part in the FA Cup that season, scoring in a second-round match at Boston and at the next stage netting both of the goals that knocked out Second Division Bolton Wanderers. In July 1971 he moved to Bournemouth in a player exchange deal involving Eddie Rowles. He later moved to Stockport County before finishing his days in non-League football.

Appearances

	League		FA Cup		League Cup		TOTAL	
SEASON	Apps	Gls	Apps	Gls	Apps	Gls	Apps	Gls
1969–70	39+3	0	5	0	1	0	45+3	0
1970–71	43+1	4	6	3	4	1	53+1	8
TOTAL	82+4	4	11	3	5	1	98+4	8

Clayton Donaldson

Pacy, skilful forward Clayton Donaldson spent two successful Conference seasons with City after signing from Hull City in the summer of 2005. Born in Bradford on 7 February 1984, his first-team opportunities were limited with the Tigers and he had loan spells with Harrogate Town, Scarborough and Halifax Town before his move to York. Clayton made his first team debut for City on the opening day of the 2005–06 campaign, at home

to Crawley Town. He quickly settled down and scored in six successive games in September and October, thrilling the fans with his exciting skills and speed. At the end of the campaign he finished second-top scorer and was voted Clubman of the Year. In 2006–07 he top scored with 24 League goals, including a hat-trick in a 5–0 win at Cambridge United on 13 March 2007, and helped the club reach the Conference promotion Play-offs. In total he scored 44 goals in 93 League and Cup games and while with the club he represented the England non-League XI. In the summer of 2007 Donaldson moved to Scottish Premier League club Hibernian.

Appearances

	League		Play-offs		FA Cup		FA Trophy		TOTAL	
SEASON	Apps	Gls	Apps	Gls	Apps	Gls	Apps	Gls	Apps	Gls
2005–06	42	17	0	0	2	1	1	0	45	18
2006–07	43	24	2	0	2	1	1	1	48	26
TOTAL	85	41	2	0	4	2	2	1	93	44

Richard Duckworth

Dick Duckworth was a very experienced campaigner, having played for Oldham Athletic, Chesterfield, Southport, Chester and Rotherham United before joining City in July 1936. His strong and resolute play in defence was an important

factor in City's success in the late 1930s. Dick took over the captaincy during the 1937–38 season and his strong leadership played a big part as City reached the quarter-finals of the FA Cup. He left the club for Newark Town in 1939 after 109 League and Cup appearances but returned 11 years later to take over as manager. (See York City Managers.)

Appearances

	League		FA Cup		Others		TOTAL	
SEASON	Apps	Gls	Apps	Gls	Apps	Gls	Apps	Gls
1936–37	40	0	7	0	3	0	50	0
1937–38	37	0	9	0	1	0	47	0
1938–39	11	0	1	0	0	0	12	0
TOTAL	88	0	17	0	4	0	109	0

David Dunmore

Born in Whitehaven on 8 February 1934, David Dunmore moved to York as a youngster and was a product of local football, joining City from the noted Cliftonville minor League side that proved a good breeding team for the Bootham Crescent club in the 1940s and 1950s. Dave turned professional in 1952 and made his Football League debut for the club aged 18 in a Division Three North game on the last day of the 1951–52 season, scoring against Crewe Alexandra in a 3–0 win. The powerfully built centre-forward made steady progress the following season, and in 1953–54 he attracted the attention of several leading clubs with his strong and at times explosive finishing, including a hat-trick in a win over Mansfield Town

in October 1953. Dunmore had 20 League goals to his credit when he was transferred to Tottenham Hotspur in February 1954 shortly after his 20th birthday for a then club record fee received of £10,500. Much of this cash was used in the summer of 1954 to help build the side that reached the semi-final of the FA Cup, knocking out Spurs in the fifth round. Dunmore spent over 11 years playing in London: six years at Spurs, one season with West Ham United and four years at Leyton Orient, helping the Brisbane Road club win promotion to Division One. Dunmore returned to York in the summer of 1965 for £5,000 and spent two seasons with the club before moving into non-League football, which included a spell with Scarborough. In his Football League career he made 396 appearances and scored 132 goals, 38 of which were for City.

Appearances

	League		FA Cup		League Cup		TOTAL	
SEASON	Apps	Gls	Apps	Gls	Apps	Gls	Apps	Gls
1951–52	1	1	0	0	0	0	1	1
1952–53	16	4	1	0	0	0	17	4
1953–54	31	20	1	1	0	0	32	21
1965–66	38+1	8	0	0	2	2	40+1	10
1966–67	23+1	5	6	0	2	0	31+1	5
TOTAL	109+2	38	8	1	4	2	121+2	41

Darren Edmondson

A hard-tackling and committed right-back, Darren Edmondson gave the club good service in their last four seasons in the Football League. He

was born in Coniston on 4 November 1970, was a trainee with Carlisle United and turned professional in 1990. He made over 250 senior appearances for the Cumbrians before moving to Huddersfield Town in 1997. Signed by Terry Dolan in March 2000, he made his debut that month in a home game against Hartlepool United and his experience proved invaluable in the closing weeks of that campaign as City pulled clear of the relegation zone and avoided the drop to the Conference. A very sound defender, he was at his best in a wing-back role and scored five goals in a 12-match spell in 2002–03 as City pushed for a promotion Play-off position. One of these was a spectacular effort in a win at Bristol Rovers in March 2003. Darren captained the side in 2003–04 but injuries limited his appearances and he was released at the end of that season. He made a total of 147 League and Cup appearances for City.

Appearances

	League		FA Cup		League Cup		Others		TOTAL	
SEASON	Apps	Gls	Apps	Gls	Apps	Gls	Apps	Gls	Apps	Gls
1999–00	7	0	0	0	0	0	0	0	7	0
2000–01	22+1	0	2	0	2	0	0	0	26+1	0
2001–02	34+2	0	5	0	1	0	0	0	40+2	0
2002–03	37+1	5	2	0	1	0	1	0	41+1	5
2003–04	26+1	1	1	0	1	0	0	0	28+1	1
TOTAL	126+5	6	10	0	5	0	1	0	142+5	6

Thomas Fenoughty

One of the club's all-time stalwarts, Tom Fenoughty played in both the Midland League and the Football League, at Fulfordgate and Bootham Crescent, and gave City seven years' excellent service. He was born in Rotherham on 7 July 1905 and joined City from Rotherham United in February 1927, making his debut on 5 March 1927 in the Midland League at home to Lincoln City reserves. The skilful, attacking inside-forward made 93 senior appearances prior to the club's election to the Football League and quickly established himself at the higher level. In 1929–30 he netted a total of 20 goals, including five in the FA Cup as City reached the third round of the competition for the first time. Tom went on to become the first player in the club's history to score 100 goals in all competitions, and his final tally was 104 in 252 League and Cup games. City reluctantly released Fenoughty early in 1934 because of financial problems. The player, who had earlier been granted a testimonial match against Leeds United, offered to loan his benefit cheque to assist the club: a fine gesture from a fine clubman. Tom returned to his former club Rotherham United and later played for Gainsborough Trinity. He died in 2001.

Appearances

	League		FA Cup		TOTAL	
SEASON	Apps	Gls	Apps	Gls	Apps	Gls
1926–27*	12	8	0	0	12	8
1927–28*	35	18	5	1	40	19
1928–29*	35	15	6	1	41	16
1929–30	29	15	6	5	35	20
1930–31	38	17	3	0	41	17
1931–32	30	13	1	0	31	13
1932–33	30	9	1	0	31	9
1933–34	20	2	1	0	21	2
TOTAL	229	97	23	7	252	104

* Midland League

William (Billy) Fenton

One of the club's most exciting players, left-winger Billy Fenton thrilled the Bootham Crescent crowds in the 1950s with his pace and goalscoring feats. Born in Hartlepool on 23 June 1926, he started his professional career at Blackburn Rovers in 1948 and made a number of League appearances for the Ewood Park club before joining City in May 1951 for a small fee. He made his debut on the opening day of the 1951–52 campaign at Lincoln City and netted 31 League goals that season, beating the scoring record of 29 that Reg Baines set in the early 1930s. Billy was a key member of the 1954–55 side that reached the FA Cup semi-finals, and he scored vital goals in the wins over Blackpool and Tottenham Hotspur. He also figured in the FA Cup runs of 1955–56 and 1957–58. His best scoring feat

came when he netted four goals in a 5–4 win at Carlisle United in November 1954. He went on to make 278 League and Cup appearances, and his total of 124 goals is the club's third-highest behind Norman Wilkinson and Keith Walwyn. He left City at the end of the 1957–58 campaign to join Scarborough and coached in local football after finishing his playing career. A part-time player, he was a draughtsman by trade. He died suddenly in April 1973, aged 46, but his name lives on – the Billy Fenton Memorial Trophy is presented annually to the Clubman of the Year.

Appearances

	League		FA Cup		TOTAL	
SEASON	Apps	Gls	Apps	Gls	Apps	Gls
1951–52	45	31	3	0	48	31
1952–53	44	25	1	0	45	25
1953–54	37	8	1	1	38	9
1954–55	44	22	8	3	52	25
1955–56	29	12	4	1	33	13
1956–57	37	15	1	0	38	15
1957–58	21	5	3	1	24	6
TOTAL	257	118	21	6	278	124

Alan Fettis

One of the best 'keepers to represent the club, Alan Fettis was Clubman of the Year in his two full seasons at Bootham Crescent. Born in Belfast on 1 February 1971, Alan joined Hull City from Irish club Ards in 1991 and played in over 150 games for the Tigers before moving to Nottingham Forest in 1996. A year later he went to Blackburn Rovers but, despite winning 25 caps for Northern Ireland, first-team opportunities were limited at Ewood Park. In March 2000, Terry Dolan, his former boss at Boothferry Park, snapped him up and he made his debut that month away at Peterborough United. Alan kept eight clean sheets in the last 13 matches of that season, playing a crucial part as City avoided the drop out of the Football League. A safe handler of the ball and brave and agile, he missed just one League game during the next two campaigns, and the excellent 'keeper became a great favourite with the fans. After 140 senior games, Fettis was released in the midst of City's financial problems in January 2003 and returned to Hull. He later played for Macclesfield Town and Bury.

Appearances

	League		FA Cup		League Cup		Others		TOTAL	
SEASON	Apps	Gls	Apps	Gls	Apps	Gls	Apps	Gls	Apps	Gls
1999–00	13	0	0	0	0	0	0	0	13	0
2000–01	46	0	4	0	1	0	0	0	51	0
2001–02	45	0	6	0	1	0	0	0	52	0
2002–03	21	0	2	0	1	0	0	0	24	0
TOTAL	125	0	12	0	3	0	0	0	140	0

Gary Ford

One of the best and most consistent players produced by the club was local lad Gary Ford, who was born in York on 8 February 1961. Gary was on

schoolboy forms with Hull City but upon leaving school in 1977 he joined York City as an apprentice, at the same time as John Byrne. He made his debut as a 17-year-old in a Division Four encounter at Reading on 21 October 1978 before turning professional on his 18th birthday. The talented right-sided midfielder quickly established himself in the senior side and was a permanent fixture from 1980 until 1987. He played a key role in the 1983–84 Division Four Championship-winning side and in the FA Cup runs in the two following campaigns. City's 'Mr Consistency' did not miss a single home game between September 1981 and April 1986, and in January 1986 he became the second-youngest player to reach 300 League games for the club with only Chris Topping bettering this feat. Gary netted 64 goals, one of the most famous of which was in February 1986 when he gave City the lead in the fifth round of the FA Cup against Liverpool. In June 1987 he was transferred to Leicester City for £25,000 and later moved to Port Vale, helping the Valiants win promotion to Division Two (Championship). He later played for Mansfield Town and had a spell playing in Norway. Gary made a total of 435 senior appearances for City, putting him fifth in the all-time list, and his total of 36 FA Cup games has only been exceeded by Norman Wilkinson.

Appearances

	League		FA Cup		League Cup		Others		TOTAL	
SEASON	Apps	Gls	Apps	Gls	Apps	Gls	Apps	Gls	Apps	Gls
1978–79	32+1	4	5	1	0	0	0	0	37+1	5
1979–80	26+3	2	3	0	2	0	0	0	31+3	2
1980–81	41+2	4	2	0	4	1	0	0	47+2	5
1981–82	40+1	8	3	1	2	0	0	0	45+1	9
1982–83	45	11	4	2	2	0	0	0	51	13
1983–84	46	11	3	0	2	1	1	0	52	12
1984–85	44	5	6	0	4	2	3	0	57	7
1985–86	40	4	7	3	4	0	2	0	53	7
1986–87	45	4	3	0	4	0	3	0	55	4
TOTAL	359+7	53	36	7	24	4	9	0	428+7	64

Thomas Forgan

One of the best and arguably the most popular goalkeepers to play for York City is Tommy Forgan, who made 428 League and Cup appearances – a club record for a 'keeper – in his 12 seasons at Bootham Crescent. Forgan was born in Middlesbrough on 12 October 1929 and joined Hull City in 1949. In his five years at Boothferry Park he made a handful of League appearances

but was chiefly understudy to the legendary Tigers 'keeper Billy Bly. He moved to York in the summer of 1954 and made his debut on the opening day of the famous 1954–55 campaign at Wrexham, which resulted in a 6–2 win. Tommy was an immediate success with his safe handling and, at times, spectacular keeping. He missed the opening two rounds of the run to the FA Cup semi-final through injury but returned to save a penalty in the win at Blackpool. Apart from 1957–58, when he missed most of the season because of injury, he was a virtual ever present from 1954 until 1962. He did not miss a game in the 1958–59 promotion season and went on to play a big part in the promotion success of 1964–65. Forgan left the club in 1966 and played for Gainsborough Trinity, and then in local York football into his 40s. He emigrated with his family to Perth, Australia, in 1974.

Appearances

	League		FA Cup		League Cup		TOTAL	
SEASON	Apps	Gls	Apps	Gls	Apps	Gls	Apps	Gls
1954–55	39	0	6	0	0	0	45	0
1955–56	41	0	5	0	0	0	46	0
1956–57	46	0	3	0	0	0	49	0
1957–58	12	0	0	0	0	0	12	0
1958–59	46	0	1	0	0	0	47	0
1959–60	32	0	3	0	0	0	35	0
1960–61	41	0	6	0	1	0	48	0
1961–62	38	0	1	0	5	0	44	0
1962–63	30	0	4	0	0	0	34	0
1963–64	20	0	1	0	2	0	23	0
1964–65	29	0	0	0	0	0	29	0
1965–66	14	0	0	0	2	0	16	0
TOTAL	388	0	30	0	10	0	428	0

Stan Fox

One of City's stalwarts in the 1930s, Stan Fox served the club well in his seven years at York. Fox was born in Sheffield on 4 July 1906 and was on the books of Sheffield United and Bury before joining City in October 1931. He made his debut at Fulfordgate in a Northern Section game against New Brighton on 27 February 1932. A versatile player, he was mostly used in midfield but could always be relied on whatever position he filled, and he was an excellent clubman. Fox figured in the FA Cup run in 1936–37 when the club reached the fourth round for the first time. In recognition of his services, Stan was granted a benefit match against Southport in May 1938. He made 151 League and Cup appearances and netted five goals. Upon leaving the club at the end of the 1937–38 season, Fox lived and worked in York and died in 1979, aged 73.

Appearances

	League		FA Cup		Others		TOTAL	
SEASON	Apps	Gls	Apps	Gls	Apps	Gls	Apps	Gls
1931–32	5	0	0	0	0	0	5	0
1932–33	12	2	0	0	0	0	12	2
1933–34	19	1	0	0	2	0	21	1
1934–35	35	1	2	0	3	0	40	1
1935–36	36	0	0	0	1	0	37	0
1936–37	24	0	3	0	3	1	30	1
1937–38	5	0	0	0	1	0	6	0
TOTAL	136	4	5	0	10	1	151	5

Marco Gabbiadini

Born in Nottingham on 20 January 1968 to an Italian father and English mother, Marco was brought up in York and joined the club as an apprentice in 1984. He made his senior debut aged 17 as a substitute in a Third Division League One game at home to Bolton Wanderers on 28 March 1985. Marco scored on his full debut on the opening day of the 1985–86 campaign in a win over Plymouth Argyle at Bootham Crescent, and the talented forward made steady progress. His pace, strength and powerful shooting greatly impressed manager Denis Smith, who before the end of that season urged England boss Bobby Robson to call him up to the Under-21 squad before Italy made a claim. In November 1986 he became the youngest player to score a hat-trick for the club in a senior game when he accomplished that feat in a Freight Rover Trophy match against Darlington, one of 12 goals netted that term. It was no great surprise that Marco was one of Denis Smith's first signings for new club Sunderland in September 1987. The initial fee was £80,000 and the forward finished top marksman that campaign as the Roker Park club won the Third Division Championship. In his four years with the Black Cats he helped the club reach the First Division (Premiership) and was capped for England at Under-21 level. As part of the transfer deal in 1987,

York chairman Michael Sinclair and manager Bobby Saxton inserted a clause that City would receive a 25 per cent share of any sell-on fee, and when Marco moved to Crystal Palace in 1991 the club banked over £300,000. Gabbiadini went on to play for Derby County and Oxford United and had a spell in Greece prior to returning to Bootham Crescent in February 1998, where he stayed until the end of that season. He later played for Darlington, Northampton Town and Hartlepool before ending his playing days in 2004. Gabbiadini made 78 senior appearances for City and scored 19 goals in a career spanning 659 League games and 222 goals.

Appearances

	League		FA Cup		League Cup		Others		TOTAL	
SEASON	Apps	Gls	Apps	Gls	Apps	Gls	Apps	Gls	Apps	Gls
1984–85	0+1	0	0	0	0	0	0	0	0+1	0
1985–86	10+12	4	0	0	0+1	0	2	0	12+13	4
1986–87	24+5	9	0	0	2+2	0	2	3	28+7	12
1987–88	8	1	0	0	2	1	0	0	10	2
1997–98	5+2	1	0	0	0	0	0	0	5+2	1
TOTAL	47+20	15	0	0	4+3	1	4	3	55+23	19

Samuel Gledhill

Sammy Gledhill gave the club several seasons of excellent service in a career that included the war years. Born in Castleford on 7 July 1913, he joined City as an amateur in August 1936, turning professional the following month and making his Football League debut in a Division Three North game at Port Vale on 10 October 1936. A versatile player, chiefly at half-back, he always gave 100 per cent, and by 1938 had established himself in the senior side in the last season before the outbreak of war. A part-time player throughout his footballing career, Sammy was a miner and therefore available to play for City throughout the war. Some of his best football was played during this period and he made well over 200 wartime appearances, receiving a benefit in 1943. He figured in the club's League War Cup (North) run in 1942–43, when they reached the semi-finals, and the FA Cup in 1945–46, when they got to the fourth round. When peacetime football resumed, Gledhill played for another three seasons before retiring in 1949 after 135 League and Cup appearances. A loyal clubman, he helped with the coaching of the juniors and scouted for City for many years. One amusing story regarding Sammy dates back to

January 1937, when City were involved in a gruelling FA Cup tie at the Vetch Field. They played in shocking conditions and it was decided to stay overnight. However, Sammy overslept, the team left without him and he arrived home alone several hours later. He was a very good baseball player and once represented a Rest of England side in the 1930s. He died in 1994, aged 81.

Appearances

	League		FA Cup		Others		TOTAL	
SEASON	Apps	Gls	Apps	Gls	Apps	Gls	Apps	Gls
1936–37	9	5	0	0	0	0	9	5
1937–38	16	0	0	0	1	1	17	1
1938–39	34	0	1	0	0	0	35	0
1945–46	0	0	8	1	0	0	8	1
1946–47	28	1	1	0	0	0	29	1
1947–48	32	0	1	0	0	0	33	0
1948–49	4	0	0	0	0	0	4	0
TOTAL	123	6	11	1	1	1	135	8

Walter Gould

Wally Gould was a fast and direct winger and a popular character at Bootham Crescent in the early 1960s, scoring 27 goals in 138 League and Cup games for the club. He was born in Rotherham on 25 September 1938, started his professional career at Sheffield United in 1958 and joined City early in 1961, making his debut in a Fourth Division game at home to Oldham Athletic on 18 February 1961. Equally at home on either flank, Wally was a

regular in City's attack in his three years with the club and figured in the side's run to the League Cup quarter-finals in 1961–62. A very lively player with an eye for goal, he was second-top marksman in 1962–63. Midway through the 1963–64 campaign he moved to Brighton & Hove Albion and helped the Seagulls win the Fourth Division Championship the following season, when they beat City to the title by just one point. Gould later played and coached in South Africa for many years and was later on the coaching staff at Stoke City.

Appearances

	League		FA Cup		League Cup		TOTAL	
SEASON	Apps	Gls	Apps	Gls	Apps	Gls	Apps	Gls
1960–61	13	3	0	0	0	0	13	3
1961–62	40	5	1	0	7	1	48	6
1962–63	42	11	3	0	2	1	47	12
1963–64	25	6	1	0	4	0	30	6
TOTAL	120	25	5	0	13	2	138	27

Stephen Griffiths

Although in the twilight of his career when he joined City in 1951 aged 37, Steve Griffiths was an influential figure in his two seasons at Bootham Crescent. He was born in Barnsley on 23 February 1914 and started his professional career with Chesterfield in 1934 before moving to Halifax Town. He joined FA Cup holders Portsmouth in the summer of 1939 and played for Pompey in the 1942 War Cup Final at Wembley, when they lost to Brentford. After the war Griffiths played for Aldershot and Barnsley before joining City in June 1951. The clever, scheming ball-playing inside-forward was made captain and led the side to finishes of 10th and fourth in Division Three North, their highest-ever placing in the Football League at the time. Upon the death of the City manager Charles Spencer in February 1953, Griffiths applied unsuccessfully for the job and left the club at the end of that season after making 78 senior appearances and scoring 12 goals. He later became a publican and died in 1998.

Appearances

	League		FA Cup		TOTAL	
SEASON	Apps	Gls	Apps	Gls	Apps	Gls
1951–52	40	6	3	0	43	6
1952–53	34	6	1	0	35	6
TOTAL	74	12	4	0	78	12

Wayne Hall

Fourth in City's all-time appearance list with 438 games, Wayne Hall gave the club 12 years' outstanding service. Born in Rotherham on 25 October 1968, he joined City on trial in 1988–89 having previously played for Hatfield Main, and made substitute appearances in the last two games of that season. He turned professional and made his full debut on the opening day of the 1989–90 season. Originally a left-sided midfielder, he was converted to left-back and was virtually first choice at number three throughout the 1990s. Known affectionally as 'Ginner' because of the colour of his hair, he became a cult figure at Bootham Crescent and wrote himself into the club's history books when he netted the fifth and final penalty in the shoot-out against Crewe Alexandra at Wembley in May 1993, which clinched promotion. A consistent and reliable defender, he was quick in the tackle and netted 11 goals for City, including a memorable equaliser in a televised FA Cup tie against Tranmere Rovers in December 1991. A virtual ever present in the mid-1990s he helped the club win promotion and reach the Second Division (League One) Play-offs in 1993–94 and record League Cup triumphs over Manchester United and Everton. As a reward for his loyal service, Wayne received a richly deserved testimonial year that included a match against Middlesbrough in August 2000. Hall was released at the end of the 2000–01 season and will be remembered as one of the club's great stalwarts.

Appearances

	League		Play-offs		FA Cup		League Cup		Others		TOTAL	
SEASON	Apps	Gls	Apps	Gls	Apps	Gls	Apps	Gls	Apps	Gls	Apps	Gls
1988–89	0+2	0	0	0	0	0	0	0	0	0	0+2	0
1989–90	22+5	3	0	0	0+1	0	1	0	1	0	24+6	3
1990–91	46	1	0	0	3	0	2	0	3	0	54	1
1991–92	36+1	3	0	0	3	1	1+1	0	2	0	42+2	4
1992–93	42	1	3	0	1	0	2	0	2	0	50	1
1993–94	45	0	2	0	2	0	2	0	3	1	54	1
1994–95	33+4	0	0	0	0	0	2	0	1	0	36+4	0
1995–96	21+2	0	0	0	0	0	5	0	2	0	28+2	0
1996–97	12+1	0	0	0	1	0	2	0	0	0	15+1	0
1997–98	31+1	0	0	0	1	0	4	0	1	0	37+1	0
1998–99	26+1	1	0	0	0	0	2	0	1	0	29+1	1
1999–00	23	0	0	0	1	0	2	0	0	0	26	0
2000–01	16+3	0	0	0	1+1	0	2	0	0+1	0	19+5	0
TOTAL	353+20	9	5	0	13+2	1	27+1	0	16+1	1	414+24	11

Sean Haslegrave

Hard-tackling and committed midfielder Sean Haslegrave was a key man in City's Fourth Division Championship-winning side of 1983–84. He moved to Bootham Crescent just prior to the start of that record-breaking campaign and went on to give the club four years' excellent service. Born in Stoke-on-Trent on 7 June 1951, he turned professional with his home-town club in 1968 and went on to play for Nottingham Forest, Preston North End and Crewe Alexandra, amassing over

300 League appearances before joining City. Sean always played with drive and determination and figured in the FA Cup triumphs in the mid-1980s. He qualified as an FA coach and took over the captaincy when Roger Jones retired in 1985. After playing in a total of 172 games, Haslegrave left the club in 1987 and became player-coach and then assistant manager at Torquay United.

Appearances

	League		FA Cup		League Cup		Others		TOTAL	
SEASON	Apps	Gls	Apps	Gls	Apps	Gls	Apps	Gls	Apps	Gls
1983–84	24+2	0	0	0	1+1	0	0+1	0	25+4	0
1984–85	42	0	6	0	4	0	2	0	54	0
1985–86	37+2	0	4	0	4	0	0+1	0	45+3	0
1986–87	34+1	0	1	0	2	0	3	0	40+1	0
TOTAL	137+5	0	11	0	11+1	0	5+2	0	164+8	0

Edward (Ted) Hathway

Ted Hathway gave City six years' outstanding service in the 1930s and scored 43 goals in 250 League and Cup appearances. He was born in Bristol in 1912 and was on the books of both Bristol clubs and Bolton Wanderers, but did not make his Football League debut before joining City in the summer of 1933. He played his first match for the club at home to Halifax Town on 14 October 1933 and was a regular in the side until May 1939, chiefly playing at left-half. A strong and reliable player, he possessed a terrific shot from a dead ball and scored a number of goals direct from free-kicks. Ted played in all the FA Cup triumphs of 1936–37 and 1937–38 – a total of 16 ties. He returned to his native Bristol on the outbreak of war and in 1943 received a well-deserved benefit from City in recognition of his services.

Appearances

	League		FA Cup		Others		TOTAL	
SEASON	Apps	Gls	Apps	Gls	Apps	Gls	Apps	Gls
1933–34	31	14	1	0	3	1	35	15
1934–35	41	6	3	1	3	0	47	7
1935–36	39	6	1	0	1	0	41	6
1936–37	40	7	7	1	3	2	50	10
1937–38	25	1	9	0	0	0	34	1
1938–39	42	4	1	0	0	0	43	4
TOTAL	218	38	22	2	10	3	250	43

Alan Hay

Scottish defender Alan Hay was one of manager Denis Smith's signings in the summer of 1982 and went on to become City's regular left-back during the club's League and Cup successes of the mid-1980s. Born in Dunfermline on 28 November 1958, he joined Bolton Wanderers from Scottish junior football in 1977 but did not make his Football League debut until he moved to Bristol City the following year. Alan spent four years at Ashton Gate and made his debut at York on the opening day of the 1982–83 season. A hard tackler,

he was very reliable and consistent, and a virtual ever present in his first three seasons. He figured prominently in the Fourth Division Championship campaign of 1983–84 and the FA Cup run the following term. At the end of 1985–86 he was transferred to Tranmere Rovers and then, after a period back in Scotland, he had a second spell with City in December 1988. He later moved to Sunderland and finished his League days with Torquay United. Hay made 182 League and Cup appearances for the club and netted four goals.

Appearances

	League		FA Cup		League Cup		Others		TOTAL	
SEASON	Apps	Gls	Apps	Gls	Apps	Gls	Apps	Gls	Apps	Gls
1982–83	42	1	4	0	2	0	0	0	48	1
1983–84	42	1	3	0	2	0	0	0	47	1
1984–85	42+3	0	6	1	4	0	3	0	55+3	1
1985–86	21	1	3	0	2	0	1+1	0	27+1	1
1988–89	1	0	0	0	0	0	0	0	1	0
TOTAL	148+3	3	16	1	10	0	4+1	0	178+4	4

Ian Helliwell

Centre-forward Ian Helliwell was signed from Matlock Town for £10,000 in October 1987 and served the club well, scoring 48 goals in 183 senior appearances in nearly four seasons, and he played manfully during what was a lean period for the club. Born in Rotherham on 7 November 1962, he had spent over four years with the Northern Premier League club and proved a useful marksman by notching 68 goals. He made his City debut at Sunderland in a Division Three (League One) encounter on 24 October 1987, and although he was unable to help the club avoid relegation that season, the tall centre-forward added height and authority to the attack. Ian was a virtual ever present in his time at York and was top scorer and Clubman of the Year in 1988–89. The following campaign he was leading marksman again with 19 League and Cup goals, including a hat-trick in a 7–1 win over Hartlepool United in the Leyland DAF Cup. In August 1991 he was transferred to Scunthorpe United for £80,000 and went on to play for Rotherham United, Stockport County and Burnley.

Appearances

	League		FA Cup		League Cup		Others		TOTAL	
SEASON	Apps	Gls	Apps	Gls	Apps	Gls	Apps	Gls	Apps	Gls
1987–88	32	8	0	0	0	0	1	0	33	8
1988–89	41	11	1	0	2	0	3	0	47	11
1989–90	44+2	14	1	0	4	1	2+1	4	51+3	19
1990–91	41	7	3	0	2	0	3	3	49	10
TOTAL	158+2	40	5	0	8	1	9+1	7	180+3	48

Thomas Heron

Talented left-back Tommy Heron spent five seasons with the club in the 1960s and his enthusiastic and skilful play made him a firm favourite with the fans. He was born in Irvine, Ayrshire, on 31 March 1936 and signed by Manchester United from Irish club Portadown in 1958, making his Football League debut for the Red Devils shortly after the Munich air disaster. His first-team appearances were limited at Old Trafford, however, and he joined City in the summer of 1961. Heron made his debut for the club on the opening day of the 1961–62 campaign at Bradford City and missed just seven League games in his first four seasons. A player with attacking instincts, he had been an outside-left in his early days but was converted to full-back while at Manchester United, although he did play some games for City on the left wing. Tommy helped the club reach the quarter-finals of the League Cup in 1961–62 and played a full part in the promotion-winning side of 1964–65. He went on to make 216 League and Cup appearances,

netting six goals before leaving the club in June 1966 to join non-League Altrincham.

Appearances

	League		FA Cup		League Cup		TOTAL	
SEASON	Apps	Gls	Apps	Gls	Apps	Gls	Apps	Gls
1961–62	44	0	1	0	7	0	52	0
1962–63	39	3	4	0	2	0	45	3
1963–64	46	3	1	0	4	0	51	3
1964–65	46	0	2	0	1	0	49	0
1965–66	17	0	0	0	2	0	19	0
TOTAL	192	6	8	0	16	0	216	6

Ian Holmes

A clever and skilful midfielder, Ian Holmes took a little time to establish himself at the club but he became a firm favourite with the fans, and his partnership with Barry Lyons on the right side of midfield played a big part as City won promotion to the second tier of English football for the first time in 1974. He was born in Wombwell on 8 December 1950 and turned professional with Sheffield United in 1968 but found first-team opportunities limited at Bramall Lane. Holmes moved to York in July 1973, making his debut on the opening day of the 1973–74 campaign in a 4–2 win at Charlton Athletic. He was a penalty-kick expert and showed great coolness under pressure,

never more so than when netting a stoppage-time winner against Bristol Rovers in a vital promotion clash in March 1974. Holmes was an ever present in City's first season in Division Two and went on to total 180 League and Cup appearances and 35 goals. In October 1977 he teamed up with his former City boss Tom Johnston when he signed for Huddersfield Town for £10,000. Holmes later became player-coach at Gainsborough Trinity.

Appearances

	League		FA Cup		League Cup		TOTAL	
SEASON	Apps	Gls	Apps	Gls	Apps	Gls	Apps	Gls
1973–74	27+4	5	0+1	0	1+2	1	28+7	6
1974–75	42	9	2	0	1	0	45	9
1975–76	30+1	6	1	0	2	0	33+1	6
1976–77	39+2	7	5	3	3	1	47+2	11
1977–78	14	3	0	0	3	0	17	3
TOTAL	152+7	30	8+1	3	10+2	2	170+10	35

Derek Hood

One of the most popular and versatile players to wear City's colours, Derek Hood gave outstanding service in over eight years at Bootham Crescent in the 1980s. Born in Washington, Co. Durham on 17 December 1958, he served his apprenticeship at West Bromwich Albion and Hull City before turning professional with the Tigers in 1977. Derek joined City in February 1980 for a bargain fee of £2,000 and made his debut that month in a

Fourth Division game at home to Halifax Town. The energetic and hard-working player went on to amass 354 League and Cup appearances. In addition, he was twice an ever present (1981–82 and 1982–83) and was voted Clubman of the Year in the latter campaign. Injury caused him to miss the start of the following season but he returned to play a vital role as the club won the Fourth Division Championship. Equally comfortable either at full-back or in midfield, Hood continued to serve the club well and figured in the FA Cup runs of 1984–85 and 1985–86. He left the club in May 1988 and a testimonial match against a past City side was played in November that year – a just benefit for a fine and loyal club stalwart.

Appearances

	League		FA Cup		League Cup		Others		TOTAL	
SEASON	Apps	Gls	Apps	Gls	Apps	Gls	Apps	Gls	Apps	Gls
1979–80	16	1	0	0	0	0	0	0	16	1
1980–81	42	0	2	0	1	0	0	0	45	0
1981–82	46	8	3	0	2	0	0	0	51	8
1982–83	46	7	4	2	2	0	0	0	52	9
1983–84	33+1	4	3	0	1	0	1	0	38+1	4
1984–85	27+3	4	2+1	0	0+2	0	3	0	32+6	4
1985–86	29+2	1	5	0	2+1	0	1	0	37+3	1
1986–87	24+3	3	3	0	4	0	1+2	0	32+5	3
1987–88	24+4	4	2+1	1	4	1	1	0	31+5	6
TOTAL	287+13	32	24+2	3	16+3	1	7+2	0	334+20	36

Keith Houchen

On 26 January 1985 Keith Houchen etched his name in the club's history when he netted the dramatic late penalty winner against Arsenal in the fourth round of the FA Cup. Born in Middlesbrough on 25 July 1960, he began his professional career with Hartlepool in 1978 before moving to Orient. He signed for City in March 1984 for a fee of £15,000 and made a dramatic debut as a substitute in a Fourth Division game at Aldershot on 14 April 1984. He scored in a 4–1 win, missed a penalty and was cautioned. A talented forward with good ball skills and an eye for goal, Keith figured prominently in the 1984–85 campaign and was top scorer with 18 League and Cup goals, including a hat-trick in a 7–1 win over Gillingham in November 1984. After notching 27 goals in 88 senior appearances, he was transferred to Scunthorpe United in March 1986 for £20,000 and then moved to Coventry City. He helped the Sky Blues win the FA Cup in 1986–87, and his diving header, which clinched the trophy in a 3–2 win over Tottenham Hotspur, is regarded as one of the finest in an FA Cup Final at Wembley. Houchen later played for Hibernian and appeared in the UEFA Cup, and then Port Vale. He finished his playing days at his former club, Hartlepool, and went on to have a spell as manager at Victoria Park.

He scored 151 League goals in 534 games in his career. After hanging up his boots, Houchen worked in the media in the North East, which included reporting on City matches.

Appearances

	League		FA Cup		League Cup		Others		TOTAL	
SEASON	Apps	Gls	Apps	Gls	Apps	Gls	Apps	Gls	Apps	Gls
1983–84	1+6	1	0	0	0	0	0	0	1+6	1
1984–85	35	12	5	3	3	2	2	1	45	18
1985–86	20+5	6	4+2	0	3	1	2	1	29+7	8
TOTAL	56+11	19	9+2	3	6	3	4	2	75+13	27

George Howe

One of the heroes of the 1954–55 FA Cup side, George Howe gave the club splendid service at left-back and missed only 15 League games out of a possible 322 in seven seasons (1954–61). Born in Wakefield on 10 January 1924, he joined Huddersfield Town during the war and went on to make 40 League appearances before moving to City in the summer of 1954. George made his debut on the opening day of the memorable 1954–55 campaign and instantly became a fixture in City's defence thanks to his coolness, consistency and fine positional play. A highlight of his career came in January 1955 when he kept the legendary Stanley Matthews quiet in the famous FA Cup win at Blackpool. Howe played in all the FA Cup triumphs of the mid-1950s and the promotion-winning side of 1958–59. His last term at York was spent in the reserves as he helped with the development of the younger players, and he left the club in May 1962 after appearing in 338 League and Cup games. In November 1971 Howe became the first member of the famous 'Happy Wanderers' side to die, aged 47.

Appearances

	League		FA Cup		League Cup		TOTAL	
SEASON	Apps	Gls	Apps	Gls	Apps	Gls	Apps	Gls
1954–55	46	0	8	0	0	0	54	0
1955–56	44	0	5	0	0	0	49	0
1956–57	45	0	2	0	0	0	47	0
1957–58	44	0	5	0	0	0	49	0
1958–59	36	0	1	0	0	0	37	0
1959–60	46	0	3	0	0	0	49	0
1960–61	46	0	6	0	1	0	53	0
TOTAL	307	0	30	0	1	0	338	0

William (Billy) Hughes

One of the finest wingers in the club's history, Billy Hughes was the regular wearer of the number-seven shirt from 1951 to 1961 and played in 380 League and Cup games, putting him 10th in the all-time appearance list. Born in Glasgow on 3 March 1929 he was an amateur on Newcastle

United's books and was spotted while doing his National Service at nearby RAF Rufforth. Billy signed professional terms for City in May 1951 and played for the club in the Festival of Britain games that month against Irish sides Sligo Rovers and Transport. Upon the departure of John Linaker to Hull City, he made his Football League debut at Rochdale on 20 October 1951 and immediately established himself in the side. A very skilful ball player, he was the old-school dribbling type of winger and figured in all the major FA Cup ties in the mid-1950s, and in the promotion campaign of 1958–59. He missed the start of the 1954–55 campaign having returned to his native Scotland but was persuaded to return, and so played his full part in the run to the FA Cup semi-finals. He scored a total of 58 goals and his last game was on 30 September 1961, by coincidence at Spotland: the ground were he had started his City senior career 10 years earlier. Like so many ex-City players he continued to live and work in the York area and played for a number of seasons in local football. He died in 2003, aged 74.

Appearances

	League		FA Cup		League Cup		TOTAL	
SEASON	Apps	Gls	Apps	Gls	Apps	Gls	Apps	Gls
1951–52	33	4	0	0	0	0	33	4
1952–53	32	6	0	0	0	0	32	6
1953–54	25	2	1	0	0	0	26	2
1954–55	33	5	8	0	0	0	41	5
1955–56	39	7	5	1	0	0	44	8
1956–57	24	4	2	0	0	0	26	4
1957–58	32	7	5	0	0	0	37	7
1958–59	42	7	1	0	0	0	43	7
1959–60	46	7	3	1	0	0	49	8
1960–61	41	5	5	1	1	0	47	6
1961–62	2	1	0	0	0	0	2	1
TOTAL	349	55	30	3	1	0	380	58

Barry Jackson

A colossus at the heart of City's defence from 1958 to 1970, Barry Jackson holds the club appearance record of 539 League and Cup games – a total that is unlikely to be beaten. Born in Askrigg, North Yorkshire, on 2 February 1938, he moved with his family to York as a youngster and was another player who developed through the ranks of local minor league club Cliftonville. Barry joined City as an amateur in the summer of 1956 and starred in a public pre-season practice match in August 1956, Reds versus Blues, in front of a crowd of 7,099. He turned professional in December that year and his

first two seasons with the club were spent in the reserve side. He made his senior debut on the opening day of the 1958–59 season at Oldham in City's first-ever game in Division Four and made an immediate impact by helping the club win promotion that term. A virtual ever present for 12 seasons, 6ft 4in Jackson was a commanding and imposing figure who played with tremendous wholeheartedness and spirit. He captained the side on a number of occasions and helped the club reach the quarter-finals of the League Cup in 1961–62, and another promotion success in 1964–65. As a youngster he played chiefly at centre-forward, making a few appearances in this position at senior level and scoring a total of 10 goals for the club. A fully committed player who always gave 100 per cent, he occasionally found himself in trouble with referees. He was sent off in a Fourth Division game at Scunthorpe United in January 1970, shortly after three outstanding displays against Cardiff City in the FA Cup in which he completely snuffed out rising young Welsh star John Toshack. He received an eight-week ban and was unable to win back his place in the team. Nonetheless, Barry was awarded a richly deserved testimonial game against Hull City in February 1970. He was released at the end of that season and, after a short spell at Scarborough in

1970–71, hung up his boots. Without doubt a City legend – a great clubman and a giant in every respect – he was voted York City's all-time favourite player in a poll conducted by the PFA as part of their centenary celebrations in 2007.

Appearances

	League		FA Cup		League Cup		TOTAL	
SEASON	Apps	Gls	Apps	Gls	Apps	Gls	Apps	Gls
1958–59	34	0	1	0	0	0	35	0
1959–60	37	0	3	0	0	0	40	0
1960–61	43	2	5	0	0	0	48	2
1961–62	42	1	1	0	7	1	50	2
1962–63	45	2	4	0	1	0	50	2
1963–64	38	0	1	0	4	0	43	0
1964–65	44	0	2	0	1	0	47	0
1965–66	45	0	1	0	3	0	49	0
1966–67	46	1	6	0	4	0	56	1
1967–68	42	1	1	0	1	0	44	1
1968–69	40+1	1	2	0	1	0	43+1	1
1969–70	25	1	7	0	1	0	33	1
TOTAL	481+1	9	34	0	23	1	538+1	10

Samuel Johnson

Left-back Sam Johnson was one of the players recruited during the summer of 1929 as the club prepared for their first season in the Football League. He made his debut in the opening game at Wigan Borough on 31 August 1929 and, for City's first three campaigns in the League, he was a regular in the defence, impressing with his cool and constructive play. Johnson was born in Kidsgrove, Staffordshire, on 19 October 1901, joined Stoke City in 1924 and moved to Swindon Town prior to signing for City. He went on to make 137 senior appearances for the club and figured in the side that reached the third round of the FA Cup in successive seasons, taking First Division sides Newcastle United and Sheffield United to replays. Johnson left the club in 1933 and, after a short spell back at Swindon, returned to York, where he became a publican. In 1937 Sam became City's reserve-team trainer, a position he was to hold until the 1960s. He died in 1975, aged 73.

Appearances

	League		FA Cup		TOTAL	
SEASON	Apps	Gls	Apps	Gls	Apps	Gls
1929–30	37	0	6	0	43	0
1930–31	36	0	5	0	41	0
1931–32	38	0	1	0	39	0
1932–33	13	0	1	0	14	0
TOTAL	124	0	13	0	137	0

Barry Jones

Equally at home at right-back or in the centre of defence, Barry Jones served the club well and won the Clubman of the Year award in successive seasons (1998–99 and 1999–2000). Born in Prescot on 30 June 1970, Jones was on the books of

Liverpool before joining Wrexham in 1992 and made nearly 250 senior appearances in five years with the Welsh club. He was signed by City in December 1997 for a fee of £40,000 and quickly settled in the defence. Very steady and reliable, Barry was a strong tackler and good in the air. He was very popular with the fans and captained the side in 1998–99, making a total of 145 League and Cup appearances before moving to Southport in 2001.

Appearances

	League		FA Cup		League Cup		Others		TOTAL	
SEASON	Apps	Gls	Apps	Gls	Apps	Gls	Apps	Gls	Apps	Gls
1997–98	23	2	0	0	0	0	0	0	23	2
1998–99	44+1	2	3	0	2	0	1	0	50+1	2
1999–00	35+2	1	1	0	2	0	0	0	38+2	1
2000–01	28+1	0	0	0	2	1	0	0	30+1	1
TOTAL	130+4	5	4	0	6	1	1	0	141+4	6

Christopher Jones

Chris Jones joined the club from Walsall in the summer of 1973 and scored on his debut on the opening day of the 1973–74 campaign, in a 4–2 win at Charlton Athletic. This victory heralded a very successful season for City as they went on to win promotion to Division Two (Championship) for the first time in their history. One of the key factors was the striking partnership between Chris, who top scored with 20 League and Cup goals, and Jimmy Seal. His experience in attack and his marksmanship stood City in good stead in their first season at the higher level and he finished second-top scorer with 12 goals. He twice bagged a brace against Fulham, who were FA Cup runners-up that season, as City completed a double over the Cottagers and scored two at Carrow Road as City won 3–2 at Norwich, who went on to win promotion to Division One (Premiership). Chris also netted the winner against Cardiff City in August 1974 as City recorded their first-ever victory in the Second Division, and he played an important role as City experienced their best and most successful time in the Football League. He went on to score 37 goals in 107 League and Cup appearances before joining Huddersfield Town in August 1976. Born in Altrincham on 19 November 1945, Jones joined Manchester City as a junior and turned professional in 1964. He made his Football League debut for the Maine Road club in 1966–67 before moving to Swindon Town, helping them

win promotion from Division Three in 1968–69. Jones later played for Doncaster Rovers and Rochdale and finished his playing days with Rowntree Mackintosh in the North Eastern Counties League. He became chairman of the York Football Coaches' Association and a summariser on City matches for BBC Radio York.

Appearances

	League		FA Cup		League Cup		TOTAL	
SEASON	Apps	Gls	Apps	Gls	Apps	Gls	Apps	Gls
1973–74	41	18	2	2	5	0	48	20
1974–75	36+1	12	2	0	0	0	38+1	12
1975–76	17	4	0	0	3	1	20	5
TOTAL	94+1	34	4	2	8	1	106+1	37

Roger Jones

Arguably the best all-round goalkeeper to represent York City was Roger Jones, who captained the club when they won their first major honour – Fourth Division champions – in 1983–84. Jones was born in Upton-on-Severn, Worcestershire, on 8 November 1946 and made his Football League debut with Bournemouth despite starting his professional career in 1964 at Portsmouth. While at Dean Court he was capped at Under-23 level for England and went on to play for Blackburn Rovers, Newcastle United, Stoke City and Derby County, before becoming one of

Denis Smith's captures in the summer of 1982. He made his debut on the opening day of the 1982–83 campaign at home to Torquay United. Roger gave the club three seasons' great service, and his command of the goal area and positional play made him an outstanding 'keeper. He made 141 League and Cup appearances for City before leaving the club in 1985, and he was subsequently on the coaching staff at Sunderland. In a long and illustrious career, Jones played in 693 Football League games. Roger is pictured with the Fourth Division Canon League trophy in May 1984.

Appearances

	League		FA Cup		League Cup		Others		TOTAL	
SEASON	Apps	Gls	Apps	Gls	Apps	Gls	Apps	Gls	Apps	Gls
1982–83	42	0	3	0	2	0	0	0	47	0
1983–84	41	0	3	0	1	0	1	0	46	0
1984–85	39	0	2	0	4	0	3	0	48	0
TOTAL	122	0	8	0	7	0	4	0	141	0

Robert (Roy) Kay

Roy Kay was the regular left-back and captain in his four years with the club (1978–1982), serving City splendidly in this time. Born in Edinburgh on 24 October 1949, he made his mark in Scottish football and spent nine seasons with Hearts, gaining a Scottish FA Cup runners'-up medal in 1976 and also appearing in the European Cup-

Winners' Cup. He then had one season at Celtic, representing them in the European Cup, before coming to Bootham Crescent in the summer of 1978. Roy made his debut for City on the opening day of the 1978–79 season at Rochdale and proved to be a most consistent and reliable defender, impressing with his coolness and positional play. He could also play in the centre of the defence or in midfield when needed. A fine clubman, Kay totalled 183 senior games for City before his release in 1982, and he was a virtual ever present in his four seasons at York.

Appearances

	League		FA Cup		League Cup		TOTAL	
SEASON	Apps	Gls	Apps	Gls	Apps	Gls	Apps	Gls
1978–79	46	0	5	0	2	0	53	0
1979–80	41	3	3	0	2	0	46	3
1980–81	36	1	2	0	4	0	42	1
1981–82	37	4	3	0	2	0	42	4
TOTAL	160	8	13	0	10	0	183	8

Dean Kiely

One of the club's top 'keepers, Dean Kiely joined City in May 1990, having previously been on the books of West Bromwich Albion as a junior and Coventry City, and he represented England at Under-15, 16 and 17 level. Born on 10 October 1970 in Salford, Dean made his senior debut in a Freight Rover Trophy match against Bury on 22 January 1991 and his League debut four days later at home to Hartlepool United. An excellent shot-stopper and good handler of the ball, he had

established himself as first-choice 'keeper by the promotion campaign of 1992–93 and had an outstanding season, crowned by his penalty save in the shoot-out against Crewe Alexandra at Wembley in May 1993. As City reached the Second Division (League One) Play-offs the following season, he kept 20 clean sheets, equalling a club record. He had made 239 League and Cup appearances by the time he moved to Bury in August 1996 for a tribunal fee of £125,000. Kiely moved on to Charlton Athletic for £1 million in 1999 and was first-choice 'keeper in six seasons at the Valley, five of them in the Premiership. He then played for Portsmouth and joined West Bromwich Albion after a spell on loan at Luton Town. Kiely helped the Baggies win promotion back to the top flight in 2007–08 and by the end of that campaign had made 650 Football League appearances in his career and won nine caps for the Republic of Ireland, the country of his father's birth.

Appearances

	League		Play-offs		FA Cup		League Cup		Others		TOTAL	
SEASON	Apps	Gls	Apps	Gls	Apps	Gls	Apps	Gls	Apps	Gls	Apps	Gls
1990–91	17	0	0	0	0	0	0	0	1	0	18	0
1991–92	21	0	0	0	0	0	0	0	1	0	22	0
1992–93	40	0	3	0	0	0	2	0	1	0	46	0
1993–94	46	0	2	0	2	0	2	0	3	0	55	0
1994–95	46	0	0	0	2	0	2	0	2	0	52	0
1995–96	40	0	0	0	0	0	3	0	3	0	46	0
TOTAL	210	0	5	0	4	0	9	0	11	0	239	0

George Lee

Local lad George Lee made only 37 Football League appearances for City but was one of the finest players to have been produced by the club. Born in York on 4 June 1919, the club were so keen to capture George that secretary Billy Sherrington sat with his parents until after midnight so that he could sign on the dotted line on his 17th birthday. The left-winger made his debut on 24 April 1937 at home to Oldham Athletic and was blooded slowly, chiefly playing for the reserves. But by 1938–39, at the age of 19, he had established himself in the senior side. It was during the war years that George's footballing career blossomed and he benefitted greatly from having guest player Bert 'Sailor' Brown, the England and Charlton Athletic inside-forward, playing alongside him. The pair became the finest club wing partnership in north-east England, and City reached the League War

Cup (North) semi-finals in 1942–43. During the war, George made 153 appearances and scored 90 times, so completing 100 goals for the club. A natural left-sided player, he had craft, ball control and pace, together with a fine shot. During the latter part of the war, military service took him abroad and he was not demobbed until 1947. He played in only one game in 1946–47 and was transferred to Nottingham Forest in August 1947 for a then club record fee received of £7,500. In 1949 Lee moved to West Bromwich Albion and spent nine years with the Baggies, helping them win the FA Cup in 1953–54. He was later trainer-coach at the Hawthorns and held a similar post at Norwich City from 1963 until 1987. He died in Norwich in April 1991, aged 71.

Appearances

	League		FA Cup		TOTAL	
SEASON	Apps	Gls	Apps	Gls	Apps	Gls
1936–37	2	0	0	0	2	0
1937–38	4	3	0	0	4	3
1938–39	30	8	1	0	31	8
1945–46	0	0	1	1	1	1
1946–47	1	0	0	0	1	0
TOTAL	37	11	2	1	39	12

Barry Lyons

One of City's stars in the 1970s, Barry Lyons was a very skilful right-sided midfield player who played a big part in the club's promotion to Division Two (Championship) in 1974. Born in Shirebrook on 14 March 1945, he turned professional with Rotherham United in 1962 before moving to Nottingham Forest in 1966. He topped 200 League games (mostly in the old First Division) for the Midlanders and was signed by City boss Tom Johnston in September 1973, after a period on loan, for a then club record fee paid of £12,000. He made an immediate impact with his class and skill, and his experience stood City in good stead in the Second Division in 1974–75 when Barry had the distinction of scoring City's first-ever goal at this level. He made 98 senior appearances for the club and scored 11 goals before moving to Darlington in 1976. Lyons returned to Bootham Crescent in 1979 as youth coach and took over as manager in March 1980 (see chapter on York City managers). Dismissed in December 1981, he resumed his youth-team duties but left the club in July 1982. After leaving football he worked in insurance and became a hotelier in York.

Appearances

	League		FA Cup		League Cup		TOTAL	
SEASON	Apps	Gls	Apps	Gls	Apps	Gls	Apps	Gls
1973–74	40	5	2	0	5	0	47	5
1974–75	30+5	4	2	1	1	0	33+5	5
1975–76	10	1	0	0	3	0	13	1
TOTAL	80+5	10	4	1	9	0	93+5	11

Jonathan McCarthy

Exciting right-winger Jon McCarthy thrilled City crowds in five seasons at Bootham Crescent with his pace, skill and tenacity. Jon was born in Middlesbrough on 18 August 1970 and made his Football League debut as a non-contract player in 1988 for Hartlepool United, managed by John Bird. He then studied at Nottingham University, where he gained a Sports Science and Administration degree and played for Shepshed Charterhouse. In March 1990 Bird, now City boss, signed McCarthy on a part-time basis and gave him his debut as a substitute in a Fourth Division game at home to Gillingham on 29 September 1990. He turned professional in March 1991 and, that summer, won a bronze medal as a member of the Great Britain team in the World Student Games held in Sheffield. By 1991–92 McCarthy was established in the City attack, and he was Clubman of the Year that season. His electrifying pace and close ball control was a big factor as City won promotion the following

season and then the Second Division (League One) Play-offs in 1993–94. Jon was again voted Clubman of the Year in 1994–95 but was transferred to Port Vale in August 1995 for £450,000, after making 233 League and Cup appearances and scoring 38 goals. He moved to Birmingham City for £1. 5 million in 1997 and was capped 18 times for Northern Ireland, qualifying through parentage. He returned to Port Vale and played one game back in City colours in November 2002. Jon finished his League days with Carlisle United and then played for Hucknall Town and Northwich Victoria.

Appearances

	League		Play-offs		FA Cup		League Cup		Others		TOTAL	
SEASON	Apps	Gls	Apps	Gls	Apps	Gls	Apps	Gls	Apps	Gls	Apps	Gls
1990–91	26+1	2	0	0	3	0	0	0	1	1	30+1	3
1991–92	42	6	0	0	3	1	2	1	2	1	49	9
1992–93	42	7	3	0	1	0	2	0	2	0	50	7
1993–94	44	7	2	0	2	1	2	0	3	1	53	9
1994–95	44	9	0	0	2	1	2	0	2	0	50	10
2002–03	1	0	0	0	0	0	0	0	0	0	1	0
TOTAL	199+1	31	5	0	11	3	8	1	10	3	233+1	38

Ian McDonald

A very talented left-sided midfield player, Ian McDonald was a virtual ever present in his four years at Bootham Crescent. Born in Barrow-in-Furness on 10 May 1953 he turned professional with his home-town club in 1971 and after a spell with Workington was signed by Liverpool in 1974 for £33,000. A very bright future was predicted for him, but unfortunately he suffered a serious injury in his first game for the reserves at Anfield and was not able to establish himself on Merseyside. He moved to Mansfield Town in 1975, helping the Stags win promotion from the Fourth Division, and then joined City in November 1977 for £7,000. Ian made his debut in a home game against Southport that month and immediately proved a reliable and consistent performer, with his skilful play and specialist penalty-kicks. Clubman of the Year in 1979–80, he was top scorer the following season and went on to play in 195 League and Cup games, scoring 31 goals before moving to Aldershot in November 1981 in a player-exchange deal with Malcolm Crosby. McDonald made 340 Football League appearances for the Shots and had a spell as player-manager before the Hampshire club dropped out of the League in 1992.

Appearances

	League		FA Cup		League Cup		TOTAL	
	Apps	Gls	Apps	Gls	Apps	Gls	Apps	Gls
1977–78	30	2	1	0	0	0	31	2
1978–79	43	6	5	0	1	0	49	6
1979–80	46	8	3	1	2	0	51	9
1980-81	46	11	2	0	4	1	52	12
1981–82	10	2	0	0	2	0	12	2
TOTAL	175	29	11	1	9	1	195	31

Edward (Ted) MacDougall

One of the most prolific marksmen in the country in the 1960s and 1970s, Ted MacDougall made his Football League debut for City. He turned professional with Liverpool but had not made his senior debut at Anfield when manager Tom Lockie signed him in the summer of 1967 for a reported fee of £5,000. Ted netted on his first appearance for the club at home to Workington on the opening day of the 1967–68 campaign, and he was leading scorer in his two seasons at Bootham Crescent, totalling 40 goals in 90 League and Cup appearances. A strong player with good all-round ability, he was very sharp in front of goal: he hit one hat-trick for City in March 1968 at home to Port Vale and, in April 1969, netted in six successive Fourth Division games, scoring seven times. In the summer of 1969 he was transferred to Bournemouth for £10,000, later teaming up with his former City colleague Phil Boyer and, in three years on the south coast, he scored 103 goals in 146 League games and also hit nine goals in an FA Cup tie against Margate. MacDougall went on to play for Manchester United, West Ham United, Norwich City and Southampton and was capped for Scotland seven times. In his career he scored 256 goals in 535 Football League games.

Appearances

SEASON	League		FA Cup		League Cup		TOTAL	
	Apps	Gls	Apps	Gls	Apps	Gls	Apps	Gls
1967–68	38	15	1	0	1	0	40	15
1968–69	46	19	3	4	1	2	50	25
TOTAL	84	34	4	4	2	2	90	40

David McGurk

The central-defender signed for City in August 2006, having spent the previous season on loan from Darlington. He had had a short spell on loan in 2004–05 playing his first game for the club on 18 September 2004 at home to Northwich Victoria. David McGurk was born in Middlesbrough on 30 September 1982 and joined Darlington as a youngster, turning professional in 2002. A very composed and talented defender, he has been a virtual ever present in his time at York and was a key figure in the defence that reached the promotion Play-offs in 2006–07. David maintained his consistent form the following season, helping the club reach the semi-finals of the FA Trophy, and he was voted Clubman of the Year in 2007–08.

Appearances

SEASON	League		Play-offs		FA Cup		FA Trophy		Others		TOTAL	
	Apps	Gls	Apps	Gls	Apps	Gls	Apps	Gls	Apps	Gls	Apps	Gls
2004–05	5+1	0	0	0	0	0	0	0	0	0	5+1	0
2005–06	36	2	0	0	2	0	1	0	0	0	39	2
2006–07	38	0	2	0	0	0	1	0	0	0	41	0
2007–08	46	1	0	0	2	0	7	0	1	0	56	1
TOTAL	125+1	3	2	0	4	0	9	0	1	0	141+1	3

Andre (Andy) McMillan

One of the best right-backs to represent the club was Andy McMillan, City's regular number two throughout the 1990s. His total of 492 League and Cup appearances is bettered only by Barry Jackson in the history of the club. Born in Bloemfontein, South Africa, on 22 June 1968 to English parents, Andy played junior international football for Zimbabwe. The family returned to England in 1986 and McMillan had trials with Hull City, Tottenham Hotspur and Preston North End before coming to York in August 1987. The young defender made his Football League debut as a substitute in a Division Three (League One) match at home to Mansfield Town on 28 December 1987, and he immediately made an impact with his style and coolness. Andy had an extended run in the senior side in the second half of that season but missed nearly all the following campaign through injury. By 1990, however, he had firmly established himself in the defence and for the next nine years was a virtual ever present. Between October 1991 and March 1995 McMillan played in 154 successive League games. His understanding and partnership with right-winger Jon McCarthy was an important part of City's success from 1992 to 1995, as the club gained promotion and reached the Second Division (League One) Play-offs. Ever reliable and consistent, the cultured player was voted best right-back in Division Three by his fellow professionals in 1992–93 and was Clubman of the Year in 1995–96. He was granted a richly deserved testimonial season in 1998–99, which featured a game against Leeds United in July 1999. Upon leaving the club that year, McMillan had a spell in Scotland with Ayr United and helped them reach the semi-finals of the Scottish Cup in 1999–2000 before returning to play local football in the York area. Ever popular, McMillan was one of the finest players to appear for City.

Appearances

	League		Play-offs		FA Cup		League Cup		Others		TOTAL	
SEASON	Apps	Gls	Apps	Gls	Apps	Gls	Apps	Gls	Apps	Gls	Apps	Gls
1987–88	20+2	0	0	0	0	0	0	0	0	0	20+2	0
1988–89	0+2	0	0	0	0	0	0	0	0	0	0+2	0
1989–90	21+4	0	0	0	1	0	1	0	2	0	25+4	0
1990–91	45	1	0	0	3	0	2	0	3	0	53	1
1991–92	41	1	0	0	3	0	2	0	2	0	48	1
1992–93	42	0	3	0	1	0	2	0	2	0	50	0
1993–94	46	0	2	0	2	0	2	0	2	0	54	0
1994–95	39+4	1	0	0	2	0	2	0	2	0	45+4	1
1995–96	46	1	0	0	1	0	5	0	5	0	57	1
1996–97	46	0	0	0	3	0	5	0	2	0	56	0
1997–98	30	1	0	0	0	0	4	0	0	0	34	1
1998–99	33	0	0	0	2	0	2	0	1	0	38	0
TOTAL	409+12	5	5	0	18	0	27	0	21	0	480+12	5

John MacPhail

One of the best centre-halves to appear for City was John MacPhail, a key figure at the heart of defence during the club's successful days in the mid-1980s. Born on 7 December 1955 in Dundee, he joined Sheffield United in 1979 and made 135 League appearances for the Blades before moving to City in February 1983, initially on loan. He made his debut that month at Peterborough United, and for three seasons John was a kingpin and commanding figure in the side thanks to his keen tackling and overall ability. A tremendous header of the ball, he also scored a number of vital goals and was a huge influence in the record-breaking 1983–84 Division Four Championship side and the FA Cup runs in the following campaigns. Very popular with the fans, he was voted Clubman of the Year in both 1983–84 and 1984–85. MacPhail scored 29 goals in 173 League and Cup appearances for the club. In July 1986 he moved to Bristol City and teamed up with his

former City boss Denis Smith at Sunderland the following year. There, MacPhail helped the Roker Park club win promotion from Division Three to Division One (Premiership) in three seasons. He finished his playing days at Hartlepool United with a spell as player-manager. In a distinguished playing career, MacPhail made 596 League appearances and scored 58 goals.

Appearances

	League		FA Cup		League Cup		Others		TOTAL	
SEASON	Apps	Gls	Apps	Gls	Apps	Gls	Apps	Gls	Apps	Gls
1982–83	11+1	2	0	0	0	0	0	0	11+1	2
1983–84	46	10	3	0	2	0	1	0	52	10
1984–85	42	5	6	1	4	2	3	1	55	9
1985–86	42	7	7	0	4	1	1	0	54	8
TOTAL	141+1	24	16	1	10	3	5	1	172+1	29

John Mackin

A talented and polished right-back, John Mackin gave the club four years' excellent service and was a key figure in the promotion season of 1970–71. A Glaswegian, he was born on 18 November 1943 and signed for Northampton Town in 1963, making his League debut for the Cobblers in the First Division in 1965–66. After a short spell on loan at Lincoln City he moved to Bootham Crescent in September 1969, making his debut that month in a Fourth Division encounter at Workington, and he quickly became a fixture in

City's defence. Sound and consistent, John figured in the FA Cup runs of 1969–70 and 1970–71 and was a reliable penalty taker. Mackin played in 184 senior games for the club and scored eight goals. In the summer of 1973, he moved to non-League Corby Town as player-manager.

Appearances

	League		FA Cup		League Cup		TOTAL	
SEASON	Apps	Gls	Apps	Gls	Apps	Gls	Apps	Gls
1969–70	36+1	0	5	0	0	0	41+1	0
1970–71	46	2	6	1	4	0	56	3
1971–72	46	5	3	0	4	0	53	5
1972–73	29+2	0	1	0	1	0	31+2	0
TOTAL	157+3	7	15	1	9	0	181+3	8

Christopher Marples

Born in Chesterfield on 3 August 1964, Chris Marples started his professional career with his home-town club and helped the Spireites win the Fourth Division Championship in 1984–85. He moved to Stockport County then joined City in July 1988 for £28,000, a club record fee for a goalkeeper. A very sound custodian and safe handler, Chris missed only one game in his first two seasons at Bootham Crescent. In 1989–90 he was voted Clubman of the Year and was elected Fourth Division 'keeper of the season by his fellow professionals. By 1992, however, he had

lost his place to rising star Dean Kiely and, after 166 senior appearances, returned to his former club Chesterfield before moving into non-League football. Marples was an excellent cricketer and kept wicket for Derbyshire in the County Championship in the mid-1980s.

Appearances

	League		FA Cup		League Cup		Others		TOTAL	
SEASON	Apps	Gls	Apps	Gls	Apps	Gls	Apps	Gls	Apps	Gls
1988–89	45	0	1	0	2	0	3	0	51	0
1989–90	46	0	1	0	4	0	3	0	54	0
1990–91	29	0	3	0	2	0	2	0	36	0
1991–92	16	0	3	0	2	0	0	0	21	0
1992–93	2	0	1	0	0	0	1	0	4	0
TOTAL	138	0	9	0	10	0	9	0	166	0

John (Jack) Middlemiss

One of City's stalwarts in the Midland League days of the 1920s was Jack Middlemiss, who made a then club record 259 League and Cup appearances. Born on 17 January 1896 in Easington, Co. Durham, he played for Blyth Spartans and Hull City before moving to Fulfordgate in the summer of 1923. He made his Midland League debut at home to Scunthorpe United on 25 August 1923 and was a virtual ever present in the City side for six seasons, mostly at left-half. He only scored five goals but one of those was in City's first-ever game in the FA Cup in September 1923 when, in an extra preliminary round, Castleford and Allerton United were beaten 2–1 at Fulfordgate. Only three players in the club's history have bettered Middlemiss's total of 31 FA Cup appearances – Norman Wilkinson, Gary Ford and Barry Jackson. In April 1929 Jack was rewarded with a testimonial match against Middlesbrough – the first-ever City player to be so honoured – and he received the then sizeable amount of £111. Middlemiss left the club in July 1929 just prior to City's baptism in the Football League, and returned to his former club Blyth. The first of City's great and loyal servants, he died in April 1984 aged 88.

Appearances

	League		FA Cup		TOTAL	
SEASON	Apps	Gls	Apps	Gls	Apps	Gls
1923–24	33	0	5	1	38	1
1924–25	35	0	2	0	37	0
1925–26	36	0	4	0	40	0
1926–27	36	3	7	0	43	3
1927–28	43	0	6	0	49	0
1928–29	45	1	7	0	52	1
TOTAL	228	4	31	1	259	5

Ronald Mollatt

A hard-working and enthusiastic half-back, Ron Mollatt spent five seasons with the club and was a popular character. He was born in Edwinstowe, Nottinghamshire, on 24 February 1932 and turned professional with Leeds United in 1950. While at Elland Road, Ron made a number of senior appearances and became a close friend of the legendary Welsh star John Charles, and was even best man at his wedding. He joined City in the summer of 1955 and made his debut at home to Gateshead in a Division Three North fixture on 3 December 1955. In the following campaign Mollatt established himself in City's midfield, and he went on to play an important part in the 1958–59 promotion season. An aggressive and hard-tackling player, he made 125 League and Cup appearances for the club before moving to Bradford City in 1960. He was later involved in local football and managed York Railway Institute FC in the Northern Counties East League for several years. Ron died in 2001.

Appearances

	League		FA Cup		TOTAL	
SEASON	Apps	Gls	Apps	Gls	Apps	Gls
1955–56	13	0	0	0	13	0
1956–57	36	0	0	0	36	0
1957–58	21	0	0	0	21	0
1958–59	33	1	0	0	33	1
1959–60	21	0	1	0	22	0
TOTAL	124	1	1	0	125	1

Graeme Murty

Born in Saltburn on 13 November 1974, Graeme Murty joined the club through the Youth Training Scheme in 1991 and helped the City youngsters reach the quarter-finals of the FA Youth Cup in 1992–93, losing to Manchester United. He turned professional in 1993 and made his senior debut in an Autoglass Trophy match at home to Hartlepool United on 9 November 1993. Later that term he made his Football League debut in a Second Division (League One) game at Port Vale. He was blooded gently and by 1995–96 the pacy and enthusiastic right-sided midfielder had established himself at senior level. He played in the League Cup triumph at Manchester United that season and, the following year, netted one of the goals that knocked Everton out of the competition. Graeme was switched to full-back and greatly impressed with his tackling and all-round ability. He was signed by Reading in the summer of 1998 for a then club record fee received of £700,000 after making a total of 141 appearances for City. Murty figured in the Royals' rise from Division Two (League One) and captained the side as they won promotion to the Premiership in 2006. At the start of their second season at the top level, he approached 300 League appearances for the Berkshire club. He was also capped for Scotland, the country of his father's birth.

Appearances

	League		FA Cup		League Cup		Others		TOTAL	
SEASON	Apps	Gls	Apps	Gls	Apps	Gls	Apps	Gls	Apps	Gls
1993–94	1	0	0	0	0	0	1	0	2	0
1994–95	17+3	2	0	0	0	0	0	0	17+3	2
1995–96	31+4	2	0	0	3	0	3+1	0	37+5	2
1996–97	25+2	2	3+1	0	5	1	1+1	0	34+4	3
1997–98	32+2	1	2	0	2	1	1	0	37+2	2
TOTAL	106+11	7	5+1	0	10	2	6+2	0	127+14	9

Lee Nogan

Vastly experienced forward and former Welsh international Lee Nogan joined City from Luton Town in February 2001 and made his debut at home to Exeter City that month, when the club were at the bottom of the Football League. He made an immediate impact with his all-round skill which, together with six goals in the closing weeks of that campaign, helped the club pull clear of the relegation zone. Born on 21 May 1969 in Cardiff, Nogan served his apprenticeship with Oxford United and turned professional in 1987, making his Football League debut in 1987–88. He went on to play for Watford, Reading, Grimsby Town, Darlington and Luton Town, and was capped for Wales twice. Lee was a virtual ever present in City's attack in their last three seasons in the Football League, finishing second-top scorer in 2001–02 and top marksman in 2003–04. Lee was a tireless worker and led the line in fine style with the ability to hold the ball. He served the club well in what were difficult times and, in the summer of 2003, was appointed assistant manager to Chris Brass.

Nogan figured in the first half of the club's first season in the Conference but left City in February 2005 after making a total of 183 League and Cup appearances and scoring 37 goals. He later managed Whitby Town. Overall, he played in 561 Football League games and scored 114 goals.

Appearances

	League		FA Cup		FA Trophy		League Cup		Others		TOTAL	
SEASON	Apps	Gls	Apps	Gls	Apps	Gls	Apps	Gls	Apps	Gls	Apps	Gls
2000–01	16	6	0	0	0	0	0	0	0	0	16	6
2001–02	40+2	13	5	0	0	0	1	0	1	0	47+2	13
2002–03	39+7	5	2	0	0	0	1	0	1	1	43+7	6
2003–04	38+1	8	1	1	0	0	1	0	0+1	0	40+2	9
2004–05*	18+4	3	1	0	0+1	0	0	0	2	0	21+5	3
TOTAL	151+14	35	9	1	0+1	0	3	0	4+1	1	167+16	37

* Conference

Emmanuel (Manny) Panther

Born in Glasgow, Manny Panther started his professional career at St Johnstone before joining Partick Thistle, and he also had a spell on loan with Brechin City prior to his move to York before the start of the 2005–06 campaign. Manny made his debut at home to Crawley Town on 13 August 2005 and immediately made a big impact in City's midfield. A fully committed player with strength and talent, he captained the side to the promotion Play-offs in 2006–07 and led the team to the semi-finals of the FA Trophy the following campaign. At his best when making strong driving runs from midfield, his form dipped a little towards the

end of the 2007–08 season and he was released at the end of his contract in May 2008 after making 136 senior appearances and moved to Exeter City.

Appearances

	League		Play-offs		FA Cup		FA Trophy		Others		TOTAL	
SEASON	Apps	Gls	Apps	Gls	Apps	Gls	Apps	Gls	Apps	Gls	Apps	Gls
2005–06	36+1	0	0	0	0	0	0	0	0	0	36+1	0
2006–07	42+2	3	2	0	2	0	1	0	0	0	47+2	3
2007–08	36+4	1	0	0	2	0	6+1	0	1	0	45+5	1
TOTAL	114+7	4	2	0	4	0	7+1	0	1	0	128+8	4

Alfred Patrick

Fourth in the club's all-time scoring list is Alf Patrick, who netted 117 goals in 241 League and Cup appearances and was leading marksman in the first four post-war seasons. Born on 25 September 1921 in York, he signed professional terms for City in September 1946 after the war, during which he served in the Royal Engineers in the Italian campaign. After a prolific scoring spell with the reserves, he made his Football League debut at the age of 25 and scored in a 3–2 win over Stockport County at Bootham Crescent on 2 November 1946. From then until April 1953 he was the leading figure in City's attack, and during that post-war boom time for football, he thrilled the big crowds with his scoring feats, pace and tremendous wholehearted enthusiasm. Alf's best season was in 1948–49, when he chalked up 27 goals, including five in a memorable 6–1 win over Rotherham United on 20 November 1948 – the only time a City player has achieved this feat in the Football League. That season he also netted twice in a 3–2 win at Hull in front of over 40,000 at Boothferry Park. Together with the five-goal haul plus four against Halifax Town in August 1947, Alf also hit hat-tricks on four other occasions, thus equalling Reg Baines's tally of six Football League hat-tricks for the club. During the 1951–52 season he became the first player to score 100 League goals in peacetime football for the club. His last term at York (1953–54) was spent in the reserve side and he left for Scarborough in 1954, although injury ended his career early the following year. Patrick later returned to Bootham Crescent, helping train and coach the youngsters in a third team that operated in the Yorkshire League. A very good local cricketer, he played for Dringhouses for many years. Alf always gave 100 per cent for his local club and, without doubt, is one of the most popular and best-liked players to have worn the number-nine shirt for City.

Appearances

	League		FA Cup		TOTAL	
SEASON	Apps	Gls	Apps	Gls	Apps	Gls
1946–47	23	17	1	0	24	17
1947–48	27	19	0	0	27	19
1948–49	41	26	3	1	44	27
1949–50	37	14	1	0	38	14
1950–51	33	9	4	4	37	13
1951–52	36	15	3	2	39	17
1952–53	31	9	1	1	32	10
TOTAL	228	109	13	8	241	117

Matthew Patrick

Matt Patrick gave the club 11 years' stalwart service and along with his namesake, Alf, was one of the most popular players in the immediate post-war seasons. Born in Slamanan, Angus, on 13 June 1919, he was on the books of Cowdenbeath prior to the outbreak of war. During the hostilities, when based at York, he made a number of guest appearances for City. Just before the start of the 1946–47 season he left his native Scotland and signed for City, making his debut on the opening day of that first peacetime campaign. Matt was to prove an outstanding capture with his versatility and all-round ability. The stocky and hard-working player was at home in either defence, midfield or attack and went on to make 261 League and Cup appearances and score 48 goals. In 1950–51 he was top scorer with 14 League and Cup

goals. His first-team playing days ended in 1954, but Patrick went on to give three more years' valuable service, playing for both the reserves and third team, and helping and encouraging the younger players. An outstanding clubman, Matt continued to live and work in York after hanging up his boots. He died in 2005.

Appearances

	League		FA Cup		TOTAL	
SEASON	Apps	Gls	Apps	Gls	Apps	Gls
1946–47	31	1	1	0	32	1
1947–48	42	8	1	0	43	8
1948–49	35	14	3	0	38	14
1949–50	38	9	1	0	39	9
1950–51	45	13	4	1	49	14
1951–52	10	2	2	0	12	2
1952–53	18	0	0	0	18	0
1953–54	29	0	1	0	30	0
TOTAL	248	47	13	1	261	48

Nigel Pepper

A powerhouse midfielder, Nigel Pepper was a mainstay in the City side for almost seven seasons and notched 45 goals in 281 League and Cup games. Nigel was born in Rawmarsh, Rotherham, on 25 April 1968, turned professional with his home-town club in 1986 and moved to York four years later in an exchange deal which took Steve Spooner to Millmoor. He made his City debut at home to Maidstone United on 25 August 1990 and quickly made his mark with his forceful tackling and tigerish displays. Nigel sometimes earned the wrath of referees and was sent off three times in 1990–91, all of the red cards coming against Darlington! A key man in the promotion-winning team of 1992–93, he became the club's penalty-kick expert and netted 19 out of 22 spot-kicks

during his time at York. Pepper was always in the thick of the action giving 100 per cent, and he figured in the League Cup triumphs against Manchester United and Everton in the mid-1990s. Apart from 1993–94, when he missed a good deal of the campaign owing to injury, he was a virtual ever present during his time at Bootham Crescent. At the end of February 1997 he was transferred to Bradford City for £100,000 and, at the time of his departure, the midfielder was leading scorer with 12 League goals to his credit that term. He later played for Aberdeen and Scunthorpe United before injury cut short his career.

Appearances

	League		Play-offs		FA Cup		League Cup		Others		TOTAL	
SEASON	Apps	Gls	Apps	Gls	Apps	Gls	Apps	Gls	Apps	Gls	Apps	Gls
1990–91	38+1	3	0	0	3	1	0+1	0	2	0	43+2	4
1991–92	33+2	4	0	0	3	0	2	0	1	0	39+2	4
1992–93	34	8	3	0	0	0	2	0	0	0	39	8
1993–94	18+5	0	0+1	0	2	0	2	0	3	0	25+6	0
1994–95	35	4	0	0	0	0	2	1	2	0	39	5
1995–96	39+1	9	0	0	1	0	4	1	3	0	47+1	10
1996–97	26+3	12	0	0	3	1	4+1	1	1	0	34+4	14
TOTAL	223+12	40	3+1	0	12	2	16+2	3	12	0	266+15	45

Ernest Phillips

An outstanding right-back and captain, Ernie Phillips led the City side in the club's glory days in the mid-1950s, and his fine leadership took the club to the brink of Wembley in 1955. Phillips was born in North Shields on 29 November 1923 and joined Manchester City in 1947. He made 80 League appearances while at Maine Road before being transferred to Hull City in 1951, in a move

which involved Don Revie going to Manchester. Ernie was signed by manager Jimmy McCormick and made his debut in the sensational 6–2 win at Wrexham in August 1954. A fine tackler – he perfected the sliding tackle – and fine distributor of the ball, he was a virtual ever present in his time with the club and did not miss a game in his first two seasons. A model professional, he led the side with distinction and sportsmanship and played in 183 senior games for the club, including all of the 19 FA Cup ties during his successful period with City. Phillips left the club in 1958 and moved back to his first club Ashington, later becoming player-manager of Bridlington Town. Ernie died in 2004.

Appearances

	League		FA Cup		TOTAL	
SEASON	Apps	Gls	Apps	Gls	Apps	Gls
1954–55	46	1	8	0	54	1
1955–56	46	0	5	0	51	0
1956–57	36	0	1	0	37	0
1957–58	36	1	5	0	41	1
TOTAL	164	2	19	0	183	2

John (Jack) Pinder

One of City's all-time greats, right-back Jack Pinder's playing career with the club spanned 19 years (1929–1948) and, including wartime appearances, over 400 games. Born on 1 December 1912 in Acomb, York, he played for York Boys, Yorkshire Boys and then England Boys, captaining his country against Scotland at Hampden Park in 1927. Interestingly, future England star Raich

Carter was playing in the same team. Jack signed for City in 1929 and turned professional in February 1930, when the club were based at Fulfordgate and had just been elected to the Football League. He made his senior debut on 5 September 1932 in a Division Three North game at Stockport County. In 1934–35 he established himself in the first team and from then until the outbreak of war was a regular in the defence. A no-nonsense, hard-tackling player, he figured prominently in the 1937–38 FA Cup run to the quarter-finals. Perhaps his most memorable game was against West Bromwich Albion in the fourth round. Jack put through his own goal early in the match and was then injured but typically battled on and, in the last five minutes, saw two of his free-kicks converted by Reg Baines to earn a famous 3–2 victory. A part-time player throughout his career – he was a railway telegraphist – he continued to play regularly for the club during the war and made 173 appearances from 1939 to 1946. He figured in the club's run to the 1942–43 League War Cup (North) semi-finals and the FA Cup successes in 1945–46. When peacetime football resumed in 1946–47, he was a regular in the defence again and netted four goals from the penalty spot. Pinder's last senior outing for City was at New Brighton in March 1948, when he reached 229 Football League and FA Cup appearances. He became the first player to receive two benefit matches, against Grimsby Town in 1938 and Huddersfield Town in 1946. After his playing days he continued to help the club for many years as a coach and scout. Jack retained a great love and affection for his local club and was one of the first to join the supporters' trust in 2002. He attended the fan's forum and various functions right up to his death in August 2004 at the age of 91 – a true legend of York City.

Appearances

	League		FA Cup		Others		TOTAL	
SEASON	Apps	Gls	Apps	Gls	Apps	Gls	Apps	Gls
1932–33	19	0	0	0	0	0	19	0
1933–34	4	0	0	0	0	0	4	0
1934–35	33	0	3	0	3	0	39	0
1935–36	20	0	1	0	0	0	21	0
1936–37	19	0	7	0	0	0	26	0
1937–38	31	0	5	0	1	0	37	0
1938–39	23	0	1	0	0	0	24	0
1945–46	0	0	8	0	0	0	8	0
1946–47	40	4	1	0	0	0	41	4
1947–48	10	0	0	0	0	0	10	0
TOTAL	199	4	26	0	4	0	229	4

Brian Pollard

Fast and direct winger Brian Pollard had two successful spells with the club and twice helped City win promotion. Born in York on 22 May 1954, he won five England Youth caps when a youngster on City's books, and he turned professional in March 1972. He made his League debut that month aged 17 in a Third Division (League One) game at home to Rotherham United, and his lively play soon impressed operating down either flank. Brian figured prominently in the promotion campaign of 1973–74 and played 40 games in the club's two seasons in Division Two (Championship). In 1976–77 he was top scorer and voted Clubman of the Year, before being transferred to Watford in November 1977 for a then club record fee received of £33,000. He helped Watford, then under the chairmanship of Elton John and manager Graham Taylor, win promotion from the Fourth to the Second Division. Pollard then moved to Mansfield Town before returning to Bootham Crescent in September 1981. The following term he netted 19 goals to finish second-top scorer and played a big part in the Division Four Championship campaign of 1983–84. In total, he made 302 League and Cup appearances and netted 68 goals by the time he left the club in 1984. Pollard later played for Chesterfield and Hartlepool United before joining non-League North Ferriby United.

Appearances

	League		FA Cup		League Cup		Others		TOTAL	
SEASON	Apps	Gls	Apps	Gls	Apps	Gls	Apps	Gls	Apps	Gls
1971–72	4	0	0	0	0	0	0	0	4	0
1972–73	30	7	3	1	0	0	0	0	33	8
1973–74	21+6	4	2	0	5+1	1	0	0	28+7	5
1974–75	11+1	1	0	0	0	0	0	0	11+1	1
1975–76	27+1	5	1	0	0	0	0	0	28+1	5
1976–77	41+3	12	4+1	1	3	0	0	0	48+4	13
1977–78	17	5	0	0	3	0	0	0	20	5
1981–82	25+1	3	3	2	0	0	0	0	28+1	5
1982–83	44+2	17	4	2	2	0	0	0	50+2	19
1983–84	29+1	6	3	0	2	1	1	0	35+1	7
TOTAL	249+15	60	20+1	6	15+1	2	1	0	285+17	68

Andrew (Andy) Provan

A lively and tricky winger, Andy Provan served the club well in his four years at Bootham Crescent and was an important member of the side that won promotion in 1964–65, finishing second-top scorer with 18 goals. Born on New Year's Day 1944 in Greenock, he was on the books of Barnsley before joining City just prior to the start of that successful 1964–65 season. Andy scored on his debut in the opening-day win over Rochdale and was an ever present that term, impressing with his pace and opportunism. A cheeky little player, he was a firm favourite with the fans and could operate on either flank but played chiefly down the left wing. In a win over Bradford Park Avenue in

September 1966 he scored an unorthodox goal that was typical of the player. He sprinted onto a through-ball, dribbled around the advancing goalkeeper and then, dropping on all fours, lay on the ground at full stretch to head the ball into the unguarded net. It took the crowd a few moments to realise it was a goal! Provan went on to score 54 times in 179 senior games before he was transferred to Chester in August 1968. He later played for Wrexham, Southport and Torquay United and also had a spell playing in the States.

Appearances

	League		FA Cup		League Cup		TOTAL	
SEASON	Apps	Gls	Apps	Gls	Apps	Gls	Apps	Gls
1964–65	46	18	2	1	1	0	49	19
1965–66	26	2	1	0	3	1	30	3
1966–67	40+1	15	6	1	3	2	49+1	18
1967–68	44	13	1	0	1	0	46	13
1968–69	3	1	0	0	1	0	4	1
TOTAL	159+1	49	10	2	9	3	178+1	54

Kevin Randall

Born in Ashton-under-Lyne, Manchester, on 20 August 1945, Kevin Randall was, for a number of seasons, one of the most consistent scorers in the Football League. He made his debut with Bury in 1965–66 and moved to Chesterfield the following season. Randall spent five seasons at Saltergate and helped them gain promotion to the Third Division in 1970. He then moved to Notts County and figured in their promotion to the Second Division in 1973 before moving to Mansfield and helping the Stags win the Third Division Championship in 1977. City signed him from Town for £8,000 in October 1977, and he scored twice on his debut that month in a home win over Doncaster Rovers. A very skilful player who led the line well with his ability to hold the ball, Kevin proved popular at Bootham Crescent, and in 1980 he was appointed youth coach and assistant manager. Upon the departure of Barry Lyons in December 1981 he took over as caretaker manager, but three months later he was relieved of his duties and left the club. He made a total of 118 appearances for City and scored 31 goals. After a spell as manager of Goole Town, he was appointed coach and then manager of Chesterfield but was dismissed from that post in November 1988 and joined the coaching staff at Mansfield. He later returned to Chesterfield as assistant manager and coach and helped the Spireites reach the FA Cup semi-final in 1996–97.

Appearances

	League		FA Cup		League Cup		TOTAL	
SEASON	Apps	Gls	Apps	Gls	Apps	Gls	Apps	Gls
1977–78	29+1	8	1	0	0	0	30+1	8
1978–79	37+5	10	5	2	0	0	42+5	12
1979–80	21+5	7	3	1	2	1	26+5	9
1980–81	9	2	0	0	0	0	9	2
TOTAL	96+11	27	9	3	2	1	107+11	31

Shaun Reid

A hard-working and determined midfielder, Shaun Reid served the club well in what were lean times in the late 1980s and early 1990s. The brother of

Peter Reid, of England and Everton fame, Shaun was born in Huyton, Liverpool, on 13 October 1965 and turned professional with Rochdale in 1983. He moved to City in December 1988 for a fee of £32,500 and made his debut in a Fourth Division encounter at Scarborough on Boxing Day. He captained the side during his time with the club and was industrious and a strong tackler. Reid totalled 122 League and Cup games and scored eight times before returning to Rochdale in 1992. He later played for Bury and Chester City.

Appearances

	League		FA Cup		League Cup		Others		TOTAL	
SEASON	Apps	Gls	Apps	Gls	Apps	Gls	Apps	Gls	Apps	Gls
1988–89	24	2	0	0	0	0	0	0	24	2
1989–90	24+1	4	0	0	3	0	0	0	27+1	4
1990–91	28+1	0	1	0	2	0	3	1	34+1	1
1991–92	28	1	3	0	2	0	2	0	35	1
TOTAL	104+2	7	4	0	7	0	5	1	120+2	8

James (Jimmy) Rudd

One of the finest ball players and entertainers to appear for York City, Jimmy Rudd thrilled Bootham Crescent crowds in the early post-war period. He was born in Dublin on 25 October 1919 and joined Manchester City before the war. Rudd

was signed by York City in March 1947 and immediately struck up a brilliant left-wing partnership with Sid Storey. Jimmy's ball skills and wizardry made him an exciting and outstanding personality, and he scored 24 goals in 87 League and Cup games for the club. In February 1949 he was transferred to Leeds United and later played for Rotherham United, Scunthorpe United and Workington, with whom he finished his League career in 1952–53. Jimmy's playing days ended at Northwich Victoria and, upon retiring, he made his home in Manchester. He died in December 1985.

Appearances

	League		FA Cup		TOTAL	
SEASON	Apps	Gls	Apps	Gls	Apps	Gls
1946–47	17	9	0	0	17	9
1947–48	41	8	1	0	42	8
1948–49	25	6	3	1	28	7
TOTAL	83	23	4	1	87	24

William (Billy) Rudd

Nephew of Jimmy, Billy Rudd without doubt inherited a lot of his uncle's footballing skills. Born in Manchester on 13 December 1941, he played for Manchester Boys and Lancashire Boys alongside

Nobby Stiles, the future Manchester United and England World Cup star. After trials at Old Trafford and Arsenal, Rudd joined Stalybridge Celtic in 1958 then signed for Birmingham City the following year. He made 24 First Division appearances for the Blues before moving to Bootham Crescent in November 1961, and although he made his debut that month in a home game against Accrington Stanley, the match was later deleted from the record books following the Lancashire club's demise. His first official game was on 13 January 1962 at home to Gillingham. In four seasons with the club (1962–66), Billy missed only three League games and captained the side in the promotion campaign of 1964–65. A skilful inside-forward, Rudd proved a fine leader and was an outstanding player during his time with City, making 212 League and Cup appearances and scoring 31 goals. Rudd was transferred to Grimsby Town in the summer of 1966 and went on to play for Rochdale and Bury, ending his League days in 1976–77. In a long and excellent career, he made a total of 574 League appearances and netted 68 goals.

Appearances

	League		FA Cup		League Cup		TOTAL	
SEASON	Apps	Gls	Apps	Gls	Apps	Gls	Apps	Gls
1961–62	12	3	0	0	1	0	13	3
1962–63	44	8	4	0	2	0	50	8
1963–64	46	7	1	0	4	1	51	8
1964–65	46	9	2	0	1	0	49	9
1965–66	45	3	1	0	3	0	49	3
TOTAL	193	30	8	0	11	1	212	31

Richard (Ricky) Sbragia

Born in Lennoxtown, Glasgow, on 26 May 1956, Ricky Sbragia served his apprenticeship with Birmingham City and signed professional forms in June 1974. He made his League debut in 1974–75 and then moved to Walsall in October 1978. Sbragia helped the Saddlers gain promotion to the Third Division in 1979–80 and in the summer of 1980 was transferred to Blackpool, who were then in the Second Division (Championship). After two years at Bloomfield Road, new City boss Denis Smith signed him in the summer of 1982. Ricky made his debut on the opening day of the 1982–83 campaign at home to Torquay United in a Fourth Division game, and he soon established himself in the heart of the defence, striking up a magnificent partnership with John MacPhail in the Fourth Division Championship season of 1983–84. He did not score many goals, but one of the highlights of his career came when he netted the equaliser against Liverpool in the FA Cup fifth round in 1984–85. Injuries limited his appearances and in 1987 he retired, after playing 179 senior games, to concentrate on coaching duties. Sbragia was given the responsibility of looking after the junior and intermediate players at Bootham Crescent. He gained his full coaching badge and guided City's youngsters to the quarter-finals of the FA Youth Cup in 1992–93. Among the players who

developed under his guidance were Graeme Murty and Richard Cresswell. Sbragia left the club in 1994 and took over as youth team coach at Sunderland, where he spent a number of years before joining the backroom staff at Manchester United. Later, he was an assistant first-team coach at Bolton Wanderers before returning to Sunderland in a coaching capacity.

Appearances

	League		FA Cup		League Cup		Others		TOTAL	
SEASON	Apps	Gls	Apps	Gls	Apps	Gls	Apps	Gls	Apps	Gls
1982–83	46	1	4	0	2	0	0	0	52	1
1983–84	45	4	3	1	2	0	1	0	51	5
1984–85	25	2	6	1	3	0	0	0	34	3
1985–86	7	0	2	1	0	0	0	0	9	1
1986–87	26	0	2	0	4	0	1	0	33	0
TOTAL	149	7	17	3	11	0	2	0	179	10

Peter Scott

Full-back Peter Scott became the second York City player to receive international honours while with the club. Born in Liverpool on 19 September 1952, he served his apprenticeship with Everton and signed full-time professional forms at Goodison Park in July 1970. Scott made his First Division debut in 1971–72 and went on to make 44 League appearances for the Toffeemen. In December 1975 Wilf McGuinness brought him to City for a fee in the region of £11,000, and he made his debut that month in a Second Division (Championship) game at home to Hull City. A strong, hard-tackling defender, he was an England Youth international but was capped for Northern Ireland 10 times at full international level, with seven of those caps won while he was at Bootham Crescent. After playing in 114 League and Cup games, he was transferred to Aldershot for £30,000 in March 1979 and spent four seasons with the Hampshire club.

Appearances

	League		FA Cup		League Cup		TOTAL	
SEASON	Apps	Gls	Apps	Gls	Apps	Gls	Apps	Gls
1975–76	19	0	2	0	0	0	21	0
1976–77	24+1	0	3	0	3	0	30+1	0
1977–78	45	3	1	0	3	0	49	3
1978–79	11	0	0	0	2	0	13	0
TOTAL	99+1	3	6	0	8	0	113+1	3

James Seal

Born in Walton near Wakefield on 9 December 1950, Jimmy Seal joined Wolves as a junior and signed professional forms in March 1968. He made one First Division appearance while at Molineux before moving to Walsall during the 1969–70 campaign and then Barnsley in the summer of 1971. Seal spent one season at Oakwell and moved to Bootham Crescent for a fee of £6,000 plus Kevin McMahon in July 1972. Jimmy made his debut for the club on the opening day of the 1972–73 campaign, but he took time to settle down and only scored three goals in his first season. The

following season, however, he formed a fine striking partnership with Chris Jones and netted 17 League goals as City were promoted to the second tier of English football. In 1974–75 he was top scorer with 17 goals again as the club held their own in the Second Division, and he scored a magnificent goal to earn a 1–1 draw at Highbury in the third round of the FA Cup. A very popular and likeable personality, he netted 48 goals in 183 League and Cup games for the club. In November 1976 Seal was transferred to Darlington and spent three seasons at Feethams, finishing his League career with Rochdale in 1979–81. He made his home in York and played in local football for a number of years.

Appearances

	League		FA Cup		League Cup		TOTAL	
SEASON	Apps	Gls	Apps	Gls	Apps	Gls	Apps	Gls
1972–73	29+2	3	3	1	1	0	33+2	4
1973–74	43+1	17	2	0	5	0	50+1	17
1974–75	41	17	2	1	1	0	44	18
1975–76	34+5	5	2	1	3	2	39+5	8
1976–77	5+1	1	0	0	3	0	8+1	1
TOTAL	152+9	43	9	3	13	2	174+9	48

Stephen Senior

Born in Sheffield on 15 May 1963, Steve Senior joined York as an apprentice in 1979. After making good progress with the intermediates and reserves, he signed professional terms on his 18th birthday, shortly after making his first-team debut as a substitute at Aldershot on 25 April 1981. Steve was

nursed along gently and by 1983–84 had established himself at right-back. He was ever-present in the Championship-winning side until breaking his leg at Aldershot in April 1984. He made a full recovery and regained his place in the first team the following season, playing his part in the FA Cup runs of 1984–85 and 1985–86. A very talented defender, in his last four seasons at Bootham Crescent he was a vital cog in the back four, making a total of 206 League and Cup appearances. In May 1987 Senior was transferred to Northampton Town for £15,000, and a few months later he moved on to Wigan Athletic and then Preston North End.

Appearances

	League		FA Cup		League Cup		Others		TOTAL	
SEASON	Apps	Gls	Apps	Gls	Apps	Gls	Apps	Gls	Apps	Gls
1980–81	1+2	0	0	0	0	0	0	0	1+2	0
1981–82	14+3	1	3	0	0	0	0	0	17+3	1
1982–83	6+4	1	0	0	0	0	0	0	6+4	1
1983–84	39	1	3	0	2	0	1	1	45	2
1984–85	28	0	5	0	0+1	0	4	0	37+1	0
1985–86	33+1	3	6	0	2	0	2	0	43+1	3
1986–87	37	0	3	0	3	0	3	0	46	0
TOTAL	158+10	6	20	0	7+1	0	10	1	195+11	7

John Simpson

John Simpson served York City splendidly, first as a player (1948–54) and then as a physiotherapist (1977–83). Born in Hull on 27 October 1918, he spent a lifetime in football. He played for Hull City Boys while at school then joined Hull City as an amateur, playing a number of times for the Tigers' reserve team. After trials with Huddersfield Town, he signed professional terms in 1936 and made a number of First Division appearances for the Leeds Road club. During the war, Simpson was in the Army Physical Training Corps and guested for several clubs. He also captained the Southern Command side. After the war he rejoined Huddersfield and in March 1948 was signed by City for a then record fee paid of £1,000, making his debut that month at home to Southport. For the next six seasons, John gave the club excellent service at left-back. A hard-tackling, no-nonsense player, his chief attributes were his great fitness and speed. His playing days ended in 1954 after 220 senior appearances, and he spent nine years as coach with Hull City. Simpson moved to Hartlepool, first as coach and then manager. In 1971 he joined Cambridge United as coach and

physiotherapist and in the summer of 1977 was appointed trainer and physiotherapist at Bootham Crescent. For six seasons he carried out these duties in meticulous and dedicated fashion, and he was rewarded with a testimonial match against Leeds United in May 1983, which attracted a crowd of over 3,000. He died in 2000.

Appearances

	League		FA Cup		TOTAL	
SEASON	Apps	Gls	Apps	Gls	Apps	Gls
1947–48	10	0	0	0	10	0
1948–49	39	0	3	0	42	0
1949–50	22	0	1	0	23	0
1950–51	41	0	4	0	45	0
1951–52	44	0	3	0	47	0
1952–53	29	0	1	0	30	0
1953–54	22	0	1	0	23	0
TOTAL	207	0	13	0	220	0

Joseph Spence

The son of a famous England and Manchester United player, Joe Spence was born in Salford on 13 October 1925. He began his footballing days with Buxton and signed for Chesterfield in 1948. He did not appear in the first team while at Saltergate and moved to York in July 1950. A polished and cool defender, he made his City debut on 13 October 1950 in a Division Three North game at New Brighton. Spence played at either right-back or centre-half and was virtually ever present in seasons 1951–52 and 1952–53, totalling

115 League and Cup games for City. He left the club in the summer of 1954 and moved to Gainsborough Trinity in the Midland League.

Appearances

	League		FA Cup		TOTAL	
SEASON	Apps	Gls	Apps	Gls	Apps	Gls
1950–51	10	0	1	0	11	0
1951–52	43	0	3	0	46	0
1952–53	45	0	1	0	46	0
1953–54	12	0	0	0	12	0
TOTAL	110	0	5	0	115	0

Ronald Spence

Apart from a three-year break in the early 1960s, Ron Spence served York City from 1948 to 1975, first as an outstanding wing-half and then as trainer and physiotherapist. Born in Spennymoor on 7 January 1927, Spence was playing for Rossington Colliery in South Yorkshire when spotted by City, and he joined the club in March 1948. Ron made his debut at home to Barrow on 24 April 1948, and after establishing himself in the first team by 1950 he was a fixture in the side for six seasons. A fine attacking half-back and tireless worker, Spence was an integral part of the great 1954–55 side. However, a serious knee injury, sustained in a match against Barrow in March 1956, was to sideline him for 18 months. In typical fashion, he fought his way back to fitness and was in the side that played Birmingham and Bolton in

the FA Cup in 1957–58. He made his last League appearance in November 1958 and ended his playing days with the club in May 1960 with 306 senior games under his belt and 26 goals, including a hat-trick in a win over Wrexham in February 1950. After a spell with Scarborough, Spence returned to Bootham Crescent in the summer of 1963 and served the club as trainer, coach and physiotherapist for 12 years. In September 1975 he retired from football and went into the licensing trade. One of the club's outstanding stalwarts, he died in 1996, aged 69.

Appearances

	League		FA Cup		TOTAL	
SEASON	Apps	Gls	Apps	Gls	Apps	Gls
1947–48	1	0	0	0	1	0
1948–49	15	0	0	0	15	0
1949–50	6	4	0	0	6	4
1950–51	32	6	4	0	36	6
1951–52	44	2	3	0	47	2
1952–53	46	2	1	0	47	2
1953–54	34	7	1	0	35	7
1954–55	46	2	8	1	54	3
1955–56	36	2	5	0	41	2
1956–57	0	0	0	0	0	0
1957–58	9	0	3	0	12	0
1958–59	11	0	1	0	12	0
TOTAL	280	25	26	1	306	26

Peter Spooner

One of the heroes of the 1937–38 FA Cup run, Peter Spooner had two spells with York City in the 1930s. Born in Hepscott in the North East on 30 August 1910, he played for Newbiggin United and Ashington, and had trials with Newcastle United before signing for Bradford in 1930. Spooner joined City from Park Avenue in the summer of 1931, and after making his debut on 5 September 1931 at Rotherham United, the talented outside-left quickly impressed. In May 1933 he was transferred to Sheffield United for a fee of £500 and joined former teammate Reg Baines at Bramall Lane. Peter returned to Bootham Crescent two years later and for the next three seasons was City's regular number 11. In the 1937–38 FA Cup run he scored one of the goals which beat Coventry in the third round, and he netted the winner in the fifth-round victory over Middlesbrough. He was almost the match-winner in the quarter-final tie against Huddersfield, but his header was cleared off the line. The clever and talented winger played in 212 League and Cup games and scored 48 goals. In May 1939 he left the club and joined Gateshead just before the outbreak of war.

Appearances

	League		FA Cup		Others		TOTAL	
SEASON	Apps	Gls	Apps	Gls	Apps	Gls	Apps	Gls
1931–32	22	2	0	0	0	0	22	2
1932–33	35	11	1	1	0	0	36	12
1935–36	42	7	1	0	1	0	44	7
1936–37	41	12	7	3	3	0	51	15
1937–38	37	10	9	2	0	0	46	12
1938–39	12	0	0	0	1	0	13	0
TOTAL	189	42	18	6	5	0	212	48

Paul Stancliffe

Central-defender Paul Stancliffe had the honour and distinction of leading York City out at Wembley on the club's first visit to the stadium in May 1993. Born in Sheffield on 5 May 1958, he started his professional career with Rotherham United in 1976 before joining Sheffield United in 1983 for a fee of £100,000, topping 275 League appearances for both clubs. After a short spell at Wolverhampton Wanderers, Paul was signed by City boss John Bird in the summer of 1991 and made captain. He made his debut at Rochdale on the opening day of the 1991–92 campaign but injuries caused him to miss much of that season. However, the following term the experienced and commanding centre-half led the side to promotion via the Play-offs at Wembley. Stancliffe, who marshalled the defence in fine style, led the side to the Second Division (League One) Play-offs in 1993–94, during which time he was appointed player-coach. He played his last game in November 1994 in an FA Cup replay at Rotherham, the ground where he had made his senior debut almost 20 years earlier. Stancliffe became the youth-team coach in 1997 and helped guide City's youngsters to the last 16 of the FA Youth Cup in 1998–99, losing to West Ham United. He totalled 103 senior appearances for City and is pictured with the Division Three Play-off trophy in 1993. He left the club in the mid-2000s and joined the coaching staff at Doncaster Rovers.

Appearances

	League		Play-offs		FA Cup		League Cup		Others		TOTAL	
SEASON	Apps	Gls	Apps	Gls	Apps	Gls	Apps	Gls	Apps	Gls	Apps	Gls
1991–92	16+2	1	0	0	0	0	1	0	0	0	17+2	1
1992–93	41	1	3	0	1	0	1	0	2	0	48	1
1993–94	28	1	2	0	0	0	0	0	0	0	30	1
1994–95	4	0	0	0	2	0	0	0	0	0	6	0
TOTAL	89+2	3	5	0	3	0	2	0	2	0	101+2	3

Gordon Staniforth

Born in Hull on 23 May 1957, Gordon Staniforth represented Hull, Yorkshire and England Schoolboys. He joined his home-town club as an apprentice and signed professional terms in 1974. Having made a number of Second Division appearances for the Tigers, Staniforth joined York on loan midway through the 1976–77 season, and a month later in January 1977 he was signed for a fee of £7,500. Gordon made his debut on 27 December 1976 at Sheffield Wednesday in a Third Division (League One) encounter. He was an instant success and was a fine attacking player, chiefly down the left. He had considerable flair and skill and was leading scorer in 1977–78 and 1978–79, winning the Clubman of the Year award in each of these seasons. He recorded hat-tricks at home to Port Vale in May

1979 and at Wigan Athletic in September 1979. The following month Staniforth was transferred to Carlisle United for a then club record fee received of £120,000 and later moved to Plymouth Argyle in 1983, helping the Devon club reach the FA Cup semi-finals in 1983–84. His next port of call was Newport County, and he returned to Bootham Crescent in October 1987 to play on a non-contract basis for the rest of the season. Gordon made a total of 164 League and Cup appearances for City, netting 40 goals. In 1988–89 he played for North Ferriby and, for the second time in his career, came close to a Wembley appearance when the Humberside club narrowly lost to Tamworth in the FA Vase semi-finals. Gordon Staniforth finally hung up his boots, and in the summer of 1989 he was appointed community officer at York City FC and steward of the social club at Bootham Crescent. A PFA North Regional coach, he later became involved in coaching at York University.

Appearances

	League		FA Cup		League Cup		TOTAL	
SEASON	Apps	Gls	Apps	Gls	Apps	Gls	Apps	Gls
1976–77	28	3	0	0	0	0	28	3
1977–78	46	12	1	0	3	1	50	13
1978–79	45	15	5	4	2	0	52	19
1979–80	9	3	0	0	2	1	11	4
1987–88	15+4	1	4	0	0	0	19+4	1
TOTAL	143+4	34	10	4	7	2	160+4	40

Alan Stewart

Signed from Huddersfield Town in August 1949 for what was reported as the then second highest fee paid in York City's history, Alan Stewart was a tall, commanding figure at the heart of City's defence in the 1950s. Born in Newcastle on 24 July 1922, he joined Huddersfield during the war and made a number of First Division appearances while at Leeds Road. Alan made his debut at the start of the 1949–50 season at Barrow and soon established himself in City's defence. He overcame a series of bad injuries – he missed the whole of the 1952–53 campaign but returned to play an important role in the memorable 1954–55 season. During the Cup run, Stewart had outstanding games against Stan Mortensen (Blackpool) and Len Duquemin (Spurs), and he was a stalwart in defence. His cut head in the semi-final replay against Newcastle proved a big handicap, as the side went down to defeat. Without doubt one of the best 'stoppers' and headers of the ball to wear

City's colours, he received a benefit from the club in 1955. Stewart, who made 231 League and Cup appearances for the club, hung up his boots in 1957 and died in 2004.

Appearances

	League		FA Cup		TOTAL	
SEASON	Apps	Gls	Apps	Gls	Apps	Gls
1949–50	29	0	1	0	30	0
1950–51	30	0	4	0	34	0
1951–52	20	0	2	0	22	0
1952–53	0	0	0	0	0	0
1953–54	28	1	0	0	28	1
1954–55	35	0	8	0	43	0
1955–56	46	0	5	0	51	0
1956–57	20	0	3	0	23	0
TOTAL	208	1	23	0	231	1

Sidney Storey

Sid Storey was perhaps the best bargain York City ever bought. He joined from Wombwell in May 1947 for £100, and in nine splendid seasons he made 354 League and Cup appearances and scored 42 goals. Born at Darfield, South Yorkshire, on Christmas Day 1919, Storey was a coal miner and played his early football for mining sides Ardsley Welfare and Grimethorpe Athletic. He played some wartime games for Huddersfield Town and then joined Wombwell Athletic. A small inside-forward with tremendous talent and skills, he was regarded at one time as the best ball-player in the Northern Section. For nine seasons, Sid was a first-team regular and a key man in City's attack in 1954–55. He netted vital goals in the wins at Blackpool and

Bishop Auckland, and it was a big blow when injury caused him to miss the semi-final against Newcastle at Hillsborough. He did play in the replay but missed several games at the end of that season, which upset promotion hopes. Storey received a benefit in 1955, but at the end of the following campaign he was rather surprisingly given a free transfer. The club sent him a letter thanking him for his 'fine football' and recorded in the club minute book his 'outstanding service and loyalty'. He joined Second Division Barnsley before moving on to Accrington Stanley and Bradford, ending his playing days at Park Avenue when he was 40. He returned to Bootham Crescent in 1960 in the capacity of trainer-coach and served in this position for three years. Throughout his playing days, Sid had remained a coal miner. In his later years he worked for the West Yorkshire Bus Company as a driver. He was without doubt one of the most skilful inside-forwards to play for the club.

Appearances

	League		FA Cup		TOTAL	
SEASON	Apps	Gls	Apps	Gls	Apps	Gls
1946–47	3	0	0	0	3	0
1947–48	41	12	1	0	42	12
1948–49	35	6	3	0	38	6
1949–50	28	1	1	0	29	1
1950–51	39	8	2	0	41	8
1951–52	39	1	3	0	42	1
1952–53	44	3	1	0	45	3
1953–54	36	3	1	0	37	3
1954–55	28	4	7	2	35	6
1955–56	37	2	5	0	42	2
TOTAL	330	40	24	2	354	42

Barry Swallow

An outstanding centre-half and captain, Barry Swallow led City from the Fourth to the Second Division (Championship) in the early 1970s. He was born at Arksey, near Doncaster, on 2 July 1942 and turned professional with his home-town club in 1959. Swallow went on to play for Crewe Alexandra, Barnsley and Bradford City before joining City in October 1969, making his debut the following month in an FA Cup tie against Whitby Town. For over six seasons the talented and skilful player starred in the heart of City's defence and went on to make 312 League and Cup appearances and score 27 goals. Barry skippered the side to promotion to the Third Division in 1970–71 and to the second tier of English football in 1973–74. In the latter campaign he was voted by his fellow professionals as Division Three's centre-half and captain for the season. Swallow finished his playing days at the end of the 1975–76 season and was granted a testimonial match against an All Star XI including Bobby and Jack Charlton and Peter Lorimer. In August 1981 he became a City director and had a spell as caretaker manager from March to May 1982, during which time he was instrumental in bringing Denis Smith to York. In the late 1980s he had another period as caretaker

boss prior to the appointment of John Bird. He was voted City's Player of the Millennium, but sadly his popularity diminished because of his involvement, as a director of Bootham Crescent Holdings, in the off-field traumas in the early 2000s.

Appearances

	League		FA Cup		League Cup		TOTAL	
SEASON	Apps	Gls	Apps	Gls	Apps	Gls	Apps	Gls
1969–70	28	3	7	2	0	0	35	5
1970–71	44	5	5	0	4	0	53	5
1971–72	46	5	3	1	4	1	53	7
1972–73	43+1	2	3	0	1	0	47+1	2
1973–74	46	3	2	1	6	1	54	5
1974–75	37	2	2	0	1	0	40	2
1975–76	24	1	2	0	3	0	29	1
TOTAL	268+1	21	24	4	19	2	311+1	27

Gary Swann

Local lad Gary Swann had two successful seasons in City's midfield in the early 1990s, helping the club win promotion via the Play-offs in 1992–93 and reach the Second Division Play-offs the following year. Born in York on 11 April 1962, Swann began his professional career with Hull City before moving to Preston North End and had 385 Football League games under his belt before signing for City in the summer of 1992. A hard-working and creative midfielder, he was a key player, and although he only scored two goals in the promotion campaign, it should be noted that these were in the Play-off semi-final second leg against Bury and in the Final at Wembley against Crewe Alexandra. The following season, Gary played another big role as City just missed out on promotion to Division One (Championship). An influential figure in the City side in his time with the club, Swann made 95 senior appearances. He moved to Scarborough in 1994 and later played in Hong Kong. Gary is pictured celebrating his goal against Bury, which sent City to Wembley.

Appearances

	League		Play-offs		FA Cup		League Cup		Others		TOTAL	
SEASON	Apps	Gls	Apps	Gls	Apps	Gls	Apps	Gls	Apps	Gls	Apps	Gls
1992–93	38	0	3	2	1	0	2	0	2	0	46	2
1993–94	44	4	2	0	0	0	2	0	1	0	49	4
TOTAL	82	4	5	2	1	0	4	0	3	0	95	6

Arthur (Archie) Taylor

Born in Doncaster on 7 November 1939, Archie Taylor played for his home-town club as an amateur before signing professional forms with Bristol City in 1958. He made his League debut in 1959–60 and went on to play for Barnsley, Mansfield Town, Goole Town and Hull City before joining Halifax Town in 1963. Archie had a short spell with Bradford City before moving to Bootham Crescent in October 1968, scoring on his

debut that month in a home game against Bradford Park Avenue. Archie had tremendous pace, a fierce shot and the ability to play on either flank, making him a firm favourite with the fans. Taylor played an important part in the 1970–71 promotion season, making 39 appearances, but he was not retained at the end of the campaign and moved on to non-League football with Gainsborough Trinity and then Frickley Colliery. Taylor played a total of 112 senior games for the club and scored nine goals.

Appearances

	League		FA Cup		League Cup		TOTAL	
SEASON	Apps	Gls	Apps	Gls	Apps	Gls	Apps	Gls
1968–69	30	3	3	0	0	0	33	3
1969–70	27	1	5	1	0	0	32	2
1970–71	36+3	4	4	0	4	0	44+3	4
TOTAL	93+3	8	12	1	4	0	109+3	9

Desmond Thompson

The son of former City goalkeeper George Thompson, who played for the club in the Midland League in 1926–27, Des Thompson was born in Southampton on 4 December 1928. He had been on the books of Scunthorpe United and Gainsborough Trinity before City signed him from South Yorkshire club Dinnington in January 1951. After only three games in the reserves, he won a place in the senior side, making his debut on 10 February 1951 in a Division Three North game at Halifax Town. In his one and a half years at Bootham Crescent, he was the regular first-choice 'keeper. Very agile and a sound handler of the ball, Des was an outstanding goalkeeper and, as a result, soon attracted the attention of leading clubs. In November 1952 he was transferred to First Division Burnley for the sizeable fee of £7,350 after making 83 League and Cup appearances. Thompson spent over seven years at Turf Moor before joining Sheffield United in 1955. He stayed nine years with the Blades, mostly as understudy to England international Alan Hodgkinson, before retiring from the League scene in 1964. He finished his playing days with Buxton. His brother George was also a goalkeeper of note in the 1950s and 1960s, with Scunthorpe, Preston North End and Carlisle United.

Appearances

	League		FA Cup		TOTAL	
SEASON	Apps	Gls	Apps	Gls	Apps	Gls
1950–51	19	0	0	0	19	0
1951–52	42	0	3	0	45	0
1952–53	19	0	0	0	19	0
TOTAL	80	0	3	0	83	0

Oliver Thompson

Oliver Thompson joined York in June 1929 from Queen's Park Rangers and captained the side in their first three seasons of League football. A very

constructive left-half and an able skipper, his experience was invaluable in those important early days in the Football League, and Ollie also figured in the FA Cup triumphs of 1929–30 and 1930–31. He made 133 League and Cup appearances for City. Born in Gateshead on 11 May 1900, Thompson played for Spennymoor before entering League football with Chesterfield in 1922. He then spent two seasons with QPR before moving to Fulfordgate. After leaving City, Thompson joined Halifax Town and returned to Chesterfield in 1933. He was to stay at Saltergate as trainer until the 1960s. He died in 1975.

Appearances

	League		FA Cup		TOTAL	
SEASON	Apps	Gls	Apps	Gls	Apps	Gls
1929–30	42	0	6	0	48	0
1930–31	39	0	5	0	44	0
1931–32	40	2	1	0	41	2
TOTAL	121	2	12	0	133	2

Christopher Topping

An outstanding central-defender, Chris Topping gave the club 10 years' fine service, during which time he showed remarkable consistency. Born locally at Bubwith on 6 March 1951, he became City's first apprentice professional in 1967, and manager Tom Johnston gave the 17-year-old his Football League debut on 28 December 1968 in a Fourth Division game at home to Newport County. The following week he played his first FA Cup tie in a third-round match at Bootham Crescent against First Division (Premiership) Stoke City. Chris turned professional in March 1969 and quickly established himself at senior level. Following in the footsteps of Barry Jackson, he was a dominant and commanding figure in the heart of the defence with his keen tackling and strength in the air. He was a key figure in the promotion-winning sides of 1970–71 and 1973–74, and in the club's first season in the second tier he was voted Clubman of the Year. Along with 'keeper Graeme Crawford, he played in every one of City's games in the Second Division and, from September 1970 until April 1978, he played in 355 consecutive League games – a record sequence for the club. His final tally of 463 senior appearances has been bettered only by Jackson and Andy McMillan. Topping was transferred to Huddersfield Town in May 1978 for a fee of £20,000 and later played for Scarborough, before having a spell as player-manager with Northallerton Town.

Appearances

	League		FA Cup		League Cup		TOTAL	
SEASON	Apps	Gls	Apps	Gls	Apps	Gls	Apps	Gls
1968–69	22	1	1	0	0	0	23	1
1969–70	32+2	1	1	0	0	0	33+2	1
1970–71	42	3	6	0	4	0	52	3
1971–72	46	0	3	0	4	1	53	1
1972–73	46	0	3	0	1	0	50	0
1973–74	46	1	2	0	6	0	54	1
1974–75	42	2	2	0	1	0	45	2
1975–76	42	0	2	0	3	0	47	0
1976–77	46	0	5	0	3	0	54	0
1977–78	46	3	1	0	3	1	50	4
TOTAL	410+2	11	26	0	25	2	461+2	13

Stephen Tutill

Another in the line of outstanding local central-defenders, Steve Tutill amassed 366 senior appearances in his City career, which spanned over 11 years. Born on 1 October 1969 in York, he won eight caps for England Schoolboys and joined City as an associate schoolboy. Steve made his senior debut as a 17-year-old substitute at Rochdale in the Associate Members' Cup in January 1987, and his Football League baptism came the following season. A broken ankle sustained in December 1987 was a setback but, after turning professional the following month, the determined young

defender made a quick recovery and was a fixture in the heart of City's defence by 1989–90. In 1990–91 Tutill was voted Clubman of the Year. A strong tackler and excellent in the air, he unfortunately missed much of the 1992–93 promotion campaign, chiefly because of injury. The following campaign, however, Steve was an ever present and skippered the side to a place in the Second Division (League One) promotion Play-offs, also figuring in the League Cup run of 1995–96 in which Manchester United were vanquished. Tutill was rewarded with a richly deserved testimonial year, and a benefit game against Middlesbrough in July 1997 attracted a crowd of 7,123. A fine stalwart for the club, he moved to Darlington in 1997–98 and finished his League days at Chesterfield.

Appearances

	League		Play-offs		FA Cup		League Cup		Others		TOTAL	
SEASON	Apps	Gls	Apps	Gls	Apps	Gls	Apps	Gls	Apps	Gls	Apps	Gls
1986–87	0	0	0	0	0	0	0	0	0+1	0	0+1	0
1987–88	20+1	0	0	0	4	0	2	0	1+1	0	27+2	0
1988–89	21+1	1	0	0	1	0	1	0	1	0	24+1	1
1989–90	42	0	0	0	1	0	3	0	3	1	49	1
1990–91	42	0	0	0	3	0	2	0	3	0	50	0
1991–92	39	1	0	0	3	0	1	0	2	0	45	1
1992–93	6+2	0	0+1	0	0	0	1	0	0	0	7+3	0
1993–94	46	4	2	0	2	0	2	0	3	0	55	4
1994–95	37+2	0	0	0	0	0	2	0	1	0	40+2	0
1995–96	25	0	0	0	1	0	5	0	5	0	36	0
1996–97	13+2	0	0	0	3+1	0	1	0	1	0	18+3	0
1997–98	2	0	0	0	0	0	1	0	0	0	3	0
TOTAL	293+8	6	2+1	0	18+1	0	21	0	20+2	1	354+12	7

Dennis Walker

Born in Northwich on 26 October 1944, Dennis Walker joined Manchester United from school and turned professional in 1961. He made one Football League appearance for the Old Trafford club at the end of the 1962–63 season, becoming United's first black player. Dennis signed for City in April 1964 and made his debut on 22 August 1964 at home to Rochdale. Playing initially at inside-forward, he made an explosive beginning to his career at Bootham Crescent, topping the scoring charts in early October with 12 goals in 15 matches. He then

switched to his customary left-half position, and his skilful, constructive midfield play was an important factor as City swept to promotion to the Third Division. Walker spent a further three years at York with variable success, but he was never quite able to maintain the form and promise of his first season. In total he netted 19 goals in 169 League and Cup games for the club. In the summer of 1968 he moved to Cambridge United, then in the Southern League, and was with them when they were elected to the Football League in 1970. He later played for Poole Town and died in 2003.

Appearances

	League		FA Cup		League Cup		TOTAL	
SEASON	Apps	Gls	Apps	Gls	Apps	Gls	Apps	Gls
1964–65	44	15	1	0	0	0	45	15
1965–66	41	2	1	0	3	0	45	2
1966–67	32	0	6	0	3	0	41	0
1967–68	32+5	2	1	0	0	0	33+5	2
TOTAL	149+5	19	9	0	6	0	164+5	19

Keith Walwyn

Second in the club's all-time scoring list is Keith Walwyn, who netted 140 goals in 291 League and Cup games over six magnificent years for City in the 1980s. Born in Nevis in the West Indies on 17 February 1956, Keith was signed by City boss Barry Lyons from Chesterfield in June 1981 for the bargain fee of £4,000. His first-team chances at Saltergate had been limited but his impact at York was immediate, and he scored on his debut on 29 August 1981 at Tranmere in a win on opening day of the season. The big centre-forward led the City attack with great success and was one of the most feared and respected strikers in the lower leagues. Apart from 1984–85, when he missed a number of games through injury, he notched over 20 goals per season, and the ever-popular striker was voted Clubman of the Year in 1981–82 and 1986–87. Keith netted 25 goals in the Fourth Division Championship campaign of 1983–84, when he struck up an outstanding partnership up front with John Byrne. Walwyn also figured in the FA Cup runs in the mid-1980s, when the club twice reached the fifth round. He twice recorded hat-tricks – at home to Mansfield Town in the League in November 1982 and at Sunderland in the League Cup in 1986. Utterly fearless, he was very strong in the air and would run through the proverbial brick wall. Walwyn

was an outstanding figure in his time at Bootham Crescent and a much-loved player who always gave 100 per cent effort. In 1987 he moved to Blackpool for a tribunal-fixed fee of £35,000 and later played for Carlisle United and Kettering Town. Keith died in April 2003 at the early age of 47, but his name lives on through the Keith Walwyn Vice Presidents' Lounge at the ground, a hospitality suite officially opened by his widow Liz in August 2006. A true legend, Keith was a great favourite of City fans, and his scoring feats will never be forgotten.

Appearances

	League		FA Cup		League Cup		Others		TOTAL	
SEASON	Apps	Gls	Apps	Gls	Apps	Gls	Apps	Gls	Apps	Gls
1981–82	44	23	3	2	2	0	0	0	49	25
1982–83	41	21	4	2	2	1	0	0	47	24
1983–84	45	25	1	0	2	0	1	0	49	25
1984–85	27	9	6	2	4	1	0	0	37	12
1985–86	46	22	7	4	4	3	0	0	57	29
1986–87	42	19	3	1	4	4	3	1	52	25
TOTAL	245	119	24	11	18	9	4	1	291	140

Edwin (Ted) Wass

Ted Wass gave York City splendid and dedicated service throughout the 1930s. He played at full-back in the early part of his footballing career, but by the time of the great FA Cup runs (1936–38) he

had been converted to centre-half and developed into a great 'stopper'. Born near Chesterfield in 1910, he was the younger brother of Horace, who for many years played with great distinction for the Spireites. Ted was also on Chesterfield's books before moving to York in September 1931, and he made his debut on 2 January 1932 at Tranmere Rovers. Within two years Wass had established himself in the first team, and for five seasons he was a regular in City's defence and a key man in the FA Cup triumphs. Wass was granted a benefit match in May 1939, when Newcastle United provided the opposition, and he totalled 253 senior games for the club. Throughout his City days, Wass was a part-time professional and lived and worked in Chesterfield as an engineer. During the war he served in the Royal Navy and suffered serious wounds when his minesweeper was sunk off Crete. He died in 1955.

Appearances

	League		FA Cup		Others		TOTAL	
SEASON	Apps	Gls	Apps	Gls	Apps	Gls	Apps	Gls
1931–32	1	0	0	0	0	0	1	0
1932–33	10	0	0	0	0	0	10	0
1933–34	39	0	1	0	3	0	43	0
1934–35	33	0	3	0	1	0	37	0
1935–36	40	0	1	0	1	0	42	0
1936–37	39	0	7	0	3	0	49	0
1937–38	41	0	9	0	1	0	51	0
1938–39	19	0	1	0	0	0	20	0
TOTAL	222	0	22	0	9	0	253	0

James Weir

A Glaswegian born on 12 April 1939, Jimmy Weir joined Fulham from Clydebank Juniors in 1957. He made only a handful of League appearances while at Craven Cottage and moved to York in June 1960, making his City debut on the opening day of the 1960–61 campaign at home to Millwall. A very skilful ball-player, he could operate on either wing but appeared predominately on the left. He was a fine opportunist and had an outstanding second season, netting 28 goals in 41 League outings. Weir hit two hat-tricks that term – at home to Crewe Alexandra in October 1961 and at Workington in April 1962, when City just failed to gain promotion. That term he also helped the club reach the quarter-finals of the League Cup. Jimmy was a lively character and very popular with the fans – a match-winner. In total he netted 39 goals in 95 senior appearances. Weir was transferred to Mansfield Town in September 1962 and later played for Luton Town, Tranmere Rovers and Scarborough.

Appearances

	League		FA Cup		League Cup		TOTAL	
SEASON	Apps	Gls	Apps	Gls	Apps	Gls	Apps	Gls
1960–61	36	10	6	0	0	0	42	10
1961–62	41	28	1	0	6	1	48	29
1962–63	5	0	0	0	0	0	5	0
TOTAL	82	38	7	0	6	1	95	39

Norman Wharton

Born at Askham, near Barrow, on 28 July 1903, Norman Wharton was City's first-choice 'keeper for the last three seasons before the war. He had been with a number of clubs before moving to York, starting his playing career with his hometown club in 1922, then moving to Preston before returning to Holker Street in 1927. He was transferred to Sheffield United in 1928 for a fee of £250 and joined Norwich City three years later. Wharton won a Third Division South Championship medal with the Canaries in 1933–34, and in May 1935 he teamed up with Doncaster Rovers. A year later he was signed by City, making his debut on 29 August 1936 at Halifax Town and immediately establishing himself in the senior side. Arguably the best goalkeeper to play for the club before the war, he figured in all 16 FA Cup ties played in 1936–37 and 1937–38. Norman's finest display was in the fourth-round tie at Swansea in January 1937, when he gave a magnificent exhibition of goalkeeping in a goalless draw. He made 138 senior appearances for the club and moved to Leeds United in August 1939. An electrician by trade, Wharton was quite a character. He took life very seriously and in the dressing-room would talk on every subject under the sun, switching from politics to religion and so on in a flash, and he was the victim of many a leg pull. He died in July 1961 shortly before his 58th birthday.

Appearances

	League		FA Cup		Others		TOTAL	
SEASON	Apps	Gls	Apps	Gls	Apps	Gls	Apps	Gls
1936–37	42	0	7	0	3	0	52	0
1937–38	41	0	9	0	1	0	51	0
1938–39	34	0	1	0	0	0	35	0
TOTAL	117	0	17	0	4	0	138	0

Norman Wilkinson

Without a doubt one of the most loyal and outstanding players to appear for York City, Norman Wilkinson gave 12 years' fine service to the club. Born in Alnwick on 16 February 1931, he played for Hull City as an amateur while in the RAF in 1953–54. Wilkinson joined York City in May 1954 and scored twice on his debut in the famous 6–2 victory at Wrexham on the opening day of the 1954–55 season. The youngest member of the semi-final team, his finest hour came when he netted twice in the 3–1 victory over Tottenham Hotspur in the fifth round. Norman figured in two promotion-winning campaigns – 1958–59 and 1964–65 – and netted three League hat-tricks in his City career. His total of 127 League goals and an overall aggregate of 143 goals make him the leading scorer in City's history. His chief attributes

were his skill in the air, his outstanding positional play and his ability to create space and openings for his colleagues, but he will be particularly remembered for his fine sportsmanship and club loyalty. He played in 401 League and Cup games for the club before leaving in 1966, and no other City player has matched his record of 39 FA Cup appearances. In recognition of his fine service, Wilkinson was presented with an inscribed gold watch by the City directors in May 1966. After leaving Bootham Crescent, he played for Annfield Plain in the Wearside League but retained his links with the club, acting as a scout in the North East. Throughout his playing career, he was a part-time professional with a boot-and-shoe repair business.

Appearances

	League		FA Cup		League Cup		TOTAL	
SEASON	Apps	Gls	Apps	Gls	Apps	Gls	Apps	Gls
1954–55	39	19	8	4	0	0	47	23
1955–56	27	10	5	1	0	0	32	11
1956–57	38	17	3	1	0	0	41	18
1957–58	41	10	5	2	0	0	46	12
1958–59	27	9	1	0	0	0	28	9
1959–60	37	14	3	0	0	0	40	14
1960–61	35	11	6	4	1	0	42	15
1961–62	18	3	1	0	4	0	23	3
1962–63	38	15	4	2	0	0	42	17
1963–64	27	10	1	2	3	0	31	12
1964–65	23	9	2	0	0	0	25	9
1965–66	4	0	0	0	0	0	4	0
TOTAL	354	127	39	16	8	0	401	143

Alan Woods

A popular, talented and industrious midfield player, Alan Woods spent six seasons at Bootham Crescent in the 1960s. Born in Doncaster on 15 February 1937, Woods was capped for England Schoolboys and England Youth, and a teammate at both levels was Duncan Edwards. Woods joined Tottenham Hotspur as a junior and signed professional forms on his 17th birthday. He played in six First Division games for Spurs before being transferred to Swansea Town in December 1956. After three and a half years at Vetch Field, he moved to York in June 1960. He scored on his City debut at home to Millwall on 20 August 1960 and was a most consistent player. Alan missed only 21 League games in his first five seasons with City, and he was a key man at wing-half in the promotion season of 1964–65. He totalled 259 League and Cup games for the club before leaving Bootham Crescent in 1966, later playing for Boston United

and Gainsborough Trinity. His son, Neil, who was on the club's books as a schoolboy, went on to play for Doncaster Rovers, Glasgow Rangers and Ipswich Town and played for City in 1998–99.

Appearances

	League		FA Cup		League Cup		TOTAL	
SEASON	Apps	Gls	Apps	Gls	Apps	Gls	Apps	Gls
1960–61	46	1	6	0	1	0	53	1
1961–62	42	1	1	0	7	0	50	1
1962–63	38	0	4	0	2	0	44	0
1963–64	37	2	1	0	3	0	41	2
1964–65	44	0	2	0	1	0	47	0
1965–66	20+1	0	1	0	2	0	23+1	0
TOTAL	227+1	4	15	0	16	0	258+1	4

John Woodward

Born in Glasgow on 10 January 1949, John Woodward was a Scottish Youth international. He was spotted by Arsenal while playing for Glasgow junior side Possilpark, and he joined the Gunners in January 1966. He was to make only a handful of senior appearances in a five-and-a-half-year stay at Highbury before being signed by City in July 1971. Woodward made his debut on 18 October 1971 at home to Torquay United. A versatile utility player who could operate in either defence or midfield, he took a little while to settle down at Bootham Crescent. John established himself in the senior side the following season and in the 1973–74 promotion campaign played an important part in the team's success. He was a virtual ever present in

the line up that term and scored twice in the opening day win at Charlton. A somewhat underrated performer, he served the club well and went on to complete seven seasons with the club, making 191 League and Cup appearances. Woodward left City in 1978 but continued to live in York and played in local soccer for many years.

Appearances

	League		FA Cup		League Cup		TOTAL	
SEASON	Apps	Gls	Apps	Gls	Apps	Gls	Apps	Gls
1971–72	10+4	0	0+1	0	0+1	0	10+6	0
1972–73	35+3	2	3	0	0	0	38+3	2
1973–74	38+2	4	2	0	6	0	46+2	4
1974–75	12+5	0	2	0	0	0	14+5	0
1975–76	33+1	0	2	0	1	0	36+1	0
1976–77	17	0	0	0	3	0	20	0
1977–78	7	0	0	0	3	0	10	0
TOTAL	152+15	6	9+1	0	13+1	0	174+17	6

Peter Wragg

Born in Rotherham on 12 January 1931, Peter Wragg was an England Schoolboy international and joined his home-town club as a junior. He signed professional terms in April 1948 and spent four and a half years at Millmoor before his transfer to Sheffield United in January 1953. He went on to play 56 League games for the Blades, most of them in the First Division, and scored 17 goals. Just prior to the start of the 1956–57 campaign, he was signed by manager Sam Bartram for the sizeable fee of £4,000, and he made his debut on the opening day of the campaign at Accrington Stanley. Wragg gave City seven seasons' outstanding service and was a most versatile player, equally at home at centre-forward, inside-forward or half-back. He was leading scorer twice, in 1958–59 and 1960–61, netted three hat-tricks and is one of only five players to score four goals for the club in a Football League match, achieving that feat in a 5–1 win at Crewe in January 1961. A fully qualified FA coach, Peter captained the side in the 1958–59 promotion season and went on to make 297 League and Cup appearances. His tally of 87 goals puts him ninth in the all-time scoring list. Wragg was transferred to Bradford City in 1963 and spent two seasons at Valley Parade. He continued to live in York and for some time helped to run Haxby FC in the York & District Football League. He died in 2004.

Appearances

	League		FA Cup		League Cup		TOTAL	
SEASON	Apps	Gls	Apps	Gls	Apps	Gls	Apps	Gls
1956–57	46	8	3	1	0	0	49	9
1957–58	42	11	5	1	0	0	47	12
1958–59	41	14	1	0	0	0	42	14
1959–60	39	3	3	0	0	0	42	3
1960–61	32	22	6	0	1	0	39	22
1961–62	42	15	1	0	7	5	50	20
1962–63	22	5	4	2	2	0	28	7
TOTAL	264	78	23	4	10	5	297	87

York City Managers

John Collier

July 1928 to May 1930 and May 1933 to March 1937

John 'Jock' Collier was appointed the first official manager of York City in July 1928, prior to the start of what was to be the club's last season in the Midland League.

Born in Dysart, Fifeshire, on 1 February 1897, Collier played for Inverkeithing Juniors and had trials for the Scottish Junior international team. He signed for Raith Rovers and then, in the summer of 1920, was transferred to Hull City. A hard-tackling right-half, he made 169 League appearances in six years with Hull and captained the side for a couple of seasons before moving to Queen's Park Rangers in 1926.

Collier joined York City as player-manager, but a broken ankle ended his playing days after only two senior appearances. He was at the helm as City successfully bridged the gap between non-League and Third Division football, but at the end of the first season of League soccer he left York to become a publican. Collier retained an interest in City's affairs, and in May 1933 he was reappointed manager. City's fortunes were at a low ebb, but under Collier's leadership steady progress was made as York continued to establish themselves at League level. In 1936–37 they progressed to the fourth round of the FA Cup. Collier was very much involved in the coaching side of the game that season, but in March 1937 he announced his retirement from football and went into a business partnership with one of his brothers in Scotland. Sadly, he was troubled by ill health and was only 43 when he died in Hull in December 1940.

George William Sherrington

May 1930 to May 1933

If anyone can claim the title 'Mr York City' it is George William (Billy) Sherrington. Born in Blaydon, Tyneside, on 18 November 1890, he moved to York shortly after World War One to take up a senior civil service post in the record office of the armed forces.

A keen football enthusiast, he was one of the founder members of the club in 1922 and one of the original directors. In 1924 he took over the role of honorary secretary and, inheriting a legacy of administrative problems, did a tremendous amount of work to help steer the club through difficult times in the mid-1920s. When the club gained election to the Football League in 1929 the secretarial duties increased, and in February 1930 he was appointed full-time secretary and relinquished his position as a director.

Upon the resignation of Jock Collier the following month he stepped into the breach, and combined his job as secretary with that of manager for three years. During this time the club moved from Fulfordgate to Bootham Crescent. From September 1954 to March 1956, he worked alongside trainer Tom Lockie in a dual caretaker managerial role, and they helped guide City to the FA Cup semi-finals.

Sherrington went on to complete 37 years as secretary and in 1951 was awarded the Football League's long service medal. Upon his retirement in 1961, many tributes were made to his outstanding

and tireless service to the club and he received a television set from the directors and a set of cut glass.

A truly outstanding and much-respected figure in the club's history, Sherrington was appointed York City's first-ever vice-president and in 1966 became president. He died in the summer of 1977, aged 86.

Thomas Mitchell

March 1937 to February 1950

Born in Spennymoor on 30 September 1899, Thomas Morris Mitchell played junior football in the North East with Tudhoe United, Spennymoor United and Blyth Spartans before signing for Newcastle United in 1920. He spent six seasons at St James's Park before joining Leeds United. In five years with the Yorkshire club, the left-winger made nearly 150 League appearances, helping them win promotion to the First Division in 1928. He moved to City in September 1931 and in two seasons made 24 League and Cup appearances for the club, scoring five goals. He netted City's first-ever goal at Bootham Crescent in a 2–2 draw against Stockport County on 31 August 1932.

Tom temporarily retired from football at the end of the 1932–33 campaign but returned to the club in March 1937 when he was appointed manager. He was to hold the position for 13 years, the longest spell in the club's history, and in his first full season he guided City to the quarter-finals of the FA Cup. A qualified FA coach, he made frequent summer coaching visits to Scandinavia. He served in the RAF during the war and was stationed in Norway. At the end of hostilities he returned to take charge of City again before resigning in February 1950 to concentrate on his business interests, which included a sports outfitters shop in York.

Tom was a City director from 1961 to 1969 and died in November 1984, aged 85.

Richard Duckworth

March 1950 to October 1952

Dick Duckworth was no stranger to Bootham Crescent when he was appointed manager in March 1950 – 12 years earlier he had captained the City side that reached the sixth round of the FA Cup.

Born in Bacup on 6 June 1906 to a former England and Manchester United star, he played at right-half, the same position as his father. Duckworth began his career with Second Division Oldham Athletic before moving to Chesterfield. In three seasons at Saltergate he was an ever-present, helping the Derbyshire club win promotion to the Second Division in 1930–31. He subsequently played for Southport, Chester and Rotherham United before joining City in 1936. Duckworth spent three seasons at Bootham Crescent, where his strong and forceful wing-half play had a big influence on City's success during that period.

He was player-manager at Newark at the outbreak of war and, after hostilities had ended, became coach at Chesterfield. At the time of his City appointment, Duckworth was the chief northern scout of Birmingham City.

In just over two full seasons at Bootham Crescent, he lifted the club from the foot of the Northern Section to a position in the top four. He left to take over at Stockport County in October 1952 and remained in charge at Edgeley Park until 1956, later managing Darlington and Scunthorpe United. He died in 1983, aged 76.

Charles Spencer

November 1952 to February 1953

Born in Washington, County Durham, on 4 December 1899, Charles William Spencer had an illustrious playing career as a centre-half with Newcastle United in the 1920s. He made 175 League and Cup appearances for the Magpies, winning an FA Cup-winners' medal in 1924 and a League Championship medal three years later. He was also capped twice for England. Spencer moved to Manchester United in 1928 and then became player-coach of Tunbridge Wells in 1930 and player-manager of Wigan Athletic in 1932.

Spencer was appointed manager of Grimsby Town in 1937, a position he held for 14 years before ill health forced him to retire. During most of his time at Blundell Park the Mariners were in the First Division, and in 1939 they reached the FA Cup semi-finals.

Recovered from illness, he had a spell in charge of Hastings United before his appointment as manager at Bootham Crescent in November 1952. Sadly, his health declined again and in February 1953 he died, aged 53, after less than three months in office.

James McCormick

June 1953 to September 1954

Born in Rotherham on 26 September 1912, James McCormick was a right-winger who made his Football League debut with his home-town club in the early 1930s. He played for Chesterfield before having six successful seasons with Tottenham Hotspur, making 137 League appearances and scoring 26 goals. After the war he appeared for Fulham, Lincoln City and Crystal Palace before ending his playing days.

McCormick went on to gain extensive coaching experience in Norway, Malta and Turkey, and at the time of his appointment as City boss in the summer of 1953 he was coach and assistant trainer at Sheffield United.

During what was to be McCormick's only full season at York, local centre-forward Dave Dunmore was sold to Tottenham Hotspur for a then club record fee received of £10,750. It was with this money that he recruited Arthur Bottom, Norman Wilkinson, Tommy Forgan, Ernie Phillips and George Howe, and the new look City side made a sensational start to the 1954–55 season with a 6–2 win at Wrexham. A 1–0 win over Hartlepools United followed but then came a 3–2 home defeat at the hands of Scunthorpe United. A dispute regarding team selection followed between McCormick and the board of directors. This was not resolved, and early in September 1954 McCormick's resignation was accepted and his contract cancelled by mutual consent. What followed is history, as the team which he had largely built went on to reach the semi-finals of the FA Cup.

In January 1968 Jimmy McCormick was killed in a road accident while on holiday in Spain, aged 55. At the time of his death he was a licensee of a public house in Hertfordshire.

Samuel Bartram

March 1956 to July 1960

Following the dramatic resignation of Jimmy McCormick, York City went 18 months without a manager. During this period – arguably the most successful in their history from a playing point of view – managerial affairs were looked after by trainer Tom Lockie and secretary Billy Sherrington. In March 1956, however, the board announced the appointment of Sam Bartram, the former Charlton Athletic goalkeeper who had spent 22 years at The Valley.

It was a popular choice as Bartram had guested for City during the war with great distinction, making 75 appearances and scoring three goals from the penalty spot.

Born in Simonside, County Durham, on 22 January 1914, Sam signed for Charlton in 1934 and helped the London club gain promotion from Division Three South to the First Division in successive seasons in the mid-1930s. After the war he played in successive FA Cup Finals for Charlton, gaining a winners' medal in 1946–47. In total he made 579 League appearances in goal for Athletic, the last at the age of 42 in March 1956, and he was generally regarded as the best goalkeeper never to be capped for England.

During his four-year reign at Bootham Crescent, Bartram experienced mixed fortunes. In 1957–58 City reached the fourth round of the FA Cup, knocking out First Division Birmingham City 3–0 en route, and narrowly failed on goal average to become founder members of the new national Third Division. The following campaign, however, they gained promotion for the first time in their history when they finished third in

Division Four, although they suffered immediate relegation in 1959–60.

In July 1960 City released Bartram, who took over as manager of Luton Town. He spent two years in charge at Kenilworth Road and then became involved in sports journalism, reporting on football for the *Sunday People.* He died suddenly in London in July 1981, aged 67.

Thomas Lockie

July 1960 to October 1967

Upon the departure of Sam Bartram, City turned to their loyal servant Tom Lockie to fill the managerial position at Bootham Crescent. Born in Duns, Scotland, on 13 January 1906, Lockie started his career with his home-town club before joining Glasgow Rangers, where he spent four years, mostly playing for the reserves.

A tall, commanding centre-half, Lockie went on to play for Leith Athletic and Barnsley before joining York City in 1933. He spent one season with the club, then played for Accrington Stanley and Mansfield Town before returning to Bootham Crescent as reserve-team trainer in 1936.

Lockie was soon promoted to first-team trainer and obtained qualifications for the treatment of players. He was very much involved with the team that reached the quarter-finals of the FA Cup in 1937–38 and did a tremendous amount of work to help the club during those difficult days of the war. A qualified FA coach, he was granted a testimonial

match in 1951–52, in which City played a Football League XI.

Following Jimmy McCormick's departure in September 1954, Lockie shared the managerial duties with Billy Sherrington and played a considerable part in team affairs as City embarked on one of the most glorious chapters in their history.

In his first two years as manager in his own right, York narrowly missed promotion back to the Third Division, but this was followed by a couple of disappointing campaigns and an application for re-election to the Football League in 1963–64. The following season was an outstanding one, however, with some of the best football seen at York since the FA Cup glory days of 10 years earlier. Playing exciting and attacking football, the side won promotion to the Third Division, finishing just one point behind champions Brighton. The club suffered immediate relegation in 1965–66 and the following season had to apply again for re-election. The start of the 1967–68 campaign was disastrous and, with the club at the bottom of the Fourth

Division without a win in 12 games, Lockie was dismissed in October 1967, the first City manager to suffer this fate. He was in charge for 332 Football League games, more than any other manager in the club's history, winning 120 and drawing 67.

Upon leaving City he spent a number of years working in the wages office at Rowntree Mackintosh. He lived in the village of New Earswick, near York, for over 40 years and died in July 1977 at the age of 71.

Joseph Shaw

November 1967 to August 1968

The choice of Joe Shaw as the next City manager was a popular one. Shaw had enjoyed an outstanding 21–year career with Sheffield United as a fine, ball-playing centre-half. He captained the Blades for a number of seasons and toured Australia with an FA representative side in 1952, as well as representing the Football League on a number of occasions.

Born in Marton, South Yorkshire, on 23 June 1928, he made well over 600 League appearances for United. In his last two seasons at Bramall Lane he assisted manager John Harris by looking after the Intermediate and Central League sides. One of Shaw's first moves after arriving at York was to appoint as coach a former Sheffield United colleague, Billy Hodgson. After the nightmare start to 1967–68, results improved, and by early April City had climbed to 14th position. A bad slump in the closing weeks followed, however, and to everyone's bitter disappointment another re-election bid had to be made.

During the summer, a number of signings were made, notably Phil Boyer from Derby County, and hopes were high for the new season. However, on 16 August 1968, Joe Shaw made the shock announcement of his resignation for personal reasons. His wife had a woollen and baby clothes shop in Sheffield and they were having difficulty selling this and purchasing a new house in the York area. This had been causing him considerable worry and he had found the constant travelling a problem. Shaw later returned to football and managed Chesterfield from 1973 to 1976, and he died in November 2007, aged 79.

Thomas Johnston

October 1968 to January 1975

Scotsman Tom Johnston is arguably the most successful manager in York City's history. He took over with the club in the lower reaches of the Fourth Division and, although he could not help avoid another re-election application in May 1969, he was to pilot City to the old Second Division (Championship) for the first, and so far only, time in their history.

Thomas Deans Johnston was born near Coldstream on 30 December 1918 and he spent his English playing career with Nottingham Forest and Notts County, making a total of 332 League appearances and scoring 112 goals, chiefly as a left-winger. He was in the Notts County side that lost to City in the quarter-finals of the FA Cup in 1955 and was reserve for Scotland four times before he hung up his boots in 1957.

A fully qualified FA coach, Johnston spent four years in Finland with the Valkeakosken Harka club, who won the Finnish Cup during his regime. Upon returning to England he was appointed manager of Rotherham United, and while at Millmoor he took United to the first-ever Football League Cup Final

when they were runners-up to Aston Villa in 1961. He later became manager of Grimsby Town and Huddersfield Town and took over as York City's chief on 31 October 1968.

A strong disciplinarian, Johnston gradually improved the squad and after finishing in mid-table in 1969–70, City gained promotion the following year. The next two seasons saw York avoid relegation only on goal-average, but in 1973–74 they astounded the football world by finishing third and winning promotion to the Second Division.

The manager had built an almost impregnable defence led by Barry Swallow. New signings Barry Lyons, from Forest, and Ian Holmes, from Sheffield United, brought skill and inventiveness to the midfield, in which former Hull City player Ian Butler also starred. Up front, Jimmy Seal and Chris Jones provided the scoring power. It was a glorious season and a marvellous achievement by the team under Johnston's leadership.

York were holding their own in the higher grade and had held Arsenal to a draw in the FA Cup at Highbury when it was announced early in January 1975 that the manager had asked to be released from his new four-year contract, which still had three years and two months to run.

Huddersfield Town, struggling near the foot of the Third Division, wanted his services and after some controversy over his contract he was allowed to go to Leeds Road as general manager. An official statement made by City read as follows: 'York City FC has accepted, with reluctance, the resignation of Mr T.D. Johnston from his position as manager of the club with effect from January 11 1975. The directors would like to place on record their appreciation of the services rendered to the club by Mr Johnston during his period as manager and wish him success in his new appointment.' His second spell at Huddersfield was to last two seasons.

Tom Johnston brought considerable success to Bootham Crescent during his six-year stay and did very well in transfer deals, achieving just the right blend in his team. Often described as a 'dour and canny Scot', his period as manager was not without controversy. During the 1972–73 season a major row developed between the players and Johnston, which amounted to a vote of no-confidence in their manager. The matter was eventually resolved by the directors and Tom Johnston went on to create history for York City. He died in 1994.

Wilfred McGuinness

February 1975 to October 1977

One of the most illustrious names to manage York City was Wilf McGuinness, but unfortunately he presided over a bad period in which the club slumped from the Second to Fourth Division. At the time of his departure they were in the bottom four of the Football League.

Born in Manchester on 25 October 1937, McGuinness was an outstanding wing-half and one of Manchester United's 'Busby Babes'. He captained Manchester, Lancashire and England schools and joined Manchester United on the same day as Bobby Charlton in January 1953. He helped United win the FA Youth Cup three times in the mid-1950s and made his Football League debut for the Red Devils in 1955, aged 17. Injury caused him to miss the ill-fated trip to Munich in February 1958 but his career was cut short by a broken leg in the early 1960s, soon after being capped twice for England. He went on to coach the England Youth team and helped Sir Alf

Ramsey with his preparations for the 1966 World Cup.

He was promoted from reserve-team trainer with Manchester United to chief coach and was later appointed to succeed Sir Matt Busby as manager. After only a short spell in charge, however, (and with the shadow of Busby never far way) he was relieved of the post and spent three years in Greece, managing Aris Salonika.

He was appointed manager of York City on 15 February 1975 and helped City stay in the Second Division. From then on, however, it was all downhill as the club finished 21st in the table in 1975–76 and bottom of the Third Division in 1976–77. He was unable to check the slide, and when he was dismissed on 20 October 1977 City were 22nd in the Fourth Division. During his period with the club, York won only 27 League matches out of 113 and suffered 60 defeats.

A most likeable and friendly man, it was very sad that Wilf McGuinness did not have success at York. He later became chief coach and physiotherapist at Bury.

Charles Wright

November 1977 to March 1980

Charles George Wright became the fourth Scotsman and second former Charlton Athletic goalkeeper to manage York City when he was appointed on 22 November 1977. A Glaswegian, he was born on 11 December 1938 and started his playing days with Morton before a spell with Glasgow Rangers. While doing his National Service in Hong Kong, Wright represented that country in an international match against Peru. His English clubs were Workington, Grimsby Town, Charlton and Bolton Wanderers, and he made a total of 535 League appearances. Wright was a qualified FA coach and became youth coach and looked after the reserve team at Bolton before his move to York.

Wright could not prevent City having to seek re-election in May 1978, but in his first full season there was a considerable improvement and the club finished 10th. In 1979–80 fortunes dipped again and the side was struggling in the lower reaches of the Fourth Division when he was sacked on 18 March 1980.

A hard-working manager, he was never able to quite rebuild the side that had dropped from the

Second Division to the Fourth in the mid-1970s. A very loyal man, Wright was at times outspoken and his colourful language was not to everyone's liking. He saw his side win 35 of 111 League games, and after coaching on the continent he managed Bolton Wanderers from January to December 1985. Upon leaving Burnden Park, Wright moved to London, where he ran his own transport café.

Barry Lyons

March 1980 to December 1981

Upon the departure of Charlie Wright, youth coach and former City player Barry Lyons was appointed caretaker manager. The re-election threat was beaten off, the side finished 17th, and on 4 May 1980 Lyons was officially appointed manager.

Born in Shirebrook on 14 March 1945, he began his career with Rotherham and moved to Nottingham Forest, for whom he made over 200 League appearances. He was transferred to York City in September 1973 for a then record club fee

paid of £12,000, and he played a big part in the side's promotion drive to the Second Division with his skilful play on the right side of midfield. He had the distinction of scoring City's first-ever goal in the Second Division in a 1–1 home draw against Aston Villa. In total he made 98 senior appearances and scored 11 goals before leaving Bootham Crescent for Darlington at the end of the 1975–76 season. He retired as a player in 1979 and returned to York as youth coach in June that year.

The team made a good start to his first full season as manager and were unbeaten in their first seven League and Cup games. A bad slump followed and City finished bottom of the Football League in 92nd position.

During the summer of 1981 he signed a player who was to have a big influence in the years ahead – Keith Walwyn from Chesterfield – but City continued to struggle in the lower half of the table and on 8 December 1981 Barry Lyons was relieved of his duties. He resumed as youth-team coach but finally left the club in July 1982 and took up employment outside football. After working as an insurance salesman he became a hotelier in York.

Denis Smith

May 1982 to May 1987

For the second half of the 1981–82 season, York City utilised the services of two caretaker managers. Former player and youth coach Kevin Randall was in charge until early March 1982, then club director Barry Swallow was put in control of team matters until the end of a season in which City finished 17th. One of Swallow's first acts was to obtain, on a month's loan, the Stoke City centre-half Denis Smith, who was approaching the end of his playing career.

Born in Stoke on 19 November 1947, Smith made over 400 League appearances for the Potters and won a League Cup-winners' medal in 1971–72. On 12 May 1982 it was announced that the experienced defender was to become York City's first player-manager since Jock Collier in the 1920s.

Smith chose the former Fulham and Norwich City striker Viv Busby as player-coach and his right-hand man, and a new era was ushered in at Bootham Crescent. A new defence was recruited

and City rose to seventh place in 1982–83. The manager hung up his boots at the start of the following season, which was to be a historic one for York City as they won their first major title – the Fourth Division Championship.

It was a record-breaking campaign as City became the first club in League history to reach 100 points, under the three points for a win system. The next two seasons were also successful: the side finished eighth and seventh in the Third Division and on each occasion reached the fifth round of the FA Cup, losing to Liverpool in replays at Anfield. City knocked out Arsenal in the fourth round en route to this stage in 1984–85.

After four good campaigns, the 1986–87 season was disappointing and relegation was only just avoided. On a salary reported to be £45,000 per annum, Smith was believed to be the highest-paid Third Division manager at the time, but at the end of May 1987 he accepted the vacant manager's job at Sunderland. After compensation of £20,000 was agreed between the clubs he moved to Roker Park, along with Viv Busby. Although the last months of the Smith-Busby regime at Bootham Crescent turned a little sour, the pair did an excellent job overall and put the club back on the footballing map. City won 105 and drew 54 of the 230 League games under their control. In their first season in charge at Roker Park, Sunderland won the Third Division Championship. The Rokermen went on to reach the First Division under Smith, but following immediate relegation he was dismissed at the end of 1991. He was later manager of Bristol City, Oxford United and West Bromwich Albion inj the 1990s, and Wrexham from October 2001 until January 2007.

Robert Saxton

June 1987 to September 1988

When Bobby Saxton became York City manager on 9 June 1987, he was faced with the monumental task of virtually rebuilding the side in a matter of a few weeks. Experienced players Keith Walwyn, Gary Ford and Steve Senior had left Bootham Crescent, and when training for the new season resumed in mid-July only three players had signed contracts.

Eventually a squad was acquired but almost inevitably the team struggled and relegation was

on the cards from the opening day. New signings were made during the summer of 1988 and when City started their first season back in the Fourth Division since 1984, hopes were reasonably high. A disastrous start was made, however, and with only one point from the opening four games and the side at the bottom of the League, Saxton resigned on 17 September. He blamed himself for putting the players under too much pressure and openly admitted that he did not know what to do next. During his time as manager, York won only eight of 50 League games.

Born in Doncaster on 6 September 1943, Saxton's playing career was spent as a central-defender with Derby County, Plymouth Argyle and Exeter City. He went on to manage the two latter clubs and then Blackburn Rovers. He had a good deal of success at Ewood Park, narrowly failing to win promotion to the First Division. Rovers fortunes then slumped and he was sacked in December 1986 and had a short spell coaching at Preston before joining City.

Upon leaving York he became assistant manager at Preston North End and then assistant boss to Jim Smith at Newcastle United. He was later on the coaching staff at Blackpool and then Sunderland.

John Bird

October 1988 to October 1991

Barry Swallow was again summoned as caretaker boss after Bobby Saxton's dramatic departure. Vital points were gained, which lifted City off the foot of the table, and on 10 October 1988 John Charles Bird became the 15th person to hold the official post of manager of York City. Like Saxton he was Doncaster-born, on 9 June 1948, and had started his playing days with his home-town club. A centre-half, Bird went on to play for Preston North End, Newcastle United and Hartlepool United and managed the latter before his City appointment. Assisted by coach Alan Little, he set about the recovery and rescue job, and at the end of his first season he had lifted City to 11th position.

For the first half of the 1989–90 season the team were well placed in the promotion race and hopes were high. A bad run in the New Year – both with results and injuries – saw them falter,

and although results improved in the closing weeks the final position of 13th was undoubtedly very disappointing to the manager.

The death of striker David Longhurst in September 1990 was a terrible blow but by the start of the following season Bird was laying the foundation of a strong side with the acquisition of Dean Kiely, Wayne Hall, Ray Warburton, Paul Stancliffe, Nigel Pepper and Jon McCarthy – all players who were to play a big part in the promotion success of 1992–93. However, a bad start to the 1991–92 campaign, partly due to injury problems, led to the dismissal of Bird in October 1991 with the side near the bottom of Division Four after just two wins in 11 games.

He later joined Doncaster on the coaching side and in the mid-1990s had a spell as manager of Conference club Halifax Town. Upon leaving the Shay he became an insurance salesman and then developed his lifelong hobby of painting and sketching as a business. A talented artist, he has had a number of his works displayed at the Tate Gallery.

John Ward

October 1991 to March 1993

Born in Lincoln on 7 April 1951, John Patrick Ward was relatively unknown when he was appointed the new City boss in October 1991.

As a forward he netted 91 goals in 223 Football League appearances for his home-town club and helped the Imps win promotion from Division Four in 1975–76. He later had spells with Watford, Grimsby Town and again at Sincil Bank before his playing days ended in the early 1980s.

Ward then concentrated on coaching and became assistant to Graham Taylor at Aston Villa. When Taylor became the England manager Ward helped coach the national youth side. Upon arriving at Bootham Crescent, Ward kept on John Bird's assistant Alan Little as his number two. Very articulate and a keen tactician, Ward settled well into his first managerial job and developed the side left by Bird. In the summer of 1992 he made a key signing when Paul Barnes was acquired from Stoke City for £50,000. Ward was very keen on community relations and with the fans, and he helped raise money for the Family Stand.

City made a great start to the 1992–93 season and led the table up to Christmas. A midterm slump followed but City were back on the promotion trail when Ward accepted a lucrative offer from Bristol Rovers and left Bootham Crescent in March 1993.

Sacked by Rovers in 1996, he had a spell as assistant boss at Burnley before taking over the managerial reins at Bristol City. He later spent a number of seasons as assistant chief and coach at Wolverhampton Wanderers before his appointment as manager of Cheltenham Town in November 2003. Ward subsequently guided the club to promotion to League One in 2005–06 and took over as boss at Carlisle United during the 2007–08 campaign, helping the Cumbrians reach the Play-offs.

Alan Little

March 1993 to March 1999

Since moving to Bootham Crescent with John Bird in October 1988, Alan Little had been second in command at City. Upon the departure of John Ward he was promoted to the managerial role, and after just two months in charge he had the honour

of leading City out at Wembley and to promotion via the Play-offs. In a thrilling encounter, Crewe Alexandra were beaten on penalties after extra-time.

The following season (1993–94) Little and his appointed assistant, former skipper Paul Stancliffe, guided City to the Division Two (League One) Play-offs, where they narrowly lost in the semi-finals to Stockport County, thus just missing out on a second successive trip to Wembley.

In 1994–95 the side finished in the top half of the table, but only a dramatic win at Brighton on the last day of the season enabled them to avoid relegation in the following campaign. The 1995–96 season was notable, however, for a famous Coca-Cola Cup triumph over Manchester United with a famous 3–0 first leg win at Old Trafford. The following season Alan Little presided over another League Cup shock as Everton were vanquished but again City just avoided the drop.

By now, star players Dean Kiely, Paul Barnes and Jon McCarthy had all been transferred and by the late 1990s City's fortunes continued to slide.

In July 1998 Little was rewarded for 10 years' dedicated service by a testimonial game against Middlesbrough, which attracted a crowd of over 6,000. In the first half of this season City showed good form and at the turn of the year were in 10th place. Then came a dramatic slump, and a run of 10 games without a win led to the dismissal of Little on 15 March 1999. He had become the fourth longest-serving manager in the club's history. In announcing his dismissal with deep regret, the directors stated that 'this was his 11th season as one of the most honest and loyal servants and managers this club has ever had'. Little had been in charge for 324 League and Cup games, winning 113 and losing 119.

Born in Horden on 5 February 1955, Alan Little served his apprenticeship along with brother Brian at Aston Villa. A hard-tackling midfielder, he went on to play with Southend United, Barnsley, Doncaster Rovers, Torquay United and Halifax Town before finishing his playing days at Hartlepool United in 1986. He was assistant to manager John Bird at the Victoria Ground prior to their move to York. Upon leaving City, Little went on to have managerial spells at Southend United and Halifax Town.

Neil Thompson

March 1999 to February 2000

Left-back Neil Thompson was made caretaker manager following Alan Little's departure. The experienced defender had joined City from Barnsley in March 1998. Born in Beverley on 2 October 1963, he had previously been with Hull City, Scarborough and Ipswich Town, making over 200 League appearances for the Tractor Boys.

Despite just failing in his bid to save the club from relegation to Division Three (League Two) – only a defeat away to Manchester City on the last day of the campaign sealed their fate – he was appointed manager in May 1999. His assistant was Adie Shaw, the former head of City's youth development.

Back in the basement League for the first time since 1993, City struggled to make an impact, and with the club languishing in 21st position Thompson was relieved of his duties on 10 February 2000.

Thompson, who made 46 senior appearances for City and scored nine goals, later went to Boston United, where he had a spell as manager.

Terence Dolan

February 2000 to May 2003

City next turned to Terry Dolan to fill the hot seat. Unlike Neil Thompson, who had no previous managerial experience, Dolan had been in charge of Bradford City, Rochdale and Hull City.

In his six years at Boothferry Park (1991–97), he led Hull to promotion to Division Two (League One) in 1991–92. Faced with mounting financial problems, the Tigers were relegated in 1996 and Dolan was relieved of his duties in the summer of 1997. Prior to his appointment at Bootham Crescent he was the reserve team manager at Huddersfield Town.

Terence Peter Dolan was born in Bradford on 11 June 1950 and spent his playing career as a midfielder with Bradford City, Bradford Park Avenue, Huddersfield Town and Rochdale.

One of Dolan's first signings at York was Northern Ireland goalkeeper Alan Fettis, who had previously been with Hull City, Nottingham Forest and Blackburn Rovers. He also brought in loan signings Peter Hawkins from Wimbledon and Mark Bower from Bradford City, and City rallied to pull clear of the relegation zone. Midway through the following season, City once again faced the threat of dropping into the Conference, and in February 2001 were at the bottom of the table. Again Dolan rallied his forces and they finished the season in 14th position.

In 2002–03, amid mounting problems off the pitch regarding the club's very existence, City experienced their best playing season since 1994–95. At the end of March they occupied an automatic promotion place and Play-off hopes remained alive until the penultimate game. Their final placing was 10th.

At the end of May 2003 the new City board of directors announced that Terry Dolan and Adie Shaw, who had retained his assistant manager's role, had been given notice under their contracts that they would be leaving the club. The official statement issued by the club said: 'The decision was taken to benefit the long-term financial position of the club and is considered to be in the best interests of York City Football Club. The board of directors would like to thank Terry Dolan and Adie Shaw for their service and wish them both well for the future.'

Dolan had done a steady job under difficult circumstances in his three years-plus at York. He later managed Guiseley.

Christopher Brass

May 2003 to November 2004

Chris Brass, born in Easington on 24 July 1975, was appointed player-manager on 4 June 2003 aged just 27, making him the youngest managerial appointment by a Football League club since 1946, when Ivor Broadis became player-manager of Carlisle United, aged 23.

Brass, at home in midfield or defence, had joined City in March 2001 from Burnley after seven seasons and over 170 senior appearances at Turf Moor. A very enthusiastic and committed person on and off the field, he and his assistant Lee Nogan made a flying start as City won their opening four games in the 2003–04 campaign. In January 2004 the club were 10th in the table, but a dreadful sequence of 20 games without a win (five draws and 15 defeats) saw City finish bottom of the table. Seventy-five years' proud membership of the Football League was thus ended as City dropped into the Conference.

Brass recruited a number of experienced players as City embarked on their first season of non-League football since 1929. The side failed to make an impact, however, and following a home defeat at the hands of Forest Green Rovers on 6 November 2004, which left the club fourth from bottom of the Conference, Brass was dismissed as manager. A very passionate and hard-working individual, he had paid the price of having achieved just 14 wins and 18 draws from 67 senior games in charge.

He continued to play for the club until serious leg injury sustained in a home game against Burton Albion at the end of December 2004 ended his first-team playing days at York.

After loan spells with Harrogate Town and Southport, Brass resumed his Football League career with Bury in 2006, later coaching the junior side at Gigg Lane.

Vivian Busby

November 2004 to February 2005

In September 2004 Viv Busby returned to the club after 17 years to assist manager Chris Brass and player-coach Lee Nogan.

Since leaving Bootham Crescent along with Denis Smith in 1987, he had been assistant boss at Sunderland, manager at Hartlepool United and a coach with Sheffield United, Everton, Ethnikos (Greece), Fulham and Swindon Town. He also had to overcome serious illness.

When Brass was relieved of his managerial duties, Busby was appointed caretaker manager. Results did not improve greatly, and following defeat at Burton Albion in the FA Trophy, Busby offered to step down. This was not accepted, but on 10 February 2005 he left the club by mutual consent. His 14 matches in charge resulted in four wins and two draws.

Born in High Wycombe on 19 June 1949, Vivian Dennis Busby was a striker in his playing days. He appeared in the FA Cup Final for Fulham in 1974–75 and his other clubs included Luton Town, Norwich City, Stoke City and Blackburn Rovers. He played for Tulsa in the US before finishing his playing days with City in 1983–84.

William McEwan

February 2005 to November 2007

With City languishing in the lower regions of the Conference, Billy McEwan was named as the new boss on 10 February 2005, the club's third manager in a turbulent season.

City's fifth Scottish manager, William Johnston McGowan McEwan was born in Cleland near Motherwell on 20 June 1951 and started his playing career with Hibernian. As a midfielder he went on to play for Brighton & Hove Albion, Chesterfield, Mansfield Town, Peterborough United and Rotherham United, making 301 Football League appearances.

His first coaching position was as youth team boss at Sheffield United in 1984, and he had a spell in charge of the senior side at Bramall Lane before taking over as manager of Rotherham United in 1988. In his first full season in charge at Millmoor he led the club to the Fourth Division Championship, but in 1991 he was sacked and had spells as manager at Darlington and then assistant boss at Scarborough. McEwan then spent nine years coaching at Derby County prior to his move to York.

Billy's first task with City was to avoid relegation from the Conference and this was just achieved, with a final position of 17th. The following campaign his rebuilt side, which included new signings Manny Panther, Mark Convery and striker Clayton Donaldson, finished eighth. Despite losing leading scorer Andy Bishop, who moved to Bury in May 2006, McEwan guided City to the Conference promotion Play-offs in 2006–07, when they finished fourth. They lost narrowly to Morecambe in the semi-finals, thus just missing out on a return to the Football League. McEwan won the Conference Manager of the Month award twice that season, the club's most successful for over 10 years.

For the second successive year McEwan lost the services of his leading marksman, when Scottish Premiership club Hibernian exploited a transfer loophole when signing Clayton Donaldson without a fee. For the third year running the manager set about rebuilding the side but a bad start was made to the 2007–08 campaign, with just five points collected from the first 10 games. Results improved but home form remained poor and successive defeats at KitKat Crescent against Havant & Waterlooville in the FA Cup and Salisbury City, which made it seven reverses in 10 home League games, marked the end of McEwan's tenure on 19 November 2007. In the York City board statement, tribute was made to Billy's hard work and dedication and the fact that he was instrumental in turning around the playing fortunes of the club. But the board went on to say 'The football industry is very much a result-based business and it is therefore felt a fresh approach is needed to take the club out of our current – 19th in the Conference – predicament.'

A forthright disciplinarian, McEwan left the club in a position in the Conference similar to when he arrived, but in almost three years at York he had enjoyed two successful seasons and had instilled a professional attitude both on and off the field. He won 49 and drew 30 of his 121 Conference games in charge.

Upon his departure, his assistant Colin Walker was appointed caretaker manager.

Colin Walker

December 2007 to present day

Following a run of five wins and one draw in his six games as caretaker boss, Colin Walker was officially appointed manager on Boxing Day 2007. He went on to make the best-ever start by a City boss and did not taste defeat until February 2008, when the side lost in a penalty shoot-out against Northwich Victoria in the Setanta Shield – a sequence of 14 unbeaten games. In the League he presided over a run of 11 unbeaten matches and was Blue Square Premier Manager of the Month for December 2007. Colin piloted the club to the semi-finals of the FA Trophy, but League form dipped in the closing weeks and the final position was 14th.

Born in Rotherham on 1 May 1958, Walker began his career with Barnsley and made his Football League debut in 1980–81. The forward went on to play for Doncaster Rovers, Cambridge United and Sheffield Wednesday, and he had loan spells with Darlington and Torquay United.

He moved to New Zealand with his family and was capped 34 times and scored 18 goals while there with Gisborne City. Upon his return he had spells as a coach at Barnsley and at Leeds United's academy before being recruited to City's backroom staff in 2005.

York City's Football League Record Against Other Clubs (1929–2004)

	Season	HOME							AWAY							TOTAL						
Opponents	first met	P	W	D	L	F	A	PTS	P	W	D	L	F	A	PTS	P	W	D	L	F	A	PTS
Accrington Stanley	1929–30	24	13	6	5	46	25	32	24	3	3	18	22	60	9	48	16	9	23	68	85	41
Aldershot	1958–59	22	11	6	5	42	21	32	22	7	7	8	28	39	26	44	18	13	13	70	60	58
Aston Villa	1971–72	2	0	1	1	1	2	1	2	0	0	2	0	5	0	4	0	1	3	1	7	1
Barnet	1991–92	5	3	1	1	6	5	10	5	2	0	3	11	12	6	10	5	1	4	17	17	16
Barnsley	1932–33	11	1	4	6	10	19	6	11	1	2	8	6	15	4	22	2	6	14	16	34	10
Barrow	1929–30	30	16	5	9	57	37	37	30	11	8	11	37	39	30	60	27	13	20	94	76	67
Birmingham City	1994–95	1	1	0	0	2	0	3	1	0	0	1	2	4	0	2	1	0	1	4	4	3
Blackburn Rovers	1971–72	4	3	0	1	4	2	6	4	0	0	4	0	13	0	8	3	0	5	4	15	6
Blackpool	1974–75	17	8	4	5	22	16	28	17	5	3	9	23	23	18	34	13	7	14	45	39	46
Bolton Wanderers	1971–72	7	2	1	4	7	10	7	7	2	2	3	7	11	6	14	4	3	7	14	21	13
Boston United	2002–03	2	1	1	0	3	1	4	2	0	0	2	0	5	0	4	1	1	2	3	6	4
Bournemouth	1959–60	21	11	4	6	31	18	33	21	4	6	11	22	40	15	42	15	10	17	53	58	48
Bradford City	1937–38	31	11	9	11	47	43	31	31	8	9	14	41	61	25	62	19	18	25	88	104	56
Bradford P A	1950–51	16	11	1	4	40	15	23	16	5	3	8	20	24	13	32	16	4	12	60	39	36
Brentford	1959–60	19	8	6	5	25	22	27	19	4	5	10	24	40	15	38	12	11	15	49	62	42
Brighton and Hove	1963–64	12	5	1	6	15	13	14	12	3	2	7	11	22	10	24	8	3	13	26	35	24
Bristol City	1974–75	11	2	3	6	8	15	8	11	0	4	7	9	21	4	22	2	7	13	17	36	12
Bristol Rovers	1965–66	19	8	5	6	22	21	27	19	6	5	8	21	26	21	38	14	10	14	43	47	48
Burnley	1984–85	10	4	4	2	16	10	16	10	2	4	4	12	24	10	20	6	8	6	28	34	26
Bury	1957–58	14	5	6	3	16	12	19	14	2	1	11	14	32	7	28	7	7	14	30	44	26
Cambridge United	1970–71	9	8	0	1	22	7	22	9	2	4	3	10	10	10	18	10	4	4	32	17	32
Cardiff City	1974–75	8	3	3	2	16	11	11	8	1	2	5	9	18	5	16	4	5	7	25	29	16
Carlisle United	1929–30	40	19	15	6	80	42	59	40	7	15	18	48	71	33	80	26	30	24	128	113	92
Charlton Athletic	1972–73	3	0	1	2	2	5	1	3	1	0	2	6	6	2	6	1	1	4	8	11	3
Chelsea	1975–76	1	0	1	0	2	2	1	1	0	1	0	0	0	1	2	0	2	0	2	2	2
Cheltenham Town	1999–2000	4	0	0	4	2	9	0	4	1	2	1	3	6	5	8	1	2	5	5	15	5
Chester City	1931–32	38	20	12	6	78	41	56	38	7	10	21	44	101	26	76	27	22	27	122	142	82
Chesterfield	1929–30	38	15	12	11	58	39	46	38	5	10	23	38	66	21	76	20	22	34	96	105	67
Colchester United	1959–60	12	9	1	2	31	9	25	12	2	3	7	9	18	9	24	11	4	9	40	27	34
Coventry City	1958–59	2	0	2	0	1	1	2	2	0	0	2	2	7	0	4	0	2	2	3	8	2
Crewe Alexandra	1929–30	44	25	9	10	104	57	64	44	13	11	20	66	90	40	88	38	20	30	170	147	104
Crystal Palace	1958–59	3	1	1	1	3	4	3	3	0	1	2	0	2	1	6	1	2	3	3	6	4
Darlington	1929–30	49	31	12	6	113	47	82	49	11	12	26	53	84	36	98	42	24	32	166	131	118
Derby County	1955–56	4	1	2	1	4	5	4	4	0	0	4	3	7	0	8	1	2	5	7	12	4
Doncaster Rovers	1929–30	33	11	11	11	53	50	37	33	9	7	17	39	53	29	66	20	18	28	92	103	66
Exeter City	1958–59	18	8	3	7	34	26	22	18	5	0	13	19	33	12	36	13	3	20	53	59	34

Opponents	Season first met	HOME P	W	D	L	F	A	PTS	AWAY P	W	D	L	F	A	PTS	TOTAL P	W	D	L	F	A	PTS
Fulham	1974–75	7	3	1	3	8	10	8	7	2	2	3	8	10	7	14	5	3	6	16	20	15
Gateshead *	1929–30	23	12	8	3	43	29	32	23	4	10	9	25	39	18	46	16	18	12	68	68	50
Gillingham	1958–59	18	7	6	5	30	21	25	18	4	7	7	16	21	18	36	11	13	12	46	42	43
Grimsby Town	1951–52	19	2	10	7	21	28	14	19	2	4	13	14	39	8	38	4	14	20	35	67	22
Halifax Town	1929–30	46	24	16	6	108	53	71	46	15	15	16	62	65	49	92	39	31	22	170	118	120
Hartlepool United	1929–30	47	26	13	8	91	41	70	47	11	10	26	60	91	37	94	37	23	34	151	132	107
Hereford United	1973–74	12	8	1	3	28	13	23	12	2	4	6	10	16	10	24	10	5	9	38	29	33
Huddersfield Town	1973–74	7	2	1	4	7	13	6	7	3	1	3	8	10	8	14	5	2	7	15	23	14
Hull City	1930–31	25	9	7	9	32	29	28	25	6	8	11	27	40	22	50	15	15	20	59	69	50
Kidderminster Harriers	2000–01	4	2	1	1	2	1	7	4	1	0	3	5	12	3	8	3	1	4	7	13	10
Leyton Orient	1974–75	11	6	2	3	19	13	20	11	4	3	4	10	13	15	22	10	5	7	29	26	35
Lincoln City	1929–30	37	19	11	7	52	35	57	37	8	9	20	48	74	29	74	27	20	27	100	109	86
Luton Town	1966–67	7	1	3	3	14	13	5	7	0	0	7	4	21	0	14	1	3	10	18	34	5
Macclesfield Town	1998–99	6	2	0	4	4	10	6	6	2	3	1	6	5	9	12	4	3	5	10	15	15
Maidstone United	1989–90	3	0	2	1	1	2	2	3	0	0	3	4	7	0	6	0	2	4	5	9	2
Manchester City	1998–99	1	1	0	0	2	1	3	1	0	0	1	0	4	0	2	1	0	1	2	5	3
Manchester United	1974–75	1	0	0	1	0	1	0	1	0	0	1	1	2	0	2	0	0	2	1	3	0
Mansfield Town	1932–33	34	22	5	7	75	45	54	34	9	6	19	37	71	27	68	31	11	26	112	116	81
Middlesbrough	1986–87	1	1	0	0	3	1	3	1	0	0	1	1	3	0	2	1	0	1	4	4	3
Millwall	1958–59	10	6	2	2	21	16	16	10	2	2	6	14	21	7	20	8	4	8	35	37	23
Nelson	1929–30	2	2	0	0	4	0	4	2	1	0	1	6	5	2	4	3	0	1	10	5	6
New Brighton	1929–30	15	14	0	1	36	9	28	15	4	2	9	22	29	10	30	18	2	10	58	38	38
Newport County	1959–60	15	12	1	2	30	8	28	15	3	6	6	19	22	12	30	15	7	8	49	30	40
Northampton Town	1958–59	20	8	5	7	27	24	26	20	2	7	11	20	41	12	40	10	12	18	47	65	38
Norwich City	1959–60	2	1	0	1	2	2	2	2	1	0	1	3	3	2	4	2	0	2	5	5	4
Nottingham Forest	1974–75	2	1	1	0	4	3	3	2	0	0	2	1	3	0	4	1	1	2	5	6	3
Notts County	1964–65	16	4	6	6	26	27	14	16	2	4	10	15	34	9	32	6	10	16	41	61	23
Oldham Athletic	1935–36	29	15	10	4	49	21	40	29	4	7	18	35	71	16	58	19	17	22	84	92	56
Oxford United	1962–63	12	5	2	5	13	16	14	12	3	3	6	14	20	10	24	8	5	11	27	36	24
Peterborough Utd	1960–61	18	10	4	4	29	20	30	18	3	5	10	16	33	14	36	13	9	14	45	53	44
Plymouth Argyle	1971–72	13	4	6	3	14	11	17	13	2	5	6	11	18	10	26	6	11	9	25	29	27
Portsmouth	1974–75	5	4	0	1	12	8	8	5	1	1	3	5	10	3	10	5	1	4	17	18	11
Port Vale	1929–30	23	13	4	6	42	22	32	23	3	7	13	24	44	14	46	16	11	19	66	66	46
Preston North End	1976–77	6	2	1	3	5	6	7	6	1	0	5	8	16	3	12	3	1	8	13	22	10
Queen's Park Rangers	1959–60	2	1	1	0	4	3	3	2	0	1	1	2	7	1	4	1	2	1	6	10	4
Reading	1959–60	10	2	4	4	12	13	9	10	1	2	7	4	14	5	20	3	6	11	16	27	14
Rochdale	1929–30	50	23	11	16	86	71	61	50	20	7	23	72	77	52	100	43	18	39	158	148	113
Rotherham United	1929–30	29	15	7	7	58	34	42	29	6	5	18	32	62	20	58	21	12	25	90	96	62
Rushden and Diamonds	2001–02	2	0	1	1	0	1	1	2	0	0	2	1	5	0	4	0	1	3	1	6	1
Scarborough	1988–89	5	3	1	1	8	3	10	5	1	2	2	7	8	5	10	4	3	3	15	11	15
Scunthorpe United	1950–51	28	13	4	11	39	33	35	28	7	6	15	29	48	22	56	20	10	26	68	81	57
Sheffield United	1981–82	1	0	0	1	3	4	0	1	0	0	1	0	4	0	2	0	0	2	3	8	0

	Season	HOME							AWAY							TOTAL						
Opponents	first met	P	W	D	L	F	A	PTS	P	W	D	L	F	A	PTS	P	W	D	L	F	A	PTS
Sheffield Wednesday	1974–75	2	1	0	1	3	2	2	2	0	0	2	2	6	0	4	1	0	3	5	8	2
Shrewsbury Town	1950–51	16	8	4	4	21	14	25	16	2	3	11	14	29	8	32	10	7	15	35	43	33
Southampton	1959–60	3	1	2	0	5	4	4	3	0	0	3	2	7	0	6	1	2	3	7	11	4
Southend United	1959–60	19	10	4	5	27	21	29	19	4	6	9	17	28	15	38	14	10	14	44	49	44
Southport	1929–30	32	17	6	9	62	36	40	32	9	11	12	43	47	29	64	26	17	21	105	83	69
Stockport County	1929–30	42	20	11	11	66	48	54	42	7	6	29	41	88	23	84	27	17	40	107	136	77
Stoke City	1998–99	1	0	1	0	2	2	1	1	0	0	1	0	2	0	2	0	1	1	2	4	1
Sunderland	1974–75	3	1	0	2	3	6	3	3	0	0	3	2	7	0	6	1	0	5	5	13	3
Swansea City	1965–66	16	10	3	3	28	15	28	16	6	4	6	19	21	21	32	16	7	9	47	36	49
Swindon Town	1959–60	7	4	1	2	9	7	11	7	0	1	6	7	24	1	14	4	2	8	16	31	12
Torquay United	1958–59	21	7	12	2	26	20	29	21	7	5	9	28	31	22	42	14	17	11	54	51	51
Tranmere Rovers	1929–30	37	21	5	11	63	28	48	37	7	10	20	44	80	27	74	28	15	31	107	108	75
Walsall	1931–32	23	10	6	7	28	26	31	23	3	6	14	22	51	13	46	13	12	21	50	77	44
Watford	1958–59	7	1	4	2	5	9	6	7	2	3	2	12	14	7	14	3	7	4	17	23	13
West Bromwich Albion	1974–75	2	0	0	2	1	4	0	2	0	1	1	2	4	1	4	0	1	3	3	8	1
Wigan Athletic	1978–79	10	4	3	3	16	12	14	10	2	3	5	14	20	8	20	6	6	8	30	32	22
Wigan Borough	1929–30	2	1	0	1	6	3	2	2	1	0	1	3	3	2	4	2	0	2	9	6	4
Wimbledon	1977–78	4	0	1	3	3	10	1	4	0	0	4	5	11	0	8	0	1	7	8	21	1
Wolverhampton W	1985–86	1	1	0	0	2	1	3	1	0	0	1	2	3	0	2	1	0	1	4	4	3
Workington	1951–52	17	7	7	3	31	17	21	17	1	6	10	13	27	8	34	8	13	13	44	44	29
Wrexham	1929–30	47	26	14	7	87	49	73	47	7	16	24	58	89	33	94	33	30	31	145	138	106
Wycombe Wanderers	1994–95	5	4	1	0	9	1	13	5	1	1	3	4	7	4	10	5	2	3	13	8	17
Yeovil Town	2003–04	1	0	0	1	1	2	0	1	0	0	1	0	3	0	2	0	0	2	1	5	0
GRAND TOTALS		**1526**	**734**	**396**	**396**	**2591**	**1713**	**2101**	**1526**	**328**	**378**	**820**	**1719**	**2828**	**1160**	**3052**	**1062**	**774**	**1216**	**4310**	**4541**	**3261**

** Note: Gateshead were known as South Shields in 1929–30.*

City's League Record 1922–2008

		Home					Away								
SEASON	P	W	D	L	F	A	W	D	L	F	A	PTS	POS	TOP SCORER	AVE ATT
MIDLAND LEAGUE															
1922–23	42	9	6	6	37	28	2	6	13	19	42	34	19	Elliott 16	
1923–24	42	6	9	6	29	24	4	4	13	19	47	33	19	Charlesworth 12	
1924–25	28	7	4	3	23	15	3	6	5	16	21	30	6	Miller 17	
1925–26	40	12	6	2	51	27	2	1	17	23	67	35	16	O'Cain 12	
1926–27	38	12	6	1	63	22	4	7	8	33	46	45	6	Flood 17	
1927–28	44	16	1	5	59	32	6	6	10	38	41	51	7	Fenoughty 19	
1928–29	50	17	4	4	74	39	5	9	11	32	60	57	9	Cowie 49	
FOOTBALL LEAGUE DIVISION THREE NORTH															
1929–30	42	11	7	3	43	20	4	9	8	34	44	46	6	Bottrill 18	5,279
1930–31	42	15	3	3	59	30	3	3	15	26	52	42	12	Fenoughty 17	3,906
1931–32	40	14	3	3	49	24	4	4	12	27	57	43	9	Baines 29	4,330
1932–33	42	10	4	7	51	38	3	2	16	21	54	32	20	Baines 29	4,370
1933–34	42	11	5	5	44	28	4	3	14	27	46	38	12	Dando 25	4,361
1934–35	42	12	5	4	50	20	3	1	17	26	62	36	15	Dando 21	3,902
1935–36	42	10	8	3	41	28	3	4	14	21	67	38	16	Speed 13	3,721
1936–37	42	13	3	5	54	27	3	8	10	25	43	43	12	Thompson 24	5,257
1937–38	42	11	4	6	40	25	5	6	10	30	43	42	11	Baines 23	5,957
1938–39	42	8	5	8	37	34	4	3	14	27	58	32	20	Mortimer 22	5,544
Suspended due to war															
1946–47	42	6	4	11	35	42	8	5	8	32	39	37	15	A. Patrick 17	6,900
1947–48	42	8	7	6	38	25	5	7	9	27	35	40	13	A. Patrick 19	9,006
1948–49	42	11	3	7	49	28	4	6	11	25	46	39	14	A. Patrick 26	10,412
1949–50	42	6	7	8	29	33	3	6	12	23	37	31	22	A. Patrick 14	8,016
1950–51	46	7	12	4	37	24	5	3	15	29	53	39	17	M. Patrick 13, Linaker 13	7,478
1951–52	46	16	4	3	53	19	2	9	12	20	33	49	10	Fenton 31	7,968
1952–53	46	14	5	4	35	16	6	8	9	25	29	53	4	Fenton 25	8,654
1953–54	46	8	7	8	39	32	4	6	13	25	54	37	22	Dunmore 20	5,636
1954–55	46	13	5	5	43	27	11	5	7	49	36	58	4	Bottom 31	9,630
1955–56	46	12	4	7	44	24	7	5	11	41	48	47	11	Bottom 31	10,291
1956–57	46	14	4	5	43	21	7	6	10	32	40	52	7	Bottom 21	9,414
1957–58	46	11	8	4	40	26	6	4	13	28	50	46	13	Farmer 12	7,270
FOOTBALL LEAGUE DIVISION FOUR															
1958–59	46	12	10	1	37	17	9	8	6	36	35	60	3	Wragg 14	8,124
FOOTBALL LEAGUE DIVISION THREE															
1959–60	46	11	5	7	38	26	2	7	14	19	47	38	21	Edgar 15	7,507
FOOTBALL LEAGUE DIVISION FOUR															
1960–61	46	17	3	3	50	14	4	6	13	30	46	51	5	Wragg 22	6,900
1961–62	44	17	2	3	62	19	3	8	11	22	34	50	6	Weir 28	6,890

		Home					Away								
SEASON	P	W	D	L	F	A	W	D	L	F	A	PTS	POS	TOP SCORER	AVE ATT
1962–63	46	12	6	5	42	25	4	5	14	25	37	43	14	Wilkinson 15	4,515
1963–64	46	9	3	11	29	26	5	4	14	23	40	35	22	Wilkinson 10	3,937
1964–65	46	20	1	2	63	21	8	5	10	28	35	62	3	Aimson 26	7,185
FOOTBALL LEAGUE DIVISION THREE															
1965–66	46	5	7	11	30	44	4	2	17	23	62	27	24	Aimson 17	5,921
FOOTBALL LEAGUE DIVISION FOUR															
1966–67	46	11	5	7	45	31	1	6	16	20	48	35	22	Spencer 18	3,776
1967–68	46	9	6	8	44	30	2	8	13	21	38	36	21	MacDougall 15	4,578
1968–69	46	12	8	3	36	25	2	3	18	17	50	39	21	MacDougall 19	3,883
1969–70	46	14	7	2	38	16	2	7	14	17	46	46	13	Mahon 10, McMahon 10	3,951
1970–71	46	16	6	1	45	14	7	4	12	33	40	56	4	Aimson 26	4,962
FOOTBALL LEAGUE DIVISION THREE															
1971–72	46	8	8	7	32	22	4	4	15	25	44	36	19	Aimson 16	5,597
1972–73	46	8	10	5	24	14	5	5	13	18	32	41	18	Pollard 7, Rowles 7	3,792
1973–74	46	13	8	2	37	15	8	11	4	30	23	61	3	Jones 18	6,600
FOOTBALL LEAGUE DIVISION TWO															
1974–75	42	9	7	5	28	17	5	3	13	23	38	38	15	Seal 17	8,828
1975–76	42	8	3	10	28	34	2	5	14	11	37	28	21	Cave 8	5,189
FOOTBALL LEAGUE DIVISION THREE															
1976–77	46	7	8	8	24	34	3	4	16	26	55	32	24	Pollard 12	2,986
FOOTBALL LEAGUE DIVISION FOUR															
1977–78	46	8	7	8	27	31	4	5	14	23	38	36	22	Staniforth 12	2,139
1978–79	46	11	6	6	33	24	7	5	11	18	31	47	10	Staniforth 15	2,935
1979–80	46	9	6	8	35	34	5	5	13	30	48	39	17	Eccles 9	2,703
1980–81	46	10	2	11	31	23	2	7	14	16	43	33	24	McDonald 11	2,162
1981–82	46	9	5	9	45	37	5	3	15	24	54	50	17	Walwyn 23	2,362
1982–83	46	18	4	1	59	19	4	9	10	29	39	79	7	Walwyn 21	3,243
1983–84	46	18	4	1	58	16	13	4	6	38	23	101	1	Byrne 27	5,008
FOOTBALL LEAGUE DIVISION THREE															
1984–85	46	13	5	5	42	22	7	4	12	28	35	69	8	Banton 12, Houchen 12	5,550
1985–86	46	16	4	3	49	17	4	7	12	28	41	71	7	Walwyn 22	4,111
1986–87	46	11	8	4	34	29	1	5	17	21	50	49	20	Walwyn 19	3,432
1987–88	46	4	7	12	27	45	4	2	17	21	46	33	23	Banton 16	2,754
FOOTBALL LEAGUE DIVISION FOUR															
1988–89	46	10	8	5	43	27	7	5	11	19	36	64	11	Helliwell 11	2,613
1989–90	46	10	5	8	29	24	6	11	6	26	29	64	13	Helliwell 14	2,615
1990–91	46	8	6	9	21	23	3	7	13	24	34	46	21	Helliwell 7	2,511
1991–92	42	6	9	6	26	23	2	7	12	16	35	40	19	Blackstone 8, Naylor 8	2,506
FOOTBALL LEAGUE DIVISION THREE															
1992–93	42	13	6	2	41	15	8	6	7	31	30	75	4	Barnes 21	3,946
FOOTBALL LEAGUE DIVISION TWO															
1993–94	46	12	7	4	33	13	9	5	9	31	27	75	5	Barnes 24	4,633

		Home					Away								
SEASON	P	W	D	L	F	A	W	D	L	F	A	PTS	POS	TOP SCORER	AVE ATT
1994–95	46	13	4	6	37	21	8	5	10	30	30	72	9	Barnes 16	3,685
1995–96	46	8	6	9	28	29	5	7	11	30	44	52	20	Barnes 15	3,538
1996–97	46	8	6	9	27	31	5	7	11	20	37	52	20	Pepper 12, Tolson 12	3,359
1997–98	46	9	7	7	26	21	5	10	8	26	37	59	16	Rowe 11	3,850
1998–99	46	6	8	9	28	33	7	3	13	28	47	50	21	Cresswell 16	3,645
FOOTBALL LEAGUE DIVISION THREE															
1999–2000	46	7	10	6	21	21	5	6	12	18	32	52	20	Conlon 11	3,048
2000–01	46	9	6	8	23	26	4	7	12	19	37	52	17	McNiven 8	3,026
2001–02	46	11	5	7	26	20	5	4	14	28	47	57	14	Proctor 14	3,144
2002–03	46	11	9	3	34	24	6	6	11	18	29	66	10	Duffield 13	4,176
2003–04	46	7	6	10	22	29	3	8	12	13	37	44	24	Nogan 8	3,963
FOOTBALL CONFERENCE															
2004–05	42	7	6	8	22	23	4	4	13	17	43	43	17	A. Bishop 11	2,333
2005–06	42	10	5	6	36	26	7	7	7	27	22	63	8	A. Bishop 22	2,871
2006–07	46	10	6	7	29	22	13	5	5	36	23	80	4	Donaldson 24	2,859
FOOTBALL CONFERENCE (BLUE SQUARE PREMIER)															
2007–08	46	8	5	10	33	34	9	6	8	38	40	62	14	Sodje, 14 Woolford 14	2,258

Football League Record

Elected to Football League in 1929

68 seasons in the League

Old Division Two	2 seasons
Division Two	6 seasons
Old Division Three	10 seasons
Division Three	6 seasons
Division Three North	22 seasons
Division Four	22 seasons

	P	*W*	*D*	*L*	*F*	*A*	*Pts*
Home	1526	734	396	396	2591	1713	2101
Away	1526	328	378	820	1719	2828	1160
Total	3052	1062	774	1216	4310	4541	3261

Football League Record at Bootham Crescent

P	*W*	*D*	*L*	*F*	*A*	*Pts*
1464	694	383	387	2440	1639	2008

1922–23

Midland League

	P	W	D	L	F	A	Pts
Sheffield Wednesday (R)	42	28	7	7	88	37	63
Doncaster Rovers	42	26	9	7	72	28	61
Worksop Town	42	26	5	11	86	45	57
Denaby United	42	24	9	9	76	48	57
Grimsby United (R)	42	21	9	12	77	58	51
Scunthorpe United	42	18	13	11	65	58	49
Wath Athletic	42	18	10	14	59	38	46
Notts County (R)	42	16	12	14	76	55	44
Boston Town	42	18	8	16	61	46	44
Nottingham Forest (R)	42	16	11	15	74	60	43
Rotherham Co. (R)	42	18	6	18	56	52	42
Hull City (R)	42	14	13	15	63	63	41
Mansfield Town	42	17	6	19	79	64	40
Barnsley (R)	42	14	12	16	67	65	40
Wombwell Town	42	12	14	15	50	63	38
Castleford Town	42	14	8	20	56	79	36
Mexborough	42	11	13	18	44	63	35
York City	42	11	12	19	56	70	34
Gainsborough Tr.	42	8	8	26	42	111	24
Rotherham Town	42	8	6	28	45	105	22
Lincoln City (R)	42	7	7	28	39	114	21

Did you know that?

The club was formed in May 1922 and made an immediate application to join the Football League. Not surprisingly, this failed – they received just one vote – and they were elected to the Midland League.

As the new ground at Fulfordgate was not ready in time, City played their first two home games at Mille Crux, Haxby Road, the ground of Rowntree & Co. Ltd, the confectionery manufacturers.

The club were formed too late to enter this season's FA Cup competition but did reach the Final of the North Riding Senior Cup when they lost 4–2 to Middlesbrough reserves at Ayresome Park.

Joe Hulme made his debut for the club. Transferred to Blackburn Rovers the following season, he later played for Arsenal. In the 1930s he won League and Cup honours for the Gunners and won nine caps for England. He played in four FA Cup Finals.

Match No.	Date		Venue	Opponents	Result		Scorers	Attend.
1	Sep	6	A	Notts County Reserves	L	2–4	Smith, Woods	
2		9	H	Lincoln City Reserves	W	3–2	Acklam, Elliott, Woods	
3		16	H	Boston Town	L	2–4	Woods, Lemons	
4		20	H	Mansfield Town	W	4–1	Moult, Woods, Lemons, J. Harron	
5		25	A	Rotherham Town	D	2–2	Moult, J. Harron	
6		30	A	Wombwell	D	1–1	Ellliott	
7	Oct	7	H	Barnsley Reserves	W	1–0	Woods (pen)	
8		14	A	Boston Town	L	0–2		
9		18	H	Denaby United	W	1–0	Moult	
10		21	A	Barnsley Reserves	L	0–1		
11		28	H	Nottingham Forest Reserves	D	0–0		
12	Nov	4	A	Worksop Town	L	0–1		
13		25	A	Mexborough	W	1–0	Woods	
14		29	H	Rotherham Town	W	5–1	Elliott (3), Woods (2)	
15	Dec	2	H	Notts County Reserves	D	2–2	Elliott, J. Harron	
16		9	A	Gainsborough Trinity	D	0–0		
17		16	H	Wombwell	W	2–1	Albrecht, J. Harron	
18		23	A	Denaby United	L	3–4	Moult, Elliott, Woods	
19		25	A	Castleford Town	D	1–1	Elliott	
20		26	H	Castleford Town	W	3–0	Moult, Elliott, Woods	
21	Jan	13	A	Rotherham County Reserves	L	0–2		
22		17	H	Scunthorpe United	D	2–2	Lemons, J. Harron	
23		20	H	Chesterfield Reserves	W	3–0	Bowe (2), Moult	
24	Feb	3	H	Doncaster Rovers	L	0–2		
25		17	H	Gainsborough Trinity	W	2–0	Maskill, Elliott	
26		28	H	Hull City Reserves	L	0–2		
27	Mar	3	A	Hull City Reserves	D	2–2	Woods (2, 1 pen)	
28		14	A	Lincoln City Reserves	W	4–2	Elliott (2), Woods, Lemons	
29		24	A	Sheffield Wednesday Reserves	D	0–0		
30		30	A	Doncaster Rovers	L	1–3	Lemons	
31		31	A	Chesterfield Reserves	L	0–2		
32	Apr	2	H	Rotherham County Reserves	L	0–1		
33		3	A	Wath Athletic	L	0–2		
34		7	H	Sheffield Wednesday Reserves	L	1–2	Elliott	
35		11	H	Grimsby Town Reserves	D	2–2	Elliott (2)	
36		14	A	Grimsby Town Reserves	L	0–2		
37		18	H	Wath Athletic	D	0–0		
38		19	A	Scunthorpe United	L	0–3		
39		21	H	Mexborough	D	1–1	Lucas	
40		26	A	Nottingham Forest Reserves	L	2–5	Charlesworth (2)	
41		28	H	Worksop Town	L	3–5	Lynch, Elliott, Acklam	
42	May	5	A	Mansfield Town	L	0–3		

A

Holmes	Thorpe	Lynch	Smith	Acklam	Elliott	Moult	Woods	Lemons	Harron J.	Maskill T.	Lickley	Harron G.	Albrecht	Bowe	Dale	Tindale	Dinsdale	Lucas	Barrett	Howarth	Quinlan	Allison	Charlesworth	Tomes	Hulme	Boot	Kay W. A.	
2	3	4	5	6	7	8	9	10	11																			1
2	3	4	5	6	8		9	10	11	7																		2
2	3	4	5	6	8		9	10	11	7																		3
	3	2	5			8	9	10	11	4	6	7																4
	3	2	5			8	9	10	11	4	6	7																5
	3	2	5		7	8	9	10	11	4	6																	6
	3	2	5	6	7	8	9	10	11	4																		7
	3	2	5	6	7	8		10	11	4			9															8
	3	2	5	6	7	8	9	10	11	4																		9
	3	2	5	6	7	8	9	10	11	4																		10
	3	2	5	6	8	7	9	10	11	4																		11
	3	2	5	6	8		9	10	11	7	4																	12
	3	2	5	6	8	7	9	10	11	4																		13
	3	2	5		8		9	10	11	4	6			7														14
	3	2	5	4	8		9	10	11	7	6																	15
	3	2	5	6	8	7	9	10	11	4																		16
	3	2	5	6	8	7		10	11	4			9															17
	3	2		6	7	8	9	10	11	4	5																	18
	3	2	5	6	7	8	9	10	11	4																		19
	3	2	5	6	7	8	9	10	11	4																		20
	3	2	5		8		9	10	11	4					6	7												21
	3	2	5	6	8	7	9	10	11	4																		22
	3	2	5	6	9	8		10	11	4				7														23
7	3	2	5	6	8		9	10	11	4																		24
	3	2	5	6	8			10	11	4						7	9											25
2	3		5	9	8			10	11	4					6	7												26
2	3		5	6	8		9	10	11	4						7												27
	3	2	5	6	8		9	10		4						7		11										28
2	3		5	6	8		9	10		4						7		11										29
2	3		5	6	8		9	10		4									7	11								30
2	3		5		8		9	10		4					6	7					11							31
2	3		5		8		9	10		4					6	7					11							32
2	3		5		8		9	10		4					6	7					11							33
2	3		5	6	8		11	10		4						7						9						34
	3	2	5	6	8		11	10		4						7						9						35
	3	2	5	6	8		11	10		4						7						9						36
	3	2	5	6	8			10		4						7		11					9					37
	3	2	5		8		9	10		4								11						6	7			38
3		2	5		8			10		4					6	7		11					9					39
2	3	4	5	10	8					6								11					9		7			40
	3	4	5	10	8					6								11					9		7	1	2	41
	3		5	6	8			10		4						11							9		7	1	2	42
14	41	33	41	32	40	17	32	40	27	41	7	2	2	2	6	15	1	7	1	1	3	3	5	1	4	2	2	
		1	1	2	16	6	13	5	5	1			1	2				1					2					

Charlie Elliott, top scorer.

Nick Hendry, goalkeeper.

Joe Hulme, one of the most famous players in the club's Midland League days.

Billy Smith, City's first ever captain.

1923–24

Midland League

	P	W	D	L	F	A	Pts
Mansfield Town	42	31	6	5	98	31	68
Grimsby Town (R)	42	25	6	11	99	46	56
Worksop Town	42	25	4	13	93	54	54
Mexborough	42	22	7	13	78	64	51
Notts County (R)	42	21	8	13	83	51	50
Scunthorpe United	42	21	7	14	55	49	49
Sutton Town	42	21	6	15	86	68	48
Denaby United	42	21	6	15	78	62	48
Hull City (R)	42	19	8	15	70	48	46
Nottingham Forest (R)	42	18	9	15	52	52	45
Chesterfield	42	19	5	18	64	64	43
Boston Town	42	16	10	16	64	62	42
Gainsborough Tr.	42	16	8	18	55	62	40
Barnsley (R)	42	15	9	18	58	57	39
Doncaster Rovers (R)	42	14	9	19	58	63	37
Rotherham Co. (R)	42	15	7	20	60	75	37
Wath Athletic	42	14	8	20	57	85	36
Wombwell Town	42	12	10	20	47	74	34
York City	42	10	13	19	48	71	33
Lincoln City	42	13	3	26	46	81	29
Castleford Town	42	8	5	29	39	116	21
Rotherham Town	42	7	4	31	42	95	18

Did you know that?

En route to the game at Grimsby in December they crossed the Humber by ferry to New Holland. The boat went off course and hit a sandbank, and the City party were stuck mid-river. A late arrival at New Holland caused the match to start nearly an hour late. The game finished in almost total darkness, and City lost 9–0!

Joe Hulme, who went on to play in four FA Cup Finals for Arsenal in the 1930s, made his first appearance in the competition in a first round qualifying match at Mexborough.

City made their first appearance in the FA Cup when they beat Castleford & Allerton United in the extra preliminary round. Scorer of the club's first ever FA Cup goal was Tommy Rippon, who had played for Grimsby Town in the Football League before World War One.

Match No.	Date		Venue	Opponents	Result		Scorers	Atten
1	Aug	25	H	Scunthorpe United	D	0–0		
2	Sep	1	A	Doncaster Rovers Reserves	W	1–0	Elliott	
3		5	A	Sutton Town	L	0–2		
4		12	H	Denaby Town	D	1–1	Elliott (pen)	
5		15	A	Lincoln City Reserves	W	1–0	Rippon	
6		29	A	Scunthorpe United	L	1–4	Elliott	
7	Oct	13	H	Wombwell	W	2–1	Charlesworth (2)	
8		18	A	Hull City Reserves	D	0–0		
9		27	H	Sutton Town	W	3–1	Tindale, Albrecht, Charlesworth	
10	Nov	10	A	Rotherham Town	D	1–1	Albrecht	
11		15	A	Notts County Reserves	L	1–2	Charlesworth	
12		17	H	Mexborough	L	1–2	Hulme (pen)	
13		22	A	Nottingham Forest Reserves	L	0–1		
14		24	A	Mexborough	L	1–2	Elliott	
15	Dec	1	H	Lincoln City Reserves	L	0–1		
16		8	A	Mansfield Town	L	2–5	Charlesworth, Davison	
17		15	H	Grimsby Town Reserves	D	2–2	Charlesworth, Davison	
18		22	A	Grimsby Town Reserves	L	0–9		
19		25	H	Castleford Town	D	1–1	Elliott	
20		26	A	Castleford Town	L	0–2		
21		29	H	Nottingham Forest Reserves	D	0–0		
22	Jan	5	H	Hull City Reserves	D	1–1	Pattie	
23		12	A	Wombwell	L	0–2		
24		19	H	Gainsborough Trinity	L	1–3	Albrecht	
25		23	H	Wath Athletic	D	1–1	Charlesworth	
26		26	A	Gainsborough Trinity	L	0–3		
27	Feb	13	H	Barnsley Reserves	D	1–1	Hulme (pen)	
28		16	H	Notts County Reserves	W	2–0	Acklam, Rippon	
29		20	H	Doncaster Rovers Reserves	L	0–2		
30		23	A	Rotherham County Reserves	W	5–0	Rippon (3), Hulme (pen), Charlesworth	
31		27	H	Mansfield Town	D	1–1	Smith	
32	Mar	6	A	Barnsley Reserves	W	3–0	Acklam (2), Elliott	
33		8	H	Boston Town	L	0–1		
34		15	A	Denaby United	D	1–1	Marshall	
35		22	H	Rotherham County Reserves	L	3–4	Acklam (3)	
36	Apr	5	H	Worksop Town	W	3–1	Acklam (2), Marshall	
37		12	A	Worksop Town	L	1–7	Marshall	
38		18	A	Wath Athletic	L	0–1		
39		19	H	Chesterfield Reserves	W	4–0	Charlesworth (2), Acklam, Rippon	
40		22	A	Chesterfield Reserves	D	0–0		
41		26	A	Boston Town	L	1–5	Elliott	
42	May	3	H	Rotherham Town	W	2–0	Charlesworth (2)	

FA Cup

Ex Pr	Sep	8	H	Castleford & Allerton Utd	W	2–1	Rippon, Middlemiss	
Pre		22	A	Cudworth	W	1–0	Davison	
1Q	Oct	6	H	Mexborough	D	1–1	Elliott	
r		11	A	Mexborough	D	1–1*	Elliott	
2r		15	N	Mexborough	L	1–3	Rippon	

* After extra-time. Second replay staged at Doncaster.

Shaw	MacMurray	Reed	Smith	Middlemiss	Tindale	Elliott	Charlesworth	Rippon	Davison	Hulme	Wood	Dennis	Acklam	Bowe	Jones	Appleton	Hendry	Albrecht	Walker	Dale	Pattie	Shann	Maskill G.	Marshall	Atkinson	Clarke	Surtees	Flanagan	Glover	Roberts	Cross	Kay W. A	
2	3	4	5	6	7	8	9	10	11																								1
2	3	4	5	6	7	8	9	10	11																								2
2	3	4	5	6		8	9	10	11	7																							3
2	5	4		6		8		10	11	7	3	9																					4
2	5	4		6		8		10	11	7	3	9																					5
2	5	4		6		8	9	10	11	7	3																						6
	3		5			8	9	10	11		2		4	7	6																		7
2	3	4	5		7		9		11	8			6			10																	8
2	3	4	5	6	7		9	10	11								1	8															9
2	3	4	5		7		9	10	11				6					8	1														10
2	3	4	5				9		11	7			6			10		8	1														11
2	3	4	5				9		11	7			6			10		8	1														12
2	3	4				8	9	10	11	7			6					5	1														13
2	3	5		6		8	9	10	11	7			4						1														14
2	3	5		6		8	9		11	7			4					10	1														15
2	3		5	6		8	9		11	7			4					10	1														16
2	3		5	6	7		9	10	11	8			4						1														17
2	3			6		8	9	10	11	7			4					5	1														18
	3			6		8	9	10	11	7	2		4				1	5															19
2	3			6		8	9	10	11	7			4				1	5															20
	3			6		8		10	11	7	2		4				1			5	9												21
	3		5	6		8		10	11	7	2		4				1				9												22
	3		5	6		8		10	11	7	2		4				1				9												23
2	3		5	6		8	9			11			4				1	10				7											24
	3		5	6			9	10	11	7	2		8				1						4										25
2	3		10				9		11						6			8	1	5				4	7								26
	3	4	5	6				10		7	2		8				1				9					11							27
	3	4	5	6				10	11	7	2		8				1				9												28
	3	4	5	6				10		7	2		8				1	11			9												29
	3	4	5	6			9	10	11	7	2		8				1																30
	3	4	5	6		8		9	11		2						1										7	10					31
	3	4	5	6		8		10	7		2		9				1	11															32
	3	4	5	6		9		10	7		2		8						1									11					33
	3	4	5	6		10			7		2		8				1							9				11					34
	3	4	5	6			7						8			10	1							9				11	2				35
	3	2	5	6			7	10	11				8										4	9						1			36
	3	2	5	6			7	10	11				8										4	9						1			37
2	3	4	5	6				10	11				8										7	9						1			38
2	3	4		6			9	10	11				8					5		1	7												39
	3	4	5				9	10	11		7							6						2						1	8		40
	3	4				8		10					9		11			5		6				2						1	7		41
	3	5		6			9	10	11				8										4						2	1	7		42
22	42	30	29	33	6	23	28	33	37	24	18	2	32	1	3	4	16	16	11	3	6	1	5	8	1	1	1	5	2	7	4		
			1		1	7	12	6	2	3			9					3			1			3									

Shaw	MacMurray	Reed	Smith	Middlemiss	Tindale	Elliott	Charlesworth	Rippon	Davison	Hulme	Wood	Dennis	Acklam	Bowe	Jones	Appleton	Hendry	Albrecht	Walker	Dale	Pattie	Shann	Maskill G.	Marshall	Atkinson	Clarke	Surtees	Flanagan	Glover	Roberts	Cross	Kay W. A	
2	3	4	5	6	7	8	9	10	11																								ExPr
2	3	4	5	6		8	7	10	11			9																					Pre
2	3	4	5	6		8	9	10	11	7																							1Q
2	3	4	5	6	7	8	9	10	11																								r
	3	4	5	6	7	8	9	10	11																							2	2r
4	5	5	5	5	3	5	5	5	5	1		1																				1	
				1		2		2	1																								

Progamme cover from 5 January 1924 against Hull City.

Jack Middlemiss.

1924–25

Midland League

	P	W	D	L	F	A	Pts
Mansfield Town	28	20	4	4	82	27	44
Boston Town	28	17	5	6	56	36	39
Gainsborough Tr.	28	14	7	7	47	38	35
Worksop Town	28	14	4	10	51	42	32
Lincoln City (R)	28	14	4	10	40	40	32
York City	28	10	10	8	39	36	30
Scunthorpe United	28	12	5	11	45	41	29
Mexborough	28	9	9	10	49	49	27
Denaby United	28	9	8	11	41	38	26
Wath Athletic	28	10	4	14	43	46	24
Castleford Town	28	9	5	14	47	61	23
Rotherham Town	28	10	2	16	43	46	22
Frickley Colliery	28	6	9	13	35	61	21
Sutton Town	28	7	4	17	40	66	18
Wombwell Town	28	5	8	15	31	59	18

Did you know that?

In the summer of 1924 the old established Midland League faced a bombshell. Eight reserve XIs of the Football League clubs who had competed in the competition withdrew and formed the Midland Combination. Only Lincoln City retained their reserve side in the League. At such short notice and to ensure a full complement of fixtures, two competitions were formed. The first competition ended in February and this was followed by two subsidiary North and South sections. City finished sixth in the main competition and second in the regionalised section so enjoying their best campaign to date.

Reg Baines, who was to prove a most prolific scorer for the club in the 1930s helping City reach the last eight of the FA Cup in 1937–38, had his first spell at York. A teammate was his elder brother Joe.

A defender, Lester Marshall, was converted to centre-forward and netted five goals in the FA Cup win over Horsforth. In January 1925 he was transferred to Football League club Lincoln City for a fee of £100. Three years later he returned to the club. Another transfer was centre-half Fred Walker to Tottenham Hotspur.

Match No.	Date	Venue	Opponents	Result		Scorers	Attend.
1	Sep 10	H	Scunthorpe United	W	1–0	Miller	
2	13	A	Sutton Town	L	0–5		
3	24	H	Worksop Town	W	2–0	Cleasby, Miller	
4	27	A	Frickley Colliery	W	3–0	Brooke, Miller, Elliott	
5	Oct 9	A	Worksop Town	D	2–2	Walker, Miller	
6	11	H	Sutton Town	D	1–1	Elliott	
7	18	H	Castleford Town	W	5–2	Marshall (5)	
8	25	A	Wath Athletic	D	1–1	Miller	
9	Nov 1	A	Lincoln City Reserves	D	1–1	Cleasby	
10	8	H	Wombwell Town	D	1–1	Miller	
11	13	A	Castleford Town	L	0–1		
12	22	H	Frickley Colliery	D	2–2	Marshall (2)	
13	Dec 6	A	Gainsborough Trinity	L	0–3		
14	17	H	Wath Athletic	W	1–0	Brown	
15	20	H	Mexborough	L	1–2	Laws (pen)	
16	26	H	Denaby United	W	4–1	Laws (2), Brown, Albrecht	
17	27	A	Denaby United	W	4–2	Miller (3), Brown	
18	Jan 1	A	Rotherham Town	L	0–1		
19	10	H	Rotherham Town	W	2–0	Miller, Laws	
20	17	H	Gainsborough Trinity	L	0–1		
21	24	A	Wombwell Town	D	1–1	Laws	
22	31	H	Lincoln City Reserves	W	2–1	Miller, Brown	
23	Feb 5	A	Boston Town	W	2–0	Laws (pen), Smith	
24	7	A	Scunthorpe United	D	1–1	Miller	
25	14	A	Mansfield Town	L	0–2		
26	18	H	Mansfield Town	L	0–3		
27	21	A	Mexborough	D	1–1	J. Baines	
28	28	H	Boston Town	D	1–1	Smith	

North Subsidiary Competition

Match No.	Date	Venue	Opponents	Result		Scorers	Attend.
29	Mar 5	A	Wath Athletic	L	2–4	Walker (2)	
30	7	A	Castleford Town	W	3–1	Albrecht (2), Brown	
31	14	A	Frickley Colliery	W	1–0	Brown	
32	21	H	Frickley Colliery	W	2–0	Walker, Allbrecht	
33	25	H	Denaby United	W	1–0	R. Baines	
34	28	A	Wombwell Town	L	0–1		
35	Apr 4	A	Mexborough	L	0–1		
36	11	H	Wombwell Town	D	2–2	Walker, Miller (pen)	
37	13	A	Rotherham Town	W	3–1	Miller (2), Walker	
38	18	A	Denaby United	L	1–6	Miller	
39	22	H	Wath Athletic	W	2–0	J. Baines, Walker	
40	25	H	Mexborough	D	1–1	Laws	
41	29	H	Rotherham Town	D	0–0		
42	May 2	H	Castleford Town	W	3–1	Walker, J. Baines, Miller	
							A

FA Cup

Match No.	Date	Venue	Opponents	Result		Scorers	Attend.
ExPr	Sep 6	H	Guiseley	W	1–0	Cleasby	3
Pre	20	H	Horsforth	W	7–1	Marshall (5), Miller (2)	3,
1Q	Oct 4	H	Wombwell Town	L	1–2	Miller	4,
							A

Wood	Baines J.	Albrecht	Rutherford	Jones	Elliott	Blyth	Miller	Cleasby	O'Cain	Maskill G.	Baines R.	Glover	Marshall	Brooke	Sayles	Thirlbeck	Kendall	Middlemiss	Tindale	Walker	Laws	Croft	Kay W.A.	Brown	Kay F.	Furnell	Ashdown	Hewitt	Smith W.	Acklam	Bowe	
2	3	4	5	6	7	8	9	10	11																							1
2	3	6	5		7		8	10	11	4	9																					2
	3	6	5		7		8	10	11	4		2	9																			3
	3	6	5		7		8		11	4		2	9	10																		4
			5		7		10		11						2	3	4	6	8	9												5
			5		7		10		11	4					2	3		6	8	9												6
			5		7		8	10	11	4			9		2	3		6														7
	3	10	5		7		8		11	4			9		2			6														8
3					7		8	10	11	4			9		2			6		5												9
3					7		8	10		4			9		2			6		5	11											10
3							8	10		4			9		2			6		5	11	7										11
3					7		10	8		4			9		2			6		5	11											12
3		4			7		10	8					9		2			6		5	11											13
		4						10					9		3			6		5	11		2	7	8							14
					7			10		4			9		2	3		6		5	11			8								15
3		10			7		9			4					2			6		5	11			8								16
3		8					10			4			9		2			6		5	11			7								17
3		10					8			4			9		2					5	11			7		1	6					18
3		10			7		9			4					2			6		5	11			8								19
3		2			7		9			4								6		5	11			8				10				20
3		8					9			4					2			6		5	11			7				10				21
3		8					9	10		4					2			6		5	11			7								22
3	10	4					8								2			6		5	11			7					9			23
3							8	10		4		2						6		5	11			7					9			24
3		4						10				2						6		5	11			7					9	8		25
3		4					8	10							2			6		5	11			7						9		26
3	10	6								4					2					5	11			7					9	8		27
3	10	6								4					2					5	11			7					9	8		28
3	9	11					10			4					2			6		5				7						8		29
3		8					10			4	9	2						6		5	11			7								30
3		8					10			4	9	2						6		5	11			7								31
		8					10			4	9	2			3			6		5	11			7								32
		8					10			4	9	2			3			6		5	11			7								33
		8					10	7		4		2			3			6		5	11			9								34
		4					10	8			9	2			3			6		5	11			7								35
							10	8		4	9	2			3			6		5	11			7								36
							10	8		4	9	2			3			6		5	11			7								37
		8					10	9		4		2			3			6		5	11			7								38
	9	8					10			4		2			3			6		5	11			7								39
	9	8			7		10			4		2			3			6		5	11											40
	9						10			4	8	2			3			6		5	11										7	41
	9	8			7		10			4		2			3			6		5	11											42
23	13	30	8	1	18	1	37	20	9	34	9	17	13	1	33	4	1	35	2	36	32	1	1	26	1	1	1	2	5	5	1	
	3	4			2		17	2			1		7	1							8	7			6					2		

Wood	Baines J.	Albrecht	Rutherford	Jones	Elliott	Blyth	Miller	Cleasby	O'Cain	Maskill G.	Baines R.	Glover	Marshall	Brooke	Sayles	Thirlbeck	Kendall	Middlemiss	Tindale	Walker	Laws	Croft	Kay W.A.	Brown	Kay F.	Furnell	Ashdown	Hewitt	Smith W.	Acklam	Bowe	
2	3		5		7		9	10	11	4								6												8		ExPr
	3	4	5		7		8	10	11				9		2			6														Pre
	3	6	5		7		8		11	4		2	9	10																		1Q
1	3	2	3		3		3	2	3	2		1	2	1	1			2												1		
							3	1					5																			

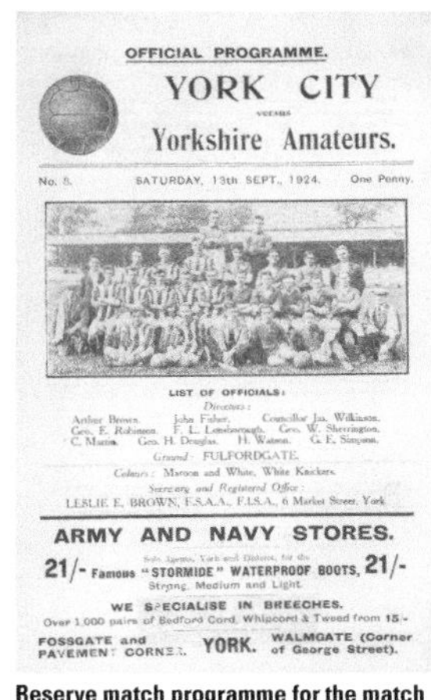

Reserve match programme for the match against Yorkshire Amateurs on 13 September 1924.

1925–26

Midland League

	P	W	D	L	F	A	Pts
Mexborough	40	25	7	8	111	53	57
Mansfield Town	40	23	7	10	120	54	53
Boston Town	40	21	10	9	98	43	52
Lincoln City (R)	40	20	10	10	102	57	50
Denaby United	40	20	7	13	95	63	47
Wath Athletic	40	19	9	12	98	72	47
Scunthorpe United	40	19	9	12	86	78	47
Newark Town	40	16	9	15	94	88	41
Alfreton Town	40	17	7	16	99	102	41
Loughborough Cor.	40	17	5	18	86	82	39
Worksop Town	40	14	10	16	82	82	38
Wombwell Town	40	14	9	17	73	89	37
Long Eaton	40	14	8	18	82	94	36
Grantham	40	15	6	19	71	94	36
Sutton Town	40	15	6	19	68	102	36
York City	40	14	7	19	74	94	35
Gainsborough Tr.	40	13	8	19	58	85	34
Shirebrook	40	14	4	22	81	106	32
Ilkeston United	40	12	7	21	57	91	31
Frickley Colliery	40	11	7	22	61	99	29
Castleford Town	40	10	2	28	62	130	22

Match No.	Date	Venue	Opponents	Result		Scorers	Atten
1	Aug 29	H	Boston Town	D	1–1	Holland	
2	31	A	Worksop Town	L	1–3	Holland	
3	Sep 5	A	Loughborough Corinthians	L	1–5	Ranby	
4	9	H	Worksop Town	L	1–2	Holland	
5	12	A	Boston Town	L	0–3		
6	16	A	Gainsborough Trinity	L	0–1		
7	26	H	Alfreton Town	W	6–0	Holland (4), Cleasby (2)	
8	Oct 8	A	Mexborough	W	2–1	Ranby, Loughran (pen)	
9	10	H	Loughborough Corinthians	W	2–0	Cleasby, Holland	
10	24	A	Newark Town	L	3–5	Holland, Albrecht, Laws	
11	Nov 7	H	Ilkeston United	W	3–0	Holland, Laws, Ranby	
12	14	H	Frickley Colliery	D	2–2	O'Cain, Ranby	
13	21	A	Alfreton Town	L	1–5	Jones	
14	28	H	Long Eaton	D	2–2	Holland, Loughran (pen)	
15	Dec 5	A	Shirebrook	W	5–3	Riley (3), Laws, Harron	
16	12	H	Scunthorpe United	D	1–1	O'Cain	
17	19	A	Scunthorpe United	L	1–2	Riley	
18	25	A	Castleford Town	L	0–2		
19	26	H	Castleford Town	W	2–1	Harron, Riley	
20	Jan 1	A	Wath Athletic	L	1–3	O'Cain	
21	2	H	Newark Town	L	2–4	Harron, Ranby	
22	9	A	Long Eaton	D	1–1	Riley	
23	23	H	Lincoln City Reserves	D	1–1	Loughran (pen)	
24	Feb 6	H	Grantham	W	3–1	Loughran (pen), Richardson, Laws	
25	13	H	Shirebrook	W	3–1	Loughran, O'Cain, Riley	
26	20	H	Wombwell Town	W	4–1	R. Baines (3), Loughran	
27	27	A	Wombwell Town	L	0–4		
28	Mar 6	H	Mansfield Town	D	2–2	Clayton (2)	
29	11	A	Grantham	L	1–3	Laws	
30	13	H	Sutton Town	W	4–2	R. Baines, Ranby, Stonehouse, Laws	
31	17	H	Gainsborough Trinity	W	4–2	Clayton (2), R. Baines, Laws	
32	20	A	Mansfield Town	L	1–5	Stonehouse	
33	27	A	Frickley Colliery	L	1–2	R. Baines	
34	Apr 2	A	Denaby United	L	1–5	Laws	
35	5	H	Denaby United	W	3–2	Richardson (2), O'Cain	
36	10	H	Wath Athletic	W	3–1	O'Cain (2), Laws	
37	17	A	Lincoln City Reserves	L	1–6	O'Cain	
38	19	A	Ilkeston United	L	1–2	O'Cain	
39	24	H	Mexborough	W	2–1	O'Cain (2)	
40	May 1	A	Sutton Town	L	1–6	O'Cain	

FA Cup

	Date	Venue	Opponents	Result		Scorers
Pre	Sep 23	H	Maltby Main *	W	5–3	Cleasby (2), Holland (2), Laws
1Q	Oct 3	H	Wombwell	W	5–0	Holland (3), Ranby, Loughran (pen)
2Q	17	H	Castleford Town	W	3–0	Cleasby, Holland, Ranby
3Q	31	A	Wath Athletic	L	1–4	Loughran

* Match on 19 September abandoned after 71 minutes with City leading 7–0.

Did you know that?

On 21 November 1925 City travelled to Alfreton and were one player short. The City party stopped at a pub and recruited a person by the name of Jones who was having a drink. He was reputed to be a good player and scored City's only goal in a 5–1 defeat.

City's FA Cup preliminary round match at Maltby Main was abandoned after 71 minutes owing to a violent thunderstorm. At the time City were winning 7–0! The tie was replayed four days later at Fulfordgate, and City won 5–3.

George Richardson, who made 14 appearances this season, played for Huddersfield Town in the 1920 FA Cup Final when they were runners-up to Aston Villa.

Sayles	Drew	Maskill G.	Loughran	Middlemiss	Laws	Acklam	Holland	Cleasby	Harron	Albrecht	Sandiland	Ranby	Baines J.	Miller	Baines R.	Glover	O'Cain	Clayton	Jones	Riley	Horrocks	Lodge	Martindale	Kay F.	Brown	Richardson	Stonehouse	Barnicle	Kay E.	Martin	Noble	Bell	Daniels	Dennis	Tillotson	
2	3	4	5	6	7	8	9	10	11																											1
2	3	4	6		7	8	9	10	11	5																										2
2	3		5	6	7		9		11	4	8	10																								3
2		4	6		11		9		7	5	8	10	3																							4
2		4	5	6	11	8			7			10	3	9																						5
2		4	5	6	11				7	8		10	3		9																					6
2		4	5	6	11		9	10	7			8	3																							7
2		4	5	6	11		9	10	7			8	3																							8
2		4	5	6	11		9	10	7			8	3																							9
2		4	5	6	11		9		7	10		8	3																							10
3		4	5	6	11		9		7			8				2	10																			11
3		4	5	6	11		9		7			8				2	10																			12
3		4		6	11		9		7			8				2		5	10																	13
3		4	10	6	11		9		7			8				2		5																		14
3			5	6	11				7			8				2	10	4		9																15
3		4	5	6	11				7			8				2	10			9																16
3			5	6	11				7			8				2	10	4		9	1															17
3			5	6	11				7			8			9	2	10	4			1															18
3			5	6	11				7			8				2	10	4		9	1															19
			5	6	11				7			8				2	10	4			1	3	9													20
			5	6	11				7	4		8				2		10			1	3		9												21
			5	6	11				7			8				2	10	4		9	1	3														22
			5	6	11				7			8				2	10	4		9	1	3														23
			5	6	11							8				2		4		10	1	3			7	9										24
			5	6	11											2	8	4		10	1	3			7	9										25
			5	6	11							8			9	2		4		10	1	3			7											26
		4	5	6	11							8			9	2		10			1	3			7											27
		4	5	6	11							10			9	2		8			1	3			7											28
		4	5		11					6		10			9	2		8				3			7											29
			5	6	11							10			9	2		4			1	3			7		8									30
		4	5	6	11							10			9	2		8				3			7			1								31
		4							7	5													2				9	1	6	8	10	11	3			32
		4	5	6	11							7			9			8				3	2			10		1								33
		4	5	6	11							10						8				3	2			9		1						7		34
		4	5	6	11					2		10					8	3								9								7		35
			5	6	11					4					10	2	8				1	3				9								7		36
	9	4	5	6								10				2	8				1	3				11								7		37
		4	5	6	11							10				2	8				1	3				9								7		38
		4	5	6	11							10				2	8					3				9									7	39
			5	6	11							10	4			2	8					3			7	9		1								40
19	4	25	38	36	38	3	12	5	24	10	2	35	8	1	10	26	17	21	1	9	16	19	4	1	9	10	2	5	1	1	1	1	1	5	1	
			6		9		11	3	3	1		6			6		12	4	1	7						3	2									

Sayles	Drew	Maskill G.	Loughran	Middlemiss	Laws	Acklam	Holland	Cleasby	Harron	Albrecht	Sandiland	Ranby	Baines J.	
2	3		5	6	11		9	10	7	4		8		Pre
2		4	5	6	11		9	10	7			8	3	1Q
2	3	4	5	6	11		9	10	7			8		2Q
2	3	4	5	6	11		9		7	10		8		3Q
4	3	3	4	4	4		4	3	4	2		4	1	
			2		1		6	3				2		

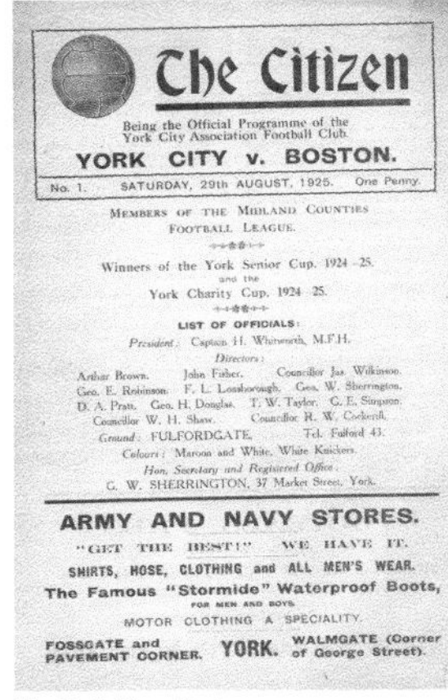
The Citizen
Being the Official Programme of the York City Association Football Club.
YORK CITY v. BOSTON.
No. 1. SATURDAY, 29th AUGUST, 1925. One Penny.
Members of the Midland Counties Football League.
Winners of the York Senior Cup, 1924–25, and the York Charity Cup, 1924–25.
LIST OF OFFICIALS:
President: Captain H. Whitworth, M.F.H.
Directors:
Ground: FULFORDGATE.
ARMY AND NAVY STORES.
"GET THE BEST!" WE HAVE IT.
SHIRTS, HOSE, CLOTHING and ALL MEN'S WEAR.
The Famous "Stormide" Waterproof Boots,
MOTOR CLOTHING A SPECIALITY.
FOSSGATE and PAVEMENT CORNER. YORK. WALMGATE (Corner of George Street).

The York City v Boston programme, 29 August 1925.

1926–27

Midland League

	P	W	D	L	F	A	Pts
Scunthorpe United	38	28	4	6	121	44	60
Boston Town	38	21	7	10	128	64	49
Gainsborough Tr.	38	22	5	11	85	63	49
Wath Athletic	38	21	4	13	76	63	46
Mexborouh Athletic	38	20	6	12	97	81	46
York City	38	16	13	9	96	68	45
Loughborough Cor.	38	20	5	13	94	76	45
Lincoln City (R)	38	18	7	13	94	70	43
Denaby United	38	18	4	16	88	59	40
Shirebrook	38	19	2	17	112	96	40
Worksop Town	38	17	5	16	95	87	39
Frickley Colliery	38	14	9	15	80	84	37
Ilkeston Town	38	13	7	18	73	95	33
Grantham	38	12	8	18	84	76	32
Heanor Town	38	13	6	19	70	99	32
Newark Town	38	13	6	19	67	95	32
Long Eaton	38	12	7	19	72	105	31
Alfreton Town	38	8	5	25	59	143	21
Wonbwell Town	38	7	6	25	57	111	20
Sutton Town	38	8	4	26	67	136	20

Match No.	Date	Venue	Opponents	Result		Scorers	Attend
1	Aug 28	H	Loughborough Corinthians	D	1–1	Flood	
2	Sep 1	H	Worksop Town	W	2–0	Flood, Middlemiss	
3	4	A	Alfreton Town	L	1–3	Albrecht	
4	11	H	Alfreton Town	W	7–0	Duckham (5), Flood (2)	
5	15	A	Ilkeston United	L	2–3	Ranby, O'Cain	
6	18	A	Shirebrook	L	1–4	Loughran (pen)	
7	23	A	Grantham	D	1–1	Richards	
8	25	H	Ilkeston United	W	6–0	Flood (4), Richards, Harvey	
9	Oct 9	A	Wombwell Town	D	1–1	Merritt	
10	11	A	Denaby United	L	1–3	Ranby	
11	23	H	Wath Athletic	W	7–1	Flood (3), Ranby (2), O'Cain, Loughran	
12	Nov 6	H	Boston Town	D	0–0		
13	20	H	Denaby United	W	2–1	Duckham, Middlemiss	
14	Dec 4	H	Heanor Town	D	4–4	Flood (3, 1 pen), Merritt	
15	18	H	Shirebrook	W	5–2	Clayton (2), Ranby (2), Merritt	
16	25	A	Scunthorpe United	D	2–2	Merritt, Loughran	
17	27	H	Scunthorpe United	L	1–2	Merritt	
18	Jan 1	H	Sutton Town	W	1–0	Clancey	
19	8	A	Frickley Colliery	W	3–1	Thompson (3)	
20	22	A	Gainsborough Trinity	D	3–3	Flood, Loughran (pen), Thompson	
21	Feb 5	H	Wombwell Town	W	7–1	Clayton (3), Flood (2), Harvey, Merritt	
22	12	A	Wath Athletic	W	2–0	Thompson, Ranby	
23	Mar 5	H	Lincoln City Reserves	D	4–4	Ranby (2), Redfern, Thompson	
24	12	A	Boston Town	D	3–3	Merritt, Fenoughty, Thompson	
25	16	H	Grantham	D	1–1	Fenoughty	
26	19	H	Mexborough Athletic	D	2–2	Merritt (2)	
27	26	A	Newark Town	W	1–0	Fenoughty	
28	31	A	Worksop Town	L	1–6	Fenoughty	
29	Apr 2	H	Gainsborough Trinity	W	3–2	Clayton (2), Fenoughty	
30	9	A	Lincoln City Reserves	L	0–2		
31	16	H	Newark Town	W	5–0	Clayton (2), Ranby, Merritt, Fenoughty	
32	18	H	Long Eaton	W	2–1	Ranby, Merrritt	
33	19	A	Long Eaton	D	3–3	Ranby (2), Noble	
34	23	A	Mexborough Athletic	L	3–4	O'Cain (2), Clayton	
35	26	A	Heanor Town	D	1–1	Noble	
36	27	A	Sutton Town	W	4–1	Duckham, Middlemiss, O'Cain, Loughran	
37	30	H	Frickley Colliery	W	3–0	Fenoughty (2), Ranby	
38	May 4	A	Loughborough Corinthians	L	0–5		

A

FA Cup

1Q	Oct 2	H	Guisborough Belmont	W	5–0	Clayton (3), Ranby, Loughran	2,
2Q	16	H	South Bank	W	4–0	Merritt (2), Flood, Duckham	3,
3Q	31	H	Whitby United	D	0–0		3,
r	Nov 3	H*	Whitby United	W	2–1	Flood, Ranby	2,
4Q	13	A	Ilkeston United	W	5–1	Clayton (2), Ranby, Loughran, Duckham	3,
1	Dec 1	H	Worksop Town #	W	4–1	Merritt (2), Ranby, Harvey	2,
2	11	A	Grimsby Town	L	1–2	Harvey	11,

* Replay staged at York.

A

Match on 27 November abandoned (due to fog) after 70 mins with the score 1–1.

Did you know that?

George Thompson was the regular first-choice 'keeper this season. In the summer of 1927 he was transferred to Second Division Southampton. In the early 1950s his son Des played for City.

Inside-forward Tom Fenoughty made his debut this campaign, making over 250 senior appearances for the club and scoring over 100 goals spanning the transition to the Football League and the move from Fulfordgate to Bootham Crescent.

For the first time City reached the first round proper of the FA Cup, losing in the second round away to Second Division Grimsby Town in what was their first meeting with a Football League club.

Flynn	Daniels	Maskill G.	Richards	Loughran	Harvey	Ranby	Flood	Duckham	Richardson	Middlemiss	O'Cain	Albrecht	Merritt	Clayton	Kay T.	Redfern	Shanks	Thompson R.	Clancey	Fenoughty	Furnell	Noble	Hill	Everest	
2	3	4	5	6	7	8	9	10	11																1
2	3	4		5		8	9	10	11	6	7														2
2	3	4		5	7	8	9	10		6		11													3
2	3	4		5	7	8	9	10	11	6															4
2	3	4		5		8	9	10	11	6	7														5
2	3	4		5	7	8	9	10		6			11												6
2	3		9	5			8	10		6			11	4	7										7
2	3	4	9	5	7		8	10		6			11												8
2	3	4		5	7	10		9		6	8		11												9
2	3	4		5	7	10		9		6	8		11												10
2	3			5	7	10	8			6	9		11			4									11
2				5	7	10		8		6			11	9		4	3								12
2				5	7	10		8		6			11	9		4	3								13
2				5	7	10	8			6			11	9		4	3								14
2		8		5	7	10				6			11	9		4	3								15
2		8		5	7	10				6			11	9		4	3								16
2		4		5	7	10				6	8		11	9		3									17
2	3			5	7	10	8			6						4		9	11						18
2	3			5	7		8			6			11	10		4		9							19
2	3			5	7	10	8			6			11			4		9							20
2	3			5	7	10	8			6			11	9		4									21
2	3			5	7	10	8			6			11			4		9							22
2	3			5	7	10				6			11			4		9		8					23
2	3	4			7	10				6			11			5		9		8					24
2				5		10				6			11			4	3	9		8	1	7			25
2				5	7	10				6			11	8		4	3	9							26
2				5	7	10				6			11			4	3	9		8					27
2				5		10				6			11			4	3	9		8		7			28
2		4			7	10				6			11	9		5	3			8					29
2	3				7	10				6		4	11	9		5				8					30
2	3			4		10				6			11	9		5				8		7			31
2	3	4				10				6			11	9		5				8		7			32
2	3			4		10								9		5				8		7	6	11	33
2		4			11	10				6	8			9		5	3					7			34
2		4				10				6		8	11	9		5	3					7			35
2		4		5				11		6	7	8		9			3					10			36
2	3			5	7	10		8		6		11				4				9					37
2	3			5	7	10		8		6		11				4				9					38
38	24	18	3	32	28	34	15	15	4	36	8	6	27	18	1	27	13	10	1	12	1	8	1	1	
			2	5	2	14	17	7		3	5	1	11	10		1		7	1	8		2			

Flynn	Daniels	Maskill G.	Richards	Loughran	Harvey	Ranby	Flood	Duckham	Richardson	Middlemiss	O'Cain	Albrecht	Merritt	Clayton	Kay T.	Redfern	Shanks	Thompson R.	Clancey	Fenoughty	Furnell	Noble	Hill	Everest	
2	3	4		5	7	8		10		6			11	9											1Q
2	3			5	7	10	8	9		6	4		11												2Q
2	3			5	7	10	8			6	9		11			4									3Q
2				5		10	8	9		6			11	7		4	3								r
2				5	7	10		8		6			11	9		4	3								4Q
2				5	7	10	8			6			11	9		4	3								1
2				5	7	10		8		6			11	9		4	3								2
7	3	1		7	6	7	4	5		7	2		7	5		5	4								
				2	2	4	2	2					4	5											

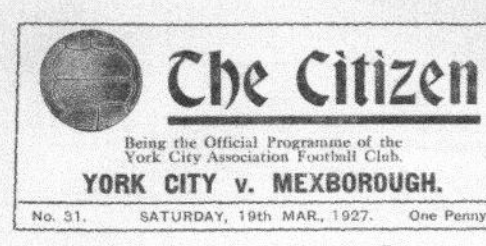

The Citizen

Being the Official Programme of the York City Association Football Club.

YORK CITY v. MEXBOROUGH.

No. 31. SATURDAY, 19th MAR., 1927. One Penny.

Members of the Midland Counties Football League and Yorkshire League.

Winners of the York Charity Cup, 1925–26.
F.A. Cup, 2nd Round, 1926–27.

LIST OF OFFICIALS:

President: Captain H. Whitworth, M.F.H.

Directors:
John Fisher. Arthur Brown. Councillor Jas. Wilkinson.
Geo. E. Robinson. Geo. W. Sherrington. D. A. Pratt.
Geo. H. Douglas. G. E. Simpson. Councillor W. H. Shaw.
H. Rusholme. A. H. Shaw. W. H. McAdams.

Ground: FULFORDGATE. Tel. Fulford 43.

Colours: Maroon and White, White Knickers.

Hon. Secretary and Registered Office:
G. W. SHERRINGTON, 37 Market Street, York.

ARMY AND NAVY STORES.
"GET THE BEST!" WE HAVE IT.
SHIRTS, HOSE, CLOTHING and ALL MEN'S WEAR.
The Famous "Stormide" Waterproof Boots, FOR MEN AND BOYS.
MOTOR CLOTHING A SPECIALITY.
FOSSGATE and PAVEMENT CORNER. YORK. WALMGATE (Corner of George Street).

The York City v Mexborough programme, 19 March 1927.

George Thompson, goalkeeper.

1927–28

Midland League

	P	W	D	L	F	A	Pts
Gainsborough Tr.	44	29	7	8	141	62	65
Scarborough	44	26	7	11	108	61	59
Nottingham Forest (R)	44	23	8	13	127	84	54
Notts County (R)	44	24	5	15	143	81	53
Lincoln City	44	23	7	14	126	99	53
Wath Athletic	44	24	4	16	94	74	52
York City	44	22	7	15	97	73	51
Shirebrook	44	23	5	16	108	89	51
Scunthorpe United	44	23	4	17	118	85	50
Mansfield Town	44	19	11	14	118	97	49
Worksop Town	44	20	9	15	97	101	49
Grimsby Town (R)	44	20	8	16	93	83	48
Grantham	44	17	11	16	88	102	45
Denaby United	44	19	6	19	76	82	44
Boston Town	44	16	11	17	79	87	43
Stavely Town	44	16	10	18	98	109	42
Mexborough Atheltic	44	14	9	21	84	112	37
Frickley Colliery	44	15	5	24	84	107	35
Loughborough Cor.	44	14	7	23	76	104	35
Wombwell Town	44	12	7	25	70	107	31
Heanor Town	44	10	5	29	66	155	25
Ilkeston United	44	8	5	31	75	133	21
Newark Town	44	8	4	32	60	139	20

Did you know that?

On 8 March 1928 City recorded their biggest ever away win when they beat Nottingham Forest reserves 7–1.

The FA Cup tie against Scarborough drew a then record crowd of 6,422 to Fulfordgate.

At the end of the season City made their third application for election to the Football League and received just seven votes, one more than the previous year.

Match No.	Date	Venue	Opponents	Result		Scorers	Attend
1	Aug 27	H	Worksop Town	W	3–1	Fenoughty (2), Merritt	
2	31	H	Grantham	L	1–2	Merritt	
3	Sep 3	A	Frickley Colliery	L	2–3	Waite, Merritt	
4	10	H	Grimsby Town Reserves	W	4–2	Tyson (2), Merritt, Fenoughty	
5	17	A	Newark Town	W	3–1	Hammerton, Fenoughty, Merritt	
6	24	H	Heanor Town	W	7–1	Hammerton (4), Waite, Ranby, Fenoughty	
7	Oct 8	H	Nottingham Forest Reserves	L	1–2	Hammerton	
8	22	H	Wombwell Town	W	4–2	Merritt (2), Albrecht (2)	
9	Nov 5	H	Staveley Town	W	5–2	Merritt (2), Albrecht (2), Ranby	
10	19	A	Wath Athletic	L	0–2		
11	Dec 3	A	Denaby United	D	2–2	Merritt, Hooper	
12	10	H	Frickley Colliery	W	4–2	Hammerton (2), Merritt, Hooper	
13	17	A	Heanor Town	L	1–2	Ranby	
14	26	A	Scarborough	L	1–3	Merritt	
15	27	H	Scarborough	W	2–0	Merritt, Hammerton	
16	31	A	Grimsby Town Reserves	W	1–0	Hammerton	
17	Jan 2	H	Gainsborough Trinity	L	0–3		
18	7	H	Wath Athletic	W	3–1	Hammerton (2), Merritt	
19	14	A	Mansfield Town	L	1–5	Waite	
20	19	A	Notts County Reserves	D	2–2	Hammerton, Waite	
21	21	H	Ilkeston United	W	4–1	Ranby (2), Hammerton (2)	
22	26	A	Wombwell Town	W	2–1	Clayton, Levick	
23	28	A	Gainsborough Trinity	L	1–4	Ranby	
24	Feb 8	H	Denaby United	W	3–1	Hammerton, Waite, Everest	
25	11	H	Scunthorpe United	W	2–1	Simms, Ranby	
26	15	H	Mansfield Town	L	2–5	Hammerton (2)	
27	18	H	Loughborough Corinthians	D	1–1	Loughran	
28	25	A	Loughborough Corinthians	L	1–4	Fenoughty	
29	29	H	Mexborough Athletic	W	4–2	Fenoughty (3), Jones	
30	Mar 3	A	Scunthorpe United	W	1–0	Albrecht	
31	8	A	Nottingham Forest Reserves	W	7–1	Noble (3), Waite (2), Fenoughty, Albrecht	
32	10	A	Boston Town	D	0–0		
33	17	H	Newark Town	W	3–0	Waite, Ranby, Albrecht	
34	23	A	Mexborough Athletic	W	4–0	Fenoughty (2), Albrecht, Everest	
35	24	A	Ilkeston United	D	1–1	Fenoughty	
36	31	H	Notts County Reserves	W	2–1	Ranby, Albrecht	
37	Apr 6	A	Worksop Town	L	2–3	Fenoughty, Albrecht	
38	7	H	Shirebrook	W	1–0	Fenoughty	
39	9	A	Shirebrook	L	0–2		
40	14	A	Grantham	D	2–2	Simms, Fenoughty	
41	21	H	Boston Town	L	0–1		
42	25	A	Staveley Town	L	3–4	Ranby (2), Noble	
43	28	H	Lincoln City Reserves	W	3–1	Fenoughty (2), Everest	
44	May 5	A	Lincoln City Reserves	D	1–1	Everest	

FA Cup

	Date	Venue	Opponents	Result		Scorers	Attend
1Q	Oct 1	H	Whitby United	W	4–0	Hammerton (2), Waite, Ranby	2
2Q	15	H	Scarborough	D	1–1	Hammerton	6
r	19	A	Scarborough	W	4–0	Albrecht, Merritt (2), Clayton	4
3Q	29	H	Stockton Malleable	W	7–1	Merritt (2) Albrecht (2), Ranby (2), Levick	2
4Q	Nov 12	A	Shildon	D	1–1	Fenoughty	3
r	16	H	Shildon	L	1–2	Ranby	4

Flynn	Daniels	Loughran	Levick	Middlemiss	Waite	Fenoughty	Hammerton	Ranby	Merritt	Harvey	Page	Clayton	Tyson	Albrecht	Hooper	Noble	Robinson	Furnell	Precious	Everest	Simms	Hill	Jones	
2	3	4	5	6	7	8	9	10	11															1
2	3	4	5	6	9	8		10	11	7														2
2		4	5	6	7	8		10	11		3	9												3
2		4	5	6	7	8	9		11		3		10											4
2		4	5	6	7	8	9	10	11		3													5
2		4	5	6	7	8	9	10	11		3													6
2		4	5	6	7	8	9	10	11		3													7
2		4	5	6	7			10	11		3	8		9										8
2		4	5	6	7	8		10	11		3			9										9
2		4		6	7	9		10	11		3	5			8									10
2		4	5	6			9	10	11		3				8	7								11
2		4	5	6	7		9	10	11		3				8									12
2		4	5	6	7		9	10	11		3				8									13
		4	5	6	7		9	10	11		3				8		2							14
2		4	5	6	7		9	10	11		3				8			1						15
2		4	5	6	7	8	9	10	11		3													16
2		4	5	6	7	8	9	10	11		3													17
2			5	6		8	9		11		3	10				7			4					18
2	3		5	6	7	8	9	10	11			4												19
2	3	4	5	6	7	8	9	10	11									1						20
2	3	4	5	6	7	8	9	10	11									1						21
2	3	4	5	6	7	8		10				9						1		11				22
2	3	4	5	6	7	8	9	10										1		11				23
2	3	4	5	6	7		9	10				8								11				24
2	3	4	5	6	7			10				8								11	9			25
2	3	4	5	6	7		11	10				8									9			26
2		4	5	6	7	8	11	10			3							1			9			27
2	3	5		6		8	9	10						4		7				11				28
2	3		5	6		8		10						11		7						4	9	29
2	3		5	6		8	11	10						9		7			4					30
2	3		5	6	11	8		10						9		7			4					31
2	3		5	6	11	8		10						9		7			4					32
2	3		5	6	11	8		10						9		7			4					33
	3		5	6	11	8		10						2		7			4	9				34
2	3		5	6	11	8		10						9		7			4					35
2	3		5	6	11	8		10						9		7			4					36
2	3		5	6	11	8		10						9		7			4					37
2	3		5		11	8		10				6		9		7			4					38
2	3		5	6	11	8		10						9		7			4					39
2			5	6	11	8		10			3	4				7					9			40
2	3		5	6	11	8		10				4				7					9			41
2			5	6	11	8		10			3					7			4		9			42
2	3			6	11	8		10						5		7			4	9				43
2	3		5	6	11	8		10								7			4	9				44
42	25	26	41	43	39	35	22	42	21	1	19	12	1	15	6	19	1	6	14	8	6	1	1	
		1	1		8	18	18	11	14			1	2	10	2	4				4	2		1	

Flynn	Daniels	Loughran	Levick	Middlemiss	Waite	Fenoughty	Hammerton	Ranby	Merritt	Harvey	Page	Clayton	Tyson	Albrecht	
2		4	5	6	7	8	9	10	11		3				1Q
2		4	5	6	7	8	9	10	11		3				2Q
2		4	5	6	7			10	11		3	8		9	r
2		4	5	6	7	8		10	11		3			9	3Q
2		4	5	6	7	8		10	11		3			9	4Q
2		4	5	6	7	8		10	11		3			9	r
6		6	6	6	6	5	2	6	6		6	1		4	
			1		1	1	3	4	4			1		3	

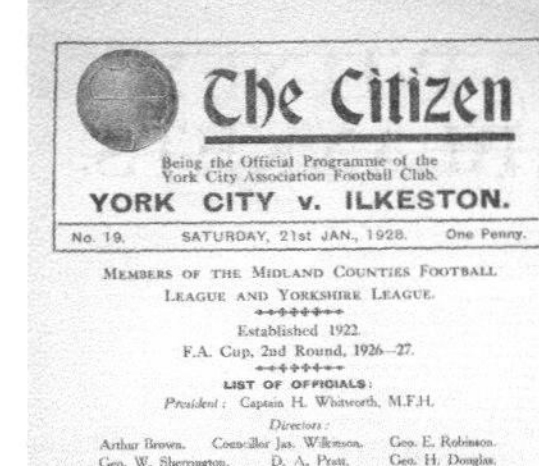
The Citizen

Being the Official Programme of the York City Association Football Club.

YORK CITY v. ILKESTON.

No. 19. SATURDAY, 21st JAN., 1928. One Penny.

MEMBERS OF THE MIDLAND COUNTIES FOOTBALL LEAGUE AND YORKSHIRE LEAGUE.

Established 1922.

F.A. Cup, 2nd Round, 1926–27.

LIST OF OFFICIALS:

President: Captain H. Whitworth, M.F.H.

Directors:

Arthur Brown. Councillor Jas. Wilkinson. Geo. E. Robinson.
Geo. W. Sherrington. D. A. Pratt. Geo. H. Douglas.
G. E. Simpson. W. H. Shaw. H. Rusholme.
A. H. Shaw. W. H. McAdam.

Ground: FULFORDGATE. Tel. Fulford 43.

Colours: Maroon and White, White Knickers.

Hon. Secretary and Registered Office: G. W. SHERRINGTON, 37 Market Street, York.

ARMY AND NAVY STORES.

"GET THE BEST!" WE HAVE IT.

SHIRTS, HOSE, CLOTHING and ALL MEN'S WEAR.

THE FAMOUS "RE-ZIST-WET" WATERPROOF BOOTS, FOR MEN AND BOYS.

MOTOR CLOTHING A SPECIALITY.

FOSSGATE and PAVEMENT CORNER. YORK. WALMGATE (Corner of George Street).

The York City v Ilkeston programme, 21 January 1928.

Sam Ranby.

1928–29

Midland League

Manager: John Collier

	P	W	D	L	F	A	Pts
Mansfield Town	50	31	10	9	133	72	72
Gainsborough Tr.	50	25	13	12	94	54	63
Lincoln City (R)	50	29	5	16	118	80	63
Hull City (R)	50	26	10	14	101	84	62
Grantham	50	25	10	15	113	79	60
Boston United	50	27	5	18	96	72	59
Scarborough	50	25	8	17	115	91	58
Notts County (R)	50	21	15	14	91	75	57
York City	50	22	13	15	106	99	57
Grimsby Town (R)	50	24	6	20	109	95	54
Scunthorpe United	50	20	14	16	98	96	54
Barnsley (R)	50	18	17	15	95	79	53
Nottingham Forest	50	20	12	18	101	74	52
Frickley Colliery	50	22	8	20	93	87	52
Denaby United	50	22	7	21	86	86	51
Chesterfield (R)	50	19	9	22	69	81	47
Shirebrook	50	19	8	23	112	113	46
Doncaster Rovers (R)	50	19	7	24	92	97	45
Wath Athletic	50	16	12	22	97	104	44
Mexborough Athletic	50	15	12	23	81	105	42
Newark Town	50	16	9	25	82	118	41
Rotherham United (R)	50	18	4	28	99	125	40
Stavely Town	50	15	8	27	102	142	38
Loughborough Cor.	50	13	6	31	75	117	32
Wombwell Town	50	12	8	30	80	136	32
Worksop Town	50	10	6	34	69	140	26

Did you know that?

In July 1928 John 'Jock' Collier was appointed the first official manager of the club. He joined as player-manager, but a broken ankle ended his playing days after just two games for the club. He had previously played for Hull City and Queen's Park Rangers.

This season was remarkable for the scoring feats of Scottish centre-forward Jimmy Cowie. He netted 56 goals in 56 League and Cup appearances, and at the end of the season, along with winger Dick Merritt, was selected for the Rest of the Midland League against champions Mansfield Town in a special challenge match.

On 3 June 1929, at the fourth attempt, City were elected to the Football League, taking the place of Ashington.

Match No.	Date	Venue	Opponents	Result		Scorers	Attend
1	Aug 23	H	Shirebrook	W	2–1	Fenoughty (2)	
2	Sep 1	A	Shirebrook	W	2–0	Cowie, Ranby	
3	5	H	Notts County Reserves	L	3–6	Fenoughty (2), Cowie	
4	8	H	Newark Town	W	5–1	Ranby (2), Cowie (2), Opp. og	
5	15	A	Newark Town	L	0–1		
6	20	A	Notts County Reserves	D	1–1	Cowie	
7	22	H	Frickley Colliery	D	1–1	Charnley	
8	Oct 3	H	Scunthorpe United	W	3–1	Duthie (2), Cowie	
9	6	H	Rotherham United Reserves	W	3–2	Forrest, Duthie, Cowie	
10	17	H	Mansfield Town	L	0–1		
11	20	A	Boston Town	L	0–6		
12	31	H	Staveley Town	W	4–2	Roberts (3), Charnley	
13	Nov 3	H	Hull City Reserves	W	6–1	Cowie (5), Ranby	
14	6	A	Grimsby Town Reserves	L	0–3		
15	11	A	Frickley Colliery	L	1–6	Cowie	
16	17	H	Mexborough Athletic	L	1–2	Fenoughty	
17	Dec 1	A	Mansfield Town	L	1–2	Cowie (pen)	
18	15	H	Loughborough Corinthians	D	1–1	Forrest	
19	22	A	Mexborough Athletic	W	2–1	Lacy (2)	
20	25	A	Scarborough	L	0–5		
21	26	H	Scarborough	W	4–1	Cowie (2), Roberts, Middlemiss	
22	29	H	Chesterfield Reserves	W	3–2	Cowie, Roberts, Forrest	
23	Jan 1	A	Wath Athletic	D	1–1	Cowie	
24	3	A	Nottingham Forest Reserves	D	0–0		
25	5	A	Loughborough Corinthians	W	1–0	Lacy	
26	12	H	Grimsby Town Reserves	D	2–2	Cowie, Forrest	
27	19	A	Worksop Town	L	2–4	Merritt, Ranby	
28	26	H	Barnsley Reserves	W	5–2	Cowie (2), Ranby (2), Forrest	
29	31	A	Scunthorpe United	L	2–3	Cowie, Merritt	
30	Feb 7	A	Hull City Reserves	D	2–2	Cowie (2, 1 pen)	
31	9	H	Denaby United	D	2–2	Cowie, Charnley	
32	16	A	Denaby United	D	2–2	Cowie, Clayton	
33	23	H	Worksop Town	W	8–2	Cowie (6), Fenoughty (2)	
34	Mar 2	H	Boston Town	W	4–0	Cowie (4)	
35	9	A	Wombwell Town	L	0–4		
36	13	H	Grantham	L	1–2	Fenoughty	
37	16	A	Rotherham United Reserves	W	7–2	Ranby, Cowie (4), Fenoughty (2)	
38	20	A	Staveley Town	D	2–2	Cowie, Forrest	
39	23	H	Lincoln City Reserves	W	4–3	Merritt (3), Cowie	
40	29	H	Doncaster Rovers Reserves	W	3–1	Cowie, Fenoughty, Merritt	
41	Apr 1	A	Doncaster Rovers Reserves	D	1–1	Fenoughty	
42	6	A	Barnsley Reserves	L	1–5	Forrest	
43	11	A	Grantham	D	2–2	Fenoughty, Ranby	
44	13	H	Wombwell Town	W	3–2	Cowie (2), Roberts	
45	17	H	Wath Athletic	W	3–1	Cowie (2), Fenoughty	
46	20	A	Chesterfield Reserves	D	1–1	Fenoughty	
47	22	A	Gainsborough Trinity	W	1–0	Charnley	
48	27	H	Nottingham Forest Reserves	W	2–0	Cowie (2)	
49	29	A	Lincoln City Reserves	L	0–6		
50	May 1	H	Gainsborough Trinity	W	1–0	Duthie	

A

1 own-goal

FA Cup

1Q	Sep 29	H	Stockton	W	7–1	Cowie (6), Ranby	3,
2Q	Ocy 13	H	Normanby Magnestie	W	2–1	Forrest, Charnley	2,
3Q	27	H	Bridlington	W	3–0	Duthie (2), Ranby	2,
4Q	Nov 10	A	Jarrow	D	0–0		5,
r	14	H	Jarrow	D	2–2*	Merritt, Cowie	4,
2r	19	N#	Jarrow	W	3–2	Roberts, Merritt, Fenoughty	6,
1	24	H	Barrow	L	0–1		6,

Ap

* After extra-time.

At St James' Park, Newcastle.

Brown	Marshall	Collier	Charnley	Duthie	Forrest	Fenoughty	Cowie	Ranby	Roberts	Robinson	Precious	Middlemiss	Merritt	Albrecht	Houghton	Chown	Clayton	Addison	Bolton	Sharpe	Lacy	
2	3	4	5	6	7	8	9	10	11													1
2	3	4	5	6	7	8	9	10	11													2
3			5	6	7	8	9	10	11	2	4											3
2	3		5	6	7	8	9	10	11			4										4
2	3		5	6	7	8	9	10	11			4										5
2	3		5	6	7	8	9	10	11			4										6
2	3		5	6	7	8	9	10	11			4										7
2	3		5	8	7		9	10			6	4	11									8
2	3		5	8	7		9	10	11		6	4										9
2	3		5	6	7	8	9		11			4		10								10
2	3		5		7	8	9	10	11			4		6								11
2	3		5	6			9	10	11			4	7		8							12
2	3		5	6		8	9	10	11			4	7									13
2	3		5	6		8	9	10	11			4	7									14
2						8	9			3			7		10	1	4	5	6	11		15
2	3		5	6	10	8	9		11			4	7									16
2	3		5	6	10		9	8	11			4	7									17
2	3		5	6	8		9	10	11			4										18
2	3		5	6	7		8	10	11			4									9	19
2	3		5	6	7		8	10	11			4									9	20
2	3			6			8	10	11			4	7				5				9	21
2	3		5	6	8		9	10	11			4	7									22
2	3		5	6	8		9	10	11			4	7									23
	3		5	6	7		8	10	11			4		2							9	24
	3		5	6	7		8	10	11			4		2							9	25
2	3		5	6	7	8	9	10	11			4										26
	3		5	6	7		8	10		2		4	11								9	27
	3		5	6	7	8	9	10	11			4		2								28
	3		5	6	8		9	10	11				7	2			4					29
	3		5	6	7	8	9	10	11	2		4										30
2	3		5	6		8	9	10	11			4	7									31
2	3		5	6	7		9	10	11			4					8					32
2	3		5	6	7	8	9	10	11			4										33
	3		5	6	7	8	9	10	11	2		4										34
	3		5	6	7	8	9	10		2		4	11									35
	3		5	6	7	8	9	10	11	2		4										36
2	3		5	6	7	8	9	10				4	11									37
2	3		5	6	7	8	9	10				4	11									38
2	3		5	6	7	8	9	10				4	11									39
2	3		5	6	7	8	9	10				4	11									40
3			5	6	7	8	9	10		2		4	11									41
2	3		5	6	7	8	9	10				4	11									42
2	3		5	6	7	8	9	10	11			4										43
2	3		5	6	7	8	9	10	11			4										44
2	3		5	6	7	8	9	10	11			4										45
2	3		5	6	7	8	9	10	11			4										46
2			5	6	10	9		8	11			4	7				3					47
2	3		5	6	7	8	9	10	11			4										48
2	3		5	6	7	8	9	10	11			4										49
2	3		5	6	7	8	9	10	11			4										50
41	46	2	48	48	44	35	49	47	40	8	3	45	22	6	2	1	5	1	1	1	6	
			4	4	7	15	49	9	6			1	6				1				3	

Brown	Marshall	Collier	Charnley	Duthie	Forrest	Fenoughty	Cowie	Ranby	Roberts	Robinson	Precious	Middlemiss	Merritt	Albrecht	
2	3		5	8	7		9	10	11		4	6			1Q
2	3		5	4	7	8	9	10	11			6			2Q
2	3		5	6		8	9	10	11			4	7		3Q
2	3		5	6		8	9	10	11			4	7		4Q
2	3		5	6	10	8	9		11			4	7		r
2			5	6	10	8	9		11			4	7	3	2r
2	3		5	6	10	8	9		11			4	7		1
7	6		7	7	5	6	7	4	7		1	7	5	1	
			1	2	1	1	7	2	1				2		

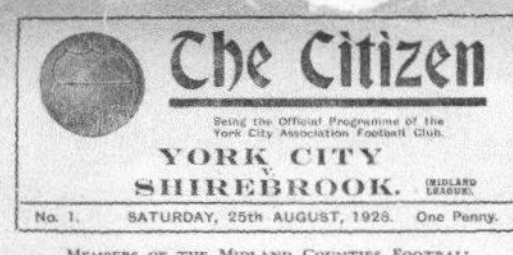
The Citizen
Being the Official Programme of the York City Association Football Club.
YORK CITY v. SHIREBROOK. (MIDLAND LEAGUE).
No. 1. SATURDAY, 25th AUGUST, 1928. One Penny.

MEMBERS OF THE MIDLAND COUNTIES FOOTBALL LEAGUE AND YORKSHIRE LEAGUE.

Established 1922.
F.A. Cup, 2nd Round, 1926–27.

LIST OF OFFICIALS:
President: Captain H. Whitworth, M.F.H.
Directors:
Arthur Brown. Councillor Jas. Wilkinson. Geo. E. Robinson.
Geo. W. Sherrington. D. A. Pratt. Geo. H. Douglas.
G. E. Simpson. N. Pratt. H. Rusholme.
Mr. J. Fisher. H. Hayhurst W. Mason.
Ground: FULFORDGATE. Tel. Fulford 43.
Colours: Maroon and White, White Knickers.
Hon. Secretary and Registered Office:
G. W. SHERRINGTON, 37 Market Street, York. Tel. York 3869.

The York City v Shirebrook programme, 25 August 1928.

Jimmy Cowie.

YORK CITY SECURE ADMISSION TO THE FOOTBALL LEAGUE.

ELECTED WITH HARTLEPOOLS UNITED TO THE NORTHERN SECTION.

HEAVY TASK AHEAD FOR THE DIRECTORS.

TEAM BUILDING AND GROUND IMPROVEMENTS AT FULFORD GATE.

YORK City were to-day elected to the Northern Section of the Third Division of the Football League.

The decision will be welcomed by all followers of Association football in this part of Yorkshire. It marks an advance in the history of the game in York which, it is hoped, may ultimately prove the stepping-stone to even greater things.

For seven years all the energies of the directorate of the city club and the supporters have been devoted to securing admission to the Football League; now that the ambition has been realised serious work will be put in hand at once to ensure that the club's ground at Fulford Gate may be thoroughly equipped and ready to receive the larger crowds that may be expected at the matches, while the directors will have to grapple with the vital problem of team building.

In the matter of the choice of players the whole future of the club is at stake, and here the directors may be trusted to exercise that wise discretion upon which everything will depend in bringing together a team capable of ensuring a successful run for the city club in the higher sphere of football shortly to be entered upon.

SUCCESS AFTER SEVEN YEARS' ENDEAVOUR.

Newspaper article celebrating the admission of York City into the Football League.

1929–30

Division Three North

Manager: John Collier

	P	W	D	L	F	A	Pts
Port Vale	42	30	7	5	103	37	67
Stockport County	42	28	7	7	106	44	63
Darlington	42	22	6	14	108	73	50
Chesterfield	42	22	6	14	76	56	50
Lincoln City	42	17	14	11	83	61	48
York City	42	15	16	11	77	64	46
South Shields	42	18	10	14	77	74	46
Hartlepools United	42	17	11	14	81	74	45
Southport	42	15	13	14	81	74	43
Rochdale	42	18	7	17	89	91	43
Crewe Alexandra	42	17	8	17	82	71	42
Tranmere Rovers	42	16	9	17	83	86	41
New Brighton	42	16	8	18	69	79	40
Doncaster Rovers	42	15	9	18	62	69	39
Carlisle United	42	16	7	19	90	101	39
Accrington Stanley	42	14	9	19	84	81	37
Wrexham	42	13	8	21	67	88	34
Wigan Borough	42	13	7	22	60	88	33
Nelson	42	13	7	22	51	80	33
Rotherham United	42	11	8	23	67	113	30
Halifax Town	42	10	8	24	44	79	28
Barrow	42	11	5	26	41	98	27

Match No.	*Date*	*Venue*	*Opponents*	*Result*		*Scorers*	*Attend*
1	Aug 31	A	Wigan Borough	W	2–0	Cowie, Stockill	8
2	Sep 4	H	Wrexham	D	0–0		8
3	7	H	Carlisle United	D	2–2	Gardner (2)	7
4	11	A	Wrexham	D	1–1	Davis	6
5	14	A	Nelson	L	1–3	Cowie	4
6	18	H	New Brighton	W	3–0	Bottrill (2), Evans	5
7	21	H	Southport	L	0–4		5
8	28	A	Crewe Alexandra	D	2–2	Beck, Gardner	5
9	Oct 5	H	Chesterfield	D	1–1	Cowie	4
10	12	H	Stockport County	L	1–2	Bottrill	6
11	19	A	Lincoln City	L	0–3		5
12	26	H	Tranmere Rovers	D	0–0		3
13	Nov 2	A	Halifax Town	D	2–2	Bottrill (2, 1 pen)	4
14	9	H	Rotherham United	W	3–0	Fenoughty, Cowie, Millar	3
15	23	H	South Shields	D	2–2	Gardner (2)	3
16	Dec 7	H	Darlington	D	1–1	Millar	4
17	21	H	Doncaster Rovers	D	2–2	Gardner, Opp. og	2
18	25	A	Barrow	D	0–0		2
19	26	H	Barrow	W	3–1	Evans, Fenoughty, Bottrill	7
20	28	H	Wigan Borough	W	4–0	Bottrill (3), Gardner	4
21	Jan 1	A	New Brighton	D	1–1	Fenoughty	5
22	4	A	Carlisle United	D	2–2	Fenoughty, Bottrill	7
23	18	H	Nelson	W	1–0	Bottrill	5
24	25	A	Southport	L	0–1		3
25	Feb 1	H	Crewe Alexandra	W	4–2	Millar (3), Bottrill	4
26	8	A	Chesterfield	L	0–3		4
27	15	A	Stockport County	W	3–2	Beck, Gardner, Fenoughty	9
28	22	H	Lincoln City	W	1–0	Gardner	5
29	Mar 1	A	Tranmere Rovers	D	4–4	Gardner, Fenoughty, Millar, Bottrill	4
30	5	A	Accrington Stanley	D	1–1	Evans	2
31	8	H	Halifax Town	W	3–0	Evans, Fenoughty, Millar	4
32	15	A	Rotherham United	W	5–2	Fenoughty (2), Bottrill (2), Gardner	2
33	22	H	Rochdale	W	6–0	Gardner (2), Fenoughty (2), Millar, Bottrill	4
34	29	A	South Shields	L	1–4	Fenoughty	2
35	Apr 2	A	Hartlepools United	L	1–3	Aitken	4
36	5	H	Accrington Stanley	W	2–0	Sharpe, Fenoughty	4
37	12	A	Darlington	L	2–5	Beck (pen), Millar	6
38	18	A	Port Vale	D	1–1	Gardner	15
39	19	H	Hartlepools United	W	4–1	Evans (2), Gardner, Bottrill	2
40	21	H	Port Vale	L	0–2		10
41	26	A	Doncaster Rovers	W	3–0	Fenoughty (2), Evans	4
42	May 3	A	Rochdale	L	2–4	Gardner, Bottrill	1
							A
						1 own-goal	

FA Cup

4Q	Nov 16	A	Scarborough	W	3–1	Bottrill (2), Cowie	8
1	30	H	Tranmere Rovers	D	2–2	Fenoughty (2)	5
r	Dec 5	A	Tranmere Rovers	W	1–0	Fenoughty	4
2	14	A	Southend United	W	4–1	Davis, Gardner, Fenoughty (2)	11
3	Jan 11	A	Newcastle United	D	1–1	Gardner	38
r	15	H	Newcastle United	L	1–2	Evans	12
							A

Did you know that?

City's first-ever match in the Football League marked the debut of the youngest-ever player to appear for the club in a senior competitive game. Local lad Reg Stockill was 15 years, 281 days old when he played at Wigan Borough on 31 August 1929, and he scored City's first-ever League goal in their 2–0 success. He later played for Arsenal and Derby County.

Only three players who had appeared in the Midland League side of 1928–29 played this season in the first team: Jimmy Cowie, Tom Fenoughty and George Sharpe.

City's first-ever League hat-trick was recorded by inside-forward Billy Bottrill in the return game against Wigan on 28 December 1929. He finished top scorer this season and at the end of the campaign joined Wolverhampton Wanderers, helping them win promotion to the First Division in 1931–32.

City's position of sixth in the table was their highest until 1952–53 when they finished in fourth place.

The average home crowd for this first season of League football was 5,279.

City appeared in the fourth qualifying round of the FA Cup this season. It was to be the last time they were to play at this stage until 2004–05 when they were in the Conference.

They reached the third round of the competition and met First Division opposition for the first time when they played Newcastle United.

Archibald	Johnson	Beck	Davis	Thompson	Evans	Gardner	Cowie	Smiles	Stockill	Millar	Bottrill	Fenoughty	Glidden	Gallacher	Brooks	Sharpe	Aitken	Ridley	No.
2	3	4	5	6	7	8	9	10	11										1
2	3	4	5	6	7	8	9	10		11									2
2	3	4	5	6	7	8	9			11	10								3
2	3	4	5	6	7	8				11	9	10							4
2	3	4	5	6	7	8	9			11	10								5
2	3	4	5	6	7					11	10		8	9					6
2	3	4	5	6	7		9			11	10		8						7
2	3	4	5	6	7	8	9	11			10								8
2	3	4	5	6	7	8	9	11			10								9
2	3	4	5	6	7	8		10		11	9								10
2	3	4	5	6	7	8		10		11	9								11
	3	4	5	6	7			10		11	9			8	2				12
	3	4	5	6	7		9			11	10	8			2				13
2	3	4	5	6	7		9			11	10	8							14
	3	4	5	6	7	8	9			11		10			2				15
	3		5	6	7		9			11	10	4		8	2				16
	3	4	5	6	7	9					8	10			2	11			17
	3	4	5	6	7	9				11	8	10			2				18
	3	4	5	6	7	9				11	8	10			2				19
	3	4	5	6	7	9				11	8	10			2				20
	3	4	5	6	7	9				11	8	10			2				21
	3	4	5	6	7		9			11	8	10			2				22
	3	4	5	6	7	9				11	8	10			2				23
	3	4	5	6	7	9				11	8	10			2				24
	3	4	5	6						11	8	10			2	7	9		25
	3	4	5	6						11	8	10			2	7	9		26
	3	4	5	6	7	9				11	8	10			2				27
	3	4	5	6	7	9				11	8	10			2				28
	3	4	5	6	7	9				11	8	10			2				29
	3	4	5	6	7	9				11	8	10			2			1	30
	3	4	5	6	7	9				11	8	10			2				31
	3	4	5	6	7	9				11	8	10			2				32
	3	4	5	6	7	9				11	8	10			2				33
	3	4	5	6	7	9				11	8	10			2				34
	3	4	5	6			9	7		11	8				2		10		35
	3	4	5	6		9				11	8	10			2	7			36
	3	4	5	6		9				11	8	10			2	7			37
3		4	5	6	7	9				11	8	10			2				38
3		4		5	7	10	9				8	6			2	11			39
3		4	5	6	7					11	8				2	10	9	1	40
3		4	5	6	7	9				11	8	10			2			1	41
3		4	5	6	7	9				11	8	10			2			1	42
17	37	41	41	42	37	31	14	8	1	37	39	29	2	3	30	7	4	4	
		3	1		7	16	4		1	9	18	15				1	1		

Archibald	Johnson	Beck	Davis	Thompson	Evans	Gardner	Cowie	Smiles	Stockill	Millar	Bottrill	Fenoughty	Glidden	Gallacher	Brooks	Sharpe	Aitken	Ridley	No.
	3	4	5	6	7		9		11		8	10			2				4Q
	3	4	5	6	7		9			11	8	10			2				1
	3	4	5	6	7		9			11	8	10			2				r
	3	4	5	6	7	9				11	8	10			2				2
	3	4	5	6	7	9				11	8	10			2				3
	3	4	5	6	7	9				11	8	10			2				r
	6	6	6	6	6	3	3		1	5	6	6			6				
			1		1	2	1				2	5							

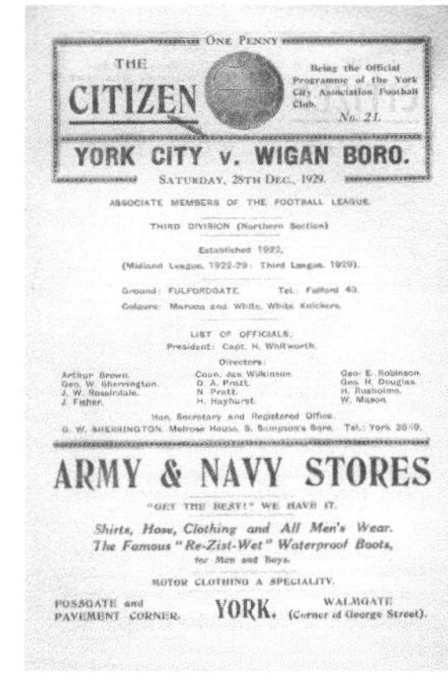
ONE PENNY
THE CITIZEN
Being the Official Programme of the York City Association Football Club.
No. 21.
YORK CITY v. WIGAN BORO.
SATURDAY, 28TH DEC., 1929.
ASSOCIATE MEMBERS OF THE FOOTBALL LEAGUE.
THIRD DIVISION (Northern Section)
ARMY & NAVY STORES
"GET THE BEST!" WE HAVE IT.
Shirts, Hose, Clothing and All Men's Wear.
The Famous "Re-Zist-Wet" Waterproof Boots, for Men and Boys.
MOTOR CLOTHING A SPECIALITY.
FOSSGATE and PAVEMENT CORNER. YORK. WALMGATE (Corner of George Street).

The York City v Wigan Borough. programme, 28 December 1929.

Reg Stockill.

1930–31

Division Three North

Manager-secretary: G.W. Sherrington

	P	W	D	L	F	A	Pts
Chesterfield	42	26	6	10	102	57	58
Lincoln City	42	25	7	10	102	59	57
Wrexham	42	21	12	9	94	62	54
Tranmere Rovers	42	24	6	12	111	74	54
Southport	42	22	9	11	88	56	53
Hull City	42	20	10	12	99	55	50
Stockport County	42	20	9	13	77	61	49
Carlisle United	42	20	5	17	98	81	45
Gateshead	42	16	13	13	71	73	45
Wigan Borough	42	19	5	18	76	86	43
Darlington	42	16	10	16	71	59	42
York City	42	18	6	18	85	82	42
Accrington Stanley	42	15	9	18	84	108	39
Rotherham United	42	13	12	17	81	83	38
Doncaster Rovers	42	13	11	18	65	65	37
Barrow	42	15	7	20	68	89	37
Halifax Town	42	13	9	20	55	89	35
Crewe Alexandra	42	14	6	22	66	93	34
New Brighton	42	13	7	22	49	76	33
Hartlepools United	42	12	6	24	67	86	30
Rochdale	42	12	6	24	62	107	30
Nelson	42	6	7	29	43	113	19

Did you know that?

Jimmy Cowie made his last appearance for the club this season. He signed off with five goals in three matches in February, including a hat-trick in a win against Hartlepools United.

As in the previous campaign Reg Stockill only played in the opening League game of the season. He moved to Scarborough in March 1931 prior to his transfer to Highbury two months later.

The aggregate of 167 goals this season (F85 A82) remains a record for the club while in the Football League.

The FA Cup third-round replay against First Division Sheffield United on 14 January 1931 drew Fulfordgate's all-time attendance and receipts records of 12,721 and £1,059.

Average home League crowd was 3,906. The crowd of 1,735 against New Brighton on 25 April 1931 was the smallest-ever at Fulfordgate for a Football League game.

Match No.	Date		Venue	Opponents	Result		Scorers	Attend
1	Aug	30	A	Rotherham United	L	1–2	Beck (pen)	6
2	Sep	3	A	Wrexham	L	2–3	Gardner, Laycock	6
3		6	H	Chesterfield	D	2–2	Beck (pen), Fenoughty	5
4		10	H	Tranmere Rovers	W	3–1	Fenoughty, Gardner, D. Kelly	3
5		13	A	Barrow	W	2–1	Fenoughty, Gardner	7,
6		18	A	Tranmere Rovers	L	1–4	Evans	3
7		20	H	Southport	W	3–1	Beck (pen), Fenoughty, Gardner	4,
8		27	A	Accrington Stanley	L	2–4	Gardner (2)	4
9	Oct	4	H	Rochdale	W	3–0	Fenoughty, Sharpe, Laycock	4
10		11	A	Crewe Alexandra	L	1–5	Fenoughty	3
11		18	H	Stockport County	L	1–2	Jenkinson	4
12		25	A	Doncaster Rovers	W	2–0	Evans, Fenoughty	4
13	Nov	1	H	Halifax Town	W	4–1	Beck (2), Fenoughty, D. Kelly	3
14		8	A	Darlington	L	0–3		4
15		15	H	Nelson	W	3–0	Ellis, J. Kelly, D. Kelly	3
16		22	A	Wigan Borough	L	1–3	J. Kelly	4
17	Dec	6	A	Lincoln City	L	1–4	J. Kelly	5,
18		20	A	New Brighton	L	3–5	Gardner, Laycock, D. Kelly	2
19		25	H	Carlisle United	W	4–0	Gardner (2), Beck, Laycock	4
20		26	A	Carlisle United	L	0–2		7
21		27	H	Rotherham United	D	1–1	Tomlinson	4
22	Jan	1	A	Gateshead	L	1–2	Gardner	4
23		3	A	Chesterfield	L	1–3	Laycock	4
24		17	H	Barrow	W	4–2	Evans (2), Fenoughty, J. Kelly	3,
25	Feb	4	H	Hartlepools United	W	4–2	Cowie (3), Millar	1
26		7	A	Rochdale	D	2–2	Evans, Cowie	2,
27		14	H	Crewe Alexandra	W	4–3	Laycock (2), Cowie, Millar	3,
28		17	A	Southport	L	0–1		2,
29		21	A	Stockport County	D	0–0		4,
30		28	H	Doncaster Rovers	W	4–2	D. Kelly (2), Fenoughty, McCabe	3
31	Mar	7	A	Halifax Town	D	0–0		2,
32		14	H	Darlington	W	2–1	Fenoughty (2)	4,
33		18	H	Hull City	W	3–2	Beck (pen), McCabe, Laycock	3,
34		21	A	Nelson	W	5–2	Fenoughty (2), McCabe, Laycock, D. Kelly	1
35		28	H	Wigan Borough	L	2–3	Beck, Laycock	2,
36	Apr	3	H	Gateshead	W	4–3	Beck, Fenoughty, McCabe, Laycock	4,
37		4	A	Hartlepools United	L	0–3		3,
38		6	H	Accrington Stanley	W	3–1	Fenoughty, McCabe, Laycock	4,
39		11	H	Lincoln City	D	1–1	Fenoughty	6,
40		18	A	Hull City	L	1–3	Brewis	4,
41		25	H	New Brighton	W	4–1	McCabe (2), Brewis, Millar	1,
42	May	2	H	Wrexham	L	0–1		2,
								A

FA Cup

1	Nov	29	H	Gresley Rovers	W	3–1	Evans, Laycock, J. Kelly	4,
2	Dec	13	A	Nelson	D	1–1	Brewis	3,
r		18	H	Nelson	W	3–2 *	Laycock (2), Sharpe	2,
3	Jan	10	A	Sheffield United	D	1–1	Laycock	31,
r		14	H	Sheffield United	L	0–2		12,
								A

*First replay on 17 December abandoned (due to bad weather) after 70 minutes with City leading 2–0.

Brooks	Johnson	Beck	Davis	Thompson	Evans	Fenoughty	Gardner	Laycock	Stockill	Kelly D.	Kelly J.	Brewis	Sharpe	Archibald	Ridley	Jenkinson	Duthie	Ellis	Cowie	Tomlinson	Millar	McCabe	Loughran	
2	3	4	5	6	7	8	9	10	11															1
2	3	4	5	6	7	8	9	10		11														2
2	3	4	5	6	7	8				11	10	9												3
2	3	4	5		7	8	9			11			10	6										4
2	3	4	5		7	8	9			11			10	6										5
2	3	4	5		7	8	9			11			10	6										6
2	3	4	5	6	7	8	9			11			10											7
2	3	4	5	6	7	8	9			11			10											8
2	3	4	5	6	7	8	9	10					11											9
2	3	4	5	6	7	8	9	10					11											10
2	3	5		6		10	9					8	11		1	7	4							11
2	3	4	5	6	7	8	9			11			10											12
2	3	4	5	6	7	8	9			11			10											13
2	3	4	5	6	7	8	9			11			10											14
2	3	4	5	6	7	8				11	10							9						15
2	3	4	5	6	7	8					11							9	10					16
2	3	4	5	6		8		10			11		9			7								17
2	3	4	5	6			9	10		11			8					7						18
2	3	5		6	7		9	8					10		1		4			11				19
2	3	5		6	7		9	8					10		1		4			11				20
2		5		6	7		9	8					10	3	1		4			11				21
2	3	5		6	7	10	9	8							1		4				11			22
2	3	5		6		10	9	8		7					1		4				11			23
2	3	4	5	6	7	10		8			9										11			24
2	3	4	5	6	7	10		8											9		11			25
2	3	5		6	7	10		8									4		9		11			26
2	3	5		6	7	10		8									4		9		11			27
2		5		6	7	10	9	8						3			4				11			28
2	3	5		6		10		8		7	9						4				11			29
2	3	5		6		10		8		7							4				11	9		30
2	3	5		6		10		8		7							4				11	9		31
2	3	5		6		10		8		7							4				11	9		32
2	3	5		6		10		8		7							4				11	9		33
2	3	5		6		10		8		7							4				11	9		34
2	3	5		6		10		8		7							4				11	9		35
2	3	5		6	7	10		8							1		4				11	9		36
2	3			6	7	10		8							1		4				11	9	5	37
2	3	5		6	7	10		8							1		4				11	9		38
2		5		6	7	10		8						3	1		4				11	9		39
2		5		6	7	10						8		3	1		4				11	9		40
2		5		6		10				7		8		3	1		4				11	9		41
2		4	5	6		10				7		8		3	1						11	9		42
42	36	41	20	39	29	38	20	27	1	22	6	5	16	9	13	2	22	3	4	3	21	13	1	
		9			5	17	10	12		7	4	2	1			1		1	5	1	3	7		

Brooks	Johnson	Beck	Davis	Thompson	Evans	Fenoughty	Gardner	Laycock	Stockill	Kelly D.	Kelly J.	Brewis	Sharpe	Archibald	Ridley	Jenkinson	Duthie	Ellis	Cowie	Tomlinson	Millar	McCabe	Loughran	
2	3	4	5	6	7	10		8			9							11						1
2	3	4	5	6				10		7	9	8					11							2
2	3	4	5	6			9	10		7		8	11											r
2	3	4	5	6	7	10	9	8													11			3
2	3	4	5	6	7	10	9	8													11			r
5	5	5	5	5	3	3	3	5		2	2	2	1				1	1			2			
					1			4			1	1	1											

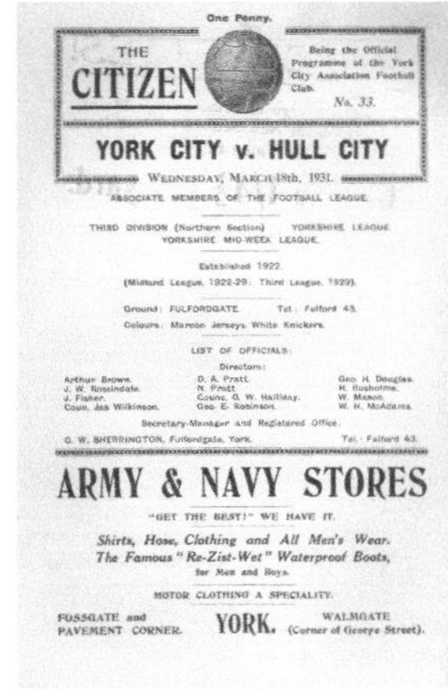
One Penny.
THE CITIZEN
Being the Official Programme of the York City Association Football Club.
No. 33.
YORK CITY v. HULL CITY
WEDNESDAY, MARCH 18th, 1931.
ASSOCIATE MEMBERS OF THE FOOTBALL LEAGUE.
THIRD DIVISION (Northern Section) YORKSHIRE LEAGUE
YORKSHIRE MID-WEEK LEAGUE.
Established 1922.
(Midland League, 1922-29; Third League, 1929).
Ground: FULFORDGATE. Tel.: Fulford 43.
Colours: Maroon Jerseys, White Knickers.
LIST OF OFFICIALS:
Directors:
Arthur Brown. D. A. Pratt. Geo. H. Douglas.
J. W. Rossindale. N. Pratt. H. Rusholme.
J. Fisher. Coune. G. W. Halliday. W. Mason.
Coun. Jas Wilkinson. Geo. E. Robinson. W. H. McAdams.
Secretary-Manager and Registered Office.
G. W. SHERRINGTON, Fulfordgate, York. Tel.: Fulford 43.
ARMY & NAVY STORES
"GET THE BEST!" WE HAVE IT.
Shirts, Hose, Clothing and All Men's Wear.
The Famous "Re-Zist-Wet" Waterproof Boots,
for Men and Boys.
MOTOR CLOTHING A SPECIALITY.
FOSSGATE and PAVEMENT CORNER. YORK. WALMGATE (Corner of George Street).

The York City v Hull City programme, 18 March 1931.

Tom Fenoughty.

1931–32

Division Three North

Manager-secretary: G.W. Sherrington

	P	W	D	L	F	A	Pts
Lincoln City	40	26	5	9	106	47	57
Gateshead	40	25	7	8	94	48	57
Chester	40	21	8	11	78	60	50
Tranmere Rovers	40	19	11	10	107	58	49
Barrow	40	24	1	15	86	59	49
Crewe Alexandra	40	21	6	13	95	66	48
Southport	40	18	10	12	58	53	46
Hull City	40	20	5	15	82	53	45
York City	40	18	7	15	76	81	43
Wrexham	40	18	7	15	64	69	43
Darlington	40	17	4	19	66	69	38
Stockport County	40	13	11	16	55	53	37
Hartlepools United	40	16	5	19	78	100	37
Accrington Stanley	40	15	6	19	75	80	36
Doncaster Rovers	40	16	4	20	59	80	36
Walsall	40	16	3	21	57	85	35
Halifax Town	40	13	8	19	61	87	34
Carlisle United	40	11	11	18	64	79	33
Rotherham United	40	14	4	22	63	72	32
New Brighton	40	8	8	24	38	76	24
Rochdale	40	4	3	33	48	135	11

Match No.	Date		Venue	Opponents	Result		Scorers	Attend
1	Aug	29	H	Tranmere Rovers	W	3–2	Brewis, McCabe, Fenoughty	5
2	Sep	2	H	Southport	L	1–2	Brewis	2
3		5	A	Rotherham United	W	1–0	McCabe	6
4		9	A	Gateshead	L	0–6		14
5		12	H	Stockport County	W	1–0	Fenoughty	4
6		16	H	Gateshead	W	3–2	Brewis (2), McDonald	6
7		19	A	Accrington Stanley	L	1–2	McCabe	4
8		26	H	Wrexham	W	3–2	Kelly (2), Thompson	4
9	Oct	3	A	Carlisle United	D	1–1	Baines	5
10		10	H	Crewe Alexandra	D	3–3	Fenoughty (2), Kelly	3
11		17	A	New Brighton	W	2–0	Baines (2, 1 pen)	2
12		24	H	Barrow	W	1–0	McDonald	3
13		31	A	Hull City	W	3–2	Baines (2), Mitchell	7
14	Nov	7	H	Lincoln City	D	1–1	Baines	4
15		14	A	Chester	L	0–3		7
16		21	H	Hartlepools United	W	3–1	Baines (2, 1 pen), Brewis	4
17	Dec	5	H	Darlington	W	3–0	Brewis (2), McDonald	4
18		12	A	Walsall	D	2–2	Brewis, Baines	3
19		19	H	Walsall	W	2–0	Kelly (2)	3
20		25	A	Doncaster Rovers	L	0–1		4
21		26	H	Doncaster Rovers	L	1–2	McDonald	8
22	Jan	1	A	Southport	L	0–3		6
23		2	A	Tranmere Rovers	D	2–2	Baines (2)	5
24		16	H	Rotherham United	W	2–0	Baines, Fenoughty	3
25		23	A	Stockport County	L	2–3	Baines, Fenoughty	5
26		30	H	Accrington Stanley	W	1–0	Fenoughty	3
27	Feb	6	A	Wrexham	L	1–2	Brewis	3
28		13	H	Carlisle United	L	2–4	Baines, Fenoughty	2
29		20	A	Crewe Alexandra	L	1–8	Baines	6
30		27	H	New Brighton	W	4–0	Baines (3), Jenkinson	3
31	Mar	5	A	Barrow	L	1–3	Fenoughty	4
32		12	H	Hull City	D	0–0		5
33		19	A	Lincoln City	D	1–1	Opp. og	7
34		25	H	Rochdale	W	5–2	Jenkinson (2), Baines (2), Thompson	5
35		26	H	Chester	W	3–1	Spooner, Jenkinson, Baines	5
36		28	A	Rochdale	W	5–3	Baines (3), Spooner, Fenoughty	1
37	Apr	2	A	Hartlepools United	L	2–7	Baines, Fenoughty	2
38		16	A	Darlington	L	1–4	Baines	2
39		23	H	Halifax Town	W	7–2	Baines (3), McDonald (2), Jenkinson, Fenoughty	2
40		28	A	Halifax Town	L	1–4	Fenoughty	1
								A
							1 own-goal	

FA Cup

1	Nov	28	A	New Brighton	L	1–3	McDonald	3
								A

Did you know that?

Two notable signings for this campaign were Scottish players Tommy McDonald and Joe Harris from Newcastle United. Inside-forward McDonald helped United win the FA Cup in 1923–24 and the First Division Championship three years later and made over 350 appearances for the Magpies. Half-back Harris had been capped twice for Scotland in 1921 while with Partick Thistle and then played for Middlesbrough before joining Newcastle, where he also figured in their title-winning season. He died while still on City's books after a short illness in October 1933 aged 37.

Another newcomer was left-winger Tom Mitchell who arrived from Leeds United. He only had a short playing career at Bootham Crescent but was to be an influential figure with the club and was manager from 1937 to 1950 and was on the board of directors in the 1960s.

Also making their debuts this term were defender Ted Wass, who gave the club eight seasons' stalwart service, figuring in the FA Cup exploits of 1937–38, and utility player Stan Fox, who was to serve City splendidly in the 1930s. Peter Spooner was signed from Bradford Park Avenue and the left-winger also had a big part to play in the club's fortunes in two spells at York.

The end of the season saw the departure of defence stalwarts Oliver Thompson, City's captain in their first three years in the Football League, Harry Beck and Jack Brooks.

Reg Baines returned to the club and scored on his League debut at Carlisle on 3 October 1931. He went on to net 29 League goals that term, a feat he emulated the following campaign, to create a new club seasonal scoring tally in the Football League. This record stood until 1951–52 when Billy Fenton scored 31 times.

Archibald	Johnson	Jones	Beck	Thompson	Kelly	Brewis	McCabe	Fenoughty	McDonald	Brooks	Spooner	Mitchell	Baines	Harris	Blackburn	Wass	Jenkinson	Thornton	Fox	
2	3	4	5	6	7	8	9	10	11											1
2	3	4	5	6	7	8	9	10	11											2
		4	5	6	7	8	9	3	10	2	11									3
	3	4	5	6	7	8	9		10	2	11									4
	3	4	5	6	7	8	9	10	11	2										5
	3	4	5	6	7	8	9	10	11	2										6
	3	4	5	6	7		9	8	10	2		11								7
	3	4	5	6	7		9	8	10	2		11								8
	3	4	5	6	7	8			10	2		11	9							9
	3	4	5	6	7			8	10	2		11	9							10
	3	4	5	6	7			8	10	2		11	9							11
2	3		5	6	7			8	10			11	9	4						12
2	3		5	6	7			8	10			11	9	4						13
2	3		5	6	7			8	10		11		9	4						14
2	3		5	6	7			8	10			11	9	4						15
2	3		5	6	7	8			11				9	4	10					16
2	3		5	6	7	8			10			11	9	4						17
2	3		5	6	7	8			10		11		9	4						18
2	3		5	6	7	8			10			11	9	4						19
2	3		5	6	7	8			10			11	9	4						20
2	3		5	6	7	8			10			11	9	4						21
2	3	4	5	6	7	8		10			11		9							22
2			5	6	7	8		4	10		11		9			3				23
2	3		5	6	7	8		10			11		9	4						24
2	3		5	6		8		10			11		9	4			7			25
2	3		5	6		8		10			11		9	4			7			26
2	3		5	6		8		10			11		9	4			7			27
2	3		5	6		8		10			11		9	4			7			28
	3			6		8		5	10	2	11		9	4			7			29
2	3			6	8				10		11		9	5			7	1	4	30
2	3			6				8	10		11		9	5			7	1	4	31
2	3		4	6				8	10		11		9	5			7	1		32
2	3		4	6				8	10		11		9	5			7	1		33
2	3		4	6	8				10		11		9	5			7	1		34
2	3		5	6				8	10		11		9				7	1	4	35
2	3		5	6				8	10		11		9				7	1	4	36
2	3		4	6				8	10		11		9	5			7	1		37
2	3		4	6				8	10				9	5			7	1	11	38
2	3		4	6				8	10		11		9	5			7	1		39
2	3		4	6				8	10		11		9	5			7	1		40
30	38	12	37	40	26	21	8	30	34	10	22	12	32	25	1	1	16	11	5	
				2	5	9	3	13	6		2	1	29				5			

Archibald	Johnson	Jones	Beck	Thompson	Kelly	Brewis	McCabe	Fenoughty	McDonald	Brooks	Spooner	Mitchell	Baines	Harris	Blackburn	Wass	Jenkinson	Thornton	Fox	
2	3		5	6	7			8	10			11	9	4						1
1	1		1	1	1			1	1			1	1	1						
									1											

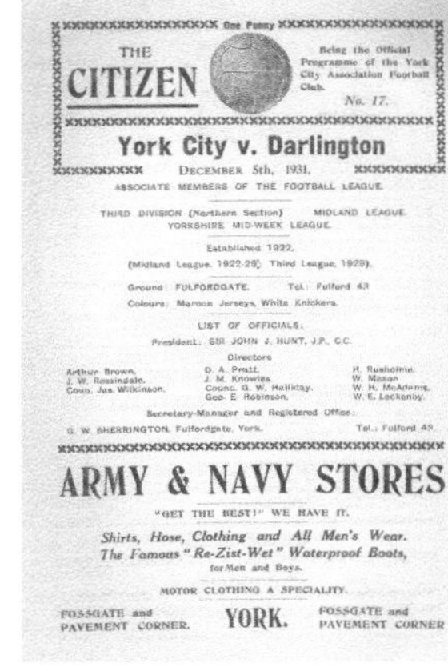
One Penny

THE CITIZEN

Being the Official Programme of the York City Association Football Club.

No. 17.

York City v. Darlington

December 5th, 1931.

ASSOCIATE MEMBERS OF THE FOOTBALL LEAGUE.

THIRD DIVISION (Northern Section) MIDLAND LEAGUE
YORKSHIRE MID-WEEK LEAGUE.

Established 1922.

(Midland League, 1922-29; Third League, 1929).

Ground: FULFORDGATE. Tel.: Fulford 43

Colours: Maroon Jerseys, White Knickers.

LIST OF OFFICIALS.

President: SIR JOHN J. HUNT, J.P., C.C.

Directors

Arthur Brown, J. W. Rossindale, Coun. Jas. Wilkinson, D. A. Pratt, J. M. Knowles, Counc. G. W. Halliday, Geo. E. Robinson, H. Rusholme, W. Mason, W. H. McAdams, W. E. Leckenby.

Secretary-Manager and Registered Office:

G. W. SHERRINGTON, Fulfordgate, York. Tel.: Fulford 43

ARMY & NAVY STORES

"GET THE BEST!" WE HAVE IT.

Shirts, Hose, Clothing and All Men's Wear.
The Famous "Re-Zist-Wet" Waterproof Boots, for Men and Boys.

MOTOR CLOTHING A SPECIALITY.

FOSSGATE and PAVEMENT CORNER. YORK. FOSSGATE and PAVEMENT CORNER

The York City v Darlington programme, 5 December 1931.

Reg Baines.

In April 1932 the club announced the move to Bootham Crescent, and City signed off from Fulfordgate with a 7–2 win over Halifax Town on 23 April 1932 when Reg Baines hit his third hat-trick of the season.

The home match against Carlisle United on 13 February 1932 was attended by the Archbishop of York Dr W. Temple. The event was described as unique in the history of football, as no evidence had been found that any other archbishop of York or Canterbury had been to a Football League game before. There was no divine intervention, however, as City lost 4–2!

Average League attendance for the last season at Fulfordgate was 4,330.

1932–33

Division Three North

Manager-secretary: G.W. Sherrington

	P	W	D	L	F	A	Pts
Hull City	42	26	7	9	100	45	59
Wrexham	42	24	9	9	106	51	57
Stockport County	42	21	12	9	99	58	54
Chester	42	22	8	12	94	66	52
Walsall	42	19	10	13	75	58	48
Doncaster Rovers	42	17	14	11	77	79	48
Gateshead	42	19	9	14	78	67	47
Barnsley	42	19	8	15	92	80	46
Barrow	42	18	7	17	60	60	43
Crewe Alexandra	42	20	3	19	80	84	43
Tranmere Rovers	42	17	8	17	70	66	42
Southport	42	17	7	18	70	67	41
Accrington Stanley	42	15	10	17	78	76	40
Hartlepools United	42	16	7	19	87	116	39
Halifax Town	42	15	8	19	71	90	38
Mansfield Town	42	14	7	21	84	100	35
Rotherham United	42	14	6	22	60	84	34
Rochdale	42	13	7	22	58	80	33
Carlisle United	42	13	7	22	51	75	33
York City	42	13	6	23	72	92	32
New Brighton	42	11	10	21	63	88	32
Darlington	42	10	8	24	66	109	28

Did you know that?

This was the first season at Bootham Crescent, with Tom Mitchell scoring the club's first League goal at the new ground on 31 August 1932 against Stockport County.

Right-back Jack Pinder, who captained England Schoolboys in 1927, made his debut in the return game against Stockport on 5 September 1932. He went on to give the club several years' splendid service, making his last League appearance in March 1948.

At the end of the season Reg Baines and Peter Spooner were both transferred to Sheffield United for fees of £500.

In May 1933 John Collier was reappointed as manager.

The average home League crowd at the new ground was 4,370.

Match No.	Date	Venue	Opponents	Result		Scorers	Attend
1	Aug 27	A	Crewe Alexandra	L	0–1		6
2	31	H	Stockport County	D	2–2	Mitchell, Baines (pen)	8,
3	Sep 3	H	Rochdale	L	2–6	Fenoughty, Mitchell	4
4	5	A	Stockport County	L	0–2		6,
5	10	A	Southport	L	1–5	Baines	5
6	17	H	Mansfield Town	W	4–3	Baines (3, 1 pen), Fenoughty	4
7	24	A	Rotherham United	L	0–1		4
8	Oct 1	H	Accrington Stanley	D	0–0		4
9	8	A	New Brighton	W	1–0	Baines	2
10	15	H	Chester	W	3–1	McDonald (2), Baines	5
11	22	H	Gateshead	D	2–2	Baines, Spooner	6,
12	29	A	Walsall	L	2–4	Baines, Spooner	3,
13	Nov 5	H	Wrexham	L	2–3	T. Maskill, Baines	5,
14	12	A	Tranmere Rovers	W	3–2	Baines (2), Spooner	3
15	19	H	Halifax Town	W	5–3	Fenoughty (2), Spooner (2), McDonald	3
16	Dec 3	H	Barnsley	W	3–2	Baines, McDonald, Spooner	3,
17	17	H	Doncaster Rovers	L	2–3	Fox, Baines	3
18	24	A	Darlington	L	0–3		4
19	27	A	Barrow	L	0–1		3,
20	31	H	Crewe Alexandra	W	4–0	Baines (2), McDonald, T. Maskill	3
21	Jan 7	A	Rochdale	W	4–1	Baines (2), Fenoughty, Spooner	3,
22	14	A	Hartlepools United	L	2–4	Donaldson, Baines	3,
23	28	A	Mansfield Town	L	0–3		4,
24	Feb 4	H	Rotherham United	W	4–3	Spooner (2), Baines, T. Maskill	3,
25	11	A	Accrington Stanley	L	0–5		2,
26	18	H	New Brighton	W	3–0	Spooner (2), Jenkinson	2,
27	Mar 4	A	Gateshead	D	2–2	Jenkinson, Fenoughty	3
28	11	H	Walsall	W	4–2	Baines (2), Fenoughty, Jenkinson	4,
29	18	A	Wrexham	L	1–3	Baines	7,
30	25	H	Tranmere Rovers	L	0–1		3,
31	29	A	Chester	L	0–5		7
32	Apr 1	A	Halifax Town	L	0–2		2,
33	5	H	Barrow	W	3–1	Baines (3)	2,
34	8	H	Hartlepools United	D	1–1	Baines	3,
35	14	A	Carlisle United	L	1–5	Fenoughty	6,
36	15	A	Barnsley	D	1–1	Jenkinson	4,
37	17	H	Carlisle United	L	0–1		4,
38	22	H	Hull City	L	1–2	Baines	8,
39	26	H	Southport	L	0–1		2
40	29	A	Doncaster Rovers	L	2–3	Jenkinson, Baines	4,
41	May 1	A	Hull City	L	1–2	Jenkinson	19,
42	6	H	Darlington	W	6–1	Fox, Jenkinson (2), Mitchell (2), Fenoughty	3,
							A

FA Cup

1	Nov 26	H	Scarborough	L	1–3	Spooner	8,
							A

Archibald	Johnson	Maskill G.	Harris	Bolton	Williams	Fenoughty	Baines	McDonald	Mitchell	Fox	Pinder	Turnbull	Spooner	Spargo	Wass	Donaldson	Fawcett	Greener	Camidge	Jenkinson	Moore	Maskill T.	
2	3	4	5	6	7	8	9	10	11														1
2	3	4	5	6	7	8	9	10	11														2
2		4	5	6		8	9	10	11	7					3								3
			4	6				10	11	8	2	9	7	5	3								4
			4	6	7		9	10	11		2		7	5	3								5
2	3		4	6	7	8	9	10					11	5									6
2	3			6	7	8	9	10					11	5								4	7
2	3		4			8	9	10					11	5		7	1					6	8
2	3		4			8	9	10					11	5		7	1					6	9
2			4			8	9	10		3			11	5		7	1					6	10
2	3		4			8	9	10					11	5		7	1					6	11
2			4			8	9	10		3			11	5		7	1					6	12
2	3		4			8	9	10					11	5		7	1					6	13
	3		4			8	9	10					11	5		7	1	6				2	14
	3		4			8	9	10					11	5		7	1	6				2	15
	3		4			8	9	10					11	5		7	1	6				2	16
	3		4				9	10		8			11	5		7	1	6				2	17
2			4		7		9	10			3		11	5			1		8			6	18
2			4				9	10			3		11	5		7	1	8				6	19
2			4				9	10			3		11	5		7	1	8				6	20
2			4			6	9	10			3		11	5		7	1	8					21
2			4			6	9	10			3		11	5		7	1	8					22
2			4				9	10			3		11	5		7	1	8				6	23
2			4				9	10			3		11	5		7	1	8				6	24
2			4		7	6	9	10			3		11	5			1	8					25
2			4			6	9	10			3		11	5			1	8		7			26
2			4			8	9	10			3		11	5			1			7		6	27
2			4			8	9	10			3		11	5			1			7		6	28
2			4			8	9	10			3		11	5			1			7		6	29
2			4			8	9	10			3		11	5			1			7		6	30
2			4				9	10					11	5			1	8	3	7		6	31
2			4				9	10	6				11	5	3		1	8		7			32
2			4				9	10	6		3		11	5			1	8		7			33
2			4				9	10	6		3		11	5			1	8		7			34
			4			3	9	10	11		2			5			1	8		7		6	35
			5			10	9			4					3	2	1	8		7	11	6	36
			5			10	9			4					3	2	1	8		7	11	6	37
2			5			8	9	10		4	11						1	6		7		3	38
	2					8	9	10		4			11		5		1	6		7		3	39
						8	9	10		4			11	5	2		1	6		7		3	40
						8		10	9	4			11	5	2		1	6		7		3	41
						8		10	9	4			11	5	2		1	6		7		3	42
29	13	3	37	7	7	30	39	40	11	12	19	1	35	35	10	18	35	24	2	17	2	29	
						9	29	5	4	2			11			1				8		3	

Archibald	Johnson	Maskill G.	Harris	Bolton	Williams	Fenoughty	Baines	McDonald	Mitchell	Fox	Pinder	Turnbull	Spooner	Spargo	Wass	Donaldson	Fawcett	Greener	Camidge	Jenkinson	Moore	Maskill T.	
	3		4			8	9	10					11	5		7	1	6				2	1
	1		1			1	1	1					1	1		1	1	1				1	
													1										

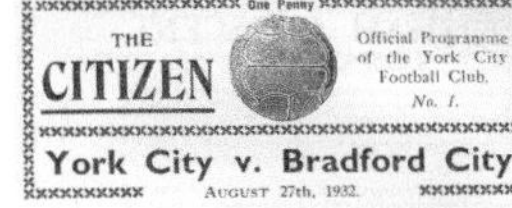
THE CITIZEN — One Penny — Official Programme of the York City Football Club. No. 1.
York City v. Bradford City
AUGUST 27th, 1932.
ASSOCIATE MEMBERS OF THE FOOTBALL LEAGUE.
Established 1922.
Ground: BOOTHAM CRESCENT. Tel.: York 4447
Colours: Chocolate and Cream Shirts, White Knickers
President: SIR JOHN J. HUNT, J.P., C.C.
Directors
Arthur Brown (Chairman) H. Rusholme (Vice Chairman)
Coun. G. W. Halliday. J. W. Rosindale. J. M. Knowles. W. Mason.
W. H. McAdoo. D. A. Pratt. S. M. Gawthorpe. W. E. Leckenby.
A. H. Shaw. L. F. Lonsborough.
Secretary-Manager and Registered Office:
G. W. SHERRINGTON, Bootham Crescent, York.
ARMY & NAVY STORES
"GET THE BEST!" WE HAVE IT.
Shirts, Hose, Clothing and All Men's Wear.
The Famous "Re-Zist-Wet" Waterproof Boots,
for Men and Boys.
MOTOR CLOTHING A SPECIALITY.
FOSSGATE and PAVEMENT CORNER. YORK. FOSSGATE and PAVEMENT CORNER.

The York City v Bradford City programme, 27 August 1932. This was a reserve game, the first-ever match staged at Bootham Crescent.

Jack Pinder.

1933–34

Division Three North

Manager: John Collier

	P	W	D	L	F	A	Pts
Barnsley	42	27	8	7	118	61	62
Chesterfield	42	27	7	8	86	43	61
Stockport County	42	24	11	7	115	52	59
Walsall	42	23	7	12	97	60	53
Doncaster Rovers	42	22	9	11	83	61	53
Wrexham	42	23	5	14	102	73	51
Tranmere Rovers	42	20	7	15	84	63	47
Barrow	42	19	9	14	116	94	47
Halifax Town	42	20	4	18	80	91	44
Chester	42	17	6	19	89	86	40
Hartlepools United	42	16	7	19	89	93	39
York City	42	15	8	19	71	74	38
Carlisle United	42	15	8	19	66	81	38
Crewe Alexandra	42	15	6	21	81	97	36
New Brighton	42	14	8	20	62	87	36
Darlington	42	13	9	20	70	101	35
Mansfield Town	42	11	12	19	81	88	34
Southport	42	8	17	17	63	90	33
Gateshead	42	12	9	21	76	110	33
Accrington Stanley	42	13	7	22	65	101	33
Rotherham United	42	10	8	24	53	91	28
Rochdale	42	9	6	27	53	103	24

Match No.	Date	Venue	Opponents	Result		Scorers	Attend
1	Aug 26	H	Walsall	D	2–2	Wilcockson, Ivory	5
2	30	A	Crewe Alexandra	L	3–5	Dando (2), Lockie	4
3	Sep 2	A	Hartlepools United	L	0–2		5
4	6	H	Crewe Alexandra	W	4–1	Wilcockson, Fenoughty, Dando, Opp. og	5
5	9	A	Chester	D	1–1	Jenkinson	7
6	16	H	Doncaster Rovers	L	1–2	Ivory (pen)	6
7	23	A	Barrow	D	2–2	Dawson, Dando	5
8	30	H	Carlisle United	W	4–1	Dando (2), Fenoughty, Ivory	5
9	Oct 7	A	Stockport County	L	1–2	Fox	5
10	14	H	Halifax Town	W	1–0	Jenkinson	5
11	21	H	Mansfield Town	W	1–0	Hathway	5
12	28	A	Barnsley	L	0–1		5
13	Nov 4	H	Tranmere Rovers	W	1–0	Jenkinson	4
14	18	H	Chesterfield	L	1–2	Dando	6
15	Dec 2	H	Gateshead	D	1–1	Hathway	3
16	9	A	Darlington	L	0–4		2
17	16	H	Southport	W	1–0	Dando	2
18	23	A	Wrexham	W	3–2	Dando (2), Lax	3
19	25	H	Rotherham United	L	0–1		3
20	26	A	Rotherham United	L	2–3	Lax (2)	6
21	30	A	Walsall	L	0–1		5
22	Jan 1	A	Southport	D	0–0		3
23	6	H	Hartlepools United	L	1–3	Dando	4
24	20	H	Chester	W	3–2	Hathway (2, 2 pens), Ivory	4
25	24	A	Accrington Stanley	L	1–4	Hathway	1
26	27	A	Doncaster Rovers	L	1–3	Ivory	4
27	Feb 3	H	Barrow	W	6–1	Hathway (3), Dando (2), Jenkinson	2
28	10	A	Carlisle United	L	2–3	Wilcockson, Ivory	3
29	17	H	Stockport County	D	2–2	Scott, Ivory	5
30	20	A	Rochdale	W	6–3	Wilcockson (2), Dando (2), Ivory, Hathway	
31	24	A	Halifax Town	L	0–3		5
32	Mar 3	A	Mansfield Town	W	2–0	Jenkinson, Hathway	4
33	10	H	Barnsley	D	1–1	Jenkinson	2
34	17	A	Tranmere Rovers	L	0–3		2
35	24	H	Rochdale	W	6–1	Dando (3), Hathway (2), Lax	3
36	30	H	New Brighton	W	2–1	Dando (2)	5
37	31	A	Chesterfield	L	0–2		10
38	Apr 2	A	New Brighton	L	1–2	Dando	3
39	7	H	Accrington Stanley	W	3–2	Dando (2), Lax	3
40	14	A	Gateshead	W	2–0	Hathway, Dando	1
41	21	H	Darlington	D	1–1	Ivory	3
42	May 5	H	Wrexham	L	2–4	Hathway, Dando	2

A

1 own-goal

FA Cup

1	Nov 25	H	Hartlepools United	L	2–3	Lax, Jenkinson	6

A

Northern Section Cup

1	Jan 13	H	Hartlepools United	W	2–1	Lax, Dando	3
2	Mar 7	H	Carlisle United	W	2–1	Dando, Wilcockson	2
3	21	A	Darlington	L	3–4	Dando (2), Hathway	2

A

Did you know that?

Newcomers this season included centre-half Tom Lockie, half-back Ted Hathway and centre-forward Maurice Dando.

Lockie, who had previously been with Glasgow Rangers, was signed from Barnsley. This was his only season as a player for City, but he returned to Bootham Crescent in 1936 and for 31 years gave the club stalwart service as reserve-team trainer, coach and then manager.

Hathway joined the club from Bolton Wanderers and was a virtual ever present for the six seasons he was at York, figuring in all 16 FA Cup ties in 1936–37 and 1937–38.

A former Bristol Rovers player, Dando netted twice on his debut at Crewe on 30 August 1933 and finished top marksman.

For the third successive season City fell at the first hurdle in the FA Cup and as an economy measure released Tom Fenoughty in January 1934. He had been with the club since 1927 and he joined Rotherham United.

The average home League crowd was 4,361.

The crowd of 800 on 20 February 1934 at Rochdale was the smallest-ever to watch City in a Football League game.

Match	Pinder	Dawson	Scott	Lockie	Wilcockson	Jenkinson	Ivory	Clayson	Fenoughty	King	Dando	Fox	Wass	Bonass	Wightman	Slicer	Hathway	Lax	Burrows	Strain	Whitelaw
1	2	3	4	5	6	7	8	9	10	11											
2	2	3	4	5	6	7	8	11	10		9										
3	2			5	6	7	8		10		9	4	3	11							
4		3	5		6	7	8		10		9	4	2	11							
5		3	5		6	7	8		10		9	4	2	11							
6		3	5			7	8		10		9	4	2	11	6						
7		3	5		6	7	8		10		9	4	2	11							
8		3	5		6	7	8		10		9	4	2			11					
9		3	5		6	7	8		10		9	4	2			11					
10		3	5		6	7	8		10		9		2			11	4				
11		3	5		6	7	8		10		9		2			11	4				
12		3	5		6	7		8	10		9	4	2			11					
13		3	5		6	7		8	10		9		2		4	11					
14		3	5		6	7		8			9		2		10		4	11			
15		3	5		6	7			10		9	4	2				8	11			
16		3	5		6	7		8			9	4	2				10	11			
17		3		5	6	7			10		9	4	2				8	11			
18		3		5	6	7			10		9	4	2				8	11			
19		3		5	6	7			10		9	4	2				8	11	1		
20	2	3	4	5	6				10		9	7					8	11	1		
21		3		5	6	7			10		9	4	2				8	11			
22		3		5	6	7			10		9	4	2				8	11			
23		3	4	5	6		8				9	7	2				10	11			
24		3	4	5	6	7	8				9		2				10	11			
25		3	4	5	6	7	8				9		2				10	11			
26		3	4	5	6		8	7			9		2				10	11			
27		3	4	5	6	7	8				9		2				10	11			
28		3	4	5	6	7	8				9		2				10	11			
29		3	4	5	6	7	8				9		2				10	11			
30			4	5	6	7	8				9		2				10	11		3	
31			4	5	6	7	8				9		2				10	11		3	
32				5	6	7	8				9	4	2				10	11		3	
33			4	5	6	7	8				9		2				10	11		3	
34			4	5	6	7	8				9		2				10	11		3	
35			4	5	6	7	8				9		2				10	11		3	
36			4	5	6	7	8				9		2				10	11		3	
37			4	5		7	8				9		2		6		10	11		3	
38			4	5		7	8				9		2		6		10	11		3	
39			4	5	6	7	8				9		2				10	11		3	
40			4	5	6		8				9		2				10	11		3	7
41			4	5	6		8				9		2				10	11		3	7
42				5	6	7	8				9	4	2	11			10		1	3	
Apps	4	28	34	29	39	37	31	7	20	1	41	19	39	6	5	6	31	28	3	13	2
Goals		1	1	1	5	6	9		2		25	1					14	5			

Match	Pinder	Dawson	Scott	Lockie	Wilcockson	Jenkinson	Ivory	Clayson	Fenoughty	King	Dando	Fox	Wass	Bonass	Wightman	Slicer	Hathway	Lax	Burrows	Strain	Whitelaw
1		3	5			7	8		10		9		2		6		4	11			
Apps		1	1			1	1		1		1		1		1		1	1			
Goals						1												1			

Match	Pinder	Dawson	Scott	Lockie	Wilcockson	Jenkinson	Ivory	Clayson	Fenoughty	King	Dando	Fox	Wass	Bonass	Wightman	Slicer	Hathway	Lax	Burrows	Strain	Whitelaw
1		3	4	5	6	7					9	8	2				10	11			
2				5	6	7	8				9	4	2				10	11		3	
3			4	5	6	7	8				9		2				10	11		3	
Apps		1	2	3	3	3	2				3	2	3				3	3		2	
Goals					1						4						1	1			

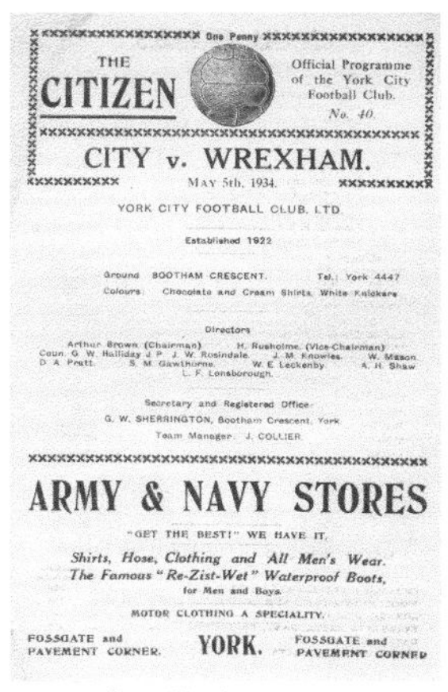
THE CITIZEN
One Penny
Official Programme of the York City Football Club. No. 40.
CITY v. WREXHAM.
May 5th, 1934.
YORK CITY FOOTBALL CLUB, LTD.
ARMY & NAVY STORES
"GET THE BEST!" WE HAVE IT.
Shirts, Hose, Clothing and All Men's Wear.
The Famous "Re-Zist-Wet" Waterproof Boots,
MOTOR CLOTHING A SPECIALITY.
FOSSGATE and PAVEMENT CORNER. YORK. FOSSGATE and PAVEMENT CORNER.

The York City v Wrexham programme, 5 May 1934.

Tom Lockie.

1934–35

Division Three North

Manager: John Collier

	P	W	D	L	F	A	Pts
Doncaster Rovers	42	26	5	11	87	44	57
Halifax Town	42	25	5	12	76	67	55
Chester	42	20	14	8	91	58	54
Lincoln City	42	22	7	13	87	58	51
Darlington	42	21	9	12	80	59	51
Tranmere Rovers	42	20	11	11	74	55	51
Stockport County	42	22	3	17	90	72	47
Mansfield Town	42	19	9	14	75	62	47
Rotherham United	42	19	7	16	86	73	45
Chesterfield	42	17	10	15	71	52	44
Wrexham	42	16	11	15	76	69	43
Hartlepools United	42	17	7	18	80	78	41
Crewe Alexandra	42	14	11	17	66	86	39
Walsall	42	13	10	19	81	72	36
York City	42	15	6	21	76	82	36
New Brighton	42	14	8	20	59	76	36
Barrow	42	13	9	20	58	87	35
Accrington Stanley	42	12	10	20	63	89	34
Gateshead	42	13	8	21	58	96	34
Rochdale	42	11	11	20	53	71	33
Southport	42	10	12	20	55	85	32
Carlisle United	42	8	7	27	51	102	23

Did you know that?

The 7–0 win over Carlisle United on 27 April 1935 was to remain City's biggest League victory until 1957.

Maurice Dando again top scored and at the end of the season was transferred to Chesterfield, helping the Spireites win promotion to Division Two in 1935–36.

Goalkeeper Joe Cunningham joined the club from Walsall. He had kept goal for the Saddlers in their famous FA Cup win over Arsenal in 1933.

Another notable newcomer was centre-half Bill Routledge, who had previously been on the books of Crystal Palace and Chelsea.

Tommy McDonald, then City's assistant trainer, came out of retirement to play his last game for the club on 23 March 1935 at Rotherham, aged 39.

For the first time since 1930–31 City reached the third round of the FA Cup, and on 12 January 1935 Bootham Crescent staged its first big game when First Division Derby County won 1–0 in front of a then record crowd of 13,612.

The average home League crowd numbered 3,902.

Match No.	Date	Venue	Opponents	Result		Scorers	Attend
1	Aug 25	A	Darlington	L	0–2		5
2	29	H	Stockport County	W	3–1	Bowater (2), Dando	5
3	Sep 1	H	Lincoln City	L	1–2	Dando	5
4	3	A	Stockport County	D	0–0		10
5	8	H	New Brighton	W	1–0	Bowater	4
6	15	A	Chester	L	1–5	Dando	8
7	22	H	Southport	W	3–1	Jenkins, Eyres, Dando	3
8	29	A	Doncaster Rovers	L	1–4	Fox	5
9	Oct 6	H	Hartlepools United	W	3–1	Speed, Eyres, Dando	4
10	13	A	Crewe Alexandra	L	2–3	Barnes, Eyres	3
11	20	A	Tranmere Rovers	L	0–4		7
12	27	H	Wrexham	D	0–0		4,
13	Nov 3	A	Halifax Town	L	3–5	Jenkins (2), Dando	9
14	10	H	Rotherham United	W	5–0	Dando (3), Eyres, Bowater	3,
15	17	A	Walsall	W	3–2	Jenkins (2), Eyres	6,
16	Dec 1	A	Mansfield Town	L	1–5	Bowater	5
17	15	A	Carlisle United	L	0–4		2
18	22	H	Rochdale	L	0–1		3
19	25	H	Accrington Stanley	W	5–2	Jenkins (2), Dando, Hathway, Bowater	3,
20	26	A	Accrington Stanley	L	2–5	Dando, Bowater	3
21	29	H	Darlington	W	2–1	Dando, Hathway	4,
22	Jan 5	A	Lincoln City	L	1–3	Hathway (pen)	3
23	19	A	New Brighton	L	2–4	Dando (2)	2
24	26	H	Chester	D	1–1	Bowater	24
25	Feb 2	A	Southport	W	3–0	Speed, Eyres, Dando	2
26	9	H	Doncaster Rovers	L	1–2	Dando	6
27	16	A	Hartlepools United	L	1–3	Opp. og	2
28	23	H	Crewe Alexandra	W	7–3	Johnson (2), Dando (2), Hathway (2), Eyres	3,
29	Mar 2	H	Tranmere Rovers	D	0–0		5
30	9	A	Wrexham	L	0–2		3,
31	16	H	Halifax Town	L	0–1		4
32	23	A	Rotherham United	L	1–4	Jenkins	5
33	27	H	Chesterfield	D	1–1	Tucker	1
34	30	H	Walsall	W	4–1	Hughes (3), Bowater	2
35	Apr 3	H	Barrow	D	1–1	Bowater	2
36	6	A	Chesterfield	L	1–3	Bowater	2
37	13	H	Mansfield Town	W	2–1	Hughes, Eyres	3
38	19	A	Gateshead	L	1–2	Eyres	3
39	20	A	Barrow	W	3–0	Jenkins (2), Hughes	3
40	22	H	Gateshead	W	3–0	Eyres (2), Hathway (pen)	4,
41	27	H	Carlisle United	W	7–0	Dando (3), Eyres (2), Pawson, Opp. og	2,
42	May 4	A	Rochdale	L	0–2		5,
							A
						2 own-goals	

FA Cup

1	Nov 24	A	Burton Town	W	3–2	Hathway, Jenkins, Bowater	6
2	Dec 8	H	New Brighton	W	1–0	Speed	6,
3	Jan 12	H	Derby County	L	0–1		13,
							A

Northern Section Cup

1	Jan 2	A	Gateshead	D	2–2	Dando, Jenkins	2,
r	30	H	Gateshead	W	3–1	Dando, Hughes, Bowater	2,
2	Feb 20	A	Hartlepools United	L	0–4		1,
							A

Wass	Turner A.	Turner R.	Routledge	Speed	Jenkins	Eyres	Dando	Hathway	Bowater	Fox	Pinder	Barnes	Hughes	Bullock	Johnson	McDonald	Tucker	Pawson	
2	3	4	5	6	7	8	9	10	11										1
3			5	6		8	9	10	11	4	2	7							2
3			5	6		8	9	10	11	4	2		7						3
3			5	6		8	9	10	11	4	2	7							4
3			5	6		8		10	11	4	2	7	9						5
3			5	6		8	9	10	11	4	2	7							6
			5	6	7	8	9	3	11	4	2		10						7
	3		5	6	7	8	9	10	11	4	2								8
3			5	6		8	9	10	11	4	2	7							9
3		4	5			8	9	10	11	6	2	7							10
3		4	5		7	8	9	10	11	6		2							11
3		4	5	6	7	8	9	10	11	2									12
3			5	6	7	8	9	10	11	2		4							13
3			5	6	7	8	9	10	11	4	2								14
3			5	6	7	8	9	10	11	4	2								15
3			5	6	7	8	9	10	11		2	4							16
3			5	6	7	8	9	10	11		2		4						17
		4	5	6	7	8	9		10	3	2			11					18
3			5	6	7	8	9	10	11	4	2								19
3			5	6	7	8	9	10	11	4	2								20
3			5	6	7	8	9	10		4	2			11					21
2	3		5	6	7	8	9	10	11	4									22
3			5	6	7	8	9	10		4	2			11					23
3			5	6	7	8	9	10	11	4	2								24
3			5	6	7	8	9	10	11	4	2								25
3			5	6	7	8	9	10	11	4	2								26
3			5	6	7	8	9	10		4	2	11							27
3			5	6		8	9	10		4	2			11	7				28
3			5	6		8	9	10		4	2		11		7				29
3			5	6			9	10		4	2		8	11	7				30
3			5	6			9	10		4	2		8	11	7				31
3		5		6	7		9	10		4	2	8				11			32
2	3			5	8		9	6	11	4			10				7		33
2	3			5			9	6	11	4		8	10				7		34
	3		5	6		8	9	2	11	4		7	10						35
2	3			5	7	8	9	10	11	4			6						36
3				5	7	8	9	10	11	4	2		6						37
	3		5	6	7	8	9	10	11		2		4						38
	3	4	5	6	7	8	9	10			2		11						39
	3	4	5	6	7	8	9	10			2		11						40
	3	4	5	6		8	9	10			2	7						11	41
	3		5	6	7	8	9	10		4	2	11							42
33	12	9	37	40	28	37	41	41	30	35	33	15	15	6	4	1	2	1	
				2	10	13	21	6	11	1		1	5		2		1	1	

Wass	Turner A.	Turner R.	Routledge	Speed	Jenkins	Eyres	Dando	Hathway	Bowater	Fox	Pinder	Barnes	Hughes	Bullock	Johnson	McDonald	Tucker	Pawson	
3			5	6	7	8	9	10	11	4	2								1
3			5	6	7	8	9	4	11		2		10						2
3			5	6	7	8	9	10		4	2			11					3
3			3	3	3	3	3	3	2	2	3		1	1					
				1	1			1	1										

Wass	Turner A.	Turner R.	Routledge	Speed	Jenkins	Eyres	Dando	Hathway	Bowater	Fox	Pinder	Barnes	Hughes	Bullock	Johnson	McDonald	Tucker	Pawson	
	3		5	6	7	8	9	10	11	4	2								1
	3		5		7	8	9	6	11	4	2		10						r
3			5	6	7	8	9	10	11	4	2								2
1	2		3	2	3	3	3	3	3	3	3		1						
					1		2		1				1						

Jack Eyres.

Maurice Dando.

1935–36

Division Three North

Manager: John Collier

	P	W	D	L	F	A	Pts
Chesterfield	42	24	12	6	92	39	60
Chester	42	22	11	9	100	45	55
Tranmere Rovers	42	22	11	9	93	58	55
Lincoln City	42	22	9	11	91	51	53
Stockport County	42	20	8	14	65	49	48
Crewe Alexandra	42	19	9	14	80	76	47
Oldham Athletic	42	18	9	15	86	73	45
Hartlepools United	42	15	12	15	57	61	42
Accrington Stanley	42	17	8	17	63	72	42
Walsall	42	16	9	17	79	59	41
Rotherham United	42	16	9	17	69	66	41
Darlington	42	17	6	19	74	79	40
Carlisle United	42	14	12	16	56	62	40
Gateshead	42	13	14	15	56	76	40
Barrow	42	13	12	17	58	65	38
York City	42	13	12	17	62	95	38
Halifax Town	42	15	7	20	57	61	37
Wrexham	42	15	7	20	66	75	37
Mansfield Town	42	14	9	19	80	91	37
Rochdale	42	10	13	19	58	88	33
Southport	42	11	9	22	48	90	31
New Brighton	42	9	6	27	43	102	24

Did you know that?

Left-winger Peter Spooner returned to the club from Sheffield United and was an ever present along with new signing Harold Green, an outside-right from Bristol City.

The attack was led by another newcomer Duncan Lindsay. A Scot, he had previously been with Newcastle United and Bury and had joined City from Barrow.

A total of 95 League goals were conceded this season and this figure has only been exceeded once in the club's history (106 in 1965–66).

On 1 February 1936 they suffered their heaviest-ever defeat when they went down 0–12 at Chester.

The average home League crowd was 3,721. The attendance of 1,811 on 29 February 1936 against Rotherham United was the smallest pre-war at Bootham Crescent.

In the first round of the FA Cup they crashed out of the competition, losing 5–1 at home to non-League Burton Town.

Match No.	Date	Venue	Opponents	Result		Scorers	Attend
1	Aug 31	H	Stockport County	L	0–4		6
2	Sep 2	A	Chesterfield	D	2–2	Banfield, Hathway	6
3	7	A	Crewe Alexandra	L	1–2	Speed	4
4	11	H	Chesterfield	D	1–1	Hathway	5
5	14	H	Accrington Stanley	D	1–1	Speed	3
6	18	H	New Brighton	W	2–0	Speed, Green	3
7	21	A	Southport	W	1–0	Green	2
8	28	H	Chester	L	1–2	Hathway	4
9	Oct 5	A	Lincoln City	L	2–3	Lawie, Banfield	5
10	12	H	Rochdale	W	2–1	Speed, Green	4
11	19	H	Halifax Town	D	2–2	Green (2)	3
12	26	A	Oldham Athletic	L	2–6	Banfield (2)	4
13	Nov 2	H	Wrexham	D	1–1	Lindsay	4
14	9	A	Rotherham United	L	0–5		7
15	16	H	Mansfield Town	W	7–5	Banfield, Hughes (2), Spooner (2), Lindsay, Green	3
16	23	A	Hartlepools United	L	2–4	Speed, Hathway	4
17	Dec 7	A	Walsall	L	0–6		6
18	21	A	Gateshead	D	0–0		2
19	26	H	Darlington	W	4–1	Speed (2), Lindsay, Spooner	3
20	28	A	Stockport County	L	2–3	Speed (2)	6
21	Jan 2	A	Darlington	L	0–3		4
22	4	H	Crewe Alexandra	W	4–1	Green (2), Speed (pen), Routledge	3
23	11	H	Carlisle United	W	2–0	Hughes, Hathway	4
24	18	A	Accrington Stanley	L	2–7	Speed, Spooner	2
25	Feb 1	A	Chester	L	0–12		3
26	8	H	Lincoln City	W	2–1	Hughes, Spooner	3
27	15	A	Rochdale	W	3–2	Speed, Hughes, Spooner	4
28	22	A	Halifax Town	L	0–2		3
29	29	H	Rotherham United	W	2–1	Hughes (2)	1
30	Mar 7	A	Wrexham	L	0–1		1
31	14	H	Oldham Athletic	W	3–1	Speed (pen), Banfield, Spooner	3
32	18	H	Southport	D	0–0		2
33	21	A	Mansfield Town	L	0–5		4
34	28	H	Hartlepools United	D	2–2	Gray, Banfield	2
35	Apr 4	A	Carlisle United	D	0–0		4
36	10	H	Barrow	L	1–2	Banfield	5
37	11	H	Walsall	D	0–0		2
38	13	A	Barrow	D	1–1		3
39	18	A	Tranmere Rovers	L	1–3	Lindsay	5
40	22	H	Tranmere Rovers	W	2–0	Banfield, Hathway	3
41	25	H	Gateshead	D	2–2	Lindsay (2)	2
42	May 2	A	New Brighton	W	2–0	Lindsay (2)	1

A

FA Cup

1	Nov 30	H	Burton Town	L	1–5	Lindsay (pen)	6

A

Northern Section Cup

1	Oct 9	A	Darlington	L	2–3	Speed, Lawie	1

A

Pinder	Young	Fox	Routledge	Speed	Green	Banfield	Graham	Lawie	Spooner	Hathway	Wass	Lindsay	Gray	Legge	Hughes	Robinson	Craven	
2	3	4	5	6	7	8	9	10	11									1
2	3	4	5	6	7	8	9		11	10								2
2		4	5	6	7	8	9		11	10	3							3
2		4	5	6	7	8		9	11	10	3							4
2		4	5	6	7	8		9	11	10	3							5
2		4	5	6	7	8	9		11	10	3							6
2		4	5	6	7	8	9		11	10	3							7
2		4	5	6	7	8	9		11	10	3							8
2		4	5		7	8	9	10	11	6	3							9
2			5	6	7	8		10	11	4	3	9						10
2		4	5	6	7	8			11	10	3	9						11
2		4	5	6	7	8			11	10	3	9						12
2			5	6	7	8			11	10	3	9	4					13
			5	6	7	8		10	11	4	2	9		3				14
			5	6	7	8			11	4	2	9		3	10			15
2			5	6	7			10	11	4	3	9			8			16
2		4		5	7				11	6	3	9	8		10			17
2		4	5	8	7				11	10	3	9		6				18
2		4	5	8	7				11	10	3	9		6				19
2		4	5	8	7				11	10	3	9		6				20
2		4	5		7				11	8	3	9		6	10			21
		4	5	6	7				11	8	2	9		3		10		22
		4	5	6	7				11	8	2			3	9	10		23
		4	5	6	7				11	8	2	9		3		10		24
		2	8	6	7			4	11	8	5	9		3				25
		4	5	6	7				11	8	2	9		3	10			26
		4	5	6	7	8			11	10	2			3	9			27
		4	5	6	7	8			11	10	2	9		3				28
		4	5		7	8			11	10	2	9		3	6			29
		4	5	6	7	8			11		2	9		3	10			30
		4	5	6	7	8			11		2	9		3	10			31
		4	5	6	7	8			11	10	2			3	9			32
		4	5	6	7	8			11	2	3	9			10			33
		4	5	6	7	8			11	10	2		9	3			1	34
		4	5	6	7	8		10	11	9	2			3			1	35
		4	5	6	7	8		10	11	9	2			3			1	36
		4	5	6	7				11	9	2		8	3	10			37
		4	5	6	7	8			11	10	2			3	9			38
		4	5	6	7	8			11	10	2	9		3				39
		4	5	6	7	8			11	10	2	9		3				40
		4	5	6	7	8			11	10	2	9		3				41
2			8	6	7	10			11	4	5	9		3				42
20	2	36	41	39	42	30	7	10	42	39	40	25	4	26	14	3	3	
			1	13	8	10		1	7	6		8	1		7			

Pinder	Young	Fox	Routledge	Speed	Green	Banfield	Graham	Lawie	Spooner	Hathway	Wass	Lindsay	Gray	Legge	Hughes	Robinson	Craven	
2			5	6	7			8	11	4	3	10			9			1
1			1	1	1			1	1	1	1	1			1			
												1						

Pinder	Young	Fox	Routledge	Speed	Green	Banfield	Graham	Lawie	Spooner	Hathway	Wass	Lindsay	Gray	Legge	Hughes	Robinson	Craven	
		2	5	6	7	8	9	10	11	4	3							1
		1	1	1	1	1	1	1	1	1	1							
				1				1										

Bill Routledge.

Fred Speed.

1936–37

Division Three North

Manager: John Collier

	P	W	D	L	F	A	Pts
Stockport County	42	23	14	5	84	39	60
Lincoln City	42	25	7	10	103	57	57
Chester	42	22	9	11	87	57	53
Oldham Athletic	42	20	11	11	77	59	51
Hull City	42	17	12	13	68	69	46
Hartlepools United	42	19	7	16	75	69	45
Halifax Town	42	18	9	15	68	63	45
Wrexham	42	16	12	14	71	57	44
Mansfield Town	42	18	8	16	91	76	44
Carlisle United	42	18	8	16	65	68	44
Port Vale	42	17	10	15	58	64	44
York City	42	16	11	15	79	70	43
Accrington Stanley	42	16	9	17	76	69	41
Southport	42	12	13	17	73	87	37
New Brighton	42	13	11	18	55	70	37
Barrow	42	13	10	19	70	86	36
Rotherham United	42	14	7	21	78	91	35
Rochdale	42	13	9	20	69	86	35
Tranmere Rovers	42	12	9	21	71	88	33
Crewe Alexandra	42	10	12	20	55	83	32
Gateshead	42	11	10	21	63	98	32
Darlington	42	8	14	20	66	96	30

Did you know that?

There was an upturn in City's fortunes, with new players Norman Wharton, Dick Duckworth and Malcolm Comrie all making an impact and figuring prominently in the FA Cup successes that saw the club reach the fourth and sixth rounds in consecutive campaigns.

Wharton was a goalkeeper who had helped Norwich City win Division Three (South) in 1933–34 and was signed from Doncaster Rovers.

Centre-half Dick Duckworth joined from Rotherham United and was later to manage City (1950–52), while inside-forward Comrie had previously been with Manchester City, Burnley and Crystal Palace.

Half-back Sammy Gledhill, who had joined the club as an amateur, made his senior debut on 10 October 1936 at Port Vale. A miner, he played for City throughout the war, and his last season at Bootham Crescent was 1948–49.

Also making his City debut during this term was right-winger Fred Scott from Bradford Park Avenue, and at the end of the campaign 17-year-old local lad George Lee, who was destined for a big future, made his first appearance on the left wing. Both these players were to sign for Nottingham Forest just after the war.

Top marksman was Welshman Albert Thompson, who averaged a goal a game in his 24 League appearances. He had been a regular soldier and was with Bradford Park Avenue before joining City in October 1936. He left for Swansea Town at the end of the season.

The game against Chester at Bootham Crescent on 19 September 1936 attracted a then record home League crowd of 10,629.

The average home League crowd was 5,257.

In the FA Cup City reached the fourth round for the first time in their history and, in knocking out Second Division Bradford City at the third stage, beat opposition from a higher League for the first time.

Former City player Tom Mitchell took over the managerial reins in March 1937.

Match No.	Date	Venue	Opponents	Result		Scorers	Attenda
1	Aug 29	A	Halifax Town	W	2–1	Hathway (pen), Hughes	8,
2	Sep 2	H	Tranmere Rovers	W	4–0	Spooner (2), Hathway, Nicol	7,
3	5	H	Mansfield Town	D	1–1	Agar	7,
4	7	A	Tranmere Rovers	D	0–0		5,
5	12	A	Crewe Alexandra	D	2–2	Nicol, Spooner	4,
6	19	H	Chester	L	0–2		10,
7	26	A	Rochdale	L	0–3		4,
8	Oct 3	H	Barrow	L	1–2	Hewitson	5,
9	10	A	Port Vale	D	1–1	Spooner	7,
10	17	H	Rotherham United	W	4–3	Spooner (2), Hughes, Comrie	3,
11	24	A	Stockport County	L	0–6		9,
12	31	H	Wrexham	L	3–4	Thompson (2, 1 pen), Comrie	4,
13	Nov 7	A	Darlington	D	1–1	Thompson	3,
14	14	H	Gateshead	W	2–0	Hathway, Thompson	5,
15	21	A	Hull City	L	0–1		7,
16	Dec 5	A	Lincoln City	L	1–3	Agar	4,
17	19	A	Oldham Athletic	D	2–2	Thompson (2)	5,
18	25	H	Hartlepools United	W	4–1	Hughes (2), Thompson (2)	7,
19	26	H	Halifax Town	W	4–0	Agar, Hughes, Thompson, Spooner	6,
20	28	A	Hartlepools United	L	0–2		2,
21	Jan 1	A	Carlisle United	D	1–1	Legge (pen)	9,
22	2	A	Mansfield Town	W	2–1	Hathway (2)	4,
23	9	H	Crewe Alexandra	L	2–3	Hughes, Thompson	5,
24	23	A	Chester	L	1–3	Nicol	4,
25	Feb 6	A	Barrow	D	2–2	Thompson, Spooner	3,
26	10	H	Rochdale	W	4–1	Comrie (2), Agar, Thompson	2,
27	13	H	Port Vale	L	1–2	Comrie	4,
28	20	A	Rotherham United	D	2–2	Thompson, Spooner	4,
29	27	H	Stockport County	W	2–1	Legge, Spooner	3,
30	Mar 6	A	Wrexham	L	0–2		2,
31	13	H	Darlington	W	3–0	Thompson (3)	3,
32	20	A	Gateshead	L	2–3	Hathway (2)	2,
33	26	A	Southport	W	4–1	Whitelaw (2), Thompson (2)	5,
34	27	H	Hull City	D	1–1	Thompson	6,
35	29	H	Southport	W	4–0	Thompson (2), Whitelaw, Comrie	6,
36	Apr 3	A	New Brighton	L	1–4	Whitelaw	3,
37	10	H	Lincoln City	D	0–0		5,
38	14	H	Accrington Stanley	W	4–2	Gledhill (2), Scott (2)	3,
39	17	A	Accrington Stanley	L	1–2	Gledhill	2,
40	21	H	New Brighton	W	2–1	Gledhill, Spooner	3,
41	24	H	Oldham Athletic	W	3–1	Comrie (2), Gledhill	4,
42	May 1	H	Carlisle United	W	5–2	Thompson (3), Scott, Spooner	3

Ap

FA Cup

1	Nov 28	H	Hull City	W	5–2	Agar (3), Thompson (2)	7,
2	Dec 12	A	Southend United	D	3–3	Spooner, Thompson (2)	11,
r	16	H	Southend United	W	2–1*	Comrie, Spooner	6,
3	Jan 16	A	Bradford City	D	2–2	Comrie, Spooner	13,
r	20	H	Bradford City	W	1–0	Nicol	12,
4	30	A	Swansea Town	D	0–0		12,
r	Feb 3	H	Swansea Town	L	1–3	Hathway	11,

* After extra-time.

Ap

Northern Section Cup

1	Sep 16	H	Hull City	W	3–2	Hughes (2), Fox	7,
2	Mar 17	H	Hatlepools United	W	5–0	Whitelaw (2), Thompson, Comrie, Hathway	1,
3	Apr 7	A	Darlington	L	2–3	Hathway, Scott	1,

Ap

Wass	Legge	Fox	Duckworth	Hathway	Agar	Hughes	Nicol	Comrie	Spooner	Hewitson	Porritt	Denholme	Pinder	Gledhill	Young	Thompson	Scott	Whitelaw	Lee	
2	3	4	5	6	7	8	9	10	11											1
2	3	4	5	6	7	8	9	10	11											2
2	3	4	5	6	7	8	9	10	11											3
2	3	4	5	6	7	8	9	10	11											4
2	3	4	5	6	7	8	9	10	11											5
2	3	4	5	6	7	8	9	10	11											6
2	3	4	5	6		8		10	11	9	7									7
2	3	4	5	6	7			10	11	9		8								8
5	3		4	6	7		9	10	11				2	8						9
	3	4	5	6	7	9		10	11				2	8						10
	3		5		7	8	9	10	11				2	4	6					11
3			5		7	8		10	11				2	4	6	9				12
5			4	6	7	8		10	11				2		3	9				13
5			4	6	7	8		10	11				2		3	9				14
5	3		4	6	7	8		10	11				2			9				15
5	3		4	6	7	8		10	11				2			9				16
5	3		4	6	7	8		10			11		2			9				17
5	3		4	6	7	8		10	11				2			9				18
5	3		4	6	7	8		10	11				2			9				19
5	3		4	6	7	8		10	11				2			9				20
5	3		4	6	7	8	9	10	11				2							21
5	3		4	6		8	9	10	11				2	7						22
5	3		4	6	7	8		10	11				2			9				23
	3	4	5	6	7	8	9	10	11						2					24
5	3		4	6	7	8		10	11				2			9				25
5	3		4	6	7	8		10	11				2			9				26
5	3		4	6		8		10	11				2			9	7			27
5	3		4	6		8		10	11				2			9	7			28
5	3	2	4	6		8		10	11							9	7			29
5	3	2	4	6		8		10	11							9	7			30
5	3	2	4	6				10	11							9	7	8		31
5	3	2	4	6				10	11							9	7	8		32
5	3	2		6				10	11		4					9	7	8		33
5	3	2		6				10	11		4					9	7	8		34
5	3	2	4	6				10	11							9	7	8		35
5	3	2	4	6				10	11							9	7	8		36
5	3	2	4	6				10	11							9	7	8		37
5	3	2	4	6				10	11					9			7	8		38
5		2	4	6				10	11			3		9			7	8		39
5		2	4	6				10	11			3		9			7	8		40
5		2	4	6				8	10			3		9			7		11	41
5	3	2	4	6				8	10							9	7		11	42
39	36	24	40	40	24	28	11	42	41	2	4	4	19	9	5	24	16	10	2	
	2			7	4	6	3	8	12	1				5		24	3	4		
5	3		4	6	7	8		10	11				2			9				1
5	3		4	6	7	8		10	11				2			9				2
5	3		4	6	7	8		10	11				2			9				r
5	3	6	4	8		7	9	10	11				2							3
5	3		4	6		7	9	10	11				2			8				r
5	3	6	4	8		7	9	10	11				2							4
5	3	6	4	8		7		10	11				2			9				r
7	7	3	7	7	3	7	3	7	7				7			5				
				1	3		1	2	3							4				
2		4	5	6	7	8	9	10	11						3					1
5	3	2	4	8				10	11							9	7	6		2
5	3	2	4	8				10	11							9	7	6		3
3	2	3	3	3	1	1	1	3	3						1	2	2	2		
		1		2		2		1								1	1	2		

Peter Spooner.

George Lee.

1937–38

Division Three North

Manager: Tom Mitchell

	P	W	D	L	F	A	Pts
Tranmere Rovers	42	23	10	9	81	41	56
Doncaster Rovers	42	21	12	9	74	49	54
Hull City	42	20	13	9	80	43	53
Oldham Athletic	42	19	13	10	67	46	51
Gateshead	42	20	11	11	84	59	51
Rotherham United	42	20	10	12	68	56	50
Lincoln City	42	19	8	15	66	50	46
Crewe Alexandra	42	18	9	15	71	53	45
Chester	42	16	12	14	77	72	44
Wrexham	42	16	11	15	58	63	43
York City	42	16	10	16	70	68	42
Carlisle United	42	15	9	18	57	67	39
New Brighton	42	15	8	19	60	61	38
Bradford City	42	14	10	18	66	69	38
Port Vale	42	12	14	16	65	73	38
Southport	42	12	14	16	53	82	38
Rochdale	42	13	11	18	67	78	37
Halifax Town	42	12	12	18	44	66	36
Darlington	42	11	10	21	54	79	32
Hartlepools United	42	10	12	20	53	80	32
Barrow	42	11	10	21	41	71	32
Accrington Stanley	42	11	7	24	45	75	29

Did you know that?

Reg Baines rejoined the club, and other signings included full-back Claude Barrett from Port Vale and right-winger Albert 'Sam' Earl from Rhyl Athletic.

These players all figured in the famous FA Cup run to the quarter-finals.

Including replays, City played at home in all six rounds – a unique experience – and from the third round onwards Bootham Crescent's attendance record was beaten, culminating in the all-time record figure of 28,123 on 5 March 1938.

Stan Fox finished his playing days with the club, and other departures at the end of the season included Reg Baines and Malcolm Comrie.

The average home League attendance of 5,957 was then the highest in the club's history.

Match No.	Date	Venue	Opponents	Result		Scorers	Attend
1	Aug 28	A	Rochdale	D	0–0		8
2	Sep 1	H	Doncaster Rovers	W	2–0	Comrie (2)	8
3	4	H	Rotherham United	W	4–1	Hathway, Scott, Baines, Spooner	7
4	11	A	Chester	L	3–4	Baines (3)	7
5	14	A	Southport	W	3–2	Spooner (2), Scott	5
6	18	H	Accrington Stanley	D	1–1	Scott	7
7	25	A	Carlisle United	L	1–2	Comrie	6
8	Oct 2	H	Halifax Town	D	1–1	Comrie	6
9	9	A	Tranmere Rovers	W	2–1	Baines, Spooner	8
10	16	A	Oldham Athletic	L	2–6	Comrie (2)	7
11	23	H	Darlington	L	1–2	Hughes	3
12	30	A	Port Vale	L	2–3	Scott, Hughes	5
13	Nov 6	H	Crewe Alexandra	L	1–2	Spooner	3
14	13	A	Barrow	W	2–1	Baines, Hughes	4
15	20	H	Wrexham	W	2–1	Baines (2)	4
16	Dec 4	H	Lincoln City	W	3–1	Scott, Hughes, Baines (pen)	3
17	18	H	New Brighton	W	3–1	Hughes, Baines, Comrie	4
18	25	A	Gateshead	D	2–2	Hughes, Spooner	10
19	27	H	Gateshead	W	5–1	Baines (2), Spooner (2), Earl	9
20	Jan 1	H	Rochdale	L	0–5		5
21	12	A	Hartlepools United	D	0–0		2,
22	15	A	Rotherham United	L	0–3		6
23	26	H	Chester	W	4–0	Earl (2), Baines, Comrie	3,
24	29	A	Accrington Stanley	W	2–1	Earl, Spooner	3
25	Feb 5	H	Carlisle United	W	3–1	Baines (2), Spooner	6
26	14	A	Halifax Town	D	2–2	Carr (2)	1,
27	19	H	Tranmere Rovers	W	2–0	Hughes (2)	6
28	26	H	Oldham Athletic	D	0–0		8,
29	Mar 12	H	Port Vale	D	2–2	Baines (2)	7
30	16	A	Darlington	D	2–2	Scott (2)	2,
31	19	A	Crewe Alexandra	L	2–4	Baines, Comrie	4
32	26	H	Barrow	L	1–2	Baines	4
33	Apr 2	A	Wrexham	D	1–1	Comrie	3
34	9	H	Hartlepools United	W	1–0	Baines	3
35	15	H	Bradford City	W	3–1	Comrie (2), Baines	7
36	16	A	Lincoln City	L	0–2		7
37	19	A	Bradford City	W	1–0	Baines	7
38	23	H	Hull City	L	0–1		9
39	25	A	Hull City	L	1–3	Lee	15,
40	30	A	New Brighton	L	1–3	Baines	2
41	May 2	A	Doncaster Rovers	L	1–2	Lee	15,
42	7	H	Southport	L	1–2	Lee	4,
							A

FA Cup

1	Nov 27	H	Halifax Town	D	1–1	Hughes	7,
r	Dec 1	A	Halifax Town	W	1–0	Baines	6,
2	11	A	Clapton Orient	D	2–2	Scott, Comrie	7,
r	15	H	Clapton Orient	W	1–0	Hughes	7,
3	Jan 8	H	Coventry City	W	3–2	Spooner, Hughes, Earl	13,
4	22	H	West Bromwich Albion	W	3–2	Baines (3)	18,
5	Feb 12	H	Middlesbrough	W	1–0	Spooner	23,
6	Mar 5	H	Huddersfield Town	D	0–0		28,
r	9	A	Huddersfield Town	L	1–2	Baines	58,
							A

Northern Section Cup

1	Sep 20	A	Halifax Town	L	1–4	Gledhill	1,
							A

Pinder	Legge	Duckworth	Wass	Hathway	Scott	Earl	Baines	Comrie	Spooner	Fox	Gledhill	Young	Denholme	Hughes	Barrett	Porritt	McCartney	Carr	Lee	Milton	Milner	
2	3	4	5	6	7	8	9	10	11													1
2	3	4	5	6	7	8	9	10	11													2
2	3	4	5	6	7	8	9	10	11													3
2	3	4	5	6	7	8	9	10	11													4
2	3	4	5		7	8	9	10	11	6												5
2	3	4	5		7	8	9	10	11	6												6
2	3	4	5		7	8	9	10	11		6											7
2	3	4	5	6	7	8	9	10	11													8
	3		5	4	7	8	9	10	11			2	6									9
	3		5	4	7	8	9	10	11			2	6									10
	3	4	5	6	7	8		10	11			2		9								11
2	3	4	5	6	7		9	10	11					8								12
2		4	5	6	7		9	10	11					8	3							13
	3		5	6		8	9		11		4			10	2	7						14
	3	4	5	6		8	9		11					10	3		7					15
	3	4	5	6	7		9	10	11					8	2							16
	3	4	5	6			9	10	11					8	2	7						17
	3	4	5	6		7	9	10	11					8	2							18
	3	4	5	6		7	9	10	11					8	2							19
	3	4	5	6		7	9	10	11					8	2							20
2		5		4		7		10	11				6	8	3			9				21
2		4	5	6		7	9	10	11					8	3							22
2		4	5	6		7	9	10	11					8	3							23
2			5	6		7	9	10	11		4			8	3							24
2		4	5	6		7	9	10	11					8	3							25
	3	4	5		7	8			11	2	6			10				9				26
2		4	5	6		7	9	10	11					8	3							27
2		4	5	6		7	9	10	11					8	3							28
2		4	5			7	9	10	11		6			8	3							29
2		4	5		7	8	9		11		6			10	3							30
2		4	5	6	7	8	9	10	11						3							31
2		4	5			7	9	10	11		6			8	3							32
2		4	5			7	9	10	11		6			8	3							33
2		4	5			8	9	10	11		6				3	7						34
2		4	5			8	9	10	11		6				3	7						35
2			5			7	9	10	11	4	6			8	3							36
2		4	5			7	9	10	11		6			8	3							37
2		4	5		11	7	9	10			6			8	3							38
2		4	5		7	8	9	10			6				3				11			39
2		4	5		7	8	9	10			6				3				11			40
2		4	5		7	8	9	10			6				3				11			41
2		4	5		7	8	9			6					3				11	1	10	42
31	20	37	41	25	22	38	39	37	37	5	16	3	3	25	29	4	1	2	4	1	1	
				1	7	4	23	12	10					8				2	3			

Pinder	Legge	Duckworth	Wass	Hathway	Scott	Earl	Baines	Comrie	Spooner	Fox	Gledhill	Young	Denholme	Hughes	Barrett	Porritt	McCartney	Carr	Lee	Milton	Milner	
	3	4	5	6	7		9	10	11					8	2							1
	3	4	5	6	7		9	10	11					8	2							r
	3	4	5	6	7		9	10	11					8	2							2
	3	4	5	6	7		9	10	11					8	2							r
2		4	5	6		7	9	10	11					8	3							3
2		4	5	6		7	9	10	11					8	3							4
2		4	5	6		7	9	10	11					8	3							5
2		4	5	6		7	9	10	11					8	3							6
2		4	5	6		7	9	10	11					8	3							r
5	4	9	9	9	4	5	9	9	9					9	9							
					1	1	5	1	2					3								

Pinder	Legge	Duckworth	Wass	Hathway	Scott	Earl	Baines	Comrie	Spooner	Fox	Gledhill	Young	Denholme	Hughes	Barrett	Porritt	McCartney	Carr	Lee	Milton	Milner	
2	3	4	5		7	8			11	6	9										10	1
1	1	1	1		1	1			1	1	1										1	
											1											

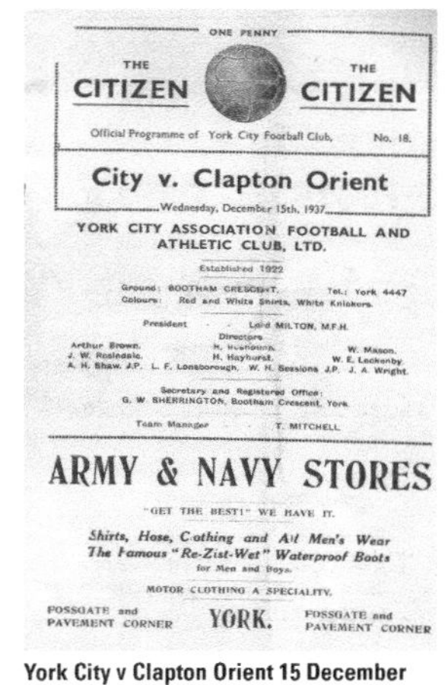

York City v Clapton Orient 15 December 1937 programme cover.

Jimmy Hughes.

1938–39

Division Three North

Manager: Tom Mitchell

	P	W	D	L	F	A	Pts
Barnsley	42	30	7	5	94	34	67
Doncaster Rovers	42	21	14	7	87	47	56
Bradford City	42	22	8	12	89	56	52
Southport	42	20	10	12	75	54	50
Oldham Athletic	42	22	5	15	76	59	49
Chester	42	20	9	13	88	70	49
Hull City	42	18	10	14	83	74	46
Crewe Alexandra	42	19	6	17	82	70	44
Stockport County	42	17	9	16	91	77	43
Gateshead	42	14	14	14	74	67	42
Rotherham United	42	17	8	17	64	64	42
Halifax Town	42	13	16	13	52	54	42
Barrow	42	16	9	17	66	65	41
Wrexham	42	17	7	18	66	79	41
Rochdale	42	15	9	18	92	82	39
New Brighton	42	15	9	18	68	73	39
Lincoln City	42	12	9	21	66	92	33
Darlington	42	13	7	22	62	92	33
Carlisle United	42	13	7	22	66	111	33
York City	42	12	8	22	64	92	32
Hartlepools United	42	12	7	23	55	94	31
Accrington Stanley	42	7	6	29	49	103	20

Did you know that?

City signed centre-forward Bob Mortimer from Blackburn Rovers for a then club record fee of £300.

On 4 March 1939 Bert Brenen scored on his debut at Chester. A schoolteacher and part-time professional, he spent 12 seasons with the club including the war years. Although chiefly a midfielder, he played in every position for City including 'keeper in a wartime game.

As a reward for their Cup exploits of 1937–38 City were invited by the Dutch FA to visit Holland. They played the Dutch National XI in Rotterdam in October 1938 and lost 8–2 to a team that had previously beaten Arsenal.

City were also exempt to the third round of the FA Cup. The next time this happened was in the club's days in the old Second Division in the mid-1970s.

At the end of what was to be the last season of peacetime football for seven years, several players left the club including Norman Wharton, Dick Duckworth, Sam Earl, Jimmy Hughes, Peter Spooner and Ted Wass.

The average home League crowd for this last season before the war was 5,544.

Match No.	Date	Venue	Opponents	Result		Scorers	Attend
1	Aug 27	A	Doncaster Rovers	L	0–1		13
2	31	H	Darlington	D	1–1	Mortimer	6
3	Sep 3	H	Rotherham United	L	0–1		5
4	6	A	Southport	D	1–1	Firth	6
5	10	A	Rochdale	D	2–2	Scott, Hughes	5
6	17	H	Halifax Town	W	3–0	Mortimer (2), Earl	6
7	24	H	Wrexham	W	1–0	Mortimer	6
8	Oct 1	A	Gateshead	W	3–2	Mortimer (2), Lee	8
9	8	H	Hartlepools United	W	2–0	Mortimer, Earl	6
10	15	A	New Brighton	L	2–3	Mortimer, Lee	5
11	22	H	Barrow	L	2–3	Scott, Earl	6
12	29	A	Chester	L	1–5	Hughes	7
13	Nov 5	H	Bradford City	L	0–1		5
14	12	A	Hull City	L	0–2		8
15	19	H	Lincoln City	L	1–3	Mortimer	5
16	26	A	Barnsley	L	0–1		10
17	Dec 3	H	Accrington Stanley	D	2–2	Hathway (pen), Lee	4
18	10	A	Bradford City	L	0–6		5
19	17	H	Oldham Athletic	W	4–1	Mortimer (2), Milner, Lee	5
20	24	H	Doncaster Rovers	D	2–2	Hughes, Earl	6
21	26	H	Crewe Alexandra	W	4–1	Mortimer (2), Earl, Lee	8
22	27	A	Crewe Alexandra	L	2–8	Mortimer, Lee	7
23	31	A	Rotherham United	L	0–2		6
24	Jan 14	H	Rochdale	L	0–7		3
25	21	A	Halifax Town	L	1–2	Mortimer	3
26	28	A	Wrexham	W	3–1	Mortimer (2), Scott	3
27	Feb 4	H	Gateshead	D	1–1	Hughes	5
28	11	A	Hartlepools United	L	2–3	Porritt, Scott	3
29	18	H	New Brighton	W	2–0	Mortimer (2)	4
30	25	A	Barrow	L	0–2		5
31	Mar 4	H	Chester	D	2–2	Mortimer, Brenen	4
32	18	H	Hull City	W	1–0	Mortimer	5
33	25	A	Lincoln City	D	3–3	Porritt, Mortimer, Brenen	4
34	Apr 1	H	Stockport County	L	1–2	Hathway	5
35	7	A	Carlisle United	W	3–1	Hathway, Scott, Brenen	5
36	8	A	Accrington Stanley	L	1–3	Hathway	2
37	10	H	Carlisle United	W	4–1	Milner (2), Brenen (pen), Lee	5
38	15	H	Barnsley	L	2–3	Milner, Opp. og	6
39	22	A	Oldham Athletic	L	0–6		3
40	24	A	Stockport County	L	1–3	Hawkins	2
41	29	A	Darlington	W	2–1	Scott, Porritt	3
42	May 6	H	Southport	L	2–3	Brenen, Lee	3
							A
						1 own-goal	

FA Cup

Match No.	Date	Venue	Opponents	Result		Scorers	Attend
3	Jan 11	H	Millwall	L	0–5		6
							A

Pinder	Barrett	Duckworth	Wass	Hathway	Reynolds	Firth	Mortimer	Earl	Spooner	Milner	Scott	Hughes	Springett	Gledhill	Lee	Hamer	Porritt	Milton	Kelly	Hawkins	Denholme	Flatley	Brenen	Chappell	
2	3	4	5	6	7	8	9	10	11																1
2	3	4	5	6	7	8	9	10	11																2
2	3	4	5	6		8	9		11	10	7														3
	3		5	6		8	9		11		7	10	2	4											4
2	3		5	6			9	8	11		7	10		4											5
2			5	6			9	8			7	10		4	11	3									6
2			5	4			9	8			7	10		6	11	3									7
2			5	4			9	8			7	10		6	11	3									8
2			5	4			9	8			7	10		6	11	3									9
	2	4	5	6			9	8			7	10			11	3									10
2			5	4			9	8			7	10		6	11	3									11
	2		5	4			9				8	10		6	11	3	7								12
2	3		5	4			9				8	10		6	11		7	1							13
2	3	4	5	6	7		9				8	10			11			1							14
2		4	5	6			9	7	11		8	10				3		1							15
2	3	4	5	6		8			11		7	10		9											16
2	3	4	5	6			9				7	10		8	11										17
2	3	4	5	6		8	9				7	10			11										18
				4			9	7		10		8	2	6	11				3	5					19
				4			9	7		10		8	2	6	11			1	3	5					20
				4			9	7		10		8	2	6	11				3	5					21
2				4			9	7		10		8		6	11				3	5					22
2		5		4			9	7		10		8		6	11				3						23
2		4	5	6			9			10	7			8	11			1	3						24
				4			9	8			7	10	2	6	11				3	5					25
				4			9	8	11		7	10	2	6					3	5					26
				4			9	8	11		7	10	2	6					3	5					27
2				4				10	11		7	9		6			8		3		5				28
				4			9		11		7		2	6			8		3	5		10			29
				4			9		11		7		2	6			8		3	5		10			30
				4			9				7		2	6	11		10		3	5			8		31
				4			9				7		2	6	11		10		3	5			8		32
				4			9				7		2	6	11		10		3	5			8		33
				4			9				7		2	6	11		10		3	5			8		34
				4							7		2	6	11		10		3	5		9	8		35
				4							7		2	6	11		10		3	5		9	8		36
				4						9	7		2	6	11		10		3	5			8		37
				4						9	7		2	6	11		10		3	5			8		38
2				4				7		9				6	11		10		3	5			8		39
2				4			9				7			6	11		10	1	3	5			8		40
2				4			9				7			6	11		10	1	3	5			8		41
2				4			9				7				11		10	1	3	5			8	6	42
23	12	11	19	42	3	6	35	20	12	10	34	24	17	34	30	8	17	8	24	21	1	4	12	1	
				4		1	22	5		4	6	4			8		3			1			5		

Pinder	Barrett	Duckworth	Wass	Hathway	Reynolds	Firth	Mortimer	Earl	Spooner	Milner	Scott	Hughes	Springett	Gledhill	Lee	Hamer	Porritt	Milton	Kelly	Hawkins	Denholme	Flatley	Brenen	Chappell	
2		4	5	6			9	7				8		10	11				3						3
1		1	1	1			1	1				1		1	1				1						

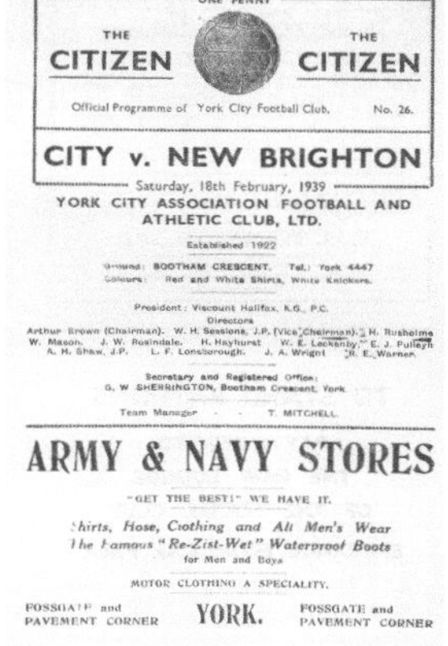
ONE PENNY

THE CITIZEN THE CITIZEN

Official Programme of York City Football Club. No. 26.

CITY v. NEW BRIGHTON

Saturday, 18th February, 1939

YORK CITY ASSOCIATION FOOTBALL AND ATHLETIC CLUB, LTD.

Established 1922

Ground: BOOTHAM CRESCENT. Tel.: York 4447

Team Manager - - T. MITCHELL

ARMY & NAVY STORES

"GET THE BEST!" WE HAVE IT.

Shirts, Hose, Clothing and All Men's Wear

The Famous "Re-Zist-Wet" Waterproof Boots for Men and Boys

MOTOR CLOTHING A SPECIALITY.

FOSSGATE and PAVEMENT CORNER YORK. FOSSGATE and PAVEMENT CORNER

York City v New Brighton 18 February 1939 programme cover.

How City Were Surprised

FINE FOOTBALL BY DUTCH XI

Afterwards Picked For International

By "CITIZEN"

YORK CITY officials and players will have pleasant memories of their first Continental match, except for the fact that they were so heavily beaten by the Dutch National XI at Rotterdam, yesterday.

An adverse score of eight goals to two was rather disappointing to the York party, who had hoped to give their Dutch opponents a closer game. There are certain circumstances, however, to be taken into consideration in reviewing the match.

In the first place, despite all that one has heard about the development of Association football on the Continent, one has to see it to really believe what progress has been made. I must frankly admit that York City had a shock. They met a team that was collectively much faster and whose sense of positional play was infinitely more highly developed than their own.

The football played by this Dutch side in the first 25 minutes was a surprise. In that period they outplayed City to score five goals, and the creditable feature of the game from the York point of view was that afterwards the team rallied well enough to make the game interesting.

Still, allowing for their faults on the City side, the Dutch players did produce football comparable to many a First Division team here at home. The Dutch selectors were so pleased that they picked the team that played against City to represent Holland against Denmark at Copenhagen later in the month. So City at least can claim to have met Holland's full strength.

Newspaper cutting regarding the trip to Holland in October 1938 in recognition of the 1937–38 FA Cup run.

1939–40

Football League North East

Match No.	Date	Venue	Opponents	Result		Scorers
1	Aug 26	H	Chester	D	2–2	Allen (2)
2	28	A	Rotherham United	L	1–2	Thompson (pen)
3	Sep 2	A	Rochdale	L	0–1	

Acting Manager: Arthur Wright

Following the outbreak of war on 3 September the Football League programme was abandoned and the above fixtures were expunged from the records.

	P	W	D	L	F	A	Pts
Huddersfield Town	20	15	4	1	54	22	34
Newcastle Utd	20	12	0	8	58	39	24
Bradford PA	19	10	2	7	44	38	22
Middlesbrough	20	9	4	7	49	42	22
Leeds Utd	18	9	3	6	36	27	21
Bradford City	19	9	3	7	41	36	21
Hull City	20	8	1	11	35	41	17
York City	20	8	1	11	36	51	17
Darlington	19	6	3	10	44	56	15
Hartlepools Utd	20	6	1	13	27	47	13
Halifax Town	19	3	2	14	28	53	8

1	Oct 21	H	Middlesbrough	L	1–3	Stockill
2	28	A	Newcastle United	L	2–9	Allen, Lee
3	Nov 11	H	Hull City	W	3–1	Lee (2), Stockill
4	18	A	Halifax Town	W	4–1	Allen, Stockill (pen), Lee, Sherwood
5	25	H	Leeds United	D	1–1	Lee
6	Dec 2	A	Bradford City	L	1–2	Stockill
7	9	H	Darlington	W	2–1	Lee, Porritt
8	25	A	Hartlepools United	W	2–1	Lee, Opp. og
9	Mar 16	H	Halifax Town	W	3–1	Porritt (2), G. Hodgson
10	23	A	Leeds United	L	1–3	Brenen
11	25	A	Hull City	L	1–4	Brenen
12	30	H	Bradford City	L	0–1	
13	Apr 6	A	Darlington	L	3–5	Stockill, Lee, Hawkins
14	17	H	Newcastle United	L	2–4	Hydes (2)
15	May 4	H	Bradford PA	W	3–2	Lee (2), G. Hodgson
16	18	H	Hartlepools United	W	2–1	Lee, Hydes
17	25	A	Bradford PA	W	3–2	Gledhill, Hydes, Stockill
18	29	H	Huddersfield Town	L	1–2*	Hydes (pen)
19	Jun 1	A	Middlesbrough	L	1–6	Lee
20	3	A	Huddersfield Town	L	0–1	

* Match abandoned (due to storm) after 58 mins. Result stood.

North War Cup

Pre	Apr 13	H	Bradford City	W	6–4	Hydes (3), Lee, Roberts, Wardle
1 (1)	20	H	Hull City	D	1–1	Gallacher
1 (2)	27	A	Hull City	L	0–1	

Did you know that?

Former England forward Fred Tilson was signed in the summer of 1939 from Northampton Town. Capped four times, he gained FA Cup and Division One Championship medals while with Manchester City. He scored twice in the 1934 FA Cup Final when Manchester City beat Portsmouth 2–1.

Guest players in this first season of wartime football included former players Reg Stockill (Luton Town), Jack Everest (Barnsley) and most notably Scottish footballing legend Hughie Gallacher. Born in 1903, Gallacher had an illustrious career and was a prolific scorer, and his clubs included Newcastle United, with whom he won a Division One Championship medal in 1926–27, Chelsea and Derby County. Wee Hughie (5ft 5in) was capped 20 times for Scotland and was a temperamental and fiery character as well as being very skilful.

Owing to artic weather, City did not play a competitive game from Christmas Day until 16 March, and the season was extended into June.

Kelly	Boyle	Hathway	Hawkins	Gledhill	Scott	Allen	Thompson	Tilson	Lee	
2	3	4	5	6	7	8	9	10	11	1
2	3	4	5	6	7	8	9	10	11	2
2	3	4	5	6	7	8	9	10	11	3
3	3	3	3	3	3	3	3	3	3	
						2	1			

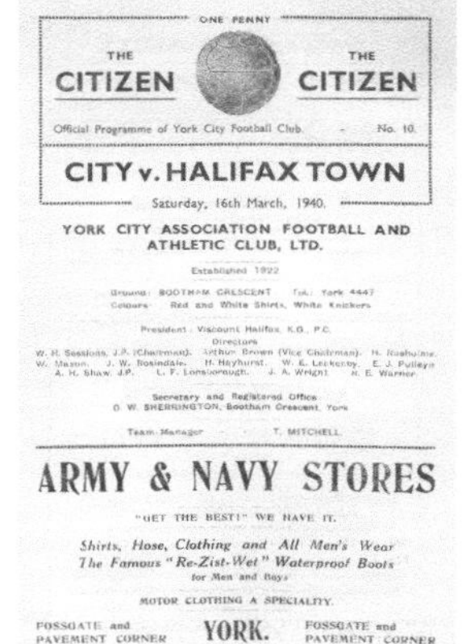

York City v Halifax Town 16 March 1940 programme cover.

ame	Apps	Goals
llen, W.	6	2
ntonio, G.R.*	1	
arkas, T.*	1	
oyle, M.J.	10	
renen, A.	11	2
ollier, A.	23	
verest, J.*	11	
erguson, R.	16	
allacher, H.	2	1
ledhill, S.	18	1
awkins, J.	19	1
odgson, G.*	6	2
odgson, J.*	1	
ogg, F.*	3	
urst, J.*	2	
ydes, A.*	8	8
ee, G.	23	13
cMahon, H.*	1	
ilner, L.	2	
ilton, S.	7	
inder, J.J.	13	
orritt, W.	11	3
oberts, S.G.*	5	1
caife, G.*	5	
herwood, G.W.*	7	1
tephens, A.*	1	
tockill, R.R.*	16	6
ilson, S.F.	1	
ardle, G.*	10	1
hite, N.*	1	
offinden, R.S.	12	
wn-goals		1
otal Goals		**43**

Guest Players

1940–41

Football League North

Acting Manager: Arthur Wright

	P	W	D	L	F	A	Ave
Preston North End	29	18	7	4	81	37	2.189
Chesterfield	35	20	6	9	76	40	1.900
Manchester City	35	18	10	7	104	55	1.890
Barnsley	30	18	4	8	86	49	1.775
Everton	34	19	7	8	85	51	1.666
Blackpool	20	13	3	4	56	34	1.646
Halifax Town	30	10	13	7	64	51	1.254
Manchester Utd	35	14	8	13	80	65	1.249
Lincoln City	27	13	7	7	65	53	1.226
Newcastle Utd	23	12	0	11	49	41	1.195
Huddersfield Town	33	11	6	16	69	58	1.189
Middlesbrough	27	16	1	10	84	71	1.183
New Brighton	26	15	1	10	97	82	1.182
Burnley	35	17	7	11	62	53	1.169
Leeds Utd	30	13	8	9	62	54	1.148
Liverpool	37	15	6	16	91	82	1.109
Wrexham	29	15	5	9	78	71	1.098
Chester	35	14	6	15	94	89	1.056
Doncaster Rovers	32	15	7	10	77	74	1.040
Oldham Athletic	37	17	4	16	78	77	1.012
Grimsby Town	27	12	2	13	60	63	0.952
Bradford PA	31	9	7	15	64	74	0.864
Rotherham Utd	29	12	5	12	48	57	0.842
Blackburn Rovers	32	9	10	13	49	60	0.816
Bury	38	10	8	20	80	100	0.800
Bolton Wanderers	16	6	2	8	31	40	0.775
Tranmere Rovers	25	9	5	11	67	90	0.744
Sheffield Utd	25	6	6	13	44	60	0.733
Bradford City	29	8	3	18	72	99	0.727
Rochdale	32	12	5	15	64	92	0.695
Southport	28	7	2	19	61	88	0.693
York City	25	7	4	14	49	71	0.690
Hull City	23	8	3	12	44	67	0.656
Sheffield Wednesday	30	9	6	15	50	78	0.641
Stockport County	29	9	5	15	54	93	0.580
Crewe Alexandra	24	2	3	19	32	84	0.380

Did you know that?

Among this season's guest players was utility player Matt Patrick from Scottish club Cowdenbeath. After the war he signed for City and gave the club many years' outstanding service. Also making his debut this season was his namesake Alf. A local lad, the centre-forward was to have a fine career with City in the post war period with his goalscoring feats.

Other notable players to wear City colours this campaign were George Eastham (England and Blackpool) and Tommy Dawson (Charlton Athletic). The latter went on to make over 100 wartime appearances for City and scored 48 goals. In 1947 he gained an FA Cup-winners' medal with Charlton.

Tom Holley, former Leeds United centre-half, also guested. After the war he became a notable sports journalist.

Match No.	Date	Venue	Opponents	Result		Scorers	Attend
1	Aug 31	H	Middlesbrough	W	4–3	Porritt (2), Brenen, M. Patrick	3
2	Sep 7	A	Middlesbrough	L	1–2	Brenen	2
3	14	H	Hull City	W	4–1	Brenen (2), M. Patrick (2)	3
4	21	A	Rotherham United	L	0–3		2
5	28	A	Hull City	W	3–1	Brenen (2), M. Patrick	1
6	Oct 5	H	Lincoln City	L	1–2	Lee	3
7	12	A	Lincoln City	L	2–4	M. Patrick, Little	2
8	19	H	Rotherham United	W	3–1	M. Patrick, Brenen, Lee	2
9	26	A	Halifax Town	L	1–2	Lee	3
10	Nov 2	A	Bradford City	L	2–8	M. Patrick, Robinson	
11	9	A	Newcastle United	L	0–3		3
12	16	A	Middlesbrough	L	4–6	Little, Halton, Dawson, Gledhill	1
13	23	H	Newcastle United	W	3–0	Lee (2), Robinson (pen)	2
14	30	H	Halifax Town	D	2–2	Robinson, Brenen	1
15	Dec 7	H	Bradford City	W	5–2	Lee (2), Gledhill (2), Walsh	1
16	14	H	Doncaster Rovers	L	1–4	Walsh	2
17	21	A	Doncaster Rovers	L	2–9	Mennie (2)	2
18	25	A	Chesterfield	L	0–2		3
19	28	H	Bradford PA	D	0–0		2
20	Jan 11	A	Bradford PA	L	2–4	Brenen, Lee	2
21	25	H	Hull City	D	3–3	Lee (3)	2
22	Apr 12	H	Grimsby Town	W	3–2	Brenen (2), Dawson	3
23	14	A	Barnsley	D	1–1	Dawson	2
24	28	A	Grimsby Town	L	0–2		2
25	May 24	H	Middlesbrough	L	2–4	Lee, Brenen	2

League North War Cup

Round	Date	Venue	Opponents	Result		Scorers	Attend
Pre (1)	Feb 1	H	Sheffield Wednesday	W	7–0	Brenen (4), Lee (2), Dawson	2
Pre (2)	8	A*	Sheffield Wednesday	L	1–2	Halton	1
1 (2)	15	H	Bradford PA	W	3–2	Dawson (2), Little	2
1 (2)	22	A*	Bradford PA	W	4–3	Lee (2), Flinton, Gledhill	1
2 (2)	Mar 1	H	Newcastle United	D	1–1	Robinson	4
2 (2)	8	A*	Newcastle United	L	1–4	Dawson	6

* Played at The Old Show Ground, Scunthorpe United.

ame	Apps	Goals
argh, G.W.*	10	
easley, A.*	1	
renen, A.	26	16
awson, T.	13	7
astham, G.R.*	4	
verest, J.*	6	
allon, J.	1	
erguson, R.	23	
inton, W.	2	1
edhill, S.	31	4
alton, R.L.*	12	2
awkins, J.	10	
odgson, S*	22	
olley, T.*	1	
ydes, A.*	1	
epson, A.*	8	
ones, G.	26	
elly, J.E.	2	
ee, G.	28	16
evesley, L.*	10	
ttle, G.*	22	3
cGowen, J.*	1	
ennie, F.*	4	2
ortimer, G.	1	
atrick, A.	1	
atrick, M.*	15	7
earson, J.	1	
nder, J.J.	24	
orritt, W.	11	2
obinson, E.*	13	4
cott, F.H.	1	
tockill, R.R.*	4	
urtees, J.*	2	
alsh, W.*	3	2
offinden, R.S.*	1	
otal Goals		66

Guest Players

Matt Patrick.

1941–42

Football League North

Acting Manager: Arthur Wright

	P	W	D	L	F	A	Pts
Blackpool	18	14	1	3	75	19	29
Lincoln City	18	13	3	2	54	28	29
Preston North End	18	13	1	4	57	18	27
Mancester Utd	18	10	6	2	79	27	26
Stoke City	18	12	2	4	75	36	26
Everton	18	12	2	4	61	31	26
Blackburn Rovers	18	10	6	2	40	24	26
Liverpool	18	11	4	3	66	44	26
Gateshead	18	9	5	4	39	35	23
Sunderland	18	9	4	5	50	30	22
Huddersfield Town	18	10	1	7	48	33	21
Bradford PA	18	8	5	5	33	28	21
Grimsby Town	18	7	6	5	41	31	20
Barnsley	18	8	4	6	39	31	20
Newcastle Utd	18	7	6	5	46	39	20
Sheffield Utd	18	7	4	7	39	38	18
Burnley	18	6	6	6	36	40	18
Halifax Town	18	7	3	8	29	41	17
Oldham Athletic	18	6	4	8	40	49	16
Rochdale	18	6	4	8	28	52	16
Chesterfield	18	5	5	8	27	31	15
Chester	18	6	3	9	45	53	15
Middlesbrough	18	6	3	9	44	56	15
Leeds Utd	18	7	1	10	36	46	15
Doncaster Rovers	18	6	2	10	39	46	14
Bradford City	18	5	4	9	32	42	14
Rotherham Utd	18	6	2	10	33	47	14
New Brighton	18	4	6	8	39	75	14
Tranmere Rovers	18	5	3	10	35	60	13
York City	18	4	4	10	41	55	12
Mansfield Town	18	6	0	12	29	50	12
Bolton Wanderers	18	3	5	10	35	48	11
Southport	18	5	1	12	33	61	11
Bury	18	3	3	12	37	59	9
Wrexham	18	2	5	11	40	69	9
Stockport County	18	2	2	14	34	73	6

Match No.	Date	Venue	Opponents	Result		Scorers	Atten
1	Aug 30	A	Leeds United	L	0–2		
2	Sep 6	H	Leeds United	W	1–0	Brenen	
3	13	H	Middlesbrough	W	9–5	Lee (4), Brenen (2), G. Brown (pen), Bradley, Dawson	
4	20	A	Middlesbrough	L	2–5	R. Brown, Dawson	
5	27	A	Newcastle United	L	3–5	Brenen (3)	
6	Oct 4	H	Newcastle United	D	2–2	Dawson (2)	
7	11	H	Bradford City	D	3–3	Dawson (2), Gledhill	
8	18	A	Bradford City	W	2–0	Lee, Marshall	
9	25	A	Huddersfield Town	L	1–5	Lee	
10	Nov 1	H	Huddersfield Town	L	1–5	Bentall	
11	8	A	Lincoln City	D	3–3	Lee (2), Brenen	
12	15	H	Lincoln City	W	4–2	Lee (2), Brenen (2)	
13	22	H	Gateshead	L	3–4	Lee (2), Dean	
14	29	A	Gateshead	L	0–1		
15	Dec 6	A	Sunderland	L	2–4	Porritt, G. Jones	
16	13	H	Sunderland	L	1–4	Melaniphy	
17	20	H	Bradford PA	L	2–3	Melaniphy, Rudd	
18	25	A	Bradford PA	D	2–2	Marshall, Bradley	

League North War Cup (Qualifying Competition)

Match No.	Date	Venue	Opponents	Result		Scorers	Atten
1	Dec 27	A	Grimsby Town	D	0–0		
2	Jan 3	H	Grimsby Town	W	3–2	Lee (2), R. Brown	
3	10	A	Gateshead	L	2–3	Sargent (2)	
4	17	H	Gateshead	D	3–3	Lee (2 pens), Dryden	
5	31	A	Middlesbrough	D	3–3	Livingstone, W. Jones, R. Brown	
6	Feb 14	A	Sunderland	L	3–8	G. Jones, Lee, Brenen	
7	28	A	Bolton Wanderers	L	3–4	Lee (2), Brenen	
8	Mar 14	H	Sunderland	D	2–2	Brenen, Lee	
9	21	H	Middlesbrough	D	1–1	McGarry	
10	28	H	Bolton Wanderers	W	2–1	Sargent, Lee	

City failed to qualify for the competition proper.

Combined Counties Cup

Match No.	Date	Venue	Opponents	Result		Scorers	Atten
Q	Apr 11	H	Chesterfield	W	3–1	Lee, Brenen (2)	
Q	18	A	Halifax Town	D	1–1	Livingstone	
Q	25	H	Huddersfield Town	D	2–2	Livingstone (2)	
1	May 9	H	Bradford City	W	2–1	Brenen (2)	
SF	16	H	Middlesbrough	W	4–1	Lee, Brenen, O'Donnell (2)	
F (1)	23	H	Halifax Town	W	2–0	Lee (2)	
F (2)	30	A	Halifax Town	L	3–4	Lee, Brenen, O'Donnell	

City won the competition 5–4 on aggregate.

Did you know that?

One of the most famous players in English football between the wars – William Ralph (Dixie) Dean – made an appearance for City this season. A goalscoring legend, he netted 349 League goals in 399 games for Everton, including 60 in 1927–28, and won League and FA Cup medals with the Toffeemen. He was capped for England 16 times. True to form, he scored in his one game for the club in a 4–3 home defeat against Gateshead.

Another star to play for the club this term was Raich Carter. The inside-forward played for England before and after the war and was capped 13 times. He gained League and FA Cup honours while with Sunderland in the mid-1930s and won an FA Cup-winners' medal with Derby County after hostilities ended and then was player-manager at Hull City.

Scottish international Frank O'Donnell (Preston NE and Aston Villa) made his debut this season and, over three campaigns with the club, scored 15 goals in 14 appearances.

Bert (Sailor) Brown (Charlton Athletic) began a very successful association with the club. The skilful inside-forward gained his nickname because of his rolling gait, and over three seasons he made over 50 appearances and scored 16 goals. He formed an outstanding partnership with local lad left-winger George Lee and played in a number of wartime internationals for England.

Irishman Jimmy Rudd (Manchester City) guested for City, which was a prelude to the early post-war period when the exciting wingman starred for the club.

me	Apps	Goals
kinson, J.*	7	
ntall, C.E.	3	1
adley, C.	10	2
enen, A.	28	18
own, R.A. (Sailor) *	20	3
own, G.*	3	1
tt, L.*	1	
rter, H.S. (Raich)	1	
llier, A.	3	
oke, W.H.*	18	
rbett, N.G.	1	
vis, H.*	1	
wson, T.*	14	6
an, W.R. (Dixie)	1	1
yden, H.*	1	1
ggen, E.J.*	2	
rguson, R.	16	
ankish, A.W.	6	
l, C.	1	
edhill, S.	31	1
lton, R.L.*	1	
wkins, J.	5	
ndmarsh, J.W.*	1	
dgson, J.V.*	31	
nes, G.	28	2
nes, W.H.*	5	1
slin, P.J.*	11	
mp, D.J.*	2	
e, G.	31	26
vingstone, A.*	8	4
arshall, C.R.	3	2
cGarry, T.*	4	1
cInnes, J.S.*	2	
elaniphy, E.M.*	5	2
Donnell, F.*	3	3
tterson, G.L.*	1	
nder, J.J.	18	
rritt, W.	10	1
msden, B.*	1	
agan, C.M.	3	
dfern, R.*	4	
dd, J.*	1	1
rgent, F.A.	7	3
addell, W.*	4	
aller, H.*	1	
lson, J.W.	13	
oodhead, C.	14	
tal Goals		**80**

Guest Players

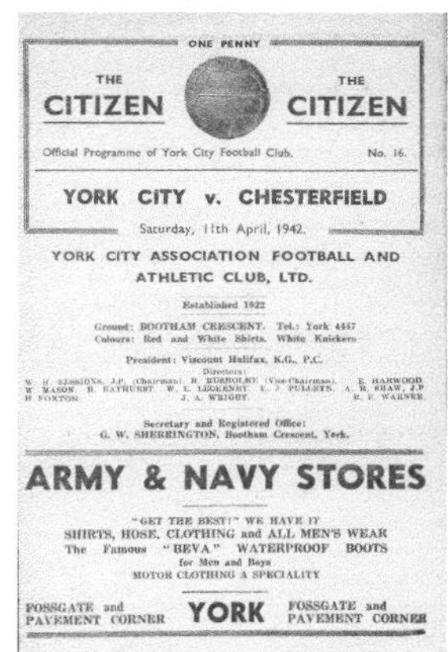
ONE PENNY

THE CITIZEN THE CITIZEN

Official Programme of York City Football Club. No. 16.

YORK CITY v. CHESTERFIELD

Saturday, 11th April, 1942.

YORK CITY ASSOCIATION FOOTBALL AND ATHLETIC CLUB, LTD.

Established 1922

Ground: BOOTHAM CRESCENT. Tel.: York 4447
Colours: Red and White Shirts. White Knickers

President: Viscount Halifax, K.G., P.C.

Directors:

Secretary and Registered Office:
G. W. SHERRINGTON, Bootham Crescent, York.

ARMY & NAVY STORES

"GET THE BEST!" WE HAVE IT
SHIRTS, HOSE, CLOTHING and ALL MEN'S WEAR
The Famous "BEVA" WATERPROOF BOOTS
for Men and Boys
MOTOR CLOTHING A SPECIALITY

FOSSGATE and PAVEMENT CORNER YORK FOSSGATE and PAVEMENT CORNER

York City v Chesterfield 11 April 1942 programme cover.

Jimmy Rudd.

1942–43

Football League North

Acting Manager: Arthur Wright, Tom Lockie

	P	W	D	L	F	A	Pts
Blackpool	18	16	1	1	93	28	33
Liverpool	18	14	1	3	70	34	29
Sheffield Wednesday	18	12	3	3	61	26	27
Manchester Utd	18	12	2	4	58	26	27
Huddersfield Town	18	10	6	2	52	32	26
Stoke City	18	11	3	4	36	25	25
Coventry City	18	10	5	3	28	16	25
Southport	18	11	3	4	64	42	25
Derby County	18	11	2	5	51	37	24
Bradford PA	18	8	7	3	46	21	23
Lincoln City	18	9	5	4	58	36	23
Halifax Town	18	10	3	5	39	27	23
Gateshead	18	10	3	5	52	45	23
Aston Villa	18	10	2	6	47	33	22
Everton	18	10	2	6	52	41	22
Grimsby Town	17	8	5	4	42	31	21
York City	18	9	3	6	47	36	21
Blackburn Rovers	18	9	3	6	56	43	21
Barnsley	18	8	5	5	39	30	21
Sheffield Utd	18	7	6	5	45	35	20
Birmingham	18	9	2	7	27	30	20
Sunderland	18	8	3	7	46	40	19
Chester	18	7	4	7	43	40	18
Walsall	18	6	5	7	33	31	17
Northampton Town	18	8	1	9	38	44	17
Newcastle Utd	18	6	4	8	51	52	16
Chesterfield	18	5	6	7	30	34	16
WBA	18	6	4	8	35	43	16
Notts County	18	7	2	9	34	57	16
Manchester City	18	7	1	10	46	47	15
Nottingham Forest	18	6	3	9	38	39	15
Burnley	18	5	5	8	35	45	15
Leicester City	18	5	4	9	32	37	14
Bury	18	6	2	10	53	81	14
Stockport County	18	5	3	10	34	55	13
Rotherham Utd	18	4	5	9	28	41	13
Tranmere Rovers	18	5	3	10	36	63	13
Wolverhampton Wanderers	18	5	2	11	28	41	12
Crewe Alexandra	18	5	2	11	43	64	12
Middlesbrough	18	4	4	10	30	50	12
Rochdale	18	5	2	11	34	57	12
Wrexham	18	5	1	12	43	67	11
Leeds Utd	18	3	4	11	28	45	10
Oldham Athletic	18	4	2	12	29	54	10
Bradford City	18	4	2	12	30	62	10
Bolton Wanderers	18	3	3	12	31	52	9
Doncaster Rovers	17	3	3	11	23	41	9
Mansfield Town	18	2	4	12	25	65	8

Match No.	Date	Venue	Opponents	Result		Scorers	Attend
1	Aug 29	H	Gateshead	L	1–2	Knight	3
2	Sep 5	A	Gateshead	W	4–1	Knight (2), O'Donnell (2)	3,
3	12	A	Sunderland	D	0–0		7
4	19	H	Sunderland	L	0–3		4
5	26	H	Middlesbrough	D	2–2	Lee, O'Donnell	3
6	Oct 3	A	Middlesbrough	W	3–2	Brown, Lee, F. Scott	3
7	10	H	Newcastle United	W	4–3	O'Donnell (4)	4
8	17	A	Newcastle United	D	3–3	F. Scott, Gledhill, Brown	5
9	24	H	Grimsby Town	W	5–2	F. Scott, Lee, O'Donnell, Compton (2)	3
10	31	A	Grimsby Town	W	1–0	Knight	2
11	Nov 7	A	Bradford City	W	3–1	Lee, Brown, O'Donnell	3
12	14	H	Bradford City	W	9–1	Knight (3), O'Donnell, Brown, Lee, Gledhill, F. Scott, Opp. og	4,
13	21	A	Leeds United	L	1–2	Lee	4
14	28	H	Leeds United	W	3–1	Lee (2, 1 pen), O'Donnell	4
15	Dec 5	H	Bradford PA	L	3–6	Lee (2, 1 pen), Tutill	2,
16	12	A	Bradford PA	L	1–3	Brown	2,
17	19	H	Rotherham United	W	2–1	Brown, Lee	2,
18	25	A	Rotherham United	L	2–3	Lee, Marshall	6

League North War Cup (Qualifying Competition)

Match No.	Date	Venue	Opponents	Result		Scorers	Attend
1	Dec 26	H	Doncaster Rovers	D	3–3	Lee (2), A. Scott	4,
2	Jan 2	A	Doncaster Rovers	W	5–3	F. Scott (3), Lee (pen), Brenen	2,
3	16	A	Newcastle United	L	1–3	Brenen	5,
4	23	H	Sunderland	W	4–0	Lee (2, 1 pen), Knight, Brown	5,
5	30	A	Sunderland	W	5–4	Lee (2, 1 pen), Knight, Brenen, Campbell	7,
6	Feb 6	A	Gateshead	L	2–3	Brenen, Shimwell	4,
7	13	H	Gateshead	W	2–0	Lee (pen), Campbell	5,
8	20	A	Middlesbrough	W	5–1	Lee (2), Brenen, F. Scott, Hodgson	2
9	27	H	Middlesbrough	W	6–0	Brenen (3, 1 pen), Lee, Brown, Hodgson	5,

League North War Cup (Proper)

Match No.	Date	Venue	Opponents	Result		Scorers	Attend
1 (1)	Mar 6	A	Newcastle United	L	2–3	Lee, Brown	19,
1 (2)	13	H	Newcastle United	W	2–0	Wilson, Brenen	11,
2 (1)	20	H	Bradford PA	W	2–1	Brenen, Lee	10
2 (2)	27	A	Bradford PA	W	3–0	F. Scott, Dawson, Brenen	12,
3 (1)	Apr 3	H	Chesterfield	W	2–0	Brown, McCormack	14,
3 (2)	10	A	Chesterfield	W	2–0	McCormack, F. Scott	16,
SF (1)	17	A	Sheffield Wednesday	L	0–3		35,
SF (2)	24	H	Sheffield Wednesday	D	1–1	Lee (pen)	16,

Football League North (additional fixture)

Match No.	Date	Venue	Opponents	Result		Scorers	Attend
1	May 1	H	Newcastle United	D	5–5	Brenen (2, 1 pen), Campbell (2), Stone	2,

Did you know that?

City's most successful campaign saw them reach the semi-finals of the League North War Cup in front of the club's biggest wartime crowds.

Charlton Athletic goalkeeper Sam Bartram started his three-year association with the club, making his debut in a home win over Newcastle United on 10 October 1942.

Arsenal star Leslie Compton scored twice on his debut in a 5–2 home win over Grimsby Town on 24 October 1942. Brother of cricket legend Denis, he won his first cap for England at centre-half aged 38.

Eddie Shimwell (Blackpool) made one guest appearance. The full-back went to play in three FA Cup Finals for the Tangerines after the war, including the famous Matthews match of 1953.

On 17 October 1942 Bootham Crescent hosted a representative match between the Football League and the Northern Command. Playing at left-back for the League was City's highly rated youngster Gordon Jones. Striken by illness the following year, he died in January 1947.

Midway through the season, director and acting manager Arthur Wright had to resign owing to ill health. He had been instrumental in bringing a number of notable guest payers to Bootham Crescent and had played a big part in keeping the club operating in the early war years with his tireless efforts. One of York's leading chemists, he died in June 1943.

me	Apps	Goals
rnard, R.	1	
rtram, S.*	22	
ll, R.	1	
ck, A.*	1	
wden, A.J.	1	
enen, A.	21	13
own, R.A. (Sailor) *	28	10
mpbell, R.*	13	4
mpton, L.H.	3	2
ultate, C.	1	
llen, J.	1	
wson, T.*	8	1
erson, W.*	1	
rinton, R.*	1	
guson, R.	11	
ster, L.J.	1	
edhill, S.	32	2
wkins, J.	3	
dgson, S.*	30	2
nes, G.	28	
ight, J.*	20	9
ng, F.J.*	1	
e, A.H.*	2	
e, G.	35	26
ingstone, A.*	1	
rshall, C.R.	3	1
Cormack, C.J.*	5	2
Phee, M.G.*	1	
lls, D.*	1	
lner, L.	1	
rdey, H.*	3	
Donnell, F.*	10	11
arson, W.	1	
der, J.J.	26	
llard, H.*	5	
well, A.*	1	
agan, C.M.	3	
nderson, T.*	1	
ott, A.T.	1	1
ott, F.H.	29	10
mwell, E.*	1	1
elman, I.*	1	
one, J.*	1	1
ill, N.A.	1	1
lson, J.W.*	34	1
vn-goals		1
tal Goals		**99**

Guest Players

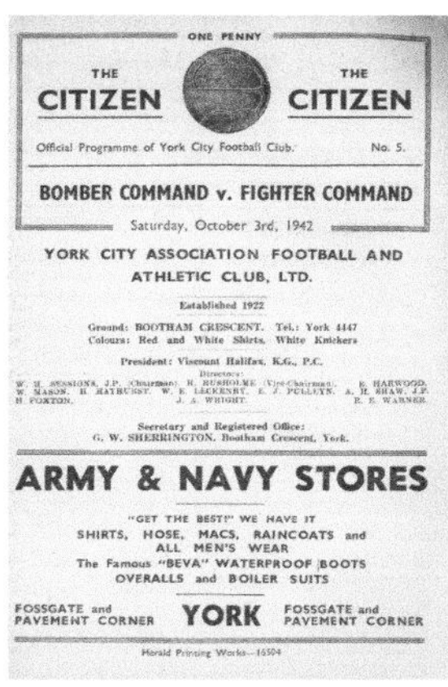

Bomber Command v Fighter Command 3 October 1942 programme cover.

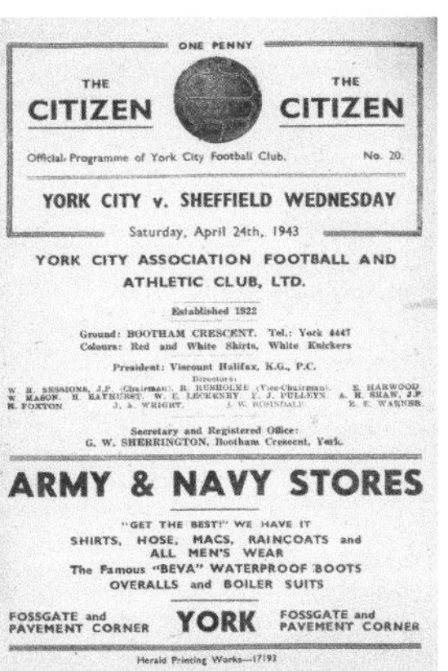

York City v Sheffield Wednesday 24 April 1943 programme cover.

1943–44

Football League North

Acting Manager: Tom Lockie

	P	W	D	L	F	A	Pts
Blackpool	18	12	4	2	56	20	28
Manchester Utd	18	13	2	3	56	30	28
Liverpool	18	13	1	4	76	26	27
Doncaster Rovers	18	11	5	2	45	25	27
Bradford PA	18	11	4	3	65	28	26
Huddersfield Town	18	12	2	4	48	25	26
Northampton Town	18	10	5	3	43	25	25
Aston Villa	18	11	3	4	43	27	25
Sunderland	18	10	3	5	46	30	23
Harlepools Utd	18	10	3	5	44	31	23
Everton	18	9	4	5	60	34	22
Blackburn Rovers	18	10	2	6	47	32	22
Rochdale	18	10	2	6	43	41	22
Sheffield Utd	18	8	5	5	30	25	21
Lincoln City	18	8	4	6	51	40	20
Birmingham	18	8	4	6	38	31	20
Manchester City	18	9	2	7	38	35	20
Mansfield Town	18	9	2	7	32	33	20
Derby County	18	8	4	6	43	45	20
Chester	18	9	2	7	40	43	20
Grimsby Town	18	8	3	7	32	36	19
WBA	18	8	3	7	42	44	19
Gateshead	18	8	2	8	40	51	18
Burnley	18	5	7	6	24	22	17
Walsall	18	5	7	6	27	31	17
Nottingham Forest	18	6	5	7	33	39	17
Leeds Utd	18	6	5	7	38	50	17
Leicester City	18	6	4	8	33	30	16
Darlington	18	6	4	8	49	48	16
Rotherham Utd	18	7	2	9	38	42	16
York City	18	7	2	9	35	40	16
Halifax Town	18	6	4	8	27	36	16
Southport	18	7	2	9	33	51	16
Stoke City	18	6	3	9	40	35	15
Chesterfield	18	7	1	10	29	31	15
Oldham Athletic	18	7	1	10	30	44	15
Stockport County	18	5	5	8	24	43	15
Coventry City	18	4	6	8	25	23	14
Newcastle Utd	18	5	4	9	32	37	14
Sheffield Wednesday	18	5	4	9	29	34	14
Middlesbrough	18	4	6	8	35	52	14
Wolverhampton Wanderers	18	5	3	10	30	42	13
Bury	18	6	1	11	31	44	13
Barnsley	18	5	2	11	32	42	12
Bradford City	18	4	3	11	27	47	11
Wrexham	18	5	1	12	43	63	11
Notts County	18	4	3	11	26	53	11
Bolton Wanderers	18	5	0	13	24	46	10
Tranmere Rovers	18	4	1	13	39	71	9
Crewe Alexandra	18	4	1	13	29	62	9

Match No.	Date	Venue	Opponents	Result		Scorers	Attendance
1	Aug 28	A	Grimsby Town	L	2–3	Woodgate, Stone	1
2	Sep 4	H	Grimsby Town	W	2–0	Dawson, Dunn	4
3	11	A	Gateshead	L	0–3		3
4	18	H	Gateshead	W	5–1	Billington (3), Woodgate, Fenton	4
5	25	H	Newcastle United	W	2–0	Lee, Dawson	5
6	Oct 2	A	Newcastle United	D	1–1	Lee	9
7	9	H	Hartlepools United	W	2–0	Dunn, Scott	5
8	16	A	Hartlepools United	L	1–4	Dawson	5
9	23	A	Darlington	L	2–4	Wilson (pen), Brenen	8
10	30	H	Darlington	W	5–2	Billington (3), Lee (pen), Fenton	4
11	Nov 6	A	Middlesbrough	D	1–1	O'Donnell	3
12	13	H	Middlesbrough	W	5–3	A. Walker (3), Dawson, Killourhy	5
13	20	H	Leeds United	L	1–3	Dawson	4
14	27	A	Leeds United	L	0–1		4
15	Dec 4	A	Bradford PA	L	1–6	Dawson	4
16	11	H	Bradford PA	L	2–4	McDonald, Billington	4
17	18	A	Rotherham United	L	1–3	McDonald	3
18	25	H	Rotherham United	W	2–1	Woodgate, Dawson	3

League War North Cup (Qualifying Competition)

Match No.	Date	Venue	Opponents	Result		Scorers	Attendance
1	Dec 27	H	Huddersfield Town	W	2–1	Billington (2)	8
2	Jan 1	A	Huddersfield Town	W	3–0	R. Brown, Billington (2)	4
3	8	A	Bradford City	L	1–4	Billington	3
4	15	H	Bradford City	W	3–1*	Lee, Killourhy, Billington	2
5	22	A	Barnsley	L	1–2	Killourhy	4
6	29	H	Barnsley	W	2–0	Killourhy (2)	5
7	Feb 5	H	Bradford PA	L	0–1		6
8	12	A	Bradford PA	L	1–4	Lee	6
9	19	A	Leeds United	L	1–2	Hawkins	7
10	26	H	Leeds United	W	8–1	Lee (2), Billington (2), Hawkins (2), Killourhy, Litchfield	5

* Match abandoned (due to fog) after 60 mins. Result stood.

League War North Cup (Competition Proper)

Match No.	Date	Venue	Opponents	Result		Scorers	Attendance
1 (1)	Mar 4	H	Barnsley	W	4–1	Lee (2), Litchfield, Killourhy	7
1 (2)	11	A	Barnsley	L	1–3	Hawkins	14
2 (1)	18	H	Bradford PA	L	1–5	Billington	11
2 (2)	25	A	Bradford PA	L	1–2	Billington	12

Combined Counties Cup

Match No.	Date	Venue	Opponents	Result		Scorers	Attendance
1 (1)	Apr 1	A	Halifax Town	L	1–4	Hawkins	2
1 (2)	8	H	Halifax Town	D	1–1	Hawkins	5

Football League North (additional fixtures)

Match No.	Date	Venue	Opponents	Result		Scorers	Attendance
1	Apr 15	A	Chesterfield	L	0–2		2
2	22	H	Chesterfield	D	1–1	R. Brown	3
3	29	A	Sheffield Wednesday	L	1–2	Scott	5
4	May 6	H	Sheffield Wednesday	W	4–3	T. Brown (2), Wilson (pen), Dawson	2

Did you know that?

Notable guest player this term was inside-forward Benny Fenton, who made his debut on the opening day at Grimsby Town. Described as one of London's greatest football characters, he played for West Ham United, Charlton Athletic and Millwall, and after the war he was manager at the Den for many years.

Half-back Joe Harvey made his debut on the last day of the season at home to Sheffield Wednesday. He went on to captain Newcastle United in successive FA Cup Final wins in the early 1950s and later managed the Magpies.

Young local goalkeeper Peter Pickering played his first game on 15 April 1944 at Chesterfield. He was to make his mark in the immediate post-war period.

George Lee, who had topped the scoring charts in each of the previous four campaigns, joined the army in March 1944 and this was to limit his future City appearances.

me	Apps	Goals
rnard, R.	6	
rtram, S.*	30	
ntall, C.E.	2	
lington, H.J.R.*	17	17
wden, A.J.	3	
enen, A.	20	1
own, R.A. (Sailor) *	6	2
own, T.	1	2
mpbell, R.	26	
llier, A.	1	
vies, C.J.*	1	
wson, T.*	33	8
oley, G.W.*	1	
nn, R.*	8	2
nton, B.*	8	2
rguson, R.	6	
zsimons, M.J.*	2	
rde, S.	3	
edhill, S.	34	
rvey, J.*	1	
stie, A.*	1	
wkins, G.H.*	12	6
k, L.D.	4	
, D.*	1	
hnston, A.*	1	
lourhy, M.	24	7
k, J.*	1	
ott, H.*	1	
wson, J.R.	5	
e, G.	31	9
chfield, E.*	3	2
vell, C.*	1	
kinson, J.*	2	
rtin, J. *	3	
ssey, A.W.	4	
cDonald, J.C.*	2	2
cMenemy, H.*	1	
lligan, G.H.*	1	
Donnell, F.*	1	1
kering, P.B.	1	
nder, J.J.	33	
ole, B.	1	
yner, H.J.	2	
ynolds, G.A.C.*	13	
vage, R.E.*	2	
ott, F.H.	9	2
one, F.H.*	2	1
ompson, H.*	1	
ndall, J.E.	2	
lker, A.	5	3
lker, C.H.*	7	
lson, J.W.*	17	2
thington, R.*	1	
oodgate, T.J.*	14	3
tal Goals		**72**

Guest Players

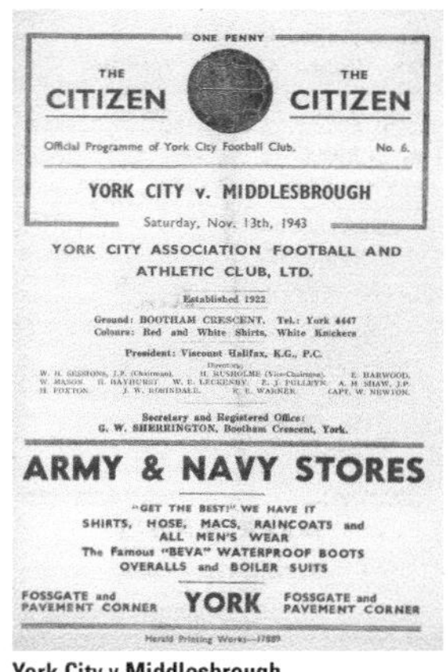

York City v Middlesbrough
13 November 1943 programme cover.

1944–45

Football League North

Acting Manager: Tom Lockie

	P	W	D	L	F	A	Pts
Huddersfield Town	18	14	3	1	50	22	31
Derby County	18	14	1	3	54	19	29
Sunderland	18	12	4	2	52	25	28
Aston Villa	18	12	3	3	54	19	27
Everton	18	7	2	4	58	25	26
Wrexham	18	11	3	4	40	18	25
Doncaster Rovers	18	12	0	6	48	27	24
Bolton Wanderers	18	9	6	3	34	22	24
Bradford PA	18	10	4	4	45	31	24
Manchester City	18	9	4	5	53	31	22
Stoke City	18	9	4	5	37	25	22
Birmingham City	18	8	6	4	30	21	22
Barnsley	18	10	2	6	42	32	22
Rotherham Utd	18	9	4	5	31	25	22
WBA	18	9	4	5	36	30	22
Liverpool	18	9	3	6	41	30	21
Grimsby Town	18	9	3	6	37	29	21
Halifax Town	18	8	5	5	30	29	21
Chester	18	9	3	6	45	45	21
Burnley	18	8	4	6	39	27	20
Blackpool	18	9	2	7	53	38	20
Leeds Utd	18	9	2	7	53	42	20
Sheffield Wednesday	18	9	2	7	34	30	20
Chesterfield	18	8	3	7	30	19	19
Darlington	18	9	1	8	52	45	19
Wolverhampton Wanderers	18	7	5	6	31	27	19
Rochdale	18	7	5	6	35	33	19
Crewe Alexandra	18	9	1	8	43	41	19
Blackburn Rovers	18	7	4	7	30	29	18
Manchester Utd	18	8	2	8	40	40	18
Preston North End	18	7	4	7	26	28	18
Walsall	18	5	6	7	27	29	16
Gateshead	18	7	2	9	45	53	16
Northampton Town	18	5	6	7	30	38	16
Newcastle Utd	18	7	1	10	51	38	15
Sheffield Utd	18	6	3	9	27	25	15
Hartlepools Utd	18	7	1	10	41	47	15
Oldham Athletic	18	7	1	10	28	36	15
Mansfield Town	18	6	3	9	31	40	15
Nottingham Forest	18	5	5	8	22	34	15
Coventry City	18	6	2	10	23	42	14
York City	18	6	1	11	49	52	13
Middlesbrough	18	5	3	10	34	57	13
Bradford City	18	6	1	11	35	60	13
Accrington Stanley	18	5	2	11	29	46	12
Port Vale	18	5	2	11	22	36	12
Bury	18	5	2	11	28	48	12
Stockport County	18	5	1	12	33	70	11
Hull City	18	4	3	11	23	60	11
Southport	18	3	4	11	32	55	10
Lincoln City	18	4	2	12	32	56	10
Leicester City	18	3	4	11	23	46	10
Tranmere Rovers	18	2	1	15	20	53	5
Notts County	18	2	1	15	19	62	5

Match No.	Date		Venue	Opponents	Result		Scorers	Attend
1	Aug	26	H	Hartlepools United	W	3–1	Dawson, Wrigglesworth, Taylor	4
2	Sep	2	A	Hartlepools United	L	0–5		4
3		9	A	Huddersfield Town	L	1–2	Haddington	4
4		16	H	Huddersfield Town	L	1–3	Dawson	5
5		23	A	Hull City	L	0–1		7
6		30	H	Hull City	W	1–0	Hawkins	4
7	Oct	7	H	Darlington	W	2–0	Hawkins, Dix	4
8		14	A	Darlington	L	4–6	Dawson (2), Dix, Sutherland	6
9		21	A	Gateshead	L	2–4	Scott (2)	1
10		28	H	Gateshead	W	10–2	Hawkins (4), Dix (3), Scott (2), Dawson	4
11	Nov	4	H	Bradford PA	W	4–1	Dix, Thompson (2), Dawson (pen)	6
12		11	A	Bradford PA	L	3–5	Thompson (2), Dawson	7
13		18	H	Sunderland	L	3–5	Dawson (2, 1 pen), Riddle	8
14		25	A	Sunderland	D	3–3	M. Wilson, J. Wilson, Thompson	11
15	Dec	2	H	Middlesbrough	W	5–1	Dawson (2), Hawkins (2), Thompson	4
16		9	A	Middlesbrough	L	3–4	Dawson (3)	3
17		16	A	Leeds United	L	1–3	Dix	5
18		23	H	Leeds United	L	3–6	Dawson, Hawkins, Bowden	4

League North War Cup (Qualifying Competition)

Match No.	Date		Venue	Opponents	Result		Scorers	Attend
1	Dec	25	H	Hull City	W	5–1	Bowden (2), Dawson, Hawkins, Woollett	2
2		30	A	Hull City	L	1–6	J. Wilson (pen)	4
3	Jan	6	A	Bradford PA	L	2–4	Thompson, J. Wilson (pen)	7
4		20	H	Leeds United	L	0–5		1
5		27	A	Leeds United	L	3–4	Bates, Riddle, Opp. og	6
6	Feb	3	A	Barnsley	L	1–2	J. Wilson (pen)	10
7		10	H	Barnsley	W	5–1	Hawkins (3), Nettleton, Johnson	4
8		17	H	Bradford City	D	2–2	Johnson (2)	4
9		24	A	Bradford City	L	0–3		6
10	Mar	3	H	Bradford PA	W	6–1	Dawson (3), Scott, Nettleton, Bartram (pen)	3

City failed to qualify for the competition proper.

Football League North (additional fixtures)

Match No.	Date		Venue	Opponents	Result		Scorers	Attend
1	Mar	10	A	Hartlepools United	D	1–1	Johnson	2
2		24	H	Huddersfield Town	W	1–0	Nettleton	3
3		31	A	Huddersfield Town	L	0–1		3
4	Apr	2	A	Darlington	L	3–7	Hawkins (2), Dix	3
5		7	A	Sunderland	D	0–0		5
6		14	H	Sunderland	W	4–2	Johnson (2), J. Wilson (pen), Nettleton	2
7	May	19	A	Darlington	L	2–4	Maddison, Johnson	3
8		21	H	Middlesbrough	W	5–3	Hawkins (2), Nettleton, Dawson, Maddison	3

Tyne, Wear & Tees Cup

Match No.	Date		Venue	Opponents	Result		Scorers	Attend
1 (1)	Apr	21	H	Darlington	W	2–0	Bartram (2 pens)	4
1 (2)		28	A	Darlington	D	2–2	Hawkins (2)	4
2 (1)	May	5	H	Sunderland	W	2–1	Hawkins (2)	4
2 (2)		12	A	Sunderland	L	1–6	Dawson	6

Did you know that?

No fewer than 57 players appeared for the club this term, with centre-half Joe Wilson an ever present. The former Newcastle United, Southend United, Brentford and Reading player had guested regularly for City since February 1942 when he made his deb in a game at Sunderland.

In total he made 114 wartime appearances and netted eight goals.

On 28 October 1944 City recorded their biggest-ever score when they netted 10 times against Gateshead.

On 9 December 1944 Bootham Crescent hosted a game between Bradford and Gateshead, as Park Avenue was being used for a representative match between the Football Association and British Army.

Ever popular 'keeper Sam Bartram scored three goals from the penalty spot, including two in a win over Darlington on 21 April 1945.

ame	Apps	Goals
annister, K.*	24	
arclay, R.*	7	
arron, J.*	1	
artram, S.*	23	3
ates, D.	2	1
onass, A.E.*	1	
owden, A.J.	3	3
rown, T.	1	
ampbell, R.*	4	
ockcroft, W.	1	
oyne, C.*	1	
unningham, L.*	2	
alby, M.	1	
awson, T.*	27	21
ix, R.*	15	8
llis, N.*	1	
erguson, R.	12	
oxcroft, G.	1	
ledhill, S.	40	
addington, R.*	1	1
alton, R.L.*	1	
arvey, J.*	1	
atfield, B.*	1	
awkins, G.H.*	32	21
ays, C.J.	1	
ohnson, J.W.*	14	7
awson, J.R.	24	
ee, G.	3	
achin, A.H.*	1	
addison, R.	2	2
akinson, J.*	1	
ilton, S.	1	
ulvaney, J.	3	
urphy, G.*	1	
ettleton, E.	15	5
akes, L.*	1	
liver, J.	1	
ckering, P.B.	2	
inder, J.J.	31	
oole, B.	21	
ayner, H.J.	1	
iddle, A.*	3	2
obbins, P.	14	
cott, F.H.	19	5
mith, C.J.*	6	
tocker, J.N.*	1	
utherland, H.	2	1
aylor, A.*	1	1
hompson, H.	15	7
alshaw, K.*	1	
atmough, D.	2	
estlake, F.A.*	2	
ilson, J.W.*	40	5
ilson, M.*	6	1
oods, P.*	1	1
oollett, C.*	1	1
rigglesworth, W.	3	1
wn-goals		1
otal Goals		**97**

Guest Players

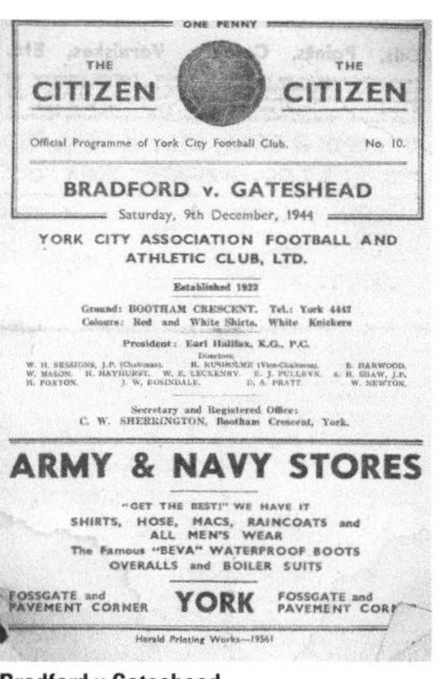

Bradford v Gateshead
9 December 1944 programme cover.

Sam Bartram.

1945–46

Football League North East

Acting Manager: Tom Lockie

LEAGUE	P	W	D	L	F	A	Pts
Rotherham Utd	18	12	2	4	56	28	26
Darlington	18	12	2	4	61	36	26
Gateshead	18	11	2	5	51	34	24
Doncaster Rovers	18	8	4	6	34	35	20
York City	18	6	6	6	34	34	18
Halifax Town	18	7	4	7	39	46	18
Bradford City	18	6	4	8	45	40	16
Carlisle Utd	18	5	3	10	34	58	13
Lincoln City	18	4	2	12	34	54	10
Hartlepools Utd	18	3	3	12	22	45	9

CUP	P	W	D	L	F	A	Pts
Doncaster Rovers	10	6	3	1	24	15	15
Carlisle Utd	10	7	0	3	30	17	14
Bradford City	10	4	3	3	27	22	11
Hartlepools Utd	10	4	3	3	25	21	11
Gateshead	10	4	2	4	21	23	10
Darlington	10	5	0	5	26	31	10
Rotherham Utd	10	3	2	5	24	26	8
York City	10	2	4	4	16	18	8
Halifax Town	10	2	4	4	15	18	8
Lincoln City	10	2	1	7	21	38	5

Did you know that?

The opening day of the last season of wartime football marked the debut of local centre-forward Ian Winters. He scored in a 3–3 home draw against Carlisle United and went on to net 16 goals in 17 appearances.

At the end of the campaign long-serving full-back Jack Pinder received a second benefit when Huddersfield Town played in a testimonial match at York. Along with Bert Brenen and Sam Gledhill, he had played for City throughout the war years. Between them they totalled more than 500 appearances during this period.

For the first and only time the FA Cup was on a two-leg basis. Figuring in City's run to the fourth round was centre-half Alf Young, who had played for Huddersfield Town in the 1938 FA Cup Final against Preston North End. Also in the side was inside-forward Harry Thompson, who was signed from Sunderland in December 1945 for an undisclosed record fee. He had previously played for Wolverhampton Wanderers before a £7,500 transfer move to Roker Park in 1938. He never settled at York and in 1946 was released and later played for Northampton Town.

Match No.	Date	Venue	Opponents	Result		Scorers
1	Aug 25	H	Carlisle United	D	3–3	Winters, Gledhill, Nettleton
2	Sep 1	A	Carlisle United	W	2–0	Winters, Dawson
3	8	A	Gateshead	W	3–1	Winters (3)
4	15	H	Gateshead	W	2–1	Dawson, Winters
5	22	H	Darlington	L	3–4	Maddison, Winters, Dawson
6	29	A	Darlington	L	1–3	Winters
7	Oct 6	H	Halifax Town	D	0–0	
8	13	A	Halifax Town	L	1–3	Nettleton
9	20	H	Lincoln City	W	3–0	Winters (2), Nettleton
10	27	A	Lincoln City	D	2–2	Winters, Dawson
11	Nov 3	A	Hartlepools United	W	2–0	Winters (2)
12	10	H	Hartlepools United	W	5–2	Porritt, Routledge, Dawson, Gledhill, Opp. og
13	Dec 1	A	Doncaster Rovers	D	1–1	Robbins
14	22	A	Rotherham United	L	2–3	Cooke, Scott
15	25	H	Bradford City	D	2–2	Robbins, Winters
16	26	A	Bradford City	L	0–6	
17	29	H	Doncaster Rovers	L	1–2	Cooke
18	Feb 20	H	Rotherham United	D	1–1	Allen

Division North Cup (Qualifying Group East)

1	Jan 12	H	Carlisle Unitd	L	1–2	Winters
2	19	A	Carlisle United	L	1–3	Scott
3	Feb 2	H	Doncaster Rovers	L	1–3	Gledhill
4	9	A	Bradford City	D	0–0	
5	16	H	Bradford City	D	2–2	Allen, Iddon
6	23	A	Halifax Town	W	1–0	Allen
7	Mar 2	H	Halifax Town	D	1–1	Allen
8	9	H	Lincoln City	W	6–2	Thompson (3), Mahon, Winters
9	13	A	Lincoln City	D	2–2	Allen, Iddon
10	16	A	Doncaster Rovers	L	1–3	Pinder (pen)

Third Division North Cup (Competition Proper)

1 (1)	Mar 23	A	Accrington Stanley	L	0–1	
1 (2)	30	H	Accrington Stanley	W	3–1	Allen (2), Scott
2 (1)	Apr 6	A	Chester	L	0–4	
2 (2)	13	H	Chester	W	1–0	Allen

Division Three North (East) (additional fixtures)

1	Apr 19	H	Doncaster Rovers	W	5–1	Scott (2), Brenen, Allen (2)
2	22	A	Doncaster Rovers	D	1–1	Allen
3	27	H	Hartlepools United	L	2–3	Opp. og, Allen
4	May 4	A	Hartlepools United	L	2–6	Porritt (2)

FA Cup

1 (1)	Nov 17	A	Halifax Town	L	0–1	
1 (2)	24	H	Halifax Town	W	4–2	Lee, Gledhill (pen), Scott (2)
2 (1)	Dec 8	A	Bishop Auckland	W	2–1	Maddison, Winters
2 (2)	15	H	Bishop Auckland	W	3–0	Winters, Brenen, Robbins
3 (1)	Jan 5	A	Chesterfield	D	1–1	Mahon
3 (2)	9	H	Chesterfield	W	3–2*	Winters (2), Opp. og
4 (1)	26	A	Sheffield Wednesday	L	1–5	Scott (pen)
4 (2)	30	H	Sheffield Wednesday	L	1–6	Allen

* After extra-time.

1 own-goal

ne	Apps	Goals
n, W.	20	12
nitage, L.C.*	2	
tall, C.E.	13	
on, D.H.*	1	
r, J.A.*	5	
throyd, S.	1	
vden, A.J.	3	
tley, G.W.*	6	
nen, A.	21	1
ier, A.	8	
ke, W.H.*	6	2
iels, J.*	2	
vson, T.*	9	5
gleby, G.*	1	
on, G.*	1	
some, W.	5	
guson, R.	22	
dhill, S	33	3
en, S.	3	
ner, A.	1	
on, H.*	11	2
son, J.R.	1	
, G.	2	
ddison, R.	1	1
non, J.	11	2
Mahon, E.	1	
tleton, E.	11	3
ver, H.S.*	1	
ne, E.G.H.*	1	
ering, P.B.	10	
der, J.J.	28	1
le, B.	6	
ritt, W.	11	3
an, C.M.	1	
bins, P.	26	2
gers, C.	25	
tledge, A.	8	1
tt, F.H.	19	5
mpson, H.	19	3
nbull, R.*	1	
ker, F.	1	
son, J.W.*	10	
ters, I.A.	17	16
ng, A.	11	
n-goals		2
al Goals		**64**

uest Players

Pinder	Poole	Gledhill	Bentall	Rodgers	Scott	Robbins	Winters	Green	Routledge	Reagan	Lee	Young	Maddison	Brenen	Thompson	Mahon	Allen	Porritt	
2	3	4	5	6	7	8	9	10	11										1 (1)
2	3	4	5	6	8	10	9			7	11								1 (2)
2	3	4		6	8	10	9			7		5	11						2 (1)
2	3	4		6	7	10	9		11			5		8					2 (2)
2		6		3	7	8	9					5		4	10	11			3 (1)
2		6		3	7	8	9					5		4	10	11			3 (2)
2		6		3	7	8	9					5		4	10	11			4 (1)
2		6	5	3	7	8								4	10		9	11	4 (2)
8	4	8	3	8	8	8	7	1	2	2	1	5	1	5	4	3	1	1	
		1			3	1	4				1		1	1		1	1		

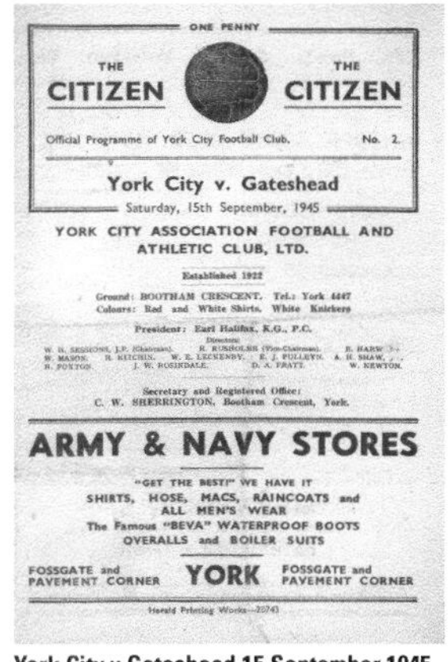

York City v Gateshead 15 September 1945 programme cover.

1946–47

Division Three North

Manager: Tom Mitchell

	P	W	D	L	F	A	Pts
Doncaster Rovers	42	33	6	3	123	40	72
Rotherham United	42	29	6	7	114	53	64
Chester	42	25	6	11	95	51	56
Stockport County	42	24	2	16	78	53	50
Bradford City	42	20	10	12	62	47	50
Rochdale	42	19	10	13	80	64	48
Wrexham	42	17	12	13	65	51	46
Crewe Alexandra	42	17	9	16	70	74	43
Barrow	42	17	7	18	54	62	41
Tranmere Rovers	42	17	7	18	66	77	41
Hull City	42	16	8	18	49	53	40
Lincoln City	42	17	5	20	86	87	39
Hartlepools United	42	15	9	18	64	73	39
Gateshead	42	16	6	20	62	72	38
York City	42	14	9	19	67	81	37
Carlisle United	42	14	9	19	70	93	37
Darlington	42	15	6	21	68	80	36
New Brighton	42	14	8	20	57	77	36
Oldham Athletic	42	12	8	22	55	80	32
Accrington Stanley	42	14	4	24	56	92	32
Southport	42	7	11	24	53	85	25
Halifax Town	42	8	6	28	43	92	22

Match No.	Date		Venue	Opponents	Result		Scorers	Attend
1	Aug	31	H	Chester	D	4–4	Carr (2), Allen, Nettleton	7
2	Sep	4	H	Rotherham United	L	2–3	Allen (2)	5
3		7	A	Rochdale	W	1–0	Allen	8
4		11	H	Lincoln City	L	2–4	Winters, Nettleton	6
5		14	A	Tranmere Rovers	L	1–2	Allen	6
6		21	H	Darlington	W	3–0	Pinder (pen), Forster, Jackson	7
7		28	A	Hull City	D	2–2	Allen, Winters	22
8	Oct	5	H	Gateshead	W	3–1	Allen (2), Jackson	8
9		12	A	Hartlepools United	D	1–1	Brenen	9
10		19	H	Doncaster Rovers	L	1–4	Pinder (pen)	15
11		26	A	Wrexham	L	1–3	Park	5
12	Nov	2	H	Stockport County	W	3–2	Pinder (pen), Forster, A. Patrick	6
13		9	A	Oldham Athletic	D	2–2	Allen, A. Patrick	9
14		16	H	Bradford City	L	0–3		8
15		23	A	Barrow	W	1–0	Bradley	4
16	Dec	7	A	Carlisle United	W	2–1	Porritt (2)	11
17		25	A	Southport	W	3–0	A. Patrick (2), Allen	5
18		26	H	Southport	D	1–1	Pinder (pen)	10
19		28	A	Chester	L	0–6		7
20	Jan	1	A	Rotherham United	L	1–6	Carr	14
21		4	H	Rochdale	L	2–3	Gledhill, Allen	5
22		11	H	Accrington Stanley	L	0–1		2
23		18	H	Tranmere Rovers	L	0–1		5
24		25	A	Darlington	L	1–3	A. Patrick	7
25	Feb	1	H	Hull City	W	3–0	A. Patrick (2), Allen	7
26	Mar	22	A	Bradford City	L	2–3	Allen, A. Patrick	9
27		29	H	Barrow	L	0–2		5
28	Apr	4	A	Crewe Alexandra	L	0–2		7,
29		7	H	Crewe Alexandra	L	2–3	A. Patrick (2)	6
30		12	H	Carlisle United	D	2–2	Rudd (2, 1 pen)	6,
31		19	A	Halifax Town	W	3–0	A. Patrick (2), Rudd	3
32		26	H	New Brighton	L	1–2	Bradley	4,
33	May	3	A	Lincoln City	D	2–2	A. Patrick, Rudd	6
34		10	H	Hartlepools United	L	1–4	Butt	4
35		14	A	Accrington Stanley	W	2–1	A. Patrick (2)	3,
36		17	A	New Brighton	W	3–0	M. Patrick, A. Patrick, Rudd (pen)	4
37		21	H	Oldham Athletic	W	1–0	A. Patrick	4
38		24	A	Gateshead	W	2–1	Winters (2)	8
39		26	H	Halifax Town	W	2–0	Rudd (2)	5
40		27	H	Wrexham	D	2–2	Winters, Rudd	4
41		31	A	Stockport County	L	2–4	Winters, Rudd	5
42	Jun	7	A	Doncaster Rovers	D	0–0		15
								A

FA Cup

1	Dec	14	H	Scunthorpe United	L	0–1		7,
								A

Did you know that?

The 1946–47 season marked the resumption of peacetime football, and of the side that played in the opening game at home to Chester there were four survivors that had appeared in the match at Rochdale on 2 September 1939 prior to the outbreak of World War Two – Bob Ferguson, Sam Gledhill, Fred Scott and Bill Allen.

City used 34 players this term, which remained a club record until the new millennium.

Winger Fred Scott was transferred to Nottingham Forest in September 1946 for a club record fee received of £3,000.

Notable debuts included Matt Patrick (H) Chester 31 August, Alf Patrick (H) Stockport County 2 November, Jimmy Rudd (A) Bradford City 22 March and Sid Storey (H) Wrexham 27 May.

Two Polish Army players made appearances – goalkeeper Edouard Wojtczak and left-winger Eryk Kubicki. The former was an outstanding skater who starred in ice shows after the war. He once walked from York to London on skates to publicise a show.

The winter of 1947 was one of the worst of the 20th century. City did not play between 1 February and 22 March, and the Football League season was extended into June.

Average League attendance at Bootham Crescent was 6,900.

Midland League club Scunthorpe United knocked City out of the FA Cup. It was to be 40 years before the club next lost at home to non-League opposition in the FA Cup (1986–87 Caernarfon Town).

Pinder	Gledhill	Brenen	Roberts	Collier	Scott	Carr	Allen	Patrick M.	Nettleton	Rodgers	Jackson	Porritt	Duthoit	Winters	Reagan	Jowett	Park	Forster	Kubicki	Wojtczak	Porteous	Patrick A.	Bradley	Lee	Gargan	Butt	Rudd	Greenwell	Bentall	Pickering	Lawson	Storey	
2	3	4	5	6	7	8	9	10	11																								1
2	3	4		6	7	8	9	10	11	5																							2
2		5		6		8	9	10	11	3	4	7																					3
2		5		6			8	10	11	3	4		7	9																			4
2	6	5		4			8				10		3	9	7	11																	5
2	3	4		6			8		11		10			9			5	7															6
2	3	10		4			8	11			6			9			5	7															7
2	6	10		4			9				8		3				5	7	11														8
2	6	10		4			9				8		3				5	7	11														9
2	6	8		4			9	10					3				5	7	11														10
2	3	4					9	10			8						5	7	11	1	6												11
2		4					8	10		3							5	7	11	1	6	9											12
2	4	5					8	11		3								7		1	6	9	10										13
2		4					8	11		3							5	7		1	6	9	10										14
2		4					8	11		3		7					5				6	9	10										15
2		4					8	11		3		7					5				6	9	10										16
2		4					8	11		3		7					5				6	9	10										17
2		4					8	7		3							5				6	9	10	11									18
2		4					8	11		3		7					5				6	9	10										19
2		4				10	8	11		3		7					5				6	9											20
2	4					10	8	11				7	3	9			5				6												21
2						10	8				6	11	3	9			5	7							4								22
2	4						9	11			10	7	3				5				6					8							23
2	4					8		10	11			7	3				5				6	9											24
2	4						8		11	3		7					5				6	9				10							25
2	4						8			3		7					5				6	9				10	11						26
2	4	5					8			3		7									6	9				10	11						27
2		5					8			3		7									6	9				10	11	4					28
	4	5					8	7		3			2								6	9				10	11						29
	4	5						7		3			2								6	9	10			8	11						30
2	4	5						7					3							1	6	9	10			8	11						31
2		4						7					3				5			1	6	9	10			8	11						32
2		4						7					3	10			5			1	6	9				8	11						33
2	3	4						7						10						1	6	9				8	11		5				34
2	4	5						7		3	6			10								9				8	11			1			35
2	4	5						7		3	6			10								9				8	11			1			36
2	4	5						7		3	6			10								9				8	11			1			37
2	4	5					9	7		3	6			10												8	11			1			38
2	4	5					9	7		3	6			10												8	11			1			39
2	4	5					9			3	6			8													11			1	7	10	40
2	4	5					9	7		3	6			8													11			1		10	41
2	4	5					9			3	6	7		8													11			1		10	42
40	28	36	1	10	2	7	33	31	7	26	18	15	14	16	1	1	22	10	5	8	23	23	10	1	1	16	17	1	1	8	1	3	
4	1	1				3	13	1	2		2	2		6			1	2				17	2			1	9						
2	6	4					8	11		3	10	7					5					9											1
1	1	1					1	1		1	1	1					1					1											

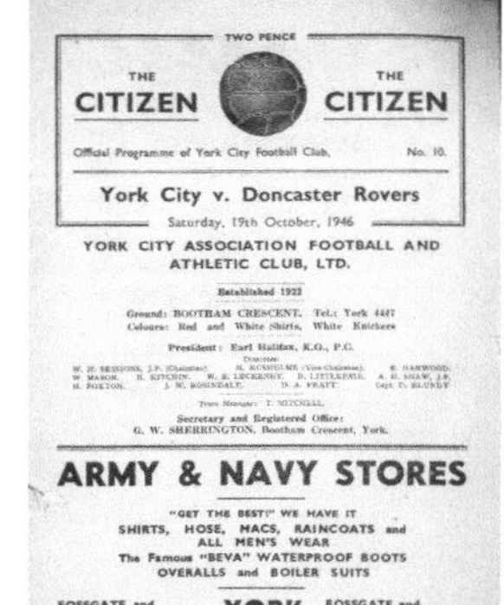
TWO PENCE

THE CITIZEN THE CITIZEN

Official Programme of York City Football Club. No. 10.

York City v. Doncaster Rovers

Saturday, 19th October, 1946

YORK CITY ASSOCIATION FOOTBALL AND ATHLETIC CLUB, LTD.

Established 1922

Ground: BOOTHAM CRESCENT. Tel.: York 4447

Colours: Red and White Shirts, White Knickers

President: Earl Halifax, K.G., P.C.

Team Manager: T. MITCHELL

Secretary and Registered Office: G. W. SHERRINGTON, Bootham Crescent, York.

ARMY & NAVY STORES

"GET THE BEST!" WE HAVE IT

SHIRTS, HOSE, MACS, RAINCOATS and ALL MEN'S WEAR

The Famous "BEVA" WATERPROOF BOOTS

OVERALLS and BOILER SUITS

FOSSGATE and PAVEMENT CORNER YORK FOSSGATE and PAVEMENT CORNER

Herald Printing Works—23148

York City v Doncaster Rovers 19 October 1946 programme cover.

Fred Scott.

CLUB NOTES

Everybody connected with football will welcome the resumption on normal lines to-day. For the City club, it means a return to the Northern Section as we knew it before the war, with all the keen competition associated with it in the struggle for the one promotion place which is granted by the Football League.

It is almost a completely new start for the majority of clubs, and to-day there will be many new faces in the teams. So far as the City club is concerned, we have probably fewer newcomers than most clubs. The management has taken the view that it is better to rely on players whose ability they know, rather than run undue risks in too many new men who have yet to prove themselves.

There is no doubt that there is a general shortage of players in the country, and this is likely to continue because of the effect of national service on youths of 18, which deprives clubs of likely lads at an age when they usually develop.

The seven years war gap also means that many of the older players have dropped out of the game, and many more are likely to do so at the end of the present season. In short, it is a season of reconstruction, and at the moment few would try and prophesy how teams are likely to fare.

Captain of the City team this season is Bert Brenen, and we are confident that under his leadership the team will settle down and do well. If weaknesses are obvious after the early games, the management will endeavour to cure them, and given the right sort of support, they feel that the City club will take its rightful place in the football boom which is expected.

Club notes on the opening day of the season.

1947–48

Division Three North

Manager: Tom Mitchell

	P	W	D	L	F	A	Pts
Lincoln City	42	26	8	8	81	40	60
Rotherham United	42	25	9	8	95	49	59
Wrexham	42	21	8	13	74	54	50
Gateshead	42	19	11	12	75	57	49
Hull City	42	18	11	13	59	48	47
Accrington Stanley	42	20	6	16	62	59	46
Barrow	42	16	13	13	49	40	45
Mansfield Town	42	17	11	14	57	51	45
Carlisle United	42	18	7	17	88	77	43
Crewe Alexandra	42	18	7	17	61	63	43
Oldham Athletic	42	14	13	15	63	64	41
Rochdale	42	15	11	16	48	72	41
York City	42	13	14	15	65	60	40
Bradford City	42	15	10	17	65	66	40
Southport	42	14	11	17	60	63	39
Darlington	42	13	13	16	54	70	39
Stockport County	42	13	12	17	63	67	38
Tranmere Rovers	42	16	4	22	54	72	36
Hartlepools United	42	14	8	20	51	73	36
Chester	42	13	9	20	64	67	35
Halifax Town	42	7	13	22	43	76	27
New Brighton	42	8	9	25	38	81	25

Match No.	Date	Venue	Opponents	Result		Scorers	Atten
1	Aug 23	A	Mansfield Town	W	2–1	A. Patrick, Storey	
2	25	H	Carlisle United	D	2–2	Butt, A. Patrick	
3	30	H	Halifax Town	W	6–0	A. Patrick (4), M. Patrick (2)	
4	Sep 4	A	Carlisle United	D	1–1	Jackson (pen)	
5	6	H	Oldham Athletic	W	1–0	Rudd	
6	10	H	Rotherham United	W	2–0	Rudd (2)	
7	13	A	Tranmere Rovers	L	2–4	M. Patrick, Rudd	
8	20	H	Darlington	L	0–2		
9	27	A	Gateshead	D	0–0		
10	Oct 4	H	Hartlepools United	W	4–0	Allen (2), M. Patrick, Winters	
11	11	A	Rochdale	L	0–3		
12	18	H	New Brighton	W	3–1	Allen (2), M. Patrick	
13	25	A	Southport	L	1–2	Storey	
14	Nov 1	H	Lincoln City	L	0–1		
15	8	A	Accrington Stanley	L	0–1		
16	15	H	Hull City	D	2–2	Pyle, Winters	
17	22	A	Stockport County	L	2–4	Brenen, Winters	
18	Dec 6	A	Barrow	L	0–1		
19	20	H	Mansfield Town	L	1–2	Winters	
20	26	H	Chester	W	2–0	A. Patrick (2)	
21	27	A	Chester	W	3–2	A. Patrick (3)	
22	Jan 1	A	Rotherham United	L	2–3	Jackson (2, 1 pen)	
23	3	A	Halifax Town	W	1–0	Rudd	
24	10	H	Bradford City	D	3–3	M. Patrick, Storey, Rudd	
25	17	A	Oldham Athletic	D	2–2	Storey (2)	
26	24	H	Wrexham	D	1–1	M. Patrick	
27	31	H	Tranmere Rovers	L	1–2	Little	
28	Feb 7	A	Darlington	D	1–1	A. Patrick	
29	14	H	Gateshead	W	3–1	A. Patrick, Storey, Rudd	
30	21	A	Hartlepools United	D	2–2	A. Patrick (2)	
31	28	H	Rochdale	D	0–0		
32	Mar 6	A	New Brighton	L	1–2	Storey	
33	13	H	Southport	D	3–3	Little, A. Patrick, Storey	
34	20	A	Lincoln City	D	0–0		
35	26	A	Crewe Alexandra	W	3–1	A. Patrick (2), M. Patrick	
36	27	H	Accrington Stanley	L	1–2	Pyle	
37	29	H	Crewe Alexandra	L	0–1		
38	Apr 3	A	Hull City	D	1–1	Storey	
39	10	H	Stockport County	W	3–2	Brenen, Storey, Rudd	
40	17	A	Bradford City	W	3–1	Storey (2), A. Patrick	
41	24	H	Barrow	D	0–0		
42	May 1	A	Wrexham	L	0–3		

FA Cup

1	Nov 29	H	Rochdale	L	0–1		

Did you know that?

Prior to the start of the season left-winger George Lee was transferred to Nottingham Forest for a new club record fee received of £7,500. He teamed up with outside-right Fred Scott, who had left York a year earlier, and another former colleague and wartime mentor Bert (Sailor) Brown.

Unbeaten after six games, City topped the Northern Section table on 10 September.

Notable newcomers this campaign included full-back John Simpson, who became the club's first £1,000 signing when he was recruited from Huddersfield Town in March 1948.

Two other players who were to have a long career at York made their debuts – defender Percy Andrews (A) Carlisle United 4 September 1947 and half-back Ron Spence (H) Barrow 24 April 1948.

Full-back Jack Pinder played his last senior game for the club on 6 March 1948 at New Brighton. He had made his debut in September 1932 and, including wartime appearances, played in over 400 games for the club.

Goalkeeper Peter Pickering, who saved no less than seven penalties in a three-month spell of the season, moved to Chelsea in May 1948 for £6,750, reputed then to be the second-highest fee paid for a 'keeper.

Average home League attendance rose to 9,006.

Pinder	McDermott	Jackson	Brenen	Browne	Patrick M.	Butt	Patrick A.	Storey	Rudd	Gale	Andrews	Gledhill	Hamby	Dutholt	Allen	Winters	Pyle	Little	Brown	Simpson	Pears	Spence	
2	3	4	5	6	7	8	9	10	11														1
2	3	4	5	6	7	8	9	10	11														2
	3	4	2	6	7	8	9	10	11	5													3
	3	4		6	7	8	9	10	11	5	2												4
	3	4	2	6	7	8	9	10	11	5													5
	3	6	2		7	8	9	10	11	5		4											6
	3	6	2		7	8	9	10	11	5		4											7
		6	2		7	8	9	10	11	5		4	3										8
		6	4		7	8		10	11	5		3		2	9								9
		6	4		7			10	11	5		3		2	9	8							10
		6	4		7			10	11	5		3		2	9	8							11
		6	4		7			10	11	5		3		2	9	8							12
		6	4		7			10	11	5		3		2	9	8							13
		6	4		7			10	11	5		3		2	9	8							14
		6	4		7		9	10	11	5		3		2		8							15
		6	4		7			10	11	5		3		2		9	8						16
		6	4		7			10	11	5		3		2	8	9							17
		6	4		7			10	11	5		3		2		9	8						18
			4		7			8	11	5		3		2	6	9	10						19
			4		10		9		11	5		3		2	6	8		7					20
			4		8		9	10	11	5		3		2	6			7					21
		6	4		8		9	10	11	5		3		2				7					22
		6	4		8		9	10	11	5		3		2				7					23
2			4		8		9	10	11	5		3			6			7					24
2		9	4		8			10	11	5		3			6			7					25
2		9	4		8			10	11	5		3			6			7					26
		9	4		8			10	11	5		3		2	6			7					27
2			4		11		9	10		5		3			6		8	7					28
2			4		8		9	10	11	5		3			6			7					29
2			4		8		9	10	11	5		3			6			7					30
2		9	4		8			10	11	5		3			6			7					31
2			4		8		9	10	11	5		3			6			7					32
			4		8		9	10	11	5					6			7	2	3			33
			4		7		9	10	11	5					6		8		2	3			34
			4		7		9	10	11	5					6		8		2	3			35
			4		7		9	10	11	5					6		8		2	3			36
			8		7		9	10	11	5		4			6				2	3	1		37
		9	8		7			10	11	5		4			6				2	3			38
			8		7		9	10	11	5		4			6				2	3			39
			8		7		9	10	11	5		4			6				2	3			40
			8		7		9	10	11	5		2			6					3		4	41
			4		8		9	10	11	5					6			7	2	3			42
10	7	25	41	5	42	9	27	41	41	40	1	32	1	16	29	11	7	15	9	10	1	1	
		3	2		8	1	19	12	8						4	4	2	2					

Pinder	McDermott	Jackson	Brenen	Browne	Patrick M.	Butt	Patrick A.	Storey	Rudd	Gale	Andrews	Gledhill	Hamby	Dutholt	Allen	Winters	Pyle	Little	Brown	Simpson	Pears	Spence	
		6	4		7			10	11	5		3		2	8	9							1
		1	1		1			1	1	1		1		1	1	1							

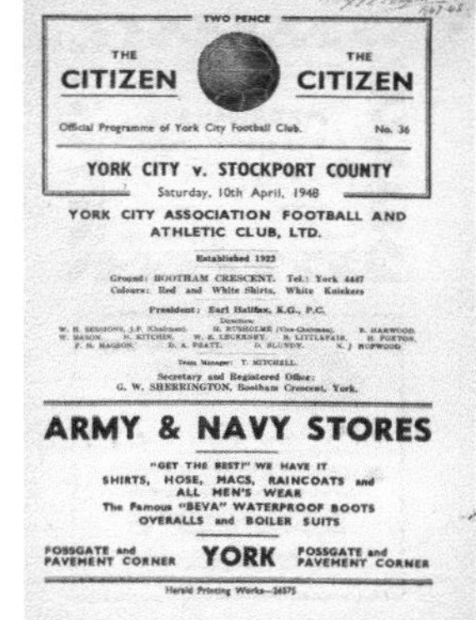
TWO PENCE
THE CITIZEN THE CITIZEN
Official Programme of York City Football Club. No. 36
YORK CITY v. STOCKPORT COUNTY
Saturday, 10th April, 1948
YORK CITY ASSOCIATION FOOTBALL AND ATHLETIC CLUB, LTD.
ARMY & NAVY STORES
SHIRTS, HOSE, MACS, RAINCOATS and ALL MEN'S WEAR
OVERALLS and BOILER SUITS
FOSSGATE and PAVEMENT CORNER YORK FOSSGATE and PAVEMENT CORNER

York City v Stockport County 10 April 1948 programme cover.

Peter Pickering.

1948–49

Division Three North

Manager: Tom Mitchell

	P	W	D	L	F	A	Pts
Hull City	42	27	11	4	93	28	65
Rotherham United	42	28	6	8	90	46	62
Doncaster Rovers	42	20	10	12	53	40	50
Darlington	42	20	6	16	83	74	46
Gateshead	42	16	13	13	69	58	45
Oldham Athletic	42	18	9	15	75	67	45
Rochdale	42	18	9	15	55	53	45
Stockport County	42	16	11	15	61	56	43
Wrexham	42	17	9	16	56	62	43
Mansfield Town	42	14	14	14	52	48	42
Tranmere Rovers	42	13	15	14	46	57	41
Crewe Alexandra	42	16	9	17	52	74	41
Barrow	42	14	12	16	41	48	40
York City	42	15	9	18	74	74	39
Carlisle United	42	14	11	17	60	77	39
Hartlepools United	42	14	10	18	45	58	38
New Brighton	42	14	8	20	46	58	36
Chester	42	11	13	18	57	56	35
Halifax Town	42	12	11	19	45	62	35
Accrington Stanley	42	12	10	20	55	64	34
Southport	42	11	9	22	45	64	31
Bradford City	42	10	9	23	48	77	29

Did you know that?

It was the height of the post-war soccer boom, with huge crowds throughout the country. City's average League crowd of 10,412 remains a club record.

The all-time record home League crowd at York (21,010) on 23 April 1949 saw the visit of Northern Section champions elect Hull City.

Alf Patrick created a new club individual scoring record in the Football League when he netted five times against then League leaders Rotherham United on 20 November 1948.

In the first half of the campaign City won eight successive League games at home, scoring 31 goals in the process and conceding just four.

Sam Gledhill ended his first-team playing days on 16 October 1948 at Barrow. He had made his debut 12 years earlier and, including wartime appearances, played in over 350 games for City.

In September 1948 the club announced the purchase of Bootham Crescent, which had been on lease since 1932.

Match No.	Date	Venue	Opponents	Result		Scorers	Attenda
1	Aug 21	H	Crewe Alexandra	L	1–3	A. Patrick	10
2	23	A	Southport	W	2–0	Brigham (pen), Pyle	10
3	28	A	Halifax Town	W	2–1	Storey, M. Patrick	10
4	30	H	Southport	L	1–3	Storey	9
5	Sep 4	A	Stockport County	D	1–1	Storey	12
6	8	A	Chester	L	1–4	Storey	6
7	11	H	Carlisle United	W	6–0	Ivey (2), M. Patrick, A. Patrick, Rudd (2)	8
8	13	H	Chester	W	2–0	Ivey, M. Patrick	9
9	18	A	Gateshead	D	1–1	A. Patrick	6
10	25	H	Hartlepools United	W	4–0	A. Patrick (2), M. Patrick, Allen	10
11	Oct 2	A	Darlington	L	1–3	Rudd	11
12	9	H	Wrexham	W	5–1	M. Patrick (2), A. Patrick (2), Allen	10
13	16	A	Barrow	L	0–5		9
14	23	H	Mansfield Town	W	2–1	M. Patrick, Rudd	10
15	30	A	Tranmere Rovers	D	0–0		8
16	Nov 6	H	Oldham Athletic	W	4–0	A. Patrick (2), Brenen, Rudd	9
17	13	A	Accrington Stanley	L	1–2	Brigham (pen)	3
18	20	H	Rotherham United	W	6–1	A. Patrick (5), Brigham (pen)	19
19	Dec 25	A	New Brighton	L	1–3	Price	4
20	26	H	New Brighton	W	2–1	A. Patrick (2)	10
21	Jan 1	H	Halifax Town	D	2–2	M. Patrick, Rudd	9
22	8	H	Doncaster Rovers	L	2–3	Brigham (pen), Price	11
23	15	H	Stockport County	W	4–0	A. Patrick (3), Allen	5
24	22	A	Carlisle United	D	3–3	M. Patrick (2), Ivey	9
25	29	A	Crewe Alexandra	L	0–2		6
26	Feb 5	H	Gateshead	L	0–1		9
27	12	A	Bradford City	D	2–2	Hindle (2)	9
28	19	A	Hartlepools United	W	3–2	Brigham (pen), M. Patrick, A. Patrick	8
29	26	H	Darlington	L	2–5	M. Patrick, A. Patrick	10
30	Mar 5	A	Wrexham	D	3–3	A. Patrick (2), Storey	3
31	12	H	Barrow	W	2–0	Hindle, Ivey	8
32	19	A	Mansfield Town	L	0–3		8
33	26	H	Tranmere Rovers	W	1–0	M. Patrick	6
34	Apr 2	A	Oldham Athletic	L	0–4		16
35	6	A	Hull City	W	3–2	A. Patrick (2), Ivey	40
36	9	H	Accrington Stanley	D	1–1	M. Patrick	8
37	15	H	Rochdale	D	1–1	Storey	12
38	16	A	Rotherham United	L	1–2	Ivey	14
39	18	A	Rochdale	L	0–2		7
40	23	H	Hull City	L	1–3	A. Patrick	21
41	30	A	Doncaster Rovers	L	0–1		7
42	May 7	H	Bradford City	L	0–2		5
							A

FA Cup

1	Nov 27	H	Runcorn	W	2–1	Brigham (pen), Rudd	10
2	Dec 11	A	Southport	D	2–2*	Ivey, A. Patrick	10
r	18	H	Southport	L	0–2		12
							A

* After extra-time.

Match	Brigham	Gledhill	Peart	Gale	Allen	Patrick M.	Brenen	Patrick A.	Storey	Rudd	Spence	Burton	Pyle	Simpson	Brown	Ivey	Jackson	Price	Pears	Middleton	Hindle	Woollett	Duthoit	Porter	Andrews
1	2	3	4	5	6	7	8	9	10	11															
2	2		3	5		8	6	9		11	4	7	10												
3	2		6	5		7	4	9	10	11			8	3											
4	2		6	5		7	4	9	10	11			8	3											
5		2		5		8	6	9	10	11	4	7		3											
6				5	6	8		9	10	11	4	7		3	2										
7	2			5		8	6	9	10	11	4			3		7									
8	2			5		8	6	9	10	11	4			3		7									
9	2			5	10	8	6	9		11	4			3		7									
10	2			5	10	8	6	9		11	4			3		7									
11	2			5	10	8	6	9		11	4			3		7									
12	2	6	4	5	10	8		9		11				3		7									
13	2	6		5	10	8	4	9		11				3		7									
14	2			5	6	8	4	9	10	11				3		7									
15	2			5	6		4	9	10	11				3		7	8								
16	2			5	6		8	9	10	11				3		7	4								
17	2				6		5	9	10	11	8			3		7	4								
18	2			5	6	8	4	9	10	11				3		7									
19	2			5	6	8	4		10	11				3		7		9							
20	2			5	6	8	4	9	10	11				3		7			1						
21	2			5	6	8	4	9	10	11				3		7			1						
22	2			5	6	8	4	9		11				3		7		10							
23	2			5	8	7	6	9	10		4			3		11									
24	2			5	6	8	4	9	10	11				3		7									
25	2			5	6	8	4	9	10	11				3		7									
26	2			5	8		6	9	10	11	4			3		7									
27	2			5	6		4	9	10					3		7				1	8	11			
28	2			5	6	7		9	10		4			3		11				1	8				
29	2			5	6	7	4	9	10					3		11				1	8				
30	2			5	6	7	4	9	10											1	8	11	3		
31	2			5	6	7	4	9	10					3		11				1	8				
32	2			5	6	7	4	9	10					3		11				1	8				
33				5	6	7	4	9	10					3	2	11				1	8				
34				5	6	7	4	9	10					3	2	11				1				8	
35				5	6	8	4	9	10					3	2	7				1	11				
36				5	6	8	4	9	10					3	2	7				1	11				
37					6	8	4	9	10					3	2	7				1	11				5
38				5			6	9	10		4			3	2	7				1	8	11			
39					6		4	9	10					3	2	7				1	8	11			5
40					6	8	4	9	10					3	2	7				1	11				5
41						8	6	9	10		4			3	2	7				1	11				5
42						8		9	10		4			3	2	7				1	11			6	5
	30	4	5	36	33	35	38	41	35	25	15	3	3	39	11	35	3	2	2	16	15	4	1	2	5
	5				3	14	1	26	6	6			1			7		2			3				

Match	Brigham	Gledhill	Peart	Gale	Allen	Patrick M.	Brenen	Patrick A.	Storey	Rudd	Spence	Burton	Pyle	Simpson	Brown	Ivey	Jackson	Price	Pears	Middleton	Hindle	Woollett	Duthoit	Porter	Andrews
1	2			5	6	8	4	9	10	11				3		7									
2	2			5	6	8	4	9	10	11				3		7									
r	2			5	6	8	4	9	10	11				3		7									
	3			3	3	3	3	3	3	3				3		3									
	1							1		1						1									

TWO PENCE
THE CITIZEN
THE CITIZEN
Official Programme of York City Football Club. No. 37
CITY v. HULL CITY
23rd April, 1949
YORK CITY ASSOCIATION FOOTBALL AND ATHLETIC CLUB, LTD.
Ground: BOOTHAM CRESCENT.
ARMY & NAVY STORES
"GET THE BEST?" WE HAVE IT
SHIRTS, HOSE, MACS, RAINCOATS and ALL MEN'S WEAR
The Famous "BEVA" WATERPROOF BOOTS
OVERALLS and BOILER SUITS
FOSSGATE and PAVEMENT CORNER YORK FOSSGATE and PAVEMENT CORNER

York City v Hull City 23 April 1949 programme cover.

Alf Patrick.

Newspaper cutting.

York City Purchase Bootham Crescent Ground

YORK CITY Association Football and Athletic Club, Ltd., which has held the Bootham-crescent ground on a lease since 1932, has now purchased the ground. Shareholders of the company were told of this important development at the annual meeting, held in the City Social Club last night.

Mr. W. H. Sessions, the chairman, announced that an agreement for the purchase of the ground had been signed, and said he felt that the club now owned one of the best ground in the Third Division.

1949–50

Division Three North

Manager: Tom Mitchell

	P	W	D	L	F	A	Pts
Doncaster Rovers	42	19	17	6	66	38	55
Gateshead	42	23	7	12	87	54	53
Rochdale	42	21	9	12	68	41	51
Lincoln City	42	21	9	12	60	39	51
Tranmere Rovers	42	19	11	12	51	48	49
Rotherham United	42	19	10	13	80	59	48
Crewe Alexandra	42	17	14	11	68	55	48
Mansfield Town	42	18	12	12	66	54	48
Carlisle United	42	16	15	11	68	51	47
Stockport County	42	19	7	16	55	52	45
Oldham Athletic	42	16	11	15	58	63	43
Chester	42	17	6	19	70	79	40
Accrington Stanley	42	16	7	19	57	62	39
New Brighton	42	14	10	18	45	63	38
Barrow	42	14	9	19	47	53	37
Southport	42	12	13	17	51	71	37
Darlington	42	11	13	18	56	69	35
Hartlepools United	42	14	5	23	52	79	33
Bradford City	42	12	8	22	61	76	32
Wrexham	42	10	12	20	39	54	32
Halifax Town	42	12	8	22	58	85	32
York City	42	9	13	20	52	70	31

Match No.	Date	Venue	Opponents	Result		Scorers	Atten
1	Aug 20	A	Barrow	L	2–3	M. Patrick, A. Patrick	
2	24	A	Lincoln City	L	0–1		1
3	27	H	Crewe Alexandra	D	1–1	Coop	1
4	29	H	Lincoln City	L	1–2	Coop	
5	Sep 3	A	Tranmere Rovers	L	0–1		
6	5	H	Mansfield Town	D	3–3	Brenen, Ivey, Walker	
7	10	H	Halifax Town	W	3–1	M. Patrick, A. Patrick, Walker	
8	12	A	Mansfield Town	L	0–1		1
9	17	H	Oldham Athletic	L	0–1		
10	24	A	Wrexham	L	0–2		
11	Oct 1	H	Accrington Stanley	W	2–1	A. Patrick (2)	
12	8	A	Rochdale	L	1–3	M. Patrick	
13	15	H	Bradford City	D	1–1	Allen	
14	22	A	Chester	W	3–2	Benson, A. Patrick, Collins	
15	29	H	Southport	L	0–1		
16	Nov 5	A	Stockport County	L	1–3	Birch	1
17	12	H	Doncaster Rovers	L	0–3		1
18	19	A	Gateshead	D	1–1	Walker	
19	Dec 3	A	Darlington	D	1–1	Walker	
20	17	H	Barrow	W	2–0	Allen, A. Patrick	
21	24	A	Crewe Alexandra	D	3–3	A. Patrick (2), Walker	
22	26	H	Carlisle United	D	1–1	Walker	1
23	27	A	Carlisle United	L	3–4	Walker (2), M. Patrick	1
24	31	H	Tranmere Rovers	W	1–0	Benson	
25	Jan 14	A	Halifax Town	W	2–1	M. Patrick, Walker	
26	21	A	Oldham Athletic	L	0–2		1
27	28	H	Hartlepools United	L	0–2		
28	Feb 4	H	Wrexham	W	5–0	Spence (3, 2 pens), A. Patrick (2)	
29	11	H	New Brighton	W	2–1	A. Patrick (2)	
30	18	A	Accrington Stanley	D	0–0		
31	25	H	Gateshead	L	1–5	Spence (pen)	
32	Mar 4	A	Hartlepools United	L	0–2		
33	11	H	Chester	L	2–3	Allen, Benson	
34	18	A	Southport	D	1–1	Storey	
35	25	H	Stockport County	D	1–1	M. Patrick	
36	Apr 1	A	Doncaster Rovers	D	1–1	A. Patrick	1
37	7	H	Rotherham United	L	0–3		1
38	8	H	Rochdale	D	2–2	A. Patrick, M. Patrick	
39	10	A	Rotherham United	L	1–2	M. Patrick	
40	15	A	Bradford City	W	2–0	M. Patrick, Coop	1
41	22	H	Darlington	D	1–1	Coop	
42	May 6	A	New Brighton	L	1–3	Ivey	

FA Cup

1	Nov 26	A	Gateshead	L	1–3	Birch	

Did you know that?

In February 1950 Tom Mitchell resigned as manager. He had held the position since March 1937.

In March 1950 the death was announced of City's first trainer Hughie (Spud) Murphy at the age of 64.

For the first time in the club's history they had to apply for re-election. At the end of the season, however, the League was extended to 92 clubs so City, along with Halifax Town, Newport County and Millwall at the bottom of the Northern and Southern sections, were re-elected without having to enter a ballot. The four newcomers were Scunthorpe United, Shrewsbury Town, Gillingham and Colchester United.

For the fourth successive season Alf Patrick was top scorer, and one notable newcomer was centre-half Alan Stewart, who had been signed from Huddersfield Town. He made his debut on the opening day of the campaign at Barrow. Defender Eric Burgin also made his debut that day and in his two seaons at York contested the number-five spot with Stewart. A good cricketer, he was a pace bowler and played a number of games for Yorkshire in the early 1950s.

Half-back Bill Allen, who joined the club in 1939, moved to Scunthorpe United at the end of the campaign. Including wartime appearances he played over 150 games for the club.

Average League attendance at Bootham Cresecnt was 8,016.

Stewart	Simpson	Spence	Burgin	Allen	Ivey	Patrick M.	Patrick A.	Hindle	Coop	Brenen	Brown	Storey	Duthoit	Thompson	Collins	Brigham	Walker	Andrews	Benson	Birch	Jackson	Grant	Porter	
2	3	4	5	6	7	8	9	10	11															1
2	3		5	6	7	8	9	10	11	4														2
	3		5	6	7	8	9		11	4	2	10												3
	3		5	6	7	8	9		11	4	2	10												4
	3		5	6	7		9		11	4			2	8	10									5
	3		5	6	11	7	9			4				8		2	10							6
	3		5	6	11	7	9	8		4						2	10							7
	3		5	6		7	9	8	11	4			2				10							8
	3		5	6	11	7	9			4		10		8		2								9
	3		5	6	11	7	9			4			2	8			10							10
	3		5	6	11	7	9			4		10	2	8										11
	3		5	6	11	7	9			4		10	2	8										12
5				6	7	10	9			4				8		2	11	3						13
5				6			9			4		8			10	2		3	7	11				14
5				6			9			4		8			10	2		3	7	11				15
5		4		8			9			6		10				2		3	7	11				16
5				6	7	8				4		10				2	9	3		11				17
5					7	8				6		10				2	9	3		11	4			18
5				6	7	8	9			4						2	10	3		11				19
5				6	7	8	9			4						2	10	3		11				20
5				6	11	8	9			4						2	10	3	7					21
5				6	11	8	9			4						2	10	3	7					22
5				6		8	9			4		11				2	10	3	7					23
5				6	11	8	9			4						2	10	3	7					24
			5	6		11				4		10			8	2	9	3	7					25
			5	6		11				4		10			8	2	9	3	7					26
				6	7	11				5					10	2	9	3	8		4			27
5	3	8		6		11	9			4		10						2	7					28
5	3	8		6		11	9			4		10						2	7					29
5	3	8		6		11	9			4		10						2	7					30
5	3	8		6		11	9			4		10						2	7					31
5	3			6		11	9			4		10		8				2	7					32
5				6		11	9			4		8			10	2		3	7					33
5				6		11	9			4		8			10	2		3	7			1		34
5						11	9			4		8			10	2		3	7			1	6	35
5	3					11	9			4		8			10	2			7			1	6	36
5	3			10		11	9			4		8				2			7				6	37
5					7	11	9			4		8				2		3			10		6	38
5					7	11	9			4		8				2		3			10		6	39
5	3				7	10	9		11	4		8						2					6	40
5	3				7	10	9		11	4		8						2					6	41
5	3			6	7	10	9		11	4		8				2								42
29	22	6	14	35	25	38	37	4	9	41	2	28	5	8	10	26	16	27	20	7	4	3	7	
		4		3	2	9	14		4	1		1			1		9		3	1				

Stewart	Simpson	Spence	Burgin	Allen	Ivey	Patrick M.	Patrick A.	Hindle	Coop	Brenen	Brown	Storey	Duthoit	Thompson	Collins	Brigham	Walker	Andrews	Benson	Birch	Jackson	Grant	Porter	
5	3				7	8	9			6		10				2				11	4			1
1	1				1	1	1			1		1				1				1	1			
																				1				

'Spud' Murphy.

Newspaper cutting.

YORK CITY MANAGER TO RESIGN

BY " CITIZEN "

MR. TOM MITCHELL, manager of York City Football Club, to-day intimated to the club that he does not desire his contract to be renewed when his existing agreement ends. Mr. Mitchell is on contract with the club until the end of the present season in May.

This will end a long association with the club, which began as a player in 1931 and as manager in 1937.

1950–51

Division Three North

Manager: Dick Duckworth

	P	W	D	L	F	A	Pts
Rotherham United	46	31	9	6	103	41	71
Mansfield Town	46	26	12	8	78	48	64
Carlisle United	46	25	12	9	79	50	62
Tranmere Rovers	46	24	11	11	83	62	59
Lincoln City	46	25	8	13	89	58	58
Bradford Park Avenue	46	23	8	15	90	72	54
Bradford City	46	21	10	15	90	63	52
Gateshead	46	21	8	17	84	62	50
Crewe Alexandra	46	19	10	17	61	60	48
Stockport County	46	20	8	18	63	63	48
Rochdale	46	17	11	18	69	62	45
Scunthorpe United	46	13	18	15	58	57	44
Chester	46	17	9	20	62	64	43
Wrexham	46	15	12	19	55	71	42
Oldham Athletic	46	16	8	22	73	73	40
Hartlepools United	46	16	7	23	64	66	39
York City	46	12	15	19	66	77	39
Darlington	46	13	13	20	59	77	39
Barrow	46	16	6	24	51	76	38
Shrewsbury Town	46	15	7	24	43	74	37
Southport	46	13	10	23	56	72	36
Halifax Town	46	11	12	23	50	69	34
Accrington Stanley	46	11	10	25	42	101	32
New Brighton	46	11	8	27	40	90	30

Did you know that?

City made their worst-ever start to a season when they crashed to a 7–2 defeat at Tranmere Rovers (coincidentally, in the return game between the clubs in April, City recorded their best win of the season 4–0). Making his one and only appearance in goal for City that day at Prenton Park was Jimmy Pegg, who had previously been with Torquay United and Manchester United.

Also making their City debuts on the opening day were right-winger John Linaker and half-back/inside-forward Gordon Brown, who had both been signed from Nottingham Forest.

Goalkeeper Des Thompson played his first game on 10 February 1951 at Halifax Town. His father, George Thompson, played in goal for the club in the mid-1920s in the Midland League days.

For the first time since 1945–46 City reached the third round of the FA Cup, at which stage they lost at First Division Bolton Wanderers.

As part of the Festival of Britain celebrations a series of special matches were staged throughout the country in May 1951. For their part, City entertained League of Ireland clubs Sligo Rovers and Transport, winning 5–0 and 4–0 respectively. It was in these games that young trialist right-winger Billy Hughes made his debut.

Utility player Bert Brenen ended his City career at the end of the season, thus ending the last pre-war playing link at Bootham Crescent. He had been at the club since 1938 and including the war years made 345 appearances.

Average home League attendance was 7,478.

Match No.	Date	Venue	Opponents	Result		Scorers	Attenda
1	Aug 19	A	Tranmere Rovers	L	2–7	Brown, M. Patrick	10
2	21	H	Hartlepools United	W	3–0	Daniels (2), Storey	10,
3	26	H	Bradford PA	L	1–3	Storey	12
4	28	A	Hartlepools United	L	1–4	M. Patrick	8,
5	Sep 2	A	Oldham Athletic	D	2–2	Linaker M. Patrick	12
6	4	H	Accrington Stanley	W	3–0	M. Patrick (2), Linaker	7,
7	9	H	Wrexham	W	3–0	Ivey (2), Brenen	8
8	16	A	Scunthorpe United	W	1–0	M. Patrick	12
9	23	H	Mansfield Town	D	1–1	Ivey	9,
10	26	A	Accrington Stanley	L	0–2		7
11	30	A	Rotherham United	L	1–3	A. Patrick	6,
12	Oct 7	A	Rochdale	W	1–0	Linaker	8
13	14	H	Chester	D	2–2	Linaker, M. Patrick	8
14	21	A	New Brighton	D	0–0		3
15	28	H	Bradford City	L	1–2	A. Patrick	8
16	Nov 4	A	Gateshead	L	0–3		7,
17	11	H	Crewe Alexandra	L	1–2	Brenen	7
18	18	A	Shrewsbury Town	L	0–1		8,
19	Dec 2	A	Darlington	W	3–0	Linaker, Brown, Storey	4,
20	23	A	Bradford PA	L	0–4		9
21	25	H	Southport	W	2–0	Linaker, Brown	7
22	26	A	Southport	D	1–1	Brown	5,
23	30	H	Oldham Athletic	D	2–2	Brown, M. Patrick	5,
24	Jan 13	A	Wrexham	L	3–4	A. Patrick (2), R. Spence (pen)	5
25	20	H	Scunthorpe United	D	0–0		7,
26	27	H	Carlisle United	D	1–1	Storey	7
27	Feb 3	A	Mansfield Town	L	1–3	Storey	10
28	10	A	Halifax Town	W	3–1	R. Spence (pen), Brown, M. Patrick	8,
29	17	H	Rotherham United	D	3–3	M. Patrick (2), A. Patrick	9
30	24	H	Rochdale	D	2–2	Linaker, Brown	7,
31	Mar 3	A	Chester	L	1–3	Linaker	4
32	10	H	New Brighton	W	2–0	Linaker (2)	6,
33	17	A	Bradford City	L	2–5	R. Spence, Brown	10
34	23	H	Barrow	L	0–2		9,
35	24	H	Gateshead	D	1–1	Ivey	5
36	26	A	Barrow	L	0–2		4
37	31	A	Crewe Alexandra	W	4–2	A. Patrick (2), R. Spence, Storey	4
38	Apr 7	H	Shrewsbury Town	W	2–0	A. Patrick, Linaker	5
39	11	H	Stockport County	D	0–0		5
40	14	A	Lincoln City	L	1–2	A. Patrick	8
41	16	H	Lincoln City	D	2–2	Linaker, Brenen	6
42	21	H	Darlington	D	1–1	Linaker	6,
43	25	H	Tranmere Rovers	W	4–0	M. Patrick (2), R. Spence, Storey	6
44	28	A	Stockport County	L	0–1		5
45	May 3	A	Carlisle United	L	2–3	R. Spence, Storey	7
46	5	H	Halifax Town	D	0–0		2
							A

FA Cup

1	Nov 25	A	Bishop Auckland	D	2–2	M. Patrick, Brenen	10
r	29	H	Bishop Auckland	W	2–1	A. Patrick (2)	6
2	Dec 9	H	Tranmere Rovers	W	2–1	A. Patrick (2)	10
3	Jan 6	A	Bolton Wanderers	L	0–2		26
							A

Andrews	Simpson	Horton	Stewart	Daniels	Linaker	Brown	Patrick A.	Patrick M.	Coop	Frost	Thompson K.	Woodward	Storey	Brenen	Ivey	Spence R.	Spence J.	Ashley	Burgin	Medd	Thompson D.	Porter	Lloyd	
2	3	4	5	6	7	8	9	10	11															1
	3	4	5	6	7	8		11		1	2	9	10											2
	3	4	5	6	7	8		11		1	2	9	10											3
3		4	5	6	7	8		11		1	2	9	10											4
	3	4	5		7			8		1	2	9	10	6	11									5
	3	4	5		7		9	8		1	2		10	6	11									6
	3	4	5		7		9	8		1	2		10	6	11									7
	3	4	5		7		9	8		1	2		10	6	11									8
	3	4	5		7		9	8	10	1	2			6	11									9
2	3	4	5		7	10	9	8		1					11	6								10
2	3	4	5		7	10	9	8		1				6	11									11
3		4	5		7	10	9	8		1				2	11	6								12
3		4	5		7	10	9	8		1				2	11	6								13
	3	4	5		7	10		9		1			8	6	11		2							14
	3	4	5		7	10	9						8	6	11		2	1						15
	3	4	5		7		9	8					10	6	11		2	1						16
	3	4	5		7	8	9	11		1			10	6			2							17
2	3	4	5		7		9	11	8	1				10		6								18
2	3	4	5		7	8	9	11					10			6		1						19
2	3		5		7	8	9	11					10	4		6		1						20
2	3		5		7	8	9	11					10	4		6		1						21
2	3		5		7	8	9	11					10	4		6		1						22
2	3	4	5		7	8	9	11		1			10			6								23
2	3	4			7	8	9	11					10	5		6		1						24
2	3		5		7	8	9	11		1			10	4		6								25
2	3				7		9	8					10	4		6		1	5	11				26
2	3				7	8	9	11					10	4		6		1	5					27
	3				7	8	9	11			2		10	4		6			5		1			28
	3				7	8	9	11			2		10	4		6			5		1			29
	3				7	8	9	11			2		10	4		6			5		1			30
2	3				7	8	9	11					10	4		6			5		1			31
2	3				7	8		11					10	5		6					1	4	9	32
2	3				7	8	9	11					10	5		6					1	4		33
2	3				7	8		11				9	10	5		6					1	4		34
2	3				7		9	8					10	5	11	6					1	4		35
	3				7	11	9	8			2		10	5		6					1	4		36
	3				7		9	8			2		10	4	11	6			5		1			37
	3				7		9	8			2		10	5	11	6					1	4		38
	3				7		9	8			2		10		11	6			5		1	4		39
	3				7		9	8			2		10		11	6			5		1	4		40
	3		5		7			8					10	9	11	6	2				1	4		41
	3		5		7			8					10	9	11	6	2				1	4		42
			5		7	8		11			3		10	6		9	2				1	4		43
			5		7	8		11			3		10	6		9	2				1	4		44
	3		5		7	8		11			6		10			9	2				1	4		45
	3		5		7	8		11					10	6		9	2				1	4		46
21	41	21	30	4	46	31	33	45	3	17	19	5	39	36	19	32	10	9	9	1	19	14	1	
				2	13	8	9	13					8	3	4	6								

Andrews	Simpson	Horton	Stewart	Daniels	Linaker	Brown	Patrick A.	Patrick M.	Coop	Frost	Thompson K.	Woodward	Storey	Brenen	Ivey	Spence R.	Spence J.	Ashley	Burgin	Medd	Thompson D.	Porter	Lloyd	
2	3	4	5		7		9	11	8					10		6		1						1
	3	4	5		7	8	9	11					10			6	2	1						r
2	3		5		7	8	9	11					10	4		6		1						2
2	3		5		7	8	9	10						4	11	6		1						3
3	4	2	4		4	3	4	4	1				2	3	1	4	1	4						
							4	1						1										

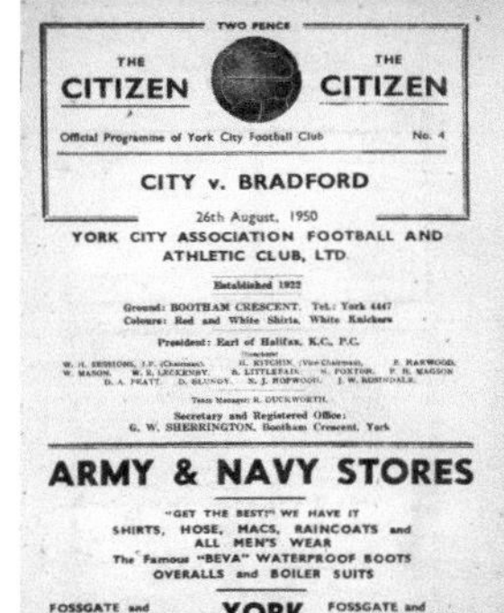
TWO PENCE
THE CITIZEN THE CITIZEN
Official Programme of York City Football Club No. 4
CITY v. BRADFORD
26th August, 1950
YORK CITY ASSOCIATION FOOTBALL AND ATHLETIC CLUB, LTD.
Established 1922
Ground: BOOTHAM CRESCENT. Tel.: York 4447
Colours: Red and White Shirts, White Knickers
President: Earl of Halifax, K.C., P.C.
Team Manager: R. DUCKWORTH.
Secretary and Registered Office: G. W. SHERRINGTON, Bootham Crescent, York
ARMY & NAVY STORES
"GET THE BEST!" WE HAVE IT
SHIRTS, HOSE, MACS, RAINCOATS and ALL MEN'S WEAR
The Famous "BEVA" WATERPROOF BOOTS
OVERALLS and BOILER SUITS
FOSSGATE and PAVEMENT CORNER YORK FOSSGATE and PAVEMENT CORNER

York City v Bradford Park Avenue 26 August 1950 programme cover.

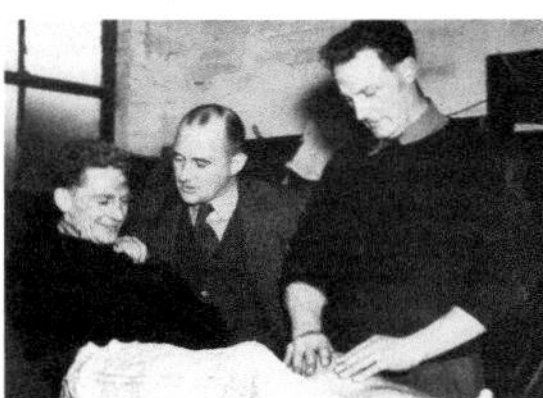

John Linaker receiving attention from manager Dick Duckworth and trainer Tom Lockie.

1951–52

Division Three North

Manager: Dick Duckworth

	P	W	D	L	F	A	Pts
Lincoln City	46	30	9	7	121	52	69
Grimsby Town	46	29	8	9	96	45	66
Stockport County	46	23	13	10	74	40	59
Oldham Athletic	46	24	9	13	90	61	57
Gateshead	46	21	11	14	66	49	53
Mansfield Town	46	22	8	16	73	60	52
Carlisle United	46	19	13	14	62	57	51
Bradford Park Avenue	46	19	12	15	74	64	50
Hartlepools United	46	21	8	17	71	65	50
York City	46	18	13	15	73	52	49
Tranmere Rovers	46	21	6	19	76	71	48
Barrow	46	17	12	17	57	61	46
Chesterfield	46	17	11	18	65	66	45
Scunthorpe United	46	14	16	16	65	74	44
Bradford City	46	16	10	20	61	68	42
Crewe Alexandra	46	17	8	21	63	82	42
Southport	46	15	11	20	53	71	41
Wrexham	46	15	9	22	63	73	39
Chester	46	15	9	22	72	85	39
Halifax Town	46	14	7	25	61	97	35
Rochdale	46	11	13	22	47	79	35
Accrington Stanley	46	10	12	24	61	92	32
Darlington	46	11	9	26	64	103	31
Workington	46	11	7	28	50	91	29

Did you know that?

Two notable additions to the forward line were made this campaign – Steve Griffiths and Billy Fenton – and they both made their debut on the opening day at Lincoln. 37-year-old inside-forward Griffiths had numbered Portsmouth and Barnsley among his previous clubs and was made skipper. Left-winger Fenton had been signed from Second Division Blackburn Rovers and went on to break the club's scoring record by netting 31 goals in his first season, thus beating Reg Baines's tally of 29 set in 1931–32 and 1932–33.

Billy Hughes made his League debut on the right wing at Rochdale on 20 October 1951.

In the game at Scunthorpe on 17 January 1952 brothers were opposing goalkeepers – Des Thompson for City and George Thompson for United.

Alf Patrick became the first City player to score 100 League goals in peacetime football when he scored against Grimsby Town on 19 April 1952.

Another local centre-forward – David Dunmore – played his first senior game on the last day of the season, and the 18-year-old scored in the 3–0 win over Crewe Alexandra.

Average home League attendance was 7,968.

Match No.	Date	Venue	Opponents	Result		Scorers	Atten
1	Aug 18	A	Lincoln City	L	1–3	Slater	1
2	20	H	Tranmere Rovers	D	1–1	Linaker	
3	25	H	Chester	W	4–2	Fenton (2), Linaker, Opp. og	
4	28	A	Tranmere Rovers	L	0–2		
5	Sep 1	H	Chesterfield	W	1–0	Fenton	
6	3	H	Southport	L	0–2		
7	8	A	Bradford City	D	3–3	Brown, M. Patrick, Fenton	1
8	11	A	Southport	L	1–2	M. Patrick	
9	15	H	Hartlepools United	W	3–1	A. Patrick (2), Fenton	
10	22	A	Oldham Athletic	L	0–2		2
11	29	H	Darlington	W	2–1	Slater (2)	
12	Oct 6	A	Halifax Town	D	1–1	A. Patrick	
13	13	H	Mansfield Town	W	3–0	Fenton (2), Linaker	
14	20	A	Rochdale	W	2–0	R. Spence, Fenton	
15	27	H	Accrington Stanley	W	6–1	Fenton (3), Brown, Griffiths, A. Patrick	
16	Nov 3	A	Carlisle United	L	1–2	Fenton	1
17	10	H	Stockport County	L	0–1		1
18	17	A	Workington	L	0–1		
19	Dec 1	A	Grimsby Town	D	0–0		1
20	8	H	Wrexham	W	4–2	Fenton (2), Griffiths, A. Patrick	
21	22	A	Chester	W	1–0	Fenton	
22	25	H	Bradford PA	W	1–0	Fenton	
23	26	A	Bradford PA	L	1–2	R. Spence	1
24	29	A	Chesterfield	L	1–2	Hughes	
25	Jan 5	H	Bradford City	W	3–1	Brown, Griffiths, Fenton	
26	17	A	Scunthorpe United	D	1–1	Fenton	
27	19	A	Hartlepools United	L	2–3	Griffiths, A. Patrick	
28	26	H	Oldham Athletic	W	5–0	A. Patrick (3), Fenton (2)	
29	Feb 9	A	Darlington	L	0–1		
30	16	H	Halifax Town	W	6–2	Hughes, A. Patrick (3), Fenton (2)	
31	23	A	Crewe Alexandra	D	0–0		
32	Mar 1	A	Mansfield Town	D	1–1	Griffiths	
33	8	H	Rochdale	D	1–1	Griffiths	
34	15	A	Accrington Stanley	L	1–2	Fenton	
35	22	H	Carlisle United	D	0–0		
36	29	A	Stockport County	L	1–3	Fenton	
37	31	H	Lincoln City	W	1–0	Storey	
38	Apr 5	H	Workington	W	5–1	Brown, A. Patrick (2), Fenton (2)	
39	11	H	Gateshead	W	1–0	Hughes	1
40	12	A	Barrow	D	0–0		
41	14	A	Gateshead	D	1–1	Fenton	
42	19	H	Grimsby Town	D	1–1	A. Patrick	1
43	21	H	Barrow	W	2–1	Fenton (2)	
44	26	A	Wrexham	D	1–1	Fenton	
45	28	H	Scunthorpe United	L	0–1		
46	May 3	H	Crewe Alexandra	W	3–0	Hughes, Dunmore, Fenton	

1 own-goal

FA Cup

	Date	Venue	Opponents	Result		Scorers	Atten
1	Nov 24	H	Bradford PA	D	1–1	A. Patrick	1
r	28	A	Bradford PA	D	1–1*	A. Patrick	
2r	Dec 3	N#	Bradford PA	L	0–4		1

* After extra-time. # At Elland Road, Leeds.

Thompson K.	Simpson	Porter	Stewart	Spence R.	Linaker	Griffiths	Slater	Storey	Fenton	Frost	Spence J.	Brown	Patrick M.	Patrick A.	Hughes	Andrews	Desmond	Dunmore	Kelly	Match
2	3	4	5	6	7	8	9	10	11											1
2	3	4	5	6	7	8	9	10	11											2
2	3	4	5	6	7	8	9	10	11											3
	3		5	6	7	8	9	10	11	1	2	4								4
	3		5	6	7	8	9	10	11	1	2	4								5
	3		5	6	7	8	9	10	11	1	2	4								6
	3		5	6	7	10			11	1	2	4	8	9						7
	3	4	5	6	7				11		2	8	10	9						8
	3		5	6	7			8	11		2	4	10	9						9
	3		5	6	7			8	11		2	4	10	9						10
	3		5	6	7		8	10	11		2	4		9						11
	3		5	6	7		8	10	11		2	4		9						12
	3		5	6	7		8	10	11		2	4		9						13
	3		5	6		8		10	11		2	4		9	7					14
	3		5	6		8		10	11		2	4		9	7					15
	3		5	6		8		10	11		2	4		9	7					16
	3		5	6		8		10	11		2	4		9	7					17
	3		5	6		8		10	11		2	4		9	7					18
	3	4	5	6		8	10		11		2			9	7					19
	3		5	6		8		10	11		2	4		9	7					20
	3			6		8		10	11		5	4		9	7	2				21
	3			6		8	9	10	11		5	4			7	2				22
	3			6		8	9	10			5	4	11		7	2				23
	3			6		8	9		11		5	4			7	2	10			24
	3			6		8		10	11		5	4		9	7	2				25
	3			6		8		10	11		5	4		9	7	2				26
	3			6		8		10	11		5	4		9	7	2				27
	3			6		8		10	11		5	4		9	7	2				28
	3			6		8		10	11		5	4		9	7	2				29
	3			6		8		10	11		5	4		9	7	2				30
	3			6		8		10	11		5	4		9	7	2				31
	3			6		8		10	11		5	4		9	7	2				32
	3			6		8		10	11		5	4		9	7	2				33
	3			6		8		10	11		5	4		9	7	2				34
	3			6		8		10	11		5	4		9	7	2				35
	3			6		8		10	11		5	4		9	7	2				36
				6		8		10	11		5	4	3	9	7	2				37
				6		8		10	11		5	4	3	9	7	2				38
	3			6		8			11		5	4	10	9	7	2				39
	3			6		8			11		5	4	10	9	7	2				40
	3			6		8			11		5	4	10	9	7	2				41
	3	6				8		10	11		5	4		9	7	2				42
	3	6				8		10	11		5	4		9	7	2				43
	3			6		8		10	11		5	4		9	7	2				44
	3			6		8		10	11		5	4		9	7	2				45
	3			6		8		10	11		5	4			7	2		9		46
3	44	7	20	44	13	40	13	39	45	4	43	42	10	36	33	26	1	1		
				2	3	6	3	1	31			4	2	15	4			1		
	3		5	6		8		10	11		2	4	7	9						1
	3		5	6		8		10	11		2	4	7	9						r
	3			6		8	7	10	11		2	4		9					5	2r
	3		2	3		3	1	3	3		3	3	2	3					1	
														2						

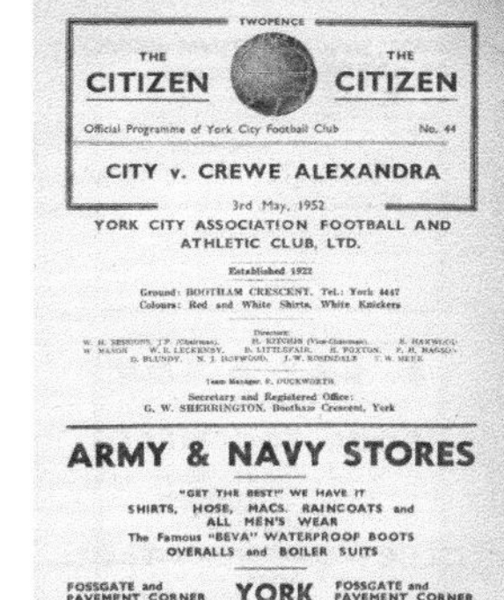

TWOPENCE
THE CITIZEN
THE CITIZEN
Official Programme of York City Football Club
No. 44
CITY v. CREWE ALEXANDRA
3rd May, 1952
YORK CITY ASSOCIATION FOOTBALL AND ATHLETIC CLUB, LTD.
ARMY & NAVY STORES
"GET THE BEST!" WE HAVE IT
SHIRTS, HOSE, MACS, RAINCOATS and ALL MEN'S WEAR
The Famous "BEVA" WATERPROOF BOOTS
OVERALLS and BOILER SUITS
FOSSGATE and PAVEMENT CORNER
YORK
FOSSGATE and PAVEMENT CORNER

York City v Crewe Alexandra 3 May 1952 programme cover.

Billy Fenton and Billy Hughes.

1952–53

Division Three North

Manager: Dick Duckworth, then Charles Spencer

	P	W	D	L	F	A	Pts
Oldham Athletic	46	22	15	9	77	45	59
Port Vale	46	20	18	8	67	35	58
Wrexham	46	24	8	14	86	66	56
York City	46	20	13	13	60	45	53
Grimsby Town	46	21	10	15	75	59	52
Southport	46	20	11	15	63	60	51
Bradford Park Avenue	46	19	12	15	75	61	50
Gateshead	46	17	15	14	76	60	49
Carlisle United	46	18	13	15	82	68	49
Crewe Alexandra	46	20	8	18	70	68	48
Stockport County	46	17	13	16	82	69	47
Tranmere Rovers	46	21	5	20	65	63	47
Chesterfield	46	18	11	17	65	63	47
Halifax Town	46	16	15	15	68	68	47
Scunthorpe United	46	16	14	16	62	56	46
Bradford City	46	14	18	14	75	80	46
Hartlepools United	46	16	14	16	57	61	46
Mansfield Town	46	16	14	16	55	62	46
Barrow	46	16	12	18	66	71	44
Chester	46	11	15	20	64	85	37
Darlington	46	14	6	26	58	96	34
Rochdale	46	14	5	27	62	83	33
Workington	46	11	10	25	55	91	32
Accrington Stanley	46	8	11	27	39	89	27

Did you know that?

A final position of fourth in Division Three North and a total of 53 points set new club records and the average home League crowd rose to 8,654.

City had two managers this term. Dick Duckworth, who had been appointed after Tom Mitchell's departure in 1950, was released from his contract in October 1952 to take over at Stockport County. His successor was the former Newcastle United and England centre-half Charles Spencer, who had previously been manager at Grimsby Town. After less than three months in charge he died in January 1953 and the post then remained vacant until the end of the season when James McCormick was appointed as the new City boss.

'Keeper Des Thompson was transferred to First Division Burnley for £7,250 in November 1952, and later that month 21-year-old local lad Mick Granger made his debut in goal in the FA Cup tie against Barrow.

Alf Patrick made his last senior appearance on 20 April 1953 away at Port Vale. He netted 117 goals in 241 League and Cup outings.

Billy Fenton again was top scorer and in two seasons had netted more than 50 goals from the left wing.

Match No.	Date	Venue	Opponents	Result		Scorers	Attend
1	Aug 23	H	Bradford PA	W	3–1	Griffiths (pen), A. Patrick, Fenton	10
2	28	A	Chester	D	1–1	A. Patrick	6
3	30	A	Oldham Athletic	L	1–2	A. Patrick	16
4	Sep 1	H	Chester	D	0–0		8
5	6	H	Mansfield Town	W	2–0	Hughes, Opp. og	8
6	10	A	Wrexham	D	1–1	Fenton	9
7	13	A	Halifax Town	D	0–0		9
8	15	H	Wrexham	W	2–1	Griffiths, A. Patrick	7
9	20	H	Accrington Stanley	W	2–0	A. Patrick, Storey	8
10	22	A	Hartlepools United	L	1–2	Griffiths	9
11	27	A	Workington	W	3–1	Fenton (2), A. Patrick	5
12	29	H	Port Vale	W	1–0	R. Spence	7
13	Oct 4	H	Chesterfield	D	0–0		9
14	11	A	Scunthorpe United	L	0–2		7
15	18	H	Stockport County	W	3–0	Fenton (2), Dunmore	9
16	25	A	Bradford City	D	1–1	Fenton	11
17	Nov 1	H	Rochdale	W	2–0	Warrender, Griffiths	9
18	8	A	Darlington	W	1–0	Fenton	7
19	15	H	Gateshead	L	1–2	Fenton	9
20	29	H	Carlisle United	W	1–0	Storey	6
21	Dec 6	A	Crewe Alexandra	L	0–3		6
22	13	H	Crewe Alexandra	W	2–1	A. Patrick, Fenton	6
23	20	A	Bradford PA	W	3–2	Hughes, A. Patrick, Fenton	6
24	26	H	Tranmere Rovers	W	2–0	Griffiths (pen), Fenton	11
25	Jan 3	H	Oldham Athletic	L	1–2	Fenton	15
26	10	H	Barrow	D	1–1	Fenton	7
27	17	A	Mansfield Town	D	1–1	Fenton	6
28	24	H	Halifax Town	D	2–2	Fenton (2)	9
29	31	A	Barrow	L	0–1		4
30	Feb 7	A	Accrington Stanley	L	0–1		4
31	14	H	Workington	L	1–3	Brown	7
32	21	A	Chesterfield	W	2–1	R. Spence, Hughes	8
33	28	H	Scunthorpe United	L	0–2		7
34	Mar 7	A	Stockport County	D	1–1	Griffiths (pen)	8
35	14	H	Bradford City	D	0–0		7,
36	21	A	Rochdale	W	3–0	Fenton (2), Hughes	6
37	28	H	Darlington	W	3–0	Fenton (2), A. Patrick	5,
38	Apr 3	A	Grimsby Town	L	1–2	Fenton	18
39	4	A	Gateshead	D	1–1	Fenton	5,
40	6	H	Grimsby Town	W	2–0	Hughes, Warrender	12
41	11	H	Hartlepools United	W	1–0	Hughes	7
42	14	A	Southport	L	0–2		4,
43	18	A	Carlisle United	D	1–1	Fenton	4
44	20	A	Port Vale	L	0–2		11
45	25	H	Southport	W	3–1	Warrender, Dunmore, Storey	6,
46	28	A	Tranmere Rovers	W	3–1	Dunmore (2), Fenton	4,
							A
						1 own-goal	

FA Cup

1	Nov 22	H	Barrow	L	1–2	A. Patrick	9,
							A

Andrews	Simpson	Brown	Spence J.	Spence R.	Hughes	Griffiths	Patrick A.	Storey	Fenton	Wheat	Patrick M.	Dunmore	Warrender	Kirby	Searson	Barritt	Ryan	Granger	
2	3	4	5	6	7	8	9	10	11										1
2	3	4	5	6	7	8	9	10	11										2
2	3	4	5	6	7	8	9	10	11										3
2	3	4	5	6	7	8	9		11	10									4
2	3	4	5	6	7	8	9	10	11										5
2	3	4	5	6	7	8	9	10	11										6
2		4	5	6	7	8	9	10	11		3								7
2		4	5	6	7	8	9	10	11		3								8
2		4	5	6	7	8	9	10		11	3								9
2		4	5	6	7	8	9	10		11	3								10
2		4	5	6		8	9	10	11		3	7							11
2		4	5	6		8	9	10	11		3	7							12
2		4	5	6		8	9	10	11		3	7							13
2	3	4	5	6	7	8	9	10	11										14
2	3	4	5	6		8		10	11			9	7						15
2	3	4	5	6		8		10	11			9	7						16
2	3	4	5	6		8		10	11			9	7						17
2	3	4	5	6		8		10	11			9	7						18
2	3		5	6		8		10	11			9	7	4					19
2		4	5	6		8	7	10	11		3				1	9			20
2		4	5	6	7	8		10	11		3				1	9			21
2		4	5	6	7	8	9	10	11		3				1				22
2		4	5	6	7	8	9	10	11		3				1				23
2		4	5	6	7	8	9	10	11		3				1				24
2		4	5	6	7	8	9	10	11		3				1				25
2		4	5	6	7	8	9	10	11		3				1				26
2	3	4	5	6		8		10	11			9	7		1				27
2	3	4	5	6		8		10	11			9			1		7		28
2	3	4	5	6		8		10	11			9			1		7		29
2	3	4	5	6		8		10	11			9			1		7		30
2		4	5	6					11	10	3	8			1	9	7		31
2		4	5	6	7			10	11		3	8			1	9			32
2		4	5	6	7	8		10	11		3				1	9			33
2	3	4	5	6	7	8	9	10	11						1				34
2	3	4	5	6	7	8	9	10	11						1				35
2	3	4	5	6	7		9	10	11				8		1				36
2	3	4	5	6	7		9	10	11				8		1				37
2	3	4	5	6	7		9	10	11				8		1				38
2	3	4	5	6	7	8	9	10	11						1				39
2	3	4	5	6	7		9	10	11				8		1				40
2	3	4	5	6	7		9	10	11				8		1				41
5	3	4		6	7		9	10	11		2		8		1				42
2	3	4	5	6	7		9	10	11				8		1				43
2	3	4	5	6	7		9	10	11				8		1				44
2	3	4	5	6	7			10	11			9	8		1				45
2	3	4	5	6	7			10	11			9	8		1				46
46	29	45	45	46	32	34	31	44	44	4	18	16	16	1	27	5	4		
		1		2	6	6	9	3	25			4	3						

Andrews	Simpson	Brown	Spence J.	Spence R.	Hughes	Griffiths	Patrick A.	Storey	Fenton	Wheat	Patrick M.	Dunmore	Warrender	Kirby	Searson	Barritt	Ryan	Granger	
2	3	4	5	6		8	7	10	11			9						1	1
1	1	1	1	1		1	1	1	1			1						1	
							1												

York City v Southport 25 April 1953 programme cover.

Captain Steve Griffiths and manager Charles Spencer with 'keeper Mick Granger prior to his debut in November 1952 in the FA Cup tie against Barrow.

1953–54

Division Three North

Manager: Jim McCormick

	P	W	D	L	F	A	Pts
Port Vale	46	26	17	3	74	21	69
Barnsley	46	24	10	12	77	57	58
Scunthorpe United	46	21	15	10	77	56	57
Gateshead	46	21	13	12	74	55	55
Bradford City	46	22	9	15	60	55	53
Chesterfield	46	19	14	13	76	64	52
Mansfield Town	46	20	11	15	88	67	51
Wrexham	46	21	9	16	81	68	51
Bradford Park Avenue	46	18	14	14	77	68	50
Stockport County	46	18	11	17	77	67	47
Southport	46	17	12	17	63	60	46
Barrow	46	16	12	18	72	71	44
Carlisle United	46	14	15	17	83	71	43
Tranmere Rovers	46	18	7	21	59	70	43
Accrington Stanley	46	16	10	20	66	74	42
Crewe Alexandra	46	14	13	19	49	67	41
Grimsby Town	46	16	9	21	51	77	41
Hartlepools United	46	13	14	19	59	65	40
Rochdale	46	15	10	21	59	77	40
Workington	46	13	14	19	59	80	40
Darlington	46	12	14	20	50	71	38
York City	46	12	13	21	64	86	37
Halifax Town	46	12	10	24	44	73	34
Chester	46	11	10	25	48	67	32

Did you know that?

After being out of action through injury since December 1951 centre-half Alan Stewart returned to first-team duty on 3 October 1953 at Port Vale.

Following his 20th birthday, centre-forward David Dunmore was transferred to Tottenham Hotspur in February 1954 for a new club record fee received of £10,500.

In November 1953 Mr W.H. Sessions stood down as chairman after 14 years. His successor was Mr H.W. (Hugh) Kitchin.

City avoided having to seek re-election by winning the last game of the season at fellow strugglers Halifax Town. In that match, long-serving utility player Matt Patrick made his last senior appearance. In eight seasons he had played in 261 League and Cup games and scored 48 goals.

Full-back John Simpson made the last of his 220 appearances on Boxing Day 1953 at Barnsley. He was later City's trainer/physiotherapist 1977–83.

Average home League crowd dropped to 5,636, the then lowest since the war.

Match No.	Date	Venue	Opponents	Result		Scorers	Attend
1	Aug 19	A	Grimsby Town	L	0–3.		16
2	22	H	Workington	D	0–0		
3	24	A	Hartlepools United	D	2–2	R. Spence (pen), Fenton	11
4	29	A	Scunthorpe United	L	0–3		
5	31	H	Hartlepools United	W	5–0	Burgess (2), Porter, Brown, Dunmore	
6	Sep 5	H	Stockport County	D	0–0		
7	7	A	Gateshead	L	0–3		
8	12	H	Southport	W	2–1	Dunmore (2)	
9	14	H	Gateshead	D	1–1	Dunmore (pen)	
10	19	A	Chester	L	1–3	Dunmore (pen)	
11	21	H	Darlington	D	3–3	Dunmore (2), Linaker	
12	26	H	Crewe Alexandra	L	0–3		
13	Oct 3	A	Port Vale	L	0–5		18
14	10	A	Wrexham	D	1–1	Fenton	
15	17	H	Mansfield Town	W	5–1	Dunmore (3), Storey, Fenton	
16	24	A	Barrow	L	1–4	Fenton	
17	31	H	Bradford City	W	3–2	Linaker, Dunmore, Opp. og	
18	Nov 7	A	Chesterfield	L	2–3	Linaker, Fenton	
19	14	H	Tranmere Rovers	D	0–0		
20	28	H	Carlisle United	L	1–3	Dunmore (pen)	
21	Dec 5	A	Accrington Stanley	L	0–2		
22	19	A	Workington	L	2–5	Dunmore, Fenton	
23	25	H	Barnsley	L	0–2		
24	26	A	Barnsley	L	1–2	Dunmore (pen)	
25	Jan 1	A	Darlington	W	3–1	Dunmore (2), Burgess	
26	2	H	Scunthorpe United	W	2–0	Storey, Burgess	
27	9	A	Rochdale	W	2–1	Storey, Dunmore	
28	16	A	Stockport County	W	1–0	Dunmore	
29	23	A	Southport	D	1–1	Dunmore	
30	30	H	Rochdale	L	1–2	Burgess	
31	Feb 6	H	Chester	W	2–1	Dunmore, Burgess	
32	13	A	Crewe Alexandra	D	1–1	Burgess	
33	24	H	Port Vale	L	0–1		
34	27	H	Wrexham	W	5–2	R. Spence (2), Linaker, Burgess, Fenton	
35	Mar 6	A	Mansfield Town	L	2–7	Burgess, R. Spence	
36	13	H	Barrow	W	5–2	Burgess (2), R. Spence (2, 1 pen), Fenton	
37	20	A	Bradford City	L	0–1		12
38	27	H	Chesterfield	L	1–3	Burgess	
39	Apr 3	A	Tranmere Rovers	D	1–1	Burgess	
40	10	H	Halifax Town	D	1–1	Stewart	
41	12	H	Grimsby Town	L	1–2	R. Spence (pen)	
42	16	H	Bradford PA	D	0–0		
43	17	A	Carlisle United	D	1–1	Burgess	
44	19	A	Bradford PA	L	0–2		
45	24	H	Accrington Stanley	L	1–2	Hughes	
46	27	A	Halifax Town	W	3–2	Warrender (2), Hughes	

1 own-goal

FA Cup

Match No.	Date	Venue	Opponents	Result		Scorers	Attend
1	Nov 21	A	Barnsley	L	2–5	Dunmore, Fenton	14

Andrews	Simpson	Brown	Spence J.	Spence R.	Hughes	Burgess	Dunmore	Warrender	Fenton	Porter	Linaker	Storey	Ware	Marlow	Stewart	Jukes	Patrick	Williams	Maddison	Bainbridge	
2	3	4	5	6	7	8	9	10	11												1
2	3	4	5	6	7	8	9	10	11												2
2	3	4	5	6	7	8	9	10	11												3
2	3	4	5	6	7	8	9	10	11												4
2	3	8	5	6		10	9	7	11	4											5
2	3	8	5	6		10	9	7	11	4											6
2	3	4	5			10	9	8	11	6	7										7
2	3	4	5			8	9		11	6	7	10									8
2	3	4	5			8	9			6	7	10	11								9
2	3	8	5	6			9		11	4	7	10									10
2	3	8	5	6			9		11	4	7	10									11
2	3	8	5	6			9		11	4	7	10									12
2	3			6	8		9		11		7	10		4	5						13
5	3			6	8		9		11		7	10		4		2					14
5	3			6	8		9		11		7	10					2	4			15
5	3	4		6	8		9		11		7	10					2				16
5	3	4		6	8		9		11		7	10					2				17
5	3	4		6	8		9		11		7	10					2				18
5	3	4		6	8		9		11		7	10					2				19
3		4		6	7	8	9		11			10			5		2		1		20
2		4		6	7	8	9		11			10			5		3		1		21
2	3	4		6	8		9		11		7	10			5				1		22
2	3	4		6	8		9		11		7	10			5						23
2	3	4		6	8		9		11		7	10			5						24
2		4				10	9				7	8	11	6	5		3				25
2		4				10	9				7	8	11	6	5		3				26
2		4				10	9				7	8	11	6	5		3				27
2		4			8	10	9				7		11	6	5		3				28
2		4			8	10	9				7		11	6	5		3				29
2		4				10	9				7	8	11	6	5		3				30
2		4				10	9				7	8	11	6	5		3				31
2		4			8	9			11		7	10		6	5		3				32
2		4			8	9			11		7	10		6	5		3				33
2		4		10		9			11		7	8		6	5		3				34
2		4		10		9			11		7	8		6	5		3				35
2		4		10		9			11		7	8		6	5		3				36
2		4		10		9			11		7	8		6	5		3				37
2		4		10		9			11		7	8		6	5		3				38
2		4		10		9			11		7	8		6	5		3		1		39
2		4		10	8	9			11		7			6	5		3		1		40
2		4		10		9			11		7	8		6	5		3		1		41
2		4		10		9			11		7	8		6	5		3		1		42
2		4		10	7	9			11			8		6	5		3		1		43
2		4		10	7	9			11			8		6	5		3		1		44
2		4		10	7	9						8	11	6	5		3		1		45
2		4		6	7			8	11			10			5		3		1	9	46
46	22	43	12	34	25	32	31	8	37	8	34	36	9	23	28	1	29	1	11	1	
		1		7	2	14	20	2	8	1	4	3			1						

Andrews	Simpson	Brown	Spence J.	Spence R.	Hughes	Burgess	Dunmore	Warrender	Fenton	Porter	Linaker	Storey	Ware	Marlow	Stewart	Jukes	Patrick	Williams	Maddison	Bainbridge	
5	3	4		6	8		9		11		7	10					2				1
1	1	1		1	1		1		1		1	1					1				
							1		1												

York City v Mansfield Town 17 October 1953 programme cover.

David Dunmore.

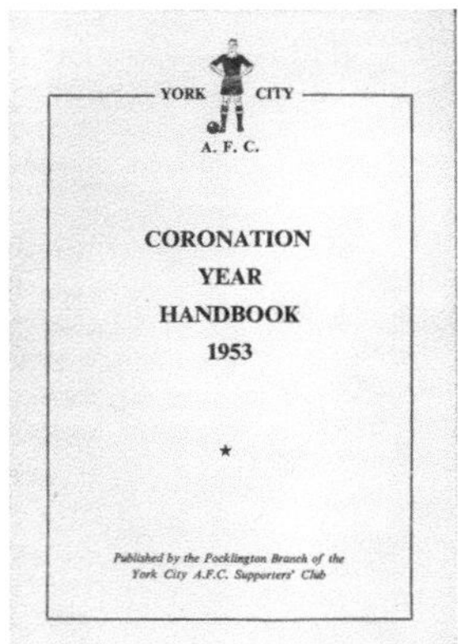

Coronation year handbook.

1954–55

Division Three North

Manager: Jim McCormick

	P	W	D	L	F	A	Pts
Barnsley	46	30	5	11	86	46	65
Accrington Stanley	46	25	11	10	96	67	61
Scunthorpe United	46	23	12	11	81	53	58
York City	46	24	10	12	92	63	58
Hartlepools United	46	25	5	16	64	49	55
Chesterfield	46	24	6	16	81	70	54
Gateshead	46	20	12	14	65	69	52
Workington	46	18	14	14	68	55	50
Stockport County	46	18	12	16	84	70	48
Oldham Athletic	46	19	10	17	74	68	48
Southport	46	16	16	14	47	44	48
Rochdale	46	17	14	15	69	66	48
Mansfield Town	46	18	9	19	65	71	45
Halifax Town	46	15	13	18	63	67	43
Darlington	46	14	14	18	62	73	42
Bradford Park Avenue	46	15	11	20	56	70	41
Barrow	46	17	6	23	70	89	40
Wrexham	46	13	12	21	65	77	38
Tranmere Rovers	46	13	11	22	55	70	37
Carlisle United	46	15	6	25	78	89	36
Bradford City	46	13	10	23	47	55	36
Crewe Alexandra	46	10	14	22	68	91	34
Grimsby Town	46	13	8	25	47	78	34
Chester	46	12	9	25	44	77	33

Did you know that?

A 6–2 win at Wrexham on the opening day heralded an outstanding campaign. Arthur Bottom, one of seven new signings making their debut that day, became the first City player to score a hat-trick in his first match for the club since a centre-forward by the name of Riley achieved the feat in December 1925 in the Midland League.

Bottom went on to score 39 League and Cup goals – a new City scoring record for a season.

Notable players also playing their first City game on 21 August 1954 were Tommy Forgan, Ernie Phillips, George Howe, and Norman Wilkinson.

Billy Fenton became the first City player since August 1947 to score four goals in a match when he achieved the feat at Carlisle United on 6 November 1954. It was in this game that Mick Granger made his League debut in goal for City.

Defender Percy Andrews played his last first-team game on 9 October 1954 at Gateshead.

City became the first side outside the top two divisions to reach an FA Cup semi-final replay.

The win at Blackpool marked the first occasion that City had beaten a club from the top division in the competition.

The attendance of 65,000 to see the first semi-final at Hillsborough is the largest ever to watch a York City game.

The average home League crowd at Bootham Crescent was 9,630.

In September 1954 manager James McCormick resigned, and first-team affairs were looked after by trainer Tom Lockie and secretary Bill Sherrington.

Match No.	Date	Venue	Opponents	Result		Scorers	Attend
1	Aug 21	A	Wrexham	W	6–2	Bottom (3), Wilkinson (2), McNab	11
2	23	H	Hartlepools United	W	1–0	McNab	10
3	28	H	Scunthorpe United	L	2–3	Wilkinson, Fenton	12
4	30	A	Hartlepools United	L	0–1		8
5	Sep 4	A	Barnsley	L	0–1		11
6	6	H	Workington	D	0–0		5
7	11	H	Bradford City	L	0–1		9
8	15	A	Workington	L	1–2	Bottom	6
9	18	A	Oldham Athletic	L	2–3	Brown, Bottom	8
10	20	H	Southport	D	1–1	Bottom (pen)	5
11	25	H	Halifax Town	W	2–1	Bottom, McNab	6
12	28	A	Southport	D	2–2	Bottom (2)	3
13	Oct 2	H	Stockport County	W	4–0	Brown, Spence, Bottom, Fenton	6
14	9	A	Gateshead	D	1–1	Bottom	6
15	16	H	Darlington	W	3–1	Wilkinson, Storey, Fenton	11
16	23	A	Chesterfield	W	3–0	Fenton (2), Hughes	10
17	30	H	Crewe Alexandra	W	3–1	Bottom (2), Wilkinson	9
18	Nov 6	A	Carlisle United	W	5–4	Fenton (4), Bottom	5
19	13	H	Chester	W	5–0	Hughes, Bottom (2), Fenton (2)	6
20	27	H	Bradford PA	L	1–2	Wilkinson	8
21	Dec 4	A	Rochdale	D	1–1	Wilkinson	4
22	18	H	Wrexham	D	3–3	Bottom (2, 2 pens), Storey	6
23	25	H	Mansfield Town	W	3–1	Bottom, Storey, Fenton	10
24	27	A	Mansfield Town	W	2–1	Bottom, Wilkinson	9
25	Jan 1	A	Scunthorpe United	W	2–1	Wilkinson, Fenton	10
26	15	H	Barnsley	L	1–3	Spence	7
27	Feb 5	H	Oldham Athletic	W	2–1	Wilkinson (2)	9
28	12	A	Halifax Town	D	3–3	Brown, Bottom, Storey	6
29	21	A	Stockport County	W	2–1	Bottom (2)	2
30	26	H	Gateshead	W	2–1	Bottom, Wilkinson	13
31	Mar 5	A	Darlington	L	0–1		10
32	16	H	Chesterfield	W	3–2	Bottom (2, 1 pen), Fenton	10
33	19	A	Crewe Alexandra	W	3–2	Wilkinson (2), Bottom	7
34	Apr 2	A	Chester	W	2–1	Bottom, Fenton	6
35	4	A	Bradford City	W	3–2	Bottom, Wilkinson, Fenton	6
36	8	H	Accrington Stanley	D	1–1	Bottom	19
37	9	H	Grimsby Town	D	0–0		12
38	11	A	Accrington Stanley	D	2–2	Bottom, Wilkinson	15
39	13	H	Carlisle United	W	2–1	Hughes, Wilkinson	8
40	16	A	Bradford PA	W	3–1	Phillips (pen), Fenton (2)	9
41	18	H	Tranmere Rovers	W	1–0	Brown	10
42	23	H	Rochdale	W	2–0	Fenton (2)	9
43	27	A	Grimsby Town	L	1–2	Fenton	7
44	30	A	Tranmere Rovers	L	0–1		6
45	May 2	H	Barrow	L	1–4	Wilkinson	8
46	5	A	Barrow	W	5–1	Brown, Wilkinson, Hughes (2), Fenton	4

A

FA Cup

1	Nov 20	H	Scarborough	W	3–2	Wilkinson, Bottom, Spence	10
2	Dec 11	A	Dorchester Town	W	5–2	Bottom (3), Wilkinson, Fenton	5
3	Jan 8	A	Blackpool	W	2–0	Storey, Fenton	26
4	29	A	Bishop Auckland	W	3–1	Bottom (2, 1 pen), Storey	15
5	Feb 19	H	Tottenham Hotspur	W	3–1	Wilkinson (2), Fenton	21
6	Mar 12	A	Notts County	W	1–0	Bottom	47
SF	Mar 26	N*	Newcastle United	D	1–1	Bottom	65
SFr	Mar 30	N#	Newcastle United	L	0–2		58

* Played at Hillsborough. # At Roker Park.

A

Phillips	Howe	Brown	Stewart	Spence	Slatter	Bottom	Wilkinson	McNab	Fenton	Charlesworth	Storey	Linaker	Bainbridge	Andrews	Hughes	Whiteside	Granger	Marlow	Wardle	Jones	Smith	
2	3	4	5	6	7	8	9	10	11													1
2	3	4	5	6	7	8	9	10	11													2
2	3	4	5	6	7	8	9	10	11													3
2	3	4	5	6	7	8	9		11	10												4
2	3	4	5	6	7	8	9		11		10											5
2	3	4	5	6	7	8	9		11		10											6
2	3	4	5	6	7	8	9		11		10											7
2	3	4	5	6		8		11			10	7	9									8
2	3	4	5	6		8	9	10	11			7										9
2	3	4	5	6		8		11			10	7	9									10
2	3	4		6	7	9		10	11		8			5								11
2	3	4		6	7	9		10	11		8			5								12
2	3	4		6		8	9		11		10			5	7							13
2	3	4		6		9			11		10			5	7	8						14
2	3	4	5	6		8	9		11		10				7							15
2	3	4	5	6	7	8	9		11						10							16
2	3	4	5	6		8	9		11		10				7							17
2	3	4	5	6		8	9		11		10				7		1					18
2	3	4	5	6		8	9		11		10				7		1					19
2	3	4	5	6		8	9		11		10				7		1					20
2	3		5	6		8	9		11		10				7		1	4				21
2	3	4	5	6		8	9		11		10				7		1					22
2	3	4	5	6		8	9		11		10				7							23
2	3	4	5	6		8	9		11		10				7							24
2	3	4	5	6		8	9		11		10				7							25
2	3	4	5	6	7	8	9		11		10											26
2	3	4		6		8	9	10	11						7				5			27
2	3	4	5	6		8	9		11		10				7							28
2	3	4	5	6		8	9		11		10				7							29
2	3	4	5	6		8	9		11		10				7							30
2	3	4	5	6	7	9		10	11						8							31
2	3	4		6		8	9		11		10				7				5			32
2	3	4	5	6		8	9		11		10				7							33
2	3			6		8	9		11		10				7				5	4		34
2	3	4		6		8	9		11		10				7				5			35
2	3	4	5	6		8	9		11		10				7							36
2	3	4	5	6		8	9	10	11						7							37
2	3	4	5	6		8	9	10	11						7							38
2	3	4	5	6			9	10	11						7	8	1					39
2	3	4	5	6			9	10	11						7	8	1					40
2	3	4	5	6			9	10	11						7	8						41
2	3	4	5	6				10	11				9		7	8						42
2	3	4	5	6			9	10	11						7	8						43
2	3	4		6	8		9	10	11						7				5			44
2	3	4		6			9	10	11						7	8			5			45
2	3	4		6			9		11			7			10	8					5	46
46	46	44	35	46	13	38	39	19	44	1	28	4	3	4	33	8	7	1	6	1	1	
1		5		2		31	19	3	22		4				5							

Phillips	Howe	Brown	Stewart	Spence	Slatter	Bottom	Wilkinson	McNab	Fenton	Charlesworth	Storey	Linaker	Bainbridge	Andrews	Hughes	Whiteside	Granger	Marlow	Wardle	Jones	Smith	
2	3	4	5	6		8	9		11		10				7		1					1
2	3	4	5	6		8	9		11		10				7		1					2
2	3	4	5	6		8	9		11		10				7							3
2	3	4	5	6		8	9		11		10				7							4
2	3	4	5	6		8	9		11		10				7							5
2	3	4	5	6		8	9		11		10				7							6
2	3	4	5	6		8	9	10	11						7							SF
2	3	4	5	6		8	9		11		10				7							SFr
8	8	8	8	8		8	8	1	8		7				8		2					
				1		8	4		3		2											

York City v Hartlepools United 23 August 1954 programme cover.

York City v Scarborough 20 November 1954 programme cover.

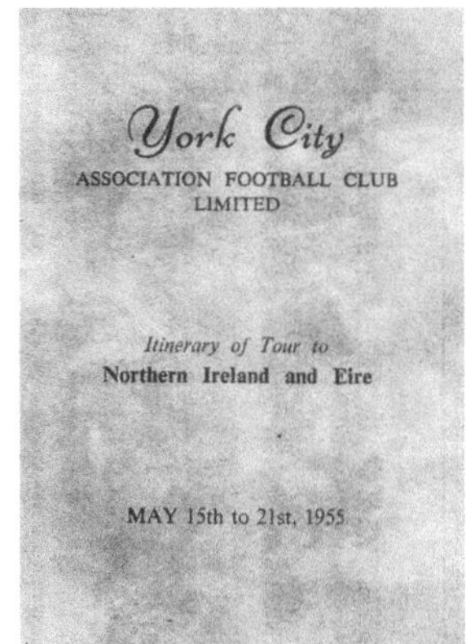

York City
ASSOCIATION FOOTBALL CLUB
LIMITED
Itinerary of Tour to
Northern Ireland and Eire
MAY 15th to 21st, 1955

Itinerary booklet cover for the Tour of Northern Ireland and Eire 15–21 May 1955.

1955–56

Division Three North

Manager: Sam Bartram

	P	W	D	L	F	A	Pts
Grimsby Town	46	31	6	9	76	29	68
Derby County	46	28	7	11	110	55	63
Accrington Stanley	46	25	9	12	92	57	59
Hartlepools United	46	26	5	15	81	60	57
Southport	46	23	11	12	66	53	57
Chesterfield	46	25	4	17	94	66	54
Stockport County	46	21	9	16	90	61	51
Bradford City	46	18	13	15	78	64	49
Scunthorpe United	46	20	8	18	75	63	48
Workington	46	19	9	18	75	63	47
York City	46	19	9	18	85	72	47
Rochdale	46	17	13	16	66	84	47
Gateshead	46	17	11	18	77	84	45
Wrexham	46	16	10	20	66	73	42
Darlington	46	16	9	21	60	73	41
Tranmere Rovers	46	16	9	21	59	84	41
Chester	46	13	14	19	52	82	40
Mansfield Town	46	14	11	21	84	81	39
Halifax Town	46	14	11	21	66	76	39
Oldham Athletic	46	10	18	18	76	86	38
Carlisle United	46	15	8	23	71	95	38
Barrow	46	12	9	25	61	83	33
Bradford Park Avenue	46	13	7	26	61	122	33
Crewe Alexandra	46	9	10	27	50	105	28

Did you know that?

For the second successive season Arthur Bottom netted 31 League goals.

On 27 December 1955 Bottom became the first City player to be sent off since the war, when he was dismissed in a home game against Mansfield Town.

During the campaign Billy Fenton, joint record holder with Bottom for League goals (31) netted in a season, reached 100 League and Cup goals for City when he scored his first goal in a win at Wrexham on 17 December 1955.

On 24 March 1956 Ron Spence suffered a serious injury that was to keep him out of first-team action until November 1957.

Inside-forward Sid Storey played his last game for the club on 14 April 1956 at Gateshead after 354 senior appearances and 42 goals.

Charlton Athletic goalkeeper and wartime guest player for City, Sam Bartram was appointed manager on 12 March 1956.

Average home League attendance was 10,291 – the second highest in the club's history – and no fewer than 10 games drew five-figure crowds.

Match No.	Date	Venue	Opponents	Result		Scorers	Attend
1	Aug 20	H	Wrexham	L	1–3	Wilkinson	12
2	24	A	Crewe Alexandra	W	2–1	Bottom, Opp. og	6
3	27	A	Halifax Town	W	4–2	Fenton (2), Hughes, Bottom	8
4	29	H	Crewe Alexandra	D	1–1	Fenton	11
5	Sep 3	H	Bradford City	L	0–2		11
6	5	A	Hartlepools United	W	1–0	Fenton	9
7	10	A	Scunthorpe United	D	1–1	Fenton	9
8	12	H	Hartlepools United	W	3–0	Colbridge, Tait, Fenton	10
9	17	H	Oldham Athletic	W	2–0	Bottom (2)	11
10	19	H	Stockport County	W	1–0	Bottom	10
11	24	A	Workington	D	0–0		5
12	28	A	Derby County	L	2–3	Bottom, Prescott	13
13	Oct 1	A	Tranmere Rovers	L	1–2	Bottom	6
14	8	H	Rochdale	L	1–2	Brown	9
15	15	A	Southport	D	3–3	Hughes, Bottom, Prescott	3
16	22	H	Grimsby Town	L	3–4	Colbridge (2), Wilkinson	14
17	29	A	Carlisle United	L	1–3	Wilkinson	6
18	Nov 5	H	Chester	W	3–0	Bottom (2), Storey	8
19	12	A	Barrow	W	1–0	Fenton	5
20	26	A	Darlington	W	4–1	Fenton (2), Hughes, Bottom	8
21	Dec 3	H	Gateshead	W	1–0	Bottom	9
22	17	A	Wrexham	W	5–4	Wilkinson (3), Fenton (2)	5
23	24	H	Halifax Town	W	5–0	Hughes (2), Bottom, Wilkinson, Colbridge	9
24	26	A	Mansfield Town	L	1–3	Spence	6
25	27	H	Mansfield Town	D	1–1	Bottom (pen)	14
26	31	A	Bradford City	L	1–3	Bottom	13
27	Jan 21	A	Oldham Athletic	D	2–2	Hughes, Wilkinson	5
28	Feb 4	H	Workington	D	1–1	Bottom (pen)	6
29	11	H	Tranmere Rovers	L	2–4	Brown, Spence	6
30	18	A	Rochdale	L	1–3	Fenton	3
31	25	H	Southport	L	0–1		9
32	Mar 3	A	Grimsby Town	L	1–2	Bottom	14
33	10	H	Carlisle United	W	3–1	Bottom (2), Hughes	9
34	14	A	Bradford PA	L	1–2	Hobson	3
35	17	A	Accrington Stanley	W	3–1	Colbridge (2), Bottom	9
36	24	H	Barrow	W	3–2	Bottom, Storey, Colbridge	8
37	30	H	Chesterfield	W	3–1	Colbridge (2), Bottom	13
38	31	A	Chester	D	2–2	Prescott, Bottom	6
39	Apr 2	A	Chesterfield	L	1–3	Bottom	9
40	7	H	Darlington	W	4–0	Bottom (2, 1 pen), Prescott, Colbridge	8
41	9	H	Scunthorpe United	D	0–0		9
42	14	A	Gateshead	L	2–3	Bottom (2)	2
43	16	H	Accrington Stanley	L	0–1		8
44	21	H	Bradford PA	W	5–0	Wilkinson (2), Bottom, Prescott, Colbridge	8
45	23	H	Derby County	W	1–0	Bottom	14
46	28	A	Stockport County	L	1–4	Bottom	9
							A
						1 own-goal	

FA Cup

1	Nov 19	A	Rochdale	W	1–0	Wilkinson	9
2	Dec 10	H	Mansfield Town	W	2–1	Bottom, Hughes	13
3	Jan 7	A	Swansea Town	W	2–1	Colbridge, Bottom	25
4	28	H	Sunderland	D	0–0		22
r	Feb 1	A	Sunderland	L	1–2	Fenton	43
							A

Phillips	Howe	Brown	Stewart	Spence	Hughes	Bottom	Wilkinson	Storey	Fenton	Prescott	Colbridge	Tait	Wardle	Mollatt	Linaker	Hobson	Granger	
2	3	4	5	6	7	8	9	10	11									1
2	3	4	5	6	7	8	9	10	11									2
2	3	4	5	6	7	8	9	10	11									3
2	3	4	5	6	7	8	9	10	11									4
2	3	4	5	6	7	8		10	11	9								5
2	3	4	5	6	7	8		10	11	9								6
2	3	4	5	6	7	8	9	10	11									7
2	3	4	5	6		8		10	11		7	9						8
2	3	4	5	6		8		10	11		7	9						9
2		4	5	6		8		10	11		7	9	3					10
2	3	4	5	6	7	8		10	11	9								11
2	3	4	5	6	7	8		10	11	9								12
2	3	4	5	6	7	8	9		11	10								13
2	3	4	5	6	7	8	9		11	10								14
2	3	4	5	6	7	8	9		11	10								15
2	3	4	5	6	7	8	9	10			11							16
2	3	4	5	6	7	8	9	10			11							17
2	3	4	5	6	7	8	9	10	11									18
2	3	4	5	6	7	8	9	10	11									19
2	3	4	5	6	7	8	9	10	11									20
2	3		5	6	7	8	9	10	11					4				21
2	3	4	5	6		8	9	10	11						7			22
2	3	4	5	6	7	8	9	10			11							23
2	3	4	5	6	7	8	9	10			11							24
2	3	4	5	6	7	8	9	10	11									25
2	3		5	6	7	8	9	10	11					4				26
2	3	4	5	6	7		9	10		8	11							27
2		4	5	6	7	8	9	10	11				3					28
2	3	4	5	6	7		9	10	11	8								29
2	3	4	5	6	10		9		11	8	7							30
2	3	4	5	6	7	8		10	11	9								31
2	3	4	5	6		8	9	10	11		7							32
2	3	4	5	6	7	9		10	11							8		33
2	3	4	5	6	7	9		10	11							8		34
2	3	4	5	6	7	9		10			11					8	1	35
2	3	4	5	6	7	9		10			11			8			1	36
2	3	4	5		7	9		10		8	11			6			1	37
2	3	4	5		7	9		10		8	11			6			1	38
2	3	4	5		7	9		10		8	11			6			1	39
2	3		5		10	9				8	11		4	6		7		40
2	3		5		8	9		10			11		4	6		7		41
2	3	4	5		8	9		10			11			6		7		42
2	3	4	5		10	9				8	11			6		7		43
2	3	4	5			8	9			10	11			6		7		44
2	3	4	5		10	8	9				11			6		7		45
2	3	4	5			8	9			10	11			6		7		46
46	44	42	46	36	39	43	27	37	29	18	22	3	4	13	1	10	5	
		2		2	7	31	10	2	12	5	11	1				1		

Phillips	Howe	Brown	Stewart	Spence	Hughes	Bottom	Wilkinson	Storey	Fenton	Prescott	Colbridge	Tait	Wardle	Mollatt	Linaker	Hobson	Granger	
2	3	4	5	6	7	8	9	10	11									1
2	3	4	5	6	7	8	9	10	11									2
2	3	4	5	6	7	8	9	10			11							3
2	3	4	5	6	7	8	9	10	11									4
2	3	4	5	6	7	8	9	10	11									r
5	5	5	5	5	5	5	5	5	4		1							
					1	2	1		1		1							

F.A. CUP — FOURTH ROUND
YORK CITY v. SUNDERLAND
SATURDAY, 28th JANUARY, 1956
OFFICIAL PROGRAMME — PRICE SIXPENCE
ARMY & NAVY STORES
"GET THE BEST!"—WE HAVE IT
SHIRTS, HOSE, MACS., RAINCOATS and
ALL MEN'S WEAR
The Famous "BEVA" WATERPROOF BOOTS
OVERALLS and BOILER SUITS
FOSSGATE and PAVEMENT CORNER
YORK
FOSSGATE and PAVEMENT CORNER

York City v Sunderland 28 January 1956 programme cover.

Clive Colbridge.

1956–57

Division Three North

Manager: Sam Bartram

	P	W	D	L	F	A	Pts
Derby County	46	26	11	9	111	53	63
Hartlepools United	46	25	9	12	90	63	59
Accrington Stanley	46	25	8	13	95	64	58
Workington	46	24	10	12	93	63	58
Stockport County	46	23	8	15	91	75	54
Chesterfield	46	22	9	15	96	79	53
York City	46	21	10	15	75	61	52
Hull City	46	21	10	15	84	69	52
Bradford City	46	22	8	16	78	68	52
Barrow	46	21	9	16	76	62	51
Halifax Town	46	21	7	18	65	70	49
Wrexham	46	19	10	17	97	74	48
Rochdale	46	18	12	16	65	65	48
Scunthorpe United	46	15	15	16	71	69	45
Carlisle United	46	16	13	17	76	85	45
Mansfield Town	46	17	10	19	91	90	44
Gateshead	46	17	10	19	72	90	44
Darlington	46	17	8	21	82	95	42
Oldham Athletic	46	12	15	19	66	74	39
Bradford Park Avenue	46	16	3	27	66	93	35
Chester	46	10	13	23	55	84	33
Southport	46	10	12	24	52	94	32
Tranmere Rovers	46	7	13	26	51	91	27
Crewe Alexandra	46	6	9	31	43	110	21

Did you know that?

A crowd of 7,099 saw the public practice match between the Reds (first team) and the Blues (second team) in August 1956. Appearing in this game was a youthful Barry Jackson, who was to make a big impact in the years ahead.

A total of £12,000 (big by 1956 values) was spent on new signings Alan Monkhouse ex-Newcastle United, Peter Wragg ex-Sheffield United and Jim Cairney from Portsmouth. The first two made their City debut on the opening day at Accrington Stanley.

On 2 February 1957 City recorded their biggest-ever win in the Football League when they beat Southport 9–1.

Arthur Bottom netted four goals in this match and topped the scoring charts for the third successive season.

The average home League crowd was 9,414 and there were six five-figure attendances at Bootham Crescent, including a record crowd to see an opening fixture (15,318) when Workington were the visitors.

Match No.	Date	Venue	Opponents	Result		Scorers	Attend
1	Aug 18	A	Accrington Stanley	L	0–3		11
2	20	H	Workington	D	2–2	Monkhouse, Colbridge	15
3	25	H	Tranmere Rovers	W	1–0	Wragg	12
4	29	A	Workington	L	2–3	Wilkinson, Wragg (pen)	9
5	Sep 1	A	Halifax Town	D	0–0		8
6	3	H	Carlisle United	W	2–0	Bottom, Fenton	11
7	8	A	Oldham Athletic	L	1–3	Hughes	8
8	15	H	Mansfield Town	W	2–0	Colbridge, Fenton	9
9	17	H	Chester	L	0–1		9
10	22	A	Southport	D	1–1	Bottom	4
11	26	A	Chester	W	4–3	Hughes, Wilkinson, Wragg, Fenton	4
12	29	H	Chesterfield	L	1–2	Bottom	8
13	Oct 6	H	Hull City	W	2–1	Wilkinson, Fenton	10
14	13	A	Barrow	W	2–1	Brown, Hughes	5
15	20	H	Scunthorpe United	L	0–2		8
16	27	A	Bradford PA	W	2–0	Wilkinson (2)	9
17	Nov 3	H	Gateshead	W	1–0	Wilkinson	7
18	10	A	Wrexham	D	1–1	Fenton	12
19	24	A	Crewe Alexandra	D	1–1	Bottom	4
20	Dec 1	H	Darlington	W	1–0	Bottom	8
21	15	H	Accrington Stanley	W	3–1	Bottom (pen), Wilkinson, Opp. og	8,
22	22	A	Tranmere Rovers	D	3–3	Bottom, Wilkinson, Wragg	3
23	25	H	Hartlepools United	D	3–3	Bottom (pen), Wilkinson, Fenton	8,
24	26	A	Hartlepools United	L	0–2		6,
25	29	H	Halifax Town	L	1–2	Fenton	8,
26	Jan 1	A	Carlisle United	L	0–2		7,
27	5	H	Bradford City	W	3–1	Bottom, Wilkinson, Fenton	10
28	12	H	Oldham Athletic	W	2–1	Bottom (2)	9,
29	19	A	Mansfield Town	L	1–4	Wragg	6
30	26	A	Bradford City	W	2–0	Hughes, Fenton	13
31	Feb 2	H	Southport	W	9–1	Bottom (4, 1 pen), Wilkinson (2) Brown, Wragg, Fenton	8
32	9	A	Chesterfield	W	4–3	Bottom (2), Hill, Fenton	16,
33	16	A	Hull City	D	1–1	Wragg	15
34	23	H	Barrow	W	1–0	Fenton	8
35	Mar 2	A	Scunthorpe United	L	1–2	Fenton	7
36	9	H	Bradford PA	L	1–2	Bottom	8
37	16	A	Gateshead	W	2–0	Brown, Bottom (pen)	4
38	23	H	Wrexham	W	1–0	Bottom	8
39	30	A	Derby County	L	0–1		21,
40	Apr 6	H	Crewe Alexandra	W	2–1	Bottom, Wilkinson	7,
41	13	A	Darlington	W	4–2	Hill (2), Wilkinson, Fenton	4,
42	19	H	Stockport County	D	0–0		11,
43	20	H	Rochdale	W	4–0	Wilkinson (3), Wragg	7,
44	22	A	Stockport County	L	0–3		7,
45	27	A	Rochdale	L	0–1		4,
46	29	H	Derby County	D	1–1	Fenton	9,
							A
						1 own-goal	

FA Cup

1	Nov 17	A	Southport	D	0–0		5
r	21	H	Southport	W	2–1	Wragg, Wilkinson	8,
2	Dec 8	A	Hull City	L	1–2	Bottom	24,
							A

Phillips	Howe	Brown	Stewart A.	Mollatt	Hughes	Bottom	Monkhouse	Wragg	Colbridge	Hobson	Wilkinson	Cairney	Fenton	Powell	Wardle	Steel	Stoddart	Hill	Stewart J.	
2	3	4	5	6	7	8	9	10	11											1
2	3	4	5	6		8	9	10	11	7										2
2	3	4	5	6		8	9	10	11	7										3
2	3	4	5	6			8	10	11	7	9									4
2	3	4	5	6	7		8	10	11		9									5
2	3	4		6	7	8	9	10				5	11							6
2	3	4		6	7	8	9	10				5	11							7
2	3	4	5	6		8	9	10	7				11							8
2	3	4	5	6		8	9	10	7				11							9
2	3	4	5	6	7	8		10			9		11							10
2	3	4	5	6	7	8		10			9		11							11
2	3	4	5	6	7	8		10			9		11							12
	3	4			7		8	6			9	5	11	10	2					13
	3	4			7	8	9	6			9	5		11	2					14
		4	5		7	8	9	6	11					10	2	3				15
	3	4	5		7	8		10			9		11		2		6			16
	3	4	5		7	8		10			9		11		2		6			17
	3	4	5			8		10			9		11		2		6	7		18
	3	4	5			8		10	11	7	9	6			2					19
	3		5	4	7	8		10		11	9	6			2					20
2	3	4	5			8		10		7	9	6	11							21
2	3	4	5			8		10		7	9	6	11							22
2	3	4	5			8		10		7	9	6	11							23
2	3	4	5	8				10		7	9	6	11							24
	3	4		6		8		10	7		9	5	11		2					25
	3	4		6		8		10			9	5	11		2				7	26
2	3	4		6		8		10		7	9	5	11							27
2	3	4		6		8		10		7	9	5	11							28
2	3	4		6		8		10		7	9	5	11							29
2	3	4		6	7	8		10			9	5	11							30
2	3	4		6		8		10			9	5	11					7		31
2	3	4		6		8		10			9	5	11					7		32
2	3	4		6		8		10			9	5	11					7		33
2	3	4		6		8		10			9	5	11					7		34
2	3	4		6		8		10			9	5	11					7		35
2	3	4		6		8		10			9	5	11					7		36
2	3	4		6	7	8		10			9	5	11							37
2	3	4		6	7	8		10			9	5	11							38
2	3	4		6	7	8		10			9	5	11							39
2	3	4		6	7	8		10			9	5	11							40
2	3	4		6	7			10			8	5	11					9		41
2	3	4		6	7			10			8	5	11					9		42
2	3	4		6	7			10			8	5	11					9		43
2	3	4		6	7			10			8	5	11					9		44
2	3			6	7	8		4			10	5	11					9		45
2	3			6	7			4	10		8	5	11					9		46
36	45	43	20	36	24	37	12	46	11	12	38	32	37	3	10	1	3	13	1	
		3			4	21	1	8	2		17		15					3		

Phillips	Howe	Brown	Stewart A.	Mollatt	Hughes	Bottom	Monkhouse	Wragg	Colbridge	Hobson	Wilkinson	Cairney	Fenton	Powell	Wardle	Steel	Stoddart	Hill	Stewart J.	
2		4	5		7	8		10			9	6	11		3					1
	3	4	5			8		10	11	7	9	6			2					r
	3	4	5		7	8		10	11		9	6			2					2
1	2	3	3		2	3		3	2	1	3	3	1		3					
						1		1			1									

SOUTHPORT FOOTBALL CLUB LTD.
Official Programme 3D. Nº 1231
Holland Toffee
Best on Earth
F.A. Challenge Cup—First Round
Southport
Versus
York City
SATURDAY, 17th NOVEMBER, 1956
Kick-off 2-15 p.m.

Southport v York City 17 November 1956 programme cover.

Jimmy Cairney.

Alan Monkhouse.

1957–58

Division Three North

Manager: Sam Bartram

	P	W	D	L	F	A	Pts
Scunthorpe United	46	29	8	9	88	50	66
Accrington Stanley	46	25	9	12	83	61	59
Bradford City	46	21	15	10	73	49	57
Bury	46	23	10	13	94	62	56
Hull City	46	19	15	12	78	67	53
Mansfield Town	46	22	8	16	100	92	52
Halifax Town	46	20	11	15	83	69	51
Chesterfield	46	18	15	13	71	69	51
Stockport County	46	18	11	17	74	67	47
Rochdale	46	19	8	19	79	67	46
Tranmere Rovers	46	18	10	18	82	76	46
Wrexham	46	17	12	17	61	63	46
York City	46	17	12	17	68	76	46
Gateshead	46	15	15	16	68	76	45
Oldham Athletic	46	14	17	15	72	84	45
Carlisle United	46	19	6	21	80	78	44
Hartlepools United	46	16	12	18	73	76	44
Barrow	46	13	15	18	66	74	41
Workington	46	14	13	19	72	81	41
Darlington	46	17	7	22	78	89	41
Chester	46	13	13	20	73	81	39
Bradford Park Avenue	46	13	11	22	68	95	37
Southport	46	11	6	29	52	88	28
Crewe Alexandra	46	8	7	31	47	93	23

Match No.	Date	Venue	Opponents	Result		Scorers	Attend
1	Aug 24	A	Hull City	W	1–0	Hughes	17
2	26	H	Bradford City	W	2–0	Bottom (2)	12
3	31	H	Barrow	D	0–0		9
4	Sep 4	A	Bradford City	L	2–3	Wragg (pen), Fenton	10
5	7	A	Oldham Athletic	W	3–2	Wilkinson (2), Colbridge	8
6	10	A	Carlisle United	L	1–2	Fenton	9
7	14	H	Bury	W	2–1	Bottom, Fenton	10
8	16	H	Carlisle United	L	0–5		6
9	21	A	Accrington Stanley	L	0–3		6
10	25	A	Bradford PA	W	2–0	Bottom, Wragg	5
11	28	H	Chester	L	1–2	Fenton	7
12	30	H	Bradford PA	W	3–0	Hughes, Robertson, Wragg	4
13	Oct 5	A	Chesterfield	L	0–2		8
14	12	H	Halifax Town	D	1–1	Robertson	6
15	19	A	Mansfield Town	L	1–2	Robertson	7
16	26	H	Gateshead	D	2–2	Wragg, Metcalfe	6
17	Nov 2	A	Darlington	L	0–2		7
18	9	H	Scunthorpe United	D	0–0		8
19	23	H	Crewe Alexandra	W	3–1	Wragg, Hughes, Robertson	6
20	30	A	Rochdale	L	1–2	Metcalfe	6
21	Dec 14	A	Stockport County	L	1–2	Robertson	10
22	21	H	Hull City	W	3–1	Wilkinson, Bottom, Fenton	7
23	25	A	Hartlepools United	D	2–2	Brown, Hughes	6
24	26	H	Hartlepools United	D	2–2	Bottom, Powell	10
25	28	A	Barrow	L	0–1		6
26	Jan 1	A	Tranmere Rovers	L	1–6	Bottom	6
27	11	H	Oldham Athletic	D	2–2	Bottom, Wilkinson	8
28	18	A	Bury	L	1–4	Farmer	8
29	Feb 1	H	Accrington Stanley	L	0–3		7
30	8	A	Chester	L	2–9	Phillips, Farmer	5
31	15	H	Chesterfield	D	3–3	Bottom (pen), Farmer, Hughes	4
32	22	A	Crewe Alexandra	W	4–3	Farmer (2), Wilkinson, Wragg	3
33	Mar 1	H	Mansfield Town	W	3–1	Hughes, Wilkinson, Wragg	6
34	22	A	Halifax Town	L	1–2	Wragg	5
35	24	A	Gateshead	D	0–0		3
36	29	H	Wrexham	L	1–2	Wragg	4
37	Apr 4	A	Southport	W	1–0	Hughes	4
38	5	A	Workington	D	0–0		4
39	7	H	Southport	W	1–0	Wilkinson	6
40	12	H	Rochdale	W	1–0	Wardle	5
41	16	A	Wrexham	D	2–2	Wilkinson, Opp. og	7
42	19	A	Scunthorpe United	W	2–1	Farmer (2)	10
43	23	H	Tranmere Rovers	W	4–0	Farmer (3), Patterson	7
44	26	H	Stockport County	D	0–0		8
45	28	H	Workington	W	3–0	Wilkinson (2), Wragg	5
46	May 1	H	Darlington	W	3–0	Farmer (2), Wragg	5
							A

FA Cup

Round	Date	Venue	Opponents	Result		Scorers	Attend
1	Nov 16	H	Chesterfield	W	1–0	Fenton	8
2	Dec 7	A	South Shields	W	3–1	Robertson, Wilkinson, Bottom	18
3	Jan 8	H	Birmingham City	W	3–0	Bottom, Wragg, Wilkinson	19
4	25	H	Bolton Wanderers	D	0–0		23
r	29	A	Bolton Wanderers	L	0–3		34
							A

Did you know that?

The last season of regional football and City failed on goal average to make the top 12 of the Northern Section, thus becoming founder members of the new Division Four. This, after a tremendous bid at the end when they went unbeaten in the last 10 games.

Two heavy defeats cost them dear. On New Year's Day 1958 they went down 6–1 at Tranmere Rovers, and on 8 February they suffered their heaviest post-war reverse when they crashed 9–2 at Chester, where they lost 12–0 (the club record defeat) almost 22 years earlier.

On 14 September 1957 17-year-old inside-forward Colin Addison made his senior debut.

Two days later the club suffered their heaviest post-war home defeat when they lost 5–0 to Carlisle United. City finished this game with nine men – 'keeper Tommy Forgan went off injured and Arthur Bottom was sent off.

Ron Spence returned to first-team action, after an absence of 18 months through injury, on 2 November 1957 at Darlington.

Arthur Bottom played his last game on 15 February 1958 prior to his transfer to Newcastle United. He scored 105 goals in 158 League and Cup games for City.

Top scorer was Terry Farmer, who was signed from Rotherham United in January 1958.

Three more of the FA Cup semi-final side made their final appearances this term. Captain Ernie Phillips bowed out at Wrexham, where he had made his debut in August 1954, on 16 April 1958. Billy Fenton's last game came earlier that month at home to Southport and Gordon Brown's came on the last day of the season. In total these players made over 800 appearances for the club in the 1950s.

Average home League attendance was 7,270.

For the third time in four seasons City progressed beyond the third round of the FA Cup. They recorded their biggest-ever win over opposition from the top division when they beat Birmingham City 3–0 in the third round before losing to eventual winners Bolton Wanderers after a replay in the next stage.

Phillips	Howe	Wragg	Cairney	Mollatt	Hughes	Bottom	Wilkinson	Robertson	Fenton	Colbridge	Brown	Johnson	Longden	Addison	Hill	Granger	Patterson	Powell	Boyes	Metcalfe	Spence	Greensmith	Farmer	Steel	Wardle	
2	3	4	5	6	7	8	9	10	11																	1
2	3	4	5	6	7	8	9		11	10																2
2	3	4	5	6	7	8	9		11	10																3
2	3	8	5	6	7		9	10	11		4															4
2	3	8	5		7		9		11	10	4	6														5
2	3	8	5				9		11	10	4	6	7													6
2	3	6	5		7	8	9		11		4			10												7
2	3	6	5		7	8			11		4			10	9											8
2		10	5	6	7			9	11		4	3		8		1										9
2	3	10	5	6	7	8	9		11		4					1										10
2	3	10		6	7	8	9		11		4	5				1										11
2	3	10		6	7		9	8	11		4	5				1										12
2	3		5	6	7		9		11		4					1	8	10								13
2	3		5	6	7		8	9	11		4			10		1										14
2	3	10	5	6	7		8	9	11		4					1										15
2	3	10	5	6			8	9							7	1			4	11						16
2	3	10			7		8	9				5				1			4	11	6					17
2	3	6			7	8	9	10	11		4	5				1										18
2	3	6			7	8	9	10	11		4	5				1										19
2	3	6			7	8	9	10			4					1			5	11						20
2	3	6			7	8	9	10			4	5				1		11								21
2	3	6			7	9	8	10	11		4	5				1										22
2	3	6			7	9	8	10			4	5				1		11								23
2	3	6				9	8	10			4	5			7	1		11								24
2	3	6		10		9	8				4		7	11		1			5							25
2	3					9	8		11		4				7	1		10	5		6					26
2	3	10			7	9	8				4	5				1					6	11				27
2	3	10			7		9				4	5				1					6	11	8			28
2		10	5		7		9				4					1					6	11	8	3		29
2	3	6	5		7	9		10			4					1						11	8			30
	3	6	5		10	9			11		4					1						7	8		2	31
2	3	10	6		7		9				4	5				1						11	8			32
2	3	10	6		7		9				4	5				1						11	8			33
2	3	4	6		7		9					5				1						11	8	10		34
2	3	10	5		7		9				4			8		1					6	11				35
2	3	10			7		9				4	5				1					6	11	8			36
	3			6	7			9				5		10		1	4					11	8		2	37
	3	10		6			9					5		11		1	4					7	8		2	38
	3	10		6			9		11			5				1	4					7	8		2	39
	3	10		6			9					5			7	1	4					11	8		2	40
2	3	10		6			9					5				1	4					11	8		7	41
	3	10		6			9					5			7	1	4					11	8		2	42
	3	10		6			9					5			7		4					11	8		2	43
	3	10		6			9					5			7		4					11	8		2	44
	3	10					9				4	5			7						6	11	8		2	45
	3	10					9				4	5			7						6	11	8		2	46
36	44	42	21	21	32	19	41	17	21	4	32	28	2	8	10	34	9	5	5	3	9	20	18	2	11	
1		11			7	9	10	5	5	1	1						1	1		2			12		1	

Phillips	Howe	Wragg	Cairney	Mollatt	Hughes	Bottom	Wilkinson	Robertson	Fenton	Colbridge	Brown	Johnson	Longden	Addison	Hill	Granger	Patterson	Powell	Boyes	Metcalfe	Spence	Greensmith	Farmer	Steel	Wardle	
2	3	6			7	8	9	10	11		4	5				1										1
2	3	7			7	8	9	10			4	5				1		11								2
2	3	10			7	8	9		11		4	5				1					6					3
2	3	10			7	8	9		11		4	5				1					6					4
2	3	10			7	8	9				4	5				1					6	11				r
5	5	5			5	5	5	2	3		5	5				5		1			3	1				
		1				2	2	1	1																	

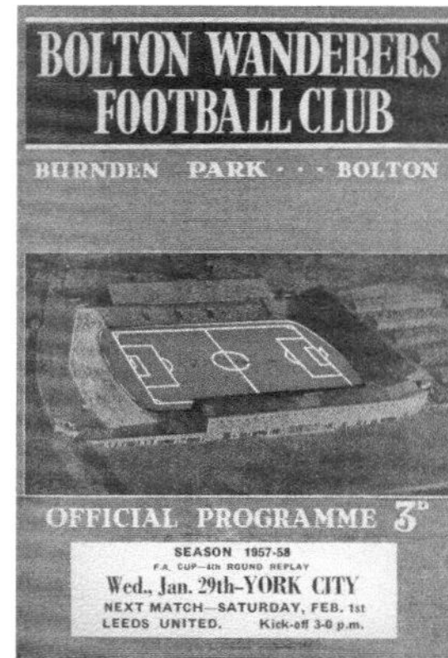

Bolton v City 29 January 1958 programme cover.

Terry Farmer.

1958–59

Division Four

Manager: Sam Bartram

	P	W	D	L	F	A	Pts
Port Vale	46	26	12	8	110	58	64
Coventry City	46	24	12	10	84	47	60
York City	46	21	18	7	73	52	60
Shrewsbury Town	46	24	10	12	101	63	58
Exeter City	46	23	11	12	87	61	57
Walsall	46	21	10	15	95	64	52
Crystal Palace	46	20	12	14	90	71	52
Northampton Town	46	21	9	16	85	78	51
Millwall	46	20	10	16	76	69	50
Carlisle United	46	19	12	15	62	65	50
Gillingham	46	20	9	17	82	77	49
Torquay United	46	16	12	18	78	77	44
Chester	46	16	12	18	72	84	44
Bradford Park Avenue	46	18	7	21	75	77	43
Watford	46	16	10	20	81	79	42
Darlington	46	13	16	17	66	68	42
Workington	46	12	17	17	63	78	41
Crewe Alexandra	46	15	10	21	70	82	40
Hartlepools United	46	15	10	21	74	88	40
Gateshead	46	16	8	22	56	85	40
Oldham Athletic	46	16	4	26	59	84	36
Aldershot	46	14	7	25	63	97	35
Barrow	46	9	10	27	51	104	28
Southport	46	7	12	27	41	86	26

Did you know that?

This was City's first-ever promotion season.

On the opening day 20-year-old centre-half Barry Jackson made his debut.

Left-winger Charlie Twissell was signed from Plymouth Argyle and played his first game on 22 November 1958 at home to Walsall. Before turning professional for the Devon club in 1957 he had been a notable amateur player, gaining several England caps and representing Great Britain in the 1956 Melbourne Olympics.

Ron Spence made his last senior appearance for the club in the match against Walsall on 22 November 1958. He made 306 League and Cup appearances and scored 26 goals.

Top marksman was skipper Peter Wragg with 14 goals.

Home average League attendance was 8,124.

For the first time since 1953–54 City fell at the first hurdle of the FA Cup.

Match No.	Date	Venue	Opponents	Result		Scorers	Attenda
1	Aug 23	A	Oldham Athletic	W	1–0	Greensmith	8
2	25	H	Southport	W	2–0	Wilkinson (2)	8,
3	30	H	Bradford PA	W	4–0	Farmer (2), Wilkinson, Wragg	8,
4	Sep 2	A	Southport	L	0–1		3,
5	6	A	Port Vale	D	2–2	Farmer (2)	10,
6	8	H	Torquay United	W	1–0	Farmer	8,
7	13	H	Crystal Palace	D	1–1	Addison	8,
8	17	A	Torquay United	D	1–1	Boyes	5,
9	20	A	Chester	D	2–2	Addison, Opp. og	8,
10	22	H	Crewe Alexandra	W	4–0	Addison (2), Hughes, Farmer	6,
11	27	H	Watford	D	0–0		8,
12	Oct 1	A	Crewe Alexandra	W	4–2	Wragg (2), Hughes, Addison	8,
13	4	A	Hartlepools United	W	5–1	Wragg (3), Hughes, Addison	9,
14	9	A	Northampton Town	W	2–1	Wragg, Addison	5,
15	11	H	Carlisle United	D	1–1	Wilkinson	9,
16	18	A	Gillingham	D	2–2	Patterson (2)	12,
17	25	H	Exeter City	L	0–2		9,
18	Nov 1	A	Coventry City	L	0–2		24,
19	8	H	Shrewsbury Town	W	2–0	Addison, Hartnett	7,
20	22	H	Walsall	W	3–2	Farmer (2), Wilkinson	7,
21	29	A	Millwall	L	2–5	Wragg, Addison	13,
22	Dec 13	A	Gateshead	L	0–1		2
23	20	H	Oldham Athletic	W	3–1	Wragg, Brownlee, Twissell	6,
24	26	H	Barrow	W	1–0	Wardle	10,
25	27	A	Barrow	W	3–2	Hughes, Addison, Powell	5,
26	Jan 3	A	Bradford PA	L	1–2	Mollatt	7,
27	24	H	Aldershot	D	0–0		7,
28	31	A	Crystal Palace	D	0–0		16,
29	Feb 7	H	Chester	D	1–1	Wragg	5,
30	14	A	Watford	W	3–2	Twissell, Farmer, Brownlee	5,
31	21	H	Hartlepools United	D	1–1	Wragg	5,
32	28	A	Carlisle United	D	0–0		3,
33	Mar 7	H	Gillingham	W	3–1	Hughes, Tait, Wragg (pen)	5,
34	14	A	Exeter City	W	2–0	Tait, Twissell	9,
35	18	A	Darlington	W	1–0	Tait	2,
36	21	H	Coventry City	D	0–0		8,
37	27	H	Workington	D	2–2	Wilkinson, Wragg	10,
38	28	A	Shrewsbury Town	D	2–2	Patterson, Twissell	9,
39	30	A	Workington	D	2–2	Wragg, Wilkinson	4,
40	Apr 4	H	Darlington	W	2–1	Wilkinson, Twissell	7,
41	11	A	Walsall	L	0–5		8,
42	15	H	Port Vale	D	0–0		9,
43	18	H	Millwall	D	3–3	Hughes, Farmer, Opp. og	7,
44	20	H	Northampton Town	W	2–1	Wilkinson, Farmer	9,
45	25	A	Aldershot	W	1–0	Farmer	2,
46	27	H	Gateshead	W	1–0	Hughes	9,
							A
						2 own-goals	

FA Cup

1	Nov 18	A	Bury	L	0–1		13,

Match on 15 November abandoned (due to fog) after 60 minutes. Result stood at 0–0. A

Wardle	Howe	Patterson	Jackson	Mollatt	Hughes	Wilkinson	Wragg	Farmer	Greensmith	Addison	Hartnett	Boyes	Spence	Powell	Ramsey	Twissell	Middleton	Brownlee	Tait	
2	3	4	5	6	7	8	9	10	11											1
2	3	4	5	6	7	8	9	10	11											2
2	3	4	5	6	7	8	9	10	11											3
2	3	4	5	6	7	8	9	10	11											4
2	3	4	5	6	7		9	8	11	10										5
2	3	4	5	6	7		9	8	11	10										6
2	3	4	5	6	7		9	8		10	11									7
2	3		5	6	7	8		9	11	10		4								8
2	3		5	6	7	8		9	11	10		4								9
2	3		5	6	7	8		9	11	10			4							10
2	3		5	6	7	8		9	11	10			4							11
2	3	4	5		7		9	8	11	10			6							12
2	3	4	5		7		9	8	11	10			6							13
2	3	4	5		7	8	9		11	10			6							14
2	3	4	5		7	8	9		11	10			6							15
2	3	4	5		7	8	9		11	10			6							16
2	3	4	5		7		9	8	11				6	10						17
2	3	4			7		9	8		10		5	6	11						18
2	3	4	5		7		9	8		10	11		6							19
	3		5		7	8	4	9		10			6		2	11				20
	3		5		7	8	4	9		10					2	11	6			21
2		4	5		7		6	8		10					3	11		9		22
2		4			7		6	8		10		5			3	11		9		23
2		4			7	8	6			10		5			3	11		9		24
2		4		6	7	8	3	9		10		5		11						25
2				6	7	8	4			10		5			3	11		9		26
2			5	6	7		4			10					3	11		9	8	27
2		4	5	6			8		11	10					3	7		9		28
2		4	5	6			10	8	11						3	7		9		29
2		4	5	6			10	8	11						3	7		9		30
2		4	5	6			10	8	11						3	7		9		31
	3	4	5	6	7		10	9							2	11			8	32
	3	4	5	6	7		10	9							2	11			8	33
	3	4	5	6	7		10	9							2	11			8	34
	3	4	5	6	7		10	9							2	11			8	35
	3	4	5	6	7	9	10			11					2				8	36
	3	4	5	6	7	9	10								2	11			8	37
	3	4		6	7	8	10	9				5			2	11				38
	3	4		6	7	8	9					5		10	2	11				39
	3	4		6	7	8	10	9				5			2	11				40
	3	4		6	7	8		9	11	10		5			2					41
	3	4	5	6	7	8	10	9						11	2					42
	3	4	5	6	7	8	10	9						11	2					43
	3	4		6	7	8	10	9				5		11	2					44
	3	4		6	7	8	10	9				5		11	2					45
	3	4		6	7	8	10	9				5		11	2					46
29	36	38	34	33	42	27	41	36	21	25	2	14	11	9	26	19	1	9	7	
1		3		1	7	9	14	12	1	10	1	1		1		5		2	3	

Wardle	Howe	Patterson	Jackson	Mollatt	Hughes	Wilkinson	Wragg	Farmer	Greensmith	Addison	Hartnett	Boyes	Spence	Powell	Ramsey	Twissell	Middleton	Brownlee	Tait	
	3		5		7	8	4	9		10	11		6		2					1
	1		1		1	1	1	1		1	1		1		1					

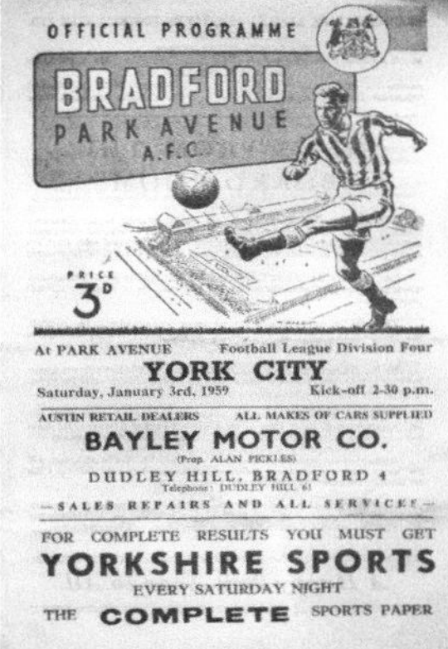

Bradford Park Avenue v York City 3 January 1959 programme cover.

Charlie Twissell.

Peter Wragg.

1959–60

Division Three

Manager: Sam Bartram

	P	W	D	L	F	A	Pts
Southampton	46	26	9	11	106	75	61
Norwich City	46	24	11	11	82	54	59
Shrewsbury Town	46	18	16	12	97	75	52
Grimsby Town	46	18	16	12	87	70	52
Coventry City	46	21	10	15	78	63	52
Brentford	46	21	9	16	78	61	51
Bury	46	21	9	16	64	51	51
Queen's Park Rangers	46	18	13	15	73	54	49
Colchester United	46	18	11	17	83	74	47
Bournemouth	46	17	13	16	72	72	47
Reading	46	18	10	18	84	77	46
Southend United	46	19	8	19	76	74	46
Newport County	46	20	6	20	80	79	46
Port Vale	46	19	8	19	80	79	46
Halifax Town	46	18	10	18	70	72	46
Swindon Town	46	19	8	19	69	78	46
Barnsley	46	15	14	17	65	66	44
Chesterfield	46	18	7	21	71	84	43
Bradford City	46	15	12	19	66	74	42
Tranmere Rovers	46	14	13	19	72	75	41
York City	46	13	12	21	57	73	38
Mansfield Town	46	15	6	25	81	112	36
Wrexham	46	14	8	24	68	101	36
Accrington Stanley	46	11	5	30	57	123	27

Did you know that?

In the summer of 1959 floodlights were installed at Bootham Crescent and were first used in the evening game against Queen's Park Rangers on 7 September 1959.

The official opening of the lights took place on 28 October 1959 when Newcastle United were the visitors for an exhibition match. The Magpies won 8–2 in front of 9,414.

City met a number of clubs for the first time in League football, and these included Southampton, Norwich City, QPR and Reading.

Top scorer was John Edgar, who had been signed in the close season from Gillingham. In the home win over Accrington Stanley on 3 October 1959 he netted three goals in six minutes – the fastest recorded hat-trick in the club's history.

Players to make their last appearances this term were midfielder Ron Mollatt, wingers Billy Hill and Ron Greensmith and forwards Terry Farmer and Johnny Powell.

Average League attendance at Bootham Crescent was 7,507.

Match No.	Date	Venue	Opponents	Result		Scorers	Attend
1	Aug 22	A	Bradford City	L	0–2		1
2	24	H	Bury	W	1–0	Edgar	
3	29	H	Coventry City	D	1–1	Twissell	
4	Sep 1	A	Bury	L	0–2		1
5	5	H	Halifax Town	L	1–2	Farmer	
6	7	H	Queen's Park Rangers	W	2–1	Edgar, Powell	1
7	12	A	Swindon Town	D	1–1	Wilkinson	1
8	14	A	Queen's Park Rangers	D	0–0		1
9	19	H	Chesterfield	W	1–0	Wilkinson	
10	21	H	Grimsby Town	D	3–3	Wilkinson (2), Powell	1
11	26	A	Newport County	L	2–3	Edgar (2)	
12	28	A	Grimsby Town	D	2–2	Hughes, Wilkinson	1
13	Oct 3	H	Accrington Stanley	W	3–0	Edgar (3)	
14	7	A	Bournemouth	L	0–2		
15	10	A	Barnsley	D	1–1	Farmer	
16	12	H	Bournemouth	W	3–2	Farmer, Wragg, Twissell	
17	17	H	Southampton	D	2–2	Wilkinson (2)	
18	24	A	Reading	L	0–1		1
19	31	H	Mansfield Town	W	2–1	Addison, Wilkinson	
20	Nov 7	A	Port Vale	L	0–2		
21	21	A	Brentford	W	2–1	Wragg, Wilkinson	1
22	28	H	Colchester United	L	2–3	Boyes, Addison	
23	Dec 12	A	Shrewsbury Town	L	0–4		
24	19	H	Bradford City	D	1–1	Tait	4
25	26	A	Tranmere Rovers	D	2–2	Tait, Edgar	1
26	28	H	Tranmere Rovers	W	3–0	Edgar (2), Opp. og	
27	Jan 2	A	Coventry City	L	2–5	Hughes, Edgar	1
28	16	A	Halifax Town	W	2–1	Wilkinson, Twissell	
29	23	H	Swindon Town	W	1–0	Addison	6
30	30	A	Southend United	D	1–1	Wilkinson	
31	Feb 6	A	Chesterfield	L	0–2		6
32	12	H	Newport County	W	2–0	Edgar (2)	7
33	27	H	Barnsley	D	0–0		6
34	Mar 5	A	Southampton	L	1–3	Edgar	20
35	12	H	Reading	L	2–3	Hughes, Wilkinson	
36	16	H	Norwich City	L	1–2	Farmer	6
37	19	A	Colchester United	D	2–2	Wilkinson (2)	
38	26	H	Port Vale	W	2–0	Hughes, Edgar	6
39	30	A	Accrington Stanley	L	0–4		
40	Apr 2	A	Norwich City	L	0–1		2
41	9	H	Brentford	L	0–1		4
42	15	H	Wrexham	W	3–0	Hughes, Wragg, Wilkinson	6
43	16	A	Mansfield Town	L	0–2		7
44	18	A	Wrexham	L	1–3	Powell	4
45	23	H	Southend United	L	2–3	Hughes (2)	4
46	30	H	Shrewsbury Town	L	0–1		4

1 own-goal

FA Cup

1	Nov 14	H	Barrow	W	3–1	Addison, Hughes, Edgar	7
2	Dec 5	A	Crook Town	W	1–0	Edgar	8
3	Jan 9	A	Bournemouth	L	0–1		14

Ramsey	Howe	Patterson	Boyes	Mollatt	Hughes	Edgar	Wilkinson	Alexander	Twissell	Granger	Battye	Jackson	Farmer	Wragg	Powell	Addison	Hill	Greensmith	Tait	Jones	
2	3	4	5	6	7	8	9	10	11												1
2	3			6	7	8		10	11	1	4	5	9								2
2	3			6	7	8		10	11	1	4	5	9								3
2	3			6	7	8		10		1	4	5		9	11						4
2	3				7	8		10		1	4	5	9	6	11						5
2	3				7	8	9			1	4	5		6	11	10					6
2	3				7	8	9			1	4	5		6	11	10					7
2	3				7	8	9			1	4	5		6	11	10					8
2	3				7	8	9				4	5		6	11	10					9
2	3				7	8	9				4	5		6	11	10					10
2	3				7	8	9				4	5		6	11	10					11
2	3				7	8	9		11	1	4	5		6		10					12
2	3				7	8	9		11	1	4	5		6		10					13
2	3				7	8			11	1	4	5	9	6		10					14
2	3	4			7	8			11	1	6	5	9	10							15
2	3	4			7	8			11	1	6	5	9	10							16
2	3	4		6	7	8	9		11	1		5		10							17
2	3	4	5		7	10	8		11	1				6			9				18
2	3	4			7	10	9		11			5		6		8					19
2	3		4		7	10	9		11			5		6		8					20
2	3		4		7	10	9		11			5		6		8					21
2	3	4	5		7	10	9		11					6		8					22
2	3		4		7	10	9					5		6		8		11			23
2	3			6	7	10	9		11			5		4					8		24
2	3			6	7	10	9		11			5		4					8		25
2	3			6	7	10	9		11			5		4					8		26
2	3			6	7	10	9		11			5		4					8		27
2	3			6	7	10	9		11			5		4		8					28
2	3		5	6	7		8		11					4		10	9				29
2	3		5		7	10	9		11		4			6		8					30
2	3		5		7	10	9		11		4			6		8					31
2	3			6	7	9		10	11			5		4		8					32
2	3			6	7	9	8	10	11			5		4							33
2	3			6	7	10						5		4	11	8	9				34
2	3			6	7	10	8		11			5		4			9				35
2	3		5	6	7	10	8						9	4		11					36
2	3		5	6	7	10	8						9	4		11					37
2	3		4		7	10	8					5	9	6		11					38
2	3			6	7	10	5		11				9	4		8					39
2	3		4		7	10	8					5		6		11			9		40
2	3		4		7		8		11			5	9	6		10					41
2	3		4	6	7	10	8					5		6		11					42
2	3		4	6	7		10					5	9			11			8		43
2	3	4		6	7		8					5			10	11	9				44
2	3	4			7	10	8					5				11	9			6	45
2	3	6	4		7	10	9		11			5				8					46
46	46	10	17	21	46	42	37	7	28	14	17	37	12	39	10	31	6	1	6	1	
			1		7	15	14		3				4	3	3	4			2		

Ramsey	Howe	Patterson	Boyes	Mollatt	Hughes	Edgar	Wilkinson	Alexander	Twissell	Granger	Battye	Jackson	Farmer	Wragg	Powell	Addison	Hill	Greensmith	Tait	Jones	
2	3		4		7	10	9		11			5		6		8					1
2	3		4		7	10	9		11			5		6		8					2
2	3			6	7	10	9		11			5		4					8		3
3	3		2	1	3	3	3		3			3		3		2			1		
					1	2										1					

YORK CITY A.F. & A.C. LTD.

No. 25 CITY v SHREWSBURY T. 30th April

CITY MUST WIN AND TRANMERE LOSE!

York City v Shrewsbury Town 30 April 1960 programme cover.

John Edgar.

1960–61

Division Four

Manager: Tom Lockie

	P	W	D	L	F	A	Pts
Peterborough United	46	28	10	8	134	65	66
Crystal Palace	46	29	6	11	110	69	64
Northampton Town	46	25	10	11	90	62	60
Bradford Park Avenue	46	26	8	12	84	74	60
York City	46	21	9	16	80	60	51
Millwall	46	21	8	17	97	86	50
Darlington	46	18	13	15	78	70	49
Workington	46	21	7	18	74	76	49
Crewe Alexandra	46	20	9	17	61	67	49
Aldershot	46	18	9	19	79	69	45
Doncaster Rovers	46	19	7	20	76	78	45
Oldham Athletic	46	19	7	20	79	88	45
Stockport County	46	18	9	19	57	66	45
Southport	46	19	6	21	69	67	44
Gillingham	46	15	13	18	64	66	43
Wrexham	46	17	8	21	62	56	42
Rochdale	46	17	8	21	60	66	42
Accrington Stanley	46	16	8	22	74	88	40
Carlisle United	46	13	13	20	61	79	39
Mansfield Town	46	16	6	24	71	78	38
Exeter City	46	14	10	22	66	94	38
Barrow	46	13	11	22	52	79	37
Hartlepools United	46	12	8	26	71	103	32
Chester	46	11	9	26	61	104	31

Did you know that?

Long-serving clubman Tom Lockie was appointed manager during the summer of 1960, following the release of Sam Bartram to take up a similar position at Luton Town. At the same time former player Sid Storey returned to Bootham Crescent as trainer.

New signings included Walter Bingley from Swindon Town, Alan Woods ex-Swansea Town and Jimmy Weir ex-Fulham, and the three made their debuts on the opening day in the home win over Millwall.

On 27 August 1960 City were winning 2–1 at Accrington Stanley, with Peter Wragg scoring twice, when the game was abandoned in the 83rd minute owing to a violent thunderstorm. The rearranged match later in the season was lost 2–0.

Colin Addison, who scored City's first-ever goal in the newly instituted Football League Cup on 10 October 1960 against Blackburn Rovers, was transferred to First Division Nottingham Forest for a then new club record fee received of £12,000 following the FA Cup defeat at Norwich.

Left-winger Wally Gould was signed from Sheffield United and made his debut at home to Oldham Athletic on 18 February 1961.

Left-back George Howe made his last senior appearance on the final day of the campaign at Crystal Palace. In seven seasons (1954–61) he had missed just 15 League games out of a possible 322.

For the second time in three seasons Peter Wragg was top scorer. In the 5–1 win at Crewe on 21 January 1961 he became only the fourth player to score four goals in a Football League match for the club.

Average home League crowd was 6,900.

At the end of the season, long-serving secretary Billy Sherrington retired having held the post for 37 years.

Match No.	Date	Venue	Opponents	Result		Scorers	Attend
1	Aug 20	H	Millwall	W	3–2	Wragg (2), Woods	7
2	22	A	Barrow	D	1–1	Wragg	7
3	29	H	Barrow	W	2–0	Weir (2)	8
4	Sep 3	H	Doncaster Rovers	D	1–1	Wilkinson	7
5	5	A	Bradford PA	D	3–3	Weir (2), Wragg (pen)	7
6	10	H	Crewe Alexandra	W	3–1	Addison, Scott, Wilkinson	6
7	12	H	Bradford PA	W	2–0	Addison, Wragg	9
8	17	A	Chester	L	1–2	Scott	5
9	21	A	Gillingham	L	2–3	Wragg, Addison	5
10	24	H	Workington	W	4–0	Addison (3), Opp. og	6
11	26	H	Gillingham	D	0–0		8
12	Oct 1	A	Oldham Athletic	L	1–3	Addison	9
13	3	H	Aldershot	W	4–1	Wragg (3), Weir	7
14	8	A	Wrexham	L	0–4		5
15	15	H	Carlisle United	W	4–0	Fountain, Hughes, Wilkinson, Wragg	4
16	22	A	Rochdale	D	0–0		4
17	29	H	Mansfield Town	W	3–2	Wragg (2), Addison	5
18	Nov 12	H	Exeter City	W	6–1	Addison (2), Hughes, Wilkinson, Wragg (pen), Weir	5
19	19	A	Peterborough United	D	1–1	Wilkinson	11
20	Dec 3	A	Darlington	L	1–2	Addison	8
21	10	H	Crystal Palace	L	0–2		6
22	17	A	Millwall	L	2–3	Wilkinson (2)	6
23	26	H	Northampton Town	L	0–1		7
24	27	A	Northampton Town	L	0–3		18
25	31	H	Accrington Stanley	W	1–0	Addison	4
26	Jan 2	A	Hartlepools United	W	3–1	Addison (2), Wragg	5
27	14	A	Doncaster Rovers	W	2–0	Hughes, Hoggart	5
28	21	A	Crewe Alexandra	W	5–1	Wragg (4), Wilkinson	8
29	Feb 4	H	Chester	W	2–0	Hughes, Wragg	4
30	10	A	Workington	L	0–2		3
31	18	H	Oldham Athletic	W	1–0	Wragg	8
32	25	H	Wrexham	W	2–1	Hughes, Wragg	4
33	Mar 4	A	Carlisle United	D	1–1	Jackson	3
34	11	H	Rochdale	W	2–0	Wragg (pen), Opp. og	5
35	13	A	Stockport County	L	0–2		5
36	18	A	Mansfield Town	W	3–1	Hoggart (2), Wilkinson	5
37	20	H	Southport	W	2–0	Wilkinson, Weir	6
38	25	H	Stockport County	D	0–0		8
39	31	H	Hartlepools United	W	4–0	Jackson (pen), Hoggart, Weir, Gould	8
40	Apr 1	A	Exeter City	L	1–2	Hoggart	5
41	8	H	Peterborough United	L	0–1		11
42	15	A	Southport	D	2–2	Wilkinson, Weir	3
43	19	A	Accrington Stanley	L	0–2		1
44	22	H	Darlington	W	4–1	Gould (2), Hoggart, Weir	4
45	26	A	Aldershot	L	1–6	Edgar	4
46	29	A	Crystal Palace	L	0–1		17

A

2 own-goals

FA Cup

1	Nov 5	H	Bradford PA	D	0–0		7
r	9	A	Bradford PA	W	2–0	Wilkinson, Addison	5
2	30	A	Tranmere Rovers	D	1–1	Wilkinson	11
r	Dec 5	H	Tranmere Rovers	W	2–1	Wilkinson (2)	10
3	Jan 7	H	Norwich City	D	1–1	Hughes	9
r	11	A	Norwich City	L	0–1		27

A

Football League Cup

1	Oct 10	H	Blackburn Rovers	L	1–2	Addison	10

A

ingley	Howe	Woods	Jackson	Jordan	Hughes	Scott	Wragg	Addison	Weir	Wilkinson	Twissell	Granger	Tait	Hoggart	Ramsey	Fountain	Boyes	Edgar	Gould	
2	3	4	5	6	7	8	9	10	11											1
2	3	4	5	6	7	8	9	10	11											2
2	3	4	5	6	7	8	9		11	10										3
2	3	4	5	6		8	9		11	10	7									4
2	3	4	5	6		8	9		11	10	7									5
2	3	4	5	6		8	9	7	11	10										6
2	3	4	5	6		8	10	7	11			1	9							7
2	3	4	5	6		8	9	7	11			1		10						8
	3	4	5		7	8	9	10	11			1			2	6				9
2	3	4	5		7	8	9	10	11							6				10
2	3	4	5		7	8		10	11				9			6				11
2	3	4	5		7	8	9	10	11							6				12
2	3	4	5		7	8	9	10	11							6				13
2	3	4	5		7	8	9	10	11							6				14
2	3	4	5		7		9	10	11	8						6				15
2	3	4	5		7		9	10	11	8						6				16
2	3	4	5		7		9	10	11	8						6				17
2	3	4			7		10	8	11	9						6	5			18
2	3	4	5		7		10	8	11	9						6				19
2	3	4	5		7		10	8	11	9						6				20
2	3	4	5		7		10	8	11	9						6				21
2	3	4			7			8	11	9						6	5	10		22
2	3	4			7	8		11		9		1				6	5	10		23
2	3	4	5		7	8	9	11		10		1				6				24
2	3	4	5		7		10	8	11	9						6				25
2	3	4	5		7		10	8	11	9						6				26
2	3	4	5		7		8				11			10		6		9		27
2	3	4	5		7		9			8	11			10		6				28
2	3	4	5		7		9			8	11			10		6				29
	3	4	5		7		9			8	11			10	2	6				30
2	3	4	5		7		9			10				8		6			11	31
2	3	4	5		7		9			10				8		6			11	32
2	3	4	5		7		9			10				8		6			11	33
2	3	4	5		7		10			9				8		6			11	34
2	3	4	5		7		10		11	9				8		6				35
2	3	4	5		7				10	9				8		6			11	36
2	3	4	5		7				10	9				8		6			11	37
2	3	4	5		7				10	9				8		6			11	38
2	3	4	5		7				10	9				8		6			11	39
2	3	4	5		7				10	9				8		6			11	40
2	3	4	5		7				10	8					9	6			11	41
2	3	4	5		7				10	9				8		6			11	42
2	3	4	5		7				10	9				8		6			11	43
2	3	4	5		7				10	9				8		6			11	44
2	3	4	5		7				11	9				8		6		10		45
2	3	4	5		7	8			11	10						6		9		46
44	46	46	43	8	41	17	32	23	36	35	6	5	2	19	3	38	3	5	13	
		1	2		5	2	22	14	10	11				6		1		1	3	

ingley	Howe	Woods	Jackson	Jordan	Hughes	Scott	Wragg	Addison	Weir	Wilkinson	Twissell	Granger	Tait	Hoggart	Ramsey	Fountain	Boyes	Edgar	Gould	
2	3	4	5		7		9	10	11	8						6				1
2	3	4	5		7		10	8	11	9						6				r
2	3	4				7	10	8	11	9						6	5			2
2	3	4	5		7		10	8	11	9						6				r
2	3	4	5		7		10	8	11	9						6				3
2	3	4	5		7		10	8	11	9						6				r
6	6	6	5		5	1	6	6	6	6						6	1			
					1			1		4										

ingley	Howe	Woods	Jackson	Jordan	Hughes	Scott	Wragg	Addison	Weir	Wilkinson	Twissell	Granger	Tait	Hoggart	Ramsey	Fountain	Boyes	Edgar	Gould	
2	3	4			7	8	9	11		10						6	5			1
1	1	1			1	1	1	1		1						1	1			
								1												

Darlington v York City 3 December 1960 programme cover.

Jack Fountain.

1961–62

Division Four

Manager: Tom Lockie

	P	W	D	L	F	A	Pts
Millwall	44	23	10	11	87	62	56
Colchester United	44	23	9	12	104	71	55
Wrexham	44	22	9	13	96	56	53
Carlisle United	44	22	8	14	64	63	52
Bradford City	44	21	9	14	94	86	51
York City	44	20	10	14	84	53	50
Aldershot	44	22	5	17	81	60	49
Workington	44	19	11	14	69	70	49
Barrow	44	17	14	13	74	58	48
Crewe Alexandra	44	20	6	18	79	70	46
Oldham Athletic	44	17	12	15	77	70	46
Rochdale	44	19	7	18	71	71	45
Darlington	44	18	9	17	61	73	45
Mansfield Town	44	19	6	19	77	66	44
Tranmere Rovers	44	20	4	20	70	81	44
Stockport County	44	17	9	18	70	69	43
Southport	44	17	9	18	61	71	43
Exeter City	44	13	11	20	62	77	37
Chesterfield	44	14	9	21	70	87	37
Gillingham	44	13	11	20	73	94	37
Doncaster Rovers	44	11	7	26	60	85	29
Hartlepools United	44	8	11	25	52	101	27
Chester	44	7	12	25	54	96	26

Did you know that?

Notable newcomers who made their City debut on the opening day were Tommy Heron from Manchester United and John Stainsby ex-Barnsley.

In November 1961 inside-forward Billy Rudd was signed from Birmingham City and scored on his official debut on 13 January 1962 at home to Gillingham. He was in the City side that beat Accrington Stanley 1–0 on 18 November 1961, but this match was expunged from the records when the Lancashire club withdrew from the League owing to financial problems in March 1962. One of Stanley's players, half-back Alex Hamilton, joined City for the closing weeks of the season.

Victory in the last game of the campaign at home to Aldershot would have ensured promotion.

Jimmy Weir was top marksman with 29 League and Cup goals, including two hat-tricks. On 2 December 1961 he netted the only goal of the game at home to Stockport County and then was sent off.

Billy Hughes played his last senior game on 30 September 1961 at Rochdale, the same ground on which he had made his debut almost exactly 10 years earlier. He netted 58 goals in 380 League and Cup outings.

'Keeper Mick Granger made his last first-team appearance at Oldham on 13 March 1962.

Average home League crowd was 6,890.

City experienced their best season in the Football League Cup, knocking out First Division Leicester City en route to the quarter-finals.

Match No.	Date	Venue	Opponents	Result		Scorers
1	Aug 19	A	Bradford City	D	2–2	Weir, Opp. og
2	21	H	Wrexham	W	3–2	Weir (2), Stainsby
3	26	H	Chesterfield	W	4–0	Weir (2), Wragg (2, 1 pen)
4	30	A	Wrexham	L	1–2	Pierce
5	Sep 2	A	Gillingham	W	2–1	Weir, Pierce
6	4	H	Exeter City	W	2–1	Wragg, Pierce
7	9	H	Millwall	L	0–1	
8	16	A	Mansfield Town	L	1–3	Gould
9	18	H	Carlisle United	D	1–1	Wragg (pen)
10	23	H	Barrow	W	5–0	Woods, Wragg, Stainsby, Pierce, Gould
11	27	A	Carlisle United	L	2–3	Hughes, Weir
12	30	A	Rochdale	L	1–3	Weir
13	Oct 2	H	Crewe Alexandra	W	4–2	Weir (3), Stainsby
14	7	H	Colchester United	W	5–0	Weir (2), Wragg (pen), Stainsby, Gould
15	11	A	Crewe Alexandra	D	0–0	
16	14	A	Chester	D	1–1	Pierce
17	21	H	Tranmere Rovers	L	1–2	Weir
18	28	A	Southport	L	1–3	Stainsby
19	Nov 11	A	Darlington	D	0–0	
20	Dec 2	H	Stockport County	W	1–0	Weir
21	9	A	Aldershot	L	0–2	
22	16	H	Bradford City	W	4–0	Wragg (2), Stainsby, Wilkinson
23	23	A	Chesterfield	D	1–1	Weir
24	26	A	Doncaster Rovers	W	2–1	Stainsby (2)
25	Jan 13	H	Gillingham	W	4–0	Stainsby (3), Rudd
26	20	A	Millwall	L	1–2	Stainsby
27	Feb 3	H	Mansfield Town	W	2–1	Stainsby, Wragg
28	10	A	Barrow	D	0–0	
29	17	H	Rochdale	W	2–1	Jackson, Weir
30	24	A	Colchester United	L	1–3	Fountain
31	Mar 3	H	Chester	W	5–1	Weir (2), Gould, Wragg, Stainsby
32	9	A	Tranmere Rovers	D	2–2	Stainsby, Weir
33	13	A	Oldham Athletic	L	0–1	
34	16	H	Southport	D	2–2	Wragg, Weir
35	19	H	Hartlepools United	W	2–0	Rudd, Weir
36	24	A	Hartlepools United	W	2–0	Francis, Rudd
37	31	H	Darlington	W	2–1	Francis (2)
38	Apr 2	H	Doncaster Rovers	W	5–2	Wragg (3), Weir, Opp. og
39	11	A	Exeter City	L	1–2	Weir
40	14	H	Oldham Athletic	W	4–1	Francis, Wragg, Wilkinson, Weir
41	20	H	Workington	W	4–0	Weir (3), Gould
42	21	A	Stockport County	L	1–2	Wilkinson
43	23	A	Workington	D	0–0	
44	28	H	Aldershot	L	0–1	

2 own-goals

FA Cup

1	Nov 4	A	Bradford City	L	0–1	

Football League Cup

1	Sep 13	H	Bristol City	W	3–0	Weir, Stainsby, Wragg
2	Cot 9	H	Leicester City	W	2–1	Wragg, Stainsby
3	Nov 15	H	Watford	D	1–1	Gould
r	21	A	Watford	D	2–2*	Wragg, Stainsby
2r	Dec 4	H	Watford	W	3–2	Francis, Wragg, Jackson
4	13	H	Bournemouth	W	1–0	Stainsby
5	Feb 7	A	Rochdale	L	1–2	Wragg (pen)

* After extra-time.

	Bingley	Heron	Woods	Jackson	Fountain	Weir	Wragg	Stainsby	Pierce	Gould	Boyes	Wilkinson	Hughes	Hoggart	Francis	Rudd	Granger	Hamilton
1	2	3	4	5	6	7	8	9	10	11								
2	2	3	4	5	6	7	8	9	10	11								
3	2	3	4	5	6	7	8	9	10	11								
4	2	3	4	5	6	7	8	9	10	11								
5	2	3	4	5	6	7	8	9	10	11								
6	2	3	4		6	7	8	9	10	11	5							
7	2	3	4	5	6	7	8	9	10	11								
8	2	3	4	5	6	7	8	9		11		10						
9	2	3	4	5	6	7	8	9	10	11								
10	2	3	4	5	6	7	8	9	10	11								
11	2	3	4	5	6	10	9		8	11			7					
12	2	3	4	5	6	10	9			11		8	7					
13	2	3	4	5	6	7	8	9		11		10						
14	2	3	4	5	6	7	8	9		11		10						
15	2	3	4		6	7	8	9		11	5			10				
16	2	3	4	5	6	7		9	8	11		10						
17	2	3		5	6	7	4	9		11		10			8			
18	2	3		5	6	7	4	9		11		10			8			
19	2	3	4	5	6	10	8	9		11					7			
20	2	3	4	5	6	10	8	9		11					7			
21	2	3	4	5	6	10	8	9		11					7			
22	2	3	4	5	6	11	8	9		7		10						
23	2	3	4	5	6	11	8	9		7		10						
24	2	3	4	5	6	11	8	9		7		10						
25	2	3	4	5	6		8	9		11					7	10		
26	2	3	4	5	6		8	9		11					7	10		
27	2	3	4	5	6		10	9		11					7	8		
28	2	3	4	5	6	11	10	9		7						8	1	
29	2	3	4	5	6	11	8	9		7						10	1	
30	2	3	4	5	6	11	8	9		7						10	1	
31	2	3	4	5	6	11	8	9		7		10					1	
32	2	3	4	5	6	11	8	9		7		10					1	
33	2	3	4	5	6	11	8	9	10	7							1	
34	2	3	4	5		11	8	9		7		10						6
35	2	3	4	5		11	8	9							7	10		6
36	2	3	4	5		11	8	9							7	10		6
37	2	3	4	5		11	8	9							7	10		6
38	2	3	4	5		11	8	9		7						10		6
39	2	3	4	5		11	8	9		7						10		6
40	2	3	4	5		11	8					9			7	10		6
41	2	3	4	5		10	8			11		9			7			6
42	2	3	4	5		10		9		11		8			7			6
43	2	3	4	5		10	8			11		9			7			6
44	2	3	4	5		10	8			11		9			7			6
	44	44	42	42	33	41	42	38	12	40	2	18	2	1	16	12	6	11
			1	1	1	28	15	15	5	5		3	1		4	3		

	Bingley	Heron	Woods	Jackson	Fountain	Weir	Wragg	Stainsby	Pierce	Gould	Boyes	Wilkinson	Hughes	Hoggart	Francis	Rudd	Granger	Hamilton
1	2	3	4	5	6	7	9			11		10			8			
	1	1	1	1	1	1	1			1		1			1			

	Bingley	Heron	Woods	Jackson	Fountain	Weir	Wragg	Stainsby	Pierce	Gould	Boyes	Wilkinson	Hughes	Hoggart	Francis	Rudd	Granger	Hamilton
1	2	3	4	5	6	7	8	9		11		10						
2	2	3	4	5	6	7	8	9		11		10						
3	2	3	4	5	6	7	8	9		11		10						
r	2	3	4	5	6	11	8	9		7		10						
2r	2	3	4	5	6	10	8	9		11					7		1	
4	2	3	4	5	6	10	8	9		11					7			
5	2	3	4	5	6		10	9		11					7	8	1	
	7	7	7	7	7	6	7	7		7		4			3	1	2	
				1		1	5	4		1					1			

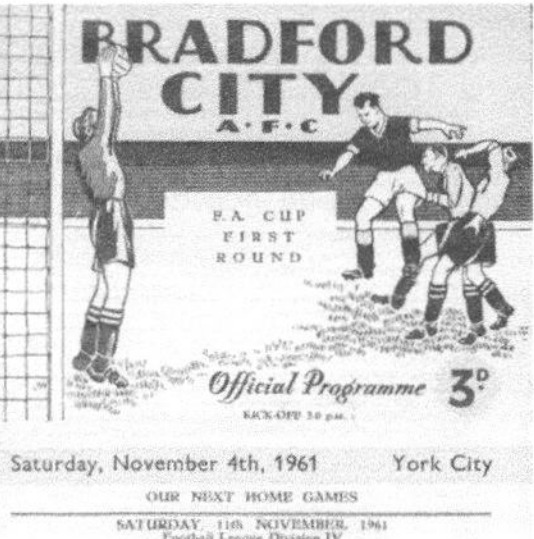

Bradford City v York City 4 November 1961 programme cover.

Jimmy Weir.

Rochdale v York City 7 February 1962 programme cover.

1962–63

Division Four

Manager: Tom Lockie

	P	W	D	L	F	A	Pts
Brentford	46	27	8	11	98	64	62
Oldham Athletic	46	24	11	11	95	60	59
Crewe Alexandra	46	24	11	11	86	58	59
Mansfield Town	46	24	9	13	108	69	57
Gillingham	46	22	13	11	71	49	57
Torquay United	46	20	16	10	75	56	56
Rochdale	46	20	11	15	67	59	51
Tranmere Rovers	46	20	10	16	81	67	50
Barrow	46	19	12	15	82	80	50
Workington	46	17	13	16	76	68	47
Aldershot	46	15	17	14	73	69	47
Darlington	46	19	6	21	72	87	44
Southport	46	15	14	17	72	106	44
York City	46	16	11	19	67	62	43
Chesterfield	46	13	16	17	70	64	42
Doncaster Rovers	46	14	14	18	64	77	42
Exeter City	46	16	10	20	57	77	42
Oxford United	46	13	15	18	70	71	41
Stockport County	46	15	11	20	56	70	41
Newport County	46	14	11	21	76	90	39
Chester	46	15	9	22	51	66	39
Lincoln City	46	13	9	24	68	89	35
Bradford City	46	11	10	25	64	93	32
Hartlepools United	46	7	11	28	56	104	25

Did you know that?

During the winter of the Big Freeze City did not play from 22 December until 8 March. In the first part of the season City collected just 16 points from 24 games and after the 'break' gained 27 points from 22 matches.

Jimmy Weir played his last game on 1 September 1962 at Mansfield and joined the Stags a few days later.

Peter Wragg made his last appearance on 8 April 1963 at Aldershot. He scored 87 times in 297 senior games.

Amateur centre-forward Jeff Barmby made two appearances. Years later, his son Nick played for Tottenham Hotspur, Everton, Liverpool and England.

Average League attendance dropped to a new post-war low – 4,515.

Match No.	Date	Venue	Opponents	Result		Scorers	Attend
1	Aug 18	A	Stockport County	D	1–1	Rudd	4
2	20	H	Crewe Alexandra	W	2–0	Wragg (2, 1 pen)	7
3	25	H	Doncaster Rovers	W	1–0	Gould	5
4	29	A	Crewe Alexandra	L	0–1		6
5	Sep 1	A	Mansfield Town	L	0–2		10
6	8	H	Workington	L	1–2	Hoggart	4
7	12	A	Chester	D	0–0		5
8	15	A	Exeter City	L	1–2	Jackson	3
9	17	H	Gillingham	L	0–3		5
10	22	H	Chesterfield	L	3–4	Gould, Stainsby, Wilkinson	2
11	26	A	Gillingham	D	0–0		6
12	29	A	Rochdale	L	0–1		3
13	Oct 1	H	Darlington	W	5–1	Wilkinson (2), Gould, Hoggart, Rudd	4
14	6	A	Southport	L	1–2	Wilkinson	3
15	13	H	Aldershot	D	0–0		3
16	18	A	Newport County	W	3–1	Hoggart, Rudd, Opp. og	5
17	26	H	Oxford United	L	1–2	Jackson	5
18	Nov 10	H	Tranmere Rovers	L	1–2	Wilkinson	3
19	12	H	Chester	D	0–0		3
20	17	A	Torquay United	L	0–1		3
21	Dec 1	A	Oldham Athletic	L	2–3	Bingley (pen), Ambler	11
22	8	H	Barrow	D	1–1	Wragg	2
23	15	H	Stockport County	W	3–1	Gould (2), Wragg	2
24	22	A	Doncaster Rovers	L	2–3	Ambler, Bingley (pen)	4
25	Mar 8	H	Newport County	W	2–0	Bingley (pen), Wilkinson	4
26	11	A	Darlington	L	1–2	Wragg	3
27	16	A	Oxford United	W	2–0	Rudd, Heron	5
28	18	H	Exeter City	D	3–3	Bingley (pen), Gould, Rudd	4
29	22	H	Breadford City	W	3–0	Wilkinson, Stainsby, Heron	4
30	25	H	Hartlepools United	W	2–0	Wilkinson, Heron	4
31	29	A	Lincoln City	W	4–2	Gould, Wilkinson, Stainsby, Opp. og	2
32	Apr 1	A	Chesterfield	D	1–1	Rudd	8
33	5	H	Torquay United	W	1–0	Bingley (pen)	4
34	8	A	Aldershot	L	1–4	Opp. og	4
35	12	H	Brentford	D	1–1	Fountain	7
36	13	A	Tranmere Rovers	L	1–2	Ambler	5
37	15	A	Brentford	L	1–2	Stainsby	15
38	20	H	Oldham Athletic	W	5–2	Stainsby (2), Gould, Wilkinson, Rudd	4
39	22	H	Lincoln City	W	3–1	Wilkinson (3)	5
40	27	A	Barrow	L	1–2	Hoggart	3
41	29	A	Hartlepools United	D	1–1	Wilkinson	2
42	May 4	H	Rochdale	W	1–0	Gould	4
43	11	H	Mansfield Town	W	2–1	Rudd, Gould	5
44	15	A	Bradford City	W	2–1	Wilkinson, Gould	1
45	18	A	Workington	L	0–3		1
46	20	H	Southport	D	1–1	Opp. og	3
							A
						4 own-goals	

FA Cup

1	Nov 3	H	Rochdale	D	0–0		4
r	6	A	Rochdale	W	2–1	Wragg, Wilkinson	6
2	24	H	Crewe Alexandra	W	2–1	Wragg, Wilkinson	6
3	Feb 13	A	Southampton	L	0–5		11
							A

Football League Cup

1	Sep 5	H	Lincoln City	D	2–2	Gould, Fountain	6
r	19	A	Lincoln City	L	0–2		4
							A

ingley	Heron	Woods	Jackson	Fountain	Gould	Wragg	Stainsby	Rudd	Weir	Moor	Boyes	Wilkinson	Moore	Hoggart	Perry	Ambler	Ashworth	Popely	Barmby	
2	3	4	5	6	7	8	9	10	11											1
2	3	4	5	6	7	8	9	10	11	1										2
2	3	4	5	6	7	8	9	10	11	1										3
2	3	4	5	6	7	8	9	10	11	1										4
2	3	4		6	7			10	11	1	5	8	9							5
2	3	4	5	6	11	8		10		1			9	7						6
2	3	4	5	6	11	8	9			1		10		7						7
2	3	4	5	6	11	8	9			1		10		7						8
2	3	4	9	6	7	10	8	11		1	5									9
	3	4	5	6	7		8	11		1		9		10	2					10
2	3	4	5	6		7	8	11		1		9		10						11
	3	4	5	6	7	8		11		1		9		10	2					12
	3	4	5	6	7		8	11		1		9		10	2					13
2	3	4	5	6	7		8	11		1		9		10						14
2	3	4	5	6	7		8	11		1		9		10						15
2	3	4	5	6	7	8		11		1		9		10						16
2	3	4	5	6	7	8		11		1		9		10						17
2	3	4	5	6	7	8		11				9				10				18
2		4	5	6	7	9		11						8	3	10				19
2	3	4	5	6	7	8		11				9				10				20
2	3	4	5	6	7	8		11				9				10				21
2	3	4	5	6	7	8		11				9				10				22
2	3	4	5	6	7	8		11				10				9				23
2	3	4	5	6	7	8		11				10				9				24
2	3	4	5	6	7	8	9	11				10								25
2	3	4	5	6	7	8	9	11				10								26
2	11	4	5	6	7		9	10				8			3					27
2	11	4	5	6	7		9	10				8			3					28
2	11	4	5	6	7		9	10				8			3					29
2	11	4	5	6	7		9	10				8			3					30
2	11	4	5	6	7		9	10				8			3					31
2		4	5	6	7		9	10				8			3	11				32
2		4	5	6	7		9	10				8			3	11				33
2		4	5	6	7	11	9	10				8			3					34
2	11	4	5	6	7		9	10				8			3					35
2	11	4	5	6			9	10				8			3	7				36
2	11	4	5	6			9	10				8			3	7				37
2	11		5	6	7		9	10				8			3		4			38
2	11		5	6	7		9	10				8			3		4			39
2	11		5	6	7		9	10						8	3		4			40
2	11		5	6			9	10				8		7	3		4			41
2			5	6	11		9	10				8		7	3		4			42
2			5	6	11			10				8		7	3	9	4			43
2			5	6	11		9	10				8		7	3		4			44
2	11		5	6	7			10				9		8	3		4			45
	3	4	5	6	11			8				9		7				2	10	46
42	39	38	45	46	42	22	31	44	5	16	2	38	2	19	23	12	8	1	1	
5	3		2	1	11	5	6	8				15		4		3				

ingley	Heron	Woods	Jackson	Fountain	Gould	Wragg	Stainsby	Rudd	Weir	Moor	Boyes	Wilkinson	Moore	Hoggart	Perry	Ambler	Ashworth	Popely	Barmby	
2	3	4	5	6		7	8	11				10					9			1
2	3	4	5	6	7	8		11				9		10						r
2	3	4	5	6	7	8		11				9				10				2
2	3	4	5	6	7	8		11				10				9				3
4	4	4	4	4	3	4	1	4				4		1		2	1			
						2						2								

ingley	Heron	Woods	Jackson	Fountain	Gould	Wragg	Stainsby	Rudd	Weir	Moor	Boyes	Wilkinson	Moore	Hoggart	Perry	Ambler	Ashworth	Popely	Barmby	
2	3	4		6	11	8		10		1	5	9		7						1
2	3	4	9	6	7	10	8	11		1	5									r
2	2	2	1	2	2	2	1	2		2	2	1		1						
				1	1															

Southampton v York City 5 January 1963 programme cover. The winter of the Big Freeze meant that this game was not played until 13 February 1963.

Tony Moor.

1963–64

Division Four

Manager: Tom Lockie

	P	W	D	L	F	A	Pts
Gillingham	46	23	14	9	59	30	60
Carlisle United	46	25	10	11	113	58	60
Workington	46	24	11	11	76	52	59
Exeter City	46	20	18	8	62	37	58
Bradford City	46	25	6	15	76	62	56
Torquay United	46	20	11	15	80	54	51
Tranmere Rovers	46	20	11	15	85	73	51
Brighton & Hove Albion	46	19	12	15	71	52	50
Aldershot	46	19	10	17	83	78	48
Halifax Town	46	17	14	15	77	77	48
Lincoln City	46	19	9	18	67	75	47
Chester	46	19	8	19	65	60	46
Bradford Park Avenue	46	18	9	19	75	81	45
Doncaster Rovers	46	15	12	19	70	75	42
Newport County	46	17	8	21	64	73	42
Chesterfield	46	15	12	19	57	71	42
Stockport County	46	15	12	19	50	68	42
Oxford United	46	14	13	19	59	63	41
Darlington	46	14	12	20	66	93	40
Rochdale	46	12	15	19	56	59	39
Southport	46	15	9	22	63	88	39
York City	46	14	7	25	52	66	35
Hartlepools United	46	12	9	25	54	93	33
Barrow	46	6	18	22	51	93	30

Did you know that?

A bad season for the club ended with them having to apply for re-election for the second time in their history and also getting embroiled in the football bribery scandal, that saw half-back and former skipper Jack Fountain found guilty and sent to prison.

Former Republic of Ireland international and Leeds United inside-forward Noel Peyton made his debut on the opening day and full-back Gerry Baker in the following game.

Wally Gould played his last match for the club on 28 December 1963 at Darlington prior to his move to Brighton.

For the second successive campaign, veteran forward Norman Wilkinson was top scorer.

Average home League crowd dropped to 3,937 and the attendance of 1,653 on 21 December 1963 for the visit of Oxford United was a then record low crowd for Bootham Crescent.

At the League AGM City received the maximum 48 votes as they were re-elected to the Football League.

Match No.	Date		Venue	Opponents	Result		Scorers
1	Aug	24	H	Rochdale	L	0–3	
2		26	A	Tranmere Rovers	L	0–1	
3		31	A	Oxford United	D	4–4	Goldie (2), J. Scott (pen), Rudd
4	Sep	7	H	Workington	L	0–1	
5		9	H	Tranmere Rovers	L	1–2	Peyton
6		14	A	Newport County	D	0–0	
7		16	H	Barrow	L	1–2	Woods
8		20	H	Stockport County	W	2–0	Woods, Gould
9		28	A	Bradford PA	W	3–1	Peyton (2), Rudd
10		30	A	Barrow	W	2–1	Hoggart, Rudd
11	Oct	5	H	Chesterfield	W	2–0	Gould, Wilkinson
12		7	H	Brighton & Hove Albion	L	2–3	Gould, Rudd
13		12	H	Hartlepools United	L	0–1	
14		17	A	Brighton & Hove Albion	L	0–3	
15		19	A	Exeter City	L	0–1	
16		22	A	Doncaster Rovers	D	0–0	
17		25	H	Southport	W	4–1	Lang (2), Gould, Wilkinson
18		28	H	Doncaster Rovers	W	3–1	Gould, Wilkinson, Rudd
19	Nov	2	A	Gillingham	L	0–1	
20		9	H	Lincoln City	D	0–0	
21		23	H	Aldershot	L	1–2	Gould
22		30	A	Carlisle United	L	0–4	
23	Dec	14	A	Rochdale	L	0–2	
24		21	H	Oxford United	L	0–2	
25		28	A	Darlington	L	2–4	Wilkinson, Opp. og
26	Jan	4	A	Bradford City	L	2–3	Wilkinson, Goldie (pen)
27		10	A	Workington	L	0–1	
28		18	H	Newport County	W	3–0	Baker (2), Goldie
29		25	H	Torquay United	D	1–1	Goldie
30	Feb	1	A	Stockport County	L	0–2	
31		8	H	Bradford PA	W	2–0	Heron, Rudd
32		15	A	Chesterfield	L	0–1	
33		22	A	Hartlepools United	W	1–0	Rudd
34		28	H	Exeter City	L	1–2	J. Scott (pen)
35	Mar	7	A	Southport	W	3–0	Wilkinson (2), Goldie
36		20	A	Lincoln City	L	2–3	Wilkinson, Goldie
37		27	H	Chester	W	1–0	J. Scott (pen)
38		28	H	Halifax Town	L	1–3	Wilkinson
39		30	A	Chester	D	1–1	Wilkinson
40	Apr	4	A	Aldershot	L	2–5	Baker (2)
41		6	H	Darlington	W	3–1	Peyton, Heron, Opp. og
42		11	H	Carlisle United	D	0–0	
43		17	A	Torquay United	W	1–0	Baker
44		20	A	Halifax Town	L	0–2	
45		25	H	Bradford City	W	1–0	Heron
46		27	H	Gillingham	L	0–1	

2 own-goals

FA Cup

1	Nov	16	H	Carlisle United	L	2–5	Wilkinson (2)

Football League Cup

1	Sep	4	A	Doncaster Rovers	D	0–0	
r		23	H	Doncaster Rovers	W	3–0	Lang, Rudd, Baker
2		25	H	Lincoln City	D	1–1	Peyton
r	Oct	14	A	Lincoln City	L	0–2	

Wealthall	Heron	Ashworth	Jackson	Fountain	Scott J.	Peyton	Goldie	Rudd	Gould	Baker	Boyes	Moor	Woods	Hoggart	Meecham	Wilkinson	Lang	Scott M.	Barnby	Popely	Wolstenholme	
2	3	4	5	6	7	8	9	10	11													1
	3	4		6	7	8	9	10	11	2	5											2
	3	4	5	6	7	8	9	10	11	2												3
	3	4	5	6	7	8	9	10	11	2												4
	3	6	5			8		10	11	2		1	4	7	9							5
	3	6	5			8		10	11	2		1	4	7	9							6
	3	6	5			8		10	11	2		1	4	7	9							7
	3	6	5				9	10	7	2		1	4			8	11					8
2	3		5	6		8		10	7			1	4			9	11					9
2	3		5	6				10	7			1	4	8	9		11					10
2	3		5	6		8		10	7			1	4			9	11					11
2	3		5	6		8		10	7			1	4			9	11					12
	3		5					10	7	2	6		4	8		9	11					13
	3	6	5					10	7	2			4		9	8	11					14
	3	6	5					10	7	2			4		9	8	11					15
2	3	6	5			8		10	7				4			9	11					16
2	3	6	5			8		10	7				4			9	11					17
2	3	6	5			8	11	10	7				4			9						18
2	3	6	5			8	11	10	7				4			9						19
	3	6	5			8		10	7	2			4			9	11					20
2	3	6	5		7	8		10	11				4			9						21
2	3	4	5		7	10		8	9								11	6				22
2	3	4	5		7	8		10	11			1				9		6				23
	3	4	5		7	8		10	11	2								6	9			24
	3		5			8	9	11	7	2			4			10		6				25
2	3		5			7	10	11		9		1	4			8		6				26
2	3		5			7	10	11		9		1	4			8		6				27
2	3		5			7	10	11		9		1	4			8		6				28
2	3		5			7	10	11		9		1	4			8		6				29
2	3					7	10	11		9	5	1	4			8		6				30
2	11				7	8	9	10		3	5	1	4					6				31
2	11				7	8	9	10		3	5	1	4					6				32
2	11				7	8	9	10		3	5	1	4					6				33
2	11				7	8	9	10		3	5	1	4					6				34
2	11				7		10	8		3	5	1	4			9		6				35
2	11				7		10	8		3	5	1	4			9		6				36
2	11		5		7		10	8		3		1	4			9		6				37
2	11		5		7		10	8		3		1	4			9		6				38
2	11		5	4		7	10	8				1				9		6		3		39
2	11		5	4	7	8		10		9		1						6		3		40
2	11		5	6	7	8		10		9			4							3	1	41
	11	2	5	6		8		10		9			4	7						3	1	42
2	11	7	5	6		8		10		9			4							3		43
2	11	6	5		7	8		10		9			4							3		44
2	11	6	5		7			10		9			4			8				3		45
2	11	6	5		7			10		9			4			8				3		46
32	46	24	38	13	21	35	22	46	25	33	9	24	37	6	6	27	12	19	1	8	2	
	3				3	4	7	7	6	5			2	1		10	2					

Wealthall	Heron	Ashworth	Jackson	Fountain	Scott J.	Peyton	Goldie	Rudd	Gould	Baker	Boyes	Moor	Woods	Hoggart	Meecham	Wilkinson	Lang	Scott M.	Barnby	Popely	Wolstenholme	
	3	6	5		7	8		10	11	2			4			9						1
	1	1	1		1	1		1	1	1			1			1						
																2						

Wealthall	Heron	Ashworth	Jackson	Fountain	Scott J.	Peyton	Goldie	Rudd	Gould	Baker	Boyes	Moor	Woods	Hoggart	Meecham	Wilkinson	Lang	Scott M.	Barnby	Popely	Wolstenholme	
	3	4	5	6		8	9	10	11	2				7								1
	3	6	5					10	7	2		1	4	8		9	11					r
	3	6	5			8		10	7	2		1	4			9	11					2
	3	6	5					10	7	2			4	8		9	11					r
	4	4	4	1		2	1	4	4	4		2	3	3		3	3					
						1		1		1							1					

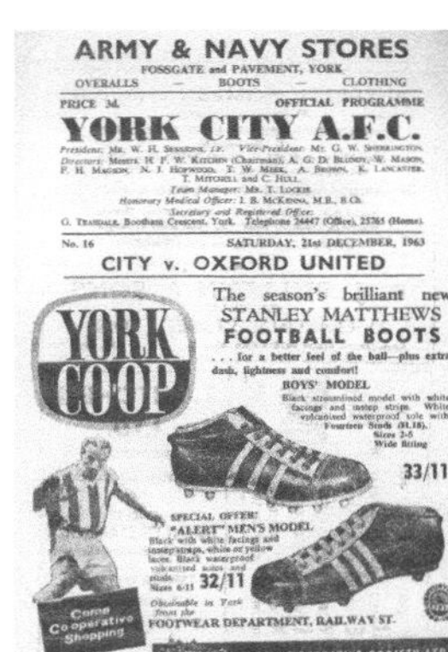

York City v Oxford United 21 December 1963 programme cover.

Noel Peyton.

1964–65

Division Four

Manager: Tom Lockie

	P	W	D	L	F	A	Pts
Brighton & Hove Albion	46	26	11	9	102	57	63
Millwall	46	23	16	7	78	45	62
York City	46	28	6	12	91	56	62
Oxford United	46	23	15	8	87	44	61
Tranmere Rovers	46	27	6	13	99	56	60
Rochdale	46	22	14	10	74	53	58
Bradford Park Avenue	46	20	17	9	86	62	57
Chester	46	25	6	15	119	81	56
Doncaster Rovers	46	20	11	15	84	72	51
Crewe Alexandra	46	18	13	15	90	81	49
Torquay United	46	21	7	18	70	70	49
Chesterfield	46	20	8	18	58	70	48
Notts County	46	15	14	17	61	73	44
Wrexham	46	17	9	20	84	92	43
Hartlepools United	46	15	13	18	61	85	43
Newport County	46	17	8	21	85	81	42
Darlington	46	18	6	22	84	87	42
Aldershot	46	15	7	24	64	84	37
Bradford City	46	12	8	26	70	88	32
Southport	46	8	16	22	58	89	32
Barrow	46	12	6	28	59	105	30
Lincoln City	46	11	6	29	58	99	28
Halifax Town	46	11	6	29	54	103	28
Stockport County	46	10	7	29	44	87	27

Did you know that?

City's second promotion success was watched by an average home League crowd of 7,185, which was almost double that of the previous campaign.

Newcomers to the City attack were Dennis Walker, Andy Provan and Paul Aimson, and they all made their debut on the opening day. The latter, who was signed from Manchester City, finished top marksman with 30 goals, which was the best tally since 1955–56.

A new club record was set in mid-term, with seven consecutive wins culminating in a 7–1 home win over Chesterfield on Boxing Day 1964.

The home record of 20 wins and one draw was the best in City's history, and the last 14 games of the season at Bootham Crescent were all won: P21 W20 D1 L2 F63 A21.

Match No.	Date	Venue	Opponents	Result		Scorers	Attend
1	Aug 22	H	Rochdale	W	2–1	Aimson, Provan	4
2	24	A	Hartlepools United	D	2–2	Walker (2, 2 pens)	6
3	29	A	Millwall	D	1–1	Walker	8
4	31	H	Hartlepools United	D	0–0		5
5	Sep 5	H	Bradford City	W	5–2	Walker (2, 1 pen), Aimson (2), Provan	3
6	7	A	Barrow	W	2–0	Weddle, Aimson	4
7	12	A	Chester	L	1–4	Provan	6
8	14	H	Barrow	W	2–0	Walker, Aimson	5
9	18	H	Torquay United	L	1–2	Aimson	6
10	25	A	Stockport County	W	2–1	Walker, Aimson	4
11	28	H	Brighton & Hove Albion	W	2–1	Walker (2)	8
12	Oct 3	A	Notts County	L	1–3	Opp. og	6
13	6	A	Brighton & Hove Albion	L	1–3	Walker	14
14	9	H	Doncaster Rovers	W	4–2	Walker (2), Provan, Aimson	11
15	12	H	Oxford United	W	2–1	Provan, Aimson	8
16	17	A	Aldershot	L	0–1		4
17	21	A	Oxford United	L	0–2		6
18	24	H	Bradford PA	L	0–1		7
19	27	A	Halifax Town	D	1–1	Walker	2
20	31	A	Southport	W	1–0	Aimson	2
21	Nov 7	H	Wrexham	W	2–1	Aimson, Provan	4
22	21	H	Darlington	W	2–1	Wilkinson, Provan	4
23	28	A	Crewe Alexandra	W	3–2	Weddle, Wilkinson, Aimson	2
24	Dec 12	A	Rochdale	W	2–1	Wilkinson, Rudd	3
25	19	H	Millwall	W	3–1	Aimson (2), Weddle	4
26	26	H	Chesterfield	W	7–1	Aimson (2), Provan (2), Weddle, Rudd, Wilkinson	6
27	28	A	Chesterfield	D	1–1	Provan	6
28	Jan 2	A	Bradford City	W	2–1	Wilkinson, Aimson	4
29	16	H	Chester	W	3–2	Provan (2), Walker	5
30	23	A	Torquay United	W	3–1	Wilkinson, Aimson, Provan	6
31	29	A	Tranmere Rovers	L	1–2	Aimson	13
32	Feb 6	H	Stockport County	W	3–0	Weddle, Aimson, Rudd	5
33	13	H	Notts County	W	2–1	Walker (pen), Rudd	6
34	20	A	Doncaster Rovers	L	3–4	Wilkinson, Aimson, Rudd	8
35	27	H	Aldershot	W	1–0	Provan (pen)	5
36	Mar 1	H	Newport County	W	5–1	Provan (2), Wilkinson, Aimson, Opp. og	5
37	6	A	Bradford PA	D	0–0		13
38	12	H	Southport	W	3–2	Weddle (2), Aimson	9
39	20	A	Wrexham	L	0–2		3
40	26	H	Tranmere Rovers	W	4–0	Weddle (3), Baker	13
41	Apr 3	A	Darlington	L	0–1		6
42	9	H	Crewe Alexandra	W	3–1	Rudd (2), Aimson	8
43	16	A	Lincoln City	W	1–0	Weddle	6
44	17	A	Newport County	L	0–2		2
45	19	H	Lincoln City	W	3–0	Wilkinson, Rudd, Provan	10
46	24	H	Halifax Town	W	4–0	Aimson (2), Rudd, Provan	12
							A
						2 own-goals	

FA Cup

1	Nov 14	H	Bangor City	W	5–1	Aimson (3), Provan, Weddle	5
2	Dec 5	A	Chesterfield	L	1–2	Aimson	7
							A

Football League Cup

1	Sep 2	A	Bradford City	L	0–2		2
							A

Wealthall	Heron	Woods	Jackson	Ashworth	Weddle	Walker	Aimson	Rudd	Provan	Povey	Wilkinson	Peyton	Baker	Hamstead	Forgan	
2	3	4	5	6	7	8	9	10	11							1
2	3		5	6		4	9	10	11	7	8					2
2	3		5	6	7	4	9	10	11		8					3
2	3	4	5	6	7		9	10	11			8				4
2	3	4	5	6	7	8	9	10	11							5
	3	4	5	6	7	8	9	10	11				2			6
	3	4	5	6	7	8	9	10	11				2			7
2	3	4		6		8	9	10	7				5	11		8
2	3	4		6		8	9	10	7				5	11		9
	3	4	5	6		8	9	10	7				2	11		10
	3	4	5	6		8	9	10	7				2	11		11
	3	4	5	6		8	9	10	7				2	11		12
	3	4	5	6		8	9	10	7				2	11	1	13
	3	4	5	6		8	9	10	7				2	11	1	14
	3	4	5	6		8	9	10	7				2	11	1	15
	3	4	5	6		8	9	10	7				2	11	1	16
	3	4	5	6		8	9	10	7				2	11	1	17
	3	4	5	6		8	9	10	11	7			2		1	18
	3	4	5	6		8	9	10	11	7			2			19
	3	4	5	6		8	9	10	7				2	11		20
	3	4	5	6	7	8	9	10	11				2			21
	3	4	5	6	7		9	10	11		8		2			22
	3	4	5		7	6	9	10	11		8		2			23
	3	4	5		7	6	9	10	11		8		2		1	24
	3	4	5		7	6	9	10	11		8		2		1	25
	3	4	5		7	6	9	10	11		8		2		1	26
	3	4	5		7	6	9	10	11		8		2		1	27
	3	4	5			6	9	10	7		8		2	11	1	28
	3	4	5		7	6	9	10	11		8		2		1	29
	3	4	5		7	6	9	10	11		8		2		1	30
	3	4	5			6	9	10	7		8		2	11	1	31
	3	4	5		7	6	9	10	11		8		2		1	32
	3	4	5		7	6	9	10	11		8		2		1	33
	3	4	5		7	6	9	10	11		8		2		1	34
	3	4	5		7	6	9	10	11		8		2		1	35
	3	4	5		7	6	9	10	11		8		2		1	36
	3	4	5		7	6	9	10	11		8		2		1	37
	3	4	5		7	6	9	10	11		8		2		1	38
	3	4	5		7	6	9	10	11		8		2		1	39
2	3	4	5		7	6		10	11		8		9		1	40
	3	4	5		7	6	9	10	11			8	2		1	41
	3	4	5	8	7	6	9	10	11				2		1	42
	3	4	5	8	7	6	9	10	11				2		1	43
	3	4	5	8	7	6	9	10	11				2		1	44
	3	4	5		7	6	9	10	11		8		2		1	45
	3	4	5		7	6	9	10	11		8		2		1	46
8	46	44	44	25	30	44	45	46	46	3	23	2	41	13	29	
					11	15	26	9	18		9		1			

Wealthall	Heron	Woods	Jackson	Ashworth	Weddle	Walker	Aimson	Rudd	Provan	Povey	Wilkinson	Peyton	Baker	Hamstead	Forgan	
	3	4	5	6	7		9	10	11		8		2			1
	3	4	5		7	6	9	10	11		8		2			2
	2	2	2	1	2	1	2	2	2		2		2			
					1		4		1							

Wealthall	Heron	Woods	Jackson	Ashworth	Weddle	Walker	Aimson	Rudd	Provan	Povey	Wilkinson	Peyton	Baker	Hamstead	Forgan	
2	3	4	5	6	7		9	10	11			8				1
1	1	1	1	1	1		1	1	1			1				

York City v Tranmere 26 March 1965 programme cover.

Derek Weddle.

1965–66

Division Three

Manager: Tom Lockie

	P	W	D	L	F	A	Pts
Hull City	46	31	7	8	109	62	69
Millwall	46	27	11	8	76	43	65
Queen's Park Rangers	46	24	9	13	95	65	57
Scunthorpe United	46	21	11	14	80	67	53
Workington	46	19	14	13	67	57	52
Gillingham	46	22	8	16	62	54	52
Swindon Town	46	19	13	14	74	48	51
Reading	46	19	13	14	70	63	51
Walsall	46	20	10	16	77	64	50
Shrewsbury Town	46	19	11	16	73	64	49
Grimsby Town	46	17	13	16	68	62	47
Watford	46	17	13	16	55	51	47
Peterborough United	46	17	12	17	80	66	46
Oxford United	46	19	8	19	70	74	46
Brighton & Hove Albion	46	16	11	19	67	65	43
Bristol Rovers	46	14	14	18	64	64	42
Swansea Town	46	15	11	20	81	96	41
Bournemouth	46	13	12	21	38	56	38
Mansfield Town	46	15	8	23	59	89	38
Oldham Athletic	46	12	13	21	55	81	37
Southend United	46	16	4	26	54	83	36
Exeter City	46	12	11	23	53	79	35
Brentford	46	10	12	24	48	69	32
York City	46	9	9	28	53	106	27

Did you know that?

Notable capture this term was midfielder Eamon Dunphy from Manchester United, and he made his debut on 27 August 1965 at home to Grimsby Town. After 26 senior appearances he was transferred to Millwall in January 1966. During his time at York he became the first player to win a full international cap while with the club when he represented the Republic of Ireland against Spain in November 1965 in a World Cup qualifying game.

Centre-forward David Dunmore returned to the club after 11 years.

John Pearson became City's first-ever substitute when he replaced Tommy Heron in the Grimsby game on 27 August.

Leading scorer Paul Aimson was transferred to Bury in March 1966.

The last two members of the semi-final side of 1954–55 played their last games for the club – Tommy Forgan and Norman Wilkinson. The goalkeeper's last appearance was on 13 March 1966 at home to Oxford United and the latter's was at home to Reading on 6 May 1966. Between them they made 829 senior appearances, and Wilkinson's total of 143 goals remains a club record.

Also departing at the end of the season were Billy Rudd, Tommy Heron, Alan Woods and Ken Boyes.

The total number of League goals conceded was 106 – a new club record.

Average home League crowd was 5,921. The attendance of 19,420 on 12 March 1966 was the third highest-ever League crowd at Bootham Crescent.

For the first time since 1946–47 City lost to non-League opposition when they went down at South Shields.

Match No.	Date	Venue	Opponents		Result	Scorers	Attend
1	Aug 21	A	Shrewsbury Town	L	1–4	Aimson	5
2	23	H	Swindon Town	L	0–2		9
3	27	H	Grimsby Town	D	1–1	Aimson	8
4	Sep 4	A	Brentford	W	1–0	Dunphy	10
5	10	H	Bristol Rovers	L	1–5	Aimson	9
6	13	A	Southend United	W	3–2	Aimson (2), Pearson	10
7	18	A	Hull City	W	4–1	Aimson (3), Dunmore	20
8	25	A	Oxford United	L	1–4	Pearson	6
9	Oct 1	H	Swansea Town	W	5–1	Provan (2), Pearson, Aimson, Rudd	8
10	4	H	Southend United	L	0–3		9
11	9	H	Queen's Park Rangers	D	2–2	Pearson, Rudd	6
12	15	A	Brighton & Hove Albion	L	1–3	Aimson	14
13	19	A	Swindon Town	L	0–6		12
14	30	A	Watford	L	2–3	Aimson, Opp. og	8
15	Nov 5	H	Oldham Athletic	D	2–2	Walker, Dunmore	5
16	19	H	Millwall	W	2–1	Dunmore, Aimson (pen)	5
17	27	A	Peterborough United	L	0–1		6
18	Dec 4	H	Scunthorpe United	L	1–3	Walker	4
19	11	A	Reading	L	0–3		6
20	17	H	Brighton & Hove Albion	L	0–1		3
21	27	H	Workington	D	3–3	Dunphy (2), Aimson	6
22	Jan 1	A	Queen's Park Rangers	L	2–7	Aimson (2)	7
23	8	H	Gillingham	L	1–2	Aimson	4
24	15	A	Scunthorpe United	L	1–4	Opp. og	3
25	21	H	Watford	W	1–0	Weddle	4
26	29	H	Shrewsbury Town	D	2–2	Weddle, Cunliffe	4
27	Feb 5	A	Grimsby Town	L	1–3	Aimson	7
28	12	H	Bournemouth	L	0–2		3
29	26	A	Bristol Rovers	D	0–0		8
30	Mar 5	A	Bournemouth	L	0–1		5
31	12	H	Hull City	L	1–2	Rudd	19
32	15	A	Workington	L	1–2	Cunliffe	3
33	18	H	Oxford United	L	1–4	Dunmore (pen)	4
34	25	A	Swansea Town	L	2–7	Morton, Opp. og	6
35	28	H	Brentford	D	1–1	Morton	2
36	Apr 8	H	Mansfield Town	W	2–1	Hawksby, Dunmore (pen)	3
37	9	H	Exeter City	W	2–0	Dunmore (2, 1 pen)	2
38	11	A	Mansfield Town	L	1–4	Hawksby	4
39	16	A	Millwall	L	0–2		14
40	23	H	Peterborough United	D	1–1	Dunmore	3
41	25	H	Walsall	L	0–3		2
42	30	A	Exeter City	W	2–0	Burden (2)	3
43	May 6	H	Reading	L	1–2	Hamstead	2
44	10	A	Oldham Athletic	L	0–3		9
45	17	A	Walsall	L	0–2		6
46	21	A	Gillingham	D	0–0		5

A

S

3 own-goals

FA Cup

1	Nov 12	A	South Shields	L	1–3	Aimson (pen)	7

A

Football League Cup

1	Sep 1	A	Lincoln City	D	2–2	Dunphy, Aimson	3
r	7	H	Lincoln City	W	4–2	Dunmore (2), Aimson (2)	7
2	22	A	Millwall	L	1–4	Provan	7

A

Note:

One substitute allowed from this season in the Football League. Substitute No. 12, player substituted in bold.

Substitutes allowed in the FA Cup from 1968–69.

Baker	Heron	Woods	Jackson	Walker	Weddle	Dunmore	Aimson	Rudd	Provan	Dunphy	Pearson	Fallon	Cunliffe	Hamstead	Wealthall	Morton	Popely	Wilkinson	Hawksby	Boyes	Hague	Burden	Wolstenholme	
2	3	4	5	6	7	8	9	10	11															1
2	3	4	5	6	7	8	9	10	11															2
2	**3**	4	5	6		7	9	10	11	8	12													3
2	3		5	6	7	8	9	10	11	4														4
2	3	12	5	6	7	8	9	10	11	4														5
2	3		5	6		8	9	10	11	4	7	1												6
2		4	5	3		8	9	10	11	6	7	1												7
2		4	5	3		8	9	10	11	6	7	1												8
2	3		5	6		8	9	10	11	4	7	1												9
2	3		5	6		8	9	10	11	4	7	1												10
2	3		5	6			9	10	11	4	7	**1**	8	12										11
		4	5	3		8	9	10	11	6	7	1			2									12
	3	4	5	6			9	10	11	8	7	1			2									13
2	3	4	5	6			9	10	11	8	7	1												14
2	**3**	4	5	6		9	8	7	11	10		1				12								15
2			5	6		8	9	10	7	4		1				11	3							16
		2	5	6		8	9	10	7	4		1				11	3							17
2	3		5	6		8	9	10		4	7	1				11								18
3		2	5			9	11	10		4	**7**	1	12	6				8						19
3	11	2	5				9	10	7	4		1		6				8						20
2	3	4	5	6	7		9	10		8		1		11										21
2	3	4	5	6	7		9	10		8		1		11										22
2			5	6	7	4	9	10		8		1		11	3									23
2		4	5		7	6	9	10		8		1		11	3									24
2		4	5	8	7	6	9	10						11	3									25
2		4	5	8	7	6	9						10	11	3									26
2		4	5		7	6	9	10					8	11	3									27
2		4	5		7	6	9	10	11				8		3									28
2			5	6	7	4	9	10	11				8		3									29
2			5	6	7	4	9	10	11				8		3									30
2			5	6		4	9	10	**7**				8	12	3				11					31
2			5	6		4	9	10					8		3	7			11					32
2			5	4		9		10					8	6	3	7			11					33
2	11	4	5	6		9		10				1			3	7			8					34
4				6		9		10	**7**			1			2	11	3		8	5	12			35
4			5	6		9		10				1		11	2	7	3		8					36
4			5	6		9		10			7	1		11	2		3		8					37
4			5	6		9		10			7	1		11	2		3		8					38
4			5	6		9		10			7	1		11	2		3		8					39
4			5	6		9		10	7			1		11	2		3		8					40
4			5	6		9		10	7			1		11	2		3		8					41
4			5	6				10	**7**			1		12	2		3	8	11			9		42
4			5	6		12		10				1		11	2		3	**8**	7			9		43
4			5	6		8		10				1	7		2		3		11			9		44
4			5	6		9		10				1	7	11	2		3		8					45
4			5	6		9		10				1		7	2	11	3		8					46
43	17	20	45	41	14	38	32	45	26	22	14	32	11	19	26	9	14	4	16	1		3		
		1				1					1		1	3		1					1			
				2	2	8	17	3	2	3	4		2	1		2			2			2		

Baker	Heron	Woods	Jackson	Walker	Weddle	Dunmore	Aimson	Rudd	Provan	Dunphy	Pearson	Fallon	Cunliffe	Hamstead	Wealthall	Morton	Popely	Wilkinson	Hawksby	Boyes	Hague	Burden	Wolstenholme	
2		4	5	3	7		9	10	11	6	8	1												1
1		1	1	1	1		1	1	1	1	1	1												
							1																	

Baker	Heron	Woods	Jackson	Walker	Weddle	Dunmore	Aimson	Rudd	Provan	Dunphy	Pearson	Fallon	Cunliffe	Hamstead	Wealthall	Morton	Popely	Wilkinson	Hawksby	Boyes	Hague	Burden	Wolstenholme	
2	3	4	5	6			9	10	11	8	7													1
2	3		5	6	7	8	9	10	11	4														r
2		4	5	3		8	9	10	11	6	7												1	2
3	2	2	3	3	1	2	3	3	3	3	2												1	
						2	3		1	1														

York City v Reading 6 May 1966 programme cover.

Ken Boyes.

Eamon Dunphy.

1966–67

Division Four

Manager: Tom Lockie

	P	W	D	L	F	A	Pts
Stockport County	46	26	12	8	69	42	64
Southport	46	23	13	10	69	42	59
Barrow	46	24	11	11	76	54	59
Tranmere Rovers	46	22	14	10	66	43	58
Crewe Alexandra	46	21	12	13	70	55	54
Southend United	46	22	9	15	70	49	53
Wrexham	46	16	20	10	76	62	52
Hartlepools United	46	22	7	17	66	64	51
Brentford	46	18	13	15	58	56	49
Aldershot	46	18	12	16	72	57	48
Bradford City	46	19	10	17	74	62	48
Halifax Town	46	15	14	17	59	68	44
Port Vale	46	14	15	17	55	58	43
Exeter City	46	14	15	17	50	60	43
Chesterfield	46	17	8	21	60	63	42
Barnsley	46	13	15	18	60	64	41
Luton Town	46	16	9	21	59	73	41
Newport County	46	12	16	18	56	63	40
Chester	46	15	10	21	54	78	40
Notts County	46	13	11	22	53	72	37
Rochdale	46	13	11	22	53	75	37
York City	46	12	11	23	65	79	35
Bradford Park Avenue	46	11	13	22	52	79	35
Lincoln City	46	9	13	24	58	82	31

Did you know that?

Following the previous season's relegation City finished in the bottom four and had to make their third application for re-election to the Football League. They were duly re-elected with 45 votes out of a possible 48.

Phil Burrows, ex-Manchester City, made his York City debut on the opening day.

Leading scorer was another newcomer Tommy Spencer, who had previously been with Southampton.

In November and December City suffered eight successive League defeats – a club record.

The away record of one win and six draws was then the worst in the club's history.

The average home League crowd of 3,776 was the worst since the war.

City played six FA Cup ties but did not progress beyond the second round.

They met Middlesbrough in a total of five Cup games (FA Cup and Football League Cup).

Match No.	Date	Venue	Opponents	Result		Scorers	Attend
1	Aug 20	H	Chesterfield	D	1–1	Hawksby	5
2	26	A	Stockport County	L	1–3	Spencer (pen)	7
3	Sep 2	H	Rochdale	D	1–1	Provan	5
4	4	H	Halifax Town	W	4–3	Provan (2), Jackson, Opp. og	4
5	10	A	Southport	L	0–2		4
6	16	H	Notts County	W	4–1	Dunmore (2, 1 pen), Burrows, Spencer	4
7	24	A	Chester	L	1–3	Spencer	5
8	27	A	Halifax Town	L	1–2	Goodchild	2
9	30	H	Bradford PA	W	3–1	Horrey, Dunmore (pen), Provan	5
10	Oct 7	H	Hartlepools United	D	1–1	Horrey	5
11	15	A	Exeter City	L	1–3	Hawksby	4
12	17	A	Barrow	D	1–1	Dunmore	4
13	22	H	Bradford City	W	4–1	Horrey, Dunmore, Spencer, Provan	5
14	28	A	Tranmere Rovers	L	1–2	Horrey	6
15	Nov 4	H	Southend United	W	2–1	Opp. og, Spencer	4
16	12	A	Wrexham	D	1–1	Spencer	9
17	14	H	Barrow	L	1–2	Opp. og	4
18	19	H	Aldershot	L	1–2	Provan	2
19	Dec 3	H	Barnsley	L	0–3		3
20	10	A	Newport County	L	2–4	Spencer, Goodchild	1
21	17	A	Chesterfield	L	0–1		3
22	26	A	Crewe Alexandra	L	0–2		5
23	27	H	Crewe Alexandra	L	0–2		2
24	31	H	Stockport County	L	1–2	Goodchild	2
25	Jan 14	H	Southport	W	2–0	Burrows, Spencer	3
26	21	A	Notts County	L	0–2		4
27	Feb 4	H	Chester	D	1–1	Spencer	3
28	11	A	Bradford PA	L	0–1		4,
29	18	A	Brentford	D	1–1	Provan	7
30	25	A	Hartlepools United	L	2–4	Caulfield, Provan (pen)	6
31	Mar 3	H	Exeter City	L	2–4	Horrey, Goodchild	3
32	11	H	Brentford	D	0–0		1
33	18	A	Bradford City	L	0–1		4
34	24	A	Lincoln City	D	2–2	Turner, Spencer	7
35	25	H	Luton Town	W	5–1	Provan 2, Collinson, Spencer, Goodchild	1,
36	27	H	Lincoln City	W	3–1	Spencer, Caulfield, Opp. og	3
37	31	A	Southend United	L	1–2	Provan	8
38	Apr 7	H	Wrexham	W	4–0	Spencer (2), Turner (pen), Provan	3
39	10	H	Port Vale	W	3–1	Provan, Spencer, Hawksby	3,
40	15	A	Aldershot	D	0–0		3
41	21	H	Tranmere Rovers	L	0–1		4,
42	24	A	Port Vale	L	1–4	Spencer	2,
43	28	A	Barnsley	W	1–0	Spencer	5,
44	May 2	A	Rochdale	D	2–2	Provan, Spencer	2,
45	5	H	Newport County	W	2–1	Provan, Goodchild	2,
46	13	A	Luton Town	L	1–5	Hawksby	5,
							A
							S
						4 own-goals	

FA Cup

1	Nov 26	H	Morecambe	D	0–0		5,
r	Dec 5	A	Morecambe	D	1–1*	Spencer	6,
2r	8	N#	Morecambe	W	1–0	Spencer	4,
2	Jan 7	A	Middlesbrough	D	1–1	Provan	20
r	11	H	Middlesbrough	D	0–0*		14,
2r	16	N~	Middlesbrough	L	1–4	Horrey	21,
							A

* After extra-time. # At Maine Road, Manchester.

~ At St James' Park, Newcastle.

Football League Cup

1	Aug 24	A	Middlesbrough	D	0–0		9,
r	29	12	Middlesbrough	W	2–1	Provan, Spencer (pen)	4,
2	Sep 13	H	Chesterfield	W	3–2	Spencer (2), Provan	4,
3	Oct 4	H	Blackburn Rovers	L	0–2		8,
							A

Wealthall	Turner	Wolstenholme	Jackson	Burrows	Horrey	Walker D.	Spencer	Hawksby	Goodchild	Dunmore	Provan	Baker	Brookes	Walker M.	Popely	Coyne	Caulfield	Collinson	
2	3	4	5	6	7	8	9	10	11										1
2	3	4	5	6	7	8	9	10	11										2
2	3	4	5	6	7		9	10		8	11								3
2	3		5	6		4	9	10	7	8	11								4
2	3		5	6		4	9	10	7	8	11								5
	3		5	6	7	4	9	10		8	11	2							6
	3		5	6	7	4	9	10			11	2	8						7
	3		5	6		4	9	10	7	8	11	2							8
	3	4	5	6	7		9	10		8	11	2							9
	3	4	5	6	7		9	10		8	11	2							10
4	3		5	6	7		9	10		8	11	2							11
4	3		5	6	7		9	10		8	11	2		1					12
4	3		5	6	7		9	10		8	**11**	2		1	12				13
4	3		5	6	7		9	10		8	11	2		1					14
	3		5	6	7	4	9	10		8	11	2		1					15
	3		5	6	7	4	9	10		8	11	2		1					16
	3		5	6	7	4	9	10		8	11	2		1					17
	3	4	5	6			9	10	7	8	11			1	2				18
	3		5	6	7	4	9	10		8	11	2		1					19
	3		5	6	7	4	9	11	10	8		2		1					20
	3		5	6	7	4	9	11	10	8		2		1					21
	3		5	6	7	4		**11**	10	8	12	2		1		9			22
	3	4	5	6	7				10	8	11	2		1		9			23
	3	4	5	6	7		9	8	10		11	2		1					24
	3		5	6	7	4	8		10	9	11	2		1					25
	3	4	5	10	7	6	8	11		9		2		1					26
	3	4	5	6	7	8	12		10		11	2		1			**9**		27
	3	4	5	6	7		9		10		11	2		1			8		28
	3		5	6	7		9		10		11	2		1			8	4	29
	3		5	6	7		**9**		10	12	11	2		1			8	4	30
	3		5	6	7				9	10	11	2		1			8	4	31
	3		5		7	6		10	9		11	2					8	4	32
	3		5	**6**	7	8	12	10			11	2					9	4	33
	3		5		7	6	9	10	8		11	2						4	34
	3		5		7	6	9	10	8		11	2						4	35
	3		5		7	6	9	10			11	2					8	4	36
	3		5		7	6	9	10			11	2					8	4	37
	3		5		7	6	9	10	8		11	2						4	38
	3		5		7	6	9	10	8		11	2						4	39
	3		5		7	6	9	10	8		11	2						4	40
	3		5		7	6	9	10	8		11	2						4	41
	3		5		7	6	9	10	8		11	2						4	42
	3		5		7	6	9	10	8		11	2						4	43
	3		5	12	7	6	9	10	8		**11**	2						4	44
	3		5		7	6	9	10	8		11	2						4	45
	3		5		7	6	9	10	8		11	2						4	46
9	46	11	46	32	42	32	40	39	29	23	40	40	1	20	1	2	9	18	
				1			2			1	1				1				
	2		1	2	5		18	4	6	5	15						2	1	

Wealthall	Turner	Wolstenholme	Jackson	Burrows	Horrey	Walker D.	Spencer	Hawksby	Goodchild	Dunmore	Provan	Baker	Brookes	Walker M.	Popely	Coyne	Caulfield	Collinson	
	3		5	6		4	9	10	7	8	11			1	2				1
	3		5	6	7	4	9		10	8	11	2		1					r
	3		5	6	7	4	9		10	8	11	2		1					2r
	3	4	5	6	7	8			10	9	11	2		1					2
	3	4	5	6	7	8			10	9	11	2		1					r
2	3	4	5	6	7	8			10	9	11			1					2r
1	6	3	6	6	5	6	3	1	6	6	6	4		6	1				
					1		2				1								

Wealthall	Turner	Wolstenholme	Jackson	Burrows	Horrey	Walker D.	Spencer	Hawksby	Goodchild	Dunmore	Provan	Baker	Brookes	Walker M.	Popely	Coyne	Caulfield	Collinson	
2	3	4	5	6	7	8	9	10	11										1
2	3	4	5	6	7	8	9	10			11								r
	3		5	6	7	4	9	10		8	11	2							2
	3	4	5	6	7		9	10		8	11	2							3
2	4	3	4	4	4	3	4	4	1	2	3	2							
							3				2								

York City v Middlesbrough 29 August 1966 programme cover.

Tommy Spencer.

1967–68

Division Four

Manager: Tom Lockie, then Joe Shaw

	P	W	D	L	F	A	Pts
Luton Town	46	27	12	7	87	44	66
Barnsley	46	24	13	9	68	46	61
Hartlepools United	46	25	10	11	60	46	60
Crewe Alexandra	46	20	18	8	74	49	58
Bradford City	46	23	11	12	72	51	57
Southend United	46	20	14	12	77	58	54
Chesterfield	46	21	11	14	71	50	53
Wrexham	46	20	13	13	72	53	53
Aldershot	46	18	17	11	70	55	53
Doncaster Rovers	46	18	15	13	66	56	51
Halifax Town	46	15	16	15	52	49	46
Newport County	46	16	13	17	58	63	45
Lincoln City	46	17	9	20	71	68	43
Brentford	46	18	7	21	61	64	43
Swansea Town	46	16	10	20	63	77	42
Darlington	46	12	17	17	47	53	41
Notts County	46	15	11	20	53	79	41
Port Vale	46	12	15	19	61	72	39
Rochdale	46	12	14	20	51	72	38
Exeter City	46	11	16	19	45	65	38
York City	46	11	14	21	65	68	36
Chester	46	9	14	23	57	78	32
Workington	46	10	11	25	54	87	31
Bradford Park Avenue	46	4	15	27	30	82	23

Did you know that?

For the first time in 31 years City changed their strip and sported an all white kit.

Centre-forward Ted MacDougall was signed from Liverpool for a fee of £5,000 and scored on his debut in the opening game. He finished top scorer with 15 goals.

City failed to win any of their opening 13 League games – then the worst start in their history.

Tom Lockie became the first City manager to be sacked when he was dismissed on 16 October 1967. He had served the club as trainer, coach, physiotherapist and then manager for over 30 years. His successor was Joe Shaw, the Sheffield United centre-half.

City, watched by an average home League crowd of 4,578, again finished in the bottom four but were re-elected with 46 votes out of a possible 48.

For the first time City were knocked out in the first round of both Cup competitions.

May 1968 marked the end of an era with the retirement of *Yorkshire Evening Press* journalist Wilf Meek, who had reported on City for 46 years since their formation in 1922. His successor was Malcolm Huntington.

Match No.	Date	Venue	Opponents	Result		Scorers
1	Aug 19	H	Workington	D	1–1	MacDougall
2	26	A	Rochdale	L	2–3	Spencer, Provan
3	Sep 2	H	Brentford	L	0–1	
4	5	A	Newport County	L	1–2	Alderson
5	9	A	Bradford PA	D	1–1	Provan
6	16	H	Doncaster Rovers	L	1–2	Alderson
7	23	A	Luton Town	L	1–3	MacDougall
8	25	H	Newport County	L	0–1	
9	30	H	Southend United	D	2–2	Provan (2)
10	Oct 3	A	Swansea Town	D	1–1	MacDougall
11	7	A	Halifax Town	L	1–2	Provan
12	14	H	Bradford City	L	0–1	
13	21	A	Crewe Alexandra	D	0–0	
14	23	H	Swansea Town	W	2–1	Horrey, Opp. og
15	28	H	Notts County	W	4–2	Burrows, Horrey, Ross, Walker
16	Nov 4	A	Port Vale	L	0–1	
17	11	H	Chester	W	4–1	Ross (2), MacDougall, Provan
18	14	A	Brentford	L	1–3	MacDougall
19	18	A	Chesterfield	L	1–3	Hawksby
20	25	H	Exeter City	W	4–0	Ross (2), Burrows, MacDougall
21	Dec 2	A	Darlington	L	1–3	Horrey
22	16	A	Workington	D	1–1	Provan
23	23	H	Rochdale	W	4–1	MacDougall (2), Provan, Opp. og
24	26	H	Barnsley	D	1–1	MacDougall
25	30	A	Barnsley	L	0–1	
26	Jan 19	A	Doncaster Rovers	L	0–2	
27	27	A	Lincoln City	W	3–1	Collinson, Ross, Spencer
28	Feb 3	H	Luton Town	D	1–1	Ross
29	10	A	Southend United	W	1–0	Spencer
30	17	H	Wrexham	W	3–1	Ross (2), Provan
31	24	H	Chesterfield	L	0–2	
32	Mar 2	A	Bradford City	D	0–0	
33	9	H	Lincoln City	W	1–0	Ross
34	16	H	Crewe Alexandra	D	1–1	Walker (pen)
35	23	A	Notts County	D	1–1	Jackson
36	25	H	Bradford PA	W	6–2	Ross (2), MacDougall (2), Horrey, Provan
37	30	H	Port Vale	W	5–1	MacDougall (3), Baker, Opp. og
38	Apr 6	A	Chester	D	1–1	Provan
39	12	A	Hartlepools United	L	0–1	
40	13	H	Halifax Town	L	1–2	Ross
41	15	H	Hartlepools United	L	0–2	
42	20	A	Exeter City	L	1–3	Alderson
43	22	H	Aldershot	L	2–3	Alderson, Provan
44	27	H	Darlington	D	1–1	Ross
45	May 4	A	Aldershot	D	2–2	MacDougall, Provan
46	11	A	Wrexham	L	1–3	Alderson

3 own-goals

FA Cup

1	Dec 9	H	Doncaster Rovers	L	0–1	

Football League Cup

1	Aug 23	A	Darlington	L	0–1	

Joy	Turner	Collinson	Jackson	Burrows	Alderson	Ross	Spencer	MacDougall	Provan	Walker D.	Baker	Hawksby	Horrey	Fellows	Walker M.	Hodgson	Spratt	Woodall	
2	3	4	5	6	7	8	9	10	11										1
2	3		5	6	7	8	9	10	11	4									2
2	3	4	5		7	8	9	10	11	6									3
2	3	4	5		7	8	9	10	11	6									4
	3		5	6	7	8		9	11	4	2	10							5
	3		5	6	7	9		10	11	4	2	8							6
	3		5	6	7		9	8		4	2	10	11						7
	3		5	6	7		9	8		**4**	2	10	11	12					8
	3	4	5	6		8		9	11		2	10	7						9
	3	4	5	6		8		9	11	12	**2**	10	7		1				10
	3	4	**5**	6		8		9	11	12	2	10	7		1				11
	3		5	6		8		9	11	4	2	10	7		1				12
	3	4	5	6	12			9	11	8	2	**10**	7		1				13
	3	4	5	6		10	9	8	11		2		7		1				14
	3	4	5	6		8		9	11	12	2	**10**	7		1				15
	3	4	5	6		10		9	11	8	2		7		1				16
	3	4	5	6		8		9	11	10	2		7		1				17
	3	**4**	5	6		8		9	11	10	2	12	7		1				18
2	3			4		8	12	9	11	6	5	**10**	7		1				19
12	3		**5**	4		8	10	9	11	6	2		7		1				20
2	3			4		8		9	11	6	5	10	7		1				21
2	3			6	7		9		11	4	5	8			1	10			22
2	3		5	6	7			9	11	4		8			1	10			23
2	3			6	7	12		9	11	4	5	8			1	10			24
	3		5	6	7			9	11	4	2	8			1	10			25
	3		5	6				9	11	4	2	**8**	7	12	1	10			26
	3	4	5	6		8	9		11		2		7		1	10			27
	3	4	5	6		8	9		11		2		7		1	10			28
12	3	4	5			8	9		11	6	2		**7**		1	10			29
	3	4	5	12		8	9		11	6	2		**7**		1	10			30
	3	4	5			8	9	7	11	6	2				1	10			31
	3		5			8		9	11	6	2		7		1	10	4		32
	3		5			8		9	11	6	2		7		1	10	4		33
	3		5			8		9	11	6	2		7		1	10	4		34
	3		5			8		9	11	6	2		7		1	10	4		35
	3		5			8		9	11	6	2		7		1	10	4		36
	3		5			8		9	11	6	2		7		1	10	4		37
	3		5			8		9	11	6	2		7		1	10	4		38
9	3		5			8			11	6	2		7		1	10	4		39
	3		5	12		8		9	11	6	2		7		1	10	4		40
			5	6	3	8		9	11		2		7		1	10	4		41
3			5	6	7	8			11	12	2				1	10	4	**9**	42
3			5	6	7	8			11	12	2				1	10	4	**9**	43
3			5	6	**7**	8		9	11		2	12			1	10	4		44
	3		5	6	12	**8**		9	11		2		7		1	10	4		45
	3		5	6	8			9	11		2		7		1	10	4		46
13	42	17	42	32	17	37	14	38	44	32	41	17	32		37	25	15	2	
2				2	2	1	1			5		2		2					
		1	1	2	5	14	3	15	13	2	1	1	4						

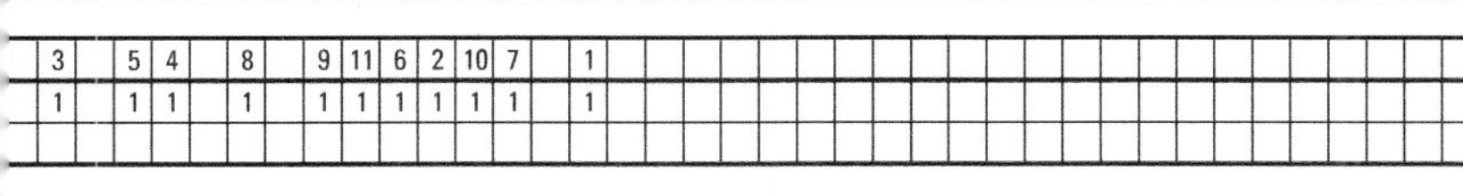

Joy	Turner	Collinson	Jackson	Burrows	Alderson	Ross	Spencer	MacDougall	Provan	Walker D.	Baker	Hawksby	Horrey	Fellows	Walker M.	Hodgson	Spratt	Woodall	
	3		5	4		8		9	11	6	2	10	7		1				1
	1		1	1		1		1	1	1	1	1	1		1				

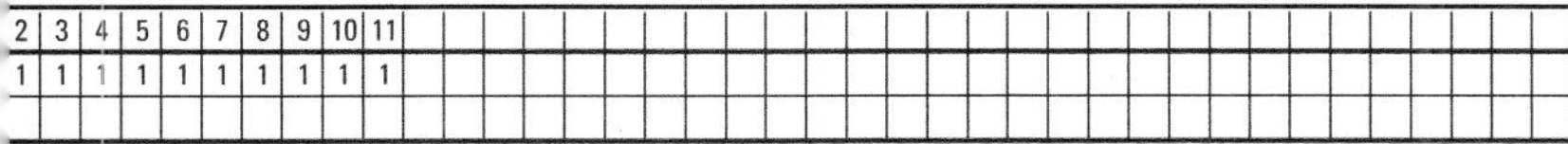

Joy	Turner	Collinson	Jackson	Burrows	Alderson	Ross	Spencer	MacDougall	Provan	Walker D.	Baker	Hawksby	Horrey	Fellows	Walker M.	Hodgson	Spratt	Woodall	
2	3	4	5	6	7	8	9	10	11										1
1	1	1	1	1	1	1	1	1	1										

York City v Brentford 2 September 1967 programme cover.

Mike Walker.

1968–69

Division Four

Manager: Joe Shaw, then Tom Johnston

	P	W	D	L	F	A	Pts
Doncaster Rovers	46	21	17	8	65	38	59
Halifax Town	46	20	17	9	53	37	57
Rochdale	46	18	20	8	68	35	56
Bradford City	46	18	20	8	65	46	56
Darlington	46	17	18	11	62	45	52
Colchester United	46	20	12	14	57	53	52
Southend United	46	19	13	14	78	61	51
Lincoln City	46	17	17	12	54	52	51
Wrexham	46	18	14	14	61	52	50
Swansea Town	46	19	11	16	58	54	49
Brentford	46	18	12	16	64	65	48
Workington	46	15	17	14	40	43	47
Port Vale	46	16	14	16	46	46	46
Chester	46	16	13	17	76	66	45
Aldershot	46	19	7	20	66	66	45
Scunthorpe United	46	18	8	20	61	60	44
Exeter City	46	16	11	19	66	65	43
Peterborough United	46	13	16	17	60	57	42
Notts County	46	12	18	16	48	57	42
Chesterfield	46	13	15	18	43	50	41
York City	46	14	11	21	53	75	39
Newport County	46	11	14	21	49	74	36
Grimsby Town	46	9	15	22	47	69	33
Bradford Park Avenue	46	5	10	31	32	106	20

Did you know that?

Phil Boyer was signed from Derby County in the close season and made his debut on the opening day, teaming up with Ted MacDougall in a partnership that was to continue in the years ahead at Bournemouth and Norwich. The latter, who moved to the Dean Court club at the end of the season, again finished top marksman.

Manager Joe Shaw resigned on 16 August 1968 for personal reasons, and Tom Johnston took over the reigns at the end of October.

Left-winger Andy Provan played his last game on 24 August 1968 prior to his move to Chester.

Full-back Gerry Baker played his last game on 7 December 1968 against Morecambe in the FA Cup and ended his career because of injury.

Later that month 17-year-old Chris Topping, the club's first apprentice professional, made his debut at home to Newport County.

In the last home game of the season against Halifax Town, referee Roy Harper collapsed and died.

Average League attendance was 3,883 as City made their third successive bid for re-election, which was successful with 45 votes out of a possible 48 at the League's AGM.

For the first time since 1960–61 City reached the third round of the FA Cup, and their 6–0 win at South Shields was their biggest-ever away victory in the competition.

Match No.	Date	Venue	Opponents	Result		Scorers	Attend
1	Aug 10	A	Chester	L	0–2		7
2	17	H	Doncaster Rovers	D	1–1	Ross	5,
3	24	A	Chesterfield	D	1–1	Provan	7
4	26	H	Bradford City	D	1–1	Coleman	5
5	31	H	Peterborough United	W	2–1	Boyer, Hodgson	4
6	Sep 7	A	Colchester United	L	0–1		3
7	14	H	Scunthorpe United	W	2–1	MacDougall, Hodgson	5,
8	16	A	Port Vale	L	0–3		3
9	21	A	Brentford	L	1–5	Boyer	8
10	28	H	Rochdale	D	0–0		3
11	Oct 5	H	Bradford PA	W	4–2	MacDougall (2), Taylor, Sweenie	5
12	9	A	Bradford City	L	0–5		5,
13	12	A	Lincoln City	L	0–3		7
14	19	H	Southend United	D	1–1	Ross	3,
15	26	A	Newport County	D	1–1	Boyer	2
16	28	H	Exeter City	L	0–2		2,
17	Nov 4	H	Aldershot	W	2–1	Ross (2)	2
18	9	A	Grimsby Town	L	0–3		3
19	23	A	Notts County	D	0–0		3
20	30	H	Darlington	D	1–1	Ross	5
21	Dec 14	H	Lincoln City	D	1–1	Ross	2,
22	20	A	Southend United	W	2–1	MacDougall, Boyer	9
23	28	H	Newport County	D	0–0		2,
24	Jan 11	A	Halifax Town	W	4–0	MacDougall, Carr, Coleman, Boyer	5
25	18	H	Grimsby Town	L	2–5	MacDougall (pen), Coleman	3
26	25	A	Aldeshot	L	0–2		6
27	Feb 24	H	Wrexham	W	1–0	Spratt	3,
28	Mar 7	A	Doncaster Rovers	L	1–2	MacDougall	12,
29	10	H	Workington	W	2–1	Topping, MacDougall	3,
30	15	H	Chesterfield	W	3–1	MacDougall (2, 1 pen), Boyer	3,
31	18	A	Swansea Town	L	1–2	Boyer	2
32	22	A	Peterborough United	L	1–2	MacDougall	4,
33	26	A	Bradford PA	L	0–1		2
34	29	H	Colchester United	W	2–0	Boyer (2)	3
35	Apr 4	H	Port Vale	W	3–1	Sibbald (2, 1 pen), Taylor	4,
36	5	A	Rochdale	L	1–2	MacDougall	6
37	9	A	Exeter City	L	0–5		4,
38	12	H	Brentford	W	2–1	MacDougall, Hewitt	3
39	16	A	Wrexham	L	1–2	MacDougall	3
40	18	A	Scunthorpe United	L	1–2	MacDougall	2
41	21	A	Darlington	L	2–3	MacDougall, Taylor	4
42	23	H	Notts County	W	2–0	Burrows, MacDougall	3
43	28	H	Chester	W	4–2	MacDougall (2), Jackson, Hewitt	3
44	30	A	Workington	L	0–2		1
45	May 2	H	Swansea Town	L	0–2		3
46	5	H	Halifax Town	D	0–0		4,
							A
							S

FA Cup

1	Nov 16	A	South Shields	W	6–0	Ross (3), MacDougall (2), Baker (pen)	6
2	Dec 7	H	Morecambe	W	2–0	MacDougall (2)	5
3	Jan 4	H	Stoke City	L	0–2		11,
							A
							S

Football League Cup

1	Aug 14	H	Barnsley	L	3–4	MacDougall (2), Spratt	5
							A
							S

Baker	Kelly	Carr	Jackson	Burrows	Boyer	Hodgson	MacDougall	Ross	Provan	Spratt	Walker	Coleman	Shepherd	Dale	Taylor	Sweenie	Richardson	Topping	Tunks	Sibbald	Hewitt	Andrews	Pennick	
2	3	4	5	6	7	8	9	10	11															1
	3	2	5	6	7	8	9	10	11	4														2
	3	2	5	6	7	8	9	10	11	4	1													3
2	3	4	5		7	11	9	8		10	1	6												4
2	3	4	5		7	11	9	8		10	1	6												5
2	3	4	5		7	11	9			10		6	8											6
2	3		5	6	11	10	9	8				4	7											7
2	3		5	6	11	10	9	8				4	7											8
2	3	4	5	6	11	10	9	8		12			**7**											9
2	3	4	5	6	7	**10**	9	8				12		11										10
2	3	5		6	8	4	9							11	7	10								11
2	3	5		6	8	4	9							11	7	10								12
	2	5	12	6	8	10	9			4				**11**	7		3							13
	2	4	5	6	8		9	10						11	7		3							14
2		4	5	6	11	8	9								7	10	3							15
2		**4**	5	6	11	8	9	12							7	10	3							16
2		4	5	6	11	10	9	8							7		3							17
2		4	5	6	11	10	**9**	8		12					7		3							18
2		4	5	6	11	10	9	8							7		3							19
2		4	5	6	11	10	9	8							7		3							20
	2	4	5	6	11	10	9	8							7		3							21
	2	4	5	6	11	10	9								7	8	3							22
	2			6	11	10	9	12		4					**7**	8	3	5						23
	2	4		6	11	10	9					8			7		3	5						24
	2	4	7	6	11	10	9			12		**8**					3	5						25
	2	4	5	6	11	10	9	7		8							3							26
	2		5	6	11	10	9			8					**7**		3	4	1	12				27
	2		5	6	11	10	9			**8**					7		3	4	1	12				28
			5	6	11	10	9	7		8							3	4	1	2				29
		8	5	6	11	10	9								7		3	4	1	2				30
	3	8	5	6	11		9								7			4		2	10			31
	12	8	5	6	11	7	9										3	4		2	**10**			32
		4	5	6	11	8	9								7		3			2	10			33
		4	5		11	8	9								7		3	6		2	10			34
		4	5		11	8	9					12			7		3	6		2	10			35
		4	5		11	8	9					12			**7**		3	6		2	10	1		36
		12	5	6	11	8	9					7					3	4		2	**10**	1		37
	3		5	6	11	8	9								7			4		2	10	1		38
	3		5	6	11	8	9								7			4		2	10	1		39
	3	4		6	11	8	**9**	12					10		7			5		2		1		40
	3		5	6	11	8	9	10							7			4		2		1		41
	3		5	6	11	8	9								7			4		2	10	1		42
	3		5	6	11	8	9	12							**7**			4		2	10	1		43
	3		5	6	11	8	9	7										4		2	10	1		44
	3		5	6	11	8	9								7			4		2	10	1		45
		4	5	3	11	8	9								**7**			6		2	10	1	12	46
6	31	32	40	40	46	44	46	19	3	11	3	8	5	5	30	6	24	22	4	18	14	11		
	1	1	1					4		3		3								2			1	
		1	1	1	9	2	19	6	1	1		3			3	1		1		2	2			

Baker	Kelly	Carr	Jackson	Burrows	Boyer	Hodgson	MacDougall	Ross	Provan	Spratt	Walker	Coleman	Shepherd	Dale	Taylor	Sweenie	Richardson	Topping	Tunks	Sibbald	Hewitt	Andrews	Pennick	
2		4	5	6	11	10	9	8							7		3							1
2		4	5	6	11	10	9	8							7		3							2
	2	4		6	11	10	9	8							7		3	5						3
2	1	3	2	3	3	3	3	3							3		3	1						
1							4	3																

Baker	Kelly	Carr	Jackson	Burrows	Boyer	Hodgson	MacDougall	Ross	Provan	Spratt	Walker	Coleman	Shepherd	Dale	Taylor	Sweenie	Richardson	Topping	Tunks	Sibbald	Hewitt	Andrews	Pennick	
	2	4	5	6	7	8	9	10	11	12							**3**							1
	1	1	1	1	1	1	1	1	1								1							
										1														
							2			1														

SOUTH SHIELDS
Association Football Club Ltd.
Simonside Hall, Season 1968-69

Today's Visitors
YORK CITY
F.A. CUP 1st ROUND

SATURDAY, 16th NOVEMBER
Kick-off 3-0 p.m.

South Shields v York City 16 November 1968 programme cover.

Billy Hodgson

OFFICIAL PROGRAMME 1/-

F.A. CUP - THIRD ROUND
YORK C. v STOKE C.
SATURDAY, 4th JAN., 1969
KICK-OFF 3.00 p.m.

York City v Stoke City 4 January 1969 programme cover.

1969–70

Division Four

Manager: Tom Johnston

	P	W	D	L	F	A	Pts
Chesterfield	46	27	10	9	77	32	64
Wrexham	46	26	9	11	84	49	61
Swansea Town	46	21	18	7	66	45	60
Port Vale	46	20	19	7	61	33	59
Brentford	46	20	16	10	58	39	56
Aldershot	46	20	13	13	78	65	53
Notts County	46	22	8	16	73	62	52
Lincoln City	46	17	16	13	66	52	50
Peterborough United	46	17	14	15	77	69	48
Colchester United	46	17	14	15	64	63	48
Chester	46	21	6	19	58	66	48
Scunthorpe United	46	18	10	18	67	65	46
York City	46	16	14	16	55	62	46
Northampton Town	46	16	12	18	64	55	44
Crewe Alexandra	46	16	12	18	51	51	44
Grimsby Town	46	14	15	17	54	58	43
Southend United	46	15	10	21	59	85	40
Exeter City	46	14	11	21	57	59	39
Oldham Athletic	46	13	13	20	60	65	39
Workington	46	12	14	20	46	64	38
Newport County	46	13	11	22	53	74	37
Darlington	46	13	10	23	53	73	36
Hartlepool	46	10	10	26	42	82	30
Bradford Park Avenue	46	6	11	29	41	96	23

Did you know that?

Paul Aimson returned to the club in August 1969, and his first game back that month against Exeter City drew a crowd of 6,200, almost double the previous attendance.

City's four wins and one draw in the opening five games represented their best start to a Football League season.

Seventeen-year-old goalkeeper Ron Hillyard made his debut on 25 October 1969 at Peterborough.

During the season, centre-half Barry Swallow was signed from Bradford City, and he made his debut in an FA Cup tie against Whitby Town on 15 November 1969.

Barry Jackson's career with City ended at the end of the season after an all-time club record 539 League and Cup appearances. His last game was at home to Notts County on 31 January 1970. Earlier that month he had been sent off at Scunthorpe.

Average home League attendance was 3,951.

City won just twice on their travels and in four seasons had managed only seven victories in 92 away games.

They reached the fourth round of the FA Cup for the first time since 1957–58.

At the third stage they knocked out Second Division (Championship) Cardiff City in a second replay.

Match No.	Date		Venue	Opponents	Result		Scorers	Atten
1	Aug	9	A	Newport County	W	2–1	Mahon (2)	
2		16	H	Lincoln City	W	2–0	McMahon, Jackson	
3		23	A	Hartlepool	D	2–2	Hewitt, Topping	
4		25	H	Exeter City	W	1–0	Mahon	
5		30	H	Swansea Town	W	3–0	McMahon (2), Aimson	
6	Sep	6	A	Wrexham	L	0–4		
7		13	H	Bradford PA	W	4–1	Hodgson, McMahon, Burrows, Mahon	
8		15	A	Chesterfield	L	1–3	Opp. og	
9		20	A	Workington	D	1–1	Aimson	
10		27	H	Scunthorpe United	W	3–2	McMahon (2), Mahon	
11		29	H	Darlington	W	2–1	Aimson, McMahon	
12	Oct	4	A	Notts County	W	2–0	Mahon, McMahon	
13		8	A	Lincoln City	L	0–4		
14		11	H	Port Vale	L	0–1		
15		18	H	Colchester United	W	4–2	Opp. og, Boyer (2), Mahon	
16		25	A	Peterborough United	L	1–3	Mahon	
17	Nov	1	H	Northampton Town	D	1–1	Boyer	
18		8	A	Oldham Athletic	L	1–3	Hewitt	
19		22	H	Southend United	W	1–0	Stainwright	
20		26	A	Aldershot	L	1–4	Mahon	
21		29	A	Chester	L	0–3		
22	Dec	13	A	Bradford PA	L	0–2		
23		26	H	Hartlepool	D	0–0		
24		27	A	Swansea Town	L	1–2	Sibbald	
25	Jan	17	A	Scunthorpe United	D	1–1	Boyer	
26		31	H	Notts County	L	1–2	Sibbald (pen)	
27	Feb	7	A	Port Vale	D	1–1	Sibbald	
28		9	H	Workington	W	1–0	McMahon	
29		21	H	Oldham Athletic	D	0–0		
30		28	A	Colchester United	L	0–3		
31	Mar	2	H	Grimsby Town	D	1–1	Mahon	
32		9	A	Brentford	D	0–0		
33		13	H	Chester	D	0–0		
34		18	A	Crewe Alexandra	L	0–3		
35		21	A	Grimsby Town	D	0–0		
36		27	H	Peterborough United	W	3–0	Boyer (2), Aimson	
37		28	H	Brentford	W	4–2	Aimson (3), Boyer	
38		31	A	Northampton Town	D	2–2	Aimson, Hewitt	
39	Apr	4	A	Exeter City	L	1–2	McMahon	
40		7	H	Aldershot	W	2–0	Taylor, Sibbald	
41		13	H	Chesterfield	D	1–1	Boyer	
42		17	H	Crewe Alexandra	D	0–0		
43		21	H	Newport County	W	2–1	Swallow (2)	
44		24	H	Wrexham	W	2–1	Swallow, Boyer	
45		27	A	Darlington	L	0–1		
46	May	1	A	Southend United	L	0–1		

2 own-goals

FA Cup

1	Nov	15	H	Whitby Town	W	2–0	Aimson, Sibbald	
2	Dec	6	A	Bangor City	D	0–0		
r		10	H	Bangor City	W	2–0	Mahon, Boyer	
3	Jan	3	H	Cardiff City	D	1–1	Boyer	
r		12	A	Cardiff City	D	1–1*	Taylor	
2r		15	N#	Cardiff City	W	3–1*	Swallow (2), Aimson	
4		24	A	Middlesbrough	L	1–4	Boyer	

* After extra-time. # At St Andrews, Birmingham.

Football League Cup

1	Aug	13	A	Darlington	L	0–3		

Sibbald	Kelly	Davidson	Jackson	Burrows	Mahon	Stainwright	McMahon	Hodgson	Hewitt	Topping	Taylor	Boyer	Widdowson	Aimson	Mackin	Hillyard	Morritt	Swallow	McArthur	Maloney	
2	3	4	5	6	**7**	8	9	10	11	12											1
2		4	5	3	**11**		9	10	12	6	7	8									2
2		4	5	3			9	10	11	6	7	8	1								3
2			5	3	11		8	4	10	6		7		9							4
2		4	5	3	11		8	10		6		7		9							5
2		4	5	3	**11**		8	10	12	6		7		9							6
2		4	5	3	11	12	**8**	10		6		7		9							7
2		4	5	3	11			10		6	7	8		9							8
2		4	5	6	11	8		10				7		9	3						9
2		4	5	6	11		8	10				7		9	3						10
2		4	5	6	11		8	10				7		9	3						11
2			5	6	11	12	**8**	10		4		7		9	3						12
2		12	5	6	11		8	10		**4**		7		9	3						13
2		4	5	6			8	10		12	7	11		9	3						14
2		4	5	12	11		7	10		**6**		8	1	9	3						15
2		4	5	6	11		8	10				7		9	3	1					16
2		4	5	6	**11**		8	10	12			7		9	3	1					17
2		4	5	6	12		8	10	**11**			7		9	3		1				18
2		4	5	3		8	9	11			7				10		1	6			19
2		4	5	3	8		9	11		7					10		1	6			20
2		4	5	3	7		9	11				8			10		1	6			21
2		4	5	3	11		**9**	10			7	8			12		1	6			22
2		4	5	3	11		9	10			7			8			1	6			23
2		10		3	**11**	9	12			5	7	8			4		1	6			24
4		10	5	3					11		7	8		9	2		1	6			25
4		10	5	3	11		8				7			9	2		1	6			26
4		10		3	11		9			6	7	8			2		1	5			27
4		10		3			9		11	6	**7**	8		12	2		1	5			28
4		10		3			**9**		11	6	7	8		12	2		1	5			29
4		12		3			9		11	6	**7**	8		10	2		1	5			30
		4		3	11					6	7	8		10	2		1	5	9		31
4				3	**11**	9		10	12	6	7	8			2		1	5			32
4				3	11	9		10		6	7	8			2		1	5			33
4		8		3			9	10		6	**7**	11		12	2		1	5			34
4		8		3				10		6	7	11		9	2		1	5			35
4		8		3				10		6	7	11		9	2		1	5			36
4		8		3				10		6	7	11		9	2		1	5			37
4		8		3					10	6	7	11		9	2		1	5			38
4		8		3			12		10	6	7	**11**		9	2		1	5			39
4		8		3					10	6	7	11		9	2		1	5			40
4		8		3					10	6	7	11		9	2		1	5			41
4		12		3	8		9		10	6	**7**	11			2		1	5			42
4		8		3	7		9		11	6		12			2	1		5		**10**	43
4		10		3	12		7		**11**	6		8		9	2		1	5			44
4		8		3			10		7	6		11		**9**	2		1	5		12	45
4		10		3			9		**8**	6	7	11		12	2		1	5			46
45	1	39	25	45	27	6	32	29	17	32	27	40	2	29	36	3	28	28	1	1	
		3		1	2	2	2		4	2		1		4	1					1	
4			1	1	10	1	10	1	3	1	1	9		8			3				

Sibbald	Kelly	Davidson	Jackson	Burrows	Mahon	Stainwright	McMahon	Hodgson	Hewitt	Topping	Taylor	Boyer	Widdowson	Aimson	Mackin	Hillyard	Morritt	Swallow	McArthur	Maloney	
2			5	3	7		8	10	11					9	4		1	6			1
2			5	3	11	8	9	10		4		7					1	6			2
2		4	5	3	11		9	10			7	8					1	6			r
4		10	5	3				12	**11**		7	8		9	2		1	6			3
4		10	5	3				12	**11**		7	8		9	2		1	6			r
4		**10**	5	3				11	12		7	8		9	2		1	6			2r
4		10	5	3				11			7	8		9	2		1	6			4
7		5	7	7	3	1	3	5	3	1	5	6		5	5		7	7			
								2	1												
1					1						1	3		2				2			

Sibbald	Kelly	Davidson	Jackson	Burrows	Mahon	Stainwright	McMahon	Hodgson	Hewitt	Topping	Taylor	Boyer	Widdowson	Aimson	Mackin	Hillyard	Morritt	Swallow	McArthur	Maloney	
2	3	4	5	6	7	8	9	10	11												1
1	1	1	1	1	1	1	1	1	1												

York City A.F.C.
Testimonial Match for
Gerry Baker
City
v
The Happy Wanderers
Bootham Crescent, Monday, October 20, 1969
KICK-OFF 7-15 P.M.

York City v The Happy Wanderers 20 October 1969 testimonial game programme cover.

Ron Hillyard.

OFFICIAL PROGRAMME 1/-
F.A. CUP 3rd ROUND
CARDIFF CITY
Saturday, January 3rd, 1970
KICK OFF 3 p.m.
No. 15

York City v Cardiff City 3 January 1970 programme cover.

1970–71

Division Four

Manager: Tom Johnston

	P	W	D	L	F	A	Pts
Notts County	46	30	9	7	89	36	69
Bournemouth	46	24	12	10	81	46	60
Oldham Athletic	46	24	11	11	88	63	59
York City	46	23	10	13	78	54	56
Chester	46	24	7	15	69	55	55
Colchester United	46	21	12	13	70	54	54
Northampton Town	46	19	13	14	63	59	51
Southport	46	21	6	19	63	57	48
Exeter City	46	17	14	15	67	68	48
Workington	46	18	12	16	48	49	48
Stockport County	46	16	14	16	49	65	46
Darlington	46	17	11	18	58	57	45
Aldershot	46	14	17	15	66	71	45
Brentford	46	18	8	20	66	62	44
Crewe Alexandra	46	18	8	20	75	76	44
Peterborough United	46	18	7	21	70	71	43
Scunthorpe United	46	15	13	18	56	61	43
Southend United	46	14	15	17	53	66	43
Grimsby Town	46	18	7	21	57	71	43
Cambridge United	46	15	13	18	51	66	43
Lincoln City	46	13	13	20	70	71	39
Newport County	46	10	8	28	55	85	28
Hartlepool	46	8	12	26	34	74	28
Barrow	46	7	8	31	51	90	22

Did you know that?

This was City's third promotion season.

On 29 January 1971, following the defeat at Southend United, City were 10th in the table with the following record: P26 W12 D4 L10 F39 A33 Pts28.

Then followed an unbeaten run of 16 games, which established a new club record.

Albert Johanneson, former Leeds United winger, made his debut on the opening day.

Phil Boyer played his last game on 19 December 1970 at home to Crewe Alexandra prior to his £20,000 transfer (new club record) to Bournemouth.

In front of Bootham Crescent's biggest crowd for five seasons (14,321) Oldham Athletic won 1–0. It was City's first home defeat since 31 January 1970, a club record run of 36 League and Cup games.

Paul Aimson was top marksman, and the average home League crowd was 4,962.

During the campaign Aimson netted in seven consecutive League games, equalling the club-record sequences of Jimmy Cowie in 1928–29, Billy Fenton in 1952–53 and Arthur Bottom in 1954–55.

Match No.	Date	Venue	Opponents	Result		Scorers	Attend
1	Aug 15	H	Notts County	D	0–0		4
2	22	A	Crewe Alexandra	W	4–3	Aimson (2), Taylor, Boyer	2
3	29	H	Lincoln City	W	2–0	Aimson, Boyer	4
4	31	H	Workington	W	1–0	Boyer	5
5	Sep 5	A	Northampton Town	L	2–3	Aimson, Boyer	7
6	12	H	Chester	D	1–1	Boyer	3
7	19	A	Scunthorpe United	W	1–0	Davidson	3
8	23	A	Peterborough United	L	1–2	Sibbald	4
9	26	H	Bournemouth	D	1–1	Boyer	3
10	Oct 3	A	Darlington	L	0–2		2,
11	9	H	Southport	W	2=0	Johanneson, Boyer	3,
12	12	H	Barrow	W	4–3	Taylor, Aimson (2), Topping	4,
13	17	A	Notts County	L	1–2	Johanneson	7
14	19	A	Colchester United	L	0–1		4,
15	24	A	Grimsby Town	L	1–3	Hewitt	4
16	30	H	Newport County	W	1–0	Aimson	3,
17	Nov 6	A	Stockport County	L	0–1		4,
18	9	A	Brentford	L	4–6	Aimson (2), Hewitt, Opp. og	5,
19	13	H	Aldershot	W	3–1	Boyer, Aimson (2)	3,
20	27	H	Southend United	W	3–0	Johanneson, Swallow, Boyer	3,
21	Dec 5	A	Exeter City	W	2–0	Mackin (pen), Aimson	4,
22	19	H	Crewe Alexandra	W	1–0	Aimson	3,
23	26	A	Hartlepool	L	1–2	McMahon	2,
24	Jan 9	A	Barrow	W	2–0	Taylor, Davidson	2
25	16	H	Colchester United	D	1–1	McMahon	3,
26	29	A	Southend United	L	0–1		5,
27	Feb 6	H	Exeter City	D	2–2	McMahon (2)	3,
28	13	A	Cambridge United	D	1–1	Swallow	4,
29	20	H	Brentford	D	0–0		3,
30	26	A	Newport County	W	3–0	Henderson (2), Aimson	1,
31	Mar 1	H	Cambridge United	W	3–0	McMahon (2), Aimson	2
32	5	H	Grimsby Town	W	4–1	Swallow, Mackin (pen), Aimson, McMahon	3
33	8	H	Peterborough United	W	2–1	Aimson (2)	5,
34	13	A	Aldershot	W	1–0	Topping	4
35	15	A	Oldham Athletic	D	1–1	Aimson	9,
36	19	H	Stockport County	W	2–1	McMahon, Aimson	6
37	27	H	Northampton Town	W	4–1	McMahon (2), Aimson, Swallow	7,
38	Apr 3	A	Lincoln City	W	5–4	McMahon, Burrows, Swallow, Aimson, Davidson	4,
39	9	H	Darlington	W	2–0	Aimson, Taylor	10,
40	10	H	Hartlepool	W	4–0	Swallow, McMahon, Topping, Aimson	7,
41	12	A	Chester	D	1–1	Aimson	7,
42	16	A	Southport	D	2–2	Davidson, McMahon	2,
43	19	H	Oldham Athletic	L	0–1		14,
44	24	H	Scunthorpe United	W	2–0	Aimson, Chambers	5,
45	27	A	Workington	L	0–1		1
46	May 1	A	Bournemouth	L	0–4		12,
							A
							S
						1 own-goal	

FA Cup

1	Nov 21	A	Tamworth	D	0–0		4
r	23	H	Tamworth	W	5–0	Aimson (3), Boyer, Hewitt	5,
2	Dec 12	A	Boston United	W	2–1	Davidson, Mackin (pen)	6
3	Jan 2	H	Bolton Wanderers	W	2–0	Davidson (2)	10
4	23	H	Southampton	D	3–3	McMahon, Hewitt, Aimson	13,
r	Feb 1	A	Southampton	L	2–3	Aimson, Johanneson	25,
							A
							S

Football League Cup

1	Aug 14	A	Hartlepool	W	3–2	Boyer (2), Johanneson	3,
2	Sep 9	H	Northampton Town	D	0–0		5,
r	14	A	Northampton Town	D	1–1*	Davidson	7,
2r	28	N#	Northampton Town	L	1–2	Boyer	2,
							A
							S

* After extra-time. # At Villa Park, Birmingham.

Mackin	Burrows	Sibbald	Swallow	Topping	Taylor	Boyer	Aimson	Davidson	Johanneson	McMahon	Thompson	Maloney	Hewitt	Hillyard	Newman	Henderson	Jones	Smith	Chambers	
2	3	4	5	6	**7**	8	9	10	11	12										1
2	6	4	5		7	8	9	10	11		3									2
2	6	4	5		7	8	9	10	11		3									3
2	6	4	5		7	8	9	10	11		3									4
2	6	4	5		**7**	8	9	10	11	12	3									5
2	3	4	5	6	7	8		10	11	9										6
2	3	4	5	6	7	8		10	11	9										7
2	3	4	5	6	7	8	9	10	**11**	12										8
2	3	4	5	6	7	8		10	11	9										9
2	3		5	6	7	8		4	11	**9**		12	10							10
2	3		5	6	7	8	9	4	11				10	1						11
2	3		5	6	7	8	9	4	11				10	1						12
2	3	12	5	6	7	8	9	**4**	11				10	1						13
2	3		5	6	7	8	9	4	11				10	1						14
2	3	12	5	6	7	8	9	**4**	11				10	1						15
2	3	4	5	6	7	8	9		11				10	1						16
2	3		5	6		8	9	12					10		4	**7**	11			17
2	3		**5**	6		8	9					12	10		4	7	**11**			18
2	3			5		8	9	4					10	1	4	7	11			19
2	3		5	6	7	8	9	4	**11**				10	1	12					20
2	3		5	6	7	8	9	4					10	1		11				21
2	3		5	6	7	8	9	4					10	1		11				22
2	3		5	6			9	4		8			10	1		7		11		23
2	3		5	6	11		9	4		8			10	1		7				24
2	3		5	6	7		9	4		8			10	1		11				25
2	3		5	6			9	4	11	8		12	**10**	1		7				26
2	3		5	6	12		9	4	11	8			10	1		**7**				27
2	3		5	6	7		9	4	11	8			10	1						28
2	3		5	6	7		9	4	11	8			10	1						29
2	3	12	5	6			**9**	4	11	8			10	1		7				30
2	3		5	6	12		9	4	**11**	8			10	1		7				31
2	3		5	6	11		9	4		8			**10**	1		7		12		32
2	3		5	6	11		9	4		8			10	1		7				33
2	3		5	6	11		9	4		8			10	1		**7**			12	34
2	3		5	6	11		9	4		8			10	1		7				35
2	**3**		5	6	11		9	4		8			10	1		7			12	36
2	3		5	6	11		9	4		8			10	1		7				37
2	3		5	6	11		9	4		8			10	1		**7**			12	38
2	3		5	6	11		9	4		8			10	1		7				39
2	3		5	6	11		9	4		8			10	1		7				40
2	3		5	6	11		9	4		8			10	1		7				41
2	3		5	6	11		9	4		8			10	1		7				42
2	3		5	6	7		9	4	11	**8**			10	1					12	43
2	3		5	6			9	4	**11**	8			10	1		7			12	44
2	3		**5**	6	12		9	4		8			10	1		7			11	45
2	6	3		5	11		9	8		12			10	1		7			**4**	46
46	46	11	44	42	36	22	42	43	25	27	4		37	34	3	26	3	1	2	
		3			3			1		4		3			1			1	5	
2	1	1	6	3	4	9	26	4	3	13			2			2			1	
2	3			5		8	9	4					10	1	6	7	11			1
2	3		5	6	7	8	9	4					10	1			11			r
2	3		5	6	11	8	9	4					10	1		7				2
2	3		5	6			9	4	11	8			10	1		7				3
2	3		5	6	7		9	4	11	8			10	1						4
2	3		5	6	**7**		9	4	11	8			10	1		12				r
6	6		5	6	4	3	6	6	3	3			6	6	1	3	2			
																1				
1						1	5	3	1	1			2							
2	3	4	5	**6**	7	8	9	10	11	12										1
2	3	4	5	6	7	8		10	11	9										2
2	3	4	5	6	7	8	9	10	11											r
2	3	4	5	6	7	8		10	11	9										2r
4	4	4	4	4	4	4	2	4	4	2										
										1										
						3		1	1											

OFFICIAL PROGRAMME 5p
INCLUDING FOOTBALL LEAGUE REVIEW
FOOTBALL LEAGUE DIVISION IV
Today's Visitors
OLDHAM ATHLETIC
Monday, April 19th, 1971
KICK OFF 7-30 p.m.
No. 25

York City v Oldham Athletic 19 April 1971 programme cover.

Kevin McMahon.

Albert Johanneson.

1971–72

Division Three

Manager: Tom Johnston

	P	W	D	L	F	A	Pts
Aston Villa	46	32	6	8	85	32	70
Brighton & Hove Albion	46	27	11	8	82	47	65
Bournemouth	46	23	16	7	73	37	62
Notts County	46	25	12	9	74	44	62
Rotherham United	46	20	15	11	69	52	55
Bristol Rovers	46	21	12	13	75	56	54
Bolton Wanderers	46	17	16	13	51	41	50
Plymouth Argyle	46	20	10	16	74	64	50
Walsall	46	15	18	13	62	57	48
Blackburn Rovers	46	19	9	18	54	57	47
Oldham Athletic	46	17	11	18	59	63	45
Shrewsbury Town	46	17	10	19	73	65	44
Chesterfield	46	18	8	20	57	57	44
Swansea City	46	17	10	19	46	59	44
Port Vale	46	13	15	18	43	59	41
Wrexham	46	16	8	22	59	63	40
Halifax Town	46	13	12	21	48	61	38
Rochdale	46	12	13	21	57	83	37
York City	46	12	12	22	57	66	36
Tranmere Rovers	46	10	16	20	50	71	36
Mansfield Town	46	8	20	18	41	63	36
Barnsley	46	9	18	19	32	64	36
Torquay United	46	10	12	24	41	69	32
Bradford City	46	11	10	25	45	77	32

Did you know that?

In the first season back in Division Three since 1966, City avoided relegation on goal average.

City's back four of John Mackin, Barry Swallow, Chris Topping and Phil Burrows were all ever presents.

Goalkeeper Graeme Crawford was signed from Sheffield United and made his debut on 5 November 1971 at Tranmere Rovers.

Seventeen-year-old winger Brian Pollard made his Football League debut on 31 March 1972 at home to Rotherham United.

Paul Aimson again led the scoring charts, and the average home League crowd of 5,597 was the highest for six years.

Match No.	Date	Venue	Opponents	Result		Scorers	Atten
1	Aug 14	H	Bristol Rovers	D	0–0		
2	21	A	Halifax Town	L	1–3	McMahon	
3	28	H	Plymouth Argyle	L	2–3	Henderson, Aimson	
4	31	A	Oldham Athletic	L	0–1		
5	Sep 4	A	Brighton & Hove Albion	W	2–0	Aimson (2)	1
6	11	H	Wrexham	D	1–1	Aimson	
7	18	A	Bolton Wanderers	W	1–0	Calloway	1
8	25	H	Walsall	W	2–0	McMahon (2)	
9	29	A	Bradford City	L	1–3	Aimson	
10	Oct 2	A	Rotherham United	D	1–1	Opp. og	
11	9	H	Shrewsbury Town	D	1–1	Henderson	
12	16	A	Bristol Rovers	L	4–5	McMahon, Aimson, Mackin (2, 2 pens)	
13	18	H	Torquay United	W	3–1	Aimson, McMahon, Calloway	
14	23	A	Port Vale	L	3–4	Henderson, Mackin, McMahon	
15	30	H	Notts County	L	0–2		
16	Nov 5	A	Tranmere Rovers	L	0–2		
17	13	H	Barnsley	D	1–1	McMahon	
18	27	H	Mansfield Town	L	1–2	Swallow	
19	Dec 4	A	Bournemouth	D	2–2	Rowles, Swallow	1
20	18	H	Brighton & Hove Albion	L	1–2	Rowles	
21	27	A	Chesterfield	L	1–2	Burluraux	
22	Jan 1	H	Bolton Wanderers	D	0–0		
23	8	A	Plymouth Argyle	L	0–4		
24	15	A	Blackburn Rovers	L	0–3		
25	21	H	Bradford City	W	3–1	McMahon, Henderson, Aimson	
26	24	H	Swansea City	D	1–1	Burrows	
27	29	A	Torquay United	W	1–0	Aimson	
28	Feb 5	A	Aston Villa	L	0–1		2
29	12	H	Port Vale	W	2–1	Aimson (2)	
30	19	A	Notts County	D	2–2	Rowles, Lally	1
31	26	H	Tranmere Rovers	W	5–0	Rowles (2), Wann, Lally, Aimson	
32	Mar 4	A	Barnsley	L	1–2	Mackin (pen)	
33	10	A	Shrewsbury Town	L	1–2	Opp. og	
34	14	A	Swansea City	L	1–2	Burrows	
35	18	H	Halifax Town	D	1–1	Mackin (pen)	
36	20	H	Rochdale	W	2–0	Swallow, Calloway	
37	25	A	Wrexham	L	0–2		
38	31	H	Rotherham United	W	2–0	Rowles (2)	
39	Apr 1	H	Chesterfield	W	4–1	Aimson (3), Swallow	
40	4	A	Walsall	L	1–2	Aimson	
41	8	H	Aston Villa	L	0–1		
42	15	A	Mansfield Town	D	0–0		
43	17	A	Rochdale	W	2–1	Burrows, Henderson	
44	22	H	Bournemouth	L	0–2		
45	24	H	Oldham Athletic	D	0–0		
46	29	H	Blackburn Rovers	L	0–1		

2 own-goals

FA Cup

1	Nov 20	H	Grimsby Town	W	4–2	Opp. og, Henderson, Swallow, McMahon	6
2	Dec 11	A	Rotherham United	D	1–1	Rowles	8
r	13	H	Rotherham United	L	2–3*	McMahon, Chambers	10

* After extra-time.

1 own-goal

Football League Cup

1	Aug 18	A	Darlington	W	1–0	Henderson	4
2	Sep 8	H	Middlesbrough	D	2–2	McMahon, Henderson	10
r	14	A	Middlesbrough	W	2–1	Calloway, Henderson	21
3	Oct 5	A	Sheffield United	L	2–3	Swallow, Topping	29

Mackin	Burrows	Calloway	Swallow	Topping	Chambers	McMahon	Aimson	Hewitt	Johanneson	Henderson	Rowles	Lally	Woodward	Crawford	Burluraux	Morritt	Maloney	Murray	Wann	Rioch	Yeats	Pollard	De Placido	
2	3	4	5	6	**7**	8	9	10	11	12														1
2	3	4	5	6	7	8	9	10		11														2
2	3	4	5	6	7	8	9	10		**11**	12													3
2	3	4	5	6		8	9	10		11		7												4
2	3	4	5	6		8	9	10		11		7												5
2	3	8	5	6		9	10	11		7		4												6
2	3	10	5	6		8	9	11		7		4												7
2	3	8	5	6		9	10	11		7		4												8
2	3	10	5	6		8	9	11		7		4												9
2	3	10	5	6		8	9	11		7		4												10
2	3	10	5	6		8	9	11		7		4												11
2	3	10	5	6		8	9	11		7		**4**	12											12
2	3	10	5	6	12	8	9	**11**		7			4											13
2	3	10	5	6	11	8	9			**7**		12	4											14
2	3	10	5	6		8	9	11		7		4												15
2	3	10	5	6		8	9	**11**		7		4	12	1										16
2	3	10	5	6	12	8	9			**7**	11	4		1										17
2	3	10	5	6	12	8	9			**7**	11	4		1										18
2	3		5	6	7	9	10			11	8	4												19
2	3		5	6	**10**	12	9			7	8	4			11									20
2	3	10	5	6			9	**11**			8	4			7	1	12							21
2	3	10	5	6		9		11			8	4		1	7									22
2	3		5	6		8	9	**11**		7	12		4	1			10							23
2	3	10	5	6			9			7	**8**	4	12	1				11						24
2	3	10	5	6		8	9			7		4		1				11						25
2	3	10	5	6		8	9			7		4		1				11						26
2	3	8	5	6		9	10			7		4		1					11					27
2	3	10	5	6		8	9				12	4		1				**7**	11					28
2	3	8	5	6			9			7	10	4		1					11					29
2	3	**8**	5	6			9			7	10	4		1					11	12				30
2	3	10	5	6			9			7	8	4		1					11					31
2	3		5	6		9				7	8	4	12	1			**10**		11					32
2	3	10	5	6						7	8	4		1					11		9			33
2	3	10	5	6			12			7	8	4		1					11		**9**			34
2	3	10	5	6			9			7	8		4	1					11					35
2	3	10	5	6			9			7	8		4	1					11					36
2	3	10	5	6			9			**7**	8	12	4	1					11					37
2	3	10	5	6			9				8	4		1					11			**7**	12	38
2	3	10	5	6			9				8	4		1					11			**7**	12	39
2	3	10	5	6			9				8	4		1					11			**7**	12	40
2	3	10	5	6			9				8	4		1					11			7		41
2	3	10	5	6			9			7	8	4		1					11					42
2	3	10	5	6		12	9			7	8		4	1					**11**					43
2	3	10	5	6			9			7	8	12	4	1					**11**					44
2	3	10	5	6			9			**7**	8		4	1					11				12	45
2	3	10	5	6			9	11			8	12	4	1									**7**	46
46	46	42	46	46	6	26	42	19	1	37	25	33	10	28	3	1	2	4	19		2	4	1	
					3	2	1			1	3	4	4				1			1			4	
5	3	3	4			8	16			5	7	2			1				1					

Mackin	Burrows	Calloway	Swallow	Topping	Chambers	McMahon	Aimson	Hewitt	Johanneson	Henderson	Rowles	Lally	Woodward	Crawford	Burluraux	Morritt	Maloney	Murray	Wann	Rioch	Yeats	Pollard	De Placido	
2	3	10	5	6		8	9			7	11	4												1
2	3		5	6	7	9	10			11	8	4												2
2	3		5	6	7	**9**	10			11	8	4	12											r
3	3	1	3	3	2	3	3			3	3	3												
													1											
			1		1	2				1	1													

Mackin	Burrows	Calloway	Swallow	Topping	Chambers	McMahon	Aimson	Hewitt	Johanneson	Henderson	Rowles	Lally	Woodward	Crawford	Burluraux	Morritt	Maloney	Murray	Wann	Rioch	Yeats	Pollard	De Placido	
2	3	4	5	6	7	8	**9**	10		11			12											1
2	3	10	5	6		8	9	11		7		4												2
2	3	10	5	6		8	9	11		7		4												r
2	3	10	5	6		**8**	9	11		7	12	4												3
4	4	4	4	4	1	4	4	4		4		3												
											1		1											
		1	1	1		1				3														

York City v Blackburn Rovers 29 April 1972 programme cover.

Dennis Wann.

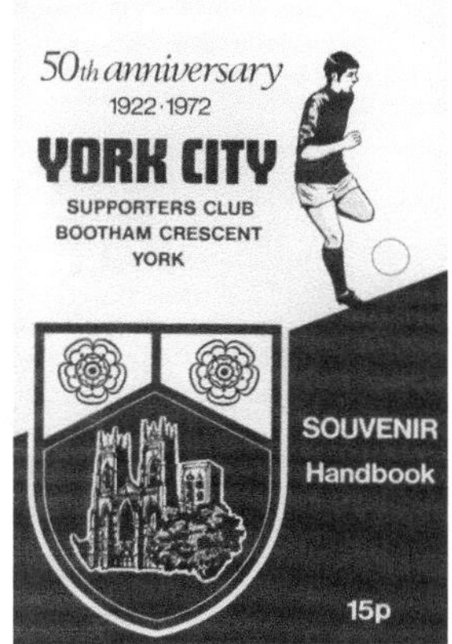

50th anniversary souvenir handbook.

1972–73

Division Three

Manager: Tom Johnston

	P	W	D	L	F	A	Pts
Bolton Wanderers	46	25	11	10	73	39	61
Notts County	46	23	11	12	67	47	57
Blackburn Rovers	46	20	15	11	57	47	55
Oldham Athletic	46	19	16	11	72	54	54
Bristol Rovers	46	20	13	13	77	56	53
Port Vale	46	21	11	14	56	69	53
Bournemouth	46	17	16	13	66	44	50
Plymouth Argyle	46	20	10	16	74	66	50
Grimsby Town	46	20	8	18	67	61	48
Tranmere Rovers	46	15	16	15	56	52	46
Charlton Athletic	46	17	11	18	69	67	45
Wrexham	46	14	17	15	55	54	45
Rochdale	46	14	17	15	48	54	45
Southend United	46	17	10	19	61	54	44
Shrewsbury Town	46	15	14	17	46	54	44
Chesterfield	46	17	9	20	57	61	43
Walsall	46	18	7	21	56	66	43
York City	46	13	15	18	42	46	41
Watford	46	12	17	17	43	48	41
Halifax Town	46	13	15	18	43	53	41
Rotherham United	46	17	7	22	51	65	41
Brentford	46	15	7	24	51	69	37
Swansea City	46	14	9	23	51	73	37
Scunthorpe United	46	10	10	26	33	72	30

Did you know that?

City again avoided the drop on goal average, but only by winning the last game of the season at Rotherham United.

Jimmy Seal, ex-Barnsley, made his debut on the opening day at home to Grimsby Town.

City failed to win any of their opening 11 games, which included eight matches without scoring.

During the campaign City were involved in nine goalless draws.

Paul Aimson was transferred to Bournemouth in March 1973, and his last game for the club was at home to Bolton Wanderers on 5 March. In two spells at York he netted 113 goals (fifth-highest scorer in City's history) in just under 250 senior appearances.

Phil Burrows was an ever present for the third successive season.

Average League crowd at Bootham Crescent was 3,792.

Match No.	Date	Venue	Opponents	Result		Scorers	Attend
1	Aug 12	H	Grimsby Town	D	0–0		6
2	19	A	Port Vale	L	1–2	Rowles	4
3	26	H	Notts County	D	1–1	Taylor	4
4	28	H	Rotherham United	L	0–1		4
5	Sep 2	A	Charlton Athletic	L	0–1		5
6	9	H	Bournemouth	D	0–0		3
7	15	A	Tranmere Rovers	L	0–1		3
8	18	H	Watford	D	0–0		3
9	23	H	Oldham Athletic	D	0–0		2
10	26	A	Shrewsbury Town	L	0–1		2
11	30	A	Wrexham	L	1–3	Wann	5
12	Oct 7	A	Bristol Rovers	W	2–1	Stone, Aimson	7
13	9	H	Blackburn Rovers	W	1–0	Swallow	3
14	14	H	Chesterfield	W	2–0	Burrows, Rowles	3
15	21	A	Scunthorpe United	L	0–1		3
16	24	A	Plymouth Argyle	D	1–1	Seal	8
17	28	H	Walsall	D	0–0		3
18	Nov 4	H	Shrewsbury Town	W	2–1	Seal, Rowles	2
19	11	A	Watford	D	2–2	Rowles, Lally	6
20	25	A	Brentford	L	0–2		7
21	Dec 2	H	Southend United	W	2–0	Pollard, Wann	2
22	23	H	Swansea City	W	3–0	Pollard (2), Wann	2
23	26	A	Oldham Athletic	D	1–1	Wann	9
24	30	H	Port Vale	D	0–0		3
25	Jan 6	A	Notts County	L	0–1		6
26	20	H	Charlton Athletic	D	1–1	Pollard	2
27	27	A	Bournemouth	W	3–2	Aimson, Stone (2)	11
28	29	A	Swansea City	W	3–1	Rowles, Aimson, Opp. og	3
29	Feb 3	A	Blackburn Rovers	L	0–2		8
30	10	H	Tranmere Rovers	W	4–1	Woodward (pen), Swallow, Pollard, Aimson	3
31	17	A	Grimsby Town	W	2–1	Rowles, Aimson	12
32	24	H	Halifax Town	W	2–1	Rowles, Woodward	3
33	Mar 3	H	Bristol Rovers	D	0–0		4
34	5	H	Bolton Wanderers	L	0–1		9
35	10	A	Chesterfield	D	0–0		3
36	13	A	Halifax Town	L	0–1		1
37	17	H	Scunthorpe United	W	3–1	Pollard, Lally, Taylor	2
38	19	A	Rochdale	L	0–1		2
39	24	A	Walsall	D	0–0		4
40	26	H	Plymouth Argyle	L	1–2	Pollard	3
41	31	H	Brentford	L	0–1		2
42	Apr 7	A	Southend United	L	0–3		7
43	14	H	Rochdale	L	1–2	Stone	2
44	20	H	Wrexham	D	1–1	Lally	2
45	21	A	Bolton Wanderers	L	0–3		19
46	28	A	Rotherham United	W	2–1	Stone, Seal	3
							A
							S
						1 own-goal	

FA Cup

1	Nov 18	H	Mansfield Town	W	2–1	Rowles, Seal	4
2	Dec 9	A	Bangor City	W	3–2	Rowles, Burrows, Pollard	3
3	Jan 13	H	Oxford United	L	0–1		8
							A
							S

Football League Cup

1	Aug 16	A	Notts County	L	1–3	Calloway	8
							A
							S

Mackin	Burrows	Calloway	Swallow	Topping	Pollard	Seal	Aimson	Wann	Taylor	Woodward	Rowles	Lally	Hillyard	Yeats	Stone	Crangle	De Placido	Thompson	Calvert	
2	3	4	5	6	7	8	9	10	11											1
2	3	4	5	6		9		10	11	**7**	8	12								2
2	3	4	5	6			9	10	11	12	8	**7**								3
2	3	4	5	6		**7**	9	10	11		8	12								4
2	3	11	5	6	7		9	10		12	**8**	4	1							5
2	3		5	6			9	10	11	7		4		8						6
	3	8	12	6		**7**	9	10	11	5		4			2					7
	3	4		6		8	9	10	11	5					2	7				8
12	3	4		6		**8**	9	10	11	5					2	7				9
7	3		5	6		9		10	11	5	8				2					10
4	3		5	6		8	9	10	**11**		7	12			2					11
2	10	4	5	6		**8**	9	11			7			12	3					12
2	10	4	5	6		8	9	11			7				3					13
2	10	4	5	6		8		11			7			9	3					14
2	10	4	5	6		8		11		12	7			**9**	3					15
	3		5	6	7	8		11		10	9	4			2					16
	3		5	6	**7**	9		11	12	8	10	4			2					17
	3		5	6	7	8		11		9	10	4			2					18
	3		5	6	7	8		11		9	10	4			2					19
	3	12	5	6	7	9		11		**8**	10	4			2					20
	3		5	6	7	8	12	11		10	**9**	4			2					21
12	3		5	6	7	8		11		10	9	**4**			2					22
4	3		5	6	7	**8**	12	11		10	9				2					23
4	3		5	6	7	8				10	9	11			2					24
4	3		5	6	7	8	12			10	**9**	11			2					25
	3		5	6	7		10		11		9	4			2		8			26
	3		5	6	7		10		11	8	9	4			2					27
	3		5	6	7		10		11	8	9	4			2					28
	3		5	6	7	12	10		11	8	9	4			**2**					29
2	3		5	6	7		10		11	8	9	4								30
2	3		5	6	7		10		11	8	9	4								31
2	3		5	6	7		10		11	8	9	4								32
2	3		5	6	7		10		11	8	9	4								33
	3		5	6	7		10		11	8	9	4			2					34
	3		5	6	7	10			**11**	8	9	4	1		2			12		35
	3		5	6	7	10			11	8	9	4	1		**2**			12		36
2	3		5	6	7				11	8		4	1	9				10		37
2	3		5	6	7				11	8	12	4		**9**				10		38
2	3		5	6	7				**11**	8	12	4		9				10		39
2	3		5	6	7	11				8	9						12	**10**	4	40
2	3		5	6	7	10			12	8	9						11		4	41
2	3		5	6		11			10	8	**7**				9		12		4	42
2	3		5	6	7	**10**			11	8		4			9				12	43
2	3		5	6						**8**	10	4			9	11	12		7	44
2	3		5	6		12					10	7			9	11	**8**		4	45
2	3		5	6	7	**11**				10	12	4			9				8	46
29	46	12	43	46	30	29	20	23	26	35	36	31	4	6	31	4	3	4	6	
2		1	1			2	3		2	3	3	3		1			3	2	1	
	1		2		7	3	5	4	2	2	7	3			5					

Mackin	Burrows	Calloway	Swallow	Topping	Pollard	Seal	Aimson	Wann	Taylor	Woodward	Rowles	Lally	Hillyard	Yeats	Stone	Crangle	De Placido	Thompson	Calvert	
	3		5	6	7	8		11		10	9	4			2					1
	3		5	6	**7**	**8**	12	11		10	9	4			2					2
4	3		5	6	7	8	12			10	9	11			2					3
1	3		3	3	3	3		2		3	3	3			3					
							2													
	1				1	1					2									

Mackin	Burrows	Calloway	Swallow	Topping	Pollard	Seal	Aimson	Wann	Taylor	Woodward	Rowles	Lally	Hillyard	Yeats	Stone	Crangle	De Placido	Thompson	Calvert	
2	3	4	5	6		8		10	11			12		9		**7**				1
1	1	1	1	1		1		1	1					1		1				
												1								
		1																		

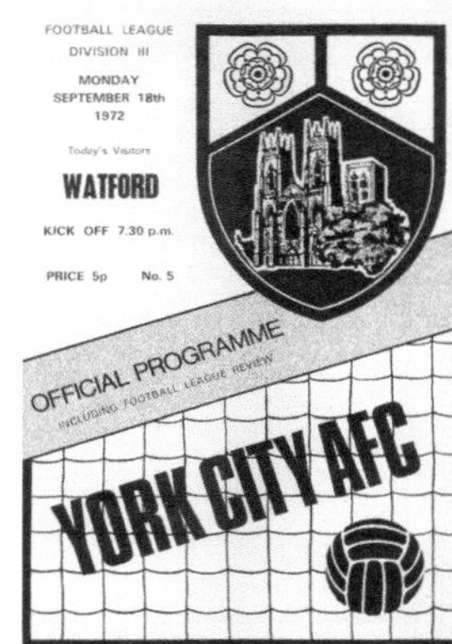

York City v Watford 18 September 1972 programme cover.

John Stone.

1973–74

Division Three

Manager: Tom Johnston

	P	W	D	L	F	A	Pts
Oldham Athletic	46	25	12	9	83	47	62
Bristol Rovers	46	22	17	7	65	33	61
York City	46	21	19	6	67	38	61
Wrexham	46	22	12	12	63	43	56
Chesterfield	46	21	14	11	55	42	56
Grimsby Town	46	18	15	13	67	50	51
Watford	46	19	12	15	64	56	50
Aldershot	46	19	11	16	65	52	49
Halifax Town	46	14	21	11	48	51	49
Huddersfield Town	46	17	13	16	56	55	47
Bournemouth	46	16	15	15	54	58	47
Southend United	46	16	14	16	62	62	46
Blackburn Rovers	46	18	10	18	62	64	46
Charlton Athletic	46	19	8	19	66	73	46
Walsall	46	16	13	17	57	48	45
Tranmere Rovers	46	15	15	16	50	44	45
Plymouth Argyle	46	17	10	19	59	54	44
Hereford United	46	14	15	17	53	57	43
Brighton & Hove Albion	46	16	11	19	52	58	43
Port Vale	46	14	14	18	52	58	42
Cambridge United	46	13	9	24	48	81	35
Shrewsbury Town	46	10	11	25	41	62	31
Southport	46	6	16	24	35	82	28
Rochdale	46	2	17	27	38	94	21

Did you know that?

City won promotion to the Second Division (Championship) for the first time in their history by finishing third in the table. This was the first season of three up and three down in the top three divisions.

New signings Ian Holmes (Sheffield United), Chris Jones (Walsall) and Ian Butler (Hull City) made their debuts in the opening day win at Charlton Athletic.

Barry Lyons, signed from Nottingham Forest, played his first game at home to Port Vale on 15 September 1973.

From 8 September 1973 to 19 January 1974 City were unbeaten in the League – a club-record run of 21 games – and they lost only six matches all season to set another club record.

On 29 September 1973 Jack Howarth scored for Aldershot at Bootham Crescent. In the return game at the Recreation Ground on 22 December Howarth netted again, but in between time City went 11 games (17 hours 19 minutes) without conceding a goal, thus equalling Millwall's record set in 1926.

The club's first-ever home Sunday fixture was on 10 February 1974 against Watford.

City appeared for the first time on BBC's *Match of the Day* on 6 April 1974 when their game at Hereford was televised.

City's average home crowd rose to 6,228 and the game against Oldham, which clinched promotion, attracted 15,583.

Phil Burrows, who had not missed a game in five seasons, was voted City's first-ever Clubman of the Year. During the summer of 1974 he was transferred to Plymouth Arygle.

Match No.	Date	Venue	Opponents	Result		Scorers	Attend
1	Aug 25	A	Charlton Athletic	W	4–2	Woodward (2), Seal, Jones	4
2	Sep 1	H	Halifax Town	D	1–1	Jones	4
3	8	A	Blackburn Rovers	L	0–4		8
4	10	H	Walsall	D	1–1	Butler	3
5	15	H	Port Vale	W	3–1	Swallow (2), Seal	3
6	19	A	Chesterfield	W	2–0	Pollard, Jones	5
7	22	A	Watford	D	1–1	Pollard	6
8	29	H	Aldershot	W	3–1	Seal, Lyons (2)	3
9	Oct 1	H	Chesterfield	D	0–0		5
10	6	A	Cambridge United	D	0–0		4
11	12	H	Wrexham	W	1–0	Peachey	5
12	16	A	Walsall	D	0–0		5
13	20	A	Bristol Rovers	D	0–0		8
14	27	H	Tranmere Rovers	W	2–0	Swallow, Seal	4
15	Nov 3	A	Brighton & Hove Albion	D	0–0		16
16	10	H	Southend United	W	1–0	Jones	8
17	12	H	Hereford United	D	0–0		7
18	17	A	Shrewsbury Town	W	2–0	Jones, Peachey	1
19	Dec 8	H	Southport	W	4–0	Seal, Jones, Pollard, Peachey	2
20	22	A	Aldershot	D	2–2	Seal, Woodward	3
21	26	H	Grimsby Town	D	1–1	Woodward (pen)	5
22	29	H	Blackburn Rovers	W	1–0	Pollard	6
23	Jan 5	H	Rochdale	W	2–1	Jones, Seal	3
24	12	A	Port Vale	D	2–2	Burrows, Holmes	3
25	19	H	Charlton Athletic	L	0–1		4
26	Feb 3	A	Rochdale	W	3–1	Jones (2), Seal	2
27	10	H	Watford	D	2–2	Seal, Holmes	7
28	20	A	Wrexham	L	0–1		6
29	24	H	Cambridge United	W	2–0	Seal, Opp. og	7
30	Mar 2	A	Grimsby Town	W	2–1	Seal, Lyons (pen)	7
31	6	H	Bournemouth	W	4–1	Topping, Jones, Lyons (pen), Seal	10
32	9	A	Tranmere Rovers	D	0–0		2
33	12	A	Oldham Athletic	L	1–2	Burrows	15
34	16	H	Bristol Rovers	W	2–1	Jones, Holmes (pen)	11
35	24	A	Southend United	D	3–3	Jones (2), Seal	6
36	27	A	Bournemouth	W	3–1	Jones, Seal, Holmes	7
37	30	H	Brighton & Hove Albion	W	3–0	Burrows, Jones (2)	7
38	Apr 3	H	Plymouth Argyle	D	1–1	Seal	8
39	6	A	Hereford United	D	0–0		7
40	12	H	Huddersfield Town	W	2–1	Holmes (pen), Jones	9
41	13	H	Shrewsbury Town	L	0–1		7
42	16	A	Huddersfield Town	W	1–0	Seal	7
43	19	A	Southport	D	1–1	Lyons	1
44	27	H	Oldham Athletic	D	1–1	Jones	15
45	30	A	Halifax Town	L	1–2	Hunter	4
46	May 6	A	Plymouth Argyle	W	2–0	Seal, Opp. og	5

A

S

2 own-goals

FA Cup

1	Nov 24	H	Mansfield Town	D	0–0		4
r	Dec 10	A	Mansfield Town	L	3–5	Jones (2), Swallow	4

A

S

Football League Cup

1	Aug 29	H	Huddersfield Town	W	1–0	Opp. og	6
2	Oct 9	H	Aston Villa	W	1–0	Peachey	7
3	31	A	Orient	D	1–1	Swallow	12
r	Nov 6	H	Orient	W	2–1*	Holmes, Butler	11
4	21	H	Manchester City	D	0–0		15
r	Dec 5	A	Manchester City	L	1–4	Pollard	17

* After extra-time.

A

S

1 own-goal

Stone	Burrows	Taylor	Swallow	Topping	Holmes	Woodward	Seal	Jones	Butler	Pollard	Hillyard	Calvert	Lyons	Wilson	Peachey	Hunter	Wann	Robb	
2	3	4	5	6	7	8	9	10	11										1
2	3	7	5	6	8		9	10	11	4									2
2	3	7	5	6	**4**	8	9	10	11	12									3
2	3	**4**	5	6		8	9	10	11	7	1	12							4
2	3		5	6		8	9	10		7	1	4	11						5
2	3		5	6		8	9	10		7		4	11						6
2	3		5	6		8	9	10		7		4	11						7
2	3		5	6		8	9	10	12	7		**4**	11						8
2	3		5	6		8	9		11	7			4	10					9
2	3		5	6		8	**9**		11	7		12	4	10					10
2	3		5	6		8			11	7		10	4		9				11
2	3		5	6		8	12		11	7		**10**	4		9				12
2	3		5	6		8	9		11	7		**8**	4		12				13
2	3		5	6		8	9	10	11	7			4						14
2	3		5	6		8	9	10		7		11	4						15
2	3		5	6		8	9	10	11	7			4						16
2	3		5	6	12	8	9	10	11	**7**			4						17
2	3		5	6	**7**	8		10	11	12			4		9				18
2	3		5	6	12	8	9	**10**		7		4			11				19
2	3		5	6	12	8	9	10		7		**11**	4						20
2	3		5	6		8	9	10		7		11	4						21
	3		5	6		8	9	10		7		11	4			2			22
2	3		5	6	12	8	9	10		**7**		11	4						23
2	3		5	6	7	8	9	10				11	4						24
2	3		5	6	**7**	8	9	10		12		11	4						25
2	3		5	6	4	11	9	10				8	7						26
2	3		5	6	4	**11**	9	10		12		8	7						27
2	3		5	6	4	11	9	10		12	1	8	**7**						28
2	3		5	6	4		9	10				8	7				11		29
2	3		5	6	4	12	9	10				8	7				**11**		30
2	3		5	6	4		9	10				8	7				11		31
2	3		5	6	4		9	10				8	7				11		32
2	3		5	6	4	12	9	10				8	7				**11**		33
2	3		5	6	4	11	9	10				8	7						34
2	3		5	6	4	**11**	9	10		12		8	7						35
2	3		5	6	4	11	9	10				8	**7**		12				36
2	3		5	6	4	11	9	10				8	7						37
2	3		5	6	4	11	9	10				8	7						38
2	3		5	6	4	11	9	10	12	**7**		8							39
2	3		5	6	4	**11**	9	10	12			8	7						40
2	3		5	6	4		9	10	11			8	7						41
2	3		5	6	4	8	9	10	11				7						42
2	3		5	6	4	8	9	10	11				7						43
	3		5	6	4	8	9	10	11			2	7						44
	3		5	6	4	8	9	10	11				7			2			45
2	3		5	6	4		9	10	11				7					8	46
43	46	4	46	46	27	38	43	41	19	21	3	32	40	2	4	2	5	1	
					4	2	1		3	6		2			2				
	3		3	1	5	4	17	18	1	4			5		3	1			

Stone	Burrows	Taylor	Swallow	Topping	Holmes	Woodward	Seal	Jones	Butler	Pollard	Hillyard	Calvert	Lyons	Wilson	Peachey	Hunter	Wann	Robb	
2	3		5	6	12	8	9	10		7			**4**		11				1
2	3		5	6		8	9	10		7		4	11						r
2	2		2	2		2	2	2		2		1	2		1				
					1														
			1					2											

Stone	Burrows	Taylor	Swallow	Topping	Holmes	Woodward	Seal	Jones	Butler	Pollard	Hillyard	Calvert	Lyons	Wilson	Peachey	Hunter	Wann	Robb	
2	3	4	5	6	7	**8**	9	10	11	12									1
2	3		5	6		8			11	7		10	4		9				2
2	3		5	6		8	9	10	11	7			4						3
2	3		5	6	12	8	9	**10**	11	7			4						r
2	3		5	6	12	8	**9**	10		7			4		11				4
2	3		5	6		8	**9**	10		7		12	4		11				r
6	6	1	6	6	1	6	5	5	4	5		1	5		3				
					2					1		1							
			1		1				1	1					1				

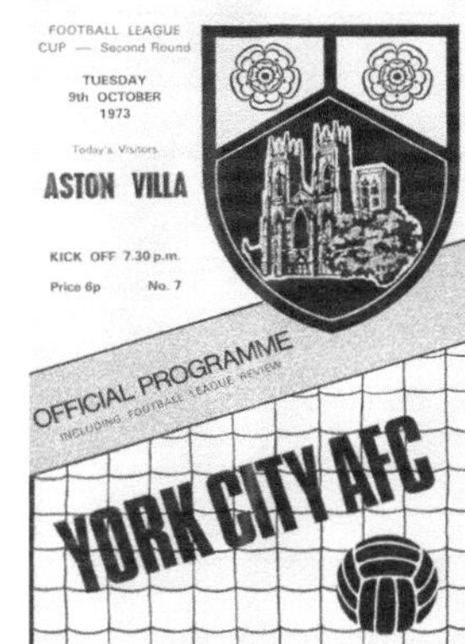

York City v Aston Villa 9 October 1973 programme cover.

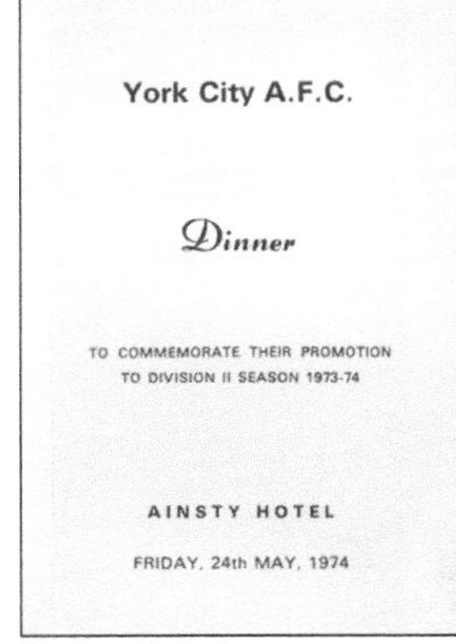

Dinner card invitation to commemorate York's promotion to the Second Division.

Ian Butler.

1974–75

Division Two

Manager: Tom Johnston, then Wilf McGuinness

	P	W	D	L	F	A	Pts
Manchester United	42	26	9	7	66	30	61
Aston Villa	42	25	8	9	79	32	58
Norwich City	42	20	13	9	58	37	53
Sunderland	42	19	13	10	65	35	51
Bristol City	42	21	8	13	47	33	50
West Bromwich Albion	42	18	9	15	54	42	45
Blackpool	42	14	17	11	38	33	45
Hull City	42	15	14	13	40	53	44
Fulham	42	13	16	13	44	39	42
Bolton Wanderers	42	15	12	15	45	41	42
Oxford United	42	15	12	15	41	51	42
Orient	42	11	20	11	28	39	42
Southampton	42	15	11	16	53	54	41
Notts County	42	12	16	14	49	59	40
York City	42	14	10	18	51	55	38
Nottingham Forest	42	12	14	16	43	55	38
Portsmouth	42	12	13	17	44	54	37
Oldham Athletic	42	10	15	17	40	48	35
Bristol Rovers	42	12	11	19	42	64	35
Millwall	42	10	12	20	44	56	32
Cardiff City	42	9	14	19	36	62	32
Sheffield Wednesday	42	5	11	26	29	64	21

Did you know that?

City's first-ever season in the second tier of English football and an average home League crowd of 8,828 – the highest since 1956–57 – saw them finish a respectable 15th.

City crossed swords for the first time in League football this campaign with the likes of Aston Villa, Sunderland, Nottingham Forest, Sheffield Wednesday, Fulham, West Bromwich Albion and Manchester United. Only six years earlier, while the Red Devils were winning the European Cup, City were having to apply for re-election to the Football League.

Following the 3–2 win at Oldham on 19 October 1974 City moved up to fifth in the table, their highest-ever placing in the League.

City did the double over Norwich City, who won promotion, and Fulham, who reached the FA Cup Final.

The biggest-ever crowd to watch City in a League game was on 29 March 1975 when 46,802 saw United win 2–1 at Old Trafford.

Manager Tom Johnston was released from his contract to join Huddersfield Town in January 1975 after over six years in charge. His successor was Wilf McGuinness.

Clubman of the Year was Chris Topping, who had not missed a game since September 1970.

Match No.	Date	Venue	Opponents	Result		Scorers	Attend.
1	Aug 17	H	Aston Villa	D	1–1	Lyons	9
2	24	A	Oxford United	L	1–3	Jones	6,
3	27	H	Cardiff City	W	1–0	Jones	6
4	31	H	Notts County	D	2–2	Seal (2)	6
5	Sep 7	A	Fulham	W	2–0	Jones (2)	7,
6	14	H	Sunderland	L	0–1		14
7	17	H	Oxford United	D	1–1	Holmes (pen)	7,
8	21	A	Blackpool	D	1–1	Seal	7
9	24	A	Bristol City	D	0–0		11
10	28	H	Portsmouth	W	3–0	Seal, Holmes, Wann	6,
11	Oct 5	A	West Bromwich Albion	L	0–2		11,
12	12	H	Bristol Rovers	W	3–0	Seal (2), Hinch	6,
13	16	A	Cardiff City	L	2–3	Holmes (2, 2 pens)	5
14	19	A	Oldham Athletic	W	3–2	Lyons, Holmes, Seal	12,
15	26	H	Bolton Wanderers	L	1–3	Holmes (pen)	9
16	Nov 1	H	Orient	L	0–1		8
17	9	A	Sheffield Wednesday	L	0–3		12
18	16	H	Millwall	W	2–1	Jones, Seal	6
19	23	A	Nottingham Forest	L	1–2	Jones	10,
20	30	H	Norwich City	W	1–0	Seal	7
21	Dec 7	A	Southampton	L	1–2	Seal	13
22	14	A	Aston Villa	L	0–4		15
23	21	H	Manchester United	L	0–1		15
24	26	A	Sunderland	L	0–2		35
25	28	H	Hull City	W	3–0	Holmes (2, 2 pens), Swallow	10
26	Jan 10	H	Southampton	D	1–1	Topping	9
27	18	A	Norwich City	W	3–2	Seal, Jones (2)	23
28	31	H	Sheffield Wednesday	W	3–0	Lyons (2), Butler	10
29	Feb 8	A	Orient	L	0–1		6
30	14	H	Nottingham Forest	D	1–1	Seal	7
31	22	A	Millwall	W	3–1	Jones (2), Cave	9
32	Mar 1	A	Notts County	L	1–2	Seal	8
33	8	H	Bristol City	W	1–0	Pollard	7,
34	15	A	Portsmouth	L	0–1		9
35	22	H	Fulham	W	3–2	Jones (2), Holmes (pen)	7,
36	29	A	Manchester United	L	1–2	Seal	46
37	31	A	Hull City	L	0–2		10,
38	Apr 1	H	Blackpool	D	0–0		8,
39	5	A	Bolton Wanderers	D	1–1	Seal	7
40	12	H	West Bromwich Albion	L	1–3	Seal	8,
41	19	A	Bristol Rovers	W	3–1	Topping, Swallow, Seal	11
42	26	H	Oldham Athletic	D	0–0		10,
							A
							S

FA Cup

3	Jan 4	A	Arsenal	D	1–1	Seal	27,
r	7	H	Arsenal	L	1–3*	Lyons	15,
							A
							S

* After extra-time

Football League Cup

1	Aug 21	H	Huddersfield Town	L	0–2		5,
							A
							S

Stone	Oliver	Holmes	Swallow	Topping	Lyons	Cave	Seal	Jones	Butler	Hinch	Wann	Peachey	Hunter	Ogden	Calvert	Woodward	Robb	Pollard	Coop	Taylor	
2	3	4	5	6	7	8	**9**	10	11	12											1
2	3	4	5	6	7	8		10		9	11										2
2	3	4	5	6	7	8	9	10			11										3
2	3	4	5	6	7	**8**	9	10		12	11										4
2	3	4	5	6	7	8	9	10	11												5
2	3	4	5	6	7	8	9	10	11	12											6
	3	4	5	6	7	8	9	10	11			3									7
	3	4	**5**	6	7	8	9	10	11	12			2								8
	3	4	5	6	7	8	9	**10**		12	11		2								9
	3	4	5	6	7	8	9			10	11		2								10
	3	4	5	6	7	8	9			10	11		2								11
	2	4	5	6	7	8	9			10	11			3							12
	2	4	5	6	7	8	9			10	**11**			3	12						13
	2	4	5	6	7	8	9			10	**11**			3		12					14
	3	4	5	6	7	8	9	12		**10**	11				2						15
	3	4	5	6	**7**	8	9	10	11						2	12					16
		4		6		8	9	10	11			3			2	7	5	12			17
	3	4		6		8	9	10	11							12	5	7	2		18
		4	5	6	11	8	9	10					2			7			3		19
		4	5	6	7	8	9	10					2			11			3		20
		4	5	6	11	8	9	10					2		12	**7**			3		21
		4	5	6	7	11	**9**	10		12			2	3		8					22
		4	5	6	12	11	9	10		7			2	3		**8**					23
		4	5	6	12	11	9	**10**		7			2	3		8					24
		4	5	6	7		9	10	11					3	2	8					25
	3	4	5	6	7	8	9	**10**	11	12					2						26
	3	4	5	6	7	8	9	10	**11**						2	12					27
	3	4	5	6	7	8	9	10	11						2						28
	3	4	5	6	7	8	9	10	11						2						29
	3	4		6	7	8	9	10	11						2		5				30
	3	4	**5**	6		8	9	10	11						2	12		7			31
	3	4		6		**8**	9	10	11		12				2	5		7			32
	3	4		6	11	8	9	10							2	5		7			33
	3	4	5	6	11	8	9	10							2			7			34
	3	4	5	6		8	9	10	11						2			7			35
	3	4	5	6	12	8	9	**10**	11						2			7			36
	3	4	5	6	12	8	9	**10**	11						2			7			37
	3	4	5	6		8	9	10	11						2			7			38
	3	4	5	6		8	9	10	11						2			7			39
	3	4	5	6	12	**8**	9	10	11						2			7			40
	3	4	5	6	7		9	10	11						2	8					41
	3	4	**5**	6	7		9	10	11						2	8				12	42
6	34	42	37	42	30	39	41	36	24	9	10	2	10	7	21	12	3	11	4		
					5			1		7	1				2	5		1		1	
		9	2	2	4	1	17	12	1	1	1							1			

Stone	Oliver	Holmes	Swallow	Topping	Lyons	Cave	Seal	Jones	Butler	Hinch	Wann	Peachey	Hunter	Ogden	Calvert	Woodward	Robb	Pollard	Coop	Taylor	
		4	5	6	7		9	10	11					3	2	8					3
	12	4	5	6	7		9	10	11					3	2	**8**					r
		2	2	2	2		2	2	2					2	2	2					
	1																				
					1		1														

Stone	Oliver	Holmes	Swallow	Topping	Lyons	Cave	Seal	Jones	Butler	Hinch	Wann	Peachey	Hunter	Ogden	Calvert	Woodward	Robb	Pollard	Coop	Taylor	
2	3	4	5	6	7	8	9		11	10											1
1	1	1	1	1	1	1	1		1	1											

York City v Manchester United 21 December 1974 programme cover.

Peter Oliver.

1975–76

Division Two

Manager: Wilf McGuinness

	P	W	D	L	F	A	Pts
Sunderland	42	24	8	10	67	36	56
Bristol City	42	19	15	8	59	35	53
West Bromwich Albion	42	20	13	9	50	33	53
Bolton Wanderers	42	20	12	10	64	38	52
Notts County	42	19	11	12	60	41	49
Southampton	42	21	7	14	66	50	49
Luton Town	42	19	10	13	61	51	48
Nottingham Forest	42	17	12	13	55	40	46
Charlton Athletic	42	15	12	15	61	72	42
Blackpool	42	14	14	14	40	49	42
Chelsea	42	12	16	14	53	54	40
Fulham	42	13	14	15	45	47	40
Orient	42	13	14	15	37	39	40
Hull City	42	14	11	17	45	49	39
Blackburn Rovers	42	12	14	16	45	50	38
Plymouth Argyle	42	13	12	17	48	54	38
Oldham Athletic	42	13	12	17	57	68	38
Bristol Rovers	42	11	16	15	38	50	38
Carlisle United	42	12	13	17	45	59	37
Oxford United	42	11	11	20	39	59	33
York City	42	10	8	24	39	71	28
Portsmouth	42	9	7	26	32	61	25

Did you know that?

City's second season of Second Division football ended in relegation, with home average League crowds slipping to 5,189.

New opposition this term was Chelsea, and both games between the clubs ended in draws.

Notable newcomer was Northern Ireland international Eric McMordie, who scored on his debut in the opening game.

Chris Calvert played his last game for City at home to Notts County on 13 September 1975 and was transferred to Sheffield United for a new record fee received of £30,000.

During the season, City twice had sequences of seven successive defeats.

Their best results were a 2–1 home win over Southampton, who went on to win the FA Cup that season, and a 2–1 success at Bolton Wanderers.

Barry Swallow made his last appearance for City on 7 February 1976 at home to Luton Town. He twice led the club to promotion and played in 312 League and Cup games and scored 27 goals.

Micky Cave was top scorer and Clubman of the Year.

The total number of League goals scored (39) set a new club low.

Match No.	Date	Venue	Opponents	Result		Scorers	Atten
1	Aug 16	H	Portsmouth	W	2–1	Lyons, McMordie	
2	23	A	Bristol Rovers	L	1–2	Downing	
3	30	H	Bolton Wanderers	L	1–2	Jones	
4	Sep 6	A	West Bromwich Albion	D	2–2	Seal, Jones	1
5	13	H	Notts County	L	1–2	McMordie	
6	20	A	Plymouth Argyle	D	1–1	Seal	1
7	23	A	Orient	L	0–1		
8	27	H	Oxford United	W	2–0	Swallow, Wann	
9	Oct 4	A	Chelsea	D	0–0		1
10	11	A	Oldham Athletic	L	0–2		
11	18	H	Bristol City	L	1–4	Cave	
12	21	H	Charlton Athletic	L	1–3	Jones	
13	25	A	Southampton	L	0–2		1
14	Nov 1	H	Sunderland	L	1–4	Jones	1
15	4	A	Luton Town	L:	0–4		
16	8	A	Carlisle United	L	0–1		
17	15	H	Fulham	W	1–0	Holmes (pen)	
18	22	A	Bristol City	L	1–4	Seal	1
19	29	A	Nottingham Forest	L	0–1		1
20	Dec 6	H	Hull City	L	1–2	Seal	
21	13	H	Bristol Rovers	D	0–0		
22	20	A	Portsmouth	W	1–0	Hinch	
23	26	H	Blackburn Rovers	W	2–1	Holmes (pen), Hosker	
24	27	A	Blackpool	D	0–0		
25	Jan 10	A	Notts County	L	0–4		1
26	17	H	West Bromwich Albion	L	0–1		
27	31	A	Charlton Athletic	L	2–3	Cave, Pollard	
28	Feb 7	H	Luton Town	L	2–3	Holmes (pen), Pollard	
29	14	H	Carlisle United	L	1–2	Holmes	
30	21	A	Fulham	L	0–2		
31	24	H	Orient	L	0–2		
32	28	H	Southampton	W	2–1	Cave, Hinch	
33	Mar 13	H	Oldham Athletic	W	1–0	Cave	
34	20	H	Nottingham Forest	W	3–2	Hinch, Pollard (2)	
35	27	A	Hull City	D	1–1	Cave	
36	30	A	Sunderland	L	0–1		3
37	Apr 3	A	Oxford United	L	0–1		
38	10	H	Plymouth Argyle	W	3–1	Holmes, Pollard, Cave	
39	13	A	Bolton Wanderers	W	2–1	Hinch, Cave	1
40	17	A	Blackburn Rovers	L	0–4		
41	19	H	Blackpool	D	1–1	Holmes	
42	24	H	Chelsea	D	2–2	Seal, Cave	

FA Cup

3	Jan 3	H	Hereford United	W	2–1	Seal, Hosker	
4	24	H	Chelsea	L	0–2		1

Football League Cup

1 (1)	Aug 20	A	Bradford City	L	0–2		
1 (2)	26	H	Bradford City	W	3–0	Seal (2), Jones	
2	Sep 10	H	Liverpool	L	0–1		1

	Oliver	Downing	Holmes	Swallow	Topping	Lyons	Cave	Seal	Jones	McMordie	Woodward	Calvert	Stone	Pollard	Wann	Hinch	Hunter	Creamer	Hosker	Scott	Taylor	James
1	2	3	4	5	6	7	8	9	10	11												
2	2	3	**4**	5	6	7	8	9	10	11	12											
3		3	4	5	6	7	8	9	10	11		2										
4		3		5	6	7	8	9	10	11	4	2										
5		3	12	5	6	7	8	9	10	11	**4**	2										
6		3		5	6			9	10	11	4		2	7	8							
7		3		5	6			9	10	**11**	4		2	7	8	12						
8		3		5	6		4	9	10	11			2	7	8							
9		3		5	6		4	9	10	11			2	7	8							
10		3		5	6		4	9	**10**	11			2	7	8	12						
11	2	3	**4**	5	6	11	8	9		10				7			12					
12	2	3			5		4	9	10	11	8			7			6					
13	2	3			5		4	9	10		8			7	11		6					
14	2	3			5		4	9	10		8			7	11		6					
15	2	3	8	5	6		4	9	10					7	11							
16		11	8	5	6	7		9	**10**	4	3							2	12			
17		11	8	5	6	7		9	10	4	3							2				
18		11	8	5	6	**7**		9		4	3					10		2	12			
19		11	8	5	6	**7**		9		4	3					10		2	12			
20		11	8	5	6			9	**10**	4	3					12			7	2		
21		**11**	8	5	6		12	9		4	3					10			7	2		
22			8	5	6		11	9		4	3					10	2		7			
23		11	8	5	6		12	9		4	**3**					10	2		7			
24		**3**		5	6		8	9		4				12		10	2		7		11	
25		11	8	5	6			9		4	3					10			7	2		
26					6		10	12		**4**	3			11		9	8		7	2		5
27			**8**	5	6		10	9		11	3			7			12			2		4
28			**8**	5	6		10	9		11	3		2	7					12			4
29			4		6		8	9		10	3			7					11	2		5
30			4		6		8	9		10	3			7					11	2		5
31			4		6		8	9		10	3			7		12			**11**	2		5
32		3	4		6		8			11	10			7		9				2		5
33		3	4		6		8			11	10			7		9				2		5
34		3	4		6		8			11	10			7		9				2		5
35		3	**4**		6		8	12		11	10			7		9				2		5
36		3	4		6		8	12		11	10			**7**		9				2		5
37		3	**4**		5		8	12		11	6			7		9			10	2		
38		3	**4**		6		8	12		11	10			7		9				2		5
39		3	4		5		8	10		11	6			7		9				2		
40		3	4		5		8	10		**11**	6			7		9			12	2		
41		3	4		6		8	11			10			7		9				2		5
42		3	4		6		8	11			10			7		9				2		5
	7	35	30	24	42	10	32	34	17	37	33	3	6	27	8	19	7	4	11	19	1	14
			1				2	5			1			1		4	2		5			
		1	6	1		1	8	5	4	2				5	1	4			1			

	Oliver	Downing	Holmes	Swallow	Topping	Lyons	Cave	Seal	Jones	McMordie	Woodward	Calvert	Stone	Pollard	Wann	Hinch	Hunter	Creamer	Hosker	Scott	Taylor	James
3		11	8	5	6			9		4	3					10			7	2		
4				5	6		4	9		12	3			11		**10**	8		7	2		
		1	1	2	2		1	2		1	2			1		2	1		2	2		
										1												
								1											1			

	Oliver	Downing	Holmes	Swallow	Topping	Lyons	Cave	Seal	Jones	McMordie	Woodward	Calvert	Stone	Pollard	Wann	Hinch	Hunter	Creamer	Hosker	Scott	Taylor	James
1 (1)	2	3	4	5	6	7	8	9	10	11												
1 (2)		3	4	5	6	7	8	9	10	11		2										
2		3		5	6	7	8	9	10	11	4	2										
	1	3	2	3	3	3	3	3	3	3	1	2										
								2	1													

York City v Nottingham Forest 20 March 1976 programme cover.

Eric McMordie.

Jim Hinch.

1976–77

Division Three

Manager: Wilf McGuinness

	P	W	D	L	F	A	Pts
Mansfield Town	46	28	8	10	78	42	64
Brighton & Hove Albion	46	25	11	10	83	40	61
Crystal Palace	46	23	13	10	68	40	59
Rotherham United	46	22	15	9	69	44	59
Wrexham	46	24	10	12	80	54	58
Preston North End	46	21	12	13	64	43	54
Bury	46	23	8	15	64	59	54
Sheffield Wednesday	46	22	9	15	65	55	53
Lincoln City	46	19	14	13	77	70	52
Shrewsbury Town	46	18	11	17	65	59	47
Swindon Town	46	15	15	16	68	75	45
Gillingham	46	16	12	18	55	64	44
Chester	46	18	8	20	48	58	44
Tranmere Rovers	46	13	17	16	51	53	43
Walsall	46	13	15	18	57	65	41
Peterborough United	46	13	15	18	55	65	41
Oxford United	46	12	15	19	55	65	39
Chesterfield	46	14	10	22	56	64	38
Port Vale	46	11	16	19	47	71	38
Portsmouth	46	11	14	21	53	70	36
Reading	46	13	9	24	49	73	35
Northampton Town	46	13	8	25	60	75	34
Grimsby Town	46	12	9	25	45	69	33
York City	46	10	12	24	50	89	32

Did you know that?

Back in Division Three City suffered another relegation and for the first time in the club's League history the average home attendance dropped below 3,000 (2,986).

City's 7–2 defeat at Brighton on 18 September 1976 was featured on BBC's *Match of the Day.*

Jimmy Seal made his last appearance in City colours at Wrexham on 1 November 1976.

Gordon Staniforth joined the club from Hull City, and his debut was at Sheffield Wednesday on 27 December 1976.

Chris Topping was an ever present for the sixth successive season and made his 300th consecutive League appearance on 9 April 1977 at Lincoln City.

Graeme Crawford made his last appearance in goal on 16 April 1977 at Northampton Town. At the end of the season he moved to Scunthorpe United.

Top scorer and Clubman of the Year was Brian Pollard.

Match No.	Date	Venue	Opponents	Result		Scorers	Attenda
1	Aug 21	A	Crystal Palace	L	0–1		14,
2	28	H	Bury	D	2–2	Cave, Seal	2,
3	Sep 4	A	Peterborough United	L	0–3		6,
4	7	H	Tranmere Rovers	W	1–0	Cave	2,
5	11	H	Mansfield Town	L	0–1		2,
6	18	A	Brighton & Hove Albion	L	2–7	Hinch, Pollard	15,
7	25	H	Oxford United	W	2–1	Young, Hinch	2,
8	Oct 2	A	Preston North End	L	2–4	Holmes, Hinch	6,
9	9	H	Rotherham United	D	1–1	Holmes	3,
10	16	A	Grimsby Town	L	0–1		4,
11	23	H	Chester	L	0–2		2,
12	26	H	Northampton Town	L	1–4	Cave	2,
13	30	A	Chesterfield	L	0–2		4,
14	Nov 1	A	Wrexham	D	1–1	Cave	6,
15	6	H	Port Vale	W	1–0	Pollard	1,
16	13	A	Walsall	W	2–1	Downing, Hope	5,
17	27	H	Shrewsbury Town	L	0–3		2,
18	Dec 18	H	Portsmouth	L	1–4	Pollard	2,
19	27	A	Sheffield Wednesday	L	2–3	Holmes, Pollard	22,
20	Jan 8	H	Gillingham	D	2–2	Pollard (2)	2,
21	22	H	Crystal Palace	W	2–1	Galvin (2)	3,
22	25	H	Chesterfield	W	2–1	Staniforth, Galvin	2,
23	31	A	Tranmere Rovers	D	4–4	Staniforth (2), Opp. og, Hope	2,
24	Feb 5	A	Bury	L	2–4	Opp. og, Pollard	4,
25	7	A	Port Vale	W	2–0	James, Pollard	4,
26	12	H	Peterborough United	W	2–1	Hinch, Pollard	3,
27	16	A	Reading	D	1–1	Galvin	4,
28	19	A	Mansfield Town	L	1–4	Pollard	7,
29	22	H	Lincoln City	D	2–2	Galvin, Holmes	2,
30	26	H	Brighton & Hove Albion	L	0–1		4,
31	Mar 5	A	Oxford United	W	2–0	Pollard, Opp. og	4,
32	12	H	Preston North End	L	0–2		3,
33	19	A	Rotherham United	D	1–1	Holmes	7,
34	26	H	Grimsby Town	D	1–1	Hinch	2,
35	29	A	Swindon Town	L	1–5	Holmes	5,
36	Apr 2	A	Chester	L	0–1		3,
37	9	A	Lincoln City	L	0–2		6,
38	11	H	Sheffield Wednesday	L	0–2		5,
39	12	H	Wrexham	D	0–0		2,
40	16	A	Northampton Town	L	0–3		5,
41	19	H	Swindon Town	W	4–2	Galvin, Hinch, Pollard, Hope	1,
42	23	H	Walsall	D	0–0		2,
43	30	A	Shrewsbury Town	L	1–2	Hinch	2,
44	May 3	A	Gillingham	L	0–2		3,
45	7	H	Reading	D	1–1	Holmes	1,
46	14	A	Portsmouth	L	1–3	Hope	14,
							Ap
							Su
						3 own-goals	

FA Cup

1	Nov 20	A	Dudley Town	D	1–1	Cave	5,
r	23	H	Dudley Town	W	4–1	Holmes (2, 1 pen), Cave, Pollard	2,
2	Dec 11	A	Rotherham United	D	0–0		7,
r	14	H	Rotherham United	D	1–1*	Holmes (pen)	3,
2r	21	A	Rotherham United	L	1–2*	Hinch	6,
							Ap
							Su

* After extra-time.

Football League Cup

1 (1)	Aug 14	H	Barnsley	D	0–0		3,
1 (2)	17	A	Barnsley	D	0–0*		4,
r	24	H	Barnsley	L	1–2*	Holmes (pen)	3,
							Ap
							Su

* After extra-time.

Scott	Hunter	James	Topping	Woodward	Pollard	Holmes	Seal	Cave	Hosker	Taylor	Hinch	Joy	Downing	Walker	Young	McMordie	Hope	Galvin	Staniforth	Hutt	Bell	Morris	Neenan	
2	3	4	5	6	7	8	9	10	11															1
2	3	4	5	6	7	8	9	10	**11**	12														2
2	3	4	5	6	7	**8**		10	11	12	9													3
2		4	5	3	7	8		10	11		9	6												4
2		4	5	3	7	8	12	10	**11**		9	6												5
2		4	5	3	7	8	11	10			9	**6**	12											6
2	3	4	5	6	7			10			9	11		1	8									7
2	3	4	5	**6**	7	12		10			9	11		1	8									8
2	3	4	5		7	6		10			9	11			8									9
2	3		5	6	7		**10**	11			9	4	12		8									10
2	3		5	6	7	4		10	12		9		11		**8**									11
2	3		5	6	7	4		10			9		11		8									12
2	**3**		5	6		12		10			9	4	11		8	7								13
2		5	6		12	4	9	10				3	11		8	**7**								14
2		5	6		12	4		10			9	3	11		8	**7**								15
2		5	6		12	4		10				3	11		8	7	9							16
2		5	6		7	4						3	11		10	8	9							17
	2	5	6		7	4		10	12			**3**	11		8		9							18
2	6		5		7	4							3		8		9	10	11					19
	6		5		7	4		8				3			2		9	10	11					20
		5	6		7	4		8				3			2		9	10	11					21
12		5	6		7	4		8				3			2		9	10	**11**					22
		5	6		7	4		8				3			2		9	10	11					23
		5	6		7	4		8			12	3			2		**9**	10	11					24
		4	6		7	8		9							2			10	11	3	5			25
		4	6		7	8					9				2			10	11	3	5			26
		4	6		7	8					9				2			10	11	3	5			27
		4	6		7	8					9				2			10	11	3	5			28
		4	6		7	8					9				2			10	11	3	5			29
	4	5	6		7	8					9				2			10	11	3				30
2	4	5	6		7	8					9							10	11	3				31
2	4	**5**	6		7	8					9							10	11	3		12		32
2	4	5	6		7	8					9							10	11	3				33
	4	5	6		7	8					9				2			10	**11**	3		12		34
	4	5	6		7	8					9				2			10	11	3		12		35
2	4	5	6			**8**							12		10			9	11	3		7		36
2	4	5	6		**7**	8									10		9		11	3		12		37
2	4	5	6		7	8					9				10				11	3		12		38
	2	5	6		7	8					9				4			10	11	3				39
	2	**5**	6	4	7						9				8		12	10	11	3				40
	4		5	6	7						9				2		8	10	11	3			1	41
	4		5	6	7						**9**				2		8	10	11	3		12	1	42
	4		5	6	7	10					9				2		8		11	3			1	43
	2	5	6	**4**	7	10			12	11							8		9	3			1	44
	2	5	6		7	10				11					4		8		9	3			1	45
	2	5	6		7	10			12	11					4		8		9	3			1	46
24	30	37	46	17	41	39	5	23	5	3	28	18	9	2	36	5	16	22	28	22	5	1	6	
1					3	2	1		4	2	1		3				1					6		
		1			12	7	1	4			7		1		1		4	6	3					

Scott	Hunter	James	Topping	Woodward	Pollard	Holmes	Seal	Cave	Hosker	Taylor	Hinch	Joy	Downing	Walker	Young	McMordie	Hope	Galvin	Staniforth	Hutt	Bell	Morris	Neenan	
2		5	6		12	4		10			9	3	11		8	**7**								1
2		5	6		7	4		9				3	11		10	8								r
	2	5	6		7	4		10	12			3	**11**		8		9							2
	2	5	6		7	4		10				3	11		8		9							r
2	3	**5**	6		7	4		10	11		12				8		9							2r
3	3	5	5		4	5		5	1		1	4	4		5	2	3							
					1				1		1													
					1	3		2			1													

Scott	Hunter	James	Topping	Woodward	Pollard	Holmes	Seal	Cave	Hosker	Taylor	Hinch	Joy	Downing	Walker	Young	McMordie	Hope	Galvin	Staniforth	Hutt	Bell	Morris	Neenan	
2		4	5	6	7	8	9	10					3			11								1 (1)
2	3	4	5	6	7	8	9	10	11															1 (2)
2	3	4	5	6	7	8	9	10	11															r
3	2	3	3	3	3	3	3	3	2				1			1								
						1																		

York City v Swindon Town 19 April 1977 programme cover.

Joe Neenan.

1977–78

Division Four

Manager: Wilf McGuinness, then Charlie Wright

	P	W	D	L	F	A	Pts
Watford	46	30	11	5	85	38	71
Southend United	46	25	10	11	66	39	60
Swansea City	46	23	10	13	87	47	56
Brentford	46	21	14	11	86	54	56
Aldershot	46	19	16	11	67	47	54
Grimsby Town	46	21	11	14	57	51	53
Barnsley	46	18	14	14	61	49	50
Reading	46	18	14	14	55	52	50
Torquay United	46	16	15	15	57	56	47
Northampton Town	46	17	13	16	63	68	47
Huddersfield Town	46	15	15	16	63	55	45
Doncaster Rovers	46	14	17	15	52	65	45
Wimbledon	46	14	16	16	66	67	44
Scunthorpe United	46	14	16	16	50	55	44
Crewe Alexandra	46	15	14	17	50	69	44
Newport County	46	16	11	19	65	73	43
Bournemouth	46	14	15	17	41	51	43
Stockport County	46	16	10	20	56	56	42
Darlington	46	14	13	19	52	59	41
Halifax Town	46	10	21	15	52	62	41
Hartlepool United	46	15	7	24	51	84	37
York City	46	12	12	22	50	69	36
Southport	46	6	19	21	52	76	31
Rochdale	46	8	8	30	43	85	24

Did you know that?

Wilf McGuinness was dismissed as manager on 20 October 1977, and his successor was Charlie Wright.

New signing Kevin Randall from Mansfield Town scored twice on his debut at home to Doncaster Rovers on 28 October 1977.

Brian Pollard was transferred to Watford in November 1977 for a record fee received of £33,000. His last game was at home to Southport on 12 November. Making his debut in this match was Ian McDonald.

Chris Topping was an ever present for the seventh successive season. He had played in 355 consecutive League games, and in May 1978 joined Huddersfield Town. In total he made 463 senior appearances, the third-highest for the club, and the move severed the last link with City's Second Division days.

Gordon Staniforth was top scorer and Clubman of the Year.

Average home League attendance dropped to a new all-time record low of 2,139 as City had to make their sixth application for re-election. The club received a massive vote of confidence at the League AGM and topped the ballot with a maximum 49 votes.

The attendance of 1,339 for the last game of the season was then the smallest-ever home crowd.

For only the second time in their history City fell at the first hurdle in both Cup competitions, losing to non-League Wigan Athletic in the FA Cup.

Match No.	Date	Venue	Opponents	Result		Scorers	Attend
1	Aug 20	H	Aldershot	L	1–2	Opp. og	1
2	27	A	Watford	W	3–1	Pollard, Hope, Taylor	7
3	Sep 2	H	Stockport County	W	2–1	Staniforth, Holmes (pen)	2
4	6	A	Newport County	L	1–2	Hope	2
5	10	H	Grimsby Town	L	1–2	Opp. og	1
6	13	A	Bournemouth	L	1–2	Holmes	2
7	16	A	Southend United	D	0–0		7
8	24	H	Huddersfield Town	D	1–1	Hoy	2
9	27	H	Reading	W	2–0	Staniforth, Pollard	1
10	Oct 1	A	Barnsley	L	1–2	Pollard	4
11	5	A	Crewe Alexandra	L	0–1		2
12	7	H	Darlington	L	1–2	Pollard	2
13	15	A	Swansea City	D	1–1	Hope	5
14	21	H	Rochdale	D	2–2	Hutt, Holmes	1
15	28	H	Doncaster Rovers	W	2–1	Randall (2)	3
16	Nov 5	A	Brentford	L	0–1		5
17	12	H	Southport	W	2–1	Pollard, Opp. og	2
18	19	A	Wimbledon	L	1–2	Topping	2
19	Dec 3	H	Torquay United	D	0–0		1
20	10	A	Northampton Town	D	1–1	Staniforth	3
21	26	H	Hartlepool United	W	1–0	Novacki	3
22	27	A	Scunthorpe United	L	1–2	Scott	3
23	31	H	Brentford	W	3–2	Staniforth, Randall, Young	2
24	Jan 2	A	Halifax Town	L	0–2		3
25	7	H	Newport County	W	2–0	Scott, Staniforth (pen)	1
26	14	A	Aldershot	D	1–1	Randall	3
27	21	H	Watford	L	0–4		4
28	27	A	Stockport County	L	0–2		4
29	Feb 4	A	Grimsby Town	L	2–3	Staniforth, Scott	3
30	24	H	Barnsley	L	1–2	Randall	3
31	28	H	Southend United	L	1–2	Staniforth (pen)	1
32	Mar 4	A	Darlington	W	2–0	Topping (2)	1
33	7	H	Bournemouth	D	0–0		1
34	11	H	Swansea City	W	2–1	Staniforth (2, 2 pens)	2
35	14	A	Hartlepool United	L	2–4	Randall, Staniforth	3
36	18	A	Rochdale	W	2–1	Randall (2)	1
37	24	H	Scunthorpe United	L	0–2		2
38	28	A	Doncaster Rovers	D	1–1	Hope	2
39	31	H	Halifax Town	D	1–1	Novacki	1
40	Apr 4	H	Crewe Alexandra	D	1–1	McDonald	1
41	7	A	Southport	L	1–4	Novacki	1
42	11	A	Huddersfield Town	W	2–1	Staniforth (pen), McDonald	2
43	15	H	Wimbledon	D	1–1	Staniforth (pen)	1
44	22	A	Torquay United	L	0–3		1
45	26	A	Reading	L	0–1		2
46	29	H	Northampton Town	L	0–3		1
							A
							S
						3 own-goals	

FA Cup

1	Nov 26	A	Wigan Athletic	L	0–1		6
							A
							S

Football League Cup

1 (1)	Aug 13	A	Rotherham United	L	0–3		2
1 (2)	16	H	Rotherham United	W	3–0	Topping, Hoy, Staniforth	1
r	23	H	Rotherham United	D	1–1*	James	2
							A
							S

* After extra-time. Rotherham won 6–5 on penalties.

Scott	Hutt	Young	Topping	James	Pollard	Holmes	Hope	Woodward	Staniforth	Hoy	Taylor	Hunter	Mitchell	Brown	Randall	Clements	McDonald	Novacki	Bainbridge	
2	3	4	5	6	7	8	9	**10**	11	12										1
2	3		5	6	7	8	9		11	4	10									2
2	3		5	6	7	8	**9**		11	4	10	12								3
2	3		5	6	7	8	9		11	**4**	10	12								4
2	**3**	4	5	6	7	8	9		11		10	12								5
2			5	6	7	8	10	4	11	12		3	**9**							6
2	3		5	6	7	8	9	4	11	10										7
2	3	12	5	6	7	8	**9**	4	11	10										8
2	**3**	9	5	6	7	8		4	11	10			12							9
2	3	9	5	6	7	**8**		4	11	10			12							10
2		3	5	6	7	8		**4**	11	12	10	9		1						11
2	3	4	5	6	7	8			11	12	**10**	9		1						12
2	3	4	5	6	7	8	9		11			10		1						13
2	3	4	5	6	7	8			11	10		9		1						14
2	3	4	5	6	7				11	10		8		1	9					15
2	3	4	5	6	7				11	10		8		1	9					16
4	3	12	5	**6**	7		8		11					1	9	2	10			17
4	3	7	5	6			**8**		11			12		1	9	2	10			18
4	3	8	5	6					11		7			1	9	2	10			19
4	3	8	5	6					11		7			1	9	2	10			20
4	3	8	5	6					11					1	9	2	10	7		21
4	3	8	5	6					11					1	9	2	10	7		22
4	3	8	5	6					11					1	9	2	10	7		23
4	3	8	5	6					11					1	9	2	10	7		24
4	3		5	6			12		11		**8**			1	9	2	10	7		25
4	3	8	5	6			12		11					1	9	2	10	**7**		26
4	3		5	6			12		11			8		1	9	2	10	**7**		27
4	3		5	6			12		11			8		1	9	2	10	**7**		28
4	3		5	6			12		11			8		1	9	2	10	**7**		29
	3	8	5				4		11			6		1	9	2	10	7		30
4	3	8	5				7		11			6		1	9	2	10			31
4	3	8	5	6			9		11					1		2	10	7		32
4	3	8	5	6			9		11					1		2	10	7		33
4	3	8	5	6			9		11					1	12	2	10	**7**		34
4	3	8	5	6			**9**		11					1	7	2	10	12		35
4	3	8	5	**6**					11			12		1	9	2	10	7		36
4	3	8	5						11			6		1	9	2	10	7		37
4	3		5				12		11			8		1	9	2	10	7	**6**	38
4	3		5						11		12	8		1	9	2	**10**	7	6	39
4	3		5						11			8		1	9	2	10	7	6	40
4	3		5	6			8		11		12			1	**9**	2	10	7		41
4	3		5						11			8		1	9	2	10	7	6	42
4	3		5				12		11			8		1	9	2	10	7	6	43
4		3	5						11		12	8			9	**2**	10	7	6	44
4		8	5	**6**					11		12	3			9	2	10	7		45
4		2	5						11		8	3			9		10	7	6	46
45	41	29	46	36	17	14	18	7	46	10	10	21	1	33	29	29	30	24	7	
		2					7			4	4	5	2		1			1		
3	1	1	3		5	3	4		12	1	1				8		2	3		

Scott	Hutt	Young	Topping	James	Pollard	Holmes	Hope	Woodward	Staniforth	Hoy	Taylor	Hunter	Mitchell	Brown	Randall	Clements	McDonald	Novacki	Bainbridge	
4	3	8	5	6					11		12	**7**		1	9	2	10			1
1	1	1	1	1					1			1		1	1	1	1			
											1									

Scott	Hutt	Young	Topping	James	Pollard	Holmes	Hope	Woodward	Staniforth	Hoy	Taylor	Hunter	Mitchell	Brown	Randall	Clements	McDonald	Novacki	Bainbridge	
2	3	**4**	5	6	7	8	9	10	11		12									1 (1)
2	3	4	5	6	7	8	9	**10**	11	12										1 (2)
2	3		5	6	7	8	9	**10**	11	4	12									r
3	3	2	3	3	3	3	3	3	3	1										
										1	2									
			1	1					1	1										

YORK CITY
WELCOME
WIMBLEDON
Football League Division Four
Season 1977/78
Saturday 15th April, 1978
Kick Off 3.00 p.m.
Match No. 23
Official Programme 10p
YORK CITY
ASSOCIATION FOOTBALL CLUB

York City v Wimbledon 15 April 1978 programme cover.

Brian Pollard.

1978–79

Division Four

Manager: Charlie Wright

	P	W	D	L	F	A	Pts
Reading	46	26	13	7	76	35	65
Grimsby Town	46	26	9	11	82	49	61
Wimbledon	46	25	11	10	78	46	61
Barnsley	46	24	13	9	73	42	61
Aldershot	46	20	17	9	63	47	57
Wigan Athletic	46	21	13	12	63	48	55
Portsmouth	46	20	12	14	62	48	52
Newport County	46	21	10	15	66	55	52
Huddersfield Town	46	18	11	17	57	53	47
York City	46	18	11	17	51	55	47
Torquay United	46	19	8	19	58	65	46
Scunthorpe United	46	17	11	18	54	60	45
Hartlepool United	46	13	18	15	57	66	44
Hereford United	46	15	13	18	53	53	43
Bradford City	46	17	9	20	62	68	43
Port Vale	46	14	14	18	57	70	42
Stockport County	46	14	12	20	58	60	40
Bournemouth	46	14	11	21	47	48	39
Northampton Town	46	15	9	22	64	76	39
Rochdale	46	15	9	22	47	64	39
Darlington	46	11	15	20	49	66	37
Doncaster Rovers	46	13	11	22	50	73	37
Halifax Town	46	9	8	29	39	72	26
Crewe Alexandra	46	6	14	26	43	90	26

Did you know that?

Left-back Roy Kay, formerly with Hearts and Celtic, made his debut on the opening day.

Seventeen-year-old Gary Ford made his Football League debut on 21 October 1978 at Reading.

Central-defender Steve James missed the whole of the season through injury.

For the second successive campaign Gordon Staniforth was top marksman and Clubman of the Year.

On 7 May 1979 against Port Vale Staniforth became the first City player to score a League hat-trick since April 1972.

The average League attendance was 2,935.

City reached the fourth round of the FA Cup for the first time since 1970–71. They lost at that stage to reigning First Division (Premiership) champions and European Cup-winners elect Nottingham Forest.

Match No.	Date	Venue	Opponents	Result		Scorers	Attend
1	Aug 19	A	Rochdale	W	2–1	Staniforth, Randall	1
2	22	H	Portsmouth	W	5–3	Staniforth (2, 1 pen), Randall (2), Loggie	2
3	26	H	Doncaster Rovers	D	1–1	Randall	3
4	Sep 2	A	Barnsley	L	0–3		8
5	9	H	Northampton Town	W	1–0	Staniforth	2
6	12	A	Halifax Town	W	1–0	Randall	1
7	15	A	Stockport County	L	0–2		6
8	23	H	Wigan Athletic	L	0–1		3
9	26	H	Hereford United	W	1–0	Randall	2
10	30	A	Newport County	D	1–1	Loggie	3
11	Oct 7	H	Wimbledon	L	1–4	Loggie	3
12	14	A	Bradford City	L	1–2	Randall	4
13	17	H	Torquay United	D	0–0		2
14	21	A	Reading	L	0–3		12
15	28	H	Scunthorpe United	W	1–0	Staniforth	1
16	Nov 4	A	Huddersfield Town	L	0–1		3
17	11	H	Barnsley	L	0–1		6
18	18	A	Doncaster Rovers	W	2–1	Randall, Wellings	2
19	Dec 9	A	Bournemouth	W	2–1	Clements, Staniforth	3
20	23	A	Grimsby Town	L	0–3		4
21	26	H	Hartlepool United	D	1–1	Faulkner	3
22	Feb 3	A	Hereford United	L	0–1		3
23	24	H	Bradford City	D	2–2	Staniforth, Loggie	4
24	28	A	Wigan Athletic	D	1–1	Loggie	5
25	Mar 3	H	Reading	L	0–1		2
26	6	A	Darlington	W	1–0	Staniforth	1
27	10	A	Scunthorpe United	W	3–2	Randall (2), Clements	2
28	13	H	Halifax Town	W	2–0	Loggie, Staniforth	2
29	20	H	Newport County	L	1–2	Staniforth	2
30	24	A	Portsmouth	D	1–1	Loggie	9
31	27	H	Rochdale	W	2–1	Opp. og, McDonald	2
32	31	H	Aldershot	D	1–1	McDonald	2
33	Apr 3	A	Northampton Town	L	0–1		1
34	7	A	Port Vale	D	0–0		2
35	13	H	Grimsby Town	D	0–0		5
36	14	A	Hartlepool United	D	1–1	McDonald	2
37	16	H	Darlington	W	5–2	Staniforth, Ford, Loggie, Stronach, McDonald	2
38	21	A	Crewe Alexandra	W	1–0	Stronach	1
39	25	A	Torquay United	L	0–3		1
40	28	H	Bournemouth	W	2–1	McDonald, Staniforth (pen)	2
41	May 1	H	Crewe Alexandra	W	1–0	Ford	2
42	5	A	Aldershot	L	0–1		3
43	7	H	Port Vale	W	4–0	Staniforth (3, 1 pen), McDonald	2
44	11	A	Wimbledon	L	1–2	Ford	3
45	14	H	Stockport County	W	1–0	Wellings	2
46	19	H	Huddersfield Town	L	1–3	Ford	2
							A
							S
						1 own-goal	

FA Cup

1	Nov 25	H	Blyth Spartans	D	1–1	Pugh	5
r	28	A	Blyth Spartans	W	5–3*	Wellings, Clements, Ford, Randall, Staniforth	3
2	Dec 16	H	Scarborough	W	3–0	Faulkner, Staniforth (2)	7
3	Jan 9	H	Luton Town	W	2–0	Staniforth, Randall	6
4	27	A	Nottingham Forest	L	1–3	Wellings	25
							A
							S

* After extra-time.

Football League Cup

1 (1)	Aug 12	A	Grimsby Town	L	0–2		3
1 (2)	15	H	Grimsby Town	L	0–3		2
							A
							S

Scott	Kay	Young	Faulkner	Clements	Stronach	Randall	Loggie	McDonald	Staniforth	Warnock	Wellings	Bainbridge	Collier	Walsh	Brown	Ford	Pugh	
2	3	4	5	6	7	8	9	10	**11**	12								1
2	3	7	5	6	4	8	9	10	11									2
2	3	7	5	6	4	8	9	10	11									3
2	3	7	5	6	**4**	8	9	10	11		12							4
2	3	7	5	6	4	8	9	10	11									5
2	3	7		6	4	8	9	10	11			5						6
2	3	7		6	4	8	9	10	11			5						7
2	3	7	5	6	10	8	9		11				4	12				8
	2	7	5	6		8	9	10	11				4	3				9
	2	7	5	6	12	8	9	10	**11**				4	3				10
	2	7	5	6	**8**	9	10		11		12		4	3				11
7	2		5	6		8	9	10	11				4	3				12
7	2		5	6	4	8	9	10	11					3	1			13
4	2		5	6	10	8	**9**		11	12				3	1	7		14
	2		5	6	4	8	9	10	11					3	1	7		15
	2		5	6		8	9	10	11	12				**3**	1	7	4	16
	2		5	6		8	9	10	11	**7**				3	1	12	4	17
	2		5	6		8		10	11		9			3	1	7	4	18
	2		5	6		8		10	11		9			3	1	7	4	19
	2		5	6		8		10	11		9			3	1	7	4	20
	2		5	6		8	12	10	11		**9**			3	1	7	4	21
	2		5	6		8		10	11		9			3	1	7	4	22
	2		5	6		12	8	10	11		**9**			3	1	7	4	23
	2		5	6		8	9	10	11					3		7	4	24
	2		5	6		8	9	10	11		12			3		**7**	4	25
	2		5	6		8	**9**	10	11		12			3		7	4	26
	2		5	6		8	9	10	11					3		7	4	27
	2		5	6		8	9	10	11					3		7	4	28
	2		5	6		8	9	10	11					3		7	4	29
	2		5	6			9	10	11		8			3		7	4	30
	2		5	6	12	**8**	9	10	11					3		7	4	31
	2		5	6		8	9	10	11					3		7	4	32
	2		5	6	12	8	**9**	10	11					3		7	4	33
	2		5	6		8	9	10	11					3	1	7	4	34
	2		5	6		8	9	10	11					3	1	7	4	35
	2		5	6	12	**8**	9	10	11					3	1	7	4	36
	2		5	6	8		9	10	11					3	1	7	4	37
	2		5	6	8		9	10	11					3	1	7	4	38
	2		5	6	8		9	10	11					3	1	7	4	39
	2		5	6	8	12	**9**	10	11					3	1	7	4	40
	2		5	6	8	**9**	12	10	11					3	1	7	4	41
	2		5	6	**8**	12	9	10	11					3	1	7	4	42
	2		5	6	8	**9**		10	11		12			3	1	7	4	43
	2		5	6	8	12		10	11		**9**			3	1	7	4	44
	2		5	6	8	11		10			9			3	1	7	4	45
	2		5	6	**8**	12		10	11		9			3	1	7	4	46
1	46	11	44	46	22	37	36	43	45	1	10	2	5	38	24	32	31	
					4	5	2			3	5			1		1		
			1	2	2	10	8	6	15		2					4		

Scott	Kay	Young	Faulkner	Clements	Stronach	Randall	Loggie	McDonald	Staniforth	Warnock	Wellings	Bainbridge	Collier	Walsh	Brown	Ford	Pugh	
	2		5	6		9		10	11		8			3	1	7	4	1
	2		5	6		9		10	11		8			3	1	**7**	4	r
	2		5	6		8		10	11		9			3	1	7	4	2
	2		5	6		8	9	10	11					3	1	7	4	3
	2		5	6		8	**9**	10	11		12			3	1	7	4	4
	5		5	5		5	2	5	5		3			5	5	5	5	
											1							
			1	1		2			4		2					1	1	

Scott	Kay	Young	Faulkner	Clements	Stronach	Randall	Loggie	McDonald	Staniforth	Warnock	Wellings	Bainbridge	Collier	Walsh	Brown	Ford	Pugh	
2	3	4	5	6	8		9		11	7				10				1 (1)
2	3	4	5	6	7		9	10	11		12			**8**				1 (2)
2	2	2	2	2	2		2	1	2	1				2				
											1							

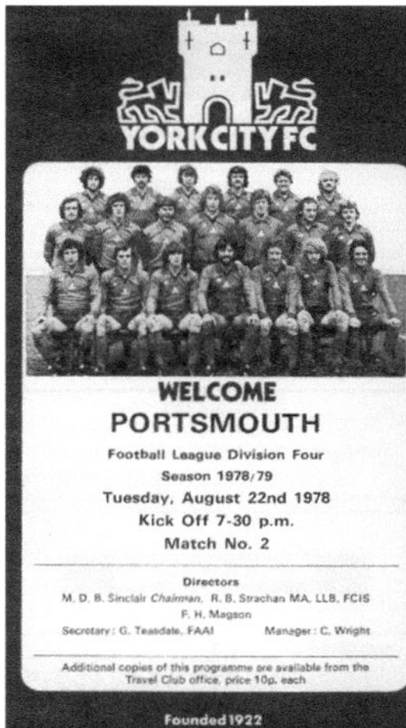

YORK CITY FC
WELCOME
PORTSMOUTH
Football League Division Four
Season 1978/79
Tuesday, August 22nd 1978
Kick Off 7-30 p.m.
Match No. 2
Directors
M. D. B. Sinclair Chairman, R. B. Strachan MA, LLB, FCIS
F. H. Magson
Secretary: G. Teasdale, FAAI
Manager: C. Wright
Additional copies of this programme are available from the Travel Club office, price 10p. each
Founded 1922
York City Association Football & Athletic Club Limited
Bootham Crescent, York YO3 7AQ

York City v Portsmouth 22 August 1978 programme cover.

Steve Faulkner.

1979–80

Division Four

Manager: Charlie Wright, then Barry Lyons

	P	W	D	L	F	A	Pts
Huddersfield Town	46	27	12	7	101	48	66
Walsall	46	23	18	5	75	47	64
Newport County	46	27	7	12	83	50	61
Portsmouth	46	24	12	10	91	49	60
Bradford City	46	24	12	10	77	50	60
Wigan Athletic	46	21	13	12	76	61	55
Lincoln City	46	18	17	11	64	42	53
Peterborough United	46	21	10	15	58	47	52
Torquay United	46	15	17	14	70	69	47
Aldershot	46	16	13	17	62	53	45
Bournemouth	46	13	18	15	52	51	44
Doncaster Rovers	46	15	14	17	62	63	44
Northampton Town	46	16	12	18	51	66	44
Scunthorpe United	46	14	15	17	58	75	43
Tranmere Rovers	46	14	13	19	50	56	41
Stockport County	46	14	12	20	48	72	40
York City	46	14	11	21	65	82	39
Halifax Town	46	13	13	20	46	72	39
Hartlepool United	46	14	10	22	59	64	38
Port Vale	46	12	12	22	56	70	36
Hereford United	46	11	14	21	38	52	36
Darlington	46	9	17	20	50	74	35
Crewe Alexandra	46	11	13	22	35	68	35
Rochdale	46	7	13	26	33	79	27

Did you know that?

The former Leeds United and Scotland star Peter Lorimer made 32 appearances this season and scored nine goals. His debut was on 8 September 1979 against Peterborough United, but his last match in City colours, on 1 March 1980 at home to Tranmere Rovers, was marred when he was sent off.

Eighteen-year-old John Byrne made his debut, when coming on as substitute, on 25 August 1979 at home to Lincoln City.

Gordon Staniforth moved to Carlisle United in October 1979 for a record fee received of £120,000. The previous month he had netted three goals in a 5–2 win at Wigan – the first away hat-trick in the League since September 1965.

Graeme Crawford returned to the club, and his first game was on 26 January 1980 at home to Crewe Alexandra.

Derek Hood, who arrived from Hull City, made his debut at home to Halifax Town on 12 February 1980.

Manager Charlie Wright was sacked in March 1980 and Barry Lyons took over, initially on a caretaker basis.

City's victory at Port Vale on 19 April 1980 was their 200th away win in the Football League.

Average home League attendance was 2,703.

Clubman of the Year was Ian McDonald.

Match No.	Date	Venue	Opponents	Result		Scorers	Attenc
1	Aug 18	A	Hereford United	L	1–3	Randall	
2	21	H	Darlington	W	3–1	McDonald (2), Ford	
3	25	H	Lincoln City	L	0–2		
4	Sep 1	A	Newport County	L	0–2		
5	8	H	Peterborough United	L	0–2		
6	15	A	Wigan Athletic	W	5–2	Staniforth (3), Loggie, Lorimer	
7	18	A	Scunthorpe United	L	1–6	McDonald	
8	22	H	Stockport County	D	2–2	Wellings, Lorimer	
9	29	A	Portsmouth	L	2–5	Eccles, Kay	
10	Oct 2	H	Scunthorpe United	W	2–0	Byrne, Eccles	
11	6	H	Rochdale	W	3–2	Eccles, Byrne, Wellings	
12	9	A	Darlington	L	1–2	Wellings	
13	12	H	Bournemouth	D	1–1	Lorimer	
14	19	A	Tranmere Rovers	W	2–1	Randall, Lorimer	
15	23	H	Doncaster Rovers	L	1–3	Eccles	
16	27	A	Huddersfield Town	D	2–2	Eccles (2)	
17	Nov 2	H	Hereford United	W	3–1	Lorimer, Eccles, Randall	
18	6	A	Doncaster Rovers	L	0–2		
19	10	A	Torquay United	L	3–4	Randall, Eccles, Wellings	
20	17	H	Bradford City	D	2–2	Randall, Kay	
21	Dec 1	H	Port Vale	W	5–1	Lorimer (2), Clements, Randall, McDonald	
22	8	A	Aldershot	D	2–2	Randall, Wellings	
23	21	H	Walsall	L	0–1		
24	26	A	Hartlepool United	L	1–3	Loggie	
25	29	A	Lincoln City	D	1–1	Clements	
26	Jan 5	A	Northampton Town	L	0–2		
27	12	H	Newport County	W	2–1	Kay, Lorimer	
28	26	H	Crewe Alexandra	D	2–2	McDonald (pen), Loggie	
29	Feb 2	H	Wigan Athletic	L	1–2	Opp. og	
30	8	A	Stockport County	L	0–1		
31	12	H	Halifax Town	D	2–2	Faulkner (2)	
32	16	H	Portsmouth	W	1–0	Hood	
33	23	A	Bournemouth	D	0–0		
34	Mar 1	H	Tranmere Rovers	L	0–1		
35	5	A	Peterborough United	L	1–2	Faulkner	
36	8	H	Huddersfield Town	L	0–4		
37	14	A	Rochdale	W	2–0	Wellings, McDonald	
38	22	H	Torquay United	W	1–0	Eccles	
39	29	A	Bradford City	W	2–1	McDonald, Ford	
40	Apr 1	A	Walsall	L	1–3	Faulkner	
41	5	H	Hartlepool United	W	2–1	Walsh (2)	
42	7	A	Halifax Town	D	1–1	Pugh	
43	12	H	Northampton Town	L	1–2	Faulkner	
44	19	A	Port Vale	W	2–1	Clements, Wellings	
45	26	H	Aldershot	D	1–1	McDonald (pen)	
46	May 3	A	Crewe Alexandra	L	0–2		

1 own-goal

FA Cup

1	Nov 24	H	Mossley	W	5–2	Randall, Eccles, Byrne, Lorimer, McDonald (pen)	
2	Dec 15	A	Bury	D	0–0		
r	18	H	Bury	L	0–2		

Football League Cup

(1)	Aug 11	A	Mansfield Town	L	0–1		
1 (2)	14	H	Mansfield Town	W	3–2*	Randall, Clements, Staniforth	

* After extra-time. Mansfield won on away goals.

Kay	Walsh	Pugh	Faulkner	Clements	Ford	Randall	Stronach	McDonald	Staniforth	Byrne	James	Lorimer	Wellings	Loggie	Neenan	Kamara	Eccles	Harrison	McGhie	Ferebee	Crawford	Hood	Taylor	Leaf	
2	3	4	5	6	7	8	9	10	11																1
2	3	4	5	6	7	8	9	10	11																2
2	3	4	5	6	7	8	**9**	10	11	12															3
2	3	4		6	7	8	9	10	11		5														4
2	3	**4**	5		7	9		10	11		6	8	12												5
2	3	6	5		7			10	11			8	9	4											6
2	3	6	5	12	7			10	11			8	9	**4**											7
3		12	5	6				10	11	**7**		8	9	4	1	2									8
3		4	5					10	11		6	8	7		1	2	9								9
3		4		6		12		10		**7**	5	8	11		1	2	9								10
3		4		6				10		7	5	8	11		1	2	9								11
3		4		6				10		7	5	8	11		1	2	9								12
2	3	4		6		12		10		**7**	5	8	11		1		9								13
3		4		6		7		10			5	8	11		1	2	9								14
3		4		6		7		10			5	8	11		1	2	9								15
3		**4**		6		12	8	10			5	7	11		1	2	9								16
3				6	12	7	4	10			**5**	8	11			2	9								17
3			5	6	7	12	4	10				8	11			**2**	9								18
3			5	2	12	7	4	10			**6**	8	11				9								19
2			5	6	4	7		10				8	11		1		9	3							20
2				6	**4**	7		10		12	5	8	11		1		9	3							21
2				6	4	7		10		12	5	8	11		1		**9**	3							22
2				6	4	7		10			5	8	11	9	1			3							23
2		12		6	4	7		10			5	8	**11**	9	1			3							24
2		4		6				10			5	8		11			9	3	**7**	12					25
2		4		6				10			5	8		11			9	3	**7**	12					26
2	3	4	5	6		7		10				8		11	1		9								27
2	3	4	5	6		7		10				8	12	11			**9**				1				28
2	3		5	6		7		10				8		**11**			9		4	12	1				29
2	3	4	5	6		**7**		10				8		12			9		11		1				30
	3	4	5	6				10				8					9		11	7	1	2			31
	3	**4**	5	6		12		10				8					9		11	7	1	2			32
	3		5	6	4	8		10									9		11	7	1	2			33
	3		5	6	12	4		10				8					9		11	**7**	1	2			34
3		12	5	6	4	**8**		10					7				9		11		1	2			35
3			5	6	4			10		12			7	**8**			9		11		1	2			36
3		8	5	6	4			10					7				9		11		1	2			37
3		8	5	6	4			10					7				**9**		11	12	1	2			38
3		8	5	6	4			10					7				9		11		1	2			39
3		8	5	6	4			10					7				9		11		1	2			40
3	12	8	5	6	4			10					7				9		**11**		1	2			41
3	11	8	5	6	4			10					7				9				1	2			42
3	11	8	5	6	4			10					**7**				9			12	1	2			43
3		8	5	6	4			10					7				9		11		1	2			44
		8	5	6	4			10					7				9		11			2	1	3	45
6	3	12	**5**		4			10									9	8	11	7		2	1		46
41	19	31	31	41	26	21	8	46	9	5	18	29	30	11	15	10	36	8	18	5	17	16	2	1	
	1	4		1	3	5				4			2	1						5					
3	2	1	5	3	2	7		8	3	2		8	7	3			9					1			

Kay	Walsh	Pugh	Faulkner	Clements	Ford	Randall	Stronach	McDonald	Staniforth	Byrne	James	Lorimer	Wellings	Loggie	Neenan	Kamara	Eccles	Harrison	McGhie	Ferebee	Crawford	Hood	Taylor	Leaf	
2			**5**	6	4	7		10		12		8	11		1		9	3							1
2				6	4	7		10			5	8	11	9	1			3							2
2			12	6	4	7		10		**9**	5	8	11		1			3							r
3			1	3	3	3		3		1	2	3	3	1	3		1	3							
			1							1															
						1		1		1		1					1								

Kay	Walsh	Pugh	Faulkner	Clements	Ford	Randall	Stronach	McDonald	Staniforth	Byrne	James	Lorimer	Wellings	Loggie	Neenan	Kamara	Eccles	Harrison	McGhie	Ferebee	Crawford	Hood	Taylor	Leaf	
2	3	4	5	6	7	8	12	10	11					**9**											(1)
2	3	4	5	6	7	8	9	10	11																(2)
2	2	2	2	2	2	2	1	2	2					1											
							1																		
				1		1			1																

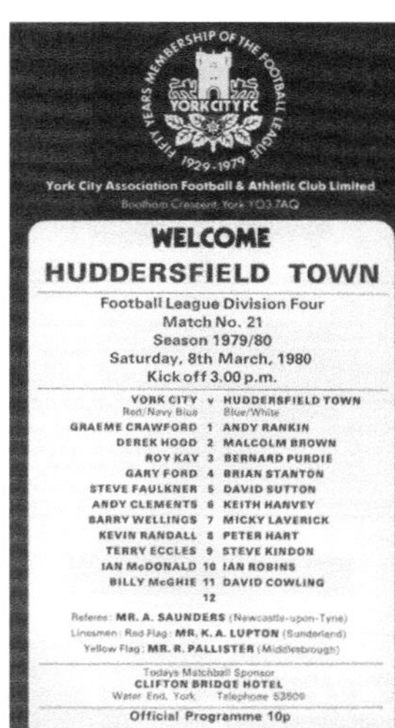

FIFTY YEARS MEMBERSHIP OF THE FOOTBALL LEAGUE
YORK CITY FC
1929-1979
York City Association Football & Athletic Club Limited
Bootham Crescent, York YO3 7AQ
WELCOME
HUDDERSFIELD TOWN
Football League Division Four
Match No. 21
Season 1979/80
Saturday, 8th March, 1980
Kick off 3.00 p.m.
YORK CITY v HUDDERSFIELD TOWN
Red/Navy Blue Blue/White
GRAEME CRAWFORD 1 ANDY RANKIN
DEREK HOOD 2 MALCOLM BROWN
ROY KAY 3 BERNARD PURDIE
GARY FORD 4 BRIAN STANTON
STEVE FAULKNER 5 DAVID SUTTON
ANDY CLEMENTS 6 KEITH HANVEY
BARRY WELLINGS 7 MICKY LAVERICK
KEVIN RANDALL 8 PETER HART
TERRY ECCLES 9 STEVE KINDON
IAN McDONALD 10 IAN ROBINS
BILLY McGHIE 11 DAVID COWLING
12
Referee: MR. A. SAUNDERS (Newcastle-upon-Tyne)
Linesmen: Red Flag: MR. K. A. LUPTON (Sunderland)
Yellow Flag: MR. R. PALLISTER (Middlesbrough)
Todays Matchball Sponsor
CLIFTON BRIDGE HOTEL
Water End, York Telephone 53809
Official Programme 10p

York City v Huddersfield Town 8 March 1980 programme cover.

Gordon Staniforth celebrates his hat-trick feat at Wigan Athletic in September 1979.

Peter Lorimer.

1980–81

Division Four

Manager: Barry Lyons

	P	W	D	L	F	A	Pts
Southend United	46	30	7	9	79	31	67
Lincoln City	46	25	15	6	66	25	65
Doncaster Rovers	46	22	12	12	59	49	56
Wimbledon	46	23	9	14	64	46	55
Peterborough United	46	17	18	11	68	54	52
Aldershot	46	18	14	14	43	41	50
Mansfield Town	46	20	9	17	58	44	49
Darlington	46	19	11	16	65	59	49
Hartlepool United	46	20	9	17	64	61	49
Northampton Town	46	18	13	15	65	67	49
Wigan Athletic	46	18	11	17	51	55	47
Bury	46	17	11	18	70	62	45
Bournemouth	46	16	13	17	47	48	45
Bradford City	46	14	16	16	53	60	44
Rochdale	46	14	15	17	60	70	43
Scunthorpe United	46	11	20	15	60	69	42
Torquay United	46	18	5	23	55	63	41
Crewe Alexandra	46	13	14	19	48	61	40
Port Vale	46	12	15	19	57	70	39
Stockport County	46	16	7	23	44	57	39
Tranmere Rovers	46	13	10	23	59	73	36
Hereford United	46	11	13	22	38	62	35
Halifax Town	46	11	12	23	44	71	34
York City	46	12	9	25	47	66	33

Did you know that?

For the first time in the club's history City finished 92nd in the Football League.

Their seventh and last application for re-election was successful, and they received 46 votes out of a possible 52.

Newcomer Eddie Blackburn made his debut in goal on the opening day and went on to become Clubman of the Year.

'Keeper Mick Astbury made his senior debut on 18 November 1980. Aged 16 years and 298 days, he became the then second youngest player to appear for City.

During the second half of the campaign City suffered 10 defeats in 11 League outings, equalling the worst-ever sequences of 1946–47 and 1975–76.

Average home League crowd was 2,162, and the attendance for the last game against Northampton of 1,167 was the smallest-ever for a Football League match at Bootham Crescent.

For the first time since 1975–76 City reached the second round of the Football League Cup.

Match No.	Date	Venue	Opponents	Result		Scorers
1	Aug 16	H	Bournemouth	W	4–0	Eccles, McDonald, Ford, Byrne
2	18	A	Mansfield Town	W	1–0	Eccles
3	23	H	Torquay United	D	0–0	
4	30	A	Hereford United	D	1–1	Ford
5	Sep 5	A	Southend United	L	0–3	
6	13	H	Hartlepool United	L	0–1	
7	19	A	Northampton Town	L	0–2	
8	23	H	Tranmere Rovers	W	4–1	Kay, Ford, Faulkner, Eccles
9	27	H	Doncaster Rovers	L	0–1	
10	29	A	Tranmere Rovers	L	0–5	
11	Oct 4	H	Port Vale	W	4–1	McDonald (2), Byrne, Eccles
12	7	A	Halifax Town	L	1–3	Smith
13	11	A	Lincoln City	D	1–1	Smith
14	18	H	Stockport County	W	1–0	McDonald
15	21	H	Darlington	L	1–2	Smith
16	25	A	Wimbledon	L	0–3	
17	29	A	Wigan Athletic	L	0–1	
18	Nov 1	H	Scunthorpe United	W	1–0	Eccles
19	4	H	Halifax Town	D	1–1	Eccles
20	8	A	Crewe Alexandra	D	1–1	McGhie
21	11	H	Mansfield Town	W	2–0	Smith, Byrne
22	15	A	Bournemouth	D	1–1	Clements
23	Dec 6	A	Bradford City	D	1–1	Opp. og
24	20	H	Aldershot	W	4–1	McDonald, Eccles (2), Ford
25	26	A	Bury	L	0–2	
26	27	H	Rochdale	L	1–2	Smith
27	Jan 3	A	Darlington	D	0–0	
28	10	H	Wigan Athletic	W	2–1	McDonald, Richards
29	17	A	Peterborough United	L	0–3	
30	24	H	Hereford United	L	1–2	Craig
31	Feb 7	A	Hartlepool United	L	0–1	
32	14	H	Southend United	L	0–1	
33	20	A	Doncaster Rovers	L	2–3	Opp. og, Eccles
34	Mar 7	A	Port Vale	L	0–2	
35	14	H	Lincoln City	W	1–0	Pugh
36	20	A	Stockport County	L	0–2	
37	24	H	Peterborough United	L	1–2	Randall
38	28	H	Wimbledon	L	0–1	
39	Apr 4	A	Scunthorpe United	L	2–3	Byrne, Randall
40	8	A	Torquay United	W	2–1	Smith, McDonald
41	11	H	Crewe Alexandra	W	2–0	McDonald (pen), Byrne
42	14	H	Bury	L	0–1	
43	18	A	Rochdale	L	2–3	McDonald (2, 1 pen)
44	25	A	Aldershot	D	1–1	McDonald
45	May 2	H	Bradford City	L	0–3	
46	5	H	Northampton Town	L	1–2	Byrne

2 own-goals

FA Cup

1	Nov 23	A	Tranmere Rovers	D	0–0	
r	25	H	Tranmere Rovers	L	1–2*	Byrne

* After extra-time.

Football League Cup

1 (1)	Aug 9	H	Hartlepool United	W	2–1	Ford, McDonald
1 (2)	11	A	Hartlepool United	D	0–0	
2 (1)	27	H	Bristol Rovers	W	2–1	Richards, Opp. og
2 (2)	Sep 3	A	Bristol Rovers	L	0–1*	

* After extra-time. Bristol Rovers won on away goals.

1 own-goal

Match	Kay	Walsh	Richards	Faulkner	Craig	Ford	Byrne	Eccles	McGhie	McDonald	Smith	Hood	Ferebee	Millar	Clements	Astbury	Stanley	Randall	Pugh	Senior
1	2	3	4	5	6	7	8	9	10	11										
2	2	3	4	5	6	7		9	10	11	8									
3	2	3	4	5	6	7		9	10	11	8									
4	2	3	4	5	6	7		9	10	11	8									
5	2	3	4	5	6	7	12	**9**		11	8	10								
6	2	3	4	5	6	7	**8**	9		11		10	12							
7	2	3	4	5	6	**7**		9		11	8	10		12						
8	3		4	5	6	7		9		10	8	2		11						
9	3		4	5	6	7		9		10	8	2		11						
10	3		4	5	6	7		9		10	8	2		**11**	12					
11	3	12			6	7	**8**	9		10	4	2		11	5					
12	3	12			6	7	8	9		10	4	**2**		11	5					
13	3	12			6	7	8	**9**		10	4	2		11	5					
14	3	12			6	7	**8**			10	4	2	9	11	5					
15	3	12			6	7	8			10	4	2	**9**	11	5					
16	3	7			6		8	9		10	4	2		11	5					
17	3	7			6	12	8	9		10	**4**	2		11	5					
18	3	7	11		6	4	8	9		10		2			5					
19	3	7	11		6	4	8	9		10		2			5					
20	3	11			6	12	8	9	**7**	10	4	2			5					
21	3	12			6		8	9	7	10	**4**	2		11	5					
22	3	4			6	7	8	9	11	10		2			5	1				
23	3	4			6	7	8	9	**11**	10	12	2			5					
24	3	4			6	7		9	11	10	8	2			5					
25	3	4			6	**7**	12	9	11	10	8	2			5					
26	3	11			6	7	8	9		10	8	2			5					
27	3	11	12		6	7	8		4	10	**9**	2			5					
28	3	11	9		6	7	8		4	10		2			5					
29	3	11	9		6	**7**	8		4	10	12	2			5					
30	3	**11**	9		6	7	8		4	10	12	2			5					
31	3				6	7	8	9	4	10	11	2			5					
32	3		4		6	7	8	9		10	11	2			5					
33	3	11		4	6		8	9		10	7	2			5					
34		3	11	4	6	7	8	9		10		2			5					
35		3		5	**6**	7	8		12	10		2					4	9	11	
36		3		5	6	7	8			10		2					4	9	11	
37		3		5	6	7	8			10		2					4	9	11	
38		3			6	7	8			10		2			5		4	9	11	
39		3			6	7	8		12	10		2			5		**4**	9	11	
40		3			6	7	8		4	10	12	2			5			**9**	11	
41		3			6	7	8		4	10	12	2			5			**9**	11	
42		3			6	7	8		4	10	12	2			**5**			9	11	
43		3			6	7	**8**		4	10	12	2			5			9	11	
44	2	3			6	7	8		**11**	10	9	5					4			12
45	2	3			6	7	8			**10**	9	5					4		11	12
46	3				6	7	8			10	9	5					4		11	2
Appearances	36	34	17	15	46	41	36	28	20	46	27	42	2	11	30	1	8	9	11	1
Substitute appearances		6	1			2	2		2		7		1	1	1					2
Goals	1		1	1	1	4	6	9	1	11	6				1			2	1	

Round	Kay	Walsh	Richards	Faulkner	Craig	Ford	Byrne	Eccles	McGhie	McDonald	Smith	Hood	Ferebee	Millar	Clements	Astbury	Stanley	Randall	Pugh	Senior
1	3	4			6	7	8	9	11	10		2			5					
r	3	4			6	7	**8**	9	11	10		2		12	5					
Appearances	2	2			2	2	2	2	2	2		2			2					
Substitute appearances														1						
Goals							1													

Round	Kay	Walsh	Richards	Faulkner	Craig	Ford	Byrne	Eccles	McGhie	McDonald	Smith	Hood	Ferebee	Millar	Clements	Astbury	Stanley	Randall	Pugh	Senior
1(1)	2	3	4	5	6	7		9	10	11	8									
1(2)	2	3	4	5	6	7		9	10	11	8									
2(1)	2	3	4	5	6	7	12	9	**10**	11	8									
2(2)	2	3	4	5	6	**7**	12	9		11	8	10								
Appearances	4	4	4	4	4	4		4	3	4	4	1								
Substitute appearances							2													
Goals			1			1				1										

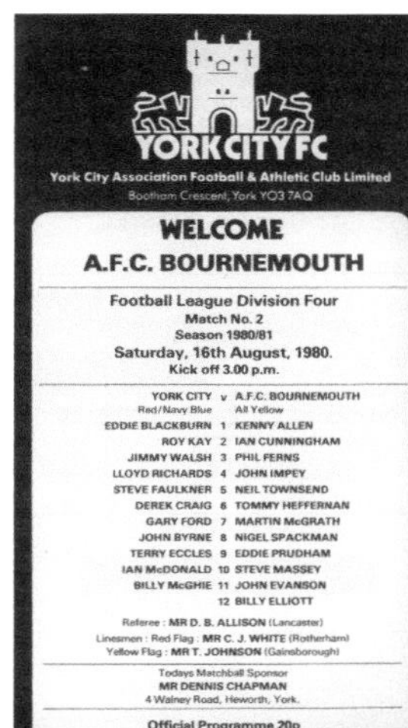
YORK CITY FC
York City Association Football & Athletic Club Limited
Bootham Crescent, York YO3 7AQ

WELCOME
A.F.C. BOURNEMOUTH

Football League Division Four
Match No. 2
Season 1980/81
Saturday, 16th August, 1980.
Kick off 3.00 p.m.

YORK CITY	v	A.F.C. BOURNEMOUTH
Red/Navy Blue		All Yellow
EDDIE BLACKBURN	1	KENNY ALLEN
ROY KAY	2	IAN CUNNINGHAM
JIMMY WALSH	3	PHIL FERNS
LLOYD RICHARDS	4	JOHN IMPEY
STEVE FAULKNER	5	NEIL TOWNSEND
DEREK CRAIG	6	TOMMY HEFFERNAN
GARY FORD	7	MARTIN McGRATH
JOHN BYRNE	8	NIGEL SPACKMAN
TERRY ECCLES	9	EDDIE PRUDHAM
IAN McDONALD	10	STEVE MASSEY
BILLY McGHIE	11	JOHN EVANSON
	12	BILLY ELLIOTT

Referee : MR D. B. ALLISON (Lancaster)
Linesmen : Red Flag : MR C. J. WHITE (Rotherham)
Yellow Flag : MR T. JOHNSON (Gainsborough)

Todays Matchball Sponsor
MR DENNIS CHAPMAN
4 Walney Road, Heworth, York.

Official Programme 20p

York City v AFC Bournemouth 16 August 1980 programme cover.

Mick Astbury.

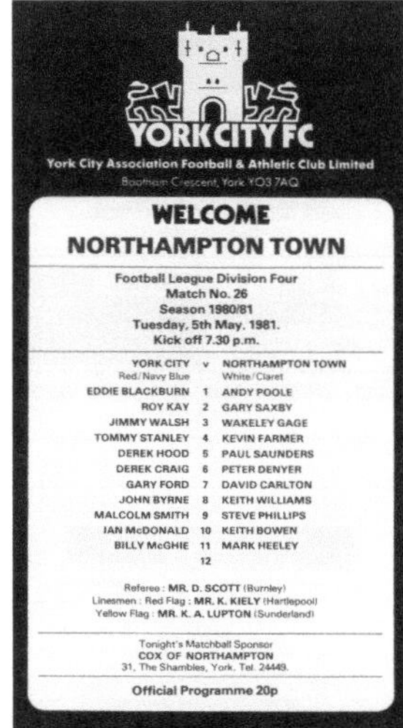
YORK CITY FC
York City Association Football & Athletic Club Limited
Bootham Crescent, York YO3 7AQ

WELCOME
NORTHAMPTON TOWN

Football League Division Four
Match No. 26
Season 1980/81
Tuesday, 5th May, 1981.
Kick off 7.30 p.m.

YORK CITY	v	NORTHAMPTON TOWN
Red/Navy Blue		White/Claret
EDDIE BLACKBURN	1	ANDY POOLE
ROY KAY	2	GARY SAXBY
JIMMY WALSH	3	WAKELEY GAGE
TOMMY STANLEY	4	KEVIN FARMER
DEREK HOOD	5	PAUL SAUNDERS
DEREK CRAIG	6	PETER DENYER
GARY FORD	7	DAVID CARLTON
JOHN BYRNE	8	KEITH WILLIAMS
MALCOLM SMITH	9	STEVE PHILLIPS
IAN McDONALD	10	KEITH BOWEN
BILLY McGHIE	11	MARK HEELEY
	12	

Referee : MR. D. SCOTT (Burnley)
Linesmen : Red Flag : MR. K. KIELY (Hartlepool)
Yellow Flag : MR. K. A. LUPTON (Sunderland)

Tonight's Matchball Sponsor
COX OF NORTHAMPTON
31, The Shambles, York. Tel. 24449.

Official Programme 20p

York City v Northampton 5 May 1981 programme cover.

1981–82

Division Four

Manager: Barry Lyons, then Kevin Randall, then Barry Swallow (the last two were caretaker managers)

	P	W	D	L	F	A	Pts
Sheffield United	46	27	15	4	94	41	96
Bradford City	46	26	13	7	88	45	91
Wigan Athletic	46	26	13	7	80	46	91
Bournemouth	46	23	19	4	62	30	88
Peterborough United	46	24	10	12	71	57	82
Colchester United	46	20	12	14	82	57	72
Port Vale	46	18	16	12	56	49	70
Hull City	46	19	12	15	70	61	69
Bury	46	17	17	12	80	59	68
Hereford United	46	16	19	11	64	58	67
Tranmere Rovers	46	14	18	14	51	56	60
Blackpool	46	15	13	18	66	60	58
Darlington	46	15	13	18	61	62	58
Hartlepool United	46	13	16	17	73	84	55
Torquay United	46	14	13	19	47	59	55
Aldershot	46	13	15	18	57	68	54
York City	46	14	8	24	69	91	50
Stockport County	46	12	13	21	48	67	49
Halifax Town	46	9	22	15	51	72	49
Mansfield Town	46	13	10	23	63	81	47
Rochdale	46	10	16	20	50	62	46
Northampton Town	46	11	9	26	57	84	42
Scunthorpe United	46	9	15	22	43	79	42
Crewe Alexandra	46	6	9	31	29	84	27

Did you know that?

This was the first season of three points for a win, and City had three different managers. Barry Lyons departed in December and, in the second half of the campaign, first Kevin Randall and then Barry Swallow had spells as caretaker boss.

New signing Keith Walwyn from Chesterfield scored on his debut on the opening day and went on to be Clubman of the Year and the first City player to top 20 League goals since 1970–71.

Brian Pollard returned to the club and his first game back was at home to Bournemouth on 22 September 1981.

Ian McDonald played his last game at home to Blackpool on 20 October 1981 after making 195 senior appearances.

The second goal scored by Keith Walwyn in the 3–0 home win over Colchester United on 5 March 1982 was the club's 3,000th in the Football League. It was also City's 500th home League victory.

Denis Smith, on loan from Stoke City, made his City debut at home to Hull City on 16 March 1982.

The 6–0 win over Crewe Alexandra on 23 April 1982 was City's biggest since Boxing Day 1964.

Roy Kay made his last appearance on the final day of the season. He played in 183 League and Cup games for the club.

Average home League crowd was 2,362.

For the sixth time since their election to the League in 1929 City lost to non-League opposition in the FA Cup and on this occasion the first-ever time in a replay.

Match No.	Date	Venue	Opponents	Result		Scorers	Atten
1	Aug 29	A	Tranmere Rovers	W	2–0	Walwyn, Hood	
2	Sep 4	H	Northampton Town	W	2–1	Waldron, Walwyn	
3	12	A	Bradford City	L	2–6	Walwyn, Byrne	
4	18	H	Hartlepool United	L	1–2	Walwyn	
5	22	H	Bournemouth	L	0–1		
6	26	A	Torquay United	L	2–3	Walwyn, Pollard	
7	29	A	Aldershot	W	1–0	Pollard	
8	Oct 3	H	Sheffield United	L	3–4	Walwyn, Ford, McDonald (pen)	
9	9	H	Darlington	D	2–2	McDonald, Walwyn	
10	16	A	Colchester United	L	0–4		
11	20	H	Blackpool	L	0–4		
12	24	A	Peterborough United	W	1–0	Walwyn	
13	31	H	Hereford United	L	3–4	Pollard, Ford, Hedley	
14	Nov 3	A	Hull City	L	0–2		
15	7	A	Scunthorpe United	W	3–0	Ford, Walwyn (2)	
16	14	H	Wigan Athletic	D	0–0		
17	28	A	Crewe Alexandra	D	1–1	Walwyn	
18	Dec 5	H	Stockport County	D	2–2	Walwyn, Kay	
19	Jan 23	H	Tranmere Rovers	L	1–3	Senior	
20	30	A	Hartlepool United	L	2–3	Crosby (2)	
21	Feb 2	H	Bury	D	0–0		
22	6	H	Bradford City	L	0–3		
23	9	A	Bournemouth	L	1–5	Hood	
24	13	A	Sheffield United	L	0–4		1
25	19	H	Torquay United	D	1–1	Kay	
26	22	H	Port Vale	W	2–0	Ford, Hood (pen)	
27	28	A	Darlington	L	1–3	Aitken	
28	Mar 5	H	Colchester United	W	3–0	Hood (pen), Walwyn (2)	
29	10	A	Blackpool	L	1–3	Walwyn	
30	13	H	Peterborough United	W	4–3	Kay (2), Laverick, Byrne	
31	16	H	Hull City	L	1–3	Walwyn	
32	20	A	Hereford United	L	1–2	Aitken	
33	23	A	Northampton Town	L	0–5		
34	26	H	Scunthorpe United	W	3–1	Walwyn, Hood (pen), Opp. og	
35	Apr 2	A	Wigan Athletic	L	2–4	Byrne, D. Smith	
36	5	A	Mansfield Town	W	2–0	Laverick, Ford	
37	10	H	Mansfield Town	W	2–1	Walwyn, Ford	
38	12	A	Rochdale	L	0–2		
39	16	A	Stockport County	L	1–4	Laverick	
40	23	H	Crewe Alexandra	W	6–0	Laverick, Walwyn (2), Ford, Byrne, Hood (pen)	
41	27	H	Rochdale	L	1–2	Walwyn	
42	May 1	A	Port Vale	D	0–0		
43	4	H	Aldershot	W	4–0	Walwyn, Ford, Byrne, Hood	
44	7	H	Halifax Town	W	4–0	Opp. og, Walwyn, Byrne, Hood (pen)	
45	11	A	Halifax Town	D	0–0		
46	15	A	Bury	L	1–3	Opp. og	

3 own-goals

FA Cup

1	Nov 21	A	Stafford Rangers	W	2–1	Ford, Walwyn
2	Dec 12	H	Altrincham	D	0–0	
r	Jan 2	A	Altrincham	L	3–4	Pollard (2), Walwyn

Football League (Milk) Cup

1 (1)	Sep 1	A	Sheffield United	L	0–1	
1 (2)	15	H	Sheffield United	D	1–1	Byrne

Kay	Flood	Hood	Croft	Dawson	Ford	Byrne	Walwyn	McDonald	Waldron	McGhie	Craig	Senior	Pollard	Smith M.	Bentham	Stanley	Hedley	Crosby	Czuczman	Laverick	Astbury	Sweeney	Aitken	Fell	Smith D.	
2	3	4	5	6	7	8	9	10	11																	1
2	3	4	5	6	7	**8**	9	10	11	12																2
2	3	4	5	6	7	8	9	10	**11**	12																3
2	3	4		6	7	8	9	10		**6**	5	12														4
2	3	4	5	6		**8**	9					12	7	10	11											5
3		4	5	6		8	9	10				2	7		11											6
3		4	5	6		8	9	10				**2**	7		11	12										7
2	3	4	5	6	8		9	10					7		11											8
2	3	4	5	6	8		9	10					7		11											9
	3	2	5	6		8	9	10					7		11		4									10
	3	2	5	6	12	**8**	9	10					7		11		4									11
3		2	5	6	8		9				10		7		11		4									12
3		2	5	6	8	**9**					10	12	7		11		4									13
3		8	5	6	10						4	2	9		11		7									14
	3	8	5	6	10		9					2	7		11			4								15
6	3	5			10		9					2	7		11	4		8								16
6	3	4			10	12	9					2	7		**11**			8	5							17
6	3	4			10		9					2	7		11			8	5							18
3		5		6	10		9					2	7		11			8		4						19
3		5		6	10		9					2	7		**11**	12		8		4	1					20
3		5		6			9					2	7		11			8		4	1					21
3		5		6	7	10	9					2			11			8		4	1					22
3		5		6	7	**10**	9					2			11	12		8		4	1					23
3	12	4		6	7	10	9				5	2				11		**8**								24
8		4		3	10		9								11	7			5			2	6			25
8		4		3	10		9									7			5	11		2	6			26
4		2		3	10		9									7		8	5	11			6			27
		4		3	10		9											8	5	11		2	6	7		28
6		**4**		3	10	8	9				5				12	2				11				7		29
7		4		3	10	8	9				5									11		**2**	6	12		30
7		4		3	10	8	9													11	1	2	6	12	5	31
7		4		3	10	8	9													11	1	2	6		5	32
7		4		3		8	9											10	**5**	11	1	2	6	12		33
		4		3	7	**10**	9											12	6	11	1	2	8		5	34
		4		3	7	10	9											12	6	**11**	1	2	8		5	35
		4		3	7	10	9											12	**6**	11	1	2	8		5	36
		4		3	8		9						7					10		11	1	2	6		5	37
		4		3	8		9						7					10		11	1	2	6		5	38
4		5		6	8		9					2	7		3			10		11	1					39
3		4		2	7	8	9											10	5	11			6			40
6		4		2	7	8	9						12		3			10	**5**	11						41
3	12	4		6	10	8	9						7					**2**	5	11						42
3		4		2	10	8	9						7						5	11			6			43
3		4		2	10	8	9						7						5	11			6			44
3		4		2	10	8	9						7						5	11	1		6			45
3		4		2	10	8	9						7					12	5	11	1		6			46
37	13	46	14	43	40	28	44	10	3	1	7	14	25	1	22	6	5	19	17	26	15	12	18	2	7	
	2				1	1				2		3	1		1	3		4						3		
4		8			8	6	23	2	1			1	3				1	2		4			2		1	

Kay	Flood	Hood	Croft	Dawson	Ford	Byrne	Walwyn	McDonald	Waldron	McGhie	Craig	Senior	Pollard	Smith M.	Bentham	Stanley	Hedley	Crosby	Czuczman	Laverick	Astbury	Sweeney	Aitken	Fell	Smith D.	
6	3	5			10		9					2	7		11	4		8								1
6	3	4			10		9					2	7		11			8	5							2
6	3	4		5	10		9					2	7		11			8								r
3	3	3		1	3		3					3	3		3	1		3	1							
					1		2						2													

Kay	Flood	Hood	Croft	Dawson	Ford	Byrne	Walwyn	McDonald	Waldron	McGhie	Craig	Senior	Pollard	Smith M.	Bentham	Stanley	Hedley	Crosby	Czuczman	Laverick	Astbury	Sweeney	Aitken	Fell	Smith D.	
2	3	4	5	6	7	8	9	10	11																	1 (1)
2	3	4		6	7	8	9	10		11	5															1 (2)
2	2	2	1	2	2	2	2	2	1	1	1															
						1																				

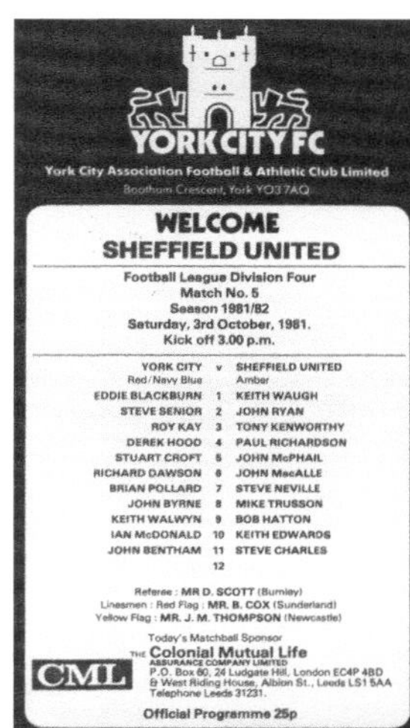

York City v Sheffield United 3 October 1981 programme cover.

Keith Walwyn.

York City v Altrincham 21 December 1981 programme cover.

1982–83

Division Four

Manager: Denis Smith

	P	W	D	L	F	A	Pts
Wimbledon	46	29	11	6	96	45	98
Hull City	46	25	15	6	75	34	90
Port Vale	46	26	10	10	67	34	88
Scunthorpe United	46	23	14	9	71	42	83
Bury	46	23	12	11	74	46	81
Colchester United	46	24	9	13	75	55	81
York City	46	22	13	11	88	58	79
Swindon Town	46	19	11	16	61	54	68
Peterborough United	46	17	13	16	58	52	64
Mansfield Town	46	16	13	17	61	70	61
Halifax Town	46	16	12	18	59	66	60
Torquay United	46	17	7	22	56	65	58
Chester	46	15	11	20	55	60	56
Bristol City	46	13	17	16	59	70	56
Northampton Town	46	14	12	20	65	75	54
Stockport County	46	14	12	20	60	79	54
Darlington	46	13	13	20	61	71	52
Aldershot	46	12	15	19	61	82	51
Tranmere Rovers	46	13	11	22	49	71	50
Rochdale	46	11	16	19	55	73	49
Blackpool	46	13	12	21	55	74	49
Hartlepool United	46	13	9	24	46	76	48
Crewe Alexandra	46	11	8	27	53	71	41
Hereford United	46	11	8	27	42	79	41

Did you know that?

1982 marked the diamond jubilee of the founding of the club and the 50th anniversary of the move to Bootham Crescent.

The new managerial team of Denis Smith and Viv Busby were in charge.

Smith was sent off in the game at Hull City on 7 September 1982.

Newcomers making their debut on the opening day were skipper Roger Jones, Chris Evans, Alan Hay and Ricky Sbragia.

John MacPhail, ex-Sheffield United, made his City debut at Peterborough United on 5 February 1983.

Keith Walwyn again top scored and Clubman of the Year was Derek Hood.

From 30 October until 15 March City won 13 successive League and Cup games at Bootham Crescent, scoring 47 goals in the process.

In League and Cup football City scored exactly 100 goals.

The average home League crowd of 3,243 was the highest since 1975–76

In a 0–0 draw against Swindon Town on 26 March 1983 City failed to score at home for the first time since 6 February 1982 – a run of 30 games.

The victory over Rochdale on 2 April 1983 gave City their 2,000th point in the Football League since their election in 1929.

Match No.	Date	Venue	Opponents	Result		Scorers	Attend
1	Aug 28	H	Torquay United	D	1–1	Hood (pen)	1
2	Sep 4	A	Northampton Town	D	1–1	Laverick	2
3	7	A	Hull City	L	0–4		3
4	11	H	Tranmere Rovers	W	2–1	Hood (pen), Walwyn	1
5	19	A	Scunthorpe United	D	0–0		2
6	25	H	Peterborough United	D	1–1	Ford	1
7	28	H	Halifax Town	W	3–2	Laverick, Ford, Busby	1
8	Oct 2	A	Hereford United	D	0–0		2
9	9	A	Bristol City	D	2–2	Byrne, Ford	3
10	16	H	Wimbledon	L	1–4	Pollard	2
11	19	A	Blackpool	D	1–1	Walwyn	2
12	22	A	Stockport County	L	1–2	Walwyn	2
13	30	H	Hartlepool United	W	5–1	Hood, Crosby, Walwyn, Ford, Pollard	1
14	Nov 2	A	Crewe Alexandra	L	1–2	Smith	1
15	6	H	Aldershot	W	4–0	Pollard (2, 1 pen), Byrne (2)	1
16	13	A	Swindon Town	L	2–3	Ford, Walwyn	4
17	37	H	Mansfield Town	W	6–1	Walwyn (3), Pollard (2), Crosby	2
18	Dec 3	A	Colchester United	D	0–0		2
19	18	A	Chester	W	1–0	Walwyn	1
20	27	H	Bury	W	3–1	Opp. og, Pollard (pen), Walwyn	5
21	28	A	Rochdale	L	0–1		2
22	Jan 1	H	Darlington	W	5–2	Smith (2), Busby, Byrne (2)	3
23	3	A	Port Vale	L	1–2	Busby	6
24	15	A	Torquay United	W	3–1	Byrne, Walwyn, Pollard	2
25	23	H	Scunthorpe United	W	2–1	Walwyn, Ford	7
26	29	A	Tranmere Rovers	L	0–3		1
27	Feb 5	A	Peterborough United	D	2–2	Hood, Pollard (pen)	2
28	15	H	Blackpool	W	2–0	Ford, Byrne	2
29	19	H	Bristol City	W	3–0	Byrne (2), Pollard	2
30	26	A	Wimbledon	L	3–4	Opp. og, Walwyn, Hay	2
31	Mar 1	H	Crewe Alexandra	W	2–0	Smith, Walwyn	2
32	5	H	Stockport County	W	3–1	Ford, Pollard (2, 1 pen)	2
33	12	A	Hartlepool United	L	0–2		1
34	15	H	Northampton Town	W	5–2	Ford (2), Walwyn, Pollard, Hood	2
35	19	A	Aldershot	W	3–2	Byrne, Walwyn (2)	1
36	26	H	Swindon Town	D	0–0		3
37	Apr 2	H	Rochdale	W	1–0	Walwyn	3
38	4	A	Bury	L	1–2	Walwyn	3
39	9	H	Colchester United	W	3–0	Busby, Pollard (pen), Senior	2
40	15	A	Halifax Town	D	2–2	Pollard (pen), Sbragia	2
41	19	H	Hull City	W	1–0	Byrne	9
42	23	H	Chester	W	1–0	MacPhail	3
43	30	A	Mansfield Town	D	2–2	Ford, Walwyn	2
44	May 2	H	Port Vale	D	0–0		4
45	7	H	Hereford United	W	5–1	Pollard (2), Opp. og, Hood, MacPhail	2
46	14	A	Darlington	W	3–1	Byrne, Hood, Walwyn	1
							A
							S
						3 own-goals	

FA Cup

1	Nov 20	H	Bury	W	3–1	Hood, Ford, Walwyn	3
2	Dec 11	A	Hartlepool United	D	1–1	Pollard	3
r	14	H	Hartlepool United	W	4–0	Hood, Pollard, Byrne, Ford	4
3	Jan 8	A	Crystal Palace	L	1–2	Walwyn	7
							A
							S

Football League (Milk) Cup

1 (1)	Aug 31	H	Lincoln City	W	2–1	Walwyn, Byrne	1
1 (2)	Sep 15	A	Lincoln City	L	1–3	Opp. og	2
							A
							S
						1 own-goal	

Evans	Hay	Sbragia	Hood	Laverick	Pollard	Ford	Busby	Byrne	Crosby	Senior	Smith	Walwyn	Dawson	Stanley	Astbury	MacPhail	King	
2	3	4	5	6	7	8	**9**	10	11	12								1
2	3	4	6	11	7	8		10			5	9						2
2	3	4	6	11	7	8		10			5	9						3
2	3	4	6	11	7	8		10			5	9						4
2	3	4	5	11	**7**	8		10	6	12		9						5
2	3	4	5	11	**7**	8		10	6	12		9						6
2	3	4	5	11	7	8	12	**10**	6			9						7
2	3	4	5	11	7	8		10	6			9						8
2		4	5		7	8	12	10	6	**11**		9	3					9
2		4	5	11	7	8	12	10	6			9	**3**					10
2		4	3	11	7	8	10		6		5	9						11
2		4	3	11	7	8	**10**	12	6		5	9						12
2	3	4	6		11	7		10	8		5	9						13
2	3	4	6		11	7		10	8		5	9						14
2	3	4	6		11	7		10	8		5	9						15
2	3	4	6		11	7		10	8		5	9						16
2	3	4	6		11	7		10	8		5	9						17
2	3	4	6		11	7		10	8		5	9						18
2	3	4	6	11	7	10			8		5	9						19
2	3	4	6	12	11	7	10		8		5	**9**						20
2	3	4	6		11	7	**9**	10	8		5			12				21
2	3	4	6	12	11	7	9	10	**8**		5				1			22
2	3	4	6	12	11	7	9	10	8		5				1			23
2	3	4	6		11	7		10	8		5	9						24
2	3	4	6		11	7		10	8		5	9						25
2	3	**4**	6		11	7	12	10	8		5	9						26
2	3	4	6		12	7		10	8		5	9				11		27
2	3	4	6		11	7		10	8		**5**	9				12		28
2	3	4	6		11	7		10	8		5	9						29
2	3	4	6		12	7		10	8		5	9				**11**		30
2	3	4	6		11	7		10	8		5	9						31
2	3	4	6		11	7		10	8		5	9						32
2	3	4	6		11	7		10	8		5	9			1			33
2	3	4	6		11	7		10	8		5	9			1			34
2	3	4	6		11	7		10	8		5	9						35
2	3	4	6		11	7		10	8		5	9						36
2	3	4	6		11	7	12	10	**8**		5	9						37
2	3	4	6		11	7	12	10		**8**		9				5		38
2	3	4	6		11	7	9	10		8						5		39
2	3	4	6		11		7	10		**8**		9				5	12	40
2	3	4	6		11	7		10		8		9				5		41
2	3	4	6		11	7		10		8		9				5		42
2	3	4	6		11	7		10	8			9				5		43
2	3	4	6		11	**7**	12	10	8			9				5		44
2	3	4	6		11	7		10	8			9				5		45
2	3	4	6		11	7		**10**	8	12		9				5		46
46	42	46	46	12	44	45	9	42	38	6	30	41	2		4	11		
				3	2		7	1		4				1		1	1	
	1	1	7	2	17	11	4	12	2	1	4	21				2		

Evans	Hay	Sbragia	Hood	Laverick	Pollard	Ford	Busby	Byrne	Crosby	Senior	Smith	Walwyn	Dawson	Stanley	Astbury	MacPhail	King	
2	3	4	6		11	7		10	8		5	9						1
2	3	4	6		11	7		10	8		5	9						2
2	3	4	6		11	7		10	8		5	9						r
2	3	4	6		11	7		10	8		5	9			1			3
4	4	4	4		4	4		4	4		4	4			1			
			2		2	2		1				2						

Evans	Hay	Sbragia	Hood	Laverick	Pollard	Ford	Busby	Byrne	Crosby	Senior	Smith	Walwyn	Dawson	Stanley	Astbury	MacPhail	King	
2	3	4	6	11	7	8		10			5	9						1 (1)
2	3	4	6	11	7	8		10			5	9						1 (2)
2	2	2	2	2	2	2		2			2	2						
								1				1						

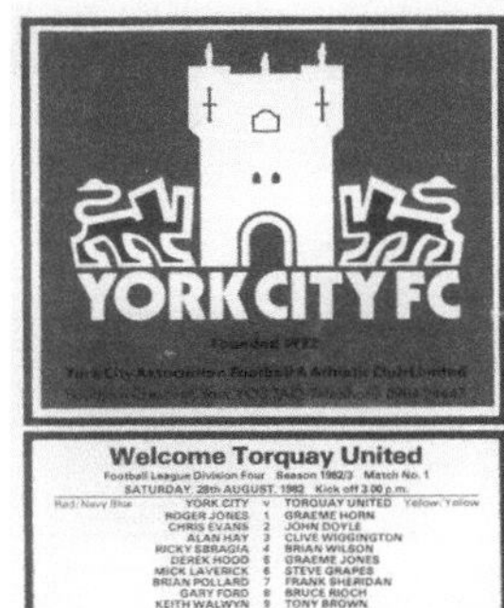

York City v Torquay United 28 August 1982 programme cover.

Chris Evans.

1983–84

Division Four

Manager: Denis Smith

	P	W	D	L	F	A	Pts
York City	46	31	8	7	96	39	101
Doncaster Rovers	46	24	13	9	82	54	85
Reading	46	22	16	8	84	56	82
Bristol City	46	24	10	12	70	44	82
Aldershot	46	22	9	15	76	69	75
Blackpool	46	21	9	16	70	52	72
Peterborough United	46	18	14	14	72	48	68
Colchester United	46	17	16	13	69	53	67
Torquay United	46	18	13	15	59	64	67
Tranmere Rovers	46	17	15	14	53	53	66
Hereford United	46	16	15	15	54	53	63
Stockport County	46	17	11	18	60	64	62
Chesterfield	46	15	15	16	59	61	60
Darlington	46	17	8	21	49	50	59
Bury	46	15	14	17	61	64	59
Crewe Alexandra	46	16	11	19	56	67	59
Swindon Town	46	15	13	18	58	56	58
Northampton Town	46	13	14	19	53	78	53
Mansfield Town	46	13	13	20	66	70	52
Wrexham	46	11	15	20	59	74	48
Halifax Town	46	12	12	22	55	89	48
Rochdale	46	11	13	22	52	80	46
Hartlepool United	46	10	10	26	47	85	40
Chester City	46	7	13	26	45	82	34

Did you know that?

City won their first major honour when they finished runaway Division Four champions and became the first-ever Football League club to reach 100 points.

New club records set were most wins (31), most away wins (13) and most goals (96).

City were never out of the top two and went top on 29 October 1983 and were never again headed.

For the second successive season they only lost once at home, and their record at Bootham Crescent was identical to 1982–83, namely W18 D4 L1.

They had gone unbeaten at home in the League from 16 October 1982 until 12 November 1983.

Twice they won five successive away League games.

The game against Darlington on 11 February 1984 was the 1,000th Football League game at Bootham Crescent.
(P1,000 W496 D249 L255 F1,802 A1,141)

John Byrne topped the scoring chart, and for the first time since 1954–55 City had two players who netted over 20 League goals in a season.

Clubman of the Year was John MacPhail.

The average League attendance was 5,008 and the crowd of 11,297 to see the visit of Doncaster Rovers on 8 April 1984 was the biggest at York for eight years.

Match No.	Date	Venue	Opponents	Result		Scorers
1	Aug 27	A	Stockport County	W	2–0	MacPhail, Byrne
2	Sep 3	H	Rochdale	W	2–0	Ford, Walwyn
3	6	H	Peterborough United	W	2–0	Pollard, Byrne
4	10	A	Chesterfield	L	1–2	Walwyn
5	17	H	Chester City	W	4–1	Byrne (3), MacPhail
6	24	A	Darlington	D	0–0	
7	27	A	Doncaster Rovers	D	2–2	Byrne, Walwyn
8	Oct 1	H	Blackpool	W	4–0	Byrne (2), Walwyn (2)
9	7	H	Colchester United	W	3–0	MacPhail, Pollard (pen), Walwyn
10	15	A	Swindon Town	L	2–3	Walwyn (2)
11	18	A	Bristol City	L	0–1	
12	22	H	Reading	D	2–2	Pollard, Sbragia
13	29	A	Northampton Town	W	2–1	Walwyn (2)
14	Nov 1	H	Wrexham	W	3–2	Sbragia, Pollard (2, 1 pen)
15	5	A	Crewe Alexandra	W	3–0	Walwyn (2), Byrne
16	12	H	Torquay United	L	2–3	Hood, Ford
17	26	A	Hartlepool United	W	3–2	Byrne (2), Sbragia
18	Dec 3	H	Aldershot	W	2–0	Byrne, Pearce
19	17	H	Hereford United	W	4–0	Ford (2), Pearce, Byrne
20	26	A	Halifax Town	W	2–1	Walwyn (2)
21	27	H	Tranmere Rovers	D	1–1	Senior
22	31	A	Bury	W	3–1	Walwyn, Byrne (2)
23	Jan 2	H	Mansfield Town	W	2–1	Ford, Hay
24	14	H	Stockport County	W	3–1	Hood (pen), MacPhail, Walwyn
25	31	H	Chesterfield	W	1–0	Byrne
26	Feb 4	A	Blackpool	L	0–3	
27	11	H	Darlington	W	2–0	MacPhail, Ford
28	18	H	Northampton Town	W	3–0	Walwyn, Pollard (pen), Byrne
29	25	A	Reading	L	0–1	
30	28	A	Wrexham	D	0–0	
31	Mar 3	H	Bristol City	D	1–1	Opp. og
32	6	H	Crewe Alexandra	W	5–2	Walwyn (2), Byrne, Sbragia, Pearce
33	10	A	Torquay United	W	3–1	Ford, Walwyn, Byrne
34	19	A	Colchester United	W	3–1	MacPhail, Walwyn, Pearce
35	24	H	Swindon Town	W	2–0	Walwyn, Ford
36	27	A	Rochdale	W	2–0	Byrne (2)
37	Apr 1	A	Peterborough United	W	2–0	MacPhail, Byrne
38	8	H	Doncaster Rovers	D	1–1	Ford
39	14	A	Aldershot	W	4–1	MacPhail, Houchen, Byrne, Pearce
40	18	A	Chester	D	1–1	Hood
41	20	H	Halifax Town	W	4–1	Byrne (3), Walwyn
42	23	A	Tranmere Rovers	W	1–0	Ford
43	28	H	Hartlepool United	W	2–0	Walwyn (2)
44	May 5	A	Mansfield Town	W	1–0	MacPhail
45	7	H	Bury	W	3–0	Byrne, Hood, Ford
46	12	A	Hereford United	L	1–2	MacPhail

1 own-goal

FA Cup

1	Nov 19	A	Macclesfield Town	D	0–0	
r	22	H	Macclesfield Town	W	2–0	Sbragia, Byrne
2	Dec 13	H	Rochdale	L	0–2	

Football League (Milk) Cup

1 (1)	Aug 30	H	Grimsby Town	W	2–1	Ford, Pollard
1 (2)	Sep 13	A	Grimsby Town	L	0–2*	

* After extra-time.

Senior	Hay	Sbragia	MacPhail	Hood	Ford	Crosby	Walwyn	Byrne	Pollard	Haslegrave	Astbury	Evans	Busby	Pearce	Chippendale	Houchen	
2	3	4	5	6	7	8	9	10	11								1
2	3	4	5		7	8	9	10	11	6							2
2	3	4	5		7	8	9	10	11	6							3
2	3	4	5		7	8	9	10	11	6	1						4
2	3	4	5		7	8	9	10	11	6	1						5
2	3	4	5		**7**	8	9	10	11	6		12					6
2	3	4	5		7	8	9	10	11	6							7
2	3	4	5		7	8	9	10	11	6							8
2	3	4	5		7	8	9	10	11	6							9
2	3	4	5		7	8	9	10	11	6	1						10
6	3	4	5		7	8	**9**	10	11		1	2	12				11
6	3	4	5	12	7	8	9	10	11			**2**					12
2	3	4	5	6	7	8	9	10	11			12					13
3		4	5	6	7	8	**9**	10	11			2	12				14
3		4	5	6	7	**8**	9	10	11			2	12				15
8	3	4	5	6	7		9	10	11			2					16
9	3	4	5	6	7	8		10				2		**11**	12		17
2	3	4	5		7	8	9	10		**6**		12		11			18
2	3	4	5	6	7	8	9	10						11			19
2	3	4	5	**6**	7	8	9	10	11						12		20
6	3	4	5		7	8	9	10				2		11			21
2	3	4	5	**6**	7	8	9	10	11						12		22
2	3	4	5	6	7	8	9	10	**11**					12			23
2	3	4	5	6	7	8	9	10						11			24
2	3	4	5	**6**	**7**	8	9	10	11	12							25
2	3	4	5	6	7	8	9	10	11								26
2	3	4	5	6	7	8	9	10	11		1						27
3		4	5	6	7	8	9	10	11			2					28
3		4	5	6	7	8	9	10	**11**	12		2					29
2	3	4	5	6	7	8	9	10						11			30
2	3	4	5	6	7	8	9	10						11			31
2	3	4	5	6	7		9	10		8				11			32
2	3	4	5	6	7		9	10		8				11			33
2	3	4	5	6	7		9	10		8				11			34
2	3	4	5	6	7		9	10		8				11			35
2	3	4	5	6	7		9	10	12	8				**11**			36
2	3	4	5	6	7		9	10	11	8							37
2	3	4	5	6	7		9	10		8				11			38
2	3	4	5	6	7		9	10		8				11		12	39
	3	4	5	6	7		9	10		8		2		11			40
	3	4	5	6	7		9	10	11	**8**		2				12	41
	3	4	5	6	7		9	10	11	**8**		2				12	42
	3	4	5	6	7		9	10	**11**	8		2				12	43
	3	4	5	6	7	8	**9**	10	11			2				12	44
	3		5	4	7		9	10		8		2		11	12	**6**	45
	3	4	5	6	7		9	**10**		8		2		11		12	46
39	42	45	46	33	46	31	45	46	29	24	5	16		17		1	
				1					1	2		3	3	1	4	6	
1	1	4	10	4	11		25	27	6					5		1	

Senior	Hay	Sbragia	MacPhail	Hood	Ford	Crosby	Walwyn	Byrne	Pollard	Haslegrave	Astbury	Evans	Busby	Pearce	Chippendale	Houchen	
2	3	4	5	6	7	8		10	11				9				1
2	3	4	5	6	7	8		10	**11**			12	9				r
2	3	4	5	6	7	8	9	10	11								2
3	3	3	3	3	3	3	1	3	3				2				
												1					
		1						1									

Senior	Hay	Sbragia	MacPhail	Hood	Ford	Crosby	Walwyn	Byrne	Pollard	Haslegrave	Astbury	Evans	Busby	Pearce	Chippendale	Houchen	
2	3	4	5	**6**	7	8	9	10	11	12							1 (1)
2	3	4	5		7	8	9	**10**	11	6	1	12					1 (2)
2	2	2	2	1	2	2	2	2	2	1	1						
										1		1					
					1				1								

York City v Bury 7 May 1984 programme cover.

John Byrne.

Division IV winners trophy.

1984–85

Division Three

Manager: Denis Smith

	P	W	D	L	F	A	Pts
Bradford City	46	28	10	8	77	45	94
Millwall	46	26	12	8	73	42	90
Hull City	46	25	12	9	78	49	87
Gillingham	46	25	8	13	80	62	83
Bristol City	46	24	9	13	74	47	81
Bristol Rovers	46	21	12	13	66	48	75
Derby County	46	19	13	14	65	54	70
York City	46	20	9	17	70	57	69
Reading	46	19	12	15	68	62	69
Bournemouth	46	19	11	16	57	46	68
Walsall	46	18	13	15	58	52	67
Rotherham United	46	18	11	17	55	55	65
Brentford	46	16	14	16	62	64	62
Doncaster Rovers	46	17	8	21	72	74	59
Plymouth Argyle	46	15	14	17	62	65	59
Wigan Athletic	46	15	14	17	60	64	59
Bolton Wanderers	46	16	6	24	69	75	54
Newport County	46	13	13	20	55	67	52
Lincoln City	46	11	18	17	50	51	51
Swansea City	46	12	11	23	53	80	47
Burnley	46	11	13	22	60	73	46
Orient	46	11	13	22	51	76	46
Preston North End	46	13	7	26	51	100	46
Cambridge United	46	4	9	33	37	95	21

Did you know that?

Back in Division Three for the first time since 1977, City went top on 2 October 1984, unbeaten after eight games, their best-ever start to a Football League campaign. The match that day against Bristol Rovers marked the 100th League game of the Smith/Busby regime and their record reads: P100 W59 D23 L18 F200 A104 Pts200.

City lost the next game at home to Bristol City – only their second League defeat at Bootham Crescent since October 1982.

John Byrne was transferred to First Division (Premiership) Queen's Park Rangers in October 1984 for £100,000 and made his last appearance on the 13th of that month at Bradford City. He netted 64 goals in 199 senior games for the club.

Dale Banton was signed for a club record fee of £50,000 from Aldershot in November 1984 and made his debut that month at Lincoln.

Debutants this season also included Tony Canham, who scored on his League debut on 2 March 1985 at home to Brentford, and Marco Gabbiadini, who came on as a substitute later that month against Bolton Wanderers.

The average League crowd at home was 5,550, the best since 1974–75.

The attendance of 10,442 for the visit of Bradford City was the last occasion of a five-figure League crowd at Bootham Crescent.

John MacPhail was Clubman of the Year for the second successive season.

City played a club record 14 Cup ties this season and progressed beyond the fourth round of the FA Cup for the first time since 1954–55.

The 7–0 reverse away to Liverpool in the fifth-round replay was City's biggest-ever defeat in the FA Cup.

Match No.	Date	Venue	Opponents	Result		Scorers	Attend
1	Aug 25	H	Walsall	D	1–1	Walwyn	4
2	Sep 1	A	Swansea City	W	3–1	Walwyn (2), Byrne	4
3	8	H	Newport County	W	2–0	MacPhail (pen), Houchen	4
4	15	A	Orient	W	3–1	Walwyn, Byrne, Nicholson	2
5	18	A	Plymouth Argyle	D	1–1	Walwyn	4
6	25	H	Cambridge United	W	3–2	Opp. og (2), Ford	4
7	29	A	Wigan Athletic	W	2–1	Walwyn, Houchen	3
8	Oct 2	H	Bristol Rovers	W	1–0	Walwyn	7
9	6	H	Bristol City	L	0–2		4
10	13	A	Bradford City	L	0–1		5
11	20	H	Millwall	D	1–1	Sbragia	4
12	23	A	Bournemouth	L	0–4		2
13	27	A	Brentford	L	1–2	Ford	4
14	Nov 3	H	Gillingham	W	7–1	Houchen (3), Opp. og, Pearce (2), Walwyn	2
15	6	A	Bolton Wanderers	L	1–2	Hood	4
16	11	H	Doncaster Rovers	W	3–1	Houchen (2), Ford	8
17	24	A	Lincoln City	L	1–2	Banton	2
18	Dec 1	H	Reading	D	2–2	Houchen, Hood	4
19	15	A	Rotherham United	L	1–4	Banton	4
20	19	A	Preston North End	W	4–2	MacPhail, Houchen, Pearce, Banton	2
21	26	H	Burnley	W	4–0	Banton (2), Houchen, Ford	6
22	29	H	Hull City	L	1–2	Walwyn	9
23	Jan 1	A	Derby County	L	0–1		16
24	12	H	Swansea City	W	1–0	Nicholson	5
25	Feb 2	H	Wigan Athletic	W	2–0	Ford, Pearce	10
26	9	A	Cambridge United	W	4–0	Banton (2), MacPhail (pen), Sbragia	1
27	12	H	Plymouth Argyle	D	0–0		4
28	23	A	Gillingham	L	0–1		5
29	26	A	Walsall	L	0–3		5
30	Mar 2	H	Brentford	W	1–0	Canham	4
31	5	H	Bournemouth	W	4–1	Hood, MacPhail (pen), Banton, Opp. og	4
32	9	A	Millwall	L	0–1		7
33	17	H	Bradford City	L	1–2	Butler	10
34	20	A	Newport County	D	1–1	Nicholson	1
35	23	A	Bristol City	L	0–1		8
36	29	H	Bolton Wanderers	L	0–3		4
37	Apr 2	H	Orient	W	2–1	Banton, Hood	3
38	6	A	Burnley	D	1–1	Houchen	3
39	8	H	Derby County	D	1–1	MacPhail	6
40	15	A	Doncaster Rovers	L	0–3		3
41	21	H	Lincoln City	W	2–1	Houchen, Butler	3
42	27	A	Reading	W	2–1	Banton, Nicholson	2
43	May 3	H	Rotherham United	W	3–0	Ward (2), Banton	3
44	6	A	Hull City	W	2–0	Banton, Ward	15
45	11	H	Preston North End	L	0–1		4
46	14	A	Bristol Rovers	D	1–1	Butler	3
							A
							S

FA Cup

						4 own-goals	
1	Nov 17	H	Blue Star	W	2–0	Walwyn, Houchen	3
2	Dec 8	A	Hartlepool United	W	2–0	MacPhail, Houchen	8
3	Jan 5	H	Walsall	W	3–0	Butler, Walwyn, Hay	5
4	26	H	Arsenal	W	1–0	Houchen (pen)	10
5	Feb 16	H	Liverpool	D	1–1	Sbragia	13
r	20	A	Liverpool	L	0–7		43
							A
							S

Football League (Milk) Cup

1 (1)	Aug 28	A	Doncaster Rovers	W	3–2	Byrne (2), Ford	4
1 (2)	Sep 4	H	Doncaster Rovers	W	5–0	MacPhail (2, 1 pen), Byrne, Houchen, Ford	5
2 (1)	25	H	Queen's Park Rangers	L	2–4	Houchen, Walwyn	10
2 (2)	Oct 9	A	Queen's Park Rangers	L	1–4	Chippendale	7
							A
							S

Match	Evans	Hay	Sbragia	MacPhail	Haslegrave	Ford	Houchen	Walwyn	Byrne	Nicholson	Hood	Pearce	Atkinson	Chippendale	Butler	Banton	Senior	Crosby	Astbury	Richards	Canham	Gabbiadini	Ward
1	2	3	4	5	6	7	**8**	9	10	11	12												
2	2	3	4	5	6	7	**8**	9	10	11	12												
3	2	3	4	5	6	7	8	9	10	11													
4	2	3	4	5	6	7	8	9	10	11													
5	2	3	4	5	6	7	8	9	10	**11**	12												
6	2	3	4	5	6	7	8	9	10	11													
7	2	3	4		6	7	8	9	10		5	11											
8	2	3		5	6	7	**8**	9	10		4	11	12										
9	2	3	4	5	6	7		9	10	11	**8**		12										
10	2	3		5	6	7		9	10	11			4	8									
11	2	3	4	5	6	7	10	9			8	**11**			12								
12	2	3	4	5	6	7	10	9			**8**	11			12								
13	2	**3**	4	5	6	7	10	9			8	11			12								
14	2	3	4	5	6	7	10	9			8	11											
15	2	3	4	5	6	7	10	9		12	8	**11**											
16	2	3	4	5	6	7	10	9			8	11											
17	2	3	4	5	6	7	10	9				11				8							
18	2	3	4		6	7	10	9			5	11				8							
19		3	4	5	6	7	10	9				11				12	2	**8**					
20		3	4	5	6	7	10	9				11				8	2						
21		3	4	5	6	7	10	9				11				8	2		1				
22		3	4		6	7	10	9				11				8	2		1	5			
23		3	4		6	7	10	9				11				8	2		1	5			
24		3	4	5	6	7	10	**9**		11			12			8	2		1				
25		3	4	5	6	7	**10**	9				11	12			8	2		1				
26		3	4	5	6	7						11	10		9	8	2		1				
27		3	4	5	6	7						11	10		9	8	2		1				
28		3		5	6	7		9			10	11				8	2			4			
29		3		5	6	7		**9**			10	11			12	8	2			4			
30		3		5	6	7					10			12	9	8	2			**4**	11		
31		3		5	6	7					10				9	8	2	4			11		
32		3		5	6	7					10			12	9	8	2	4			**11**		
33		3		5	6	7	10			11	4				9	8	2						
34		3		5	6					11	4			7	9	8	2	10					
35		3		5	**6**					11	4	7			9	8	2	10		12			
36		3		5	6	7	9			11	10					**8**	2			4		12	
37		3		5	6	7	9			11	4	10				8	2						
38		3		5		7	9			11	4	**10**			12	8	2	6					
39		3		5	6	7	9			11	4				12	**8**	2	10					
40		3		5	6	7	9			11	4				12	8	2	**10**					
41	3	12		5	6	7	10			**11**	4				9	8	2						
42	3			5	6	7	10			11	4				9	8	2						
43	3	12		5	6	7	10			11	4					8	2						**9**
44	3	12		5		7	10			11	**4**					8	2	6					9
45	3	4		5		7	10			11					12	8	2	6					**9**
46	3	4		5		7	10			**11**					12	8	2	6					9
	4	42	25	42	42	44	35	27	10	23	27	23	3	2	10	29	28	11	7	6	3		4
		3								1	3		4	2	9	1				1		1	
			2	5		5	12	9	2	4	4	4			3	12					1		3
1	2	3	4	5	6	7	10	9			8	11											
2		3	4	5	6	7	10	9				11					2	8					
3		3	4	5	6	7	10	9		11					8		2		1				
4		3	4	5	6	7	10	9				11			8		2		1				
5		3	4	5	6	7		9			10	11			8		2		1				
r		3	4	5	6	7	**10**	9			12	11			8		2		1				
	1	6	6	6	6	6	5	6		1	2	5			4		5	1	4				
											1												
		1	1	1			3	2							1								
1 (1)	2	3	4	5	6	7	8	9	10	11													
1 (2)	2	3	4	5	**6**	7	8	9	10	11	12												
2 (1)	2	3	4	5	6	7	8	9	10	**11**	12												
2 (2)	2	3		5	**6**	7		9	10	11			4	8			12						
	4	4	3	4	4	4	3	4	4	4			1	1									
											2						1						
				2		2	2	1	3					1									

York City v QPR 25 September 1984 programme cover.

Dale Banton.

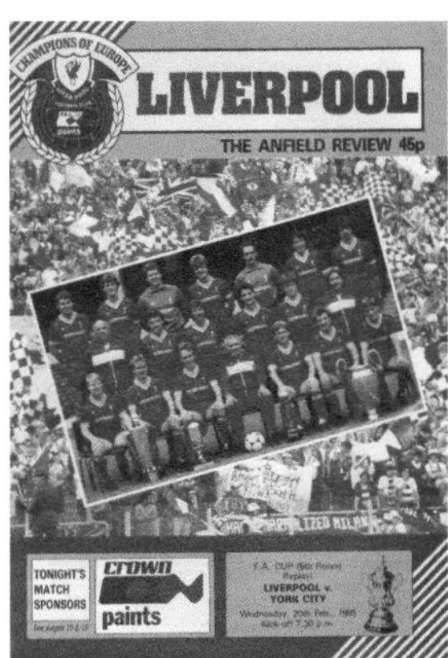

Liverpool v York City 20 February 1985 programme cover.

1985–86

Division Three

Manager: Denis Smith

	P	W	D	L	F	A	Pts
Reading	46	29	7	10	67	51	94
Plymouth Argyle	46	26	9	11	88	53	87
Derby County	46	23	15	8	80	41	84
Wigan Athletic	46	23	14	9	82	48	83
Gillingham	46	22	13	11	81	54	79
Walsall	46	22	9	15	90	64	75
York City	46	20	11	15	77	58	71
Notts County	46	19	14	13	71	60	71
Bristol City	46	18	14	14	69	60	68
Brentford	46	18	12	16	58	61	66
Doncaster Rovers	46	16	16	14	45	52	64
Blackpool	46	17	12	17	66	55	63
Darlington	46	15	13	18	61	78	58
Rotherham United	46	15	12	19	61	59	57
Bournemouth	46	15	9	22	65	72	54
Bristol Rovers	46	14	12	20	51	75	54
Chesterfield	46	13	14	19	61	64	53
Bolton Wanderers	46	15	8	23	54	68	53
Newport County	46	11	18	17	52	65	51
Bury	46	12	13	21	63	67	49
Lincoln City	46	10	16	20	55	77	46
Cardiff City	46	12	9	25	53	83	45
Wolverhampton W	46	11	10	25	57	98	43
Swansea City	46	11	10	25	43	87	43

Did you know that?

This was City's 50th playing season in the Football League, and for the fifth successive campaign they finished higher in the competition.

New signing Simon Mills from Sheffield Wednesday made his debut on the opening day and was Clubman of the Year.

Chris Evans played his last game on 17 September 1985 and moved to Darlington.

A 7–0 win over the Quakers on 5 October 1985 equalled their second-ever best victory in the Football League.

During the season Gary Ford became only the 10th player to make 300 League appearances for the club, and top scorer Keith Walwyn completed 100 goals for City.

John MacPhail played his last game for City on the final day of the campaign.

The average home League crowd was 4,111.

For only the fourth time in their history, City reached the fifth round of the FA Cup and for the second successive season bowed out at Anfield in a replay.

To reach that stage they had the unique experience of being drawn at home to non-League opposition in four successive rounds.

Match No.	Date		Venue	Opponents	Result		Scorers	Atten
1	Aug	17	H	Plymouth Argyle	W	3–1	Canham, Walwyn, Gabbiadini	
2		24	A	Bury	L	2–4	MacPhail (pen), Walwyn	
3		26	H	Wigan Athletic	W	4–1	Walwyn (2), Ford (2)	
4		31	A	Wolverhampton Wanderers	L	2–3	MacPhail (pen), Walwyn	
5	Sep	7	H	Cardiff City	D	1–1	Evans	
6		14	A	Blackpool	W	2–0	Walwyn, Canham	
7		17	A	Notts County	L	1–3	Walwyn	
8		21	H	Bristol City	D	1–1	MacPhail (pen)	
9		28	A	Gillingham	W	2–1	Banton, McAughtrie	
10	Oct	1	H	Bolton Wanderers	W	3–0	Houchen (2), Banton	
11		5	H	Darlington	W	7–0	Canham (3,1pen), Walwyn (2), Houchen, Senior	
12		12	A	Chesterfield	L	0–1		
13		19	A	Derby County	L	1–2	Houchen (pen)	1
14		22	H	Bournemouth	W	2–1	Walwyn, Ford	
15		26	H	Rotherham United	W	2–1	Banton (2)	
16	Nov	2	A	Bristol Rovers	W	1–0	Banton	
17		6	A	Newport County	D	1–1	Mills	
18		9	H	Reading	L	0–1		
19		24	A	Lincoln City	W	4–3	Banton (2), Senior, Walwyn	
20		30	H	Brentford	W	1–0	Walwyn	
21	Dec	14	A	Swansea City	L	0–1		
22		20	H	Bury	D	0–0		
23		26	H	Doncaster Rovers	L	0–1		
24	Jan	1	A	Walsall	L	1–3	MacPhail	
25		11	H	Wolverhampton Wanderers	W	2–1	Houchen, Banton	
26		18	A	Plymouth Argyle	D	2–2	Walwyn (2)	
27		31	A	Cardiff City	L	1–2	Walwyn	
28	Feb	4	A	Bournemouth	L	0–2		
29		8	H	Derby County	L	1–3	Houchen (pen)	
30		22	A	Bristol City	D	2–2	MacPhail (pen), Canham	
31	Mar	1	H	Gillingham	W	2–0	Opp. og (2)	
32		4	A	Bolton Wanderers	D	1–1	Walwyn	
33		9	A	Darlington	L	0–1		
34		12	H	Bristol Rovers	W	4–0	Canham (2), Walwyn, Gabbiadini	
35		15	H	Chesterfield	W	2–0	Hood, Gabbiadini	
36		18	A	Wigan Athletic	L	0–1		
37		22	A	Rotherham United	L	1–4	Gabbiadini	
38		29	H	Walsall	W	1–0	Walwyn	
39		31	A	Doncaster Rovers	D	1–1	Hay	
40	Apr	5	H	Newport County	W	3–1	Walwyn (2), Canham	
41		12	A	Reading	D	0–0		
42		19	H	Lincoln City	W	2–1	Canham, MacPhail (pen)	
43		22	H	Notts County	D	2–2	Walwyn, MacPhail (pen)	
44		26	A	Brentford	D	3–3	Banton (pen), Mills, Senior	
45	May	3	H	Swansea City	W	3–1	Walwyn, Banton, Canham	
46		6	H	Blackpool	W	3–0	Canham (2), Banton	

2 own-goals

Hood	Evans	McAughtrie	MacPhail	Haslegrave	Ford	Gabbiadini	Walwyn	Houchen	Canham	Mills	Banton	Senior	Hay	Leaning	Sbragia	Pearce	Butler	McKenzie	Murphy	
2	3	4	5	6	7	**8**	9	10	11	12										1
2	3	4	5	6	7		9	**10**	11		8	12								2
2	3	**4**	5	6	7	12	9		11	10	8									3
2	3	4	5	6	7		9	12	**11**	10	8									4
2	3	4	5	**6**	7		9	12	11	10	8									5
2	3	4	5	6	7		9		11	10	8									6
2	3	4	5	**6**	7		9	12	11	10	8									7
		4	5	6	7	12	9	10	11	8		**2**	3							8
		4	5	6	7		9	10	11		8	2	3							9
		4	5	6	7		9	10	11		8	2	3							10
12		**4**	5	6	7		9	10	11		8	2	3							11
		4	5	6	7		9	10	11		8	2	3							12
		4	5	6	7		9	10	11		8	2	3							13
		4	5	6	7	12	9		11	**10**	8	2	3							14
		4	5	6	7		9		11	10	8	2	3							15
		4	5	6	7		9	12	11	10	8	2	3							16
		4	5	6	7		9		11	10	8	2	3	1						17
			5	6	7		9	12	**11**	10	8	2	3	1	4					18
12			5		7		**9**	10		6	8	2	3	1	4	11				19
			5		7		9	10		6	8	2	3	1	4	11				20
		4	5		7		9	10		6	8	2	3	1		11				21
2		4	5		7	12	9	10		6	8		3	1		**11**				22
		4	5		7	12	9	10		6	8	2	3	1		**11**				23
3		4	5	6	7	12	9	10	11		**8**	2		1						24
3		4	5	12	7		**9**	10	11	6	8	2		1						25
3		4	5		7		9	10	11	6	8	2		1						26
3		4	5		7		9	10	11	6	8	2		1						27
3		4	5	12	7		9	10	**11**	6	8	2		1						28
3		4	5	6	7		9	11	12	10	**8**	2		1						29
3		4	5	6	7		9		11	10	**8**	2		1			12			30
3		4	5	6	7	12	9		11	10		2		1			**8**			31
5		4		6	7	12	9		11	10		2	3	1			**8**			32
5		4		6	7	12	9	8	11	10		**2**	3	1						33
3		4	5	**6**	7	8	9		11	10				1			12	2		34
3		4	5	6	7	8	9		11	10				1				2		35
3		4	5	6	7	**8**	9		11	10				1			12	2		36
3		4	5	6	7	8	9		**11**	10				1			12	2		37
3		4	5	6	7	8	9		11	10		2		1			12			38
		4	5	6	7	8	9		**11**	10		2	3	1			12			39
2		4		6		8	9		11	10	12		3	1	5		**7**			40
		4	5	6	7	**8**	9		11	10	12	2	3	1						41
3		4	5	6		12	9		11		**8**	2		1		10	7			42
3			5	6		12	9		11		8	2		1	4	**10**	7			43
3		4		6			9		11	10	8	2		1	5		7			44
3			5	6		12	9		11	**10**	8	2		1	4		7			45
3		4	5	6		8	9		11		10	2		1			7			46
29	7	41	42	37	40	10	46	20	40	35	33	33	21	30	7	7	8	4		
2				2		12		5	1	1	2	1					6			
1	1	1	7		4	4	22	6	13	1	11	3	1							

York City v Darlington 5 October 1985 programme cover.

Simon Mills.

1985–86

Cont.

FA Cup

Match No.	Date	Venue	Opponents	Result		Scorers	Attend
1	Nov 16	H	Morecambe	D	0–0		3
r	19	N#	Morecambe	W	2–0	Sbragia, Walwyn	1
2	Dec 7	H	Whitby Town	W	3–1	Ford, Walwyn, Pearce	6
3	Jan 4	H	Wycombe Wanderers	W	2–0	Walwyn (2)	5
4	25	H	Altrincham	W	2–0	Banton, Ford	8
5	Feb 15	H	Liverpool	D	1–1	Ford	12
r	18	A	Liverpool	L	1–3*	Canham	29

N# At Maine Road, Manchester. * After extra-time.

Football League (Milk) Cup

Match No.	Date	Venue	Opponents	Result		Scorers	Attend
1 (1)	Aug 20	H	Lincoln City	W	2–1	Walwyn, McAughtrie	3
1 (2)	Sep 4	A	Lincoln City	W	2–1	MacPhail (pen), Walwyn	2
2 (1)	24	A	Grimsby Town	D	1–1	Walwyn	2
2 (2)	Oct 8	H	Grimsby Town	L	2–3	Houchen (pen), Banton	5

Tony Canham and Keith Walwyn watch as a shot goes over the Bristol City crossbar in the 1–1 draw at Bootham Cresent in September 1985.

ood	Evans	McAughtrie	MacPhail	Haslegrave	Ford	Gabbiadini	Walwyn	Houchen	Canham	Mills	Banton	Senior	Hay	Leaning	Sbragia	Pearce	Butler	McKenzie	Murphy	
			5	6	7		9	12	**11**	10	8	2	3	1	4					1
			5		7		9	10		6	8	2	3	1	4	11				r
2		4	5		7		9	10		6	8		3	1		11				2
3		4	5	6	7		9	10	11		8	2		1						3
3		4	5		7		9	10	11	6	8	2		1						4
3		4	5	6	7		9		11	10	8	2		1						5
3		4	5	**6**	7		9	12	11	10	8	2		1						r
5		5	7	4	7		7	4	5	6	7	6	3	7	2	2				
								2												
					3		4		1		1				1	1				

ood	Evans	McAughtrie	MacPhail	Haslegrave	Ford	Gabbiadini	Walwyn	Houchen	Canham	Mills	Banton	Senior	Hay	Leaning	Sbragia	Pearce	Butler	McKenzie	Murphy	
2	3	4	5	6	7	12	9	10	11		**8**									1 (1)
2	3	4	5	6	7		9		11	10	8									1 (2)
2		4	5	6	7		9	10	11	**8**		2	3							2 (1)
		4	5	6	7		9	10	11		8	2	3							2 (2)
2	2	4	4	4	4		4	3	4	2	3	2	2							
						1														
		1	1				3	1			1									

John McPhail.

sigings Simon Mills and David McAughtrie are given a warm welcome to Bootham Crescent by manager Denis Smith and h Viv Busby.

1986–87

Division Three

Manager: Denis Smith

	P	W	D	L	F	A	Pts
Bournemouth	46	29	10	7	76	40	97
Middlesbrough	46	28	10	8	67	30	94
Swindon Town	46	25	12	9	77	47	87
Wigan Athletic	46	25	10	11	83	60	85
Gillingham	46	23	9	14	65	48	78
Bristol City	46	21	14	11	63	36	77
Notts County	46	21	13	12	77	56	76
Walsall	46	22	9	15	80	67	75
Blackpool	46	16	16	14	74	59	64
Mansfield Town	46	15	16	15	52	55	61
Brentford	46	15	15	16	64	66	60
Port Vale	46	15	12	19	76	70	57
Doncaster Rovers	46	14	15	17	56	62	57
Rotherham United	46	15	12	19	48	57	57
Chester City	46	13	17	16	61	59	56
Bury	46	14	13	19	54	60	55
Chesterfield	46	13	15	18	56	69	54
Fulham	46	12	17	17	59	77	53
Bristol Rovers	46	13	12	21	49	75	51
York City	46	12	13	21	55	79	49
Bolton Wanderers	46	10	15	21	46	58	45
Carlisle United	46	10	8	28	39	78	38
Darlington	46	7	16	23	45	77	37
Newport County	46	8	13	25	49	86	37

Did you know that?

Average League attendance at Bootham Crescent dropped to 3,432 as City just avoided the drop. This was the first and only season of promotion and relegation Play-offs, and Bolton Wanderers were demoted following a Play-off defeat against Fourth Division Aldershot.

Ricky Sbragia played his last game for the club on 20 April 1987 at home to Blackpool.

Making their last appearances for City on the final day of the season were Gary Ford (435 games, 64 goals) and Keith Walwyn (291 games, 140 goals).

For the first time in their Football League history City lost at home in a replay to non-League opposition in the FA Cup.

At the end of the season the managerial team of Denis Smith and Viv Busby moved to Sunderland.

Match No.	Date	Venue	Opponents	Result		Scorers	Atten
1	Aug 23	H	Darlington	W	3–1	Hood (pen), Canham, Ford	
2	30	A	Carlisle United	D	2–2	Banton, Walwyn	
3	Sep 6	H	Bristol Rovers	W	1–0	Canham	
4	13	A	Port Vale	W	3–2	Walwyn (2), Gabbiadini	
5	16	A	Gillingham	L	0–2		
6	20	H	Bury	W	1–0	Hood	
7	27	A	Doncaster Rovers	L	1–3	Gabbiadini	
8	30	H	Bournemouth	W	2–0	Walwyn (2)	
9	Oct 4	H	Mansfield Town	L	1–3	Ford	
10	11	A	Bristol City	L	0–3		
11	18	A	Brentford	L	1–3	Banton	
12	21	H	Chester City	D	1–1	Canham	
13	25	H	Rotherham United	W	2–1	Walwyn, Banton	
14	Nov 1	A	Swindon Town	L	1–3	Banton	
15	4	A	Newport County	D	1–1	Walwyn	
16	8	H	Chesterfield	D	1–1	Gabbiadini	
17	22	H	Walsall	L	1–5	Hood (pen)	
18	29	A	Bolton Wanderers	L	1–3	Gabbiadini (pen)	
19	Dec 13	A	Notts County	L	1–5	Canham	
20	20	H	Fulham	D	1–1	Gabbiadini (pen)	
21	26	A	Blackpool	L	1–2	Gabbiadini (pen)	
22	27	H	Wigan Athletic	D	1–1	Canham	
23	Jan 1	H	Middlesbrough	W	3–1	Butler, Walwyn (2)	
24	23	A	Bristol Rovers	L	0–1		
25	Feb 7	H	Gillingham	W	2–1	Walwyn, Gabbiadini	
26	14	A	Bury	L	0–1		
27	21	H	Doncaster Rovers	D	1–1	Banton	
28	24	A	Darlington	D	2–2	Ford, Gabbiadini	
29	28	A	Bournemouth	L	0–3		
30	Mar 3	H	Swindon Town	L	0–3		
31	7	A	Rotherham United	D	0–0		
32	14	H	Brentford	W	2–1	Walwyn, Gabbiadini	
33	18	A	Chester City	L	1–2	Canham	
34	21	H	Bristol City	D	1–1	Canham	
35	24	A	Walsall	L	2–3	Canham, Mills	
36	28	A	Mansfield Town	D	1–1	Walwyn	
37	31	H	Carlisle United	W	2–0	Walwyn (2)	
38	Apr 4	A	Chesterfield	L	0–1		
39	11	H	Newport County	W	3–0	Ford, Walwyn (2)	
40	14	H	Port Vale	L	1–4	Banton (pen)	
41	18	A	Middlesbrough	L	1–3	Walwyn	1
42	20	H	Blackpool	D	1–1	Pickering	
43	25	A	Fulham	L	0–1		
44	May 2	H	Bolton Wanderers	W	2–1	Butler, Canham	
45	4	A	Wigan Athletic	L	2–3	Walwyn (2)	
46	9	H	Notts County	D	1–1	Butler	

FA Cup

1	Nov 15	H	Crewe Alexandra	W	3–1	Mills, Banton, Walwyn
2	Dec 6	A	Caernarfon Town	D	0–0	
r	9	H	Caernarfon Town	L	1–2	Canham

Football League (Littlewoods) Cup

1 (1)	Aug 26	A	Sunderland	W	4–2	Mills, Walwyn (3)
1 (2)	Sep 2	H	Sunderland	L	1–3*	Walwyn
2 (1)	23	H	Chelsea	W	1–0	Canham
2 (2)	Oct 7	A	Chelsea	L	0–3	

* After extra-time. City won on away goals.

Senior	Hood	Sbragia	Pickering	Haslegrave	Ford	Banton	Walwyn	Mills	Canham	Butler	McKenzie	Gabbiadini	Murray	McAughtrie	Whitehead	Pearce	Smallwood	Lowey	Costello	Tutill	
2	3	4	5	6	7	8	9	10	11												1
2	3	4	5	6		8	9	10	11	7											2
	3	4	5	**6**	7		9	10	11	12	2	8									3
	3	4	5		7	8	9	10	11		2	6									4
2	3	4	5		7	8	9	10	11			6									5
2	3	4	5		7	8	9	10	11		12	**6**									6
2	3	4	5		7	8	9	10	11			6									7
2	3	4	5		7	8	9	10	11			**6**	12								8
2	3	4	5		7	**8**		10	11	12		6	9								9
2	6	4			7	8		10	11	12	3	**9**		5							10
2	6		**5**		7	8		10	11	12	3	9		4							11
2	3				7	8		10	11	9		12	**6**	4	5						12
2	3				7	8	9	10	11					4	5	6					13
2	3			6	7	8	9	10	11					4	5						14
2	3			6	7	**8**	9	10				12		4	5	11					15
2	3			6	7	**8**	9	10				12		4	5	11					16
2	3			6	7	**8**	9	10	11			12		4	5						17
2				**6**	7		9	10	12		3	8		4	5	11	1				18
2	3	4		12	7		9	10	11			**8**		5		6	1				19
2		4		6	7		9	10	11	12		**8**		5		3					20
2		4		6	7		9	10	11			8		5		3					21
2		4		6	7		9	10	11	12		8		**5**		3					22
2	12	4	5	6	7		9	10	11	8						3					23
2	12	4	5	6	7		9		11	**8**		10				3					24
2	11	4	5	6	7		9	10				8				3					25
2	11	4	**5**	6	7	12	9	10				8				3					26
2	11	4	**5**	6	7	12	9	10				8				3					27
2	11	4	5	6	**7**	12	9	10				8				3					28
2	11	4	5	6	**7**	12	9	10				8				3					29
2		4		6	7	8	9	10	11						5	3					30
2		4	12	6	7		9	10	11			8			5	**3**					31
			4	6	7		9	10	11		2	8			5	3					32
			4	6	7		9	10	11		2	8			5	3					33
3	12		4	6	7		9	10	11		2	**8**		5							34
3			4	6	7	8	9	10	**11**		2			5		12					35
2			4	6	7	8	9	10	11					5		3					36
2			4	6	7	8	9	10	11					5		3					37
2			4	6	7	8	9	10	**11**					5		3		12			38
2			4	6	7	8	9	10	11					5		3					39
2		4	5	6	7	8	9	10	**11**							3		12			40
		4	5	6	7	**8**	9	10	12		2					3		11			41
3		4	5	**6**	7		9	10	11	8	2						1	12			42
			4		7	12	9	10		8	2			5		3	1	6	**11**		43
			4	6	7		9	10	11	8	2			5		3	1				44
			4	6	7		9	10	11	8	**2**	12		5		3	1				45
	4			6	7		9	10	11	8				5		3	1	2			46
37	24	26	31	34	45	24	42	45	36	9	14	24	2	23	11	29	7	3	1		
	3		1	1		5			2	6	1	5	1			1		3			
	3		1		4	6	19	1	9	3		9									

Senior	Hood	Sbragia	Pickering	Haslegrave	Ford	Banton	Walwyn	Mills	Canham	Butler	McKenzie	Gabbiadini	Murray	McAughtrie	Whitehead	Pearce	Smallwood	Lowey	Costello	Tutill	
2	3			6	7	8	9	10	11					4	5						1
2	3	4			7	**8**	9	10	11	12				5		6	1				2
2	3	4			7	**8**	9	10	11	12				5		6	1				r
3	3	2		1	3	3	3	3	3					3	1	2	2				
										2											
						1	1	1	1												

Senior	Hood	Sbragia	Pickering	Haslegrave	Ford	Banton	Walwyn	Mills	Canham	Butler	McKenzie	Gabbiadini	Murray	McAughtrie	Whitehead	Pearce	Smallwood	Lowey	Costello	Tutill	
2	3	4	5	6	**7**	8	9	10	11			12									1 (1)
2	3	**4**	5	6	7	8	9	10	11			13		12							1 (2)
	3	4	5		7	8	9	10	11		2	6									2 (1)
2	3	4	5		7	8	9	10	11	13	12	**6**									2 (2)
3	4	4	4	2	4	4	4	4	4		1	2									
										1	1	2		1							
							4	1	1												

York City v Caernarfon Town 9 December 1986 programme cover.

Andy Leaning.

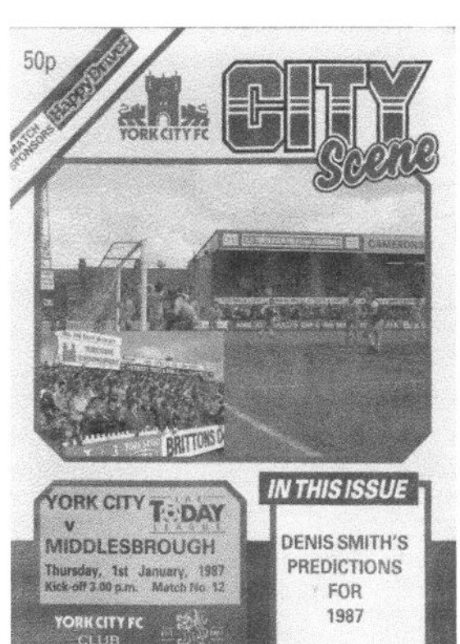

York City v Middlesbrough 1 January 1987 programme cover.

1987–88

Division Three

Manager: Bobby Saxton

	P	W	D	L	F	A	Pts
Sunderland	46	27	12	7	92	48	93
Brighton & Hove Albion	46	23	15	8	69	47	84
Walsall	46	23	13	10	68	50	82
Notts County	46	23	12	11	82	49	81
Bristol City	46	21	12	13	77	62	75
Northampton Town	46	18	19	9	70	51	73
Wigan Athletic	46	20	12	14	70	61	72
Bristol Rovers	46	18	12	16	68	56	66
Fulham	46	19	9	18	69	60	66
Blackpool	46	17	14	15	71	62	65
Port Vale	46	18	11	17	58	56	65
Brentford	46	16	14	16	53	59	62
Gillingham	46	14	17	15	77	61	59
Bury	46	15	14	17	58	57	59
Chester City	46	14	16	16	51	62	58
Preston North End	46	15	13	18	48	59	58
Southend United	46	14	13	19	65	83	55
Chesterfield	46	15	10	21	41	70	55
Mansfield Town	46	14	12	20	48	59	54
Aldershot	46	15	8	23	64	74	53
Rotherham United	46	12	16	18	50	66	52
Grimsby Town	46	12	14	20	48	58	50
York City	46	8	9	29	48	91	33
Doncaster Rovers	46	8	9	29	40	84	33

Did you know that?

Statistically, this was City's worst season as a Football League club, With fewest wins (8), most defeats (29) and least points (33 or 25 under the old system).

City did not win until their 16th game on 31 October 1987, the club's worst-ever start to a campaign.

The run of away League games without a win was extended to 38 (six draws, 32 defeats) before they were successful at Aldershot on 5 March 1988. Their previous victory on their travels had been at Port Vale on 13 September 1986.

Marco Gabbiadini played his last game at Gillingham prior to his move to Sunderland for £80,000.

Steve Tutill made his full League debut in the following game at home to Doncaster Rovers.

Andy McMillan made his senior debut when coming on as a substitute at home to Mansfield Town on 28 December 1987.

Gordon Staniforth returned after a gap of eight years, and his first game back was at Sunderland on 24 October 1987.

No fewer than 31 players were utilised compared with 18 in the Fourth Division Championship season of four years earlier. Derek Hood, the only surviving member of that successful side, played his last game for the club on 25 April 1988 against Northampton, after 354 senior appearances and 36 goals.

Dale Banton was leading marksman and Clubman of the Year.

Average home League attendance was 2,754.

Match No.	Date	Venue	Opponents	Result		Scorers	Attend.
1	Aug 15	A	Brighton & Hove Albion	L	0–1		6
2	22	H	Notts County	L	3–5	Whitehead, Canham, Banton	2
3	29	A	Chester City	L	0–1		2
4	31	H	Walsall	L	1–3	Banton	2
5	Sep 5	A	Port Vale	L	1–2	Canham	2
6	12	H	Preston North End	D	1–1	Hood (pen)	3
7	16	A	Bristol Rovers	L	1–2	Banton	3
8	19	A	Gillingham	L	1–3	M. Gabbiadini	5
9	26	H	Doncaster Rovers	D	1–1	Cook (pen)	2
10	29	H	Blackpool	L	1–3	Buchanan	2
11	Oct 3	A	Wigan Athletic	D	1–1	Banton (pen)	2
12	10	A	Fulham	L	1–3	Buchanan	4
13	17	H	Aldershot	D	2–2	Banton (2)	1
14	20	H	Rotherham United	L	1–2	Hood (pen)	1
15	24	A	Sunderland	L	2–4	Banton, Mills	19
16	31	H	Chesterfield	W	1–0	Banton	2
17	Nov 4	A	Northampton Town	D	0–0		4
18	7	H	Bury	D	1–1	Helliwell	2
19	21	A	Grimsby Town	L	1–5	Mills	2
20	28	H	Southend United	L	0–3		2
21	Dec 12	A	Bristol City	L	2–3	Banton (2)	6
22	18	H	Brentford	D	1–1	Clegg	1
23	26	A	Doncaster Rovers	L	0–2		2
24	28	H	Mansfield Town	D	2–2	Banton (pen), Helliwell	2
25	Jan 1	H	Chester City	W	2–0	Clegg, Wilson	2
26	2	A	Preston North End	L	0–3		6
27	9	A	Notts County	L	0–3		5
28	16	H	Gillingham	L	0–2		2
29	30	A	Walsall	L	1–2	Banton	4
30	Feb 6	H	Port Vale	L	2–3	Himsworth, Banton	2
31	13	A	Mansfield Town	L	1–2	Helliwell	2
32	20	H	Brighton & Hove Albion	L	0–2		2
33	27	H	Wigan Athletic	W	3–1	Helliwell, Banton (2)	2
34	Mar 1	A	Blackpool	L	1–2	Bradshaw	2
35	5	A	Aldershot	W	2–1	Helliwell, Hood	2
36	12	H	Fulham	L	1–3	Hood (pen)	2
37	19	A	Chesterfield	L	1–2	Himsworth	1
38	26	H	Sunderland	W	2–1	Helliwell, Banton	9
39	Apr 2	A	Bury	W	1–0	Clegg	2
40	4	H	Grimsby Town	L	0–2		3
41	8	A	Rotherham United	W	1–0	Branagan	2
42	15	H	Bristol Rovers	L	0–4		1
43	25	H	Northampton Town	D	2–2	Howlett (2)	2
44	29	A	Southend United	L	1–3	Helliwell	3
45	May 2	H	Bristol City	L	0–1		2
46	7	A	Brentford	W	2–1	Helliwell, Staniforth	4
							A
							S

FA Cup

1	Nov 14	H	Burton Albion	D	0–0		3
r	18	A	Burton Albion	W	2–1	Hood (pen), Mills	4
2	Dec 5	H	Hartlepool United	D	1–1	Wilson	3
r	9	A	Hartlepool United	L	1–3	Banton	4
							A
							S

Football League (Littlewoods) Cup

1 (1)	Aug 18	A	Halifax Town	D	1–1	M. Gabbiadini	1
1 (2)	25	H	Halifax Town	W	1–0	Hood (pen)	2,
2 (1)	Sep 23	A	Leeds United	D	1–1	Buchanan	11
2 (2)	Oct 6	H	Leeds United	L	0–4		6,
							A
							S

Note: Two substitutes were allowed from this season in the Football League. First substitute No. 12, player substituted in bold. Second substitute No. 13, player substituted underlined. Two substitutes introduced in the FL Cup the previous season.

McKenzie	Johnson	Wilson	Whitehead	Clegg	Himsworth	Hood	Gabbiadini M.	Butler	Canham	Banton	Kitching	Tutill	Smallwood	Cook	Mills	Branagan	Buchanan	Costello	Downing	Helliwell	Staniforth	Bradshaw	Brough	Stowell	Spofforth	McMillan	Rogers	Gabbiadini R.	Howlett	
2	3	4	5	6	**7**	8	9	10	11	12	13																			1
2	3	4	5	6		8	**9**	7	11	10	12																			2
2	3	4	5	6		8	9	7	**11**	10		12																		3
2	3	4	5	6		12	9	**7**	11	10			1	8																4
7	3	4	5	6		2	9		11	10			1	8	12															5
	3	4	5	6		2	9		11	10				8	7															6
7	3	**4**	5	6		2	9		12	10				8	11															7
7	3		5	6	12	2	9			10	**4**			8	11															8
12	3	4	5		11					**10**		6		8	7	2	9													9
9	3	4	5		11	8					12	6			7	2	10													10
	3	4	5	6						10	8	11			7	2	9													11
	3	4	5	6				12		10		11			8	2	9	**7**												12
	3	4	5	6						10		11			8	2	9		7											13
7	3	4		6		5				10		11			8	2	9													14
7	3	4	5	6		13				10		11			8	2				9	12									15
	3	4	5	6						10		11			8	2				9	7									16
	3	4	5	6		2						11			8		10			9	7									17
	3	4	5	6		2				10		11			8					9	7									18
			5	6		**3**				10	4	11			8	2				9	7	12	13							19
		4	5		**11**	3				10		6			7	2				9	12	8								20
	3	4	5	12	13	2			11	10		**6**	1		7					9		8								21
	3	4	5	6	13				11	10			1		8	12				9	7	2								22
		4	5	6	7	3				10	12					2				9	11	**8**		1						23
		4	5	6	7					10	8					2		13		9	11			1	**3**	12				24
		4	**5**	6	7						10					2				9	11	8		1		12	3			25
		4		6	**7**						10					2		12		9	11	8		1		5	3	13		26
		4	5	12	7					10						2				9	11	8		1		6	**3**			27
	3	4	5	6	7						10									9	11	8		1		2				28
	3	4	5		7				11	10			1							9	13	**8**				2	12		6	29
	3	4	5		8				**11**	10	13		1							9	12					2	6		**7**	30
	3	4			8	5			11	10										9						2	6		7	31
	3	**4**	5		11				13	10						6				9		8				2	12		**7**	32
	4				11	5			12	10						3				9		8			**6**	2			7	33
	4				**11**	5			12	10						3				9		8			6	2			7	34
	3			4	11	5				10						6				9		8				2			7	35
	3			4	11	5				10						6				9		8				2			7	36
	3	13		4	11	5			12	10						6				**9**		8				2			7	37
	3			4	11					10		5				6				9		8				2			7	38
	3	13		4	11	12			10			**5**				6				9		8				2			7	39
	3	12	13	4	11	5			10							6				9		**8**				2			7	40
	3	10		4	11	5										6				9		8				2			7	41
	3	10		4	11	12						5				**6**				9		8				2			7	42
	3	**10**		4	11	6					12	5								9	2	8							7	43
	3			4	11							5				6				9	10	8				2			7	44
6	3			4	11							5								9	10	8				2			7	45
6	3			4	11							5								9	10	8				2			7	46
12	39	33	29	35	28	24	8	4	13	32	7	20	6	6	17	27	7	1	1	32	15	24		6	3	20	5		18	
1		3	1	2	3	4		1	5	1	6	1			1	1		2			4	1	1			2	2	1		
		1	1	3	2	4	1		2	16				1	2	1	2			8	1	1							2	

McKenzie	Johnson	Wilson	Whitehead	Clegg	Himsworth	Hood	Gabbiadini M.	Butler	Canham	Banton	Kitching	Tutill	Smallwood	Cook	Mills	Branagan	Buchanan	Costello	Downing	Helliwell	Staniforth	Bradshaw	Brough	Stowell	Spofforth	McMillan	Rogers	Gabbiadini R.	Howlett	
	3	4		6		5				10	2	11			8						7		9							1
		4	5	6		3				10		11			8	2					7		9							r
	3	4	5							10		6	1		7	2					11	8	9							2
	3	4	5			12				10		6	1		7	**2**					11	8	9							r
	3	4	3	2		2				4	1	4	2		4	3					4	2	4							
						1																								
		1				1				1					1															

McKenzie	Johnson	Wilson	Whitehead	Clegg	Himsworth	Hood	Gabbiadini M.	Butler	Canham	Banton	Kitching	Tutill	Smallwood	Cook	Mills	Branagan	Buchanan	Costello	Downing	Helliwell	Staniforth	Bradshaw	Brough	Stowell	Spofforth	McMillan	Rogers	Gabbiadini R.	Howlett	
2	3		5	6		8	9	7	11	10	4																			1 (1)
2	3	4	5	6		8	9	7	11	10																				1 (2)
9	3	4	5		11	2				10	**7**	6			8		12													2 (1)
	3	4	5	6		2				10	8	11			7		9													2 (2)
3	4	3	4	3	1	4	2	2	2	4	3	2			2		1													
																	1													
						1	1										1													

York City v Leeds United 6 October 1987 programme cover.

Gary Howlett.

1988–89

Division Four

Manager: Bobby Saxton, then John Bird

	P	W	D	L	F	A	Pts
Rotherham United	46	22	16	8	76	35	82
Tranmere Rovers	46	21	17	8	62	43	80
Crewe Alexandra	46	21	15	10	67	48	78
Scunthorpe United	46	21	14	11	77	57	77
Scarborough	46	21	14	11	67	52	77
Leyton Orient	46	21	12	13	86	50	75
Wrexham	46	19	14	13	77	63	71
Cambridge United	46	18	14	14	71	62	68
Grimsby Town	46	17	15	14	65	59	66
Lincoln City	46	18	10	18	64	60	64
York City	46	17	13	16	62	63	64
Carlisle United	46	15	15	16	53	52	60
Exeter City	46	18	6	22	65	68	60
Torquay United	46	17	8	21	45	60	59
Hereford United	46	14	16	16	66	72	58
Burnley	46	14	13	19	52	61	55
Peterborough United	46	14	12	20	52	74	54
Rochdale	46	13	14	19	56	82	53
Hartlepool United	46	14	10	22	50	78	52
Stockport County	46	10	21	15	54	52	51
Halifax Town	46	13	11	22	69	75	50
Colchester United	46	12	14	20	60	78	50
Doncaster Rovers	46	13	10	23	49	78	49
Darlington	46	8	18	20	53	76	42

Did you know that?

Manager Bobby Saxton, after just over one year in charge, resigned in the first month of the campaign. John Bird was his successor, with Alan Little his assistant.

Dale Banton moved to Walsall for £80,000, and his last game was at Grimsby Town on 22 October 1988.

Andy McMillan missed most of the season through injury.

Wayne Hall made his debut on the left wing when coming on as a substitute in the last two games of the season.

A feature of the season was the fact that City won away against the top three clubs of the division.

Top scorer Ian Helliwell was Clubman of the Year.

Average League attendance at Bootham Crescent was 2,613.

For the third time in their history City fell at the first hurdle of both major Cup competitions.

Match No.	Date	Venue	Opponents	Result		Scorers	Attenc
1	Aug 27	A	Colchester United	L	0–1		
2	Sep 3	H	Carlisle United	D	1–1	Banton (pen)	
3	10	A	Burnley	L	0–6		
4	17	H	Scunthorpe United	L	1–2	Howlett	
5	20	H	Hartlepool United	L	2–3	Bradshaw, Banton	
6	24	A	Peterborough United	W	1–0	Helliwell	
7	Oct 1	H	Halifax Town	W	5–3	Butler, Bradshaw, Canham, Banton (pen), Howlett	
8	4	A	Leyton Orient	L	0–4		
9	7	A	Tranmere Rovers	W	1–0	Canham	
10	15	H	Darlington	W	4–1	Butler (2), Canham, Banton	
11	22	A	Grimsby Town	L	0–2		
12	25	H	Doncaster Rovers	D	1–1	Dunn	
13	29	A	Wrexham	L	1–2	Smith	
14	Nov 5	H	Torquay United	D	1–1	Eli	
15	8	H	Crewe Alexandra	W	3–0	Dunn, Johnson, Wilson	
16	11	A	Stockport County	L	2–3	Dunn, Smith	
17	26	A	Rochdale	L	0–2		
18	Dec 3	H	Hereford United	W	4–1	Helliwell (2), Canham, Himsworth	
19	16	H	Rotherham United	D	1–1	Spooner	
20	26	A	Scarborough	D	0–0		
21	31	A	Exeter City	L	0–2		
22	Jan 2	H	Lincoln City	W	2–1	Smith, Dixon	
23	14	A	Carlisle United	D	0–0		
24	21	H	Colchester United	W	2–0	Dixon, Howlett	
25	28	A	Scunthorpe United	L	2–4	Canham (2)	
26	Feb 4	A	Hartlepool United	W	1–0	Helliwell	
27	11	H	Peterborough United	W	5–1	Helliwell (2), Spooner, Canham, Dixon	
28	18	H	Tranmere Rovers	L	0–1		
29	25	A	Darlington	D	2–2	Dixon, Helliwell	
30	28	A	Doncaster Rovers	W	2–1	Greenough, Smith	
31	Mar 4	H	Grimsby Town	L	0–3		
32	14	H	Wrexham	W	1–0	Spooner (pen)	
33	18	H	Burnley	D	0–0		
34	25	A	Lincoln City	L	1–2	Himsworth	
35	27	H	Scarborough	D	0–0		
36	Apr 1	A	Rotherham United	W	1–0	Canham	
37	4	A	Cambridge United	D	1–1	Reid	
38	8	H	Exeter City	W	3–1	Spooner, Dunn, Helliwell	
39	14	A	Halifax Town	D	0–0		
40	22	H	Leyton Orient	D	1–1	Dunn	
41	25	A	Torquay United	L	0–2		
42	29	H	Rochdale	D	3–3	Canham, Tutill, Dunn	
43	May 1	A	Crewe Alexandra	W	2–1	Reid, Helliwell	
44	6	A	Hereford United	W	2–1	Smith, Howlett	
45	9	H	Cambridge United	L	1–2	Spooner (pen)	
46	13	H	Stockport County	W	2–0	Helliwell (2)	

FA Cup

1	Nov 19	A	Halifax Town	L	0–1		

Football League (Littlewoods) Cup

1 (1)	Aug 30	H	Sunderland	D	0–0		
1 (2)	Sep 6	A	Sunderland	L	0–4		

Bradshaw	Johnson	Wilson	Fazackerley	Smith	Howlett	Spooner	Helliwell	Banton	Himsworth	Canham	Branagan	Clegg	Tutill	Butler	Hotte	Dunn	Shaw	McMillan	Morris	Eli	Greenough	Dixon	Hay	Reid	Endersby	Hurlstone	Barratt	Hall	Match
2	3	**4**	5	6	7	8	9	10	11	12																			1
			6		7	8	9	10	**11**	4	2	3	5	12															2
4	3	12	6	5	7		9	10	11		2	**8**		13															3
4	3		6		7		9	**10**	11		2		5	12	8														4
2	4		6		8		9	10		11	3	12	**5**	7															5
2	4		6	5	8		9	10		11	3			7															6
2	4		6		8		9	10		**11**	3		5	7	12														7
2	4		6	12	8		9	10		11	3		**5**	7															8
2	4		6		8		9	10		11	3		5	7															9
2	4	12	6		8		9	10		11	3		**5**	7		13													10
2	4	13	6		8		**9**	10		11	3	5		7		12													11
2	4	12	6	5					**10**	11	3			7		9	8	13											12
2	4	12	6	5					**10**	11	3			7		9	8	13											13
2	3	4	6	5					**7**	11						10	8		9	12									14
2	3	4	6	5						11						10	8		9	7									15
2	3	4	6	**5**					13	11	12					10	8		9	7									16
	3	4		6			9		7	11			5						12	8	2	**10**							17
4	3			6		8	9		7	11			5								2	10							18
4				6		8	9		7	11	2										5	10	3						19
2	3			6		8	9		7	11											5	10		4					20
2	3			6		8	9		7	11											5	10		4					21
2	3			6		8	9		**7**	11						12					5	10		4					22
2	3			6		8	9			11						7					5	10		4					23
2	3			6	12	8	9			11						**7**					5	10		4					24
2	3			6	**7**	8	9		12	11											5	10		4					25
2	3			6		8	9		7	11											5	10		4					26
2	3			6	4	8	9		7	11											5	10							27
2	3			6	4	8	9		**7**	11						12					5	10							28
2	3			6	4	8	9		7	11											5	10							29
2	3			6		8	9		7	11											5	10		4					30
2	3			6	7	8	9		11				13			12					5	**10**		4					31
2	3			6		8	9		11							7					5	**10**		4	1	12			32
2	3			6		8	9		7							12					5	10		4		**11**			33
2	3			6		8	9		7	11											5	10		4					34
2	3					8	9		10	**11**			6			12					5			4			7		35
2	3					8	9		**10**	11			6			12					5			4			7		36
	3					8	9		10	11			6			**7**					5	12		4			2		37
	3					8	9		10	11			6			7					5			4			2		38
	3					8	9		10	11			6			7					5			4			2		39
	3					8	9		10	11			6			7					5			4			2		40
	3				12	8	9		10	11			6			**7**					5			4			2		41
	3				12	8	9		**10**	11			6			7					5			4			2		42
	3			5	10	8	9			11			6			7								4			2		43
	3			5	10	8	9			11			6			7								4			2		44
	3			5	10	8	9			11			6			**7**								4			2	12	45
	3			5	**10**	8	9			11			6			7								4			2	12	46
34	44	5	16	30	20	31	41	11	30	40	13	3	21	9	1	18	5		3	3	26	18	1	24	1	1	12		
		5		1	3				2	1	1	1	1	3	1	8		2	1	1		1				1		2	
2	1	1		5	4	5	11	4	2	9			1	3		6				1	1	4		2					

Bradshaw	Johnson	Wilson	Fazackerley	Smith	Howlett	Spooner	Helliwell	Banton	Himsworth	Canham	Branagan	Clegg	Tutill	Butler	Hotte	Dunn	Shaw	McMillan	Morris	Eli	Greenough	Dixon	Hay	Reid	Endersby	Hurlstone	Barratt	Hall	Match
	3	8	6		12		9			11	2		5	7		**10**				4									1
	1	1	1				1			1	1		1	1		1				1									
					1																								

Bradshaw	Johnson	Wilson	Fazackerley	Smith	Howlett	Spooner	Helliwell	Banton	Himsworth	Canham	Branagan	Clegg	Tutill	Butler	Hotte	Dunn	Shaw	McMillan	Morris	Eli	Greenough	Dixon	Hay	Reid	Endersby	Hurlstone	Barratt	Hall	Match
2	3		6		7	8	9	10	11		4		5																1 (1)
2			6		7	8	9	10	11		3	5		4															1 (2)
2	1		2		2	2	2	2	2		2	1	1	1															

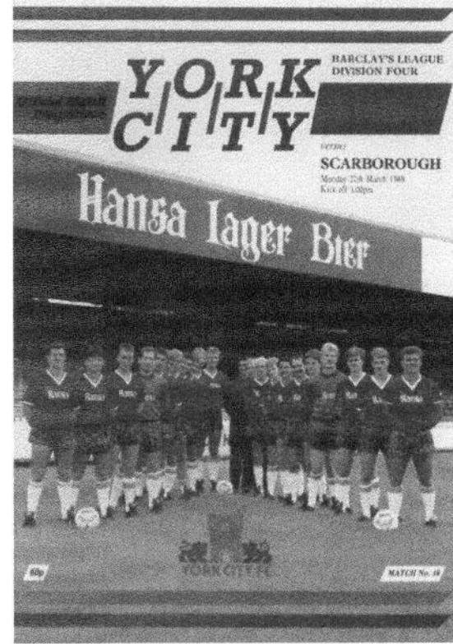

York City v Scarborough 27 March 1989 programme cover.

Paul Johnson.

1989–90

Division Four

Manager: John Bird

	P	W	D	L	F	A	Pts
Exeter City	46	28	5	13	83	48	89
Grimsby Town	46	22	13	11	70	47	79
Southend United	46	22	9	15	61	48	75
Stockport County	46	21	11	14	68	62	74
Maidstone United	46	22	7	17	77	61	73
Cambridge United	46	21	10	15	76	66	73
Chesterfield	46	19	14	13	63	50	71
Carlisle United	46	21	8	17	61	60	71
Peterborough United	46	17	17	12	59	46	68
Lincoln City	46	18	14	14	48	48	68
Scunthorpe United	46	17	15	14	69	54	66
Rochdale	46	20	6	20	52	55	66
York City	46	16	16	14	55	53	64
Gillingham	46	17	11	18	46	48	62
Torquay United	46	15	12	19	53	66	57
Burnley	46	14	14	18	45	55	56
Hereford United	46	15	10	21	56	62	55
Scarborough	46	15	10	21	60	73	55
Hartlepool United	46	15	10	21	66	88	55
Doncaster Rovers	46	14	9	23	53	60	51
Wrexham	46	13	12	21	51	67	51
Aldershot	46	12	14	20	49	69	50
Halifax Town	46	12	13	21	57	65	49
Colchester United	46	11	10	25	48	75	43

Did you know that?

Newcomers included central-defender Ray Warburton from Rotherham United, who made his debut on the opening day, and forward David Longhurst, who was signed from Peterborough United in January 1990 for £30,000.

City lost more times at home than away, and only once before had this happened (1946–47).

Chris Marples was Clubman of the Year, the first 'keeper since Eddie Blackburn in 1980–81 to win the award.

Top scorer for the second season running was Ian Helliwell.

Average home League attendance was almost identical to 1988–89 at 2,615.

Match No.	Date	Venue	Opponents	Result		Scorers	Attend
1	Aug 19	A	Southend United	L	0–2		2
2	26	H	Peterborough United	W	1–0	Hall	2
3	Sep 1	A	Stockport County	D	2–2	Howlett, Helliwell	2
4	9	H	Rochdale	W	1–0	Spooner (pen)	2
5	16	A	Lincoln City	D	0–0		4
6	23	H	Grimsby Town	L	0–1		3
7	26	A	Burnley	D	1–1	Warburton	7
8	30	H	Wrexham	W	1–0	Dunn	2
9	Oct 7	H	Cambridge United	W	4–2	Barratt, Dixon, Helliwell, Spooner	2
10	13	A	Colchester United	W	2–0	Himsworth (2)	3
11	17	H	Aldershot	D	2–2	Helliwell, Dixon	2
12	21	A	Hartlepool United	W	2–1	Himsworth, Howlett	2
13	28	H	Doncaster Rovers	W	2–1	Dixon, Warburton	2
14	31	A	Scunthorpe United	D	1–1	Helliwell	3
15	Nov 4	H	Torquay United	D	1–1	Kelly (pen)	2
16	11	A	Maidstone United	L	0–1		2
17	24	A	Scarborough	W	3–1	Helliwell, Howlett, Barratt	3
18	Dec 9	H	Gillingham	W	1–0	Canham	2
19	16	A	Chesterfield	D	0–0		3
20	26	H	Halifax Town	L	0–2		3
21	30	H	Hereford United	L	1–2	Dixon	2
22	Jan 1	A	Carlisle United	L	1–2	Kelly (pen)	6
23	13	A	Peterborough United	D	1–1	Hall	2
24	20	H	Southend United	W	2–1	Helliwell (2)	2
25	27	H	Colchester United	W	3–1	Longhurst (2), Reid	2
26	Feb 3	A	Grimsby Town	L	0–3		5
27	6	A	Rochdale	W	1–0	Helliwell	1
28	10	H	Lincoln City	D	0–0		2
29	13	H	Stockport County	L	0–3		2
30	17	A	Gillingham	D	0–0		3
31	24	H	Scarborough	L	1–2	Helliwell	3
32	Mar 3	A	Exeter City	L	1–3	Reid	4
33	6	A	Wrexham	L	0–2		1
34	10	H	Burnley	L	1–3	Reid (pen)	3
35	16	A	Cambridge United	D	2–2	Howlett, Hall	4
36	24	A	Aldershot	D	2–2	Spooner, Helliwell	1
37	31	H	Hartlepool United	D	1–1	Reid	2
38	Apr 2	H	Exeter City	W	3–0	Barratt, Canham, Helliwell	2
39	7	A	Doncaster Rovers	W	2–1	Spooner, Himsworth	2
40	10	H	Scunthorpe United	L	0–1		2
41	14	H	Carlisle United	L	0–1		2
42	16	A	Halifax Town	D	2–2	Canham, Helliwell	1
43	21	H	Chesterfield	W	4–0	Barratt, Helliwell, Dunn, Spooner	2
44	25	A	Hereford United	W	2–1	Helliwell, Barratt	2
45	28	H	Maidstone United	D	0–0		2
46	May 5	A	Torquay United	D	1–1	Spooner	1

A
S

FA Cup

1	Nov 18	H	Grimsby Town	L	1–2	Warburton	4

A
S

Football League (Littlewoods) Cup

1 (1)	Aug 23	A	Hartlepool United	D	3–3	Colville (2), Helliwell	1
1 (2)	29	H	Hartlepool United	W	4–1	Warburton, Spooner (3)	2
2 (1)	Sep 20	H	Southampton	L	0–1		4
2 (2)	Oct 3	A	Southampton	L	0–2		8

A
S

Barratt	Kelly	Reid	Greenough	Warburton	Howlett	Spooner	Helliwell	Colville	Hall	Dunn	Tutill	Dixon	Canham	McMillan	Himsworth	Heathcote	Longhurst	Naylor	Ord	Madden	Crossley	
2	3	4	5	6	7	8	9	10	**11**	12												1
2	3	4	12	6	7	8	9	10	11		**5**											2
2	3	4		6	7	8	9	10	**11**	12	5											3
2	3	**4**		6	7	8	9	10	12		5	11										4
2	3	4		6	7	8	9	10		11	5											5
2	3	4		6	7	8	9	10	12	**11**	5											6
2	3			6	7	8	9	10	11	13	5		**4**	12								7
4	3			6	7	8	9	**10**		11	5	12		2								8
2	3	4		6	7	8	9				5	10			11							9
4	3			6	7	8	9				5	10	12	2	**11**							10
4	3			6	7	8	9				5	10	12	2	**11**							11
4	3			6	7	8	9				5	10		2	11							12
4	3			6	7	8	9				5	10	12	2	**11**							13
4	3			6	7	8	9	12		**10**	5			2	11							14
4	3			6	7	8	9	**10**		13	5		12	2	11							15
4	3			6	7	8	9				5	12	10	2	11							16
4	3			6	7	8	9				5	10	11	2								17
4	3			6	7	8	9				5	10	11	2								18
4	3			6	7	8	9				5	10	**11**	2	12							19
4	3			6	**7**	8	9		12		5	10	11	2	13							20
2	3			6	7	8	9	13			5	10	11	12	4							21
2	3			6	7	8	12	9			5	10	11		**4**							22
2	3				7		12	**9**	8	13	5	10	11		4	6						23
2	3			6	7		9	13	**8**		5	12	11			4	10					24
8	3	**4**		6	7		9		12		5		11			2	10					25
2	3	4		6	7	8	9				5		11				10					26
2	3	4		6	7	8	9	12			5		11				**10**					27
2	3	4		6	7	8	9	10			5		11									28
2	3	**4**		6	7	8	9	10	12	13	5		11									29
2	3			6	7	8	9	**10**	4		5		11					12				30
2	3	4		6	7		9	10	8				**11**		12				5			31
2	3	4	6		**7**		9		8			10	12		11				5			32
2	3	**4**			12	8	9		11		5	13	7						6	10		33
2	3	4		6	7	8	9				**5**		11	12	13					10		34
2	3	4		6	7	8	9		11		5				10							35
2				6	7	8	9		3		5	10	11		**4**					12		36
2		4		6	**7**	8	9		3	13	5		11	12	10							37
7		4		6		8	9		3	10	5		11	2								38
7		4		6		8	9		3	**10**	5		11	2	12							39
7		4		6		8	9		3	**10**	5		11	2	12							40
7		4		6	13	8	9	12	3				11	2						**10**	5	41
7				6	4	8	9	**10**	3	12	5		11	2	13							42
7		12		6	4	8	9		3	10	5		**11**	2								43
7		4		6	11	8	9	12	3	**10**	5			2								44
7		4		6	**11**	8	9	13	3	10	5		12	2								45
7				6	4	8	9	**10**	3		5		11	2	12							46
46	35	24	2	43	41	41	44	17	22	10	42	15	28	21	15	3	4		3	3	1	
		1	1		2		2	7	5	8		4	6	4	8			1		1		
5	2	4		2	4	6	14		3	2		4	3		4		2					

Barratt	Kelly	Reid	Greenough	Warburton	Howlett	Spooner	Helliwell	Colville	Hall	Dunn	Tutill	Dixon	Canham	McMillan	Himsworth	Heathcote	Longhurst	Naylor	Ord	Madden	Crossley	
4	3			6	7	**8**	9		12		5	10	11	2								1
1	1			1	1	1	1				1	1	1	1								
									1													
				1																		

Barratt	Kelly	Reid	Greenough	Warburton	Howlett	Spooner	Helliwell	Colville	Hall	Dunn	Tutill	Dixon	Canham	McMillan	Himsworth	Heathcote	Longhurst	Naylor	Ord	Madden	Crossley	
2	3	4	5	6	7	8	9	10		11												1 (1)
2	3	4		6	7	8	9	10	11		5											1 (2)
2	3	4		6	7	8	9	**10**		11	5	12										2 (1)
4	3			6	7	8	**9**	12		11	5	10		2								2 (2)
4	4	3	1	4	4	4	4	3	1	3	3	1		1								
								1				1										
				1		3	1	2														

York City v Burnley 16 March 1990 programme cover.

Steve Spooner.

1990–91

Division Four

Manager: John Bird

	P	W	D	L	F	A	Pts
Darlington	46	22	17	7	68	38	83
Stockport County	46	23	13	10	84	47	82
Hartlepool United	46	24	10	12	67	48	82
Peterborough United	46	21	17	8	67	45	80
Blackpool	46	23	10	13	78	47	79
Burnley	46	23	10	13	70	51	79
Torquay United	46	18	18	10	64	47	72
Scunthorpe United	46	20	11	15	71	62	71
Scarborough	46	19	12	15	59	56	69
Northampton Town	46	18	13	15	57	58	67
Doncaster Rovers	46	17	14	15	56	46	65
Rochdale	46	15	17	14	50	53	62
Cardiff City	46	15	15	16	43	54	60
Lincoln City	46	14	17	15	50	61	59
Gillingham	46	12	18	16	57	60	54
Walsall	46	12	17	17	48	51	53
Hereford United	46	13	14	19	53	58	53
Chesterfield	46	13	14	19	47	62	53
Maidstone United	46	13	12	21	66	71	51
Carlisle United	46	13	9	24	47	89	48
York City	46	11	13	22	45	57	46
Halifax Town	46	12	10	24	59	79	46
Aldershot	46	10	11	25	61	101	41
Wrexham	46	10	10	26	48	74	40

Did you know that?

The season was overshadowed when striker David Longhurst collapsed and died during a game against Lincoln City at Bootham Crescent on 8 September 1990. The match was abandoned.

Making their debuts this term were Nigel Pepper on the opening day, Jon McCarthy when he made a substitute appearance at home to Gillingham on 29 September 1990, Dean Kiely in the Leyland DAF Trophy on 22 January 1991 and Steve Bushell as a substitute on 15 February 1991 at Northampton.

Nigel Pepper was sent off three times on each occasion against Darlington – twice in League matches and in the FA Cup tie at Feethams.

Ian Helliwell made his final appearance on the last day of the season at Torquay. He was top scorer again, but his tally of only seven League goals equalled the club lowest individual record for a season (1972–73). Just prior to the start of 1991–92 he was transferred to Scunthorpe United.

Steve Tutill was Clubman of the Year.

Average home League attendance was 2,511.

Match No.	Date	Venue	Opponents	Result		Scorers
1	Aug 25	H	Maidstone United	L	0–1	
2	Sep 1	A	Hereford United	L	0–2	
3	18	A	Darlington	D	0–0	
4	22	H	Doncaster Rovers	W	3–1	Warburton, Helliwell, Canham
5	29	H	Gillingham	D	1–1	Howlett (pen)
6	Oct 2	A	Chesterfield	D	2–2	Helliwell, Opp. og
7	6	A	Burnley	D	0–0	
8	13	H	Cardiff City	L	1–2	Warburton
9	16	A	Hartlepool United	W	1–0	Helliwell
10	20	H	Halifax Town	D	3–3	Helliwell, Howlett, Dunn
11	23	A	Walsall	D	1–1	Howlett
12	26	A	Stockport County	L	0–2	
13	Nov 3	H	Torquay United	D	0–0	
14	10	A	Carlisle United	L	0–1	
15	24	H	Northampton Town	L	0–1	
16	Dec 1	H	Scunthorpe United	D	2–2	Canham, Naylor
17	15	A	Peterborough United	L	0–2	
18	21	H	Aldershot	W	2–0	Helliwell (2)
19	29	A	Wrexham	W	4–0	Blackstone (3), Warburton
20	Jan 1	H	Blackpool	L	0–1	
21	5	A	Scarborough	D	2–2	Pepper (pen), Canham
22	12	H	Hereford United	W	1–0	Warburton
23	19	A	Maidstone United	L	4–5	Pepper (pen), Blackstone, Helliwell, Barratt
24	26	H	Hartlepool United	D	0–0	
25	Feb 2	H	Darlington	L	0–1	
26	5	A	Doncaster Rovers	D	2–2	Blackstone, McCarthy
27	15	A	Northampton Town	L	1–2	Hall
28	23	H	Carlisle United	W	2–0	Naylor, Dunn
29	26	H	Lincoln City	W	1–0	Dunn
30	Mar 2	A	Scunthorpe United	L	1–2	Blackstone
31	9	H	Peterborough United	L	0–4	
32	12	H	Chesterfield	L	0–2	
33	16	A	Gillingham	D	0–0	
34	19	A	Cardiff City	L	1–2	Canham
35	23	H	Burnley	W	2–0	McMillan, Naylor
36	26	A	Lincoln City	L	1–2	Lister
37	30	H	Rochdale	L	0–2	
38	Apr 1	A	Aldershot	W	1–0	Opp. og
39	6	H	Wrexham	D	0–0	
40	13	A	Blackpool	L	0–1	
41	16	A	Rochdale	L	1–2	Naylor
42	19	A	Halifax Town	L	1–2	Canham
43	23	H	Scarborough	W	2–0	Canham, McCarthy
44	26	H	Walsall	W	1–0	Naylor
45	May 4	H	Stockport County	L	0–2	
46	11	A	Torquay United	L	1–2	Pepper

2 own-goals

FA Cup

1	Nov 17	A	Darlington	D	1–1	Canham
r	19	H	Darlington	W	1–0	Canham
2	Dec 17	A	Mansfield Town	L	1–2	Pepper

Football League (Rumbelows) Cup

1 (1)	Aug 28	H	Wrexham	L	0–1
1 (2)	Sep 4	A	Wrexham	L	0–2

McMillan	Hall	Reid	Tutill	Warburton	Barratt	Pepper	Helliwell	Longhurst	Canham	Howlett	Dunn	Himsworth	Weatherhead	McCarthy	Blackstone	Cooper	Naylor	Cook	Kiely	Hart	Bushell	Crossley	Curtis	Lister	Grayson	Bradshaw	Wood	
2	3	**4**	5	6	7	8	9	10	11	12	13																	1
2	3	4	5	6	**7**	12	9	10		8	13	11																2
2	3	4	5			7	9		11	8	10		6															3
2	3	4	5	6		7	9		11	8	10																	4
2	3	4	5	6		7	9		11	8	**10**			12														5
2	3	4	**5**	6			9		11	8	7		12		10													6
2	3	4		6		7	9		11	8	**10**		5		12													7
2	3	4		6		**7**	9		11	8	10		5		12													8
2	3	4		6		7	9		11	8			5		10													9
2	3	4		6		7	9		11	8	12		5		**10**													10
2	3	4	5	6		7	9		11	8	10																	11
2	3	4	5	6		7	9		**11**	8	10	12																12
2	3	4	5	6		7	9		**11**	8	10				12													13
2	3	4	5	6		7	9		11	12	**10**				13	8												14
2	3	12	5	6		7	9		11	8				4		**10**	13											15
2	3	4	5	6			9		11					7			10	8										16
2	3	4	5	6	12	7	9		11					10			13	**8**										17
2	3	4	5	6		7	9		11					8			**10**	12										18
2	3	**4**	5	6	12	7			11		10			8	9													19
2	3	4	5	6		7			11		10			**8**	9			12										20
2	3	4	5	6	7	8	9		11						10													21
2	3	**4**	5	6	7	8	9		11		13				10			12										22
2	3		5	**6**	7	8	9		11		12				10			4										23
2	3	4	5		6	7	9		11	8					10				1									24
2	3	4	5		6	7	9		11	8	12				**10**				1									25
2	3	4	5		6	7	9		**11**		12			8	10				1									26
2	3	4	5		7		9				10		12	8			11		1	**6**	13							27
2	3	**4**	5		7		9		13		10			8			11		1		12	6						28
2	3	4	5		7		9				10			**8**			11		1		12	6						29
2	3		5		7		9				10		8		12		11		1		4	**6**						30
2	3		5		7		**9**				10			8	12		11		1		4	6	13					31
2	3	4	5		6	7	**9**		13		12			8	10		11		1									32
2	3		5		7	4	9		11		12			8			**10**							6				33
2	3		5		7	4	9		11					8			10							6				34
2	3		5		7	**4**	9		11		12			8			10							6				35
2	3		5		7	4	9		11		13			8			10				12			**6**				36
2	3		5		7	4	9		11					8	13		10				12	6						37
2	3		5		7	4	9		11					6	10								**8**		12			38
2	3		5			4	9		11		12			6	13		10		1		8		**7**					39
2	3		5		6	4	9		11		12			7	10				1		**8**							40
2	3		5		6	4	**9**		11					7	10		12		1		8							41
2	3		5		6	4			11		12			7	10		**9**		1		8					13		42
2	3		5		6	4			11					7	10		9		1		8							43
2	3		5		6	4			11		12			7	10		**9**		1		8							44
2	3		5		6	4	9		11					7	**10**				1		8		12					45
	3		5		**2**	7	6		11		10			8	9				1		4		12				13	46
45	46	28	42	22	27	38	41	2	39	15	18	1	6	26	20	2	17	3	17	1	10	5	2	4				
		1			2	1			2	2	15	1	2	1	8		3	3			5		3		1	1	1	
1	1			4	1	3	7		6	3	3			2	6		5							1				

McMillan	Hall	Reid	Tutill	Warburton	Barratt	Pepper	Helliwell	Longhurst	Canham	Howlett	Dunn	Himsworth	Weatherhead	McCarthy	Blackstone	Cooper	Naylor	
2	3		5	6		7	9		11	8	10			4				1
2	3		5	6		7	9		11	8	10			4				r
2	3	4	5	6	13	7	9		11		12			8			**10**	2
3	3	1	3	3		3	3		3	2	2			3			1	
					1						1							
						1			2									

McMillan	Hall	Reid	Tutill	Warburton	Barratt	Pepper	Helliwell	Longhurst	Canham	Howlett	Dunn	Himsworth	
2	3	4	5	6	7		9	10		8		11	1 (1)
2	3	4	5	6		12	9	10	7	8	13	**11**	1 (2)
2	2	2	2	2	1		2	2	1	2		2	
						1					1		

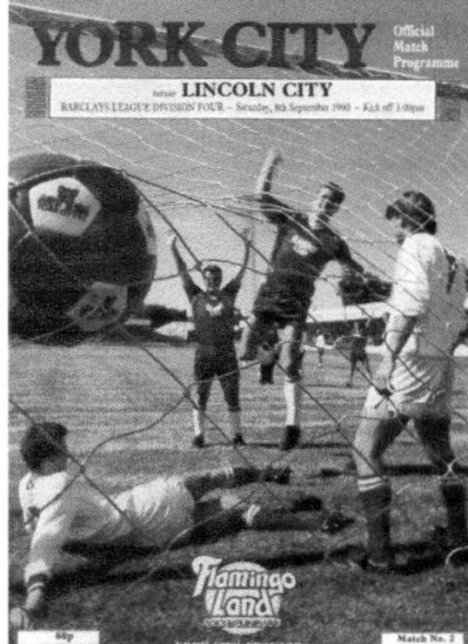

York City v Lincoln City 8 September 1990 programme cover.

David Longhurst.

Memorial Service
at Bootham Crescent, York.
Conducted by
Canon John H. Armstrong S.B.St.J. B.A. Dip.Th.

David John Longhurst
15th January 1965 - 8th September 1990

Saturday 15th September, 1990
3.00 p.m.

1991–92

Division Four

Manager: John Bird, then John Ward

	P	W	D	L	F	A	Pts
Burnley	42	25	8	9	79	43	83
Rotherham United	42	22	11	9	70	37	77
Mansfield Town	42	23	8	11	75	53	77
Blackpool	42	22	10	10	71	45	76
Scunthorpe United	42	21	9	12	64	59	72
Crewe Alexandra	42	20	10	12	66	51	70
Barnet	42	21	6	15	81	61	69
Rochdale	42	18	13	11	57	53	67
Cardiff City	42	17	15	10	66	53	66
Lincoln City	42	17	11	14	50	44	62
Gillingham	42	15	12	15	63	53	57
Scarborough	42	15	12	15	64	68	57
Chesterfield	42	14	11	17	49	61	53
Wrexham	42	14	9	19	52	73	51
Walsall	42	12	13	17	48	58	49
Northampton Town	42	11	13	18	46	57	46
Hereford United	42	12	8	22	44	57	44
Maidstone United	42	8	18	16	45	56	42
York City	42	8	16	18	42	58	40
Halifax Town	42	10	8	24	34	75	38
Doncaster Rovers	42	9	8	25	40	65	35
Carlisle United	42	7	13	22	41	67	34

Did you know that?

Paul Stancliffe made his debut on the opening day.

Following a 1–1 draw in the Autoglass Trophy against Carlisle United in front of 957, the then smallest-ever recorded home attendance, John Bird was dismissed as manager and his successor was John Ward.

The total of eight League wins equalled the club record low set in 1987–88.

Ian Blackstone was top scorer with 11 League and Cup goals.

Jon McCarthy, who was the only ever present, was Clubman of the Year.

Average home League attendance was 2,506.

For the sixth successive season the club failed to reach the third round of the FA Cup, the worst sequence since their election to the Football League in 1929.

Match No.	Date	Venue	Opponents	Result		Scorers	Attend
1	Aug 17	A	Rochdale	D	1–1	Naylor	2
2	24	H	Gillingham	D	1–1	Naylor	2
3	30	A	Halifax Town	D	0–0		2
4	Sep 3	H	Blackpool	W	1–0	McCarthy	2
5	7	H	Chesterfield	L	0–1		2
6	17	A	Hereford United	L	1–2	Stancliffe	3
7	21	H	Wrexham	D	2–2	Naylor, Canham	1
8	28	A	Maidstone United	L	0–1		1
9	Oct 5	H	Scarborough	W	4–1	Canham, Naylor, Tutill, McCarthy	2
10	12	A	Barnet	L	0–2		4
11	19	H	Lincoln City	D	1–1	McCarthy	1
12	25	A	Rotherham United	L	0–4		4
13	Nov 2	H	Walsall	W	2–0	Reid, Hall	1
14	5	A	Burnley	L	1–3	McCarthy	7
15	8	A	Doncaster Rovers	W	1–0	Canham	2
16	30	A	Scunthorpe United	L	0–1		2
17	Dec 14	H	Cardiff City	L	1–3	Canham	1
18	21	A	Gillingham	D	1–1	Barratt	2
19	26	H	Rochdale	L	0–1		2
20	28	H	Halifax Town	D	1–1	Hall	2
21	Jan 1	A	Blackpool	L	1–3	Pepper	3
22	4	H	Mansfield Town	L	1–2	McCarthy	2
23	11	A	Northampton Town	D	2–2	Pepper, Canham	3
24	18	H	Carlisle United	W	2–0	Barratt (2)	1
25	Feb 8	H	Rotherham United	D	1–1	Hall	3
26	11	H	Scunthorpe United	W	3–0	Blackstone, Pepper (2, 1 pen)	2
27	15	A	Cardiff City	L	0–3		8
28	22	H	Northampton Town	D	0–0		2
29	25	A	Crewe Alexandra	L	0–1		3
30	29	A	Mansfield Town	L	2–5	McCarthy, Atkin	3
31	Mar 3	A	Carlisle United	D	1–1	Blackstone	1
32	7	H	Crewe Alexandra	D	1–1	McMillan	2
33	14	A	Walsall	D	1–1	Blackstone	2
34	18	A	Lincoln City	D	0–0		1
35	21	H	Doncaster Rovers	D	1–1	Blackstone	2
36	Apr 4	A	Chesterfield	W	3–1	Blackstone, Naylor (2)	2
37	11	H	Hereford United	W	1–0	Blackstone	1
38	18	A	Wrexham	L	1–2	Naylor	2
39	20	H	Maidstone United	D	1–1	Naylor	1
40	25	A	Scarborough	L	0–1		2
41	28	H	Burnley	L	1–2	Blackstone	7
42	May 2	H	Barnet	L	1–4	Blackstone	2

A
S

FA Cup

1	Nov 16	A	Bridlington Town	W	2–1	Blackstone (2)	1
2	Dec 7	H	Tranmere Rovers	D	1–1	Hall	4
r	17	A	Tranmere Rovers	L	1–2	McCarthy	5

A
S

Football League (Rumbelows) Cup

1 (1)	Aug 20	A	Bolton Wanderers	D	2–2	McCarthy, Blackstone	3
1 (2)	27	H	Bolton Wanderers	L	1–2	Canham	2

A
S

McMillan	Crosby	Reid	Tutill	Stancliffe	McCarthy	Pepper	Blackstone	Naylor	Canham	Marples	Atkin	Hall	Osborne	Barratt	Warburton	Curtis	Gosney	McLoughlin	Tilley	Bushell	Shepstone	
2	3	4	5	6	7	8	9	10	11													1
2	3	4	5	6	7	8	9	10	11	1												2
2	3	4	5		8	7	9			1	6	**11**	10	12								3
2	3	4	5		8	7			11	1			9	10	6							4
2	3	4	5		8	7		12	11	1			**9**	10	6							5
2	3	4	5	6	8	7			11	1		12	**9**	10								6
2		4	5		8	7		9	11	1	6	3	12	**10**								7
		4	5		8	7		**10**	11	1	6	3	9	2		12						8
2		4	5		8	7		**10**	11	1	6	3	12			9						9
2		4	5	6	8	7		10	11	1	13	3	12			**9**						10
2		4	5		8	7		13	11		6	3	9	12		**10**	1					11
2		4	5		8	7		12	11		6	3		**10**		9	1					12
2	3	4	5		8	7	9				6	10		11			1					13
2	3	4	5		8	7	**9**		11		6	10				12	1					14
2	3	4	5		8	7	9		**11**		6	10		12			1					15
2	3	4	5		8	7	9		11	1	6	10										16
2	3	4	5		8	7	9	12	11	1	6	**10**										17
2	3	4	5		8	7			11	1	6	10		9								18
2	**3**	4			8	7	12		11	1	6	10		9	5							19
2	3	4			8	7	12		11	1	6	10		**9**	5							20
2	3	4			8	7	12		11	1	6	10		**9**	5							21
2	3	4	5		8	7	9		11	1		10			6							22
2	3	4	5		8	7			**11**		13			10	6			9	12			23
2	3	4	5		8				11		6	10		7					9			24
2	3	4	5	13	8		12		11		6	10		**7**					9			25
2	3		5		8	7	11				6	10		12					**9**	4		26
2	3		5	13	8	7	11				6	10		12					**9**	4		27
2	3		5	6	8	7	**11**	12				10							9	4		28
2	3		5	6	8	7	11	12				10		**9**						4		29
2	3		5	6	8	7	11	**9**	12		13	10								4		30
2	3		5	6	8	7	9		11			10								4		31
2			5	6	8	7	9	12	11		13	3								**4**	10	32
2		4	5		8	7	9		11		6	3							12		**10**	33
2		4	5		8	7	9		11		6	3			12					**10**		34
2		**4**	5		8	7	9		11		6	3			13				10	12		35
2			5	6	8		11	9			7	3							10	4		36
2			5	6	8		11	9			7	3				12			**10**	4		37
2			5	6	8		11	9			7	3		12					**10**	4		38
2			5	6	8	12	11	9			7	3							10	**4**		39
2			5	6	8		11	9	12		7	3							**10**	4		40
2			5	6	8		11	9			7	3							10	4		41
2			5	6	8	13	11	9	12		7	3							**10**	4		42
41	25	28	39	16	42	33	26	14	28	16	29	36	6	15	7	4	5	1	13	15	2	
				2		2	4	7	3		4	1	3	6	2	3			2	1		
1		1	1	1	6	4	8	8	5		1	3		3								

McMillan	Crosby	Reid	Tutill	Stancliffe	McCarthy	Pepper	Blackstone	Naylor	Canham	Marples	Atkin	Hall	Osborne	Barratt	Warburton	Curtis	Gosney	McLoughlin	Tilley	Bushell	Shepstone	
2	3	4	5		8	7	9			1	6	10		11								1
2	3	4	5		8	7	**9**	12	11	1	6	10										2
2	3	4	5		8	7	9		11	1	6	10										r
3	3	3	3		3	3	3		2	3	3	3		1								
								1														
					1		2					1										

McMillan	Crosby	Reid	Tutill	Stancliffe	McCarthy	Pepper	Blackstone	Naylor	Canham	Marples	Atkin	Hall	Osborne	Barratt	Warburton	Curtis	Gosney	McLoughlin	Tilley	Bushell	Shepstone	
2	3	4	5	**6**	8	7	9	10	11	1	12	13										1 (1)
2	3	4			8	7	9		**11**	1	5	6	10			12						1 (2)
2	2	2	1	1	2	2	2	1	2	2	1	1	1									
											1	1				1						
					1		1		1													

York City v Maidstone United 20 April 1992 programme cover.

Ian Blackstone.

1992–93

Division Three

Manager: John Ward, then Alan Little

	P	W	D	L	F	A	Pts
Cardiff City	42	25	8	9	77	47	83
Wrexham	42	23	11	8	75	52	80
Barnet	42	23	10	9	66	48	79
York City	42	21	12	9	72	45	75
Walsall	42	22	7	13	76	61	73
Crewe Alexandra	42	21	7	14	75	56	70
Bury	42	18	9	15	63	55	63
Lincoln City	42	18	9	15	57	53	63
Shrewsbury Town	42	17	11	14	57	52	62
Colchester United	42	18	5	19	67	76	59
Rochdale	42	16	10	16	70	70	58
Chesterfield	42	15	11	16	59	63	56
Scarborough	42	15	9	18	66	71	54
Scunthorpe United	42	14	12	16	57	54	54
Darlington	42	12	14	16	48	53	50
Doncaster Rovers	42	11	14	17	42	57	47
Hereford United	42	10	15	17	47	60	45
Carlisle United	42	11	11	20	51	65	44
Torquay United	42	12	7	23	45	67	43
Northampton Town	42	11	8	23	48	74	41
Gillingham	42	9	13	20	48	64	40
Halifax Town	42	9	9	24	45	68	36

Did you know that?

Notable newcomers included Paul Barnes, a £50,000 signing from Stoke City, and he scored on his debut in an opening day win against Shrewsbury Town. It was the first time since 1986–87 that City had started with a victory.

Also making his debut that day was Gary Swann from Preston North End.

The campaign opened with four straight wins – a club record start.

In the 5–1 win over Scunthorpe United on 27 February 1993 Paul Barnes became the first City player to score four goals in a match for over 32 years. He also hit a hat-trick in the 5–1 win at Barnet on 13 March 1993. This was the first game in charge for Alan Little following the departure of John Ward to Bristol Rovers. In total Barnes netted 21 League goals and was top marksman.

Clubman of the Year was skipper Paul Stancliffe.

Average League attendance at Bootham Crescent was 3,946, the highest since 1985–86.

For the first time in their history City figured in the promotion Play-offs and triumphed on their first visit to Wembley. The semi-final attendance of 9,206 against Bury was the best since the visit of Liverpool in February 1986.

City fell at the first hurdle in each of the three Cup competitions for the first time.

Match No.	Date	Venue	Opponents	Result		Scorers
1	Aug 18	H	Shrewsbury Town	W	2–0	Warburton, Barnes
2	22	A	Lincoln City	W	1–0	Barnes
3	29	H	Wrexham	W	4–0	Blackstone, Pepper (pen), Borthwick, Barnes
4	Sep 1	H	Torquay United	W	2–1	Pepper (pen), Warburton
5	5	A	Walsall	L	1–3	Warburton
6	12	A	Carlisle United	W	2–1	Pepper (pen), McCarthy
7	15	H	Hereford United	W	4–2	Borthwick (2), Blackstone, McCarthy
8	19	H	Colchester United	W	2–0	Blackstone (2)
9	25	A	Darlington	W	1–0	Blackstone
10	Oct 3	H	Doncaster Rovers	D	1–1	Pepper (pen)
11	10	A	Scunthorpe United	W	2–1	McCarthy, Pepper (pen)
12	17	H	Rochdale	W	3–0	Barnes, Borthwick (2)
13	31	A	Bury	D	1–1	Borthwick
14	Nov 7	H	Barnet	W	2–0	Barnes, Pepper (pen)
15	21	A	Northampton Town	L	3–4	Hall, Blackstone (2)
16	28	H	Crewe Alexandra	W	3–1	Atkin (2), Blackstone
17	Dec 12	H	Chesterfield	D	0–0	
18	19	A	Scarborough	L	2–4	Barnes, Canham
19	26	A	Cardiff City	D	3–3	Blackstone (2), Barnes
20	29	H	Halifax Town	D	1–1	Barnes
21	Jan 9	A	Hereford United	D	1–1	Borthwick
22	16	H	Darlington	D	0–0	
23	19	H	Carlisle United	D	2–2	Borthwick, Barnes
24	22	A	Colchester United	D	0–0	
25	26	A	Wrexham	L	0–3	
26	30	H	Lincoln City	W	2–0	Stancliffe, Canham
27	Feb 6	A	Shrewsbury Town	D	1–1	Canham
28	13	H	Walsall	L	0–1	
29	20	A	Torquay United	L	0–1	
30	27	H	Scunthorpe United	W	5–1	Barnes (4), Blackstone
31	Mar 5	A	Doncaster Rovers	W	1–0	Blackstone
32	9	H	Gillingham	D	1–1	Barnes
33	13	A	Barnet	W	5–1	Barnes (3), Blackstone, Opp. og
34	20	H	Bury	L	1–2	McCarthy
35	23	A	Crewe Alexandra	L	1–3	McCarthy
36	26	H	Northampton Town	W	2–1	Canham, Blackstone
37	Apr 2	A	Gillingham	W	4–1	Blackstone, Barnes (2), McCarthy
38	6	A	Chesterfield	D	1–1	Barnes
39	10	H	Cardiff City	W	3–1	McCarthy, Blackstone, Pepper
40	12	A	Halifax Town	W	1–0	Barnes
41	17	H	Scarborough	W	1–0	Pepper (pen)
42	24	A	Rochdale	L	0–1	

1 own-goal

Play-offs

SF	May 16	A	Bury	D	0–0	
SF	19	H	Bury	W	1–0	Swann
F	29	N#	Crewe Alexandra	D	1–1*	Swann

\# At Wembley. * After extra-time, City won 5–3 on penalties.

FA Cup

1	Nov 14	H	Stockport County	L	1–3	Canham

Football League (Coca-Cola) Cup

1 (1)	Aug 18	A	Chesterfield	L	0–2	
1 (2)	25	H	Chesterfield	D	0–0	

McMillan	Hall	Pepper	Stancliffe	Warburton	McCarthy	Borthwick	Barnes	Swann	Blackstone	Canham	Atkin	Barratt	Tutill	Jordan	Marples	Bushell	Tilley	Naylor	
2	3	4	5	6	7	8	9	10	**11**	12									1
2	3	4	**5**	6	7	8	9	10	11		12								2
2	3	4	**5**	6	7	8	9	10	11		12								3
2	3	4	5	6	7	8	9	10	11										4
2	3	4	5	6	7	**8**	9	10	11	12									5
2	3	4	5	6	7	8	9	10	**11**		12								6
2	3	4	5	6	7	8	9	10	11										7
2	3	4	5	6	7	8	9	10	11										8
2	3	4	5	6	**7**	8	9	10	11			12							9
2	3	4	5		7	8	9	10	11		6								10
2	3	4	5		**7**	8	9	10	11	12	6		13						11
2	3	4	5		7	8	9	10	**11**	12	6			13					12
2	3	4	5		7	8	9	10	**11**	12	6								13
2	3	4	5		7	8	9	10	**11**	12	6								14
2	3		5		7	8	9	10	11		6				1	4			15
2	3		5		7	8	9	10	**11**	12	6				1	4			16
2	3		5	12	7	8	9	10	11		6					**4**			17
2	3	4	5		7	**8**	9	10	11	13	6						12		18
2	3	4	5		7	8	9	10	11		6								19
2	3	4	5		7	**8**	9	10	11		6						12		20
2	3	4	5		7	8	9	10	**11**	12	6								21
2	3	4	5		7	8	9	10	**11**	12	6								22
2	3	4	**5**		7	8	9	10	11	12	6								23
2	3	4	5		7	**8**	9	10		11			6					12	24
2	3	4	5		7	**8**	9	10		11			6					12	25
2	3	4	5		7		**9**		12	11		13	6			10	8		26
2	3	4	5		7		9			11		12	6			**10**	8		27
2	3	4	**5**		7				9	11		12	6			10	8	13	28
2	3	4			7				12	11	5	13	6			10	**8**	9	29
2	3	4	5		7	8	9	10	11		6								30
2	3	4	5		7	**8**	9	10	11	12	6								31
2	3	4	5		7	**8**	9	10	11	12	6								32
2	3	4	5		7		9	10	11	8	6								33
2	3	4	5		7	13	9	10	11	8	6	12							34
2	3		5		7		9	10	11	8	6	4							35
2	3		5		7		9	10	11	8	6	4							36
2	3		5		7		9	10	11	8	6	4							37
2	3		5		7	12	9	10	11	8	6	**4**	13						38
2	3	4	5		7	12	9	10	**11**	8	6								39
2	3	4	5		7		9	10	11	8	6								40
2	3	4	5		7	12	9	10	**11**	8	6								41
2	3		5		7	12	9	10	11	8	6					**4**			42
42	42	34	41	9	42	28	40	38	37	16	28	4	6		2	8	4	1	
				1		5			2	13	3	6	2	1			2	3	
	1	8	1	3	7	8	21		16	4	2								

McMillan	Hall	Pepper	Stancliffe	Warburton	McCarthy	Borthwick	Barnes	Swann	Blackstone	Canham	Atkin	Barratt	Tutill	Jordan	Marples	Bushell	Tilley	Naylor	
2	3	4	5		7		9	10	11	8	6								SF
2	3	4	5		7	12	9	10	**11**	8	6								SF
2	3	4	**5**		7		9	10	11	8	6		12						F
3	3	3	3		3		3	3	3	3	3								
						1							1						
								2											

McMillan	Hall	Pepper	Stancliffe	Warburton	McCarthy	Borthwick	Barnes	Swann	Blackstone	Canham	Atkin	Barratt	Tutill	Jordan	Marples	Bushell	Tilley	Naylor	
2	3		5		7	8	9	10		11	6			4	1				1
1	1		1		1	1	1	1		1	1			1	1				
										1									

McMillan	Hall	Pepper	Stancliffe	Warburton	McCarthy	Borthwick	Barnes	Swann	Blackstone	Canham	Atkin	Barratt	Tutill	Jordan	Marples	Bushell	Tilley	Naylor	
2	3	4	5	6	7	**8**	9	10	12	11									1 (1)
2	3	4		6	7	8	9	10	11				5					12	1 (2)
2	2	2	1	2	2	2	2	2	1	1			1						
									1									1	

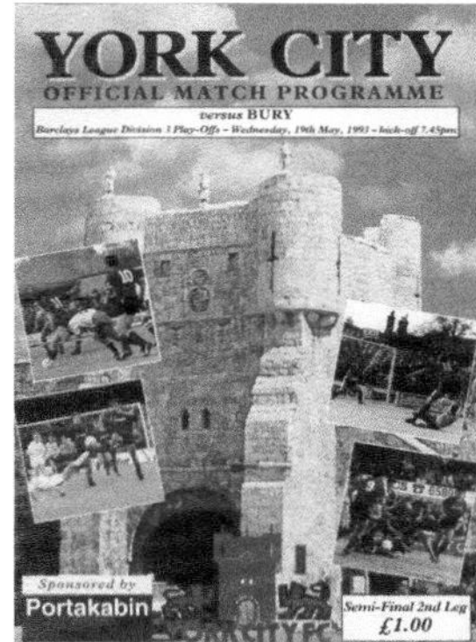

York City v Bury 19 May 1993 programme cover.

Dean Kiely with teammates Paul Stancliffe, Paul Atkin and Andy McMillan celebrate the victory over Bury in the Play-off semi-final.

1993–94

Division Two

Manager: Alan Little

	P	W	D	L	F	A	Pts
Reading	46	26	11	9	81	44	89
Port Vale	46	26	10	10	79	46	88
Plymouth Argyle	46	25	10	11	88	56	85
Stockport County	46	24	13	9	74	44	85
York City	46	21	12	13	64	40	75
Burnley	46	21	10	15	79	58	73
Bradford City	46	19	13	14	61	53	70
Bristol Rovers	46	20	10	16	60	59	70
Hull City	46	18	14	14	62	54	68
Cambridge United	46	19	9	18	79	73	66
Huddersfield Town	46	17	14	15	58	61	65
Wrexham	46	17	11	18	66	77	62
Swansea City	46	16	12	18	56	58	60
Brighton & Hove Albion	46	15	14	17	60	67	59
Rotherham United	46	15	13	18	63	60	58
Brentford	46	13	19	14	57	55	58
Bournemouth	46	14	15	17	51	59	57
Leyton Orient	46	14	14	18	57	71	56
Cardiff City	46	13	15	18	66	79	54
Blackpool	46	16	5	25	63	75	53
Fulham	46	14	10	22	50	63	52
Exeter City	46	11	12	23	52	83	45
Hartlepool United	46	9	9	28	41	87	36
Barnet	46	5	13	28	41	86	28

Did you know that?

For the second successive campaign City figured in the promotion Play-offs and narrowly failed to reach the second tier for the second time in their history.

The 5–0 win at Blackpool on 28 December 1993 was City's biggest-ever away victory in the Football League.

Ray Warburton's last senior appearance was at home to Mansfield Town in the Autoglass Trophy on 4 December 1993.

Graeme Murty made his Football League debut on 21 April 1994 at Port Vale.

Gary Swann and Ian Blackstone both made their final appearances for the club in the Play-off game at Stockport County.

Only 13 League goals were conceded at Bootham Crescent, a new club record, and 20 clean sheets equalled the record of 1983–84.

Paul Barnes was leading scorer and Clubman of the Year.

Average home League attendance of 4,633 was the highest since 1984–85.

For the second year running City were knocked out of all three Cup competitions in the first round.

Match No.	Date	Venue	Opponents	Result		Scorers	Attend
1	Aug 14	H	Swansea City	W	2–1	Barnes (2)	4
2	21	A	Exeter City	W	2–1	Swann, Naylor	2
3	28	H	Rotherham United	D	0–0		4
4	31	A	Bournemouth	L	1–3	Canham	4
5	Sep 4	A	Leyton Orient	L	0–2		3
6	11	H	Brighton & Hove Albion	W	3–1	McCarthy (2), Swann	3
7	14	H	Stockport County	L	1–2	Tutill	3
8	18	A	Fulham	W	1–0	Barnes	3
9	25	A	Hartlepool United	W	2–0	McCarthy, Barratt	3
10	Oct 2	H	Cardiff City	W	5–0	Cooper (2), Swann, Barnes, McCarthy	3
11	9	H	Huddersfield Town	L	0–2		6
12	16	A	Plymouth Argyle	L	1–2	Barnes	5
13	23	H	Brentford	L	0–2		3
14	30	A	Bradford City	D	0–0		6
15	Nov 2	H	Bristol Rovers	L	0–1		3
16	6	A	Burnley	L	1–2	Barnes	10
17	20	H	Barnet	D	1–1	Bushell	2
18	27	A	Wrexham	D	1–1	Tutill	3
19	Dec 11	H	Exeter City	W	3–0	Barnes (2, 2 pens), Cooper	2
20	18	A	Swansea City	W	2–1	Cooper, Barnes	2
21	27	H	Hull City	D	0–0		8
22	28	A	Blackpool	W	5–0	Barnes (2), Cooper, Canham, Barratt	4
23	Jan 1	H	Port Vale	W	1–0	Barnes	5
24	3	A	Reading	L	1–2	Opp. og	7
25	8	A	Cambridge United	W	2–0	Barnes, Tutill	3
26	15	H	Plymouth Argyle	D	0–0		4
27	22	A	Huddersfield Town	L	2–3	Barnes (2)	6
28	29	H	Bradford City	D	1–1	Bushell	5
29	Feb 5	A	Brentford	D	1–1	Barnes	6
30	12	H	Cambridge United	W	2–0	Barnes (2)	3
31	19	A	Rotherham United	L	1–2	Blackstone	3
32	26	H	Leyton Orient	W	3–0	Blackstone (2), Barnes	3
33	Mar 5	A	Brighton & Hove Albion	L	0–2		8
34	12	H	Fulham	W	2–0	McCarthy, Barnes (pen)	3
35	15	A	Stockport County	W	2–1	Barnes (2)	3
36	19	H	Hartlepool United	W	3–0	McCarthy, Barnes, Tutill	3
37	22	H	Bournemouth	W	2–0	Stancliffe, Blackstone	3
38	26	A	Cardiff City	D	0–0		4
39	29	H	Reading	W	1–0	Swann	5
40	Apr 2	A	Hull City	D	1–1	McCarthy	8
41	4	H	Blackpool	W	2–1	Bushell, Blackstone	5
42	16	A	Bristol Rovers	W	1–0	Bushell	5
43	21	A	Port Vale	L	1–2	Cooper	8
44	23	H	Burnley	D	0–0		8
45	30	A	Barnet	W	3–1	Barnes, Blackstone (2)	2
46	May 7	H	Wrexham	D	1–1	Canham	5
							A
							S

Play-offs

						1 own-goal	
SF	May 15	H	Stockport County	D	0–0		8
SF	18	A	Stockport County	L	0–1		6
							A
							S

FA Cup

1	Nov 13	A	Burnley	D	0–0		10
r	30	H	Burnley	L	2–3	Canham, McCarthy	5
							A
							S

Football League (Coca-Cola) Cup

1 (1)	Aug 17	A	Rochdale	L	0–2		1
1 (2)	24	H	Rochdale	D	0–0		2
							A
							S

McMillan	Hall	Pepper	Tutill	Atkin	McCarthy	Cooper	Barnes	Swann	Canham	Naylor	Barratt	Warburton	Blackstone	Bushell	Stancliffe	Murty	Jordan	
2	3	4	5	6	7	**8**	9	10	11	12	13							1
2	3	4	5	6	7	8		**10**	11	**9**	12	13						2
2	3	4	5	6	7	8		10	11	**9**			12					3
2	3	4	5	6	7	8	**9**	**10**	11		13		12					4
2	3	4	5	6	7	8	9	10	11									5
2	3	4	5	6	7		9	10	**11**	8			12	13				6
2	3	4	5	6	7	8	9	10					11					7
2	3	4	5	6	7	8	9	10			12		**11**					8
2	3	4	5	6	7	8	9	10			11							9
2	3	**4**	5	6	7	8	9	10			11		12					10
2	3	4	5	6	7	8	9	10		12	**11**							11
2	3	4	5	6	7	**8**	9	10			11		12					12
2	3	4	5	**6**	7	8	9	10			12		11					13
2	3	4	5		7	8	9	10				6	11					14
2	3	4	5		7	8	9	10				6	11					15
2	3	4	5		7	8	9	10			12	6	**11**					16
2	3	4	5		7	8			11	9		6		10				17
2	3	4	5		7	8			11	9		6		10				18
2	3		5		7	8	9	4	11					10	6			19
2	3		5		7	8	9	4	**11**		12			10	6			20
2	3		5		7	8	9	4	11					10	6			21
2	3		5		7	8	9	4	11		12			**10**	6			22
2	3		5		**7**	8	9	4	11		12			10	6			23
2	3		5		7	**8**	9	4	11		12			10	6			24
2	3		5		7	**8**	9	4	11		12			10	6			25
2	3		5		7		9	4	11				8	10	6			26
2	3	12	5		7		9	4	11				8	**10**	6			27
2	3		5		7		9	4	11				8	10	6			28
2			5		7	8	9	4	3				11	10	6			29
2	3	13	5		7	**8**	9	4	11				12	10	6			30
2	3	12	5		7		9	**4**	11				8	10	6			31
2	3		5		7		9	4	11				8	10	6			32
2	3	13	5		7		9	4	11	12			**8**	10	6			33
2	3		5		7		9	4	11				8	10	6			34
2	3		5		7		9	4	**11**		12		8	10	6			35
2	3		5		7		9	4	11				8	10	6			36
2	3		5		7		9	4	11				8	10	6			37
2	3		5		7		9	4	11		12		**8**	10	6			38
2	3		5		7		9	4	11				8	10	6			39
2	3		5		7		9	4	11				8	10	6			40
2	3		5		**7**		9	4	11	13	12		8	10	6			41
2	3		5	13		12	9	4	11		7		**8**	10	6			42
2	3		5			8	9	4	11				12	10	6	**7**		43
2	3		5		7	**8**	9	4	11				12	10	6			44
2	3		5		7		9	4	11				8	10	6			45
2	3	12	5		7		9	4	11	13			8	**10**	6			46
46	45	18	46	13	44	28	42	44	36	5	5	5	24	30	28	1		
		5		1		1				5	14	1	8	1				
			4		7	6	24	4	3	1	2		7	4	1			
2	3		5		7	12	9	4	11				**8**	10	6			SF
2	3	12	5		**7**		9	4	11				8	10	6			SF
2	2		2		2		2	2	2				2	2	2			
		1				1												

McMillan	Hall	Pepper	Tutill	Atkin	McCarthy	Cooper	Barnes	Swann	Canham	Naylor	Barratt	Warburton	Blackstone	Bushell	Stancliffe	Murty	Jordan	
2	3	4	5		7	8			11		9	6		10				1
2	3	4	5		7		9		11	**8**		6	12	10				r
2	2	2	2		2	1	1		2	1	1	2		2				
													1					
					1				1									
2	3	4	5	6	7	8	**9**	10	11	12								1 (1)
2	3	4	5	6	7	8		10	11	9								1 (2)
2	2	2	2	2	2	2	1	2	2	1								
										1								

York City v Stockport County 15 May 1994 programme cover.

Paul Barnes.

1994–95

Division Two

Manager: Alan Little

	P	W	D	L	F	A	Pts
Birmingham City	46	25	14	7	84	37	89
Brentford	46	25	10	11	81	39	85
Crewe Alexandra	46	25	8	13	80	68	83
Bristol Rovers	46	22	16	8	70	40	82
Huddersfield Town	46	22	15	9	79	49	81
Wycombe Wanderers	46	21	15	10	60	46	78
Oxford United	46	21	12	13	66	52	75
Hull City	46	21	11	14	70	57	74
York City	46	21	9	16	67	51	72
Swansea City	46	19	14	13	57	45	71
Stockport County	46	19	8	19	63	60	65
Blackpool	46	18	10	18	64	70	64
Wrexham	46	16	15	15	65	64	63
Bradford City	46	16	12	18	57	64	60
Peterborough United	46	14	18	14	54	69	60
Brighton & Hove Albion	46	14	17	15	54	53	59
Rotherham United	46	14	14	18	57	61	56
Shrewsbury Town	46	13	14	19	54	62	53
Bournemouth	46	13	11	22	49	69	50
Cambridge United	46	11	15	20	52	69	48
Plymouth Argyle	46	12	10	24	45	83	46
Cardiff City	46	9	11	26	46	74	38
Chester City	46	6	11	29	37	84	29
Leyton Orient	46	6	8	32	30	75	26

Did you know that?

For the second successive season City won 5–0 at Blackpool (18 April 1995), thus equalling the club record away victory.

For the third successive campaign Paul Barnes topped the scoring charts and hit two hat-tricks during the season.

Two notable departures at the end of the season were wingmen Jon McCarthy and Tony Canham, who both made their final appearances on the last day at Peterborough United.

McCarthy, who was Clubman of the Year, was transferred to Port Vale in August 1995 for a then club record fee received of £450,000.

Canham was released after 413 senior appearances, the then fifth-highest in the club's history.

Average home League attendance was 3,685.

For the third successive campaign City fell at the first hurdle in the FA Cup, and not since 1985–86 had they progressed beyond the second round of any of the Cups.

Match No.	Date	Venue	Opponents	Result		Scorers
1	Aug 13	H	Crewe Alexandra	L	1–2	Cooper
2	20	A	Bristol Rovers	L	1–3	McCarthy
3	27	H	Cardiff City	D	1–1	Barnes
4	31	A	Brighton & Hove Albion	L	0–1	
5	Sep 3	A	Bournemouth	W	4–1	Barnes (3), McCarthy
6	10	H	ShrewsburyTown	W	3–0	Barnes, Pepper, Naylor
7	13	H	Brentford	W	2–1	Pepper, Jordan
8	17	A	Bradford City	D	0–0	
9	24	A	Swansea City	D	0–0	
10	Oct 1	H	Stockport County	L	2–4	Barnes (pen), Naylor
11	8	H	Peterborough United	D	1–1	McCarthy
12	15	A	Rotherham United	L	1–2	Pepper
13	22	H	Chester City	W	2–0	McCarthy, Barnes
14	29	A	Wycombe Wanderers	D	0–0	
15	Nov 1	A	Hull City	L	0–3	
16	5	H	Huddersfield Town	W	3–0	Baker, Naylor, Barnes
17	19	A	Leyton Orient	W	1–0	Barnes
18	26	H	Plymouth Arygle	W	1–0	McCarthy
19	Dec 10	H	Bristol Rovers	L	0–3	
20	16	A	Crewe Alexandra	L	1–2	Barnes (pen)
21	26	H	Blackpool	W	4–0	Barnes (3), Naylor
22	28	A	Cambridge United	L	0–1	
23	Jan 2	A	Oxford United	W	2–0	Naylor, Opp. og
24	7	A	Chester City	W	4–0	Barnes, Jordan, McCarthy, Opp. og
25	14	H	Birmingham City	W	2–0	McCarthy, Canham
26	Feb 4	A	Plymouth Arygle	W	2–1	Baker, Naylor
27	7	H	Wrexham	L	0–1	
28	18	A	Birmingham City	L	2–4	Baker, McCarthy
29	21	H	Leyton Orient	W	4–1	Opp. og, Baker (2), Naylor
30	25	A	Stockport County	W	3–2	Baker, Pepper, Opp. og
31	28	A	Huddersfield Town	L	0–3	
32	Mar 4	H	Swansea City	L	2–4	Canham, Barnes
33	7	H	Bournemouth	W	1–0	Jordan
34	11	A	Cardiff City	W	2–1	Naylor (2)
35	14	H	Wycombe Wanderers	D	0–0	
36	18	H	Brighton & Hove Albion	W	1–0	Barnes
37	21	A	ShrewsburyTown	L	0–1	
38	25	H	Bradford City	D	0–0	
39	Apr 1	A	Brentford	L	0–3	
40	4	H	Hull City	W	3–1	Baker (2), Murty
41	8	A	Wrexham	D	1–1	Peverell
42	15	H	Cambridge United	W	2–0	Barras, McMillan
43	18	A	Blackpool	W	5–0	Baker (2, 1 pen), Bushell, McCarthy, Murty
44	22	H	Oxford United	L	0–2	
45	29	H	Rotherham United	W	2–0	Baker (2, 1 pen)
46	May 6	A	Peterborough United	D	1–1	Baker

4 own-goals

FA Cup

1	Nov 12	H	Rotherham United	D	3–3	Naylor (2), McCarthy
r	22	A	Rotherham United	L	0–3	

Football League (Coca-Cola) Cup

1 (1)	Aug 16	A	Burnley	L	0–1	
1 (2)	23	H	Burnley	D	2–2	Pepper, Cooper

McMillan	Hall	Pepper	Tutill	Stancliffe	McCarthy	Cooper	Barnes	Bushell	Canham	Naylor	Barras	Atkin	Jordan	Simpson	Wilson	Baker	Murty	Williams	Barratt	Peverell	Scaife	
2	3	4	5	6	7	8	**9**	10	11	12												1
2	3	4	5		7	8	9	10	11		**6**	12										2
2	3	4	5		7	8	9	10	11		6											3
2	3	4	5		7	8	9	**10**	11		6	12										4
2	12	4	5		7	8	9		11		6	3	**10**									5
2	12	4	5		7	8	9		11	13	**6**	3	10									6
2		4	5		7	8	9		**11**		12	6	10	3								7
2	3	4	5		7	**8**	9			12	6	11	10									8
2	3	4	5		7	8	9				6	11	10									9
2	3	4	5		7		9		12	8	6	**11**	10									10
2		4	5		7		9		11	8	6		10		3							11
2		4	5		7		9		11	8	6		**10**		3	12						12
2		4	5		7		9		11	8	6		10		3							13
2	12	4	**5**		7		9		11	8	6		10		3							14
2	3	4		5	7		9		11	8	6		**10**			12						15
2	3	4		5	7		9		**11**	8	6		12			10						16
2				5	7		9		11	**8**	6	4	12		3	10						17
2		4			7		9		11	**8**	6	5	12		3	10						18
2	3	4	13		7		9		11	12	6	5	**8**			10						19
2	3	4	12		7		9		11		6	**5**	8			10	13					20
2	3	4	5		7		9		11	8		6	**10**				12	13				21
2	3	4	5		7		9		11	8		6	10									22
2	11	4	5		7		9			8		6	10		3							23
2	11	4	5		7		9			**8**		6	10		3	12	13					24
2	11	4	5		7				12			6	10		3	9	**8**					25
2	11	4	5		7				12	13		6	10		3	9	**8**					26
2	11	4	5		7		12		13	8		6	10		3	**9**						27
2	13	4	5		7		**9**		11	8		6	10		3	12						28
2		4	5		7				11	8		6			3	9	10					29
2	10	4	5						11			6	**8**		3	9			12	7		30
2	10	4	5		7		8		11		12	**6**			3	9				13		31
2		**4**	5		7		8		11			6	10		3	9			12			32
	3		5		7		**8**		11	12	13	6	10			9	4		2			33
	3		5		7		8			11	12	6	**10**			9	4		2			34
12	11		5				8			**10**		6	7		3	9	4		2			35
12	11		5		**7**		9			13		6	4		3	10	8		2			36
12	11		5		7		9					6	4		**3**	10	8		2			37
12	**11**	4	5		7		9			10	6				3	13	8		2			38
2		**4**	5		7		9	8			6	13			3	10	11		12			39
2	3		5		7			8		**9**	6		4			10	11			12		40
2	3				7			**4**	12	10	6	5	8			9	11			13		41
2	3		5		7			**4**	11		6		8			9	10			12	13	42
2	3		5		7			**4**	11		6		8			9	10			12		43
	3		**5**		7				11	13	6	12	4			9	10		2	8		44
2	3	4			7		**8**		11		6	5	13			9	10			12		45
2	3	4			7			**8**	11		6	5			12	9	10			13		46
39	33	35	37	4	44	9	35	10	30	21	27	30	33	1	21	25	17		7	2		
4	4		2				1		5	8	4	4	4		1	5	3	1	3	7	1	
1		4			9	1	16	1	2	9	1		3			13	2			1		

McMillan	Hall	Pepper	Tutill	Stancliffe	McCarthy	Cooper	Barnes	Bushell	Canham	Naylor	Barras	Atkin	Jordan	Simpson	Wilson	Baker	Murty	Williams	Barratt	Peverell	Scaife	
2				5	7		9		11	8	6	4			3	10						1
2				5	7		9		11	8	6	4			3	10						r
2				2	2		2		2	2	2	2			2	2						
					1					2												

McMillan	Hall	Pepper	Tutill	Stancliffe	McCarthy	Cooper	Barnes	Bushell	Canham	Naylor	Barras	Atkin	Jordan	Simpson	Wilson	Baker	Murty	Williams	Barratt	Peverell	Scaife	
2	3	4	5		7	8	9	10	11		6											1 (1)
2	3	4	5		7	8	9	10	11		6											1 (2)
2	2	2	2		2	2	2	2	2		2											
		1				1																

York City v Huddersfield Town 5 November 1994 programme cover.

Jon McCarthy.

1995–96

Division Two

Manager: Alan Little

	P	W	D	L	F	A	Pts
Swindon Town	46	25	17	4	71	34	92
Oxford United	46	24	11	11	76	39	83
Blackpool	46	23	13	10	67	40	82
Notts County	46	21	15	10	63	39	78
Crewe Alexandra	46	22	7	17	77	60	73
Bradford City	46	22	7	17	71	69	73
Chesterfield	46	20	12	14	56	51	72
Wrexham	46	18	16	12	76	55	70
Stockport County	46	19	13	14	61	47	70
Bristol Rovers	46	20	10	16	57	60	70
Walsall	46	19	12	15	60	45	69
Wycombe Wanderers	46	15	15	16	63	59	60
Bristol City	46	15	15	16	55	60	60
Bournemouth	46	16	10	20	51	70	58
Brentford	46	15	13	18	43	49	58
Rotherham United	46	14	14	18	54	62	56
Burnley	46	14	13	19	56	68	55
Shrewsbury Town	46	13	14	19	58	70	53
Peterborough United	46	13	13	20	59	66	52
York City	46	13	13	20	58	73	52
Carlisle United	46	12	13	21	57	72	49
Swansea City	46	11	14	21	43	79	47
Brighton & Hove Albion	46	10	10	26	46	69	40
Hull City	46	5	16	25	36	78	31

Did you know that?

Paul Stephenson signed from Millwall and made his debut on the opening day.

'Keeper Andy Warrington made his first senior appearance at home to Manchester United on 3 October 1995 in the Coca-Cola Cup, following injury to Dean Kiely, who thus missed his first game since December 1992.

Midfielder Adrian Randall was signed from Burnley in December 1995 for a club record fee paid of £140,000, and his first game was at Rotherham United on 6 January 1996.

Richard Cresswell made his Football League debut when coming on as a substitute at Brentford on 20 January 1996. He scored his first League goal at Bradford City on 2 March 1996 and this was Paul Barnes's last game in City colours.

Barnes was transferred to Birmingham City for a reported fee of £350,000. He made 179 League and Cup appearances for the club and scored 85 goals, putting him in City's top 10 leading marksmen.

Gary Bull joined the club from Birmingham City and on 30 March 1996 scored three goals at Wrexham, the last recorded hat-trick for City in the Football League. He was the fourth City player in post-war football to achieve this feat at the Racecourse Ground (Arthur Bottom 1954, Norman Wilkinson 1955, Ian Blackstone 1990).

City avoided relegation by winning at Brighton in a rearranged game on a Thursday morning (9 May 1996). Dean Kiely made his last City appearance in this game. The original match on 27 April was abandoned because of a crowd disturbance.

Clubman of the Year was Andy McMillan.

Average home League attendance was 3,538.

Triumph came in the Coca-Cola Cup against Manchester United, but for the fourth successive season City failed to reach the second round of the FA Cup.

Match No.	Date	Venue	Opponents	Result		Scorers	Attend
1	Aug 12	H	Brentford	D	2–2	Baker, Barnes	3
2	19	A	Swindon Town	L	0–3		7
3	26	H	Crewe Alexandra	L	2–3	Baker, Barnes	3
4	29	A	Chesterfield	L	1–2	Pepper	3
5	Sep 3	A	Oxford United	L	0–2		4
6	9	H	Bristol Rovers	L	0–1		4
7	12	H	Burnley	D	1–1	Barnes	4
8	16	A	Swansea City	W	1–0	Opp. og	2
9	23	H	Walsall	W	1–0	Barnes	3
10	30	A	Hull City	W	3–0	Barnes (2, 1 pen), Peverell	5
11	Oct 7	H	Wrexham	W	1–0	Barras	3
12	14	A	Shrewsbury Town	L	1–2	Pepper	2
13	21	H	Bristol City	L	0–1		3
14	28	A	Peterborough United	L	1–6	Baker	4
15	31	A	Wycombe Wanderers	L	1–2	Barnes	4
16	Nov 4	H	Stockport County	D	2–2	Barnes (2, 1 pen)	3
17	18	A	Blackpool	W	3–1	Barnes, Matthews, Baker	4
18	25	H	Brighton & Hove Albion	W	3–1	Barnes 2, Baker	3
19	Dec 9	A	Walsall	L	0–2		3
20	16	H	Hull City	L	0–1		3
21	26	H	Bradford City	L	0–3		5
22	Jan 6	A	Rotherham United	D	2–2	Barnes (2)	2
23	13	H	Swindon Town	W	2–0	Naylor, McMillan	3
24	20	A	Brentford	L	0–2		3
25	Feb 10	H	Rotherham United	D	2–2	Pepper, Naylor	3
26	17	A	Burnley	D	3–3	Pepper (pen), Naylor, Murty	8
27	20	H	Oxford United	W	1–0	Barnes	2
28	24	H	Swansea City	D	0–0		2
29	27	A	Bristol Rovers	L	0–1		4
30	Mar 2	A	Bradford City	D	2–2	Pepper (pen), Cresswell	5
31	5	A	Crewe Alexandra	D	1–1	Murty	3
32	9	H	Carlisle United	D	1–1	Stephenson	3
33	12	A	Notts County	D	2–2	Pepper, Barras	3
34	16	A	Bournemouth	D	2–2	Barras, Pepper	3
35	23	H	Notts County	L	1–3	Bull	3
36	26	H	Bournemouth	W	3–1	Himsworth, Naylor (2)	2
37	30	A	Wrexham	W	3–2	Bull (3)	2
38	Apr 2	H	Shrewsbury Town	L	1–2	Pepper	2
39	6	H	Peterborough United	W	3–1	Naylor, Pepper, Bull	3
40	8	A	Bristol City	D	1–1	Bull	7
41	13	H	Wycombe Wanderers	W	2–1	Bull (pen), Naylor	3
42	20	A	Stockport County	L	0–3		6
43	23	A	Carlisle United	L	0–2		4
44	30	H	Chesterfield	L	0–1		2
45	May 4	H	Blackpool	L	0–2		7
46	9	A	Brighton & Hove Albion	W	3–1	Bull, Stephenson, Jordan	2

A
S

1 own-goal

FA Cup

1	Nov 12	H	Notts County	L	0–1		4

A
S

Football League (Coca-Cola) Cup

1 (1)	Aug 15	A	Rochdale	L	1–2	Baker	1
1 (2)	22	H	Rochdale	W	5–1*	Baker, Barnes (2), Pepper, Peverell	2
2 (1)	Sep 20	A	Manchester United	W	3–0	Barnes (2, 1 pen), Barras	29
2 (2)	Oct 3	H	Manchester United	L	1–3	Jordan	9
3	25	A	Queen's Park Rangers	L	1–3	Barnes	12

* After extra-time.

A
S

Note: Three substitutes were allowed from this season in the Football League. First substitute No. 12, player substituted in bold. Second substitute No. 13, player substituted underlined. Third substitute No. 14, player substituted in italics.

McMillan	Osborne	Pepper	Tutill	Barras	Murty	Jordan	Barnes	Baker	Stephenson	Williams	Atkin	Hall	Oxley	Peverell	Naylor	Matthews	Warrington	Scaife	Bushell	Curtis	Atkinson	Randall	Cresswell	Himsworth	Bull	Sharples	
2	3	**4**	5	6	7	8	9	10	11	12	13																1
2		4	5	6	12		9	10	11	8		3	**7**														2
2		4	5		7		9	10	11	8	6	3															3
2	14	**4**	5		7	12	9	10	11	8	6	*3*		13													4
2		4	5		7	12	9	10		**8**	6	3		11	13												5
2		4	5	6	7		9	**10**		8	13	3		11		12											6
2		4	5	6	7		9			8		3		10		11											7
2		4	5	6	7	12	9			8		3		10	13	**11**											8
2		4	5	6		11	9	12		8		3		10		**7**											9
2		4	5	6		11	9	12		8		3		10		7											10
2		4	5	6		11	9			8		3		**10**	12	7	1	13									11
2		4	5	6	13	**11**	9	12		8		3		10		7	1										12
2			5	6	11	**4**	9	13		8		3		10		7	1		12								13
2		12	5		11	4	9	14		**8**	6	3		10		13	1		*7*								14
2		4	5	6	*11*	13	9				14	3		10		**7**	1		8	12							15
2		4	5	6			9	10		11		3				7	1		8								16
2		4	5	6		8	9	10	11			3				7											17
2		4	5	6		8	9	10	11			3				**7**					12						18
2		**4**	5	6	13	8	9	10	11			3				7			12								19
2		4	5		7		9	**10**	11		6	3				12			8								20
2		4	5		7		**9**	12	11		6	3		13		10			8								21
2		4	5		7		9	13	**11**		6	3				10					12	8					22
2			5		7	13	9			11	6	12			10				4		**3**	8					23
2			**5**		7	13	9			11	6	12	14						4		3	8	*10*				24
2		4	5		7		9				6			12	10						3	8	**11**				25
2		4		5	7		9				6			12	10						3	8	**11**				26
2		4		5	7		9				6			14	*10*				13		3	8	**11**	12			27
2		4		5			9				6			12	**10**				7		3	8	11				28
2				5	7		9		12		6				10				4		3	8		**11**			29
2		4		5	7	13	9				6				**10**				8		3		12	11			30
2		4		5	7	13			12		6			14	*10*				8		3		9	11			31
2		4		5	7				12		6								8		3		9	**11**	10		32
2	3	4		5	7				11		6				12				8				9		**10**		33
2	3	4		5	7				11		6				12				8			13	**9**		10		34
2	3	4		5					11		6				9				12			**8**	13	7	10		35
2	3	4		5					11		6				9							8		7	10		36
2		4							11		6				9				12		3	**8**	13	7	10	5	37
2		4		6	7				11						9				8		3				10	5	38
2		4		6	7	8			11						9						3				10	5	39
2		4		6	**7**	8			11					13	9				12		3				10	5	40
2				6	7	8			11						9				4		3				10	5	41
2				6	7	8			11					13	9				**4**		3	12			10	5	42
2		4		**6**	7	8			*11*		12				9						3	14	13		10	5	43
2		4				8			11		6				**9**						3	7	12		10	5	44
2		4			12	8			**11**		6				9						3	7	13		10	5	45
2		4			7	8			11	13	6				**9**						3		12		10	5	46
46	5	39	25	32	31	18	30	11	24	16	25	21	1	11	20	14	6		17		20	13	9	7	15	10	
	1	1			4	8		7	3	2	4	2	1	9	5	3		1	6	1	2	3	7	1			
1		9		3	2	1	15	5	2					1	7	1							1	1	8		

McMillan	Osborne	Pepper	Tutill	Barras	Murty	Jordan	Barnes	Baker	Stephenson	Williams	Atkin	Hall	Oxley	Peverell	Naylor	Matthews	Warrington	Scaife	Bushell	Curtis	Atkinson	Randall	Cresswell	Himsworth	Bull	Sharples	
2	3	4	5	6		8	9	10		**11**						7	1			12							1
1	1	1	1	1		1	1	1		1						1	1										
																				1							

McMillan	Osborne	Pepper	Tutill	Barras	Murty	Jordan	Barnes	Baker	Stephenson	Williams	Atkin	Hall	Oxley	Peverell	Naylor	Matthews	Warrington	Scaife	Bushell	Curtis	Atkinson	Randall	Cresswell	Himsworth	Bull	Sharples	
2		4	5	6		**8**	9	10	11	12		3	7														1 (1)
2		4	5	**6**	7	13	9	*10*	11	8	12	3		14													1 (2)
2		4	5	6	7	11	9	12		8	13	3		**10**													2 (1)
2		4	5	6		11	**9**	12		8	7	3		10	13		1										2 (2)
2			5	**6**	11	4	9			8	12	3		10			1		7								3
5		4	5	5	3	4	5	2	2	4	1	5	1	3			2		1								
						1		2		1	3			1	1												
		1		1		1	5	2						1													

York City v Manchester United 3 October 1995 programme cover.

Paul Stephenson.

1996–97

Division Two

Manager: Alan Little

	P	W	D	L	F	A	Pts
Bury	46	24	12	10	62	38	84
Stockport County	46	23	13	10	59	41	82
Luton Town	46	21	15	10	71	45	78
Brentford	46	20	14	12	56	43	74
Bristol City	46	21	10	15	69	51	73
Crewe Alexandra	46	22	7	17	56	47	73
Blackpool	46	18	15	13	60	47	69
Wrexham	46	17	18	11	54	50	69
Burnley	46	19	11	16	71	55	68
Chesterfield	46	18	14	14	42	39	68
Gillingham	46	19	10	17	60	59	67
Walsall	46	19	10	17	54	53	67
Watford	46	16	19	11	45	38	67
Millwall	46	16	13	17	50	55	61
Preston North End	46	18	7	21	49	55	61
Bournemouth	46	15	15	16	43	45	60
Bristol Rovers	46	15	11	20	47	50	56
Wycombe Wanderers	46	15	10	21	51	56	55
Plymouth Argyle	46	12	18	16	47	58	54
York City	46	13	13	20	47	68	52
Peterborough United	46	11	14	21	55	73	47
Shrewsbury Town	46	11	13	22	49	74	46
Rotherham United	46	7	14	25	39	70	35
Notts County	46	7	14	25	33	59	35

Did you know that?

Newcomer Neil Tolson from Bradford City finished top scorer with 17 League and Cup goals.

Joint leading scorer in the League was Nigel Pepper, who moved to Bradford City, and he played his last game for the club on 25 February 1997. In 281 senior appearances he netted 45 goals.

Jonathan Greening made his senior debut on 22 March 1997 when coming on as a substitute at Bournemouth.

New signing from Leeds United Mark Tinkler made his City debut at home to Plymouth Argyle on 29 March 1997.

The only ever present was skipper Tony Barras, and he was Clubman of the Year.

Average home League crowd fell for the fourth successive campaign and was 3,359.

For the first time since 1985–86 the third round of the FA Cup was reached, but at that stage they lost away to non-League Hednesford Town.

Match No.	Date		Venue	Opponents	Result		Scorers	Atten
1	Aug	17	A	Plymouth Argyle	L	1–2	Pepper (pen)	
2		24	H	Bournemouth	L	1–2	Pepper	
3		27	H	Millwall	W	3–2	Pepper (2, 1 pen), Tolson	
4		31	A	Notts County	W	1–0	Tolson	
5	Sep	7	H	Shrewsbury Town	D	0–0		
6		10	A	Preston North End	L	0–1		
7		14	A	Peterborough United	D	2–2	Bushell, Pepper	
8		21	H	Stockport County	L	1–2	Tolson	
9		28	A	Brentford	D	3–3	Tolson, Randall, Murty	
10	Oct	1	H	Bristol Rovers	D	2–2	Tolson, Randall	
11		5	H	Watford	L	1–2	Pepper (pen)	
12		11	A	Bristol City	L	0–2		
13		15	A	Crewe Alexandra	W	1–0	Himsworth	
14		19	H	Rotherham United	W	2–1	Stephenson, Pepper	
15		26	A	Chesterfield	L	0–2		
16		29	H	Wycombe Wanderers	W	2–0	Pepper (pen), Tolson	
17	Nov	2	H	Burnley	W	1–0	Murty	
18		9	A	Bury	L	1–4	Himsworth	
19		23	A	Gillingham	W	1–0	Tolson	
20		30	H	Chesterfield	D	0–0		
21	Dec	3	A	Luton Town	L	0–2		
22		14	H	Wrexham	W	1–0	Opp. og	
23		21	A	Blackpool	L	0–3		
24		28	A	Shrewsbury Town	L	0–2		
25	Jan	11	H	Brentford	L	2–4	Pepper (pen), Pouton	
26		18	A	Bristol Rovers	D	1–1	Pepper (pen)	
27		25	A	Wycombe Wanderers	L	1–3	Campbell	
28	Feb	1	H	Bury	L	0–2		
29		8	A	Burnley	W	2–1	Tolson, Jordan	
30		11	H	Walsall	L	0–2		
31		15	H	Gillingham	L	2–3	Bushell, Barras	
32		22	A	Walsall	D	1–1	Pepper (pen)	
33		25	H	Preston North End	W	3–1	Bull, Pepper, Rowe	
34	Mar	1	H	Luton Town	D	1–1	Tolson	
35		8	H	Blackpool	W	1–0	Sharples	
36		15	A	Wrexham	D	0–0		
37		22	A	Bournemouth	D	1–1	Gilbert	
38		29	H	Plymouth Argyle	D	1–1	Bushell	
39	Apr	2	A	Millwall	D	1–1	Tolson	
40		5	H	Notts County	L	1–2	Rowe	
41		8	H	Peterborough United	W	1–0	Bull	
42		12	A	Watford	L	0–4		
43		19	H	Bristol City	L	0–3		
44		22	A	Stockport County	L	1–2	Tolson	
45		26	A	Rotherham United	W	2–0	Rowe, Tolson	
46	May	3	H	Crewe Alexandra	D	1–1	Tinkler	

1 own-goal

FA Cup

1	Nov	16	A	Hartlepool United	D	0–0	
r		26	H	Hartlepool United	W	3–0	Pepper, Himsworth, Tolson
2	Dec	7	A	Preston North End	W	3–2	Barras, Tolson, Opp. og
3	Jan	13	A	Hednesford Town	L	0–1	

1 own-goal

Football League (Coca-Cola) Cup

1 (1)	Aug	20	A	Doncaster Rovers	D	1–1	Tolson	
1 (2)	Sep	3	H	Doncaster Rovers	W	2–0	Pepper, Bushell	
2 (1)		18	A	Everton	D	1–1	Tolson	1
2 (2)		24	H	Everton	W	3–2	Tolson, Bull, Murty	
3	Oct	22	H	Leicester City	L	0–2		

McMillan	Atkinson	Randall	Atkin	Barras	Himsworth	Bushell	Bull	Tolson	Stephenson	Pepper	Murty	Pouton	Cresswell	Sharples	Naylor	Williams	Hall	Campbell	Tutill	Clarke	Jordan	Rush	Prudhoe	Harrison	Rowe	Gilbert	Greening	Tinkler	Reed	
2	3	4	5	6	7	**8**	9	10	11	12	13																			1
2		4	5	6	7	**8**	*9*	10	11	12	3	13	14																	2
2		8		6	3			10	11	4	7		**9**	5	12															3
2		8		6	3	13	12	**10**	11	4	7		9	5																4
2		8		6	3		12	10	11	4	7		**9**	5																5
2		8		6	3		10	9	11	4	7			5																6
2				6	3	8	10	9	**11**	4	7			5		12														7
2		8	14	6	**3**	13	10	9	11	4	7		12	*5*																8
2		8	13	6			10	**9**	11	4	7			5			3	12												9
2		8		6			**10**	9	11	4	7			5			3	12												10
2		8	*5*	6		12	10	9	**11**	4	7						3	13	14											11
2	3	8		6		12	10	9	11	**4**	7	13							5	1										12
2		8		6	11			9		4	7		**10**				3	12	5	1										13
2		8		6	**11**		13	9	12	4	7		10				3		5	1										14
2			5	6	11	8	10	9		4	7						3			1										15
2				6	11	8	10	9		4	7						3		5	1										16
2				6	11	8	10	9		4	7						3		5	1										17
2		12		6	11	8	10		9	**4**	7	13					3		5	1										18
2				6	7	**8**	10	9	11	4	3	12							5	1										19
2		12		6	3		10	9	11	**4**	7	8							5	1										20
2	12	13		6	**3**		10	*9*	11	4	7	8	14						5	1										21
2	3		14	6	7		10	9	*11*		**8**	4	13						5	1	12									22
2	3			6			10	9	11			4	**7**					12	5	1	8									23
2	3		8	6			10	9	11	**4**		7						13	5	1	12									24
2	3			6	12		10	9	11	4	**7**	8	13						5	1										25
2	3			6	7			12	11	4		8	10	5				**9**		1										26
2	3			6	**7**		14		11	4	12	8	*10*	5				9		1	12									27
2	3			6		14	13		11	*4*	7		**10**	5				9		1	8	12								28
2				6	11	4		9			3	7		5							8	10								29
2				6	11	4		9		12	3	7	13	5				10			**8**									30
2	3		13	6	11	4	10	9				7	12	5							*8*		1	14						31
2			12	6	3	8	10		11	4		7		5									**1**		9					32
2				6	3	8	10		11	4		7		5											9					33
2				6	3	4	10	11				7		5							8				9					34
2				6	3	4	10	9				7	12	5											**8**	11				35
2				6	3	4	10	9				7		5					13		12				**8**	11				36
2				6	3	4	10	9				**7**		5							12				8	11	13			37
2				6	3	4	10	9	7					5			12								13	**11**		8		38
2				6		4	10	9	**7**					5			3				12					11		8		39
2				6		4	10		7					5			3								9	11		8		40
2				6		4	10	9	7					5			**3**				12					11	13	8		41
2	3			6		4	10	9	7					5							12					11		**8**		42
2	3			6		4	10	9	7					5												**11**	12	8		43
2			3	6		4	14	9	12					5				*10*			**11**						13	8	7	44
2			12	6	3	4	13	9	11			**7**		5											10			8		45
2	3			6	**7**	4	13	9	11																10		12	8	5	46
46	13	13	6	46	32	26	33	39	33	26	25	18	9	28			12	5	13	17	7	1	2		9	9		9	2	
	1	3	6		1	5	8	1	2	3	2	4	8		1	1	1	6	2		8	1		1	1		5			
		2		1	2	3	2	12	1	12	2	1		1				1			1				3	1		1		

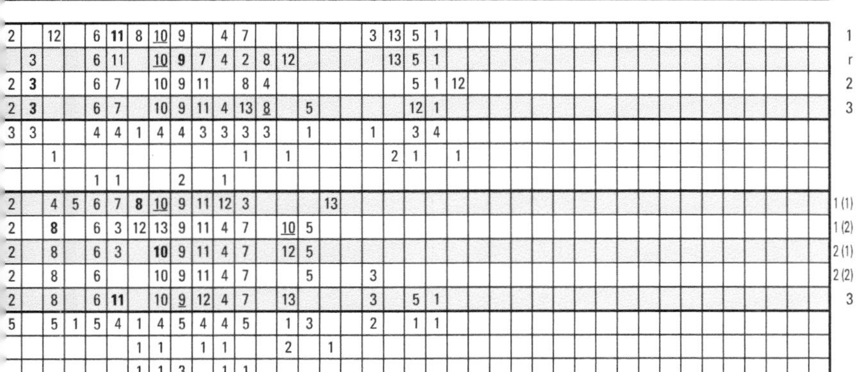

McMillan	Atkinson	Randall	Atkin	Barras	Himsworth	Bushell	Bull	Tolson	Stephenson	Pepper	Murty	Pouton	Cresswell	Sharples	Naylor	Williams	Hall	Campbell	Tutill	Clarke	Jordan	Rush	Prudhoe	Harrison	Rowe	Gilbert	Greening	Tinkler	Reed	
2		12		6	**11**	8	10	9		4	7						3	13	5	1										1
	3			6	11		10	**9**	7	4	2	8	12					13	5	1										r
2	**3**			6	7		10	9	11		8	4							5	1	12									2
2	**3**			6	7		10	9	11	4	13	8		5					12	1										3
3	3			4	4	1	4	4	3	3	3	3		1			1		3	4										
		1									1		1					2	1		1									
				1	1			2		1																				

McMillan	Atkinson	Randall	Atkin	Barras	Himsworth	Bushell	Bull	Tolson	Stephenson	Pepper	Murty	Pouton	Cresswell	Sharples	Naylor	Williams	Hall	Campbell	Tutill	Clarke	Jordan	Rush	Prudhoe	Harrison	Rowe	Gilbert	Greening	Tinkler	Reed	
2		4	5	6	7	**8**	10	9	11	12	3				13															1 (1)
2		**8**		6	3	12	13	9	11	4	7		10	5																1 (2)
2		8		6	3		**10**	9	11	4	7		12	5																2 (1)
2		8		6			10	9	11	4	7			5			3													2 (2)
2		8		6	**11**		10	9	12	4	7		13				3		5	1										3
5		5	1	5	4	1	4	5	4	4	5		1	3			2		1	1										
						1	1		1	1			2		1															
						1	1	3		1	1																			

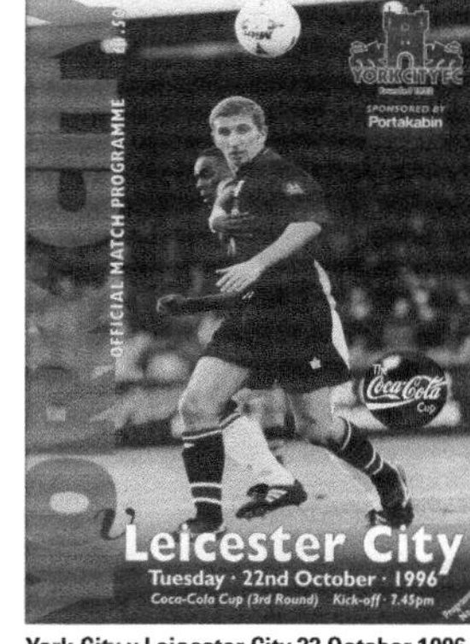

York City v Leicester City 22 October 1996 programme cover.

Mark Tinkler.

Jonathan Greening.

1997–98

Division Two

Manager: Alan Little

	P	W	D	L	F	A	Pts
Watford	46	24	16	6	67	41	88
Bristol City	46	25	10	11	69	39	85
Grimsby Town	46	19	15	12	55	37	72
Northampton Town	46	18	17	11	52	37	71
Bristol Rovers	46	20	10	16	70	64	70
Fulham	46	20	10	16	60	43	70
Wrexham	46	18	16	12	55	51	70
Gillingham	46	19	13	14	52	47	70
Bournemouth	46	18	12	16	57	52	66
Chesterfield	46	16	17	13	46	44	65
Wigan Athletic	46	17	11	18	64	66	62
Blackpool	46	17	11	18	59	67	62
Oldham Athletic	46	15	16	15	62	54	61
Wycombe Wanderers	46	14	18	14	51	53	60
Preston North End	46	15	14	17	56	56	59
York City	46	14	17	15	52	58	59
Luton Town	46	14	15	17	60	64	57
Millwall	46	14	13	19	43	54	55
Walsall	46	14	12	20	43	52	54
Burnley	46	13	13	20	55	65	52
Brentford	46	11	17	18	50	71	50
Plymouth Argyle	46	12	13	21	55	70	49
Carlisle United	46	12	8	26	57	73	44
Southend United	46	11	10	25	47	79	43

Did you know that?

Steve Tutill made his last City appearance on 16 August 1997 at home to Bristol Rovers (366 League and Cup games for the club).

City's fourth goal netted by Steve Bushell in the win over Carlisle United on 25 October 1997 was their 4,000th in the Football League.

Defender Barry Jones from Wrexham played his first game on 19 December 1997.

City's defeat at Burnley on 31 January 1998 was the first time they had conceded seven goals in a League match since September 1976.

Marco Gabbiadini returned to the club, and his first game back was at home to Watford on 21 February 1998.

Neil Thompson, ex-Ipswich Town and Barnsley, made his debut away to Wycombe Wanderers on 3 March 1998.

Graeme Murty's last full game in City colours was at Preston North End on 14 March 1998. In the summer he was transferred to Reading for a new club record fee received of £700,000.

Jonathan Greening's final appearance was at home to Fulham on 21 March 1998 prior to his transfer to Manchester United for an initial reported fee of £500,000.

Defender Graham Rennison was sent off on his debut on 4 April 1998 at Luton. Mark Tinkler was also dismissed in this game.

During the campaign Andy McMillan passed 450 senior appearances for the club.

Clubman of the Year Steve Bushell made his last appearance on 25 April 1998 at Carlisle United. In the close season he moved to Blackpool.

Rodney Rowe was top marksman.

Average League crowd at Bootham Crescent rose to 3,850.

Match No.	Date		Venue	Opponents	Result		Scorers	Attend
1	Aug	9	A	Oldham Athletic	L	1–3	Bushell	6
2		16	H	Bristol Rovers	L	0–1		3
3		23	A	Millwall	W	3–2	Rowe, Pouton, Stephenson	6
4		30	H	Gillingham	W	2–1	Rowe, Greening	2
5	Sep	2	H	Chesterfield	L	0–1		3
6		9	A	Grimsby Town	D	0–0		5
7		13	H	Burnley	W	3–1	Davis, Rowe, Tolson	5,
8		20	A	Walsall	L	0–2		2
9		27	A	Watford	D	1–1	Tolson	13,
10	Oct	4	H	Plymouth Argyle	W	1–0	Rowe	2
11		11	H	Brentford	W	3–1	Stephenson, Tinkler, Murty	2
12		17	A	Bristol City	L	1–2	Rowe	9
13		21	A	Northampton Town	D	1–1	Rowe	6
14		25	H	Carlisle United	W	4–3	Rowe, Stephenson (2), Bushell	3,
15	Nov	1	A	Wigan Athletic	D	1–1	Rowe	3
16		4	H	Preston North End	W	1–0	Tinkler	3
17		8	H	Wycombe Wanderers	W	2–0	Barras (pen), Rowe	3,
18		18	A	Fulham	D	1–1	Barras (pen)	5
19		22	A	Blackpool	L	0–1		4
20		29	H	Luton Town	L	1–2	Cresswell	3
21	Dec	2	A	Bournemouth	D	0–0		3,
22		13	H	Wrexham	W	1–0	Barras	2
23		19	A	Southend United	D	4–4	Pouton (2), Barras (pen), Tinkler	3,
24		26	H	Grimsby Town	D	0–0		7
25		28	A	Chesterfield	D	1–1	Greening	5
26	Jan	10	H	Oldham Athletic	D	0–0		4,
27		17	A	Gillingham	D	0–0		5
28		24	H	Millwall	L	2–3	Stephenson, Bull	3
29		31	A	Burnley	L	2–7	Pouton, Barras	9
30	Feb	7	H	Walsall	W	1–0	Tinkler	2,
31		14	A	Plymouth Argyle	D	0–0		4
32		21	H	Watford	D	1–1	Barras (pen)	4
33		24	H	Bristol City	L	0–1		3
34		28	A	Brentford	W	2–1	Gabbiadini, Jones	4
35	Mar	3	A	Wycombe Wanderers	L	0–1		3,
36		7	H	Wigan Athletic	D	2–2	Thompson, Bushell	3
37		10	A	Bristol Rovers	W	2–1	Jones, Cresswell	4
38		14	A	Preston North End	L	2–3	Rowe (2)	7
39		21	H	Fulham	L	0–1		4
40		28	H	Blackpool	D	1–1	Cresswell	3
41	Apr	4	A	Luton Town	L	0–3		5
42		11	H	Bournemouth	L	0–1		2
43		13	A	Wrexham	W	2–1	Thompson (pen), Cresswell	5
44		18	H	Southend United	D	1–1	Tolson	2
45		25	A	Carlisle United	W	2–1	Pouton, McMillan	3
46	May	2	H	Northampton Town	D	0–0		6
								A
								S

FA Cup

1	Nov	15	A	Southport	W	4–0	Rowe (2), Pouton, Opp. og	3
2	Dec	6	A	Wigan Athletic	L	1–2	Rowe	4
								A
								S
							1 own-goal	

Football League (Coca-Cola) Cup

1 (1)	Aug	12	A	Port Vale	W	2–1	Bushell, Bull	2,
1 (2)		26	H	Port Vale	D	1–1	Barras	3
2 (1)	Sep	16	A	Oxford United	L	1–4	Rowe	2
2 (2)		23	H	Oxford United	L	1–2	Murty	1
								A
								S

McMillan	Atkinson	Bushell	Tutill	Barras	Stephenson	Tinkler	Tolson	Bull	Pouton	Rowe	Hall	Campbell	Jordan	Rush	Reed	Cresswell	Greening	Murty	Davis	Himsworth	Warrington	Jones	Gabbiadini	Thompson	Rennison	Alderson	
2	3	4	5	6	**7**	8	9	10	11	12																	1
2		4	**5**	6	13	8		10	11	9	3	*7*	*12*	14													2
2		4		6	7	8		12	11	9	3			**10**	5	13											3
2	14	4		6	7	8		**10**	*11*	9	3				5	12	13										4
2		4			7	6			8	9	3				5	10	**11**	12									5
2		4		6	11	5	12		8	9	3					**10**		7									6
2		4		6	11	8	9	13	12	10	3							**7**	5								7
2		4		6	11	8	**9**		13	10	3			12				7	5								8
2		4		6		8	**9**	12	11	10	3				5			7									9
		4		6	7	8	9	13	**11**	10	3				5			2		12							10
2		4		6	*11*	8	**9**	13		10	3				5		12	7		14							11
2		4		6	11	8	9			10	3				5			7									12
2		4		6	11	8		9		10	3				5			7									13
2		4		6	11	8	13	**9**		10	3				5		12	7		14							14
		4		6	11	8		9	**7**	10	3				5			2		12							15
		4		6	11	**8**		9	7	10	3		12		5			2									16
		4		6	11	8		9	*7*	10	3		12		**5**		13	2		14							17
		4		6		8		**9**	7	10	3				5	12		2		11							18
	13	4		6		8			7	10	3				5	**9**	12	2		11							19
	3	4		6	11	8		**9**	7	10					5	12		2			1						20
		4		6	11	8		12	7	**10**					5	9		2		3	1						21
				6	7	8		13	4	*10*	3		12		**5**	9	14	2		11	1						22
				6	11	8		13	4	10	3					9	12	2		**7**	1	5					23
				6	11	8			4	10	3					9		2		7	1	5					24
				6	11	8			4	10	3		12			9	13	2		**7**	1	5					25
		4		6	11	5			8	10	3					**9**	12	7			1	2					26
2		4		6	**11**	8				10	3		12			9		7			1	5					27
2		4		6	11	8		13	14	10	3					**9**	12	7			1	5					28
	3	4		6	11	5		9	8	**10**			14			*12*	13	7			1	2					29
		4		6	**11**	8		9	7		3		12			13	10	2				5					30
		4		6	11	8		9	7	12	*3*		14			13	**10**	2				5					31
2		4		6	11	8		9	7									3				5	10				32
2		4		6	11	8		**9**	7	10							12	3				5					33
2		4		6	11	8			7	**9**							12	3				5	10				34
2		4		6	11	8			7								9					5	10	3			35
2		4		6	11	**8**			12	9							13	7				5	10	3			36
2		4		6	11				8	9						10		7				5		3			37
2		4		**6**	11	12			8	9			14			10	13	*7*				5		3			38
2		4				8	12	10	7	9					6		**11**					5		3			39
2		4				8	12	10	7	**9**					6	13					1	5	11	3			40
2		7				8	12		11	**9**			4			10					1	5	13	3	6		41
2		4		*6*		8	**9**		7		13		11		14	10					1	5	12	3			42
2		4				8	9		7		3		11			10					1	5		6			43
2							9		7	12	3		8		4	10				**11**	1	5		6			44
2		4				6	12		7	9	11		8			**10**				13	1	5		3			45
2						6		10	7	9	11		4		**5**			12		8	1			3		13	46
30	3	40	2	38	34	43	10	18	37	38	31	1	6	1	21	18	5	32	2	9	17	23	5	12	1		
	2				1	1	6	9	4	3	1		10	2	1	8	15	2		6			2			1	
1		3		6	5	4	3	1	5	11						4	2	1	1			2	1	2			

McMillan	Atkinson	Bushell	Tutill	Barras	Stephenson	Tinkler	Tolson	Bull	Pouton	Rowe	Hall	Campbell	Jordan	Rush	Reed	Cresswell	Greening	Murty	Davis	Himsworth	Warrington	Jones	Gabbiadini	Thompson	Rennison	Alderson	
	14	4		6	**11**	8		9	7	10	*3*				5	13		2		12							1
		4		6	11	8		12	7	10			13		5	**9**		2		3	1						2
		2		2	2	2		1	2	2	1				2	1		2		1	1						
	1							1					1			1				1							
									1	3																	

McMillan	Atkinson	Bushell	Tutill	Barras	Stephenson	Tinkler	Tolson	Bull	Pouton	Rowe	Hall	Campbell	Jordan	Rush	Reed	Cresswell	Greening	Murty	Davis	Himsworth	Warrington	Jones	Gabbiadini	Thompson	Rennison	Alderson	
2		4	5	6	12	8	13	10	11	9	3	**7**															1 (1)
2		4		6	7	8		10	11	**9**	3				5	12	13										1 (2)
2		4		6	11	5	10	12	8	**9**	3							7									2 (1)
2		4		6	**11**	8	9	10	12		3				5			7									2 (2)
4		4	1	4	3	4	2	3	3	3	4	1			2			2									
					1		1	1	1							1	1										
		1		1				1		1								1									

York City v Burnley 13 September 1997 programme cover.

Graeme Murty receives the Junior Red Player of the Year award 1997–98 from City secretary Keith Usher.

1998–99

Division Two

Manager: Alan Little, then Neil Thompson

	P	W	D	L	F	A	Pts
Fulham	46	31	8	7	79	32	101
Walsall	46	26	9	11	63	47	87
Manchester City	46	22	16	8	69	33	82
Gillingham	46	22	14	10	75	44	80
Preston North End	46	22	13	11	78	50	79
Wigan Athletic	46	22	10	14	75	48	76
Bournemouth	46	21	13	12	63	41	76
Stoke City	46	21	6	19	59	63	69
Chesterfield	46	17	13	16	46	44	64
Millwall	46	17	11	18	52	59	62
Reading	46	16	13	17	54	63	61
Luton Town	46	16	10	20	51	60	58
Bristol Rovers	46	13	17	16	65	56	56
Blackpool	46	14	14	18	44	54	56
Burnley	46	13	16	17	54	73	55
Notts County	46	14	12	20	52	61	54
Wrexham	46	13	14	19	43	62	53
Colchester United	46	12	16	18	52	70	52
Wycombe Wanderers	46	13	12	21	52	58	51
Oldham Athletic	46	14	9	23	48	66	51
York City	46	13	11	22	56	80	50
Northampton Town	46	10	18	18	43	57	48
Lincoln City	46	13	7	26	42	74	46
Macclesfield Town	46	11	10	25	43	63	43

Did you know that?

Bobby Mimms, who had kept goal for Everton in the 1986 FA Cup Final, made his debut on 15 August 1998 at home to Gillingham.

Steve Agnew played his first game for City against his former club Sunderland in the Worthington Cup on 18 August 1998.

City had two players sent off in the FA Cup tie at Wrexham – Mark Tinkler and Martin Reed. Lee Bullock made his debut in this match on 5 December 1998.

On 19 December 1998 Andrew Dawson made his debut when he came on as a substitute, and he netted the winning goal against Manchester City with virtually his first kick of the ball.

Alan Little, after exactly six years in charge, was dismissed on 15 March 1999 and Neil Thompson took over initially as caretaker player-manager.

Leading scorer Richard Cresswell, who in February 1999 became the first City player to win representative honours for England when he was capped at Under-21 level against France, was transferred to Sheffield Wednesday on 26 March for a record fee received of £950,000. His last game for City was at home to Wigan Athletic six days earlier.

City did not drop into the bottom four until the last day of the campaign when they lost at Manchester City in front of 32,471, the biggest crowd to watch York in the League since March 1976.

Clubman of the Year was captain Barry Jones.

Average home League crowd was 3,645.

Relegation brought to an end a club record equalling run of six seasons out of the bottom Division (previous 1971–77).

Andy McMillan played his last match for the club on 20 March 1999 at home to Wigan Athletic. He is second in the all time appearance list with 492 games to his credit.

Match No.	Date	Venue	Opponents	Result		Scorers
1	Aug 8	A	Preston North End	L	0–3	
2	15	H	Gillingham	D	1–1	Cresswell
3	22	A	Burnley	W	1–0	Connelly
4	29	H	Wycombe Wanderers	W	3–0	Thompson (2, 1 pen), Cresswell
5	Sep 5	H	Colchester United	L	1–2	Thompson (pen)
6	8	A	Walsall	W	3–2	Cresswell (2), Tinkler
7	12	H	Wrexham	D	1–1	Cresswell
8	19	A	Fulham	D	3–3	Agnew (2), Tolson
9	26	H	Bristol Rovers	W	1–0	Tolson
10	Oct 3	A	Blackpool	W	2–1	Thompson (pen), Jordan
11	10	H	Luton Town	D	3–3	Connelly, Cresswell (2)
12	17	A	Chesterfield	L	1–2	Cresswell
13	21	A	Millwall	L	1–3	Cresswell (pen)
14	31	A	Wigan Athletic	L	0–5	
15	Nov 4	A	Reading	L	0–1	
16	7	H	Notts County	D	1–1	Connelly
17	10	H	Macclesfield Town	L	0–2	
18	21	A	Stoke City	L	0–2	
19	28	H	Northampton Town	D	1–1	Cresswell
20	Dec 8	H	Lincoln City	W	2–1	Tolson, Opp. og
21	12	A	Bournemouth	L	1–2	Cresswell
22	19	H	Manchester City	W	2–1	Connelly, Dawson
23	26	H	Burnley	D	3–3	Hall, Rowe (2)
24	28	A	Oldham Athletic	W	2–0	Cresswell, Jones
25	Jan 2	A	Wycombe Wanderers	W	2–1	Cresswell, Jones
26	9	H	Preston North End	L	0–1	
27	16	A	Gillingham	L	1–3	Rowe
28	23	H	Reading	D	1–1	Rowe
29	30	H	Oldham Athletic	L	0–1	
30	Feb 5	A	Colchester United	L	1–2	Cresswell (pen)
31	13	H	Walsall	L	1–2	Cresswell
32	20	A	Wrexham	D	1–1	Pouton
33	27	H	Fulham	L	0–3	
34	Mar 6	A	Bristol Rovers	L	0–2	
35	13	A	Notts County	L	2–4	Rowe, Cresswell (pen)
36	20	H	Wigan Athletic	L	1–3	Jordan
37	28	A	Lincoln City	W	2–1	Williams (2)
38	Apr 3	H	Chesterfield	L	1–2	Jordan
39	6	A	Luton Town	L	1–2	Thompson
40	10	H	Millwall	W	2–1	Rowe, Thompson
41	13	A	Northampton Town	D	2–2	Williams, Jordan
42	17	H	Stoke City	D	2–2	Garratt, Jordan
43	24	A	Macclesfield Town	W	2–1	Rowe, Tinkler
44	27	H	Blackpool	W	1–0	Williams
45	May 1	H	Bournemouth	L	0–1	
46	8	A	Manchester City	L	0–4	

1 own-goal

FA Cup

1	Nov 14	A	Enfield	D	2–2	Cresswell (2)
r	24	H	Enfield	W	2–1	Jordan, Cresswell
2	Dec 5	A	Wrexham	L	1–2	Jordan

Football League (Worthington) Cup

1 (1)	Aug 11	H	Sunderland	L	0–2	
1 (2)	18	A	Sunderland	L	1–2	Thompson

McMillan	Hall	Jones	Reed	Tinkler	Thompson	Pouton	Woods	Cresswell	Garratt	Rowe	Mimms	Connelly	Prendergast	Agnew	Jordan	Tolson	Barras	Himsworth	Dawson	Carruthers	Fairclough	Williams	Skinner	Hocking	Bullock	Rennison	
2	3	4	5	6	7	8	**9**	10	11	12																	1
2	3	5		4	6	8	12	9	11	**10**	1	7	13														2
2	3	5		4	6	8	10	9	12		1	7		**11**													3
2	3	5	13	4	6	8	**10**	9	11		1	7			14	12											4
2	3	5	12	4	6	8	*10*	9	**11**		1	7			13	14											5
2	3	5		4	6	8		9			1	7		11		10											6
2		5		4	3	8		9		12	1	7		11		**10**	6										7
2		5		4	3	8		*9*	12	14	1	**7**		11	13	10	6										8
2	11	5		4	3	7		9		12	1			8		**10**	6										9
2				5	3	**8**		9	12	13	1	7		11	4	10	6										10
2	13	12		5	3			9	8	14	1	7		11	**4**	*10*	6										11
2	3	5						9	8	12	1	7		11	4	**10**	6										12
2	**3**	5		4				9	8	13	1	7	12	11		10	6										13
2		5		4	3			9	6	13	1	7	**11**	8	12	10											14
2		5		4				9	3	10		7		11	8		6										15
2		5		4				9	3	**10**		7		11	8	12	6										16
2		5		4			13	9	**3**			7		11	8	10	6	12									17
2	3	5	12	4				9	6	10		7		**11**	8												18
2		5	6	4			**10**	9	3	12	1	7		11		8											19
		2	5	4				9	3	11	1	7			8	10	6										20
		2	5	4			12	9	3	**11**	1	7			8	10	6										21
2	3	5						9	8	12	1	7			4	**10**	6	11	13								22
2	3	5						9	8	10	1	7			4		6	11									23
2	3	5		4				9		10	1	7			8		6	11									24
2	3	5		4				9		10	1	7			8		6	11									25
2	3	5		4				9	12	**10**	1	7			8	13	6	11									26
2	3	5		4				9	12	10	1	**7**			8		6	11									27
2	**3**	5				12		9	8	10	1	7			4		6	11									28
2	**3**	5				12		9	8	10	1	7			4		6	11		13							29
2	3	5		4		7		9	8	10	1			13			6	11		12							30
2	**11**	5		4	3			9		10	1			8			6	7		12							31
	11	5		4	3	7		9			1			8			6	2		10							32
2		5		4	3	7		9		12				8			6	**11**		10							33
2	**3**	5	14	4	6	7		9	11	13				*8*	12					10							34
2	3	5	**6**	12		8		9	11	10		7			4												35
2	3	4	5					9	7	12					8	**10**			13		6	11					36
	3	2	5			7			8						4	10			12		6	9	**11**				37
	3	2	*5*			7			8	13					4	10			12		6	9	**11**	14			38
		5			3	7			8	**10**	1				4	12			11		6	9		2			39
		5		8	3	7			**11**	10	1				4	12			2		6	9					40
		5		8	3	7			11	10	1				4				2		6	9					41
		5		8	3	**7**			11	10	1				4	12			2		6	9					42
		5		8	3	7			*11*	10	1				**4**	13			2		6	9	14	12			43
		5		8	3	7			11	**10**	1					12			2		6	9		4			44
		5		8	3	7			11	10	1					12			**2**		6	9	13	4			45
		5		8	**3**	13			11	10	1				4	12					6	9	7	2			46
33	26	44	8	36	24	24	5	36	33	24	35	28	1	19	27	17	24	12	7	3	11	11	3	4			
	1	1	4	1		3	3		5	15			2	1	5	11		1	4	3			2	2			
	1	2		2	6	1		16	1	7		4		2	5	3			1			4					

McMillan	Hall	Jones	Reed	Tinkler	Thompson	Pouton	Woods	Cresswell	Garratt	Rowe	Mimms	Connelly	Prendergast	Agnew	Jordan	Tolson	Barras	Himsworth	Dawson	Carruthers	Fairclough	Williams	Skinner	Hocking	Bullock	Rennison	
2		5	13	**4**				9	3	14		7		11	8	*10*	6	12									1
2		5		4			10	*9*	6	14		7	12	11	8	13		**3**									r
		5	6	4				9	3	13	1	7		11	8	10									**2**	12	2
2		3	1	3			1	3	3		1	3		3	3	2	1	1							1		
			1							3			1			1		1								1	
								3							2												

McMillan	Hall	Jones	Reed	Tinkler	Thompson	Pouton	Woods	Cresswell	Garratt	Rowe	Mimms	Connelly	Prendergast	Agnew	Jordan	Tolson	Barras	Himsworth	Dawson	Carruthers	Fairclough	Williams	Skinner	Hocking	Bullock	Rennison	
2	3	5		4	6	8		9	**11**	10		7	12														1 (1)
2	3	5		4	6	8	**10**	9	13		1	7		11		12											1 (2)
2	2	2		2	2	2	1	2	1	1	1	2		1													
									1				1			1											
					1																						

York City v Manchester City 19 December 1998 programme cover.

Rodney Rowe.

1999–2000

Division Three

Manager: Neil Thompson, then Terry Dolan

	P	W	D	L	F	A	Pts
Swansea City	46	24	13	9	51	30	85
Rotherham United	46	24	12	10	72	36	84
Northampton Town	46	25	7	14	63	45	82
Darlington	46	21	16	9	66	36	79
Peterborough United	46	22	12	12	63	54	78
Barnet	46	21	12	13	59	53	75
Hartlepool United	46	21	9	16	60	49	72
Cheltenham Town	46	20	10	16	50	42	70
Torquay United	46	19	12	15	62	52	69
Rochdale	46	18	14	14	57	54	68
Brighton & Hove Albion	46	17	16	13	64	46	67
Plymouth Argyle	46	16	18	12	55	51	66
Macclesfield Town	46	18	11	17	66	61	65
Hull City	46	15	14	17	43	43	59
Lincoln City	46	15	14	17	67	69	59
Southend United	46	15	11	20	53	61	56
Mansfield Town	46	16	8	22	50	65	56
Halifax Town	46	15	9	22	44	58	54
Leyton Orient	46	13	13	20	47	52	52
York City	46	12	16	18	39	53	52
Exeter City	46	11	11	24	46	72	44
Shrewsbury Town	46	9	13	24	40	67	40
Carlisle United	46	9	12	25	42	75	39
Chester City	46	10	9	27	44	79	39

Did you know that?

For the first time since 1993–94 City started the campaign with a win.

City's victory over Shrewsbury Town on 23 November 1999 was their 1,000th win in the Football League.

In midterm, only one win was recorded in 18 League outings, and during this time on 10 February 2000 Neil Thompson was dismissed as manager and Terry Dolan became his successor.

Former Northern Ireland international 'keeper Alan Fettis made his debut in the game at Peterborough United on 4 March 2000.

Only 39 League goals were scored, equalling the club record of 1975–76 when only 42 games were played.

Clubman of the Year for the second successive season was Barry Jones.

Top marksman was Barry Conlon in his first season with the club.

Average home League attendance of 3,048 was the smallest since 1991–92.

The total of 35 players used during the season was a new club record.

For the ninth time as a Football League club, City were knocked out of the FA Cup by non-League opposition when they lost at Hereford United.

Halifax Town had three players sent off in the game at Bootham Crescent on 29 April 2000.

Match No.	Date		Venue	Opponents	Result		Scorers	Attend
1	Aug	7	H	Swansea City	W	1–0	Atkins	3
2		14	A	Torquay United	D	0–0		3
3		21	H	Rochdale	L	0–3		3
4		28	A	Barnet	L	3–6	Atkins, Conlon (2)	1
5		30	H	Northampton Town	L	0–1		2
6	Sep	4	A	Rotherham United	L	0–1		3
7		11	H	Peterborough United	D	0–0		2
8		18	A	Exeter City	L	1–2	Hulme	2
9		25	A	Hull City	D	1–1	Opp. og	8
10	Oct	2	H	Chester City	D	2–2	M. Williams, Opp. og	2
11		9	H	Leyton Orient	W	2–1	Conlon (2)	2
12		16	A	Brighton & Hove Albion	W	1–0	Hocking	5
13		19	A	Halifax Town	W	2–0	Conlon, M. Williams	2
14		23	H	Hull City	D	1–1	Hulme	5,
15	Nov	2	A	Carlisle United	W	1–0	J. Williams	2
16		6	H	Macclesfield Town	L	0–2		2
17		12	A	Lincoln City	L	2–4	Hulme, M. Williams (pen)	2
18		23	H	Shrewsbury Town	W	1–0	Alcide	1
19		27	H	Plymouth Argyle	D	0–0		2
20	Dec	4	A	Swansea City	L	0–1		3
21		17	H	Southend United	D	2–2	M. Williams, Jordan	2
22		26	A	Hartlepool United	L	1–2	Conlon	4
23		28	H	Cheltenham Town	L	1–2	M. Williams	2,
24	Jan	8	H	Mansfield Town	L	0–1		2
25		15	H	Torquay United	D	2–2	Turley, Fox	2,
26		18	A	Darlington	D	2–2	Conlon, J. Williams	5,
27		22	A	Rochdale	L	1–2	Jones	2,
28		29	H	Barnet	W	1–0	Hocking	2
29	Feb	5	A	Northampton Town	L	0–3		4,
30		8	A	Mansfield Town	L	0–1		2
31		12	H	Rotherham United	L	1–2	Conlon	4,
32		19	A	Plymouth Argyle	L	0–2		4,
33		26	H	Exeter City	D	0–0		3,
34	Mar	4	A	Peterborough United	L	0–2		5,
35		7	A	Macclesfield Town	D	1–1	Hulme	1,
36		11	H	Carlisle United	D	1–1	Conlon	2,
37		18	A	Shrewsbury Town	W	1–0	Conlon	2,
38		21	H	Lincoln City	W	2–0	Bower, Conlon	2,
39		25	H	Hartlepool United	W	2–1	J. Williams, Alcide	4,
40	Apr	1	A	Southend United	D	0–0		3,
41		8	H	Darlington	D	0–0		5,
42		15	A	Cheltenham Town	W	1–0	Sertori	4,
43		22	H	Brighton & Hove Albion	D	0–0		3,
44		24	A	Chester City	L	0–2		3,
45		29	H	Halifax Town	W	2–0	Turley, Jordan	3,
46	May	6	A	Leyton Orient	D	0–0		4,
								A
								S
							2 own-goals	

FA Cup

1	Oct	30	A	Hereford United	L	0–1		2,
								A
								S

Football League (Worthington) Cup

1 (1)	Aug	10	H	Wigan Athletic	L	0–1		1,
1 (2)		24	A	Wigan Athletic	L	1–2	Rowe	3,
								A
								S

Hocking	Hall	Atkins	Jones	Fairclough	Dawson	Dixon	Conlon	Rowe	Bullock	Garratt	Williams M.	Williams J.	Jordan	Fox	Thompson N.	Mimms	Sertori	Hulme	Turley	Ormerod	Agnew	Alcide	Keegan	Skinner	Reed	Bower	Thompson M.	Hawkins	Fettis	Talbot	Swan	Edmondson	Darlow	
2	3	4	5	6	**7**	8	9	10	11	12	13																							1
2	3	4	5	6	7	8	9	12	11			**10**																						2
2	3	4	5	6	7	*8*	9	13	**11**	12		10	14																					3
5	3	4	13	6	2		9	12		11		**10**	8	7																				4
2	11	4	5	6				10	12			9	8	**7**	3	1																		5
2	11	4		6	12			10	13			9	8	7	**3**	1	5																	6
2	11	4		6	14		9	13		12		10		7	**3**	1	5	8																7
2	3	**4**		6			9		12	11	14	13		7		1	5	8	*10*															8
2	3	4		6			9		10					7		1	5	8	12	**11**														9
2	3	4	12	6					10	13	14			7		1	5	8	9	*11*														10
	3		2	6			13			14	10	9	*8*	**4**		1	5	7		11	12													11
12	3		2	6	7		9				**10**		4			1	5	8			11													12
12	3		2	6	7		9				**10**		4			1	5	8			11													13
	3		2	6	7		9				10		4	12		1	5	8		13	**11**													14
12	3		2	6			9				13	**10**	4	7		1	5	8		11														15
10	3		2	6			9				12		4	7		1	5	8		11														16
	3		2	6			**9**				12	10	4	7		1	5	8		11														17
	3		2	6	13		12		8			**10**	4	7		1	5			11		9												18
12	**3**		2	6	4				8			10		7		1	5			11		9												19
3			2	6	13		12					10	4	7		1	5	**8**		11		9												20
2				6	**7**						10	12	8	7		1	5				11	9	4											21
2			3				12				10	8	6	7		1	5			13	11	**9**	4											22
2			3	**6**			13				10	*8*	4	7		1	5			14	11	9	12											23
2			6				13		12		10	8	**4**	7	3	1	5				11	9												24
2	11		6				9		4		12	10		7	3	1	5		**8**					13										25
2			6		12		9		4		13	10		7		1	5		8		**11**				3									26
2	3		6		**11**		9		4		13	10	12	7		1	5		8															27
2	3		6				9		11			10	8	7		1	5								4									28
2	3		6				9		11		13	10	8	7		1	5							12	4									29
2			6		12		9		**4**		10	11	8	7	3	1	13								5									30
2			6				9				10	11	8	7		1	5							3	5									31
2			6		**11**						10	9	4			1	5	7	14					12		3	*8*							32
2			6				9		13		14	12	*8*	7			5	10								4	**11**	3						33
2			5				9		6			13					10	8			12					4	11	3	1	7				34
			5				12		6					13			9	8	7		10					4	2	3	1	**11**				35
			5				14		**6**			13		12			9	8	7		10					4	2	3	1	*11*				36
			6				9					**10**		12			8	7			11	13				4	2	3	1		5			37
			6				9		12			10					8	7			11	13				4	**2**	3	1		5			38
			6				9		12			10		14			**8**	7			11	13				4		*3*	1		5	2		39
14			5	*6*			9					**10**		12			8	7			11	13				4		3	1			2		40
			6				**9**		13					7			10	8			11	12				4		3	1		5	2		41
			6	12			9					13		*7*			10	8			11	14				4	4	3	1		5	2		42
				6			9					12	8				10				11	**7**			14	4		3	1	13	5	2		43
				6			9					10	8				14				*11*			12		4	14	3	1	**7**	5	2		44
							14					13	8						*10*		11	9			2	4	6	3	1	**7**	5		12	45
12							9						8				13		10		11				6	4	7	*3*	1		**5**	2	14	46
26	23	10	35	25	11	3	31	3	16	2	11	28	26	28	6	28	37	23	9	9	20	9	2	1	7	15	9	14	13	5	9	7		
6			2	1	6		9	4	8	5	11	8	2	6			3		2	3	2	6	1	4	1		1			1			2	
2		2	1				11				5	3	2	1			1	4	2			2				1								

Hocking	Hall	Atkins	Jones	Fairclough	Dawson	Dixon	Conlon	Rowe	Bullock	Garratt	Williams M.	Williams J.	Jordan	Fox	Thompson N.	Mimms	Sertori	Hulme	Turley	Ormerod	Agnew	Alcide	Keegan	Skinner	Reed	Bower	Thompson M.	Hawkins	Fettis	Talbot	Swan	Edmondson	Darlow	
13	3		2	6	7		9				**10**	12	4	11		1	5	8																1
	1		1	1	1		1				1		1	1		1	1	1																
1												1																						

Hocking	Hall	Atkins	Jones	Fairclough	Dawson	Dixon	Conlon	Rowe	Bullock	Garratt	Williams M.	Williams J.	Jordan	Fox	Thompson N.	Mimms	Sertori	Hulme	Turley	Ormerod	Agnew	Alcide	Keegan	Skinner	Reed	Bower	Thompson M.	Hawkins	Fettis	Talbot	Swan	Edmondson	Darlow	
2	3	4	5	6	7	8	9	10	11																									1 (1)
12	3	4	**5**	6	2		9	13		11		10	8	7																				1 (2)
1	2	2	2	2	2	1	2	1	1	1		1	1	1																				
1								1																										
								1																										

York City v Leyton Orient 9 October 1999 programme cover.

Alan Fettis.

2000–01

Division Three

Manager: Terry Dolan

	P	W	D	L	F	A	Pts
Brighton & Hove Albion	46	28	8	10	73	35	92
Cardiff City	46	23	13	10	95	58	82
Chesterfield	46	25	14	7	79	42	80
Hartlepool United	46	21	14	11	71	54	77
Leyton Orient	46	20	15	11	59	51	75
Hull City	46	19	17	10	47	39	74
Blackpool	46	22	6	18	74	58	72
Rochdale	46	18	17	11	59	48	71
Cheltenham Town	46	18	14	14	59	52	68
Scunthorpe United	46	18	11	17	62	52	65
Southend United	46	15	18	13	55	53	63
Plymouth Argyle	46	15	13	18	54	61	58
Mansfield Town	46	15	13	18	64	72	58
Macclesfield Town	46	14	14	18	51	62	56
Shrewsbury Town	46	15	10	21	49	65	55
Kidderminster Harriers	46	13	14	19	47	61	53
York City	46	13	13	20	42	63	52
Lincoln City	46	12	15	19	58	66	51
Exeter City	46	12	14	20	40	58	50
Darlington	46	12	13	21	44	56	49
Torquay United	46	12	13	21	52	77	49
Carlisle United	46	11	15	20	42	65	48
Halifax Town	46	12	11	23	54	68	47
Barnet	46	12	9	25	67	81	45

Did you know that?

City dropped to the bottom of the Football League on 17 February 2001 for the first time since 1980–81. They recovered and, with only two defeats in the last 16 games, finished 17th.

Chris Brass made his City debut at home to Lincoln City on 17 March 2001.

Clubman of the Year was Alan Fettis, while top scorer was David McNiven with 10 League and Cup goals.

A new record number of players were used – 38.

Average home League attendance was 3,026.

For only the second time since 1985–86 City reached the third round of the FA Cup.

Match No.	Date	Venue	Opponents	Result		Scorers
1	Aug 12	A	Chesterfield	L	1–4	Duffield
2	19	H	Cheltenham Town	L	0–2	
3	25	A	Carlisle United	D	1–1	Duffield (pen)
4	28	H	Barnet	W	1–0	A;cide
5	Sep 2	A	Darlington	D	1–1	Duffield (pen)
6	9	H	Scunthorpe United	W	2–0	McNiven, Agnew
7	12	H	Rochdale	L	0–2	
8	16	A	Exeter City	L	1–3	McNiven
9	23	H	Brighton & Hove Albion	L	0–1	
10	30	A	Hartlepool United	L	0–1	
11	Oct 6	H	Mansfield Town	W	2–1	McNiven, Mathie
12	14	A	Southend United	L	0–1	
13	17	A	Lincoln City	L	1–2	McNiven
14	21	H	Leyton Orient	D	1–1	Tarrant
15	24	A	Halifax Town	W	3–1	Sertori, Bullock, McNiven
16	28	H	Hull City	D	0–0	
17	Nov 4	A	Cardiff City	L	0–4	
18	11	H	Torquay United	W	3–2	Hulme (2), McNiven
19	25	A	Kidderminster Harriers	L	1–3	Bullock
20	Dec 2	H	Shrewsbury Town	W	2–1	McNiven, Hulme
21	16	A	Plymouth Argyle	L	0–1	
22	22	H	Blackpool	L	0–2	
23	26	A	Macclesfield Town	W	1–0	Iwelumo
24	Jan 13	A	Barnet	L	0–2	
25	20	H	Macclesfield Town	L	1–3	Iwelumo
26	23	H	Chesterfield	L	0–1	
27	27	A	Blackpool	L	0–1	
28	30	H	Carlisle United	D	0–0	
29	Feb 10	A	Scunthorpe United	L	0–4	
30	17	H	Exeter City	L	0–3	
31	20	A	Rochdale	W	1–0	Emmerson
32	24	A	Brighton & Hove Albion	D	1–1	Agnew
33	Mar 3	H	Hartlepool United	D	1–1	McNiven
34	6	H	Southend United	W	1–0	Nogan
35	10	A	Mansfield Town	W	3–1	Potter, Alcide, Nogan
36	13	H	Darlington	W	2–0	Richardson, Alcide
37	17	H	Lincoln City	D	0–0	
38	20	A	Cheltenham Town	D	1–1	Nogan
39	24	A	Leyton Orient	D	1–1	Nogan
40	31	H	Plymouth Argyle	L	1–2	Bower
41	Apr 14	H	Halifax Town	W	2–1	Bullock, Nogan
42	16	A	Hull City	D	0–0	
43	21	H	Cardiff City	D	3–3	Brass (pen), Nogan, Alcide
44	28	A	Torquay United	D	2–2	Basham, Potter
45	May 1	A	Shrewsbury Town	L	0–2	
46	5	H	Kidderminster Harriers	W	1–0	Alcide

FA Cup

1	Nov 19	A*	Radcliffe Borough	W	4–1	Potter, Bullock, McNiven, Jordan
2	Dec 9	H	Reading	D	2–2	McNiven, Mathie
r	19	A	Reading	W	3–1	Agnew, Alcide, Iwelumo
3	Jan 6	A	Leicester City	L	0–3	

* Gigg Lane, Bury.

Football League (Worthington) Cup

1 (1)	Aug 22	H	Stoke City	L	1–5	Jones
1 (2)	Sep 6	A	Stoke City	D	0–0	

Edmondson	Potter	Sertori	Swan	Hobson	Fox	Hulme	Conlon	Duffield	Agnew	McNiven	Hall	Alcide	Jones	Bullock	Thompson	Williams	Hocking	Jordan	Turley	Mathie	Durkan	Stamp	Reed	Tarrant	Iwelumo	Bower	Patterson	Wood	Emmerson	Nogan	Darlow	Richardson	Cooper	Brass	Basham	Howarth	
2	3	4	5	6	7	8	9	10	11	12	13																										1
2	3	4	5	6	7	8	9	10	11	13		12																									2
2	3	4		6		8		9	7	10	11	13	5	12	14																						3
2	3	4		6	12		14	9	7	10	11	13	5	8																							4
2	3	4		6		8		9	7	10	11	14	5	13		12																					5
2	3	4		6		8	13	9	7	10	11	12	5																								6
2	3	4		6		8	13		7	10	11	9	5	14		12																					7
2	3	4		6		8	13		7	10	11	9	5			14	12																				8
2		4							7	10	11	13	5	8	14	9	3	6	12																		9
2	13	4							7	10	11		5	8		12	3	6		9																	10
2	3	4							8	10	11	12		6		13	5			9	7																11
	3				12				7	10		9	2	6			5		13	8	11	4															12
	3				12		13		7	10		9	2	6			5			8	11	4															13
2	3				12		13		7	14				10			5			8	11	6	4	9													14
2	3	4							7	13				10			5	12		8	11	6		9													15
2	3	4				14			7	12			13	10			5			8	11	6		9													16
	3	4				12			7	10	13	14	2	8			5				11	6		9													17
	13	4				8				11	3	10	2	6	14		5	7						9	12												18
2	3					14				10	11		5	4			6	7		12			13	9	8												19
2	3	4				12			7	10				8			6	14		9				13	11	5											20
2	3	4				8			7	10		6						13		9					11	5	12										21
	3	4				8			7	10		12			2			13	14	9					11	5	6										22
	3	4			7					12	13	5			2			8		9		10			11		6										23
		4			12	8			7	13	3	10					2		14	9					11	5	6										24
	3	4							10	12		9					2	8	7	13					11	5	6										25
	3	4							10	12		6	5		2			13	7	9		8			11												26
		4							8	10		6	5		2				7			3			9			11	12								27
	13	4							8	10		6	5		2			14	7			3			9			11	12								28
	3	4							8	10		5	2	13					7			6			9		14	11	12								29
		4							8	10	11	5	2	7								3						6	13	9	12	14					30
									8		11		2	7	6		3		12							5			10	9		4					31
									8	14	11	12	2	7	6		3									5		13	10	9		4					32
									8	12	11	13	2	7			3									5			10	9		4	6				33
									8	10		12	2	7	11		3									5				9		4	6				34
	12			14					8	10		13	2	7	11		3									5				9		4	6				35
	3								8	12		10	4	11			6			13						5				9		7	2				36
	3								8	13		10	4	11			6			12						5				9		7	2	14			37
	3								8	13		10	4	11			6									5				9		7	2	12			38
	3			12								10	4	11			6			13						5				9		7	2	8			39
	3									12		10	4	11			6			14						5				9		7	2	8	12		40
12	3								4			10		11												5				9		7	2	8	6		41
2	3			12								10		11												5				9		7	4	8	6		42
2	3											10		11												5				9		7	4	8	6		43
2	3								12	13		10		11												5				9		7	4	8	6		44
2	3								12	10		14		11			13									5				9		7	4	8	6		45
2	3								11	10		9										12				5			13			7	4	8	6		46
22	34	26	2	8	3	11	2	6	37	25	16	24	28	29	9	1	24	6	5	13	7	12	1	6	11	21	4	4	3	16		16	14	8	6		
1	4			3	5	4	6		2	16	3	14	1	4	3	5	2	6	5	6		1	1	1	1		2	1	5		1	1		2	1		
	2	1				3		3	2	8		5		3						1				1	2	1			1	6		1		1	1		

Edmondson	Potter	Sertori	Swan	Hobson	Fox	Hulme	Conlon	Duffield	Agnew	McNiven	Hall	Alcide	Jones	Bullock	Thompson	Williams	Hocking	Jordan	Turley	Mathie	Durkan	Stamp	Reed	Tarrant	Iwelumo	Bower	Patterson	Wood	Emmerson	Nogan	Darlow	Richardson	Cooper	Brass	Basham	Howarth	
2	3	4								10	11			6			5	7		12		13		9	8												1
2	3	4				8			7	10		11		12						9		13			8	5											2
	3	4				7			11	10		12			2			13		9					8	5	6										r
	3				7	8			11	10	13	4			2		14			12					9	5	6										3
2	4	3			1	3			3	4	1	2		1	2		1	1		2				1	4	3	2										
											1	1		1			1	1		2		2															
	1								1	2		1		1				1		1					1												

Edmondson	Potter	Sertori	Swan	Hobson	Fox	Hulme	Conlon	Duffield	Agnew	McNiven	Hall	Alcide	Jones	Bullock	Thompson	Williams	Hocking	Jordan	Turley	Mathie	Durkan	Stamp	Reed	Tarrant	Iwelumo	Bower	Patterson	Wood	Emmerson	Nogan	Darlow	Richardson	Cooper	Brass	Basham	Howarth	
2	3	4		6		8	12	9	10	7	11		5	13																						1	1 (1)
2	3	13				8	12			14	11	10	5	7	6	9	4																				1 (2)
2	2	1		1		2		1	1	1	2	1	2	1	1	1	1																			1	
		1					2			1				1																							
													1																								

York City v Stoke City 22 August 2000 programme cover.

David McNiven.

2001–02

Division Three

Manager: Terry Dolan

	P	W	D	L	F	A	Pts
Plymouth Argyle	46	31	9	6	71	28	102
Luton Town	46	30	7	9	96	48	97
Mansfield Town	46	24	7	15	72	60	79
Cheltenham Town	46	21	15	10	66	49	78
Rochdale	46	21	15	10	65	52	78
Rushden & Diamonds	46	20	13	13	69	53	73
Hartlepool United	46	20	11	15	74	48	71
Scunthorpe United	46	19	14	13	74	56	71
Shrewsbury Town	46	20	10	16	64	53	70
Kidderminster Harriers	46	19	9	18	56	47	66
Hull City	46	16	13	17	57	51	61
Southend United	46	15	13	18	51	54	58
Macclesfield Town	46	15	13	18	41	52	58
York City	46	16	9	21	54	67	57
Darlington	46	15	11	20	60	71	56
Exeter City	46	14	13	19	48	73	55
Carlisle United	46	12	16	18	49	56	52
Leyton Orient	46	13	13	20	55	71	52
Torquay United	46	12	15	19	46	63	51
Swansea City	46	13	12	21	53	77	51
Oxford United	46	11	14	21	53	62	47
Lincoln City	46	10	16	20	44	62	46
Bristol Rovers	46	11	12	23	40	60	45
Halifax Town	46	8	12	26	39	84	36

Did you know that?

On the opening day City lost to League newcomers Rushden & Diamonds.

Lee Grant became the second-youngest player to appear for City when he came on as substitute on 16 April 2002 at home to Bristol Rovers. He was 16 years and 106 days old.

For the second successive season Alan Fettis was voted Clubman of the Year, and top scorer was Michael Proctor, who was on loan from Sunderland.

Average home League crowd was 3,144.

For the first time since 1985–86 City reached the fourth round of the FA Cup, knocking out Second Division (League One) Reading for the second successive season in round two. In the third round, First Division (Championship) Grimsby Town were vanquished. In the first round City were involved in their first-ever penalty shoot-out in the competition.

Match No.	Date	Venue	Opponents	Result		Scorers	Attend
1	Aug 11	H	Rushden & Diamonds	L	0–1		4
2	18	A	Torquay United	W	3–0	Bullock, Basham, Nogan	2
3	25	H	Leyton Orient	W	2–1	Nogan, Proctor	2
4	28	A	Shrewsbury Town	L	2–3	Bullock, Fielding	3
5	Sep 1	H	Halifax Town	W	1–0	Proctor	2
6	8	A	Hull City	L	0–4		9
7	15	H	Luton Town	L	1–2	Nogan	3
8	18	A	Carlisle United	L	1–2	Salvati	2
9	22	A	Bristol Rovers	D	2–2	Potter, Cooper	6
10	25	H	Plymouth Argyle	D	0–0		2
11	29	A	Lincoln City	W	3–1	Proctor (2), Brass	2
12	Oct 6	H	Exeter City	L	2–3	Bullock, Mathie	2
13	13	A	Hartlepool United	L	0–3		3
14	20	H	Southend United	W	2–1	Nogan, Proctor	2
15	23	A	Kidderminster Harriers	L	1–4	Nogan	2
16	27	H	Macclesfield United	W	1–0	Proctor	2
17	Nov 3	A	Oxford United	D	2–2	Nogan, Proctor	5
18	9	H	Scunthorpe United	L	0–2		3
19	20	H	Swansea City	L	0–2		1
20	23	A	Mansfield Town	D	1–1	Nogan	4
21	Dec 1	A	Darlington	L	1–3	Proctor	4
22	15	H	Cheltenham Town	L	1–3	Bullock	2
23	29	H	Shrewsbury Town	D	1–1	Nogan	2
24	Jan 12	H	Torquay United	D	1–1	Bullock	3
25	19	A	Rushden & Diamonds	L	0–3		4
26	22	H	Rochdale	D	0–0		2
27	29	H	Hull City	W	2–1	Proctor, Duffield	6
28	Feb 5	A	Rochdale	L	4–5	Brass, Duffield, Bullock, Proctor	2
29	9	A	Southend United	W	1–0	Parkin	3
30	12	A	Halifax Town	D	1–1	Opp. og	2
31	16	H	Hartlepool United	W	1–0	Nogan	4
32	19	A	Leyton Orient	W	2–1	Duffield, Mathie	3
33	23	A	Luton Town	L	1–2	Proctor	6
34	Mar 5	A	Plymouth Argyle	L	0–1		10
35	9	A	Cheltenham Town	L	0–4		3
36	16	H	Darlington	W	2–0	Basham, Proctor	3
37	19	A	Exeter City	L	1–2	Nogan	2
38	23	H	Kidderminster Harriers	L	0–1		2
39	26	H	Lincoln City	W	2–0	Bullock, Nogan	2
40	30	A	Macclesfield United	L	1–2	Bullock	1
41	Apr 1	H	Oxford United	W	1–0	Potter	3
42	6	A	Swansea City	W	1–0	Jones	2
43	9	H	Carlisle United	D	0–0		2
44	13	H	Mansfield Town	W	3–1	Nogan, Parkin, Proctor	5
45	16	H	Bristol Rovers	W	3–0	Opp. og, Nogan, Proctor	2
46	20	A	Scunthorpe United	L	0–1		5
							A
							S
						2 own-goals	

FA Cup

1	Nov 17	A	Colchester United	D	0–0		3
r	27	H	Colchester United	D	2–2*	Brass, Potter	2
2	Dec 8	H	Reading	W	2–0	Richardson, Potter	3
3	Jan 5	A	Grimsby Town	D	0–0		5
r	15	H	Grimsby Town	W	1–0	Opp. og	6
4	26	H	Fulham	L	0–2		7
							A
							S
						1 own-goal	

* After extra-time. City won 3–2 on penalties.

Football League (Worthington Cup)

1	Aug 21	H	Crewe Alexandra	D	2–2*	Bullock, Brass	1
							A
							S

* After extra-time. Crewe won 6–5 on penalties.

Edmondson	Potter	Hocking	Basham	Hobson	Brass	Bullock	Nogan	Proctor	Richardson	Duffield	Fielding	Cooper	O'Kane	Wood	Emmerson	Stamp	Evans	Fox	Salvati	Mathie	Maley	Smith	Darlow	Rhodes	Parkin	Wise	Brackstone	Jones	Howarth	Grant	
2	3	4	5	6	7	8	9	10	**11**	12																				1
2	3		5		7	**8**	9	10			4	6	11	12	13																2
2	3	12	**5**		7	8	9	10			4	6	11																	3
2	3		5		7	8	9	10			4	6	**11**		12																4
2	3	12	**5**		7	8	9	10	13		4	6	11																	5
2	3		5		7	8	9	10	**11**		4	6				12	13														6
2	3		5		7	8	9	10	11		4						**6**	13	12													7
2	*3*	12	**5**		7	8	9	10	11		4	13						14	6													8
2	3	5			7	8	9	10			4	6						**11**	12	13												9
2	3	4	5		7	8	9	10				6						**11**	12													10
2	3	4	5		7	8	9	10				**6**							12		11											11
2	3	**4**	5		7	8	9	10				*6*							13	14	11	12										12
					7	8	9	10	**11**		4	3						6	12	13	5	2										13
		2		13	7	8	**9**	10				6				3		11	12		5	4										14
		2	13	12	7	8	9	10	14			6				3		11			*5*	4										15
2	3	4		5	7	**8**	9	10	12			11				6																16
2	3	4		5	7	8	9	10				11									6											17
2		4		5	7	8	9	10				3			13			12			6		**11**									18
12	3	4		*5*	7	8	9	10	**11**			6									14	2	13									19
2	3	4			7		**9**	10	11			6				8				12		5											20
2	3	**4**	12		7	9		10	11			8									5	6		13								21
2	3	12	**5**		7	9		10	*11*	13		8	14								6	4											22
2	3	4	5	6	7	8	9	10	11																						23
2	3	4	**5**	6		8	9	10	11			7										12											24
2	3		5	6		8	**9**	10	11	12		7								13		4											25
2	3	4	5	6	7		9	10		12		11								**8**													26
	3	4	5	6	7		**9**	10	11	*8*		2				14				12		13											27
2	3	4	5		7	8		10	11	9						**6**				13	12												28
	3	4	5		7	**8**		10	12	9											13	2	6			11						29
	3	4	5		7	8	12	10	13	9												2	**6**			11						30
2	3	4	5		7	12	**9**	10	11	8										13					6						31
2	3	4	5			8	9	10		**11**				7						12					6						32
2	3		**5**	6	7	8	9	10		11										13					4	12					33
	3	4	5	**6**	7	8	9		11											10					2	12					34
	3	4		6	7	**8**	9	10	2					12						11					5						35
	3	2	12	**6**	7	8	*9*	10						4	13					11					5		14				36
	3	2	5		7	8	12						11	10	13					**9**					6		4				37
12	3		5		7	8	9						**11**	4	13					10					6		2				38
2	3	4			7	8	9	**10**						6						11					5		13	12			39
2	3	4			7	8	9							6						**11**					10		12	5			40
2	3	**4**			7	8	9							6				13								10	12	11	5			41
2						7	8	9	12					6	4						**11**					10	5		3			42
2						7	8	9	**10**					6	4						12					11	5		3			43
2					7		9	10					6	8				12								11	**5**	4	3			44
2								9	10					11	7				13		*8*		3			6		4	5	12	14	45
2								9	**10**				13	11	7				12		8		3			6		4	5	1		46
34	37	29	26	14	41	39	40	40	17	7	9	23	11	12		5	1	5	1	11	11	12	1		18	3	6	7	1		
2		4	3	2		1	2	1	5	4		2	1	2	6	2	1	7	7	12	2	3	1	1		3	3	1	1	1	
	2		2		2	8	13	14		3	1	1							1	2					2			1			

Edmondson	Potter	Hocking	Basham	Hobson	Brass	Bullock	Nogan	Proctor	Richardson	Duffield	Fielding	Cooper	O'Kane	Wood	Emmerson	Stamp	Evans	Fox	Salvati	Mathie	Maley	Smith	Darlow	Rhodes	Parkin	Wise	Brackstone	Jones	Howarth	Grant	
	3	4		5	7	8	9	10	12			11									**6**	2									1
2	3	5			7	14	**9**	10	11			8				4				*12*	13	6									r
2	3		5		7	8		9	10			11									6	4									2
2	3	4	5	6	**7**	8	9	10	11			12																		3
2	3	4	5	6		8	9	10	7			11																		r
2	3	4	5	**6**	7	8	9	10		12		11								13										4
5	6	5	4	4	5	5	5	6	4			5				1					2	3								
						1			1	1		1								2	1									
	2				1				1																					

Edmondson	Potter	Hocking	Basham	Hobson	Brass	Bullock	Nogan	Proctor	Richardson	Duffield	Fielding	Cooper	O'Kane	Wood	Emmerson	Stamp	Evans	Fox	Salvati	Mathie	Maley	Smith	Darlow	Rhodes	Parkin	Wise	Brackstone	Jones	Howarth	Grant	
2	3		5		7	8	9	10			4	6	**11**		12																1
1	1		1		1	1	1	1			1	1	1																		
															1															
					1	1																									

York City v Fulham 26 January 2002 programme cover.

Michael Proctor.

2002–03

Division Three

Manager: Terry Dolan

	P	W	D	L	F	A	Pts
Rushden & Diamonds	46	24	15	7	73	47	87
Hartlepool United	46	24	13	9	71	51	85
Wrexham	46	23	15	8	84	50	84
Bournemouth	46	20	14	12	60	48	74
Scunthorpe United	46	19	15	12	68	49	72
Lincoln City	46	18	16	12	46	37	70
Bury	46	18	16	12	57	56	70
Oxford United	46	19	12	15	57	47	69
Torquay United	46	16	18	12	71	71	66
York City	46	17	15	14	52	53	66
Kidderminster Harriers	46	16	15	15	62	63	63
Cambridge United	46	16	13	17	67	70	61
Hull City	46	14	17	15	58	53	59
Darlington	46	12	18	16	58	59	54
Boston United	46	15	13	18	55	56	54
Macclesfield Town	46	14	12	20	57	63	54
Southend United	46	17	3	26	47	59	54
Leyton Orient	46	14	11	21	51	61	53
Rochdale	46	12	16	18	63	70	52
Bristol Rovers	46	12	15	19	50	57	51
Swansea City	46	12	13	21	48	65	49
Carlisle United	46	13	10	23	52	78	49
Exeter City	46	11	15	20	50	64	48
Shrewsbury Town	46	9	14	23	62	92	41

Did you know that?

A total of 33 players were utilised this season, including a record number of six goalkeepers.

Early in the season Brazilian Rogerio Carvalho and Argentinian Nicolas Mazzina made appearances.

Jon McCarthy made one appearance back in City colours on 9 November 2002 at home to Leyton Orient.

Alan Fettis was transferred to Hull City, and his last game for City was at home to Swansea City on 18 January 2003.

Leading scorer Peter Duffield played his last game for the club at Hull City on 25 January 2003 prior to his move to Boston United. He started the campaign by scoring in each of the first six League games.

The supporters' trust took over the running of the club, and the first match of the new regime, on 29 March 2003 against Southend United, marked City's 3,000th game in the Football League.

The average League attendance at Bootham Crescent of 4,176 had only been bettered once since 1984–85 (1993–94).

Clubman of the Year was Chris Brass, and during the close season he was appointed player manager following the departure of Terry Dolan after three-and-a-half years in charge.

Match No.	Date	Venue	Opponents	Result		Scorers
1	Aug 10	A	Macclesfield Town	D	1–1	Duffield
2	13	H	Shrewsbury Town	W	2–1	Duffield, Parkin
3	17	H	Torquay United	W	4–3	Duffield, Nogan, Parkin (2)
4	24	A	Scunthorpe United	L	1–2	Duffield
5	26	H	Boston United	W	2–0	Duffield, Nogan
6	31	A	Swansea City	W	2–1	Bullock, Duffield (pen)
7	Sep 6	A	Bury	L	1–2	Cowan
8	14	H	Rushden & Diamonds	D	0–0	
9	17	H	Darlington	W	1–0	Parkin
10	21	A	Cambridge United	L	0–3	
11	28	H	Oxford United	L	0–1	
12	Oct 5	A	Exeter City	W	1–0	Cook
13	12	A	Southend United	L	0–1	
14	19	H	Bristol Rovers	D	2–2	Duffield (pen), Brackstone
15	26	A	Bournemouth	L	0–1	
16	29	H	Wrexham	D	1–1	Duffield
17	Nov 1	A	Hartlepool United	D	0–0	
18	9	H	Leyton Orient	W	3–2	Brass, Parkin, Bullock
19	23	A	Rochdale	W	1–0	Duffield
20	30	H	Carlisle United	W	2–1	Reddy, Duffield
21	Dec 14	A	Kidderminster Harriers	W	2–1	Brackstone, Nogan
22	20	H	Lincoln City	D	1–1	Cooper
23	26	A	Boston United	L	0–3	
24	28	H	Hull City	D	1–1	Edmondson
25	Jan 1	H	Scunthorpe United	L	1–3	Edmondson
26	11	A	Torquay United	L	1–3	Duffield (pen)
27	18	H	Swansea City	W	3–1	Duffield (2, 1 pen), Reddy
28	25	A	Hull City	D	0–0	
29	Feb 2	H	Macclesfield Town	W	2–1	Parkin, Bullock
30	8	A	Leyton Orient	W	1–0	Shandran
31	11	A	Shrewsbury Town	D	2–2	Potter, Parkin
32	15	H	Hartlepool United	D	0–0	
33	22	H	Bury	D	1–1	Parkin (pen)
34	Mar 1	A	Rushden & Diamonds	L	1–2	Bullock
35	4	A	Darlington	L	1–2	Bullock
36	8	H	Cambridge United	W	3–1	Parkin, Nogan, Shandran
37	15	H	Bournemouth	W	1–0	Parkin
38	18	A	Bristol Rovers	W	1–0	Edmondson
39	22	A	Wrexham	D	1–1	Edmondson
40	29	H	Southend United	W	2–0	Nogan, Bullock
41	Apr 12	H	Rochdale	D	2–2	Graydon (pen), Edmondson
42	15	A	Carlisle United	D	1–1	Shandran
43	19	A	Lincoln City	L	0–1	
44	21	H	Kidderminster Harriers	D	0–0	
45	26	H	Exeter City	L	0–2	
46	May 3	A	Oxford United	L	0–2	

FA Cup

1	Nov 26	H	Swansea City	W	2–1	Duffield (2)
2	Dec 7	H	Brentford	L	1–2	Bullock

Football League (Worthington) Cup

1	Sep 10	A	Sheffield United	L	0–1	

Okoli	Cowan	Jones	Smith	Hobson	Brass	Fox	Nogan	Duffield	Brackstone	Parkin	Edmondson	Mathie	Wilding	Wise	Carvalho	Bullock	Potter	Wood	Fettis	Yalcin	Mazzina	Cook	Reddy	McCarthy	Cooper	Ingham	Shandran	Graydon	Whitehead	Stockdale	
2	3	4	5	**6**	7	8	*9*	10	11	12	13	14																			1
	3	4	5	6	7		9	10	11	**8**	2	13	12																		2
12	3	4	**5**	6	7		*9*	10	11	8	2	14	13																		3
	3	**4**	5	6	7		9	10	*11*	8	2			12	13	14															4
	6		5	12	**7**		9	10	11	*8*	2				14	4	3	13													5
	6		5	14	7		9	**10**	11	8	2	12				4	*3*	13													6
	6		*5*	13	7		9	10	11	**8**	2	14			12	4	3		1												7
	3		5	6	7		9	10	11		2	**8**			13	4			1	12											8
	3		5	6	7		9	10	11	12	2	**8**				4			1												9
	3		5	6	7		9	10	11	**8**	2		12			4	13		1												10
	11		5	**6**	7		9	*10*		8	2					4	3	12	1	14	13										11
			5	6	4		**9**	*10*	7	12	2					8	3	13	1		14	11									12
	3		5	6	4		**9**	10	7	12	2					8	13		1			11									13
			5		4		14	10	7	9	2					**8**	3	*6*	1	13	12	11									14
12		4	5	**6**	7		13	10		9						8	3	2	1			11									15
		5	12		4		13	10		9	2		*7*			*8*	3	6	1	14		11									16
					4		**9**	10	7	5	2					8	3	6	1			11	12								17
					4		12	10	8	5	**2**					6	3		1			11	9	7							18
			5	6			9	10	7		2			4		8	3		1				11								19
				6	4	12	**9**	10	*7*	5	2					8	3	13	1				11								20
	13			6	**4**	14	9	10	*7*	5	2					8	3	12	1				11								21
	6					12	9	10	**7**	5	2			4		8	3		1				11		13						22
	6		12			7	9	10		**5**	2					8	3		1				11		4						23
	4		5	6		7	9	**10**			2		13			8	3	12	1				11								24
	4		**5**	6		7	9	10		11	2		13			8	3		1						12						25
	4	13		6		7	9	10		**5**	*2*			12		8	3		1				11		14						26
	4			6	7		9	10		5						8	3		1				11		2						27
	4	6			7		9	**10**		5						8	3			12			11		2	1					28
	4	6	5		7		9			10						8	3	12							2	1	**11**				29
	2	6	5		4		9			10						8	3								7	1	11				30
	2	6	5		4	12	9			10						8	3								7	1	**11**				31
	2	6	5		4	12	*9*			10		14		13		8	3								7	1	**11**				32
	6		5		7		9			10	2	13		4			3	12							8	1	11				33
		6	5		4		9			10	2					7	3								8	1	11				34
		6	5		4		9			10	2	14		12		8	3	13							**7**	1	*11*				35
	11	6	5		7		**9**			10	2					8	3								4	1	12				36
	11	6	5		7		9		12	10	2					*8*	3	14							**4**	1	13				37
	11	6	5	12	**7**		13			9	2						3	8							4	1	10				38
	11	6	5		7		13		12	9	2		14				3	8							4	1	*10*				39
			5	6	4		11		12	9	2					**8**	3	14							7	1	13	10			40
			5	6	4		9				2					8	3								7	1	11	10			41
	11		5	6	4		9				2					8	3								7		12	**10**	1		42
	11		5	6	4		9		14	10	2					8	**3**								7		12	13	1		43
	13	5		6	4		9		11	10	2						3								7	1	**8**	12			44
		5	12	**6**	4		*9*		11	10	2					8	3								*7*	1	14	13			45
	3				4	7	12		11	5				14		8		6							2	1	*10*	9		13	46
1	31	19	33	24	40	6	39	28	22	37	37	2	1	3		38	37	7	21			7	10	1	21	17	12	4	2		
2	2	1	3	4		5	7		4	4	1	8	6	5	4	1	2	12		5	3		1		3		6	3		1	
	1	1			1		5	13	3	10	5					6	1					1	2		1		3	1			

Okoli	Cowan	Jones	Smith	Hobson	Brass	Fox	Nogan	Duffield	Brackstone	Parkin	Edmondson	Mathie	Wilding	Wise	Carvalho	Bullock	Potter	Wood	Fettis	Yalcin	Mazzina	Cook	Reddy	McCarthy	Cooper	Ingham	Shandran	Graydon	Whitehead	Stockdale	
			5	6	4		9	10	7	11	2					8	3		1												1
				6	4	7	9	10	11	5	2					8	3		1												2
			1	2	2	1	2	2	2	2	2					2	2		2												
								2								1															

Okoli	Cowan	Jones	Smith	Hobson	Brass	Fox	Nogan	Duffield	Brackstone	Parkin	Edmondson	Mathie	Wilding	Wise	Carvalho	Bullock	Potter	Wood	Fettis	Yalcin	Mazzina	Cook	Reddy	McCarthy	Cooper	Ingham	Shandran	Graydon	Whitehead	Stockdale	
	3		5	6	4		**9**	10	7		2				12	8	11		1	13											1
	1		1	1	1		1	1	1		1					1	1		1												
															1					1											

York City v Rushden & Diamonds 14 September 2002 programme cover.

Peter Duffield.

Jon Parkin.

2003–04

Division Three

Manager: Chris Brass

	P	W	D	L	F	A	Pts
Doncaster Rovers	46	27	11	8	79	37	92
Hull City	46	25	13	8	82	44	88
Torquay United	46	23	12	11	68	44	81
Huddersfield Town	46	23	12	11	68	52	81
Mansfield Town	46	22	9	15	76	62	75
Northampton Town	46	22	9	15	58	51	75
Lincoln City	46	19	17	10	68	47	74
Yeovil Town	46	23	5	18	70	57	74
Oxford United	46	18	17	11	55	44	71
Swansea City	46	15	14	17	58	61	59
Boston United	46	16	11	19	50	54	59
Bury	46	15	11	20	54	64	56
Cambridge United	46	14	14	18	55	67	56
Cheltenham Town	46	14	14	18	57	71	56
Bristol Rovers	46	14	13	19	50	61	55
Kidderminster Harriers	46	14	13	19	45	59	55
Southend United	46	14	12	20	51	63	54
Darlington	46	14	11	21	53	61	53
Leyton Orient	46	13	14	19	48	65	53
Macclesfield Town	46	13	13	20	54	69	52
Rochdale	46	12	14	20	49	58	50
Scunthorpe United	46	11	16	19	69	72	49
Carlisle United	46	12	9	25	46	69	45
York City	46	10	14	22	35	66	44

Did you know that?

Player-manager Chris Brass was sent off on the opening day of the campaign as City won their first four League games, equalling the club record set in 1992–93.

Prior to his transfer to Macclesfield Town Jon Parkin's last appearance was at home to Lincoln City on 17 February 2004. Lee Bullock played his last game at home to Scunthorpe United on 9 March 2004 and moved to Cardiff City.

Following the 2–0 home win over Carlisle United on 10 January 2004 City were 10th in the table with 39 points from 26 games – 18 points clear of a relegation place.

City then failed to win any of their remaining 20 fixtures (five draws, 15 defeats), which set a new club record, and 75 years' membership of the Football League ended with relegation to the Conference.

Only 35 League goals were scored (previous lowest 39), and for the first time in the club's history they failed to score more than twice in any game.

Thirty-seven players made senior appearances, and for the fourth successive season no one was ever present.

Darren Dunning was Clubman of the Year, and leading marksman was Lee Nogan.

Average home League crowd was 3,963.

For the first time since 1993–94 City fell at the first hurdle in each Cup competition, losing on each occasion to Yorkshire opposition.

Match No.	Date		Venue	Opponents	Result		Scorers	Attend
1	Aug	9	A	Carlisle United	W	2–1	Bullock, Nogan	7
2		16	H	Northampton Town	W	1–0	Nogan	3
3		23	A	Huddersfield Town	W	1–0	Bullock	9
4		26	H	Southend United	W	2–0	Hope, George	4
5		30	A	Lincoln City	L	0–3		3
6	Sep	6	H	Rochdale	L	1–2	Wilford	3
7		13	A	Yeovil Town	L	0–3		5
8		16	H	Darlington	D	1–1	George	3
9		20	H	Bristol Rovers	W	2–1	Bullock, Wilford	3
10		27	A	Macclesfield Town	D	0–0		2
11		30	A	Bury	L	0–2		2
12	Oct	4	H	Cambridge United	W	2–0	Bullock, Brackstone	3
13		11	A	Mansfield Town	L	0–2		4
14		18	H	Boston United	D	1–1	Parkin	3
15		21	H	Oxford United	D	2–2	Nogan, Hope	3
16		25	A	Scunthorpe United	D	0–0		3
17	Nov	1	A	Cheltenham Town	D	1–1	Parkin	3
18		15	H	Doncaster Rovers	W	1–0	Dunning (pen)	5
19		22	A	Leyton Orient	D	2–2	Edmondson, Brackstone	3
20		29	H	Swansea City	D	0–0		3
21	Dec	6	A	Darlington	L	0–3		4
22		13	A	Torquay United	D	1–1	Nogan	2
23		21	H	Kidderminster Harriers	W	1–0	Bullock	2
24		26	H	Hull City	L	0–2		7
25		28	A	Rochdale	W	2–1	Nogan (2)	2
26	Jan	10	H	Carlisle United	W	2–0	Brass, Cooper	4
27		17	A	Northampton Town	L	1–2	Bullock	5
28		25	H	Huddersfield Town	L	0–2		6
29		27	A	Southend United	D	0–0		2
30	Feb	7	A	Hull City	L	1–2	Nogan	19
31		14	H	Mansfield Town	L	1–2	Nogan	4
32		17	H	Lincoln City	L	1–4	Bullock	3
33		21	A	Boston United	L	0–2		2
34	Mar	3	A	Oxford United	D	0–0		5
35		6	A	Kidderminster Harriers	L	1–4	Cooper	2
36		9	H	Scunthorpe United	L	1–3	Bell	2
37		13	H	Torquay United	D	0–0		3
38		27	A	Bristol Rovers	L	0–3		6
39	Apr	4	H	Macclesfield Town	L	0–2		3
40		9	A	Cambridge United	L	0–2		5
41		13	H	Bury	D	1–1	George	3
42		17	H	Cheltenham Town	L	0–2		3
43		20	H	Yeovil Town	L	1–2	Dunning	2
44		24	A	Doncaster Rovers	L	1–3	Dunning	7
45	May	1	H	Leyton Orient	L	1–2	Wise	3
46		8	A	Swansea City	D	0–0		6

A
S

FA Cup

1	Nov	9	H	Barnsley	L	1–2	Nogan	5

A
S

Football League (Carling) Cup

1	Aug	12	A	Rotherham United	L	1–2	Merris	2

A
S

Edmondson	Merris	Wise	Brass	Hope	Ward	Dunning	Nogan	Bullock	Fox	Cooper	Wood	George	Stewart	Downes	Brackstone	Parkin	Wilford	Crowe	Smith	Dove	Browne	Shaw	Coad	Davies	Walker	Yalcin	Dickman	Bell	Porter	Offiong	Newby	Law	Arthur	Ashcroft	Haw	
2	3	4	5	6	7	8	9	10	**11**	12	13																									1
2	3	4	5	**6**	7	8	9	10		14	12	*11*	13																							2
2	3	**4**		6	7	8	9	11		12	5	10	13																							3
2	3			6	7	8	9	11		**4**	5	*10*	14	12	13																					4
2	3			6	7	8	9	11		4	5	*10*	14	12		13																				5
	3	4	5	6	7	8	9	11		14		**10**		*2*	13		12																			6
	3	4	5	*6*	7		9	11		13	8	12	14	2			**10**																			7
	3	4	5		7	8		11		12	6	10	13	**2**			9																			8
	3		5	6	7	8		11		2	4	**10**	12				9																			9
	3		5	6	7	8		11		2	4	10					**9**	12																		10
	3		5	6	7	8		10	**11**	2	4	*9*	14					12	13																	11
	3		5	6	7	8	**9**	*11*		2	4	13			12		14	10																		12
	3	12	**5**	6	7	8	9			2	4	14				13		*10*		11																13
	3		5	6	7	8	9	**11**		2		13				10		12	4																	14
	3		5	6	7	8	9	11		2	12	13				10			4																	15
2	3		5	6	7	8	**9**	11				12				10			4																	16
2	3		5	6	7		9	11		8	12					**10**			4																	17
2	3		5	6		8	9	7							11				4		**10**	12														18
2	3		5	6		8	9	7							11				4		**10**	12														19
2	3		5	6		8	9	7							11				4		12	**10**														20
2	3		5			8	9	7		4					*11*	12			6		13	**10**	14													21
2	3		5			8	**9**	11		7						4			6		12	10														22
2	3		5			8	9	11		7						4			6			10														23
2	*3*		5		12	8	9	11		**7**						4			6		13	10		14												24
2	3		5	6	7	8	**9**	10		11					13				4			12														25
2	3		5	6	**7**	8	9	*10*		11						14			4						12	13										26
	3		5	6	*7*	8	9	10	14	2					12	4									**11**	13										27
2	3		5	6	7	8	**9**	10		11									4							12										28
2	3		5	6	7	8	12	*11*	13							**9**			4						10	14										29
2	3		5	6	7	8	**9**	10								13			4						11	12										30
13	3		5	6	*7*	8	9	12	14	2									4						11	**10**										31
2	*3*		5	4	13	8	9	7		12						14								6	11	**10**										32
	13		5	4		8	9	11		2				7					6					3	12	**10**										33
	3	4	5		7		*9*	10		12	2								13					6	11		**8**	14								34
	3	4			*7*		9	10		12	2								5					6	11	14	**8**	13								35
2	11	5			**7**	8	9	10		4	6												14	3		12		13								36
	3	5		4		8	9			7	2								6							12		11	1	**10**						37
	3	5		4		8	9			7	2								6				14			13		**11**	1	*10*	12					38
	11	4	5	6		8	9			*2*														3		14		11	1	13	10	12				39
2	11	3	5	4		8	**9**			7	13	14							6											12	*10*					40
2		**3**	5	4	12	8	9				7	11							6												10					41
2		3	**5**	4	12	8	*9*			14	7	11							6									13			10					42
2	14	3	*5*	4		8	**9**			12	7	11							6									13			10					43
2	3	4	5			8				*7*	11	9							6									13			10	12	14			44
	3	4	5			8					6	**9**	11											13		10		12	1			2	7	14		45
	3		5	4		**8**					6	13	11													9			1			2	7	10	12	46
26	42	18	39	36	27	42	38	34	2	26	21	14	2	4	4	9	4	2	26	1	2	5		6	7	5	2	3	5	2	6	2	2	1		
1	2	1			4		1	1	3	11	5	8	8	2	5	6	2	3	2		4	3	3	2	2	10		7		2	1	2	1	1	1	
1		1	1	2		3	8	7		2		3			2	2	2											1								

Edmondson	Merris	Wise	Brass	Hope	Ward	Dunning	Nogan	Bullock	Fox	Cooper	Wood	George	Stewart	Downes	Brackstone	Parkin	Wilford	Crowe	Smith	
2	3		5	6	**7**	8	9	10		*11*		13			12		14		4	1
1	1		1	1	1	1	1	1		1									1	
												1			1		1			
							1													

Edmondson	Merris	Wise	Brass	Hope	Ward	Dunning	Nogan	Bullock	Fox	Cooper	Wood	George	Stewart	
2	3	4	5	6	7	8	**9**	10			11		12	1
1	1	1	1	1	1	1	1	1			1			
													1	
	1													

York City v Leyton Orient 1 May 2004 programme cover.

Darren Dunning.

2004–05

Conference

Manager: Chris Brass, then Viv Busby, then Billy McEwan

	P	W	D	L	F	A	Pts
Barnet	42	26	8	8	90	44	86
Hereford United	42	21	11	10	68	41	74
Carlisle United	42	20	13	9	74	37	73
Aldershot	42	21	10	11	68	52	73
Stevenage Borough	42	22	6	14	65	52	72
Exeter City	42	20	11	11	71	50	71
Morecambe	42	19	14	9	69	50	71
Woking	42	18	14	10	58	45	68
Halifax Town	42	19	9	14	74	56	66
Accrington Stanley	42	18	11	13	72	58	65
Dagenham & Redbridge	42	19	8	15	68	60	65
Crawley Town	42	16	9	17	50	50	57
Scarborough	42	14	14	14	60	46	56
Tamworth	42	14	11	17	53	63	53
Northwich Victoria	42	14	10	18	58	72	52
Gravesend & Northfleet	42	13	11	18	58	64	50
Burton Albion	42	13	11	18	50	66	50
York City	42	11	10	21	39	66	43
Canvey Island	42	9	15	18	53	65	42
Forest Green Rovers	42	6	15	21	41	81	33
Farnborough	42	6	11	25	35	89	29
Leigh RMI	42	4	6	32	31	98	18

Did you know that?

This was City's first season in non-League football since 1928–29.

Following the home defeat at the hands of Forest Green Rovers on 6 November 2004 Chris Brass was dismissed as manager. He continued as a player, but the home match against Burton Albion on 29 December 2004 marked his last senior appearance owing to a serious injury.

Viv Busby took over the reins, but in February 2005 Billy McEwan was appointed, and his first match in charge was 12 February at Forest Green.

Lee Nogan's last appearance was at home to Aldershot Town on 6 February 2005.

The 6–0 defeat at Carlisle United on 12 April 2005 was City's biggest since September 1988.

Clubman of the Year was Dave Merris, and leading scorer was Andy Bishop.

Average home Conference attendance was 2,333 (the club had two lower figures in the Football League 1977–78, 1980–81).

For the second successive season City did not win a Cup tie.

For the first time since 1927–28 City did not reach the first-round proper of the FA Cup.

Match No.	Date	Venue	Opponents	Result		Scorers
1	Aug 14	A	Aldershot Town	L	0–2	
2	17	H	Tamworth	W	2–0	Groves, P.D. Robinson
3	21	H	Hereford United	L	0–3	
4	28	A	Gravesend & Northfleet	L	0–4	
5	31	H	Accrington Stanley	L	0–1	
6	Sep 4	A	Dagenham & Redbridge	W	3–0	Groves, Dunning (2)
7	11	A	Crawley Town	L	0–1	
8	18	H	Northwich Victoria	D	0–0	
9	21	H	Leigh RMI	D	1–1	Dunning (pen)
10	25	A	Burton Albion	W	2–0	Groves, Bishop
11	Oct 2	H	Stevenage Borough	W	3–1	Bishop, Nogan, Brass
12	5	A	Morecambe	L	1–2	Yalcin
13	9	A	Farnborough Town	D	1–1	Bishop
14	16	H	Canvey Island	D	0–0	
15	23	A	Barnet	L	0–4	
16	Nov 6	H	Forest Green Rovers	L	1–3	Bishop
17	20	A	Woking	L	0–1	
18	27	H	Carlisle United	W	2–1	Nogan, Merris
19	Dec 7	H	Halifax Town	D	1–1	Donovan
20	11	A	Northwich Victoria	L	0–3	
21	18	H	Crawley Town	W	3–1	Grant, P. Robinson, Bishop
22	26	A	Scarborough	L	1–5	Grant
23	28	H	Burton Albion	L	1–2	P. Robinson
24	Jan 2	H	Scarborough	L	0–2	
25	8	A	Stevenage Borough	D	2–2	Maloney, Webster
26	22	H	Morecambe	W	1–0	Bishop (pen)
27	29	A	Leigh RMI	W	3–0	Bishop (2), Nogan
28	Feb 6	H	Aldershot Town	L	0–2	
29	12	A	Forest Green Rovers	D	1–1	Bishop
30	19	H	Woking	L	0–2	
31	22	A	Exeter City	W	1–0	Merris
32	Mar 1	H	Barnet	W	2–1	Donovan, Maloney
33	5	H	Exeter City	L	1–2	Maloney
34	14	A	Halifax Town	L	0–2	
35	19	A	Tamworth	L	0–1	
36	28	A	Accrington Stanley	D	2–2	Maloney, Bishop
37	Apr 2	H	Gravesend & Northfleet	D	0–0	
38	9	A	Hereford United	L	0–2	
39	12	A	Carlisle United	L	0–6	
40	16	H	Dagenham & Redbridge	D	0–0	
41	19	A	Canvey Island	L	0–4	
42	23	H	Farnborough Town	W	4–0	Bishop, Stewart, Yalcin, P.D. Robinson

FA Cup

4Q	Oct 30	A	Carlisle United	L	1–3	Dunning (pen)

	Brass	Smith	Groves	Clarke	Davis	Pearson	Dunning	Robinson P.D.	Bishop	Stewart	Yalcin	Law	Arthur	Merris	Donovan	Nogan	Porter	Stockdale	Harrison	McGurk	Coad	Davies	Haw	Staley	Grant	Ashcroft	Robinson P.	Webster	Maloney	Constable	Jackson	Armstrong
1	2	3	4	5	6	7	8	**9**	10	11	12	13																				
2	7	3	4	5	6		8	9	**10**	11	12	2	13																			
3	7	3	4	5	6		8	9	10	**11**	12	2		13																		
4	2	**3**	4	5	6		8	*9*	10	11		12		13	7	14																
5	5		4		6		8	14	*10*	**11**	13	2		3	7	9	1	12														
6	5		4		6	*7*	8	13	10		12	2		3	11	**9**		1	14													
7	6		4	5		7	8	13	10		14	2		3	**11**	*9*		1	12													
8	6		4			7	8	9	10		12	2		3		**11**		1		5												
9	**6**		4			7	8	9	10	12	13	2		3		11		1		5												
10			4			6	8	**7**	10	11		2		3		9		1	12	5												
11	12		4			6	8	7	10	11	13	2		3		**9**		1		5												
12	12		4			6	8	7	10	11	14	**2**		3		*9*		1		5	13											
13	2	13	4			5	8	7	10	11	12			3		**9**		1				6										
14	2		4			5	8	7		11	**10**			3		9		1		13		6	12									
15	2	14	4			*5*	8	**9**	10	11	12			3				1			7	6	13									
16	2		4			5	8		10	11	9			3	12	**9**		1				6		13								
17	5		4				8		10		12			11	**7**	9		1				3		2	6							
18	5		4						**10**		12	13		11	7	9		1				3		2	6	8						
19	*5*		4				13	12			**10**	14		11	7	9		1				3		2	6	8						
20	5		4				8	13	10					11	7	**9**		1				3		2	6		12					
21	2	3	4				8		10		12			11	7			1				6			5		**9**					
22	2	3	4				8	12	10					11	7			1				6			5		**9**					
23	**5**		4				8	13	10					11	7	14	1					3		2	*6*		9	12				
24		3	4				8	12	**10**			14		11	7	13	1							2			9	6	*5*			
25		**3**	4				8		10					11	7	13	1							2	12		9	6	5			
26			4				8		10			13		11	7	**9**	1					6		2			12		5	3		
27			4				8		10		13			11	7	**9**	1					3		2			12	6	5			
28			4						10		12	14		11	7	9	1					3		*2*			13	6	5	**8**		
29			4				8	**9**	10		12	2		11	7		1					3						6	5			
30		3	4				8	9	10		12	2		11	7		1							13				**6**	5			
31			4				8	9	10			2		11	7		1					3						6	5			
32		3	4				8	9	10			2		11	7		1											6	5			
33		3	4				8	9	**10**			2		11	7		1										13	6	5		12	
34		*3*	4		14		8	12	10		13	2		11	7		1											6	5		**9**	
35		**3**	12		4		8	*9*			13	2		11	7		1										14	6	5		10	
36		**3**	12		6		8	13	10		*4*	2		11	7		1											14	5		9	
37		*3*	14		6		8	12	**10**		4	2		11	7		1										13				9	5
38		**3**	12		6		8	9		13	4	2		11	7		1														10	5
39			4		5		**8**	9	13	12	4	2		11	7		1														10	3
40			6		5		8	**9**	10	11	4	2		3	7			1													12	
41			6		5			9	10	11	4	**2**		3	7			1										8			13	12
42		13	6		5			14	10	11	4	**2**		3	7			1										*8*			9	12
	20	16	38	5	14	12	37	22	37	15	10	24		38	30	18	18	20		5	1	16		10	7	2	5	13	13	2	7	3
	2	3	4		1		1	12	1	3	21	7	1	2	1	4		1	3	1	1		2	2	1		7	2			3	2
	1		3				3	2	11	1	2			2	2	3									2		2	1	4			

	Brass	Smith	Groves	Clarke	Davis	Pearson	Dunning	Robinson P.D.	Bishop	Stewart	Yalcin	Law	Arthur	Merris	Donovan	Nogan	Porter	Stockdale	Harrison	McGurk	Coad	Davies	Haw	Staley	Grant	Ashcroft	Robinson P.	Webster	Maloney	Constable	Jackson	Armstrong
4Q	5		4				8		10	11	12		13	3		9		1			**7**	6		2								
	1		1				1		1	1				1		1		1			1	1		1								
											1		1																			
							1																									

York City v Tamworth 17 August 2004 programme cover.

Andy Bishop.

2005–06

Conference

Manager: Billy McEwan

	P	W	D	L	F	A	Pts
Accrington Stanley	42	28	7	7	76	45	91
Hereford United	42	22	14	6	59	33	80
Grays Athletic	42	21	13	8	94	55	76
Halifax Town	42	21	12	9	55	40	75
Morecambe	42	22	8	12	68	41	74
Stevenage Borough	42	19	12	11	62	47	69
Exeter City	42	18	9	15	65	48	63
York City	42	17	12	13	63	48	63
Burton Albion	42	16	12	14	50	52	60
Dagenham & Redbridge	42	16	10	16	63	59	58
Woking	42	14	14	14	58	47	56
Cambridge United	42	15	10	17	51	57	55
Aldershot	42	16	6	20	61	74	54
Canvey Island	42	13	12	17	47	58	51
Kidderminster Harriers	42	13	11	18	39	55	50
Gravesend & Northfleet	42	13	10	19	45	57	49
Crawley Town	42	12	11	19	48	55	47
Altrincham	42	10	11	21	40	71	41
Southport	42	10	10	22	36	68	40
Forest Green Rovers	42	8	14	20	49	62	38
Tamworth	42	8	14	20	32	63	38
Scarborough	42	9	10	23	40	66	37

Did you know that?

Joe O'Neill became the first City player since Arthur Bottom in August 1954 to score a hat-trick on his debut when he scored three times at Southport on 16 August 2005. He also became the first City player to bag a hat-trick since March 1996.

City's 5–0 win over Altrincham was their biggest home victory since September 1993.

The sequence of six straight wins in February and March was the best run since 1983–84.

Clubman of the Year Clayton Donaldson became the first player since Tony Barras in 1996–97 to start every League and Cup game.

Top scorer Andy Bishop became only the second-ever City player to top the divisional scoring charts when he finished leading Conference marksman (Arthur Bottom was Division Three North top scorer in 1954–55).

For only the second time since 1994–95 City finished in the top half of their division.

City utilised 30 players during the campaign, the lowest since 1998–99.

Average home Conference attendance was 2,871.

Match No.	Date	Venue	Opponents	Result		Scorers	Atteno
1	Aug 13	H	Crawley Town	D	0–0		2
2	16	A	Southport	W	4–1	O'Neill (3), Convery	1
3	20	A	Grays Athletic	D	1–1	A. Bishop	1
4	26	H	Woking	W	2–1	A. Bishop (pen), Dudgeon	2
5	29	A	Halifax Town	L	0–1		2
6	Sep 2	H	Cambridge United	W	1–0	Donaldson	2
7	10	A	Forest Green Rovers	W	2–1	Dudgeon, Convery	
8	17	H	Altrincham	W	5–0	O'Neill, Donaldson, Dudgeon, A. Bishop, Stewart	2
9	20	H	Dagenham & Redbridge	D	1–1	Donaldson	2
10	24	A	Aldershot Town	L	1–2	Donaldson	2
11	27	A	Tamworth	W	3–0	Donaldson (2), Convery	1
12	Oct 1	H	Exeter City	W	4–2	A. Bishop (2, 1 pen), Stewart, Donaldson	3
13	8	A	Gravesend & Northfleet	D	2–2	Donaldson, A. Bishop	1
14	15	H	Canvey Island	W	2–1	Convery, A. Bishop	3
15	29	A	Accrington Stanley	L	1–2	A. Bishop	2
16	Nov 12	H	Burton Albion	L	0–1		2
17	19	A	Kidderminster Harriers	D	0–0		1
18	26	A	Morecambe	L	0–2		1
19	Dec 10	A	Hereford United	L	0–1		1
20	26	H	Scarborough	W	3–1	A. Bishop, Donaldson, McGurk	4
21	31	H	Morecambe	D	1–1	Convery	2
22	Jan 2	A	Scarborough	D	2–2	A. Bishop (2)	4
23	7	A	Crawley Town	W	1–0	Dudgeon	1
24	10	H	Stevenage Borough	L	0–1		2
25	21	H	Grays Athletic	L	1–2	O'Neill	2
26	24	H	Southport	D	0–0		2
27	28	A	Woking	L	0–2		1
28	Feb 12	H	Aldershot Town	W	3–2	Convery, A. Bishop, Donaldson	2
29	18	A	Exeter City	W	3–1	Dudgeon, N. Bishop, A. Bishop	3
30	21	H	Tamworth	W	2–1	A. Bishop, Donaldson	2
31	25	H	Forest Green Rovers	W	5–1	A. Bishop (3, 1 pen), McGurk, Thomas	2
32	Mar 7	A	Dagenham & Redbridge	W	2–0	Donaldson, A. Bishop	
33	11	H	Gravesend & Northfleet	W	1–0	Dudgeon	2
34	18	A	Canvey Island	D	1–1	Dunning	
35	25	H	Accrington Stanley	L	2–4	Donaldson, A. Bishop	3
36	Apr 1	A	Burton Albion	D	0–0		2
37	4	A	Altrincham	W	3–0	Donaldson (2), A. Bishop	1
38	9	H	Kidderminster Harriers	D	2–2	A. Bishop (pen), Donaldson	3
39	14	A	Cambridge United	L	0–2		3
40	17	H	Halifax Town	L	0–2		4
41	22	A	Stevenage Borough	D	1–1	Donaldson	2
42	29	H	Hereford United	L	1–3	A. Bishop	2

A

S

FA Cup

4Q	Oct 22	A	Gainsborough Trinity	W	4–0	A. Bishop (2, 1 pen), Donaldson, Convery	1
1	Nov 5	H	Grays Athletic	L	0–3		3

A

S

Price	Peat	Mallon	Hotte	McGurk	Convery	Panther	Donaldson	Mansaram	Dunning	Bishop A.	Stewart	O'Neill	Merris	Dudgeon	Yalcin	Webster	Palmer	Andrews	Bertos	Horwood	Barwick	Stockdale	Craddock	N'Toya	Bishop N.	Thomas	Rhodes	Kamara	
2	3	**4**	5	6	7	8	9	10	11	12	13																		1
2	3		5	6	7	8	9	**10**	4	12	13	11	14																2
2	3		5	6	7	8	9	**10**	4	12		11	13																3
2	3			6	7	8	9	**10**	4	12		11		5	13														4
2	3		5	6	7	8	9		**4**	10	13	11			12														5
2	3		5	6	7	8	9	12	4	10		**11**			13														6
2		12		6	7	8	9		*4*	**10**		11	3	5	14	13													7
2				6	7	8	9		4	*10*	14	**11**	3	5	13		12												8
2				6	7	8	9		4	10		11	3	5															9
2				6	**7**	8	9		4	10	12	11	3	5			13												10
2				6	7	8	9		4	10	**11**	12	3	5			13												11
2				6	7	8	9		4	10	**11**	12	3	5															12
2			12	6	7	8	9		4	10	13	11	3	**5**															13
2	14		**5**	6	7	8	9		4	10	13	11	*3*	12															14
2		13		6	7		9		4	10	12	**11**	3	5	8														15
2		13		6	7		9		4	10	12	**11**	3		8			5											16
2		13		6	7		9		4	10		12	3		8			5	**11**										17
2				6	7		9		4	10		13						3	11	5	8	12							18
				6	12		9		4		13	10		5	**8**			2	11	3	7	1							19
			5	6	7	12	9		4	10	13	11	14					2		*3*	**8**								20
			5	6	7	8	9		4	10		11	12					2		**3**									21
			5		**7**	8	9		4	10		11	3	6	12			2	13										22
			5		7	8	**9**		4	10	12	11	3	6				2											23
			5		7	8	9		4	10	13	**11**	3	6				2	12										24
			5		**7**	8	9		4			11	3	6	12								2	10					25
	13		5		7	8	9		4	12		11	3	6									2	**10**					26
	13		5		**7**	8	9		4	10		11	3	6									2	12					27
	3			6	7	8	9		11	10	12			5									2		**4**				28
	3			6	7	**8**	9		11	10		13		5		12									4	2			29
	3			6	7	8	9		11	**10**	13	12		5											4	2			30
	3		14	6	7	8	9		**11**	10	12	13		*5*											4	2			31
	3		5	6	7	8	9		11	10															4	2			32
	3			6	7	8	9		**11**	10		12	13	5											4	2			33
2	3			6	7	8	9		11	10			13	5											4	**2**			34
2	3		12	6	7	8	9		11	10		13		**5**											*4*	14			35
2	3			6	7	8	9		11	10				5											4	12			36
	3			6	7	8	9		*11*	10		12		5											**4**	2	13	14	37
	3			6	7	8	9		**11**	10	13	12		5											4	2			38
	3		14	6	7	8	9		**11**	10	12	13		5											4	*2*			39
			5	2	12	8	9		**11**	10	13	11	3	6												4			40
2	3			6	12	8	9			10		11		5		13									7	**4**			41
	3			6	13	8	9		11	10		7	12	5											4	*2*		14	42
[illegible]	20	1	16	36	38	36	42	4	41	35	2	25	18	30	4			9	3	4	3	1	4	2	14	12			
1	3	4	4		4	1		1		5	19	12	7	1	7	3	3		2			1		1		2	1	2	
				2	6		17		1	22	2	5		6											1	1			

Price	Peat	Mallon	Hotte	McGurk	Convery	Panther	Donaldson	Mansaram	Dunning	Bishop A.	Stewart	O'Neill	Merris	Dudgeon	Yalcin	Webster	Palmer	Andrews	Bertos	Horwood	Barwick	Stockdale	Craddock	N'Toya	Bishop N.	Thomas	Rhodes	Kamara	
2	**3**	14		6	7		9		4	10	13	*11*	12	5	8														4Q
2		13		6	7		9		*4*	10	12	**11**	3	5	8	14													1
2	1			2	2		2		2	2		2	1	2	2														
		2									2		1			1													
					1		1			2																			

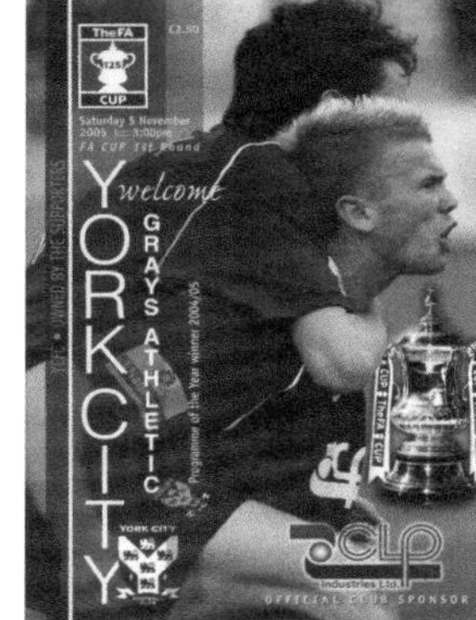

York City v Grays Athletic 5 November 2005 programme cover.

Mark Convery.

2006–07

Conference

Manager: Billy McEwan

	P	W	D	L	F	A	Pts
Dagenham & Redbridge	46	28	11	7	93	48	95
Oxford United	46	22	15	9	66	33	81
Morecambe	46	23	12	11	64	46	81
York City	46	23	11	12	65	45	80
Exeter City	46	22	12	12	67	48	78
Burton Albion	46	22	9	15	52	47	75
Gravesend & Northfleet	46	21	11	14	63	56	74
Stevenage Borough	46	20	10	16	76	66	70
Aldershot	46	18	11	17	64	62	65
Crawley Town	46	17	12	17	52	52	63
Kidderminster Harriers	46	17	12	17	43	50	63
Weymouth	46	18	9	19	56	73	63
Rushden & Diamonds	46	17	11	18	58	54	62
Northwich Victoria	46	18	4	24	51	69	58
Forest Green Rovers	46	13	18	15	59	64	57
Woking	46	15	12	19	56	61	57
Halifax Town	46	15	10	21	55	62	55
Cambridge United	46	15	10	21	57	66	55
Grays Athletic	46	13	13	20	56	55	52
Stafford Rangers	46	14	10	22	49	71	52
Altrincham	46	13	12	21	53	67	51
Tamworth	46	13	9	24	43	61	48
Southport	46	11	14	21	57	67	47
St Albans City	46	10	10	26	57	89	40

Did you know that?

For the third time in their history City figured in the promotion Play-offs. They recorded 23 League wins, more than any season since 1983–84.

The 5–0 win at Cambridge United on 13 March 2007 equalled the club's biggest away League victory since 1929 (Blackpool 1993–94 and 1994–95).

The away record of 13 wins and five draws was the best in their history, and this season was only the third time that City won more away games than at home (1946–47 and 1998–99 were the previous occasions).

The final tally of 80 points was the second-highest in the club's history.

Twenty clean sheets were kept, equalling the club record set in 1983–84 and 1993–94.

Top scorer Clayton Donaldson's haul of 24 League goals was the best since Paul Barnes hit 24 in 1993–94. His overall total of 26 goals was the highest since 1985–86.

Donaldson and Clubman of the Year Neal Bishop made their last appearances for the club in the Play-off match at Morecambe prior to their moves to Hibernian and Barnet respectively.

Average home Conference attendance was 2,859.

For the first time in 75 years, an Archbishop of York attended a City home match when Dr John Sentamu watched the Stevenage fixture on 27 March 2007.

Match No.	Date	Venue	Opponents	Result		Scorers	Atten
1	Aug 12	H	Exeter City	D	0–0		
2	15	A	Stevenage Borough	W	2–1	Donaldson, Bowey	
3	19	A	Gravesend & Northfleet United	W	1–0	Donaldson	
4	25	H	Burton Albion	W	3–2	Donaldson, Convery, Peat	
5	28	A	Rushden & Diamonds	W	1–0	Donaldson	
6	Sep 1	H	Stafford Rangers	D	0–0		
7	9	A	Crawley Town	L	0–3		
8	12	H	Morecambe	L	2–3	Woolford, Donaldson (pen)	
9	16	H	Kidderminster Harriers	W	1–0	Donaldson	
10	19	A	Woking	W	2–1	Woolford (2)	
11	23	H	Southport	D	2–2	Farrell, Opp. og	
12	30	A	Oxford United	L	0–2		
13	Oct 3	A	Northwich Victoria	W	2–1	Donaldson, Peat	
14	6	H	Aldershot Town	W	1–0	Convery	
15	10	H	Cambridge United	L	1–2	Donaldson	
16	14	A	St Albans City	L	2–4	Farrell (2)	
17	21	A	Tamworth	D	2–2	Donaldson (2)	
18	Nov 5	H	Altrincham	W	1–0	Donaldson	
19	18	A	Weymouth	W	2–1	Panther, Goodliffe	
20	25	H	Dagenham & Redbridge United	L	2–3	Woolford, Donaldson	
21	Dec 2	A	Forest Green Rovers	W	1–0	Donaldson	
22	9	A	Grays Athletic	D	0–0		
23	23	H	Halifax Town	W	2–0	Donaldson (2, 1 pen)	
24	29	H	Woking	L	0–1		
25	Jan 1	A	Morecambe	W	3–1	Donaldson, Farrell, Bowey	
26	6	H	Crawley Town	W	5–0	Donaldson (2, 1 pen), Bowey, Panther, Farrell	
27	20	A	Kidderminster Harriers	L	1–2	Farrell	
28	23	A	Halifax Town	D	1–1	Woolford	
29	27	H	Grays Athletic	D	2–2	Bowey, McMahon	
30	Feb 3	H	Tamworth	L	0–2		
31	10	A	Altrincham	W	4–0	Bishop, Bowey, Brodie, Woolford	
32	17	H	Weymouth	W	1–0	Bowey	
33	24	A	Dagenham & Redbridge United	L	1–2	Bishop	
34	Mar 3	H	Forest Green Rovers	D	0–0		
35	6	H	Northwich Victoria	W	2–1	Opp. og, Woolford	
36	10	A	Aldershot Town	W	2–0	Farrell, Panther	
37	13	A	Cambridge United	W	5–0	Farrell, Donaldson (3), Kovacs	
38	17	H	St Albans City	D	0–0		
39	24	A	Exeter City	D	1–1	Farrell	
40	27	H	Stevenage Borough	L	0–1		
41	31	H	Gravesend & Northfleet United	L	0–2		
42	Apr 7	A	Burton Albion	W	2–1	Woolford, Farrell	
43	10	H	Rushden & Diamonds	W	3–1	Donaldson (2), Bowey	
44	14	A	Stafford Rangers	D	0–0		
45	21	A	Southport	W	1–0	Donaldson (pen)	
46	28	H	Oxford United	W	1–0	Bishop	

2 own-goals

Play-offs

SF	May 4	H	Morecambe	D	0–0		
SF	7	A	Morecambe	L	1–2	Bowey (pen)	

FA Cup

4Q	Oct 28	A	Newcastle Benfield	W	1–0	Donaldson (pen)	
1	Nov 11	H	Bristol City	L	0–1		

Craddock	Peat	Bishop	McGurk	Dudgeon	Convery	Panther	Donaldson	Farrell	Bowey	Lloyd	Greenwood	Webster	Woolford	McMahon	Reid	Parslow	Foster	Goodliffe	Stamp	Maidens	Elvins	Brodie	Kovacs	James	Purkiss	Bell	
2	3	4	5	6	7	8	9	10	11																		1
2	**3**	4	5	6	7	8	9	*10*	11	12	13	14															2
2	3	*4*	5	6	7	8	**9**	10	11	13	12	14															3
2	3	4	5	6	7	8	9	10	11																		4
2	3	4	5	6	7	8	9	**10**	11		12																5
2	3	4	5	6	7	8	9	10			**11**		12	13													6
2	3	4	5	6	*7*	8	9	10					**11**	14	12	13											7
2	**3**	4	5	*6*	7	8	9	10		12			11	13	1	14											8
2		4	5		12		9	**10**	8	3			11	7		6											9
2		4	**5**	12	13		9	10	8	3			11	7		6											10
2	5	4			12	13	9	10	8	3			11	**7**		6											11
2		**4**	5		13	8	9	10	11	3			12	7		6											12
2	3	12	5			4	9	10	8			13	11	**7**		6											13
2	3	13			7	4	9	10	8				**11**	12		6	5										14
2	3				7	4	9	10	8	12			11			6	5										15
2	3	14			12	*4*	9	10	8	13			11	**7**		6	5										16
	3	7				4	9	8	11	2						5	12	**6**	10								17
2		7				12	9	8	4	3			11				5	6	**10**								18
2	3	7	5			4	**9**	10	8				11					6	12								19
2		7	5			4	9	10	8	*3*	12		11	14				6	13								20
2		**7**	5			4	9	10	8	3			11	12				6	13								21
	3	7	5			4	9	10	8	2			**11**					6	12								22
14	3	7	5	13		4	*9*	8	11	2			12					6	**10**								23
13	3	7	5			4	9	10	**8**	2			11					6	12								24
2		7				4	9	8	**11**	3			13	12		5		6	10								25
2		7				4	9	**8**	*11*	3	14		12	13		5		6	10								26
2		4	5			8	9	10	11	3	13		12			14		*6*		**7**							27
2		4	5			8		9	11	3			10	7		6											28
2	12	4	5	13		8		9	11	3			10	*7*		6				14							29
12	**3**	4	5	6		8		9	11	2			*7*	13						14	10						30
2		4	5	13		8	9	7	*11*	3			14			6					**10**	12					31
2		4	5			*8*	9	7	11	3			13	14		6					**10**	12					32
2	13	4	5			8	9	7	*11*	3			12			6					14	**10**					33
2		4	5			8	9	13	11	3			7								**10**	12	6				34
2	12	4	5		7	8	*9*	10	11	**3**			13								14		6				35
2	3	4	5		**7**	8	9	10	11				12								13		6				36
2	3	4	5		*7*	8	9	10		12	13		11								14		6				37
	3	4	5		**7**	8	9	10	11	2			13								14	*12*	6				38
		4	5		14	8	9	*7*	11		2		13									**10**	6	3	12		39
		4	5		7	*8*	9	10	**11**				12	14								13	6	3	2		40
		4	5			8	9	12	11		14		7									**10**	6	3	*2*	13	41
		4	5			8	9	10	**11**		13		7			6						12		3	2		42
		4	5		12	8	9	10	**11**		14		7			6						13		3	2		43
		4	5		13	8	9	10	**11**				7			6						12		3	2		44
		4	5			8	9	10	11				7			6								3	2		45
		4	5		13	8	9	*10*	11	12			7			6						14		3	**2**		46
32	22	42	38	9	15	42	43	44	42	23	2		26	8	1	21	4	11	5	1	4	3	8	8	7		
3	3	3		4	9	2		2		7	10	3	14	11	1	3	1		5	2	5	9			1	1	
	2	3			2	3	24	10	7				8	1				1				1	1				

Craddock	Peat	Bishop	McGurk	Dudgeon	Convery	Panther	Donaldson	Farrell	Bowey	Lloyd	Greenwood	Webster	Woolford	McMahon	Reid	Parslow	Foster	Goodliffe	Stamp	Maidens	Elvins	Brodie	Kovacs	James	Purkiss	Bell	
		4	5			8	9	**10**	11	2			7			6						12		3			SF
	12	4	5		13	8	*9*	10	11	2			7			6						14		**3**			SF
		2	2			2	2	2	2	2			2			2								2			
	1				1																	2					
									1																		

Craddock	Peat	Bishop	McGurk	Dudgeon	Convery	Panther	Donaldson	Farrell	Bowey	Lloyd	Greenwood	Webster	Woolford	McMahon	Reid	Parslow	Foster	Goodliffe	Stamp	Maidens	Elvins	Brodie	Kovacs	James	Purkiss	Bell	
2		7				4	9	8	11	3	12		13				5	6	10								4Q
2		7				4	9	**10**	8	3			11				5	6	12								1
2		2				2	2	2	2	2			1				2	2	1								
											1		1						1								
							1																				

York City v Morecambe 4 May 2007 programme cover.

Clayton Donaldson.

2007–08

Blue Square Premier (Conference)

Manager: Billy McEwan, then Colin Walker

	P	W	D	L	F	A	Pts
Aldershot	46	31	8	7	82	48	101
Cambridge Utd	46	25	11	10	68	41	86
Torquay	46	25	9	12	82	57	84
Exeter	46	22	17	7	83	58	83
Burton Albion	46	23	12	11	79	56	81
Stevenage	46	24	7	15	82	55	79
Histon	46	20	12	14	76	67	72
Forest Green	46	19	14	13	76	59	71
Oxford United	46	20	11	15	56	48	71
Grays Ath	46	19	13	14	58	47	70
Ebbsfleet	46	19	12	15	65	61	69
Salisbury	46	18	14	14	70	60	68
Kidderminster	46	19	10	17	74	57	67
York City	46	17	11	18	71	74	62
Crawley Town	46	19	9	18	73	67	60
R'den & Dmnds	46	15	14	17	55	55	59
Woking	46	12	17	17	53	61	53
Weymouth	46	11	13	22	53	73	46
N'wich Vic.	46	11	12	23	52	77	45
Halifax	46	12	16	18	61	70	42
Altrincham	46	9	14	23	56	82	41
Farsley Celtic	46	10	9	27	48	86	39
Stafford	46	5	10	31	42	99	25
Droylsden	46	5	9	32	46	103	24

Did you know that?

For the second successive season City won more games on their travels than at home, and midway through the campaign they created a club record of seven successive away victories in Cup and League.

For the 13th successive campaign, City failed to win at least half of their home League games.

The average League attendance of 2,258 was the third lowest in the club's history, and the crowd of 763 on 6 February 2008,for the game against Northwich Victoria in the Setanta Shield,was the smallest ever to see a first-team competitive home fixture.

A total of 11 Cup games were played and only twice before has this been exceeded. In 1984–85 City figured in 14 Cup ties and played in 13 in 1985–86.The tally of 23 Cup goals has been bettered just once when 25 were scored in 1984–85.

For the first time, five players scored 10 goals or more in a season for the club – Onome Sodje and Martyn Woolford 17 apiece, Richard Brodie and Craig Farrell with 14 each and Nicky Rowe scored 10.

The 6–0 win over Rushall Olympic equalled the club's biggest-ever victory in the FA Cup, and Craig Farrell's hat-trick in this match was the first for City in the competition since 1970–71, when Paul Aimson achieved the feat against Tamworth.

The crowd of 455 at Stafford Rangers on 8 April 2008 is the lowest recorded attendance to watch City in a League match. Four days later against Woking in a home game City had three players sent off – Darren Craddock, Tom Evans and Stuart Elliott – to create an unenviable new club record.

Match No.	Date		Venue	Opponents	Result		Scorers	Attend
1	Aug	11	H	Cambridge United	L	1-2	Farrell (pen)	3
2		14	A	Burton Albion	L	3-4	Woolford, Sodje, Farrell (pen)	1
3		20	A	Exeter City	D	1-1	Sodje	4
4		24	H	Forest Green Rovers	L	0-2		2
5		27	A	Northwich Victoria	W	1-0	Brayson	1
6		30	H	Rushden & Diamonds	L	2-3	Brodie, Woolford	2
7	Sep	4	H	Altrincham	D	2-2	Brodie, Brayson	2
8		8	A	Kidderminster Harriers	L	0-3		1
9		15	H	Stevenage Borough	L	0-2		2
10		18	A	Aldershot Town	L	0-2		2
11		22	A	Grays Athletic	W	2-0	Sodje, Elliott	1
12		27	H	Halifax Town	W	3-2	Sodje, Woolford, Meechan	2
13		30	A	Oxford United	D	1-1	Sodje	4
14	Oct	6	H	Histon	L	1-4	Wroe	2
15		9	H	Stafford Rangers	W	2-0	Elliott, McBreen	1
16		13	A	Woking	W	3-0	Sodje 2, Woolford	1
17		21	H	Torquay United	L	0-1		2
18	Nov	4	A	Farsley Celtic	W	4-1	McBreen, Brayson, Farrell 2	1
19		17	H	Salisbury City	L	1-3	Brayson	2
20		24	A	Weymouth	W	2-1	Kelly, Farrell	1
21	Dec	1	H	Crawley Town	D	1-1	Sodje	2
22		8	A	Ebbsfleet United	W	2-1	Sodje, Woolford	
23		26	H	Droylsden	W	2-1	Farrell (pen), Kelly	3
24		29	H	Weymouth	W	2-0	Woolford, McGurk	2
25	Jan	1	A	Droylsden	W	4-3	Panther, Farrell, Brodie 2	1
26		5	H	Kidderminster Harriers	D	2-2	Sodje, Farrell	2
27		19	A	Altrincham	D	2-2	Woolford 2	1
28		26	H	Aldershot Town	W	2-0	Brodie, Woolford	3
29	Feb	9	H	Grays Athletic	W	2-0	Wroe (pen), Fortune-West	2
30		12	A	Halifax Town	D	2-2	Sodje, Woolford	2
31		16	A	Histon	L	1-3	Wroe (pen)	1
32	Mar	1	A	Cambridge United	L	0-2		3
33		4	H	Burton Albion	D	0-0		1
34		10	H	Exeter City	W	3-2	Woolford, Parslow, Sodje	1
35		18	A	Forest Green Rovers	W	2-1	Wroe, Robinson	
36		22	A	Rushden & Diamonds	D	1-1	Brodie	1
37		25	H	Northwich Victoria	D	1-1	Brodie	1
38		29	H	Ebbsleet United	L	0-1		2
39	Apr	1	A	Stevenage Borough	L	2-3	Wroe 2 (1pen)	1
40		5	A	Crawley Town	L	1-6	Woolford	
41		8	A	Stafford Rangers	W	4-0	Woolford, Brodie, Elliott, Robinson	
42		12	H	Woking	L	2-3	Sodje 2	2
43		15	H	Oxford United	L	0-1		1
44		19	A	Torquay United	D	0-0		2
45		22	H	Farsley Celtic	W	4-1	Woolford, Fortune-West, Brodie 2	1
46		26	A	Salisbury City	L	0-3		1

A

S

FA Cup

R4Q	Oct	27	H	Rushall Olympic	W	6-0	Sodje 2, Farrell 3, Wroe	1
1	Nov	10	H	Havant & Waterlooville	L	0-1		2

A

S

Setanta Shield

4	Dec	22	A	Stafford Rangers	W	2-0 *	Brodie,Sodje	
5	Feb	6	H	Northwich Victoria	D	3-3 **	Brodie 2,Woolford	

* After extra-time **After extra-time. City lost 3–2 on penalties.

A

S

urkiss	Robinson	Elliott	McGurk	Jones	Brayson	Panther	Farrell	Beardsley	Woolford	Greenwood	Sodje	Brodie	Meechan	Craddock	Parslow	Hutchinson	Kelly	Henderson	Wroe	Hegarty	Fry	McBreen	Lloyd	Rusk	Fortune-West	Duncum	Hall	Mimms	Boyes	Rhodes	Turnbull	Shepherd	McWilliams	Beadle	
2	3	4	5	6	**7**	8	9	*10*	11	12	13	14																							1
2	3		5	6	12	8	7	14	11	4	**9**	*10*	13																						2
2	3		5		13	8		14	11	7	9	*10*		**2**	6	4																			3
2	3		5			**8**	13	*10*	11		9	14	7	2	6	4																			4
4	3	4	5		7		12		11	8	**9**	10		*2*	6	13																			5
2	3	4	6		*9*	**8**	7	13	11	12	14	10					5																		6
2	3	4	6		9	8	7		11		12	**10**					5	1																	7
2	3	4	6		13	8	14		11	7	9	*10*		12			5	1																	8
	3		6		9	8			7		12	**10**		2	13		5	1	4	11															9
	3		6			8		**10**	7		9	12		2			5	1	4	11															10
2	3	4	6		14	8		**10**	11		9	12		13			5	1	*7*																11
2		4	6		10	8			11		9		12	3			5	1	**7**		13														12
2	3	4	6		10	**8**			11		9		7				5	1	12		13														13
2	3	4	6		10	12			11		13		7				5		**8**		14	*9*													14
	3	4	6		7	8			11		**10**	12	13	2			5					9													15
	3	4	6		7	8			11		10	12		2			5				13	**9**													16
	3	4	6		7	8			11		10	12	13	2			5					**9**													17
	3	4	6		7	8	12		**11**		*10*	14		2			5		13			9													18
	3	4	6		9	8	10		11	12	13	14		**2**			*5*		7																19
2	3	13	4		9	8	*10*		11		14			**2**	6		5		7																20
	3	13	4		**9**	8	10	14	11		12			*2*	6		5		7																21
2	3	7	4			8	10		11		9			13	6		5		12																22
2		**7**	4			8	10		11		9	13			6		5		12				3												23
2		7	4			8	10		11		9	13			6		5		12				**3**												24
2		7	4		14	8	10		11		**9**	12			6		5		13				3												25
3		4	6		14	*8*	10		11		9	13		12	2		**5**		7																26
3		4	5		**10**	8			11		9	12		2	6				7				13												27
		4	5			8	12		10			**9**		3	6				7				11	2											28
2		4	5			8			*10*		13	**9**		3	6				7				11	14	12										29
7		4	5			12	14		11		*10*			**2**	6				8				3	13	9										30
2		4	5				12		10		13	14		3	6				8				**11**	7	*9*										31
2		4	5			12	7		10		*9*	14		3	6		13		8				**11**												32
2	**3**		4			8			13		14	10			6		5		4					11	*9*	12									33
2	3	12	5			*8*			11		10	9			6		13		4					14		**7**									34
2	3	7	4						11		12	*9*			6		5		10				13	**7**	14										35
2	3	7	4			13			11		10	9		12	6		**5**						14	*8*											36
2	3	**7**	5			8			11		10	9		4	6				12						13										37
2	3	12	5			*8*			11		10	9			6				4					14	13		**7**								38
2	13	8	5						11		12	9		4	6				10				3	*7*	14			1							39
2		8	5						11		12	*9*		4	6				10				**3**	7	14		13	1							40
2	3	7	5			8			11		**10**	9		4	*6*				13				14						12						41
2		7	5			**8**			11		10	9		4	6								3					14				*12*	13		42
2			5			8			11		7	**10**			6										9			1	13			12	3	4	43
2	14		5			8			**10**		12	13		3	6									7	9								*11*	4	44
2			5			8			**11**		10	12			6									7	9							13	3	4	45
2	12		4						11		13	10			6		5							7	*9*				14				**3**	8	46
3	28	32	46	2	16	36	13	4	45	4	29	21	3	25	30	2	25	7	21	2		5	11	10	7	1	1	3					4	4	
4	3	4			6	4	7	4	1	3	16	18	4	5	1	1	2		8		4		4	4	6	1	1	1	3			3	1		
	2	3	1		4	1	8		14		14	10	1		1		2		6			2			2										

urkiss	Robinson	Elliott	McGurk	Jones	Brayson	Panther	Farrell	Beardsley	Woolford	Greenwood	Sodje	Brodie	Meechan	Craddock	Parslow	Hutchinson	Kelly	Henderson	Wroe	Hegarty	Fry	McBreen	Lloyd	Rusk	Fortune-West	Duncum	Hall	Mimms	Boyes	Rhodes	Turnbull	Shepherd	McWilliams	Beadle	
	3	4	6		7	8	12		11		*10*	**9**		2			5		13											14					R4Q
	3	4	6		**7**	8	9		11		10	12		2			*5*		13											14					1
	2	2	2		2	2	1		2		2	1		2			2																		
							1					1							2											2					
							3				2								1																

urkiss	Robinson	Elliott	McGurk	Jones	Brayson	Panther	Farrell	Beardsley	Woolford	Greenwood	Sodje	Brodie	Meechan	Craddock	Parslow	Hutchinson	Kelly	Henderson	Wroe	Hegarty	Fry	McBreen	Lloyd	Rusk	Fortune-West	Duncum	Hall	Mimms	Boyes	Rhodes	Turnbull	Shepherd	McWilliams	Beadle	
2		7				8	**9**		11		10	12		4	6		5		13				3												4
2		13	5				9		11			10		*4*	6				12		**7**		3								8	14			5
2		1	1			1	2		2		1	1		2	2		1				1		2								1				
		1										1							2													1			
									1		1	3																							

York City v Torquay 15 March 2008 FA Trophy Semi-Final programme cover.

Onome Sodje and Richard Brodie greet City's goal in the semi-final against Torquay.

Colin Addison with former teammates in September 2007, exactly 50 years after he had made his City debut. From left to right: George Patterson, Des Hardcastle, Charlie Ware, Colin Addison, Don Nixon, Barrie Tait, John Powell, Charlie Twissell, Alan Woods, Mick Granger, Dave Dunmore and Jimmy Weir.

The Associate Members' Cup

This Trophy was launched in the 1983–84 season as the Associate Members' Cup (AMC) for teams in the old Third and Fourth Divisions. The AMC was initially organised into mini-Leagues of three clubs, who played each other in knock-out stages, and it was split into two regions (North and South). In 1996–97 the competition became a straight knock-out tournament. From 2000–01 to 2004–05 seven clubs f the Nationwide Conference also played in the competition.

1983–84

Associate Members' Cup

Match No.	Date	Venue	Opponents	Result		Scorers	Atten
1	Feb 21	H	Hull City	L	1–2	Senior	

1984–85

Associate Members' Cup

Match No.	Date	Venue	Opponents	Result		Scorers	Atten
1 (1)	Jan 22	A	Doncaster Rovers	D	0–0		
1 (2)	Feb 5	H	Doncaster Rovers	W	2–0	Butler, Banton	
2	Mar 12	H	Chesterfield	W	1–0	Butler	
3	Apr 22	H	Lincoln City	L	2–3	MacPhail, Houchen (pen)	

1985–86

Associate Members' Cup

Match No.	Date	Venue	Opponents	Result		Scorers	Atten
Grp	Jan 14	H	Rotherham United	D	0–0		
Grp	29	A	Hartlepool United	L	2–3	Houchen (pen), Butler	

1986–87

Associate Members' Cup

Match No.	Date	Venue	Opponents	Result		Scorers	Atten
Grp	Nov 25	H	Darlington	W	4–1	Gabbiadini (3), Walwyn	
Grp	Jan 6	A	Rochdale	D	1–1	Canham	
1	27	H	Mansfield Town	L	0–1		

1987–88

Associate Members' Cup

Match No.	Date	Venue	Opponents	Result		Scorers	Atten
Grp	Oct 13	H	Darlington	L	3–4	Mills, Banton, Whitehead	
Grp	Nov 24	A	Chesterfield	L	0–2		

Senior	Hay	Sbragia	MacPhail	Hood	Ford	Crosby	Walwyn	Byrne	Pollard	Haslegrave	Astbury	Evans	Busby	Pearce	Chippendale	Houchen	
3		4	5	6	7	**8**	9	10	11	12		2					1
1		1	1	1	1	1	1	1	1			1					
										1							
1																	

Evans	Hay	Sbragia	MacPhail	Haslegrave	Ford	Houchen	Walwyn	Byrne	Nicholson	Hood	Pearce	Atkinson	Chippendale	Butler	Banton	Senior	Crosby	Astbury	Richards	Canham	Gabbiadini	Ward	
	3		5			10			**11**			6	7	9	8	2		1	4	12			(1)
	3		5		**7**					6		10	12	9	8	2			4	11			(2)
13	3			6	7				11	5	12		10	**9**	8	2			4				2
3			5	6	7	10			**11**	4				9	8	2						12	3
1	3		3	2	3	2			3	3		2	2	4	4	4		1	3	1			
1											1		1							1		1	
			1			1								2	1								

Hood	Evans	McAughtrie	MacPhail	Haslegrave	Ford	Gabbiadini	Walwyn	Houchen	Canham	Mills	Banton	Senior	Hay	Leaning	Sbragia	Pearce	Butler	McKenzie	Murphy	
3		4	5	13	7	**9**		10	11	6	8	2	12	1						Grp
		4			7	9		10	11	6	8	2	3	1			13	12	**5**	Grp
1		2	1		2	2		2	2	2	2	2	1	2					1	
				1									1				1	1		
								1									1			

Senior	Hood	Sbragia	Pickering	Haslegrave	Ford	Banton	Walwyn	Mills	Canham	Butler	McKenzie	Gabbiadini	Murray	McAughtrie	Whitehead	Pearce	Smallwood	Lowey	Costello	Tutill	
3	13			6	7		**9**	10	12		2	8		4	5	11					Grp
2	8		4	6	7		**9**	10	11						5	3			12	13	Grp
2	12	4	5	6	7		9		11	**8**		10				3					1
3	1	1	2	3	3		3	2	2	1	1	2		1	2	3					
	2								1										1	1	
							1		1			3									

McKenzie	Johnson	Wilson	Whitehead	Clegg	Himsworth	Hood	Gabbiadini M.	Butler	Canham	Banton	Kitching	Tutill	Smallwood	Cook	Mills	Branagan	Buchanan	Costello	Downing	Helliwell	Staniforth	Bradshaw	Brough	Stowell	Spofforth	McMillan	Rogers	Gabbiadini R.	Howlett	
	3	4	5	6		11		**7**		9		12			8	2	10													Grp
		4	5	6	11					10		3			7	2				9		8								Grp
	1	2	2	2	1	1		1		2		1			2	2	1			1		1								
												1																		
			1							1					1															

1988–89

Associate Members' Cup

Match No.	Date	Venue	Opponents	Result		Scorers	Attenda
Grp	Nov 22	H	Burnley	L	0–2		1,
Grp	Dec 13	A	Hartlepool United	W	2–0	Dixon (2)	1,
1	Jan 7	A	Scarborough	L	1–3	Canham	2,

A
S

1989–90

Associate Members' Cup

Match No.	Date	Venue	Opponents	Result		Scorers	Attenda
Grp	Nov 7	H	Hartlepool United	W	7–1	Helliwell (3), Canham (2), Spooner, Tutill	1
Grp	Dec 12	A	Rotherham United	L	1–3	Kelly (pen)	1,
1	Jan 9	A	Halifax Town	D	1–1*	Helliwell	1

* Halifax won 7–6 on penalties.

A
S

1990–91

Associate Members' Cup

Match No.	Date	Venue	Opponents	Result		Scorers	Attenda
Grp	Nov 6	A	Grimsby Town	W	3–1	Helliwell, Reid, Blackstone	1,
Grp	27	H	Darlington	W	3–2	McCarthy, Helliwell (2)	1
1	Jan 22	H	Bury	L	1–2	Blackstone	1,

A
S

1991–92

Associate Members' Cup

Match No.	Date	Venue	Opponents	Result		Scorers	Attenda
Grp	Oct 22	H	Carlisle United	D	1–1	McCarthy	
Grp	Jan 7	A	Stockport County	L	0–3		1

A
S

1992–93

Associate Members' Cup

Match No.	Date	Venue	Opponents	Result		Scorers	Attenda
Grp	Dec 1	A	Doncaster Rovers	L	1–2	Canham	1
Grp	8	H	Hull City	D	0–0		2

A
S

1993–94

Associate Members' Cup (Autoglass Trophy)

Match No.	Date	Venue	Opponents	Result		Scorers	Attenda
Grp	Oct 19	A	Darlington	W	1–0	Barnes	1
Grp	Nov 9	H	Hartlepool United	W	2–0	Bushell, Hall	1
1	Dec 4	H	Mansfield Town	D	1–1*	McCarthy	1

* After extra-time. Mansfield won 5–4 on penalties.

A
S

Bradshaw	Johnson	Wilson	Fazackerley	Smith	Howlett	Spooner	Helliwell	Banton	Himsworth	Canham	Branagan	Clegg	Tutill	Butler	Hotte	Dunn	Shaw	McMillan	Morris	Eli	Greenough	Dixon	Hay	Reid	Endersby	Hurlstone	Barratt	Hall	
	3	4	6				9		12	11			5				**8**			7	2	10							Grp
4	3			6		8	9		7	11	2										5	10							Grp
2	3	4		6		8	9		**7**	11						12					5	10							1
2	3	2	1	2		2	3		2	3	1		1				1			1	3	3							
									1							1													
										1												2							

Barratt	Kelly	Reid	Greenough	Warburton	Howlett	Spooner	Helliwell	Colville	Hall	Dunn	Tutill	Dixon	Canham	McMillan	Himsworth	Heathcote	Longhurst	Naylor	Ord	Madden	Crossley	
4	3			6	7	8	9	12		13	5		11	2	10							Grp
4	3			6	7	8	9	13			5	10	11	**2**	12							Grp
2	3				7		13	9	8	12	5	10	11		**4**	6						1
3	3			2	3	2	2	1	1		3	2	3	2	2	1						
							1	2		2					1							
	1					1	4				1		2									

McMillan	Hall	Reid	Tutill	Warburton	Barratt	Pepper	Helliwell	Longhurst	Canham	Howlett	Dunn	Himsworth	Weatherhead	McCarthy	Blackstone	Cooper	Naylor	Cook	Kiely	Hart	Bushell	Crossley	Curtis	Lister	Grayson	Bradshaw	Wood	
2	3	**4**	5	6			9		11	8	10				7												12	Grp
2	3	4	5	6		7	9		11	**8**				10			12											Grp
2	3	4	5		6	7	9		11	8					10				1									1
3	3	3	3	2	1	2	3		3	3	1			1	2				1									
																	1										1	
		1					3							1	2													

McMillan	Crosby	Reid	Tutill	Stancliffe	McCarthy	Pepper	Blackstone	Naylor	Canham	Marples	Atkin	Hall	Osborne	Barratt	Warburton	Curtis	Gosney	McLoughlin	Tilley	Bushell	Shepstone	
2		4	5		8	7		9	11		6	3		10			1					Grp
2	3	4	5		8		**9**	12	11			10		7	6							Grp
2	1	2	2		2	1	1	1	2		1	2		2	1		1					
								1														
					1																	

McMillan	Hall	Pepper	Stancliffe	Warburton	McCarthy	Borthwick	Barnes	Swann	Blackstone	Canham	Atkin	Barratt	Tutill	Jordan	Marples	Bushell	Tilley	Naylor	
2	3		5		7	8	9	10	**11**	12	6				1	4			Grp
2	3		5		7	**8**		10	11		6					4	9	12	Grp
2	2		2		2	2	1	2	2		2				1	2	1		
										1								1	
										1									

McMillan	Hall	Pepper	Tutill	Atkin	McCarthy	Cooper	Barnes	Swann	Canhan	Naylor	Barratt	Warburton	Blackstone	Bushell	Stancliffe	Murty	Jordan	
2	3	4	5	6	7		9	10			11		8					Grp
	3	4	5		7	8	**9**		12		2	6		10		11	13	Grp
2	3	4	5		7	**8**	9		11	12		6		10				1
2	3	3	3	1	3	2	3	1	1		2	2	1	2		1		
									1	1							1	
	1				1		1							1				

1994–95

Associate Members' Cup (Auto Windscreens Shield)

Match No.	Date	Venue	Opponents	Result		Scorers
Grp	Oct 18	A	Huddersfield Town	L	0–3	
Grp	Nov 8	H	Bradford City	D	2–2	Barnes, Baker

1995–96

Associate Members' Cup (Auto Windscreens Shield)

Match No.	Date	Venue	Opponents	Result		Scorers
Grp	Oct 17	A	Wrexham	L	0–1	
Grp	Nov 7	H	Mansfield Town	W	1–0	Barras
1	28	A	Scunthorpe United	W	3–0	Barnes (2), Stephenson
2	Jan 9	H	Notts County	W	1–0	Williams
SF	Feb 13	A	Rotherham United	L	1–4	Peverell

1996–97

Associate Members' Cup (Auto Windscreens Shield)

Match No.	Date	Venue	Opponents	Result		Scorers
2	Jan 21	H	Preston North End	W	1–0	Himsworth
3	Feb 4	H	Carlisle United	L	0–2	

(Drew a bye in the first round)

1997–98

Associate Members' Cup (Auto Windscreens Shield)

Match No.	Date	Venue	Opponents	Result		Scorers
2	Jan 6	A	Blackpool	D	1–1*	Rowe

* After extra-time. Blackpool won 10–9 on penalties. (Drew a bye in the first round)

1998–99

Associate Members' Cup (Auto Windscreens Shield)

Match No.	Date	Venue	Opponents	Result		Scorers
2	Jan 5	A	Halifax Town	L	2–4	Rowe, Tolson

(Drew a bye in the first round)

1999–2000

Associate Members' Cup (Auto Windscreens Shield)

Match No.	Date	Venue	Opponents	Result		Scorers
1	Dec 7	H	Hull City	L	0–1	

McMillan	Hall	Pepper	Tutill	Stancliffe	McCarthy	Cooper	Barnes	Bushell	Canham	Naylor	Barras	Atkin	Jordan	Simpson	Wilson	Baker	Murty	Williams	Barratt	Peverell	Scaife	
2		4	5		7		9		11	8	6	12	**10**		3	13						Grp
2	3	4			7		9		11	8	6	5				10						Grp
2	1	2	1		2		2		2	2	2	1	1		1	1						
												1				1						
							1									1						

McMillan	Osborne	Pepper	Tutill	Barras	Murty	Jordan	Barnes	Baker	Stephenson	Williams	Atkin	Hall	Oxley	Peverell	Naylor	Matthews	Warrington	Scaife	Bushell	Curtis	Atkinson	Randall	Cresswell	Himsworth	Bull	Sharples	
2			5	6	4	**11**	9	10		8		3				7	1		12								Grp
2	3	4	5	6		12	9	10		11				14		*7*	1		**8**	13							Grp
2		4	5	6	13	**8**	9	*10*	11			3		14		7			12								1
2			5		7	12	9	10		8	6			**11**					4		3						2
2		4	5	12	7	13	9		14		6			*10*					8		3		**11**				SF
5	1	3	5	3	3	2	5	4	1	3	2	2		2		3	2		3		2		1				
				1	1	3			1					2					2	1							
				1			2		1	1				1													

McMillan	Atkinson	Randall	Atkin	Barras	Himsworth	Bushell	Bull	Tolson	Stephenson	Pepper	Murty	Pouton	Cresswell	Sharples	Naylor	Williams	Hall	Campbell	Tutill	Clarke	Jordan	Rush	Prudhoe	Harrison	Rowe	Gilbert	Greening	Tinkler	Reed	
2	**3**			6	7				11	4	12	8	10					9	5	1										2
2	3			6	11	4		12	13		7			5				*9*			8	**10**		14						3
2	2			2	2	1			1	1	1	1	1	1				2	1	1	1	1								
								1	1		1													1						
					1																									

McMillan	Atkinson	Bushell	Tutill	Barras	Stephenson	Tinkler	Tolson	Bull	Pouton	Rowe	Hall	Campbell	Jordan	Rush	Reed	Cresswell	Greening	Murty	Davis	Himsworth	Warrington	Jones	Gabbiadini	Thompson	Rennison	Alderson	
	13	4				6			7	**10**	3		8		5	9	11	2			1					12	2
		1				1			1	1	1		1		1	1	1	1			1						
	1																									1	
										1																	

McMillan	Hall	Jones	Reed	Tinkler	Thompson	Pouton	Woods	Cresswell	Garratt	Rowe	Mimms	Connelly	Prendergast	Agnew	Jordan	Tolson	Barras	Himsworth	Dawson	Carruthers	Fairclough	Williams	Skinner	Hocking	Bullock	Rennison	
2	3	5		4				9	12	10	1	**7**			8	13	6	11									2
1	1	1		1				1		1	1	1			1		1	1									
									1							1											
										1						1											

Hocking	Hall	Atkins	Jones	Fairclough	Dawson	Dixon	Conlon	Rowe	Bullock	Garratt	Williams M.	Williams J.	Jordan	Fox	Thompson N.	Mimms	Sertori	Hulme	Turley	Ormerod	Agnew	Alcide	Keegan	Skinner	Reed	Bower	Thompson M.	Hawkins	Fettis	Talbot	Swan	Edmondson	Darlow	
2				6	3		12					10	4	7		1	5	8		**11**		9												1
1				1	1							1	1	1		1	1	1		1		1												
							1																											

Match No.	Date	Venue	Opponents		Result	Scorers	Attenda

2000–01

Associate Members' Cup (LDV Vans Trophy)

1	Jan 9	H	Darlington	L	0–4		1,

A

S

2001–02

Associate Members' Cup (LDV Vans Trophy)

1	Oct 16	A	Notts County	L	0–2		1

A

S

2002–03

Associate Members' Cup (LDV Vans Trophy)

1	Oct 22	A	Lincoln City	L	3–4	Cook (pen), Nogan, Parkin	1

A

S

2003–04

Associate Members' Cup (LDV Vans Trophy)

1	Oct 14	A	Halifax Town	L	1–2	Dunning (pen)	1

A

S

2004–05

Associate Members' Cup (LDV Vans Trophy)

1	Sep 29	H	Blackpool	L	0–2		1

A

S

Edmondson	Potter	Sertori	Swan	Hobson	Fox	Hulme	Conlon	Duffield	Agnew	McNiven	Hall	Alcide	Jones	Bullock	Thompson	Williams	Hocking	Jordan	Turley	Mathie	Durkan	Stamp	Reed	Tarrant	Iwelumo	Bower	Patterson	Wood	Emmerson	Nogan	Darlow	Richardson	Cooper	Brass	Basham	Howarth	
		4			7	8			11	**10**	14	5			3				12	9		*6*				13	2									1	1
		1			1	1			1	1		1			1					1		1					1									1	
											1								1							1											

Edmondson	Potter	Hocking	Basham	Hobson	Brass	Bullock	Nogan	Proctor	Richardson	Duffield	Fielding	Cooper	O'Kane	Wood	Emmerson	Stamp	Evans	Fox	Salvati	Mathie	Maley	Smith	Darlow	Rhodes	Parkin	Wise	Brackstone	Jones	Howarth	Grant	
		3	13		7		9	10			4	6				**11**		8		12	5	2							1		1
		1			1		1	1			1	1				1		1			1	1							1		
			1																	1											

Okoli	Cowan	Jones	Smith	Hobson	Brass	Fox	Nogan	Duffield	Brackstone	Parkin	Edmondson	Mathie	Wilding	Wise	Carvalho	Bullock	Potter	Wood	Fettis	Yalcin	Mazzina	Cook	Reddy	McCarthy	Cooper	Ingham	Shandran	Graydon	Whitehead	Stockdale	Howarth	
3		4	5		12		9			8	2		10				6	7				11									1	1
1		1	1				1			1	1	1	1				1	1				1									1	
					1																											
							1			1												1										

Edmondson	Merris	Wise	Brass	Hope	Ward	Dunning	Nogan	Bullock	Fox	Cooper	Wood	George	Stewart	Downes	Brackstone	Parkin	Wilford	Crowe	Smith	Dove	Browne	Shaw	Coad	Davies	Walker	Yalcin	Dickman	Bell	Porter	Offiong	Newby	Law	Arthur	Ashcroft	Haw	
	13	5		6		8	14			2		12		3	7	9	*10*		4	**11**																1
		1		1		1				1				1	1	1	1		1	1																
	1						1					1																								
						1																														

Brass	Smith	Groves	Clarke	Davis	Pearson	Dunning	Robinson P.D.	Bishop	Stewart	Yalcin	Law	Arthur	Merris	Donovan	Nogan	Porter	Stockdale	Harrison	McGurk	Coad	Davies	Haw	Staley	Grant	Ashcroft	Robinson P.	Webster	Maloney	Constable	Jackson	Armstrong	
		4			6	8	7	10	11	13	2		3		9		1	12	5													1
		1			1	1	1	1	1		1		1		1		1		1													
										1								1														

Conference Cup

2004–05

Conference (Gladwish Sales) Cup

Match No.	Date	Venue	Opponents	Result		Scorers	Attenc
3 (N)	Jan 25	A	Accrington Stanley	L	1–2*	Bishop	

* After extra-time.

FA Trophy

2004–05

FA Trophy

Match No.	Date	Venue	Opponents	Result		Scorers	Attenc
3	Jan 15	A	Burton Albion	L	0–3		

2005–06

FA Trophy

Match No.	Date	Venue	Opponents	Result		Scorers	Attenc
1	Dec 17	H	Northwich Victoria	L	1–2	A. Bishop	

2006–07

FA Trophy

Match No.	Date	Venue	Opponents	Result		Scorers	Attenc
1	Dec 16	A	Morecambe	L	1–2	Donaldson	

2007–08

FA Trophy

Match No.	Date	Venue	Opponents	Result		Scorers	Attenc
1	Dec 15	A	Altrincham	W	3-1	Farrell, Lloyd, Wroe	
2	Jan 12	H	Grays Athletic	D	1-1	Farrell (pen)	
rep	22	A	Grays Athletic	W	4-1	Wroe 2, Woolford, Brodie (pen)	
3	Feb 3	A	Farsley Celtic	W	2-0	Woolford, Farrell	
4	23	A	Rushden & Diamonds	W	1-0	Parslow	
SF1/1	Mar 7	A	Torquay United	L	0-2		
SF1/2	15	H	Torquay United	W	1-0	Opp. og	

1 own-goal

Brass	Smith	Groves	Clarke	Davis	Pearson	Dunning	Robinson P.D.	Bishop	Stewart	Yalcin	Law	Arthur	Merris	Donovan	Nogan	Porter	Stockdale	Harrison	McGurk	Coad	Davies	Haw	Staley	Grant	Ashcroft	Robinson P.	Webster	Maloney	Constable	Jackson	Armstrong	
		4				8	13	10					11	7	**9**	1					3		2			12		5	6			3(N)
		1				1		1					1	1	1	1					1		1					1	1			
							1																			1						
								1																								

Brass	Smith	Groves	Clarke	Davis	Pearson	Dunning	Robinson P.D.	Bishop	Stewart	Yalcin	Law	Arthur	Merris	Donovan	Nogan	Porter	Stockdale	Harrison	McGurk	Coad	Davies	Haw	Staley	Grant	Ashcroft	Robinson P.	Webster	Maloney	Constable	Jackson	Armstrong	
		4				8	14	*10*					11	7	13	1					12		2	5		9	**3**	6				3
		1				1		1					1	1		1							1	1		1	1	1				
							1								1						1											

Price	Peat	Mallon	Hotte	McGurk	Convery	Panther	Donaldson	Mansaram	Dunning	Bishop A.	Stewart	O'Neill	Merris	Dudgeon	Yalcin	Webster	Palmer	Andrews	Bertos	Horwood	Barwick	Stockdale	Craddock	N'Toya	Bishop N.	Thomas	Rhodes	Kamara	
				6	7		9		4	10	13			5				2	11	3	8	**1**							1
				1	1		1		1	1				1				1	1	1	1	1							
											1																		
										1																			

Craddock	Peat	Bishop	McGurk	Dudgeon	Convery	Panther	Donaldson	Farrell	Bowey	Lloyd	Greenwood	Webster	Woolford	McMahon	Reid	Parslow	Foster	Goodliffe	Stamp	Maidens	Elvins	Brodie	Kovacs	James	Purkiss	Bell	
12	3		5			4	*9*	10	8	2	13	14	11	**7**				6									1
	1		1			1	1	1	1	1			1	1				1									
1											1	1															
							1																				

Purkiss	Robinson	Elliott	McGurk	Jones	Brayson	Panther	Farrell	Beardsley	Woolford	Greenwood	Sodje	Brodie	Meechan	Craddock	Parslow	Hutchinson	Kelly	Henderson	Wroe	Hegarty	Fry	McBreen	Lloyd	Rusk	Fortune-West	Duncan	Hall	Mimms	Boyes	Rhodes	Turnbull	Shepherd	McWilliams	Beadle	
2		7	4			8	9	13	11		10				6		5		12				3												1
2			4		12	8	*9*		**11**		10			14	6		5		7				3								13				2
2		4	5			8			10		12	9		**3**	6				7				11												rep
2		4	5			*8*	12		10		13	**9**			6				7		3		11								14				3
2		7	5			12	9		11		10	13		4	6				8				3												4
2		*7*	4			8	*9*		11		12	14			6		**5**		10				3			13									SF1/1
2	3	4	5			**8**	9		11		10	12			6				7										13						SF1/2
7	1	6	7			6	5		7		4	2		2	7		3		6		1		6												
					1	1	1	1			3	3		1					1							1			1		2				
							3		2			1			1				3				1												

Record Against Non-League opposition in FA Cup (1929–2004)

Season	Round	Opposition	Venue		Result
1929–30	4Q	Scarborough	A	W	3–1
1930–31	1	Gresley Rovers	H	W	3–1
1932–33	1	Scarborough	H	L	1–3
1934–35	1	Burton Town	A	W	3–2
1935–36	1	Burton Town	H	L	1–5
1945–46	2(1)	Bishop Auckland	H	W	3–0
	2(2)	Bishop Auckland	A	W	2–1
1946–47	1	Scunthorpe United	H	L	0–1
1948–49	1	Runcorn	H	W	2–1
1950–51	1	Bishop Auckland	A	D	2–2
	R	Bishop Auckland	H	W	2–1
1954–55	1	Scarborough	H	W	3–2
	2	Dorchester Town	A	W	5–2
	4	Bishop Auckland	A	W	3–1
1957–58	2	South Shields	A	W	3–1
1959–60	2	Crook Town	A	W	1–0
1964–65	1	Bangor City	H	W	5–1
1965–66	1	South Shields	A	L	1–3
1966–67	1	Morecambe	H	D	0–0
	R	Morecambe	A	D	1–1
	2R	Morecambe	N	W	1–0
1968–69	1	South Shields	A	W	6–0
	2	Morecambe	H	W	2–0
1969–70	1	Whitby Town	H	W	2–0
	2	Bangor City	A	D	0–0
	R	Bangor City	H	W	2–0
1970–71	1	Tamworth	A	D	0–0
	R	Tamworth	H	W	5–0
	2	Boston United	A	W	2–1
1972–73	2	Bangor City	A	W	3–2
1976–77	1	Dudley Town	A	D	1–1
	R	Dudley Town	H	W	4–1
1977–78	1	Wigan Athletic	A	L	0–1
1978–79	1	Blyth Spartans	H	D	1–1
	R	Blyth Spartans	A	W	5–3
	2	Scarborough	H	W	3–0
1979–80	1	Mossley	H	W	5–2
1981–82	1	Stafford Rangers	A	W	2–1
	2	Altrincham	H	D	0–0
	R	Altrincham	A	L	3–4
1983–84	1	Macclesfield Town	A	D	0–0
	R	Macclesfield Town	H	W	2–0
1984–85	1	Blue Star	H	W	2–0
1985–86	1	Morecambe	H	D	0–0
	R	Morecambe	N	W	2–0
	2	Whitby Town	H	W	3–1
	3	Wycombe Wanderers	H	W	2–0
	4	Altrincham	H	W	2–0
1986–87	2	Caernarfon Town	A	D	0–0
	R	Caernarfon Town	H	L	1–2
1987–88	1	Burton Albion	H	D	0–0
	R	Burton Albion	A	W	2–1
1991–92	1	Bridlington Town	A	W	2–1
1996–97	3	Hednesford Town	A	L	0–1
1997–98	1	Southport	A	W	4–0
1998–99	1	Enfield	A	D	2–2
	R	Enfield	H	W	2–1
2000–01	1	Radcliffe Borough	A	W	4–1

High-Scoring Games
(Six or more goals)

Season	Opponents	Venue	Result
For			
	MIDLAND LEAGUE		
1925–26	Alfreton Town	H	6–0
1926–27	Alfreton Town	H	7–0
1926–27	Ilkeston Town	H	6–0
1926–27	Wath Athletic	H	7–1
1926–27	Wombwell Town	H	7–1
1927–28	Heanor Town	H	7–1
1927–28	Nottingham Forest Reserves	A	7–1
1928–29	Hull City Reserves	H	6–1
1928–29	Worksop Town	H	8–2
1928–29	Rotherham United Reserves	A	7–2
	FOOTBALL LEAGUE		
1929–30	Rochdale	H	6–0
1931–32	Halifax Town	H	7–2
1932–33	Darlington	H	6–1
1933–34	Barrow	H	6–1
1933–34	Rochdale	A	6–3
1933–34	Rochdale	H	6–1
1934–35	Crewe Alexandra	H	7–3
1934–35	Carlisle United	H	7–0
1935–36	Mansfield Town	H	7–5
1947–48	Halifax Town	H	6–0
1948–49	Carlisle United	H	6–0
1948–49	Rotherham United	H	6–1
1951–52	Accrington Stanley	H	6–1
1951–52	Halifax Town	H	6–2
1954–55	Wrexham	A	6–2
1956–57	Southport	H	9–1
1960–61	Exeter City	H	6–1
1964–65	Chesterfield	H	7–1
1967–68	Bradford Park Avenue	H	6–2
1981–82	Crewe Alexandra	H	6–0
1982–83	Mansfield Town	H	6–1
1984–85	Gillingham	H	7–1
1985–86	Darlington	H	7–0

Season	Opponents	Venue	Result
Against			
	MIDLAND LEAGUE		
1923–24	Grimsby Town Reserves	A	0–9
1923–24	Worksop Town	A	1–7
1924–25	Denaby United	A	1–6
1925–26	Lincoln City Reserves	A	1–6
1925–26	Sutton Town	A	1–6
1926–27	Worksop Town	A	1–6
1928–29	Notts County Reserves	H	3–6
1928–29	Boston Town	A	0–6
1928–29	Frickley Colliery	A	1–6
1928–29	Lincoln City Reserves	A	0–6
	FOOTBALL LEAGUE		
1931–32	Gateshead	A	0–6
1931–32	Crewe Alexandra	A	2–8
1931–32	Hartlepools United	A	2–7
1932–33	Rochdale	H	2–6
1935–36	Oldham Athletic	A	2–6
1935–36	Walsall	A	0–6
1935–36	Accrington Stanley	A	2–7
1935–36	Chester	A	0–12
1936–37	Stockport County	A	0–6
1937–38	Oldham Athletic	A	2–6
1938–39	Bradford City	A	0–6
1938–39	Crewe Alexandra	A	2–8
1938–39	Rochdale	H	0–7
1938–39	Oldham Athletic	A	0–6
1946–47	Chester	A	0–6
1946–47	Rotherham United	A	1–6
1950–51	Tranmere Rovers	A	2–7
1953–54	Mansfield Town	A	2–7
1957–58	Tranmere Rovers	A	1–6
1957–58	Chester	A	2–9
1960–61	Aldershot	A	1–6
1965–66	Swindon Town	A	0–6
1965–66	Queen's Park Rangers	A	2–7
1965–66	Swansea Town	A	2–7

Season	Opponents	Venue	Result
For			
	FA CUP		
1924–25	Horsforth	H	7–1
1927–28	Stockton Malleable	H	7–1
1928–29	Stockton	H	7–1
1968–69	South Shields	A	6–0
2007–08	Rushall Olympic	H	6–0
	ASSOCIATE MEMBERS' CUP		
1989–90	Hartlepool United	H	7–1

Season	Opponents	Venue	Result
Against			
1970–71	Brentford	A	4–6
1976–77	Brighton & Hove Albion	A	2–7
1979–80	Scunthorpe United	A	1–6
1981–82	Bradford City	A	2–6
1988–89	Burnley	A	0–6
1995–96	Peterborough United	A	1–6
1997–98	Burnley	A	2–7
1999–2000	Barnet	A	3–6
	CONFERENCE		
2004–05	Carlisle United	A	0–6
2007–08	Crawley Town	A	1–6
	FA CUP		
1945–46	Sheffield Wednesday	H	1–6
1984–85	Liverpool	A	0–7

York City Hat-tricks

Player	Goals	Opponents	Venue	Season
		MIDLAND LEAGUE		
C. Elliott	3	Rotherham Town	H	1922–23
T. Rippon	3	Rotherham County R	A	1923–24
B. Acklam	3	Rotherham County R	H	1923–24
L. Marshall	5	Castleford Town	H	1924–25
J. Miller	3	Denaby United	A	1924–25
R. Holland	4	Alfreton Town	H	1925–26
Riley	3	Shirebrook	A	1925–26
R. Baines	3	Wombwell	H	1925–26
L. Duckham	5	Alfreton Town	H	1926–27
C. Flood	4	Ilkeston United	H	1926–27
C. Flood	3	Wath Athletic	H	1926–27
C. Flood	3	Heanor Town	H	1926–27
R. Thompson	3	Frickley Colliery	A	1926–27
A. Clayton	3	Wombwell	H	1926–27
J. Hammerton	4	Heanor Town	H	1927–28
T. Fenoughty	3	Mexborough Athletic	H	1927–28
R. Noble	3	Nottingham Forest R	A	1927–28
J. Roberts	3	StaveleyTown	H	1928–29
J. Cowie	5	Hull City R	H	1928–29
J. Cowie	6	Worksop Town	H	1928–29
J. Cowie	4	Boston Town	H	1928–29
J. Cowie	4	Rotherham United R	A	1928–29
R. Merritt	3	Lincoln City R	H	1928–29
		FOOTBALL LEAGUE		
W. Bottrill	3	Wigan Borough	H	1929–30
W. Millar	3	Crewe Alexandra	H	1929–30
J. Cowie	3	Hartlepools United	H	1930–31
R. Baines	3	New Brighton	H	1931–32
R. Baines	3	Rochdale	A	1931–32
R. Baines	3	Halifax Town	H	1931–32
R. Baines	3	Mansfield Town	H	1932–33
R. Baines	3	Barrow	H	1932–33
E. Hathway	3	Barrow	H	1933–34
M. Dando	3	Rochdale	H	1933–34
M. Dando	3	Rotherham United	H	1934–35
J. Hughes	3	Walsall	H	1934–35
M. Dando	3	Carlisle United	H	1934–35
A. Thompson	3	Darlington	H	1936–37
A. Thompson	3	Carlisle United	H	1936–37
R. Baines	3	Chester	A	1937–38
A. Patrick	4	Halifax Town	H	1947–48

Player	Goals	Opponents	Venue	Season
A. Patrick	3	Chester	A	1947–48
A. Patrick	5	Rotherham United	H	1948–49
A. Patrick	3	Stockport County	H	1948–49
R. Spence	3	Wrexham	H	1949–50
W. Fenton	3	Accrington Stanley	H	1951–52
A. Patrick	3	Oldham Athletic	H	1951–52
A. Patrick	3	Halifax Town	H	1951–52
D. Dunmore	3	Mansfield Town	H	1953–54
A. Bottom	3	Wrexham	A	1954–55
W. Fenton	4	Carlisle United	A	1954–55
N. Wilkinson	3	Wrexham	A	1955–56
A. Bottom	4	Southport	H	1956–57
N. Wilkinson	3	Rochdale	H	1956–57
T. Farmer	3	Tranmere Rovers	H	1957–58
P. Wragg	3	Hartlepools United	A	1958–59
J. Edgar	3	Accrington Stanley	H	1959–60
C. Addison	3	Workington	H	1960–61
P. Wragg	3	Aldershot	H	1960–61
P. Wragg	4	Crewe Alexandra	A	1960–61
J. Weir	3	Crewe Alexandra	H	1961–62
J. Stainsby	3	Gillingham	H	1961–62
P. Wragg	3	Doncaster Rovers	H	1961–62
J. Weir	3	Workington	H	1961–62
N. Wilkinson	3	Lincoln City	H	1962–63
D. Weddle	3	Tranmere Rovers	H	1964–65
P. Aimson	3	Hull City	A	1965–66
E. MacDougall	3	Port Vale	H	1967–68
P. Aimson	3	Brentford	H	1969–70
P. Aimson	3	Chesterfield	H	1971–72
G. Staniforth	3	Port Vale	H	1978–79
G. Staniforth	3	Wigan Athletic	A	1979–80
K. Walwyn	3	Mansfield Town	H	1982–83

Player	Goals	Opponents	Venue	Season
J. Byrne	3	Chester City	H	1983–84
J. Byrne	3	Halifax Town	H	1983–84
K. Houchen	3	Gillingham	H	1984–85
A. Canham	3	Darlington	H	1985–86
I. Blackstone	3	Wrexham	A	1990–91
P. Barnes	4	Scunthorpe United	H	1992–93
P. Barnes	3	Barnet	A	1992–93
P. Barnes	3	Bournemouth	A	1994–95
P. Barnes	3	Blackpool	H	1994–95
G. Bull	3	Wrexham	A	1995–96
		CONFERENCE		
J. O'Neill	3	Southport	A	2005–06
A. Bishop	3	Forest Green Rovers	H	2005–06
C. Donaldson	3	Cambridge United	A	2006–07
		FA CUP		
L. Marshall	5	Horsforth	H	1924–25
R. Holland	3	Wombwell	H	1925–26
A. Clayton	3	Guisborough Belmont	H	1926–27
J. Cowie	6	Stockton	H	1928–29
A. Agar	3	Hull City	H	1936–37
R. Baines	3	West Bromwich Albion	H	1937–38
A. Bottom	3	Dorchester Town	A	1954–55
P. Aimson	3	Bangor City	H	1964–65
T. Ross	3	South Shields	A	1968–69
P. Aimson	3	Tamworth	H	1970–71
C. Farrell	3	Rushall Olympic	H	2007–08
		FL CUP		
K. Walwyn	3	Sunderland	A	1986–87
S. Spooner	3	Hartlepool United	H	1989–90
		ASSOCIATE MEMBERS' CUP		
M. Gabbiadini	3	Darlington	H	1986–87
I. Helliwell	3	Hartlepool United	H	1989–90

Top 10 Players

TOP 10 APPEARANCE LIST

	League	Cup	Total
B. Jackson	481 +1	57	538 +1
A. McMillan	409 +12	71	480 +12
C. Topping	410 +2	51	461 +2
W. Hall	353 +20	61 +4	414 +24
G. Ford	359 +7	69	428 +7
T. Forgan	388	40	428
A. Canham	309 +38	62 +4	371 +42
N. Wilkinson	354	47	401
P. Burrows	333 +4	53	386 +4
W. Hughes	349	31	380

TOP 10 SCORERS

	League	Cup	Total
N. Wilkinson	127	16	143
K. Walwyn	119	21	140
W. Fenton	118	6	124
A. Patrick	109	8	117
P. Aimson	98	15	113
A. Bottom	92	13	105
T. Fenoughty	*97	7	104
R. Baines	*88	5	93
P. Wragg	78	9	87
P. Barnes	76	9	85

* includes Midland League

Clubman of the Year

(The Billy Fenton Memorial Trophy)

Season	*Winner*
1973–74	Phil Burrows
1974–75	Chris Topping
1975–76	Micky Cave
1976–77	Brian Pollard
1977–78	Gordon Staniforth
1978–79	Gordon Staniforth
1979–80	Ian McDonald
1980–81	Eddie Blackburn
1981–82	Keith Walwyn
1982–83	Derek Hood
1983–84	John MacPhail
1984–85	John MacPhail
1985–86	Simon Mills
1986–87	Keith Walwyn
1987–88	Dale Banton
1988–89	Ian Helliwell
1989–90	Chris Marples
1990–91	Steve Tutill
1991–92	Jon McCarthy
1992–93	Paul Stancliffe
1993–94	Paul Barnes
1994–95	Jon McCarthy
1995–96	Andy McMillan
1996–97	Tony Barras
1997–98	Steve Bushell
1998–99	Barry Jones
1999–2000	Barry Jones
2000–01	Alan Fettis
2001–02	Alan Fettis
2002–03	Chris Brass
2003–04	Darren Dunning
2004–05	David Merris
2005–06	Clayton Donaldson
2006–07	Neal Bishop
2007–08	David McGurk

Top 20 Football League Appearances

Surname	Forenames	Position	Played From	To	Apps	Sub	Gls	Total
JACKSON	Charles Barry	Centre-half	1958	1970	481	1	9	482
McMILLAN	Andre (Andy)	Right-back	1987	1999	409	12	5	421
TOPPING	Christopher	Central-defender	1968	1978	410	2	11	412
FORGAN	Thomas Carr	Goalkeeper	1954	1966	388	0	0	388
HALL	Wayne	Left-back	1989	2001	353	20	9	373
FORD	Gary	Midfield	1978	1987	359	7	53	366
WILKINSON	Norman Francis	Centre-forward	1954	1966	354	0	127	354
HUGHES	William (Billy)	Right-winger	1951	1962	349	0	55	349
CANHAM	Anthony (Tony)	Winger	1985	1995	309	38	57	347
BURROWS	Philip Arthur	Left-back	1966	1974	333	4	14	337
STOREY	Sidney	Inside-left	1947	1956	330	0	40	330
BROWN	Gordon Steele	Inside-forward/Half-back	1950	1958	322	0	25	322
HOWE	George	Left-back	1954	1961	307	0	0	307
TUTILL	Stephen Alan	Central-defender	1987	1997	293	8	6	301
HOOD	Derek	Full-back/Midfield	1980	1988	287	13	32	300
SPENCE	Ronald	Left-half	1948	1958	280	0	25	280
SWALLOW	Barry Ernest	Centre-half	1969	1976	268	1	21	269
WRAGG	Peter	Forward/Midfield	1956	1963	264	0	78	264
FENTON	William (Billy)	Left-winger	1951	1958	257	0	118	257
CRAWFORD	Peter Graeme	Goalkeeper	1971	1977				
			& 1980	1980	252	0	0	252

Top 20 FA Cup Appearances

Surname	Forenames	Position	Played From	To	Apps	Sub	Gls	Total
WILKINSON	Norman Francis	Centre-forward	1954	1966	39	0	16	39
FORD	Gary	Midfield	1978	1987	36	0	7	36
JACKSON	Charles Barry	Centre-half	1958	1970	34	0	0	34
MIDDLEMISS	John (Jack)	Half-back	1923	1929	31	0	1	31
BURROWS	Philip Arthur	Left-back	1966	1974	31	0	1	31
FORGAN	Thomas Carr	Goalkeeper	1954	1966	30	0	0	30
HUGHES	William (Billy)	Right-winger	1951	1962	30	0	3	30
HOWE	George	Left-back	1954	1961	30	0	0	30
BROWN	Gordon Steele	Inside-forward/Half-back	1950	1958	29	0	0	29
TOPPING	Christopher	Central-defender	1968	1978	26	0	0	26
SPENCE	Ronald	Left-half	1948	1958	26	0	1	26
PINDER	James John (Jack)	Right-back	1932	1948	26	0	0	26
STOREY	Sidney	Inside-left	1947	1956	24	0	2	24
HOOD	Derek	Full-back/Midfield	1980	1988	24	2	3	26
SWALLOW	Barry Ernest	Centre-half	1969	1976	24	0	4	24
WALWYN	Keith	Centre-forward	1981	1987	24	0	11	24
FENOUGHTY	Thomas	Inside-forward	1926	1934	23	0	7	23
WRAGG	Peter	Forward/Midfield	1956	1963	23	0	4	23
STEWART	Alan Victor	Centre-half	1949	1957	23	0	0	23
WASS	Edwin (Ted)	Full-back/Centre-half	1932	1939	22	0	0	22
HATHWAY	Edward Albert	Left-half/Inside-left	1933	1939	22	0	2	22

City's Internationals

The following players have gained representative honours while with York City:

England

Richard Cresswell: 1 Under-21 cap – 9 February 1999 v France (Derby).

Northern Ireland

Peter Scott: 7 full caps – 24 March 1976 v Israel (Tel Aviv), 8 May 1976 v Scotland (Hampden Park), 11 May 1976 v England (Wembley), 14 May 1976 v Wales (Swansea), 13 May 1978 v Scotland (Hampden Park), 16 May 1978 v England (Wembley), 19 May 1978 v Wales (Wrexham).

Republic of Ireland

Eamon Dunphy: 1 full cap – 10 November 1965 v Spain (World Cup Qualifying match in Paris).

Scotland

Graeme Law: capped at Under-19 level in 2002–03.

Turkey

Lev Yalcin: capped at Under-19 level in 2003–04.

Wales

Michael Walker: 3 Under-23 caps – 22 February 1967 v Northern Ireland (Belfast), 1 November 1967 v England (Swansea), 20 March 1968 v Northern Ireland (Cardiff).

The following four players gained England Youth caps:
Brian Pollard: 1971 and 1972.
Cliff Calvert: 1972.
Mike De Placido: 1972.
Russell Howarth: 1999.

Steve Tutill was capped for England Schoolboys in 1985 and 1986 while with the club as an associate schoolboy.

Gordon Jones played for a Football League XI in a wartime representative game against Northern Command staged at Bootham Crescent in October 1942.

Andy Bishop represented the England non-League XI in 2004–05 and 2005–06.
David Stockdale represented the England non-League XI in 2004–05.
Clayton Donaldson represented the England non-League XI in 2006–07.
Neal Bishop represented the England non-League XI in 2006–07.
Danny Parslow represented the Wales non-League XI in 2006–07 and 2007–08.
Martyn Woolford represented the England non-League XI in 2007–08.

FA Youth Cup

City's best season in the FA Youth Cup was in 1992–93 when they reached the quarter-finals of the competition. In earlier rounds City had knocked out Newcastle United, West Bromwich Albion and Leyton Orient and were drawn away to Manchester United in the last eight. United could boast the likes of David Beckham, Paul Scholes, Gary Neville and Keith Gillespie in their youth squad, with Andy Warrington, Graeme Murty and Scott Jordan among City's youngsters. The game was played at Old Trafford on 8 March 1993 when a crowd of 4,937 saw United win 5–0 with goals from Gary Neville, John O'Kane, Robert Savage, Richard Irving and David Beckham. The sides lined up as follows:

United: Whitmarsh, O'Kane (Brown), Riley, Casper, Neville, Gillespie, Rawlinson (Savage), Beckham, Irving, Scholes, Thornley.

City: Warrington, Gosling, Dooley, Thomlinson, Mockler, Jordan, Roberts, Murty, Falk (Bowker), Medforth, Simpson.

United lost in the Final that season to Leeds United 4–1 on aggregate. In the victorious Leeds side was Mark Tinkler who was later to join City.

Another good run in the competition was in 1998–99 when they reached the last 16 of the competition. En route to this stage City knocked out Burscough, Wigan Athletic, Stoke City and Ipswich Town, and they were drawn at home to West Ham United in round five. The game was staged at Bootham Crescent on 16 March 1999 when a crowd of just under 1,000 saw a 1–1 draw. The Hammers, who had Joe Cole and Michael Carrick in their line up, took the lead after 28 minutes through Michael Ferrante, but City fought back and West Ham's 'keeper Steve Bywater made a fine save to thwart James Turley. After the break City's skipper Peter Batchelor headed against the bar before Christian Fox hit a spectacular 25-yard equaliser in the 86th minute. There was drama in stoppage time when Fox was sent off for handball, but the subsequent penalty, taken by Carrick, was saved by 'keeper John Mohan. The teams lined up:

City: Mohan, Fox, Urwin, Bullock, Batchelor, Fielding, Thompson (Hakami), Walters, Dibie, Turley, Dufton.

West Ham: Bywater, Newton, Byrne, Forbes, Iriekpen, Angus, Briggs (Omonua), Ferrante (Uddin), Cole, Garcia, Carrick.

The Hammers won the replay 5–0 at Upton Park and went on to win the competition that season, beating Coventry City 9–0 on aggregate in the Final.

City's complete record of results in the competition

Season	Round	Matches
2007–08	Prelim	York City 4 Dunston FB 0
	1QR	York City 4 Whitley Bay 0
	2QR	Seaham 2 York City 5
	3QR	York City v West Allotment Celtic (w/o)
	1	York City 5 Dinnington 1
	2	Bury 0 York City 2
	3	Chester City 3 York City 0

Season	Round	Matches
2006–07	1QR	Ryton 0 York City 1
	2QR	York City 3 Selby Town 2
	3QR	Dunston FB 0 York City 2
	1	York City 1 Leigh RMI 1 (5–3 pens)
	2	York City 0 Chester City 1
2005–06	1QR	York City 4 Marine 1
	2QR	Trafford 2 York City 2 (1–4 pens)
	3QR	Dunston FB 3 York City 2

Season	Round	Matches
2004–05	1QR	Dunston FB 4 York City 0
2003–04	1	York City 1 Hull City 0
	2	York City 0 Macclesfield Town 1
2002–03	1	Macclesfield Town 0 York City 1
	2	Tranmere Rovers 2 York City 0
2001–02	1	York City 0 Hartlepool United 3
2000–01	1	Mansfield Town 0 York City 4
	2	Darlington 0 York City 0
	rep	York City 1 Darlington 1 (5–4 pens)
	3	York City 1 Huddersfield Town 1
	rep	Huddersfield Town 0 York City 1
	4	Wolverhampton W. 2 York City 1
1999–2000	1	Carlisle United 0 York City 2
	2	Scunthorpe United 0 York City 0
	rep	York City 1 Scunthorpe United 3
1998–99	1	Burscough 2 York City 3
	2	Wigan Athletic 0 York City 3
	3	Stoke City 0 York City 3
	4	Ipswich Town 1 York City 1
	rep	York City 2 Ipswich Town 0
	5	York City 1 West Ham United 1
	rep	West Ham United 5 York City 0
1997–98	1	Huddersfield Town 1 York City 2
	2	York City 0 Middlesbrough 1
1996–97	2	Oldham Athletic 3 York City 0
1995–96	2	Oldham Athletic 3 York City 2
1994–95	2	York City 0 Birmingham City 0
	rep	Birmingham City 0 York City 2
	3	Sheffield United 1 York City 0
1993–94	2	York City 0 Blackburn Rovers 0
	rep	Blackburn Rovers 1 York City 1
	2nd rep	Blackburn Rovers 2 York City 1

Season	Round	Matches
1992–93	1	Carlisle United 1 York City 1
	rep	York City 2 Carlisle United 0
	2	York City 2 Newcastle United 0
	3	West Bromwich Albion 1 York City 1
	rep	York City 2 West Bromwich Albion 0
	4	York City 2 Leyton Orient 0
	QF	Manchester United 5 York City 0
1991–92	1	York City 1 Blackburn Rovers 1
	rep	Blackburn Rovers 4 York City 3
1990–91	1QR	York City 1 Scarborough 0
	2QR	Rotherham United 1 York City 2
	1	York City 3 Sunderland 0
	2	Hull City 1 York City 1
	rep	York City 1 Hull City 2
1989–90	Prelim	Rotherham United 2 York City 2
	rep	York City 3 Rotherham United 4
1988–89	1QR	York City 2 Bedlington Terriers 0
	2QR	Carlisle United 2 York City 1
1987–88	1	York City 1 Burnley 2
1986–87	1	Hull City 3 York City 0
1985–86	1	Oldham Athletic 1 York City 1
	rep	York City 5 Oldham Athletic 2
	2	York City 3 Doncaster Rovers 2
	3	York City 1 Sheffield United 2
1984–85	1	Darlington 0 York City 3
	2	York City 0 Barnsley 2
1983–84	1	York City 4 Rochdale 1
	2	York City 4 Billingham Town 3
	3	York City 0 Liverpool 2
1982–83	1	York City 1 Grimsby Town 0
	2	York City 0 Sunderland 2
1981–82	Prelim	Stockton v York City (walkover)
	1QR	York City 2 Bradford City 1
	2QR	Darlington 1 York City 3
	1	York City 0 Barnsley 5

Season	Round	Matches
1980–81	Prelim	West End BC 2 York City 4
	1QR	York City 12 Tyne BC 0
	2QR	York City 10 Farsley Celtic 0
	1	Hartlepool United 2 York City 1
1979–80	1	Hartlepool United 2 York City 2
	rep	York City 2 Hartlepool United 3
1978–79	1	Hull City 2 York City 0
1977–78	1	New Hartley Juniors 1 York City 5
	2	Rotherham United 2 York City 0
1976–77	1	Lincoln City 0 York City 2
	2	York City 3 Leeds United 3
	rep	Leeds United 2 York City 0
1975–76	1	York City 2 Scunthorpe United 0
	2	York City 0 Grimsby Town 3

Season	Round	Matches
1974–75	1	Bradford City 0 York City 3
	2	York City 0 Sunderland 8
1973–74	1	Hartlepool United 3 York City 1
1972–73	1	York City 7 Hartlepool United 0
	2	Sheffield United 3 York City 2
1971–72	2QR	Leeholme U Jnrs 0 York City 6
	1	Chesterfield 4 York City 3
1970–71	1	Middlesbrough 6 York City 1
1969–70	1	York City 2 Bradford City 0
	2	Bradford PA 1 York City 0

Members of the 1992–93 side that reached the quarter-final of the FA Youth Cup.

Graeme Murty.

Andy Warrington.

NORTH RIDING SENIOR CUP

Since their formation in 1922, York City have competed in this competition and have won the trophy on 10 occasions. In their first season (1922–23) they lost in the Final away to Middlesbrough reserves. After their election to the Football League in 1929, they invariably fielded their reserves in the competition but in recent years have on occasions been represented by the senior side.

Their biggest win in the tournament was in 1924–25 when they beat Grangetown St Mary's 11–1, and the biggest crowd to watch City in the NRSC was in August 1997 when 12,500 saw Middlesbrough win 3–1 at the Riverside Stadium. The biggest home attendance was in May 1953 when Stockton beat City 2–1 in the Final in front of 3,433.

One notable game was in December 1955 when in a first round tie City lost 1–0 at Middlesbrough, with Brian Clough the scorer.

Clubs City have met in the competition over the years include: Skinningrove Iron and Steel Works, South Bank, Loftus, Scarborough Penguins, Carlin How, Redcar Albion, Head Wrightsons, Acklam Works, Marske United, ICI Wilton and Pickering Town.

City's North Riding Senior Cup Successes

1950 Middlesbrough (A) 3–0

J. Frost, J. Brown, J. Duthoit, R. Spence, E. Burgin, A. Jackson, G. Ivey, J. Coop, T. Walker, A. Collins, J. Birch

Scorers: Ivey 2, Walker

1957 Scarborough (H) 2–1 (replay – after a 0–0 draw away)

M. Granger, E. Wardle, R. Steel, D. Hardcastle, A. Stewart, T. Stoddart, A. Hobson, J. Stewart, A. Monkhouse, C. Colbridge, Fenwick

Scorers: Monkhouse, J. Stewart

In August 1970 City beat Billingham Synthonia to win the North Riding Senior Cup. City director Dr Angus McLeod presents the trophy to skipper Tommy Thompson.

1970 Billingham Synthonia (H) 2–1 (replay – after a 0–0 draw at home)
M. Gadsby, Swales, T. Thompson, Solan, K. Newman, P. Hearnshaw, C. Dale (Barber), P. Maloney, S. Tasker, R. Hewitt, D. Jones
Scorer: Hewitt 2

1979 Middlesbrough (H) 2–1
J. Neenan, A. Kamara, R. Kay, D. Pugh, S. Faulkner, S. James (J. Byrne), G. Ford, D. Loggie, B. Wellings, I. McDonald, G. Staniforth
Scorers: Loggie, Faulkner

1986 Whitby Town (A) 1–0
A. Leaning, A. Hay, D. Hood, R. Sbragia, S. Senior (S. McKenzie), M. Gabbiadini, M. Butler, D. Banton, K. Walwyn, A. Pearce, A. Canham
Scorer: M. Gabbiadini

1989 Stockton (A) 1–0
S. Endersby, R. Greenough, A. McMillan, C. Ashworth, K. Smith, S. Tutill, A. Barratt, D. Bradshaw, G. Himsworth, A. Dean, I. Dunn
Scorer: Dunn

1996 Scarborough (A) 3–2
D. Kiely, A. McMillan, P. Atkinson, S. Bushell, P. Atkin, A. Barras, G. Himsworth (G. Murty), A. Randall (S. Jordan), N. Tolson, G. Bull, P. Stephenson
Scorers: Tolson 2, Stephenson

1999 Whitby Town (A) 4–2
R. Mimms, C. Fox (A. McMillan), N. Thompson, M. Atkins, G. Rennison, M. Tinkler, C. Skinner, A. Pouton, M. Williams, R. Rowe, M. Garratt
Scorers: Pouton 2, Rowe, Atkins

2000 Scarborough (A) 1–0
R. Howarth, M. Hocking, J. Keegan, P. Vasey (L. Wood), M. Thompson, W. Hall, J. Williams, M. Williams, C. Alcide (B. Rhodes), L. Bullock, A. Dawson
Scorer: J. Williams

2006 Northallerton Town (H) 3–1
A. Reid, N. Kamara (M. Walsh), D. Hollingsworth, M. Hotte, D. Merris, B. Stewart, B. Webster, N. Holmes, A. Taylor (D. Phillips), C. Wrigley (M. Holt), A. Rhodes
Scorers: Rhodes, Holmes, Wrigley

EAST RIDING SENIOR CUP

Represented chiefly by their reserve side, the club entered this competition from 1926 to 1931 and twice won the trophy.

In 1928–29 they beat Beverley White Star 2–0 at home in a replay and the following campaign defeated Hull City 2–1 in a replay at Fulfordgate.

Player Records –
Midland League 1922–29

Surname	Forenames	Position	Career Start	Career Finish	Midland League Apps	Midland League Goals	FA Cup Apps	FA Cup Goals	Total Apps	Total Goals
ACKLAM	Bernard	Left-half	1922	1926	72	11	1	0	73	11
ADDISON		Centre-half	1928	1929	1	0	0	0	1	0
ALBRECHT	Frederick Bernard	Centre-forward	1922	1929	85	20	9	3	94	23
ALLISON	C.H.	Outside-left	1922	1923	3	0	0	0	3	0
APPLETON	A. Edward	Inside-left	1923	1924	4	0	0	0	4	0
ASHDOWN	John Terence	Left-half	1924	1925	1	0	0	0	1	0
ATKINSON	E.	Outside-right	1923	1924	1	0	0	0	1	0
BAINES	Joseph Cecil	Left-back	1924	1926	21	3	4	0	25	3
BAINES *	Reginald	Centre-forward	1924	1926	19	7	0	0	19	7
BARNICLE	P.	Goalkeeper	1925	1926	5	0	0	0	5	0
BARRETT	John	Outside-right	1922	1923	1	0	0	0	1	0
BELL	J.	Outside-left	1925	1926	1	0	0	0	1	0
BLYTHE	G.	Inside-right	1924	1925	1	0	0	0	1	0
BOLTON	Walter	Left-half	1928	1929	1	0	0	0	1	0
BOOT	Leonard George	Goalkeeper	1922	1924	10	0	5	0	15	0
BOWE	Wilfred Henry	Outside-right	1922	1925	4	2	0	0	4	2
BROOKE		Inside-left	1924	1925	1	1	1	0	2	1
BROWN	Herbert Edward	Outside-right	1924	1926	35	6	0	0	35	6
BROWN	Thomas Frank	Right-back	1928	1929	41	0	7	0	48	0
CHARLESWORTH	Arthur Laurence	Centre-forward	1922	1924	33	14	5	0	38	14
CHARNLEY	Samuel	Centre-half	1928	1929	48	4	7	1	55	5
CHOWN	Reginald Percy	Goalkeeper	1928	1929	1	0	0	0	1	0
CLANCEY	James Ronald	Outside-left	1926	1927	1	1	0	0	1	1
CLARKE		Outside-left	1923	1924	1	0	0	0	1	0
CLAYTON	Arthur	Centre-half	1925	1929	57	16	6	6	63	22
CLEASBY	Harold	Inside-left	1924	1926	25	5	5	4	30	9
COLLIER	John C.	Right-half	1928	1929	2	0	0	0	2	0
COWIE *	James	Centre-forward	1928	1929	49	49	7	7	56	56
CROFT		Outside-right	1924	1924	1	0	0	0	1	0
CROSS	Robert S.	Outside-right	1924	1925	4	0	0	0	4	0
CROWTHER	George Edward	Goalkeeper	1927	1928	38	0	6	0	44	0
DALE	Stanley	Left-half	1923	1924	9	0	0	0	9	0
DANIELS	David	Left-back	1926	1928	50	0	3	0	53	0
DAVISON	Thomas Norman	Outside-left	1923	1924	37	2	5	1	42	3
DENNIS	Percy	Centre-forward	1923	1924						
			& 1925	1926	7	0	1	0	8	0
DINSDALE	William Arthur	Centre-forward	1923	1923	1	0	0	0	1	0
DREW		Left-back	1925	1926	4	0	3	0	7	0
DUCKHAM	Leonard	Inside-left	1926	1927	15	7	5	2	20	9
DUTHIE *	John Flett	Left-half	1928	1929	48	4	7	2	55	6
ELLIOTT	Charles	Outside-right	1922	1925	81	25	8	2	89	27
EVEREST	John	Outside-left	1926	1928	9	4	0	0	9	4
FENOUGHTY *	Thomas	Inside-right	1926	1929	82	41	11	2	93	43
FLANAGHAN	Henry Nixon	Inside-left	1924	1924	5	0	0	0	5	0
FLOOD	Charles William	Centre-forward	1926	1927	15	17	4	2	19	19
FLYNN	Andrew	Right-back	1926	1928	80	0	13	0	93	0
FORREST	George	Outside-right	1928	1929	44	7	5	1	49	8
FURNELL	Albert Edward	Goalkeeper	1924	1928	27	0	4	0	31	0
GLOVER	Frederick	Right-back	1923	1926	45	0	1	0	46	0

Surname	Forenames	Position	Career Start	Career Finish	Midland League Apps	Midland League Goals	FA Cup Apps	FA Cup Goals	Total Apps	Total Goals
HAMMERTON	John Daniel	Centre-forward	1927	1928	22	18	2	3	24	21
HARRON	George	Outside-right	1922	1923	2	0	0	0	2	0
HARRON	Joseph	Outside-left	1922	1923						
			1925	1926	51	8	4	0	55	8
HARVEY	Edmund Martin	Outside-right	1926	1927	28	2	6	2	34	4
HENDRY	Conal Nicholson	Goalkeeper	1922	1924	56	0	0	0	56	0
HEWITT		Inside-left	1924	1925	2	0	0	0	2	0
HILL	Thomas	Left-half	1926	1928	2	0	0	0	2	0
HOLLAND	R.	Centre-forward	1925	1926	12	11	4	6	16	17
HOLMES	Thomas Arthur	Right-back	1922	1923	14	0	0	0	14	0
HOOPER	Charles	Inside-right	1927	1928	6	2	0	0	6	2
HORROCKS		Goalkeeper	1925	1926	16	0	0	0	16	0
HOUGHTON		Inside-right	1928	1929	2	0	0	0	2	0
HOWARTH	C.	Outside-left	1923	1923	1	0	0	0	1	0
HULME	Joseph Harold	Outside-right	1922	1924	28	3	1	0	29	3
JONES		Inside-left	1925	1925	1	1	0	0	1	1
JONES	Harold	Left-half	1923	1928	5	1	0	0	5	1
KAY	Eric Newbald	Left-half	1925	1926	1	0	0	0	1	0
KAY	Frederick Robert	Inside-right	1924	1926	2	0	0	0	2	0
KAY	Thornton Lambert	Outside-right	1926	1926	1	0	0	0	1	0
KAY	William Arthur	Right-back	1922	1925	3	0	1	0	4	0
KENDALL	John Robert	Right-half	1924	1925	1	0	0	0	1	0
LACY		Centre-forward	1928	1929	6	3	0	0	6	3
LAWS	Joseph Minto	Outside-left	1924	1926	70	16	4	1	74	17
LEMONS	Charles George	Inside-left	1922	1923	40	5	0	0	40	5
LEVICK	Oliver	Centre-half	1927	1928	41	1	6	1	47	2
LICKLEY	Arthur	Left-half	1922	1923	7	0	0	0	7	0
LODGE	James William	Left-back	1925	1926	19	0	0	0	19	0
LOUGHRAN *	James	Centre-half	1925	1928	96	12	17	4	113	16
LUCAS	C.	Outside-left	1923	1923	5	1	0	0	5	1
LYNCH	Walter	Right-half	1922	1923	33	1	0	0	33	1
MacMURRAY	Campbell	Left-back	1923	1924	42	0	5	0	47	0
MARSHALL	Lester	Right-half	1923	1925						
			& 1928	1929	67	10	8	5	75	15
MARTIN		Inside-right	1926	1926	1	0	0	0	1	0
MARTINDALE	George	Right-back	1925	1926	4	0	0	0	4	0
MASKILL *	George	Right-half	1923	1927	82	0	6	0	88	0
MASKILL *	Thomas	Outside-right	1922	1923	41	1	0	0	41	1
MERRITT	Richard	Outside-left	1926	1929	70	31	18	10	88	41
MIDDLEMISS	John (Jack)	Left-half	1923	1929	228	4	31	1	259	5
MILLER	James	Centre-forward	1924	1926	38	17	3	3	41	20
MOULT	Harold	Inside-right	1922	1923	17	6	0	0	17	6
NOBLE	Raymond	Inside-left	1925	1928	28	6	0	0	28	6
O'CAIN	James	Outside-left	1924	1927	34	17	5	0	39	17
PAGE	George	Left-back	1927	1928	19	0	6	0	25	0
PATTIE	A.S.	Centre-forward	1923	1924	6	1	0	0	6	1
PRECIOUS	George W.	Right-half	1927	1929	17	0	1	0	18	0
QUINLAN	Jack	Outside-left	1923	1923	3	0	0	0	3	0
RANBY	Samuel	Inside-left	1925	1929	158	40	21	12	179	52
REDFERN	Levi	Right-half	1926	1927	27	1	5	0	32	1
REED	Percy	Right-half	1923	1924	30	0	5	0	35	0
RICHARDS		Centre-half	1926	1927	3	2	0	0	3	2
RICHARDSON	George Edward	Centre-forward	1926	1926	14	3	0	0	14	3
RILEY		Centre-forward	1925	1926	9	7	0	0	9	7
RIPPON	Thomas	Inside-left	1923	1924	33	6	5	2	38	8
ROBERTS	F.	Goalkeeper	1923	1924	7	0	0	0	7	0
ROBERTS	Joseph	Outside-left	1928	1929	40	6	7	1	47	7
ROBERTSON	David Vallance	Goalkeeper	1928	1929	49	0	7	0	56	0

			Career		Midland League		FA Cup		Total	
Surname	**Forenames**	**Position**	**Start**	**Finish**	**Apps**	**Goals**	**Apps**	**Goals**	**Apps**	**Goals**
ROBINSON	Ernest George	Right-back	1927	1929	9	0	0	0	9	0
RUTHERFORD	John	Centre-half	1924	1925	8	0	3	0	11	0
SANDIFORD	Robert	Inside-right	1925	1925	2	0	0	0	2	0
SAYLES	George	Right-back	1924	1925	52	0	5	0	57	0
SHANKS	Robert	Left-back	1926	1927	13	0	4	0	17	0
SHANN		Outside-right	1923	1924	1	0	0	0	1	0
SHARPE *	George William	Outside-left	1928	1929	1	0	0	0	1	0
SHAW	Gilbert J.	Right-back	1923	1924	22	0	4	0	26	0
SIMMS	Ernest	Centre-forward	1928	1928	6	2	0	0	6	2
SMITH	J.	Goalkeeper	1924	1925	41	0	3	0	44	0
SMITH	William Thomas	Centre-half	1922	1925	75	4	5	0	80	4
STONEHOUSE		Inside-right	1926	1926	2	1	0	0	2	1
SURTEES	Joseph	Outside-right	1923	1924	1	0	0	0	1	0
THIRLBECK		Left-back	1924	1924	4	0	0	0	4	0
THOMPSON	George Herbert	Goalkeeper	1926	1927	37	0	7	0	44	0
THOMPSON	Robert	Centre-forward	1926	1927	10	7	0	0	10	7
THORPE	Edwin	Left-back	1922	1923	41	0	0	0	41	0
TILLOTSON	Joe	Outside-right	1926	1926	1	0	0	0	1	0
TINDALE	Richard	Outside-right	1922	1923	21	1	3	0	24	1
TINDALL	J.	Inside-right	1924	1925	2	0	0	0	2	0.
TOMES	A.	Right-half	1923	1923	1	0	0	0	1	0
TYSON		Inside-left	1927	1927	1	2	0	0	1	2
WAITE	George	Outside-right	1927	1928	39	8	6	1	45	9
WALKER	E.	Goalkeeper	1923	1924	11	0	0	0	11	0
WALKER	Frederick	Centre-half	1924	1925	36	8	0	0	36	8
WOOD	Donald	Left-back	1923	1925	41	0	1	0	42	0
WOODS	Jack	Centre-forward	1922	1923	32	13	0	0	32	13

* also played for City in the Football League (see following section)

Player Records – Football League 1929–2004

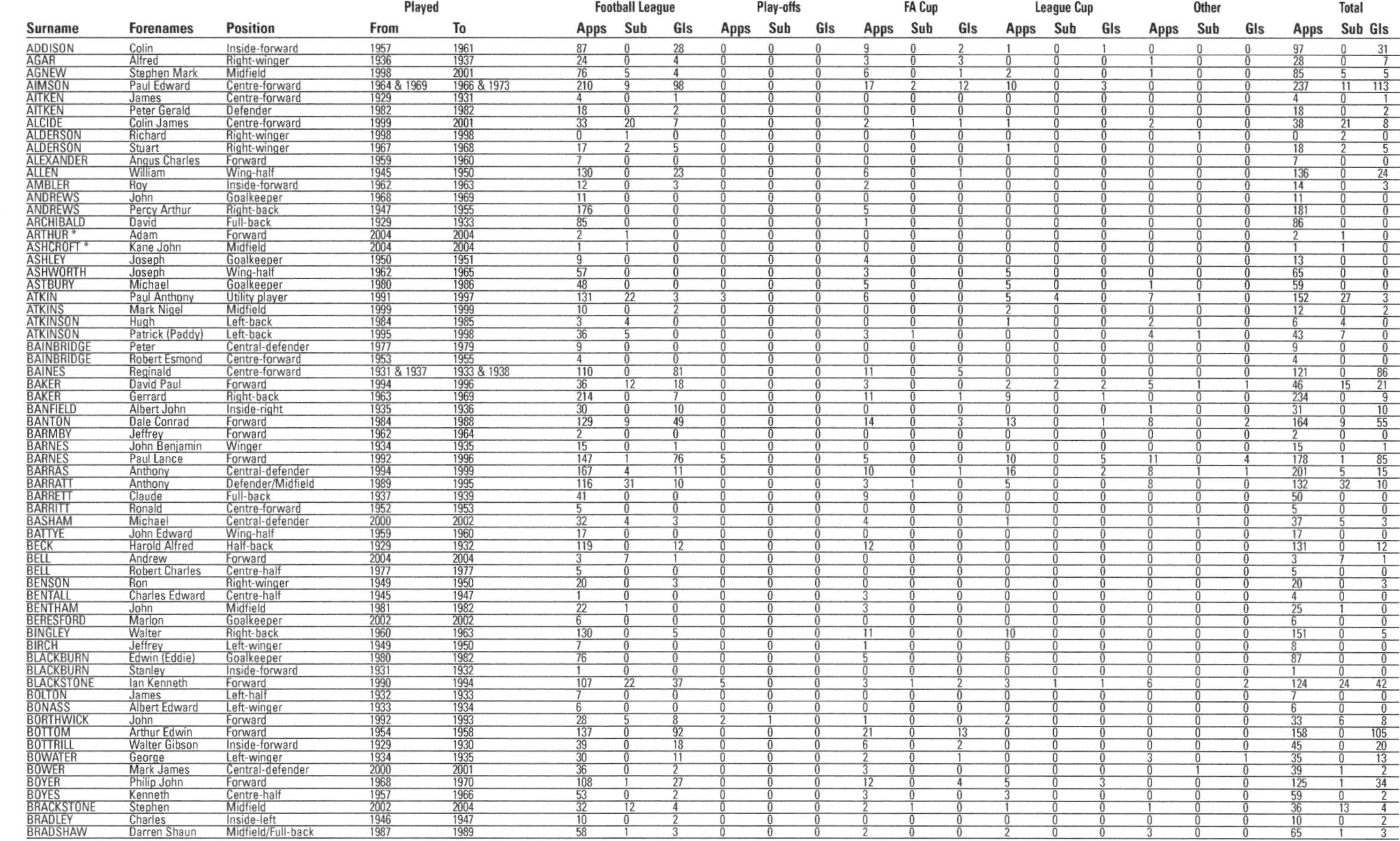

Surname	Forenames	Position	Played		Football League			Play-offs			FA Cup			League Cup			Other			Total		
			From	To	Apps	Sub	Gls	Apps	Sub	Gls	Apps	Sub	Gls	Apps	Sub	Gls	Apps	Sub	Gls	Apps	Sub	Gls
ADDISON	Colin	Inside-forward	1957	1961	87	0	28	0	0	0	9	0	2	1	0	1	0	0	0	97	0	31
AGAR	Alfred	Right-winger	1936	1937	24	0	4	0	0	0	3	0	3	0	0	0	1	0	0	28	0	7
AGNEW	Stephen Mark	Midfield	1998	2001	76	5	4	0	0	0	6	0	1	2	0	0	1	0	0	85	5	5
AIMSON	Paul Edward	Centre-forward	1964 & 1969	1966 & 1973	210	9	98	0	0	0	17	2	12	10	0	3	0	0	0	237	11	113
AITKEN	James	Centre-forward	1929	1931	4	0	1	0	0	0	0	0	0	0	0	0	0	0	0	4	0	1
AITKEN	Peter Gerald	Defender	1982	1982	18	0	2	0	0	0	0	0	0	0	0	0	0	0	0	18	0	2
ALCIDE	Colin James	Centre-forward	1999	2001	33	20	7	0	0	0	2	1	1	1	0	0	2	0	0	38	21	8
ALDERSON	Richard	Right-winger	1998	1998	0	1	0	0	0	0	0	0	0	0	0	0	0	1	0	0	2	0
ALDERSON	Stuart	Right-winger	1967	1968	17	2	5	0	0	0	0	0	0	1	0	0	0	0	0	18	2	5
ALEXANDER	Angus Charles	Forward	1959	1960	7	0	0	0	0	0	0	0	0	0	0	0	0	0	0	7	0	0
ALLEN	William	Wing-half	1945	1950	130	0	23	0	0	0	6	0	1	0	0	0	0	0	0	136	0	24
AMBLER	Roy	Inside-forward	1962	1963	12	0	3	0	0	0	2	0	0	0	0	0	0	0	0	14	0	3
ANDREWS	John	Goalkeeper	1968	1969	11	0	0	0	0	0	0	0	0	0	0	0	0	0	0	11	0	0
ANDREWS	Percy Arthur	Right-back	1947	1955	176	0	0	0	0	0	5	0	0	0	0	0	0	0	0	181	0	0
ARCHIBALD	David	Full-back	1929	1933	85	0	0	0	0	0	1	0	0	0	0	0	0	0	0	86	0	0
ARTHUR *	Adam	Forward	2004	2004	2	1	0	0	0	0	0	0	0	0	0	0	0	0	0	2	1	0
ASHCROFT *	Kane John	Midfield	2004	2004	1	1	0	0	0	0	0	0	0	0	0	0	0	0	0	1	1	0
ASHLEY	Joseph	Goalkeeper	1950	1951	9	0	0	0	0	0	4	0	0	0	0	0	0	0	0	13	0	0
ASHWORTH	Joseph	Wing-half	1962	1965	57	0	0	0	0	0	3	0	0	5	0	0	0	0	0	65	0	0
ASTBURY	Michael	Goalkeeper	1980	1986	48	0	0	0	0	0	5	0	0	5	0	0	1	0	0	59	0	0
ATKIN	Paul Anthony	Utility player	1991	1997	131	22	3	3	0	0	6	0	0	5	4	0	7	1	0	152	27	3
ATKINS	Mark Nigel	Midfield	1999	1999	10	0	2	0	0	0	0	0	0	2	0	0	0	0	0	12	0	2
ATKINSON	Hugh	Left-back	1984	1985	3	4	0	0	0	0	0	0	0	1	0	0	2	0	0	6	4	0
ATKINSON	Patrick (Paddy)	Left-back	1995	1998	36	5	0	0	0	0	3	1	0	0	0	0	4	1	0	43	7	0
BAINBRIDGE	Peter	Central-defender	1977	1979	9	0	0	0	0	0	0	0	0	0	0	0	0	0	0	9	0	0
BAINBRIDGE	Robert Esmond	Centre-forward	1953	1955	4	0	0	0	0	0	0	0	0	0	0	0	0	0	0	4	0	0
BAINES	Reginald	Centre-forward	1931 & 1937	1933 & 1938	110	0	81	0	0	0	11	0	5	0	0	0	0	0	0	121	0	86
BAKER	David Paul	Forward	1994	1996	36	12	18	0	0	0	3	0	0	2	2	2	5	1	1	46	15	21
BAKER	Gerrard	Right-back	1963	1969	214	0	7	0	0	0	11	0	1	9	0	1	0	0	0	234	0	9
BANFIELD	Albert John	Inside-right	1935	1936	30	0	10	0	0	0	0	0	0	0	0	0	1	0	0	31	0	10
BANTON	Dale Conrad	Forward	1984	1988	129	9	49	0	0	0	14	0	3	13	0	1	8	0	2	164	9	55
BARMBY	Jeffrey	Forward	1962	1964	2	0	0	0	0	0	0	0	0	0	0	0	0	0	0	2	0	0
BARNES	John Benjamin	Winger	1934	1935	15	0	1	0	0	0	0	0	0	0	0	0	0	0	0	15	0	1
BARNES	Paul Lance	Forward	1992	1996	147	1	76	5	0	0	5	0	0	10	0	5	11	0	4	178	1	85
BARRAS	Anthony	Central-defender	1994	1999	167	4	11	0	0	0	10	0	1	16	0	2	8	1	1	201	5	15
BARRATT	Anthony	Defender/Midfield	1989	1995	116	31	10	0	0	0	3	1	0	5	0	0	8	0	0	132	32	10
BARRETT	Claude	Full-back	1937	1939	41	0	0	0	0	0	9	0	0	0	0	0	0	0	0	50	0	0
BARRITT	Ronald	Centre-forward	1952	1953	5	0	0	0	0	0	0	0	0	0	0	0	0	0	0	5	0	0
BASHAM	Michael	Central-defender	2000	2002	32	4	3	0	0	0	4	0	0	1	0	0	0	1	0	37	5	3
BATTYE	John Edward	Wing-half	1959	1960	17	0	0	0	0	0	0	0	0	0	0	0	0	0	0	17	0	0
BECK	Harold Alfred	Half-back	1929	1932	119	0	12	0	0	0	12	0	0	0	0	0	0	0	0	131	0	12
BELL	Andrew	Forward	2004	2004	3	7	1	0	0	0	0	0	0	0	0	0	0	0	0	3	7	1
BELL	Robert Charles	Centre-half	1977	1977	5	0	0	0	0	0	0	0	0	0	0	0	0	0	0	5	0	0
BENSON	Ron	Right-winger	1949	1950	20	0	3	0	0	0	0	0	0	0	0	0	0	0	0	20	0	3
BENTALL	Charles Edward	Centre-half	1945	1947	1	0	0	0	0	0	3	0	0	0	0	0	0	0	0	4	0	0
BENTHAM	John	Midfield	1981	1982	22	1	0	0	0	0	3	0	0	0	0	0	0	0	0	25	1	0
BERESFORD	Marlon	Goalkeeper	2002	2002	6	0	0	0	0	0	0	0	0	0	0	0	0	0	0	6	0	0
BINGLEY	Walter	Right-back	1960	1963	130	0	5	0	0	0	11	0	0	10	0	0	0	0	0	151	0	5
BIRCH	Jeffrey	Left-winger	1949	1950	7	0	0	0	0	0	1	0	0	0	0	0	0	0	0	8	0	0
BLACKBURN	Edwin (Eddie)	Goalkeeper	1980	1982	76	0	0	0	0	0	5	0	0	6	0	0	0	0	0	87	0	0
BLACKBURN	Stanley	Inside-forward	1931	1932	1	0	0	0	0	0	0	0	0	0	0	0	0	0	0	1	0	0
BLACKSTONE	Ian Kenneth	Forward	1990	1994	107	22	37	5	0	0	3	1	2	3	1	1	6	0	2	124	24	42
BOLTON	James	Left-half	1932	1933	7	0	0	0	0	0	0	0	0	0	0	0	0	0	0	7	0	0
BONASS	Albert Edward	Left-winger	1933	1934	6	0	0	0	0	0	0	0	0	0	0	0	0	0	0	6	0	0
BORTHWICK	John	Forward	1992	1993	28	5	8	2	1	0	1	0	0	2	0	0	0	0	0	33	6	8
BOTTOM	Arthur Edwin	Forward	1954	1958	137	0	92	0	0	0	21	0	13	0	0	0	0	0	0	158	0	105
BOTTRILL	Walter Gibson	Inside-forward	1929	1930	39	0	18	0	0	0	6	0	2	0	0	0	0	0	0	45	0	20
BOWATER	George	Left-winger	1934	1935	30	0	11	0	0	0	2	0	1	0	0	0	3	0	1	35	0	13
BOWER	Mark James	Central-defender	2000	2001	36	0	2	0	0	0	3	0	0	0	0	0	0	1	0	39	1	2
BOYER	Philip John	Forward	1968	1970	108	1	27	0	0	0	12	0	4	5	0	3	0	0	0	125	1	34
BOYES	Kenneth	Centre-half	1957	1966	53	0	2	0	0	0	3	0	0	3	0	0	0	0	0	59	0	2
BRACKSTONE	Stephen	Midfield	2002	2004	32	12	4	0	0	0	2	1	0	1	0	0	1	0	0	36	13	4
BRADLEY	Charles	Inside-left	1946	1947	10	0	2	0	0	0	0	0	0	0	0	0	0	0	0	10	0	2
BRADSHAW	Darren Shaun	Midfield/Full-back	1987	1989	58	1	3	0	0	0	2	0	0	2	0	0	3	0	0	65	1	3

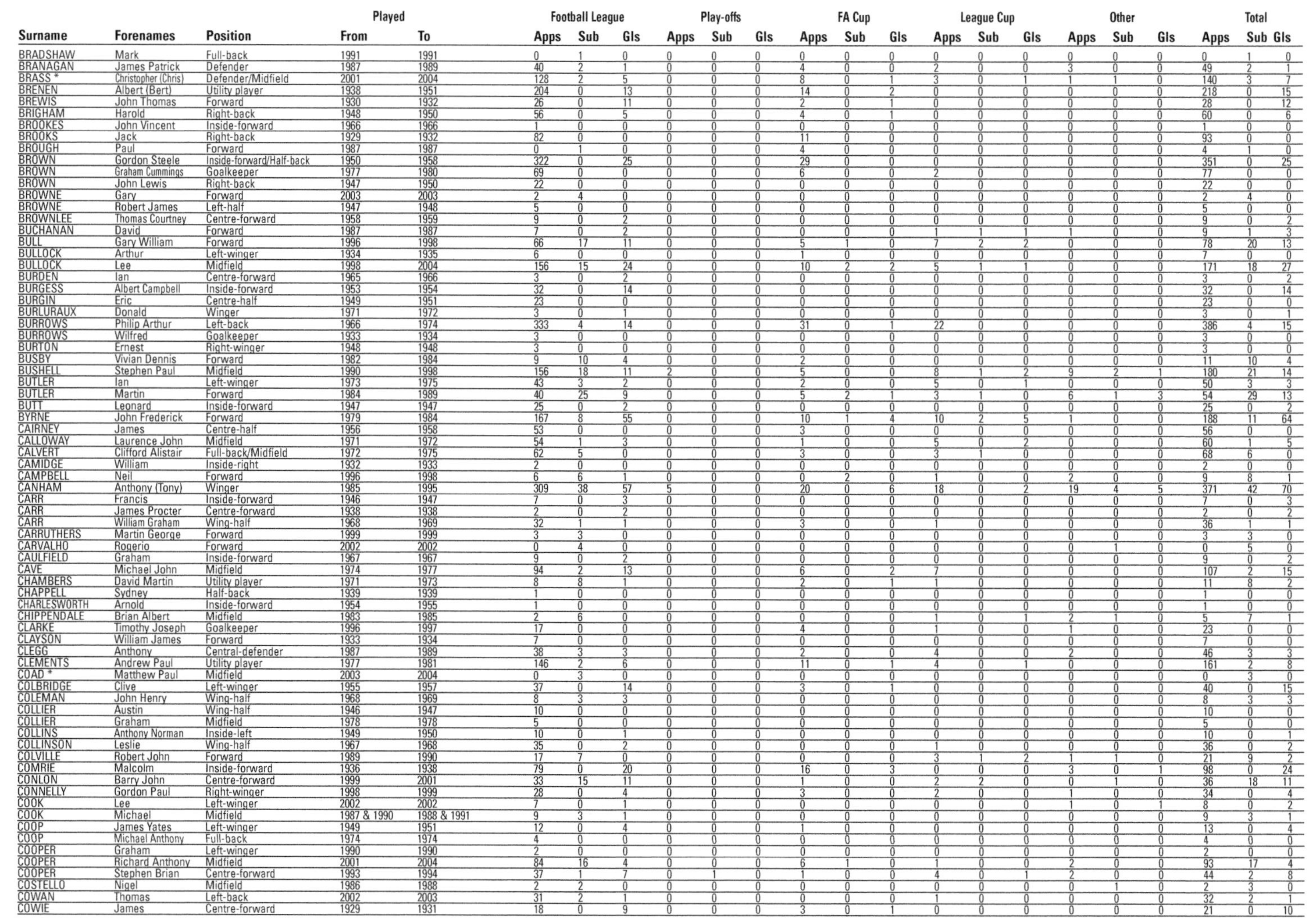

			Played		Football League			Play-offs			FA Cup			League Cup			Other			Total		
Surname	Forenames	Position	From	To	Apps	Sub	Gls	Apps	Sub	Gls	Apps	Sub	Gls	Apps	Sub	Gls	Apps	Sub	Gls	Apps	Sub	Gls
BRADSHAW	Mark	Full-back	1991	1991	0	1	0	0	0	0	0	0	0	0	0	0	0	0	0	0	1	0
BRANAGAN	James Patrick	Defender	1987	1989	40	2	1	0	0	0	4	0	0	2	0	0	3	0	0	49	2	1
BRASS *	Christopher (Chris)	Defender/Midfield	2001	2004	128	2	5	0	0	0	8	0	1	3	0	1	1	1	0	140	3	7
BRENEN	Albert (Bert)	Utility player	1938	1951	204	0	13	0	0	0	14	0	2	0	0	0	0	0	0	218	0	15
BREWIS	John Thomas	Forward	1930	1932	26	0	11	0	0	0	2	0	1	0	0	0	0	0	0	28	0	12
BRIGHAM	Harold	Right-back	1948	1950	56	0	5	0	0	0	4	0	1	0	0	0	0	0	0	60	0	6
BROOKES	John Vincent	Inside-forward	1966	1966	1	0	0	0	0	0	0	0	0	0	0	0	0	0	0	1	0	0
BROOKS	Jack	Right-back	1929	1932	82	0	0	0	0	0	11	0	0	0	0	0	0	0	0	93	0	0
BROUGH	Paul	Forward	1987	1987	0	1	0	0	0	0	4	0	0	0	0	0	0	0	0	4	1	0
BROWN	Gordon Steele	Inside-forward/Half-back	1950	1958	322	0	25	0	0	0	29	0	0	0	0	0	0	0	0	351	0	25
BROWN	Graham Cummings	Goalkeeper	1977	1980	69	0	0	0	0	0	6	0	0	2	0	0	0	0	0	77	0	0
BROWN	John Lewis	Right-back	1947	1950	22	0	0	0	0	0	0	0	0	0	0	0	0	0	0	22	0	0
BROWNE	Gary	Forward	2003	2003	2	4	0	0	0	0	0	0	0	0	0	0	0	0	0	2	4	0
BROWNE	Robert James	Left-half	1947	1948	5	0	0	0	0	0	0	0	0	0	0	0	0	0	0	5	0	0
BROWNLEE	Thomas Courtney	Centre-forward	1958	1959	9	0	2	0	0	0	0	0	0	0	0	0	0	0	0	9	0	2
BUCHANAN	David	Forward	1987	1987	7	0	2	0	0	0	0	0	0	1	1	1	1	0	0	9	1	3
BULL	Gary William	Forward	1996	1998	66	17	11	0	0	0	5	1	0	7	2	2	0	0	0	78	20	13
BULLOCK	Arthur	Left-winger	1934	1935	6	0	0	0	0	0	1	0	0	0	0	0	0	0	0	7	0	0
BULLOCK	Lee	Midfield	1998	2004	156	15	24	0	0	0	10	2	2	5	1	1	0	0	0	171	18	27
BURDEN	Ian	Centre-forward	1965	1966	3	0	2	0	0	0	0	0	0	0	0	0	0	0	0	3	0	2
BURGESS	Albert Campbell	Inside-forward	1953	1954	32	0	14	0	0	0	0	0	0	0	0	0	0	0	0	32	0	14
BURGIN	Eric	Centre-half	1949	1951	23	0	0	0	0	0	0	0	0	0	0	0	0	0	0	23	0	0
BURLURAUX	Donald	Winger	1971	1972	3	0	1	0	0	0	0	0	0	0	0	0	0	0	0	3	0	1
BURROWS	Philip Arthur	Left-back	1966	1974	333	4	14	0	0	0	31	0	1	22	0	0	0	0	0	386	4	15
BURROWS	Wilfred	Goalkeeper	1933	1934	3	0	0	0	0	0	0	0	0	0	0	0	0	0	0	3	0	0
BURTON	Ernest	Right-winger	1948	1948	3	0	0	0	0	0	0	0	0	0	0	0	0	0	0	3	0	0
BUSBY	Vivian Dennis	Forward	1982	1984	9	10	4	0	0	0	2	0	0	0	0	0	0	0	0	11	10	4
BUSHELL	Stephen Paul	Midfield	1990	1998	156	18	11	2	0	0	5	0	0	8	1	2	9	2	1	180	21	14
BUTLER	Ian	Left-winger	1973	1975	43	3	2	0	0	0	2	0	0	5	0	1	0	0	0	50	3	3
BUTLER	Martin	Forward	1984	1989	40	25	9	0	0	0	5	2	1	3	1	0	6	1	3	54	29	13
BUTT	Leonard	Inside-forward	1947	1947	25	0	2	0	0	0	0	0	0	0	0	0	0	0	0	25	0	2
BYRNE	John Frederick	Forward	1979	1984	167	8	55	0	0	0	10	1	4	10	2	5	1	0	0	188	11	64
CAIRNEY	James	Centre-half	1956	1958	53	0	0	0	0	0	3	0	0	0	0	0	0	0	0	56	0	0
CALLOWAY	Laurence John	Midfield	1971	1972	54	1	3	0	0	0	1	0	0	5	0	2	0	0	0	60	1	5
CALVERT	Clifford Alistair	Full-back/Midfield	1972	1975	62	5	0	0	0	0	3	0	0	3	1	0	0	0	0	68	6	0
CAMIDGE	William	Inside-right	1932	1933	2	0	0	0	0	0	0	0	0	0	0	0	0	0	0	2	0	0
CAMPBELL	Neil	Forward	1996	1998	6	6	1	0	0	0	0	2	0	1	0	0	2	0	0	9	8	1
CANHAM	Anthony (Tony)	Winger	1985	1995	309	38	57	5	0	0	20	0	6	18	0	2	19	4	5	371	42	70
CARR	Francis	Inside-forward	1946	1947	7	0	3	0	0	0	0	0	0	0	0	0	0	0	0	7	0	3
CARR	James Procter	Centre-forward	1938	1938	2	0	2	0	0	0	0	0	0	0	0	0	0	0	0	2	0	2
CARR	William Graham	Wing-half	1968	1969	32	1	1	0	0	0	3	0	0	1	0	0	0	0	0	36	1	1
CARRUTHERS	Martin George	Forward	1999	1999	3	3	0	0	0	0	0	0	0	0	0	0	0	0	0	3	3	0
CARVALHO	Rogerio	Forward	2002	2002	0	4	0	0	0	0	0	0	0	0	0	0	0	1	0	0	5	0
CAULFIELD	Graham	Inside-forward	1967	1967	9	0	2	0	0	0	0	0	0	0	0	0	0	0	0	9	0	2
CAVE	Michael John	Midfield	1974	1977	94	2	13	0	0	0	6	0	2	7	0	0	0	0	0	107	2	15
CHAMBERS	David Martin	Utility player	1971	1973	8	8	1	0	0	0	2	0	1	1	0	0	0	0	0	11	8	2
CHAPPELL	Sydney	Half-back	1939	1939	1	0	0	0	0	0	0	0	0	0	0	0	0	0	0	1	0	0
CHARLESWORTH	Arnold	Inside-forward	1954	1955	1	0	0	0	0	0	0	0	0	0	0	0	0	0	0	1	0	0
CHIPPENDALE	Brian Albert	Midfield	1983	1985	2	6	0	0	0	0	0	0	0	1	0	1	2	1	0	5	7	1
CLARKE	Timothy Joseph	Goalkeeper	1996	1997	17	0	0	0	0	0	4	0	0	1	0	0	1	0	0	23	0	0
CLAYSON	William James	Forward	1933	1934	7	0	0	0	0	0	0	0	0	0	0	0	0	0	0	7	0	0
CLEGG	Anthony	Central-defender	1987	1989	38	3	3	0	0	0	2	0	0	4	0	0	2	0	0	46	3	3
CLEMENTS	Andrew Paul	Utility player	1977	1981	146	2	6	0	0	0	11	0	1	4	0	1	0	0	0	161	2	8
COAD *	Matthew Paul	Midfield	2003	2004	0	3	0	0	0	0	0	0	0	0	0	0	0	0	0	0	3	0
COLBRIDGE	Clive	Left-winger	1955	1957	37	0	14	0	0	0	3	0	1	0	0	0	0	0	0	40	0	15
COLEMAN	John Henry	Wing-half	1968	1969	8	3	3	0	0	0	0	0	0	0	0	0	0	0	0	8	3	3
COLLIER	Austin	Wing-half	1946	1947	10	0	0	0	0	0	0	0	0	0	0	0	0	0	0	10	0	0
COLLIER	Graham	Midfield	1978	1978	5	0	0	0	0	0	0	0	0	0	0	0	0	0	0	5	0	0
COLLINS	Anthony Norman	Inside-left	1949	1950	10	0	1	0	0	0	0	0	0	0	0	0	0	0	0	10	0	1
COLLINSON	Leslie	Wing-half	1967	1968	35	0	2	0	0	0	0	0	0	1	0	0	0	0	0	36	0	2
COLVILLE	Robert John	Forward	1989	1990	17	7	0	0	0	0	0	0	0	3	1	2	1	1	0	21	9	2
COMRIE	Malcolm	Inside-forward	1936	1938	79	0	20	0	0	0	16	0	3	0	0	0	3	0	1	98	0	24
CONLON	Barry John	Centre-forward	1999	2001	33	15	11	0	0	0	1	0	0	2	2	0	0	1	0	36	18	11
CONNELLY	Gordon Paul	Right-winger	1998	1999	28	0	4	0	0	0	3	0	0	2	0	0	1	0	0	34	0	4
COOK	Lee	Left-winger	2002	2002	7	0	1	0	0	0	0	0	0	0	0	0	1	0	1	8	0	2
COOK	Michael	Midfield	1987 & 1990	1988 & 1991	9	3	1	0	0	0	0	0	0	0	0	0	0	0	0	9	3	1
COOP	James Yates	Left-winger	1949	1951	12	0	4	0	0	0	1	0	0	0	0	0	0	0	0	13	0	4
COOP	Michael Anthony	Full-back	1974	1974	4	0	0	0	0	0	0	0	0	0	0	0	0	0	0	4	0	0
COOPER	Graham	Left-winger	1990	1990	2	0	0	0	0	0	0	0	0	0	0	0	0	0	0	2	0	0
COOPER	Richard Anthony	Midfield	2001	2004	84	16	4	0	0	0	6	1	0	1	0	0	2	0	0	93	17	4
COOPER	Stephen Brian	Centre-forward	1993	1994	37	1	7	0	1	0	1	0	0	4	0	1	2	0	0	44	2	8
COSTELLO	Nigel	Midfield	1986	1988	2	2	0	0	0	0	0	0	0	0	0	0	0	1	0	2	3	0
COWAN	Thomas	Left-back	2002	2003	31	2	1	0	0	0	0	0	0	1	0	0	0	0	0	32	2	1
COWIE	James	Centre-forward	1929	1931	18	0	9	0	0	0	3	0	1	0	0	0	0	0	0	21	0	10

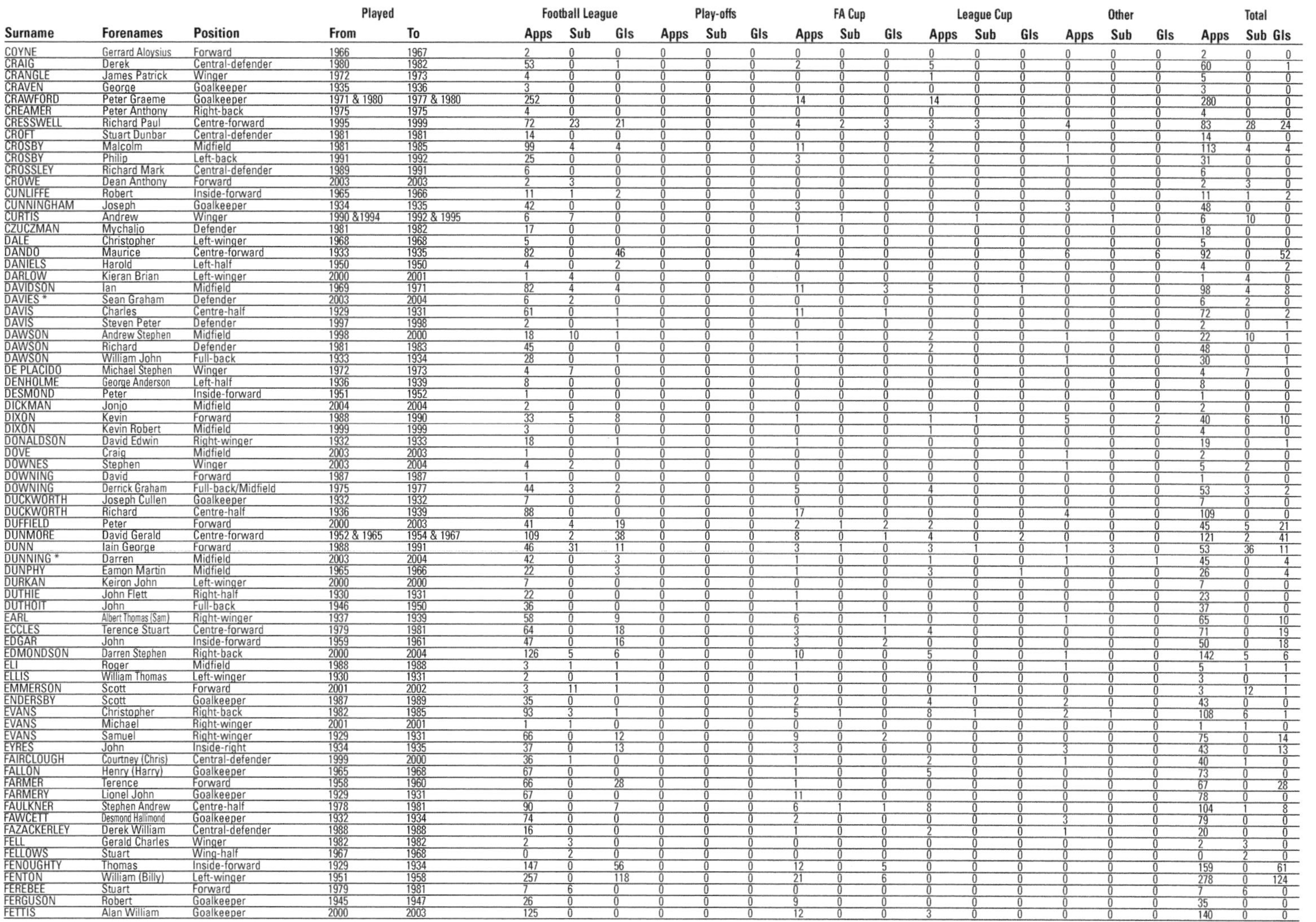

Surname	Forenames	Position	Played From	Played To	Football League Apps	Football League Sub	Football League Gls	Play-offs Apps	Play-offs Sub	Play-offs Gls	FA Cup Apps	FA Cup Sub	FA Cup Gls	League Cup Apps	League Cup Sub	League Cup Gls	Other Apps	Other Sub	Other Gls	Total Apps	Total Sub	Total Gls
COYNE	Gerrard Aloysius	Forward	1966	1967	2	0	0	0	0	0	0	0	0	0	0	0	0	0	0	2	0	0
CRAIG	Derek	Central-defender	1980	1982	53	0	1	0	0	0	2	0	0	5	0	0	0	0	0	60	0	1
CRANGLE	James Patrick	Winger	1972	1973	4	0	0	0	0	0	0	0	0	1	0	0	0	0	0	5	0	0
CRAVEN	George	Goalkeeper	1935	1936	3	0	0	0	0	0	0	0	0	0	0	0	0	0	0	3	0	0
CRAWFORD	Peter Graeme	Goalkeeper	1971 & 1980	1977 & 1980	252	0	0	0	0	0	14	0	0	14	0	0	0	0	0	280	0	0
CREAMER	Peter Anthony	Right-back	1975	1975	4	0	0	0	0	0	0	0	0	0	0	0	0	0	0	4	0	0
CRESSWELL	Richard Paul	Centre-forward	1995	1999	72	23	21	0	0	0	4	2	3	3	3	0	4	0	0	83	28	24
CROFT	Stuart Dunbar	Central-defender	1981	1981	14	0	0	0	0	0	0	0	0	0	0	0	0	0	0	14	0	0
CROSBY	Malcolm	Midfield	1981	1985	99	4	4	0	0	0	11	0	0	2	0	0	1	0	0	113	4	4
CROSBY	Philip	Left-back	1991	1992	25	0	0	0	0	0	3	0	0	2	0	0	1	0	0	31	0	0
CROSSLEY	Richard Mark	Central-defender	1989	1991	6	0	0	0	0	0	0	0	0	0	0	0	0	0	0	6	0	0
CROWE	Dean Anthony	Forward	2003	2003	2	3	0	0	0	0	0	0	0	0	0	0	0	0	0	2	3	0
CUNLIFFE	Robert	Inside-forward	1965	1966	11	1	2	0	0	0	0	0	0	0	0	0	0	0	0	11	1	2
CUNNINGHAM	Joseph	Goalkeeper	1934	1935	42	0	0	0	0	0	3	0	0	0	0	0	3	0	0	48	0	0
CURTIS	Andrew	Winger	1990 &1994	1992 & 1995	6	7	0	0	0	0	0	1	0	0	1	0	0	1	0	6	10	0
CZUCZMAN	Mychalio	Defender	1981	1982	17	0	0	0	0	0	1	0	0	0	0	0	0	0	0	18	0	0
DALE	Christopher	Left-winger	1968	1968	5	0	0	0	0	0	0	0	0	0	0	0	0	0	0	5	0	0
DANDO	Maurice	Centre-forward	1933	1935	82	0	46	0	0	0	4	0	0	0	0	0	6	0	6	92	0	52
DANIELS	Harold	Left-half	1950	1950	4	0	2	0	0	0	0	0	0	0	0	0	0	0	0	4	0	2
DARLOW	Kieran Brian	Left-winger	2000	2001	1	4	0	0	0	0	0	0	0	0	0	0	0	0	0	1	4	0
DAVIDSON	Ian	Midfield	1969	1971	82	4	4	0	0	0	11	0	3	5	0	1	0	0	0	98	4	8
DAVIES *	Sean Graham	Defender	2003	2004	6	2	0	0	0	0	0	0	0	0	0	0	0	0	0	6	2	0
DAVIS	Charles	Centre-half	1929	1931	61	0	1	0	0	0	11	0	1	0	0	0	0	0	0	72	0	2
DAVIS	Steven Peter	Defender	1997	1998	2	0	1	0	0	0	0	0	0	0	0	0	0	0	0	2	0	1
DAWSON	Andrew Stephen	Midfield	1998	2000	18	10	1	0	0	0	1	0	0	2	0	0	1	0	0	22	10	1
DAWSON	Richard	Defender	1981	1983	45	0	0	0	0	0	1	0	0	2	0	0	0	0	0	48	0	0
DAWSON	William John	Full-back	1933	1934	28	0	1	0	0	0	1	0	0	0	0	0	1	0	0	30	0	1
DE PLACIDO	Michael Stephen	Winger	1972	1973	4	7	0	0	0	0	0	0	0	0	0	0	0	0	0	4	7	0
DENHOLME	George Anderson	Left-half	1936	1939	8	0	0	0	0	0	0	0	0	0	0	0	0	0	0	8	0	0
DESMOND	Peter	Inside-forward	1951	1952	1	0	0	0	0	0	0	0	0	0	0	0	0	0	0	1	0	0
DICKMAN	Jonjo	Midfield	2004	2004	2	0	0	0	0	0	0	0	0	0	0	0	0	0	0	2	0	0
DIXON	Kevin	Forward	1988	1990	33	5	8	0	0	0	1	0	0	1	1	0	5	0	2	40	6	10
DIXON	Kevin Robert	Midfield	1999	1999	3	0	0	0	0	0	0	0	0	1	0	0	0	0	0	4	0	0
DONALDSON	David Edwin	Right-winger	1932	1933	18	0	1	0	0	0	1	0	0	0	0	0	0	0	0	19	0	1
DOVE	Craig	Midfield	2003	2003	1	0	0	0	0	0	0	0	0	0	0	0	1	0	0	2	0	0
DOWNES	Stephen	Winger	2003	2004	4	2	0	0	0	0	0	0	0	0	0	0	1	0	0	5	2	0
DOWNING	David	Forward	1987	1987	1	0	0	0	0	0	0	0	0	0	0	0	0	0	0	1	0	0
DOWNING	Derrick Graham	Full-back/Midfield	1975	1977	44	3	2	0	0	0	5	0	0	4	0	0	0	0	0	53	3	2
DUCKWORTH	Joseph Cullen	Goalkeeper	1932	1932	7	0	0	0	0	0	0	0	0	0	0	0	0	0	0	7	0	0
DUCKWORTH	Richard	Centre-half	1936	1939	88	0	0	0	0	0	17	0	0	0	0	0	4	0	0	109	0	0
DUFFIELD	Peter	Forward	2000	2003	41	4	19	0	0	0	2	1	2	2	0	0	0	0	0	45	5	21
DUNMORE	David Gerald	Centre-forward	1952 & 1965	1954 & 1967	109	2	38	0	0	0	8	0	1	4	0	2	0	0	0	121	2	41
DUNN	Iain George	Forward	1988	1991	46	31	11	0	0	0	3	1	0	3	1	0	1	3	0	53	36	11
DUNNING *	Darren	Midfield	2003	2004	42	0	3	0	0	0	1	0	0	1	0	0	1	0	1	45	0	4
DUNPHY	Eamon Martin	Midfield	1965	1966	22	0	3	0	0	0	1	0	0	3	0	1	0	0	0	26	0	4
DURKAN	Keiron John	Left-winger	2000	2000	7	0	0	0	0	0	0	0	0	0	0	0	0	0	0	7	0	0
DUTHIE	John Flett	Right-half	1930	1931	22	0	0	0	0	0	1	0	0	0	0	0	0	0	0	23	0	0
DUTHOIT	John	Full-back	1946	1950	36	0	0	0	0	0	1	0	0	0	0	0	0	0	0	37	0	0
EARL	Albert Thomas (Sam)	Right-winger	1937	1939	58	0	9	0	0	0	6	0	1	0	0	0	1	0	0	65	0	10
ECCLES	Terence Stuart	Centre-forward	1979	1981	64	0	18	0	0	0	3	0	1	4	0	0	0	0	0	71	0	19
EDGAR	John	Inside-forward	1959	1961	47	0	16	0	0	0	3	0	2	0	0	0	0	0	0	50	0	18
EDMONDSON	Darren Stephen	Right-back	2000	2004	126	5	6	0	0	0	10	0	0	5	0	0	1	0	0	142	5	6
ELI	Roger	Midfield	1988	1988	3	1	1	0	0	0	1	0	0	0	0	0	1	0	0	5	1	1
ELLIS	William Thomas	Left-winger	1930	1931	2	0	1	0	0	0	1	0	0	0	0	0	0	0	0	3	0	1
EMMERSON	Scott	Forward	2001	2002	3	11	1	0	0	0	0	0	0	0	1	0	0	0	0	3	12	1
ENDERSBY	Scott	Goalkeeper	1987	1989	35	0	0	0	0	0	2	0	0	4	0	0	2	0	0	43	0	0
EVANS	Christopher	Right-back	1982	1985	93	3	1	0	0	0	5	1	0	8	1	0	2	1	0	108	6	1
EVANS	Michael	Right-winger	2001	2001	1	1	0	0	0	0	0	0	0	0	0	0	0	0	0	1	1	0
EVANS	Samuel	Right-winger	1929	1931	66	0	12	0	0	0	9	0	2	0	0	0	0	0	0	75	0	14
EYRES	John	Inside-right	1934	1935	37	0	13	0	0	0	3	0	0	0	0	0	3	0	0	43	0	13
FAIRCLOUGH	Courtney (Chris)	Central-defender	1999	2000	36	1	0	0	0	0	1	0	0	2	0	0	1	0	0	40	1	0
FALLON	Henry (Harry)	Goalkeeper	1965	1968	67	0	0	0	0	0	1	0	0	5	0	0	0	0	0	73	0	0
FARMER	Terence	Forward	1958	1960	66	0	28	0	0	0	1	0	0	0	0	0	0	0	0	67	0	28
FARMERY	Lionel John	Goalkeeper	1929	1931	67	0	0	0	0	0	11	0	0	0	0	0	0	0	0	78	0	0
FAULKNER	Stephen Andrew	Centre-half	1978	1981	90	0	7	0	0	0	6	1	1	8	0	0	0	0	0	104	1	8
FAWCETT	Desmond Hallimond	Goalkeeper	1932	1934	74	0	0	0	0	0	2	0	0	0	0	0	3	0	0	79	0	0
FAZACKERLEY	Derek William	Central-defender	1988	1988	16	0	0	0	0	0	1	0	0	2	0	0	1	0	0	20	0	0
FELL	Gerald Charles	Winger	1982	1982	2	3	0	0	0	0	0	0	0	0	0	0	0	0	0	2	3	0
FELLOWS	Stuart	Wing-half	1967	1968	0	2	0	0	0	0	0	0	0	0	0	0	0	0	0	0	2	0
FENOUGHTY	Thomas	Inside-forward	1929	1934	147	0	56	0	0	0	12	0	5	0	0	0	0	0	0	159	0	61
FENTON	William (Billy)	Left-winger	1951	1958	257	0	118	0	0	0	21	0	6	0	0	0	0	0	0	278	0	124
FEREBEE	Stuart	Forward	1979	1981	7	6	0	0	0	0	0	0	0	0	0	0	0	0	0	7	6	0
FERGUSON	Robert	Goalkeeper	1945	1947	26	0	0	0	0	0	9	0	0	0	0	0	0	0	0	35	0	0
FETTIS	Alan William	Goalkeeper	2000	2003	125	0	0	0	0	0	12	0	0	3	0	0	0	0	0	140	0	0

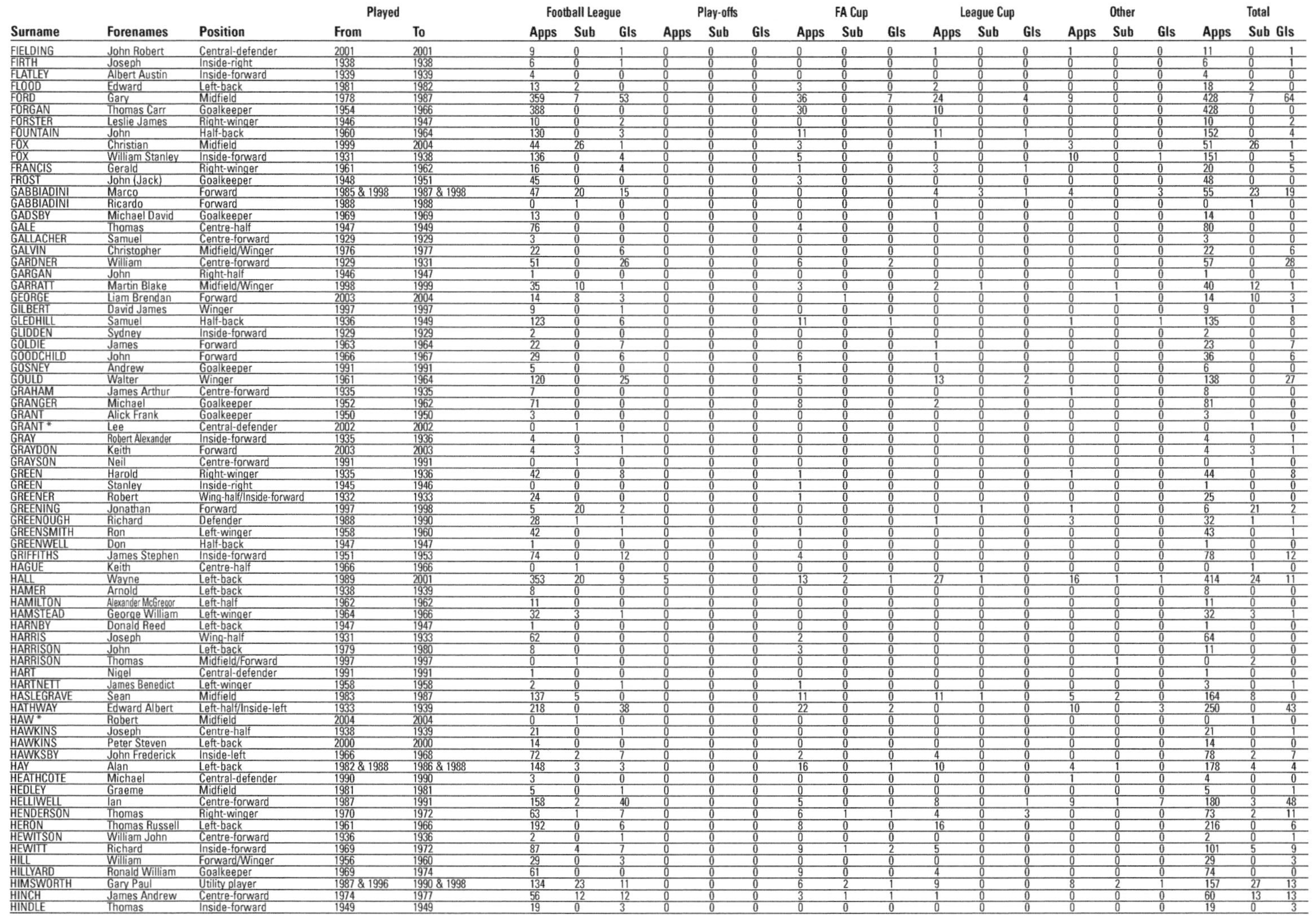

Surname	Forenames	Position	Played From	Played To	Football League Apps	Football League Sub	Football League Gls	Play-offs Apps	Play-offs Sub	Play-offs Gls	FA Cup Apps	FA Cup Sub	FA Cup Gls	League Cup Apps	League Cup Sub	League Cup Gls	Other Apps	Other Sub	Other Gls	Total Apps	Total Sub	Total Gls
FIELDING	John Robert	Central-defender	2001	2001	9	0	1	0	0	0	0	0	0	1	0	0	1	0	0	11	0	1
FIRTH	Joseph	Inside-right	1938	1938	6	0	1	0	0	0	0	0	0	0	0	0	0	0	0	6	0	1
FLATLEY	Albert Austin	Inside-forward	1939	1939	4	0	0	0	0	0	0	0	0	0	0	0	0	0	0	4	0	0
FLOOD	Edward	Left-back	1981	1982	13	2	0	0	0	0	3	0	0	2	0	0	0	0	0	18	2	0
FORD	Gary	Midfield	1978	1987	359	7	53	0	0	0	36	0	7	24	0	4	9	0	0	428	7	64
FORGAN	Thomas Carr	Goalkeeper	1954	1966	388	0	0	0	0	0	30	0	0	10	0	0	0	0	0	428	0	0
FORSTER	Leslie James	Right-winger	1946	1947	10	0	2	0	0	0	0	0	0	0	0	0	0	0	0	10	0	2
FOUNTAIN	John	Half-back	1960	1964	130	0	3	0	0	0	11	0	0	11	0	1	0	0	0	152	0	4
FOX	Christian	Midfield	1999	2004	44	26	1	0	0	0	3	0	0	1	0	0	3	0	0	51	26	1
FOX	William Stanley	Inside-forward	1931	1938	136	0	4	0	0	0	5	0	0	0	0	0	10	0	1	151	0	5
FRANCIS	Gerald	Right-winger	1961	1962	16	0	4	0	0	0	1	0	0	3	0	1	0	0	0	20	0	5
FROST	John (Jack)	Goalkeeper	1948	1951	45	0	0	0	0	0	3	0	0	0	0	0	0	0	0	48	0	0
GABBIADINI	Marco	Forward	1985 & 1998	1987 & 1998	47	20	15	0	0	0	0	0	0	4	3	1	4	0	3	55	23	19
GABBIADINI	Ricardo	Forward	1988	1988	0	1	0	0	0	0	0	0	0	0	0	0	0	0	0	0	1	0
GADSBY	Michael David	Goalkeeper	1969	1969	13	0	0	0	0	0	0	0	0	1	0	0	0	0	0	14	0	0
GALE	Thomas	Centre-half	1947	1949	76	0	0	0	0	0	4	0	0	0	0	0	0	0	0	80	0	0
GALLACHER	Samuel	Centre-forward	1929	1929	3	0	0	0	0	0	0	0	0	0	0	0	0	0	0	3	0	0
GALVIN	Christopher	Midfield/Winger	1976	1977	22	0	6	0	0	0	0	0	0	0	0	0	0	0	0	22	0	6
GARDNER	William	Centre-forward	1929	1931	51	0	26	0	0	0	6	0	2	0	0	0	0	0	0	57	0	28
GARGAN	John	Right-half	1946	1947	1	0	0	0	0	0	0	0	0	0	0	0	0	0	0	1	0	0
GARRATT	Martin Blake	Midfield/Winger	1998	1999	35	10	1	0	0	0	3	0	0	2	1	0	0	1	0	40	12	1
GEORGE	Liam Brendan	Forward	2003	2004	14	8	3	0	0	0	0	1	0	0	0	0	0	1	0	14	10	3
GILBERT	David James	Winger	1997	1997	9	0	1	0	0	0	0	0	0	0	0	0	0	0	0	9	0	1
GLEDHILL	Samuel	Half-back	1936	1949	123	0	6	0	0	0	11	0	1	0	0	0	1	0	1	135	0	8
GLIDDEN	Sydney	Inside-forward	1929	1929	2	0	0	0	0	0	0	0	0	0	0	0	0	0	0	2	0	0
GOLDIE	James	Forward	1963	1964	22	0	7	0	0	0	0	0	0	1	0	0	0	0	0	23	0	7
GOODCHILD	John	Forward	1966	1967	29	0	6	0	0	0	6	0	0	1	0	0	0	0	0	36	0	6
GOSNEY	Andrew	Goalkeeper	1991	1991	5	0	0	0	0	0	1	0	0	0	0	0	0	0	0	6	0	0
GOULD	Walter	Winger	1961	1964	120	0	25	0	0	0	5	0	0	13	0	2	0	0	0	138	0	27
GRAHAM	James Arthur	Centre-forward	1935	1935	7	0	0	0	0	0	0	0	0	0	0	0	1	0	0	8	0	0
GRANGER	Michael	Goalkeeper	1952	1962	71	0	0	0	0	0	8	0	0	2	0	0	0	0	0	81	0	0
GRANT	Alick Frank	Goalkeeper	1950	1950	3	0	0	0	0	0	0	0	0	0	0	0	0	0	0	3	0	0
GRANT *	Lee	Central-defender	2002	2002	0	1	0	0	0	0	0	0	0	0	0	0	0	0	0	0	1	0
GRAY	Robert Alexander	Inside-forward	1935	1936	4	0	1	0	0	0	0	0	0	0	0	0	0	0	0	4	0	1
GRAYDON	Keith	Forward	2003	2003	4	3	1	0	0	0	0	0	0	0	0	0	0	0	0	4	3	1
GRAYSON	Neil	Centre-forward	1991	1991	0	1	0	0	0	0	0	0	0	0	0	0	0	0	0	0	1	0
GREEN	Harold	Right-winger	1935	1936	42	0	8	0	0	0	1	0	0	0	0	0	1	0	0	44	0	8
GREEN	Stanley	Inside-right	1945	1946	0	0	0	0	0	0	1	0	0	0	0	0	0	0	0	1	0	0
GREENER	Robert	Wing-half/Inside-forward	1932	1933	24	0	0	0	0	0	1	0	0	0	0	0	0	0	0	25	0	0
GREENING	Jonathan	Forward	1997	1998	5	20	2	0	0	0	0	0	0	0	1	0	1	0	0	6	21	2
GREENOUGH	Richard	Defender	1988	1990	28	1	1	0	0	0	0	0	0	1	0	0	3	0	0	32	1	1
GREENSMITH	Ron	Left-winger	1958	1960	42	0	1	0	0	0	1	0	0	0	0	0	0	0	0	43	0	1
GREENWELL	Don	Half-back	1947	1947	1	0	0	0	0	0	0	0	0	0	0	0	0	0	0	1	0	0
GRIFFITHS	James Stephen	Inside-forward	1951	1953	74	0	12	0	0	0	4	0	0	0	0	0	0	0	0	78	0	12
HAGUE	Keith	Centre-half	1966	1966	0	1	0	0	0	0	0	0	0	0	0	0	0	0	0	0	1	0
HALL	Wayne	Left-back	1989	2001	353	20	9	5	0	0	13	2	1	27	1	0	16	1	1	414	24	11
HAMER	Arnold	Left-back	1938	1939	8	0	0	0	0	0	0	0	0	0	0	0	0	0	0	8	0	0
HAMILTON	Alexander McGregor	Left-half	1962	1962	11	0	0	0	0	0	0	0	0	0	0	0	0	0	0	11	0	0
HAMSTEAD	George William	Left-winger	1964	1966	32	3	1	0	0	0	0	0	0	0	0	0	0	0	0	32	3	1
HARNBY	Donald Reed	Left-back	1947	1947	1	0	0	0	0	0	0	0	0	0	0	0	0	0	0	1	0	0
HARRIS	Joseph	Wing-half	1931	1933	62	0	0	0	0	0	2	0	0	0	0	0	0	0	0	64	0	0
HARRISON	John	Left-back	1979	1980	8	0	0	0	0	0	3	0	0	0	0	0	0	0	0	11	0	0
HARRISON	Thomas	Midfield/Forward	1997	1997	0	1	0	0	0	0	0	0	0	0	0	0	0	1	0	0	2	0
HART	Nigel	Central-defender	1991	1991	1	0	0	0	0	0	0	0	0	0	0	0	0	0	0	1	0	0
HARTNETT	James Benedict	Left-winger	1958	1958	2	0	1	0	0	0	1	0	0	0	0	0	0	0	0	3	0	1
HASLEGRAVE	Sean	Midfield	1983	1987	137	5	0	0	0	0	11	0	0	11	1	0	5	2	0	164	8	0
HATHWAY	Edward Albert	Left-half/Inside-left	1933	1939	218	0	38	0	0	0	22	0	2	0	0	0	10	0	3	250	0	43
HAW *	Robert	Midfield	2004	2004	0	1	0	0	0	0	0	0	0	0	0	0	0	0	0	0	1	0
HAWKINS	Joseph	Centre-half	1938	1939	21	0	1	0	0	0	0	0	0	0	0	0	0	0	0	21	0	1
HAWKINS	Peter Steven	Left-back	2000	2000	14	0	0	0	0	0	0	0	0	0	0	0	0	0	0	14	0	0
HAWKSBY	John Frederick	Inside-left	1966	1968	72	2	7	0	0	0	2	0	0	4	0	0	0	0	0	78	2	7
HAY	Alan	Left-back	1982 & 1988	1986 & 1988	148	3	3	0	0	0	16	0	1	10	0	0	4	1	0	178	4	4
HEATHCOTE	Michael	Central-defender	1990	1990	3	0	0	0	0	0	0	0	0	0	0	0	1	0	0	4	0	0
HEDLEY	Graeme	Midfield	1981	1981	5	0	1	0	0	0	0	0	0	0	0	0	0	0	0	5	0	1
HELLIWELL	Ian	Centre-forward	1987	1991	158	2	40	0	0	0	5	0	0	8	0	1	9	1	7	180	3	48
HENDERSON	Thomas	Right-winger	1970	1972	63	1	7	0	0	0	6	1	1	4	0	3	0	0	0	73	2	11
HERON	Thomas Russell	Left-back	1961	1966	192	0	6	0	0	0	8	0	0	16	0	0	0	0	0	216	0	6
HEWITSON	William John	Centre-forward	1936	1936	2	0	1	0	0	0	0	0	0	0	0	0	0	0	0	2	0	1
HEWITT	Richard	Inside-forward	1969	1972	87	4	7	0	0	0	9	1	2	5	0	0	0	0	0	101	5	9
HILL	William	Forward/Winger	1956	1960	29	0	3	0	0	0	0	0	0	0	0	0	0	0	0	29	0	3
HILLYARD	Ronald William	Goalkeeper	1969	1974	61	0	0	0	0	0	9	0	0	4	0	0	0	0	0	74	0	0
HIMSWORTH	Gary Paul	Utility player	1987 & 1996	1990 & 1998	134	23	11	0	0	0	6	2	1	9	0	0	8	2	1	157	27	13
HINCH	James Andrew	Centre-forward	1974	1977	56	12	12	0	0	0	3	1	1	1	0	0	0	0	0	60	13	13
HINDLE	Thomas	Inside-forward	1949	1949	19	0	3	0	0	0	0	0	0	0	0	0	0	0	0	19	0	3

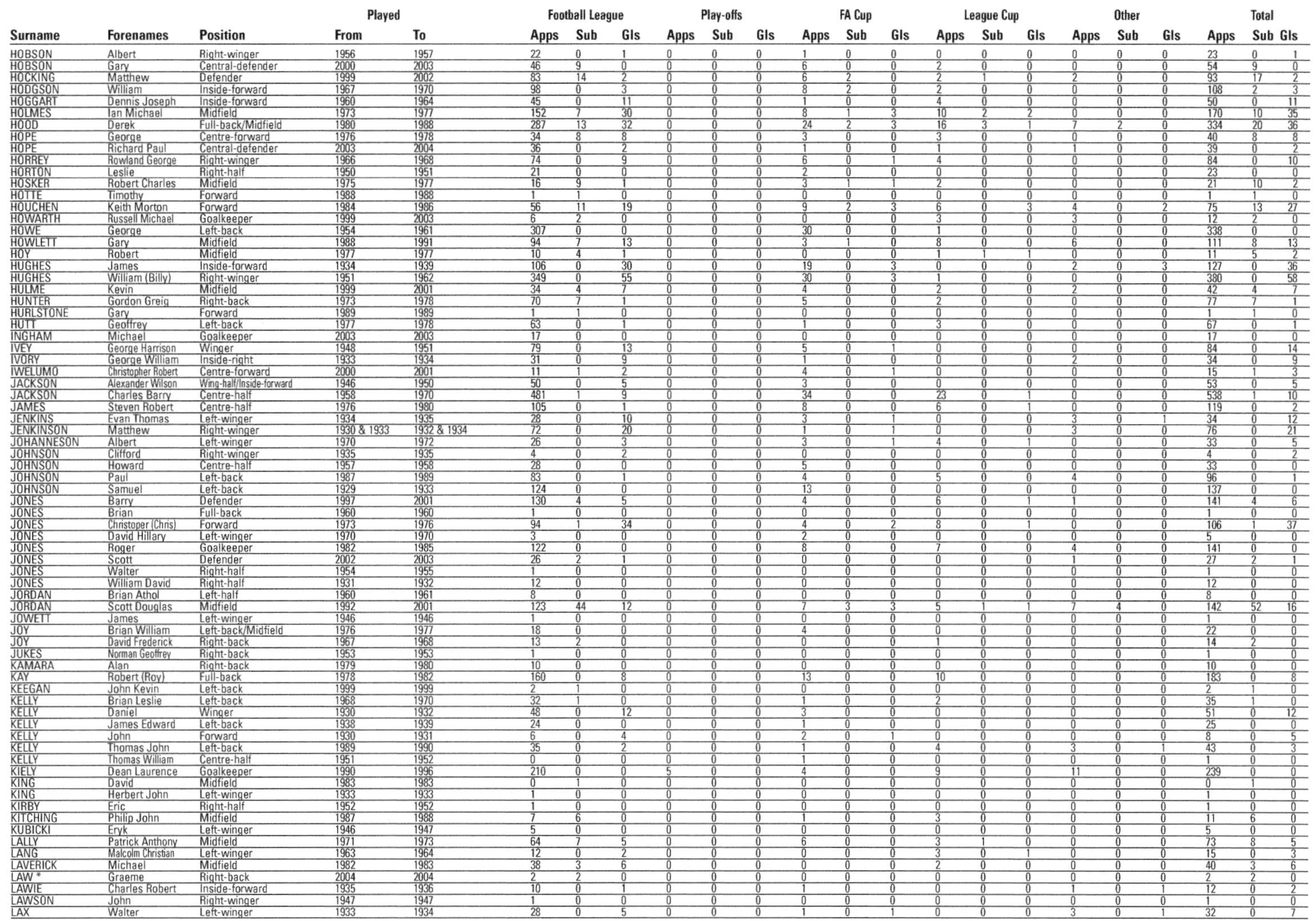

			Played		Football League			Play-offs			FA Cup			League Cup			Other			Total		
Surname	**Forenames**	**Position**	**From**	**To**	**Apps**	**Sub**	**Gls**	**Apps**	**Sub**	**Gls**	**Apps**	**Sub**	**Gls**	**Apps**	**Sub**	**Gls**	**Apps**	**Sub**	**Gls**	**Apps**	**Sub**	**Gls**
HOBSON	Albert	Right-winger	1956	1957	22	0	1	0	0	0	1	0	0	0	0	0	0	0	0	23	0	1
HOBSON	Gary	Central-defender	2000	2003	46	9	0	0	0	0	6	0	0	2	0	0	0	0	0	54	9	0
HOCKING	Matthew	Defender	1999	2002	83	14	2	0	0	0	6	2	0	2	1	0	2	0	0	93	17	2
HODGSON	William	Inside-forward	1967	1970	98	0	3	0	0	0	8	2	0	2	0	0	0	0	0	108	2	3
HOGGART	Dennis Joseph	Inside-forward	1960	1964	45	0	11	0	0	0	1	0	0	4	0	0	0	0	0	50	0	11
HOLMES	Ian Michael	Midfield	1973	1977	152	7	30	0	0	0	8	1	3	10	2	2	0	0	0	170	10	35
HOOD	Derek	Full-back/Midfield	1980	1988	287	13	32	0	0	0	24	2	3	16	3	1	7	2	0	334	20	36
HOPE	George	Centre-forward	1976	1978	34	8	8	0	0	0	3	0	0	3	0	0	0	0	0	40	8	8
HOPE	Richard Paul	Central-defender	2003	2004	36	0	2	0	0	0	1	0	0	1	0	0	1	0	0	39	0	2
HORREY	Rowland George	Right-winger	1966	1968	74	0	9	0	0	0	6	0	1	4	0	0	0	0	0	84	0	10
HORTON	Leslie	Right-half	1950	1951	21	0	0	0	0	0	2	0	0	0	0	0	0	0	0	23	0	0
HOSKER	Robert Charles	Midfield	1975	1977	16	9	1	0	0	0	3	1	1	2	0	0	0	0	0	21	10	2
HOTTE	Timothy	Forward	1988	1988	1	1	0	0	0	0	0	0	0	0	0	0	0	0	0	1	1	0
HOUCHEN	Keith Morton	Forward	1984	1986	56	11	19	0	0	0	9	2	3	6	0	3	4	0	2	75	13	27
HOWARTH	Russell Michael	Goalkeeper	1999	2003	6	2	0	0	0	0	0	0	0	3	0	0	3	0	0	12	2	0
HOWE	George	Left-back	1954	1961	307	0	0	0	0	0	30	0	0	1	0	0	0	0	0	338	0	0
HOWLETT	Gary	Midfield	1988	1991	94	7	13	0	0	0	3	1	0	8	0	0	6	0	0	111	8	13
HOY	Robert	Midfield	1977	1977	10	4	1	0	0	0	0	0	0	1	1	1	0	0	0	11	5	2
HUGHES	James	Inside-forward	1934	1939	106	0	30	0	0	0	19	0	3	0	0	0	2	0	3	127	0	36
HUGHES	William (Billy)	Right-winger	1951	1962	349	0	55	0	0	0	30	0	3	1	0	0	0	0	0	380	0	58
HULME	Kevin	Midfield	1999	2001	34	4	7	0	0	0	4	0	0	2	0	0	2	0	0	42	4	7
HUNTER	Gordon Greig	Right-back	1973	1978	70	7	1	0	0	0	5	0	0	2	0	0	0	0	0	77	7	1
HURLSTONE	Gary	Forward	1989	1989	1	1	0	0	0	0	0	0	0	0	0	0	0	0	0	1	1	0
HUTT	Geoffrey	Left-back	1977	1978	63	0	1	0	0	0	1	0	0	3	0	0	0	0	0	67	0	1
INGHAM	Michael	Goalkeeper	2003	2003	17	0	0	0	0	0	0	0	0	0	0	0	0	0	0	17	0	0
IVEY	George Harrison	Winger	1948	1951	79	0	13	0	0	0	5	0	1	0	0	0	0	0	0	84	0	14
IVORY	George William	Inside-right	1933	1934	31	0	9	0	0	0	1	0	0	0	0	0	2	0	0	34	0	9
IWELUMO	Christopher Robert	Centre-forward	2000	2001	11	1	2	0	0	0	4	0	1	0	0	0	0	0	0	15	1	3
JACKSON	Alexander Wilson	Wing-half/Inside-forward	1946	1950	50	0	5	0	0	0	3	0	0	0	0	0	0	0	0	53	0	5
JACKSON	Charles Barry	Centre-half	1958	1970	481	1	9	0	0	0	34	0	0	23	0	1	0	0	0	538	1	10
JAMES	Steven Robert	Centre-half	1976	1980	105	0	1	0	0	0	8	0	0	6	0	1	0	0	0	119	0	2
JENKINS	Evan Thomas	Left-winger	1934	1935	28	0	10	0	0	0	3	0	1	0	0	0	3	0	1	34	0	12
JENKINSON	Matthew	Right-winger	1930 & 1933	1932 & 1934	72	0	20	0	0	0	1	0	1	0	0	0	3	0	0	76	0	21
JOHANNESON	Albert	Left-winger	1970	1972	26	0	3	0	0	0	3	0	1	4	0	1	0	0	0	33	0	5
JOHNSON	Clifford	Right-winger	1935	1935	4	0	2	0	0	0	0	0	0	0	0	0	0	0	0	4	0	2
JOHNSON	Howard	Centre-half	1957	1958	28	0	0	0	0	0	5	0	0	0	0	0	0	0	0	33	0	0
JOHNSON	Paul	Left-back	1987	1989	83	0	1	0	0	0	4	0	0	5	0	0	4	0	0	96	0	1
JOHNSON	Samuel	Left-back	1929	1933	124	0	0	0	0	0	13	0	0	0	0	0	0	0	0	137	0	0
JONES	Barry	Defender	1997	2001	130	4	5	0	0	0	4	0	0	6	0	1	1	0	0	141	4	6
JONES	Brian	Full-back	1960	1960	1	0	0	0	0	0	0	0	0	0	0	0	0	0	0	1	0	0
JONES	Christoper (Chris)	Forward	1973	1976	94	1	34	0	0	0	4	0	2	8	0	1	0	0	0	106	1	37
JONES	David Hillary	Left-winger	1970	1970	3	0	0	0	0	0	2	0	0	0	0	0	0	0	0	5	0	0
JONES	Roger	Goalkeeper	1982	1985	122	0	0	0	0	0	8	0	0	7	0	0	4	0	0	141	0	0
JONES	Scott	Defender	2002	2003	26	2	1	0	0	0	0	0	0	0	0	0	1	0	0	27	2	1
JONES	Walter	Right-half	1954	1955	1	0	0	0	0	0	0	0	0	0	0	0	0	0	0	1	0	0
JONES	William David	Right-half	1931	1932	12	0	0	0	0	0	0	0	0	0	0	0	0	0	0	12	0	0
JORDAN	Brian Athol	Left-half	1960	1961	8	0	0	0	0	0	0	0	0	0	0	0	0	0	0	8	0	0
JORDAN	Scott Douglas	Midfield	1992	2001	123	44	12	0	0	0	7	3	3	5	1	1	7	4	0	142	52	16
JOWETT	James	Left-winger	1946	1946	1	0	0	0	0	0	0	0	0	0	0	0	0	0	0	1	0	0
JOY	Brian William	Left-back/Midfield	1976	1977	18	0	0	0	0	0	4	0	0	0	0	0	0	0	0	22	0	0
JOY	David Frederick	Right-back	1967	1968	13	2	0	0	0	0	0	0	0	1	0	0	0	0	0	14	2	0
JUKES	Norman Geoffrey	Right-back	1953	1953	1	0	0	0	0	0	0	0	0	0	0	0	0	0	0	1	0	0
KAMARA	Alan	Right-back	1979	1980	10	0	0	0	0	0	0	0	0	0	0	0	0	0	0	10	0	0
KAY	Robert (Roy)	Full-back	1978	1982	160	0	8	0	0	0	13	0	0	10	0	0	0	0	0	183	0	8
KEEGAN	John Kevin	Left-back	1999	1999	2	1	0	0	0	0	0	0	0	0	0	0	0	0	0	2	1	0
KELLY	Brian Leslie	Left-back	1968	1970	32	1	0	0	0	0	1	0	0	2	0	0	0	0	0	35	1	0
KELLY	Daniel	Winger	1930	1932	48	0	12	0	0	0	3	0	0	0	0	0	0	0	0	51	0	12
KELLY	James Edward	Left-back	1938	1939	24	0	0	0	0	0	1	0	0	0	0	0	0	0	0	25	0	0
KELLY	John	Forward	1930	1931	6	0	4	0	0	0	2	0	1	0	0	0	0	0	0	8	0	5
KELLY	Thomas John	Left-back	1989	1990	35	0	2	0	0	0	1	0	0	4	0	0	3	0	1	43	0	3
KELLY	Thomas William	Centre-half	1951	1952	0	0	0	0	0	0	1	0	0	0	0	0	0	0	0	1	0	0
KIELY	Dean Laurence	Goalkeeper	1990	1996	210	0	0	5	0	0	4	0	0	9	0	0	11	0	0	239	0	0
KING	David	Midfield	1983	1983	0	1	0	0	0	0	0	0	0	0	0	0	0	0	0	0	1	0
KING	Herbert John	Left-winger	1933	1933	1	0	0	0	0	0	0	0	0	0	0	0	0	0	0	1	0	0
KIRBY	Eric	Right-half	1952	1952	1	0	0	0	0	0	0	0	0	0	0	0	0	0	0	1	0	0
KITCHING	Philip John	Midfield	1987	1988	7	6	0	0	0	0	1	0	0	3	0	0	0	0	0	11	6	0
KUBICKI	Eryk	Left-winger	1946	1947	5	0	0	0	0	0	0	0	0	0	0	0	0	0	0	5	0	0
LALLY	Patrick Anthony	Midfield	1971	1973	64	7	5	0	0	0	6	0	0	3	1	0	0	0	0	73	8	5
LANG	Malcolm Christian	Left-winger	1963	1964	12	0	2	0	0	0	0	0	0	3	0	1	0	0	0	15	0	3
LAVERICK	Michael	Midfield	1982	1983	38	3	6	0	0	0	0	0	0	2	0	0	0	0	0	40	3	6
LAW *	Graeme	Right-back	2004	2004	2	2	0	0	0	0	0	0	0	0	0	0	0	0	0	2	2	0
LAWIE	Charles Robert	Inside-forward	1935	1936	10	0	1	0	0	0	1	0	0	0	0	0	1	0	1	12	0	2
LAWSON	John	Right-winger	1947	1947	1	0	0	0	0	0	0	0	0	0	0	0	0	0	0	1	0	0
LAX	Walter	Left-winger	1933	1934	28	0	5	0	0	0	1	0	1	0	0	0	3	0	1	32	0	7

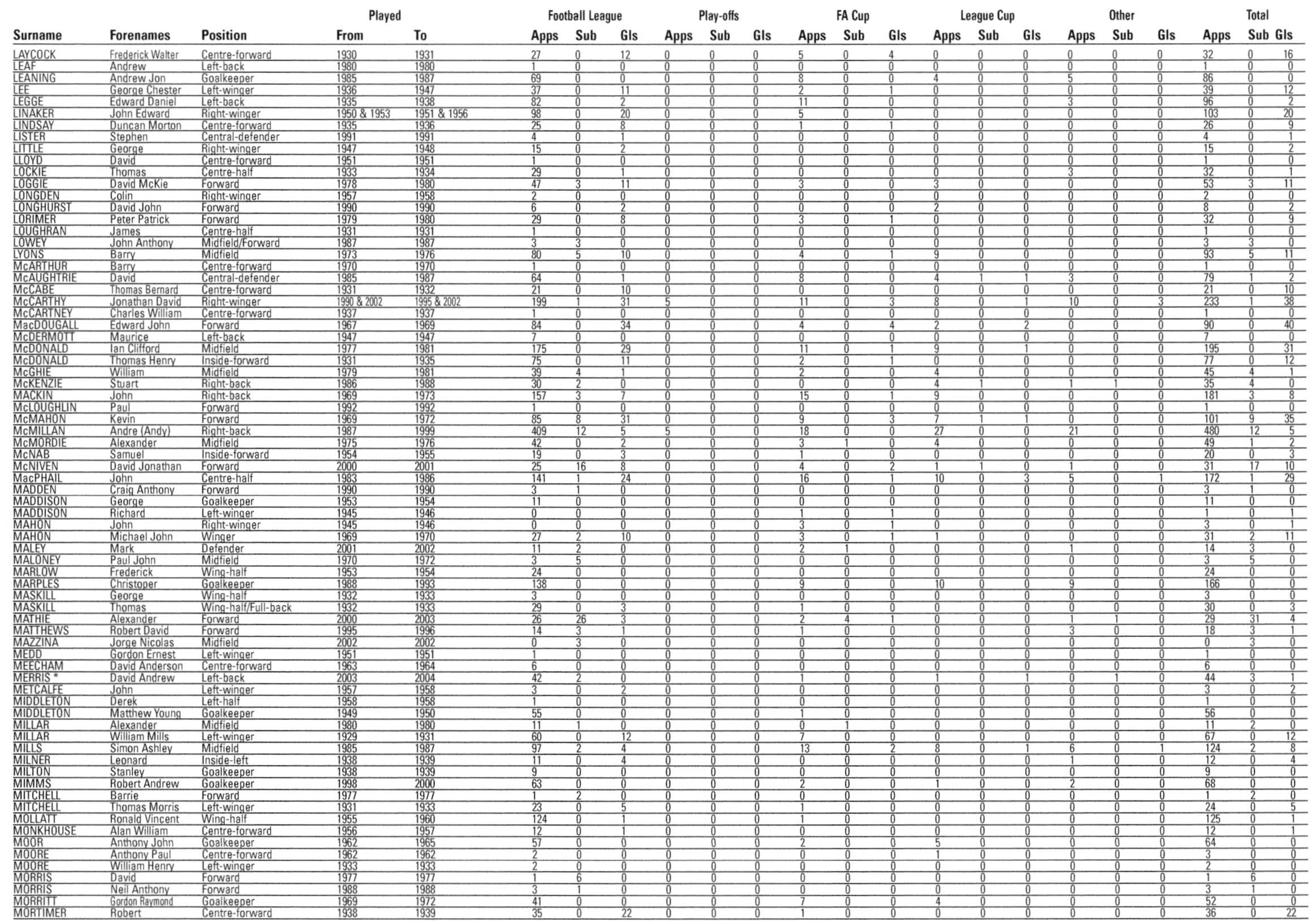

Surname	Forenames	Position	Played From	To	Football League Apps	Sub	Gls	Play-offs Apps	Sub	Gls	FA Cup Apps	Sub	Gls	League Cup Apps	Sub	Gls	Other Apps	Sub	Gls	Total Apps	Sub	Gls
LAYCOCK	Frederick Walter	Centre-forward	1930	1931	27	0	12	0	0	0	5	0	4	0	0	0	0	0	0	32	0	16
LEAF	Andrew	Left-back	1980	1980	1	0	0	0	0	0	0	0	0	0	0	0	0	0	0	1	0	0
LEANING	Andrew Jon	Goalkeeper	1985	1987	69	0	0	0	0	0	8	0	0	4	0	0	5	0	0	86	0	0
LEE	George Chester	Left-winger	1936	1947	37	0	11	0	0	0	2	0	1	0	0	0	0	0	0	39	0	12
LEGGE	Edward Daniel	Left-back	1935	1938	82	0	2	0	0	0	11	0	0	0	0	0	3	0	0	96	0	2
LINAKER	John Edward	Right-winger	1950 & 1953	1951 & 1956	98	0	20	0	0	0	5	0	0	0	0	0	0	0	0	103	0	20
LINDSAY	Duncan Morton	Centre-forward	1935	1936	25	0	8	0	0	0	1	0	1	0	0	0	0	0	0	26	0	9
LISTER	Stephen	Central-defender	1991	1991	4	0	1	0	0	0	0	0	0	0	0	0	0	0	0	4	0	1
LITTLE	George	Right-winger	1947	1948	15	0	2	0	0	0	0	0	0	0	0	0	0	0	0	15	0	2
LLOYD	David	Centre-forward	1951	1951	1	0	0	0	0	0	0	0	0	0	0	0	0	0	0	1	0	0
LOCKIE	Thomas	Centre-half	1933	1934	29	0	1	0	0	0	0	0	0	0	0	0	3	0	0	32	0	1
LOGGIE	David McKie	Forward	1978	1980	47	3	11	0	0	0	3	0	0	3	0	0	0	0	0	53	3	11
LONGDEN	Colin	Right-winger	1957	1958	2	0	0	0	0	0	0	0	0	0	0	0	0	0	0	2	0	0
LONGHURST	David John	Forward	1990	1990	6	0	2	0	0	0	0	0	0	2	0	0	0	0	0	8	0	2
LORIMER	Peter Patrick	Forward	1979	1980	29	0	8	0	0	0	3	0	1	0	0	0	0	0	0	32	0	9
LOUGHRAN	James	Centre-half	1931	1931	1	0	0	0	0	0	0	0	0	0	0	0	0	0	0	1	0	0
LOWEY	John Anthony	Midfield/Forward	1987	1987	3	3	0	0	0	0	0	0	0	0	0	0	0	0	0	3	3	0
LYONS	Barry	Midfield	1973	1976	80	5	10	0	0	0	4	0	1	9	0	0	0	0	0	93	5	11
McARTHUR	Barry	Centre-forward	1970	1970	1	0	0	0	0	0	0	0	0	0	0	0	0	0	0	1	0	0
McAUGHTRIE	David	Central-defender	1985	1987	64	0	1	0	0	0	8	0	0	4	1	1	3	0	0	79	1	2
McCABE	Thomas Bernard	Centre-forward	1931	1932	21	0	10	0	0	0	0	0	0	0	0	0	0	0	0	21	0	10
McCARTHY	Jonathan David	Right-winger	1990 & 2002	1995 & 2002	199	1	31	5	0	0	11	0	3	8	0	1	10	0	3	233	1	38
McCARTNEY	Charles William	Centre-forward	1937	1937	1	0	0	0	0	0	0	0	0	0	0	0	0	0	0	1	0	0
MacDOUGALL	Edward John	Forward	1967	1969	84	0	34	0	0	0	4	0	4	2	0	2	0	0	0	90	0	40
McDERMOTT	Maurice	Left-back	1947	1947	7	0	0	0	0	0	0	0	0	0	0	0	0	0	0	7	0	0
McDONALD	Ian Clifford	Midfield	1977	1981	175	0	29	0	0	0	11	0	1	9	0	1	0	0	0	195	0	31
McDONALD	Thomas Henry	Inside-forward	1931	1935	75	0	11	0	0	0	2	0	1	0	0	0	0	0	0	77	0	12
McGHIE	William	Midfield	1979	1981	39	4	1	0	0	0	2	0	0	4	0	0	0	0	0	45	4	1
McKENZIE	Stuart	Right-back	1986	1988	30	2	0	0	0	0	0	0	0	4	1	0	1	1	0	35	4	0
MACKIN	John	Right-back	1969	1973	157	3	7	0	0	0	15	0	1	9	0	0	0	0	0	181	3	8
McLOUGHLIN	Paul	Forward	1992	1992	1	0	0	0	0	0	0	0	0	0	0	0	0	0	0	1	0	0
McMAHON	Kevin	Forward	1969	1972	85	8	31	0	0	0	9	0	3	7	1	1	0	0	0	101	9	35
McMILLAN	Andre (Andy)	Right-back	1987	1999	409	12	5	5	0	0	18	0	0	27	0	0	21	0	0	480	12	5
McMORDIE	Alexander	Midfield	1975	1976	42	0	2	0	0	0	3	1	0	4	0	0	0	0	0	49	1	2
McNAB	Samuel	Inside-forward	1954	1955	19	0	3	0	0	0	1	0	0	0	0	0	0	0	0	20	0	3
McNIVEN	David Jonathan	Forward	2000	2001	25	16	8	0	0	0	4	0	2	1	1	0	1	0	0	31	17	10
MacPHAIL	John	Centre-half	1983	1986	141	1	24	0	0	0	16	0	1	10	0	3	5	0	1	172	1	29
MADDEN	Craig Anthony	Forward	1990	1990	3	1	0	0	0	0	0	0	0	0	0	0	0	0	0	3	1	0
MADDISON	George	Goalkeeper	1953	1954	11	0	0	0	0	0	0	0	0	0	0	0	0	0	0	11	0	0
MADDISON	Richard	Left-winger	1945	1946	0	0	0	0	0	0	1	0	1	0	0	0	0	0	0	1	0	1
MAHON	John	Right-winger	1945	1946	0	0	0	0	0	0	3	0	1	0	0	0	0	0	0	3	0	1
MAHON	Michael John	Winger	1969	1970	27	2	10	0	0	0	3	0	1	1	0	0	0	0	0	31	2	11
MALEY	Mark	Defender	2001	2002	11	2	0	0	0	0	2	1	0	0	0	0	1	0	0	14	3	0
MALONEY	Paul John	Midfield	1970	1972	3	5	0	0	0	0	0	0	0	0	0	0	0	0	0	3	5	0
MARLOW	Frederick	Wing-half	1953	1954	24	0	0	0	0	0	0	0	0	0	0	0	0	0	0	24	0	0
MARPLES	Christoper	Goalkeeper	1988	1993	138	0	0	0	0	0	9	0	0	10	0	0	9	0	0	166	0	0
MASKILL	George	Wing-half	1932	1933	3	0	0	0	0	0	0	0	0	0	0	0	0	0	0	3	0	0
MASKILL	Thomas	Wing-half/Full-back	1932	1933	29	0	3	0	0	0	1	0	0	0	0	0	0	0	0	30	0	3
MATHIE	Alexander	Forward	2000	2003	26	26	3	0	0	0	2	4	1	0	0	0	1	1	0	29	31	4
MATTHEWS	Robert David	Forward	1995	1996	14	3	1	0	0	0	1	0	0	0	0	0	3	0	0	18	3	1
MAZZINA	Jorge Nicolas	Midfield	2002	2002	0	3	0	0	0	0	0	0	0	0	0	0	0	0	0	0	3	0
MEDD	Gordon Ernest	Left-winger	1951	1951	1	0	0	0	0	0	0	0	0	0	0	0	0	0	0	1	0	0
MEECHAM	David Anderson	Centre-forward	1963	1964	6	0	0	0	0	0	0	0	0	0	0	0	0	0	0	6	0	0
MERRIS *	David Andrew	Left-back	2003	2004	42	2	0	0	0	0	1	0	0	1	0	1	0	1	0	44	3	1
METCALFE	John	Left-winger	1957	1958	3	0	2	0	0	0	0	0	0	0	0	0	0	0	0	3	0	2
MIDDLETON	Derek	Left-half	1958	1958	1	0	0	0	0	0	0	0	0	0	0	0	0	0	0	1	0	0
MIDDLETON	Matthew Young	Goalkeeper	1949	1950	55	0	0	0	0	0	1	0	0	0	0	0	0	0	0	56	0	0
MILLAR	Alexander	Midfield	1980	1980	11	1	0	0	0	0	0	1	0	0	0	0	0	0	0	11	2	0
MILLAR	William Mills	Left-winger	1929	1931	60	0	12	0	0	0	7	0	0	0	0	0	0	0	0	67	0	12
MILLS	Simon Ashley	Midfield	1985	1987	97	2	4	0	0	0	13	0	2	8	0	1	6	0	1	124	2	8
MILNER	Leonard	Inside-left	1938	1939	11	0	4	0	0	0	0	0	0	0	0	0	1	0	0	12	0	4
MILTON	Stanley	Goalkeeper	1938	1939	9	0	0	0	0	0	0	0	0	0	0	0	0	0	0	9	0	0
MIMMS	Robert Andrew	Goalkeeper	1998	2000	63	0	0	0	0	0	2	0	0	1	0	0	2	0	0	68	0	0
MITCHELL	Barrie	Forward	1977	1977	1	2	0	0	0	0	0	0	0	0	0	0	0	0	0	1	2	0
MITCHELL	Thomas Morris	Left-winger	1931	1933	23	0	5	0	0	0	1	0	0	0	0	0	0	0	0	24	0	5
MOLLATT	Ronald Vincent	Wing-half	1955	1960	124	0	1	0	0	0	1	0	0	0	0	0	0	0	0	125	0	1
MONKHOUSE	Alan William	Centre-forward	1956	1957	12	0	1	0	0	0	0	0	0	0	0	0	0	0	0	12	0	1
MOOR	Anthony John	Goalkeeper	1962	1965	57	0	0	0	0	0	2	0	0	5	0	0	0	0	0	64	0	0
MOORE	Anthony Paul	Centre-forward	1962	1962	2	0	0	0	0	0	0	0	0	1	0	0	0	0	0	3	0	0
MOORE	William Henry	Left-winger	1933	1933	2	0	0	0	0	0	0	0	0	0	0	0	0	0	0	2	0	0
MORRIS	David	Forward	1977	1977	1	6	0	0	0	0	0	0	0	0	0	0	0	0	0	1	6	0
MORRIS	Neil Anthony	Forward	1988	1988	3	1	0	0	0	0	0	0	0	0	0	0	0	0	0	3	1	0
MORRITT	Gordon Raymond	Goalkeeper	1969	1972	41	0	0	0	0	0	7	0	0	4	0	0	0	0	0	52	0	0
MORTIMER	Robert	Centre-forward	1938	1939	35	0	22	0	0	0	1	0	0	0	0	0	0	0	0	36	0	22

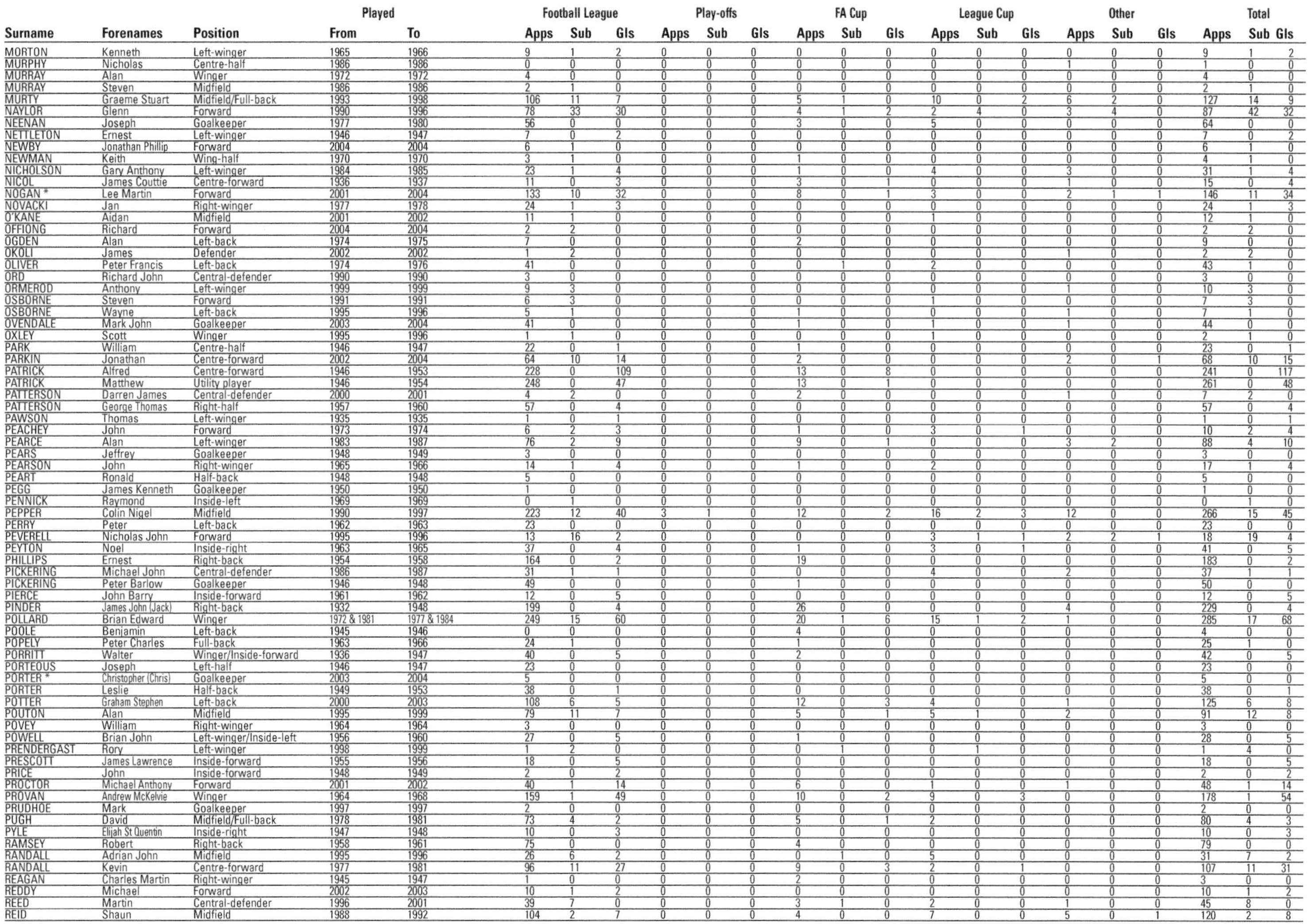

Surname	Forenames	Position	Played From	Played To	Football League Apps	Football League Sub	Football League Gls	Play-offs Apps	Play-offs Sub	Play-offs Gls	FA Cup Apps	FA Cup Sub	FA Cup Gls	League Cup Apps	League Cup Sub	League Cup Gls	Other Apps	Other Sub	Other Gls	Total Apps	Total Sub	Total Gls
MORTON	Kenneth	Left-winger	1965	1966	9	1	2	0	0	0	0	0	0	0	0	0	0	0	0	9	1	2
MURPHY	Nicholas	Centre-half	1986	1986	0	0	0	0	0	0	0	0	0	0	0	0	1	0	0	1	0	0
MURRAY	Alan	Winger	1972	1972	4	0	0	0	0	0	0	0	0	0	0	0	0	0	0	4	0	0
MURRAY	Steven	Midfield	1986	1986	2	1	0	0	0	0	0	0	0	0	0	0	0	0	0	2	1	0
MURTY	Graeme Stuart	Midfield/Full-back	1993	1998	106	11	7	0	0	0	5	1	0	10	0	2	6	2	0	127	14	9
NAYLOR	Glenn	Forward	1990	1996	78	33	30	0	0	0	4	1	2	2	4	0	3	4	0	87	42	32
NEENAN	Joseph	Goalkeeper	1977	1980	56	0	0	0	0	0	3	0	0	5	0	0	0	0	0	64	0	0
NETTLETON	Ernest	Left-winger	1946	1947	7	0	2	0	0	0	0	0	0	0	0	0	0	0	0	7	0	2
NEWBY	Jonathan Phillip	Forward	2004	2004	6	1	0	0	0	0	0	0	0	0	0	0	0	0	0	6	1	0
NEWMAN	Keith	Wing-half	1970	1970	3	1	0	0	0	0	1	0	0	0	0	0	0	0	0	4	1	0
NICHOLSON	Gary Anthony	Left-winger	1984	1985	23	1	4	0	0	0	1	0	0	4	0	0	3	0	0	31	1	4
NICOL	James Couttie	Centre-forward	1936	1937	11	0	3	0	0	0	3	0	1	0	0	0	1	0	0	15	0	4
NOGAN *	Lee Martin	Forward	2001	2004	133	10	32	0	0	0	8	0	1	3	0	0	2	1	1	146	11	34
NOVACKI	Jan	Right-winger	1977	1978	24	1	3	0	0	0	0	0	0	0	0	0	0	0	0	24	1	3
O'KANE	Aidan	Midfield	2001	2002	11	1	0	0	0	0	0	0	0	1	0	0	0	0	0	12	1	0
OFFIONG	Richard	Forward	2004	2004	2	2	0	0	0	0	0	0	0	0	0	0	0	0	0	2	2	0
OGDEN	Alan	Left-back	1974	1975	7	0	0	0	0	0	2	0	0	0	0	0	0	0	0	9	0	0
OKOLI	James	Defender	2002	2002	1	2	0	0	0	0	0	0	0	0	0	0	1	0	0	2	2	0
OLIVER	Peter Francis	Left-back	1974	1976	41	0	0	0	0	0	0	1	0	2	0	0	0	0	0	43	1	0
ORD	Richard John	Central-defender	1990	1990	3	0	0	0	0	0	0	0	0	0	0	0	0	0	0	3	0	0
ORMEROD	Anthony	Left-winger	1999	1999	9	3	0	0	0	0	0	0	0	0	0	0	1	0	0	10	3	0
OSBORNE	Steven	Forward	1991	1991	6	3	0	0	0	0	0	0	0	1	0	0	0	0	0	7	3	0
OSBORNE	Wayne	Left-back	1995	1996	5	1	0	0	0	0	1	0	0	0	0	0	1	0	0	7	1	0
OVENDALE	Mark John	Goalkeeper	2003	2004	41	0	0	0	0	0	1	0	0	1	0	0	1	0	0	44	0	0
OXLEY	Scott	Winger	1995	1996	1	1	0	0	0	0	0	0	0	1	0	0	0	0	0	2	1	0
PARK	William	Centre-half	1946	1947	22	0	1	0	0	0	1	0	0	0	0	0	0	0	0	23	0	1
PARKIN	Jonathan	Centre-forward	2002	2004	64	10	14	0	0	0	2	0	0	0	0	0	2	0	1	68	10	15
PATRICK	Alfred	Centre-forward	1946	1953	228	0	109	0	0	0	13	0	8	0	0	0	0	0	0	241	0	117
PATRICK	Matthew	Utility player	1946	1954	248	0	47	0	0	0	13	0	1	0	0	0	0	0	0	261	0	48
PATTERSON	Darren James	Central-defender	2000	2001	4	2	0	0	0	0	2	0	0	0	0	0	1	0	0	7	2	0
PATTERSON	George Thomas	Right-half	1957	1960	57	0	4	0	0	0	0	0	0	0	0	0	0	0	0	57	0	4
PAWSON	Thomas	Left-winger	1935	1935	1	0	1	0	0	0	0	0	0	0	0	0	0	0	0	1	0	1
PEACHEY	John	Forward	1973	1974	6	2	3	0	0	0	1	0	0	3	0	1	0	0	0	10	2	4
PEARCE	Alan	Left-winger	1983	1987	76	2	9	0	0	0	9	0	1	0	0	0	3	2	0	88	4	10
PEARS	Jeffrey	Goalkeeper	1948	1949	3	0	0	0	0	0	0	0	0	0	0	0	0	0	0	3	0	0
PEARSON	John	Right-winger	1965	1966	14	1	4	0	0	0	1	0	0	2	0	0	0	0	0	17	1	4
PEART	Ronald	Half-back	1948	1948	5	0	0	0	0	0	0	0	0	0	0	0	0	0	0	5	0	0
PEGG	James Kenneth	Goalkeeper	1950	1950	1	0	0	0	0	0	0	0	0	0	0	0	0	0	0	1	0	0
PENNICK	Raymond	Inside-left	1969	1969	0	1	0	0	0	0	0	0	0	0	0	0	0	0	0	0	1	0
PEPPER	Colin Nigel	Midfield	1990	1997	223	12	40	3	1	0	12	0	2	16	2	3	12	0	0	266	15	45
PERRY	Peter	Left-back	1962	1963	23	0	0	0	0	0	0	0	0	0	0	0	0	0	0	23	0	0
PEVERELL	Nicholas John	Forward	1995	1996	13	16	2	0	0	0	0	0	0	3	1	1	2	2	1	18	19	4
PEYTON	Noel	Inside-right	1963	1965	37	0	4	0	0	0	1	0	0	3	0	1	0	0	0	41	0	5
PHILLIPS	Ernest	Right-back	1954	1958	164	0	2	0	0	0	19	0	0	0	0	0	0	0	0	183	0	2
PICKERING	Michael John	Central-defender	1986	1987	31	1	1	0	0	0	0	0	0	4	0	0	2	0	0	37	1	1
PICKERING	Peter Barlow	Goalkeeper	1946	1948	49	0	0	0	0	0	1	0	0	0	0	0	0	0	0	50	0	0
PIERCE	John Barry	Inside-forward	1961	1962	12	0	5	0	0	0	0	0	0	0	0	0	0	0	0	12	0	5
PINDER	James John (Jack)	Right-back	1932	1948	199	0	4	0	0	0	26	0	0	0	0	0	4	0	0	229	0	4
POLLARD	Brian Edward	Winger	1972 & 1981	1977 & 1984	249	15	60	0	0	0	20	1	6	15	1	2	1	0	0	285	17	68
POOLE	Benjamin	Left-back	1945	1946	0	0	0	0	0	0	4	0	0	0	0	0	0	0	0	4	0	0
POPELY	Peter Charles	Full-back	1963	1966	24	1	0	0	0	0	1	0	0	0	0	0	0	0	0	25	1	0
PORRITT	Walter	Winger/Inside-forward	1936	1947	40	0	5	0	0	0	2	0	0	0	0	0	0	0	0	42	0	5
PORTEOUS	Joseph	Left-half	1946	1947	23	0	0	0	0	0	0	0	0	0	0	0	0	0	0	23	0	0
PORTER *	Christopher (Chris)	Goalkeeper	2003	2004	5	0	0	0	0	0	0	0	0	0	0	0	0	0	0	5	0	0
PORTER	Leslie	Half-back	1949	1953	38	0	1	0	0	0	0	0	0	0	0	0	0	0	0	38	0	1
POTTER	Graham Stephen	Left-back	2000	2003	108	6	5	0	0	0	12	0	3	4	0	0	1	0	0	125	6	8
POUTON	Alan	Midfield	1995	1999	79	11	7	0	0	0	5	0	1	5	1	0	2	0	0	91	12	8
POVEY	William	Right-winger	1964	1964	3	0	0	0	0	0	0	0	0	0	0	0	0	0	0	3	0	0
POWELL	Brian John	Left-winger/Inside-left	1956	1960	27	0	5	0	0	0	1	0	0	0	0	0	0	0	0	28	0	5
PRENDERGAST	Rory	Left-winger	1998	1999	1	2	0	0	0	0	0	1	0	0	1	0	0	0	0	1	4	0
PRESCOTT	James Lawrence	Inside-forward	1955	1956	18	0	5	0	0	0	0	0	0	0	0	0	0	0	0	18	0	5
PRICE	John	Inside-forward	1948	1949	2	0	2	0	0	0	0	0	0	0	0	0	0	0	0	2	0	2
PROCTOR	Michael Anthony	Forward	2001	2002	40	1	14	0	0	0	6	0	0	1	0	0	1	0	0	48	1	14
PROVAN	Andrew McKelvie	Winger	1964	1968	159	1	49	0	0	0	10	0	2	9	0	3	0	0	0	178	1	54
PRUDHOE	Mark	Goalkeeper	1997	1997	2	0	0	0	0	0	0	0	0	0	0	0	0	0	0	2	0	0
PUGH	David	Midfield/Full-back	1978	1981	73	4	2	0	0	0	5	0	1	2	0	0	0	0	0	80	4	3
PYLE	Elijah St Quentin	Inside-right	1947	1948	10	0	3	0	0	0	0	0	0	0	0	0	0	0	0	10	0	3
RAMSEY	Robert	Right-back	1958	1961	75	0	0	0	0	0	4	0	0	0	0	0	0	0	0	79	0	0
RANDALL	Adrian John	Midfield	1995	1996	26	6	2	0	0	0	0	1	0	5	0	0	0	0	0	31	7	2
RANDALL	Kevin	Centre-forward	1977	1981	96	11	27	0	0	0	9	0	3	2	0	1	0	0	0	107	11	31
REAGAN	Charles Martin	Right-winger	1945	1947	1	0	0	0	0	0	2	0	0	0	0	0	0	0	0	3	0	0
REDDY	Michael	Forward	2002	2003	10	1	2	0	0	0	0	0	0	0	0	0	0	0	0	10	1	2
REED	Martin	Central-defender	1996	2001	39	7	0	0	0	0	3	1	0	2	0	0	1	0	0	45	8	0
REID	Shaun	Midfield	1988	1992	104	2	7	0	0	0	4	0	0	7	0	0	5	0	1	120	2	8

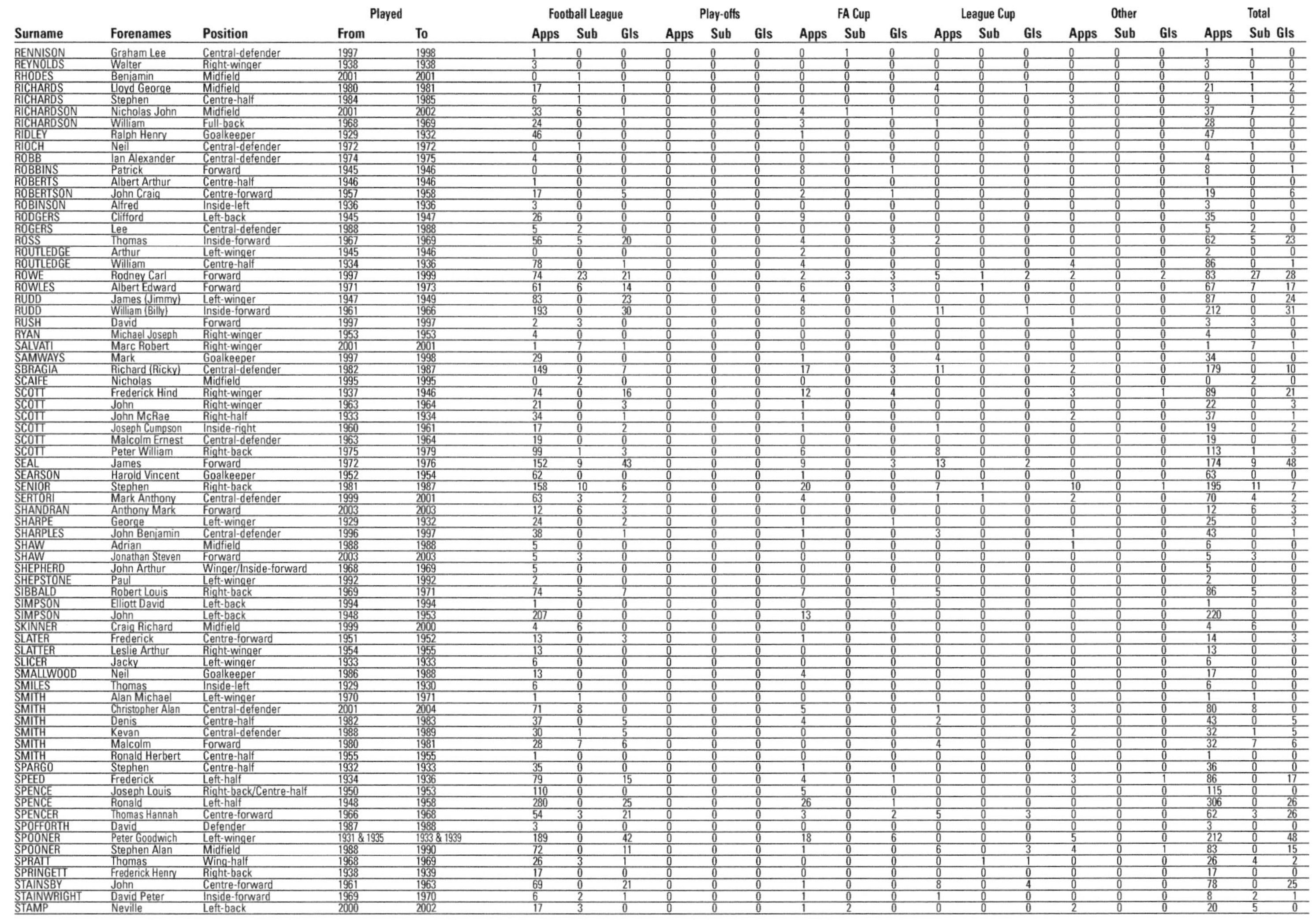

			Played		Football League			Play-offs			FA Cup			League Cup			Other			Total		
Surname	**Forenames**	**Position**	**From**	**To**	**Apps**	**Sub**	**Gls**	**Apps**	**Sub**	**Gls**	**Apps**	**Sub**	**Gls**	**Apps**	**Sub**	**Gls**	**Apps**	**Sub**	**Gls**	**Apps**	**Sub**	**Gls**
RENNISON	Graham Lee	Central-defender	1997	1998	1	0	0	0	0	0	0	1	0	0	0	0	0	0	0	1	1	0
REYNOLDS	Walter	Right-winger	1938	1938	3	0	0	0	0	0	0	0	0	0	0	0	0	0	0	3	0	0
RHODES	Benjamin	Midfield	2001	2001	0	1	0	0	0	0	0	0	0	0	0	0	0	0	0	0	1	0
RICHARDS	Lloyd George	Midfield	1980	1981	17	1	1	0	0	0	0	0	0	4	0	1	0	0	0	21	1	2
RICHARDS	Stephen	Centre-half	1984	1985	6	1	0	0	0	0	0	0	0	0	0	0	3	0	0	9	1	0
RICHARDSON	Nicholas John	Midfield	2001	2002	33	6	1	0	0	0	4	1	1	0	0	0	0	0	0	37	7	2
RICHARDSON	William	Full-back	1968	1969	24	0	0	0	0	0	3	0	0	1	0	0	0	0	0	28	0	0
RIDLEY	Ralph Henry	Goalkeeper	1929	1932	46	0	0	0	0	0	1	0	0	0	0	0	0	0	0	47	0	0
RIOCH	Neil	Central-defender	1972	1972	0	1	0	0	0	0	0	0	0	0	0	0	0	0	0	0	1	0
ROBB	Ian Alexander	Central-defender	1974	1975	4	0	0	0	0	0	0	0	0	0	0	0	0	0	0	4	0	0
ROBBINS	Patrick	Forward	1945	1946	0	0	0	0	0	0	8	0	1	0	0	0	0	0	0	8	0	1
ROBERTS	Albert Arthur	Centre-half	1946	1946	1	0	0	0	0	0	0	0	0	0	0	0	0	0	0	1	0	0
ROBERTSON	John Craig	Centre-forward	1957	1958	17	0	5	0	0	0	2	0	1	0	0	0	0	0	0	19	0	6
ROBINSON	Alfred	Inside-left	1936	1936	3	0	0	0	0	0	0	0	0	0	0	0	0	0	0	3	0	0
RODGERS	Clifford	Left-back	1945	1947	26	0	0	0	0	0	9	0	0	0	0	0	0	0	0	35	0	0
ROGERS	Lee	Central-defender	1988	1988	5	2	0	0	0	0	0	0	0	0	0	0	0	0	0	5	2	0
ROSS	Thomas	Inside-forward	1967	1969	56	5	20	0	0	0	4	0	3	2	0	0	0	0	0	62	5	23
ROUTLEDGE	Arthur	Left-winger	1945	1946	0	0	0	0	0	0	2	0	0	0	0	0	0	0	0	2	0	0
ROUTLEDGE	William	Centre-half	1934	1936	78	0	1	0	0	0	4	0	0	0	0	0	4	0	0	86	0	1
ROWE	Rodney Carl	Forward	1997	1999	74	23	21	0	0	0	2	3	3	5	1	2	2	0	2	83	27	28
ROWLES	Albert Edward	Forward	1971	1973	61	6	14	0	0	0	6	0	3	0	1	0	0	0	0	67	7	17
RUDD	James (Jimmy)	Left-winger	1947	1949	83	0	23	0	0	0	4	0	1	0	0	0	0	0	0	87	0	24
RUDD	William (Billy)	Inside-forward	1961	1966	193	0	30	0	0	0	8	0	0	11	0	1	0	0	0	212	0	31
RUSH	David	Forward	1997	1997	2	3	0	0	0	0	0	0	0	0	0	0	1	0	0	3	3	0
RYAN	Michael Joseph	Right-winger	1953	1953	4	0	0	0	0	0	0	0	0	0	0	0	0	0	0	4	0	0
SALVATI	Marc Robert	Right-winger	2001	2001	1	7	1	0	0	0	0	0	0	0	0	0	0	0	0	1	7	1
SAMWAYS	Mark	Goalkeeper	1997	1998	29	0	0	0	0	0	1	0	0	4	0	0	0	0	0	34	0	0
SBRAGIA	Richard (Ricky)	Central-defender	1982	1987	149	0	7	0	0	0	17	0	3	11	0	0	2	0	0	179	0	10
SCAIFE	Nicholas	Midfield	1995	1995	0	2	0	0	0	0	0	0	0	0	0	0	0	0	0	0	2	0
SCOTT	Frederick Hind	Right-winger	1937	1946	74	0	16	0	0	0	12	0	4	0	0	0	3	0	1	89	0	21
SCOTT	John	Right-winger	1963	1964	21	0	3	0	0	0	1	0	0	0	0	0	0	0	0	22	0	3
SCOTT	John McRae	Right-half	1933	1934	34	0	1	0	0	0	1	0	0	0	0	0	2	0	0	37	0	1
SCOTT	Joseph Cumpson	Inside-right	1960	1961	17	0	2	0	0	0	1	0	0	1	0	0	0	0	0	19	0	2
SCOTT	Malcolm Ernest	Central-defender	1963	1964	19	0	0	0	0	0	0	0	0	0	0	0	0	0	0	19	0	0
SCOTT	Peter William	Right-back	1975	1979	99	1	3	0	0	0	6	0	0	8	0	0	0	0	0	113	1	3
SEAL	James	Forward	1972	1976	152	9	43	0	0	0	9	0	3	13	0	2	0	0	0	174	9	48
SEARSON	Harold Vincent	Goalkeeper	1952	1954	62	0	0	0	0	0	1	0	0	0	0	0	0	0	0	63	0	0
SENIOR	Stephen	Right-back	1981	1987	158	10	6	0	0	0	20	0	0	7	1	0	10	0	1	195	11	7
SERTORI	Mark Anthony	Central-defender	1999	2001	63	3	2	0	0	0	4	0	0	1	1	0	2	0	0	70	4	2
SHANDRAN	Anthony Mark	Forward	2003	2003	12	6	3	0	0	0	0	0	0	0	0	0	0	0	0	12	6	3
SHARPE	George	Left-winger	1929	1932	24	0	2	0	0	0	1	0	1	0	0	0	0	0	0	25	0	3
SHARPLES	John Benjamin	Central-defender	1996	1997	38	0	1	0	0	0	1	0	0	3	0	0	1	0	0	43	0	1
SHAW	Adrian	Midfield	1988	1988	5	0	0	0	0	0	0	0	0	0	0	0	1	0	0	6	0	0
SHAW	Jonathan Steven	Forward	2003	2003	5	3	0	0	0	0	0	0	0	0	0	0	0	0	0	5	3	0
SHEPHERD	John Arthur	Winger/Inside-forward	1968	1969	5	0	0	0	0	0	0	0	0	0	0	0	0	0	0	5	0	0
SHEPSTONE	Paul	Left-winger	1992	1992	2	0	0	0	0	0	0	0	0	0	0	0	0	0	0	2	0	0
SIBBALD	Robert Louis	Right-back	1969	1971	74	5	7	0	0	0	7	0	1	5	0	0	0	0	0	86	5	8
SIMPSON	Elliott David	Left-back	1994	1994	1	0	0	0	0	0	0	0	0	0	0	0	0	0	0	1	0	0
SIMPSON	John	Left-back	1948	1953	207	0	0	0	0	0	13	0	0	0	0	0	0	0	0	220	0	0
SKINNER	Craig Richard	Midfield	1999	2000	4	6	0	0	0	0	0	0	0	0	0	0	0	0	0	4	6	0
SLATER	Frederick	Centre-forward	1951	1952	13	0	3	0	0	0	1	0	0	0	0	0	0	0	0	14	0	3
SLATTER	Leslie Arthur	Right-winger	1954	1955	13	0	0	0	0	0	0	0	0	0	0	0	0	0	0	13	0	0
SLICER	Jacky	Left-winger	1933	1933	6	0	0	0	0	0	0	0	0	0	0	0	0	0	0	6	0	0
SMALLWOOD	Neil	Goalkeeper	1986	1988	13	0	0	0	0	0	4	0	0	0	0	0	0	0	0	17	0	0
SMILES	Thomas	Inside-left	1929	1930	6	0	0	0	0	0	0	0	0	0	0	0	0	0	0	6	0	0
SMITH	Alan Michael	Left-winger	1970	1971	1	1	0	0	0	0	0	0	0	0	0	0	0	0	0	1	1	0
SMITH	Christopher Alan	Central-defender	2001	2004	71	8	0	0	0	0	5	0	0	1	0	0	3	0	0	80	8	0
SMITH	Denis	Centre-half	1982	1983	37	0	5	0	0	0	4	0	0	2	0	0	0	0	0	43	0	5
SMITH	Kevan	Central-defender	1988	1989	30	1	5	0	0	0	0	0	0	0	0	0	2	0	0	32	1	5
SMITH	Malcolm	Forward	1980	1981	28	7	6	0	0	0	0	0	0	4	0	0	0	0	0	32	7	6
SMITH	Ronald Herbert	Centre-half	1955	1955	1	0	0	0	0	0	0	0	0	0	0	0	0	0	0	1	0	0
SPARGO	Stephen	Centre-half	1932	1933	35	0	0	0	0	0	1	0	0	0	0	0	0	0	0	36	0	0
SPEED	Frederick	Left-half	1934	1936	79	0	15	0	0	0	4	0	1	0	0	0	3	0	1	86	0	17
SPENCE	Joseph Louis	Right-back/Centre-half	1950	1953	110	0	0	0	0	0	5	0	0	0	0	0	0	0	0	115	0	0
SPENCE	Ronald	Left-half	1948	1958	280	0	25	0	0	0	26	0	1	0	0	0	0	0	0	306	0	26
SPENCER	Thomas Hannah	Centre-forward	1966	1968	54	3	21	0	0	0	3	0	2	5	0	3	0	0	0	62	3	26
SPOFFORTH	David	Defender	1987	1988	3	0	0	0	0	0	0	0	0	0	0	0	0	0	0	3	0	0
SPOONER	Peter Goodwich	Left-winger	1931 & 1935	1933 & 1939	189	0	42	0	0	0	18	0	6	0	0	0	5	0	0	212	0	48
SPOONER	Stephen Alan	Midfield	1988	1990	72	0	11	0	0	0	1	0	0	6	0	3	4	0	1	83	0	15
SPRATT	Thomas	Wing-half	1968	1969	26	3	1	0	0	0	0	0	0	0	1	1	0	0	0	26	4	2
SPRINGETT	Frederick Henry	Right-back	1938	1939	17	0	0	0	0	0	0	0	0	0	0	0	0	0	0	17	0	0
STAINSBY	John	Centre-forward	1961	1963	69	0	21	0	0	0	1	0	0	8	0	4	0	0	0	78	0	25
STAINWRIGHT	David Peter	Inside-forward	1969	1970	6	2	1	0	0	0	1	0	0	1	0	0	0	0	0	8	2	1
STAMP	Neville	Left-back	2000	2002	17	3	0	0	0	0	1	2	0	0	0	0	2	0	0	20	5	0

			Played		Football League			Play-offs			FA Cup			League Cup			Other			Total		
Surname	**Forenames**	**Position**	**From**	**To**	**Apps**	**Sub**	**Gls**	**Apps**	**Sub**	**Gls**	**Apps**	**Sub**	**Gls**	**Apps**	**Sub**	**Gls**	**Apps**	**Sub**	**Gls**	**Apps**	**Sub**	**Gls**
STANCLIFFE	Paul Ian	Central-defender	1991	1994	89	2	3	5	0	0	3	0	0	2	0	0	2	0	0	101	2	3
STANIFORTH	Gordon	Left Wing/Midfield	1976 & 1987	1979 & 1988	143	4	34	0	0	0	10	0	4	7	0	2	0	0	0	160	4	40
STANLEY	Thomas	Midfield	1981	1983	14	4	0	0	0	0	1	0	0	0	0	0	0	0	0	15	4	0
STEEL	Richard	Left-back	1956	1958	3	0	0	0	0	0	0	0	0	0	0	0	0	0	0	3	0	0
STEPHENSON	Paul	Winger	1995	1998	91	6	8	0	0	0	5	0	0	9	2	0	2	2	1	107	10	9
STEWART	Alan Victor	Centre-half	1949	1957	208	0	1	0	0	0	23	0	0	0	0	0	0	0	0	231	0	1
STEWART *	Bryan William	Left-winger	2003	2004	2	8	0	0	0	0	0	0	0	0	1	0	0	0	0	2	9	0
STEWART	John Barry	Right-winger	1957	1957	1	0	0	0	0	0	0	0	0	0	0	0	0	0	0	1	0	0
STOCKDALE *	David Adam	Goalkeeper	2003	2004	0	1	0	0	0	0	0	0	0	0	0	0	0	0	0	0	1	0
STOCKILL	Reginald Robert	Winger	1929	1930	2	0	1	0	0	0	1	0	0	0	0	0	0	0	0	3	0	1
STODDART	Terence	Left-half	1956	1956	3	0	0	0	0	0	0	0	0	0	0	0	0	0	0	3	0	0
STONE	John George	Right-back	1972	1976	86	0	5	0	0	0	5	0	0	7	0	0	0	0	0	98	0	5
STOREY	Sidney	Inside-left	1947	1956	330	0	40	0	0	0	24	0	2	0	0	0	0	0	0	354	0	42
STOWELL	Michael	Goalkeeper	1987	1988	6	0	0	0	0	0	0	0	0	0	0	0	0	0	0	6	0	0
STRAIN	David	Left-back	1934	1934	13	0	0	0	0	0	0	0	0	0	0	0	2	0	0	15	0	0
STRONACH	Peter	Midfield	1978	1979	30	4	2	0	0	0	0	0	0	3	1	0	0	0	0	33	5	2
SWALLOW	Barry Ernest	Centre-half	1969	1976	268	1	21	0	0	0	24	0	4	19	0	2	0	0	0	311	1	27
SWAN	Peter Harold	Central-defender	2000	2000	11	0	0	0	0	0	0	0	0	0	0	0	0	0	0	11	0	0
SWANN	Gary	Midfield	1992	1994	82	0	4	5	0	2	1	0	0	4	0	0	3	0	0	95	0	6
SWEENEY	Gerald	Right-back	1982	1982	12	0	0	0	0	0	0	0	0	0	0	0	0	0	0	12	0	0
SWEENIE	Thomas Thornton	Midfield	1968	1968	6	0	1	0	0	0	0	0	0	0	0	0	0	0	0	6	0	1
TAIT	Barrie Stuart	Forward	1959	1960	15	0	5	0	0	0	1	0	0	0	0	0	0	0	0	16	0	5
TAIT	Peter	Centre-forward	1955	1955	3	0	1	0	0	0	0	0	0	0	0	0	0	0	0	3	0	1
TALBOT	Paul Michael	Midfield	2000	2000	5	1	0	0	0	0	0	0	0	0	0	0	0	0	0	5	1	0
TARRANT	Neil Kenneth	Forward	2000	2000	6	1	1	0	0	0	1	0	0	0	0	0	0	0	0	7	1	1
TAYLOR	Arthur (Archie)	Winger	1968	1971	93	3	8	0	0	0	12	0	1	4	0	0	0	0	0	109	3	9
TAYLOR	Paul Anthony	Midfield	1973	1973	4	0	0	0	0	0	0	0	0	1	0	0	0	0	0	5	0	0
TAYLOR	Philip Anthony	Left-winger	1975	1978	14	7	1	0	0	0	0	1	0	0	2	0	0	0	0	14	10	1
TAYLOR	Richard Herbert	Goalkeeper	1980	1980	2	0	0	0	0	0	0	0	0	0	0	0	0	0	0	2	0	0
TAYLOR	Richard William	Left-winger	1972	1973	26	2	2	0	0	0	0	0	0	1	0	0	0	0	0	27	2	2
THOMPSON	Albert	Centre-forward	1936	1937	24	0	24	0	0	0	5	0	4	0	0	0	2	0	1	31	0	29
THOMPSON	Desmond	Goalkeeper	1951	1952	80	0	0	0	0	0	3	0	0	0	0	0	0	0	0	83	0	0
THOMPSON	George Brian	Inside-forward	1973	1973	4	2	0	0	0	0	0	0	0	0	0	0	0	0	0	4	2	0
THOMPSON	Harold	Inside-forward	1945	1946	0	0	0	0	0	0	4	0	0	0	0	0	0	0	0	4	0	0
THOMPSON	Kenneth Hurst	Right-back	1950	1951	22	0	0	0	0	0	0	0	0	0	0	0	0	0	0	22	0	0
THOMPSON	Mark	Right-back	1999	2001	18	4	0	0	0	0	2	0	0	1	0	0	1	0	0	22	4	0
THOMPSON	Neil	Left-back	1997	2000	42	0	8	0	0	0	0	0	0	2	0	1	0	0	0	44	0	9
THOMPSON	Oliver	Left-half	1929	1932	121	0	2	0	0	0	12	0	0	0	0	0	0	0	0	133	0	2
THOMPSON	Ronald	Inside-right	1949	1950	8	0	0	0	0	0	0	0	0	0	0	0	0	0	0	8	0	0
THOMPSON	Thomas William	Left-back	1970	1970	4	0	0	0	0	0	0	0	0	0	0	0	0	0	0	4	0	0
THORNTON	Richard	Goalkeeper	1932	1932	11	0	0	0	0	0	0	0	0	0	0	0	0	0	0	11	0	0
TILLEY	Darren	Forward	1992	1993	17	4	0	0	0	0	0	0	0	0	0	0	1	0	0	18	4	0
TINKLER	Mark	Midfield	1997	1999	88	2	7	0	0	0	5	0	0	6	0	0	2	0	0	101	2	7
TOLSON	Neil	Centre-forward	1995	1999	66	18	18	0	0	0	6	1	2	7	2	3	0	2	1	79	23	24
TOMLINSON	Robert	Left-winger	1930	1930	3	0	1	0	0	0	0	0	0	0	0	0	0	0	0	3	0	1
TOPPING	Christopher	Central-defender	1968	1978	410	2	11	0	0	0	26	0	0	25	0	2	0	0	0	461	2	13
TUCKER	William	Right-winger	1935	1935	2	0	1	0	0	0	0	0	0	0	0	0	0	0	0	2	0	1
TUNKS	Roy	Goalkeeper	1969	1969	4	0	0	0	0	0	0	0	0	0	0	0	0	0	0	4	0	0
TURLEY	James	Forward	1999	2001	14	7	2	0	0	0	0	0	0	0	0	0	0	1	0	14	8	2
TURNBULL	John	Centre-forward	1932	1932	1	0	0	0	0	0	0	0	0	0	0	0	0	0	0	1	0	0
TURNER	Arthur	Left-back	1934	1935	12	0	0	0	0	0	0	0	0	0	0	0	2	0	0	14	0	0
TURNER	Kenneth	Left-back	1966	1968	88	0	2	0	0	0	7	0	0	2	0	0	0	0	0	97	0	2
TURNER	Robert Frewin	Right-half	1934	1935	9	0	0	0	0	0	0	0	0	0	0	0	0	0	0	9	0	0
TUTILL	Stephen Alan	Central-defender	1987	1997	293	8	6	2	1	0	18	1	0	21	0	0	20	2	1	354	12	7
TWISSELL	Charles Herbert	Left-winger	1958	1961	53	0	8	0	0	0	3	0	0	0	0	0	0	0	0	56	0	8
WALDRON	Alan	Midfield	1981	1981	3	0	1	0	0	0	0	0	0	1	0	0	0	0	0	4	0	1
WALKER	Dennis Alan	Inside-right/Midfield	1964	1968	149	5	19	0	0	0	9	0	0	6	0	0	0	0	0	164	5	19
WALKER	Justin Matthew	Midfield	2004	2004	7	2	0	0	0	0	0	0	0	0	0	0	0	0	0	7	2	0
WALKER	Michael Stewart	Goalkeeper	1966	1968	60	0	0	0	0	0	7	0	0	0	0	0	0	0	0	67	0	0
WALKER	Stuart	Goalkeeper	1976	1976	2	0	0	0	0	0	0	0	0	0	0	0	0	0	0	2	0	0
WALKER	Terence	Forward	1949	1950	16	0	9	0	0	0	0	0	0	0	0	0	0	0	0	16	0	9
WALSH	James Thomas	Left-back	1978	1981	91	8	2	0	0	0	7	0	0	8	0	0	0	0	0	106	8	2
WALWYN	Keith	Centre-forward	1981	1987	245	0	119	0	0	0	24	0	11	18	0	9	4	0	1	291	0	140
WANN	John Dennis	Left-winger/Midfield	1971	1976	65	1	7	0	0	0	2	0	0	1	0	0	0	0	0	68	1	7
WARBURTON	Raymond	Central-defender	1989	1994	86	4	9	0	0	0	6	0	1	8	0	1	7	0	0	107	4	11
WARD	Mitchum	Midfield	2003	2004	27	4	0	0	0	0	1	0	0	1	0	0	0	0	0	29	4	0
WARD	Warren	Forward	1984	1985	4	0	3	0	0	0	0	0	0	0	0	0	0	1	0	4	1	3
WARDLE	Ernest	Defender	1955	1959	60	0	2	0	0	0	3	0	0	0	0	0	0	0	0	63	0	2
WARE	Charles	Left-winger	1953	1954	9	0	0	0	0	0	0	0	0	0	0	0	0	0	0	9	0	0
WARNOCK	Neil	Winger	1978	1978	1	3	0	0	0	0	0	0	0	1	0	0	0	0	0	2	3	0
WARRENDER	Robert	Inside-forward/Winger	1952	1954	24	0	5	0	0	0	0	0	0	0	0	0	0	0	0	24	0	5
WARRINGTON	Andrew Clifford	Goalkeeper	1995	1999	61	0	0	0	0	0	4	0	0	7	0	0	4	0	0	76	0	0
WASS	Edwin (Ted)	Full-back/Centre-half	1932	1939	222	0	0	0	0	0	22	0	0	0	0	0	9	0	0	253	0	0
WEALTHALL	Barrington Arthur	Right-back	1963	1966	75	0	0	0	0	0	1	0	0	3	0	0	0	0	0	79	0	0

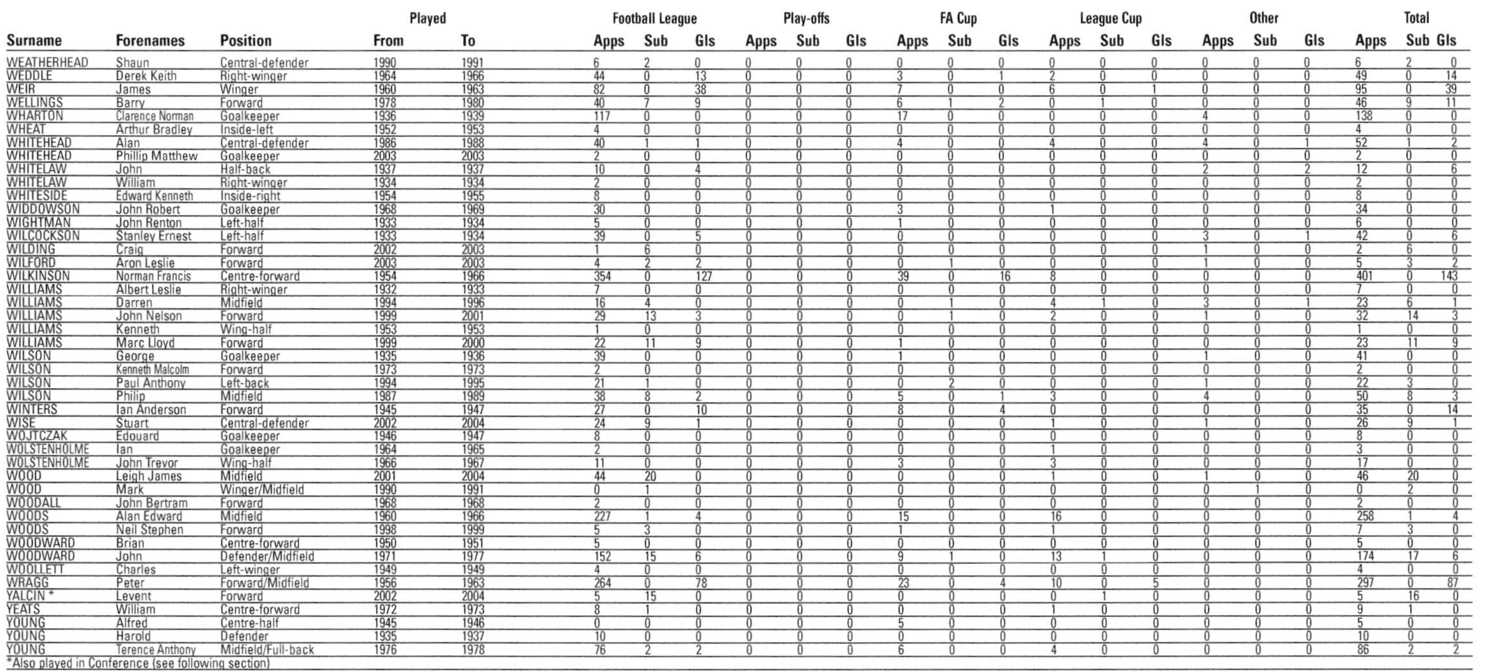

Surname	Forenames	Position	Played From	Played To	Football League Apps	Football League Sub	Football League Gls	Play-offs Apps	Play-offs Sub	Play-offs Gls	FA Cup Apps	FA Cup Sub	FA Cup Gls	League Cup Apps	League Cup Sub	League Cup Gls	Other Apps	Other Sub	Other Gls	Total Apps	Total Sub	Total Gls
WEATHERHEAD	Shaun	Central-defender	1990	1991	6	2	0	0	0	0	0	0	0	0	0	0	0	0	0	6	2	0
WEDDLE	Derek Keith	Right-winger	1964	1966	44	0	13	0	0	0	3	0	1	2	0	0	0	0	0	49	0	14
WEIR	James	Winger	1960	1963	82	0	38	0	0	0	7	0	0	6	0	1	0	0	0	95	0	39
WELLINGS	Barry	Forward	1978	1980	40	7	9	0	0	0	6	1	2	0	1	0	0	0	0	46	9	11
WHARTON	Clarence Norman	Goalkeeper	1936	1939	117	0	0	0	0	0	17	0	0	0	0	0	4	0	0	138	0	0
WHEAT	Arthur Bradley	Inside-left	1952	1953	4	0	0	0	0	0	0	0	0	0	0	0	0	0	0	4	0	0
WHITEHEAD	Alan	Central-defender	1986	1988	40	1	1	0	0	0	4	0	0	4	0	0	4	0	1	52	1	2
WHITEHEAD	Phillip Matthew	Goalkeeper	2003	2003	2	0	0	0	0	0	0	0	0	0	0	0	0	0	0	2	0	0
WHITELAW	John	Half-back	1937	1937	10	0	4	0	0	0	0	0	0	0	0	0	2	0	2	12	0	6
WHITELAW	William	Right-winger	1934	1934	2	0	0	0	0	0	0	0	0	0	0	0	0	0	0	2	0	0
WHITESIDE	Edward Kenneth	Inside-right	1954	1955	8	0	0	0	0	0	0	0	0	0	0	0	0	0	0	8	0	0
WIDDOWSON	John Robert	Goalkeeper	1968	1969	30	0	0	0	0	0	3	0	0	1	0	0	0	0	0	34	0	0
WIGHTMAN	John Renton	Left-half	1933	1934	5	0	0	0	0	0	1	0	0	0	0	0	0	0	0	6	0	0
WILCOCKSON	Stanley Ernest	Left-half	1933	1934	39	0	5	0	0	0	0	0	0	0	0	0	3	0	1	42	0	6
WILDING	Craig	Forward	2002	2003	1	6	0	0	0	0	0	0	0	0	0	0	1	0	0	2	6	0
WILFORD	Aron Leslie	Forward	2003	2003	4	2	2	0	0	0	0	1	0	0	0	0	1	0	0	5	3	2
WILKINSON	Norman Francis	Centre-forward	1954	1966	354	0	127	0	0	0	39	0	16	8	0	0	0	0	0	401	0	143
WILLIAMS	Albert Leslie	Right-winger	1932	1933	7	0	0	0	0	0	0	0	0	0	0	0	0	0	0	7	0	0
WILLIAMS	Darren	Midfield	1994	1996	16	4	0	0	0	0	0	1	0	4	1	0	3	0	1	23	6	1
WILLIAMS	John Nelson	Forward	1999	2001	29	13	3	0	0	0	0	1	0	2	0	0	1	0	0	32	14	3
WILLIAMS	Kenneth	Wing-half	1953	1953	1	0	0	0	0	0	0	0	0	0	0	0	0	0	0	1	0	0
WILLIAMS	Marc Lloyd	Forward	1999	2000	22	11	9	0	0	0	1	0	0	0	0	0	0	0	0	23	11	9
WILSON	George	Goalkeeper	1935	1936	39	0	0	0	0	0	1	0	0	0	0	0	1	0	0	41	0	0
WILSON	Kenneth Malcolm	Forward	1973	1973	2	0	0	0	0	0	0	0	0	0	0	0	0	0	0	2	0	0
WILSON	Paul Anthony	Left-back	1994	1995	21	1	0	0	0	0	0	2	0	0	0	0	1	0	0	22	3	0
WILSON	Philip	Midfield	1987	1989	38	8	2	0	0	0	5	0	1	3	0	0	4	0	0	50	8	3
WINTERS	Ian Anderson	Forward	1945	1947	27	0	10	0	0	0	8	0	4	0	0	0	0	0	0	35	0	14
WISE	Stuart	Central-defender	2002	2004	24	9	1	0	0	0	0	0	0	1	0	0	1	0	0	26	9	1
WOJTCZAK	Edouard	Goalkeeper	1946	1947	8	0	0	0	0	0	0	0	0	0	0	0	0	0	0	8	0	0
WOLSTENHOLME	Ian	Goalkeeper	1964	1965	2	0	0	0	0	0	0	0	0	1	0	0	0	0	0	3	0	0
WOLSTENHOLME	John Trevor	Wing-half	1966	1967	11	0	0	0	0	0	3	0	0	3	0	0	0	0	0	17	0	0
WOOD	Leigh James	Midfield	2001	2004	44	20	0	0	0	0	0	0	0	1	0	0	1	0	0	46	20	0
WOOD	Mark	Winger/Midfield	1990	1991	0	1	0	0	0	0	0	0	0	0	0	0	0	1	0	0	2	0
WOODALL	John Bertram	Forward	1968	1968	2	0	0	0	0	0	0	0	0	0	0	0	0	0	0	2	0	0
WOODS	Alan Edward	Midfield	1960	1966	227	1	4	0	0	0	15	0	0	16	0	0	0	0	0	258	1	4
WOODS	Neil Stephen	Forward	1998	1999	5	3	0	0	0	0	1	0	0	1	0	0	0	0	0	7	3	0
WOODWARD	Brian	Centre-forward	1950	1951	5	0	0	0	0	0	0	0	0	0	0	0	0	0	0	5	0	0
WOODWARD	John	Defender/Midfield	1971	1977	152	15	6	0	0	0	9	1	0	13	1	0	0	0	0	174	17	6
WOOLLETT	Charles	Left-winger	1949	1949	4	0	0	0	0	0	0	0	0	0	0	0	0	0	0	4	0	0
WRAGG	Peter	Forward/Midfield	1956	1963	264	0	78	0	0	0	23	0	4	10	0	5	0	0	0	297	0	87
YALCIN *	Levent	Forward	2002	2004	5	15	0	0	0	0	0	0	0	0	1	0	0	0	0	5	16	0
YEATS	William	Centre-forward	1972	1973	8	1	0	0	0	0	0	0	0	1	0	0	0	0	0	9	1	0
YOUNG	Alfred	Centre-half	1945	1946	0	0	0	0	0	0	5	0	0	0	0	0	0	0	0	5	0	0
YOUNG	Harold	Defender	1935	1937	10	0	0	0	0	0	0	0	0	0	0	0	0	0	0	10	0	0
YOUNG	Terence Anthony	Midfield/Full-back	1976	1978	76	2	2	0	0	0	6	0	0	4	0	0	0	0	0	86	2	2

*Also played in Conference (see following section)

Player Records – Conference League 2004–2008

			Played		Conference League			Play-offs			FA Cup			FA Trophy			Other			Total		
Surname	Forenames	Position	From	To	Apps	Sub	Gls	Apps	Sub	Gls	Apps	Sub	Gls	Apps	Sub	Gls	Apps	Sub	Gls	Apps	Sub	Gls
ANDREWS	Lee	Defender	2005	2006	9	0	0	0	0	0	0	0	0	1	0	0	0	0	0	10	0	0
ARMSTRONG	Kyle	Defender	2005	2005	3	2	0	0	0	0	0	0	0	0	0	0	0	0	0	3	2	0
ARTHUR	Adam	Forward	2004	2005	0	1	0	0	0	0	0	1	0	0	0	0	0	0	0	0	2	0
ASHCROFT	Kane John	Midfield	2004	2005	2	0	0	0	0	0	0	0	0	0	0	0	0	0	0	2	0	0
BARWICK	Terry	Midfield	2005	2006	3	0	0	0	0	0	0	0	0	1	0	0	0	0	0	4	0	0
BEADLE	James	Defender	2008	To Date	4	0	0	0	0	0	0	0	0	0	0	0	0	0	0	4	0	0
BEARDSLEY	Chris	Forward	2007	2008	4	4	0	0	0	0	0	0	0	0	1	0	0	0	0	4	5	0
BELL	Phillip	Forward	2007	2007	0	1	0	0	0	0	0	0	0	0	0	0	0	0	0	0	1	0
BISHOP	Andrew (Andy)	Centre-forward	2004	2006	72	6	33	0	0	0	3	0	2	2	0	1	2	0	1	79	6	37
BISHOP	Neal	Midfield	2006	2007	56	3	4	2	0	0	2	0	0	0	0	0	0	0	0	60	3	4
BOWEY	Steve	Midfield	2006	2007	42	0	7	2	0	1	2	0	0	1	0	0	0	0	0	47	0	8
BOYES	Adam	Forward	2008	To Date	0	3	0	0	0	0	0	0	0	0	1	0	0	0	0	0	4	0
BRASS	Christopher (Chris)	Defender/Midfield	2004	2005	20	2	1	0	0	0	1	0	0	0	0	0	0	0	0	21	2	1
BRAYSON	Paul	Forward	2007	2008	16	6	4	0	0	0	2	0	0	0	1	0	0	0	0	18	7	4
BRODIE	Richard	Centre-forward	2007	To Date	24	27	11	0	0	0	1	1	0	2	3	1	1	1	3	28	32	15
BERTOS	Leo	Midfield	2005	2006	3	2	0	0	0	0	0	0	0	1	0	0	0	0	0	4	2	0
CLARKE	Christopher (Chris)	Defender	2004	2005	5	0	0	0	0	0	0	0	0	0	0	0	0	0	0	5	0	0
COAD	Matthew Paul	Midfield	2004	2005	1	1	0	0	0	0	1	0	0	0	0	0	0	0	0	2	1	0
CONSTABLE	Robert	Midfield	2005	2005	2	0	0	0	0	0	0	0	0	0	0	0	1	0	0	3	0	0
CONVERY	Mark	Midfield	2005	2007	53	13	8	0	1	0	2	0	1	1	0	0	0	0	0	56	14	9
CRADDOCK	Darren	Full-back	2006	2008	61	8	0	0	0	0	4	0	0	2	2	0	2	0	0	69	10	0
CRICHTON	Paul	Goalkeeper	2004	2004	4	0	0	0	0	0	0	0	0	0	0	0	0	0	0	4	0	0
DAVIES	Sean Graham	Defender	2004	2005	16	0	0	0	0	0	1	0	0	0	1	0	1	0	0	18	1	0
DAVIS	Steve	Central-defender	2004	2005	14	1	0	0	0	0	0	0	0	0	0	0	0	0	0	14	1	0
DONOVAN	Kevin	Midfield	2004	2005	30	1	2	0	0	0	0	0	0	1	0	0	1	0	0	32	1	2
DUNNING	Darren	Midfield	2004	2006	78	1	4	0	0	0	3	0	1	2	0	0	2	0	0	85	1	5
DONALDSON	Clayton	Centre-forward	2005	2007	85	0	41	2	0	0	4	0	2	2	0	1	0	0	0	93	0	44
DUDGEON	James	Central-defender	2005	2007	40	5	6	0	0	0	2	0	0	1	0	0	0	0	0	43	5	6
DUNCUM	Sam	Winger	2008	2008	1	1	0	0	0	0	0	0	0	0	1	0	0	0	0	1	2	0
ELLIOTT	Stuart	Midfield	2007	2008	32	4	3	0	0	0	2	0	0	6	0		1	1	0	41	5	3
ELVINS	Rob	Forward	2007	2007	4	5	0	0	0	0	0	0	0	0	0	0	0	0	0	4	5	0
EVANS	Thomas (Tom)	Goalkeeper	2006	2008	81	0	0	2	0	0	4	0	0	8	0	0	2	0	0	97	0	0
FARRELL	Craig	Forward	2006	To Date	57	9	18	2	0	0	3	1	3	6	1	1	2	0	0	70	11	21
FORTUNE-WEST	Leo	Centre-forward	2008	2008	7	6	2	0	0	0	0	0	0	0	0	0	0	0	0	7	6	2
FOSTER	Luke	Central-defender	2006	2006	4	1	0	0	0	0	2	0	0	0	0	0	0	0	0	6	1	0
FRY	Russell	Midfield	2007	2008	0	4	0	0	0	0	0	0	0	1	0	0	1	0	0	2	4	0
GOODLIFFE	Jason	Central-defender	2006	2007	11	0	1	0	0	0	2	0	0	1	0	0	0	0	0	14	0	1
GRANT	Lee	Central-defender	2004	2005	7	1	2	0	0	0	0	0	0	1	0	0	0	0	0	8	1	2
GREENWOOD	Ross	Midfield	2006	2008	4	3	0	0	0	0	0	0	0	0	0	0	0	0	0	4	3	0
GROVES	Paul	Midfield/Defender	2004	2005	38	4	3	0	0	0	1	0	0	1	0	0	2	0	0	42	4	3
HALL	Chris	Winger	2008	2008	1	1	0	0	0	0	0	0	0	0	0	0	0	0	0	1	1	0
HARRISON	Gerry	Midfield	2004	2004	0	3	0	0	0	0	0	0	0	0	0	0	0	1	0	0	4	0
HAW	Robert	Midfield	2004	2005	0	2	0	0	0	0	0	0	0	0	0	0	0	0	0	0	2	0
HEGARTY	Nicholas	Left Midfield	2007	2007	2	0	0	0	0	0	0	0	0	0	0	0	0	0	0	2	0	0
HENDERSON	Stephen	Goalkeeper	2007	2007	7	0	0	0	0	0	0	0	0	0	0	0	0	0	0	7	0	0
HORWOOD	Evan	Defender	2005	2006	4	0	0	0	0	0	0	0	0	1	0	0	0	0	0	5	0	0

			Played		Conference League			Play-offs			FA Cup			FA Trophy			Other			Total		
Surname	**Forenames**	**Position**	**From**	**To**	**Apps**	**Sub**	**Gls**	**Apps**	**Sub**	**Gls**	**Apps**	**Sub**	**Gls**	**Apps**	**Sub**	**Gls**	**Apps**	**Sub**	**Gls**	**Apps**	**Sub**	**Gls**
HOTTE	Mark	Central-defender	2005	2006	16	4	0	0	0	0	0	0	0	0	0	0	0	0	0	16	4	0
HUTCHINSON	Joseph	Defender	2007	2007	2	1	0	0	0	0	0	0	0	0	0	0	0	0	0	2	1	0
JACKSON	Ben	Forward	2005	2005	7	3	0	0	0	0	0	0	0	0	0	0	0	0	0	7	3	0
JAMES	Craig	Left-back	2007	2007	8	0	0	2	0	0	0	0	0	0	0	0	0	0	0	10	0	0
JONES	Carl	Defender	2007	2008	2	0	0	0	0	0	0	0	0	0	0	0	0	0	0	2	0	0
KAMARA	Nathan	Defender	2005	2006	0	2	0	0	0	0	0	0	0	0	0	0	0	0	0	0	2	0
KELLY	Darren	Central-defender	2007	To Date	25	2	2	0	0	0	2	0	0	3	0	0	1	0	0	31	2	2
KOVACS	Janos	Central-defender	2007	2007	8	0	1	0	0	0	0	0	0	0	0	0	0	0	0	8	0	1
LAW	Graeme	Right-back	2004	2005	24	7	0	0	0	0	0	0	0	0	0	0	1	0	0	25	7	0
LLOYD	Anthony	Defender	2006	2008	34	1	0	2	0	0	2	0	0	7	0	1	2	0	0	47	11	1
McBREEN	Daniel	Forward	2007	2007	5	0	2	0	0	0	0	0	0	0	0	0	0	0	0	5	0	2
McGURK	David	Central-defender	2004	To Date	125	1	3	2	0	0	4	0	0	9	0	0	1	0	0	141	1	3
McMAHON	Lewis	Midfield	2006	2007	8	11	1	0	0	0	0	0	0	1	0	0	0	0	0	9	11	1
McWILLIAMS	Andy	Defender	2008	To Date	4	1	0	0	0	0	0	0	0	0	0	0	0	0	0	4	1	0
MAIDENS	Michael	Right Midfield	2007	2007	1	2	0	0	0	0	0	0	0	0	0	0	0	0	0	1	2	0
MALLON	Ryan	Forward	2005	2006	1	4	0	0	0	0	0	2	0	0	0	0	0	0	0	1	6	0
MALONEY	Jonathan	Central-defender	2004	2005	13	0	4	0	0	0	0	0	0	1	0	0	1	0	0	15	0	4
MANSARAM	Darren	Forward	2005	2005	4	1	0	0	0	0	0	0	0	0	0	0	0	0	0	4	1	0
MEECHAN	Alex	Midfield	2007	2008	3	4	1	0	0	0	0	0	0	0	0	0	0	0	0	3	4	1
MERRIS	David Andrew	Left-back	2004	2006	56	9	2	0	0	0	2	1	0	1	0	0	2	0	0	61	10	2
MIMMS	Josh	Goalkeeper	2008	To Date	3	1	0	0	0	0	0	0	0	0	0	0	0	0	0	3	1	0
NOGAN	Lee Martin	Forward	2004	2005	18	4	3	0	0	0	1	0	0	0	1	0	2	0	0	21	5	3
N'TOYA	Teham	Forward	2006	2006	2	1	0	0	0	0	0	0	0	0	0	0	0	0	0	2	1	0
O'NEILL	Joe	Forward	2005	2006	25	12	5	0	0	0	2	0	0	0	0	0	0	0	0	27	12	5
PALMER	Jermaine	Forward	2005	2005	0	3	0	0	0	0	0	0	0	0	0	0	0	0	0	0	3	0
PANTHER	Emmanuel (Manny)	Midfield	2005	2008	114	7	4	2	0	0	4	0	0	7	1	0	1	0	0	128	8	4
PARSLOW	Daniel	Central-defender	2006	To Date	51	4	1	2	0	0	0	0	0	7	0	1	2	0	0	62	4	2
PEARSON	Gary	Defender	2004	2004	12	0	0	0	0	0	0	0	0	0	0	0	1	0	0	13	0	0
PEAT	Nathan	Left-back	2005	2007	42	6	2	0	1	0	1	0	0	1	0	0	0	0	0	44	7	2
PORTER	Christopher (Chris)	Goalkeeper	2004	2006	59	0	0	0	0	0	2	0	0	1	1	0	1	0	0	63	1	0
PRICE	Jamie	Right-back	2005	2006	21	1	0	0	0	0	2	0	0	0	0	0	0	0	0	23	1	0
PURKISS	Ben	Right-back	2007	To Date	40	5	0	0	0	0	0	0	0	7	0	0	2	0	0	49	5	0
REID	Arran	Goalkeeper	2005	2006	1	1	0	0	0	0	0	0	0	0	0	0	0	0	0	1	1	0
RHODES	Alex	Forward	2006	2008	0	1	0	0	0	0	0	2	0	0	0	0	0	0	0	0	3	0
ROBINSON	Mark	Left-back	2007	To Date	28	3	2	0	0	0	2	0	0	1	0	0	0	0	0	31	3	2
ROBINSON	Paul	Forward	2004	2005	5	7	2	0	0	0	0	0	0	1	0	0	0	1	0	6	8	2
ROBINSON	Paul Derrick	Forward	2004	2005	22	12	2	0	0	0	0	0	0	0	1	0	1	1	0	23	14	2
RUSK	Simon	Midfield	2008	To Date	10	4	0	0	0	0	0	0	0	0	0	0	0	0	0	10	4	0
SHEPHERD	Liam	Midfield	2008	To Date	0	3	0	0	0	0	0	0	0	0	0	0	0	1	0	0	4	0
SMITH	Shaun	Left-back	2004	2005	16	3	0	0	0	0	0	0	0	0	0	0	0	0	0	16	3	0
SODJE	Onome	Forward	2007	To Date	29	16	14	0	0	0	2	0	2	4	3	0	1	0	1	36	19	17
STALEY	Michael	Defender	2004	2005	10	2	0	0	0	0	1	0	0	1	0	0	1	0	0	13	2	0
STAMP	Darryn	Forward	2006	2007	5	5	0	0	0	0	1	1	0	0	0	0	0	0	0	6	6	0
STEWART	Bryan William	Left-winger	2004	2006	17	22	3	0	0	0	1	2	0	0	1	0	1	0	0	19	25	3
STOCKDALE	David Adam	Goalkeeper	2004	2006	21	2	0	0	0	0	1	0	0	1	0	0	1	0	0	24	2	0
WEBSTER	Byron	Midfield	2004	2007	13	7	1	0	0	0	0	1	0	1	1	0	0	0	0	14	9	1
WOOLFORD	Martyn	Midfield/Winger	2006	To Date	71	15	22	2	0	0	3	1	0	8	0	2	2	0	1	86	16	25
WROE	Nicholas (Nicky)	Midfield	2007	2008	21	8	6	0	0	0	0	2	1	6	1	3	0	2	0	27	13	10
THOMAS	Stephen	Defender	2005	2006	12	2	1	0	0	0	0	0	0	0	0	0	0	0	0	12	2	1
TURNBULL	Phillip	Midfield	2007	2008	0	0	0	0	0	0	0	0	0	0	2	0	1	0	0	1	2	0
YALCIN	Levent	Midfield/Forward	2004	2006	14	28	2	0	0	0	2	1	0	0	0	0	0	1	0	16	30	2

ND - #0173 - 090625 - C0 - 240/170/30 - PB - 9781780911335 - Gloss Lamination